Pragmatics

Pragmatics——————————

A Reader

Edited by Steven Davis

New York Oxford OXFORD UNIVERSITY PRESS 1991

Oxford University Press

Oxford   New York   Toronto
Delhi   Bombay   Calcutta   Madras   Karachi
Petaling Jaya   Singapore   Hong Kong   Tokyo
Nairobi   Dar es Salaam   Cape Town
Melbourne   Auckland

and associated companies in
Berlin   Ibadan

Library of Congress Cataloging-in-Publication Data
Pragmatics : a reader / edited by Steven Davis.
p. cm.   ISBN 0-19-505898-4
1. Pragmatics.
2. Linguistics.
I. Davis, Steven, 1937–
P99.4.P72P736   1991   306.4′4—dc20
90-34054

Printing 9 8 7 6 5 4 3 2 1

Printed in the United States of America
on acid-free paper

Contents

VIII Psychology and Pragmatics

Introduction

The term 'pragmatics' was first introduced in *Foundations of the Theory of Signs* by Charles W. Morris, who contrasts it with semantics and syntax. For Morris

> syntax [is] the study of the syntactical relations of signs to one another in abstraction from the relations of signs to objects or to interpreters; . . . semantics deals with the relation of signs to designata and so to objects which they may or do denote [and] 'pragmatics' is designated the science of the relation of signs to their interpreters. (1971, pp. 28, 35, 43)

Morris's use of 'sign' here is a bit confusing, since syntax studies the grammatical relations of morphemes[1] (for example, 'the'), which are not signs. Let us replace Morris's 'sign' with 'linguistic unit,' which applies to morphemes, phrases, and sentences. With this change we can take Morris to claim that syntax is the study of the grammatical relations of linguistic units to one another, and the grammatical structures of phrases and sentences that result from these grammatical relations; that semantics is the study of the relation of linguistic units to the world; and that pragmatics is the study of the relation of linguistic units to their users. Expanding his definition, Morris tells us that pragmatics is the study of "the biotic aspects of semiosis, that is, . . . [the study of] all the psychological, biological, and sociological phenomena which occur in the functioning of signs" (1971, p. 43). The problem with this broad view of pragmatics is that it is too inclusive to be of much use. Using this definition, pragmatics has as its domain any human activity involving language, and thus includes almost all human activity, from baseball to the stock market. The consequence is that all the human sciences become part of pragmatics. On this view, then, pragmatics is not on the same level as semantics and syntax, when these are construed as theories constructed to account for various aspects of a speaker's linguistic ability. Nor can pragmatics be regarded as a field of study, like linguistics or sociology. What groups various activities and theories together in one field of study is that they share a set of questions or a methodology. But there is no common methodology or set of questions that groups together in a natural class the full range of the human sciences in which language is involved. Economics and socio-linguistics, for example, have very little in common to justify their inclusion in the same field of study. For 'pragmatics' to be a useful term, its domain must be restricted. Let us take a fresh look at the problem.

Pragmatic theories can be considered in two ways. On the first view, a pragmatic theory is part of a theory of a speaker's linguistic competence. As such, it is part of a psychological theory that plays a role in accounting for what speakers tacitly know which enables them to understand and to use sentences of their language. On the second view, pragmatics is not part of a theory of competence. It is a theory that attempts to account for a range of pragmatic facts[2] without making any commitment to whether the theory is psychologically realized. A clear view of this sort is held by Richard Montague, who claims that pragmatics is a branch of "mathematics, not of psychology" (1974, p. 2). Space does not allow me to argue for the first view, which I shall adopt here. I shall regard pragmatics as part of a theory of competence and, as such, take it to be psychologically realized.

We carry on conversations, and most of the time we are able to understand one another. How do we do this? What capacities, faculties, and knowledge enable us to communicate with one another with relative ease? According to Noam Chomsky, one of the capacities we have is our knowledge of the syntactic rules of our language. These rules account both for our intuitions about whether a string of words constitutes a well-formed sentence of our language and for our knowledge of the syntactic facts of our language. For example, our intuition of the following strings of words

(1) Boy the street the down ran.
(2) Flying planes can be dangerous.

is that (1) is not well formed, and (2) is ambiguous where the ambiguity arises from the syntactic structure of the sentence. Knowing syntactic rules is hardly sufficient to enable us to carry on a conversation. We must know more; we must understand the sentences of our language. To understand our language, we also must know its semantics. Our semantic knowledge is of two sorts. We know the meanings of the words of our language and the rules that enable us to combine these meanings to form meanings of phrases and sentences. We know, for example, that if a speaker, let us call her 'Alice,' were to say,

(3) Sam threw Sally a ball.

she could mean that Sam threw Sally a spherical object, or that Sam arranged a party for Sally at which people danced and dressed in formal clothes. Therefore, we can add to our syntactic knowledge our knowledge of the meanings of the words of our language and the rules by which we can combine them to form meanings for larger units. In some cases, our knowledge is the sort illustrated by (3), where we are in a position to give 'definitions' for a word. In other cases, our knowledge of the meaning of a word may consist in our being able to use the word appropriately in a wide range of circumstances. We are hard pressed to give the meaning of 'the,' but there is no doubt that we are able to use it correctly and, thus, we can be said to know the meaning of the word. We may argue that despite our inability to give a definition for 'the' and similar words, we tacitly know their meanings. Let us call the theory that describes the knowledge we have—tacit or explicit—of the meanings of the words of our language and the rules that combine them into meanings of larger units *a theory of meaning.*

A theory of meaning does not exhaust our semantic knowledge. We also know what the terms of our language refer to and what the *truth conditions* of the declarative sentences are. For example, in saying (3), Alice knows to whom 'Sam' and 'Sally' refer, what 'throw' is true of, and the conditions under which the sentence she utters is true. In some cases, Alice's knowledge of what the terms of her language refer to consists in her ability to identify the objects to which the terms refer; in other cases, she may know no more than that a name like 'Einstein' refers to Einstein, without knowing who he is. In fact, Alice may even be mistaken about who he is; she may confuse him with Bohr. Despite this, she can use 'Einstein' to refer to Einstein. What enables her to do so is that she is part of a linguistic community extending back in time to speakers who are causally connected to Einstein (Kripke 1980, pp. 96–98).

There is a relationship between reference and truth conditions. To illustrate this, let us consider an example that is simpler than (3). Suppose Alice says,

(4) Sally is a woman.

What Alice says in uttering (4) is true just in case 'a woman' is true of the person to whom Alice refers in using 'Sally.' We shall assume that Alice knows the truth conditions of the declarative sentences of her language. Her knowledge of these truth conditions cannot be given by a list of the sentences paired with their truth conditions. She can have no such knowledge, since the declarative sentences of her language are an infinite set. Rather, her knowledge consists in knowing a finite set of rules that specify both the referent for each term of her language and the truth conditions for each declarative sentence of her language.

Truth conditions are available for only the declarative sentences of a language. Analogous conditions apply to interrogatives and imperatives. For interrogatives, *answer conditions* specify the set of possible answers to the questions they can be used to ask. For imperatives, *compliance conditions* specify the set of actions that carry out the requests and commands which they can be used to make. Let us call truth conditions, answer conditions, and compliance conditions, *satisfaction conditions,* and a theory that specifies these conditions, a *theory of satisfaction.* We shall regard a theory of satisfaction to be a theory of Alice's knowledge of the satisfaction conditions of her language. Once again, this should not be taken to imply that Alice consciously knows these conditions. If she were asked, she could not tell us what the satisfaction conditions are for certain sentences of her language. In the same way that speakers have tacit knowledge of the syntactic rules of their language, and of the rules that assign meanings to the sentences of their language, we can take it that Alice has tacit knowledge of the rules that assign satisfaction conditions to the sentences of her language. Taken together, a theory of meaning and a theory of satisfaction constitute a semantic theory for Alice's language and are part of a theory of her linguistic competence that enables her to communicate with others.

Let us digress for a moment to try to give an initial characterization of Alice's syntactic and semantic knowledge (a characterization that later will be revised), so that we can make a first attempt to distinguish it from the knowledge she has for which a pragmatic theory should give an account.

Three characteristics are often taken to be features of Alice's syntactic and semantic knowledge. First, it is held to be linguistic knowledge about the linguistic units of her language.[3] Second, it is regarded as independent of context. It is knowledge that does not depend on her knowing anything about the context in which the sentences of her language are used. Last, it is claimed that it is knowledge which is independent of her knowing her own intentions, wants, desires—her *intentional states*—which she has in saying what she does. For example, if Alice knows that 'run' is a verb and that 'ball' means *a spherical object used in games* or *a formal dance,* the knowledge she has is knowledge about English; it is not dependent on her knowing anything about the particular context of any utterance, and no reference is made to any of her intentional states. Let us call such knowledge *context-independent linguistic knowledge.* This is the sort of knowledge that Alice can be said to have in all contexts and that she can bring to bear in any context in which it is relevant in communicating with others and in understanding what they communicate to her.

Alice's context-independent linguistic knowledge does not exhaust the knowledge that enables her to communicate with others. She also knows how to use her language. As we shall see, this knowledge includes knowing the rules or maxims that govern conversation and the intentional states she must have in particular contexts which are necessary for various uses of her language. Let us call this knowledge of pragmatic facts *conversational knowledge* and take as an initial hypothesis (which we shall modify) that pragmatics is the study of conversational knowledge. It will be helpful to have before us examples of pragmatic facts. The examples clearly are not within the domain of syntax, and most of them do not appear to fall within semantics. The last example we shall consider, however, raises the question of whether a boundary can be drawn between conversational knowledge, on the one hand, and semantic knowledge, on the other. This boundary is important because if we were not able to draw a line between the two, we would not have separate sets of facts that constitute the domains of semantic theory and of pragmatic theory. Before considering the question of whether a boundary can be drawn between conversational knowledge and semantic knowledge, let us look at some examples of pragmatic facts.

Alice can play a dual role in a conversation. She can be at once speaker and hearer. Let us concentrate on her role as speaker. Suppose that in uttering

(5) I'll be in New York.

Alice is speaking literally. The sentence that Alice uttered can be used to make a promise, to declare her intention, or even to make a prediction about her future behavior. The acts that Alice can perform in uttering (5)—promising, declaring her intention, or predicting her own behavior—are called *speech acts.*

It may be thought that it is a semantic fact about (5) that it can be used to perform these speech acts. One proposal is that (5) is ambiguous and means the same as either

(6) (a) I promise that I'll be in New York.
   (b) I predict that I'll be in New York.
   (c) I declare my intention to be in New York.

Which of these (5) means can be taken to vary from context to context, but in any context it must mean one of these, if the speaker uses the sentence with one of its standard meanings. I believe that the above proposal is mistaken. The hypothesis is that (5) means the same as (6) (a), (b), and (c), and in a particular context which of these (5) means depends on which of these the speaker means by it. Let us suppose that the speaker uses (5) to mean the same as (6) (a). If (5) and (6) (a) have the same meaning, they should be true under the same satisfaction conditions. But (5) is true just in case Alice is in New York at some time after she says (5), while (6) (a) is true just in case Alice promises that she will be in New York. Since the sentences are true under different conditions, they cannot be synonymous. Thus the proposal is false.[4] This argument does not show that there is no semantic relation between (5) and the range of speech acts which it can be used to perform. But in the absence of such a proposal, I shall assume that the relationship is a pragmatic fact. Which speech act Alice performs in uttering (5) on a particular occasion depends on her knowing the rules that govern the speech acts that (5) can be used to perform, and on whether she intends in uttering (5) to be making a promise or prediction or to be declaring her intention (see Part IV).

This is not the only case in which Alice's knowledge of rules governing the use of language or her intentions on a particular occasion of utterance play a role in determining what she intends to communicate. Consider the following sentence:

(7) Sam really had a ball.

Since 'ball' is ambiguous, in uttering (7) Alice could be saying at least two things. The ambiguity of (7) is determined by the semantics of Alice's language. But her language does not determine which of these she means on a particular occasion. It is determined by what she intends the word 'ball' to mean on this occasion. In turn, her intention to mean what she does by 'ball' plays a role in determining what she says in uttering (7) (see Part II).

In the preceding examples I have assumed that Alice is being straightforward. But this need not be so. Suppose that Alice is a professor of philosophy, and she is asked to write a letter of recommendation for Sam, one of her students. She writes,

(8) Sam has good handwriting.

In so writing, Alice implies that Sam is not a very good student of philosophy. There is no semantic or syntactic connection between (8) and what Alice implies. How, then, is she able to imply what she does by including in her letter of recommendation her comments about Sam's handwriting? She does so by exploiting certain maxims of conversation that she assumes her audience takes her to be following—one of which is 'Be relevant.' In violating the maxim of relevance, as she manifestly does in writing (8), she intends that her colleague to whom she wrote the letter recognize that she has violated the maxim and that she intended to do so. Moreover, Alice intends that her colleague, in recognizing that she has manifestly violated the maxim of relevance in commenting on Sam's handwriting (which clearly is not relevant to his philosophical ability), will draw the inference that she (Alice) does not think very highly of Sam's philosophical ability. Hence, in writing (8) Alice implies that Sam is not very good at philosophy by virtue of her knowledge of the maxims of conversation, her assumption that her audience has such knowledge, and her intention that her audience recognize her intention to exploit these maxims in saying what she does[5] (see Parts II and V).

Let us change the example to illustrate another contextual feature that plays a role in determining what Alice is communicating. Suppose that Alice says,

(9) She is tired.

Alice can use instances of (9) to say different things. In part, what she says in uttering (9) depends on the person to whom she refers in using 'she.' For example, if she were to refer to Betsy, she would be saying that Betsy is tired; if she were to refer to Ellen, she would be saying that Ellen is tired. Thus Alice's ability to use expressions to refer and her intention on the particular occasion in which she utters (9) to refer to some particular person play a role in determining both that she says something and what she says on that occasion (see Part II).

We distinguished between two sorts of semantic theories: a theory of meaning and a theory of satisfaction. Part of the theory of satisfaction is a theory of truth that is supposed to specify the truth conditions for each declarative sentence of the language. The question that arises here is whether a truth theoretic semantics can specify truth conditions without in some cases making reference to the intentions of speakers? The problem is that if truth theoretic semantics were to refer to speakers' intentions, it would cross the boundary between pragmatics and semantics, since we have supposed that speakers' intentions fall within the domain of pragmatics. The result would be that the distinction between semantics and pragmatics would be blurred, and we would not have a separate domain of facts for semantics and pragmatics.

The problem is neatly illustrated by (9). Before considering this example further, it will be useful to distinguish between *speaker referent* and *semantic referent*. The semantic referent of an expression is the referent that the expression has in the language (e.g., 'dog' in English refers to dogs). The semantic referent of an expression is fixed by the conventions of the language. The speaker referent of an expression is fixed by what a speaker refers to in using the expression on a particular occasion, which is determined by what the speaker intends to refer to on that occasion. A speaker might use 'dog' on a particular occasion to refer, mistakenly, to some wolves (Kripke 1977, pp. 96–97).

Let us return to (9). Some pronouns—for example, 'she'—have no semantic referent. Their referents are not fixed by the conventions of the language but by what the speaker intends to refer to in using such terms on a particular occasion. In addition, the referent of 'she' plays a role in determining the truth conditions of (9), truth conditions that it has relative to the context in which it is used. (9) is true just in case the person to whom Alice refers is tired.

It may seem that the truth conditions for (9) can be specified in (10) independently of context and of the intentions of a particular speaker:

(10) 'She is tired' is true just in case the person to whom the speaker refers in uttering this sentence is tired.

This will not do. One of the purposes of a semantic theory for a language is to account for the logical relations among the sentences of the language. Consider the following argument:

(11) She is tired.
   She is Margaret Smith.
   _____
   Therefore, Margaret Smith is tired.

There is one interpretation of (11) in which it turns out to be valid and one in which it turns out to be invalid. If 'she' refers to the same person on both of its occurrences, then (11) is valid; if it does not, then (11) is invalid. Suppose we assume that (10) gives the truth conditions for the first sentence of the argument and that (12) gives the truth conditions for the second sentence.

(12) 'She is Margaret Smith' is true just in case the person to whom the speaker refers in using the sentence is Margaret Smith.

The problem is that (11) and (12) do not account for the interpretation of the argument in which it is valid. There is nothing in these truth conditions which guarantees that the speaker who uses the first and second sentences of the argument is the same or, even if this were the case, that the person to whom the speaker refers in using 'she' in the two sentences is the same. Thus to give the truth conditions of certain sentences of natural languages requires that the truth conditions mention particular speakers and their intentions on particular occasions for those sentences that contain expressions whose referent is not determined by the conventions of the language. Consequently, semantic theory—at least the theory of satisfaction—must make reference to particular speakers and their referential intentions.

The problem is that these latter features seem to be the mark of the pragmatic, and thus, if the theory of satisfaction makes reference to particular speakers and their referential intentions, it should be considered to be part of pragmatic theory rather than semantic theory. This means in effect that the semantics of natural languages consists only of the theory of meaning.[6] I think, however, that there is a way to avoid this consequence by distinguishing among speakers' intentions—specifically, between their referential and communicative intentions. The referential intentions of a speaker determine the semantic referents of terms whose referents are not fixed by the conventions of the language. This includes demonstratives, such as 'this' and 'that'; indexicals, such as 'she' and 'it'; and incomplete definite descriptions, such as 'the table.' Speakers' communicative intentions are the intentions speakers have to get their audience to recognize what they are trying to communicate. In the case of terms that can be used to refer to something, the speakers' communicative intentions are to get their audience to understand to what they are referring. Let us illustrate the difference between referential and communicative intentions. Suppose that there is a room full of brown tables. Alice says,

(13) That table is brown.

In saying this, Alice intends to refer to the only table that is under the window. Alice has referred to the table and said something true if the table is brown. Imagine further that Alice mutters (13) under her breath. In uttering (13) Alice need not intend that anyone understand to what she is referring and thus what she is saying. Given the situation described, it is difficult to see how anyone could understand either to what she referred or what she said. The utterance of 'that table' has no connection to what Alice is referring, except through her intention, which is not, however, manifest in what she says. Let us change the example a bit and suppose that Alice addresses (13) to an audience—for example, to Sam—and that in doing so she does not do anything to indicate to him to what table she is referring. In this context, it is natural for Sam to think that Alice wishes him to understand what she is saying and, therefore, intends that he understand to what she is referring. That is, because Alice addresses (13) to Sam, Sam has reason to think that Alice has communicative intentions. In part, for Alice to have communicative intentions is to have the intention that her audience recognize these intentions (Grice 1968, pp. 82–83). In this case, however, Sam has reason to be puzzled. The assumption that Alice has the communicative intention that Sam understand to which table she is referring is in conflict with the fact, which is mutually obvious to Sam and Alice, that on this occasion in uttering (13) Alice has not provided Sam with enough information to understand what her communicative intention is. Something is wrong with what Alice has said. For Alice to achieve her communicative intention, she must manifest it in such a way that there is a reasonable chance that her audience will recognize her intention. How this is done depends on the context. In the context described, Alice could make clear what her intention is by pointing to the table to which she is referring.

It is not necessary for Alice to have communicative intentions for her to have said something and for what she said to be true or false. In uttering (13) Alice has said something that is true if the table under the window is brown. It does not matter whether Sam understands what she said or even whether he could understand it given the information that he has in the context. In normal situations, however, in which language is used to communicate to others, the speakers' goal is to get across to their audience what they are trying to communicate. For this reason, the fulfillment of speakers' communicative intentions requires that their audience recognize what these communicative intentions are. Moreover, and more importantly for our purposes, certain uses of language require communicative intentions. Alice cannot make a promise without the intention on her part that the person to whom she makes the promise accepts it. If she says to Sam, 'I promise to take you to the party,' she must intend that he accept her offer. If he were to decline, no promise would have been made. Similarly, Alice cannot ask a question or make a request without corresponding communicative intentions. Moreover, in uttering (8) Alice cannot imply that Sam is not very good at philosophy without intending that her audience recognize that she is violating the maxim of relevance.

Perhaps we now have a way to distinguish between a theory of satisfaction and a theory of pragmatics. We can say that the former must give an account of the satisfaction conditions of sentences, including the satisfaction conditions that certain sentences have relative to a particular context of use. This requirement means that within a specification of context-relative truth conditions, a theory of satisfaction must mention the speaker's intentions where those intentions play a role in determining the referent of terms that have no semantic referent given by the conventions of the language. Pragmatics will have as its domain speakers' communicative intentions, the uses of language that require such intentions, and the strategies that hearers employ to determine what these intentions and acts are, so that they can understand what the speaker intends to communicate.

This book is divided into eight parts. Each part contains selections that bear on the distinction I have made between semantics and pragmatics. I have also included a number of selections that are central to the discussion of pragmatics. Each part is followed by a list of secondary sources which complement the selections that appear in that part.

There are a number of people whom I would like to thank for their help in the preparation of this book: Mary Bruegeman and Carolyn Bruskiewich, for assisting in the collection of the selections; Cynthia Read, my editor at Oxford University Press, for securing permission to reprint several of the selections; Lindsay Burrell and Sean Crawford, for proofreading; and Martin Hahn, Tina Hopkins, Kim Sterenly, and Norman Swartz, for suggesting changes in this Introduction. I would also like to thank the authors of the selections that appear in the book for permission to reprint their work. Lastly, I would like to thank my wife, Lysiane Gagnon, for her patience, understanding, and encouragement.

NOTES

1. A morpheme is the smallest meaningful syntactic unit of a language, for example, the past tense marker 'ed' in English.

2. In what follows I shall give a number of examples of pragmatic facts.

3. Chomsky claims that speakers are born with a great deal of innate knowledge about the form of any possible human language. If Chomsky is right about this, some of the facts that Alice knows are not just facts about English, but about language in general.

4. There are some theorists who argue that (6) (a) is neither true nor false. If this is true, it is another reason to think that (5) and (6) (a) are not synonymous.

5. For a fuller and somewhat different account of the relationship between relevance and implicature, see Sperber and Wilson, 1986.

6. Many theorists would regard this outcome as unacceptable, since they hold that there are insurmountable problems with a theory of meaning, and the only possible semantics for natural languages is a theory of satisfaction (see Quine 1961). If these theorists are right, it means that there is no distinction between pragmatics and semantics for natural languages.

REFERENCES

Grice, H. P. (1968). "Utterer's Meaning, Sentence-Meaning, and Word-Meaning." In J. Searle (ed.), (1971). *The Philosophy of Language.* Oxford: Oxford University Press, 54–70. [Reprinted in this volume, Chapter 4]

Kripke, S. (1977). "Speaker's Reference and Semantic Reference." *Midwest Studies in Philosophy* 2: 255–276. [Reprinted in this volume, Chapter 5]

Kripke, S. (1980). *Naming and Necessity.* Cambridge, Mass.: Harvard University Press.

Montague, R. (1974). *Formal Philosophy,* R. Thomason (ed). New Haven, Conn.: Yale University Press.

Morris, C. W. (1971). "Foundations of the Theory of Signs." In *Writings on the General Theory of Signs.* The Hague: Mouton, 17–74.

Quine, W.V.O. (1961). "Two Dogmas of Empiricism." In *A Logical Point of View,* 2d ed. Cambridge, Mass.: Harvard University Press, 20–46.

Sperber, D., and D. Wilson (1986). *Relevance.* Cambridge, Mass.: Harvard University Press.

FURTHER READING

Bar-Hillel, Y. (ed). (1971). *Pragmatics of Natural Language.* Dordrecht: Reidel.

Cole, P. (ed.). (1978). *Syntax and Semantics.* Vol 9: *Pragmatics.* New York: Academic Press.

Cole, P. (ed.). (1981). *Radical Pragmatics.* New York: Academic Press.

Gazdar, G. (1979). *Pragmatics: Implicature, Presupposition, and Logical Form.* New York: Academic Press.

Kates, C. A. (1980). *Pragmatics and Semantics: An Empiricist Theory.* Ithaca, N.Y.: Cornell University Press.

Leach, G. (1983). *Principles of Pragmatics.* London: Longman.

Levinson, S. C. (1983). *Pragmatics.* Cambridge: Cambridge University Press.

Parret, H., M. Sbisà, and J. Verschueren (eds.). (1981). *Possibilities and Limitations of Pragmatics.* Amsterdam: John Benjamins.

Stalnaker, R. (1972). "Pragmatics." In D. Davidson and G. Harman (eds.), *Semantics of Natural Language.* Dordrecht: Reidel.

II

Speaker Meaning and Speaker Reference

1

Referential/Attributive

KENT BACH

Since Donnellan introduced the distinction between referential and attributive uses of definite descriptions,[1] it has followed a pattern common to many philosophical distinctions. Being intuitively plausible it becomes influential, joining the ranks of accepted philosophical jargon. Meanwhile, people start questioning its initial formulation, either seeking improvements or wondering about its significance. Then critics begin suggesting that the distinction is inherently vague or even downright untenable. All that remains is to explain how people could have fallen for the distinction in the first place. Yet as in falling out of love, despite the breakup the influence continues.

Such has been the history of the referential/attributive (R/A) distinction. Donnellan's account has been severely criticized, as has his claim that the distinction undermines such theories of descriptions as Russell's and Strawson's. Critics like Kripke and Searle have denied this claim by showing the distinction not to be semantic, and have sought to explain it pragmatically.[2] I agree that the distinction is insignificant semantically, but I believe it to be genuine and important. I propose to formulate the distinction in pragmatic terms, by working within the framework of a general theory of speech acts recently developed by Bach and Harnish.[3] This formulation will apply not only to definite descriptions proper but also to the common, and commonly neglected, case of incomplete descriptions.

I. DONNELLAN'S ACCOUNT

Donnellan contrasts referential with attributive uses of descriptions in a variety of ways. Sometimes he emphasizes the role of the description in determining the object being talked about. Sometimes he focusses on the contribution of the description to the statement made in using a sentence containing it. And sometimes what seems to be decisive is how the speaker thinks of the object he is talking about. I have discerned six different ways in which Donnellan attempts to clarify the R/A distinction and will discuss them in turn. None of them does justice to the distinction, but examining them will lead us in the right direction.

Kent Bach, "Referential/Attributive," *Synthese* 49 (1981): 219–244. Copyright © 1981 by D. Reidel Publishing Company. Reprinted by permission of Kluwer Academic Publishers.

First consider Donnellan's initial formulation of the R/A distinction:

A speaker who uses a definite description attributively in an assertion[4] states something about whoever or whatever is the so-and-so. A speaker who
uses a definite description referentially in an assertion, on the other hand, uses the description to enable his audience to pick out whom or what he is
talking about and states something about that person or thing [This volume: 54].[5]

In an attributive use the description determines which individual is being talked about,
namely whatever (uniquely) fits that description. In contrast, when a speaker uses a description referentially "to enable his audience
to pick out whom or what he is talking about,"
he does not intend his audience to rely exclusively on the description, which by itself can
determine only the individual that fits it. If the
role of a description used referentially is to enable the audience to pick out the referent but
not by way of applying uniquely to that individual, just what is this role and how does a
description play it? Understanding the R/A
distinction requires spelling this out precisely.
Unfortunately, Donnellan's glosses on the distinction tend more to cloud it than to clarify it.

(1) Donnellan begins with his example of
"Smith's murderer is insane." If "Smith's
murderer" is used attributively, the statement
made is about whoever satisfies that description, regardless of who the speaker may believe that to be. Indeed, if the speaker has a
mistaken belief about who Smith's murderer
is, the statement is not about who the speaker
thinks it is about. On the other hand, if
"Smith's murderer" is being used referentially, the statement is about whoever the
speaker "has in mind," according to Donnellan, even if that individual, say the man in the
dock, is not Smith's murderer.

Intuitively there does seem to be a distinction here, but does the notion of having someone (or something) in mind really help to explain it? The problem is that a speaker who
uses "Smith's murderer" attributively and has
no beliefs about who Smith's murderer is
could still be said to have Smith's murderer in
mind, albeit only under the description
"Smith's murderer." Although I believe that

there is a fundamental difference between *de
re* and descriptive (*de dicto*) ways of thinking
about an object, I would not deny that thinking of something under a description is having
it in mind, whatever that means. Besides,
Donnellan can make his point without denying this. His point seems to be that a description used attributively determines what the
speaker is talking about by way of applying
uniquely to that individual (even if the
speaker has a false belief about who that is,
thereby having someone else in mind),
whereas in using a description referentially,
one intends to be talking about a certain individual even if that individual does not satisfy the description used. In the latter case the
speaker must think of that individual in some
other way, and it is that other way which determines the individual being talked about. So
the distinction is not between having and not
having the individual in mind but between intending to be talking about a certain individual, who may or may not satisfy the description used, and intending to be talking about
whichever individual satisfies that description.
However, this way of putting the distinction
raises the question of how to characterize the
difference in content between these two sorts
of intentions. Specifically, what is involved in
intending to be talking about a certain individual?

(2) Sometimes Donnellan seems to suggest
that a referential use of a description expresses
a *de re* belief about some individual; used attributively it expresses a *de dicto* belief. He is
not explicit on this point but his contrast between believing something about "someone in
particular" and "someone or other" [This volume: 60] suggests it. Unfortunately, whether
or not he would endorse this point is not clarified by his occasional use of the distinction
between believing of and believing that (or the
parallel distinction between saying of and saying that). The problem here is that the difference between believes-of and believes-that *ascriptions* is independent of the difference
between ascriptions of *de re* and of *de dicto*
beliefs. Sentences both of the form "*a* believes
of the *F* that it is *G*" and of the form "*a* believes that the *F* is *G*" can be used to ascribe
either *de re* or *de dicto* beliefs about the *F*
(also, whether "the *F*" in the latter form oc-

curs transparently or opaquely does not determine whether the belief ascribed is *de re* or *de dicto*). So if we wish to distinguish the two kinds of ascriptions as *de re* and *de dicto,* we should not confuse that distinction with the one between *de re* and *de dicto* beliefs.[6]

Thus, in saying that a referential use of a description is to express a belief about, or say something of, a certain particular individual, if Donnellan means that the belief expressed must be *de re,* his requirement is surely too strong. For then one could use a description referentially only to talk about an individual one was related to in a *de re* way (see note 6). However, as suggested under (1) above, it is enough that the speaker think of the referent in *some* other way, perhaps under some "fallback" description, than under the description he is using. So if he uses "the F" but thinks of the referent under the description "the F'" rather than in a *de re* way, presumably believing that the F' is the F, should it turn out that the F is not the F' he could still be using "the F" referentially to talk about the F', though he is thinking of it descriptively (in a *de dicto* way).

(3) By requiring of a referential use not that the speaker have a *de re* belief about the referent but only that he think of it in some other way, possibly descriptive, than under the description he uses, we are doing justice to Donnellan's occasional comment that only descriptions used attributively "occur essentially" in the speaker's utterance. However, this way of distinguishing attributive from referential uses is too strong, inasmuch as a speaker can use a description attributively even though another description synonymous with that one could have been used instead in making the same statement.

(4) Clearly what is essential to the speaker's statement made using a description attributively is not the description actually used but the individual concept it expresses.[7] If different definite descriptions can express the same individual concept, and surely they can, then any one of them will do. If the speaker is using a description attributively, he is talking about whichever individual fits that or any description he might have used to express the same individual concept. Contrasting an attributive with a referential use of a description in utter-

ing a sentence of the form "The ϕ is ψ," Donnellan remarks, "In the first, if nothing is the ϕ then nothing has been said to be ψ. In the second, the fact that nothing is the ϕ does not have this consequence [This volume: 55].

The trouble with this way of getting at the R/A distinction is that a description can be used attributively even when nothing is the ϕ. For surely one can use a description nonliterally and yet use it attributively, as in "The next turkey to buy a used car from us may not live to regret it." Before supposing that Donnellan was talking about literal uses only, note that he mentions examples of descriptions used referentially but not literally. For instance, one can ask "Is the king in his countinghouse?" [This volume: 57], where "the king" is used to refer to a usurper, and where the speaker does not think, and does not believe his audience thinks, this person to be the king. What Donnellan neglects to mention is that the same description could be used, again nonliterally, attributively to talk about whoever the pretender to the throne may be. The same point applies to a nonliteral but attributive use of "the man drinking a martini." Suppose that the Company prohibits drinking on the job and that a spy is ordered by his boss to go to a certain bar and deliver an envelope to the man drinking a martini. The speaker need not know who this man is—he could be anyone the Company sent—and yet believe, and intend his audience to believe, that the man, whoever he is,[8] will be drinking water in a martini glass.

Even if we restrict our attention to descriptions used literally in utterances of the form "The ϕ is ψ," it is not true that if nothing is the ϕ but "the ϕ" is being used referentially, something may have been *said* to be ψ. The speaker, thinking that a certain individual is the ϕ, may have meant to be talking about that individual, but he did not say, in uttering "The ϕ is ψ," that that individual is ψ. For example, if the speaker says "Smith's murderer is insane," thinking of the man in the dock as Smith's murderer, he is not *saying* that the man in the dock is insane but that Smith's murderer is insane. He is saying this even if it turns out that the man in the dock is not Smith's murderer. He would still have been referring to the man in the dock, whom he was stating (though not explicitly) to be insane, but he would not have been saying that the man in the dock was insane.

(5) Donnellan's point in making the remark considered under (4) is that when a speaker uses a description referentially (but literally), the referent need not fit the description. This is directly tied to our observation that in such a case the speaker thinks of the referent in some other way than under the description used. Only thus can he refer to an individual that the description does not fit, even if he believes the description to fit, for there must be some singular term "d" (possibly but not necessarily a definite description itself) such that he thinks that d is the F. Whereas if the speaker thinks of an individual only under the description used he must be using it attributively, only if he thinks of it in some other way can he use it referentially (not that he must so use it, as Donnellan [This volume: 56] observes). However, it does not follow that if the speaker does not think of the object under the description used, he is using it referentially. Not only does it not follow, it is false, as demonstrated by the case of incomplete definite descriptions used attributively.

A description "the F" is *incomplete* if there are many F's.[9] The descriptions we commonly use, like "the door" and "the doctor," are simply not specific enough to be complete, and even specific ones like "the shortest spy," though probably complete in fact, are not *semantically* complete in the sense of being satisfiable by at most one individual.[10] Those are fairly rare, like "the least prime number" and "the first president of Zimbabwe." At any rate, for our purposes what matters primarily is the speaker's belief, together with his belief about the hearer's belief (and possibly his belief about the hearer's belief about his belief), that there is no unique F, for what the speaker believes will figure in his communicative intention in using sentences of the form "The F is G." Nevertheless, it will be convenient to refer to such descriptions simply as incomplete, since most of the descriptions we use are either obviously complete or obviously incomplete to both parties.

Incomplete definite descriptions are characteristically used referentially, as in utterances of sentences like "The car won't start" or "The teacher is late." In such cases the speaker has a specific satisfier of the incomplete description in mind and intends the hearer to take him to be referring to that individual. The hearer recognizes, as intended, that the speaker does not believe exactly one individual to fit the description and proceeds, relying on what is obvious in the context, to identify which F the speaker is referring to. But incomplete definite descriptions can be used attributively as well. If the emcee of a quiz show announces, "The winner gets a trip to Hawaii," he is using "the winner" attributively, since he presumably does not know (and certainly does not intend the audience to think he knows) who the winner will be. Obviously he intends the audience to take the description as elliptical for "the winner of the game about to be played here," and had he used that description, he would have used it attributively. Having not used it, he intended the audience not to figure out which winner he had in mind but how the description he used was to be completed.

The case of incomplete definite descriptions used attributively shows that it is false that if a speaker does not think of the individual his statement is about under the description he uses, he is using the description referentially. One cannot think of an individual under an incomplete description (though of course one can think that a certain individual, thought of in some other way, fits the description), but this does not mean that one must use it referentially, for one could instead intend the audience to complete the description in a certain way, such as "the F in the room," "the F previously mentioned," or something of the form "the F which is G." All that an attributive use of an incomplete description has in common with a referential use is that the speaker's statement is not determined merely by what he says.

The notion of what a speaker says will be important for our account of the R/A distinction. Since it has already come up in our discussion of (4) and (5), a couple of points are in order now. First, what a speaker says, as opposed to what he states, in using a sentence containing a description is the same whether he is using the description referentially or attributively. The R/A distinction is, after all, between uses not senses of definite descriptions, and as Donnellan himself remarks, doubting that the R/A distinction is semantic, "Whether or not a definite description is used referentially or attributively is a function of the speaker's intentions in a particular case" [This volume: 60]. So which way the description is used affects the statement being made, not what is said (in speech act jargon, the illocutionary act, not the locutionary act). Second, as regards incomplete descriptions, though what is stated is not fully determined by what is said whether the description is used referentially or attributively, what is said is determined by the literal meaning of the sentence uttered. What is said in uttering the sentence "The winner gets a trip to Hawaii" is that the winner gets a trip to Hawaii. Of course, that is not what is stated, which is that the winner of the game being played at the time and place of the utterance gets a trip to Hawaii. By distinguishing what a speaker states from what he says, we can extend to incomplete definite descriptions the point made by such critics of Donnellan as Kripke and Searle[11] that the R/A distinction, not being semantic, poses no problem for Russell's theory of descriptions. For even if the speaker says that there is exactly one F and that it is G, as determined by the semantics of "The F is G," that is not what he is stating, except in the case of complete descriptions used attributively.

(6) This point is directly relevant to Donnellan's remark that on Russell's theory "we introduce an element of generality which ought to be absent if what we are doing is referring to some particular thing" [This volume: 62]. That is why Donnellan thinks that referential uses are not amenable to Russell's approach and why he thinks attributive uses do not involve reference at all, except "in a very weak sense." However, even if we accept Donnellan's suggestion that this "element of generality" in the speaker's intention is quite different from a genuinely referential intention, nothing follows about the semantics of sentences containing definite descriptions and no objection is raised to a unitary theory like Russell's. But the difference between these two sorts of intentions will be important for our formulation of the R/A distinction itself, construed not semantically but pragmatically, in terms of speaker's intentions.

So far we have reviewed the various ways in which Donnellan tried to elucidate the R/A distinction. Despite their plausible ring they do not really clarify the distinction, but our examination of them will help us toward a more precise formulation. Searle's recent account will be well worth examining also, but first I wish to sum up our discussion thus far by contrasting the R/A distinction with two others, neither of which it should be confused with. This will set the stage for our later formulation.

The R/A distinction should not be confused with either (a) the distinction between not making explicit and making explicit the description under which one is thinking of the individual one is talking about or (b) that between using a description to express a *de re* attitude about some individual and using it to express a *de dicto* attitude. Rather, the R/A distinction concerns the relation between the description used *or,* if that description is not (believed) complete, between its intended completion and the individual being talked about. If the individual being talked about is determined by way of uniquely fitting the description used or its intended completion, the use is attributive; if the speaker thinks of the individual being talked about under some other description or in some *de re* way *and* intends the hearer to think of the same object even if that object does not uniquely fit the description used (or its completion), the use is referential. In the latter case the hearer need not think of the object being talked about under the description used or its intended completion (since the object might not even fit); rather, the hearer is to exploit the description in some way in order to identify the referent. It is easy to confuse the R/A distinction with the other two. (a) When one uses a description referentially, one does not make (fully) explicit how one thinks of the object. However, the same is true of using an incomplete definite description attributively. (b) And when one uses a description to express a *de re* attitude, one uses it referentially. However, one can use a description referentially without intending to express a *de re* attitude.

II. SEARLE'S ACCOUNT

According to Searle[12] when one uses a (complete) definite description referentially, there are two aspects under which one thinks of the object referred to. The "secondary aspect" is expressed by the description used, but the speaker is prepared to "fall back" on some "primary aspect" [This volume: 125–128]. In contrast, a description used attributively "expresses the primary aspect under which reference is made" [This volume: 126], for here the description determines the object being talked about, its unique satisfier. A description used referentially, however, need not even be true of the referent, and the speaker need not believe it to be. Since it expresses only the secondary aspect, its purpose is not to determine the referent but to enable the hearer to pick out that object. This object, which the speaker thinks of under some primary aspect, must satisfy that aspect if the statement made in using the description is to be able to be true. Searle remarks that whether a speaker is using a description referentially or attributively, the speaker is genuinely referring. Contrary to Donnellan, who claims that to use a description attributively is to refer "in a very weak sense" at best (as noted under (6) above), Searle maintains that there is but one kind of reference involved in the two uses. The difference between the two is the difference between expressing with the description the primary aspect or merely the secondary aspect under which one thinks of the object referred to.

There are three difficulties in Searle's formulation, but none is fatal. By identifying them we can avoid them in our own formulation of the R/A distinction. First, Searle is unclear about the role of the primary aspect, under which the speaker thinks of the object. Most of his discussion suggests that the speaker, in using a description referentially, need not intend the hearer to think of the object under that aspect. Even when he says that "in the referential use of definite descriptions one performs the act of referring to an object as satisfying the primary aspect by way of performing an act of reference expressing a secondary aspect" and adds that "one's communication intentions will succeed if one's hearer grasps the primary intention on the basis of hearing the expression which expresses the secondary intention" [This volume: 125], Searle does not explicitly state that grasping the speaker's "primary intention" requires identifying the primary aspect under which

the speaker thinks of the object or that this intention contains such a requirement, but he does not deny it either. I should think that in using a description referentially one need not intend the hearer to identify the primary aspect under which one thinks of the object. That would reduce a referential use of one description, the one uttered, to an implicit attributive use of another. That is, in uttering a sentence of the form "The F is G," the speaker would be intending merely that there be a certain description "the F'" such that the hearer is to infer that the speaker is making the statement that the F' is G. However, what is really distinctive of a referential use is not that the speaker intend the hearer to identify the primary aspect under which he thinks of the object but that he intend the hearer to identify the object itself. If Searle does not mean to imply that identifying the primary intention requires identifying the primary aspect under which the speaker thinks of the object, he does not say so and does not specify what the identification comes to. Our account will spell out the content of the speaker's primary intention and specify what the hearer's identification of it consists in.

The second problem with Searle's account stems from his neglect of incomplete definite descriptions. When he says that in attributive cases "the expression uttered expresses the primary aspect under which reference is made" and that "speaker meaning and sentence meaning are the same" [This volume: 125], since incomplete descriptions can be used attributively these remarks apply only to complete descriptions (and only if used literally). However, they can be reformulated in terms of the intended completion of the description uttered, for when one uses a sentence containing an incomplete description, its intended completion expresses the primary aspect if it is being used attributively, and the speaker meaning is the same as the meaning of the sentence yielded by replacing the incomplete description used with its intended completion.

The third difficulty, again easily remedied, is that despite holding that referential uses of descriptions involve two acts of referring, one under the secondary aspect and one under the primary aspect, Searle seems to deny that two statements are being made, one associated with each act of referring. For example, he says things like "The content of the statement cannot be expressed by 'Smith's murderer is insane' for the statement can be true even though there is no 'Smith's murderer'" and describes the primary aspect as "that aspect under which reference is made that actually counts in the truth conditions of the statement" [This volume: 125], thereby implying that in using a description referentially, one is making but one statement and that the description used is not part of its content. I agree with Searle that there is such a statement and that it is made indirectly, since the description used expresses the secondary aspect not the primary aspect, but I see no reason to deny that the speaker is not also making a statement directly. Indeed, it is precisely by using "The F is G" to state directly that the F is G that a speaker states indirectly that the object he thinks of under some unexpressed primary aspect is G. Since Searle allows two acts of referring anyway, one under the secondary and one under the primary aspect, he might as well recognize a statement made directly under the secondary aspect expressed by the description used. And if it is objected that this secondary act of referring is associated not with a direct act of stating but merely with the act of saying that the F is G, the obvious reply is that if "the F" is incomplete, not "the F" but rather its completion expresses the secondary aspect. Therefore, the secondary act of referring cannot, if the description used is incomplete, be associated with the act of saying that the F is G.

III. ILLOCUTIONARY ACTS AND EXPRESSING ATTITUDES

Our later formulation of the R/A distinction will be facilitated by exploiting the general theory of speech acts recently proposed by Bach and Harnish.[13] Since the details of that theory will not matter for present purposes, it will suffice to present certain of its key concepts. Some of these are familiar, such as Grice's notion of reflexive intention[14] and Austin's distinction between locutionary, illocutionary, and perlocutionary acts.[15] Indeed, the notion of reflexive intention helps to distinguish illocutionary acts from the other kinds and is required for defining the central notion of this

theory of linguistic communication, that of *expressing* an attitude. Illocutionary acts are themselves categorized by Bach and Harnish in terms of the different attitudes they express.

Grice's notion of reflexive (R-) intention figured in his account of speaker meaning (originally dubbed "non-natural meaning") as uttering something with the intention of producing in the hearer a certain effect by means of recognition of this intention. But what sort of effect? Grice initially thought that the R-intended effect, in the case of a statement, is belief in a certain proposition, but subsequently[16] he took it to be the belief that the speaker has this belief. However, as Searle has observed, either sort of effect is perlocutionary not illocutionary, and acts of meaning (communicating) are illocutionary acts, in which "we succeed in doing what we are trying to do by getting our audience to recognize what we are trying to do," for "the characteristic intended effect of meaning is understanding."[17] As Bach and Harnish put it, the distinctive feature of communicative R-intentions is that "their fulfillment consists in their recognition" (15). Understanding what the speaker means is to recognize the attitude he is expressing, and expressing an attitude is, to generalize Searle's objection to Grice, not a matter of intending the hearer to form that attitude or even to think the speaker has it. After all, the hearer can understand the speaker without adopting any attitude about the proposition expressed and without even believing the speaker to have such an attitude. Rather, "for the speaker to *express* an attitude is for the speaker to R-intend the hearer to take the speaker's utterance as reason to think the speaker has that attitude" (15). Thus, the hearer may have, and the speaker may even realize that he has, independent reason to think the speaker does not have that attitude, so that the speaker does not expect to be taken as having that attitude; nevertheless, the speaker can express that attitude. He can still R-intend the hearer to take his utterance as *a* reason, though hardly as a conclusive reason, to think he has that attitude (57–59, 289–291).

The type of attitude expressed determines the type of illocutionary act being performed, as illustrated in detail by Bach and Harnish's taxonomy (ch. 3). Just to mention the two

simplest cases, making a statement is expressing a belief and making a request is expressing
a desire (that the hearer do a certain thing).[18]
In the sense of "express" specified above, the
speaker can express a belief or a desire that he
does not in fact have and does not intend the
hearer to take him to have; he need merely R-
intend the hearer to take his utterance as reason to think he has that belief or desire. Any
further intentions or effects are perlocutionary.

The speaker's illocutionary act of expressing
an attitude must be distinguished from his locutionary act of saying something. Even if he
is speaking literally, so that if he is expressing
any attitude, that attitude is determined by
what he is saying, still the fact that he is expressing any attitude at all (that he is trying to
communicate) is something the hearer must
infer. For he could be saying something, as in
a rehearsal or a recitation, without trying to
communicate at all. In that case he would not
be expressing any attitude and would not be
performing any illocutionary act. Another reason for distinguishing the locutionary from
the illocutionary act is to allow for nonliteral
utterances.[19] A speaker might utter "Ostriches
can't fly," thereby saying that ostriches can't
fly. If he is expressing any attitude literally, it
is the belief that ostriches can't fly. He could
be making a literal statement to that effect, but
he might not be. Instead, he might be making
a statement nonliterally, perhaps expressing
the belief that cowards make bad pilots.

Since one can perform an illocutionary act
nonliterally without performing another one
literally, the theory of speech acts must recognize the level of the locutionary act, which
provides the hearer with the core of information, determined by the semantics of the sentence used, from which, together with contextual information or what Bach and Harnish
call "mutual contextual beliefs," he is to infer
the speaker's communicative intent, i.e., identify the attitude(s) being expressed. The
"Speech Act Schema" proposed by Bach and
Harnish (chs. 2 & 4) delineates the elements
of the hearer's inference to the speaker's expressed attitude, whether he is expressing it literally and directly, nonliterally, or indirectly.
Relying on the salient information available,
linguistic and otherwise, the hearer seeks a
plausible candidate for the speaker's expressed

attitude, one that serves to explain the speaker's utterance under the circumstances. The
speaker's communicative R-intention is reasonable to the extent that, under the circumstances, it and only it is recognizable by the
hearer.

As will become clear, the case of indirect illocutionary acts is germane to our account of
referential uses of definite descriptions, but let
us for the moment avoid examples containing
descriptions. If a speaker utters "I wonder
what time it is," probably he is indirectly requesting the hearer to tell him the time, doing
so by way of directly stating that he wonders
what time it is. It is part of his R-intention that
the hearer reason that he could not, under the
circumstances, be merely making that statement and that, therefore, he must be performing some further illocutionary act, identifiable
as a request to be told the time. That is, he is
expressing not merely a belief but also,
thereby, a desire. Notice that an indirect act
need not be based on a direct act performed
literally. A speaker might utter "I'm glad
you're playing that music so loud," thereby
saying but not stating that he is glad the hearer
is playing the music very loud. Instead, he is
stating (nonliterally) the opposite, that he is
upset that the hearer is playing the music so
loud and, by way of making this direct but
nonliteral statement, requesting the hearer to
turn down the record player. Whether the indirect illocutionary act is based on a literal or
a nonliteral direct act, the hearer is to identify
it partly on the basis of supposing that under
the circumstances the speaker could not reasonably be thought merely to be performing
the direct act. That is, he is to reason that the
speaker could not be expressing one attitude,
that expressed by the direct act, without also
expressing another.

For our subsequent discussion it should be
noted that the two attitudes expressed when
one performs an indirect illocutionary act by
way of performing a direct one need not be of
different types. Whereas in the above examples, the speaker expressed a desire (made a request) by way of expressing a belief (making a
statement), both attitudes (and acts) could be
of the same type. For instance, in expressing
the belief (making the statement) that it is
raining, the speaker could be expressing the
belief (indirectly making the statement) that

there will be no game today. Similarly, in expressing the desire (requesting) that the hearer answer the door, he could be expressing the desire (requesting indirectly) that he let in Mrs. Jones.

IV. USING DESCRIPTIONS REFERENTIALLY

In uttering a sentence of the form "The F is G," one is saying, regardless of what one is stating, that the F is G. Unless "the F" is (believed) complete and being used attributively, one is not stating (expressing the belief) that the F is G, or at least not merely that. If "the F" is incomplete but used attributively, the speaker R-intends the hearer to identify a certain completion of "the F," call it "the F_c," whereby he is to be taken as stating that the F_c is G. And if he is using "the F" referentially, he thinks of the individual he is talking about in some other way than as "the F" (or as "the F_c") and R-intends to be taken as making a statement about that individual.

Each of these points will be spelled out below. For that purpose I will assume Russell's theory of descriptions to be correct, i.e., that "The F is G" is semantically equivalent to "There is exactly one F and it is G," so that if a speaker says (or states) that the F is G, he is saying (or stating) that there is exactly one F and that it is G. Although I am making this assumption for ease of exposition, I fully endorse Russell's theory as an account of the semantics of sentences containing definite descriptions. I know of no objection to it that cannot be met by distinguishing the semantics of sentences from the pragmatics of using them. In particular, the R/A distinction poses no problem for Russell's theory, as Kripke and Searle have both noted,[20] for it pertains to what the speaker states (if that is the illocutionary act he is performing), not to what he says, as determined by the semantics of what he is uttering. Also, I know of no improvement on Russell's theory. It will be convenient to refer to statements and beliefs that the F is G, where the Russellian analysis specifies their content, as "Russellian" statements and beliefs.

Let us begin with the relatively simple, though comparatively uncommon case of complete descriptions, and later extend our account to incomplete ones. If one utters "The F is G" and is thereby saying that the F is G, if one is speaking literally one is making directly the Russellian statement that the F is G. Even if one is using "the F" referentially, one is still making a Russellian statement— unless "the F" is being used nonliterally, perhaps elliptically for "the seeming F," "the thing/person commonly thought to be F," "the phoney F," or something of this sort when one does not believe or, more to the point, does not expect the hearer to believe that the object one is talking about is F. Our question is what further statement, reflecting one's primary illocutionary intent, is being made beyond the Russellian statement being made literally and directly. What is the content of this further statement, which is being made indirectly, and how is the hearer to identify that content?

If the speaker is using "the F" referentially, he must be thinking of the individual he is talking about in some other way than as the F. Let us represent this other way as the designator "d", which may but need not be a definite description, such that he believes that d is the F (or, if he is using "the F" elliptically for a description like those mentioned above, that d uniquely fits that description). However, he is not *expressing* the belief that d is the F (or that d is G), for that would involve R-intending the hearer to think of the referent as d. As we saw in examining Searle's account earlier, in using "the F" referentially the speaker does not have to R-intend the hearer to identify "d," the primary aspect under which the speaker thinks of the referent (although he might expect the hearer to do this). Rather, he R-intends the hearer to identify the referent d itself, without any specific intention about how the hearer is to think of d or about how the hearer is to think that he the speaker thinks of d. The hearer might think of d as d but he need not. He need think of d merely in some way or other and think that the speaker thinks of d in some way or other. Since the hearer need not, and is not intended to, think of d as d, the most that the hearer need do is think of the right object (namely d), which the speaker is intending, in stating that the F is G, to refer to, and thereby to state (express the belief) to be G.

Although we are talking about how the speaker and the hearer think of the object, there is no requirement that they think of it in a *de re* way. The speaker's way "*d*" of thinking of the object might be an individual concept expressible by a definite description, and the same goes for the hearer's way, call it "*d'*," of thinking of the object. What is required, rather, is that there be some object that the speaker is using "the *F*" to refer to (presumably because it is the *F*), such that it = *d* = *d'*. From this it follows that one cannot *successfully* use a description referentially to refer to nonexistent entity. One could try to use "the man in the moon" referentially ("*d*" might be "the guy Neil Armstrong left behind"), but one could succeed only if there were a man in the moon or at least somebody whom Neil Armstrong left behind. Only then could the hearer think of that individual and suppose the speaker to be thinking of him.

When a speaker uses a complete description referentially in saying that the *F* is *G*, he is making the Russellian statement and expressing the Russellian belief that there is exactly one *F* and that it is *G*, but what further statement is he making and what further belief is he thereby expressing, and how is the hearer to think of their content? As with any indirect illocutionary act, the hearer is R-intended to reason that the speaker could not, under the circumstances, be expressing merely the attitude (in this case a Russellian belief) that he is expressing directly. Suppose the speaker utters "Smith's murderer is insane," thereby saying and stating directly that the murderer of Smith is insane. If he is making this statement in a courtroom in which a crazed-looking defendant is being tried for the murder of Smith, and if this is mutually believed between the speaker and the hearer and there is no mutual belief that the man in the dock is not the murderer, then the speaker can reasonably R-intend the hearer to infer, and the hearer will infer, that there is some way in which the speaker thinks of (who he takes to be) Smith's murderer, such that the speaker is stating (indirectly) of this individual that he is insane. Perhaps the speaker is thinking of him as the man in the dock or as the man waving his arms wildly. However he may be thinking of him, what a successful referential use of "Smith's murderer" requires is that there be

some individual whom the speaker is using the description to refer to and whom the hearer thinks of as the individual being referred to. In general, successful referential use of a complete description requires, if the referent is in fact the *F*, that $(E!x) (Fx = d = d')$, where "*d*" and "*d'*" are the ways in which, respectively, the speaker and the hearer think of the *F*.

What if the individual being referred to by "the *F*" is not the *F* (assume that "the *F*" is being used literally rather than elliptically for some description containing "*F*"), so that the Russellian statement being made directly is either false or fortuitously true because some irrelevant individual is the unique *F* and happens to be *G*? If the speaker thought of the referent only as the *F*, he could not use "the *F*" to refer to something other than the *F*, but of course he would be using it attributively. In using it referentially he must have some other way of thinking of the referent; otherwise, he could not be referring to that object if it was not in fact the *F*. Let us say that this way "*d*" of thinking of the object has *priority* over "the *F*" in determining what the speaker is talking about. What this means is clear by contrast with Donnellan's remark that a description can "be used attributively even though the speaker (and his audience) believes that a certain person or thing fits the description" [This volume: 56], i.e., they have other ways of thinking of the object they take to be the *F*. But here the speaker's statement is merely the direct, Russellian statement that the *F* is *G*. In this case, even though he thinks that *d* is the *F* and even if that were false, his primary statement, the direct, Russellian one, would be unaffected, because "*d*" does not have priority over "the *F*." The only effect, if *d* were not in fact the *F* and something else was, would be that the speaker was not talking about the individual he thought he was talking about. Whatever his collateral belief about the identity of the *F*, he would be talking about the *F*, whatever it may be. But if he is using "the *F*" referentially, so that "*d*" has priority over "the *F*" in determining what his primary statement (here the indirect statement) is about, then he can be stating of *d* that it is *G* despite the fact that his direct statement is not about *d* and might fortuitously be about something else. He could still use "the *F*" to refer to *d* if *d* is the same individual as the one that the hearer, thinking of it under "d'," thinks he is talking about.

We have insisted that it is not part of the speaker's R-intention that the hearer think of d as d or take the speaker to be thinking of d as d. The whole point of using "the F" referentially is to get the hearer to think of the object one is talking about no matter how he does it. The hearer is supposed to exploit the speaker's use of "the F" to figure out which object is being talked about, and that object need not be the F. Referential success requires only that there be such an object d. Now since referential success is necessary for communicative success and that consists in the hearer's identification of the statement being made, how is the hearer to identify the belief expressed in that statement if he need not think of the object it is about as d? The speaker is expressing a belief about d that it is G but the hearer need not identify it *as* the belief that d is G, even though this is the belief being expressed. I suggest that this belief is not being expressed fully and that the content of the statement is not the full content of the belief. The speaker's R-intention is that the hearer take him as expressing not the belief that d is G but merely a belief of d that it is G, however the hearer may think of d or take the speaker to think of d. So the content of the statement is not the content of any particular belief but the common content of all beliefs of d that it is G. It is not a proposition but rather, we might say, the class of propositions about d, however d may be designated in each proposition,[21] that it is G. The hearer understands the statement being made if he takes the utterance as expressing some belief or other of d that it is G. As noted earlier, this belief about d need not be *de re* in any weighty sense, for "d" could be merely a definite description.

It would be a mistake to suppose that the speaker is expressing a belief in a singular proposition, the proposition about d that it is G. Even if there were such propositions,[22] a singular proposition is not the content of the statement made in using a description referentially. For as just remarked, the content of the statement is the common content of *all* beliefs of d that it is G. That they are all true iff d is G does not make them the same belief (beliefs with the same content), for different des-

ignators of d *might* have designated different individuals.

V. INCOMPLETE DEFINITE DESCRIPTIONS

As remarked in our discussion of Donnellan's point (5) above (in section I), incomplete definite descriptions must be reckoned with in any account of the R/A distinction but they pose no special problem for it. The distinction can be formulated in terms of the speaker's R-intended completion of "the F," such that in saying that the F is G he is directly but not literally stating that the F_c is G.[23] If he is using "the F" attributively, that is the only statement he is making, but if he is using it referentially, then there must be some "d" under which he is thinking of some object d such that he is stating indirectly of d that it is G (using "the F" to refer to it).

This straightforward extension of our formulation of the R/A distinction to incomplete descriptions would require no further discussion but for two complications. One concerns the claim that a speaker who believes "the F" to be incomplete is nevertheless saying that the F is G. The objection is that incomplete descriptions should not be given the Russellian treatment and that, therefore, what the speaker is saying is not that the F is G (construed in Russellian fashion, anyway) but something else. The other complication pertains to referential uses of incomplete descriptions. It is not obvious that there must be some R-intended completion of "the F" nor that, therefore, the speaker must be making any direct statement of the form "The F_c is G." Perhaps his primary statement, of d that it is G, can be made directly (though not literally), with "the F" being used to refer to d without the help of any completion that the hearer is R-intended to recognize. If this possibility is genuine, then it might seem that sentences containing incomplete descriptions require not Russellian but demonstrative semantic treatment. I believe this possibility is not only genuine but commonly realized, but I wish to show that no special semantic treatment is needed to account for it.

Unless a description is semantically complete, such that it could not be satisfied by more than one individual, that it is complete is not a semantic fact. There is no difference in kind regarding the semantic contributions to the sentences in which they occur between "the man who has crossed continents walking backwards" and "the table." If there were such a difference, then presumably if many men did what Pleni Wingo did and if there existed but a single table, the two descriptions would receive reverse semantic treatment. For this reason alone, I believe that incomplete definite descriptions deserve the same semantic treatment as complete ones—the difference between them is not semantic. And yet it might be objected that when one utters a sentence like "The table is bare," one is not saying that there is exactly one table and it is bare. The obvious reply is that this is not what is being stated, because the sentence is not being used literally, but it is what is being said. What is being said is determined by the semantics of the sentence used, whereas what is being stated is determined by the communicative intention of the speaker in using it. Since no one thinks there to be but one table, no one would use the sentence literally.

It might be objected further, however, that something must be wrong with any semantic account of a sentence if, given our beliefs, we never use it literally. Surely, it might be insisted, every sentence must have a literal use. Of course every sentence *can* be used literally but any sentence which is obviously false, which no one would even believe anyone else to believe, is a sentence that if used at all would not be used literally. For example, if someone uttered "Mice are bigger than elephants," he could hardly expect to be taken literally; instead, he might be stating nonliterally that small people have more character than large people. More to the present point, there are many sentences which are almost always used nonliterally as elliptical for other sentences. For example, "Ed doesn't look tired, he is tired" would likely be used with a suppressed "merely" before "look" to be inferred by the hearer, since the speaker would not be stating that Ed does not look tired but is tired anyway. Similarly, if I say "I drink only Scotch," I would be stating not that I drink nothing but Scotch but merely that the only liquor I drink is Scotch (I could state this even by uttering "I only drink Scotch," which

taken literally would mean that I do nothing else in life but drink Scotch). The phenomenon of elliptical speech is commonplace; indeed, it often seems stilted not to suppress words that can easily be inferred as expressing part of what one means, as opposed to what the uttered sentence means.[24] Using incomplete definite descriptions elliptically for their R-intended completions is just another case of this familiar phenomenon.

At this point the last-ditch objection to a Russellian treatment of incomplete descriptions might be that sometimes there is no identifiable completion of the description used. This is why Kripke suspects that Russell's theory "ultimately fails" and conjectures that they should be treated as demonstrative descriptions like "that table."[25] But the absence of an R-intended completion of a description like "the table" in a particular use requires no such demonstrative reading, countenance of which would exemplify what Kripke himself deplores as "the lazy man's approach in philosophy to posit ambiguities when in trouble."[26] All that the absence of an R-intended completion shows is that the speaker, in using a sentence like "The table is bare," is not making any direct Russellian statement involving some completion of "the table." Instead, he is using "the table" referentially in uttering "The table is bare" to make his statement about a certain individual, presumably a table, that it is bare. The act of referring is achieved either ostensively, if there is some one table at hand, or anaphorically, if a certain table were already under discussion. Notice that the demonstrative treatment, even if not symptomatic of semantic laziness, cannot account for these referential uses anyway. For whatever the details of such a treatment, surely the sentence "This table is bare" cannot be true in a given context of utterance if the object referred to is not in fact a table. And yet one can use "the table" referentially (or "this table") to refer to a certain object and make a statement about it (like "The table is bare") even if it is not in fact a table but, say, a trunk. The unitary Russellian treatment of incomplete descriptions has no trouble handling such cases, since a speaker who uses "the table" referentially in making a statement of a certain object that it is bare is not, on our account, making his statement literally anyway.

Thus, the R/A distinction applies to incomplete definite descriptions as well as to complete ones, and neither the distinction itself nor the existence of incomplete descriptions poses any problem for Russell's theory. Speakers (and hearers) are unlikely to mistake incomplete descriptions for complete ones and so are likely to use sentences containing them nonliterally, in which case what is stated is different from what is said. The distinction between illocutionary and locutionary acts is required by the theory of speech acts generally, and whereas Russell's theory applies to the contents of locutionary acts, the R/A distinction applies to the contents of illocutionary acts (statements, in the case we have focussed on). When one uses an incomplete description attributively, there is some completion one R-intends the hearer to identify so as to recognize that one is stating not that the F is G but that the F_c is G. When one uses an incomplete description referentially, there may but need not be an R-intended completion. Whether one is using it referentially or attributively, one's statement is being made nonliterally and so there is no reason to suppose that Russell's theory should account for its content. That theory concerns merely the semantic content of the sentence being used to make the statement.

VI. LOOSE ENDS: NEAR MISSES, MISFITS, AND FALLBACKS

Our examination of the R/A distinction would not be complete without mention of these three topics. First there is the case of attributive "near misses" which Donnellan mentions in connection with his point that referential uses can succeed even when the description does not fit the referent.[27] Suppose one utters "Smith's murderer is insane" without realizing that Smith died not from the assault but from heart failure. Donnellan concedes that a true statement was made, not about Smith's murderer but about Smith's assailant, but denies that "Smith's murderer" was used referentially, even though its use seems to fit his account of referential uses. Donnellan points out that although the speaker was prepared to fall back on "Smith's assailant," close in meaning to the description

used, the speaker did not have anyone in particular in mind. He was not aiming at a "particular target," says Donnellan, but at "some target or other." I do not know what it is to aim at some target or other, but I take it that Donnellan's point is that the speaker had no individual in mind but rather some property, which the description used did not quite express. So if a true statement was made using "Smith's murderer is insane," it was not made quite literally. However, I would deny that a true statement was made at all. Not realizing how Smith died, the speaker made a false statement. Apprised of the facts, he might say, "What I meant was that Smith's assailant is insane," but *that* would not be literally true. Given his ignorance, he meant what he said. Had he known how Smith died, he would have said—and meant—that Smith's assailant was insane.

Referential uses can succeed even when the description does not fit the referent, but this is not to deny that the speaker is saying and thereby directly stating that the F is G in making his indirect statement about a certain individual he thinks of as "d." He is making this direct statement even if he does not hold the belief he is expressing but believes that the hearer thinks of d that it is the F, in which case he would be exploiting what he takes to be the hearer's false belief. He is not stating that the F is G only if, taking it to be obvious that he could not mean "the F" literally, he is using it elliptically for some R-intended completion of "the F" or for some other description containing "F" like "the apparent F" or "what people suppose to be the F." The interesting case of misfits is when the speaker is using "the F" literally and does believe that d is the F. Then, in using it referentially he is talking about d even if it is not the F, for relative to his primary statement "d" has priority over "the F." Even though his direct literal statement is false (or fortuitously true) because of the misfit, he can still make an indirect statement, indeed a true statement, of d that it is G. Our account of referential uses sought to explain how this is possible, but some questions remain. What if there is no unique "d" but several ways in which the speaker thinks of the object he is referring to? If it turns out that they do not apply to the same object, what determines which one he is prepared to fall back on, hence which object he is talking about? And why do we not always express the way in which we are thinking about the object we are talking about instead of using a description referentially?

A speaker may have many ways of thinking about the object he is talking about, any one of which he is prepared to fall back on if the object is not in fact the F. There may be no unique "d" under which he thinks of it, but all of these "d_1" through "d_n" have priority over "the F" in his statement. Thus, he believes that $d_1 = \ldots = d_n$ even if he is prepared to give up the belief that $d_1(\ldots d_n) =$ the F. But what if it is false that $d_1 = \ldots = d_n$? The problem seems to be that in such a case not only does the speaker not know what he is talking about, he does not know what he is thinking about! The solution, it seems to me, lies in developing a notion of priority that applies to thoughts rather than to statements. If some of the "d_i" have priority over all the others and all apply to the same individual, then the speaker is talking about and thinking about that individual. Here I will not try to work out a solution to this problem, which is familiar from recent discussions about reference, names, and identifying descriptions.[28] An adequate theory of what it is to think about an individual must solve this problem, explaining how priorities for different designators of what one takes to be the same object are determined. My suspicion is that even relative to the overall beliefs of a given person, these priorities are not absolute but depend on the nature of the reasons that arise for giving up the belief that they all designate the same object. As far as the theory of reference is concerned, we need not solve this problem but

can say that in using a description referentially (or for that matter, in using a name[29] or a pronoun to refer), unless the designators having greatest priority in one's thinking pick out the same object (or only one has greatest priority), one's act of referring cannot succeed, since there is no unique object one is thinking about, much less talking about.

Why do we ever use descriptions referentially rather than make explicit how we are thinking of what we are talking about? For one thing, we may be thinking of it primarily in a *de re* way rather than descriptively. For another, we may be thinking of it indifferently under many descriptions, all of which we take to be satisfied by the same individual. But the main reason is that in trying to communicate we need to use a description that enables the hearer to pick out the individual we are talking about, just as Donnellan observed originally. Just how does not matter so long as it works. If we are thinking of an object in a *de re* way or under various descriptions and believe it to be (or to seem to the hearer to be) the F (or the F_c), we will use "the F" to refer to it because even though "the F" (or "the F_c") does not have priority in our thinking about the object, it is easier for the hearer to identify the object by means of "the F," because the object is visibly or otherwise obviously the F (or the F_c). Our own ways of thinking of the object may have priority for us but might be cumbersome to express and not readily usable by the hearer. As noted, successful reference to an object requires thinking of a certain object. Just what that consists in is, as is customary to say at the end of a paper, a topic for another paper.

NOTES

1. Keith Donnellan, 'Reference and Definite Descriptions,' *Philosophical Review* **75** (1966), 281–304. [Reprinted in this volume, Chapter 3]

2. Saul Kripke, 'Speaker's Reference and Semantic Reference,' *Midwest Studies in Philosophy* II (1977), pp. 255–276 [Reprinted in this volume, Chapter 5]; John Searle, 'Referential and Attributive,' in his *Expression and Meaning,* Cambridge University Press, Cambridge, England, 1979, pp. 137–161. [Reprinted in this volume, Chapter 6]

3. Kent Bach and Robert M. Harnish, *Linguistic Communication and Speech Acts,* MIT Press, Cambridge, Mass., 1979.

4. As Donnellan notes, the distinction applies to speech acts generally, but he focusses for ease of exposition on statements, as will we.

5. All references in this section are to Donnellan, *op. cit.*

6. The *de re/de dicto* distinction for ascriptions should not lead one to think that there is no such distinction for beliefs themselves, contrary to Searle, *op. cit.* [This volume: 106–108] and Daniel Dennett, 'Beyond Belief,' in Andrew Woodfield, ed., *Thought and Object,* Oxford University Press, Oxford, 1982. A powerful case for it has been made by Tyler Burge 'Belief *De Re,' Journal of Philosophy* **74** (1977), 338–362. I attempt to formulate it for the central case of perceptual belief in *'De Re* Belief and Methodological Solipsism,' to appear in Woodfield's volume. Here the following will have to suffice. A belief about an object *d* is *de dicto* just in case the content of the belief is of the form, "The *F* is . . . ," and *d* is the unique *F*. A belief about *d* is *de re* only if the subject element of content in the belief is suitably related causally to *d*. In the above paper I focus on the case in which this element is a percept of *d*. Notice that nothing in this distinction between beliefs says anything about the form of their ascription.

7. This point is made by Brian Loar, 'The Semantics of Singular Terms,' *Philosophical Studies* **30** (1976), 353–377, who suggests further, but without full explanation, that attributive uses are "generalizing" while referential uses are "identifying."

8. As is pointed out by Searle, *op. cit.* [This volume: 104–105], there is little to be gained from Donnellan's suggestion that only attributive uses take "whoever" (or "whatever") clauses, whose applicability depends not on how the description is used but on contextually relevant interests. So nothing weighty should be inferred by our use of such a clause here and occasionally later.

9. Sometimes these definite descriptions are called "improper" or "indefinite definite descriptions."

10. It will be important later to realize that except for semantically complete descriptions, whether or not a description is complete is not a semantic question but a factual one.

11. Kripke, *op. cit.* [This volume: 85–90] and Searle, *op. cit.* [This volume: 108].

12. All references in this section are to Searle, *op. cit.*

13. *Op. cit.* All references to Bach and Harnish in this section are to this work.

14. H. P. Grice, 'Meaning,' *Philosophical Review* **66** (1957), 377–388.

15. J. L. Austin, *How to do Things with Words,* Harvard University Press, Cambridge, Mass., 1962.

16. H. P. Grice, 'Utterer's Meaning and Intentions,' *Philosophical Review* **78** (1969), 147–177.

17. John Searle, *Speech Acts,* Cambridge University Press, Cambridge, England, 1969, p. 47.

18. Bach and Harnish specify further that in making a statement one also expresses the intention that the hearer have the belief expressed (42) and that in making a request one also expresses the intention that the hearer perform the desired action at least partly because of the desire (47), but these further conditions will not affect the present discussion.

19. For both reasons Searle's rejection of the locutionary act is unwarranted. See his 'Austin on Locutionary and Illocutionary Acts,' *Philosophical Review* **77** (1968), 405–424.

20. Kripke, *op. cit.* [This volume: 85–90] and Searle, 'Referential and Attributive' [This volume: 108].

Another apparent threat to Russell's theory is the case of definite descriptions being used anaphorically, as in "A philosopher/Heidegger objected vociferously. The philosopher complained that his theory was completely misunderstood." In my view, the relation between "the philosopher" and "A philosopher" (or "Heidegger") is not grammatical but pragmatic; it is being used elliptically for "the philosopher just mentioned" and falls under our general treatment of incomplete definite descriptions. Now consider "Swifty suggested stealing a car and using the car to make their getaway." Here "the car" is not being used elliptically for "the car just mentioned," inasmuch as no car was just mentioned, but for "the car they would steal" (whichever car it might turn out to be). Again we have a case of using an incomplete description elliptically, but this time there is a different R-intended completion.

21. This should be qualified for the case of *de re* beliefs, since they are not propositional, as Burge, *op. cit.,* has shown. Subsequent critics of *de re* belief, such as Dennett, *op. cit.,* seem not to have appreciated this fundamental point. I offer a nonpropositional account of the contents of perceptual beliefs in my *'De Re* Belief and Methodological Solipsism.'

22. If propositions are contents of thoughts, there are not, as deftly shown by Stephen Schiffer, 'The Basis of Reference,' *Erkenntnis* **13** (1978), 171–206, because the contents of thoughts of objects must include modes of presentation. In *'De Re* Belief and Methodological Solipsism' I argue that this does not lead to Schiffer's conclusion that there are no irreducibly *de re* beliefs about physical objects (other than oneself).

23. This and many of the following points apply also to nonliteral uses of "the *F*" as elliptical for some description containing "*F*."

24. Many kinds of sentences ordinarily used nonliterally or indirectly, including those used elliptically for others, are discussed in Bach and Harnish, *op. cit.*, chs. 9 and 10. They show how these cases can be handled neatly in pragmatic terms, without the theoretical contortions displayed in semantic treatments.

25. Kripke, *op. cit.* [This volume: 77, 90]. Christopher Peacocke supposes that definite descriptions have demonstrative readings, in 'Proper Names, Reference, and Rigid Designation,' Simon Blackburn, ed., *Meaning, Reference, and Necessity,* Cambridge University Press, Cambridge, England, 1975, pp. 109–132.

26. Kripke, *op. cit.* [This volume: 88].

27. 'Putting Humpty Dumpty Together Again,' *Philosphical Review* **77** (1968), 209.

28. Warren Ingber has pointed out that most of this discussion, regardless of which side is taken, has assumed that a user of a name (which allegedly must have descriptive backing) must have that descriptive backing in mind at the time. See his 'The Descriptional View of Referring: Its Problems and Prospects,' *Journal of Philosophy* **76** (1979), 725–738. I am making no such assumption here but recognize the need for an account of priority in thought that does not require this assumption.

29. In my view, following Loar's suggestion, *op. cit.,* p. 370, a name "*N*" is semantically equivalent to the often incomplete definite description "the bearer of '*N*'." In 'What's in a Name,' *Australasian Journal of Philosphy* **59** (1981), 371–385, I argue that the seeming rigidity of names is due to the referentiality of our implicit uses of such descriptions.

2

Implicature, Explicature, and Truth-Theoretic Semantics

ROBYN CARSTON

1 INTRODUCTION

Pragmatists have given much attention to what an utterance can convey implicitly since Grice brought it to their attention in his work on conversational implicature. Equally important, however, is the proposition explicitly expressed by the utterance of a linguistic expression, what is said, in Grice's terms, although this has been given only passing acknowledgement. Since what is said (the explicit) and what is implicated (the implicit) exhaust the (propositional) significance of the utterance, we are unlikely to have a coherent notion of the latter without consideration of the former.

In this chapter I consider the problem of distinguishing the proposition expressed (henceforth called the explicature[1]) from those implicated (implicatures). It might seem that there is no particular problem; after all, Grice and almost all those following him have assumed the explicature is the result of accessing the conventional sense of the linguistic form used plus assignment of referents to referring expressions and, occasionally, disambiguation of those words or phrases which have more

than one sense. As an initial indication that matters might not be so straightforward let us consider B's utterance in (1):

(1) A: How is Jane feeling after her first year at university?
    B: She didn't get enough units and can't continue

Let us suppose that (part at least of) A's interpretation of B's utterance is: 'Jane didn't pass enough university course units to qualify for admission to second year study, and, as a result, Jane cannot continue with university study. Jane is not feeling at all happy about this.' There are various vaguenesses and ambiguities left in this expression of the interpretation; this is inevitable in any natural language expression of an interpretation (which is itself a set of mental representations). I intend it merely to suggest the sort of interpretation A might reasonably give to this utterance. The question then is which aspects of this interpretation are explicitly expressed (that is, part of the explicature) and which are implicit (implicated)? The disambiguation of 'get' and 'units' and the referent assignment to 'she' are surely part of the explicit content, while the assumption that Jane isn't feeling happy is surely implicit. But what about 'to qualify for admission to second year study', and 'with university study' which enrich and complete the two clauses of the conjunction, and the 'as a result', linking the two conjuncts. Are these part of what is explicated or part of what is implicated? Since they are not given linguistically, one might think they must be implicated, but then what is the explicature of the utterance? It must be 'Jane didn't pass enough university course units and Jane cannot continue (something??)'. It's not clear that this constitutes a propositional form,[2] that is, it isn't possible to specify what conditions in the world must obtain for it to be true. The same difficulty applies to the implicated bits of meaning—they are nonpropositional on their own and need to be embedded in some other representation in order to be truth evaluable. What could this representation be? The best candidate would seem to be the complete form 'Jane didn't pass enough university course units to qualify for second year study', etc. But, if so, either the utterance has no explicature at all or the explicit content is duplicated by or contained within an implicature of the utterance.

I try to establish criteria for distinguishing explicature and implicature so that such apparent enigmas as the above may be resolved. On the one hand, I suggest a criterion of functional independence of explicatures, which ensures that what counts as an explicature isn't arbitrarily confined to linguistic sense plus reference assignment and disambiguation. On the other hand, we need constraints on the process of enrichment of the linguistic sense in building the explicature of the utterance, to ensure that the explicature is not overextended so as to include information properly understood as implicit. However, while it is instructive to consider such criteria, they might well be seen as rather superficial, descriptive principles, if not *ad hoc*. It would be more satisfying to find that they are consequences of some more explanatory psychological principle or principles. This is indeed so; they follow from a single principle directing utterance interpretation, the principle of relevance, which is itself embedded in a general theory of human cognition and communica-

tion, the relevance theory of Sperber & Wilson (1986);[3] so they need not be separately stated. In the light of the relevance-theoretic framework I reconsider some examples standardly treated as generalised conversational implicatures and show them instead to be cases of explicature. One nice outcome of this reanalysis is that a previously intractable problem for the semantics/pragmatics distinction dissolves, having been caused by the erroneous implicature analysis. And, finally, this work brings into high relief the mistaken assumption of many truth-theoretic semanticists that the proper domain of truth conditional semantics is natural language sentences, rather than mental language sentences. A distinction must be made between linguistic semantics and truth-theoretic semantics.

2 IMPLICATURES

Let's start with conversational implicature, which is what has galvanised work in the new field of pragmatics. Grice established the idea first by setting up a few compelling examples rather than by attempting to define the notion. One of these is given in (2) in the rather informal way that he gave it:

(2) A: Smith doesn't seem to have a girlfriend these days
    B: He's been paying a lot of visits to New York lately

B implicates that Smith has, or may have, a girlfriend in New York, an assumption he must be taken to believe in order to preserve the assumption that he is observing the maxim of relation 'Be relevant' (Grice 1975 [This volume: 311]). This example seems clear since, whatever problems we might have in clarifying the notion of explicature, we surely don't think that the assumption that Smith has a girlfriend in New York is explicitly conveyed by B's utterance. That message is conveyed implicitly, indirectly, and is clearly dependent on the particular context which includes A's preceding utterance. If the context were different, say A's preceding utterance had been 'I believe Smith's looking for a new job', then this implicit message would not be conveyed by B's utterance. This property of cancellability without creating contradiction is one of the characteristics of implicature to which Grice gives particular emphasis.

A second important property is the calculability of implicatures, that is, something isn't an implicature if it's not possible to give an account of a reasoned derivation of it based on the assumption that the speaker is observing pragmatic principles. Sperber & Wilson (1986) have developed an account of the non-demonstrative inference processes involved in the derivation of implicatures. These processes will not be explained here but one example will indicate what has to be explained:

(3) A: Have you read Susan's book?
B: I don't read autobiographies
implicated premise: Susan's book is an autobiography
implicated conclusion: B hasn't read Susan's book

A similar distinction can be made for (2):

implicated premise: If Smith's been paying a lot of visits to New York lately he's probably got a girlfriend there.
implicated conclusion: Smith's probably got a girlfriend in New York.

There are two kinds of implicature involved in the derivations: implicated premises and implicated conclusions. Once the implicated premise has been recovered, the conclusion follows by a straightforward deductive inference rule, taking the implicated premise and the explicature of the utterance as input. The real work lies in accounting for the recovery of the implicated premise in terms of a non-deductive process of hypothesis formation and confirmation.[4]

The obvious but important point here is that the explicature is distinct from the implicatures of the utterance; they do not overlap in content. In (3) the truth conditions of 'Susan's book is an autobiography' are independent of the truth conditions of 'B doesn't read autobiographies'. Implicatures have distinct propositional forms (see note 2 of this chapter) with their own truth conditions and they function independently of the explicature as the premises and conclusions of arguments. So we have a further property of any assumption conveyed by an utterance that we would want to call an implicature: as well as cancellability (without contradiction) and calculability, there is the independent functioning of these

forms in the inferences involved in deriving the full import of an utterance. Any such requirement on implicatures naturally places an identical requirement on the explicatures of the utterance. They too are assumptions which occupy independent roles in the mental life of the hearer (and no doubt of the speaker as well): they must function as autonomous premises in inferential interactions with other assumptions and must be stored in memory as separate assumptions. In fact this is the crucial property, since cancellability and calculability are properties of any and all aspects of utterance meaning which are derived pragmatically rather than via a process of linguistic decoding. Thus the results of disambiguation and reference assignment, which are standardly acknowledged as involved in establishing the explicature of an utterance, are also cancellable and calculable. This functional autonomy property decides in favour of extending the explicature of (1) to include the explanation of what Jane didn't get enough units for and what she cannot continue, since otherwise the explicature is entailed by the implicature and thus is redundant, playing no independent role in inference. This third property proves decisive later when we face problem cases, one of which is exemplified by the casual connection between the conjuncts in (1).[5] However, in the end, this property is no more than a useful heuristic, as we shall see in section 5.

Having introduced the pragmatic maxims and the notion of conversational implicature by using these highly context-dependent cases (particularised conversational implicatures), Grice went on to consider the group he calls generalised conversational implicatures. While particularised implicatures are 'carried by saying that p on a particular occasion in virtue of special features of the context,' generalised implicatures are those 'normally carried by saying that p' no matter what the context is (Grice 1975 [This volume: 313]). A set of familiar instances of these, some of which will be reconsidered in this paper, is given in (4)–(9). In each case (a) is the sentence uttered by the speaker and (b), or (b) and (c) in (9), is the generalised conversational implicature which would be standardly conveyed by an utterance of the sentence.

(4) a. She gave him her key *and* he opened the door

b. She gave him her key and then he opened the door

(5) a. Mr Jones has been insulted *and* he's going to resign
b. Mr Jones has been insulted and as a result he's going to resign

(6) a. Mrs Smith has *three* children
b. Mrs Smith has no more than three children

(7) a. *Some* of the students passed the exam
b. Not all of the students passed the exam

(8) a. She's a *competent* pianist
b. She's not a brilliant pianist

(9) a. Bill is ill *or* he's working at home
b. Bill isn't both ill and working at home
c. The speaker doesn't know whether or not Bill is ill

Grice was interested in a pragmatic explanation for these aspects of meaning as a counter to the prevailing tendency at the time to postulate a large number of distinct but related senses for a word, multiple ambiguities. Given the notion of generalised conversational implicature he could maintain that the semantics of natural language *and* is identical with logical conjunction.

3 *AND*

Let us first remove the lexical ambiguity view from the debate on the appropriate treatment of these *and* cases by quickly running through some evidence against it. Firstly, if one is going to go for ambiguity, then *and* is going to be many more than three ways ambiguous and some of these ways are actually going to contradict one another:

(10) a. Mary was in the kitchen and she was listening to the radio
b. He fell into a deep sleep and dreamed that he was flying
c. We investigated the problem and it was far more complex than expected

If we consider the examples in (10) together with the two we already have in (4) and (5) we find three different temporal notions: successivity in (4), simultaneity in (10a) and some sort of temporal containment in (10b). Then in (10c) there is some sort of resultant sense as there is in (5), but they are different: in (5) the one event is a cause of the other or at least

gives a reason for the other. But in (10c) the fact that the problem proved far more complex than expected isn't caused by our investigating it, and our investigating it isn't a reason for its being more complex than expected. The more such examples one looks at, the less plausible it seems that what we have here are a range of subtly different meanings of the word *and*. Rather, these meanings are the result of the way our minds organise information into connected scenarios or scripts, making a variety of connections amongst events and states of affairs in the world (that variety doubtless determined by innate constraints on our powers of conceptualisation). So we relate events temporally, causally and for that matter spatially (in (10a), for example, we naturally assume that the listening of the radio was going on in the kitchen) whenever it seems reasonable to do so. It seems that this must be the outcome of general properties of the mind rather than the meaning of *and*, since if we take out all the *and*s in the examples and put in instead a full-stop or a pause, we find ourselves making exactly the same temporal and causal connections.

This strongly indicates that the account of the temporal, etc., connotations be a pragmatic one. Grice has given such an account explicitly for the temporal case invoking the submaxim, 'Be orderly', of the general maxim of Manner, 'Be perspicuous'. He says '. . . if what one is engaged upon is a narrative (if one is talking about events), then the most orderly manner for a narration of events is an order that corresponds to the order in which they took place. So the meaning of the expression "He took off his trousers and he got into bed" and the corresponding expression with a logician's constant "&" would be exactly the same' (Grice 1981:186). That is, both acquire, by the act of utterance, the implication that the event related in the first conjunct took place before that related in the second one. Grice does not discuss the further causal sense of examples such as (5) and (1) and it's less easy to see how the explanation would go using his maxims. A co-operative speaker should not present a hearer with a sequence of events which any normal human being would assume to be causally connected if she does not intend this assumption to be made. A more substantial explanation than this is desirable and is possible with a properly developed principle of relevance (see section 5).

Grice has undoubtedly established a strong case for the pragmatic treatment of these aspects of conveyed meaning; it tends to be assumed that they are therefore implicated. Linguists, such as Gazdar (1979), Horn (1972, 1984) and Levinson (1983), who took up Grice's principles, have written as if any meaning not derived by linguistic decoding must be implicated. However, everyone acknowledges that deriving the explicature depends on reference assignment and disambiguation; as several people have pointed out (Katz 1972, Walker 1975 and Wilson & Sperber 1981), these are processes which are just as dependent on context and pragmatic principles as is the derivation of implicatures. So there simply is not a neat correlation between a semantics/pragmatics distinction and an explicating/implicating distinction. The (tacit) assumption of most pragmatists then is that there IS a small gap between sentence sense and explicature, but that it is entirely filled by disambiguation and reference assignment. Why should this be so? It seems a rather arbitrary and unprincipled assumption and will be shown to be in fact false. Given that the maxims make SOME contribution to determining the explicature, it is an open question how great their contribution is. In particular, given that we are rejecting the semantic ambiguity account of conjoined utterances, it is an open question whether those aspects of their interpretation that are pragmatically determined are explicated or implicated. It seems that an account at either level is possible.

A pragmatic account at the explicature level might go as follows. In determining what the speaker of (4a) has explicated, the hearer must assign a reference to each of the referring expressions, including the past tense *gave* and *opened*. Just as pragmatic principles are employed in ascertaining the referents of *she* and *he*, so they are used in assigning temporal reference. The hearer goes beyond the strict semantic content of the sentence uttered, and on the basis of contextual assumptions and pragmatic principles (say the maxims of relation and manner) recovers from (4a), at the level of explicature, a representation such as (11):

(11) She$_1$ gave him$_2$ [her$_1$ key]$_3$ at t and he$_2$ opened the door at $t + n$ using [the key]$_3$

Now this is a conceptual representation whose properties can be shown only roughly by this index-boosted linguistic representation. The indexed pronouns should be understood as indicating uniquely referring concepts rather than as simply showing coreference; one could replace the pronouns by proper names, say *Mary* and *Bill*, but, although these are more specific referring expressions than pronouns, some further means of indicating the particular Mary and the particular Bill would be necessary. t is some more or less specific time prior to the time of utterance and $t + n$ is some more or less specific time, later than t. The temporal ordering of the events described in conjuncts is thus treated as a by-product of the reference assignment process involved in determining the explicature.

The representation in (11) might reasonably be taken to imply that (4a) contains some linguistic devices referring to instants of time analogous with pronouns that make particular references. Pierre Jacob (personal communication) says that it is not at all clear that the way tensed verbs refer to times is comparable to the way pronouns refer to persons, and that (4a) does not express conjoined singular propositions with respect to times but rather existentially (hence general) conjoined propositions as in (12):

(12) ($\exists t, t'$) (She$_1$ gave him$_2$ [her$_1$ key]$_3$ at t and he$_2$ opened the door at t' with [the key]$_3$ and t precedes t')

It seems to me that this will depend on the particular context of utterance; (12) is the least specific possibility, derived in a context where all that matters is the order of some events. More often, though, hearers will narrow down the time spans to some probable period along the line from the beginning of time to the moment of utterance.

Partee (1973) finds a range of parallels in the use of pronouns and tenses. Discussing the example *I didn't turn off the stove* she says 'When uttered, for instance, halfway down the turnpike, such a sentence does not mean that there exists some time in the past at which I did not turn off the stove or that there exists no time in the past at which I turned off the stove. The sentence clearly refers to a particular time—not a particular instant, most likely, but a definite interval whose identity is generally clear from the extralinguistic context' (Partee 1973:602–3). As she acknowledges in a footnote, the narrowing down to the relevant time is explainable pragmatically, so it is not the sentence that picks out the time interval but the explicature of the utterance. The most reasonable construal of Jacob's suggestion, then, is that it concerns the linguistic sense of the sentence, which should be taken to include these time variables bound by an existential quantifier, that is (12) above without the indices and without the clause specifying temporal ordering, and that it is left to pragmatic considerations whether and to what extent the time span is specified. In this respect the semantics of tense is parallel with that of indefinite pronouns rather than personal pronouns: *Someone has eaten the cake* might be understood as some specific person, say Bill, in some contexts, and as simply indefinite in others. The linguistic device of tense does not prescribe the accessing of particular times but nor does it preclude the possibility. It may well be that neither (11) nor (12) captures this satisfactorily. However, this is a notational problem which arises whether one opts for an explicature or an implicature analysis of temporal connotations and as such does not affect the possibility of an explicature analysis.

Finally, notice that we also understand (4a) as saying that the key *he* used to open the door is the one *she* gave him, although this too goes beyond the linguistically given sense. This is simply the most plausible interpretation to give the second conjunct since the speaker has chosen to conjoin it to the first one. If she hadn't meant us to understand this, she should have supplied the information that another key was used. This completion of sense is similar to that proposed for (1), and is discussed further below.

So once the semantic ambiguity analysis is ruled out there are two pragmatic accounts possible. We need to see if there is any reason for preferring one to the other. Let's return to the traditional implicature account for (4a) and consider what the explicature of the utterance is on such an account. It must be either (11) or (12) minus the specification of $t + n$,

or t', as later than t. Then, assuming that the implicature is a conceptual representation with a propositional form, the explicature is entailed by the implicature. If the implicated assumption is stored in memory the explicated assumption need not be, since all the information given by the latter is also given by the former. Further, whatever role the explicated assumption might play in chains of reasoning the implicated assumption could also play, as well as giving rise to the extra possibilities hinging on its encoding of the temporal ordering. In other words whatever the explicature can do, so can the implicature plus more. The explicature has no function in mental life that can't be played by the implicature. By the criterion of functional independence proposed earlier, the explicature analysis of temporal sequence is favoured. It will shortly be shown that this conclusion is supported by relevance theory predictions too and that it sweeps away a problem that the implicature analysis creates.

The question now arises whether this analysis extends to the causal connotations that often accompany uses of *and*, as in (1) and (5). While some theorists seem to be willing to grant the treatment of the temporal ordering as above they baulk at the further enrichment of explicit content so as to include the causal relation between the events related in the conjuncts. The reason for this is that the former can be seen as a by-product of the reference assignment process which is necessarily involved in deriving the explicature of the utterance. Ambiguities and referring expressions can be seen as instructions given by the grammar to carry out some process of choosing or specifying in order to derive a propositional form. There is no grammatical device in (5) that sets up a further slot to be filled, or that directs any fuller articulation of the relation between the events of the two conjuncts, which might lead to the specification of a causal relation. The assumption that the relation exists is a result of general world knowledge about human feelings and behaviour, mentally represented as scripts about the nature and effects of insults and of resigning from jobs. So it might well be felt that the causal relation is implicated and not part of the explicature. We could dub the assumption guiding this decision the 'linguistic (or grammatical) direction' principle. It should be distinguished from the linguistic encoding of conceptual content. Linguistic direction includes this but also covers cases such as pronouns, tenses, and empty grammatical categories which are indicators delivered by the grammar that some pragmatic work is needed to derive some conceptual content from the context. On this principle, the causal connection is implicated because the grammar does not deliver a relational variable instructing the hearer to find a relevant connection. This is clearly at odds with the prediction made by the criterion of functional independence, which, again, would favour an explicature analysis. Before pronouncing further on this case, which raises more problems than the temporal one, let us retreat a few steps and consider a little more closely what is meant by an explicature and whether explicatures in general respect the linguistic direction principle.

4 EXPLICATURES

As already noted, most pragmatists working in the Gricean framework have adopted as a working principle the view that any pragmatically determined aspect of utterance interpretation, apart from disambiguation and reference assignment, is necessarily an implicature. The explanation for cutting things this way lies with the further assumption that the explicature must be truth-evaluable; so Grice and the Griceans are prepared to let in just whatever is necessary in addition to linguistically determined content to bring the representation up to a complete propositional form, that is, something capable of bearing a truth value. On this basis even the temporal ordering information is not strictly part of the explicature, since a truth-evaluable proposition is derived without it: (4a) can be said to be true provided the two events took place at some time in the past, never mind the order of the events. However, as a consequence of reference assignment it might be countenanced as part of the explicature.

In general the linguistic direction principle and the minimally truth-evaluable criterion coincide, the one reflecting a more linguistic turn of mind, the order a more philosophical;

both assume that the domain of grammar, sentences, and the domain of truth-conditional semantics, propositions, are essentially the same. I want to argue that neither of these is an appropriate principle for a PSYCHOLOGICALLY plausible theory of utterance interpretation, that they give only a sufficient condition for some pragmatically derived meaning to be an aspect of the explicature, not a necessary one, and that the domains of grammar and of truth-conditional semantics are not the same.

As soon as one looks at real utterances, it becomes apparent that pragmatic principles may have much more to do in establishing what has been explicated than just assigning reference and disambiguation. Supplying ellipsed material is an obvious case of underspecification by linguistic meaning, so phrasal or lexical utterances such as *On the table*, *Telephone*, are standardly instantly understood as conveying complete propositions—a large portion of which has clearly been pragmatically derived. It can be argued that this is in line with the truth-evaluability requirement and the linguistic direction requirement, since linguistic decoding might well deliver up a representation such as (13):

(13) s[NP[e] VP[V[e] PP[on the table]]]

thereby directing the supply of further material by pragmatic processing. The completion of (1) could be directed in the same way, if the verb *continue* is subcategorised for a following NP.

For my purposes the more interesting cases are those which have the following three properties: linguistic meaning, reference assignment and disambiguation DO supply a complete (hence truth-evaluable) proposition, the grammar does NOT generate variables instructing further filling in, and yet the proposition is still too underspecified to be taken as the explicature of the utterance:

(14) a. The park is some distance from where I live
     b. It will take us some time to get there

Consider (14a); the logical form of this is existentially quantified over distances and requires just reference fixing (of *I* and *the park*) to be fully propositional, that is, capable of bearing a truth value. It's doubtless generally true that there is a distance (of some length or other) between the speaker's home and the park referred to, but it's very unlikely that that's what a speaker wants to convey on a given occasion of utterance or that that's what a hearer would take her to be explicating. This is what linguistic decoding and reference assignment alone retrieve but it is seldom going to be a claim worth making; it wouldn't tell a hearer anything he didn't already know. If this was all the speaker was saying, she wouldn't be observing pragmatic principles which enjoin relevance and informativeness. The particular proposition expressed by (14a) will depend on the particular context, which must be such that it is worth remarking on the distance. One possibility is that the speaker thinks the hearer is underestimating it, in which case the explicature would be something like 'The park is further away from where I live than you think' or 'The park isn't a walkable distance from my house'.

Philosophers and pragmatists who subscribe to the principles above want to stop at the weakest propositional form with determinate truth conditions, so in the case of (14a) this would simply be the truth that there is a distance between the park and my house, and any other conveyed meaning is an implicature. But what function then does the explicature have in the mental life of the hearer? It is entailed by the implicature: if the park is further away from my house than the hearer had been assuming, it follows that it is some distance or other from my house. When this entailment relation holds between putative implicature and explicature the probability of functional independence of the two propositional forms is very low. What the hearer is going to remember from this utterance is some estimate of the distance involved, not the fact that there is a distance, and any inferences he draws on the basis of the utterance will involve the proposition concerning this amount of distance, rather than the basic proposition concerning the existence of a distance, a truism which has long been an assumption he has subscribed to. So, again in conformity with the functional independence criterion, this more fully specified proposition must be understood as explicated. The same argument applies to (14b). It's difficult to see any justification for a principle along the lines of 'use the maxims just in order to get a min-

imally truth-bearing vehicle'. This is to ignore the nature of communication and of cognition in general in the interests of a formal principle which has absolutely no bearing on human psychology.

As Diane Blakemore has impressed upon me, the building in of extra information of one sort or another is quite pervasive; consider the following examples:

(15) a. He ran to the edge of the cliff and jumped
     b. I went to the exhibition and ran into John
     c. She took the gun, walked into the garden and killed her mother
     d. I had a holiday in Austria and did some cross-country skiing

The interpretation of (15a) in most contexts of utterance will include the understanding that he jumped over the cliff although there's no linguistic expression there telling us this or requiring us to fill in a prepositional phrase. The verb *jump* is not subcategorised for an obligatory following PP. Similarly, in (15b) we would most likely assume that the place where I ran into John was the exhibition, in (15c) that the killing of the mother was with the gun and took place in the garden, and in (15d) that the skiing referred to took place in Austria, although, again, the linguistic content of the utterances does not supply this information or direct its retrieval. The same point can be made regarding the PP *with a key* which is supplied in the interpretation of (4). In each case this is simply the most natural interpretation to give and a speaker who didn't intend this would simply not be observing the maxim of relation. Since the form with the additional prepositional phrase entails the form without in each case, the criterion of functional independence would again choose the enriched form as the explicature of the utterance rather than as an implicature.

It does not seem, then, that the pragmatically derived enrichments of the linguistically given meaning are confined to following instructions delivered by the grammar, such as finding pronominal or temporal referents. Given this, the absence of a linguistic device directing retrieval of a causal relation in (5a) need not deter an enrichment along these lines in determining the explicature of the utterance. Although it is truth-evaluable without our supposing any particular connection between the events, the most natural interpretation, in the vast majority of contexts, is one in which these events are part of a scenario in which they are both temporally and causally connected. We might represent this causal connection as in 16 (which would also of course have to be temporally specified as in (11) or (12) above):

(16) [[Mr Jones]ᵢ has been insulted]ₚ and because of p [he's]ᵢ going to resign

As with (4) there are two possible pragmatic analyses. The cancellability and calculability criteria apply to all pragmatically derived material, whether at the level of explicature or implicature, so cannot help us. The tacitly assumed criteria for determining explicatures (or what is said) do not help either: both the minimal truth-evaluability criterion and the linguistic direction criterion have been shown insufficient to account for a range of cases; fulfilling them places only a lower bound on the process of enrichment. Again the functional independence criterion makes a decision: it dictates that the causally enriched (16) be understood as the explicature, since if it is taken as an implicature of the utterance the explicature is rendered redundant as it is entailed by the implicature. The same line of reasoning applies to the relation between the conjuncts in (1) when it is understood that Susan cannot continue university studies *because* she didn't pass enough course units.[6]

As Kempson (1988) points out, the indexicality of natural language has proved far more extensive than truth-theoretic semanticists originally allowed. The term indexical is usually understood as referring to linguistic expressions whose value is dependent on the context in which they are uttered. As the last few examples show, the recovery of the proposition expressed by the utterance of a linguistic form has an even stronger degree of context-dependence than indexicality; some content supplied by the context receives no direction at all from linguistic expressions.

Sperber & Wilson (1986:182) say that 'an assumption communicated by an utterance U is *explicit* (that is, is an explicature) if and only if it is a development of a logical form encoded by U'. The logical form of the linguistic expression uttered is the semantic representation (or sense) assigned to it by the grammar

and recovered in utterance interpretation by an automatic process of decoding. As we have seen, in a range of examples this logical form is frequently not fully propositional, and a hearer then has the task of completing it to recover the fully propositional form that the speaker intended to convey. While any communicated assumption is either an explicature or an implicature, it is clear that an explicature may be more or less explicit since it is a combination of linguistically encoded and contextually inferred features. There is always a linguistic contribution, but this contribution varies from near total determination of the explicature to a very small role, as shown by the following examples:

(17) a. The sun will rise at 5.25 am on May 15 1990
     b. Susan's performance isn't good enough
     c. She took it
     d. At home
     e. Later

Understanding these requires various amounts of disambiguation, reference assignment, enrichment (e.g. not good enough for what, in (b)) and completion, in accordance with the pragmatic principles. The explicature in (17a) is highly explicit while that in (c) is much less so and (e) even less.[7]

We might worry a little about what constitutes a development of a logical form. A list of allowed developments could be made: reference assignment, disambiguation, specification of vague terms, supplying empty grammatical categories with conceptual content, building in certain relations between events and states. Obviously, though, it would be better if we could find something more explanatory to say than this. The temporal and causal connections standardly derived in interpreting conjunctions such as (4) and (5), which were formerly treated as generalised conversational implicatures, now fall under the definition of explicature. What is to stop all elements of communicated meaning being interpreted as parts of the explicature? Whole further assumptions might be tacked on: for instance, it might be claimed that the explicature of (3) is 'I don't read autobiographies and Susan's book is an autobiography' (referring expressions more fully specified of course). This surely is a development of the logical form of the utterance. In other words, while truth-evaluability sets a lower bound on the process of development there doesn't seem to be an upper bound. We might try setting up constraints, such as prohibition on any development which involves a logical form independent of the original one and so has a range of entailments of its own distinct from those of the original logic form of the utterance. Alternatively, we might exclude any development which is entirely detachable by a logical rule such as *and*-elimination. It is unlikely that these will be foolproof: although 'I don't read autobiographies' and 'Susan's book is an autobiography' do have largely distinct entailments they may have some in common, 'Autobiographies exist' for instance, and in general such a constraint is likely to be too strong. While a development involving adding the proposition 'Susan's book is an autobiography' is detachable by *and*-elimination, it may be argued that the proposed explicature need not be understood as a conjunction: 'I don't read autobiographies of which Susan's book is an instance'. However, playing around any further with these possibilities is unnecessary, since the principle of relevance which drives the interpretation process can be shown to impose the supposed missing upper bound. I turn to that now.

5 THE PRINCIPLE OF RELEVANCE

One of Grice's maxims is the instruction to speakers to 'Be relevant'. He recognised that much work needed to be done to develop this principle; Sperber & Wilson (1986) have done this work. Only the merest indication of their theory can be given here (see note 3 of this chapter).

Utterances are one of a great range of stimuli that impinge on humans; they have the special property of being ostensive, that is, they call attention to themselves in a particular way. Ostensive stimuli make evident to a receiver the intention of the communicator to make it evident that she intends to inform the receiver of something. So an addressee is justified in expecting some significance from ostensive stimuli that he cannot expect from non-ostensive stimuli which he may attend to.

He cannot expect an ostensive stimulus to achieve a certain level of *relevance*.

A phenomenon is said to be relevant to an individual if it has certain cognitive effects for that individual. There are three kinds of such cognitive effects: (1) interaction with assumptions in the individual's mental context to yield new implications (Sperber & Wilson call this *contextual implications*), (2) contradiction of an existing assumption which leads to its being abandoned, and (3) providing additional evidence for an existing assumption and so strengthening the individual's confidence in it. Clearly, then, relevance is a matter of degree: the more cognitive effects a phenomenon has the more relevant it is. This is offset, however, by a factor of processing costs: one doesn't go on endlessly processing a new piece of information, checking through all one's existing assumptions to see if it interacts with them, but abandons the endeavour when the returns threaten not to offset the effort. So there are two parts to defining relevance: the more cognitive effects a phenomenon has the more relevant it is, and the less the effort required to process a phenomenon the more relevant it is.

Utterances, and ostensive stimuli in general, come with a guarantee of *optimal relevance*: a guarantee that the cognitive effects the speaker intends the stimulus to have are sufficiently great to make it worth the hearer's while to process it, and that the stimulus is the least costly in terms of processing effort that the speaker could have chosen to have these effects. Finally, then, the *principle of relevance* states: every act of ostensive communication communicates a guarantee of its own optimal relevance. In comprehending an utterance a hearer must find an interpretation which is *consistent with the principle of relevance*, where this is defined as an interpretation which 'a rational communicator might have expected to be optimally relevant to the addressee' (Sperber & Wilson 1986:166). The first interpretation which the hearer finds to be consistent with the principle of relevance is taken to be the correct one, the one intended by the speaker. Obviously the first interpretation arrived at is the least costly one in terms of processing effort so, provided it has an adequate range of cognitive (or contextual) effects and it could have been intended by the speaker,[8] it is the only interpretation consistent with the principle of relevance. There is always at most one interpretation consistent with the principle of relevance. Sperber & Wilson (1986) show that this single principle, resting on a general theory of relevance, is sufficient to account for all pragmatic aspects of utterance interpretation and that it subsumes Grice's maxims.[9]

Let us consider how this principle might constrain the process of developing logical forms into explicatures so that they are not over enriched, encroaching on the territory of implicature. Firstly, we need some idea of what's involved in incurring processing costs. Linguistic decoding takes variable amounts of processing effort dependent on length and structural complexity of the expressions used. Interpreting an utterance requires the setting up of a context of assumptions within which to assess the cognitive impact of the utterance (some subset of the set of all our pre-existing assumptions and perhaps others constructed on the spot). The processing effort required for this varies from individual to individual and from utterance to utterance, the less accessible the assumptions needed, the more the effort involved in assembling them. The interaction of the context and the explicature involves a variable number of applications of a variable number of inference rules, the more of each the greater the processing costs.

We made the reasonable assumption above that the speaker in uttering (3) was implicating the assumption that Susan's book is an autobiography and the conclusion that she hasn't read it; surely if anything qualifies as implicature these do. But the definition of explicature that we have seems to allow the attachment of these to the logical form of the utterance as part of the development process. It might seem that we need to define the notion *development of a logical form* more closely. However, this is unnecessary. The rule that derives the implicated conclusion is a synthetic one, that is, a rule which takes two separate assumptions as its input, a universal of the form 'All X are Y' (in this case, a property is predicted of all autobiographies) and a singular of the form 'n is X', where n picks out an individual (in this case, a particular autobiogra-

phy). If the explicature had been developed into a conjunction of the enriched logical form and the retrieved assumption that Susan's book is an autobiography, the conjuncts would simply have to be detached by a rule of *and*-elimination for the inference to go through. Nothing would have been gained by this development of the logical form of the utterance and a certain amount of effort would have been expended to no end, that is, the attachment of the assumption immediately followed by its detachment. Since the utterance comes with a guarantee of optimal relevance, no hearer will waste effort in this fashion when the same effects are achievable more economically. Furthermore, a hearer might well go on to draw some conclusions of his own for which the speaker can't be held responsible: for instance, he might be privately of the opinion that people who write autobiographies are egotists and thus conclude that Susan is an egotist. Once again, arriving at this conclusion depends on the independence of the assumption that Susan's book is an autobiography.[10] A wider range of cases is considered in Carston (forthcoming) to demonstrate that the principle of relevance quite generally ensures that redundant overextensions of the explicature do not occur.

Let us consider now the two pragmatic analyses of the temporal connotations of (4a): the one treating (4b) as the explicature of the utterance, the other taking it as an implicated assumption. On an implicature analysis we have a situation in which, schematising, the explicature is 'P & Q' and the implicature is 'P & then Q', that is, the implicature entails the explicature, so that any role that the explicature might have in memory or in reasoning processes could almost certainly be performed by the implicature, which is richer in content. So the principle of functional independence favours taking 'P & then Q' as the explicature of the utterance. The same goes for the causal connotations of (5a): the explicature is either 'P & Q' or 'P & then as a result Q', with the latter favoured by functional independence.

What does the criterion of consistency with the principle of relevance have to say about these cases? It is clearly more economical to derive the single assumption 'P & then Q' rather than both 'P & Q' and 'P & then Q', and whatever contextual effects 'P & Q' gives rise to so will 'P & then Q', as well as having the potential for more. Let us suppose that on a given occasion of utterance the most accessible context for interpreting (4a) is one which contains an assumption of the form 'If Q then R', say 'If he$_2$ opened the door he$_2$ must have seen the dead man' then the conclusion R, 'He$_2$ must have seen the dead man', is derived as a result of *and*-elimination performed on either 'P & Q' or 'P & then Q' with the appropriate detached assumption and the contextual assumption functioning as premises in an application of modus ponens. Let us suppose further that in deriving an adequate range of effects the proposition concerning the sequence of events is crucial, interacting with a contextual assumption of the form 'If P & then Q then S' to give the implication S. In general, whatever constitutes an adequate range of contextual effects, they can be derived entirely from the single assumption 'P & then Q', which is more economical to derive and manipulate than the two assumptions. In fact if 'P & then Q' were understood as an implicated assumption the derivation of S would follow from contextual assumptions alone. Then it would not qualify as a contextual implication since a contextual implication is defined as following from the propositional content of the utterance and the propositional content of the context together, but from neither alone (Sperber & Wilson 1986:107–8). So it would not count as a contextual effect involved in establishing the relevance of the utterance, which, however, it clearly is. So not only does the criterion of consistency with the principle of relevance predict that the explicature of the utterance is 'P & then Q' the relevance-theoretic framework actually precludes an implicature analysis.

The argument for the inclusion of the causal connotations at the level of explicature will run in exactly the same way as will any case in which a putative generalised conversational implicature renders the putative explicature of the utterance functionally inert. Clearly then the guarantee of optimal relevance subsumes the predictions of the earlier functional independence guideline. In all aspects of utterance interpretation considerations of optimal relevance play a vital constraining and enriching role.

6 A PROBLEM SOLVED

McCawley (1981:6–10) points out that a question such as:

(18) Did John get up and fall down?

might be answered either *Yes* or *No* if the hearer knows that John in fact first fell down and then got back up. His choice would depend on whether the speaker is taken to have asked a symmetric-*and* question (Did John perform these two activities?) or a consecutive-*and* question (Did John perform these two activities in that order?), a choice dependent on context. McCawley, by the way, saw this as evidence for a lexical ambiguity at work, since a standard test for ambiguity at that time was to see if a sentence could be said to be simultaneously true and false with regard to exactly the same condition in the world. We are assuming that the semantic ambiguity of *and* is no longer a viable position, and will argue in the final section that this ambiguity test does not work: truth-conditional ambiguity cannot be used to establish the semantic ambiguity of a word, resting as it does on a conflation of natural language sentences with propositional forms. Horn (1984) recognises the pragmatic processing involved in deriving the temporal connotations but, being of the pragmatic = implicature persuasion, says that a negative answer to the question must be construed as taking into account the conversational implicature associated with *and*. But this is an odd sort of thing for the answerer of a question to do. In effect, what Horn is saying is that the hearer answers an implicated question rather than what he takes to be asked at the explicit level. The relevance-theoretic treatment of such a case would of course take the asymmetric conjunction to be the explicature and the answer *No* to be addressed to the question explicitly asked.

Grice (1967) noted a similar problem with the implicature account.[11] On that account, a denial of a conjoined utterance would sometimes apply only to what has been implicated and not to what has been explicated. Taking an adaptation of his example (2), consider the following exchange, where (19a), in context implicates (20):

(19) a. A: Jones has made a lot of visits to New York lately

b. B: No he hasn't

(20) Jones probably has a girlfriend in New York

The question is whether (19b) could be taken to bear, not on the explicit content of (19a), but only on its implicature (20), leaving the truth of (19a) intact. Surely the answer is no. Yet the implicature analysis of conjunctions predicts that denials can sometimes bear only on what is implicated. So consider (21b) and (21c) as replies to (21a), for example:

(21) a. A: She gave him the key and he opened the door
    b. B: No. He opened the door before she gave him the key
    c. B: No. He opened the door and then she gave him the key

On the implicature analysis the denials in (21b) and (21c) would bear not on what has been explicated but on the alleged implicature. Both (21b) and (21c) concede that the two actions occurred, and deny only the alleged implicature that her action preceded his. Again this doesn't seem right. Only the explicature analysis of the temporal connotations, predicted by relevance theory, satisfies the intuition that these cases of denials and answers to questions do not refer to implicatures alone, totally ignoring explicit content, and it does so without having to attribute an unwarranted ambiguity to the lexical item *and*.

However, although the point holds for these particular examples it may well be that when we take a detailed look at denials there are instances where it is the implicature of an utterance that has the main relevance and that a denial response generally refers to the most highly relevant propositional form conveyed by the utterance.[12] The strongest evidence against an implicature analysis, usually presented by those who favour a lexical ambiguity, takes a slightly different form. It seems that the alleged implicatures of conjoined utterances fall within the scope of such logical operators as negation, disjunction, comparison and conditionals. Even advocates of the implicature approach, including Grice, have seen such cases as very worrying:

(22) a. If the old king died of a heart attack and a republic was declared Sam will be happy, but if a republic was declared and the old

king died of a heart attack Sam will be unhappy

(adapted from Cohen 1971)

b. He didn't steal some money and go to the bank; he went to the bank and stole some money

(adapted from Gazdar 1980)

c. It's better to meet the love of your life and get married than to get married and meet the love of your life

(D. Wilson)

d. Either she became an alcoholic and her husband left her or he left her and she became an alcoholic; I'm not sure which

As Cohen (1971) has pointed out, if *and* is simply truth-functional and the temporal and causal connotations are captured by implicatures, then (22a) and (22b) should be contradictory at the level of explicit content (instantiating 'If P then Q but if P then not Q', and 'Not P; P' respectively).[13] Similarly, (22c) should be a nonsensical (equivalent to 'It's better to P than P') and (22d) redundant (equivalent to 'either P or P'). However, these examples are not understood as contradictory or redundant. Those who wish to maintain an implicature analysis have to say that the alleged temporal and causal implicatures contribute to the truth conditions of the utterance in which they occur, that is, to the explicit content (what is said) since they follow Grice in the view that the explicature is another term for the truth-conditional content of the utterance. This conclusion sits uneasily in his general framework, where the sole determinants of explicit content are supposed to be the sense of the sentence uttered, disambiguation and reference assignment. It looks as if the implicaturist is driving himself into a corner in which the only position left to him is that the implicatures of conjoined subordinate clauses contribute to the meaning of *sentences*—not just utterances—in which they occur. This looks like a *reductio ad absurdum* of the implicature analysis.

Pragmatists generally see only two ways in which to try to cope with these facts: either to reject the implicature analysis and to find a semantic solution, the ambiguity one or Cohen's (1971) boosted semantic account (see note 13 of this chapter); or to assume that, since the implicature analysis MUST be right, some solution to the problems it raises has to be sought. However, as this chapter shows, there is a third option: a pragmatic account in which the temporal and causal connotations of conjoined utterances, along with many other aspects of nonlinguistically determined meaning, are recovered at the level of explicit content. Given this position the problems we have been contemplating disappear: if these connotations are determined at the level of explicature, then it is not surprising to find them falling within the scope of denials, negation, conditionals, disjunctions, etc., and contributing to the truth conditions of complex utterances in which they occur. Happily, as we've seen, this explicature position is independently supported and predicted by the pragmatic principles of relevance theory.

7 GENERALISED QUANTITY IMPLICATURES?

I have concentrated in this paper on a very small range of examples but the point is intended to be quite general. Pragmatic processing makes a far greater contribution to determining explicit content than has generally been assumed. One consequence for pragmatics is that it should not automatically be assumed that every pragmatically determined aspect of utterance meaning is an implicature. Many examples of generalised conversational implicature should be reconsidered in the light of relevance theory; there is not space here to deal adequately with examples (6)–(9), though a brief discussion will indicate the direction a full analysis would take.[14] The standard approach is represented by Horn (1972) who has a notion of scales of predicates arranged in order by degree of informativeness or semantic strength:

(23) a. ⟨ . . . few, some, many, most, all⟩
     b. ⟨ . . . , three, four, five . . .⟩
     c. ⟨or, and⟩

A simple sentence containing an item on the scale entails another simple sentence which differs from the first only in containing an item lower on the scale. The reverse is not the case. So (24a) entails (24b) and (24b) does not entail (24a). However, when used in conversation such sentences frequently strongly suggest the negation of sentences in which a word is re-

placed by an item higher on the scale, so (24a) strongly suggests (24c), though this is cancellable as in (24d):

(24) a. Mrs Smith has three children
     b. Mrs Smith has two children
     c. Mrs Smith does not have four children
     d. Mrs Smith has three children; indeed she has four altogether

A semantic ambiguity theorist would have to treat all number terms in all languages as having two senses: 'at least x' and 'exactly x' so that in (24d) the 'at least' sense is being used, while in (24a) it is the 'exactly' sense, thus entailing (24c). I reject this for the familiar reasons. On the pragmatic approach of Horn and others, number terms have one sense only, 'at least x', and in many contexts utterances containing them must be understood as implicating 'at most x' in order to preserve the assumption that Grice's Quantity maxim (Be as informative as required) is being observed: the two propositions together give the meaning 'exactly x'. Again this approach is based on the assumption that anything pragmatically derived (apart from reference assignment and disambiguation) is an implicature, an assumption that simply cannot be maintained as I have argued above. We have here another case where an alleged implicature entails the explicature of the utterance: 'Mrs Smith has exactly three children' entails 'Mrs Smith has at least three children', which should immediately alert us to the possibility that the supposedly implicated material is actually part of the explicature. This is the line I would wish to pursue, taking all the numerals as having a single sense, neither an 'at least', an 'at most' nor an 'exactly' sense, these being determined pragmatically at the level of explicit content. This line is again supported by examples of numerical sentences falling within the scope of logical operators:

(25) a. If there are three books by Chomsky in the shop I'll buy them all
     b. Mrs Smith doesn't have three children; she has four
     c. Mrs Smith does have three children; in fact she has four

Understood as 'exactly three books by Chomsky' the utterance in (25a) may be true while understood as 'at least three' it may be false, in the same set of circumstances. This is no problem for the explicature analysis, indeed it is predicted, while it creates an apparently unresolvable problem for the implicature approach as shown in the previous section. Similarly, the implicature approach leads to the paradox that both (25b) and (25c) are consistent statements, although at the explicit level in both cases *three* has to be understood as 'at least three'.[15] Again there is no paradox in the explicature approach, since the sense of *three* is simply augmented differently at that level in the two cases.

The same line of reasoning leads to a reanalysis of the alleged implicatures in (7)–(9) as aspects of explicit content.

8 TWO KINDS OF SEMANTICS

Grice introduced the maxims governing conversation and giving rise to implicatures in order to channel off as much of utterance meaning as possible into pragmatics, leaving as spare a semantics as possible. The semantics at issue was the sense of words in natural language such as *and, or, if*, quantifiers, etc., which seemed to diverge from that of their counterparts in formal logic. A second interest of his was to distinguish the truth conditional content of an utterance from the non–truth-conditional, that is, to determine that on the basis of which the speaker can be judged to have spoken truly or falsely. So, for example, two sentences of the forms: '*P* and *Q*' and '*P* but *Q*', are taken to have identical truth conditions although there is clearly some crucial difference in linguistic sense between the two (see note 7 of this chapter). Not all grammatically given information, then, is part of the logical form of the utterance. For Grice the first concern is simply a part of the second, so that if it can be shown that some aspect of meaning is pragmatically derived, such as the temporal and causal connotations of *and*, it is not to be attributed to the semantics of the term but is an implicature and makes no contribution to the truth conditions of the sentence/utterance.

It should be clear by now that this equation of linguistic sense with truth-conditional semantics simply won't work, that while linguistic sense makes a crucial contribution to truth conditions it almost never supplies a truth-evaluable propositional form. As long as linguistic sense and truth-conditional semantics are not distinguished, Grice's two concerns are at odds with each other, pulling in opposite directions: disambiguation, reference assignment, recovery of ellipsed material are all pragmatically driven processes, so the content derived by them should not contribute to the truth-conditional content of the utterance, but if this is so then most utterances do not have any truth conditions, a conclusion which no one would endorse.

Pragmatists in the Gricean tradition have generally followed his example, more or less equating linguistic sense and truth-conditional content (Gazdar 1979, 1980; Levinson 1983; Posner 1980) and, assuming the formula 'pragmatics = meaning − truth conditions'. But faced with examples such as (22a) to (22d), where implicatures seem to contribute to truth conditions, Gazdar (1980:11) says: 'There is increasing evidence that the semantic component of the theory [of meaning] must sometimes have access to the pragmatic properties of constituent clauses when assigning the truth conditions of compound sentences. This evidence indicates that the semantic component is not autonomous with respect to the pragmatic component.' This is certainly so where by semantics we mean truth-conditional semantics and provided 'pragmatic properties' are not equated with implicatures. Nor is it confined to examples like (22); the truth conditions of the vast majority of utterances depend on input from pragmatic processes, as practically every example above demonstrates.

However, talk of *the* semantic component is misleading, since as we've seen the semantics of a lexical item such as *and* may be unitary and unvarying while the connotations it acquires in utterances may be several and variable, those connotations contributing to the truth-conditional content of utterances. It seems then that we must distinguish two kinds of semantics, linguistic and truth conditional, the former naturally figuring only in a theory of utterance meaning, the latter taking as its domain propositional forms, whether of utterances or unspoken thoughts. Linguistic semantics is autonomous with respect to pragmatics; it provides the input to pragmatic processes and the two together make propositional forms which are the input to a truth-conditional semantics. Once this distinction is made, the compulsion to treat all pragmatically derived meaning as implicature subsides; there is no reason why pragmatics cannot contribute to the explicature, the truth-conditional content of the utterance. Whether some particular pragmatically derived meaning is an implicature or not will fall out from the process of finding the interpretation consistent with the principle of relevance.

What does it mean to give a semantic interpretation of an expression in a language? For the truth theorist the answer is obvious: if the expression is a sentence, it is to give its truth conditions; if subsentential, it is to specify the contribution it makes to the truth conditions of sentences. In discussing what constitutes the proper subject matter of semantics, Cresswell (forthcoming) asks the question what sort of ability it is that demonstrates that a speaker knows the meanings of the expressions in a given language, and answers 'The most promising candidate for such an ability seems to be the ability to distinguish situations in which a sentence is true from those in which it is false.'

Sperber & Wilson (1986:173) take a wider view: 'A formula is semantically interpreted by being put into systematic correspondence with other objects: for example, with the formulas of another language, with states of the user of the language, or with possible states of the world.' Since we are distinguishing natural language sentences and the propositional forms they may be used to express as two different kinds of entity, we might consider the semantics of each individually. Speakers and hearers map incoming linguistic stimuli onto conceptual representations (logical forms), plausibly viewed themselves as formulas in a (mental) language. The language ability—knowing English—according to this view, is then precisely what Lewis and others have derided (Kempson 1988): it is the ability to map linguistic forms onto logical forms matching to a high degree the mappings made by a certain group of others (the speakers of English). In theory this ability could exist without the further capacities involved in matching these with conditions in the world. A computer might be programmed so as to perform perfectly correct translations from English into a logical language without, as Lewis and Searle have said, knowing the first thing about the meaning (= truth conditions) of the English sentence. Distinguishing two kinds of semantics in this way—a translational kind and the truth conditional—shows further that the semantic representation of one language may be a syntactic representation in another, though the chain must end somewhere with formulas related to situations and states of the world or possible worlds.[16]

It may be a biological fact about humans that the two abilities develop in tandem, or that the linguistic ability depends on the other perceptual and pragmatic capacities for its development, but that does not make them the same ability. Cresswell is probably right that the best way to demonstrate that one has knowledge of a language is to show that one can correctly pair up utterances in that language with situations in the world. This does not of course expose the particular abilities involved in this demonstration. The main argument of this paper has been to show that a hearer must do a lot of pragmatic work (which involves quite distinct abilities from his linguistic ones),[17] on the basis of the logical form derived from the linguistic form of the utterance, before he has a representation which is truth-evaluable, and that there is even more to be done before he has THE truth-evaluable propositional form he can reasonably take the speaker to have intended to convey.

Cresswell (1982:69) gives the following as his 'most certain principle' in the field of semantics: if we have two sentences, A and B, and A is true and B is false in exactly the same situation in the world, then A and B do not mean the same. However, this is simply not true of natural language sentences:

(26) a. Mary hit Bill and Bill fell
　　　b. Bill fell and Mary hit him

The linguistic semantics of these is identical, given an unambiguous truth-functional semantics for *and* and the standard principle of semantic compositionality, yet a speaker demonstrating her knowledge of language in the way Cresswell prescribes will almost certainly judge them as not both true in the one situation (say, a situation in which Mary hit Bill and as a result he fell over). If there is any doubt about this, embedding them so that they fall within the scope of logical operators as in (22), should dispell it. So it seems that Cresswell's most certain principle is not one concerning linguistic entities but rather the propositional forms which linguistic forms may be used to express. Similarly, the truth-conditional ambiguity test mentioned in section 6 takes as its domain propositional forms rather than natural language sentences, and cannot lead to conclusions about lexical ambiguities.

The picture we end with has a clear semantics/pragmatics distinction, where semantics is understood as translations of linguistic forms into logical forms, partially articulated conceptual representations which are the output of the grammar. Natural language semantics, then, is autonomous and provides the input to pragmatics, which plays a major role in determining the explicature of an utterance as well as determining implicatures, both of which are distinct and complete propositional forms, and as such are the domain for truth-conditional semantics.[18]

NOTES

1. For the sake of a simple clear distinction between explicature and implicature I consider only literal assertions in this paper. Thus questions and imperatives are ignored, as are such figurative uses as metaphor and irony. Sperber & Wilson (1986) use the term *propositional form of the utterance* for what I am calling the explicature. Explicatures are assumptions which have two properties: they are explicitly conveyed and the speaker wants to make them manifest to the hearer (that is, available to him as assumptions he can represent to himself as true). An utterance generally has a set of explicatures: this includes the propositional form of the utterance in the case of literal assertions but does not in the case of tropes or non-assertive speech acts.

2. The term proposition is a notoriously slippery one. I sidestep the ontological issues it raises and use the term *propositional form* in the sense of Sperber & Wilson (1986:72–3). A propositional form is a well-formed formula which (a) undergoes formal logical (truth preserving) operations determined by its structure, and (b) is semantically complete in that it is capable of being true or false.

3. For summaries of relevance theory see Wilson & Sperber (1986b), Sperber & Wilson (1987) and Wilson & Sperber (1988).

4. The problem of where this implicated assumption comes from is the central unanswered question raised by the calculability requirement; it is confronted in Wilson & Sperber (1986a) and in Sperber & Wilson (1986:193–202).

5. Another characteristic mentioned by Grice is that of the indeterminacy of implicatures, which is indeed a property which distinguishes them from explicatures. The implicit import of an utterance need not comprise solely fully determinate assumptions each of which was individually communicated by the speaker. For example, the hearer of (3) might have a readily accessible assumption that people who don't read autobiographies are not much interested in other people's lives, and conclude on that basis that B isn't much interested in other people's lives. This is not a conclusion that the speaker can be held to have communicated to the hearer; while the indirectness of her answer has encouraged the hearer to access further assumptions and draw further conclusions, the hearer has the primary responsibility for the particular assumptions made and conclusions drawn.

6. In most contexts, then, an utterance of (5a) has the same propositional content as utterances of sentences in which the causal connection is recovered by linguistic decoding: for example, *Mr Jones has been insulted and as a result (or: because of this) he is going to resign.* More interesting is the case of *and so* discussed by Blakemore (1987). She argues that the meaning of *so* cannot by analysed in terms of conceptual content but rather in terms of a processing instruction to the hearer and that the causal connection frequently derived from a use of *so* illustrates one way in which an explicature may be enriched so as to satisfy that instruction.

7. Certain linguistically given (hence explicit) aspects of the utterance are not part of the explicature of the utterance because their role is not to supply conceptual content but to guide the hearer's *processing* of the utterance. They may place constraints on the sort of context in which the explicature is to be processed or

direct the inferential role of the explicature in the context. Examples of such linguistic expressions are *but, after all, anyway, so.* They have been studied in detail by Blakemore (1987).

8. Note that it's not enough that the interpretation is optimally relevant to the addressee: a hearer might hit on a readily accessible interpretation with a good range of contextual effects but have to dismiss it as what the speaker intended, perhaps because he knows that the speaker couldn't possibly have the beliefs that this interpretation depends on.

9. Wilson & Sperber (1981) deals specifically with this.

10. Furthermore, since B has chosen to answer A in this indirect way rather than simply saying *No,* which would have saved him the effort of accessing the assumption and deducing the conclusion, it follows by the principle of relevance that she is encouraging him to access further assumptions and draw further conclusions. She must have expected this indirect response to yield cognitive effects not derivable from the direct answer which would compensate for the extra processing costs. For instance she might know that A is in the throes of writing an autobiography and that he can thereby arrive at the implication that she will not read his book.

11. Grice actually raises the problem in connection with his analysis of *if,* but it carries over intact to the analysis of *and.*

12. The most likely counterexamples to a general statement that denials must refer to explicatures are ironical and metaphorical statements. See note 1. It remains to be seen whether the generalisation could be salvaged by tightening it up along the lines that a denial cannot refer to an implicature alone when the propositional form of the utterance is an explicature.

13. Given this sort of counterexample to the implicature approach Cohen (1971) advocates a semantic solution, though not the ambiguity one. He wants a single complex lexical entry for *and* incorporating temporal, causal and other features, with some (pragmatic) mechanism for cancelling features in particular contexts. Posner (1980) discusses problems with this meaning-maximalist position.

14. For a more detailed reanalysis of a range of examples standardly treated as generalised quantity implicatures see Carston (forthcoming).

15. Horn (1985) tackles this problem by analysing the negation here as metalinguistic. This looks like a promising approach and may well replace the explicature treatment in some cases; this is considered in Carston (forthcoming) where a broader notion of metarepresentation is advocated.

16. In addition to a linguistic semantics mapping linguistic forms onto concepts and a truth-conditional semantics relating propositional forms to the real world there is a third kind of semantics, a logical or conceptual role semantics, concerned with relations of entailment, contradiction, etc., amongst logical and propositional forms.

17. Fodor (1983) and Sperber & Wilson (1986) take the language processing system to be a specialised automatic decoding system. The pragmatic processing of utterances employs relatively unspecialised inferential processes and encyclopedic knowledge which are involved in processing all incoming information, whether linguistic or perceptual, and in general thought processes.

18. Even more than usual this paper has benefited from the ideas and advice of Deirdre Wilson to whom I am very grateful. Thanks also to Diane Blakemore, Max Cresswell, Pierre Jacob, Ruth Kempson, Ewan Klein, and François Recanati for comments on an earlier version.

REFERENCES

Blakemore, D. (1987). *Semantic Constraints on Relevance.* Oxford: Basil Blackwell.

Carston, R. (forthcoming). "A Reanalysis of Some Generalised Quantity Implicatures." Ms., University College, London.

Cohen, L. J. (1971). "The Logical Particles of Natural Language." In Y. Bar-Hillel (ed.), *Pragmatics of Natural Language.* Dordrecht: Reidel.

Cresswell, M. J. (1982). "The Autonomy of Semantics." In S. Peters and E. Saarinen (eds.), *Processes, Beliefs, and Questions.* Dordrecht: Reidel.

Cresswell, M. J. (forthcoming). "Basic Concepts in Semantics." In A. von Stechow (ed.), *Handbook of Semantics.*

Fodor, J. A. (1983). *Modularity of Mind.* Cambridge, Mass.: MIT Press.

Gazdar, G. (1979). *Pragmatics: Implicature, Presupposition and Logical Form.* London: Academic Press.

Gazdar, G. (1980). "Pragmatics and Logical Form." *Journal of Pragmatics* 4:1–13.

Grice, H. P. (1967). "Logic and Conversation." William James lectures, Harvard University. Unpublished.

Grice, H. P. (1975). "Logic and Conversation." In P. Cole and J. Morgan (eds.), *Syntax and Semantics.* Vol. 3: *Speech Acts.* New York: Academic Press. [Reprinted in this volume, Chapter 19]

Grice, H. P. (1981). "Presupposition and Conversational Implicature." In P. Cole (ed.), *Radical Pragmatics.* New York: Academic Press.

Horn, L. R. (1972). "On the Semantic Properties of Logical Operators." Ph.D. diss., University of California, Los Angeles.

Horn, L. R. (1984). "Ambiguity, Negation and the London School of Parsimony." In C. Jones and P. Sells (eds.), *Proceedings from North Eastern Linguistic Society XIV.*

Horn, L. R. (1985). "Metalinguistic Negation and Pragmatic Ambiguity." *Language* 61:121–174.

Katz, J. J. (1972). *Semantic Theory.* New York: Harper & Row.

Kempson, Ruth M. (1988). "Introduction." In Ruth M. Kempson (ed.), *Mental Representations: The Interface Between Language and Reality.* Cambridge: Cambridge University Press, 3–25.

Levinson, S. (1983). *Pragmatics.* Cambridge: Cambridge University Press.

McCawley, J. D. (1981). *Everything that Linguists Have Always Wanted to Know About Logic but Were Afraid to Ask.* Oxford: Basil Blackwell.

Partee, B. (1973). "Some Structural Analogies Between Tenses and Pronouns in English." *Journal of Philosophy* 70:601–609.

Posner, R. (1980). "Semantics and Pragmatics of Sentence Connectives in Natural Language." In J. Searle, F. Kiefer, and M. Bierwisch (eds.), *Speech Act Theory and Pragmatics.* Dordrecht: Reidel.

Sperber, D., and D. Wilson (1986). *Relevance: Communication and Cognition.* Oxford: Basil Blackwell.

Sperber, D., and D. Wilson (1987). "Précis of Relevance: Communication and Cognition." *Behavioral and Brain Sciences* 10:697–754.

Walker, R. (1975). "Conversational Implicatures." In S. Blackburn (ed.), *Meaning, Reference and Necessity.* Cambridge: Cambridge University Press.

Wilson, D., and D. Sperber (1981). "On Grice's Theory of Conversation." In P. Werth (ed.), *Conversation and Discourse.* London: Croom Helm.

Wilson, D., and D. Sperber (1986a). "Inference and Implicature in Utterance Interpretation." In T. Myers, K. Brown, and B. McGonigle (eds.), *Reasoning and Discourse Processes.* London: Academic Press.

Wilson, D., and D. Sperber (1986b). "Pragmatics and Modularity." In Anne M. Farley, Peter T. Farley, and Karl-Erik McCullough (eds.), *The Chicago Linguistic Society Parasession on Pragmatics and Grammatical Theory.* Chicago: Chicago Linguistics Society. [Reprinted in this volume, Chapter 35]

Wilson, D., and D. Sperber (1988). "Representation and Relevance." In Ruth M. Kempson (ed.), *Mental Representations: The Interface Between Language and Reality.* Cambridge: Cambridge University Press, 133–153.

3

Reference and Definite Descriptions

KEITH DONNELLAN

Definite descriptions, I shall argue, have two possible functions. They are used to refer to what a speaker wishes to talk about, but they are also used quite differently. Moreover, a definite description occurring in one and the same sentence may, on different occasions of its use, function in either way. The failure to deal with this duality of function obscures the genuine referring use of definite descriptions. The best-known theories of definite descriptions, those of Russell and Strawson, I shall suggest, are both guilty of this. Before discussing this distinction in use, I will mention some features of these theories to which it is especially relevant.

On Russell's view a definite description may denote an entity: "if 'C' is a denoting phrase [as definite descriptions are by definition], it may happen that there is one entity x (there cannot be more than one) for which the proposition 'x is identical with C' is true. . . . We may then say that the entity x is the denotation of the phrase 'C.' "[1] In using a definite description, then, a speaker may use an expression which denotes some entity, but this is the only relationship between that entity and the use of the definite description recognized by

Russell. I shall argue, however, that there are two uses of definite descriptions. The definition of denotation given by Russell is applicable to both, but in one of these the definite description serves to do something more. I shall say that in this use the speaker uses the definite description to *refer* to something, and call this use the "referential use" of a definite description. Thus, if I am right, referring is not the same as denoting and the referential use of definite descriptions is not recognized on Russell's view.

Furthermore, on Russell's view the type of expression that comes closest to performing the function of the referential use of definite descriptions turns out, as one might suspect, to be a proper name (in "the narrow logical sense"). Many of the things said about proper names by Russell can, I think, be said about the referential use of definite descriptions without straining senses unduly. Thus the gulf Russell thought he saw between names and definite descriptions is narrower than he thought.

Strawson, on the other hand, certainly does recognize a referential use of definite definitions. But what I think he did not see is that a

Keith Donnellan, "Reference and Definite Descriptions," *Philosophical Review* 75 (1966):281–304. Copyright © 1966 by the Philosophical Review. Reprinted by permission of the publisher and the author.

definite description may have a quite different role—may be used nonreferentially, even as it occurs in one and the same sentence. Strawson, it is true, points out nonreferential uses of definite descriptions,[2] but which use a definite description has seems to be for him a function of the kind of sentence in which it occurs; whereas, if I am right, there can be two possible uses of a definite description in the same sentence. Thus, in "On Referring," he says, speaking of expressions used to refer, "Any expression of any of these classes [one being that of definite descriptions] can occur as the subject of what would traditionally be regarded as a singular subject-predicate sentence; and would, so occurring, exemplify the use I wish to discuss."[3] So the definite description in, say, the sentence "The Republican candidate for president in 1968 will be a conservative" presumably exemplifies the referential use. But if I am right, we could not say this of the sentence in isolation from some particular occasion on which it is used to state something; and then it might or might not turn out that the definite description has a referential use.

Strawson and Russell seem to me to make a common assumption here about the question of how definite descriptions function: that we can ask how a definite description functions in some sentence independently of a particular occasion upon which it is used. This assumption is not really rejected in Strawson's arguments against Russell. Although he can sum up his position by saying, "'Mentioning' or 'referring' is not something an expression does; it is something that someone can use an expression to do,"[4] he means by this to deny the radical view that a "genuine" referring expression *has* a referent, functions to refer, independent of the context of some use of the expression. The denial of this view, however, does not entail that definite descriptions cannot be identified as referring expressions in a sentence unless the sentence is being used. Just as we can speak of a function of a tool that is not at the moment performing its function, Strawson's view, I believe, allows us to speak of the referential function of a definite description in a sentence even when it is not being used. This, I hope to show, is a mistake.

A second assumption shared by Russell's and Strawson's account of definite descriptions is this. In many cases a person who uses a definite description can be said (in some sense) to presuppose or imply that something fits the description.[5] If I state that the king is on his throne, I presuppose or imply that there is a king. (At any rate, this would be a natural thing to say for anyone who doubted that there is a king.) Both Russell and Strawson assume that where the presupposition or implication is false, the truth value of what the speaker says is affected. For Russell the statement made is false; for Strawson it has no truth value. Now if there are two uses of definite descriptions, it may be that the truth value is affected differently in each case by the falsity of the presupposition or implication. This is what I shall in fact argue. It will turn out, I believe, that one or the other of the two views, Russell's or Strawson's, may be correct about the nonreferential use of definite descriptions, but neither fits the referential use. This is not so surprising about Russell's view, since he did not recognize this use in any case, but it is surprising about Strawson's since the referential use is what he tries to explain and defend. Furthermore, on Strawson's account, the result of there being nothing which fits the description is a failure of reference.[6] This too, I believe, turns out not to be true about the referential use of definite descriptions.

II

There are some uses of definite descriptions which carry neither any hint of a referential use nor any presupposition or implication that something fits the description. In general, it seems, these are recognizable from the sentence frame in which the description occurs. These uses will not interest us, but it is necessary to point them out if only to set them aside.

An obvious example would be the sentence "The present King of France does not exist," used, say, to correct someone's mistaken impression that de Gaulle is the King of France.

A more interesting example is this. Suppose someone were to ask, "Is de Gaulle the King of France?" This is the natural form of words for a person to use who is in doubt as to whether de Gaulle is King or President of France. Given this background to the question, there seems to be no presupposition or implication that someone is the King of France. Nor is the person attempting to refer to someone by using the definite description. On the other hand, reverse the name and description in the question and the speaker probably would be thought to presuppose or imply this. "Is the King of France de Gaulle?" is the natural question for one to ask who wonders whether it is de Gaulle rather than someone else who occupies the throne of France.[7]

Many times, however, the use of a definite description does carry a presupposition or implication that something fits the description. If definite descriptions do have a referring role, it will be here. But it is a mistake, I think, to try, as I believe both Russell and Strawson do, to settle this matter without further ado. What is needed, I believe, is the distinction I will now discuss.

III

I will call the two uses of definite descriptions I have in mind the attributive use and the referential use. A speaker who uses a definite description attributively in an assertion states something about whoever or whatever is the so-and-so. A speaker who uses a definite description referentially in an assertion, on the other hand, uses the description to enable his audience to pick out whom or what he is talking about and states something about that person or thing. In the first case the definite description might be said to occur essentially, for the speaker wishes to assert something about whatever or whoever fits that description; but in the referential use the definite description is merely one tool for doing a certain job—calling attention to a person or thing—and in general any other device for doing the same job, another description or a name, would do as well. In the attributive use, the attribute of being the so-and-so is all important, while it is not in the referential use.

To illustrate this distinction, in the case of a single sentence, consider the sentence, "Smith's murderer is insane." Suppose first that we come upon poor Smith foully murdered. From the brutal manner of the killing and the fact that Smith was the most lovable person in the world, we might exclaim,

"Smith's murderer is insane." I will assume, to make it a simpler case, that in a quite ordinary sense we do not know who murdered Smith (though this is not in the end essential to the case). This, I shall say, is an attributive use of the definite description.

The contrast with such a use of the sentence is one of those situations in which we expect and intend our audience to realize whom we have in mind when we speak of Smith's murderer and, most importantly, to know that it is this person about whom we are going to say something.

For example, suppose that Jones has been charged with Smith's murder and has been placed on trial. Imagine that there is a discussion of Jones's odd behavior at his trial. We might sum up our impression of his behavior by saying, "Smith's murderer is insane." If someone asks to whom we are referring, by using this description, the answer here is "Jones." This, I shall say, is a referential use of the definite description.

That these two uses of the definite description in the same sentence are really quite different can perhaps best be brought out by considering the consequences of the assumption that Smith had no murderer (for example, he in fact committed suicide). In both situations, in using the definite description "Smith's murderer," the speaker in some sense presupposes or implies that there is a murderer. But when we hypothesize that the presupposition or implication is false, there are different results for the two uses. In both cases we have used the predicate "is insane," but in the first case, if there is no murderer, there is no person of whom it could be correctly said that we attributed insanity to him. Such a person could be identified (correctly) only in case someone fitted the description used. But in the second case, where the definite description is simply a means of identifying the person we want to talk about, it is quite possible for the correct identification to be made even though no one fits the description we used.[8] We were speaking about Jones even though he is not in fact Smith's murderer and, in the circumstances imagined, it was his behavior we were commenting upon. Jones might, for example, accuse us of saying false things of him in calling him insane and it would be no defense, I should think, that our description, "the murderer of Smith," failed to fit him.

It is, moreover, perfectly possible for our audience to know to whom we refer, in the second situation, even though they do not share our presupposition. A person hearing our comment in the context imagined might know we are talking about Jones even though he does not think Jones guilty.

Generalizing from this case, we can say, I think, that there are two uses of sentences of the form, "The ϕ is ψ." In the first, if nothing is the ϕ then nothing has been said to be ψ. In the second, the fact that nothing is the ϕ does not have this consequence.

With suitable changes the same difference in use can be formulated for uses of language other than assertions. Suppose one is at a party and, seeing an interesting-looking person holding a martini glass, one asks, "Who is the man drinking a martini?" If it should turn out that there is only water in the glass, one has nevertheless asked a question about a particular person, a question that it is possible for someone to answer. Contrast this with the use of the same question by the chairman of the local Teetotalers Union. He has just been informed that a man is drinking a martini at their annual party. He responds by asking his informant, "Who is the man drinking a martini?" In asking the question the chairman does not have some particular person in mind about whom he asks the question; if no one is drinking a martini, if the information is wrong, no person can be singled out as the person about whom the question was asked. Unlike the first case, the attribute of being the man drinking a martini is all-important, because if it is the attribute of no one, the chairman's question has no straight-forward answer.

This illustrates also another difference between the referential and the attributive use of definite descriptions. In the one case we have asked a question about a particular person or thing even though nothing fits the description we used; in the other this is not so. But also in the one case our question can be answered; in the other it cannot be. In the referential use of a definite description we may succeed in picking out a person or thing to ask a question about even though he or it does not really fit the description; but in the attributive use if nothing fits the description, no straightforward answer to the question can be given.

This further difference is also illustrated by commands or orders containing definite descriptions. Consider the order, "Bring me the book on the table." If "the book on the table" is being used referentially, it is possible to fulfill the order even though there is no book on the table. If, for example, there is a book *beside* the table, though there is none *on* it, one might bring that book back and ask the issuer of the order whether this is "the book you meant." And it may be. But imagine we are told that someone has laid a book on our prize antique table, where nothing should be put. The order, "Bring me the book on the table" cannot now be obeyed unless there is a book that has been placed on the table. There is no possibility of bringing back a book which was never on the table and having it be the one that was meant, because there is no book that in that sense was "meant." In the one case the definite description was a device for getting the other person to pick the right book; if he is able to pick the right book even though it does not satisfy the description, one still succeeds in his purpose. In the other case, there is, antecedently, no "right book" except one which fits the description; the attribute of being the book on the table is essential. Not only is there no book about which an order was issued, if there is no book on the table, but the order itself cannot be obeyed. When a definite description is used attributively in a command or question and nothing fits the description, the command cannot be obeyed and the question cannot be answered. This suggests some analogous consequence for assertions containing definite descriptions used attributively. Perhaps the analogous result is that the assertion is neither true nor false: this is Strawson's view of what happens when the presupposition of the use of a definite description is false. But if so, Strawson's view works not for definite descriptions used referentially, but for the quite different use, which I have called the attributive use.

I have tried to bring out the two uses of definite descriptions by pointing out the different consequences of supposing that nothing fits the description used. There are still other differences. One is this: when a definite description is used referentially, not only is there in some sense a presupposition or implication that someone or something fits the description, as there is also in the attributive use, but there is a quite different presupposition; the speaker presupposes of some *particular* someone or something that he or it fits the description. In asking, for example, "Who is the man drinking a martini?" where we mean to ask a question about that man over there, we are presupposing that that man over there is drinking a martini—not just that *someone* is a man drinking a martini. When we say, in a context where it is clear we are referring to Jones, "Smith's murderer is insane," we are presupposing that Jones is Smith's murderer. No such presupposition is present in the attributive use of definite descriptions. There is, of course, the presupposition that someone *or other* did the murder, but the speaker does not presuppose of someone in particular—Jones or Robinson, say—that he did it. What I mean by this second kind of presupposition that someone or something in particular fits the description—which is present in a referential use but not in an attributive use—can perhaps be seen more clearly by considering a member of the speaker's audience who believes that Smith was not murdered at all. Now in the case of the referential use of the description, "Smith's murderer," he could accuse the speaker of mistakenly presupposing both that someone or other is the murderer and that also Jones is the murderer, for even though he believes Jones not to have done the deed, he knows that the speaker was referring to Jones. But in the case of the attributive use, he can accuse the speaker of having only the first, less specific presupposition; he cannot pick out some person and claim that the speaker is presupposing that that person is Smith's murderer. Now the more particular presuppositions that we find present in referential uses are clearly not ones we can assign to a definite description in some particular sentence in isolation from a context of use. In order to know that a person presupposes that Jones is Smith's murderer in using the sentence "Smith's murderer is insane," we have to know that he is using the description referentially and also to whom he is referring. The sentence by itself does not tell us any of this.

IV

From the way in which I set up each of the previous examples it might be supposed that the important difference between the referential and the attributive use lies in the beliefs of the speaker. Does he believe of some particular person or thing that he or it fits the description used? In the Smith murder example, for instance, there was in the one case no belief as to who did the deed, whereas in the contrasting case it was believed that Jones did it. But this is, in fact, not an essential difference. It is possible for a definite description to be used attributively even though the speaker (and his audience) believes that a certain person or thing fits the description. And it is possible for a definite description to be used referentially where the speaker believes that nothing fits the description. It is true—and this is why, for simplicity, I set up the examples the way I did—that if a speaker does not believe that anything fits the description or does not believe that he is in a position to pick out what does fit the description, it is likely that he is not using it referentially. It is also true that if he and his audience would pick out some particular thing or person as fitting the description, then a use of the definite description is very likely referential. But these are only presumptions and not entailments.

To use the Smith murder case again, suppose that Jones is on trial for the murder and I and everyone else believe him guilty. Suppose that I comment that the murderer of Smith is insane, but instead of backing this up, as in the example previously used, by citing Jones's behavior in the dock, I go on to outline reasons for thinking that *anyone* who murdered poor Smith in that particularly horrible way must be insane. If now it turns out that Jones was not the murderer after all, but someone else was, I think I can claim to have been right if the true murderer is after all insane. Here, I think, I would be using the definite description attributively, even though I believe that a particular person fits the description.

It is also possible to think of cases in which the speaker does not believe that what he means to refer to by using the definite description fits the description, or to imagine cases in which the definite description is used referentially even though the speaker believes *nothing* fits the description. Admittedly, these cases may be parasitic on a more normal use; nevertheless, they are sufficient to show that such beliefs of the speaker are not decisive as to which use is made of a definite description.

Suppose the throne is occupied by a man I firmly believe to be not the king, but a usurper. Imagine also that his followers as firmly believe that he is the king. Suppose I wish to see this man. I might say to his minions, "Is the king in his countinghouse?" I succeed in referring to the man I wish to refer to without myself believing that he fits the description. It is not even necessary, moreover, to suppose that his followers believe him to be the king. If they are cynical about the whole thing, know he is not the king, I may still succeed in referring to the man I wish to refer to. Similarly, neither I nor the people I speak to may suppose that *anyone* is the king and, finally, each party may know that the other does not so suppose and yet the reference may go through.

V

Both the attributive and the referential use of definite descriptions seem to carry a presupposition or implication that there is something which fits the description. But the reasons for the existence of the presupposition or implication are different in the two cases.

There is a presumption that a person who uses a definite description referentially believes that what he wishes to refer to fits the description. Because the purpose of using the description is to get the audience to pick out or think of the right thing or person, one would normally choose a description that he believes the thing or person fits. Normally a misdescription of that to which one wants to refer would mislead the audience. Hence, there is a presumption that the speaker believes *something* fits the description—namely, that to which he refers.

When a definite description is used attributively, however, there is not the same possibility of misdescription. In the example of "Smith's murderer" used attributively, there was not the possibility of misdescribing Jones or anyone else; we were not referring to Jones

nor to anyone else by using the description. The presumption that the speaker believes *someone* is Smith's murder does not arise here from a more specific presumption that he believes Jones or Robinson or someone else whom he can name or identify is Smith's murderer.

The presupposition or implication is borne by a definite description used attributively because if nothing fits the description the linguistic purpose of the speech act will be thwarted. That is, the speaker will not succeed in saying something true, if he makes an assertion; he will not succeed in asking a question that can be answered, if he has asked a question; he will not succeed in issuing an order that can be obeyed, if he has issued an order. If one states that Smith's murderer is insane, when Smith has no murderer, and uses the definite description nonreferentially, then one fails to say anything *true.* If one issues the order "Bring me Smith's murderer" under similar circumstances, the order cannot be obeyed; nothing would count as obeying it.

When the definite description is used referentially, on the other hand, the presupposition or implication stems simply from the fact that normally a person tries to describe correctly what he wants to refer to because normally this is the best way to get his audience to recognize what he is referring to. As we have seen, it is possible for the linguistic purpose of the speech act to be accomplished in such a case even though nothing fits the description; it is possible to say something true or to ask a question that gets answered or to issue a command that gets obeyed. For when the definite description is used referentially, one's audience may succeed in seeing to what one refers even though neither it nor anything else fits the description.

V I

The result of the last section shows something to be wrong with the theories of both Russell and Strawson; for though they give differing accounts of the implication or presupposition involved, each gives only one. Yet, as I have argued, the presupposition or implication is present for a quite different reason, depending upon whether the definite description is used attributively or referentially, and exactly what presuppositions or implications are involved is also different. Moreover, neither theory seems a correct characterization of the referential use. On Russell's there is a logical entailment: "The ϕ is ψ" entails "There exists one and only one ϕ." Whether or not this is so for the attributive use, it does not seem true of the referential use of the definite description. The "implication" that something is the ϕ, as I have argued, does not amount to an entailment; it is more like a presumption based on what is *usually* true of the use of a definite description to refer. In any case, of course, Russell's theory does not show—what is true of the referential use—that the implication that *something* is the ϕ comes from the more specific implication that *what is being referred to* is the ϕ. Hence, as a theory of definite descriptions. Russell's view seems to apply, if at all, to the attributive use only.

Russell's definition of denoting (a definite description denotes an entity if that entity fits the description uniquely) is clearly applicable to either use of definite descriptions. Thus whether or not a definite description is used referentially or attributively, it may have a denotation. Hence, denoting and referring, as I have explicated the latter notion, are distinct and Russell's view recognizes only the former. It seems to me, moreover, that this is a welcome result, that denoting and referring should not be confused. If one tried to maintain that they are the same notion, one result would be that a speaker might be referring to something without knowing it. If someone said, for example, in 1960 before he had any idea that Mr. Goldwater would be the Republican nominee in 1964, "The Republican candidate for president in 1964 will be a conservative" (perhaps on the basis of an analysis of the views of party leaders) the definite description here would *denote* Mr. Goldwater. But would we wish to say that the speaker had referred to, mentioned, or talked about Mr. Goldwater? I feel these terms would be out of place. Yet if we identify referring and denoting, it ought to be possible for it to turn out (after the Republican Convention) that the speaker had, unknown to himself, referred in 1960 to Mr. Goldwater. On my view, however, while the definite description used did *denote* Mr. Goldwater (using Russell's defini-

tion), the speaker used it *attributively* and did not *refer* to Mr. Goldwater.

Turning to Strawson's theory, it was supposed to demonstrate how definite descriptions are referential. But it goes too far in this direction. For there are nonreferential uses of definite descriptions also, even as they occur in one and the same sentence. I believe that Strawson's theory involves the following propositions:

(1) If someone asserts that the ϕ is ψ he has not made a true or false statement if there is no ϕ.[9]

(2) If there is no ϕ then the speaker has failed to refer to anything.[10]

(3) The reason he has said nothing true or false is that he has failed to refer.

Each of these propositions is either false or, at best, applies to only one of the two uses of definite descriptions.

Proposition (1) is possibly true of the attributive use. In the example in which "Smith's murderer is insane" was said when Smith's body was first discovered, an attributive use of the definite description, there was no person to whom the speaker referred. If Smith had no murderer, nothing true was said. It is quite tempting to conclude, following Strawson, that nothing true *or* false was said. But where the definite description is used referentially, something true may well have been said. It is possible that something true was said of the person or thing referred to.[11]

Proposition (2) is, as we have seen, simply false. Where a definite description is used referentially it is perfectly possible to refer to something though nothing fits the description used.

The situation with proposition (3) is a bit more complicated. It ties together, on Strawson's view, the two strands given in (1) and (2). As an account of why, when the presupposition is false, nothing true or false has been stated, it clearly cannot work for the attributive use of definite descriptions, for the reason it supplies is that reference has failed. It does not then give the reason why, if indeed this is so, a speaker using a definite description attributively fails to say anything true or false if nothing fits the description. It does, however, raise a question about the referential use. Can reference fail when a definite description is used referentially?

I do not fail to refer merely because my audience does not correctly pick out what I am referring to. I can be referring to a particular man when I use the description "the man drinking a martini," even though the people to whom I speak fail to pick out the right person or any person at all. Nor, as we have stressed, do I fail to refer when nothing fits the description. But perhaps I fail to refer in some extreme circumstances, when there is nothing that *I* am willing to pick out as that to which I referred.

Suppose that I think I see at some distance a man walking and ask, "Is the man carrying a walking stick the professor of history?" We should perhaps distinguish four cases at this point. (a) There is a man carrying a walking stick; I have then referred to a person and asked a question about him that can be answered if my audience has the information. (b) The man over there is not carrying a walking stick, but an umbrella; I have still referred to someone and asked a question that can be answered, though if my audience sees that it is an umbrella and not a walking stick, they may also correct my apparently mistaken impression. (c) It is not a man at all, but a rock that looks like one; in this case, I think I still have referred to something, to the thing over there that happens to be a rock but that I took to be a man. But in this case it is not clear that my question can be answered correctly. This, I think, is not because I have failed to refer, but rather because, given the true nature of what I referred to, my question is not appropriate. A simple "No, that is not the professor of history" is at least a bit misleading if said by someone who realizes that I mistook a rock for a person. It may, therefore, be plausible to conclude that in such a case I have not asked a question to which there is a straightforwardly correct answer. But if this is true, it is not because nothing fits the description I used, but rather because what I referred to is a rock and my question has no correct answer when asked of a rock. (d) There is finally the case in which there is nothing at all where I thought there was a man with a walking stick; and perhaps here we have a genuine failure to refer at all, even though the description was used for the purpose of referring. There is no rock, nor anything else, to which I meant to refer; it was, perhaps, a trick of light that made me think

there was a man there. I cannot say of anything, "That is what I was referring to, though I now see that it's not a man carrying a walking stick." This failure of reference, however, requires circumstances much more radical than the mere nonexistence of anything fitting the description used. It requires that there be nothing of which it can be said, "That is what he was referring to." Now perhaps also in such cases, if the speaker has asserted something, he fails to state anything true or false if there is nothing that can be identified as that to which he referred. But if so, the failure of reference and truth value does not come about merely because nothing fits the description he used. So (3) may be true of some cases of the referential use of definite descriptions; it may be true that a failure of reference results in a lack of truth value. But these cases are of a much more extreme sort than Strawson's theory implies.

I conclude, then, that neither Russell's nor Strawson's theory represents a correct account of the use of definite descriptions—Russell's because it ignores altogether the referential use, Strawson's because it fails to make the distinction between the referential and the attributive and mixes together truths about each (together with some things that are false).

VII

It does not seem possible to say categorically of a definite description in a particular sentence that it is a referring expression (of course, one could say this if he meant that it *might* be used to refer). In general, whether or not a definite description is used referentially or attributively is a function of the speaker's intentions in a particular case. "The murderer of Smith" may be used either way in the sentence "The murderer of Smith is insane." It does not appear plausible to account for this, either, as an ambiguity in the sentence. The grammatical structure of the sentence seems to me to be the same whether the description is used referentially or attributively: that is, it is not syntactically ambiguous. Nor does it seem at all attractive to suppose an ambiguity in the meaning of the words; it does not appear to be semantically ambiguous. (Perhaps we could say that the sentence is pragmatically ambiguous: the distinction between roles that the description plays is a function of the speaker's intentions.) These, of course, are intuitions; I do not have an argument for these conclusions. Nevertheless, the burden of proof is surely on the other side.

This, I think, means that the view, for example, that sentences can be divided up into predicates, logical operators, and referring expressions is not generally true. In the case of definite descriptions one cannot always assign the referential function in isolation from a particular occasion on which it is used.

There may be sentences in which a definite description can be used only attributively or only referentially. A sentence in which it seems that the definite description could be used only attributively would be "Point out the man who is drinking my martini." I am not so certain that any can be found in which the definite description can be used only referentially. Even if there are such sentences, it does not spoil the point that there are many sentences, apparently not ambiguous either syntactically or semantically, containing definite descriptions that can be used either way.

If it could be shown that the dual use of definite descriptions can be accounted for by the presence of an ambiguity, there is still a point to be made against the theories of Strawson and Russell. For neither, so far as I can see, has anything to say about the possibility of such an ambiguity and, in fact neither seems compatible with such a possibility. Russell's does not recognize the possibility of the referring use, and Strawson's, as I have tried to show in the last section, combines elements from each use into one unitary account. Thus the view that there is an ambiguity in such sentences does not seem any more attractive to these positions.

VIII

Using a definite description referentially, a speaker may say something true even though the description correctly applies to nothing. The sense in which he may say something true is the sense in which he may say something true about someone or something. This sense is, I think, an interesting one that needs investigation. Isolating it is one of the byproducts of the distinction between the attributive and referential uses of definite descriptions.

For one thing, it raises questions about the notion of a statement. This is brought out by considering a passage in a paper by Leonard Linsky in which he rightly makes the point that one can refer to someone although the definite description used does not correctly describe the person:

... said of a spinster that "Her husband is kind to her" is neither true nor false. But a speaker might very well be referring to someone using these words, for he may think that someone is the husband of the lady (who in fact is a spinster). Still, the statement is neither true nor false, for it presupposes that the lady has a husband, which she has not. This last refutes Strawson's thesis that if the presupposition of existence is not satisfied, the speaker has failed to refer.[12]

There is much that is right in this passage. But because Linsky does not make the distinction between the referential and the attributive uses of definite descriptions, it does not represent a wholly adequate account of the situation. A perhaps minor point about this passage is that Linsky apparently thinks it sufficient to establish that the speaker in his example is referring to someone by using the definite description "her husband," that he *believe* that someone is her husband. This will only approximate the truth provided that the "someone" in the description of the belief means "someone in particular" and is not merely the existential quantifier, "there is someone or other." For in both the attributive and the referential use the belief that someone *or other* is the husband of the lady is very likely to be present. If, for example, the speaker has just met the lady and, noticing her cheerfulness and radiant good health, makes his remark from his conviction that these attributes are always the result of having good husbands, he would be using the definite description attributively. Since she has no husband, there is no one to pick out as the person to whom he was referring. Nevertheless, the speaker believed that *someone or other* was her husband. On the other hand, if the use of "her husband" was simply a way of referring to a man the speaker has just met whom he assumed to be the lady's husband, he would have referred to that man even though neither he nor anyone else fits the description. I think it is likely that in this passage Linsky did mean by "someone," in his description of the belief, "someone in particular." But even then, as we have seen, we have neither a sufficient nor a necessary condition for a referential use of the definite description. A definite description can be used attributively even when the speaker believes that some particular thing or person fits the description, and it can be used referentially in the absence of this belief.

My main point, here, however, has to do with Linsky's view that because the presupposition is not satisfied, the *statement* is neither true nor false. This seems to me possibly correct *if* the definite description is thought of as being used attributively (depending upon whether we go with Strawson or Russell). But when we consider it as used referentially, this categorical assertion is no longer clearly correct. For the man the speaker referred to may indeed be kind to the spinster; the speaker may have said something true about that man. Now the difficulty is in the notion of "the statement." Suppose that we know that the lady is a spinster, but nevertheless know that the man referred to by the speaker is kind to her. It seems to me that we shall, on the one hand, want to hold that the speaker said something true, but be reluctant to express this by "It is true that her husband is kind to her."

This shows, I think, a difficulty in speaking simply about "the statement" when definite descriptions are used referentially. For the speaker stated something, in this example, about a particular person, and his statement, we may suppose, was true. Nevertheless, we should not like to agree with his statement by using the sentence he used; we should not like to identify the true statement via the speaker's words. The reason for this is not so hard to find. If we say, in this example, "It is true that her husband is kind to her," *we* are now using the definite description either attributively or referentially. But we should not be subscribing to what the original speaker truly said if we use the description attributively, for it was only in its function as referring to a particular person that the definite description yields the possibility of saying something true (since the lady has no husband). Our reluctance, however, to endorse the original speaker's statement by using the definite description referentially to refer to the same person stems from quite a different consideration. For if we too were laboring under the mistaken belief that this man was the lady's husband, we could agree with the original speaker using his exact words. (Moreover, it is possible, as we have seen, deliberately to use a definite description to refer to someone we believe not to fit the description.) Hence, our reluctance to use the original speaker's words does not arise from the fact that if we did we should not succeed in stating anything true or false. It rather stems from the fact that when a definite description is used referentially there is a presumption that the speaker believes that what he refers to fits the description. Since we, who know the lady to be a spinster, would not normally want to give the impression that we believe otherwise, we would not like to use the original speaker's way of referring to the man in question.

How then would we express agreement with the original speaker without involving ourselves in unwanted impressions about our beliefs? The answer shows another difference between the referential and attributive uses of definite descriptions and brings out an important point about genuine referring.

When a speaker says, "The ϕ is ψ," where "the ϕ" is used attributively, if there is no ϕ, we cannot correctly report the speaker as having said *of* this or that person or thing that it is ψ. But if the definite description is used referentially we can report the speaker as having attributed ψ to something. And *we* may refer to what the speaker referred to, using whatever description or name suits our purpose. Thus, if a speaker says, "Her husband is kind to her," referring to the man he was just talking to, and if that man is Jones, we may report him as having said *of Jones* that he is kind to her. If Jones is also the president of the college, we may report the speaker as having said *of the president of the college* that he is kind to her. And finally, if we are talking to Jones, we may say, referring to the original speaker, "He said of you that *you* are kind to her." It does not matter here whether or not the woman has a husband or whether, if she does, Jones is her husband. If the original speaker referred to Jones, he said of him that he is kind to her. Thus where the definite description is used referentially, but does not fit what was referred to, we can report what a speaker said and agree with him by using a description or name which does fit. In doing so we need not, it is important to note, choose a description or name which the original speaker would agree fits what he was referring to. That is, we can report the speaker in the above case to have said truly of Jones that he is kind to her even if the original speaker did not know that the man he was referring to is named Jones or even if he thinks he is not named Jones.

Returning to what Linsky said in the passage quoted, he claimed that, were someone to say "Her husband is kind to her," when she has no husband, *the statement* would be neither true nor false. As I have said, this is a likely view to hold if the definite description is being used attributively. But if it is being used referentially it is not clear what is meant by "the statement." If we think about what the speaker said about the person he referred to, then there is no reason to suppose he has not said something true or false about him, even though he is not the lady's husband. And Linsky's claim would be wrong. On the other hand, if we do not identify the statement in this way, what is the statement that the speaker made? To say that the statement he made was that her husband is kind to her lands us in difficulties. For we have to decide whether in using the definite description here in the identification of the statement, we are using it attributively or referentially. If the former, then we misrepresent the linguistic performance of the speaker; if the latter, then we are ourselves referring to someone and reporting the speaker to have said something of that person, in which case we are back to the possibility that he did say something true or false of that person.

I am thus drawn to the conclusion that when a speaker uses a definite description referentially he may have stated something true or false even if nothing fits the description, and that there is not a clear sense in which he has made a statement which is neither true nor false.

I X

I want to end by a brief examination [of] a picture of what a genuine referring expression is that one might derive from Russell's views. I want to suggest that this picture is not so far

wrong as one might suppose and that strange as this may seem, some of the things we have said about the referential use of definite descriptions are not foreign to this picture.

Genuine proper names, in Russell's sense, would refer to something without ascribing any properties to it. They would, one might say, refer to the thing itself, not simply the thing in so far as it falls under a certain description.[13] Now this would seem to Russell something a definite description could not do, for he assumed that if definite descriptions were capable of referring at all, they would refer to something only in so far as that thing satisfied the description. Not only have we seen this assumption to be false, however, but in the last section we saw something more. We saw that when a definite description is used referentially, a speaker can be reported as having said something *of* something. And in reporting what it was of which he said something we are not restricted to the description he used, or synonyms of it; we may ourselves refer to it using any descriptions, names, and so forth, that will do the job. Now this seems to give a sense in which we are concerned with the thing itself and not just the thing under a certain description, when we report the linguistic act of a speaker using a definite description referentially. That is, such a definite description comes closer to performing the function of Russell's proper names than certainly he supposed.

Secondly, Russell thought, I believe, that whenever we use descriptions, as opposed to proper names, we introduce an element of generality which ought to be absent if what we are doing is referring to some particular thing. This is clear from his analysis of sentences containing definite descriptions. One of the conclusions we are supposed to draw from that analysis is that such sentences express what are in reality completely general propositions: there is a ϕ and only one such and any ϕ is ψ. We might put this in a slightly different way. If there is anything which might be identified as reference here, it is reference in a very weak sense—namely, reference to *whatever* is the one and only one ϕ, if there is any such. Now this is something we might well say about the attributive use of definite descriptions, as should be evident from the previous discussion. But this lack of particularity is absent from the referential use of definite descriptions precisely because the description is here merely a device for getting one's audience to pick out or think of the thing to be spoken about, a device which may serve its function even if the description is incorrect. More importantly perhaps, in the referential use as opposed to the attributive, there is a *right* thing to be picked out by the audience and its being the right thing is not simply a function of its fitting the description.

ACKNOWLEDGEMENTS

I should like to thank my colleagues, John Canfield, Sydney Shoemaker, and Timothy Smiley, who read an earlier draft and gave me helpful suggestions. I also had the benefit of the valuable and detailed comments of the referee for the paper, to whom I wish to express my gratitude.

NOTES

1. "On Denoting," reprinted in *Logic and Knowledge,* ed. Robert C. Marsh (London: 1956), p. 51.

2. "On Referring," reprinted in *Philosophy and Ordinary Language,* ed. Charles C. Caton (Urbana: 1963), pp. 162–163.

3. *Ibid.,* p. 162.

4. *Ibid.,* p. 170.

5. Here and elsewhere I use the disjunction "presuppose or imply" to avoid taking a stand that would side me with Russell or Strawson on the issue of what the relationship involved is. To take a stand here would be beside my main point as well as being misleading, since later on I shall argue that the presupposition or implication arises in a different way depending upon the use to which the definite description is put. This last also accounts for my use of the vagueness indicator, "in some sense."

6. In a footnote added to the original version of "On Referring" (*op. cit.,* p. 181) Strawson seems to imply that where the presupposition is false, we still succeed in referring in a "secondary" way, which seems to mean "as we could be said to refer to fictional or make-believe things." But his view is still that we cannot refer in such a case in the "primary" way. This is, I believe, wrong. For a discussion of this modification of Strawson's view see Charles E. Caton, "Strawson on Referring," *Mind,* LXVIII (1959), 539–544.

7. This is an adaptation of an example (used for a somewhat different purpose) given by Leonard Linsky in "Reference and Referents," in *Philosophy and Ordinary Language,* p. 80.

8. In "Reference and Referents" (pp. 74–75, 80), Linsky correctly points out that one does not fail to refer simply because the description used does not in fact fit anything (or fits more than one thing). Thus he pinpoints one of the difficulties in Strawson's view. Here, however, I use this fact about referring to make a distinction I believe he does not draw, between two uses of definite descriptions. I later discuss the second passage from Linsky's paper.

9. In "A Reply to Mr. Sellars," *Philosophical Review,* LXIII (1954), 216–231, Strawson admits that we do not always refuse to ascribe truth to what a person says when the definite description he uses fails to fit anything (or fits more than one thing). To cite one of his examples, a person who said, "The United States Chamber of Deputies contains representatives of two major parties," would be allowed to have said something true even though he had used the wrong title. Strawson thinks this does not constitute a genuine problem for his view. He thinks that what we do in such cases, "where the speaker's intended reference is pretty clear, is simply to amend his statement in accordance with his guessed intentions and assess the amended statement for truth or falsity: we are not awarding a truth value at all to the original statement" (p. 230).

The notion of an "amended statement," however, will not do. We may note, first of all, that the sort of case Strawson has in mind could arise only when a definite description is used referentially. For the "amendment" is made by seeing the speaker's intended reference. But this could happen only if the speaker had an intended reference, a particular person or thing in mind, independent of the description he used. The cases Strawson has in mind are presumably not cases of slips of the tongue or the like; presumably they are cases in which a definite description is used because the speaker believes, though he is mistaken, that he is describing correctly what he wants to refer to. We supposedly amend the statement by knowing to what he intends to refer. But what description is to be used in the amended statement? In the example, perhaps, we could use "the United States Congress." But this description might be one the speaker would not even accept as correctly describing what he wants to refer to, because he is misinformed about the correct title. Hence, this is not a case of deciding what the speaker meant to say as opposed to what he in fact said, for the speaker did not mean to say "the United States Congress." If this is so, then there is no bar to the "amended" statement containing any description that does correctly pick out what the speaker intended to refer to. It could be, e.g., "The lower house of the United States Congress." But this means that there is no one unique "amended" statement to be assessed for truth value. And, in fact, it should now be clear that the notion of the amended statement really plays no role anyway. For if we can arrive at the amended statement only by first knowing to what the speaker intended to refer, we can assess the truth of what he said simply by deciding whether what he intended to refer to has the properties he ascribed to it.

10. As noted earlier (note 6), Strawson may allow that one has possibly referred in a "secondary" way, but, if I am right, the fact that there is no ϕ does not preclude one from having referred in the same way one does if there is a ϕ.

11. For a further discussion of the notion of saying something true *of* someone or something, see section VIII.

12. "Reference and Referents," p. 80. It should be clear that I agree with Linsky in holding that a speaker may refer even though the "presupposition of existence" is not satisfied. And I agree in thinking this an objection to Strawson's view. I think, however, that this point, among others, can be used to define two distinct uses of definite descriptions which, in turn, yields a more general criticism of Strawson. So, while I develop here a point of difference, which grows out of the distinction I want to make, I find myself in agreement with much of Linsky's article.

13. Cf. "The Philosophy of Logical Atomism," reprinted in *Logic and Knowledge,* p. 200.

4

Utterer's Meaning, Sentence-Meaning, and Word-Meaning

H. P. GRICE

A. INTRODUCTORY REMARKS

My aim in this paper is to throw light on the connection between (a) a notion of meaning which I want to regard as basic, namely the notion which is involved in saying of someone that by (when) doing such-and-such he meant that so-and-so (in what I have called a non-natural sense of the word 'meant'), and (b) the notions of meaning involved in saying (i) that a given sentence means 'so-and-so [and] (ii) that a given word or phrase means 'so-and-so'. What I have to say on these topics should be looked upon as an attempt to provide a sketch of what might, I hope, prove to be a viable theory, rather than as an attempt to provide any part of a finally acceptable theory. The account which I shall offer of the (for me) basic notion of meaning is one which I shall not here seek to defend; I should like its approximate correctness to be assumed, so that attention may be focused on its utility, if correct, in the explication of other and (I hope) derivative notions of meaning. This enterprise forms part of a wider programme which I shall in a moment delineate, though its later stages lie beyond the limits which I have set for this paper.

The wider programme arises out of a distinction which, for purposes which I need not here specify, I wish to make within the total signification of a remark: a distinction between what the speaker has *said* (in a certain favoured, and maybe in some degree artificial, sense of 'said'), and what he has *implicated* (e.g., implied, indicated, suggested), taking into account the fact that what he has implicated may be either conventionally implicated (implicated by virtue of the meaning of some word or phrase which he has used) or nonconventionally implicated (in which case the specification of the implicature falls outside the specification of the conventional meaning of the words used). The programme is directed towards an explication of the favoured sense of 'say' and a clarification of its relation to the notion of conventional meaning.

There are six stages in the programme.

(I) To distinguish between locutions of the form 'U (utterer) meant *that* . . .' (locutions which specify what might be called 'occasion-meaning') and locutions of the form 'X (utterance-type) means " . . ."'. In locutions of the first type, meaning is specified without the use of quotation marks, whereas in locutions of the second type the meaning of a sentence, word, or phrase is specified with the aid of quotation marks. This difference is semantically important.

(II) To attempt to provide a definiens for statements of occasion-meaning, or more precisely, to provide a definiens for 'By (when) uttering x, U meant that ∗p'. Some explanatory comments are needed here.

(a) I use the term 'utter' (together with 'utterance') in an artificially wide sense, to cover any case of doing x or producing x by the performance of which U meant that so-and-so. The performance in question need not be a linguistic or even a conventionalized performance. A specificatory replacement of the dummy 'x' will in some cases be a characterization of a deed, in others a characterization of a product (e.g., a sound).

(b) '∗' is a *dummy* mood-indicator, distinct from specific mood-indicators like '⊢' (indicative or assertive) or '!' (imperative). More precisely, one may think of the schema 'Jones meant that ∗p' as yielding a full English sentence after two transformational steps:

(i) Replace '∗' by a specific mood-indicator and replace 'p' by an indicative sentence. One might thus get to

'Jones meant that ⊢ Smith will go home'.

or

'Jones meant that ! Smith will go home'.

(ii) Replace the sequence following the word 'that' by an appropriate clause in indirect speech (in accordance with rules specified in a linguistic theory). One might thus get to

'Jones meant that Smith will go home'.
'Jones meant that Smith is to go home'.

(III) To attempt to elucidate the notion of the conventional meaning of an utterance-type, or more precisely, to explicate sentences which make claims of the form 'X (utterance-type) means "∗p"', or, in case X is a non-sentential utterance-type, claims of the form 'X means " ..."', where the locution is completed by a nonsentential expression. Again, some explanatory comments are required.

(a) It will be convenient to recognize that what I shall call statements of *timeless meaning* (statements of the type 'X means " ..."', in which the specification of meaning involves quotation marks) may be subdivided into (i) statements of timeless 'idiolect-meaning', such as 'For U (in U's idiolect) X means " ..."' and (ii) statements of timeless 'language meaning', such as, 'In L (language) X means " ..."'. It will be convenient to handle these separately, and in the order just given.

(b) The truth of a statement to the effect that 'X means " ..."' is of course not incompatible with the truth of a further statement to the effect that 'X means "__"', when the two lacunae are quite differently completed. An utterance-type may have more than one conventional meaning, and any definiens which we offer must allow for this fact. 'X means " ..."' should be understood as 'One of the meanings of X is " ..."'.

(IV) In view of the possibility of multiplicity in the timeless meaning of an utterance-type, we shall need to notice, and to provide an explication of, what I shall call the *applied timeless meaning* of an utterance-type. That is, we need a definiens for the schema 'X (utterance-type) meant *here* " ..."', a schema the specifications of which announce the correct reading of X for a given occasion of utterance.

Comments. (a) We must be careful to distinguish the applied timeless meaning of X (type) with respect to a particular token x (belonging to X) from the occasion-meaning of U's utterance of x. The following are not equivalent:

(i) 'When U uttered it, the sentence "Palmer gave Nicklaus quite a beating" meant "Palmer vanquished Nicklaus with some ease" (rather than, say, "Palmer administered vigorous corporal punishment to Nicklaus.")'

(ii) 'When U uttered the sentence "Palmer gave Nicklaus quite a beating," U meant that Palmer vanquished Nicklaus with some ease.'

U might have been speaking ironically, in which case he would likely have meant that *Nicklaus* vanquished *Palmer* with some ease. In that case (ii) would clearly be false; but nevertheless (i) would still have been true.

(b) There is some temptation to take the view that the conjunction of

(i) 'By uttering X, U meant that *p' and

(ii) 'When uttered by U, X meant "*p"'

provides a definiens for 'In uttering X, U said that *p'. Indeed, if we give consideration only to utterance-types for which there are available adequate statements of timeless meaning that take the exemplary form 'X meant "*p"' (or, in the case of applied timeless meaning, the form 'X meant here "*p"'), it may even be possible to uphold the thesis that such a co-incidence of occasion-meaning and applied timeless meaning is a necessary and sufficient condition for saying that *p. But a little reflection should convince us of the need to recognize the existence of statements of timeless meaning which instantiate forms other than the cited exemplary form; there are, I think, at least some sentences whose timeless meaning is not adequately specifiable by a statement of the exemplary form. Consider the sentence 'Bill is a philosopher and he is, therefore, brave' (S_1). It would be appropriate, I think, to make a partial specification of the timeless meaning of S_1 by saying 'Part of the meaning of S_1 is "Bill is occupationally engaged in philosophical studies"'. One might, indeed, give a full specification of timeless meaning for S_1 by saying 'One meaning of S_1 includes "Bill is occupationally engaged in philosophical studies" and "Bill is courageous" and "That Bill is courageous follows from his being occupationally engaged in philosophical studies", and that is all that is included'. We might re-express this as 'One meaning of S_1 *comprises* "Bill is occupationally engaged (etc.)", "Bill is courageous", and "That Bill is courageous follows (etc.)."' It is preferable to specify the timeless meaning of S_1 in this way than to do so as follows: 'One meaning of S_1 is "Bill is occupationally engaged (etc.) and Bill is courageous and that Bill is courageous follows (etc.),"' for the latter formulation at least suggests that S_1 is synonymous with the conjunctive sentence quoted in the formulation, which does not seem to be the case.

Since it is true that *another* meaning of S_1 includes 'Bill is addicted to general reflections about life' (in place of 'Bill is occupationally engaged (etc.)'), one could have occasion to say (truly), with respect to a given utterance by U of S_1, 'The meaning of S_1 *here* comprised "Bill is occupationally engaged (etc.)", "Bill is courageous", and "That Bill is courageous follows (etc.)"', or to say 'The meaning of S_1 *here* included "That Bill is courageous follows (etc.)"'. It could also be true that when U uttered S_1 he meant (part of what he meant was) *that* that Bill is courageous follows (etc.).

Now I do not wish to allow that, in my favoured sense of 'say', one who utters S_1 will have *said* that Bill's being courageous follows from his being a philosopher, though he may well have said that Bill is a philosopher and that Bill is courageous. I would wish to maintain that the semantic function of the word 'therefore' is to enable a speaker to *indicate,* though not to *say,* that a certain consequence holds. *Mutatis mutandis,* I would adopt the same position with regard to words like 'but' and 'moreover'. My primary reason for opting for this particular sense of 'say' is that I expect it to be of greater theoretical utility than some other sense of 'say' would be. So I shall be committed to the view that applied timeless meaning and occasion-meaning may coincide, that is to say, it may be true both (i) that when U uttered X the meaning of X included '*p' and (ii) that part of what U meant when he uttered X was that *p, and yet be false that U has said, among other things, that *p. I would like to use the expression 'conventionally meant that' in such a way that the fulfillment of the two conditions just mentioned, while insufficient for the truth of 'U said that *p' will be sufficient (and necessary) for the truth of 'U conventionally meant that *p'.

(V) This distinction between what is said and what is conventionally meant creates the task of specifying the conditions in which what U conventionally meant by an utterance is also part of what U said. I have hopes of being able to discharge this task by trying:

(1) To specify conditions which will be satisfied only by a limited range of speech-acts, the members of which will thereby be stamped as specially central or fundamental.

(2) To stipulate that in uttering X, U will have said that *p, if both (i) U has Y-ed that *p, where Y-ing is a central speech-act, and (ii) X embodies some conventional device the

meaning of which is such that its presence in X indicates that its utterer is Y-ing that *p.

(3) To define, for each member Y of the range of central speech-acts, 'U has Y-ed that *p' in terms of occasion-meaning (meaning that . . .) or in terms of some important elements involved in the already provided definition of occasion-meaning.

(VI) The fulfillment of the task just outlined will need to be supplemented by an account of the elements in the conventional meaning of an utterance which are *not* part of what has been said. This account, at least for an important subclass of such elements, might take the following shape:

(1) The problematic elements are linked with certain speech-acts which are exhibited as posterior to, and such that their performance is dependent upon, some member or disjunction of members of the central range; for example, the meaning of 'moreover' would be linked with the speech-act of adding, the performance of which would require the performance of one or another of the central speech-acts.

(2) If Z-ing is such a noncentral speech-act, the dependence of Z-ing that *p upon the performance of some central speech-act would have to be shown to be of a nature which justifies a reluctance to treat Z-ing that *p as a case not merely of saying that *p, but also of saying that #p, or of saying that # *p, where '#p' or '#*p' is a representation of one or more sentential forms specifically associated with Z-ing (as "moreover" is specifically associated with the speech-act of adding).

(3) The notion of Z-ing that *p (where Z-ing is noncentral) would be explicated in terms of the notion of *meaning that* (or in terms of some important elements in the definition of that notion).

B. TREATMENT OF SOME OF THE PROBLEMS RAISED

The problems which I shall consider in the remainder of this paper are those which are presented by Stages II–IV of the programme.

Stage II

I shall offer, without arguing for it, a somewhat over-simplified account of the notion of occasion-meaning, which (as I said at the outset) I should like to be treated as if it were correct.

In my 1957 article on 'Meaning'[1] I suggested, for the schema 'U meant (non-naturally) something by uttering x', a three-clause definiens which may be compendiously reformulated as 'For some audience A, U intended his utterance of x to produce in A some effect (response) E, by means of A's recognition of that intention'. As I wish to continue to use the central idea of this definition, I shall introduce an abbreviation: 'U intends to produce in A effect E by means of A's recognition of that intention' is abbreviated to 'U *M-intends* to produce in A effect E'. ('M' for 'meaning').

The point of divergence between my current account and my 1957 account lies in the characterization of the M-intended effect (response). In the earlier account I took the view that the M-intended effect is, in the case of indicative-type utterances, that the hearer should *believe* something, and, in the case of imperative-type utterances, that the hearer should *do* something. I wish for present purposes to make two changes here.

(1) I wish to represent the M-intended effect of imperative-type utterances as being that the hearer should *intend* to do something (with of course the ulterior intention on the part of the utterer that the hearer should go on to do the act in question).

(2) I wish to regard the M-intended effect common to indicative-type utterances as being, not that the hearer should believe something (though there is frequently an ulterior intention to that effect), but that the hearer should *think that the utterer believes* something.

The effect of the first change will be that the way is opened to a simplified treatment of the M-intended effect, as being always the generation of some propositional attitude. The effect of the second change (made in order to unify the treatment of indicative-type utterances, some of which are, and some of which are not, cases of informing or telling) will be to introduce a distinction between what I might call *exhibitive* utterances (utterances by which the utterer U M-intends to impart a belief that he (U) has a certain propositional attitude) and utterances which are not only exhibitive but also what I might call *protreptic* (utterances by which U M-intends, *via* imparting a belief that he (U) has a certain propositional attitude, to induce a corresponding attitude in the hearer).

I shall now try to reformulate the account in a generalized form. Let 'A' range over audiences or hearers. Let the device '$*_\psi$' (read 'asterisk-sub-ψ') be a dummy, which represents a specific mood-indicator which corresponds to the propositional attitude ψ-ing (whichever that may be), as, for example, '$\vdash$' corresponds to believing (thinking) and '!' corresponds to intending. I can, using this device, offer the following rough definition:

D.1. 'By (when) uttering x U meant that $*_\psi p$' = df. '($\exists A$) (U uttered x M-intending (i) that A should think U to ψ that p and [in some cases only, depending on the identification of $*_\psi p$] (ii) that A should, via the fulfillment of (i), himself ψ that p)'.

It is convenient to have an abbreviated version of this definiens. Let the device 'ψ^+' (read 'ψ-dagger') be a dummy which operates as follows: in some cases the phrase 'that A should ψ^+ that p' is to be interpreted as 'that A should think U to ψ that p'; in other cases this phrase is to be interpreted as 'that A should ψ that p (via thinking U to ψ that p)'. Which interpretation is to be selected is determined by the specification of '$*_\psi p$'. We may now reformulate D.1 as follows:

D.1'. 'By (when) uttering x, U meant that $*_\psi p$' = df. '($\exists A$) (U uttered x M-intending that A should ψ^+ that p)'.

To meet all the difficulties to which my 1957 account (which was only intended as a model) is exposed, a very much more complicated definition is required. But as the examples which force the introduction of this complexity involve relatively sophisticated kinds of communication or linguistic performance, I hope that, for working purposes, the proffered definition will be adequate.

Stage III

Step (1): timeless meaning for unstructured utterance-types.

It is, I think, extremely important to distinguish two problems:

(1) What is the relation between timeless meaning (for complete utterance-types) and occasion-meaning?

(2) In the case of syntactically structured (linguistic) utterance-types, how is the timeless meaning of a complete (sentential) utterance-type related to the timeless meanings of its noncomplete structured and unstructured elements (approximately, phrases and words), and what account is to be given of timeless meaning for noncomplete utterance-types?

If we do not treat these problems separately, we shall have only ourselves to blame for the confusion in which we shall find ourselves. So initially I shall restrict myself to examining the notion of timeless meaning in its application to unstructured utterance-types. My main example will be a gesture (a signal), and it will be convenient first to consider the idea of its timeless meaning for an individual (within a signaling idiolect, so to speak), and only afterward to consider the extension of this idea to groups of individuals. We shall thus preserve for the time being the possibility of keeping distinct the ideas of having an *established* meaning and of having a *conventional* meaning.

Suppose that a particular sort of hand wave (to be referred to as "HW") for a particular individual U (within U's idiolect) means 'I know the route.' We are to look for an explication of the sentence 'For U, HW means "I know the route"' which will relate timeless meaning to occasion-meaning. As a first shot, one might suggest something like 'It is U's policy (practice, habit) to utter HW in order to *mean that* U knows the route' (where 'mean that' is to be analysed in accordance with D.1.); or more perspicuously, 'It is U's policy (practice, habit) to utter HW iff U is making an utterance by which U *means that* U knows the route.'

If we apply D.1. to this suggested definiens, we shall get the following expanded definiens: 'It is U's policy (practice, habit) to utter HW if U is making an utterance by means of which (for some A) U M-intends to effect that A thinks U to think that U knows the route'. Now, whether or not this definiens is otherwise acceptable, I wish to argue that the notion of M-intention is otiose here, and that only the notion of simple intention need be invoked; if U's policy (practice, habit) is such that his use of HW is tied to the presence of a *simple* intention to affect an audience in the way described, it will follow that when, on a given occasion, he utters HW, he will do so, on that occasion, M-intending to affect his audience in that way.

Suppose that, using only the notion of simple intention, we specify U's policy as follows: 'I (that is, utterer U) shall utter HW if I intend (want) some A to think that I think I know the route'. Now, if U is ever to have the particular intentions which will be involved in every implementation of this policy, he must (logically) be in a position, when uttering HW, to suppose that there is at least some chance that these intentions will be realized; for such a supposition to be justified, as U well knows, a given audience A must be aware of U's policy and must suppose it to apply to the utterance of HW with which U has presented him. U, then, when uttering HW on a particular occasion, must expect A to think (or at least to be in a position to think) as follows: 'U's policy for HW is such that he utters HW now with the intention that I should think that he thinks that he knows the route; in that case, I take it that he does think that he knows the route.' But to utter HW expecting A to respond in such a way *is* to utter HW M-intending that A should think that U thinks that U knows the route. So a formulation of U's policy of HW in terms of the notion of simple intention is adequate to ensure that, by a particular utterance of HW, U will *mean that* he knows the route.

We may, then, suggest a simplified definition: 'For U, HW means "I know the route"' = df. 'It is U's policy (practice, habit) to utter HW if, for some A, U intends (wants) A to think that U thinks U knows the route'. This definition, however, is doubly unacceptable. (1) For U, HW may have a second meaning; it may also mean 'I am about to leave you'. If that is so, U's policy (etc.) cannot be to utter HW *only if* U wants some A to think that U thinks U knows the route; sometimes he will be ready to utter HW wanting some A to think that U thinks that U is about to leave A. (2) U may have other ways of getting an A to think that U thinks that U knows the route (such as saying 'I know the route') and may be ready, on occasion, to employ them. That being so, U's policy (etc.) cannot be to utter HW *if* (i.e., whenever) U wants A to think that U thinks U knows the route.

To cope with these difficulties, I think I need some such idea as that of 'having a certain procedure in one's repertoire'. This idea seems to me to be intuitively fairly intelligible and to have application outside the realm of linguistic, or otherwise communicative, performances, though it could hardly be denied that it requires further explication. A faintly eccentric lecturer might have in his repertoire the following procedure: if he sees an attractive girl in his audience, to pause for half a minute and then take a sedative. His having in his repertoire this procedure would not be incompatible with his also having two further procedures: (a) if he sees an attractive girl, to put on a pair of dark spectacles (instead of pausing and taking a sedative); (b) to pause and take a sedative when he sees in his audience not an attractive girl, but a particularly distinguished colleague. Somewhat similarly, if U has in his repertoire the procedure of uttering HW if he wants an audience A to think U thinks U knows the route, this fact would not be incompatible with his having at least two further procedures: (1) to say 'I know the route' if he wants some A to think U thinks U knows the route, and (2) to utter HW if U wants some A to think U thinks he is about to leave A. So I propose the definition:

D.2. 'For U utterance-type X means (has as one of its meanings) "$*_\psi p$"' = df. 'U has in his repertoire the following procedure: to utter a token of X if U intends (wants) A to ψ^+ that p'.

We may now turn from the idea of timeless meaning within an idiolect to that of timeless meaning for a group or class of individuals. If U utters HW, his measure of expectation of success as regards effecting the intended response obviously depends (as has already been remarked) on A's knowledge of U's procedure; and normally, unless the signal is to be explained to each A, on A's repertoire containing the same procedure. So obviously each member of some group G (within which HW is to be a tool of communication) will want his procedure with respect to HW to conform to the general practice of the group. So I suggest the following rough definition:

D.3. 'For group G, utterance-type X means "$*_\psi p$"' = df. 'At least some (many) members of group G have in their repertoires the procedure of uttering a token of X if, for some A, they want A to ψ^+ that p, the retention of this procedure being for them conditional on the assumption that at least some (other) members of G have, or have had, this procedure in their repertoires'.

D.3. gets in the idea of aiming at conformity and so perhaps (derivatively) also that of *correct* and *incorrect* use of X, as distinct from the idea merely of usual or unusual use of X.

The explication of the notion of 'having a procedure in one's repertoire' is, to my mind, a task of considerable difficulty. I have felt inclined to propose, as a makeshift definition, the following:

'U has in his repertoire the procedure of . . .' = df. 'U has a standing readiness (willingness, preparedness), in some degree, to . . .', a readiness (etc.) to do something being a member of the same family (a weaker brother, so to speak) as an intention to do that thing.

But this definition would clearly be inadequate as it stands. It may well be true that, for my exceedingly prim Aunt Matilda, the expression 'he is a runt' means 'he is an undersized person', and yet quite false that she has *any* degree of readiness to utter the expression in any circumstances whatsoever. What one seems to need is the idea of her being *equipped* to use the expression, and the analysis of *this* idea is also problematic.

So for the present I shall abandon the attempt to provide a definition, and content myself with a few informal remarks. There seem to me to be three main types of cases in which one may legitimately speak of an established procedure in respect of utterance-type X:

(1) That in which X is current for some group G; that is to say, to utter X in such-and-such circumstances is part of the practice of many members of G. In that case my Aunt Matilda (a member of G) may be said to have a procedure for X, even though she herself would rather be seen dead than utter X, for she knows that some other members of G *do* have a readiness to utter X in such-and-such circumstances.

(2) That in which X is current only for U; it is only *U's* practice to utter X in such-and-such circumstances. In this case U *will* have a readiness to utter X in such-and-such circumstances.

(3) That in which X is not current at all, but the utterance of X in such-and-such circumstances is part of some system of communication which U has devised but which has never been put into operation (like the new Highway Code which I invent one day while lying in my bath). In that case U has a procedure for X in the attenuated sense that he has envisaged a possible system of practices which *would* involve a readiness to utter X in such-and-such circumstances.

Stage IV

Step (1): applied timeless meaning for unstructured utterance types.

We are now in a position to define a notion of applied timeless meaning which will apply to HW:

D.4. 'When U uttered X (type), X meant "*p"' = df. '($\exists$A) (U intended A to recognize (? and to recognize that U intended A to recognize) what U meant [occasion-meaning] by his uttering X, on the basis of A's knowledge (assumption) that, for U, X means (has as one of its meanings) "*p" [as defined by D.2.])'.

Or it can be more fully defined (let '*' and '*'' both be dummy mood-indicators):

D.4'. 'When U uttered X, X meant "*$_\psi$p"' = df. '($\exists$A) ($\exists$q) (U meant by uttering X that *'q; and U intended A to recognize (? and to recognize that he was intended to recognize) that, by uttering X, U meant that *'q *via* A's knowledge (assumption) that in U's repertoire is the procedure of uttering X if, for some A', U wants A' to ψ^+ that p)' ['p' may, or may not, represent that propositional content to which indefinite reference is made in the existential quantification of 'q'].

D.4. and of course D.4'. allow both for the case in which U meant by HW *that* he knew the route (coincidence of meaning '. . .' and meaning *that* . . .), and also for the case in which, for example, U (a criminal) has lured a victim into his car and signals (non-literally, so to speak) to his accomplice that he knows how to handle the victim. In both cases it is expected by U that the audience's understanding of the utterance of HW will be based on its knowledge that U has a certain procedure (to utter HW if U wants an audience to think that U thinks U knows the route).

Stages III and IV

Step (2): timeless and applied timeless meaning for structured utterance-types, complete and non-complete

To deal with structure utterance-types and their elements, I think I need the following apparatus.

(1) Let 'S_1 (S_2)' (read 'S_1-with-S_2') denote a sentence of which S_2 is a sub-sentence. Allow that a sentence is a sub-sentence of itself, so that S_2 may $= S_1$.

(2) Let $v[S_1$ (S_2)] (read 'v-of-S_1-with-S_2') be a particular utterance (token) of S_1 (S_2) uttered by U. $v[S_1$ (S_2)] is to be a *complete* utterance; that is, it is not to be part of $v[S_3$ (S_1 (S_2))] (not e.g., to be the utterance of a disjunct within the utterance of a disjunction).

(3) It is characteristic of sentences (a characteristic shared with phrases) that their standard meaning is consequential upon the meaning of the elements (words, lexical items) which enter into them. So I need the notion of a 'resultant procedure': as a first approximation, one might say that a procedure for an utterance-type X is a resultant procedure if it is determined by (its existence is inferable from) a knowledge of procedures (1) for particular utterance-types which are elements in X, and (2) for any sequence of utterance-types which exemplifies a particular ordering of syntactical categories (a particular syntactical form).

Now let us deal with the notion of timeless meaning in U's idiolect:

D.5. 'For U, S means "$*_\psi p$"' = df. 'U has a resultant procedure for S, namely to utter S if, for some A, U wants A to ψ^+ that p.' [D.5. parallels D.2.]

An explication of timeless meaning in a language can, perhaps, be provided by adapting D.3., but I shall not attempt this task now.

For applied timeless meaning I offer:

D.6. 'S_2 in $v[S_1$ (S_2)] meant "$*_\psi p$"' = df. '($\exists$A)($\exists$q)(U meant by $v[S_1$ (S_2)] that $*'q$, and U intended A to recognize that U meant by $v[S_1$ (S_2)] that $*'q$ at least partly on the basis of A's thought that U has a resultant procedure for S_2, namely (for suitable A') to utter S_2 if U wants A' to ψ^+ that p).' [D.6. parallels D.4'.]

So far (maybe) so good. But the notion of 'resultant procedure' has been left pretty unilluminated, and if we are to shed any light on the notion of word meaning, and its connection with 'meaning that', we ought to look at

the nature of the more fundamental procedures from which a resultant procedure descends. It would be nice to give a general schema, to show the role of word meanings (covering every type of word) in determining (in combination) sentence meanings (covering sentences of any syntactical structure). But this looks like a Herculean task (in our present state of knowledge). The best we can hope for is a sketch, for a very restricted (but central) range of word types and syntactical forms, of a fragment of what might be the kind of theory we need. Let us take as our range all or part of the range of affirmative categorical (not necessarily indicative) sentences involving a noun (or definite description) and an adjective (or adjectival phrase).

The apparatus needed (for one such attempt) would be:

(1) Suppose σ to be an indicative sentence. Then we need to be able to apply the ideas of an indicative version of σ (σ itself), an imperative version of σ, an optative version of σ, etc. (mood variations). It would be the business of some linguistic theory to equip us to apply such characterizations (so as philosophers of language we can assume this as given).

(2) We need to be able to apply some such notion as a prediction of β (adjectival) on α (nominal). 'Smith is tactful', 'Smith, be tactful', 'Let Smith be tactful', and 'Oh, that Smith may be tactful' would be required to count, all of them, as predications of 'tactful' on 'Smith'. It would again be the business of some linguistic theory to set up such a sentential characterization.

(3) Suppose we, for a moment, take for granted two species of correlation, R-correlation (referential) and D-correlation (denotational). We want to be able to speak of some particular object as an R-correlate of α (nominal), and of each member of some class as being a D-correlate of β (adjectival).

Now suppose that U has the following two procedures (P):

P.1. To utter the indicative version of σ if (for some A) U wants/intends A to think that U thinks ... (the blank being filled by the infinitive version of σ, e.g., 'Smith to be tactful'.) Also, P.1.': obtained from P.1 by substituting 'imperative'/'indicative' and 'intend'/'think that U thinks'.) [Such procedures set up correlations between moods and specifications of 'ψ^+'.]

P.2. To utter a ψ^+-correlated [cf. P.1. and P.1.'] predication of β on α if (for some A) U wants A to ψ^+ a particular R-correlate of α to be one of a particular set of D-correlates of β.

Further suppose that, for U, the following two correlations hold:

C1. Jones' dog is an R-correlate of 'Fido'.

C2. Any hairy-coated thing is a D-correlate of 'shaggy'.

Given that U has the initial procedures P.1. and P.2., we can infer that U has the resultant procedure (determined by P.1. and P.2.):

RP1: To utter the indicative version of a predication of β on α if U wants A to think U to think a particular R-correlate of α to be one of a particular set of D-correlates of β.

Given RP1 and C1, we can infer that U has:

RP2: To utter the indicative version of a predication of β on 'Fido' if U wants A to think U to think Jones' dog to be one of a particular set of D-correlates of β.

Given RP2 and C2, we can infer that U has:

RP3: To utter the indicative version of a predication of 'shaggy' on 'Fido' if U wants A to think U to think Jones' dog is one of the set of hairy-coated things (i.e., is hairy-coated).

And given the information from the linguist that 'Fido is shaggy' is the indicative version of a predication of 'shaggy' on 'Fido' (assumed), we can infer U to have:

RP4: To utter 'Fido is shaggy' if U wants A to think U to think that Jones' dog is hairy-coated. And RP4 is an interpretant of 'For U, "Fido is shaggy" means "Jones' dog is hairy-coated"'.

I have not yet provided an explication for statements of timeless meaning relating to noncomplete utterance-types. I am not in a position to provide a definiens for 'X (non-complete) means " ..."'. Indeed, I am not certain that a general form of definition *can* be provided for this schema; it may remain impossible to provide a definiens until the syntactical category of X has been given. I can, however, provide a definiens which may be adequate for *adjectival* X (e.g., 'shaggy'):

D.7. 'For U, X (adjectival) means " ..."' = df. 'U has this procedure: to utter a ψ^+-correlated predication of X on α if (for some A) U wants A to ψ^+ a particular R-correlate of α to be ...' (where the two lacunae represented by dots are identically completed).

Any specific procedure of the form mentioned in the definiens of D.7. can be shown to be a *resultant* procedure. For example, if U has P.2. and also C2., it is inferable that he has the procedure of uttering a ψ^+-correlated predication of 'shaggy' on α if (for some A) U wants A to ψ^+ a particular R-correlate of α to be one of the set of hairy-coated things, that is, that for U 'shaggy' means 'hairy-coated.'

I can now offer a definition of the notion of a *complete* utterance-type which has so far been taken for granted:

D.8. 'X is complete' = df. 'A fully expanded definiens for "X means '...'"' contains no explicit reference to correlation, other than that involved in speaking of an R-correlate of some referring expression occurring within X'. (The expanded definiens for the complete utterance-type 'He is shaggy' may be expected to contain the phrase 'a particular R-correlate of "he"'.)

Correlation. We must now stop taking for granted the notion of correlation. What does it mean to say that, for example, Jones' dog is the/a R-correlate of 'Fido'? One idea (building in as little as possible) would be to think of 'Fido' and Jones' dog as paired, in some system of pairing in which names and objects form ordered pairs. But in *one* sense of 'pair,' any one name and any one object form a pair (an ordered pair, the first member of which is the name, the second the object). We want a sense of 'paired' in which 'Fido' is paired with Jones' dog but not with Smith's cat. 'Selected pair'? But what does 'selected' mean? Not 'selected' in the sense in which an apple and an orange may be selected from a dish: perhaps in the sense in which a dog may be selected (as something with which [to which] the selector intends to do something). But in the case of the word-thing pair, do what? And what is the process of selecting?

I suggest we consider initially the special case in which linguistic and nonlinguistic items are *explicitly* correlated. Let us take this to consist in performing some act as a result of which a linguistic item or a nonlinguistic item (or items) come to stand in a relation in which they did not previously stand, and in which neither stands to noncorrelates in the other realm. Since the act of correlation *may* be a verbal act, how can this set up a relation between items?

Suppose U produces a particular utterance (token) V, which belongs to the utterance-type 'shaggy: hairy-coated things'. To be able to say that U had by V correlated 'shaggy' with each member of the set of hairy-coated things, we should need to be able to say that there is some relation R such that:

(a) By uttering V, U effected that 'shaggy' stood in R to each hairy-coated thing, and only to hairy-coated things;

(b) U uttered V *in order that,* by uttering V he should effect this. It is clear that condition (b), on which some will look askance because it introduces a reference to U's *intention* in performing his act of correlation, is required, and that condition (a) alone would be inadequate. Certainly by uttering V, regardless of his intentions, U has set up a situation in which a relation R holds exclusively between 'shaggy' and each hairy-coated thing Z, namely the relation which consists in being an expression uttered by U on a particular occasion O in conversational juxtaposition with the name of a class to which Z belongs. But by the same act, U has also set up a situation in which another relation R' holds exclusively between 'shaggy' and each *non*-hairy-coated thing Z', namely the relation which consists in being an expression uttered by U on occasion O in conversational juxtaposition with the name of the *complement* of a class to which Z' belongs. We do not, however, for our purposes, wish to think of U as having correlated 'shaggy' with each non-hairy-coated thing. The only way to ensure that R' is eliminated is to add condition (b), which confines attention to a relationship which U *intends* to set up. It looks as if intensionality is embedded in the very foundations of the theory of language.

Let us, then, express more formally the proposed account of correlation. Suppose that V = utterance-token of type '"Shaggy": hairy-coated things' (written). Then, by uttering V, U has correlated 'Shaggy' with (and only with) each hairy-coated thing $\equiv$ ($\exists$R) {(U effected by V that [$\forall$x] [R 'Shaggy' x $\equiv$ xϵy (y is a hairy-coated thing)]) & (U uttered V in order that U effect by V that [$\forall$x] . . .)}.[2]

If so understood, U will have correlated 'shaggy' with hairy-coated things only if there is an identifiable R' for which the condition specified in the definiens holds. What is such an R'? I suggest R'xy $\equiv$ x is a (word) type such that V is a sequence consisting of a token of x followed by a colon followed by an expression ('hairy-coated things') the R-correlate of

which is a set of which y is a member. R'xy holds between 'shaggy' and each hairy-coated thing given U's utterance of V. Any utterance V' of the form exemplified by V could be uttered to set up R''xy (involving V' instead of V) between any expression and each member of any set of non-linguistic items.

There are other ways of achieving the same effect. The purpose of making the utterance can be specified in the utterance: V = utterance of 'To effect that, for some R, "shaggy" has R only to each hairy-coated thing, "shaggy": hairy-coated things'. The expression of the specified R will now have 'V is a sequence *containing*' instead of 'V is a sequence *consisting of* . . .' Or U can use the performative form: 'I correlate "shaggy" with each hairy-coated thing'. Utterance of this form will at the same time set up the required relation and label itself as being uttered with the purpose of setting up such a relation.

But by whichever form an act of explicit correlation is effected, to say of it that it is (or is intended to be) an act of correlation is always to make an indefinite reference to a relationship which the act is intended to set up, and the specification of the relation involved in turn always involves a further use of the notion of correlation (e.g., as above in speaking of a set which is the correlate [R-correlate] of a particular expression [e.g., 'Hairy-coated things']). This seems to involve a regress which might well be objectionable; though 'correlation' is not used in definition of correlation, it is used in specification of an indefinite reference occurring in the definition of correlation. It might be considered desirable (even necessary) to find a way of stopping this regress at some stage. (Is this a characteristically *empiricist* demand?) If we don't stop it, can correlation even get started (if prior correlation is presupposed)? Let us try 'ostensive correlation'. In an attempted ostensive correlation of the word 'shaggy' with the property of hairy-coatedness:

(1) U will perform a number of acts in each of which he ostends an object (a_1, a_2, a_3, etc.).

(2) Simultaneously with each ostension he utters a token of the word 'shaggy.'

(3) It is his intention to ostend, and to be recognized as ostending, only objects which are either, in his view, plainly hairy-coated or are, in his view, plainly not hairy-coated.

(4) In a model sequence these intentions are fulfilled. For a model sequence to succeed in correlating the word 'shaggy' with the property of being hairy-coated, it seems necessary (and perhaps also sufficient) that there should be some relation R which holds between the word 'shaggy' and each hairy-coated thing, y, just in case y is hairy-coated. Can such a relation R be specified? Perhaps at least in a sequence of model cases, in which U's linguistic intentions are rewarded by success, it can; the relation between the word 'shaggy' and each hairy-coated object y would be the relation which holds between each plainly hairy-coated object y and the word 'shaggy' and which consists in the fact that y is a thing to which U does and would apply, rather than refuse to apply, the word 'shaggy.' In other words in a limited universe consisting of things which in U's view are either plainly hairy-coated or plainly not hairy-coated, the relation R holds only between the word 'shaggy' and each object which is for U plainly hairy-coated.

This suggestion seems not without its difficulties:

(1) It looks as if we should want to distinguish between two relations R and R'; we want U to set up a relation R which holds between the word 'shaggy' and each hairy-coated object; but the preceding account seems not to distinguish between this relation and a relation R' which holds between the word 'shaggy' and each object which is in U's view unmistakably hairy-coated. To put it another way, how is U to distinguish between 'shaggy' (which means hairy-coated) and the word 'shaggy'* (which means 'in U's view unmistakably hairy-coated')?

(2) If in an attempt to evade these troubles we suppose the relation R to be one which holds between the word 'shaggy' and each object to which U would in certain circumstances apply the word 'shaggy,' how do we specify the circumstances in question? If we suggest that the circumstances are those in which U is concerned to set up an explicit correlation between the word 'shaggy' and each member of an appropriate set of objects, our proposal becomes at once unrealistic and problematic. Normally correlations seem to grow rather than to be created, and attempts to connect such growth with potentialities of

creation may give rise to further threats of circularity.

The situation seems to be as follows:

(1) We need to be able to invoke such a resultant procedure as the following, which we will call RP12, namely to predicate β on 'Fido', when U wants A to ψ^+ that Jones' dog is a D-correlate of β; and we want to be able to say that at least sometimes such a resultant procedure may result from among other things, a *nonexplicit* R-correlation of 'Fido' and Jones' dog.

(2) It is tempting to suggest that a nonexplicit R-correlation of 'Fido' and Jones' dog *consists* in the fact that U *would*, explicitly, correlate 'Fido' and Jones' dog.

(3) But to say that U would explicitly correlate 'Fido' and Jones' dog must be understood as an elliptical way of saying something of the form 'U would explicitly correlate "Fido" and Jones' dog, *if p*'. How is 'if p' to be specified?

(4) Perhaps as 'If U were asked to give an explicit correlation for "Fido"'. But if U were actually faced with a request, he might quite well take it that he is being asked to make a stipulation, in the making which he would have an entirely free hand. If he is not being asked for a stipulation, then it must be imparted to him that his explicit correlation is to satisfy some nonarbitrary condition. But what condition can this be? Again it is tempting to suggest that he is to make his explicit correlation such as to match or fit existing procedures.

(5) In application to RP12, this seems to amount to imposing on U the demand that he should make his explicit correlation such as to yield RP12.

(6) In that case, RP12 results from a nonexplicit correlation which consists in the fact that U *would* explicitly correlate 'Fido' and Jones' dog if he wanted to make an explicit correlation which would generate relevant existing procedures, namely RP12 itself. There is an apparent circularity here. Is this tolerable?

(7) It may be tolerable inasmuch as it may be a special case of a general phenomenon which arises in connection with the explanation of linguistic practice. We can, if we are lucky, identify 'linguistic rules', so called, which are such that our linguistic practice is *as*

if we accepted these rules and consciously followed them. But we want to say that this is not just an interesting fact about our linguistic practice but also an explanation of it; and this leads us on to suppose that 'in some sense', 'implicitly', we *do* accept these rules. Now the proper interpretation of the idea that we *do* accept these rules becomes something of a mystery, if the 'acceptance' of the rules is to be distinguished from the existence of the related practices—but it seems like a mystery which, for the time being at least, we have to swallow, while recognizing that it involves us in an as yet unsolved problem.

C. CONCLUDING NOTE

It will hardly have escaped notice that my account of the cluster of notions connected with the term 'meaning' has been studded with expressions for such intensional concepts as those of intending and believing, and my partial excursions into symbolic notation have been made partly with the idea of revealing my commitment to the legitimacy of quantifying over such items as propositions. I shall make two highly general remarks about this aspect of my procedure. First, I am not sympathetic towards any methodological policy which would restrict one from the start to an attempt to formulate a theory of meaning in extensional terms. It seems to me that one should at least *start* by giving oneself a free hand to make use of any intensional notions or devices which seem to be required in order to solve one's conceptual problems, at least at a certain level, in ways which (metaphysical bias apart) reason and intuition commend. If one denies oneself this freedom, one runs a serious risk of underestimating the richness and complexity of the conceptual field which one is investigating.

Second, I said at one point that intensionality seems to be embedded in the very foundations of the theory of language. Even if this appearance corresponds with reality, one is not, I suspect, precluded from being, in at least one important sense, an extentionalist. The psychological concepts which, in my view, are needed for the formulation of an adequate theory of language may not be among the most primitive or fundamental psychological concepts (like those which apply not only to human beings but also to quite lowly animals), and it may be possible to derive (in *some* relevant sense of 'derive') the intensional concepts which I have been using from more primitive extensional concepts. Any extensionalist has to deal with the problem of allowing for a transition from an extensional to a nonextensional language; and it is by no means obvious to me that intensionality can be explained only via the idea of concealed references to language and so presupposes the concepts in terms of which the use of language has to be understood.

NOTES

1. *Philosophical Review,* LXVII (1957).

2. The definiens suggested for explicit correlation is, I think, insufficient as it stands. I would not wish to say that if A deliberately detaches B from a party, he has thereby correlated himself with B, nor that a lecturer who ensures that just one blackboard is visible to each member of his audience (and to no one else) has thereby explicit correlated the blackboard with each member of the audience, even though in each case the analogue of the suggested definiens is satisfied. To have explicitly correlated X with each member of a set K, not only must I have intentionally effected that a *particular* relation R holds between X and all those (and only those) items which belong to K, but also my purpose or end in setting up this relationship must have been to perform an act as a result of which *there will be come relation or other* which holds between X and all those (and only those) things which belong to K. To the definiens, then, we should add, within the scope of the initial quantifier, the following clause: "& U's purpose in effecting that $\forall x$ ($\ldots\ldots$) is that $(\exists R')$ $(\forall z)$ $(R'$ 'shaggy'$z \equiv z \in y$ (y is hairy-coated))."

5

Speaker's Reference and Semantic Reference[1]

SAUL KRIPKE

I am going to discuss some issues inspired by a well-known paper of Keith Donnellan, "Reference and Definite Descriptions,"[2] but the interest—to me—of the contrast mentioned in my title goes beyond Donnellan's paper: I think it is of considerable constructive as well as critical importance to the philosophy of language. These applications, however, and even everything I might want to say relative to Donnellan's paper, cannot be discussed in full here because of problems of length.

Moreover, although I have a considerable interest in the substantive issues raised by Donnellan's paper, and by related literature, my own conclusions will be methodological, not substantive. I can put the matter this way: Donnellan's paper claims to give decisive objections both to Russell's theory of definite descriptions (taken as a theory about English) and to Strawson's. My concern is *not* primarily with the question: is Donnellan right, or is Russell (or Strawson)? Rather, it is with the question: do the considerations *in Donnellan's paper* refute Russell's theory (or Strawson's)? For definiteness, I will concentrate on Donnellan versus Russell, leaving Strawson aside.

And about this issue I will draw a definite conclusion, one which I think will illuminate a few methodological maxims about language. Namely, I will conclude that the considerations in Donnellan's paper, *by themselves,* do *not* refute Russell's theory.

Any conclusions about Russell's views *per se,* or Donnellan's, must be tentative. If I were to be asked for a tentative stab about Russell, I would say that although his theory does a far better job of handling ordinary discourse than many have thought, and although many popular arguments against it are inconclusive, probably it ultimately fails. The considerations I have in mind have to do with the existence of "improper" definite descriptions, such as "the table," where uniquely specifying conditions are not contained in the description itself. Contrary to the Russellian picture, I doubt that such descriptions can always be regarded as elliptical with some uniquely specifying conditions added. And it may even be the case that a true picture will resemble various aspects of Donnellan's in important respects. But such questions will largely be left aside here.

Saul Kripke, "Speaker's Reference and Semantic Reference." In *Contemporary Perspectives in the Philosophy of Language,* edited by P. A. French et al., 6–27. Minneapolis: University of Minnesota Press, 1979. Copyright © 1979 by Saul Kripke. Reprinted by permission of the author.

I will state my preference for one substantive conclusion (although I do not feel completely confident of it either): that unitary theories, like Russell's, are preferable to theories that postulate an ambiguity. And much, though not all, of Donnellan's paper seems to postulate a (semantic) ambiguity between his "referential" and "attributive"uses. But—as we shall see—Donnellan is not entirely consistent on this point, and I therefore am not sure whether I am expressing disagreement with him even here.[3]

1. PRELIMINARY CONSIDERATIONS

Donnellan claims that a certain linguistic phenomenon argues against Russell's theory. According to Russell, if someone says, "The x such that $\phi(x)$ ψ's," he means that there is an χ which uniquest satisfies "$\phi(x)$" and that any such χ satisfies "$\psi(x)$." [I.e., $(\exists \chi)$ $(\phi!(x) \wedge \psi(x))$, where "$\phi!(x)$" abbreviates "$\phi(x) \wedge (y)(\phi(y) \supset y = x)$"]. Donnellan argues that some phenomenon of the following kind tells against Russell: Suppose someone at a gathering, glancing in a certain direction, says to his companion,

(1) "The man over there drinking champagne is happy tonight."

Suppose both the speaker and hearer are under a false impression, and that the man to whom they refer is a teetotaler, drinking sparkling water. He may, nevertheless, be happy. Now, if there is no champagne drinker over there, Russell would regard (1) as false, and Frege and Strawson would give it a truth-value gap. Nevertheless, as Donnellan emphasizes, we have a substantial intuition that the speaker said something true of the man to whom he referred in spite of his misimpression.

Since no one is really drinking champagne, the case involves a definite description that is empty, or vacuous, according to both Russell and Frege. So as to avoid any unnecessary and irrelevant entanglements of the present question with the issues that arise when definite descriptions are vacuous, I shall modify this case (and all other cases where, in Donnellan's paper, the description was vacuous).[4] Suppose that "over there," exactly one man *is* drinking

champagne, although his glass is not visible to the speaker (nor to his hearer). Suppose that he, unlike the teetotaler to whom the speaker refers, has been driven to drink precisely by his misery. Then *all* the classical theories (both Russellian and Fregean) would regard (1) as false (since exactly one man over there is drinking champagne, and he is *not* happy tonight). Now the speaker has spoken *truly* of the man to whom he refers (the teetotaler), yet this dimension is left out in all the classical analyses, which would assign falsehood to his assertion solely on the basis of the misery of *someone else* whom *no one* was talking about (the champagne drinker). Previously Linsky had given a similar example. He gave it as an empty case; once again I modify it to make the description nonvacuous. Someone sees a woman with a man. Taking the man to be her husband, and observing his attitude towards her, he says, "Her husband is kind to her," and someone else may nod. "Yes, he seems to be." Suppose the man in question is not her husband. Suppose he is her lover, to whom she has been driven precisely by her husband's cruelty. Once again both the Russellian analysis and the Fregean analysis would assess the statement as false, and both would do so on the basis of the cruelty of a man neither participant in the dialogues was talking about.

Again, an example suggested to me by a remark of L. Crocker: suppose a religious narrative (similar, say, to the Gospels) consistently refers to its main protagonist as "The Messiah." Suppose a historian wishes to assess the work for *historical accuracy*—that is, he wishes to determine whether it gives an accurate account of the life of its hero (whose identity we assume to be established). Does it matter to this question whether the hero really was the Messiah, as long as the author took him to be so, and addressed his work to a religious community that shared this belief? Surely not. And note that it is no mere "principle of charity" that is operating here. On the contrary, if someone other than the person intended were really the Messiah, and if, by a bizarre and unintended coincidence, the narrative gave a fairly true account of *his* life, we would not for that reason call it "historically true." On the contrary, we would regard the work as historically *false* if the events mentioned were false of its intended protagonist. Whether the story happened to fit the true Messiah—who may have been totally unknown to the author and even have lived after the time the work was composed—would be irrelevant. Once again, this fact seems inconsistent with the positions both of Frege and of Russell.

On the basis of such examples, Donnellan distinguishes two uses of definite descriptions. In the "attributive" use, a speaker "states something about whoever or whatever is the so-and-so." In the "referential" use, a speaker "uses the description to enable his audience to pick out whom or what he is talking about and states something about that person or thing. In the first [attributive] case, the definite description might be said to occur essentially, for the speaker wishes to assert something about whatever or whoever fits that description; but in the referential use the definite description is merely one tool for . . . calling attention to a person or thing . . . and . . . any other device for doing the same job, another description or name, would do as well."[5] For example, suppose I come upon Smith foully murdered. The condition of Smith's body moves me to say, "Smith's murderer is (must be) insane." Then we have an *attributive* use: we speak of the murderer, whoever he may be. On the other hand, suppose that Jones is on trial for Smith's murder and that I am among the spectators in the courtroom. Observing the wild behavior of the defendant at the dock, I may say, "Smith's murderer is insane." (I forgot the defendant's name, but am firmly convinced of his guilt.) Then my use is referential: whether or not Jones was the real murderer, and even if someone else was, if Jones accused me of libel, his failure to fit my description would give me no defense. All of the previous cases, (the tee-totaling "champagne" drinker, the lover taken for a husband, the false Messiah), are all referential in Donnellan's sense.

An intuitive mark of the attributive use is the legitimacy of the parenthetical comment, "whoever he is." In the first case, we may say "Smith's murderer, whoever he is, is insane," but not in the second. But we should not be misled: a definite description may be used attributively even if the speaker believes that a certain person, say, Jones, fits it, provided that he is talking about *whoever* fits, and his belief that Jones in fact fits is not relevant. In the case where I deduce the murderer's insanity

from the condition of Smith's body, I use the description attributively even if I suspect, or even am firmly convinced, that Jones is the culprit.

I have no doubt that the distinction Donnellan brings out exists and is of fundamental importance, though I do not regard it as exclusive or exhaustive. But Donnellan also believes that Russell's theory applies, if at all, only to attributive uses, and that referential uses of definite descriptions are close to proper names, even to Russell's "logically proper" names. And he appears to believe that the examples of the referential uses mentioned above are inexplicable on Russell's theory. It is these views that I wish to examine.

2. SOME ALLEGED APPLICATIONS OF THE DISTINCTION

Some alleged applications of Donnellan's distinction have entered the oral tradition, and even to an extent, the written tradition, that are not in Donnellan's paper. I will mention some that I find questionable. Unfortunately I will have to discuss these applications more briefly than the issues in question really deserve, since they are ancillary to the main theme.

2a. De Dicto–De Re

Many able people, in and out of print, have implied that Donnellan's distinction has something to do with, can be identified with, or can replace, the *de dicto–de re* distinction, or the small scope–large scope distinction in modal or intensional contexts.

"The number of planets is necessarily odd" can mean two things, depending on whether it is interpreted *de dicto* or *de re*. If it is interpreted *de dicto,* it asserts that the proposition that the number of planets is odd is a necessary truth—something I take to be false (there might have been eight planets). If it is interpreted *de re,* it asserts that the actual number of planets (nine) has the property of necessary oddness (essentialists like me take this to be true). Similarly, if we say, "Jones believes that the richest debutante in Dubuque will marry him," we may mean that Jones's belief has a certain content, viz., that the richest debutante in Dubuque will marry him; or we may mean that he believes, *of* a girl who is (in fact) the richest in Dubuque, that she will marry him. The view in question suggests that the *de dicto* case is to be identified with Donnellan's *attributive* use, the *de re* with the *referential.*

Any such assimilation, in my opinion, is confused. (I don't think Donnellan makes it.) There are many objections; I will mention a few. First, the *de dicto* use of the definite description cannot be identified with either the *referential* or the *attributive* use. Here the basic point was already noticed by Frege. If a description is embedded in a *(de dicto)* intensional context, we cannot be said to be talking *about* the thing described, either *qua* its satisfaction of the description or *qua* anything else. Taken *de dicto,* "Jones believes that the richest debutante in Dubuque will marry him," can be asserted by someone who thinks (let us suppose, wrongly) that there are *no* debutantes in Dubuque; certainly then, he is in no way talking about the richest debutante, even "attributively." Similarly, "It is possible that (France should have a monarchy in 1976, and that) the King of France in 1976 should have been bald" is true, if read *de dicto;* yet we are not using "the King of France in 1976" attributively to speak of the King of France in 1976, for there is none. Frege concluded that "the King of France in 1976" refers, in these contexts, to its ordinary sense; at any rate, if we wish to speak of "reference" here, it cannot be to the nonexistent king. Even if there were such a king, the quoted assertion would say nothing about *him,* if read *de dicto:* to say that *he* might have been bald, would be *de re* (indeed, this *is* the distinction in question).

Second, and even more relevantly, Donnellan's referential use cannot be identified with the *de re* use. (I think Donnellan would agree.) Suppose I have no idea how many planets there are, but (for some reason) astronomical theory dictates that that number must be odd. If I say, "The number of planets (whatever it may be) is odd," my description is used attributively. If I am an essentialist, I will also say, "The number of planets (whatever it may be) is necessarily odd," on the grounds that all odd numbers are necessarily odd; and my usage is just as attributive as in the first case. In "Smith's murder, whoever he may be, is

known to the police, but they're not saying," or, more explicitly, "The police know concerning Smith's murderer, whoever he is, that he committed the murder; but they're not saying who he is," "Smith's murderer" is used attributively, but is *de re.*

Finally: Russell wished to handle the *de dicto–de re* distinction by his notion of the *scope* of a description. Some have suggested that Donnellan's referential–attributive distinction can replace Russell's distinction of scope. But *no* twofold distinction can do this job. Consider:

(2) The number of planets might have been necessarily even.

In a natural use, (2) can be interpreted as true; for example, there might have been exactly eight planets, in which case the number of planets would have been even, and hence necessarily even. (2), interpreted as true, is neither *de re* nor *de dicto;* that is, the definite description neither has the largest nor the smallest possible scope. Consider:

(2a) $\Diamond \Box (\exists x)$ (There are exactly x planets and x is even)

(2b) $(\exists x)$ (There are exactly x planets and $\Diamond \Box (x$ is even)).

(2c) $\Diamond (\exists x)$ (There are exactly x planets and $\Box (x$ is even)).

(2a)–(2c) give three alternative Russellian analyses of (2). (2a) gives the description the smallest possible scope *(de dicto);* it says, presumably falsely, that it might have been necessary that there was an even number of planets. (2b) gives the description the largest possible scope *(de re);* it says, still falsely, of the actual number of planets (viz., nine) that it might have been necessarily even. (2c) is the interpretation which makes (2) true. When intensional operators are iterated, intermediate scopes are possible. Three analogous interpretations are possible, say, for "Jones doubts that Holmes believes that Smith's murderer is insane"; or (using an indefinite description) for "Hoover charged that the Berrigans plotted to kidnap a high American official." (I actually read something like this last in a newspaper and wondered what was meant.)[6] This may mean: (a) there is a particular high official such that Hoover charged that the Berrigans plotted to kidnap him (largest scope, *de re,* this was the interpretation intended); or (b) Hoover charged that the Berrigans plotted as follows: let's kidnap a high official (smallest scope, *de dicto*); or (c) Hoover charged that there was a high official (whose identity may have been unknown to Hoover) whom the Berrigans planned to kidnap (intermediate scope).

As intensional (or other) constructions are iterated, there are more and more possible scopes for a definite description. No *twofold* distinction can replace Russell's notion of scope.[7] In particular, neither the *de dicto–de re* distinction nor the referential–attributive distinction can do so.

2b. Rigid Definite Descriptions

If definite descriptions $\iota x\phi(x)$, are taken as primitive and assigned reference, then the conventional nonrigid assignment assigns to such a description, with respect to each possible world, the unique object, if any, which would have ϕ'd in that world. (Forget the vacuous case, which requries a further convention.) For example, "the number of planets" denotes eight, speaking of a counterfactual situation where there would have been eight planets (and "the number of planets is even" is true of such a situation). Another type of definite description, $\iota x\phi x$, a "rigid" definite description, could be introduced semantically by the following stipulation: let $\iota x\phi x$ denote, with respect to all possible worlds, the unique object that (actually) ϕ's (then "the number of planets is odd," as interpreted, expresses a necessary truth). Both kinds of definite descriptions can obviously be introduced, theoretically, into a single formal language, perhaps by the notations just given. Some have suggested that definite descriptions, in English, are *ambiguous* between the two readings. It has further been suggested that the two types of definite descriptions, the nonrigid and the rigid, are the source of the *de dicto–de re* distinction and should replace Russell's notion of scope for the purpose. Further, it has been suggested that they amount to the same thing as Donnellan's attributive–referential distinction.[8]

My comments will be brief, so as to avoid too much excursus. Although I have an open mind on the subject, I am not yet convinced that there is any clear evidence for such an ambiguity. Being a twofold distinction, the ambiguity alleged cannot replace Russell's notion of scope, for the reasons given above. Once Russell's notion is available, it can be used to handle the *de dicto–de re* distinction; a further ambiguity seems unnecessary. More relevant to the present context, the "rigid" sense of a definite description, if it exists, cannot be identified with Donnellan's "referential" use. I take it that the identification of the referential use with the rigid definite description was inspired by some line of reasoning like this: Donnellan holds that referential descriptions are those close to proper names, even to Russell's "logically proper names." But surely proper names, or at least, Russellian "logically proper names," are rigid. Hence Donnellan's referential descriptions are just the rigid definite descriptions.

If we assume that Donnellan thinks of names as rigid, as I think of them, his referential definite descriptions *would* most plausibly be taken to refer rigidly to their referents. But it is not clear that he does agree with me on the rigidity of such reference.[9] More important, a rigid definite description, as defined above, still determines its referent via its unique satisfaction of the associated property—and this fact separates the notion of such a description from that of a referential description, as Donnellan defines it. David Kaplan has suggested that a demonstrative "that" can be used, in English, to make any definite description rigid. "That bastard—the man who killed Smith, whoever he may be— is surely insane!" The subject term rigidly designates Smith's murderer, but it is still attributive in Donnellan's sense.[10]

2c. Referential Descriptions

In "Naming and Necessity,"[11] one argument I presented against the description (or cluster-of-descriptions) theory of proper names concerned cases where the referent of a name, the person named by the name, did not satisfy the descriptions usually associated with it, and someone else did. For example, the name "Gödel" might be taken to mean "the man who proved the incompleteness of arithmetic"; but even if Gödel had been a fraud, who had proved nothing at all and had misappropriated his work from an unknown named "Schmidt," our term "Gödel" would refer to the fraud, not to the man who really satisfied the definite description. Against this it has been said that although the argument does succeed in its main purpose of refuting the description theory as a theory of reference (that is, it shows that the descriptive properties cited do not determine the referent), it does nothing to show that names are not abbreviated definite descriptions, because we could take the descriptions in question to be referential in Donnellan's sense. Referential descriptions can easily refer to things that fail to satisfy the descriptions; nothing in my argument shows that names are not synonymous with such descriptions.[12]

My reaction to such an argument may become clearer later. For the moment, (too) briefly: In the case of "Her husband is kind to her," and similar cases, "her husband" can refer to her lover, as long as we are under the misapprehension that the man to whom we refer (the lover) *is* her husband. Once we are apprised of the true facts, we will no longer so refer to him. Similarly, someone can use "the man who proved the incompleteness of arithmetic," as a referential definite description, to refer to Gödel; it might be so used, for example, by someone who had forgotten his name. If the hypothetical fraud were discovered, however, the description is no longer usable as a device to refer to Gödel; henceforth it can be used only to refer to Schmidt. We would withdraw any previous assertions using the description to refer to Gödel (unless they also were true of Schmidt). We would *not* similarly withdraw the *name* "Gödel," even after the fraud was discovered; "Gödel" would still be used to name Gödel, not Schmidt. The name and the description, therefore, are not synonymous. (See also note 27 below).

3. THE MAIN PROBLEM

3a. A Disagreement with Russell?

Do Donnellan's observations provide an argument against Russell's theory? Do his *views* contradict Russell's? One might think that if

Donnellan is right, Russell must be wrong, since Donnellan's truth conditions for statements containing referential definite descriptions differ from Russell's. Unfortunately, this is not so clear. Consider the case of "her husband is kind to her," mistakenly said of the lover. If Donnellan had roundly asserted that the quoted statement is true if and only if the *lover* is kind to her, regardless of the kindness of the husband, the issue between him and Russell would be clearly joined. But Donnellan doesn't say this: rather he says that the speaker has referred to a certain person, the lover, and said *of him* that he is kind to her. But if we ask, "Yes, but was the statement he made true?", Donnellan would hedge. For if *we* are not under the misimpression that the man the speaker referred to was her husband, *we* would not express the same assertion by "Her husband is kind to her." "If it ['her husband'] is being used referentially, it is not clear what is meant by 'the statement.' . . . To say that the statement he made was that her husband is kind to her lands us in difficulties. For we [in so reporting what the speaker said must use the definite description] either attributively or referentially. If the former, then we misrepresent the linguistic performance of the speaker; if the latter, then we ourselves are referring to someone," and ordinarily we can refer to someone as "her husband" only if we take him to be her husband.[13]

Since Donnellan does not clearly assert that the statement "her husband is kind to her" ever has non-Russellian truth conditions, he has *not,* so far, clearly contradicted Russell's theory. His argument, as he presents it, that there is a problem in reporting "the statement" is questionable, in two ways.

First, it uses the premise that if we say, "Jones said that her husband is kind to her," we ourselves must use the description attributively or referentially; but, as we saw, a definite description in indirect discourse is *neither* referential nor attributive.[14]

Second, there is an important problem about the nature of the referential–attributive distinction. Donnellan says that his distinction is neither syntactic nor semantic:

The grammatical structure of the sentence seems to me to be the same whether the description is used referentially or attributively: that is, it is not syntactically ambiguous. Nor does it seem at all attractive to suppose an ambiguity in the meaning of the words; it does not appear to be semantically ambiguous. (Perhaps we could say that the sentence is pragmatically ambiguous: the distinction between roles that the description plays is a function of the speaker's intentions.) These, of course, are intuitions; I do not have an argument for these conclusions. Nevertheless, the burden of proof is surely on the other side.[15]

Suppose for the moment that this is so. Then if the referential–attributive distinction is pragmatic, rather than syntactic or semantic, it is presumably a distinction about speech acts. There is no reason to suppose that in making an indirect discourse report on what someone else has said I myself must have similar intentions, or be engaged in the same kind of speech act; in fact, it is clear that I am not. If I say "Jones said the police were around the corner," Jones may have said it as a warning, but *I* need not say it as a warning. If the referential–attributive distinction is neither syntactic nor semantic, there is no reason, without further argument, to suppose that my usage, in indirect discourse, should match the man on whom I report, as referential or attributive. The case is quite different for a genuine semantic ambiguity. If Jones says, "I have never been at a bank," and I report this, saying, "Jones denied that he was ever at a bank," the sense I give to "bank" must match Jones's if my report is to be accurate.

Indeed, the passage seems inconsistent with the whole trend of Donnellan's paper. Donnellan suggests that there is no syntactic or semantic ambiguity in the statement, "Her husband is kind to her." He also suggests that Russell may well give a correct analysis of the attributive use but not of the referential use. Surely this is not coherent. It is not "uses," in some pragmatic sense, but *senses* of a sentence which can be analyzed. If the sentence is *not* (syntactically or) semantically ambiguous, it has only *one* analysis; to say that it has two distinct analyses is to attribute a syntactic or semantic ambiguity to it.

Donnellan's arguments for his refusal to give a truth value to the speaker's assertion, "Her husband is kind to her," seem to be fallacious. My own suggested account of the matter below—in terms of a theory of speech acts—creates no problem about "the statement"; it is simply the statement that her husband is kind to her. But Donnellan's cautious refusal to say, under the circumstances mentioned, that "Her husband is kind to her" is true, seems nevertheless to be intiutively correct. The man to whom the speaker refers is— let us suppose—kind to her. But it seems hard for us to say that when he uttered, "Her husband is kind to her," it expressed a truth, if *we* believe that her husband is unkind to her.

Now Donnellan thinks that he has refuted Russell. But all he has clearly claimed, let alone established, is that a speaker can refer to the lover and say, of him, that he is kind to her by saying "Her husband is kind to her." So, first, we can ask: *If* this claim is correct, does it conflict with Russell's views?

Second, since Donnellan's denial that he advocates a semantic ambiguity in definite descriptions seems inconsistent with much of his paper, we can try ignoring the denial, and take his paper to be arguing for such an ambiguity. Then we may ask: has Donnellan established a (semantic) ambiguity inconsistent with Russell's theory?

3b. General Remarks: Apparatus

We need a general apparatus to discuss these questions. Some of the apparatus is well known, but I review it for its intrinsic importance and interest. First, let us distinguish, following Grice,[16] between what *the speaker's words meant,* on a given occasion, and what *he meant,* in saying these words, on that occasion. For example, one burglar says to another, "The cops are around the corner." What *the words meant* is clear: the police were around the corner. But *the speaker may well have meant,* "We can't wait around collecting any more loot: Let's split!" That is not *the meaning of the words,* even on that occasion, though that is *what he meant in saying those words, on that occasion.* Suppose he had said, "The cops are inside the bank." Then on that occasion, "bank" meant a commercial bank, not a river bank, and this is relevant to what the *words* meant, on that occasion. (On other occasions, the same words might mean that the police were at a river bank.) But, if the speaker *meant* "Let's split," this is no part of the *meaning of his words,* even on that occasion.

Again (inspired by an example of Grice):[17] A magician makes a handkerchief change color. Someone says, recalling the trick, "Then he put the red handkerchief on the side of the table"; and someone else interjects, cautiously, "It *looked* red." The words meant, on that occasion, that the object referred to (the handkerchief) looked red. What we speak of when we speak of the meaning of his words, on that occasion, includes a disambiguation of the utterance. (Perhaps, on some occasions, where "it" refers to a book, a phonetically identical utterance might mean, "it looked read," well-thumbed and well-perused.) But the speaker meant, on this occasion, to suggest that perhaps the handkerchief wasn't really red, that perhaps the trick relied on some kind of illusion. (Note that, on this occasion, not only do the *words* "it looked red" mean what they mean, but also the *speaker* means that it looked red, as well as that it may not have been red. On the other hand, the speaker has no intention of producing a belief in the hearer that the handkerchief looked red, or a belief in the hearer that he (the speaker) believed it looked red. Both facts are common knowledge. The same *could* hold for "The cops are around the corner."[18] Do these examples contradict Grice's analysis of "meaning"? Grice's theory has become very complex and I am not quite sure.)

The notion of what words can mean, in the language, is semantical: it is given by the conventions of our language. What they mean, on a given occasion, is determined, on a given occasion, by these conventions, together with the intentions of the speaker and various contextual features. Finally what the speaker meant, on a given occasion, in saying certain words, derives from various further special intentions of the speaker, together with various general principles, applicable to all human languages regardless of their special conventions. (Cf. Grice's "conversational maxims.") For example, "It looks red" replaced a categorical affirmation of redness. A plausible general principle of human discourse would have it that if a second speaker insists that a stronger assertion should be replaced by a weaker one, he thereby wishes to cast doubt on the stronger assertion; whence, knowing the semantics of English, and the meaning of the speaker's words on this occasion, we can deduce what

was meant (the Gricean "coversational implicature").[19]

Let us now speak of speaker's reference and semantic reference: these notions are special cases of the Gricean notions discussed above. If a speaker has a designator in his idiolect, certain conventions of his idiolect[20] (given various facts about the world) determine the referent in the idiolect: that I call the *semantic referent* of the designator. (If the designator is ambiguous, or contains indexicals, demonstratives, or the like, we must speak of the semantic referent on a given occasion. The referent will be determined by the conventions of the language plus the speaker's intentions and various contextual features.)

Speaker's reference is a more difficult notion. Consider, for example, the following case, which I have mentioned elsewhere.[21] Two people see Smith in the distance and mistake him for Jones. They have a brief colloquy: "What is Jones doing?" "Raking the leaves." "Jones," in the common language of both, is a name of Jones; it *never* names Smith. Yet, in some sense, on this occasion, clearly both participants in the dialogue have referred to Smith, and the second participant has said something true about the man he referred to if and only if Smith was raking the leaves (whether or not Jones was). How can we account for this? Suppose a speaker takes it that a certain object a fulfills the conditions for being the semantic referent of a designator, "d." Then, wishing to say something about a, he uses "d" to speak about a; say, he says "$\phi(d)$." Then, he said, of a, on that occasion, that it ϕ'd in the appropriate Gricean sense (explicated above), he *meant* that a ϕ'd. This is true even if a is not really the semantic referent of "d." If it is not, then *that a ϕ's is* included in what he meant (on that occasion), but not in the meaning of his words (on that occasion).

So, we may tentatively define the speaker's referent of a designator to be that object which the speaker wishes to talk about, on a given occasion, and believes fulfills the conditions for being the semantic referent of the designator. He uses the designator with the intention of making an assertion about the object in question (which may not really be the semantic referent, if the speaker's belief that it fulfills the appropriate semantic conditions is in error). The speaker's referent is the thing the speaker referred to by the designator, though it may not be the referent of the designator, in his idiolect. In the example above, Jones, the man named by the name, is the semantic referent. Smith is the speaker's referent, the correct answer to the question, "To whom were you referring?"[22]

Below, the notion of speaker's reference will be extended to include more cases where existential quantification rather than designation is involved.

In a given idiolect, the semantic referent of a designator (without indexicals) is given by a *general* intention of the speaker to refer to a certain object whenever the designator is used. The speaker's referent is given by a *specific* intention, on a given occasion, to refer to a certain object. If the speaker believes that the object he wants to talk about, on a given occasion, fulfills the conditions for being the semantic referent, then he believes that there is no clash between his general intentions and his specific intentions. My hypothesis is that Donnellan's referential–attributive distinction should be generalized in this light. For the speaker, on a given occasion, may believe that his specific intention coincides with his general intention for one of two reasons. In one case (the "simple" case), his specific intention is simply to refer to the semantic referent: that is, his specific intention *is* simply his general semantic intention. (For examples, he uses "Jones" as a name of Jones—elaborate this according to your favorite theory of proper names—and, on this occasion, simply wishes to use "Jones" to refer to Jones.) Alternatively—the "complex" case—he has a specific intention, which is distinct from his general intention, but which he believes, as a matter of fact, to determine the same object as the one determined by his general intention. (For example, he wishes to refer to the man "over there" but believes that he *is* Jones.) In the "simple" case, the speaker's referent is, *by definition,* the semantic referent. In the "complex" case, they may coincide, if the speaker's belief is correct, but they need not. (The man "over there" may be Smith and not Jones.) To anticipate, my hypothesis will be that Donnellan's "attributive" use is nothing but the "simple" case, specialized to definite descriptions, and that the "referential" use is, similarly, the

"complex" case. If such a conjecture is correct, it would be wrong to take Donnellan's "referential" use, as he does, to be a use of a description as if it were a proper name. For the distinction of simple and complex cases will apply to proper names just as much as to definite descriptions.

3c. Donnellan's Argument Against Russell: Methodological and Substantive Considerations

In the light of the notions just developed, consider the argument Donnellan adduces against Russell. Donnellan points to a phenomenon which he alleges to be inexplicable on a Russellian account of English definite descriptions. He accounts for it by positing an ambiguity. Alternatively, we wish to account for the phenomenon on pragmatic grounds, encapsulated in the distinction between speaker's reference and semantic reference. How can we see whether Donnellan's phenomenon conflicts with a Russellian account?

I propose the following test for any alleged counterexample to a linguistic proposal: If someone alleges that a certain linguistic phenomenon in English is a counterexample to a given analysis, consider a hypothetical language which (as much as possible) is like English except that the analysis is *stipulated* to be correct. Imagine such a hypothetical language introduced into a community and spoken by it. *If the phenomenon in question would still arise in a community that spoke such a hypothetical language (which may not be English), then the fact that it arises in English cannot disprove the hypothesis that the analysis is correct for English.* An example removed from the present discussion: Some have alleged that identity cannot be the relation that holds between, and only between, each thing and itself, for if so, the nontriviality of identity statements would be inexplicable. If it is conceded, however, that such a relation makes sense, and if it can be shown that a hypothetical language involving such a relation would generate the same problems, it will follow that the existence of these problems does not refute the hypothesis that "identical to" stands for this same relation in English.[23]

By "the weak Russell language," I will mean a language similar to English except that the truth conditions of sentences with definite descriptions are *stipulated* to conicide with Russell's: for example, "The present King of France is bald" is to be true iff exactly one person is King of France, and that person is bald. On the weak Russell language, this effect can be achieved by assigning semantic reference to definite descriptions: the semantic referent of a definite description is the unique object that satisfies the description, if any; otherwise there is no semantic referent. A sentence of the simple subject-predicate form will be true if the predicate is true of the (semantic) referent of its subject; false, if either the subject has no semantic referent or the predicate is not true of the semantic referent of the subject.

Since the weak Russell language takes definite descriptions to be primitive designators, it is not fully Russellian. By "the intermediate Russell language," I mean a language in which sentences containing definite descriptions are taken to be abbreviations or paraphrases of their Russellian analyses: for example, "The present King of France is bald" *means* (or has a "deep structure" like) "Exactly one person is at present King of France, and he is bald," or the like. Descriptions are not terms, and are not assigned reference or meaning in isolation. The "strong Russell language" goes further: definite descriptions are actually *banned* from the language and Russellian paraphrases are used in their place. Instead of saying "Her husband is kind to her," a speaker of this language must say "Exactly one man is married to her, and he is kind to her," or even (better), "There is a unique man who is married to her, and every man who is married to her is kind to her," or the like. If Russell is right, long-windedness is the only defect of these versions.

Would the phenomenon Donnellan adduces arise in communities that spoke these languages? Surely speakers of these languages are no more infallible than we. They too will find themselves at a party and mistakenly think someone is drinking champagne even though he is actually drinking sparkling water. If they are speakers of the weak or intermediate Russell languages, they will say, "The man in the corner drinking champagne is happy tonight." They will say this precisely because *they think, though erroneously, that the Rus-*

sellian truth conditions are saitsfied. Wouldn't we say of these speakers that they are refering to the teetotaler, under the misimpression that he is drinking champagne? And, if he is happy, are they not saying of him, *truly,* that he is happy? Both answers seem obviously affirmative.

In the case of the weak Russell language, the general apparatus previously developed seems fully adequate to account for the phenomenon. The semantic referent of a definite description is given by the conditions laid down above: it is a matter of the specific conventions of the (weak) Russell language, in this case that the referent is the unique object satisfying the descriptive conditions. The speaker's referent, on the other hand, is determined by a general theory of speech acts, applicable to all languages: it is the object to which the speaker wishes to refer, and which he believes fulfills the Russellian conditions for being the semantic referent. Again, in asserting the sentence he does, the speaker means that the speaker's referent (the teetotaler) satisfied the predicate (is happy). Thus the rough theoretical apparatus above accounts fully for our intuitions about this case.

What about the other Russellian languages? Even in the strong Russell language, where explicit descriptions are outlawed, the same phenomena can occur. In fact, they occur in English in "arch" uses of existential quantification: "Exactly *one person* (or: *some* person or other) is drinking champagne in that corner, and I hear he is romantically linked with Jane Smith." The circumlocution, in English, expresses the delicacy of the topic, but the speaker's reference (in quite an ordinary sense) may well be clear, even if he in fact is drinking sparkling water. In English such circumlocutions are common only when the speaker wishes to achieve a rather arch and prissy effect, but in the strong Russell language (which of course isn't English), they would be made more common because the definite article is prohibited.

This example leads to an extension of the notion of speaker's reference. When a speaker asserts an existential quantification, $(\exists x)(\phi x \wedge \psi x)$, it may be clear which thing he has in mind as satisfying "ϕx," and he may wish to convey to his hearers that that thing satisfies "ψx." In this case, the thing in question (which may or may not actually satisfy "ϕx") is called the "speaker's referent" when he makes the existential assertion. In English, as I have mentioned, such cases ("arch" uses) are rather rare; but they can be carried off even if the existential quantification is expressed in a highly roundabout and apparently nonreferring fashion. "Not *everyone* in this room is abstaining from champagne, and any such non-abstainer. . . ."[24]

If the notion of speaker's reference applies to the strong Russell language, it can apply to the intermediate Russell language as well, since the speaker's referent of "$\psi((\iota x\phi)(x))$" is then the thing he has in mind as uniquely instantiating "$\phi(x)$" and about which he wishes to convey that it ψ's.

Since the phenomenon Donnellan cites *would* arise in all the Russell languages, if they *were* spoken, the fact that they *do* arise in English, as *actually* spoken, can be no argument that English is not a Russell language.

We may contrast the Russell languages with what may be called the D-languages. In the D-languages the apparent ambiguity between referential and attributive definite descriptions is explicitly built into the semantics of the language and affects truth conditions. (The D-languages are meant to suggest "Donnellan," but are not called the "Donnellan languages," since Donnellan, as we have seen, is "ambiguous" as to whether he posits a semantic ambiguity.) The *unambiguous D-language* contains two distinct words, "the" and "ze" (rhymes with "the"). A statement of the form ". . . the F . . ." is true if the predicate represented by the dots is true of the unique object fulfilling F (we need not specify what happens if there is no such thing; if we wish to follow Russell, take it to be false). A statement of the form ". . . ze F . . ." is to be true iff the predicate represented by the dots is true of the unique thing the speaker thinks F is true of. (Once again, we leave free what happens if there is no such thing.) *The ambiguous D-language* is like the unambiguous D-language except that "the," ambiguously, can be interpreted according to the semantics either of "the" *or* of "ze." The general impression conveyed by Donnellan's paper, in spite of his statement at one point to the contrary, is that English is the ambiguous D-language; only on such a hypothesis could we say that the "ref-

erential use" (really referential *sense*) diverges from Russell's theory. The truth-conditions of statements containing "ze," and therefore of one sense of "the" in the ambiguous D-language, *are* incompatible with Russell's theory.[25]

We have two hypotheses: one says that English is a Russell language, while the other says that English is the ambiguous D-language. Which hypothesis is preferable? Since, as we have argued, the phenomena Donnellan adduces would arise in a hypothetical society that spoke any of the Russell languages, the existence in English of such phenomena provides no argument against the hypothesis that English is a Russell language. If Donnellan had possessed a clear intuition that "Her husband is kind to her," uttered in reference to the kind lover of a woman married to a cruel husband, expressed the literal truth, then he *would* have adduced a phenomenon that conforms to the ambiguous D-language but is incompatible with any Russell language. But Donnellan makes no such assertion: he cautiously, and correctly, confines himself to the weaker claim that the speaker spoke truly of the man to whom he referred. This weaker claim, we have seen, *would* hold for a speaker of a Russell language.

So Donnellan's examples provide, in themselves, no evidence that English is the ambiguous D-language rather than a Russell language. Granting that this is so, we can ask whether there is any reason to favor the Russell language hypothesis over the D-language hypothesis. I think there are several general methodological considerations that are relevant.

The Russell language theory, or any other unitary account (that is, any account that postulates no semantic ambiguity), accounts for Donnellan's referential-attributive phenomenon by a general pragmatic theory of speech acts, applicable to a very wide range of languages; the D-language hypothesis accounts for these same phenomena by positing a semantic ambiguity. The unitary account appeals to a general apparatus that applies to cases, such as the "Smith-Jones" case, where it is completely implausible that a semantic ambiguity exists. According to the unitary account, far from the referential use constituting a special namelike use of definite descriptions, the referential–attributive distinction is simply a special case of a general distinction, applicable to proper names as well as to definite descriptions, and illustrated in practice by the (leaf-raking) Smith-Jones case. And anyone who compares the Smith-Jones case, where presumably no one is tempted to posit a special semantic ambiguity, with Donnellan's cases of definite descriptions, must surely be impressed by the similarity of the phenomena.[26]

Under these circumstances, surely general methodological principles favor the existing account. The apparatus of speaker's reference and semantic reference, and of simple and complex uses of designators, is needed *anyway,* to explain the Smith-Jones case; it is applicable to all languages.[27] Why posit a semantic ambiguity when it is both insufficient in general and superfluous for the special case it seeks to explain?[28] And why are the phenomena regarding proper names so similar to those for definite descriptions, if the one case involves no semantic ambiguity while the other does?

It is very much the lazy man's approach in philosophy to posit ambiguities when in trouble. If we face a putative counterexample to our favorite philosophical thesis, it is always open to us to protest that some key term is being used in a special sense, different from its use in the thesis. We may be right, but the ease of the move should counsel a policy of caution: Do not posit an ambiguity unless you are really forced to, unless there are really compelling theoretical or intuitive grounds to suppose that an ambiguity really is present.

Let me say a bit more in defense of this. Many philosophers, for example, have advocated a "strong" account of knowledge according to which it is very hard to know anything; stiff requirements must be satisfied. When such philosophers have been confronted with intuitive counterexamples to such strong requirements for knowledge they either have condemned them as popular and loose usages or they have asserted that "know" is being used in a different "weak" sense. The latter move—distinguishing two or more "strong" and "weak" senses of "know"— strikes me as implausible. There *are* different sense of "know," distinguished in German as

"kennen" and "wissen," and in French as "connaître" and "savoir"; a person is usually known in the one sense, a fact in the other. It is no surprise that other languages use distinct words for these various senses of "know"; there is no reason for the ambiguity to be preserved in languages unrelated to our own. But what about the uses of "know" that characteristically are followed by that-clauses, knowing that *p*? Are these ambiguous? I would be very surprised to be told that the Eskimos have two separate words, one for (say) Hintikka's "strong" sense of "know," another for his "weak" sense. Perhaps this indicates that we think of knowledge as a unitary concept, unlikely to be "disambiguated" by two separate words in any language.

We thus have two methodological considerations that can be used to test any alleged ambiguity. "Bank" is ambiguous; we would expect the ambiguity to be disambiguated by separate and unrelated words in some other languages. Why should the two separate senses be reproduced in languages unrelated to English? First, then, we can consult our linguistic intuitions, independently of any empirical investigation. Would we be surprised to find languages that used two separate words for the two alleged senses of a given word? If so, then, to that extent our linguistic intuitions are really intuitions of a unitary concept, rather than of a word that expresses two distinct and unrelated senses. Second, we can ask empirically whether languages are in fact found that contain distinct words expressing the allegedly distinct senses. If no such language is found, once again this is evidence that a unitary account of the word or phrase in question should be sought.

As far as our main question is concerned, the first of these two tests, that of our intuitive expectation, seems to me overwhelmingly to favor a unitary account of descriptions, as opposed to the ambiguity postulated in the ambiguous D-language. If English really is the ambiguous D-language, we should expect to find other languages where the referential and attributive uses are expressed by two separate words, as in the *unambiguous* D-language. I at least would find it quite surprising to learn that say, the Eskimo, used two separate words "the" and "ze," for the attributive and referential uses. To the extent that I have this intuition, to that extent I think of "the" as a unitary concept. I should have liked to be able to report that I have reinforced this guess by an actual empirical examination of other languages—the second test—but as of now I haven't done so.[29]

Several general methodological considerations favor the Russell language (or some other unitary account) against the ambiguous D-language as a model for English. First, the unitary account conforms to considerations of economy in that it does not "multiply senses beyond necessity." Second, the metalinguistic apparatus invoked by the unitary account to explain the referential–attributive distinction is an apparatus that is needed in *any case* for other cases, such as proper names. The separate referential sense of descriptions postulated by the D-language hypothesis, is an idle wheel that does no work: if it were absent, we would be able to express everything we wished to express, in the same way. Further, the resemblance between the case of descriptions and that of proper names (where presumably no one would be tempted to postulate an ambiguity) is so close that any attempt to explain the cases differently is automatically suspect. Finally, we would not expect the alleged ambiguity to be disambiguated in other languages, and this means we probably regard ourselves as possessing a unitary concept.

Aside from methodological considerations, is there any direct evidence that would favor one of our two rival accounts? As I remarked above, if we had a direct intuition that "Her husband is kind to her" could be true even when her actual husband is cruel, then we would have decisive evidence for the D-language model; but Donnellan rightly disclaims any such intuition. On the other hand, I myself feel that such a sentence expresses a falsehood, even when "her husband" is used referentially to refer to a kind man; but the popularity of Donnellan's view has made me uncertain that this intuition should be pressed very far. In the absence of such direct intuitions that would settle the matter conclusively, it would seem that the actual practice of English speakers is compatible with either model, and that only general methodological considerations favor one hypothesis rather than an-

other. Such a situation leaves me uneasy. If there really is no direct evidence to distinguish the two hypotheses, how are they different hypotheses? If two communities, one of whom spoke the ambiguous D-language and the other of whom spoke the (weak) Russell language, would be able to intermingle freely without detecting any linguistic difference, do they really speak two different languages? If so, wherein is the difference?

Two hypothetical communities, one of which was explicitly taught the ambiguous D-language and the other of which was taught the (weak) Russell language (say, in school), would have direct and differing intuitions about the truth-value of "Her husband was kind to her", but it is uncertain whether English speakers have any such intuions. If they have none, is this a respect in which English differs from both the Russell languages and the D-languages, and thus differentiates it from both? Or, on the contrary, is there a pragmatic consideration, deriving no doubt from the fact that the relevant rules of language are not explicitly taught, that will explain why we lack such intuitions (if we do) without showing that neither the D-language nor the Russell language is English?

Some commentators on the dispute between Russell and Frege and Strawson over sentences containing vacuous definite descriptions have held that no direct linguistic phenomena conclusively decide between the two views: we should therefore choose the most economical and theoretically satisfying model. But if this is so, are there really two views, and if there are, shouldn't we perhaps say that neither is correct? A hypothetical community that was explicitly taught Russellian or Frege-Strawsonian truth-conditions for sentences containing vacuous definite descriptions would have no difficulty producing direct intuitions that decide the Russell-Strawson dispute. If the commentators in question are correct, speakers of English have no such intuitions. Surely this fact, too, would be a significant fact about English, for which linguistic theory should give an account. Perhaps pragmatic considerations suffice for such an account; or, perhaps, the alleged lack of any such intuition must be accounted for by a feature built into the semantics of English itself.

In the latter case, neither the Russellian nor the Frege-Strawsonian truth-conditions would be appropriate for English. Similar considerations would apply to the issue between Donnellan and Russell.[30]

I am uncertain about these questions. Certainly it would be best if there were directly observable phenomena that differentiated between the two hypotheses. Actually I can think of one rather special and localized phenomenon that may indeed favor the Russellian hypothesis, or some other unitary hypothesis. Consider the following two dialogues:

DIALOGUE I:
  A: "Her husband is kind to her."
  B: "No, he isn't. The man you're referring to isn't her husband."
DIALOGUE II:
  A: "Her husband is kind to her."
  B: "He is kind to her, but he isn't her husband."

In the first dialogue the respondent (B) uses "he" to refer to the semantic referent of "her husband" as used by the first speaker (A); in the second dialogue the respondent uses "he" to refer to the speaker's referent. My tendency is to think that both dialogues are proper. The unitary account can explain this fact, by saying that pronominalization can pick up *either* a previous semantic reference or a previous speaker's reference.[31,32] In the case of the two contrasting dialogues, these diverge.

If English were the ambiguous D-language, the second dialogue would be easy to explain. "He" refers to the object that is both the semantic referent and the speaker's referent of "her husband." (Recall that the notions of speaker's reference and semantic reference are general notions applicable to all languages, even to the D-languages.[33]) The first dialogue, however, would be much more difficult, perhaps impossible, to explain. When A said "her husband," according to the D-language hypothesis he was using "her husband" in the referential sense. Both the speaker's referent and the semantic referent would be the kind lover; only if B had misunderstood A's use as attributive could he have used "he" to refer to the husband, but such a misunderstanding is excluded by the second part of B's utterance. If the first dialogue is proper, it seems hard to fit it into the D-language model.[34]

4. CONCLUSION

I said at the beginning that the main concern of this paper was methodological rather than substantive. I do think that the considerations in this paper make it overwhelmingly probable that an ultimate account of the phenomena behind Donnellan's distinction will make use of the pragmatic ambiguity between "simple" and "complex" uses, as I defined them above, rather than postulating an ambiguity of the D-language type. But any ultimate substantive conclusion on the issue requires a more extensive and thorough treatment than has been given here. First, I have not here examined theories that attempt to explain Donnellan's distinction as a *syntactic* ambiguity, either of scope or of restrictive and nonrestrictive clauses in deep structure.[35] Both these views, like the line suggested in the present paper, are compatible with a unitary hypothesis such as the hypothesis that English is a Russell language. Although I am not inclined to accept either of these views, some others have found them plausible and unless they are rebutted, they too indicate that Donnellan's observations cannot be taken as providing a conclusive argument against Russell without further discussion.

Second, and most important, no treatment of definite descriptions can be complete unless it examines the complete range of uses of the definite article and related linguistic phenomena. Such a treatment should attempt, as I have argued above, to make it clear why the same construction with a definite article is used for a wide range of cases. It would be wrong for me not to mention the phenomena most favorable to Donnellan's intuitions. In a demonstrative use such as "that table," it seems plausible, as I have mentioned above,[36] that the term rigidly designates its referent. It also seems plausible that the reference of such a demonstrative construction can be an object to which the descriptive adjectives in the construction do not apply (for example, "that scoundrel" may be used to refer to someone who is not, in fact, a scoundrel) and it is not clear that the distinction between speaker's reference and semantic reference should be invoked to account for this. As I also said above, it seems to me to be likely that "indefinite" definite descriptions[37] such as "the table" present difficulties for a Russellian analysis. It is somewhat tempting to assimilate such descriptions to the corresponding demonstratives (for example, "that table") and to the extent that such a temptation turns out to be plausible, there may be new arguments in such cases for the intuitions of those who have advocated a rigid vs. nonrigid ambiguity in definite descriptions, or for Donnellan's intuitions concerning the referential case, or for both.[38]

Because I have not yet worked out a complete account that satisfies me, and because I think it would be wrong to make any definitive claim on the basis of the restricted class of phenomena considered here, I regard the primary lessons of this paper as methodological. They illustrate some general methodological considerations and apparatus that I think should be applied to the problems discussed here and to other linguistic problems. They show in the present case that the argument Donnellan actually presents in his original paper shows nothing against a Russellian or other unitary account, and they make it highly probable to me that the problems Donnellan handles by semantic ambiguity should instead be treated by a general theory of speech acts. But at this time nothing more definitive can be said. I think that the distinction between semantic reference and speaker's reference will be of importance not only (as in the present paper) as a critical tool to block postulation of unwarranted ambiguities, but also will be of considerable constructive importance for a theory of language. In particular, I find it plausible that a diachronic account of the evolution of language is likely to suggest that what was originally a mere speaker's reference may, if it becomes habitual in a community, evolve into a semantic reference. And this consideration may be *one* of the factors needed to clear up some puzzles in the theory of reference.[39,40]

ACKNOWLEDGMENTS

I should like to thank Margaret Gilbert and Howard Wettstein for their assistance in the preparation of this paper.

NOTES

1. Versions of this paper—not read from the present manuscript—were given from 1971 onward to colloquia at New York University, M.I.T., the University of California (Los Angeles), and elsewhere. The present version was written on the basis of a transcript of the M.I.T. version prepared by P. A. French, T. E. Vehling, Jr., and H. K. Wettstein. Donnellan himself heard the talk at U.C.L.A., and his "Speaker Reference, Descriptions, and Anaphora," to a large extent appears to be a comment on considerations of the type mentioned here. (He does not, however, specifically refer to the present paper.) I decided *not* to alter the paper I gave in talks to take Donnellan's later views into account: largely I think the earlier version stands on its own, and the issues Donnellan raises in the later paper can be discussed elsewhere. Something should be said here, however, about the pronominalization phenomena. In his paper, Donnellan seems to think that these phenomena are incompatible with the suggestion that speaker's reference is a pragmatic notion. On the contrary, at the end of the present paper (and of the talk Donnellan heard), I emphasize these very phenomena and argue that they support this suggestion. See also note 31 below.

2. [Reprinted in this volume, Chapter 3]. See also Keith S. Donnellan, "Putting Humpty Dumpty Together Again," *The Philosophical Review,* 77 (1968): 203–215.

3. In his later paper mentioned above in note 1, Donnellan seems more clearly to advocate a semantic ambiguity; but he hedges a bit even in the later paper.

4. I will also avoid cases of "improper" descriptions, where the uniqueness condition fails. Such descriptions may or may not be important for an ultimate evaluation of Donnellan's position, but none of the arguments in his paper rest on them.

5. "Reference and Definite Descriptions" [This volume: 54]. My discussion in this paragraph and the next is based on Donnellan's paper [This volume: 54, 57–59].

6. At the time, it had not yet been revealed that Kissinger was the official in question.

7. In fact, no *n*-fold distinction can do so, for any fixed *n*. Independently of the present writer, L. Karttunen has argued similarly that no dual or *n*-fold distinction can replace scope distinctions. I discussed the

matter briefly in "Identity and Necessity," *Identity and Individuation,* ed. M. Munitz (New York: 1972), p. 149, n. 10.

8. See the papers of Stalnaker and Partee in *The Semantics of Natural Language,* eds. D. Davidson and G. Harman (Dordrecht: 1971) for such suggestions and also for some of the views mentioned in the previous section. I should emphasize that most of the stimulating discussion in these papers can be made independent of any of the identifications of Donnellan's distinction with others which are rejected here.

9. See his paper "The Contingent *A Priori* and Rigid Designators" [in which] Donnellan asks whether I think proper names (in natural language) are *always* rigid: obviously, he thinks, proper names *could* be introduced to abbreviate nonrigid definite descriptions. My view is that proper names (except perhaps, for some quirky and derivative uses, that are not used as *names*) *are* always rigid. In particular this applies to "Neptune." It would be logically possible to have single words that abbreviated nonrigid definite descriptions, but these would not be *names.* The point is not merely terminological: I mean that such abbreviated nonrigid definite descriptions would differ in an important semantical feature from (what we call) typical proper names in our actual speech. I merely state my position and do not argue it; nor can I digress to comment on the other points raised in Donnellan's paper in this volume.

10. See Kaplan's paper "Dthat." In that paper, however, he also has some tendency to confuse rigidity with Donnellan's referentiality. [In P. Cole (ed.), *Syntax and Semantics.* Vol. 9: *Pragmatics* (New York: 1978), pp. 221–253].

11. Kripke, S. "Naming and Necessity." In D. Davidson and G. Harman (eds.), *Semantics of Natural Language,* 253–355.

12. For this view, see Jerrold J. Katz, "Logic and Language: An Examination of Recent Criticisms of Intensionalism," in *Minnesota Studies in the Philosophy of Science,* vol. VII (Minneapolis: 1975), pp. 36–130. See especially sections 5.1 and 5.2. As far as proper names are concerned, Katz thinks that *other* arguments tell against the description theory even as a theory of meaning.

13. See Donnellan, "Reference and Definite Descriptions" [This volume: 61].

14. So I argued in the talks, and rightly, if Donnellan is taken literally. See note 25 below, however, for a more charitable reading, which probably corresponds to Donnellan's intent. We must, however, take descriptions to be *semantically* ambiguous if we are to maintain the reading in question: see the point raised immediately after this one.

15. "Reference and Definite Descriptions" [This volume: 60].

16. For Grice, see the following papers, which I follow loosely in a good deal of the discussion at the beginning of this section: "The Causal Theory of Perception," *Proceedings of the Aristotelian Society,* supplementary vol. 35 (1961); "Logic and Conversation" [Reprinted in this volume, Chapter 19]; "Meaning," *Philosophical Review* 66 (1957): 337–88; "Utterer's Meaning, Sentence-Meaning and Word-Meaning," *Foundations of Language* 4 (1968): 225–42 [Reprinted in this volume, Chapter 4]; "Utterer's Meaning and Intentions," *Philosophial Review* 78 (1969): 147–77.

17. In "The Causal Theory of Perception."

18. Suppose the second burglar is well aware of the proximity of the police, but procrastinates in his greed for more loot. Then the first burglar imparts no *information* by saying what he does, but simply urges the second burglar to "split."

19. Although conversational principles are applicable to *all languages,* they may apply differently to *different societies.* In a society where blunt statement was considered rude, where "it looks red" replaced "it is red" just because of such a custom, "it looks red" might carry different conversational implicatures from our own. This might be the case even though the members of the society spoke *English,* just as we do. Conversational principles are matters for the psychology, sociology, and anthropology of linguistic communities; they are applicable to these communities no matter what language they may speak, though the applicable principles may vary somewhat with the communities (and may even, to some extent, be conditioned by the fact that they speak languages with certain structures.) Often, of course, we can state widely applicable, "cross-cultural," general conversational principles. Semantic and syntactic principles, on the other hand, are matters of the conventions of a language, in whatever cultural matrix it may be spoken. *Perhaps* sometimes it is difficult to draw the line, but it exists in general nonetheless.

20. If the views about proper names I have advocated in "Naming and Necessity" are correct (Donnellan,

in fact, holds similar views), the conventions regarding names in an idiolect usually involve the fact that the idiolect is no mere idiolect, but part of a common language, in which reference may be passed from link to link.

As the present paper attests, my views on proper names in "Naming and Necessity" have no special connection with the referential–attributive distinction.

21. "Naming and Necessity," p. 343, n. 3.

22. Donnellan shows in his paper that there are "referential" uses, of a somewhat exceptional kind, where the speaker, or even both the speaker and the hearer, are aware that the description used does not apply to the thing they are talking about. For example, they use "the King," knowing him to be a usurper, but fearing the secret police. Analogous cases can be given for proper names: if Smith is a lunatic who thinks he is Napoleon, they may humor him. Largely for the sake of simplicity of exposition, I have excluded such both from the notion of speaker's reference and from Donnellan's "referential" use (and the "D-languages" below). I do not think that the situation would be materially altered if both notions were revised so as to admit these cases, in a more refined analysis. In particular, it would probably *weaken* the case for a semantic ambiguity if these cases were allowed: for they shade into ironical and "inverted commas" cases. "He is a 'fine friend' ", may be ironical (whether or not inverted commas are used in the transcription). "'The King' is still in power"; "'Napoleon' has gone to bed" are similar, whether or not explicit inverted commas are used. It is fairly clear that "fine friend," "brilliant scholar," etc., do not have ironical and inverted commas *senses:* irony is a certain form of speech act, to be accounted for by pragmatic considerations. The case for a semantic ambiguity in definite descriptions is similarly *weakened* if we include such cases as referential uses.

In ordinary discourse, we say that the speaker was referring to someone under a wide variety of circumstances, including linguistic errors, verbal slips, and deliberate misuses of language. (If Mrs. Malaprop says, "The geography teacher said that equilateral triangles are equiangular," she *refers* to the geometry teacher.) The more such phenomena one includes in the notion of speaker's reference, the further one gets from any connection of the notion with semantical matters.

23. See the discussion of "schmidentity" in "Naming and Necessity."

24. Or, using variables explicitly, "there is a person x such that . . ." Notice that in an utterance of "$(\exists x)$ $(\phi x \wedge \psi x)$," as long as it is clear *which* thing allegedly satisfying "ϕx" the speaker has in mind, there can be a speaker's referent, even if both the speaker and the hearer are aware that many things satisfy "ϕx."

25. This description of the D-languages specifies nothing about semantical features more "intensional" than truth conditions. It is plausible to assume that "ze F" is a *rigid* designator of the thing believed to be uniquely F, but this is not explicitly included in the extensional truth conditions. Nor has anything been said about the behavior of "ze F" in belief and indirect discourse contexts. *If* we stipulate that "ze F," even in such contexts, designates the thing the speaker believes uniquely F's, then indeed "Jones said that ze man she married is kind to her," will not be a proper way of reporting Jones's utterance "Ze man she married is kind to her" (even if Jones and the speaker happen to have the same belief as to who her husband is; the difficulty is more obvious if they do not.) No doubt it is this fact that lies behind Donnellan's view that, in the referential case, it is hard to speak of "the statement," even though his exposition of the matter seems to be defective. Such implications, which are not present in the Russell language, lend only further implausibility to the supposition that English is the ambiguous D-language.

To repeat note 22, actually there are many other ways, other than taking something uniquely to satisfy "F," that might be included under referential uses of "the F." The best short way to specify the semantics of "ze F" would seem to be this: "ze F" refers, in the unambiguous D-language, to what would have been the speaker's referent of "the F" in the weak Russell language (under the same circumstances)! But this formulation makes it very implausible that the ambiguous D-language is anything but a chimerical model for English.

26. There is one significant difference between the case of proper names and that of definite descriptions. If someone uses "Jones" to refer to Smith, he has *misidentified* Smith as Jones, taken Smith for someone else. To some extent I *did* think that *Jones* was raking the leaves. (I assume that "Jones" is already in his idiolect as a name of Jones. If I am introduced to an impostor and am told, "This man is none other than Albert Einstein," if I am fooled I will have *taken* him, falsely, to be Einstein. Someone else, who has never heard of Einstein before, may merely be mistaken as to the impostor's name.) On the other hand, if I think

that someone is "her husband" and so refer to him, I need not at all have confused two people. I merely think that one person possesses a property—that of being married to her—that in fact he lacks. The real husband is irrelevant.

27. In terms of this apparatus, I can sharpen the reply to Katz, note 12 above. If Schmidt had discovered the incompleteness of arithmetic but I had thought it was Gödel who did so, a complex ("referential") use of the description has a semantic reference to Schmidt but a speaker's reference to Gödel. Once I am apprised of the true facts, speaker's reference and semantic reference will coincide thereafter and I will no longer use the description to refer to Gödel. The name "Gödel," on the other hand, has Gödel as its *semantic* referent: the name will always be applied to Gödel in the presence of correct information. Whether a term would be withdrawn in the presence of correct information (without changing the language) is a good intuitive test for divergence of semantic reference and speaker's reference (disregarding the cases in note 22).

28. There is another problem for any theory of semantic ambiguity. Donnellan says that if I say "Smith's murderer is insane," solely on the basis of the grisly conditions of Smith's body, my use of "Smith's murderer" is attributive (even if I in fact have a belief as to who the murderer is), but if I say it on the basis of the supposed murderer's behavior at the dock, my use is referential. Surely, however, my reasons can be mixed; perhaps neither consideration would have sufficed by itself, but they suffice jointly. What is my use then? A user of the unambiguous D-language would have to choose between "the" and "ze." It seems very implausible to suppose that the speaker is confused and uncertain about what sense he gives to his description; but what else can we say if we suppose that English is the ambiguous D-language? (This problem arises even if the man at the dock is guilty, so that in fact there is no conflict. It is more obvious if he is innocent.)

A pragmatic theory of the referential–attributive distinction can handle such cases much more easily. Clearly there can be borderline cases between the simple and the complex use—where, to some extent the speaker wishes to speak of the semantic referent and to some extent he wishes to speak of something he believes to be the semantic referent. He need not sort out his motives carefully, since he thinks these things are one and the same!

Given such mixed motives, the speaker's reference may be partially to one thing and partially to another, even when the semantic reference is unambiguous. This is especially likely in the case of proper names, since divergences between speaker's referent and semantic referent are characteristically *misidentifications* (see note 26). Even if the speaker's referent of "Jones" in "Jones is raking the leaves" is Smith, to some extent I have said *of Jones* that he is raking the leaves. There are gradations, depending on the speaker's interests and intentions, as to what extent the speaker's reference was to Jones and to what extent it was to Smith. The problem is less common in the case of descriptions, where misidentification need not have occurred.

29. Of course these tests must be used with some caution. The mere fact that some language subdivides the extension of an English word into several subclasses, with their own separate words, and has no word for the whole extension, does not show that the English word was ambiguous (think of the story that the Eskimos have different words for different kinds of snow). If many unrelated languages preserve a single word, this in itself is evidence for a unitary concept. On the other hand, a word may have different senses that are obviously related. One sense may be metaphorical for another (though in that case, it may not really be a separate sense, but simply a common metaphor.) "Statistics" can mean both statistical data and the science of evaluating such data. And the like. The more we can explain relations among senses, and the more "natural" and "inevitable" the relationship, the more we will expect the different senses to be preserved in a wide variety of other languages.

The test, therefore, needs further exploration and refinement. It is certainly wrong to postulate an ambiguity without any explanation of some connection between the "senses" that explains why they occur in a wide variety of languages. In the referential–attributive case, I feel that any attempt to explain the connection between the referential and the attributive uses will be so close to the kind of pragmatic account offered here as to render any assumptions of distinct senses inplausible and superfluous.

30. That is, the *concept* of truth conditions is somehow inappropriate for the semantics of English. The vague uneasiness expressed in these paragraphs expresses my own rather confused occasional doubts and is ancillary to the main theme. Moore's "paradox of analysis" may be a related problem.

Quine's philosophy of language characteristically is based on a naturalistic doubt about building any "rules" or "conventions" into a language that are not recoverable from actual linguistic practices, even if such rules may be necessary to stipulate the language. In this sense, the uneasiness expressed is Quinean in spirit. I find Quine's emphasis on a naturalistic approach to some extent salutary. But I also feel that our intuitions of semantic rules as speakers should not be ignored cavalierly.

31. Geach, in his book "Reference and Generality," emended ed. (Ithaca: 1970), and elsewhere, has argued vigorously against speaking of pronominalization as picking up a previous reference. I do not wish to argue the extent to which he is right here. I use the terminology given in the text for convenience, but to the extent Geach's views are correct I think the example could presumably be reformulated to fit his scheme. I think the views expressed in this paper are very much in the spirit of Geach's remarks on definite descriptions and speaker's reference in the book just cited. See Geach's discussion, e.g., on p. 8.

32. Donnellan, in "Speaker Reference, Descriptions, and Anaphora," thinks that the fact that pronouns can pick up a previous semantic reference somehow casts doubt on a view that makes speaker's reference a nonsemantical notion. I don't see why: "he," "she," "that," etc., can, under various circumstances, refer to anything salient in an appropriate way. Being physically distinguished against its background is a property that may make an object salient; having been referred to by a previous speaker is another. In "Naming and Necessity," note 3, I suggested tentatively that Donnellan's "remarks about reference have little to do with semantics or truth conditions." The point would be put more exactly if I had said that Donnellan's distinction is not itself a semantical one, though it is relevant to semantics through pronominalization, as many other nonsemantical properties are.

Pronominalization phenomena are relevant to another point. Often one hears it argued against Russell's existential analysis of *indefinite* descriptions that an indefinite description may be anaphorically referred to by a pronoun that seems to preserve the reference of the indefinite description. I am not sure that these phenomena do conflict with the existential analysis. (I am not completely sure there are some that don't, either.) In any event, many cases can be accounted for (given a Russellian theory) by the facts that: (i) existential statements can carry a speaker's reference; (ii) pronouns can refer to the speaker's referent.

33. The use of "ze" in the unambiguous D-language is such that the semantic reference automatically coincided with the speaker's reference, but nevertheless, the notions are applicable. So are the notions of simple and complex uses of designators. However, speakers of the unambiguous D-language might be less likely ever to use "the" in a complex case: for, one might be inclined to argue, if such are their intentions, why not use "ze"?

34. Various moves might be tried, but none that I can think of seem to me to be plausible. It has been suggested to me that sometimes the respondent in a dialogue deliberately feigns to misunderstand an ambiguous phrase used by the first speaker, and that, given the supposed ambiguity of "her husband" in the ambiguous D-language, the first dialogue can be interpreted as such a case. For example, the following dialogue: "Jones put the money in a bank." "He put the money in one all right, but it wasn't a commercial bank; he was so much afraid it would be discovered that he hid it near the river." It seems implausible to me that the first dialogue in the text fits into such a very jocular model. But notice further that the joke consists in a mock *confirmation* of the first speaker's assertion. It would be rather bizarre to respond, "He didn't put the money in the bank, and it wasn't a commercial bank." The first dialogue would have to conform to such a bizzare pattern on the hypothesis in question.

Alternatively, it might be suggested that B uses "he" as a pronoun of laziness for A's "her husband," taken in the supposed referential sense. This move seems to be excluded, since B may well be in no position to use "her husband" referentially. He may merely have heard that she is married to a cruel man.

35. I believe that Karttunen has advocated the view that the referential–attributive distinction arises from a scope ambiguity; I do not know whether this has been published. Since the referential–attributive "ambiguity" arises even in simple sentences such as "Smith's murderer is insane," where there appears to be no room for any scope ambiguity, such a view seems forced to rely on acceptance of Ross's suggestion that all English assertive utterances begin with an initial "I say that," which is suppressed in "surface structure" but present in "deep structure."

For the view that derives the referential–attributive "ambiguity" from a distinction of restrictive and nonrestrictive clauses in "deep structure," see J. M. Bell, "What is Referential Opacity?" *The Journal of Philosophical Logic,* 2 (1973): 155–180. See also the work of Emmon Bach on which Bell's paper is based, "Nouns and Noun Phrases," in *Universals in Linguistic Theory,* ed. E. Bach and R. T. Harms (New York: 1968), pp. 91–122. For reasons of space I have not treated these views here. But some of my arguments that Donnellan's distinction is pragmatic apply against them also.

36. See p. 87 above; also see note 10 above.

37. The term is Donnellan's. See "Putting Humpty Dumpty Together Again," p. 204, footnote 5.

38. I believe that when Donnellan heard the present paper, he too mentioned considerations of this kind. The cases are mentioned briefly in Donnellan's paper, "Putting Humpty Dumpty together Again," *ibid.* Donnellan's paper "Speaker Reference, Descriptions and Anaphora" mentioned above also makes use of the existence of such incomplete descriptions but I do not find his arguments conclusive.

39. See the Santa Claus and Madagascar cases in "Naming and Necessity."

40. It seems likely that the considerations in this paper will also be relevant to the concept of a supposed "± Specific" distinction for indefinite descriptions, as advocated by many linguists.

6

The Pragmatics of What Is Said

FRANÇOIS RÉCANATI

1. THE GRICEAN PICTURE

According to Paul Grice, the meaning of a sentence conventionally determines, or helps to determine, what is literally said by uttering the sentence (the literal truth-conditions of the utterance); for example, the meaning of the sentence "I have not had breakfast today" determines that, if S utters the sentence on a certain day, what he thereby says is that he has had no breakfast on that day. The meaning of the sentence also determines other, non-truth-conditional aspects of utterance meaning, like those responsible for the difference between "and" and "but." In this paper, I will not be concerned with these "conventional implicatures," as Grice calls them, but only with Grice's distinction between what is said and the "conversational" implicatures of the utterance. Conversational implicatures are part of what the utterance communicates, but they are not conventionally determined by the meaning of the sentence; they are pragmatically rather than semantically determined. For example, in saying that he has had no breakfast, S may convey to his audience that he is hungry and wishes to be fed. As Grice pointed out, the generation of conversational implicatures can be accounted for by connecting them with certain general principles or "maxims" of conversation that participants in a talk-exchange are mutually expected to observe. In the Gricean framework, conversational implicatures are contextual implications of the utterance act—they are the assumptions that follow from the speaker's saying what he says together with the presumption that he is observing the maxims of conversation.

Since what is communicated includes a pragmatic, nonconventional element, viz. the conversational implicatures, the fact that a given expression receives different interpretations in different contexts does not imply that it is semantically ambiguous. The intuitive difference in meaning can be accounted for at the semantic level, by positing two different literal meanings, but it can also be accounted for at the pragmatic level, by positing a conversational implicature which in some contents combines with what is literally said. Take, for example, the sentence ⌜P or Q⌝. It can receive an inclusive or an exclusive interpretation. Instead of saying that "or" is ambigu-

François Récanati. "The Pragmatics of What Is Said," *Mind and Language* 4 (1989). Copyright © 1989 by Basil Blackwell. Reprinted by permission of the publisher and the author.

ous in English, we may consider it as unambiguously inclusive, and account for the exclusive reading by saying that in some contexts the utterance conversationally implicates that ⌜P⌝ and ⌜Q⌝ are not both true. When there is such a conversational implicature, the overall meaning of the utterance is clearly exclusive, even though what is strictly and literally said corresponds to the logical formula ⌜P ∨ Q⌝.

When an intuitive "ambiguity" can be accounted for either at the semantic level, by positing two different literal meanings, or at the pragmatic level, by positing a conversational implicature, the pragmatic account is to be preferred, according to Grice. This is the substance of the methodological principle he called "Modified Occam's Razor": *Senses are not to be multiplied beyond necessity* (Grice 1978:118–119). This is a principle of theoretical parsimony, like Occam's Razor. Pragmatic explanations, when available, are to be preferred because they are economical, in the sense that the principles and assumptions they appeal to are very general and independently motivated. By contrast, positing a semantic ambiguity is an ad hoc, costly move—a move which the possibility of a pragmatic analysis makes entirely superfluous.

The Gricean picture which I have just presented has been enormously influential, and rightly so; but it raises a problem which has been recognized only recently. The problem is connected with the notion that sentence meaning conventionally determines what is said. It must be noted from the outset that Grice is rather cautious in his formulation. Vaguely enough, he ascribes to what is said the property of being "closely related to the conventional meaning of words" (Grice 1975:44). But how closely? Recent work in pragmatics has shown that the gap between the conventional meaning of the words and what is said by uttering them is wider than was previously acknowledged. As a result, it is no longer possible to contrast "what is said" with those aspects of the interpretation of utterances that are pragmatically rather than semantically determined; for what is said turns out to be, in a large measure, pragmatically determined. Besides the conversational implicatures, which are external to (and combine with) what is said, there are other nonconventional, prag-

matic aspects of utterance meaning, which are constitutive of what is said. The specific issue I want to address in this paper is that of the criteria that can be used to distinguish conversational implicatures from pragmatic constituents of what is said; in particular, I want to discuss a proposal made by Robyn Carston in a recent paper (Carston 1988). Before doing so, however, I shall briefly identify those aspects of the Gricean picture that are inconsistent with due recognition of the pragmatic determination of what is said.

2. PRAGMATIC DETERMINANTS OF WHAT IS SAID

Grice is aware that what is said depends not only on the conventional meaning of the words but also on the context of utterance. What is said by uttering "I have not had breakfast today" depends on who is speaking and when. This is why there is a difference between the conventional meaning of words and what is said by uttering the words. The conventional meaning of the words determines, or helps to determine, what is said, but it cannot be identified with what is said.

But what does it mean to say that sentence meaning conventionally determines what is said? A common answer is that sentence meaning is a "function" from context onto propositions; it is a rule which determines, for every context, what is said by uttering the sentence in that context. Similarly, the meaning of a word like "I" is a function that takes us from a context of utterance to the semantic value of the word in that context, this semantic value (the reference of "I") being what the word contributes to the proposition expressed by the utterance. On this view, made popular by David Kaplan's work on the logic of demonstratives (Kaplan 1977), what is said by an utterance depends not only on the conventional meaning of the words but also on the context of utterance; however, recourse to the context of utterance is guided and controlled by the conventional meaning of the words. The meaning of "I" tells us what to look for in the context of utterance for a full identification of what is said; once the context is given, what is said can be automatically decoded.

Neat and attractive though it is, this view of the matter is quite unrealistic. In general, even if we know who is speaking, when, to whom, and so forth, the conventional meaning of the words falls short of supplying enough information to exploit this knowledge of the context so as to secure understanding of what is said. Consider a simple example, "He has bought John's book." To understand what is said, one must identify the intended referent of "he." At most, the conventional meaning of "he" imposes that the referent be male, but this allegedly necessary condition is certainly not sufficient and does not uniquely identify the referent in the context of utterance. The meaning of the word "he" provides no "rule," no criterion enabling one to identify the reference. The meaning of the sentence, in this case as in many others, seriously underdetermines what is said. Nor is this underdetermination limited to the reference of referring expressions. To understand what is said by "He has bought John's book," one must identify the referent of "he," of "John" and (perhaps) of "John's book." But one must also identify the relation that is supposed to hold between John and the book. According to Kay and Zimmer (1976:29), "genitive locutions present the hearer with two nouns and a metalinguistic instruction that there is a relation between these two nouns that the hearer must supply." "John's book" therefore means something like "the book that bears relation x to John." To understand what is said by means of a sentence in which the expression "John's book" occurs, this meaning must be contextually enriched by instantiating the variable "x." In other words, not only the reference but the descriptive sense of the expression "John's book" is context-dependent. Moreover, as in the case of "he," there is no rule or function taking us from the context to the relevant semantic value. The only constraint linguistically imposed on the relation between John and the book is that it be a relation between John and the book.

The purpose of this paper not being to review the literature on context-dependence, I will not proceed with further examples. I will simply assume (1) that context-dependence extends far beyond reference assignment, and (2) that it is generally "free" rather than "controlled," in the sense that the linguistic meaning of a context-sensitive expression constrains its possible semantic values but does not consist in a "rule" or "function" taking us from context to semantic value.

Up to this point we need not depart from the Gricean picture, but simply enrich it. We have three levels of meaning: sentence meaning, what is said, and what is communicated. What is communicated includes not only what is said but also the conversational implicatures of the utterance.[1] The mechanism of implicature generation suggested by Grice is intended to account for the step from what is said to what is communicated. But how are we to account for the step from sentence meaning to what is said? What bridges the gap instituted by there being a "free" type of context-dependence pervasive in natural language? Grice does not address this issue. However, as many people have suggested (e.g., Wilson & Sperber 1981:156), the pragmatic apparatus by means of which Grice accounts for conversational implicatures can also be used to account for the determination of what is said on the basis of sentence meaning. In the interpretation process, the referent of "he" and the relation between John and the book in "He has bought John's book" are selected so as to make what the speaker says consistent with the presumption that he is observing the maxims of conversation. The speaker might have meant that Jim has bought the book written by John or that Bob has bought the book sought by John. The hearer will select the interpretation that makes the speaker's utterance consistent with the presumption that he is trying to say something true and relevant.

Once the Gricean picture is enriched in the manner indicated, a problem arises. Implicit in the Gricean picture is the assumption that there are two, *and only two,* ways of accounting for prima facie ambiguities: the semantic approach, which posits a multiplicity of literal meanings, and the pragmatic approach, which posits a conversational implicature. Modified Occam's Razor provides a reason to prefer the latter approach, when it can be implemented, to the former. These two approaches correspond to the two basic levels of meaning that are distinguished in the Gricean picture: sentence meaning, which determines what is literally said, and the utterance's overall meaning, which comprises not only what is said but everything that happens to be communicated, including the conversational implicatures. The semantic approach locates the ambiguity at the level of sentence meaning, while the pragmatic approach considers that it is generated only at the level of what is communicated. But in the enriched Gricean picture, there are three basic levels of meaning rather than two: sentence meaning, what is said, and what is communicated. A pragmatic process is involved not only to get from what is said to what is communicated but also to get from sentence meaning to what is said. It follows that there are three ways of accounting for prima facie ambiguities rather than just two. Besides the semantic approach, which locates the ambiguity at the first level, that of sentence meaning, there are two pragmatic approaches, corresponding to the second and third levels of meaning (what is said and what is communicated). The classical Gricean approach considers that what is said is the same on all readings of the "ambiguous" utterance, the difference between the readings being due to a conversational implicature which, in some contexts, combines with what is literally said. The other pragmatic approach considers that the difference is a difference in what is said, even though the sentence itself is not ambiguous; this is possible owing to the semantic underdetermination of what is said.[2]

The important point is that Modified Occams' Razor does not support the approach in terms of conversational implicature as against the other pragmatic approach; it only says that a pragmatic approach is to be preferred, *ceteris paribus,* to a semantic approach. Hence, enriching the Gricean picture in the manner indicated has the result that the classical Gricean approach to multiple readings in terms of conversational implicature can no longer be justified by appealing to Modified Occam's Razor, as it could when it was assumed to be the only pragmatic alternative to a semantic approach. The classical Gricean approach is threatened by the appearance of a pragmatic rival.

Consider, as an example, Donnellan's distinction between two uses of definite descriptions. Donnellan held that what is said by an utterance of "Smith's murderer is insane" is different according to whether the description "Smith's murderer" is used attributively or referentially. On the attributive interpretation, what is said is true if and only if there is one and only one person who murdered Smith and he is insane. But if the description "Smith's murderer" is used to refer to a certain person, Jones, who is known to have murdered Smith, rather than in general to whomever murdered Smith, then the utterance is true if and only if *Jones* is insane: Jones's being the murder of Smith is no more part of the truth-condition of what is said, on this "referential" interpretation, than my being the speaker is part of the truth-condition of what I say when I utter the sentence "I am insane." This was Donnellan's view. Now a large number of competent philosophers have used the Gricean picture to argue against it. In doing so, they have taken for granted that there are only two possible approaches to Donnellan's distinction: a semantic approach, according to which the literal meaning of the sentence and, therefore, what is said, is different on the referential and the attributive reading, and a pragmatic approach, according to which what is said on both readings is the same (viz., that there is a unique murderer of Smith and he is insane), the referential reading being only distinguished at the level of what is communicated. Using Modified Occam's Razor as an argument for the pragmatic approach, they concluded that Donnellan was wrong to locate the difference between the two readings at the level of what is said. This argument against Donnellan's view is clearly fallacious; it relies on the mistaken assumption that there are only two possible accounts, a semantic account and a pragmatic account in terms of conversational implicature. But this is not so: another type of pragmatic account is possible, which incorporates Donnellan's view, according to which the difference between the referential and the attributive reading is a difference in what is said. On this approach, which I have developed elsewhere (Recanati, 1989), the sentence "Smith's murderer is insane" is not ambiguous, yet it can be used to express either a general or a singular proposition, depending on the context of utterance. Modified Occam's Razor provides no reason to prefer to this account an account in terms of conversational implicature; on the contrary, as I try to show in the paper referred to above, considerations of theoretical economy tend to favor the pragmatic account that incorporates Donnellan's view.

Another example is provided by Carston's pragmatic analysis of conjoined utterances (Carston 1988). In some contexts, a conjunctive utterance ⌐P and Q⌐, conveys the notion that the event described in the second conjunct occurred after the event described in the first conjunct; thus "They got married and had many children" is not intuitively synonymous with "They had many children and got married." However, what is strictly and literally said is in both cases the same thing, according to Grice; the temporal ordering, which is responsible for the intuitive difference between the two examples, is conversationally implicated rather than part of what is said. Modified Occam's Razor dictates that this approach be preferred to a semantic approach ascribing to "and" a temporal sense to account for this type of use and a non-temporal sense to account for other uses (such as "Jane had three children and Mary two," in which no temporal ordering is suggested). However, as Robyn Carston has shown, another pragmatic account is possible, according to which the temporal ordering is part of what is said by means of "They got married and had many children," even though "and" is ascribed a single, non-temporal sense at the semantic level.[3] Modified Occam's Razor provides no reason to prefer to this account the classical Gricean account in terms of conversational implicature.[4]

To sum up: Enriching the Gricean picture to take into account the semantic underdetermination of what is said implies rejecting an assumption implicit in the Gricean picture, namely the assumption that there are two, and only two, possible approaches to prima facie ambiguities, the semantic approach and the pragmatic approach in terms of implicature. Once this assumption is abandoned, the classical Gricean treatment of prima facie ambiguities in terms of implicature is considerably weakened; instead of enjoying the privileges of monopoly, it has to compete with another pragmatic approach. This raises a central issue, which is the main topic of this paper: that of the criteria that can be used in adjudicating between the different pragmatic approaches. When should a pragmatically determined aspect of utterance meaning be considered as a conversational implicature, and when should it be considered as constitutive of what is said? In what follows, I shall consider four possible answers to this question, i.e., four criteria that could be used to decide whether a given aspect of meaning is a conversational implicature or a pragmatic constituent of what is said.

3. THE MINIMALIST PRINCIPLE

The first possible criterion, the Minimalist Principle, can be stated as follows:

Minimalist Principle: A pragmatically determined aspect of meaning is part of what is said if and only if its determination is necessary for the utterance to express a complete proposition.

The Minimalist Principle entails what Carston (1988) calls the "linguistic direction principle." To every pragmatically determined aspect of meaning that is part of what is said, there corresponds a slot in the meaning of the sentence which must be filled for the utterance to be truth-evaluable. Context-sensitive expressions, such as "he" or the genitive, set up such slots, which in some cases at least can be represented as variables in need of contextual instantiation. It follows, by the Minimalist Principle, that the pragmatic determination of the referent of "he" and of the relation between John and the book contributes to determining what is said by uttering the sentence "He has bought John's book." By contrast, conversational implicatures are not part of what is said, because the utterance expresses a complete proposition without them. (Since conversational implicatures follow from the speaker's saying what he says, the generation of a conversational implicature presupposes that something has been said.)

Most theorists assume that to get from the meaning of the sentence to the proposition expressed, one has only to disambiguate the sentence, i.e., to select one of its possible readings, and to instantiate a few indexical variables. That semantic underdetermination goes beyond mere indexicality is often neglected, as is the fact that the contextual instantiation of many variables is "free" rather than "controlled." In other words, the gap between sentence meaning and what is said is generally underestimated. But the Minimalist Principle itself might be considered as a manifestation of the general tendency to underestimate this gap. Once it is recognized that there are more variables than just indexical variables, and that the contextual instantiation of variables is not always linguistically controlled, why not go one step further and reject the Minimalist Principle itself? Why not question the claim that nothing more is needed to go from sentence meaning to what is said than just disambiguation and variable instantiation?

Following Sperber and Wilson, but more explicitly, Robyn Carston has taken this step (Carston 1988). She thinks that the Minimalist Principle must be rejected: what it presents as a necessary and sufficient condition is only sufficient, according to her. Consider sentences (1) and (2):

(1) It will take us some time to get there.

(2) I have had breakfast.

Once the identity of the speaker and hearer, the time of utterance and the reference of "there" is determined, no further slot needs to be filled for an utterance of (1) to express a complete proposition. The proposition we get at this point is the truistic proposition that there is a lapse of time (of some length or other) between our departure, or some other point of reference, and our arrival at a certain place. But, according to Carston, who borrows this example from Sperber and Wilson (1986:189–90), this is not the proposition actually expressed; to get the latter, we need to go beyond the minimal proposition expressible by the sentence and enrich it by pragmatically specifying the relevant lapse of time as rather long (longer than expected, perhaps). This contextual specification is constitutive of what is said, yet it is not necessary for the sentence to express a definite proposition. It follows that the Minimalist Principle must be rejected. In the same way, according to Sperber and Wilson, once the identity of the speaker and the time of utterance has been fixed, (2) expresses a proposition, viz. the proposition that the speaker has had breakfast at least once before the time of utterance. This proposition, which would be true if the speaker had had breakfast twenty years earlier and never since, does not correspond to what the speaker

means to say when he utters "I have had breakfast." What the speaker says goes beyond the minimal proposition expressible, contrary to what the Minimalist Principle predicts.

In Sperber and Wilson's framework, three processes are involved in getting from sentence meaning to what is said: disambiguation, fixation of reference and enrichment. The notion of enrichment, for them, covers things as different as the determination of the relation between John and the book in "He has bought John's book" and the determination of the length of the lapse of time mentioned in "It will take us some time to get there." In the first case, the meaning of the sentence sets up a slot (representable as a variable: "He has bought the book that bears relation x to John") that must be contextually filled for the utterance to express a complete proposition. This type of enrichment I shall call "saturation"; it is not essentially different from the fixation of reference, but rather includes it as a particular case, since referential expressions themselves set up slots to be contextually filled for the utterace to express a complete proposition. In the other case, the enrichment of "some time" into something more specific is not needed for the utterance to express a complete proposition, but for the proposition expressed to correspond to what the speaker means by his utterance. The input to this second type of enrichment is a complete proposition, and the output is a richer proposition, i.e., one that entails the input proposition. I shall refer to this type of enrichment as "strengthening." Sperber and Wilson's claim that the proposition expressed is obtained from the disambiguated meaning of the sentence not only by saturation but also by strengthening is inconsistent with the Minimalist Principle, according to which the proposition expressed—what is said—just is the minimal proposition expressible by the utterance, i.e., what results from simply saturating the disambiguated meaning of the sentence.

I find Sperber and Wilson's proposal very interesting. The Minimalist Principle seems arbitrary, and there may be good reasons to get rid of it. (One such reason, perhaps, is that the Minimalist Principle leads to implausible semantic hypotheses when taken in conjunction with two principles I shall introduce later—the Availability Principle and the

Scope Principle.) Still, the matter is controversial, and I think caution is called for; the Minimalist Principle should not be dropped too lightly.

The examples given by Sperber and Wilson do not, in my opinion, require giving up the traditional framework: it is easy to handle these examples without dropping the Minimalist Principle. One obvious way to do so is to adopt the analysis in terms of conversational implicature, according to which the person who utters (2) "says" that he has had breakfast at least once, and "implicates" that this happened on the very day of utterance. (On this analysis, the proposition expressed—what is said—*is* the "minimal" proposition expressible.) Sperber and Wilson do not agree with this analysis; neither do I. The reason it seems unacceptable will be spelled out in the next section. What matters for my present purposes is that the analysis in terms of conversational implicature is not the only way to handle the examples without dropping the Minimalist Principle. Sperber and Wilson reject it because they believe that a pragmatically determined aspect of the meaning of (1) and (2) is such that:

⟨a⟩ it is constitutive of what is said, and

⟨b⟩ its determination is not necessary for the utterance to express a complete proposition.

This conjunction of ⟨a⟩ and ⟨b⟩ is inconsistent with the Minimalist Principle, which says that a pragmatically determined aspect of the meaning of an utterance is part of what is said if and only if its contextual determination is necessary for the utterance to express a complete proposition. However, the Minimalist Principle is not inconsistent with ⟨a⟩ or ⟨b⟩ taken separately. Defenders of the implicature analysis accept ⟨b⟩ but reject ⟨a⟩; they are thus able to maintain the Minimalist Principle. But there is another treatment, consistent with the Minimalist Principle: one may accept ⟨a⟩ but reject ⟨b⟩, i.e., consider that the relevant aspect of the meaning of (1) and (2) is constitutive of what is said (and therefore not a conversational implicature), while insisting that its contextual determination *is* necessary for the utterance to express a complete proposition. Let me briefly sketch this minimalist treatment of examples (1) and (2).

Both (1) and (2) can be analysed in terms of quantification. (1) quantifies over durations (it says that there is a duration *t* such that it will take us *t* to get there) and (2) quantifies over events (it says that there is a past event which is the speaker's having breakfast). Now, quantification involves a certain amount of context-dependence, because, in general, the domain of quantification has to be contextually specified. For example, it can be argued that the sentence "Everybody went to Paris," by itself, does not express a complete proposition—not even the proposition that everybody in the world went to Paris: what it says is that everybody in some domain x went to Paris, and the context helps to instantiate the variable "x." (On this view, the variable "x" may be contextually instantiated so as to make "everybody in the world" the right interpretation, but this interpretation is no less contextual than any other interpretation.[5] Suppose we accept this view. Then, in the case of (1), (2) and other utterances involving quantification, there is a slot to be filled, corresponding to the domain of quantification. It follows that the specific interpretations of (1) and (2), which Carston and Sperber and Wilson present as counterexamples to the Minimalist Principle, are perfectly consistent with the latter—one merely has to define the domain of quantification in an appropriate way. In the case of (1), we might say that the domain of quantification is a set of durations, contextually restricted to those that are long enough to be worth mentioning in connection with the process of our going there. (In this framework, the interpretation of (1) which corresponds to the so-called "minimal proposition" expressible—the propsition that it will take us "some time or other" to get there—is just the unlikely interpretation in which the domain of quantification is contextually identified with the set of all possible durations, including milliseconds.) In the case of (2), we might say that the domain of quantification is a time interval, or rather a set of happenings defined by a time interval. This allows us to account for the intuitive difference between "I've had breakfast" and "I've been to Tibet" (Sperber & Wilson 1986:189–90). In both cases, what is conveyed by virtue of linguistic meaning alone is that, in some temporal domain x prior to the time of utterance, there is a certain event, viz. the speaker's having breakfast or his going to Tibet; but in the first case, the time interval is contextually restricted to the day of utterance, while in the second case the relevant interval is more extended and covers the speaker's life (up to the time of utterance).

According to the view I have just outlined, it is a mistake to believe that (1) and (2) express complete propositions once the obvious indexical variables (identity of the speaker and hearer, time of utterance, reference of "there") have been instantiated; a slot remains to be filled, which corresponds to the domain of quantification. It follows that the Minimalist Principle can be retained even though one accepts thesis ⟨a⟩ above, i.e., even though one considers that what is said by means of (1) and (2) is that it will take us a *long* time to get there or that the speaker has had breakfast *on the day of utterance.* Far from being added to an already complete proposition, the pragmatic specifications I have just italicized result from filling a slot, a slot that must be filled in some way or other for the utterance to express a complete proposition.

Not only is it the case that (1), (2) and similar "counterexamples" to the Minimalist Principle *can* be handled in terms of saturation, without giving up minimalism, but I also believe that, in many such cases, a saturation-based account is actually preferable to an alternative account in terms of strengthening. Consider, for example, the sentence "One boy came." It can be used to say something quite specific, namely that *one of the boys in the class* came. This seems to be a typical case of strengthening: "One boy came" might be said to express the "minimal" proposition that at least one boy came, which minimal proposition is entailed by the richer proposition "At least one of the boys in the class came" (if one of the boys in the class came, then one boy came); the notion of strengthening therefore applies in a straightforward manner. But this account is not general enough, as can be seen by considering other cases, which look very similar but are far more difficult to handle in terms of strengthening. Thus, the sentence "Every boy came" can be used to say that every boy in the class came; the problem here is that the output proposition, i.e., the proposition that every boy in the class came, does not entail the input proposition, viz. the "min-

imal" proposition that every boy (i.e., every boy in the world!) came. Because of this problem, the account in terms of strengthening seems less attractive than the minimalist account in terms of a contextually variable domain of quantification.

The same type of problem arises in connection with examples such as (2). "I have had breakfast" can be used to say that the speaker has had breakfast on the day of utterance, even though, according to Sperber and Wilson, the minimal proposition expressible by this sentence is the proposition that the speaker has had breakfast at least once (but not necessarily on the day of utterance). This can be accounted for in terms of strengthening, because the proposition that the speaker has had breakfast on the day of utterance entails the proposition that he has had breakfast at least once in his life. But what about the similar utterance "I have not had breakfast"? It can be used to say that the speaker has not had breakfast on the day of utterance, but this cannot be straightforwardly accounted for in terms of strengthening, because the proposition that the speaker has had no breakfast on the day of utterance does not entail the proposition that he has never eaten breakfast in his life. Here again, because of its greater generality, the minimalist account presented above looks more attractive than the alternative account in terms of strengthening.[6]

Shall we conclude from this discussion that the Minimalist Principle is to be retained after all? That would be excessive. With respect to examples other than those I have discussed, a strengthening-based account, inconsistent with the Minimalist Principle, may well seem more attractive or plausible than a saturation-based one. My discussion merely shows that the matter is not as simple as one might think after reading Carston and Sperber and Wilson. Whether or not one should ultimately stick to the Minimalist Principle thus remains an open question.

In any event, I will now attempt to show that, even if there *were* decisive arguments in favor of the Minimalist Principle, the latter could not be used as a working criterion for distinguishing implicatures from the pragmatic aspects of what is said. In the next section, I will introduce another criterion, the Availability Principle, which is implicitly appealed to by those who reject the implicature analysis of (1) and (2). I will argue that this is the right criterion to use.

The Minimalist Principle states a biconditional: A pragmatically determinded aspect of meaning is part of what is said if and only if its determination is necessary for the utterance to express a complete proposition. It follows that the Minimalist Principle can be used to decide whether a pragmatically determined aspect of utterance meaning is part of what is said, *provided* one knows whether or not the pragmatic determination of this aspect of meaning is necessary for the utterance to express a complete proposition. The qualification is important: the Minimalist Principle per se cannot be used to tell whether a pragmatically determined aspect of meaning is part of what is said; it can be used to that effect only if a decision has already been made concerning the variables that have to be contextually instantiated for the utterance to express a complete proposition. In other words:

(M): For any (pragmatically determined) aspect *a* of the meaning of an utterance, the Minimalist Principle can be used to decide whether *a* is a conversational implicature or an integral part of what is said if and only if one already knows whether the determination of *a* is or is not necessary for the utterance to express a complete proposition, i.e., if and only if one already possesses a semantic analysis of the sentence uttered.

This immediately raises a problem. According to (M), the Minimalist Principle cannot be used to make a decision concerning what is said unless we already know precisely what the meaning of the sentence is. But this puts the cart before the horse: far from proceeding in that order, we generally start with some intuition concerning what is said (or, at least, what is communicated), and end up with a theory about what the sentence means. As I emphasize in the next section, sentence meaning is something more abstract and theoretical than what is said or what is communicated. For this reason, I believe that the Minimalist Principle does not actually provide a criterion for distinguishing implicatures from pragmatic aspects of what is said, because we do *not* possess a semantic analysis of the sentence ahead of any decision concerning what is said. The Minimalist Principle is more properly seen as pro-

viding a criterion for determining the semantic analysis of the sentence, on the basis of a prior, intuitive identification of what is said. For example, suppose that a theorist has decided in favor of ⟨a⟩ and believes, on an intuitive basis, that a certain pragmatically determined aspect of meaning is part of what is said. If he accepts the Minimalist Principle, he is led to posit a slot in the meaning of the sentence that must be filled for the utterance to express a complete proposition—a slot that corresponds to the pragmatically determined aspect of meaning which, by virtue of ⟨a⟩, he considers as part of what is said. Suppose, on the contrary, that he rejects ⟨a⟩. In this case, he must refrain from positing such a slot in the meaning of the sentence, for if there were one, the corresponding aspect of utterance meaning would be part of what is said, by virtue of the Minimalist Principle. Acceptance of the Minimalist Principle thus makes some semantic hypotheses look more attractive than others; it provides a criterion for choosing among alternative theories concerning the linguistic meaning of the sentence. This is not the same thing as a criterion for determining what is said.

Considered as a criterion for selecting hypotheses about sentence meaning, the Minimalist Principle may well be retained, at least provisionally.[7] But it does not constitute an adequate criterion for determining what is said, and we must find something else to answer this purpose. I suggest that we take a closer look at a claim I have just made: that what is said is identified on an intuitive basis. This, I believe, leads us to the criterion we are looking for.

4. THE AVAILABILITY PRINCIPLE

In the last part of section 3 I made two related claims: first, that sentence meaning is something more abstract and theoretical than what is said; second, that we have "intuitions" concerning what is said that serve as a starting point in the process of determining what the linguistic meaning of the sentence is. Although obviously related, these two claims are to be distinguished; the second is stronger than the first. I shall argue that the stronger claim provides us with a criterion for telling implicatures apart from pragmatic aspects of what is said. This criterion, stated below, I shall refer to as the "Availability Principle," because it presupposes that what is said by an utterance is available or accessible to the unsophisticated speaker-hearer. "Available" must be understood here in a strong sense: what I mean is not that what is said by an utterance is tacitly identified at some sub-doxastic level, but that it is accessible to our ordinary, conscious intuitions. The Availability Principle just says that these intuitions are to be respected:

Availability Principle: In deciding whether a pragmatically determined aspect of utterance meaning is part of what is said, that is, in making a decision concerning what is said, we should always try to preserve our pre-theoretic intuitions on the matter.

In this section, I will try to make more explicit the claim concerning the availability of what is said—the "availability hypothesis," as I shall call it; I will then show how the Availability Principle works. I will conclude that some very common assumptions of Gricean pragmatics are to be rejected if we take the Availability Principle seriously.

Let us start with the claim that sentence meaning is something more abstract and theoretical than what is said. Consider the diagram labelled Figure 6.1. Starting at the top, it shows the various steps that lead, by analytical abstraction, from what is communicated to the meaning of the sentence. The analysis thus displayed is intended to mirror the actual process of understanding the utterance, this corresponding to a bottom-up reading of the diagram. At the top (i.e., the root) of the inverted tree, "what is communicated" is the intuitive datum we, as analysts, start from; it is also the consciously accessible output of the process of pragmatic understanding. Everything that occurs below the top level is more abstract, that is, farther from the starting point of the analysis. At the bottom of the tree, we find sentence meaning, a theoretical construct representing both the output of the process of semantic decoding and the input to the process of pragmatic understanding. To say that sentence meaning is something more abstract than what is said is just a way of putting sentence meaning closer to the bottom of the tree,

while putting what is said closer to the top. In processing terms, sentence meaning is cognitively deeper and what is said shallower—they are respectively farther from and closer to the output of the process of pragmatic undersanding.

In the case of sentence meaning, abstractness and cognitive depth go hand in hand with a further property, that of conscious unavailability. Of sentence meaning we can assume only tacit (unconscious) knowledge on the part of the speaker who utters the sentence. To be sure, users of the language claim to have intuitions concerning what the sentences in their language mean; but these intuitions are not directly about their purported objects—linguistic meanings. They do not bear on the linguistic meanings of sentences, which are very abstract and unaccessible to consciousness, but on what would be said or communicated by the sentence were it uttered in a standard or easily accessible context.

Being located at an intermediate level in the diagram, what is said is cognitively shallower—less abstract—than sentence meaning. But we cannot conclude that it is more accessible to consciousness than the latter. We cannot infer, from the fact that what is said is shallower than sentence meaning, that there is between them a difference in nature such that the latter can only be cognized at the sub-doxastic level while the former is consciously accessible. The availability of what is said does not follow from its relative shallowness, i.e., from its proximity to the top level. *As an intermediate output, resulting from an advanced but nonfinal stage of unconscious pragmatic processing, what is said could be no less subdoxastic than sentence meaning.* It is, therefore, a nontrivial hypothesis that I am making when I claim that what is said is consciously

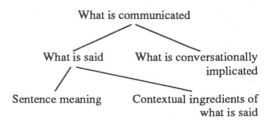

Figure 6.1

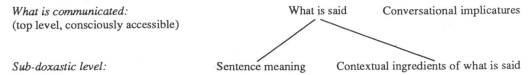

What is communicated:
(top level, consciously accessible)

Sub-doxastic level:

Figure 6.2

accessible. The availability hypothesis cannot be reduced to the claim that sentence meaning is more abstract and cognitively deeper than what is said.

To make sense of the availability hypothesis, I suggest a slight modification of the diagram in Figure 6.1. As it is, it implies that what is communicated—the object of our intuitions—is something over and above what is said and what is conversationally implicated: what is communicated is seen as the output of a specific cognitive process (the last step in the general process of pragmatic understanding) whose inputs are what is said and what is implicated. One way of understanding the claim concerning the availabiity of what is said is by rejecting this view altogether, considering that what is communicated *consists of* what is said and what is implicated, instead of being something *over and above* what is said and what is implicated. Instead of locating what is communicated at one level and what is said (as well as the implicatures) at another, I suggest that we consider "what is communicated" as simply a *name* for the level at which we find both what is said and what is implicated—the top level, characterized by conscious accessibility (Figure 6.2). On this view, the conscious availability of what is said no longer is a mystery: if what is communicated, which is consciously accessible, consists of what is said and what is implicated, then what is said cannot but be consciously accessible. In the new diagram, it is no longer suggested that there is a specific process merging what is said and what is implicated. They constitute the final output of the general process of pragmatic understanding, not an intermediate output, as Figure 6.1 suggests. What is said and what is implicated thus remains distinct, and are consciously available as distinct.[8]

It is striking that the question of the availability of what is said has never been raised in the pragmatic literature.[9] I believe it is a very

important issue. If we really have conscious access to what is said, then as theorists we have a very simple criterion for telling when a pragmatically determined aspect of meaning is part of what is said and when it is not: we merely have to check the proposal against our intuitions. This, I believe, is what most theorists have always done. Why, for example, do Sperber and Wilson claim that the proposition that the speaker has had breakfast at least once in his life is not the proposition actually expressed—what is said—by the speaker who utters (2)? Because *everybody knows* that this is not what the speaker says, under ordinary circumstances, when he utters (2). The appeal to common sense is perfectly justified once the availability hypothesis is made.

Perhaps we should consider the intuitions of the speaker instead of those of the theorist. According to the Availability Principle thus interpreted, a tentative identification of what is said has to be checked against the speaker's intuitions. In this framework, Sperber and Wilson's decision concerning example (2) can be justified as follows. We suppose that what is said by an utterance is known, at least, by the speaker (availability hypothesis). In the case of (2), if what the speaker says is that he has had breakfast at least once in his life, then the speaker does not know what he says, because he does not know that this is what he says (were he to be told, he would be very surprised); therefore, this is *not* what he says. Using the Availability Principle, we are thus able to reject the "implicature analysis" of examples (1) and (2), because it assumes an identification of what is said which is inconsistent with the speaker's intuitions. The speaker believes that what he says is that he has had breakfast *on the day of utterance;* the Availability Principle dictates that we reject all pragmatic theories inconsistent with this belief, and, in particular, the implicature analysis, which identifies what the speaker says with the proposition that he has had breakfast at least once in his life.

Before proceeding, a caveat is in order. When I claim that we have intuitions concerning what is said, I do not wish to deny that these intuitions may be fuzzy, or that we may sometimes have conflicting intuitions. (The existence of a quotational concept of "saying," to be mentioned in the next section, is but one factor among many that tend to make our intuitions fuzzy and conflicting.) What I am saying is that our intuitions are clear enough to rule out a number of analyses that are grossly inconsistent with them.

The Availability Principle can be appealed to in a number of cases to show that a tentative analysis is misguided. Consider an example mentioned earlier in this paper, the utterance "Everybody went to Paris." Under ordinary circumstances, what a speaker would mean by this is not that everybody in the absolute sense, i.e., every person in the world, went to Paris, but that everybody in some (contextually identifiable) group went to Paris. Suppose, for example, it is established that what the speaker means is that every member of the Johnson & Johnson staff went to Paris. Still, the utterance can be analyzed in two ways. The first analysis is quite straightforward: it identifies what the speaker says with what he means, i.e., with the proposition that every member of the Johnson & Johnson staff went to Paris. But there is another possible analysis. We may consider that what is literally said is that everybody in the world went to Paris, even though this is clearly not what the speaker means. A proponent of this analysis has only to assume that what the speaker says is different from what he means, i.e., that he speaks nonliterally, as in metaphor. Such an analysis has been put forward in Bach (1987) and extended to many examples, including the whole class of utterances in which an incomplete definite description occurs. Thus, Bach identifies the proposition literally expressed by the utterance "The door is closed" with the Russellian proposition "There is one and only one door in the world, and it is closed," this proposition not being what the speaker means to communicate when he utters the sentence. The Availability Principle militates against this type of analysis,

which assumes a counter-intuitive identification of what is said. The difference with genuine cases of nonliterality should be apparent. When the speaker says to the hearer, "You are the cream in my coffee," everybody would agree that what the speaker says is that the hearer is the cream in his coffee: this is clearly what he says, and it is no less clear that he is speaking nonliterally. But when the speaker says "Everybody went to Paris," or "The door is closed," it is counter-intuitive to identify what he says with the propositions that every person in the world went to Paris, or that the only door in the universe is closed. The speaker himself would not recognize those propositions as being what he said. The "nonliteral" analysis must therefore be rejected, by virtue of the Availability Principle.[10]

One important consequence of the Availability Principle is that some of the most often cited examples of conversational implicatures turn out not to be conversational implicatures after all. So-called "scalar implicatures" are a case in point. Suppose the speaker utters "John has three children," thereby communicating that John has exactly three children. It is customary to say that the proposition literally expressed by "John has three children" is the proposition that John has at least three children, even if what the speaker means to communicate by this utterance is that John has exactly three children. What is communicated (viz., that John has exactly three children) is classically accounted for by positing a conversational implicature that combines with the proposition allegedly expressed (viz., that John has at least three children). This proposal, however, does not pass the availability test, for the speaker himself would not recognize the latter proposition as being what he has said. Not being consciously available, the proposition which the classical account takes to be literally expressed cannot be identified with what is said, if we accept the Availability Principle. The latter dictates that we consider the aspect of meaning that is pragmatically determined (viz. the implicit restriction: no more than three children) as part of what is said rather than as a conversational implicature associated with what is said. The same remarks could be made with respect to other well-known examples, such as the exclusive reading of ⌜P or Q⌝, whch are often presented as prototypical cases of conversational implicature.

5. THE INDEPENDENCE PRINCIPLE

In her aforementioned paper, Robyn Carston attempts to show that many cases that have been treated as typical examples of conversational implicature are better conceived of as pragmatic aspects of what is said. Not only is she right to hold this as a general thesis; I also believe she is right with respect to particular examples, in most cases at least. This should come as no surprise: Carston certianly relies on her intuitions when she decides that a particular aspect of meaning is to be considered as an integral part of what is said, and I have argued that we do have reliable intuitions concerning what is said. Carston, however, does not hold anything like the availability hypothesis, and thus she cannot be content to rely on her intuitions. What she wants—and what she offers—is an explicit criterion for telling implicatures apart from pragmatic aspects of what is said. In this section, I shall consider the criterion she puts forward, and show that it does not work.

Those who, like Carston, reject the Minimalist Principle believe that the proposition expressed by an utterance—what is said— may be richer than what I called the "minimal proposition" expressible by the utterance. Whether or not they are right is, as I said, an open question. But Carston goes further than merely rejecting the Minimalist Principle: she puts forward an alternative principle, which entails that every communicated assumption that is richer than the minimal proposition expressible by the utterance *must* be understood as part of what is said. This principle can be stated as follows:

Independence Principle: Conversational implicatures are functionally independent of what is said; this means in particular that they do not entail, and are not entailed by, what is said. When an alleged implicature does not meet this condition, it must be considered as part of what is said.

It is not perfectly clear what Carston means by "functional independence," but it is clear that, for her, functional independence entails logical independence: as she emphasizes in her paper, an implicature will not be functionally independent of the proposition expressed if it entails, or is entailed by, the latter. It is this feature of the Independence Principle that she uses as a criterion to distinguish genuine implicatures from pragmatic aspects of what is said. Owing to this criterion, it is not possible to consider that what is said by means of (2) is that the speaker has had breakfast at least once, the fact that he has had breakfast *on the day of utterance* being only implicated. For then the implicature would entail the proposition literally expressed, contrary to what the Independence Principle requires. (If the speaker has had breakfast on the day of utterance, then he has had breakfast at least once in his life.) In the same way, it is not possible to consider that the proposition expressed by (1) is the minimal proposition that it will take us some time or other to get there, the more specific proposition that it will take us a rather *long* time to get there being only implicated; for this alleged implicature would entail the proposition expressed, and thus would not be a genuine implicature. In general, when an alleged implicature entails the proposition allegedly expressed, it must be considered as part of what is said rather than as a genuine implicature.

Using this criterion, Carston is able to show that many pragmatically determined aspects of utterance meaning that have been classified as converstional implicatures in the Gricean tradiition are better veiwed as pragmatic aspects of the proposition expressed. For example, the utterance "John has three children," used to communicate that John has exactly three children, cannot be said to express the proposition that John has at least three children, for if this was the proposition expressed, then the richer proposition—that John has exactly three children—would be an implicature, and we would have an implicature that entails the proposition expressed, in violation of the Independence Principle.[11] In this and related cases, I believe that Carston is right to say that the alleged implicature is not a genuine implicature but, rather, an aspect of the proposition expressed. However, I think the Independence Principle is to be rejected.

A first and obvious objection to the Independence Principle must be set aside. It might be argued that, in litotes, we have implicatures that entail what is said. (By saying that it is not bad, one implicates that it is excellent, and if it is excellent it cannot be bad.) This, however, is not a counterexample to Carston's Independence Principle, which is only intended to apply to literal assertions. But there are counterexamples even if we consider only literal assertions. Suppose that John says to Jim: "Someone will come and see you today— someone you have been expected for a long time. I am not permitted to reveal the identity of visitors in advance, but I take it that you see who I mean." Suppose it is clear that John means that Mrs. Robertson is going to come and see Jim. Has John said that Mrs. Robertson was going to come? No: He has said that *someone* was going to come, and has implied that it was Mrs. Robertson. The implication is very clear, but the fact that it is an implication, and not something that is explicitly said, is no less clear: as John emphasizes, he is not entitled to *say* who is going to come. Carston's principle, however, predicts that John has said, rather than simply implicated, that Mrs. Robertson was to come. For if this were an implicature, it would entail the proposition allegedly expressed (viz., that someone will come and see Jim), contrary to what the Independence Principle requires.

According to Ruth Kempson (personal communication), this is not really a counterexample to Carston's Independence Principle, because the concept of "saying" which is involved when I deny that the speaker has "said" that Mrs. Robertson was to come is not the relevant one. Certainly, there is a concept of saying such that, when I utter "I've had breakfast," I do not literally "say" that I've had breakfast *today,* because I do not utter the word "today"; what I "say" is that I have had breakfast, but I do not "say" when. In this sense of "say," it is always possible to deny that something has been said, unless the word for that thing has been explicitly pronounced. This we may refer to as the "quotational" sense of "say." The quotational sense of "say," Kempson argues, is irrelevant to the issue we are discussing, but it is critical to the Robertson example; therefore, the latter is not a real counterexample.

I am not wholly convinced by Kempson's argument, although I agree with her that the existence of a quotational sense of "say" has to be taken into account. In any event, I am willing to concede that the example is controversial. My case against the Independence Principle does not rest upon this particular example, but on general considerations to which I now turn. I shall first say what is wrong with Carston's proposal, and then use these general considerations to build up a better, and to my mind decisive, counterexample to the Independence Principle.

The problem with Carston's proposal is that, even though she constantly talks of "functional" independence, the criterion she actually uses to distinguish conversational implicatures from pragmatic aspects of what is said is the relation of *logical* independence that must hold, she believes, between a genuine implicature and what is said: basically, an implicature must not entail what is said. Now, I believe that *any* formal principle of this sort is mistaken, and cannot but make wrong predictions. This point is very general, and before giving examples connected with the Independence Principle, I should like to mention two other instances of what we might call the "formal fallacy" in pragmatics.

The first instance of the formal fallacy is a very common definition of direct and indirect speech acts. In speech-act theory sentences are taken to have a semantically determined "illocutionary act potential"; that is, they are taken to be semantically associated with an illocutionary act type. An illocutionary act performed by uttering a sentence is commonly said to be direct if and only if it falls under the illocutionary act potential of the sentence, that is, if and only if it is an instance of the illocutionary act type semantically associated with the sentence. So, given that the sentence "Can you pass the salt?" is semantically associated with the illocutionary act of asking the hearer whether he can pass the salt, an act of requesting the hearer to pass the salt, performed by uttering this sentence, can only be indirect. This same act will be direct when performed by means of the alternative sentence "Please pass the salt," which is semantically associated with the act of requesting the hearer to pass the salt.

This "formal" definition of direct and indirect illocutionary acts is seriously misguided, as the following counterexample shows. The sentence "He has come" is semantically associated with the act of conveying the information, concerning someone, that he has come; any token of this act peformed by means of this sentence must therefore be direct, in virtue of the formal definition. Now, suppose that by uttering "He has come" the speaker says that John has come; and suppose a context in which, by saying that John has come, the speaker is able to communicate another piece of information, namely that Bill has come. (For example, it is mutually known that, whenever John comes, Bill comes too, and that the point of saying that John has come is, for the speaker, to convey indirectly that Bill has come.) This is a typical case of indirect speech act: by saying something, namely that John has come, the speaker conveys something else, namely that Bill has come. Nevertheless, this indirect speech act is to be treated as direct, according to the formal definition above, just because it happens to fall under the illocutionary act potential of the sentence uttered. The formal definition obliges us to consider that the speaker has directly asserted that Bill has come, just because he has conveyed this information by uttering a sentence that could have been (but was not!) used to say that. The formal definition must therefore be rejected: what defines a speech act as direct is the way it is performed, not a formal relation of "congruence" (Gardiner 1932:142) between the speech act and the sentence uttered. To be sure, the fact that a speech act is directly performed implies that this relation holds, but it can hold also "accidentally," even though the speech act performed is indirect.

The same type of counterexample can be brought against Sperber and Wilson's definition of explicitness, understood in a certain way. Clearly, what characterizes implicatures (implicitly communicated assumptions) and explicatures (explicitly communicated assumptions) is, for Sperber and Wilson, the way they are recovered in the interpretation process: explicatures are recovered by enriching and developing a logical form encoded in the sentence uttered, while implicatures are premisses and conclusions in an inference process whose starting point is the explicature.

It follows that an explicature necessarily bears a certain formal relation to the logical form of the sentence uttered: that of being a "development" of that logical form, i.e., a generally richer and more complex form that incorporates it. But it is a mistake to use that formal property to define the explicature as opposed to the implicature, as Sperber and Wilson seem to do (Sperber & Wilson 1986:182), for it is quite possible for an implicature to have this property accidentally. Suppose that by saying "It will rain tomorrow" the speaker communicates the following explicature: that Mary believes that it will rain tomorrow. Suppose further that this explicature contextually implies that it is not the case that it will rain tomorrow, and that much of the relevance of the utterance predictably depends on this contextual implication. Then "It is not the case that it will rain tomorrow" is an implicature, according to Sperber and Wilson's ordinary characterization. But it should be treated as an explicature according to the formal definition, because "It is not the case that it will rain tomorrow" is formally a development of "It will rain tomorrow."[12]

Similar counterexamples can easily be found in connection with Carston's Independence Principle. Consider the following dialogue:

A: Was there anybody rich at the party, who might be asked to pay for the damages?
B: Jim is rich.
A: Yes, but did he go to the party?
B: I don't know, but I can tell you that if *anybody* was there, Jim was there.
A: *Somebody* was there—this I know for sure (I saw John going there). So it looks as if the damages will be paid for, after all.

The beginning of A's last reply, "Somebody was there," clearly implicates (in virtue of the premiss provided by B's last reply: "If anybody was there, Jim was there") that Jim was there and therefore (in virtue of the premiss provided by B's first reply: "Jim is rich") that a rich man was there. This implicature is what links together the beginning ("Somebody was there") and the end ("The damages will be paid for") of A's last reply. Now, the implicature that Jim was there entails what is said, namely that somebody was there. So it should be considered as part of what is said rather than as a genuine implicature, according to the Independence Principle. But, clearly, by saying that somebody was there, A is not referring to Jim in any sense; if there is any reference here (which I doubt), it would be to the person of whom the speaker knows for sure that he went to the party, namely John. So there are three candidates for the status of what is said. The most plausible is the general proposition that there was at least one person at the party. Some people believe that there is a referential use of indefinites, and are therefore prepared to argue that A was referring to John when he said "Somebody was there"; those people would perhaps conclude that A said of John that he was there. But who would accept the extraordinary conclusion, imposed by Carston's Independence Principle, that A, having John in mind and uttering "Somebody was there," has actually said that Jim was there?

On this general pattern, we might construct as many counterexamples to the Independence Principle as we may wish. This type of counterexample shows that what defines a communicated assumption as an implicature is not a formal property, and in particular not the formal property of (logical) independence with respect to the proposition expressed, but the way it is recovered in the interpretation process, i.e., not by enriching and developing a logical form encoded in the sentence, but by an inference process the starting point of which is a proposition obtained by enriching and developing an encoded logical form. To be sure, when an assumption is reached through simply enriching an encoded logical form, it cannot but entail the minimal proposition expressible by the sentence; but it could easily occur that an implicature, i.e., an assumption obtained through a totally different process, turns out to entail this minimal proposition, by accident as it were; this is not a sufficient reason to consider it as part of what is said. I conclude that the Independence Principle must be rejected.[13]

6. THE SCOPE PRINCIPLE

I shall now consider a criterion which, I think, can be used in conjunction with the Availability Principle. I shall refer to this criterion as the Scope Principle. It is based on observations that various people have made on the

behaviour of conversational implicatures in connection with logical operators. These observations tend to provide evidence for a distinction between two types of alleged implicatures: those that do and those that do not fall within the scope of logical operators. Carston devotes a section of her paper to some of these observations, showing that they can be accounted for in terms of the distinction between genuine implicatures and pragmatic aspects of what is said. Yet, when it comes to finding a criterion for deciding between the two alternative pragmatic approaches, she does not consider the Scope Principle, because of her misplaced confidence in the Independence Principle.

Consider the following pair of examples:

(3) The old king has died of a heart attack and a republic has been declared.

(4) A republic has been declared and the old king has died of a heart attack.

In (3), it is implied that the first event described (the death of the old king) occurred before the second one (the declaration of a republic). In (4) the same events are reported in a different order, and the implication is reversed; it is suggested that the death of the old king occurred after—and, perhaps, because of—the declaration of a republic. In both cases, the temporal suggestion is, for Grice, a conversational implicature, stemming from the presumption that the speaker is observing the maxim of manner: "Be perspicuous." In general, a narrative is more perspicuous if the events are reported in the order in which they occurred. The speaker's reporting a series of events in a certain order therefore implies that they occurred in that order, by virtue of the presumption that he is observing the maxim of manner. *Qua* conversatioanl implicature, the temporal suggestion is not part of what is said and makes no contribution to the truth-condition of the utterance. Thus, according to Grice, what is strictly and literally said by means of (3) and (4) is the same thing, even though there is an important difference in (conveyed) meaning between these two utterances. The truth-functionality of "and" can therefore be maintained.

L. J. Cohen (1971) raised a serious objection to that view. He pointed out the following consequence of Grice's analysis: If (3) and (4) really have the same truth-conditions and differ only at the level of conversational impli-catures, then, in Grice's framework, (5) and (6) also should have the same truth-condi-tions:

(5) If the old king has died of a heart attack and a republic has been declared, then Tom will be quite content.

(6) If a republic has been declared and the old king has died of a heart attack, then Tom will be quite content.

But, if (5) and (6) are ascribed the same truth-conditions, how are we to account for the in-tuitive difference in meaning between them? This difference is such that it is possible to as-sert (5) and to deny (6) in the same breath without contradiction. Again, we shall have to use the Gricean apparatus and say that (5) and (6) differ only at the level of conversational implicatures. This consequence is problem-atic, for it is unclear how the suggested Gri-cean analysis can be applied in the case of (5)–(6). While it may seem a good idea to say that (3) and (4) express the same proposition and differ only at the level of conversational im-plicatures, extending this type of analysis to (5) and (6) is hardly a credible move. It seems better to reject Grice's analysis, by admitting that (3) and (4) do not express the same prop-osition. This does not mean that one must fol-low Cohen in considering a semantic account of the temporal suggestion conveyed by ⌜P and Q⌝ as preferable to a pragmatic account. As Carston rightly emphasizes in her paper, Co-hen's counterexample can be handled within the type of pragmatic account she advocates, according to which the temporal suggestion conveyed by ⌜P and Q⌝ is part of what is said even though it is not part of the linguistic meaning of "and." To dispose of Cohen's ob-jection, one need only admit, as Carston does, that (3) and (4) do not express the same prop-osition.

Being counterexamples to the classical Gri-cean account but not to the other type of prag-matic account, examples such as (3)–(6) may be considered as providing a criterion for de-ciding between the two alternative pragmatic approaches, that is, for deciding whether a pragmatically determined aspect of utterance meaning must be considered as a conversa-tional implicature or as an integral part of what is said. This criterion—the Scope Princ-ple, stated below—is based on the behaviour

of an alleged implicature when the utterance which gives rise to it is embedded in a larger utterance and dominated by a logical opera-tor.

It has often been noticed that some prima facie implicatures fall within the scope of log-ical operators, while others do not. For ex-ample, when a seemingly implicature-bearing utterance is negated, sometimes the alleged implicature can be interpreted as (part of) what is negated and sometimes it cannot; when a seemingly implicature-bearing utter-ance is embedded as the antecedent of a con-ditional, sometimes the alleged implicature is an integral part of the antecedent, and some-times it is not. (5) and (6) are evidence that the alleged implicatures conveyed by (3) and (4) belong to the first category. What (5) and (6) say is that Tom will be content if the following conditions obtain: the old king has died, a re-public has been declared, *and there is a certain temporal relation between these two events.* The temporal relation allegedly implicated by (3) and (4) is an integral part of the antecedent of the conditional in (5) and (6); it falls within the scope of the conditional. In the same way, when (3) is negated, the alleged implicature falls within the scope of the negation. The ne-gation of (3) is made true if one of the follow-ing conditions fails to be satisfied: the old king has died, a republic has been declared, *and the first event occurred before the second.* Thus, one can deny (3) and thereby mean, as in (7), that the suggested order of events does not cor-resond to the facts:

(7) It is not the case that the old king has died and a republic has been declared; what is true is that a republic has been declared first and then the old king died of a heart attack.

The fact that some implicatures fall within the scope of logical operators has always been considered as raising a serious problem for pragmatics. From this fact, different theorists have drawn different conclusions. Some theo-rists (e.g., Anscombre & Ducrot 1978) have concluded that these "implicatures" cannot be implicatures in the ordinary sense of the term. Their argument can be reconstructed as fol-lows:

(a) Conversational implicatures are pragmatic con-sequences of an act of saying something.

(b) An act of saying something can be performed only by means of a complete utterance, not by means of an unasserted clause such as the antecedent of a conditional.

(c) Hence, no implicature can be generated at the sub-locutionary level, i.e., at the level of an unasserted clause such as the antecedent of a conditional.

(d) To say that an implicature falls within the scope of a logical operator is to say that it is generated at the sub-locutionary level, viz. at the level of the clause on which the logical operator operates.

(e) Hence, no implicature can fall within the scope of a logical operator.

This argument is, I think, both sound and compelling. It shows that, when an alleged implicature seems to fall within the scope of a logical operator, either it is not really an implicature, or it does not really fall within the scope of the logical operator.[14]

From the fact that some implicatures apparently fall within the scope of logical operators, other theorists (e.g., Cornulier 1984:663–664) have concluded that it is a mistake to think that implicatures cannot fall within the scope of logical operators. As Carston points out in her paper, this position is based on the assumption that all pragmatically determined aspects of meaning are conversational implicatures. If this assumption is made, and one encounters a constituent of meaning that can fall within the scope of logical operators, one has no other choice but to conclude either that this aspect of meaning is not pragmatically determined (a conclusion which Anscombre and Ducrot, contrary to Cornulier, are willing to accept), or that implicatures can fall within the scope of logical operators. If one further assumes that the relevant aspect of meaning is pragmatically determined, one is led to deny the conclusion (e) of the argument above. This is what Cornulier does. But, as we know, the assumption that all pragmatically determined aspects of meaning are implicatures is unwarranted. Conclusion (e) can therefore be maintained, even though one admits that the relevant aspect of meaning (i.e., the alleged implicature) is pragmatically rather than semantically determined.

Once the assumption that all pragmatically determined aspects of meaning are implicatures is abandoned, it turns out that far from raising a problem, operator scope provides us with a criterion for distinguishing between conversational implicatures and pragmatically determined aspects of what is said. According to this criterion, genuine implicatures are external to the proposition expressed, and it is the latter that falls within the scope of logical operators. Thus, if the utterance which gives rise to an implicature is negated or made the antecedent of a conditional, the implicature itself cannot be considered as an integral part of what is negated or of the antecedent of the conditional. If it can—if the alleged implicature turns out to fall within the scope of logical operators such as negation (as in (7)) or conditionals (as in (5) and (6))—then it is not a genuine implicature but a pragmatic constitutent of what is said. Here is a tentative formulation of the criterion:

Scope Principle: A pragmatically determined aspect of meaning is part of what is said (and, therefore, not a conversational implicature) if—and, perhaps, only if—it falls within the scope of logical operators such as negation and conditionals.

This could be tested, and weakened in various ways. I am sure that the matter is not as simple as the Scope Principle suggests, but at least it provides a starting point. Especially encouraging is the fact that the decisions it leads to concerning what is said seem to be consistent with those made by appealing to the Availability Principle. Thus the examples I mentioned earlier—"I've had breakfast," "Everybody went to Paris," "John has three children," and so forth—are all treated in the same way whether one uses the Availability Principle or the Scope Principle.

7. CONCLUSION

Everybody would agree that the saying/implicating distinction is part of the ordinary, everyday picture of linguistic communication. We commonly talk of what is "said" as opposed to what is only "implied" by means of a certain utterance, and it is that distinction which Grice undertook to elaborate (Grice 1975:43–44). Being so closely related to the everyday picture of communication, Grice's theory of conversational implicatures has strong intuitive appeal. But on a certain view of the relation between theory and common sense, the intuitive appeal of Grice's theory does not constitute very strong evidence in its favor, because it can hardly be considered as a requirement of a theory that it match our ordinary intuitions. On this view, henceforth to be called the "anti-prejudice view," there is nothing sacrosanct about our ordinary, folk concepts. If a theoretical account is consistent with our commonsensical intuitions, so much the better; if they conflict, so much the worse for common sense.

Because of this view, when the domain of Grice's theory of implicatures was extended far beyond our intuitive reach, this was hardly noticed, let alone considered to raise a problem. Not many people have observed that Grice's theory departs from our intuitions when it is applied to examples such as "John has three children," which Griceans take to express the proposition that John has at least three children and to implicate that he has no more than three children. However, there is an important difference between this example and e.g., "I've had no breakfast today," which implicates that the speaker is hungry and wishes to be fed. In the latter example, the implicature is intuitively felt to be external to what is said; it corresponds to something that we would ordinarily take to be "implied." In the former case, we are not pre-theoretically able to distinguish between the alleged two components of the meaning of the utterance—the proposition expressed (that John has at least three children) and the implicature (that he has at most three children). We are conscious only of the result of their combination, i.e., of the proposition that John has exactly three children. In this case as opposed to the other one, the theoretical distinction between the proposition expressed and the implicature does not correspond to the intuitive distinction between what is said and what is implied.

This difference between the two types of examples should have prompted the following questions: when, instead of considering intuitive examples of implied meaning, we extend the theory of implicatures to examples such as "John has three children," are we not talking of something else? If really the same thing is involved in both cases, how are we to account for the difference?[15] These were interesting questions to raise, but, because of the anti-prejudice view, they were not raised. According to this view, it is a very good thing—not something to worry about—when a theory's domain of application is extended beyond its intuitive basis. As far as Grice's theory is concerned, the intuitive basis was the everyday distinction between what is said and what is implied. Starting with this distinction, Grice did two things. First, he outlined a mechanism accounting for the generation of implied meaning; second, he tried to show that the same mechanism was at work in examples which we would not ordinarily classify as cases of implied meaning. There seems to be nothing wrong with this. That some examples of implicatures do not fall under the folk concept of implied meaning merely shows that Grice's theory has augmented our knowledge not only of the *mechanism* responsible for the phenomenon he undertook to explore, but also of the *scope* of this phenomenon.

I agree that scientific theorizing is to be freed from, rather than impeded by, intuitions and common sense, which provide only a starting point. In particular, I agree that it was a good thing to go beyond our intuitions and to show, as Grice did, that in many cases the meaning of an utterance results from an unconscious process of "meaning construction" (to use Fauconnier's suggestive phrase), an inferential process whose input is the linguistic meaning of the sentence uttered. In the case of "John has three children," there is no doubt that what this utterance communicates (that John has exactly three children) is not to be identified with the meaning of the sentence, but results from inferentially combining the latter with the presumption that the speaker has given the strongest relevant information available to him. Still, I believe there was something to worry about when the theory of implicatures was extended to examples such as this, which we would not ordinarily consider as cases of implied meaning. This does not mean that I reject the anti-prejudice view. We may at the same time accept this view and recognize that human cognition is a very special field: in this field, our intuitions are not just a first shot at a theory—something like Wittgenstein's ladder, which may be thrown away after it has been climbed up—but also *part of what the theory is about,* and as such they cannot be neglected. In the case at hand, it was a mistake to ignore our intuitions, which tell us that there is a difference between standard cases of implied meaning and the other type of alleged implicatures. This difference pointed to an important theoretical distinction, between genuine implicatures and pragmatic constituents of the proposition expressed.

The theoretical distinction itself was attainable by another route. One only has to realize that sentence meaning largely underdetermines what is said, to be forced to the conclusion that a distinction must be made between genuine implicatures and pragmatic aspects of what is said. Note that, when this route is taken, one knows *that* there is a principled distinction to be made between implicatures and pragmatic aspects of what is said, but one does not know which pragmatic aspect of the meaning of an utterance is to be treated as an implicature, and which as a constituent of what is said. Grice's "tests" for conversational implicature (cancellability, nondetachability, calculability, and so forth) test the presence of a pragmatically determined aspect of utterance meaning, but they do not tell us whether it is a genuine implicature or a constituent of what is said. New criteria have to be devised to make this decision possible.

In this paper, I have taken this route and considered various possible criteria for distinguishing implicatures from pragmatic constituents of what is said. I have considered four criteria in turn: the Minimalist Principle, the Independence Principle, the Availability Principle and the Scope Principle. I have shown that Carston's Independence Principle must be rejected, because it is an instance of a fallacy quite common in pragmatics (the "formal fallacy"). As for the Minimalist Principle, Car-

ston and Sperber and Wilson believe that it must be rejected; I have shown that the matter is not as simple as they seem to think, but I also pointed out that the Minimalist Principle could hardly be used as a working criterion. So we have to find something else. The solution I have suggested is very simple; it consists in going back to our intuitions, and using *them* as a criterion. This is the substance of the Availability Principle, which says that any decision concerning what is said and what is implicated must be consistent with our pre-theoretic intuitions on the matter. (Again, the Availability Principle is not based on a rejection of the anti-prejudice view, but on a specific cognitive hypothesis, according to which what is said is consciously accessible.) Finally, I put forward another criterion, to be used in conjunction with the Availability Principle: the Scope Principle, which says that genuine conversational implicatures cannot fall within the scope of logical operators. I am confident that, using these two criteria, it will in most cases be possible to decide whether a given aspect of meaning is a conversational implicature or a pragmatic constituent of what is said.

ACKNOWLEDGMENTS

I am indebted to Bob French, Mike Harnish, Larry Hirschfeld, Pierre Jacob, Sam Kerstein, and especially Ruth Kempson and Dan Sperber for their comments on an earlier version of this paper.

NOTES

1. The opposition between what is said and the conversational implicatures survives the claim that what is said is conventionally determined by the meaning of the senence. *Qua* assumptions following from the speaker's saying what he says, conversational implicatures are, by definition, external to what is said.

2. It may be argued that there are not only different pragmatic approaches to prima facie ambiguities, but also different semantic approaches. Thus Cohen opposes to the standard "insulationist" semantics an "interactionist" semantics in terms of which, he says, those prima facie ambiguities which Grice handles within the implicature framework can be accounted for in a way that is immune to Modified Occam's Razor (Cohen 1971:56; for a recent statement of the interactionist point of view, see Cohen 1986). I shall not address this issue in this paper; the Gricean picture will be questioned only as far as the pragmatic approach is concerned.

3. Carston's pragmatic account is, roughly, the following. To determine what is said by means of the sentence "They got married and had many children," the hearer must assign a reference to each of the referring expressions, *including the past tense "got married" and "had."* Just as pragmatic principles are employed in ascertaining the referent of "they," so, Carston says, they are used in assigning temporal reference. The hearer goes beyond the strict semantic content of the sentence uttered, and on the basis of contextual assumptions and pragmatic principles recovers from "They got married and had many children" a representation such as "John and Mary got married at t and had many children at $t + n$." "t is some more or less specific time prior

to the time of utterance and $t + n$ is some more or less specific time, later than t. The temporal ordering of the events described in the conjuncts is thus treated as a by-product of the reference assignment process involved in determining 'what is said'" (Carston 1988: [This volume: 37]). This suggested analysis raises some problem when the past tense is replaced by the present perfect, as in example (3) below, because the present perfect can hardly be considered as referring to a specific time. (In familiar terms, the present perfect is used to express general propositions of the type: "There is a time t, prior to the time of utterance, such that blah blah," while it makes sense to say that the past tense is "singular" and refers to a specific time t which must be contextually identified—with more or less precision—for the utterance to express a complete proposition.) I shall not discuss this issue in this paper; I am concerned only with the *type* of analysis Carston puts forward—a pragmatic analysis at the level of what is said. Whether or not the details of her analysis are correct is another matter.

4. In the light of Carston's suggestion concerning "and" we may reconsider Grice's use of Modified Occam's Razor against ordinary langauge philosophers, to whom he ascribed the semantic view, i.e., the notion that "and," "or," etc., are multiply ambiguous in English. The main reason why this view was ascribed to ordinary language philosophers like Strawson is the following: they held that what is said by uttering a sentence such as ⌜P or Q⌝ or ⌜P and Q⌝ varies according to the context of utterance; they considered that the truth conditions of an utterance of one of these sentences were not invariant under contextual change. Thus, ⌜P and Q⌝ is sometimes true if the event described in the second conjunct occurred before (or simultaneously with) that described in the first conjunct, and sometimes not; ⌜P or Q⌝ is sometimes true if ⌜P⌝ and ⌜Q⌝ are both true, and sometimes not. This way of putting the matter is certainly inconsistent with the classical Gricean approach, which assumes that what is said is the same on all readings, the difference being located at the level of implicatures. It was therefore natural to ascribe to ordinary philosophers the semantic approach, on the assumption that there are only two possible approaches, the semantic approach and the approach in terms of conversational implicature. However, this assumption must be abandoned, and the possibility of a pragmatic approach in terms of what is said acknowledged. Once this is done, Modified Occam's Razor no longer provides any reason to reject the claim that sentences such as ⌜P and Q⌝ can be used to say different things in different contexts; for this claim no longer implies that sentences such as ⌜P and Q⌝ are semantically ambiguous, and that "and" has a range of different senses in English. (For a fuller defence of ordinary language philosophers along these lines, see Travis 1985.)

5. For further discussion of this example, see below, section 4.

6. To save the account in terms of strengthening, the notion of *local strengthening* could be introduced. For example, in the case of "Every boy came," we might say that it is the predicate "boy" that is strengthened into "boy in the class," rather than the proposition "Every boy came" into "Every boy in the class came." This seems to work because the predicate "boy in the class" does entail the predicate "boy." In the same way, we might say that the strengthening in "I have not had breakfast" applies not to the global proposition but, within the latter, to the proposition that is negated: "I have had breakfast" is strengthened into "I have had breakfast this morning," and this is negated. However, this solution has its problems, and it does not work in all cases. Thus, in a certain context, the sentence "He put some flowers on the table" can be used to say that he put some plastic flowers on the table. The notion of global strengthening does not apply, because the proposition that he put plastic flowers on the table does not entail the proposition that he put flowers on the table; but the notion of local strengthening does not apply either, because the predicate "plastic flower" does not entail the predicate "flower." (I do not wish to imply that this example is easier to handle within a minimalist framework; it is not.)

7. I believe the Minimalist Principle has a methodological role to play, independent of its ultimate validity as a theoretical principle. In a recent paper (Recanati, 1989) I called attention to a strategy that has dominated semantics to date and impedes the progress of pragmatics: the "Anti-Contextualist Strategy," which consists in minimizing context-sensitivity. Whether true or false, the Minimalist Principle could certainly be used as part of an opposite, "contextualist" strategy, intended to counterbalance the Anti-Contextualist Strategy in an effective way.

Since, for a defender of the Minimalist Principle, what is said departs from what the sentence means only insofar as there is in the meaning of the sentence a slot to be contextually filled, he is led to posit new slots, new dimensions of semantic indeterminancy, every time the following condition obtains: the traditional slots (identity of the speaker, time of utterance, etc.) have been filled, yet it seems that the meaning of the sentence still underdetermines what is said. Thus, a minimalist is led to postulate a hidden reference to a contextually variable domain of dicourse in (1) and (2)—as well as in any quantificational utterance. It follows that there are more slots to be filled for a sentence to express a complete proposition, from the point of view of a minimalist, than there is from the point of view of someone who rejects the Minimalist Principle. Sperber and Wilson suggest that "I've had breakfast" does express a complete proposition once the identity of the speaker and the time of utterance have been fixed, a proposition which is weaker than what the speaker means to say by his utterance. This move—distinguishing the minimal proposition expressed from what the speaker says—is not open to the minimalist; therefore he must deny that the sentence, once the traditional slots have been contextually filled, expresses a complete proposition: more slots need to be filled, according to him. I conclude that the Minimalist Principle is an incentive to maximize context-sensitivity; it leads its defenders to widen the gap between linguistic meaningfulness and full propositionality. From a contextualist point of view, this is a good reason for maintaining the Minimalist Principle as far as possible. *Even if Sperber and Wilson are right and the Minimalist Principle is ultimately to be dispensed with, it still has a methodological role to play within a contextualist strategy.* For example, a contextualist might observe the following maxim: Before supposing, in a particular case, that what is said is different from the minimal proposition expressible, always try to save the Minimalist Principle by exploring the various forms of semantic indeterminacy that may possibly affect the sentence.

What I have just said shows that it is controversial to claim, as Carston does, that the Minimalist Principle is partly responsible for the usual underrating of the gap between sentence meaning and what is said. Carston believes that partisans of the Minimalist Principle "assume that the domain of grammar, sentences, and the domain of truth-conditional semantics, propositions, are essentially the same" (Carston 1988 [This volume: 39]). But this is not at all the case. Quite the contrary, defenders of the Minimalist Principle take the meaning of a sentence to be far less "propositional," much more underdetermined as far as truth-conditions are concerned, than is ordinarily supposed.

8. For simplicity's sake, the fact that the derivation of implicatures presupposes the identification of what is said (and other things as well) has not been represented in the diagram. It could have been represented by distinguishing two sub-levels within "what is communicated," what is said being input at the first sub-level and the implicatures output at the second one. (In fact, the matter is still more complicated than that, but there is no need to spell out the details here.)

9. There is an exception, though. According to Bach and Harnish (1979:29), a correct account of linguistic communication "should accord with how 'said that' is commonly ascribed." This is not very far from the Availability Principle, as Mike Harnish pointed out to me.

10. Bach (1987:chapter 4) points out that the nonliteral use of sentences such as "The door is closed" is their *standard* use; he speaks of "standardized nonliterality." He might therefore try to avoid the objection I have just raised by arguing as follows: The speaker is not conscious of having said something different from what he communicates because the sentence he uses is *standardly* used to communicate something different from the proposition literally expressed. After all, the same phenomenon occurs in cases of "standardized indirection" (Bach and Harnish 1979:192ff): when an indirect speech act is standardly performed by means of a certain type of sentence, the participants in the talk-exchange may not be conscious of the speech act directly performed (e.g., of the question in "Can you pass me the salt?").

Another defence of Bach's account would run as follows. Bach does not speak of "what is said"; he speaks of the proposition expressed by the sentence, as distinct from the proposition communicated. Despite Bach's use of the concept of "nonliterality," this distinction might be equated with Sperber and Wilson's distinction between the minimal proposition expressible by the sentence and the proposition actually expressed (what is said), rather than with the distinction which applies to genuine cases of nonliterality, viz. that between what is said and what is communicated. Thus interpreted, Bach's view would be consistent with the Availability Principle, because it would no longer involve a counter-intuitive identification of what is said. The difference between Bach's position and that of Sperber and Wilson, on that interpretation, would be this: Sperber and Wilson require that the proposition actually expressed entail the minimal proposition expressible, while Bach believes that the minimal proposition literally expressed may be enriched ("expanded," he says) in a way that does not preserve its entailments. Thus, Bach's analysis applies not only to examples such as "I've had breakfast" or "John has three children"—which he calls "nonliteral" because the proposition literally expressed by the sentence (that the speaker has had breakfast at least once, or that John has at least three chldren) is not identical with the proposition communicated (that the speaker has had breakfast this morning, or that John has exactly three children)—but also to examples such as "Everybody came to Paris" or "The door is closed," which Sperber and Wilson could not handle in terms of strengthening. "Everybody from Johnson & Johnson came to Paris" is an "expansion" of "Everybody came to Paris" in Bach's framework, but it is not an "enrichment" of the latter in Sperber and Wilson's framework. (Note that, when Sperber and Wilson first introduced their notion of enrichment, what they had in mind was probably something like Bach's "expansion," rather than the more constrained concept of strengthening.) I would certainly object to Bach's position so interpreted, but I cannot discuss these problems here.

11. There is a difficulty here. Carston considers a series of cases in which an alleged implicature entails the proposition allegedly expressed and therefore can't be a genuine implicature, by virtue of the Independence Principle. However, in many of those cases, the alleged implicature in question is not an implicature at all in the Gricean framework but rather the utterance's overall meaning, which includes what is said together with what is implicated. Thus, for a classical Gricean, "John has three children" expresses the proposition that John has (at least) three children, and in many contexts implicates that he has at most three children. When this implicature is present, the utterance communicates that John has exactly three children. It is this overall communicated meaning that implies what is said, not the implicature. The same problem arises in connection with many other examples. For a Gricean, a conjunctive utterance ⌜P and Q⌝ says that ⌜P⌝ and ⌜Q⌝ are both true and, in many contexts, implicates that the event described in the second conjunct occurred later than the event described in the first conjunct. Does this alleged implicature entail the proposition allegedly expressed, as Carston suggests? It depends on how we formulate the implicature. Carston chooses the following formulation of what is said and implicated by means of ⌜P and Q⌝ (in the classical Gricean framework):

what is said: P & Q

implicature: P & then Q.

Thus formulated, the implicature does entail the proposition expressed. But the implicature need not be formulated that way. We may consider that what is implicated is that, *if* the event P (i.e., the event described in the first conjunct) occurred at a time t and the event Q (i.e., the event described in the second conjunct) occurred at a time t', *then* t' is later than t. In this formulation the implicature does not entail what is said, namely, that these events did occur—or, more explicitly: that there is a past time t and a past time t' such that P occurs at t and Q occurs at t'. In general, it seems that the classical Gricean approach can be saved from Carston's criticism in terms of the Independence Principle simply by changing the way the implicature is formulated. As Dan Sperber pointed out to me, Carston might reply to this objection as follows. We suppose that the proposition that John has exactly three children is being communicated (this much seems to be conceded by the classical Gricean). Now, if it is communicated, either it is an implicature or it is part of what is said. The classical Gricean considers that it is not part of what is said; therefore, if it is communicated, it must be an implicature. In Sperber and Wilson's framework, it is an "implicated conclusion," i.e., something that follows from an "implicated premiss" (viz. the proposition that John has at most three children) together with the proposition expressed (viz. the proposition that John has at least three children). But this alleged implicature (that John has exactly three children) entails the proposition allegedly expressed (that John has at least three children). Therefore, by virtue of the Independence Principle, it is part of what is said. Now, if this proposition is part of what the speaker says, what a classical Gricean would consider as the implicature *stricto sensu,* namely the proposition that John has at most three children, cannot be an implicature either, for then it would be entailed by what is said. (The same argument would apply to the other examples.)

12. Sperber and Wilson could argue that, in their definition, "development" must be understood as referring not to the formal property of incorporating as a sub-part a logical form, but to the process of developing a logical form into a more complex form that has the formal property. But then they should have defined the explicature as an assumption that *results from* a development of an encoded logical form, instead of saying that an assumption communicated by an utterance is an explicature if and only if it *is* a development of a logical form encoded by the utterance. In any case, what Sperber and Wilson *mean* by "explicature" and "implicature" is quite clear, despite the ambiguity of their definition.

13. Of course, Carston might try to reformulate the Independence Principle in purely "functional" terms, with no reference whatsoever to *logical* independence. But it is not obvious that the Independence Principle, reformulated only in terms of the vague notion of functional independence, would still provide a working criterion enabling one to distinguish conversational implicatures from pragmatic aspects of what is said. In any case, when I say that the Independence Principle is to be rejected, I have in mind the criterion Carston actually uses in her paper, not an ideal reformulation of it.

14. This last remark may sound puzzling. What I have in mind is this. Suppose a sentence S and a context C such that, when S is uttered in C, the utterance conversationally implicates that grass is green. (I shall call this "the implicature of S," meaning: the implicature of an utterance of S in C.) Now, suppose that, without changing the context, S is embedded within a larger sentence S', where it is dominated by a logical operator D. For simplicity's sake, let's assume D is negation. Then, it may *seem* that the implicature of S falls within the scope of the negation: this will be so if part of what is communicated by uttering S' is that grass is *not* green. But this appearance may be accounted for without supposing that the implicature of S actually falls within the scope of D. It is logically possible that, just as the utterance of S implicates that grass is green, the utterance of S' (i.e., of the negation of S) *implicates* that grass is not green. In this case, despite appearances, the implicature that grass is green does not fall within the scope of the negation, because what is literally negated by S' is the proposition expressed by S, to the exclusion of the implicature. The latter is not literally negated—and therefore does not fall within the scope of D—but its negation happens to be conversationally implicated by uttering S'. Of course, the generation of this new implicature will have to be accounted for (it will have to be "calculable," as Grice says), and the theoretical possibility I have just mentioned will not be considered seriously unless there is an easy way to do so.

15. My account of the difference between conscious and unconscious implicatures relies on the claim that the latter are not really implicatures, but something else (pragmatic aspects of what is said). However, there are other possible accounts. For example, one can use Grice's notion of "generalized" implicatures, and argue that when an implicature is generalized (i.e., standardized, as Bach and Harnish would say), one is no longer conscious of its being external to what is said. This is a variant of the argument presented in note 10.

REFERENCES

Anscombre, J.-C., and O. Ducrot (1978). "Echelles argumentatives, échelles implicatives et lois de discours." *Semantikos* 2:43–67.

Bach, K. (1987). *Thought and Reference.* Oxford: Clarendon Press.

Bach K., and M. Harnish (1979). *Linguistic Communication and Speech Acts.* Cambridge, Mass.: MIT Press.

Carston, R. (1988). "Implicature, Explicature, and Truth-Theoretic Semantics." In R. Kempson (ed.), *Mental Representations: The Interface Between Language and Reality.* Cambridge: Cambridge University Press, 155–181. [Reprinted in this volume, Chapter 2]

Cohen, L. J. (1971). "Some Remarks on Grice's Views About the Logical Particles of Natural Language." In Y. Bar-Hillel (ed.), *Pragmatics of Natural Language.* Dordrecht: Reidel, 50–68.

Cohen, L. J. (1986). "How Is Conceptual Innovation Possible?" *Erkenntnis* 25: 221–238.

Cornulier, B. de (1984). "Pour l'analyse minimaliste de certaines expressions de quantité." *Journal of Pragmatics.* 8:661–691.

Fauconnier, G. (1985). *Mental Spaces: Aspects of Meaning Construction in Natural Language.* Cambridge, Mass.: MIT Press.

Gardiner, A. (1932). *The Theory of Speech and Language.* Oxford: Clarendon Press.

Grice, H. P. (1975). "Logic and Conversation." In P. Cole and J. L. Morgan (eds.), *Syntax and Semantics.* Vol. 3: *Speech Acts.* New York: Academic Press, 41–58. [Reprinted in this volume, Chapter 19]

Grice, H. P. (1978). "Further Notes on Logic and Conversation." In P. Cole (ed.), *Syntax and Semantics.* Vol. 9: *Pragmatics.* New York: Academic Press, 113–127.

Kaplan, D. (1977). "Demonstratives." Department of Philosophy, University of California, Los Angeles. Mimeo.

Kay, P., and K. Zimmer (1976). "On the Semantics of Compounds and Genitives in English." In R. Underhill (ed.), *Sixth California Linguistics Association Conference Proceedings.* San Diego: Campanile, 29–35.

Recanati, F. (1989). "Referential/Attributive: A Contextualist Proposal." *Philosophical Studies* [56:217–249].

Sperber, D., and D. Wilson (1986). *Relevance: Communication and Cognition.* Oxford: Blackwell.

Travis, C. (1985). "On What Is Strictly Speaking True." *Canadian Journal of Philosophy:* 15:187–229.

Wilson, D., and D. Sperber (1981). "On Grice's Theory of Conversation." In P. Werth (ed.), *Conversation and Discourse.* London: Croom Helm, 155–178.

7

Referential and Attributive[1]

JOHN R. SEARLE

Is there a distinction between referential and attributive uses of definite descriptions? I think most philosophers who approach Donnellan's[2] distinction from the point of view of the theory of speech acts, those who see reference as a type of speech act, would say that there is no such distinction and that the cases he presents can be accounted for as instances of the general distinction between speaker meaning and sentence meaning: both alleged uses are referential in the sense that they are cases of referring to objects, the only difference is in the degree to which the speaker makes his intentions fully explicit in his utterance. Such objections are in fact quite commonly made, both in the literature and in the oral tradition, but I have never seen a version of the objection I was fully satisfied with and the main aim of this article is to attempt to provide one.

1. DONNELLAN'S ACCOUNT OF THE DISTINCTION

He presents the distinction by means of certain examples, which we are supposed to be able to generalize. Suppose we come across the battered body of Smith, murdered by someone unknown to us. We might say, "Smith's murderer is insane," meaning by "Smith's murderer" not any particular person but rather, *whoever it was* that murdered Smith. This is the attributive use. But now suppose in the courtroom scene where Jones is on trial for the murder of Smith, observing his strange behavior we might say, "Smith's murderer is insane," meaning by "Smith's murderer," that man over there in the dock, Jones, who is behaving so strangely. In this case we don't mean *whoever* murdered Smith, we mean a *particular* man, the one we see in front of us. This is the referential use. A crucial feature of the distinction is that in the referential uses it doesn't matter if the definite description we use is actually true of the object we are referring to. Suppose that the man in front of us did not actually murder Smith, suppose no one murdered Smith but that he committed suicide, still in some sense at least, according to Donnellan, our statement would be true if the man we are referring to is insane. In the referential use, since we are just using the expression to pick out some object about which we then go on to say something truly or falsely

John R. Searle, "Referential and Attributive," *Monist* 62 (1979): 190–208. reprinted by permission of the publisher and the author.

it doesn't matter if the expression is true of the object. But in the attributive use, if our definite description is true of nothing, our statement cannot be true. If no one murdered Smith our statement cannot be true. Donnellan then objects to both Russell's and Strawson's theories of definite descriptions on the grounds that they both fail to account for the referential use.

Intiutively there does seem to be a distinction between these cases. What exactly is it? Donnellan nowhere give us a set of necessary and sufficient conditions for identifying each use but he does offer the following as a summary of the distinction as it applies to assertions:[3]

If a speaker S uses a definite description, "the ϕ", referentially there will be some entity e (or, at least, the speaker will intend that there should be) about which the following will be true. . . .
(1) S will have referred to e whether or not e is in fact ϕ.
(2) S will have said something true or false about e whether or not e is in fact ϕ (provided that everything is in order concerning the remainder of the speech act).
(3) S, in using "the ϕ" to refer to e, will have presupposed or implied that e is ϕ.
(4) In reporting S's speech act, it will be correct to say that he stated something about e and in reporting this to use expressions to refer to e other than "the ϕ" or synonyms of it.
Had the definite description been used attributively there would be no such entity e (nor would the speaker have intended that there should be).

Now it turns out that this characterization isn't quite right even on Donnellan's own terms because it is immediately subject to certain sorts of counterexamples, which Donnellan recognizes but does not regard as a serious challenge to his theory. Suppose that Smith died of natural causes but just before his death he was assaulted and it was the evidence of this assault that led us to attribute insanity to "Smith's murderer." Here we might say that our statement was true even though nothing satisfies the definite description "Smith's murderer." That is, in this attributive use we have a case which satisfies our conditions (1)–(4) above for the referential use, and so the distinction seems to be threatened. If we plug in "the murderer" for "the ϕ" and "the assailant" for "e" in the above formulae (1)–(4) this

case satisfies all the conditions for being referential yet it is supposed to be attributive. How can we account for these sorts of examples and still keep the distinction intact? Donnellan's answer is that this sort of a case is a "near miss" and that such cases are still quite different from genuine referential uses: "A near miss occurs with an attributive use when nothing exactly fits the description used, but some individual or other does fit a description in some sense close in meaning to the one used. It is a quite different sort of "near miss," however, that is recognized by seeing that the particular individual the speaker wanted to refer to has been described in a slightly inaccurate way." (1968, p. 290) Only in the referential cases can we "miss by a mile."

Still, the counterexamples remain a bit worrisome because at the very least we should be able to go back and rewrite conditions (1)–(4) so as to exclude these near miss attributive cases from qualifying as referential and it is not at all easy to see how to do that without using question begging formulations such as "close in meaning" or "near miss." However, at this point I am trying to present Donnellan's case in the strongest possible light and not to make objections to it. In discussing the counterexamples he introduces the following metaphor. In the referential use the speaker is aiming at a particular target, and he can be aiming at that target even if he misses it narrowly or misses it by a mile (his statement can be true of the object he is referring to even if the definite description is a near miss or is wildly inaccurate). But in the attributive case he is not aiming at a particular target; he is aiming at "some target or other" (his statement can be true only if he hits the target or scores a near miss). "Once this is seen, taking near misses into account does not blur the distinction. If anything it helps one to see what the distinction is." (1968, p. 210)

Furthermore, Donnellan is anxious to insist that the distinction is not simply a distinction between the number of beliefs that the speaker and hearer have about the object if any which satisfies the definite description. It is not merely a distinction between having a lot of beliefs about Smith's murderer in the referential case and having few in the attributive case, because even in the case where I have a lot of beliefs I can use the definite description attributively. Thus suppose I have a whole lot of beliefs about the man who I suppose won the Indianapolis 500: I believe that his name is Brown, that he is my brother-in-law, etc. Still I might make a bet expressed by the sentence "The man who won the Indianapolis 500 drove a turbine-powered car." And here I am not using the expression referentially even though I have a whole lot of beliefs about the man who I suppose satisfies it. This is proven by the fact that I might win the bet even if my brother-in-law is not the winner of the race and I might lose the bet even if he was driving a turbine-powered car, for I will win the bet if and only if the winner, whoever he is, was driving a turbine-powered car.

These last sorts of examples lead Donnellan to make what I believe is his most ambitious claim, relating to condition 4 above: In the attributive use the speaker is not really *referring* at all. Or to put it in the formal mode, in the attributive use, we in reporting his attributive use of "the ϕ" where e satisfies "the ϕ" cannot say that he referred to e or even that he *referred* to anything at all. To substantiate this claim, consider the following sort of example. Suppose that in 1960 someone had predicted on the basis of a knowledge of Republican politics, "The Republican presidential candidate in 1964 will be a conservative." Now since Goldwater, a conservative, eventually got the 1964 nomination the statement was true and the definite description used attributively was true of Goldwater. In Russell's terms it would be correct to say that the definite description *denotes* Goldwater, nonetheless according to Donnellan the speaker did not *refer to* Goldwater, nor indeed did he refer (in the sense of picking out or identifying some object) to anyone, because he didn't know who was going to be the presidential candidate, and what he meant was *whoever* is the presidential candidate will be a conservative. In the referential use, on the other hand, the speaker *has in mind* some specific object or person, and it is for this reason that we can say in reporting his speech act that he *referred* to that object or person.

There are three features of Donnellan's account that it seems to me any rival account must deal with:

1. There just seems to be an intuitively obvious difference between the referential and the attributive cases. This intuition must be accounted for.

2. Our intuitions are supported by the fact that utterances of sentences containing referential uses apparently have different truth conditions from utterances containing attributive uses. What more proof of ambiguity could one ask for?

3. There is further syntactical support for making the distinction in that the attributive uses seem to admit the insertion of "whoever" or "whatever" clauses, e.g., "Smith's murderer, whoever he is, is insane."

2. AN ALTERNATIVE ACCOUNT

The simplest way for me to discuss the foregoing account is to present an alternative explanation and show why I believe it is superior to Donnellan's account.

How is it possible for speakers to refer to objects at all? Reference is achieved with a variety of syntactical devices, among them proper names, definite descriptions and pronouns, including demonstrative pronouns. And speakers will be able to use these devices to refer to objects in virtue of standing in certain relations to the objects. For example, a speaker might know the proper name of the object, or he might know some facts about the object, or he might be able to see it in his field of vision, or he might be sitting on top of it, etc. Now there are a number of different theories in philosophy about how these various relations in which speakers stand to objects enable them to refer to objects using these various syntactical devices. It is not my aim in this article to continue the arguments between these various theories, so I will try to adopt a terminology which is neutral between them.[4] Since all these theories agree that there must be some linguistic device that the speaker uses to refer to the object we can say that whenever a speaker refers he must have some linguistic representation of the object—a proper name, a definite description, etc.—and this representation will represent the object referred to under some *aspect* or other. An utterance of "Smith's murderer" represents an object under the aspect of being Smith's murderer, "Jones" represents an object under the aspect of being Jones, "that man over there" represents an object under the aspect of being that man over there, etc. I think some of these 'aspects', such as those whose expression involves proper names, are subject to further analysis; but since I am seeking a neutral terminology here and not attempting to defend any specific theory of reference or of proper names, we can ignore this problem for present purposes. We can simply say that all reference is under an aspect, that this is a consequence of the point on which all theories agree, namely that reference always involves a linguistic representation of the object referred to, and for present purposes that will enable us to admit not only such aspects as being Smith's murderer or being that man over there, but even being Jones or being called "Jones." We can also allow that in cases of linguistic ignorance the aspect the speaker intends might not be accurately expressed by the expression he utters; for example he might erroneously suppose that Smith's name was pronounced "Schmidt" and thus when he uttered the expression "Schmidt's murderer" he was actually referring under the aspect "Smith's murderer," since that is the aspect he intended by his linguistic representation even though he did not know the correct way to express that aspect. Such cases have to be distinguished from genuine cases of mistaken identity where there really is a confusion of aspects.

There is a familiar distinction in the philosophy of language between what a sentence or an expression means and what a speaker means when he utters that sentence [or] expression. The interest of the distinction derives not from the relatively trivial fact that the speaker may be ignorant of the meaning of the sentence or expression, but from the fact that even where the speaker has perfect linguistic competence the literal sentence or expression meaning may not coincide with the speaker's utterance meaning. Some of the standard examples of this divergence are metaphor, where the speaker says one thing but means something else, irony where the speaker says one thing but means the opposite of what he says, and indirect speech acts where the speaker says one thing, means what he says, but also means something more. In my account of indirect speech acts[5] I distinguish between the speaker's primary illocutionary

act which is not literally expressed in his utterance and his secondary illocutionary act, which is literally expressed. The primary illocutionary act is performed indirectly by way of performing the secondary illocutionary act. Thus for example I might request a man to get off my foot by saying, "You are standing on my foot." In such cases I literally make a statement to the effect that the man is standing on my foot, but I don't just do that. My illocutionary intentions include the meaning of the sentence I utter but they go beyond it, because I mean not only: you are standing on my foot, but also: please get off my foot. In such cases one performs two speech acts in one utterance, because the primary illocutionary act of requesting the man to get off my foot is performed indirectly by way of performing the secondary illocutionary act of stating that he is on my foot. Now exactly how one performs the primary by way of performing the secondary is fairly complicated, but that such things commonly occur should be obvious even from this one example.

What is going on in Donnellan's so-called referential cases is simply this. Sometimes when one refers to an object one is in possession of a whole lot of aspects under which or in virtue of which one could have referred to that object, but one picks out one aspect under which one refers to the object. Usually the aspect one picks out will be one that the speaker supposes will enable the hearer to pick out the same object. In such cases, as in the indirect speech act cases, one means what one says but one means something more as well. In these cases any aspect will do, provided it enables the hearer to pick out the object. (It may even be something which both the hearer and speaker believe to be false of the object, as in the case presented by Donnellan where speaker and hearer refer to a man as "the King" even though they believe he is a usurper.) Thus, one says "Smith's murderer" but means also: that man over there, Jones, the one accused of the crime, the person now being cross-examined by the district attorney, the one who is behaving so strangely, and so on. In such cases if the aspect one picked out to refer to the object doesn't work one can fall back on some other aspect. *But notice that in every 'referential' use though the expression actually used may be false of the object re-*

ferred to and thus the object does not satisfy the aspect under which it is referred to there must always be some other aspect under which the speaker could have referred to the object and which is satisfied by the object. Furthermore, this aspect is such that if nothing satisfies it the statement cannot be true. For example, consider the referential use of the definite description in "Smith's murderer is insane," said of a man both speaker and hearer are looking at. Now they might agree that the speaker had made a true statement about *that man,* the one they are looking at even though neither he nor anyone else satisfies the definite description "Smith's murderer." So let us suppose that the speaker falls back on the aspect expressed by "the man we are both looking at." "Yes," he says, "when I said 'Smith's murderer' I was referring to the man we were both looking at. That's the man I meant, whether or not he murdered Smith." But now suppose they are not looking at anybody, that the whole experience was a hallucination. Can we still claim that what the speaker said was true? Well, we might, provided that the speaker can fall back on yet another aspect. He might say, "Even though nobody murdered Smith and we weren't looking at anybody, the man I really had in mind is the one accused by the District Attorney of murdering Smith. I was saying of that man that he was insane." But now suppose nobody satisfies the aspect expressed by being "the one accused by the District Attorney of murdering Smith." We might repeat the same procedure and get yet another aspect, but eventually we will reach bedrock. That is, eventually we will reach an aspect such that if no one satisfies it the statement cannot be true and if one person satisfies it the statement will be true or false depending on whether that person is insane. And indeed it seems to me that this point can be generalized to all of Donnellan's examples of 'referential' uses of definite descriptions: provided that the speaker's intentions are clear enough so that we can say that he really knew what he meant, then even though the aspect expressed by the expression he utters may not be satisfied by the object he "had in mind" or may not be satisfied by anything, still there must be some aspect (or collection of aspects) such that if nothing satisfies it (or them) the statement cannot be true and if some one

thing satisfies it the statement will be true or false depending on whether or not the thing that satisfies it has the property ascribed to it. Pursuing the analogy with my account of indirect speech acts, I propose to call this the *primary* aspect under which reference is made and contrast it with the *secondary* aspect. If nothing satisfies the primary aspect the speaker didn't have anything in mind, he only thought he did, and consequently his statement cannot be true. The secondary aspect is any aspect which the speaker expresses in a definite description (or other expression) and which is such that the speaker utters it in an attempt to secure reference to the object which satisfies his primary aspect, but which is not itself intended as part of the truth conditions of the statement he is attempting to make. It follows from these accounts that for every secondary aspect there must be a primary aspect, and this is true of all of Donnellan's examples: every 'referential' use is an utterance of a definite description which expresses a secondary aspect and every 'referential' use has an underlying primary aspect. Thus consider the following example from Donnellan. I might say "That man over there with champagne in his glass is happy." But suppose the man over there only had water in his glass; still what I said might be true of *that man over there* even though the definite description I used to identify him is not true of him. The primary aspect is expressed by "that man over there," the secondary aspect is expressed by "that man over there with champagne in his glass." The secondary aspect does not figure in the truth conditions (except insofar as it includes the primary aspect), the primary aspect does figure in the truth conditions: if nothing satisfies the aspect of being that man over there the statement cannot be true. All of Donnellan's referential cases are simply cases where the speaker uses a definite description that expresses a secondary aspect under which reference is made. But the fact that a definite description can be uttered to express either a secondary or primary aspect no more shows that there is an ambiguity in definite descriptions or that there are two different uses of definite descriptions than the fact that one can utter the sentence "You are standing on my foot" either in a secondary illocutionary act to request someone to get off my foot or in a primary act just to state that he is standing on my foot shows that the sentence is ambiguous or that it has two distinct uses.

Just as in the indirect speech act cases one performs the primary illocutionary act by way of performing the literal secondary illocutionary act so in the referential use of definite descriptions one performs the act of referring to an object as satisfying the primary aspect by way of performing an act of reference expressing a secondary aspect. In both cases one's communication intentions will succeed if one's hearer grasps the primary intention on the basis of hearing the expression which expresses the secondary intention. And in both cases one can succeed in one's primary intent even in certain cases where one's secondary speech act is defective in various ways. I can succeed in requesting you to get off my foot by saying "You're standing on my foot" even though you are not standing on my foot but sitting on it, and I can succeed in referring to the man we are both looking at by saying "Smith's murderer" even though neither he nor anyone else murdered Smith.

The requirement that every referential statement must have a primary aspect is simply the requirement that every such statement must have a specifiable content. If the utterance of "Smith's murderer is insane" is supposed to constitute the making of a true statement even though the person referred to is not Smith's murderer then the content of the statement must be different from the meaning of the sentence. The content of the statement cannot be expressed by "Smith's murderer is insane" for the statement can be true even though there is no "Smith's murderer." What then is the content of the statement? The answer to that question will specify the primary aspect. The specification of the statement being made—as opposed to the specification of the sentence uttered—will have to specify that aspect under which reference is made that actually counts in the truth conditions of the statement. This is an immediate consequence of the requirement that if the statement is true there must be some possible specification of exactly what statement it is that is true. And that there are two distinct reference acts being performed in these cases, a primary and a secondary, is shown by the fact that my hearer upon hearing me say in the so called referential case

"Smith's murderer is insane" can respond to my utterance by saying, "You are right in saying that the man we are both looking at is insane, but you are wrong in thinking he is Smith's murderer." In such a response the hearer accepts the statement I am making under the primary aspect, but rejects the attribution of the secondary aspect (expressed by "Smith's murderer") to the object referred to under the primary aspect (expressed by "the man we are both looking at").

This distinction between primary and secondary aspects also applies to proper names. Suppose I say, "In *Hamlet,* Shakespeare develops the character of Hamlet much more convincingly than he develops the character of Ophelia." Now suppose that Shakespeare didn't write *Hamlet,* suppose that of all the plays attributed to him, it alone was in fact written by someone else. Is my statement false? Not necessarily, for by "Shakespeare" I may simply have meant the author of *Hamlet.* "Shakespeare" may have expressed a secondary aspect, and the primary aspect may have been "author of *Hamlet*" and what I meant was, and hence the statement I made was, "the author of *Hamlet* develops the character of Hamlet more convincingly than he develops the character of Ophelia" and that statement, like Donnellan's examples of referential uses of definite descriptions, can be true even though it was not expressed exactly by the sentence I uttered and the statement made using only the aspect expressed by the sentence I uttered would be false.

What is going on in the so-called attributive uses of definite descriptions is simply this: the expression uttered expresses the primary aspect under which reference is made. Thus the statement made cannot be true if nothing satisfies that aspect and if one object satisfies that aspect the statement will be true or false depending on whether or not the object that satisfies that aspect has the property ascribed to it. In the attributive cases in short, speaker meaning and sentence meaning are the same. And in Donnellan's examples the expression uttered must express a primary aspect for one of two reasons. Either it is the only aspect in possession of the speaker (the 'attributive' example of the Smith's murder case) and consequently it is the only aspect under which the speaker can secure reference, or in those cases where the speaker is in possession of several aspects under which he could secure reference (e.g., the winner of the race case) only one of them figures crucially in the satisfaction conditions of the speech act he is performing, and that is the one he utters. Let us consider each of these cases in turn.

When we find Smith's mutilated body but have no knowledge of the identity of the murderer we have no (or very few) aspects to refer to the person about whom we wish to predicate insanity except "the murderer." Leaving aside the "near miss" cases, there is no plausible way for our utterance meaning to differ from sentence meaning because no other aspect could function as primary aspect. To see this consider a variation on Donnellan's example. Suppose that just prior to stumbling on Smith's body I, but not you, see a man running from the scene. You say, on seeing the body, "Smith's murderer is insane," I say "Yes, he certainly is insane," or even "Yes, Smith's murderer certainly is insane." Now, contrary to Donnellan, I want to argue that both your "Smith's murderer" and my "he" and my "Smith's murderer" are used to refer. Furthermore, they are used to refer under the same aspect. But your expression expresses a primary aspect, and mine may or may not express a primary aspect; I may also have meant "the man I just saw running away" and I may have meant to attribute insanity to him even if it turns out that he is not responsible for the death of Smith. I have two aspects either of which could be primary. You have only one aspect and since all referential statements have a primary aspect it must be the primary aspect of your statement.

In the bet on the outcome of the car race the speaker has a whole series of aspects but only one can be primary because only one is relevant to the satisfaction conditions of the bet. It would be possible to make the same bet using a secondary aspect to refer to the winner, provided that the speaker and hearer knew that the interest in referring to him was only that he was the winner and that the bet was being made under that aspect. Thus if you and I are both looking at the man we suppose won the race I might make the same bet by saying "I bet that guy was driving a turbine-powered car." Here "that guy" expresses a secondary aspect and "the winner of the Indianapolis 500" expresses the primary aspect. The case satisfies Donnellan's test for being referential since the person I really 'had in mind' was the winner of the race, regardless of whether or not he is 'that guy.'

We can now summarize the differences between my account and Donnellan's. On his account there are two distinct uses of definite descriptions only one of which is a use to refer. Definite descriptions thus have an ambiguity, though he allows that it may be a "pragmatic" and not a "semantic" ambiguity.[6] On my account there is no such ambiguity. All of his cases are cases where the definite description is used to refer. The only difference is that in the so-called referential cases the reference is made under a secondary aspect, and in the so-called attributive cases it is made under a primary aspect. Since every statement containing a reference must have a primary aspect, in the 'referential' use the speaker may still have referred to something that satisfies the primary aspect even though the expression uttered, which expresses a secondary aspect, is not true of that object and may not be true of anything. Whether or not the utterance of a sentence to make a statement contains a definite description used as a primary aspect or a secondary aspect depends on the intentions of the speaker; that is, it is a matter of the statement he is making and not just of the sentence he utters.

Well, what about Donnellan's stronger claim that the attributive use does not refer at all? The intuitive basis for this claim is that in such cases as my saying in 1960, "The Republican candidate in 1964 will be a conservative," I cannot have been referring to Goldwater because I had no idea who the Republican candidate would be. There was, to use Donnellan's metaphor, no particular target I was aiming at, hence I was not referring to anybody. I on the other hand want to maintain that I was indeed referring, I was referring to the Republican candidate in 1964. Now since I did not know which of the various possible people was going to be the Republican candidate, I did not know which of them I was referring to. The primary aspect of my reference was expressed by "Republican candidate in 1964" and I had no other aspects under which I could refer. But these facts do not show that my utterance was not referential. To see this imagine that I now say, "Yes, I was right way back there in 1960 when I predicted that the Republican candidate in 1964 would be a conservative, for the Republican candidate in 1964 was indeed a conservative." It seems to me that my earlier utterances of "the Republican candidate in 1964" are no more or no less referential than my later utterances. In both cases I was referring to the person who is in fact Goldwater, though in 1960 I had no way of knowing that. The main obstacle to seeing this point is the fact that, as Donnellan points out, when a person uses an expression of the form "the φ" to refer, even assuming that the φ is identical with e, we cannot always plausibly report his speech act by saying that he referred to e. Even where we know that Goldwater was the Republican presidential candidate in 1964, we can't always report his utterance of a sentence containing "the Republican presidential candidate of 1964" by saying "he referred to Goldwater." Whereas it seems in the so-called referential cases such reports are often justified. If he uttered a sentence containing "Smith's murderer" and we know that the man he had in mind was Jones we can report his speech act in the form, "He referred to Jones" and we can do this not only in cases where Smith's murderer is identical with Jones but even in cases where Jones is not Smith's murderer.

I believe that these facts have a fairly simple explanation in terms of the analysis offered earlier together with the fact that sentences of the form "S referred to x" and those of the form "S said that x is P" are intensional contexts. Substitution of expressions normally used to refer to the same object is not generally a valid form of inference for intensional contexts. The reason we are inclined to think there is a difference between the so-called attributive and referential cases is that in the referential cases we know that the speaker has several aspects in hand under which he could have referred to the referent and we are more willing to report his speech act under one of the other aspects than we are in the 'attributive' cases. If he says "Smith's murderer is insane" and we know that he knows or believes that Smith's murderer is Jones then we are more willing to report his speech act in the form, "He said that Jones was insane," than if he didn't know who Smith's murderer was when he made his statement. Indeed if we

know the primary aspect under which the reference was made it will in general be correct to report his statement under that aspect (regardless of the expression he actually used and regardless of whether the expression he actually used is true of the object that satisfies his primary aspect) since that reports the referential content of the statement he was making. In fact reports of both of the so-called referential and attributive occurrences have both intensional and extensional readings. Thus if Jones is the murderer and his friends hear that the Sheriff has said 'attributively' "Smith's murderer is insane" they might well report this to Jones as "the Sheriff says that you are insane." Similarly there are substitutions of aspects in the so-called referential cases which would be unwarranted. Thus suppose someone in 1910 says to Goldwater's mother abour the then infant Goldwater, "Mrs. Goldwater, your youngest son wants more milk." Now it is easy to imagine that this could be a 'referential' use. It might turn out that baby Goldwater was not the youngest son and still the speaker knew who he was talking about. All the same it would sound distinctly odd to say that the speaker was referring to the Republican presidential candidate of 1964 or to report his speech act by saying that he said the Republican presidential candidate of 1964 wanted more milk. But all of these facts have to do with quite familiar features of intensional contexts, deriving from the fact that when we report someone's reference we are often in varying degrees committed to reporting the aspects under which the reference was made. They do not show that in the so-called attributive cases the speaker is not referring. What they do show is that since all reference is under some aspect or other it may be misleading or even downright false to report a reference to an object under an aspect that the speaker did not in fact use and could not have used because he had no way of knowing that the object satisfying the aspects under which he did refer also satisfied the other aspect.

3. SOME RESIDUAL PROBLEMS

1. Whoever *and* Whatever.

What about the "whoever" test? Doesn't the fact that the attributive uses naturally take "whoever," "whichever" and "whatever" clauses show that there is something to the distinction beyond the distinction between primary and secondary aspects? I think not. To begin with cases that are clearly 'referential' (i.e., made under secondary aspects) can also take these clauses as in, e.g., "That man over there in the funny hat, whoever he is, is trying to break into our car!" Now the case is clearly 'referential' for it might not be a man in a funny hat but for example a woman with a strange hairdo. The applicability of these interrogative pronouns, like the notion of knowing who (or what) someone (or something) is, will always be relative to some set of interests in the context of the utterance. For example, relative to one set of interests I know who Heidegger is, relative to another set I do not. If you ask me, "Who is Klaus Heidegger?", I can say for example, "He is the Austrian słalom specialist who finished second to Stenmark in the 1977 World Cup competition"; but relative to some other sets of interests I haven't the faintest idea who he is. I couldn't pick him out of a police lineup or tell you any of the salient facts of his life, for example. And indeed when Heidegger suddenly burst on the scene in 1977 it would have been quite appropriate to say, e.g., "This guy Heidegger, whoever he is, has won yet another race." In this case as in the earlier cases, the use of "whoever" ("whatever," "whichever") indicates ignorance of, doubts about, or suspension of other aspects than the one which is expressed in the sentence. Such uses can occur more commonly with primary aspects, both because we often don't know any other aspects (as in e.g., the 'attributive', i.e., primary, use of "Smith's murderer") or when we do know of other aspects we can make it clear that they are suspended for the purpose of the utterance, they are not part of its content (as in e.g., "I bet the winner of the race, whoever he was, used a turbine-powered car").

2. The Attributive Near Misses.

We are now in a position to see what is going on in the near miss cases discussed by Donnellan. It is very unrealistic to talk, as I have been talking, as if our beliefs about the world and the aspects under which we refer to objects came in neat little packages which we could label primary or secondary aspect. In fact our beliefs come in whole messy networks, and in any situation in which we are likely to be able on the basis of observation to use an expression such as "Smith's murderer" to refer, we are also likely to have a whole lot of other aspects. Thus "Smith's assailant," "the person who left this weapon at the scene of the crime," "the person responsible for these footprints at the scene of the crime" and so on—would be possible candidates for expressing other aspects under which reference could have been made, since it is unlikely that we could have any observational evidence that there was any one to be referred to as "Smith's murderer" unless we had the sort of evidence that would enable us to refer under some of these other aspects. Even in the 'attributive' cases, we are likely to have a collection of aspects under which reference could be made, and should any one of them fail us we can fall back on the others, just as we do in the 'referential' cases; for what we really had in mind was, e.g., "the person responsible for what we observed." There is therefore no sharp dividing line between referring under a primary or a secondary aspect. As long as all goes well the question would not normally arise. Only if there is some breakdown, if for example it turns out that Smith wasn't really murdered but only assaulted, would we be forced to specify exactly what we meant, what our primary aspect was.

3. Speaker Reference and Semantic Reference.

Kripke[7] approaches Donnellan's distinction with an apparatus somewhat like mine, but it seems to me his account gets bogged down, and it may be instructive to say exactly how. He says that the distinction is between *speaker reference* and *semantic reference*. In the attributive case speaker reference and semantic reference coincide because the speaker's intention is just to refer to the semantic reference and in the referential case the speaker's reference and the semantic reference may coincide if, as the speaker believes, they both determine the same object, but they need not; if the speaker is mistaken, the semantic reference may be different from the speaker's reference (p. 264). Kripke's account couldn't be quite right as it stands, because in the 'referential' use the speaker need not even believe that the object referred to satisfies the description he uses, as Donnellan's example of referring to a usurper as "The King" illustrates. However, the distinction between speaker reference and semantic reference looks like the familiar distinction I use between speaker meaning and sentence meaning, though Kripke adopts an odd way of putting it, since reference, unlike meaning, is a speech act. In the sense in which speakers refer, expressions do not refer any more than they make promises or give orders. Still, one could explain away this difficulty very easily if one analyzed "semantic reference" in terms of aspects determined by literal meaning. Kripke starts off as if he is going to do that (p. 263) but he then goes on to try to analyze both speaker's reference and semantic reference in terms of different kinds of intentions: "In a given idiolect the semantic reference of a designator (without indexicals) is given by a *general* intention of the speaker to refer to a certain object whenever the designator is used. The speaker's referent is given by a *specific* intention, on a given occasion, to refer to a certain object." (p. 264, his italics) This is where the account bogs down. In the sense in which I really do have both general and specific intentions (e.g., I have a specific intention to drive to Berkeley tomorrow, and a general intention to drive on the right hand side of the road, *ceteris paribus,* whenever I drive in the United States) I have no such general intentions about definite descriptions. If my use of definite descriptions required such general intentions I would have to form an infinite number of them since there are an infinite number of definite descriptions I am able to use and understand in my language. Consider the definite description (without indexicals), "The man eating a ham sandwich on the top of the Empire State Building at 10 a.m., June 17, 1953." Kripke tells us that in my idiolect the semantic referent of this designator is given by my general intention to refer to a certain object whenever the designator is used. I can only say that I never formed and do not have any such general intention, and I venture to guess that you haven't either. I know what the expression means, and in so knowing I know under what conditions it would be correct to use this expression with a specific inten-

tion to perform the speech act of reference with it. That is, I know what conditions an object would have to satisfy in order that I could refer to that object as satisfying the aspects expressed in the definite descriptions. But in addition to knowing the meaning and having specific intentions on specific occasions I don't have any general intentions of the sort Kripke describes. And even supposing I did form a general intention for this case, it would be no help because there would still be literally an infinity of other cases for which I have no such general intentions. Suppose I decided to use this expression only to refer to Jones. Then in my idiolect I would indeed have a general intention which I could express by saying: "I have a general intention to refer to Jones whenever I use the expression 'the man eating a ham sandwich on top of the Empire State Building at 10 a.m. on June 17, 1953'" but that still leaves me with an infinite number of other definite descriptions for which I do not have any such general intentions. Furthermore, I don't need any such general intentions to account for my use of definite descriptions. I know the meanings of the elements of the language and the rules of their combination into larger expressions. This knowledge enables me to figure out what aspects are expressed by any new definite description I hear or form, and this knowledge I then use when I utter specific definite descriptions with specific intentions to refer to specific objects on specific occasions. What additional jobs are general intentions supposed to do? Perhaps because Kripke tries to account for Donnellan's alleged distinction in terms of what I believe is a mistaken theory of "general intentions," he fails to see that the real distinction is between primary and secondary aspects under which reference is made.

4. *DE RE* AND *DE DICTO*

Many philosophers believe the referential-attributive distinction is somehow closely related to, perhaps even identical with the *de re– de dicto* distinction. I think both distinctions are for the most part bogus. But it is instructive to see why people have believed there were such distinctions (i.e., to see what real distinctions give rise to the beliefs in these distinctions) and to see why they thought the two alleged distinctions were related or the same. I hope I have made my doubts about referential and attributive clear. My discussion of the *de dicto–de re* distinction will be much briefer; I will not try to state the whole argument, and my remarks will apply only to the distinction as it is supposed to apply to intentional states, such as belief and desire, and to speech acts and to those only as they contain references to particulars. I will, in short, not be concerned with the *de re–de dicto* distinction as it applies to modal contexts or concerns references to abstract entities, such as numbers.

I believe that the theory that there is a distinction between *de re* and *de dicto* beliefs (for example) arises from a confusion between features of reports of beliefs and features of the beliefs being reported. If I know that Ralph believes that the man he saw in the brown hat is a spy and I know that the man in the brown hat is B. J. Ortcutt I might report his belief by saying either, "About Ortcutt, Ralph believes he is a spy" or "Ralph believes that the man he saw in the brown hat is a spy."[8] The first of these reports commits me, the reporter, to the existence of an object satisfying the referential content of Ralph's belief, the second does not; and we might call these *de re reports* and *de dicto reports* respectively. But it simply does not follow from the fact that there are two different ways of *reporting* a belief that there are two different *kinds* of belief being reported. Ralph's belief is the same in the two cases. The difference is only how much I, the reporter, care to commit myself about how much of the truth conditions of his belief are in fact satisfied. The *de re–de dicto* distinction is, in short, a distinction between ways of reporting beliefs, not between different kinds of beliefs.

The simplest way to see this is to see that the distinction which I, the reporter, can make in reporting Ralph's beliefs is not one he can make when he has or gives expression to his beliefs. Suppose he says either, "About the man I saw in the brown hat, I believe he is a spy" or "I believe the man I saw in the brown hat is a spy." From his point of view there is no way he can distinguish between them. Though in the surface syntax "the man in the brown hat" lies outside the scope of "believe" in one case and not in the other, in fact the

whole of both sentences gives expression to the same content of Ralph's belief. This is even more obvious in the case of statements. Consider the statements made by Ralph in utterances of

"The man I saw in the brown hat is a spy."

and

"About the man I saw in the brown hat, he is a spy."

The truth conditions are exactly the same in each case. The reason the reporter can make a distinction that Ralph cannot make is that the reporter can decide how much of Ralph's belief he is going merely to report and how much he is going to commit himself to. In a *de dicto* report he reports the entire content of the belief and does not commit himself to the existence of an object the belief is ostensibly about. In the *de re* report, of the sort we gave above, he reports only a fragment of the belief, expressed by "is a spy," and commits himself to the existence of an object that the belief was ostensibly about, though not necessarily under the same aspect as Ralph. But Ralph is committed to the whole thing under his own aspects; that is what makes it his belief or his statement.

A great deal of effort has been wasted on the question: when does a report of a speech act or mental state entail the existence of an object that the state or act is about, when is 'exportation' a valid form of inference? The answer is: If we are just reporting the content of the belief or act, what the man believes or says, it is never valid. How could it be? From the fact that a man has a certain belief or made a certain statement nothing follows about how much of the truth conditions of his belief or statement are satisfied. One might as well ask, "When does the report of a man's belief entail that the belief is true?" In both cases one can only answer: reporting that a man has a belief with a certain content is one thing, reporting how much of it is true is something else. Reports of the first kind never entail reports of the second kind.

In addition the the distinction between *de dicto* and *de re* reports, there is furthermore a genuine distinction between general beliefs and specific beliefs as exemplified by the beliefs Ralph would express if he said respectively, "There are spies (spies exist)" and "The man in the brown hat is a spy." But this is a separate distinction independent of the distinction between *de dicto* and *de re* reports of specific beliefs.

We can now see the relations between the *de re–de dicto* distinction and the referential-attributive distinction: as standardly described in the literature, neither distinction exists. There are however some other distinctions that do exist and give rise to the illusory belief in these two distinctions; there is a distinction between reference under primary and secondary aspects and a distinction between reports of beliefs and of speech acts that commit the reporter to the existence of an object referred to and those that do not. The connection between primary and secondary reference and *de dicto* and *de re* reports is that we are more likely to make *de re* reports of secondary aspect references and more likely to make *de dicto* reports of primary aspect references. Why? Because in the report of a secondary aspect reference we know that the actual aspect expressed in the speaker's utterance was not crucial to the statement he was making and we know that he had other aspects under which he could have made the reference. In the report of a statement where reference is made explicitly under the primary aspect the report will leave out something crucial to the content of the statement if we do not report the primary aspect.

However, as we saw above in our discussion of Donnellan's condition 4, these are only tendencies and there can also be *de re* reports of primary aspect references and there can be *de dicto* reports of secondary aspect references (in the old jargon, this would amount to saying that attributive beliefs can be *de re* and referential beliefs can be *de dicto,* though I hasten to repeat that this way of expressing it is one I reject). Thus if I know the sheriff said 'attributively', "Smith's murderer is insane" and I know Jones is Smith's murderer I might indeed tell Jones, "Jones, the sheriff believes you are insane," or even report, "About Jones, the sheriff believes he is insane." Furthermore even where I know that Jones is not Smith's murderer and I know that Ralph said referentially "Smith's murderer is insane," and I know he had Jones in mind, I can still report his speech act by saying, "Ralph said that Smith's murderer is insane," for he did indeed

say just that. Both reports, though true, are misleading, for a hearer might reasonably take me to imply by the first that the sheriff said of Jones *under the aspect 'Jones'* that he was insane, and he didn't say that, he only said it of him under the aspect "Smith's murderer"; and the second might be taken to imply that the man Ralph had in mind was in fact Smith's murderer, when it wasn't. It was Jones.

Notice incidentally that if the sheriff says, in giving examples of tautologies, "Smith's murderer is Smith's murderer" and "the smallest spy is a spy," even if we know that Jones is Smith's murderer and Boris is the smallest spy we can't say to Jones, "The sheriff says you are the murderer" and to Boris, "The sheriff says you are a spy." Why not? Because in order that the sheriff be saying something about some object he referred to, it must be the case that what he says differs from the aspect under which he makes the reference; otherwise, there is no content to what is said other than that content which makes it about that which it is said.

5. RUSSELL AND STRAWSON

This whole dispute about referential and attributive grew out of the controversy between Russell and Strawson on the analysis of definite descriptions. Donnellan claims that both neglect the referential use and that in consequence there are serious weaknesses in both of their accounts. If I am right in my analysis, their accounts and the dispute between them remains untouched by Donnellan's arguments. Their accounts are properly construed as about cases in which there is no secondary aspect, where what the speaker means coincides with what he says. The fact that there are cases where the speaker means more than what he says, cases where the sentence he utters expresses a secondary aspect under which reference is made but does not express the primary aspect which counts in the truth conditions of the statement, is really quite irrelevant to the dispute between Russell and Strawson, since in such cases there will be some (actual or possible) sentence which expresses the statement that the speaker is making and that sentence will be subject to either the Russellian or the Strawsonian analysis.

NOTES

1. I am indebted to Alan Code for comments on an earlier draft of this paper.

2. Donnellan, Keith, "Reference and Definite Description," *The Philosophical Review,* 1966, p. 281–304 [Reprinted in this volume, Chapter 3], and "Putting Humpty Dumpty Back Together Again," *The Philosophical Review,* 1968, pp. 203–15.

3. 1968, cited in note 2, above, p. 206. Donnellan confines his discussion mostly to statements (as I will in this article) but the theory is intended to apply *mutatis mutandis* to other sorts of speech acts as well.

4. Perhaps in the end it will prove impossible to get a completely neutral terminology, one that is neutral between the various theories of reference. But as Donnellan does not present the referential-attributive distinction as dependent on the rest of his theory of reference, the fact that the terminology I shall employ in discussing his distinction may not sit comfortably with the rest of his theory of reference should not prevent us from making a fair examination of the distinction as he presents it. My aim in this article is to examine the referential-attributive distinction and not his whole theory of reference.

5. Searle, J. R., "Indirect Speech Acts," in Morgan and Cole (eds.), *Syntax and Semantics,* vol. 3, *Speech Acts,* 1975, Academic Press, pp. 59–82. [Reprinted in this volume, Chapter 16]

6. It is not at all clear, by the way, what a "pragmatic ambiguity" is supposed to be. "I went to the bank" is semantically ambiguous. "Flying planes can be dangerous" is syntactically ambiguous. But what is a pragmatic ambiguity? Is "You are standing on my foot" supposed to be pragmatically ambiguous because in some contexts its utterance can be more than just a statement of fact? If so, then every sentence is indefinitely "pragmatically ambiguous." If we had a notion of "pragmatic ambiguity" we would also have to have a notion of "pragmatic univocality" but in fact neither notion has any clear sense at all.

7. Kripke, S., "Speaker's Reference and Semantic Reference" in *Midwest Studies in Philosophy,* vol. II, 1977, pp. 255–76. [Reprinted in this volume, Chapter 5]

8. The example is of course Quine's in "Quantifiers and Propositional Attitudes" in Davidson and Harman (eds.), *The Logic of Grammar,* Belmont, Calif.: Dickenson, 1975, pp. 153–59.

FURTHER READING

Bertolet, R. (1986). "Donnellan's Distinction." *Australian Journal of Philosophy* 64:477–487.

Chastain, C. (1975). "Reference and Context." In K. Gunderson (ed.), *Language, Mind and Knowledge: Minnesota Studies in Philosophy VII*. Minneapolis: University of Minnesota Press, 194–269.

Clark, H. H., and C. R. Marshall (1981). "Definite Reference and Mutual Knowledge." In A. K. Joshi et al. (eds.), *Elements of Discourse Understanding*. Cambridge: Cambridge University Press, 10–63.

Devitt, M. (1981). "Donnellan's Distinction." *Midwest Studies in Philosophy* 6:511–524.

Donnellan, K. S. (1978). "Speaker Reference, Descriptions and Anaphora." In P. Cole (ed.), *Syntax and Semantics*. Vol. 9: *Pragmatics*. New York: Academic Press, 47–68.

Grandy, R., and R. Warner (eds.). (1986). *Philosophical Grounds of Rationality: Intentions, Grounds, and Ends*. Oxford: Oxford University Press.

Grice, H. P. (1969). "Utterer's Meaning and Intentions." *Philosophical Review* 78:147–177.

Grice, H. P. (1982). "Meaning Revisited." In N. V. Smith (ed.)., *Mutual Knowledge*. London: Academic Press, 223–243.

Recanati, F. (1986). "On Defining Communicative Intentions." *Mind and Language* 1:213–242.

Sainsbury, M. (1984). "Saying and Conveying." *Linguisitics and Philosophy* 7:415–432.

Shiffer, S. (1972). *Meaning*. Oxford: Clarendon Press.

Stine, G. C. (1978). "Meaning Other than What We Say and Referring." *Philosophical Studies* 33:319–337.

Travis, C. (1985). "On What Is Strictly Speaking True." *Canadian Journal of Philosophy* 15:187–229.

Ziff, P. (1967). "On H. P. Grice's Account of Meaning." *Analysis* 28:1–8.

III

Indexicals

8

On the Logic of Demonstratives

DAVID KAPLAN

In this paper I propose to outline briefly a few results of my investigations into the theory of demonstratives: words and phrases whose *intension* is determined by the contexts of their use.[1] Familiar examples of demonstratives are the nouns 'I,' 'you,' 'here,' 'now,' 'that,' and the adjectives 'actual' and 'present.' It is, of course, clear that the *extension* of 'I' is determined by the context—if you and I both say 'I' we refer to different persons. But I would now claim that the intension is also so determined. The intension of an 'eternal' term (like 'The Queen of England in 1973') has generally been taken to be represented by a function which assigns to each possible world the Queen of England in 1973 of that world. Such functions would have been called *individual concepts* by Carnap.[2] It has been thought by some—myself among others—that by analogy, the intension of 'I' could be represented by a function from speakers to individuals (in fact, the identity function). And similarly, that the intensions of 'here' and 'now' would be represented by (identity) functions on places and times. The role of contextual factors in determining the extension (with respect to such factors) of a demonstrative was thought

of as analogous to that of a possible world in determining the extension of 'The Queen of England in 1973' (with respect to that possible world). Thus an enlarged view of an intension was derived. The intension of an expression was to be represented by a function from certain factors to the extension of the expression (with respect to those factors). Originally such factors were simply possible worlds, but as it was noticed that the so-called tense operators exhibited a structure highly analogous to that of the modal operators, the factors with respect to which an extension was to be determined were enlarged to include moments of time. When it was noticed that contextual factors were required to determine the extension of sentences containing demonstratives, a still more general notion was developed and called an "index." The extension of an expression was to be determined with respect to an index. The intension of an expression was that function which assigned to every index, the extension at that index. Here is a typical passage.

The above example supplies us with a statement whose truth value is not constant but varies as a function of $i \in I$. This situation is easily appreciated in the context of time-dependent statements; that is, in the case where *I* represents the instants of time. Obviously the same statement can be true at one moment and false at another. For more general situations one must not think of the *i ε I* as anything as simple as instants of time or even possible worlds. In general we will have

$$i = (w, t, p, a, \ldots)$$

where the index *i* has many *coordinates:* for example, *w* is a *world, t* is a *time, p = (x, y, z)* is a (3-dimensional) *position* in the world, *a* is an *agent,* etc. All these coordinates can be varied, possibly independently, and thus affect the truth values of statements which have indirect reference to these coordinates. (From the Advice of a prominent logician.)

A sentence Φ was taken to be logically true if true at every index (in every 'structure'), and □Φ was taken to be true at a given index (in a given structure) just in case Φ was true at every index (in that structure).[3] Thus the familiar principle of modal generalization: if ⊨Φ, then ⊨ □Φ, is validated.

This view, in its treatment of demonstratives, now seems to me to have been technically wrong (though perhaps correctable by minor modification) and, more important, conceptually misguided.

Consider the sentence

(1) I am here now.

It is obvious that for many choices of index—i.e., for many quadruples (w, x, p, t) where w is a possible world, x is a person, p is a place, and t is a time—(1) will be false. In fact, (1) is true only with respect to those indices (w, x, p, t) which are such that in the world w, x is located at p at the time t. Thus (1) fares about on a par with

(2) David Kaplan is in Los Angeles on April 21, 1973.

(2) is contingent, and so is (1).

But here we have missed something essential to our understanding of demonstratives. Intuitively, (1) is deeply, and in some sense universally, true. One need only understand the meaning of (1) to know that it cannot be uttered falsely. No such guarantees apply to (2). A *Logic of Demonstratives* that does not reflect this intuitive difference between (1) and (2) has bypassed something essential to the logic of demonstratives.

Here is a proposed correction. Let the class of indices be narrowed to include only the *proper* ones—namely, those (w, x, p, t) such that in the world w, x *is* located at p at the time t. Such a move may have been intended originally since improper indices are like impossible worlds; no such contexts *could* exist and thus there is no interest in evaluating the extensions of expressions with respect to them. Our reform has the consequence that (1) comes out, correctly, to be logically true. Now consider

(3) □I am here now.

Since the contained sentence (namely (1)) is true at every proper index, (3) also is true at every proper index and thus also is logically true. (As would be expected by the aforementioned principle of modal generalization.)

But (3) should not be *logically* true, since it is false. It is certainly *not* necessary that I be here now. But for several contingencies, I would be working in my garden now, or even writing this in a location outside Los Angeles.

Perhaps enough has now been said to indicate that there are difficulties in attempting to assimilate the role of a *context* in a logic of demonstratives to that of a *possible world* in the familiar modal logics or a *moment of time* in the familiar tense logics.

I believe that the source of the difficulty lies in a conceptual confusion between two kinds of meaning. Ramifying Frege's distinction between sense and denotation, I would add two varieties of sense: content and character. The content of an expression is always taken *with respect to* a given context of use. Thus when I say

(4) I was insulted yesterday,

a specific content—*what I said*—is expressed. Your utterance of the same sentence, or mine on another day, would not express the same content. It is important to note that not just the truth value may change; what is said is itself different. Speaking today, my utterance of (4) will have a content roughly equivalent to that which

(5) David Kaplan is insulted on April 20, 1973

would have when spoken by you or anyone at anytime. Since (5) contains no demonstratives, its content is the same with respect to all contexts. This content is what Carnap called an 'intension' and what, I believe, has been often referred to as a 'proposition.' So my theory is that different contexts for (4) produce not just different truth values, but also different propositions.

Turning now to character, I call that component of the sense of an expression which determines how the content is determined by the context, the 'character' of an expression. Just as contents (or intensions) can be represented by functions from possible worlds to extensions, so characters can be represented by functions from contexts to contents. The character of 'I' would then be represented by *the function (or rule, if you prefer) that assigns to each context that content which is represented by the constant function from possible worlds to the agent of the context.* The latter function has been called an 'individual concept.' Note that the character of 'I' is represented by a function from contexts to individual *concepts,* not from contexts to individuals. It was the idea that a function from contexts to individuals could represent the intension of 'I' which led to the difficulties discussed earlier.

Now what is it that a competent speaker of English knows about the word 'I'? Is it the content with respect to some particular occasion of use? No. It is the character of 'I': the rule italicized above. Competent speakers recognize that the proper use of 'I' is—loosely speaking—to refer to the speaker. Thus that component of sense which I call 'character' is best identified with what might naturally be called 'meaning.'

To return, for a moment, to (1). The character (meaning) of (1) determines each of the following:

(a) In different contexts, an utterance of (1) expresses different contents (propositions).

(b) In most (if not all) contexts, an utterance of (1) expresses a contingent proposition.

(c) In all contexts, an utterance of (1) expresses a true proposition (i.e., a proposition which is true at the world of the context).

On the basis of (c), we might claim that (1) is analytic (i.e., it is true solely by virtue of its meaning). Although as we see from (b), (1) rarely or never expresses a necessary proposi-

tion. This separation of analyticity and necessity is made possible—even, I hope, plausible—by distinguishing the kinds of entities of which 'is analytic' and 'is necessary' are properly predicated: characters (meanings) are analytic, contents (propositions) are necessary.

The distinction between character and content was unlikely to be noticed before demonstratives came under consideration, because demonstrative-free expressions have a constant character, i.e., they express the same content in every context. Thus character becomes an uninteresting complication in the theory.

Although I have spoken above of contexts of utterance, my primary theoretical notion of *content with respect to a context* does not require that the agent of the context utter the expression in question. I believe that there are good reasons for taking this more general notion as fundamental.

I believe that my distinction between character and content can be used to throw light on Kripke's distinction between the a-priori and the necessary.[4] Although my distinction lies more purely within logic and semantics, and Kripke's distinction is of a more general epistemic metaphysical character, both seem to me to be of the same *structure.* (I leave this remark in a rather cryptic state.)

The distinction between content and character and the related analysis of demonstratives have certainly been foreshadowed in the literature (though they are original-with-me in the sense that I did not consciously extract them from prior sources). But to my knowledge they have not previously been cultivated to meet the standards for logical and semantical theories which currently prevail. In particular, Strawson's distinction between the significance (meaningfulness) of a sentence and the statement (proposition) expressed in a given use is clearly related.[5] Strawson recognizes that such sentences as "The *present* King of France is *now* bald" may express different propositions in different utterances, and he identifies the meaningfulness of the sentence with its potential for expressing a true or false proposition in some possible utterance. Although he does not explicitly discuss *the* meaning of the sentence, it is clear that he would not identify such a meaning with any of the propositions expressed by particular utterances. Unfortunately Strawson seems to regard the fact that sentences containing demonstratives can be used to express different propositions as immunizing such sentences against treatment by 'the logician.'

To convince myself that it is possible to conduct a consistent analysis of the semantics of demonstratives along the above lines, I have attempted to carry through the program for a version of first-order predicate logic. The result is the following Logic of Demonstratives. If my views are correct, the introduction of demonstratives into intensional logics will require more extensive reformulations than was thought to be necessary.

THE LOGIC OF DEMONSTRATIVES

The *Language* LD is based on first-order predicate logic with identity and descriptions. We deviate slightly from standard formulations in using two sorts of variables, one sort for positions and a second sort for individuals other than positions (hereafter called simply 'individuals').

Primitive Symbols for Two Sorted Predicate Logic

0. Punctuation: (,)

1. (i) An infinite set of individual variables: v_i,
   (ii) An infinite set of position variables: v_p,

2. (i) An infinite number of m-n-place predicates, for all natural numbers m, n.
   (ii) The 1-0-place predicate: Exist
   (iii) The 1-1-place predicate: Located

3. (i) An infinite number of m-n-place i-functors (functors that form terms denoting individuals)
   (ii) An infinite number of m-n-place p-functors (functors that form terms denoting positions)

4. Sentential Connectives: $\wedge$, $\vee$, $\neg$, $\rightarrow$, $\leftrightarrow$

5. Quantifiers: $\forall$, $\exists$

6. Definite Description Operator: the

7. Identity: =

Primitive Symbols for Modal and Tense Logic

8. Modal Operators: $\square$, $\diamond$

9. Tense Operators: F (it will be the case that)
   P (it has been the case that)
   G (one day ago, it was the case that)

Primitive Symbols for the Logic of Demonstratives

10. Three one place sentential operators:
    N (it is now the case that)
    A (it is actually the case that)
    Y (yesterday, it was the case that)

11. A one-place functor: dthat

12. An individual constant (0-0-place i-functor): I

13. A position constant (0-0-place p-functor): Here

The *well formed expressions* are of three kinds: formulas, position terms (p-terms), and individual terms (i-terms).

1. (i) If $\alpha \epsilon v_i$, then α is an i-term
   (ii) If $\alpha \epsilon v_p$, then α is a p-term

2. If π is an m-n-place predicate, $\alpha_1 \ldots \alpha_m$ are i-terms, and $\beta_1 \ldots \beta_n$ are p-terms, then $\pi\alpha_1 \ldots \alpha_m\beta_1 \ldots \beta_n$ is a formula

3. (i) If η is an m-n-place i-functor, $\alpha_1 \ldots \alpha_m$, $\beta_1 \ldots \beta_n$ as in 2., then $\eta\, \alpha_1 \ldots \alpha_m\beta_1 \ldots \beta_n$ is an i-term
   (ii) If η is an m-n-place p-functor, $\alpha_1 \ldots \alpha_m$, $\beta_1 \ldots \beta_n$ as in 2., then $\eta\, \alpha_1 \ldots \alpha_m \beta_1 \ldots \beta_n$ is a p-term

4. If Φ, Ψ are formulas, then $(\Phi \wedge \Psi)$, $(\Phi \vee \Psi)$, $\neg\Phi$, $(\Phi \rightarrow \Psi)$, $(\Phi \leftrightarrow \Psi)$ are formulas

5. If Φ is a formula and $\alpha \epsilon\, v_i \cup v_p$, then $\forall\alpha\Phi$, $\exists\alpha\Phi$ are formulas

6. If Φ is a formula, then
   (i) if $\alpha \epsilon\, v_i$, then the $\alpha\Phi$ is an i-term
   (ii) if $\alpha\delta\, v_p$, then the $\alpha\Phi$ is a p-term

7. If both α, β are either i-terms or p-terms, then $\alpha = \beta$ is a formula

8. If Φ is a formula, then $\square\Phi$, $\diamond\Phi$ are formulas

9. If Φ is a formula, then FΦ, PΦ, GΦ are formulas

10. If Φ is a formula, then NΦ, AΦ, YΦ are formulas

11. (i) If α is an i-term, then dthat α is an i-term
    (ii) If α is a p-term, then dthat α is a p-term

SEMANTICS FOR LD

Definition: $\mathfrak{A}$ *is an LD Structure* iff there are $\mathcal{C}\,\mathcal{W}\,\mathcal{U}\,\mathcal{P}\,\mathcal{T}\,\mathcal{I}$ such that

1. $\mathfrak{A} = \langle \mathcal{C}\mathcal{W}\mathcal{U}\mathcal{P}\mathcal{T}\mathcal{I} \rangle$

2. $\mathcal{C}$ is a nonempty set (the set of *contexts*, see 10 below)

3. If c $\epsilon\, \mathcal{C}$, then
   (i) $c_A\, \epsilon\mathcal{U}$ (the *agent* of c)
   (ii) $c_T\, \epsilon\mathcal{T}$ (the *time* of c)
   (iii) $c_P\, \epsilon\mathcal{P}$ (the *position* of c)
   (iv) $c_w\, \epsilon\mathcal{W}$ (the *world* of c)

4. $\mathcal{W}$ is a nonempty set (the set of *worlds*)

5. $\mathcal{U}$ is a nonempty set (the set of all *individuals*, see 9 below)

6. $\mathcal{P}$ is a nonempty set (the set of *positions;* common to all worlds)

7. $\mathcal{T}$ is the set of integers (thought of as the *times;* common to all worlds)

8. $\mathcal{I}$ is a function that assigns to each predicate and functor an appropriate *intension* as follows:
   (i) If π is an m-n-place predicate, $\mathcal{I}_\pi$ is a function such that for each $t\epsilon\mathcal{T}$ and $w\epsilon\mathcal{W}$, $\mathcal{I}_\pi(tw) \subseteq (\mathcal{U}^m \times \mathcal{P}^n)$
   (ii) If η is an m-n-place i-functor, $\mathcal{I}_\eta$ is a function such that for each $t\epsilon\mathcal{T}$ and $w\epsilon\mathcal{W}$, $\mathcal{I}_\eta(tw)\epsilon(\mathcal{U}\cup\{\dagger\})^{(\mathcal{U}^m \times \mathcal{P}^n)}$
   (Note: $\dagger$ is a completely alien entity, in neither $\mathcal{U}$ nor $\mathcal{P}$, which represents an 'undefined' value of the function. In a normal set theory we can take $\dagger$ to be $\{\mathcal{U}, \mathcal{P}\}$.)
   (iii) If η is an m-n-place p-functor, $\mathcal{I}_\eta$ is a function such that for each $t\epsilon\mathcal{T}$ and $w\epsilon\mathcal{W}$, $\mathcal{I}_\eta (tw)\epsilon(\mathcal{P} \cup \{\dagger\})^{(\mathcal{U}^m \times \mathcal{P}^n)}$

9. $i\epsilon\mathcal{U}$ iff $\exists t\epsilon\mathcal{T}$ $\exists w\epsilon\mathcal{W}$ $\langle i\rangle\epsilon\mathcal{I}_{\text{Exist}}(tw)$
10. If $c\epsilon\mathcal{C}$, then $\langle c_A c_P\rangle$ $\epsilon\mathcal{I}_{\text{Located}}$ $(c_T c_W)$
11. If $\langle i\ p\rangle$ $\epsilon\mathcal{I}_{\text{Located}}(tw)$, then $\langle i\rangle\epsilon\mathcal{I}_{\text{Exist}}(tw)$

Truth and Denotation in a Context

We write: $\models^{\mathfrak{A}}_{cftw} \Phi$ for

Φ when taken in the context c (under the assignment f and in the structure $\mathfrak{A}$ *is true with respect to* the time t and the world w.

We write: $|\alpha|^{\mathfrak{A}}_{cftw}$ for

The denotation of α when taken in the context c (under the assignment f and in the structure $\mathfrak{A}$) with respect to the time t and the world w.

In general we will omit the superscript '$\mathfrak{A}$', and we will assume that the structure $\mathfrak{A}$ is $\langle\mathcal{C}\mathcal{W}\mathcal{U}\mathcal{P}\mathcal{T}\mathcal{I}\rangle$.

Definition: *f is an assignment* (with respect to $\langle\mathcal{C}\mathcal{W}\mathcal{U}\mathcal{P}\mathcal{T}\mathcal{I}\rangle$) iff
$\exists$ $f_1 f_2 (f_1\epsilon\mathcal{U}^{vi}$ & $f_2\epsilon\mathcal{P}^{vp}$ & $f = f_1\cup f_2)$

Definition: $f^\alpha_x = (f \sim \{\langle\alpha\ f(\alpha)\rangle\}) \vee \{\langle\alpha\ x\rangle\}$ (i.e., the assignment which is just like f except that it assigns x to α)

For the following recursive definitions, assume that c ϵ $\mathcal{C}$, f is an assignment, $t\epsilon\mathcal{T}$, and $w\epsilon\mathcal{W}$.

1. If α is a variable, $|\alpha|_{cftw} = f(\alpha)$
2. $\models_{cftw} \pi\alpha_1 \ldots \alpha_m\beta_1 \ldots \beta_n$ iff $\langle|\alpha_1|_{cftw} \ldots |\beta_n|_{cftw}\rangle\epsilon\mathcal{I}_\pi(tw)$

3. If η is neither I nor Here (see 12, 13 below), then
$|\eta\alpha_1 \ldots \alpha_m\beta_1 \ldots \beta_n|_{cftw} =$
$$\begin{cases} \mathcal{I}\eta(tw)(\langle|\alpha_1|_{cftw} \ldots |\beta_n|_{cftw}\rangle), \text{ if} \\ \quad \text{none of } |\alpha_j|_{cftw}|\beta_k|_{cftw} \text{ are } \dagger. \\ \dagger, \text{ otherwise} \end{cases}$$

4. (i) $\models_{cftw} (\Phi\wedge\Psi)$ iff $\models_{cftw} \Phi$ & $\models_{cftw} \Psi$
   (ii) $\models_{cftw} \neg\Phi$ iff $\sim \models_{cftw} \Phi$
   etc.

5. (i) If $\alpha \epsilon v_i$, then $\models_{cftw} \forall\alpha\Phi$ iff $\forall i\epsilon\mathcal{U}$ $\models_{cf^\alpha_i tw} \Phi$
   (ii) If $\alpha \epsilon v_p$, then $\models_{cftw} \forall\alpha\Phi$ iff $\forall p\epsilon\mathcal{P}$ $\models_{cf^\alpha_p tw} \Phi$

   Similarly for $\exists\alpha\Phi$

6. (i) If $\alpha \epsilon v_i$, then $|\text{the } \alpha\Phi|_{cftw} =$
$$\begin{cases} \text{the unique i } \epsilon \mathcal{U} \text{ such that} \\ \quad \models_{cf^\alpha_i tw} \Phi, \text{ if there is such.} \\ \dagger \text{ otherwise} \end{cases}$$
   (ii) Similarly for $\alpha \epsilon v_p$

7. $\models_{cftw} \alpha = \beta$ iff $|\alpha|_{cftw} = |\beta|_{cftw}$
8. (i) $\models_{cftw} \Box\Phi$ iff $\forall w'\epsilon\mathcal{W}$ $\models_{cftw'} \Phi$
   (ii) $\models_{cftw} \Diamond\Phi$ iff $\exists w'\epsilon\mathcal{W}$ $\models_{cftw'} \Phi$
9. (i) $\models_{cftw} F\Phi$ iff $\exists t'\epsilon\mathcal{T}$ such that $t'> t$ and $\models_{cft'w} \Phi$
   (ii) $\models_{cftw} P\Phi$ iff $\exists t'\epsilon\mathcal{T}$ such that $t'< t$ and $\models_{cft'w} \Phi$
   (iii) $\models_{cftw} G\Phi$ iff $\models_{cf(t-1)w} \Phi$
10. (i) $\models_{cftw} N\Phi$ iff $\models_{cfc_T w} \Phi$
    (ii) $\models_{cftw} A\Phi$ iff $\models_{cftc_W} \Phi$
    (iii) $\models_{cftw} Y\Phi$ iff $\models_{cf(c_T - 1)w} \Phi$
11. $|\text{dthat}\alpha|_{cftw} = |\alpha|_{cfc_T c_W}$
12. $|\text{I}|_{cftw} = c_A$
13. $|\text{Here}|_{cftw} = c_P$

Remark 1: Expressions containing demonstratives will, in general, express different concepts in different contexts. We call the concept expressed in a given context the *Content* of the expression in that context. The Content of a sentence in a context is, roughly, the proposition the sentence would express if uttered in that context. This description is not quite accurate on two counts. First, it is important to distinguish an *utterance* from a *sentence-in-a-context*. The former notion is from the theory of speech acts, the latter from semantics. Utterances take time, and utterances of distinct sentences cannot be simultaneous (i.e., in the same context). But to develop a logic of demonstratives it seems most natural to be able to evaluate several premises and a conclusion all in the same context. Thus the notion of Φ being true in c and $\mathfrak{A}$ does not require an utterance of Φ. In particular, c_A need not be uttering Φ in c_W at c_T. Second, the truth of a proposition is not usually thought of as dependent on a time as well as a possible world. The time is thought of as fixed by the context. If Φ is a sentence, the more usual notion of the proposition expressed by Φ-in-c is what is here called the Content of NΦ in c.

Where Γ is either a term or a formula,
we write: $\{\Gamma\}_{cf}^{\mathfrak{A}}$ for
The Content of Γ in the context c (under the assignment f and in the structure $\mathfrak{A}$).

Definition: (i) If Φ is a formula, $\{\Phi\}_{cf}^{\mathfrak{A}}$ = that function which assigns to each tϵT and wϵW Truth, if $\underset{cftw}{\overset{\mathfrak{A}}{\vDash}}$ Φ, and Falsehood otherwise.

(ii) If α is a term, $\{\alpha\}_{cf}^{\mathfrak{A}}$ = that function which assigns to each t ϵ T and w ϵ W, $|\alpha|_{cftw}^{\mathfrak{A}}$.

Remark 2: $\underset{cftw}{\overset{\mathfrak{A}}{\vDash}}$ Φ iff $\{\phi\}_{cf}^{\mathfrak{A}}$(tw) = Truth. Roughly speaking, the sentence Φ taken in the context c is *true with respect to* t and w iff the proposition expressed by Φ-in-the-context-c would be true at the time t if w were the actual world. In the formal development of pages 140 and 141 it was smoother to ignore the conceptual break marked by the notion of *Content in a context* and to directly define *truth in a context with respect to a possible time and world.* The important conceptual role of the notion of Content is partially indicated by the following two definitions.

Definition: Φ *is true in the context c* (in the structure $\mathfrak{A}$) iff for every assignment f, $\{\Phi\}_{cf}^{\mathfrak{A}}(c_T, c_W)$ = Truth.

Definition: Φ *is valid in* LD ($\vDash \Phi$) iff for every LD structure $\mathfrak{A}$ and every context c of $\mathfrak{A}$, Φ is true in c (in $\mathfrak{A}$).

Remark 3: $\vDash (\alpha = $ dthat $\alpha)$, $\vDash$ N (Located I, Here), $\vDash$ Exist I, $\sim \vDash \Box (\alpha = $ dthat $\alpha)$, $\sim \vDash \Box$N(located I, Here), $\sim \vDash \Box$ (Exist I). In the converse direction we have the usual results in view of the fact that $\vDash(\Box\Phi\rightarrow \Phi)$.

Definition: If $\alpha_1 \ldots \alpha_n$ are all the free variables of Φ in alphabetical order, then *the closure of* Φ = AN $\forall\alpha_1 \ldots \alpha_n \Phi$.

Definition: Φ *is closed* iff Φ is equivalent (in the sense of Remark 12) to its closure.

Remark 4: If Φ is closed, then Φ is true in c (and $\mathfrak{A}$) iff for every assignment f, time t, and world w $\underset{cftw}{\overset{\mathfrak{A}}{\vDash}}$ Φ.

Definition: Where Γ is either a term or a formula, *the Content of* Γ *in the context c (in the structure $\mathfrak{A}$) is stable* iff for every assignment f, $\{\Gamma\}_{cf}^{\mathfrak{A}}$ is a constant function. (i.e., $\{\Gamma\}_{cf}^{\mathfrak{A}}$ (tw) = $\{\Gamma\}_{cf}^{\mathfrak{A}}$(t'w'), for all t, t', w w' in $\mathfrak{A}$).

Remark 5: Where Φ is a formula, α is a term, and β is a variable, each of the following has a stable Con-

tent in every context (in every structure): ANΦ, dthat α, β, I, Here.

If we were to extend the notion of Content to apply to operators, we would see that all demonstratives have a stable Content in every context. The same is true of the familiar logical constants although it does not hold for the modal and tense operators (not, at least, according to the foregoing development).

Remark 6: That aspect of the meaning of an expression which determines what its Content will be in each context, we call the *Character* of the expression. Although a lack of knowledge about the context (or perhaps about the structure) may cause one to mistake the Content of a given utterance, the Character of each well-formed expression is determined by rules of the language (such as rules 1–13 on pages 140 and 141 of this chapter) which are presumably known to all competent speakers. Our notation '$\{\Phi\}_{cf}^{\mathfrak{A}}$' for the Content of an expression gives a natural notation for the Character of an expression, namely '$\{\Phi\}$.'

Definition: Where Γ is either a term or a formula, the *Character of* Γ is that function which assigns to each structure $\mathfrak{A}$, assignment f, and context c of $\mathfrak{A}$, $\{\Gamma\}_{cf}^{\mathfrak{A}}$.

Definition: Where Γ is either a term or a formula, *the Character of* Γ *is stable* iff for every structure $\mathfrak{A}$, and assignment f the Character of Γ (under f in $\mathfrak{A}$) is a constant function. (i.e., $\{\Gamma\}_{cf}^{\mathfrak{A}} = \{\Gamma\}_{c'f}^{\mathfrak{A}}$ for all c, c' in $\mathfrak{A}$).

Remark 7: A formula or term has a stable Character iff it has the same Content in every context (for each $\mathfrak{A}$, f).

Remark 8: A formula or term has a stable Character iff it contains no essential occurrence of a demonstrative.

Remark 9: The logic of demonstratives determines a sublogic of those formulas of LD which contain no demonstratives. These formulas (and their equivalents which contain inessential occurrences of demonstratives) are exactly the formulas with a stable Character. The logic of demonstratives brings a new perspective even to formulas such as these. The sublogic of LD which concerns only formulas of stable Character is not identical with traditional logic. Even for such formulas, the familiar Principle of Necessitation (if $\vDash\Phi$, then $\vDash \Box\Phi$) fails. And so does its tense logic counterpart: if $\vDash\Phi$, then $\vDash(\neg P\neg\Phi \wedge \neg F\neg\Phi \wedge \Phi$). From the perspective of LD, validity is truth in every possible *context*. For traditional logic, validity is truth in every possible *circumstance*. Each possible context determines a possible circumstance, but it is not the case that each possible circumstance is part of a possible context. In particular, the fact that each possible context has an agent implies that any possible circumstance in which no individuals exist will not form a part of any possible context. Within LD, a possible context is represented by $\langle \mathfrak{A}, c \rangle$ and a possible circumstance by $\langle \mathfrak{A}, t, w \rangle$. To any $\langle \mathfrak{A}, c \rangle$, there corresponds $\langle \mathfrak{A}, c_T, c_W \rangle$. But it is not the case that to every $\langle \mathfrak{A}, t, w \rangle$ there exists a context c of $\mathfrak{A}$ such that $t = c_T$ and $w = c_W$. The result is that in LD such sentences as $\exists x$ Exist x and $\exists x \exists p$ Located x,p are valid, although they would not be so regarded in traditional logic, at least not in the neotraditional logic that countenances empty worlds. Using the semantical developments of pages 140 and 141, we can define this traditional sense of validity (for formulas which do not contain demonstratives) as follows. First note that by Remark 7, if Φ, has a stable Character,

$$\underset{\text{cftw}}{\overset{\mathfrak{A}}{\models}} \Phi \quad \text{iff} \quad \underset{\text{c'ftw}}{\overset{\mathfrak{A}}{\models}} \Phi$$

Thus for such formulas we can define,

Φ *is true at tw (in $\mathfrak{A}$)* iff for every assignment f and every context c $\underset{\text{cftw}}{\overset{\mathfrak{A}}{\models}} \Phi$

The neotraditional sense of validity is now definable as follows:

$\underset{\text{T}}{\models} \Phi$ iff for all structures $\mathfrak{A}$, times t, and worlds w, Φ is true at tw (in $\mathfrak{A}$).

(Properly speaking, what I have called the neotraditional sense of validity is the notion of validity now common for a quantified S5 modal tense logic with individual variables ranging over possible individuals and a predicate of existence.) Adding the subscript 'LD' for explicitness, we can now state some results.

(i) If Φ contains no demonstratives,
   if $\underset{\text{T}}{\models} \Phi$, then $\underset{\text{LD}}{\models} \Phi$

(ii) $\underset{\text{LD}}{\models} \exists x$ Exist x, but $\sim \underset{\text{T}}{\models} \exists x$ Exist x

Of course $\Box \exists x$ Exist x is not valid even in LD. Nor are its counterparts, $\neg F \neg \exists x$ Exists and $\neg P \neg \exists x$ Exists x.

This suggests that we can transcend the context-oriented perspective of LD by generalizing over times and worlds so as to capture those possible circumstances $\langle \mathfrak{A}, t, w \rangle$ which do not correspond to any possible contexts $\langle \mathfrak{A}, c \rangle$. We have the following result.

(iii) If Φ contains no demonstratives,
   $\underset{\text{T}}{\models} \Phi$ iff $\underset{\text{LD}}{\models} \Box (\neg F \neg \Phi \wedge \neg P \neg \Phi \wedge \Phi)$.

Although our definition of the neotraditional sense of validity was motivated by consideration of demonstrative-free formulas, we could apply it also to formulas containing essential occurrences of demonstratives. To do so would nullify the most interesting features of the logic of demonstratives. But it raises the question, can we express our new sense of validity in terms of the neotraditional sense? This can be done:

(iv) $\underset{\text{LD}}{\models} \Phi$ iff $\underset{\text{T}}{\models}$ AN Φ

Remark 10: Rigid designators (in the sense of Kripke) are terms with a stable Content. Since Kripke does not discuss demonstratives, his examples all have, in addition, a stable Character (by Remark 8). Kripke claims that for proper names α, β it may happen that $\alpha = \beta$, though not a priori, is nevertheless necessary. This, in spite of the fact that the names α, β may be introduced by means of descriptions α', β' for which $\alpha' = \beta'$ is not necessary. An analogous situation holds in LD. Let α', β' be definite descriptions (without free variables) such that $\alpha' = \beta'$ is not a priori, and consider the (rigid) terms: dthat α', dthat β', which are formed from them. We know that

$\models$ (dthat α' = dthat $\beta' \leftrightarrow \alpha' = \beta'$).

Thus, if $\alpha' = \beta'$ is not a priori, neither is dthat α' = dthat β'. But, since

$\models$ [dthat α' = dthat $\beta' \rightarrow$
   $\Box$ (dthat α' = dthat β')],

it may happen that dthat α' = dthat β' is necessary. The converse situation can also be illustrated in LD. Since $(\alpha = $ dthat $\alpha)$ is valid (see Remark 3), it is surely capable of being known a priori. But if α lacks a stable Content (in some context c), $\Box (\alpha = $ dthat $\alpha)$ will be false.

Remark 11: Our 0-0-place i-functors are not proper names, in the sense of Kripke, since they do not have a stable Content. But they can easily be converted by means of the stabilizing influence of dthat. Even dthat α lacks a stable Character. The process by which such expressions are converted into expressions with a stable Character is 'dubbing'—a form of definition in which context may play an essential role. The means to deal with such context-indexed definitions is not available in our object language.

There would, of course, be no difficulty in supplementing our language with a syntactically distinctive set of 0-0-place i-functors whose semantics requires them to have both a stable Character and a stable Content in every context. Variables already behave this way; what is wanted is a class of constants that behave, in these respects, like variables.

The difficulty comes in expressing the definition. My thought is that when a name, like 'Bozo,' is introduced by someone saying, in some context c*, "Let's call the Governor, 'Bozo,'" we have a context-indexed definition of the form: A $=_{c*}$ α, where A is a new constant (here, 'Bozo') and α is some term whose denotation depends on context (here, 'the Governor'). The intention of such a dubbing is, presumably, to induce the semantical clause: for all c $\{A\}_{cf}^{\mathfrak{A}} = \{\alpha\}_{c*f}$. Such a clause gives A a stable Character. The context indexing is required by the fact that the Content of α (the 'definiens') may vary from context to context. Thus the same semantical clause is not induced by taking either A = α or even A = dthat α as an axiom.

I think it likely that such definitions play a practically (and perhaps theoretically) indispensable role in the growth of language, allowing us to introduce a vast stock of names on the basis of a meager stock of demonstratives and some ingenuity in staging of demonstrations.

Perhaps such introductions should not be called 'definitions' at all, since they essentially enrich the expressive power of the language. What a nameless man may express by 'I am hungry' may be inexpressible in remote contexts. But once he says "Let's call me 'Bozo,'" his Content is accessible to us all.

Remark 12: The strongest form of logical equivalence between two formulas Φ and Φ' is sameness of Character, $\{Φ\} = \{Φ'\}$. This form of synonymy is expressible in terms of validity.

$\{Φ\} = \{Φ'\}$ iff $\vDash \Box[\neg F\neg(Φ \leftrightarrow Φ') \wedge \neg P\neg(Φ \leftrightarrow Φ') \wedge (Φ \leftrightarrow Φ')]$

[Using Remark 9 (iii) and dropping its condition, which was stated only to express the intended range of applicability of $\vDash$, we have: $\{Φ\} = \{Φ'\}$ iff $\vDash_T (Φ \leftrightarrow Φ')$.] Since definitions of the usual kind (as opposed to dubbings) are intended to introduce a short expression as a mere abbreviation of a longer one, the Character of the defined sign should be the same as the Character of the definiens. Thus, within LD, definitional axioms must take the form indicated above.

Remark 13: If β is a variable of the same sort as the term α but is not free in α, then $\{$dthat α$\} = \{$the β AN(β = α)$\}$. Thus for every formula Φ, there can be constructed a formula Φ' such that Φ' contains no occurrence of dthat and $\{Φ\} = \{Φ'\}$.

Remark 14: Y (yesterday) and G (one day ago) superficially resemble one another in view of the fact that $\vDash (YΦ \leftrightarrow GΦ)$. But the former is a demonstrative whereas the latter is an iterative temporal operator. "One day ago it was the case that one day ago it was the case that John yawned" means that John yawned the day before yesterday. But "Yesterday it was the case that yesterday it was the case that John yawned" is only a stutter.

POSSIBLE REFINEMENTS

1. The primitive predicates and functors of first-order predicate logic are all taken to be extensional. Alternatives are possible.

2. Many conditions might be added on $\mathcal{P}$; many alternatives might be chosen for $\mathcal{T}$. If the elements of $\mathcal{T}$ do not have a natural relation to play the role of <, such a relation must be added to the structure.

3. When K is a set of LD formulas, $K \vDash Φ$ is easily defined in any of the usual ways.

4. Aspects of the contexts other than c_A, c_P, c_T, and c_W would be used if new demonstratives (e.g., pointings, You, etc.) were added to the language. (Note that the subscripts A, P, T, W are external parameters. They may be thought of as functions applying to contexts, with c_A being the value of A for the context c.)

5. Special continuity conditions through time might be added for the predicate Exists.

6. If individuals lacking positions are admitted as agents of contexts, 3(iii) of page 140 should be weakened to $C_{P} \epsilon \mathcal{P} \cup \{\dagger\}$. It would no longer be the case that $\vDash$ Located I, Here. If individuals also lacking temporal location (disembodied minds?) are admitted as agents of contexts, a similar weakening is required of 3(ii). In any case it would still be true that $\vDash$ Exist I.

NOTES

1. This paper was originally composed in two parts. The formal Logic of Demonstratives was first presented at the Irvine Summer Institute in the Philosophy of Language in 1971. It was expanded in 1973. The initial discursive material was written on April 20, 1973, as part of a research proposal. This paper was intended as a companion piece to and progress report on the material in "Dthat" [*Syntax and Semantics, vol. 9: Pragmatics,* ed. Peter Cole (New York, 1978), 221–253]. A more extensive presentation occurs in my manuscript *Demonstratives.* This work was supported by the National Science Foundation.

2. Rudolf Carnap, *Meaning and Necessity* (Chicago, 1947).

3. Or possibly, just in case Φ was true at every index *that differed from the given index only in the possible world coordinate.*

4. Saul Kripke, "Naming and Necessity," in *Semantics of Natural Language,* eds. D. Davidson and G. Harman (Dordrecht, 1972).

5. Peter Strawson, *Introduction to Logical Theory* (New York, 1952).

9

Frege on Demonstratives[1]

JOHN PERRY

In "The Thought," Frege briefly discusses sentences containing such demonstratives as "today," "here," and "yesterday," and then turns to certain questions that he says are raised by the occurrence of "I" in sentences (T, 24–26). He is led to say that, when one thinks about oneself, one grasps thoughts that others cannot grasp, that cannot be communicated. Nothing could be more out of the spirit of Frege's account of sense and thought than an incommunicable, private thought. Demonstratives seem to have posed a severe difficulty for Frege's philosophy of language, to which his doctine of incommunicable senses was a reaction.

In the first part of the paper, I explain the problem demonstratives pose for Frege, and explore three ways he might have dealt with it. I argue that none of these ways provides Frege with a solution to his problem consistent with his philosophy of language. The first two are plausible as solutions, but contradict his identification of the sense expressed by a sentence with a thought. The third preserves the identification, but is implausible. In the second part, I suggest that Frege was led to his doctrine of incommunicable senses as a result of

some appreciation of the difficulties his account of demonstratives faces, for these come quickly to the surface when we think about "I." I argue that incommunicable senses won't help. I end by trying to identify the central problem with Frege's approach, and sketching an alternative.

I

Before explaining the problem posed by demonstratives, certain points about Frege's philosophy of languages need to be made.

In "On Sense and Reference," Frege introduces the notion of sense, in terms of the cognitive value of sentences. He then goes on to make two key identifications. First, he identifies the sense of a sentence with the thought it expresses. Then, he identifies the thought expressed by a sentence, and so the sense it has, with the indirect reference of the sentence in the scope of a cognitive verb.

The phrases "the sense of a sentence," "the thought expressed by a sentence," and "the indirect reference of a sentence," are not mere synonyms. They have different senses, though,

John Perry, "Frege on Demonstratives, *Philosophical Review* 86 (1977): 474–97. Copyright © 1977 by the Philosophical Review. Reprinted by permission of the publisher and the author.

if Frege's account is correct, they have the same reference. In particular, each is associated, as Frege introduces it, with a separate criterion of difference.

Sense

In the beginning of "On Sense and Reference," Frege introduces the notion of sense as a way of accounting for the difference in cognitive value of the senses of "$a = a$" and "$a = b$," even when both are true, and so made up of coreferential expressions. (SR, 56–58) So a criterion of difference for sense is:

If S and S' have differing cognitive value, then S and S' have different senses.

Dummett's explanation of sense will help us to convert this to something more helpful. He emphasizes that sense is linked to understanding and truth. The sense of an expression is "what we know when we understand it," and what we know when we understand it is something like an ideal procedure for determining its reference. (F, 293, 589ff.) In the case of a sentence, whose reference is a truth value, the sense is that we know when, roughly, we know what would have to be done—whether or not this is humanly possible—to determine whether or not it is true.

What Frege seems to have in mind at the beginning of "On Sense and Reference," then, is a situation in which some person A who understands both "$a = a$" and "$a = b$," accepts the first while rejecting, or being unsure about, the second. The assumption seems to be, that if A associated just the same ideal procedures with both sentences, he would accept the second if he accepted the first. So he must not associate the same ideal procedures with both sentences, and so, since he understands them, their senses differ. So we have:

If A understands S and S', and accepts S as true while not accepting S', then S and S' have different senses.

This criterion of difference allows that sentences might have different senses, though provably or necessarily equivalent. A complex true mathematical equation might be provably equivalent to "$2 + 3 = 5$," and yet a perfectly competent speaker might accept the latter and reject the former, having made an error in calculation. To know an ideal procedure for determining reference, is not necessarily to have carried it out, or even to be able to.

Thought

"Thought" is not just a term introduced by Frege as another way of saying, "sense of a sentence." The notion derived from Frege's untangling of the jumbled notion of a judgment, into act, thought, and truth value. The thought is, first and foremost, "that for which the question of truth arises." (T, 20–22) This is clearly intended to be a criterion of difference for thoughts:

If S is true and S' is not, S and S' express different thoughts.

Indirect Reference

Consider a report of a belief: "Copernicus believed that the planetary orbits are circles." On Frege's analysis, this is relational. "Believed that" stands for a relation, which is asserted to hold between Copernicus and whatever it is that "the planetary orbits are circles" refers to as it occurs in this sentence. Standing alone, "the planetary orbits are circles" would refer to the False, but here it clearly does not have that ordinary reference. If it did, the substitution of any false sentence at all should preserve truth of the whole report (SR, 66–67). The notion of the indirect reference of "the planetary orbits are circles," is just whatever it is, that this sentence has as reference here. (The phrase is first used in connection with indirect discourse [SR, 59].) Now if "$a R b$" is true, and "$a R c$" is not, b is not c. So we have a clear criterion of difference:

If 'A believes S' is true, and 'A believes S' ' is not, then S and S' do not have the same indirect reference.

So we have three separable criterion of difference. But Frege, as noted, identifies the sense of S the thought expressed by S, and the indirect reference of S. So we are led to a further principle:

S and S′ have different senses, if and only if they express different thoughts, and if and only if they have different indirect references.

Sense Completers

Frege takes the structure of language as a suggestive guide to the structure of senses and objects. Just as he views the sentence,

two plus two equals four

as the result of combining the complete

two

with the incomplete

( ) plus two equals four,

so he sees the sense of "two plus two equals four" as determined by the sense of "two" and the sense of "( ) plus two equals four." The sense of the latter is incomplete; the sense of the former completes it, to yield the complete sense of "two plus two equals four."

"( ) plus two equals four" could also be made into a sentence by writing "something" in the blank; similarly the sense of "( ) plus two equals four" can be completed with the sense of "something." The sense of "something," however, unlike the sense of "two," is itself also incomplete. Where "two" refers to an object, "something" refers to a concept. Two appropriately related incomplete senses can combine to form a complete sense; two complete senses cannot combine at all. (CT, 538)

Thus the class of *sense completers* for a given incomplete sense is hybrid, containing both complete and incomplete senses. But the term will be useful in what follows.

Sense Had and Sense Expressed

The structure of language is not always a sure guide to the structure of senses. Not everything we count as a sentence has a complete sense. Consider (1),

(1) Russia and Canada quarrelled when Nemtsanov defected.

"Russia and Canada quarrelled," as it occurs as a clause in (1), does not have a complete sense. (SR, 71; T, 37) It refers to a concept of times and thus must have an incomplete sense. "When Nemtsanov defected" refers to a time; the sentence is true if the time referred to falls under the concept referred to. Thus the sense of "when Nemtsanov defected" is a sense completer for the sense of "Russia and Canada quarrelled."

So the sense of the sentence "Russia and Canada quarrelled" is not a thought. Not any sentence, but only a sentence "complete in every respect" expresses a thought. (T, 37)

Now "Russia and Canada quarrelled" could be used, without a dependent clause, to express a thought. If it appeared alone, we might take it to express, *on that occasion,* the sense of

At some time or other, Russia and Canada quarrelled.

In another setting, for example after the question, "What happened when Nemtsanov defected?", the sentence would express the sense of (1). So we must, even before considering demonstratives, distinguish between the sense a sentence *has* on each occasion of use and the senses it *expresses* on various occasions of use. For an "eternal" sentence, one that really is "complete in every respect," the two will be the same; for a sentence like "Russia and Canada quarrelled," the sense *had* is incomplete: the sense *expressed* on a given occasion will be the result of completing that sense, with some sense completer available from the context of utterance. It is clearly only the sense expressed on such occasions, that Frege wants to identify with a thought.

The Problem Posed by Demonstratives

We are now in a position to see why demonstratives pose a problem for Frege.

I begin by quoting the passage in "The Thought" in which Frege discusses demonstratives in general.

often . . . the mere wording, which can be grasped by writing or the gramophone, does not suffice for the expression of the thought . . . If a time indication is needed by the present tense [as opposed to cases in which it is used to express timelessness, as in the statement of mathematical laws] one must know when the sentence was uttered to apprehend the thought correctly. Therefore, the time of utterance is part of the expression of the thought. If someone wants to say the same today as he expressed yesterday using the word 'today,' he must replace this word with 'yesterday.' Although the thought is the same its verbal expression must be different so that the sense, which would otherwise be affected by the differing times of utterance, is readjusted. The case is the same with words like 'here' and 'there.' In all such cases of mere wording, as it is given in writing, is not the complete expression of the thought, but the knowledge of certain accompanying conditions of utterance, which are used as means of expressing the thought, are needed for its correct apprehension. The pointing of fingers, hand movements, glances may belong here too. The same utterance containing the word 'I' will express different thoughts in the mouths of different men, of which some may be true, others false [T, 24].

Consider (2),

(2) Russia and Canada quarrelled today.

The sentence "Russia and Canada quarrelled" has in (2), as in (1), only an incomplete sense. So presumably "today" in (2) must somehow do what "when Nemtsanov defected" does in (1), and supply us with a completing sense. But it does not seem to do this at all.

If I uttered (2) on August 1, I expressed something true, on August 2, something false. If "today" had the same sense on August 1 as on August 2, then (2) in its entirety must have had the same sense on both occasions. If so, the sense of (2) must be incomplete, for if it were complete, its truth value could not change.

So, if "today" provides a completing sense on both days, its sense must change just at midnight. But what we know when we understand how to use "today" doesn't seem to change from day to day.

When we understand a word like "today," what we seem to know is a rule taking us from an occasion of utterance to a certain object. "Today" takes us to the very day of utterance, "yesterday" to the day before the day of utterance, "I" to the speaker, and so forth. I shall call this the *role* of the demonstrative. I take a context to be a set of features of an actual utterance, certainly including time, place, and speaker, but probably also more. Just what a context must include is a difficult question, to be answered only after detailed study of various demonstratives. The object a demonstra-

tive takes us to in a given context, I shall call its value in that context or on that occasion of use. Clearly, we must grant "today" a role, the same on both occasions of use. And we must, as clearly, give it different values on the two occasions.

Any reasonable account has to recognize that demonstratives have roles. The role of a demonstrative does not seem reducible to other notions available from Frege's philosophy. Senses do not carry us from context to references, but directly to references, the same on each occasion of use. One might suppose that "yesterday" could be thought to have just the sense of "the day before." But,

(3) Russia and Canada quarrelled the day before

does not have the same sense as (4).

(4) Russia and Canada quarrelled yesterday.

If I ask on August 5, "Did Russia and Canada quarrel August 2?" (3) would imply that they quarrelled on August 1, (4) that they quarrelled on August 4. If (3) were uttered when no day had already been mentioned, it would not express anything complete, but simply give rise to the question, "before what?" An utterance of (4) would still be fully in order.

Frege recognizes that demonstratives have roles, or at least that the context of utterance is crucial when dealing with demonstratives. He does not talk about the sense of "today" or "I" so he also seems to have recognized that the role of a demonstrative is not just a sense, as he has explained senses.

But Frege clearly thinks that, given knowledge of the accompanying conditions of utterance, we can get from an utterance of a sentence like (2) or (4) to a thought. He must have thought, then, that the demonstrative provides us not simply with an object—its value on the occasion of utterance—but with a *completing sense*. This is puzzling. Neither the unchanging role of "today," or its changing value, provides us with a completing sense. A day is not a sense, but a reference corresponding to indefinitely many senses. (SR, 71) There is no route back from reference to sense. So how do we get from the incomplete sense of "Russia and Canada quarrelled," the demonstrative "today," and the context to a thought? This is the problem demonstratives pose for Frege.

I shall first describe two options Frege might have taken, which would have excused him from the necessity of finding a completing sense. I shall argue that Frege did not take these options, and could not, given his identification of sense expressed and thought.

Sense as Roles?

Let $S(d)$ be a sentence containing a demonstrative d. Without the demonstrative, we have something, $S(\ )$, that has an incomplete sense, and so refers to a concept. This may actually still be a sentence, as when we remove "today" from (2), or it may look more like it should, as when we remove the "I" from "I am wounded."

The following scheme gives us a rule for getting from a particular context, to a truth value, for any such sentence $S(d)$.

$S(d)$ is true when uttered in context c, if and only if the value of d in c falls under the concept referred to by $S(\ )$.[2]

Such a rule is the *role of S(d)*. It is just an extension of the notion of the role of a demonstrative. Roles take us from contexts to objects. In the case of a sentence, the object is a truth value.

Thus (4) is true as uttered on August 2, if and only if August 1 is a day that falls under the concept referred to by "Russia and Canada quarrelled." "I am ill" as uttered by Lauben is true if and only if Lauben falls under the concept referred to by "( ) is ill."

The role of a sentence containing a demonstrative is clearly analogous in many ways to the sense of a sentence not containing a demonstrative. The role is a procedure for determining truth value, just as the sense is. The difference is that the role is a procedure which starts from a context.

This analogy suggests an option, which Frege might have taken. He might have identified the sense expressed by a sentence containing a demonstrative with its role. This would amount to a generalization of the notion of sense. On this view, an incomplete sense like that of "Russia and Canada quarrelled," could be completed in two ways. A sense completer, such as the sense of "when

Nemtsanov defected," gives us a complete sense of the old sort. A demonstrative, like "today," yields a sense of the new sort, a role. No complete sense of the old sort is involved at all in the utterance of a sentence containing a demonstrative, so no completing sense need be found.

But this cannot have been Frege's view. For it is clear that he thinks a thought has been expressed in the utterance of a sentence containing a demonstrative. The role of the sentence cannot be identified with the thought, for a sentence could express the same role on different occasions while having different truth-values. So by the criteria of difference for thoughts, roles are not thoughts. By the identification of the sense expreseed by a sentence and the thought expressed, roles are not the senses expressed by a sentence.

Thoughts as Information?

We can put the problem this way. (2), as uttered on August 1st, with the role of "today" fully mastered, seems to yield just this information:

(*i*) an incomplete sense, that of "Russia and Canada quarrelled";

(*ii*) an object, the day August 1st, 1976.

(*i*) and (*ii*) do not uniquely determine a thought, but only an equivalence class of thoughts. Belonging to this equivalence class will be just those thoughts obtainable by completing the sense of "Russia and Canada quarrelled" with a sense completer which determines, as reference, August 1st, 1976. I shall call thoughts related in this manner *informationally equivalent*.[3]

The second option I shall discuss, is introducing a new notion of a thought, corresponding to such a class of informationally equivalent thoughts. Since the information in (*i*) and (*ii*) is sufficient to identify such a class, without identifying any one of its members, this would explain how we can get from (*i*) and (*ii*) to a thought, without needing a completing sense.

On this view, an utterance of $S(d)$ in context c, and $S'(d')$ in context c', will express the same thought if the (incomplete) senses of

$S(\ )$ and $S'(\ )$ are the same, and if the value of d in c is the same as the value of d' in c'. Thus (2), uttered on August 1, and (4), uttered on August 2, would express the same thought. Dummett interprets Frege in this way. (F, 384) Frege's remark,

If someone wants to say the same today as he expressed yesterday using the word 'today', he must replace this with 'yesterday'. Although the thought is the same its verbal expression must be different. . . .

But this cannot have been Frege's view. This criterion actually introduces a new kind of thought, corresponding to informationally equivalent classes of thoughts of the old kind. The thought expressed by Lauben when he says "I am wounded" to Leo Peter, cannot be identified with the thought expressed by any nondemonstrative completion of the same incomplete sense in which the singular term refers to Lauben, such as

The man born on the thirteenth of September, 1875, in N. N. is wounded.

The only doctor who lives in the house next door to Rudolf Lingens is wounded.

These express different thoughts, so the thought Lauben expresses with "I am wounded" cannot be identified with *the* thought they both express; there just isn't any such thought. There is no more reason to identify it with the one than with the other, or with any other such thought. Nor can thoughts of this new type be identified with classes of thoughts of the old, for in different possible circumstances the pair, Dr. Lauben and the incomplete sense of "( ) am ill," would correspond to different sets of Fregean thoughts. If Lauben had moved, the two Fregean thoughts in question would not be informationally equivalent. We have here a radically new kind of thought, of which Frege would not have approved, even if he had seen its necessity. We have in effect made the value of the demonstrative a part of the thought. But Frege insists that only senses can be parts of senses.

Dummett remarks,

It is, of course, quite unnecessary to suppose that a thought expressible by the utterance on a particular occasion of a sentence containing a token reflexive expression can also be expressed by some 'eternal' sentence containing no such expressions. [F, 384]

But it is not only unnecessary, but impossible, on this account, that the thought should be expressed by an eternal sentence. It is not the right kind of thought for an eternal sentence to express.

Second, and closely related, this notion of a thought would violate the criteria of difference.

Suppose I am viewing the harbor from downtown Oakland; the bow and stern of the aircraft carrier *Enterprise* are visible, though its middle is obscured by a large building. The name *"Enterprise"* is clearly visible on the bow, so when I tell a visitor, "This is the *Enterprise,"* pointing towards the bow, this is readily accepted. When I say, pointing to the stern clearly several city blocks from the bow, "That is the *Enterprise, "* however, she refuses to believe me. By the criterion of difference, a different sense was expressed the first time than the second. On the present suggested criterion of identity for thoughts, the same thought was expressed; the incomplete sense was the same in both cases, and the value of the demonstratives was the *Enterprise* in both cases. To adopt this notion of a thought, Frege would have to give up the identification of sense expressed and thought expressed.

This is, of course, simply a variation on Frege's own Morning Star example. Suppose I point to Venus in the morning, and again in the evening, saying "That's the Morning Star." My listener may accept what I say the first time, and continue to think I was right, while rejecting what I say the second time. Here the *same* sentence has a different cognitive value at different times—for my listener has not changed her mind. The sentence does not have different cognitive values because the words have undergone a change of meaning, but because the sentence alone does not express the complete sense. Some supplementation is needed; here the gestures toward Venus provide it. But just what supplementation do they provide? If the supplementation were merely taken to be Venus, itself,—which is what the present proposal amounts to—then the sense of the sentence would have been supplemented in the same way on both occasions. But then we would have the same sense expressed in both occasions, in violation of the criterion of difference for senses.

Frege does not explicitly mention the demonstratives "this" and "that." So it is worth pointing out that examples can be constructed using demonstratives he does mention. For example, I might accept what you say at 11:50 p.m. when you utter "Russia and Canada quarrelled today," but disbelieve you at 12:15 a.m. when you utter "Russia and Canada quarrelled yesterday," having lost track of time.

Of course, Frege may have meant to introduce such a new notion of a thought at this point. That he does not explain it, counts against this interpretation. And what he goes on to say, in the next paragraphs, seems to make it totally implausible. There he discusses proper names, and arrives at a point where he has all the materials for this notion of a thought in his hand, so to speak, and yet passes up the opportunity to mold them into the new notion. He describes a situation in which two men express different thoughts with the sentence "Gustav Lauben has been wounded," one knowing him as the unique man born a certain day, the other as the unique doctor living in a certain house. He recognizes that these different thoughts are systematically equivalent:

The different thoughts which thus result from the same sentence correspond in their truth-value, of course; that is to say, if one is true then all are true, and if one is false then all are false.

But he insists,

Nevertheless their distinctness must be recognized.

His reason here is clearly a complex example he has just constructed, in which sentences expressing such informationally equivalent thoughts have different cognitive value:

It is possible that Herbert Garner takes the sense of the sentence 'Dr. Lauben has been wounded' to be true while, misled by false information, taking the sense of 'Gustav Lauben has been wounded' to be false. Under the assumptions given these thoughts are therefore different. [T, 25]

If demonstratives had driven Frege, three paragraphs before this, to the introduction of a class of thoughts, corresponding to a class of informationally equivalent thoughts of the old

sort, I think he would have employed it, or at least mentioned it, here.

Senses, considered to be roles, cannot be thoughts. Thoughts, considered as information, cannot be senses. If Frege is to keep his identification of sense expressed by a sentence, with thought expressed by a sentence, he must find, somewhere, a completing sense.

Demonstratives as Providing a Completing Sense

How can we extract from a demonstrative, an appropriate completing sense? Such a sense, it seems, would have to be intimately related to the sense of a unique description of the value of the demonstrative in the context of utterance. But where does such a description come from? "Today" seems to get us only to a day. And a day does not provide a particular description of itself.

In the case of proper names, Frege supposes that different persons attach different senses to the same proper name. To find the sense a person identifies with a given proper name, we presumably look at his beliefs. If he associates the sense of description D with Gustav Lauben, he should believe,

Gustav Lauben is D.

Perhaps, with demonstratives too, Frege supposes that speakers and listeners, in grasping the thought, provide the demonstrative with an appropriate sense. To understand a demonstrative, is to be able to supply a sense for it on each occasion, which determines as reference the value the demonstrative has on that occasion.[4] This is, I think, as near as we are likely to come to what Frege had in mind.

There is a problem here, with no analog in the case of proper names. One can attach the same sense to a proper name, once and for all. But, since the demonstrative takes a different value on different occasions, different senses must be supplied. So the demonstrative could not be regarded as an abbreviation, or something like an abbreviation, for some appropriate description.

But still, can we not say that for each person, the sense of the demonstrative "today" for that person on a given day, is just the sense of one of the descriptions *D* (or some combination of all the descriptions) such that on that day he believes,

Today is *D*.

One objection to this, is that we seem to be explaining the senses of sentences containing demonstratives in terms of beliefs whose natural expressions contain demonstratives. But there are three more serious problems.

The first problem might be called the *irrelevancy of belief.*[5] The sense I associate with my use of a demonstrative does not determine the thought expressed by a sentence containing that demonstrative.

Suppose I believe that today is the fourteenth of October, 1976. From that it does not follow that, when I utter

Today is sunny and bright

I express the thought

The fourteenth of October is sunny and bright.

For suppose today is really the fifteenth, cloudy, and dull. Then what I have said is wrong, whatever the weather was like on the fourteenth.

The second problem, we might call the *nonnecessity of belief.* I can express a thought with "Today is sunny and bright"—that is, say something for which the question of truth arises—whether or not I associate any correct sense at all with "today." I may have no idea at all what day it is, and not be able, without recourse to "today" or other demonstratives, to say anything about today at all, that does not describe dozens of other days equally well.

Both of these problems are illustrated by Rip Van Winkle. When he awakes on October 20, 1823, and says with conviction,

Today is October 20, 1803

the fact that he is sure he is right doesn't make him right, as it would if the thought expressed were determined by the sense he associated with "today." And, what is really the same point from a different angle, he doesn't fail to be wrong, as would be the case if "today" had to be associated with a completing sense which determined the value of "today" as reference, before the question of truth arose for sentences in which it occurs.

To state my third objection, the *nonsufficiency of belief,* I shall shift to an example using the demonstrative "I." I do so because the objection is clearest with respect to this demonstrative, and because some awareness of this problem might help explain how consideration of "I" led Frege to incommunicable senses.

Let us imagine David Hume, alone in his study, on a particular afternoon in 1775, thinking to himself, "I wrote the *Treatise.*" Can anyone *else* apprehend the thought he apprehended by thinking this? First note that what he thinks is true. So no one could apprehend the same thought, unless they apprehended a true thought. Now suppose Heimson is a bit crazy, and thinks himself to be David Hume. Alone in his study, he says to himself, "I wrote the *Treatise.*" However much his inner life may, at that moment, resemble Hume's on that afternoon in 1775, the fact remains: Hume was right, Heimson is wrong. Heimson cannot think the very thought to himself that Hume thought to himself, by using the very same sentence.

Now suppose Frege's general account of demonstratives is right. Then it seems that, by using the very same sense that Hume supplied for "I," Heimson should be able to think the same thought, without using "I," that Hume did using "I." He will just have to find a true sentence, which expresses the very thought Hume was thinking, when he thought to himself, "I wrote the *Treatise.*" But there just does not seem to be such a thought.

Suppose Heimson thinks to himself, "The author of the *Inquiries* wrote the *Treatise.*" This is ture, for the sense used to complete the sense of "( ) wrote the *Treatise*" determines Hume not Heimson as reference. But it seems clear that Hume could acknowledge "I wrote the *Treatise*" as true, while rejecting, "The author of the *Inquiries* wrote the *Treatise.*" He might have forgotten that he wrote the *Inquiries;* perhaps Hume had episodes of forgetfulness in 1775. But then the thought Heimson thinks, and the one Hume apprehended, are not the same after all, by the identification of thoughts with senses, and the criterion of difference for senses.

One might suppose that, while there is no particular sentence of this sort that must have had, for Hume, the same cognitive value as "I wrote the *Treatise*," there must be some such sentence or other that would have had the same cognitive value for him.

But I see no reason to suppose this is so. For now we have reached just the point where the first objection takes hold. There is no reason to believe we are on each occasion each equipped with some nondemonstrative equivalent of the demonstratives we use and understand. This goes for "I" as well as "today." After all, as I am imagining Heimson, he does not have any correct demonstrative free description of himself at hand. Every correct demonstrative free description he is willing to apply to himself refers to Hume instead. I'm not at all sure that I have one for myself.

To keep the identification between thought and sense intact, Frege must provide us with a completing sense. But then his account of demonstratives becomes implausible.

I I

Frege follows his general discussion of demonstratives by saying that "I" gives rise to certain questions. He then makes the point, with the examples concerning Dr. Lauben discussed above, that various persons might associate various senses with the same proper name, if the person were presented to them in various ways. This discussion seems intended to prepare the way for the startling claim about thoughts about ourselves,

Now everyone is presented to himself in a particular and primitive way, in which he is presented to no-one else. So, when Dr. Lauben thinks that he has been wounded, he will probably take as a basis this primitive way in which he is presented to himself. And only Dr. Lauben himself can grasp thoughts determined in this way. But now he may want to communicate with others. He cannot communicate a thought which he alone can grasp. Therefore, if he now says 'I have been wounded', he must use the 'I' in a sense which can be grasped by others, perhaps in the sense of 'he is speaking to you at this moment', by doing which he makes the associated conditions of his utterance serve for the expression of his thought. [T, 25–26]

Frege's doctrine appears to be this. When I use "I" to communicate, it works like other demonstratives, and perhaps could even be re-

placed by some phrase which included only other demonstratives. The sense would be completed in whatever way is appropriate for sentences containing these demonstratives. When I use "I" to think about myself, however, it has an incommunicable sense.

This is not quite right, for Frege would not have thought it necessary, in order to think about myself, to use language at all. It is at this point that Frege makes his famous remark, about how the battle with language makes his task difficult, in that he can only give his readers the thought he wants them to examine dressed up in linguistic form.

Nevertheless, it seems clear that Frege thinks there are senses, for each of us, that determine us as reference, which are incommunicable, and which would be the natural sense to associate with "I" if it did happen to be used, not merely to communicate with others, but [to] think about oneself.

I suggest this doctrine about "I" is a reaction to the problems just mentioned, the third in particular. I am not at all certain that this is so. Philosophers have come to hold somewhat similar views about the self, beliefs about oneself, and "I," without thinking as rigorously as Frege did about these matters. Perhaps Frege had adopted some such view independently of his thinking about demonstratives, and simply wished to show he could accommodate it. It seems to me more likely, however, that Frege was led to this view by his own philosophical work, in particular by some realization of the problems I have discussed for his general account, as they apply particularly to "I." All three problems turned on the failure to find a suitable description for the value of the demonstrative, whose sense would complete the sense of the sentence in just the right way. If the sense we are looking for is private and incommunicable, it is no wonder the search was in vain.

But the appeal to private and incommunicable senses cannot, I think, be a satisfactory resolution of the problem.

In the first place, I see no reason to believe that "everyone is presented to himself in a particular and primitive way." Or at least, no reason to accept this, with such a reading that it leads to incommunicable senses.

Suppose M is the private and incommunicable sense, which is to serve as the sense of

"I" when I think about myself. M cannot be a complex sense, resulting from the compounding of simpler, generally accessible senses. For it seems clear that it is sufficient, to grasp the result of such compounding, that one grasp the senses compounded. So M will have to be, as Frege says, primitive.

A sense corresponds to an aspect or mode of presentation. (SR, 57, 58) There are, I hope, ways in which I am presented to myself, that I am presented to no one else, and aspects of me that I am aware of, that no one else is aware of. But this is not sufficient for Frege's purposes.

Suppose that only I am aware of the scratchiness of a certain fountain pen. Still, "thing which is scratchy" does not uniquely pick out this pen; this pen may not be the only one which falls under the concept this phrase stands for, though perhaps the only one of which I am aware. Similarly, just because there is some aspect, such that only I am aware that I have it, and M is the sense corresponding to that aspect, it does not follow that M determines as reference a concept that only I fall under, or that *the M,* (by which I mean the result of combining the sense of "the" with M), is a sense which determines just me as reference, and can appropriately be associated with my utterances of "I."

What is needed is a primitive aspect of me, which is not simply one that only I am aware of myself as having, but that I alone have. While there are doubtless complex aspects that only I have, and primitive aspects, that only I am aware of myself as having, I see no reason to believe there are primitive aspects, that only I have. Even if there were, if they were incommunicable, I should have no way of knowing there were, since I hardly ask others if they happened to have *mine.* So I shouldn't know that *the M* determined me as reference. But I do know that I am thinking about me, when I use the word "I" in thinking to myself.

My second point in opposition to incommunicable senses, is that the third objection does not merely apply to "I," but to at least one other demonstrative, "now." However one may feel about one's private and unique aspects, Frege's doctrine must appear less plausible when it is seen that it must be extended to other demonstratives.

Suppose the department meeting is scheduled for noon, September 15, 1976. Then only at that time could we say something true with (5).

(5) The meeting starts now.

Now consider any of the informationally equivalent thoughts we might have had the day before, for example (6).

(6) The meeting starts at noon, September 15, 1976.

It seems that one could accept this [the] day before, and continue to accept it right through the meeting, without ever accepting (5), and even rejecting it firmly precisely at noon, simply by completely losing track of time. So (5) and (6) express different senses, and so different thoughts. And it seems this would be true, no matter what nondemonstrative informational equivalent we came up with instead of (6). So with "now," as with "I," it is not sufficient, to grasp the thought expressed with a demonstrative, to grasp an informational equivalent with a complete sense. Frege will have to have, for each time, a primitive and particular way in which it is presented to us at that time, which gives rise to thoughts accessible only at that time, and expressible, at it, with "now." This strikes me as very implausible. An appeal to incommunicable senses won't serve to patch up Frege's treatment.

I will conclude by sketching an alternative treatment of these problems. I try to show just how these recent examples motivate a break between sense and thought, and how, once that break is made, senses can be treated as roles, thoughts as information, and the other examples we have discussed handled.

III

Consider some of the things Hume might have thought to himself,

I am David Hume
This is Edinburgh
It is now 1775.

We would say of Hume, when he thought such things, that he knew *who* he was, *where* he was, and *when* it was. I shall call these self locating beliefs. The objections, posed in the last section to Frege's account of demonstratives, may be put in the following way: Having a self locating belief does not consist in believing a Fregean thought.

We can see that having such beliefs *could* not consist *wholly* in believing Fregean thoughts. Consider Frege's timeless realm of generally accessible thoughts. If Hume's knowing he was Hume, consisted in his believing certain true thoughts in this realm, then it would seem that anyone else could know that *he* was Hume, just by believing those same thoughts. But only Hume can know, or even truly believe, that he is Hume. Analogous remarks apply to his knowing where he was, and when it was.

Either there are some thoughts only Hume can apprehend, and his believing he is Hume consists in believing those thoughts, or self locating knowledge does not consist wholly in believing some true subset of the Fregean thoughts. Frege chose the first option; let's see what happens when we choose the second.

We accept that there is no thought only Hume can apprehend. Yet only he can know he is Hume. It must not just be the thought that he thinks, but the way that he thinks it, that sets him apart from the rest of us. Only Hume can think a true thought, by saying to himself,

I am Hume.

Self locating knowledge, then requires not just the grasping of certain thoughts, but the grasping of them via the senses of certain sentences containing demonstratives.

To firmly embed in our minds the importance that thinking a thought via one sense rather than another can have, let us consider another example. An amnesiac, Rudolf Lingens, is lost in the Stanford library. He reads a number of things in the library, including a biography of himself, and a detailed account of the library in which he is lost. He believes any Fregean thought you think might help him. He still won't know who he is, and where he is, no matter how much knowledge he piles up, until that moment when he is ready to say,

This place is aisle five, floor six, of Main Library, Stanford.

I am Rudolf Lingens.

If self locating knowledge consists not merely in believing certain thoughts, but believing them by apprehending certain senses, then senses cannot be thoughts. Otherwise it would make no sense to say that Hume and Heimson can apprehend all the same thoughts, but Hume can do so by apprehending different senses.

Let us then see how things begin to resolve themselves when this identification is given up. Let us speak of *entertaining* a sense, and apprehending a thought. So different thoughts may be apprehended, in different contexts, by entertaining the same sense (without supposing that it is an incomplete sense, somehow supplemented by a sense completer in the context), and the same thought, by entertaining different senses.

By breaking the connection between senses and thoughts, we give up any reason not to take the options closed to Frege. We can take the sense of a sentence containing a demonstrative to be a role, rather than a Fregean complete sense, and thoughts to be the new sort, individuated by object and incomplete sense, rather [than] Fregean thoughts. Though senses considered as roles, and thoughts considered as information, cannot be identified, each does its job in a way that meshes with the other. To have a thought we need an object and an incomplete sense. The demonstrative in context gives us the one, the rest of the sentence the other. The role of the entire sentence will lead us to Truth by leading us to a true thought, that is just in case the object falls under the concept determined as reference by the incomplete sense.[6]

Let us see how some of the examples we have discussed are handled.

We must suppose that both Hume and Heimson can entertain the same senses, and think the same thoughts. The difference between them is that they do not apprehend the same thoughts when they entertain the same senses. When Heimson entertains the sense of "I am the author of the *Treatise*" he apprehends the thought consisting of Heimson and the sense of "( ) is the author of the *Treatise*." This thought is false. When Hume entertains the same sense, he apprehends the thought consisting of Hume and the sense of "( ) is the author of the *Treatise*," which is true. Hume is right, Heimson is crazy.

Similarly, only at twelve noon can someone think the thought consisting of noon and the sense of "The meeting starts at ( )" by entertaining the sense of "the meeting starts now."

Why should we have a special category of self locating knowledge? Why should we care how someone apprehends a thought, so long as he does? I can only sketch the barest suggestion of an answer here. We use senses to individuate psychological states, in explaining and predicting action. It is the sense entertained, and not the thought apprehended, that is tied to human action. When you and I entertain the sense of "A bear is about to attack me," we behave similarly. We both roll up in a ball and try to be as still as possible. Different thoughts apprehended, same sense entertained, same behavior. When you and I both apprehend the thought that I am about to be attacked by a bear, we behave differently. I roll up in a ball, you run to get help. Same thought apprehended, different sense entertained, different behavior. Again, when you believe that the meeting begins on a given day at noon by entertaining, the day before, the sense of "the meeting begins tomorrow at noon," you are idle. Apprehending the same thought the next day, by entertaining the sense of "the meeting begins now," you jump up from your chair and run down the hall.

What of the indirect reference? Is the indirect reference of a sentence containing a demonstrative in the scope of such a cognitive verb, the sense or the thought?

It seems, a priori, that the "believes that" construction (to pick a particular verb) could work either way. That is,

A believes that *S*

might be designed to tell us the sense *A* entertains, or the thought *A* apprehends. The first seems a little more efficient. If we know the sense entertained, we can compute the thought apprehended, given the believer's context.

Nevertheless, it is surely the thought apprehended that is the indirect reference of a sentence containing a demonstrative in the scope of "believes." Consider (7), (8), and (9),

(7) I believe that Russia and Canada quarrelled today.

(8) Mary believed that Russia and Canada quarrelled today.

(9) Mary believed that Russia and Canada quarrelled yesterday.

Suppose Mary utters (7) on August 1, and I want to report the next day on what she believed. If I want to report the sense entertained, I should use (8). But this gives the wrong result. Clearly I would use (9). To get from the sentence embedded in (9), to the thought Mary apprehended, we take the value of the demonstrative in the context of the belief reporter, not in the context of the believer.

It has been suggested that we try to use the sense entertained by the believer in reporting his belief, whenever possible. What we have just said does not conflict with this. The point is simply that the function of thought identification dominates the function of sense identification, and when we use demonstratives, there is almost always a conflict.

There will be no conflict, when one is dealing with eternal sentences, or when one is reporting one's own current beliefs. The need for distinguishing sense from thought will not be forced to our attention, so long as we concentrate on such cases.

Let us now consider the Morning Star example.

Mary says "I believe that is the Morning Star" in the morning while pointing at Venus, and "I believe that is not the Morning Star" at night while pointing at Venus. It seems that Mary, though believing falsely, has not changed her mind, and does not believe a contradiction.

As long as we think of thoughts as senses, it will seem that anyone who understands the relevant sentences, will not believe both a thought and its negation. So long as we think of senses as thoughts, we shall think that anyone who accepts a sense at one time, and its negation at another, must have changed her mind. The correct principle is simply that no thoughtful person will accept a sense and its negation in the same context, since just by understanding the language, she should realize that she would thereby believe both a thought and its negation.

We should take "believing a contradiction," in the sense in which thoughtful people don't do it, to mean accepting senses of the forms *S* and not-*S*, relative to the same context of utterance. Mary doesn't do this; she accepts *S* in the morning, not-*S* in the evening. Has she then changed her mind? This must mean coming to disbelieve a thought once believed. We shouldn't take it to mean coming to reject a sense once accepted. I can reject "Today is sunny and bright" today, though I accepted it yesterday, without changing my mind about anything. So Mary hasn't changed her mind, either.

What she does do, is believe a thought and its negation. (Here we take the negation of a thought consisting of a certain object and incomplete sense, to be the thought consisting of the same object, and the negation of the incomplete sense.) I am inclined to think that only the habit of identifying sense and thought makes this seem implausible.

I have tried to suggest how, using the concepts of sense, thought, and indirect reference in a way compatible with the way Frege introduced them, but incompatible with his identifications, sentences containing demonstratives can be handled. I do not mean to imply that Frege could have simply made these alterations, while leaving the rest of his system intact. The idea of individuating thoughts by objects, or sequences of objects, would be particularly out of place in his system. The identification of thought with complete sense was not impulsive, but the result of pressure from many directions. I do not claim to have traced the problems that come to surface with demonstratives back to their ultimate origins in Frege's system.

I V

I have argued that Frege's identification of senses of sentences with thoughts leads to grave problems when sentences containing demonstratives are considered. The utterance of such a sentence in a context seems to yield only an incomplete sense and an object, not a complete sense of the sort a Fregean thought is supposed to be. He probably supposed that context supplies not just an object, but somehow a completing sense. There seems no place for such a sense to be found, save in the mind of the person who apprehends the thought expressed by the sentence. But to understand such a sentence, it is neither necessary nor sufficient to have grasped, and associated with the value of the demonstrative, any such sense. Frege's appeal to incommunicable senses in the case of "I," is probably an implausible attempt to deal with these problems. What is needed is to give up the identification of sense expressed with thought expressed. This would allow us to see the sense as a procedure for determining reference from a context, and the thought as identified by the incomplete sense and the value of the demonstrative. The identification of the thought, with the indirect reference of the sentence [in] the scope of a cognitive verb, need not be given up

ACKNOWLEDGMENTS

Discussions of these issues with Robert Adams, Michael Bratman, Tyler Burge, Keith Donnellan, Dagfinn Føllesdal, Alvin Goldman, Holly Goldman, David Kaplan, and Julius Moravcsik were enormously helpful. This paper was written while I was a Guggenheim Fellow, and on sabbatical leave from Stanford University. I thank both institutions for their support.

NOTES

1. The following abbreviations are used for works cited in the text. 'T' for Gottlob Frege "The Thought: A Logical Inquiry," reprinted in P. F. Strawson *Philosophical Logic* (Oxford, 1967), 17–38. This translation, by A. M. and Marcelle Quinton, appeared originally in *Mind,* Vol. 65 (1956), pp. 289–311. The original, "Der Gedanke. Eine logische Untersuchung," appeared in *Beiträge zur Philosophie des deutschen Idealismus,* I (1918), 58–77. 'SR' for Frege "On Sense and Reference," in Max Black and Peter Geach (eds.), *Translations from the Philosophical Writings of Gottlob Frege* (Oxford, 1960). Translated by Max Black. The original,

"Über Sinn und Bedeutung," appeared in *Zeitschrift für Philosophie and philosophische Kritik,* L (1892), 25–50. 'CT' for "Compound Thoughts," in E. D. Klemke (ed.), Essays on Frege. Translated by R. H. Stoothoff. The original, "Gedankenfuge," appeared in *Beiträge zur Philosophie des deutschen Idealismus,* III (1923), 36–51. 'F' for Micheal Dummett, *Frege* (London: Duckworth, 1973).

2. Here and elsewhere I assume, for the sake of simplicity of exposition, that we are considering sentences containing no more than one demonstrative. Given the notion of a sequence of objects, there would be no difficulties in extending various suggestions and options for the general case. In some of the examples I use, additional demonstratives are really needed. 'Lauben is wounded,' for example, still needs a time indication.

3. This notion is taken from A. W. Burks, "Icon, Index, and Symbol," *Philosophy and Phenomenological Research,* Vol. IX, (1949), p. 685. In this pioneering and illuminating work on demonstratives, Burks emphasizes the ineliminability of demonstratives.

4. This interpretation was suggested to me by Dagfinn Føllesdal.

5. In the three problems that follow, and the balance of the paper, I am much in debt to a series of very illuminating papers by Hector-Neri Castañeda. The fullest statement of his view is in "Indicators and Quasi-Indicators," *American Philosophical Quarterly,* Vol. 4 (1967):85–100. See also "He: A Study in the Logic of Self-Consciousness," *Ratio,* VIII (1966):130–157, and "On the Logic of Attributions of Self-Knowledge to Others," *Journal of Philosophy,* LXV (1968):439–456. All the examples of what I later call "self locating knowledge" are adaptations from Castañeda, and the difficulties they raise for Frege's account are related to points Castañeda has made.

6. The notions of the role of a sentence, and of a thought as information, are similar to the concepts of *character* and *context* in David Kaplan's "On the Logic of Demonstratives," xeroxed, UCLA Department of Philosophy. This is no accident, as my approach to these matters was formed, basically, as a result of trying to extract from this work of Kaplan's, and Kaplan himself, answers to questions posed by Castañeda's work. One should not assume that Kaplan would agree with my criticisms of Frege, my treatment of self locating knowledge, or the philosophical motivation I develop for distinguishing between sense and thought.

10

How to Bridge the Gap
Between Meaning and Reference

HOWARD K. WETTSTEIN

1. INTRODUCTION

There is a temptation, during a revolution, to
minimize the significant differences among
the revolutionary parties. The activists themselves, due to their deep and unanimous opposition to the old regime and their exhilara-
tion at recent successes, often find it difficult
to overcome the illusion of general agreement
on fundamentals. The past two decades has
been a period of revolutionary activity in the
philosophy of language. The members of the
old regime are, as it were, the proponents of
the Fregean picture of how words hook up
with the world, the idea that singular terms express descriptive concepts and refer to those
items that satisfy the concepts. Frege's perspective has been vigorously attacked by those
recently called by one anthologist "the new
theorists of reference," originally Donnellan,
Kaplan, Kripke, and Putnam. Singular terms
refer, according to the latter theorists, not by
expressing concepts but in some much more
immediate and direct way. The definite description, Frege's paradigm, has been replaced
by a new paradigm or two, the demonstrative

expression and/or the Millian proper name
that merely tags but does describe its bearer.

I plead guilty, as one of the advocates of the
newer approach, to the charge of laboring
under the illusion of agreement on fundamentals. I became suspicious, however, when
I was accused of advocating the causal theory
of reference, a view that seemed foreign to my
thinking but was supposedly central to or even
definitive of the new approach.[1] The question
I shall address, the question mentioned in the
title, will highlight profound disagreements
among the new theorists and will provide an
opportunity to further develop the direct reference approach. I shall restrict my discussion
to indexical reference, specifically to reference
by means of pronouns and demonstratives.

That there is a gap between meaning and
reference in the case of indexical expressions
has been a cornerstone of the new approach.
Consider the first person pronoun. Each of us
can use it to refer to ourselves, yet it is not ambiguous. Its lexical meaning remains constant
from your use of it to mine. I am not then the
referent of my use of 'I' simply in virtue of its
lexical meaning. There is, so to speak, not

Howard K. Wettstein, "How to Bridge the Gap Between Meaning and Reference," *Synthese* 58 (1984):63–84. Copyright © 1984 by D. Reidel Publishing Company. Reprinted by permission of Kluwer Academic Publishers.

enough to this meaning, as opposed to the meaning of, say, 'the first President of the United States,' to determine one individual rather than another. The same is true for the demonstrative 'that.' 'That' can be used to refer to anything at all. Its lexical meaning does not vary, however, from use to use. The reference of an utterance of 'that' is thus not determined solely by its meager lexical meaning. What exactly bridges the gap between the *meager* lexical meaning of such an indexical expression and its *determinate* reference? What factor(s) enter into the determination of the reference of an indexical, over and above its meaning?[2]

The answer I shall give, as a first approximation, is that the gap is to [be] bridged by features of the context of utterance. My idea is that the reference is determined by the very features which make the reference available to the auditor.[3] I shall argue for this idea by way of criticizing its two main opponents:

(1) *The causal theory of reference.* Although this title is often used sloppily to characterize the view of virtually any opponent of the Fregean description paradigm, it more accurately refers to a view about reference that parallels other causal theories in philosophy, the causal theory of perception, knowledge, and so on. The causal theorist maintains that the gap is to be bridged by the existence of a causal connection between the utterance of the indexical and the referent. Specifically, the referent of a token of 'that' is the unique item that stands in the appropriate causal relation to the production of that token.[4]

(2) *The intentional theory.* Causal theories are often championed by physicalists who see such theories as offering hope for a reduction of apparently intentional, mental phenomena in terms of physical causation. A philosopher who is disinclined to pursue such a reductionist program might insist that reference is irreducibly intentional. One form such a proposal may take yields another answer to our question. The gap between meaning and reference is bridged, on this view, by the fact that the speaker utters the indexical with the intention of communicating about a particular item he has in mind. What makes some particular book the referent of 'That is an interesting book' is not, on this view, anything about the causal history of the utterance, but rather something about the mental state of the speaker, specifically his intention to refer to the item he has in mind.[5]

One of the recurrent themes in the new theory of reference, one that it shares with the approach of Wittgenstein, is that an individualistic or agent-centered picture of language and thought is inadequate and needs to be replaced or at least supplemented by a picture that sees language as a social institution.[6] To maintain that the reference of an indexical expression is determined by the causal history of the utterance or by the referential intentions of the speaker is to maintain an individualistic view, at least by comparison with my approach. The reference of a token of 'that' is determined, on these views, by considerations *about the speaker,* specifically his causal history or intentional states. Features of the context of utterance, e.g., interactions between the speaker and addressee like pointing gestures, by means of which the addressee interprets the demonstrative utterance, play no semantic role. Such contextual cues may facilitate communication but they do not make it the case that one thing rather than another is the referent. My view, however, is that such contextual cues and indeed a whole range of extra-contextual cues, provided, e.g., by the social and cultural environment, have semantic significance. It is by means of such cues that the gap between meaning and reference is to be bridged.

Not only are natural languages *social* institutions, they are social *institutions.* I shall emphasize the institutional character of natural language in the following respect. The (or at least a) primary purpose of natural language is to allow for communication concerning the items speakers have in mind and about which they wish to inform others, ask questions, and so on.[7] Natural languages, however, like other *institutions,* e.g. the law, provide for the fulfillment of the institution's primary functions by means of a complex system of rules and conventions. The institutional rules and conventions, although their *point* is to facilitate communication, attain a life of their own once instituted. It is thus important for one who wishes to communicate his beliefs by means of

English sentences to find institutionally acceptable means for doing so. Failing to find such means, he may find himself having "said," in an institutional sense, something other than what he meant, even something other than what he succeeded in conveying. His auditor, that is, may be able to tell what he is getting at despite his having said, strictly speaking, something quite different. A frequently noted example involves a speaker's using a term, meaning by it something other than what it means in the language. Final exams in introductory philosophy courses provide many examples. I shall discuss below a less frequently noted example of the distinction between what was said, strictly speaking, and what was meant or intended. This sort of example will play a crucial role in my arguments against the intentional theory.

2. PURE INDEXICALS

Kaplan introduces a useful distinction within the class of indexical expressions.[8] I begin by considering those expressions which Kaplan classifies as "pure indexicals," e.g., 'I', 'now', 'here', and 'today'. In Section 3, I turn to Kaplan's "demonstratives," e.g., 'this', 'that', 'he', 'she.' Pure indexicals and demonstratives are similar in that both are "context sensitive", as opposed to, say, "the first President of the United States", the reference of which does not vary with the context of utterance. Indexicals are unlike demonstratives, however, in that the reference of a given indexical varies from context to context in a very regular way. 'I' always refers to what Kaplan calls the "agent" of the context, the speaker or writer. Demonstratives like 'that' exhibit no such regular variation of reference. What can be said of the reference of 'that' in every context?[9]

Let us begin with 'now'. Waiting for the babysitter to arrive I say, "The movie is starting now." 'Now' picks out a certain time.[10] How does that happen? How does the reference of 'now' get determined? Is it a matter of the right sort of causal relation holding between the referent and the utterance? Implausible. It is hard enough to think of times as *referents* let alone thinking of them as standing in causal relations. Perhaps some account can be

given according to which a time can stand in some (and indeed in *the* appropriate) causal relation to an utterance of 'now'. Causal relations between times and utterances are, in any case, a far cry from the standard examples causal theorists give to motivate their view, and it is not clear how references to times are to be accommodated. Another example: "Here I sit." Think about 'I'. What determines its reference? A causal realtion? What are the terms of this relation? Michael Devitt states that first person references are to be accounted for by the causal relations in which one stands to oneself. Devitt mentions introspection as the relevant causal process.[11] It is far from clear, however, that first person references are always, or even typically, related to introspection. Devitt's view here certainly requires detailed development and defense. Devitt, though, mentions it only in passing.

There is, in any case, a much simpler and more natural account of how the reference of a pure indexical, 'I' e.g., gets determined.[12] It is a rule of our language, internalized by every competent speaker, that 'I' refers to the agent of the context.[13] Thus I am the referent of some appropriate utterance of the first-person pronoun not because I stand in some causal relation to myself, but rather because *I uttered it*. It is then a fact about the context which bridges the gap between meaning and reference.

Am I the referent of 'I' because I uttered it, or rather because, as the intentional theorist would have it, I intended to communicate about myself, I had myself in mind?[14] My strategy against the intentional theory will be to show that a speaker who refers using 'I', refers to himself, even if he has someone other than himself in mind. Examples involving mistaken identity beliefs seem like promising terrain, examples in which a speaker believes he is someone else and intends to speak of this other person. Consider Ahern, an insane historian who believes he is de Gaulle. If we are to generate an example in which Ahern has de Gaulle in mind when he uses 'I', we need to proceed carefully for despite Ahern's crazy belief, he, like the rest of us, intends to speak of himself when he uses 'I'—at least most of the time. If someone feels uncomfortable due to the fact that he has not eaten for hours and says, "I am hungry," he presumably has himself in mind even if he is suffering from amnesia and thus "does not know who he is," and even if, like Ahern, he takes himself to be de Gaulle.[15]

Imagine, however, that Ahern is lecturing on modern European history and, in the course of speaking about de Gaulle's accomplishments, he says, ". . . and then I marched triumphantly into Paris." Such a remark may be motivated by different factors. Ahern may be bragging. The point of his remark may be that *he* did it. Alternatively his interest may be in the history of the period. His point may be that *de Gaulle* did it and he, Ahern, said "I" only because 'I', given his mistaken beliefs, seemed the contextually appropriate expression for referring to de Gaulle. We might even imagine that he was trying to keep his belief about de Gaulle's identity a secret but that he slipped and said "I", thus revealing his secret to the class. Perhaps the lecture is accompanied by a silent film of de Gaulle's return. Just as Ahern makes his remark, he points to de Gaulle. It is this history lecture case, as opposed to the bragging case, that we are after. Here Ahern has de Gaulle rather than himself in mind.[16]

What conclusions can we draw from this example? Ahern's remark, when he says, "I marched triumphantly into Paris," is, strictly speaking, false. This is not, however, to say that everything he meant was false or that everything he succeeded in communicating to his audience was false. After all, he intended to communicate that de Gaulle marched triumphantly into Paris, and he may very well have communicated this, e.g., if his students were aware of his delusion. Nevertheless, he has utilized the institutional apparatus of English to convey his beliefs and, in doing so, has asserted a false proposition. What he said, strictly speaking, was false. Two conclusions follow, both of which are damaging to the intentional theory. First, the speaker's uttering a singular term intending to communicate about something, having it in mind, is not a sufficient condition for reference to it. Ahern had de Gaulle in mind but nevertheless failed to refer to him.[17] Second, having oneself in mind is not even necessary for first person pronominal reference. Ahern referred to himself despite his failure to have himself in mind.[18]

The intentional theorist may at this point resist the idea that a speaker can use the first person pronoun competently and have someone else in mind. Ahern, since he believes he *is* de Gaulle, it may be urged, does have himself in mind.[19] Such resistance is, however, misplaced. One who wishes to speak about a particular item he has in mind but has mistaken it for a different item, will often use a singular term that conventionally applies not to his intended referent, but to the item he has confused it with. Someone says, "What is that man doing out there?" Another responds, mistaking the man they see for Jones, "It looks like Jones. Jones appears to be raking leaves." The second speaker wishes to answer a question about "the man out there". Yet due to his mistaken belief, he uses a term which fails to conventionally apply to that man.[20] Similarly, if I mistakenly take myself to be de Gaulle, I may use his name when I really want to convey information about myself, as in "De Gaulle is hungry." Given that same mistaken belief, I may use a term that applies to me, e.g., 'I' when I really want to communicate about de Gaulle. Surely the first person pronoun is not immune to this intended reference vs. conventional application phenomenon.

Nevertheless the claim that the deranged teacher has de Gaulle in mind, that de Gaulle is *the* intended referent, needs to be qualified.[21] There is surely a sense in which he also intends to communicate about himself.[22] After all, he thinks he *is* de Gaulle; he said, "*I* marched triumphantly. . . ." Why not say that the speaker, in such cases, has both individuals in mind? Indeed, I think we should say this—with one qualification: the speaker does not have them in mind equally. This may be brought out by noting that the history lecturer, who genuinely intends to be teaching about de Gaulle and is not interested in bragging, intends to communicate about himself only insofar as he takes himself to be de Gaulle. Were he to learn about his mistake (and somehow not become catatonic), he could still accomplish his communicative goal by simply substituting 'de Gaulle' for 'I'. His intending to communicate information about himself is thus a *subsidiary* intention.[23]

Cases of divergence of intended reference and conventional application often involve two havings-in-mind, one primary and one subsidiary.[24] Furthermore, when a speaker refers by using 'I', since he knows that 'I' always refers to the utterer, he will surely have himself in mind at least in the subsidiary sense. This does not, however, provide any support for the intentional theorist. The latter maintained that when the point of the historian's utterance was not to brag about himself but was to convey information about de Gaulle, then de Gaulle was the referent of 'I', that the individual had *primarily* in mind. This thesis is just what the Ahern example shows to be false.[25]

I conclude that the intentional theorist is mistaken, at least with regard to first person pronomial reference, and indeed, he is mistaken with regard to references by the other expressions Kaplan classifies as pure indexicals, e.g., 'here' and 'now', for my argument is applicable to them as well. The gap between the meaning and reference of a pure indexical is to be bridged neither by the speaker's causal connections nor by his mental states but rather by publicly available features of the context of utterance.[26]

3. DEMONSTRATIVES: CRITICAL REMARKS

The linguistic rule that governs 'I' specifies its reference in terms of a simple, noncausal, nonintentional property of the context. The singular terms with Kaplan calls "demonstratives" are quite a different matter, or so it seems. It appears to be difficult to specify the reference of 'this', 'that', 'he', or 'she,' in terms of some such property. How then does the reference of 'that', e.g., get determined?

The causal theory of reference, while it seemed so highly counterintuitive for the pure indexicals, does not seem so here. One who finds the causal-theoretic approach generally appealing in philosophy might readily suppose that the referent of "He is a nice man" is the unique man who occupies just the right place in the causal history of the utterance. Even here, however, the causal theory will not do. A speaker who is causally isolated from an entity can still refer to it by uttering a demonstrative while pointing to it. Even blindfolded and thus visually cut off from one's surroundings, one can point and say things like "That is a

tree," "That is a cow," and so on. (Imagine this occurring on a picnic with one's children.) Such guesses would be either true or false, and so one would have referred despite his lack of causal connection with the items pointed to. Colin McGinn gives an example of a factory inspector who is supposed to approve or disapprove of each car that comes off the assembly line. "That one is roadworthy," he typically says. The inspector momentarily looks away as a new car appears. He nevertheless makes the same remark with his usual gesture in the direction of the assembly line. He is not causally connected with the new car in any appropriate way but he surely refers to it. If the car is defective, he can be accused of having said something false.[27]

How about an intentional theory of demonstratives? Suppose someone says, "He is a nice man," referring to some man across the room, in a room full of people. It is not implausible to suppose that what makes one of the men in the room the referent of 'he' is that the speaker had him in mind. Nevertheless the intentional account is no more adequate here than it was in the case of the pure indexicals.

A variation on the theme of intended reference/conventional application will provide an example. A speaker wishes to say something about a certain man, Jones, who he mistakenly thinks he sees off in the distance. Jones has recently had open-heart surgery and the speaker has heard that Jones has foolishly been exerting himself raking leaves. He says, pointing to the man who he takes to be Jones but who is actually Smith, "That is a self-destructive man. He has been raking leaves against his doctor's orders." Here the speaker actually has Jones, rather than the man he sees, primarily in mind. He intends to refer to "that man over there" only insofar as he takes him to be Jones. Were he to learn of his mistake he could still accomplish his communicative end by substituting 'Jones' for 'that'.

Jones, then, is the individual he has in mind in the primary sense. Nevertheless when he says, "That is a self-destructive man," he speaks falsely, for the man he points out, Smith, is, we may assume, in excellent physical and mental health. Primary havings-in-mind, just as with the pure indexicals, are neither sufficient for determining the reference of demonstratives (since the really self-destructive Jones was not referred to), nor are such havings-in-mind necessary (since Smith, the man pointed out but out primarily intended *was* referred to).[28]

4. DEMONSTRATIVES: POSITIVE REMARKS

Reference is socially determined in a deeper way than has been allowed for even by the new theorists of reference.[29] The causal and intentional views fall short precisely because they fail to recognize the semantic significance of, e.g., the speaker's communicational interactions. The very examples which show the inadequacy of causal/intentional views, cases of "blind pointing" (the picnic example) and the recent Smith-Jones case, strongly suggest that pointing gestures not only provide cues as to the reference, they actually determine the reference.[30]

Pointing, however, is not unique in playing both roles. The reference to Smith, the man in the distance, would remain unchanged if the speaker did not point but rather took advantage of the fact that Smith was the only individual in view. The reference would remain unchanged if there were a number of people in view but Smith was somehow prominent, say he was walking towards the speaker and auditor and waving in their direction. There are a host of such contextual features that provide cues to the auditor and, at the same time, enter into the determination of reference.[31]

The semantically significant cues, moreover, are not limited to those provided by the context of utterance.[32] Just as the fact that some individual is walking toward the speaker and auditor and waving can, in the right circumstances, both indicate and determine that he is the referent, so can the fact that they were just talking about someone, or that when they last spoke their conversation was dominated by a discussion of something, or that something has dominated their attention recently, even if they have not spoken about it. "I've been thinking about it and I can actually prove that he is wrong," might open a conversation with a colleague. Jimmy Carter might wake up in the middle of the night after his debate with Reagan and say to Rosalyn, "He really beat me. I could have done much better

at that." Relevant cues then can be provided by what the addressee knows about the speaker's interest, desires, history, and so on.[33]

Semantically significant cues *can be* provided by an extremely wide range of contextual and extra-contextual factors. This is not to say, however, that every bit of information that the addressee finds helpful in interpreting the utterance is semantically significant. The auditor in the Smith-Jones case, if he knows enough, might infer that the speaker, despite pointing to Smith, really had Jones in mind. The auditor might know that the speaker had been very upset at his sick friend Jones's behavior, that the man in the distance looks like Jones but is really Smith, and so on. These latter cues have bearing on the utterance's "interpretation," in some broad sense, but they do not affect the determination of what was, strictly speaking, said. Jones, although he was indicated by these cues, is not the referent but is merely the intended referent.

What distinguishes the semantically significant cues? Notice that the cues just mentioned, the ones that might have identified Jones as the *intended* referent, were clearly not the cues that the speaker was relying on to convey his intended reference. The cue that the speaker clearly relied upon was the pointing gesture, a cue that indicated Smith and not Jones, his intended referent. This suggests that the semantically significant cues are those that the speaker relied upon. The referent is the individual *these* cues identify, whether or not this is the intended referent, the individual these cues were intended to identify.[34]

This is not quite right, however, for a speaker is sometimes responsible for unintended cues. Suppose that our speaker walks up to Smith, stares straight at him, extends his finger right in Smith's face, and says, "That is a self-destructive man." No one, as I imagine the scene, could have any doubt that the speaker intends to ostensively indicate Smith. Unfortunately for all concerned, however, our speaker was merely stretching, his mind was elsewhere, and he intended to convey his reference by more subtle background cues, cues that indeed identify Jones, his intended referent. In such a case, I am strongly inclined to suppose that the speaker is responsible for his apparent pointing gesture and that Smith, the individual apparently pointed to, is the referent. If Smith is not self-destructive, then what the speaker has said, strictly speaking, is false.[35] One who utters a demonstrative is responsible, from the point of view of the natural language institution, for making his intended reference available to his addressee, and so he is responsible for the cues that a competent and attentive addressee would take him to be exploiting. The cues for which he is responsible, those that he, to all appearances, exploits, are the cues that determine the reference.[36]

The gap between meaning and reference is to be bridged by the cues that the competent and attentive addressee will reasonably take the speaker to be exploiting. My account, although it denies that intentions determine reference, does not deny the importance of speakers' intentions. Indeed the *point* of the institutionalized conventions I have been discussing is to facilitate communication concerning the items speakers have in mind and about which they intend to inform others, ask questions, and so on. In the most usual, everyday cases, moreover, people refer to the items they intend, the items they have in mind in the primary sense, and in such cases the referent is just the intended referent. It is in the unusual cases involving misidentification in which reference and intended reference can diverge.

Intentions other than referential intentions, moreover, play an important role on my view: the speaker's reliance on certain cues, that is, his intention to utilize certain cues, discussed above, as well as the intention to address a particular audience. A competent and attentive *bystander* might reasonably interpret an utterance very differently than does the *addressee,* due to, e.g., different visual perspectives on the speaker's pointing gesture or different bits of background knowledge that they would reasonably assume the speaker to be exploiting. What the speaker says, strictly speaking, and thus his reference, is determined by the cues available to the addressee. The bystander is irrelevant. What makes a particular individual "the addressee"? Here the speaker's intention to address a particular audience comes into play. This intention does not straightforwardly determine the addressee, however, any more than did the intention to utilize certain cues straightforwardly determine the semantically significant cues. If a speaker gives every indication that he is speaking to a particular person, then the latter is the addressee even if the speaker actually intends to be speaking to someone else. The addressee is the individual who it is reasonable to take the speaker to be addressing.

We have then a noncausal, nonintentional account of the reference of demonstratives. Referential intentions, however, seem to be particularly resistant to being banished as semantic determinants; they crop up in unexpected places. Kaplan notes that

. . . whenever I point at something, from the surveyor's point of view I point at many things. When I point at my son (and say 'I love [that]'), I may also be pointing at a book he is holding, his jacket, a button on his jacket, his skin, his heart, and his dog standing behind him—from a sureveyor's point of view.[37]

Kaplan's emphasis on the surveyor's point of view encourages a misconception of our practice of pointing. One can certainly indicate an object by a pointing gesture even though the object is not geometrically along a line projected from the pointing finger. Surely, it is enough that the referent be in a vaguely defined neighborhood of such a line. Thus one can refer to a man via an utterance of 'he' and a pointing gesture even if the gesture misses his right ear by a half inch—from the surveyor's point of view.[38] But now Kaplan's indeterminancy is multiplied. Not only is pointing indeterminate along the line of the pointing finger, it is indeterminate *around* that line. One can gesture with one's head, moreover, in such a fashion that there is not even a clear line of pointing, thus complicating matters even further.

I have argued that the reference of a demonstrative utterance accompanied by a pointing gesture depends not on what the speaker has in mind but rather on what his pointing gesture indicates. The gesture, we now see, fails to indicate a unique item. How then are we to account for the determinate reference, if not by appeal [to] the speaker's referential intention? The intentional theorist would still not be vindicated, for as the Smith-Jones case of Section 3 showed, the reference of a demonstrative is not determined by what the speaker has in mind. Nevertheless, such intentions would play an important role, that of resolving the indeterminacy of pointing gestures.[39]

The indeterminacy of pointing, however, does not necessitate such an appeal to referential intentions. I agree that ostention is indeterminate. Indeed it is irremediably indeterminate. This indeterminacy is not an illusion to be overcome by finding some factor which shows us that the ostention was determinate all along, e.g., the speaker's intention or some subtle and sophisticated rules of pointing. Still, the indeterminancy creates no problem. Imagine that I point to one of several women in the room and say, "She is the author of an important paper in decision theory." My pointing gesture, we may suppose, takes us to her, to a book she is holding, to her sweater, her kidney, and so on. Nevertheless, I have referred to her. Although the pointing gesture is indeterminate, it surely provides enough of a cue *given* that the demonstrative used was 'she' and that there are no other females in the range of the pointing. Imagine an utterance of "That one is the author of an important paper in decision theory," accompanied by a gesture towards the same woman. Again the gesture, considered in isolation, is indeterminate. It is a sufficient indication, however, in the presence of additional cues, e.g., the fact that the predicate indicates that the speaker intends to talk about a person and there is no other person in the range of the pointing. Other examples we might construct would have all sorts of cues contributing to the indicated-individual calculation.

Let us consider another problem with respect to which referential intentions threaten to intrude. What if the addressee, through no fault of his own, cannot ascertain the reference? When Kaplan points in his son's direction and says, "I love that," his auditor might not be able to tell whether Kaplan means that he loves his son or, rather, exploiting the fact that Kaplan has spent a good part of the day praising the very book that his son is carrying, *The Phenomenology of Spirit,* Kaplan means that he loves the book. Even where there is no puzzle about which cues are intended, the available cues may fail to determine a unique individual. An inadvertent speaker may try to indicate an individual by an utterance of 'he,'

accompanied by a vague gesture of his head, but may fail to do so because of the presence, unnoticed by the speaker, of two men in the range of the vague gesture. Should we allow that, at least in such cases, what is referred to depends upon what the speaker had in mind? After all, the addressee will typically ask such a speaker which item he was speaking about.

It is far from obvious, however, that we should take the speaker's response to settle the question of what it was that he strictly speaking, said. The question posed to him did not concern such institutional matters. The addressee's interest, in such conversational contexts, is in which item the speaker meant, which he had in mind, and his answer should be interpreted in this light. If the speaker fails to make his reference available, his speech act is defective, and not even the best intentions can repair the defect. The speaker, strictly speaking, has not asserted anything determinant, i.e., anything at all. The defect is, of course, negligible for the practical purposes of ordinary communication since the speaker when questioned easily supplies the information about which thing he meant. Here, as in the de Gaulle case, the speaker may be able to convey his message without having said it. Cases in which the speaker fails to make the reference available to the addressee do not require us to introduce intentions as semantic determinants.

5. CONCLUSION

I shall conclude by discussing a [. . .] proposal by Colin McGinn, in 'The Mechanism of Reference,' a proposal that, like my own, gives great weight to the context of utterance in the determination of reference. Unlike my view, however, McGinn holds that the reference of indexicals and demonstratives is always determined by features of the immediate context of utterance, and never by what I have called "extra-contextual cues." Even in cases in which McGinn and I agree that the semantic determinants are features of the immediate context, our accounts of precisely how the context contributes to the determination of reference greatly differ. What is crucial, holds McGinn, are the spatio-temporal relations between "the speaker's actions and the things around him."[40] Thus, in the case of demonstratives, the pointing gesture is, for McGinn, not merely one way among many in which the context can contribute to the determination of reference, as it is for me. Indeed, McGinn proposes that the semantic rule governing demonstratives in English runs as follows: "the referent of a token of 'that F' is to be the first F to intersect the line projected from the pointing finger, i.e., the F at the place indicated—one might almost say geometrically—by the accompanying gesture."[41]

Although I agree with much in McGinn's interesting paper, I find his account of the contribution of the context implausible. I shall restrict myself to a few comments, since a full discussion is not possible here. First, McGinn formulates a rule of reference not for demonstratives like 'this' and 'that,' but rather for demonstrative phrases like 'that man.' Were one to try to formulate a McGinn-like rule for 'that' *simpliciter,* for example, "the referent of a token of 'that' is the first thing to intersect the line projected from the pointing finger," one would encounter problems. Why, for example, is the line projected from the pointing finger not stopped by the first speck of dust it hits, or the first air molecule, and so on? McGinn, as he explained in conversation, assumes that utterances of 'this' and 'that' are always elliptical for expressions of the form 'this F', and so the problem just mentioned is avoided, but it is avoided at a cost. The thesis that demonstratives like 'this' and 'that' are elliptical surely stands in need of argument, and is, to my mind at least, highly implausible.[42]

Second, as I maintain above[43] and as McGinn himself notes, pointing is quite inessential to the use of demonstratives. McGinn tries to account for this with the remark that where there is only one F around it is not important that the speaker point. "The location of the speaker's body is what serves as the paralinguistic determinant of such reference when no other or finer spatio-temporal directions are required by the hearer."[44] The inessentiality of pointing goes much deeper, however, than McGinn can allow for. Even when there are thirty men around, I may say "That one is a outrageous," or (to accommodate McGinn's view that 'that' always requires a sortal) "That

man is outrageous," without any pointing gesture, nod of the head, or anything similar. I nevertheless refer to a particular man just in case something about the communicational interaction makes it perfectly clear who is in question. Imagine that you are my addressee, that we speak often about how outrageous James Watt, the Secretary of the Interior is, and that we are at a reception for the Queen of England at which Watt is present. Further imagine that Watt is speaking into a microphone while moving around the room, so that we can hear him, but have no idea where he is at the moment. After some particularly outrageous remark of Watt's, I say "That man is outrageous." Clearly, Watt is the referent, the reference certainly seems to be a straightforward demonstrative reference, and yet nothing like a spatial relation determines the reference. Watt is the referent in virtue of the cues available to the addressee, considerations that include the fact that his voice was, so to speak, perceptually salient, you—the addressee—know that I often express this view about Watt, and so on.

Finally, a consequence of McGinn's view that I find dubious is the thesis, certainly not unique to McGinn, that one can demonstratively refer only to items to which one is in a position to point. Imagine that, with respect to the last example, immediately after Watt's speech, Watt leaves the room. Further imagine that, unlike the last case, I suppress my anger for the duration of his speech, but can hardly contain myself. Immediately after his departure I say, "That man is outrageous." Again, I take it that one has demonstratively referred to Watt, and that what makes Watt the referent is the fact that he is the individual indicated by the cues. Nor is it crucial that my remark be made immediately after the speech. You and I may be on our way home after the speech, or we may meet days later, and it may be obvious to you that I am still fuming about the speech. I may say, "That man is outrageous," realizing that it will be obvious that Watt is in question. It is plausible to suppose that we can refer demonstratively to individuals far removed from us in space and time.[45]

I have advanced what we might call a contextual account of indexical reference, now using "contextual" in the broad sense in which we speak not only of linguistic contexts but also of social and cultural ones, and using 'indexical' for the class that includes both the pure indexicals and the demonstratives. The simplest and cleanest case is that of the pure indexicals. The reference of 'I', e.g., is determined by a quite pedestrian feature of the context, namely, who is speaking. The reference of demonstratives, a much more messy business, is determined by a much more messy collection of contextual features. Reference is determined in both cases, however, by those very features of communicational interactions that make the reference available.[46]

NOTES

1. See below for the crucial distinction between the causal theory of reference, which I oppose, and the so-called "causal theory of names," with which I am sympathetic.

2. A Fregean answer, rejected by the new theorists, is that the gap is to be bridged by, so to speak, more meaning. One version of this answer is that the speaker relies on the context of utterance to supplement the meager lexical meaning of the indexical so as to yield a descriptive characterization which uniquely fits the referent. For criticisms see my papers 'Indexical Reference and Propositional Content', *Philosophical Studies* **36** (1979) and 'Demonstrative Reference and Definite Descriptions,' *Philosophical Studies* **40** (1981).

3. This answer was implicit in my earlier work on the reference of indexicals, but not fully explicit—even to me. See the two papers mentioned in note 2.

4. It is by no means obvious that the causal theory of reference is the prevailing view among the new theorists. Kripke is sometimes characterized in such terms but this seems to me at least premature and probably incorrect. New theorists typically do proffer a causal or historical-explanation theory of proper names but this is quite another matter. Kripke, e.g., in *Naming and Necessity* (Cambridge, Mass.: Harvard University Press, 1980), maintains that the use of a name by one who was not present at the dubbing involves the user's obtaining the name via a "causal chain of communication." Kripke maintains that such chains are crucial to the semantic account of, e.g., my use of 'Aristotle' (or to the semantic account of 'Aristotle' in my idiolect). This is not to say, however, that such chains are always operative. One who speaks of his own children, does not refer, at least in many everyday cases, by means of such a chain of communication. One might tell some other kind of causal story for such uses of names, but Kripke, e.g., does not do so. Adoption of a "causal theory of names" does not commit one to [a] causal theory of reference. An explicit defender of the causal theory of reference is Michael Devitt in his book *Designation* (New York: Columbia University Press, 1981).

5. While an intentional theory may be motivated by a dissatisfaction with a causal approach, it can be otherwise motivated. Indeed, the two theories may be held together, as they are by Devitt. A causal theorist can be an intentional theorist just in case he holds a causal theory of intention, i.e., the view that to have a certain object in mind is for there to be ". . . a certain sort of causal connection between his state of mind and the object" (Devitt, p. 33). Keith Donnellan, a leading advocate of the intentional theory, at least for reference by proper names, definite descriptions, and (in conversation) demonstratives, is hesitant about the causal theory. For Donnellan's general orientation see his 'Reference and Definite Descriptions', *Philosophical Review* **75** (1966) [Reprinted in this volume, Chapter 3] and 'Proper Names and Identifying Descriptions', *Semantics of Natural Language,* second ed., eds. D. Davidson and G. Harman (Dordrecht, 1972). For his hesitation about the causal theory see his 'Speaking of Nothing', *Philosophical Review* **83** (1974):3–31.

6. Putnam's remarks on the division of linguistic labor for natural kind terms and Kripke's remarks on proper names both stress the role of social interaction in determining the references of our words. See also Tyler Burge, 'Individualism and the Mental', *Midwest Studies in Philosophy* **4** (1979). I am grateful to Burge for focusing my attention on the fact that my view further socializes "reference."

7. It is a commonplace that the notion of "having in mind" stands in need of clarification. Such a task is not part of the current project and I remain neutral on how the analysis of this notion should proceed.

8. See his widely circulating, unpublished monograph *Demonstratives,* Draft 2 (UCLA Philosophy Department), esp. pp. 7–10.

9. In treating 'now', 'here', and 'today' as pure indexicals, I oversimplify for ease of exposition. I am inclined to think that 'I' is the only really *pure* indexical. The other expressions that Kaplan classifies as pure

indexicals exhibit features that make them something like hybrids of 'I' and the demonstratives. 'Now', e.g., does not simply pick out the instant of utterance (which would make it a pure indexical like 'I'), it picks out greater or lesser intervals of which this instant is always a constituent. The 'breadth' of the intervals varies with the context.

10. Or so I assume. Consistent with my project in this paper, I do not here argue against other perspectives on the roles of the singular terms I discuss, e.g., the perspective according to which 'now' means "concurrent with the present utterance". Instead I assume a nondescriptivist perspective and try to work out the most coherent way to fill out the picture.

11. See *Designation,* pp. 42–43.

12. Here I follow Kaplan in *Demonstratives.*

13. This rule should not be seen as supplying a *synonym* for 'I', e.g., 'the agent of the context', but rather as utilizing this description only, so to speak, in the meta-language, to systematically fix or specify the references of utterances of 'I'.

14. Donnellan has agreed in conversation that a Kaplan-like nonintentional account is correct *for the pure indexicals,* whereas, on his view, the havings-in-mind of the speaker are crucial for reference by names, demonstratives, and definite descriptions. I am not sure why, on his view, intentions should not also be decisive for the pure indexicals. In any case, the argument I develop here against the intentional view applies, as I argue in Section 3, to demonstratives as well.

15. David Kaplan, in his seminal paper, 'Dthat', in *Contemporary Perspectives in the Philosophy of Language,* eds. P. French, T. Uehling, and H. Wettstein (Minneapolis, 1977), states: "A person might utter: 'I am a general' intending—that is, 'having in mind'—de Gaulle, and being under the delusion that he himself was de Gaulle. But the linguistic constraints on the possible demonstrata of 'I' will not allow anyone other than de Gaulle to so demonstrate de Gaulle, no matter how hard they try (pp. 396–97)." Kaplan's example, however, does not make it clear that the speaker not only believes that he is de Gaulle, but really has the latter in mind. After all, just as in the "I am hungry" case, the speaker could say, "I am a general," believing he is de Gaulle and perhaps still have himself in mind. When I first read Kaplan's example I had this picture: the speaker utters 'I' and thinks *"de Gaulle, de Gaulle, de Gaulle."* He *tries hard,* as Kaplan says, to refer to de Gaulle. Having someone in mind, though, is surely not a matter of thinking about him actively, concentrating on him, when uttering the singular term.

16. Donnellan, in 'Proper Names and Identifying Descriptions', considers a case that is similar to my Ahern case in that a speaker uses a singular term (in Donnellan's example a proper name rather than an indexical) to refer to an individual who he misidentifies and takes to be someone else. In Donnellan's example, a student meets a man at a party who he mistakenly takes to be "J. L. Aston-Martin, the famous British philosopher." The student later describes the party to a friend and, in doing so, repeatedly used the name 'J. L. Aston-Martin'. Is the referent of the student's utterance of the name the British philosopher so-named, or rather the man at the party? Donnellan suggests that the answer depends upon the intent of the speaker. When the student says to his friend, "You'll never guess who I met last night, J. L. Aston-Martin," the point of his utterance concerns the person so-named, the famous British philosopher, and so the latter is the referent. When he says (something like), ". . . and Aston-Martin, who was by then quite drunk, tripped over Robinson's feet," his use of the name is, Donnellan says, "as it were, incidental" i.e., incidental to the point of the utterance. The point of the utterance has to do with the man the student mistakenly takes to be Aston-Martin, and the referent is the man at the party.

17. There is a sense in which Ahern did refer to de Gaulle. If he succeeded in communicating about de Gaulle, which I agree may have occurred, then he must have, in some sense, referred to him. Still, there is another sense, a preferred sense, in which he referred only to himself. If what he said, strictly speaking, was false, then his assertion was about himself. *He* is the individual whose properties are relevant to the truth or falsity of what was said. In such a case, I shall say that the speaker, while he may have intended to refer to de Gaulle, referred to himself. Alternatively, we might adopt Kripke's terminology in 'Speaker's Reference and Semantic Reference', in *Contemporary Perspectives in the Philosophy of Language,* pp. 6–27 [Reprinted in this volume, Chapter 4] and say that although the speaker has referred to de Gaulle, his words, on this occasion, do not so refer.

18. My argument here against the intentional theory depends crucially upon the intuition that what Ahern said was false. Intuitions about the truth value of what was said may be less clear in the analogous Aston-

Martin case of the note 16 above, i.e., the case in which the speaker has the man at the party in mind and the point of the utterance is to say something about *him*. Intuitions are certainly less clear with regard to some cases involving utterances of definite descriptions. See note 28 below.

19. See, e.g., Rod Bertolet's comments in 'Demonstratives and Intentions,' *Philosophical Studies* **38** (1980): 75–78.

20. This example slightly modifies Kripke's in 'Speaker's Reference and Semantic Reference'. See esp. [This volume: 83–85].

21. As do the parallel claims I made for the similar cases discussed in the last paragraph.

22. As Kripke notes in 'Speaker's Reference,' n. 28 [This volume: 94].

23. That the historian's intention to refer to himself is *subsidiary* is, no doubt, related to the fact that it is a *derivative* intention. The historian wishes to communicate about de Gaulle and must choose some linguistic means to his end. One such means, given his mistaken beliefs, is an utterance of 'I.' He knows, of course that by uttering 'I' he will refer to himself and fully intends this—as a means to his communicative end, speaking about de Gaulle. Thus his intention to communicate about himself is *derivative* from his primary intention to communicate about de Gaulle. Such a primary-derivative distinction was suggested to me by Michael McKinsey's 'Names and Intentionality', *Philosophical Review* **87**, see esp. pp. 176–177. McKinsey points out that Hector-Neri Castañeda is the father of the distinction. See Castañeda's 'Intentions and the Structure of Intending', *Journal of Philosophy* **68** (1971), esp. p. 454.

24. But not inevitably. As Kripke notes on [This volume: 93], n. 26, if one says "Smith's murderer is insane," having in mind the (innocent) man on the witness stand who is acting bizarre, the speaker has only *that guy* in mind and takes him to have a property he doesn't have, i.e., the property of having murdered Smith. He is not confusing two individuals, both of whom he has in mind.

25. Thus the Ahern example shows that having someone in mind in the primary sense is not a sufficient condition for reference to him. The Ahern example further shows that having someone in mind in the primary sense is not even a necessary condition for reference to him, for Ahern referred to himself even though he failed to have himself in mind in the primary sense.

26. 'Now,' 'here,' 'today,' and so on, since (as suggested in note 9 above) they have a "demonstrative" component, require a more complicated positive account than does 'I,' one in accordance with my remarks on demonstratives in Section 4.

27. Colin McGinn, 'The Mechanism of Reference', *Synthese* **49** (1981):157–186. The example occurs on p. 161.

28. Another example might be provided by having our deranged history lecturer try to make a point about de Gaulle, not by saying 'I' but by saying 'that one,' pointing to a student or colleague whom the lecturer takes to be de Gaulle. Kaplan in 'Dthat' provided much earlier a brilliant example of a somewhat different variety, his "Carnap-Agnew case" ('Dthat', p. 396). Notice that while intuitions about such cases, as well as about the Ahern case in Section 2 above, cases involving pure indexicals and demonstratives, are pretty clear, cases involving utterances of definite descriptions and proper names are much less so. Consider Donnellan's example in which someone says, "The man drinking the martini looks happy tonight," intending to refer to "that guy over there" who indeed looks very happy, but who, unbeknownst to the speaker, is not drinking a martini at all, but is merely drinking sparkling water in a martini glass. Another man, let us suppose, standing just off to the side, is the only man really drinking a martini in the room, and he looks quite miserable. Do we have any clear intuitions about the truth value of what was said, strictly speaking, and therefore about the reference of the definite description? Donnellan, at least as I read 'Reference and Definite Descriptions'— Donnellan has agreed in conversation that this was his intent, and he is explicit about this in his later paper 'Speaker Reference, Descriptions, and Anaphora,' in *Contemporary Perspectives in the Philosophy of Language,* pp. 28–44—thinks that what was said, the statement made, was true, and that the referent, indeed the semantic referent, is the man the speaker had in mind. (Kripke, writing only about 'Reference and Definite Descriptions,' reads Donnellan as being more cautious. See Kripke's remarks [This volume: 82], of 'Speaker's Reference and Semantic Reference'.) Kripke expresses the contrary intuition. The same dispute, supported by the same conflicting intuitive judgements, occurs with respect to proper names. See Kripke's discussion in 'Speaker's Reference' and Donnellan's in Section IX of 'Proper Names and Identifying Descriptions'. Given a lack of undisputed intuitions about such cases how might we proceed? Perhaps the arguments I have advanced are relevant, for my argument yields the result that there are at least some cases in which it is clear

that (semantic) reference is not determined by what the speaker has in mind. Donnellan, it should be remembered, was developing a quite general point, not one related to the peculiarities, say, of definite descriptions. His view that what the speaker has in mind determines the semantic reference is applied by him to names, definite descriptions, and in conversation at least, to demonstratives (see note 14 above). My arguments, at least *prima facie,* make Donnellan's general picture implausible. If semantic reference and speaker reference can diverge in the case of, say demonstratives, why can't they diverge in the case of names and descriptions? If the reference of a demonstrative does not depend upon what the speaker has in mind, why should the reference of names and descriptions so depend? (One should not conclude from this that there is nothing left to Donnellan's referential-attributive distinction. See my paper, 'Demonstrative Reference and Definite Descriptions', for Donnellan's distinction cleansed of Donnellan's views about the semantic role of havings-in-mind.)

29. For reasons of space, I cannot consider Kaplan's positive account of the determination of reference for demonstratives (presented briefly in 'Dthat' and more fully in *Demonstratives*), his "Fregean theory of demonstra*tions*" (as opposed to the "Fregean theory of demonstra*tives*," which he rejects). I shall argue in a forthcoming paper that Kaplan's view is inadequate, in part because it falls to assign a central enough place to the contextual cues and allows no place for the extra-contextual ones. Kaplan is currently developing a new approach.

30. More accurately, as we shall see, they, together with other cues, determine the reference.

31. The contextual cues go far beyond the fairly pedestrian ones mentioned in the text. When I say to my son, "That is the most disgusting thing I have ever seen," he knows that I am speaking of the dead and decaying frog he is holding. He knows this in part because of the cue provided by *the predicate* I have used. Considerations of stress and intonation are relevant as well. Cf. Stephen Isard, 'Changing the Context,' in *Formal Semantics of Natural Language,* ed. E. L. Keenen (Cambridge: Cambridge University Press, 1974).

32. See note 31 above.

33. One way to put my thesis is that the referent of 'that' is the individual that is *salient* with respect to that demonstrative utterance. The idea is that something or other must make some item salient, i.e., conspicuous or striking, with regard to each utterance of a demonstrative. I hesitate to formulate my thesis in terms of the notion of "salience," however, for doing so seems to divert attention away from the substantive thesis I am proposing and towards questions like whether the term 'salience' really captures my idea. I believe the term to be both helpful and appropriate but defending this is probably more trouble than it is worth. For a similar use of the notion of "salience" see David Lewis, 'Scorekeeping In A Language Game,' *Journal of Philosophical Logic* **8** (1979):339–359. [Reprinted in this volume, Chapter 25]

34. When I say that the speaker relies on certain cues this is not to suggest that he consciously selects them. In many contexts, it will be immediately clear to a speaker which item will be taken to be the referent and he will not bother to think about what precisely it is that will indicate this. Indeed some of these cues are very subtle and will not be easily available to him.

35. The miscommunication is, in such a case, the speaker's responsibility. In cases in which the miscommunication is the auditor's fault, e.g., he was not paying attention, the speaker will have said, strictly speaking, just what he intended to say, despite the fact that it was not understood. No doubt there are intermediate cases in which it will not be clear where to place the responsibility, and equally unclear what was, strictly speaking, said. This is, I think, as it should be since, "what is said, strictly speaking," is an institutional notion and there is little institutional utility to providing a determinate answer for such intermediate cases.

36. Discussions of the example given in this paragraph have convinced me that my intuitions here are not universally shared. The intuition that the man pointed to is the referent and that the truth value of what was said depend upon *his* properties is surely not as firm as are the intuitions about the Ahern case of Section 2, or the pointing examples in Section 3. Nor do I base my argument against the intentional theory on the present case. If my arguments in Sections 2 and 3 are correct, however, the intentional theory is no longer a contender. Given that it is not a contender, and given the sort of institutional picture that has been emerging, it seems implausible that the speaker is responsible only for those cues that he intends to communicate by. Much more plausibly, he is responsible for those that he *to all appearances* exploits.

37. 'Dthat', p. 396.

38. Nor is it clear that Kaplan could point to the dog behind his son without moving his son out of the way, despite the fact that the geometrical line from his finger passes through the dog.

39. So Kaplan concludes in 'Dthat'. This is a desperate expedient given Kaplan's program of doing the semantics of indexicals without appeal to such intentions.

40. 'The Mechanism of Reference', p. 163.

41. P. 163. McGinn's view is that this rule represents something of an idealization of our actual linguistic practice. At least part of what he means is that we do not always take such care in pointing as his rule requires, and that we will count someone as having demonstratively referred to something even if the line extending from the pointing finger misses its target by an inch or so. Nevertheless, thinks McGinn, the reference of a demonstrative is determined by the spatial relation in which the speaker stands to the referent. See his discussion of "idealization" on pp. 163–164.

42. I cannot pursue it here, but I suspect that the sort of argument I employ against Frege's view that indexicals function as surrogates for uniquely denoting definite descriptions, and against the Russellian view that "indefinite" definite descriptions like 'the table' are elliptical for uniquely denoting definite descriptions, applies against McGinn's view here as well. For the argument, see pp. 94–95 of my 'Indexical Reference and Propositional Content', and pp. 246–248 of my 'Demonstrative Reference and Definite Descriptions'.

43. See the beginning of Section 4.

44. P. 183, note 14.

45. See also the examples in the third paragraph of Section 4 above. One might try to handle all such cases, as well as the example at the end of the last paragraph of the text, as cases of anaphoric uses of demonstrative expressions. But it is hard to see how one could come up with a natural account along these lines, for one thing, since no other reference to that individual need have occurred in the prior discourse. In any case, I sometimes, perhaps often, think that it is a virtue of the account I have provided that such cases need no special treatment. Another class of cases that comes to mind here is that of "deferred ostention." A kindergarten teacher, pointing to finger-paintings done by her pupils, says, "This one is very good at writing but is not much of an artist. This one is quite good at this, but is something of a behavior problem." She thus refers with demonstratives to her pupils, by means of pointing to the paintings. Is this straightforward demonstrative reference, or rather a special category of "referring to one thing by demonstratively referring to something else (that represents it)"? My view allows us to treat such cases as straightforward demonstrative references. The referent is the pupil indicated by the cues. One of the relevant cues is the pointing gesture to the painting done by that student.

46. This paper was written while I was an NEH Fellow (1981–82) and I am grateful to the National Endowment for the Humanities, the Graduate School of the University of Minnesota, and the Office of the Academic Dean of the University of Minnesota, Morris for support. I am also grateful to the Department of Philosophy of Stanford University, and especially to its chair, John Perry, and to Patrick Suppes, Director of the Institute for the Mathematical Study of the Social Sciences at Stanford, for the hospitality shown me during 1981–82. I am especially indebted to Perry for extremely helpful discussions of the questions I discuss in this paper, as well as for his comments on earlier drafts. Others to whom I owe a special debt are David Kaplan, for hospitality and extended discussions at UCLA, and Joseph Almog for longsuffering patience with earlier versions. The final form of this paper owes much to the comments of Michael Bratman, Keith Donnellan, Evan Fales, Philippa Foot, Eli Hirsch, Ernest LePore, Julius Moravcsik, and Patrick Suppes, as well as to the comments of a number of individuals present at talks I gave on this subject at Stanford, University of California, Riverside, and the University of Notre Dame.

FURTHER READING

Bar-Hillel, Y. (1954). "Indexical Expressions." *Mind* 63:359–379.

Perry, J. (1979). "The Problem of the Essential Indexical." *Nous* 13:3–21.

Roberts, L. (1986). "The Figure–Ground Model for the Explanation of the Determination of Indexical References." *Synthese* 68:441–486.

Schiffer, S. (1981). "Indexicals and the Theory of Reference." *Synthese* 49:43–100.

Direct and Indirect Speech Acts

11

Speech Acts and Hearers' Beliefs

HERBERT H. CLARK AND THOMAS B. CARLSON

For communication to be successful, speakers must share certain knowledge, beliefs, and assumptions with the people they are talking to. Take this request:

(1) *Patricia to Eric:* Please sit down.

According to Lewis (1969), the conventions of language must be "common knowledge" between Patricia and Eric (for example, the conventions that *sit* can be used to denote sitting, *sit down* to denote sitting down, and so on). According to Schiffer (1972), what Patricia means in uttering (1) relies on her and Eric "mutually knowing or believing" that the words *Please sit down* plus other contextual information constitute good evidence that she is requesting him to sit down. Common or mutual knowledge or beliefs between speakers and addressees have also been claimed to play critical roles in assertions (Stalnaker, 1978), indirect speech acts (Clark, 1979; Cohen and Perrault, 1979), novel coinages (Clark and Clark, 1979), reference (Clark and Marshall, 1981; Nunberg, 1979) and presuppositions (Karttunen and Peters, 1975).

However, what about shared beliefs *among* hearers? Virtually all discussions of speech acts have been limited to what we will call *canonical speech acts*. In (1), there is a single speaker (Patricia) addressing a single hearer (Eric) who is fully known to the speaker, and there are no other relevant hearers. Canonical speech acts are speech acts, like (1), made by speakers to single namable addressees. In these, the question of beliefs shared by hearers doesn't even arise. But take (2):

(2) *Irving, to Pat and Mike:* Please shake hands.

Shaking hands is a joint act. For Irving to expect Pat and Mike to be able to carry it out, he must intend each of them to recognize not only what he asked of *him* but also what he has asked of the other. If they are told separately and have no guarantee the other has been told, they should realize they cannot carry out that joint act without further negotiation. Here, shared beliefs *among* the addressees appears crucial.

In this paper, we examine some common uses of language in which shared beliefs *among* bearers is critical. This is valuable in part because so little is known about speech situations with more than one hearer. Our ultimate goal, however, is to examine speech act theory in general. We argue that our findings require a rather fundamental addition to traditional theories of speech acts.

CO-ORDINATION OF ACTION

Our argument rests on an analysis of what we will call *joint acts*. A joint act is an act by two or more people who must, in general, intentionally co-ordinate their separate actions in order to succeed. Shaking hands is an everyday example, and so are rowing a boat, speaking and listening, driving down a highway, signalling in Morse code, walking in a crowd of people, meeting, and dancing (see Schelling, 1960; Lewis, 1969). What is required for joint acts to succeed? To this question, Lewis (1969) has offered an important answer. We will illustrate his solution, and expand on it, with one of the most intricate of joint acts, the playing of duets.

The Violin Duet

One evening Itzhak Perlman and Pinchas Zukerman get together to play violin duets. Perlman suggests they play Bartok's "Duet Number 38, Rumanian Whirling Dance." Zukerman agrees, and they prepare their music and violins. To start them off, Perlman lifts his violin slightly and brings it down with the gesture of a conductor, and at that moment they begin their first notes. From then on, they play according to the score, adjusting to each other auditorily and visually as they go.

The co-ordination required for this duet is indescribably complex. Perlman and Zukerman must co-ordinate: the tuning of their violins to the same pitch; the edition of the music they are playing from; whether they both begin with a down-bow or an up-bow; the point in Perlman's gesture to take as the beginning; where in the music to begin; the tempo that "allegro" implies; whether or not they are to play at the tempo as marked; whether the piece is to be conducted by Perlman or Zukerman; how loud "forte" is; how quickly to crescendo near the end; and so on. The list is so long and intricate it is a wonder Perlman and Zukerman ever manage to bring it off.

The joint act of initiating the first note is complicated enough. Imagine that Perlman has been practising his gesture to start the first note, and now he wants the gesture to be taken for real. When he gestures this time, he must believe that Zukerman will take the gesture for real (and not just practise), since Zukerman won't otherwise play the first note, and their joint act will fail. However, he recognizes that Zukerman will also not play if Zukerman believes that Perlman believes himself to be still practising, since in that case *Perlman* won't play. Perlman must believe that Zukerman believes that he, Perlman, is taking the gesture for real. This, however, is still not enough. What if Zukerman believes that he, Perlman, believes Zukerman still thinks he is practising? Zukerman won't play in that case either, since he wouldn't expect Perlman to play. That is, Perlman must believe that Zukerman believes that he, Perlman, believes that Zukerman believes that this time he is gesturing for real. It is easy to see that *in principle* Perlman should continue this reasoning *ad infinitum,* and Lewis (1969) has provided the proof.[1]

To co-ordinate their first note, therefore, Perlman and Zukerman require what Schiffer (1972) has called *mutual belief* of the proposition p that Perlman's gesture is for real this time. Let us call Perlman and Zukerman A and B. Schiffer's definition for mutual belief is this:

A and B mutually believe that $p =$ def.

(1) A believes that p.

(1′) B believes that p.

(2) A believes that B believes that p.

(2′) B believes that A believes that p.

(3) A believes that B believes that A believes that p.

(3′) B believes that A believes that B believes that p. et cetera *ad infinitum.*

This definition, with *know* in place of *believe,* is equivalent to what Lewis would call A and B's *common knowledge* of the proposition p.[2] To be more precise, however, we must talk about Perlman's and Zukerman's states of mind separately, since they are separate people with separable beliefs. As for Perlman, what he must assure himself of, technically speaking, is that he and Zukerman mutually believe that p. That is, the crucial condition is this: *A believes that A and B mutually believe that p.* The corresponding condition holds for Zukerman.

The necessity for mutual belief doesn't stop at Perlman's gesturing the start of the first note. Perlman and Zukerman must also mutually believe that they are both going to play the first note of Bartok's "Duet 38," that they are both going to down-bow, that they are both going to play mezzo forte, that they are both going to play in the key as written and not in some transposed key, and so on. Perlman and Zukerman, of course, could happen to manage these things together by accident, but then they wouldn't be performing a *joint* act. A joint act is one that the parties engage in, *intending* to do it by design and not by accident. As professionals, Perlman and Zukerman would never leave these elements to chance. Lewis's conclusion is that all genuine joint acts must be based, in principle, on mutual knowledge or beliefs.

Inferring Mutual Belief

Many people have objected to the concept of mutual knowledge or belief because of its infinity of conditions. Although "full" mutual knowledge or belief may be required for joint acts in the ideal, the argument goes, it cannot be attained in practice. A person couldn't possibly deal with the infinite number of knowledge or belief statements that are involved. Bach and Harnish (1979, p. 309), for example, say this about Lewis's and Schiffer's definitions of mutual knowledge as applied to language use:

Their definitions are not limited to three levels of belief (as Bach and Harnish's definition is) but go on indefinitely. Higher-level beliefs are in principle possible, and indeed among spies or deceptive intimates there could be divergence at the first three levels, but we think such higher-level beliefs are not possible for a whole community or large group.

Harder and Kock (1976, p. 62) offer a similar argument:

There is no logical limit to the number of levels that may be necessary to account for a given speech event. But there are psychological limits, just as, e.g., there are psychological limits on the capacity of the human brain for the embedding transformation (cf. Chomsky 1965, chapter 1). Probably not even the most subtle mind ever makes replicative as-

sumptions in speech events involving more levels than, say, six.

These objections, however, are groundless, for they rest on two false assumptions. The first is the assumption that mutual beliefs must be represented in any model of the mind as an infinite series of belief statements. This assumption is unnecessary. Mutual beliefs can be represented as mental primitives of the form *A and B mutually believe that p* along with the inference rule: *If A and B mutually believe that p, then: (a) A and B believe that p and believe that (a).* With the primitive and the inference rule, a person can truly be said to believe that A and B mutually believe that *p*. It is just that his capacity for applying the inference rule and remembering the output is limited to just a few iterations. The second false assumption is that mutual beliefs can only be inferred from infinitely many pieces of evidence, one piece per belief statement. As both Lewis and Schiffer have demonstrated, all one needs is a single piece of evidence, as long as it is of the right kind.

Consider Perlman and Zukerman once again. Perlman, to make sure his next gesture will be taken as the beginning of the first note, says to Zukerman, "On my next gesture, let us start," and Zukerman replies, "Right." In this way, Perlman and Zukerman have explicitly agreed that the next gesture will be for real. This agreement can serve as the *grounds* for their mutual belief the next gesture will be for real. It works this way:

(1) A and B have reason to believe that the agreement holds.

(2) This agreement indicates to A and B each that A and B each have reason to believe the agreement holds.

(3) The agreement indicates to A and B each that the next gesture will be for real.

Lewis has proven that these three conditions, along with some side assumptions about each other's rationality, are all Perlman and Zukerman need in order to *inductively infer* the mutual belief that Perlman's next gesture is for real. Any grounds G that satisfies these three conditions, where G is inserted in place of "the agreement," is sufficient to allow for the inductive inference of that mutual belief.

Let us call this schema the *mutual belief induction schema* (see Clark and Marshall,

1981). Notice that it produces the proposition that A and B mutually believe that p, just the mental primitive we wanted. If Perlman or Zukerman had to work out the logic of the schema each time, they might be forced to produce a set of iterated beliefs and to see that they can be iterated to infinity. But since they know the schema itself, all they need to do is find a grounds that satisfies conditions (1), (2), and (3), apply the schema, and *infer* mutual belief. The infinite character of mutual belief is never at issue.[3]

Another objection sometimes raised to mutual beliefs is that they are too exacting, too precise.[4] No one would ever infer truly mutual beliefs in practice, since no one could ever be *certain* that each of the infinitely many individual belief statements held. Instead, so the objection continues, people actually make do with something less than mutual beliefs. They rely on some sort of "shared" beliefs that vary from strong to shaky.

This objection is also groundless. It is based on the false assumption that mutual beliefs cannot vary in strength. Imagine that Perlman notices as the evening wears on that Zukerman is becoming uncharacteristically absent-minded. When they explicitly agree to begin this time, Perlman isn't completely certain that Zukerman will remember the agreement. For condition (1) in the induction schema, Perlman has reason to believe the agreement holds, but not very *good* reason. His grounds are weaker than earlier in the evening, and his belief that they mutually believe that the next gesture is for real is correspondingly weaker. That is, mutual beliefs range from weak to strong in line with the grounds on which they are based. The stronger the grounds, the stronger the mutual beliefs.

Grounds for Mutual Beliefs

Based on just this sort of argument, Clark and Marshall (1981) proposed that people ordinarily rely on certain *co-presence heuristics* for inferring mutual beliefs. At the heart of these heuristics is the idea that people seek out special kinds of evidence, apply the mutual belief induction schema, and infer mutual beliefs. The evidence, they argued, is of three basic kinds (generally in combination): physical co-presence, linguistic co-presence, and community membership.

With physical co-presence, what is sought is evidence of the "triple co-presence" of A, B, and the object of the mutual knowledge. Imagine that A and B are sitting across the table from each other staring at a candle between them and at each other beyond the candle. Each is aware simultaneously of the candle and of each other attending to the candle. This is an example *par excellence* of the triple co-presence of A, B and the candle. All A and B need do is assume that the other is attending to the candle and to his opposite simultaneously, or roughly so, and that the other is rational. Then they can each inductively infer mutual belief in the presence of the candle. Other instances of physical co-presence lead to weaker mutual beliefs, but the logic is essentially the same.

With linguistic co-presence, what is sought is the triple co-presence of A, B and the linguistic positing of the object of mutual belief. Imagine that A tells B, "I bought a candle today." Each is aware that A posited the existence of a candle by this linguistic means, and each is aware that the other was attending to the speech act. This is what is meant by "linguistic co-presence." With the right auxiliary assumptions, A and B can each use this evidence to inductively infer mutual belief in the existence of that candle.

Physical and linguistic co-presence are themselves submerged in a sea of mutual beliefs based on community membership. At the most general level, once A and B have evidence that they mutually believe they are adult humans, they can assume as mutual beliefs everything that adult humans are assumed to know or believe. This includes such generic things as that dogs are animals, objects fall because of gravity, certain causes lead to certain effects, and trees have leaves. It also includes such particular things as that the earth is round, the sun appears periodically, and the stars shine at night in the sky. Once it is mutually recognized by A and B that they are also both residents of the U.S., both residents of California, and both professors at Stanford University, they can assume a host of other mutual beliefs as well, such things as Hoover Tower is on the Stanford campus, the Stanford Bookstore is beside the Post Office, and

Sacramento is the capital of California. This source of mutual beliefs is often used in combination with physical or linguistic co-presence to infer still other mutual beliefs: like the belief that the candle that A just mentioned in conversation has a wick, even though A didn't mention that wick.[5]

These three grounds for mutual knowledge are readily apparent in Perlman's and Zukerman's co-ordination of their duet. First, they rely on physical co-presence. They use visual and auditory contact to co-ordinate their first notes, the moment by moment tempo, the successive choices of up-bow and down-bow, the intensity, the end of fermatas, and so on. Secondly, they rely on linguistic co-presence: with their spoken agreements about what piece to play, how loud to play, how certain passages should be phrased, who is to lead, and so on. And thirdly, they rely on their common membership in the community of expert violinists, whose musical training gives them common beliefs about musical notation, the manner in which violins are to be played, and all the other conventions and practices violinists know. Duet playing would be impossible without all three sources for mutual beliefs.

The Quintet

Later in the evening, Jacqueline DuPré, cello, Zubin Mehta, double bass, and Daniel Barenboim, piano, arrive and join Perlman and Zukerman in playing quintets. They decide on Schubert's *Piano Quintet, Opus 114,* which as it happens, starts with all five members playing the first chord simultaneously. As first violin, Perlman leads them off, after a few practice trials, with the gesture of his violin. Once again, there is the problem of co-ordination. What beliefs do the five of them have to have in order for Perlman's gesture to be taken this time for real?

When it was just the two of them, Perlman and Zukerman needed the mutual belief that Perlman's gesture this time was for real. Notice that mutual beliefs are defined for two people, and only two people; so how should it be extended to five? One possibility is that each of the five must have mutual beliefs with each of the others: Perlman and Zukerman must mutually believe that the gesture is for

real this time; Perlman and DuPré must mutually believe it; Zukerman and Mehta must mutually believe it; and so on. This, however, isn't enough. What if Perlman thought that Zukerman and DuPré didn't mutually believe it? Despite their mutual beliefs with him, Perlman should believe that they might not play the first note, since they weren't sure about each other. If they didn't play, of course, the first note wouldn't come off jointly. For genuine co-ordination, Perlman must believe that Zukerman and DuPré also mutually believe that the gesture is for real.

With this sort of reasoning, it is easy to show that Perlman, Zukerman, DuPré, Mehta, and Barenboim, need what Lewis (1969) defined as *common knowledge* or *belief*:

The members of a group G commonly believe that $p = $ def.

(1) The members of G believe that p.

(2) The members of G believe that the members of G believe that p.

(3) The members of G believe that the members of G believe that the members of G believe that p.

et cetera *ad infinitum.*

McCarthy (1979) has called the same notion *joint belief,* which is the source for our term joint act. Common beliefs are not just the conjunction of the mutual beliefs of pairs within a group. They encompass mutual beliefs about mutual beliefs and a good deal more.[6]

There are two points of contact between mutual and common beliefs. First, mutual beliefs are a special case of common beliefs in which the group G has only two members. We can often dispense with the term "mutual belief" and speak only about common belief (or joint belief). Secondly, all the arguments brought out earlier about the nature and source of mutual beliefs carry through, with the appropriate alterations, to common beliefs. Like mutual beliefs, common beliefs can be treated as mental primitives, and as having associated with them a rule enabling a person to infer (1), (2), (3) and so on as long as he has the time and mental capacity to do so. Also, common beliefs are beliefs that people ordinarily infer on the basis of physical co-presence, linguistic co-presence or community membership, and these inferences are made by means of a common induction schema.

Adjustable Joint Acts

Most aspects of ensemble playing are complex joint acts that require the utmost precision. Professionals like Perlman and Zukerman leave little to chance. They *know,* as they would put it, what the others are doing at all times (the co-ordination becomes second-nature) and the skill is in getting their fingers to do what they tell them to do.

Not all joint acts work this way. When Jill meets Jack, she might begin to extend her hand; when Jack realizes this, he begins to extend his hand; and the two of them adjust to each other's movements until they grasp hands in a joint handshake. Hand shaking is what we will call an *adjustable joint act.* It can be accomplished gradually, by approximation, with the participants adjusting to each other in arriving at its completion. Playing the first chord of a violin duet *could* of course be accomplished as an adjustable joint act, but it would sound like a couple of neighborhood cats picking a fight.

Even adjustable joint acts require common beliefs for their co-ordination. When Jill beings to extend her hand to Jack, she is confident that he will use her gesture as one grounds for the mutual belief that she expects them to shake hands. He is also expected to consult their common belief that (1) they are meeting; (2) in this culture, people meeting often shake hands; (3) her gesture could be the start of a handshake; (4) the handshake to be co-ordinated is the standard one; and so on. If any one of these grounds is missing, then the joint act will go awry. Jack might think that they have not yet been introduced, making a handshake inappropriate; or that in this culture, women never offer their hands first; or that she is reaching for something behind him; or that she is going to shake hands in the nonstandard way as many Americans do by grasping the base of his thumb.

Most joint acts are adjustable in one respect or another. In ensemble playing, the players adjust to the momentary intensity, pitch and tempo of their playing. Other joint acts have an even larger component of mutual adjustment. For clarity in the arguments that follow, we will avoid the adjustable aspects of joint acts, since the role that beliefs play in them is so much more complicated. Nevertheless, the arguments we will offer apply to them too insofar as common beliefs play a role in their accomplishment.

COLLECTIVE DIRECTIVES

Virtually all types of speech acts may be addressed to more than one hearer at a time. Yet, as we stated earlier, most theories of speech acts (we will call these the *standard* theories) are equipped to handle only canonical speech acts in which there is but one addressee.

Consider Searle's (1969, 1975) analysis of directives, which includes requests, commands, questions and pleas. These can be characterized, he argues, by certain conditions for their felicitous performance: their "felicity conditions." According to the "propositional content condition," for example, if an utterance is to count as a directive, the speaker must predicate a certain future act of the hearer (or more properly, the addressee). By the "essential condition," the utterance must count as an attempt to get the addressee to perform this act in accordance with the speaker's intentions.

When there is one addressee, Searle's characterization of directives seems adequate, as in (3):

(3) *Ann, to Bob:* Please bring a bottle of Glenlivet.

In uttering (3), Ann predicates of Bob the act of bringing a bottle of malt whisky, and she intends her words to count as an attempt to get Bob to do so. Problems arise when there is more than one addressee, as in (4):

(4) *Ann, to Bob and Ellen:* Please bring a bottle of Glenlivet.

Ann may have one of two distinct intentions in uttering (4). She may intend (a) that Bob and Ellen are to arrange to bring one bottle together, or (b) that each of them is to bring a bottle separately. That is, the act she is predicating is to be carried out by Bob and Ellen either (a) collectively, with one joint act of bringing, or (b) distributively, with two acts of bringing, each separate and distinct. Let us call these the *collective* and *distributive* readings, respectively.

Our claim is that standard speech act theories are incapable of accounting for the collective reading of directives. Under a collective reading, the addressees are to carry out a joint act, and for this to happen, they must commonly believe what illocutionary acts are being performed towards *all* of them. It is this last step that the standard theories cannot accommodate.

Individual Recognition

In the middle of the evening, for amusement, Perlman joins up with Isaac Stern, who has also dropped by, to play some piano pieces, with Perlman playing the right hand and Stern playing the left. Mehta offers to conduct them in "Study 119, Dance in 3/4 Time" from Bela Bartok's *Mikrokosmos,* a piece that starts with both hands playing simultaneously. Mehta practises saying *One, two, three, play* several times and finally starts them for real with the utterance in (5):

(5) *Mehta, to Perlman and Stern:* Play.

When the piece turns out to be too difficult, Perlman suggests that he play it by himself. Once again, Mehta practises his start and then utters (6), intending it to be taken for real:

(6) *Mehta, to Perlman:* Play.

With (5) and (6), we have a simple contrast. In both instances, Mehta is requesting a single act to be performed, the playing of the first chord in "Study 119." It is just that in (5) the act is a joint act performed by two people, whereas in (6) it is an individual act performed by one person. To a listener, the two acts should sound the same.

Standard speech act theories are designed to account for (6). By Searle's essential condition, Mehta's utterance counts as an attempt to get Perlman to play the first note. What about (5)? The obvious way to extend Searle's essential condition is like this: Mehta's utterance counts as an attempt to get Perlman *and* Stern to play the first note. But this statement is incomplete, for it doesn't say how Perlman and Stern are to *recognize* what they are to do.

The hearer's recognition of the speaker's intentions is an essential ingredient in all definitions of speaker's meaning (Grice, 1957, 1968; Schiffer, 1972) and illocutionary acts (Searle, 1969; Bach and Harnish, 1979). As Searle puts it, "The speaker S intends to produce an illocutionary effect IE in the hearer H by means of getting H to recognize S's intention to produce IE" (p. 47). In (6), Mehta is trying to get Perlman to recognize his intention to get Perlman to play the first note.

In (5), however, there are *two* recognizers. Mehta cannot intend Perlman and Stern *as a pair* to recognize what he wants them to do. They would have to be a Siamese twin called Perlman-and-Stern with a single mind if they were to perform such a single act of recognition. Rather, Perlman and Stern live separate mental lives, and each must recognize Mehta's intentions for himself. This assumption is no more than the commonplace idea that recognizing something is a mental act that each person must perform on his own; no one can perform it for him. We will call this the *individual recognition assumption.*

An adequate characterization of illocutionary acts, therefore, must explicate how the speaker intends *each individual hearer* to recognize his intentions. Like Mehta's request in (5), "complex" illocutionary acts must be representable, at some level of analysis, in terms of what we will call *elementary illocutionary acts.* An elementary illocutionary act is one that is intended to be recognized by one and only one hearer. The request in (6) is already an elementary illocutionary act in that it is directed at Perlman alone. In the notation we will use, what Mehta means would be represented as in (7):

(7) *Mehta, to Perlman:* 'I request of you that you play.'

To distinguish representations from utterances, we will enclose representations in single quotation marks as in (7).

Elementary illocutionary acts have two important properties, as illustrated by (7). The first is the *single-target criterion.* As the definition requires, each elementary illocutionary act must be directed at a single individual (in (7), Perlman) since recognition is an act performed only by single individuals. The second criterion, which applies only to directives, is the *target-as-agent criterion.* The act Mehta requests of Perlman must be one in which the target hearer, Perlman, is the sole agent. Mehta cannot ask Perlman to do something Stern is to do. All he could ask of Perlman is that Perlman *get* Stern to do something, which is not the same thing. This criterion follows directly from Searle's propositional content condition, which requires that the requested act be predicated of the target hearer.

To see how this analysis might work, let us consider the distributive request in (8):

(8) *Mehta, to Perlman and Stern:* Please sit down.

On the Pattern of (7), we might try to represent (8) as (9):

(9) *Mehta, to Perlman and Stern:* 'I request of the two of you that the two of you sit down.'

But (9) fails both of our criteria for elementary requests. First, it has two addressees. To remedy this, we might represent (8) as a conjunction of (10) and (10').

(10) *Mehta, to Perlman:* 'I request of you that you and Stern sit down.'

(10') *Mehta, to Stern:* 'I request of you that you and Perlman sit down.'

But (10) and (10') fail the target-as-agent criterion. Since Mehta cannot request of Perlman that Stern sit down, he also cannot request of Perlman that he *and* Stern sit down.[7] To remedy this, we might turn to the representation in (11) and (11'):

(11) *Mehta, to Perlman:* 'I request of you that you sit down.'

(11') *Mehta, to Stern:* 'I request of you that you sit down.'

By our criteria, both of these are legitimate elementary requests. Furthermore, together they capture the intuition that the distributive request in (8) is really a conjunction of elementary requests to Perlman and Stern separately. Mehta is asking each of them individually to sit down.

The point of the representation in (11) and (11') is this: It separates what Perlman is intended to recognize from what Stern is intended to recognize. We can then evaluate whether Perlman, who is privy only to (11), has all the information he needs in order to recognize what Mehta intended him to recognize, and whether the same goes for Stern, who is privy only to (11'). We require the representation of Mehta's complex illocutionary act to be one that decomposes in such a way that it spells out Mehta's two sets of intentions to recognize separately.

Collective Requests

The problem we want to solve is how to represent (5), Mehta's request of Perlman and Stern that they jointly play the first chord of Bartok's "Study 119." Mehta must obviously get both men to take part. He might do this on the pattern of (11) and (11') as in (12) and (12'):

(12) *Mehta, to Perlman:* 'I request of you that you play E, your first note.'

(12') *Mehta, to Stern:* 'I request of you that you play E sharp, your first note.'

Perlman and Stern would then play their first notes, and the piece would be off.

But with (12) and (12'), has Mehta asked Perlman and Stern to carry out a joint act? No. All he has done is ask each of them to carry out an individual act. The form of (12) and (12') is indistinguishable from the form of (11) and (11'), which are individual requests to Perlman and Stern to sit down. The problem is to distinguish between these two cases: the distributive request in (8) to sit down and the collective request in (5) to play the first chord.

Something is missing in (12) and (12'). Recall that Mehta has been practising his start and now intends it for real. When Mehta then says *play*, Perlman may himself believe that Mehta is starting them off for real, but he has no idea whether Stern believes this. If Stern doesn't, Stern won't expect to play, and the joint act won't come off. By (12), Perlman believes only that Mehta is requesting *him* to play E. If he is to take part in a joint act, he must also believe that Mehta is simultaneously requesting Stern to play E sharp. Stern, of course, would reason in the same way from (12'). The representation suggested by this reasoning is the following:

(13) a. *Mehta, to Perlman:* 'I request of you that you play E.'
     b. *Mehta, to Perlman:* 'I e-inform you of (13'a).'

(13') a. *Mehta, to Stern:* 'I request of you that you play E sharp.'
     b. *Mehta, to Stern:* 'I e-inform you of (13a).'

We will call the illocutionary acts in (13b) and (13'b) *elementary informatives* or *e-informatives.* They are called *informatives* in that they serve to inform certain hearers about other speech acts being performed. They are termed *elementary* for reasons we have already given.

With (13) and (13'), Perlman and Stern are better off than before, but they still shouldn't expect to be able to carry out a joint act. Take Perlman. He recognizes that he is being requested to play E and that Stern is being requested to play E sharp. But he should reason further, "Stern knows that *he* has been requested to play E sharp, but he may not know that *I* have been requested to play E at the same time. If he doesn't know about Mehta's request to me, he won't necessarily play, since he doesn't believe we are going to play jointly. For a joint act to come off, Mehta must inform me that he is informing Stern about his request for me to play E." Stern would reason in an analogous way. So we need to add to (13) and (13') these two illocutionary acts:

(13) c. *Mehta, to Perlman:* 'I e-inform you that I am e-informing Stern of (13a).'

(13') c. *Mehta, to Stern:* 'I e-inform you that I am e-informing Perlman of (13'a).'

The patch-up in (13c) and (13'c), however, won't succeed either. The logic here is the same as for the violin duets. What is needed is an infinite set of such e-informatives. For Perlman and Stern truly to expect to carry out the joint act of playing the first chord, they must commonly believe that they both expect to play their first notes. Mehta must *jointly* inform the two of them of what he is requesting each of them to do. This might be represented as in (14) and (14'):

(14) a. *Mehta, to Perlman:* 'I request of you that you play E.'
 b. *Mehta, to Perlman:* 'I j-inform you and Stern of (14a).'
 c. *Mehta, to Perlman:* 'I j-inform you and Stern of (14'a).'

(14') a. *Mehta, to Stern:* 'I request of you that you play E sharp.'
 b. *Mehta, to Stern:* 'I j-inform you and Perlman of (14'a).'
 c. *Mehta, to Stern:* 'I j-inform you and Perlman of (14a).'

What we mean here by *j-informative,* or *joint informative,* is the obvious extension of e-informatives to common or joint beliefs. It can be defined as follows:

S j-informs a group of hearers *G* that *p* = def.
S e-informs each hearer in *G* that he intends it to be a common belief in *G* and *S* that *p*, where *p* is that *S* is performing a particular addressee-directed illocutionary act.

Despite appearances, j-informatives are legitimate by the single-target criterion. In (14b), "I j-inform you and Stern" is really a shorthand for "I e-inform you that I intend it to be a

common belief in you, Stern, and me." We will use the shorthand for convenience.

As representations of what Perlman and Stern need, (14) and (14') fare pretty well. Perlman recognizes that he is being requested to play his first note, E. He also recognizes that he and Stern mutually believe that they are both being requested to play their first notes. He appears to have all the information from Mehta that he needs for him and Stern to coordinate their playing of the first notes successfully. The same seem to go for Stern. But even (14) and (14') don't capture the essence of the collective request in (5). To see this, we must look more closely at distributive requests.

Distributive Requests

Imagine that Mehta asks Perlman and Stern each to think of their favourite pieces of music and then he says:

(15) *Mehta, to Perlman and Stern:* Imagine the first note.

Let us assume that imagining a note cannot be done as a joint act, and so it is clear to Perlman and Stern that they are to act separately. Let us further suppose that Mehta and Perlman commonly believe that Perlman's favourite piece is Beethoven's *First,* which starts on E, and that Mehta and Stern commonly believe that Stern's favourite piece is Bach's *Brandenburg Concerto Number 1,* which starts on E sharp, or F. So Perlman recognizes that he is being requested to imagine E, and Stern that he is being requested to imagine E sharp, but neither knows what the other is being requested to imagine. In this situation, Perlman and Stern needn't know anything about the request to the other; they could be in separate recording chambers unaware that Mehta was even speaking to the other. The representation looks like this:

(16) a. *Mehta, to Perlman:* 'I request of you that you imagine E.'
 b. *Mehta, to Perlman:* 'I e-inform you of (16'a).'

(16') a. *Mehta, to Stern;* 'I request of you that you imagine E sharp.'
 b. *Mehta, to Stern:* 'I e-inform you of (16a).'

Perlman knows all he needs to know in order to do as requested, and so does Stern. Conclusion: unlike collective requests, distributive requests do not require that the several addressees be jointly informed about what each of them has been requested to do.

At first, (16) and (16′) look unnecessarily complex. When Mehta requests Perlman to imagine E, he is of course informing him that he is making that request (Schiffer, 1972). It seems unnecessary to mention the e-informative in (16b).[8] However, it *is* necessary to include the e-informative if we are to distinguish the situation just described (let us call it Situation A) from the following two situations.

Situation B. To Situation A, let us add that all three men commonly believe that Perlman's favourite piece is Beethoven's *First,* and so Mehta is informing Perlman and Stern jointly, with all the right illocutionary intentions, of his request to Perlman to imagine E. In contrast, Perlman doesn't know what Stern's favourite piece is. The representation in (16) and (16′), therefore, needs to be changed as follows:[9]

(17) a. *Mehta, to Perlman:* 'I request of you that you imagine E.'
b. *Mehta, to Perlman:* 'I j-inform you and Stern of (17a).'

(17′) a. *Mehta, to Stern:* 'I request of you that you imagine E sharp.'
b. *Mehta, to Stern:* 'I e-inform you of (17′a).'
c. *Mehta, to Stern:* 'I j-inform you and Perlman of (17a).'

Notice that for Perlman, the only thing that distinguishes Situation A from Situation B is the change in the informative. The informatives are therefore needed to distinguish Mehta's speech acts in the two situations: they are necessary parts of both representations.

Situation C. To Situtation B, let us now add the common belief among all three that Stern's favourite piece is Bach's *First Brandenburg Concerto.* The representation turns out as follows:

(18) a. *Mehta, to Perlman:* 'I request of you that you imagine E.'
b. *Mehta, to Perlman:* 'I j-inform you and Stern of (18a).'
c. *Mehta, to Perlman:* 'I j-inform you and Stern of (18′a).'

(18′) a. *Mehta, to Stern:* 'I request of you that you imagine E sharp.'
b. *Mehta, to Stern:* 'I j-inform you and Perlman of (18′a).'

c. *Mehta, to Stern:* 'I j-inform you and Perlman of (18a).'

In this situation, Perlman and Stern are each being jointly informed of what the other is being requested to do, even though they are to imagine their notes separately and not jointly.

With Situation C, we can begin to see what is wrong with the analysis of collective requests in (14) and (14′). Note that the content of (18) and (18′), which represents Mehta's distributive request, is identical (except for the verb *imagine* instead of *play*) to the content of (14) and (14′), which was intended to represent Mehta's collective request. That is, the two representations fail to distinguish collective from distributive requests.

The fault lies in the representation for the collective requests. When Mehta utters *Play* in (5), he is *not* requesting Perlman and Stern to play E and E sharp individually yet simultaneously. If he were, he would be doing nothing different from asking them to *imagine* the two notes individually yet simultaneously, which is not a joint act. Rather, what he is doing is requesting of the *pair* of them that the *pair* of them play the chord consisting of E and E sharp. This difference, though subtle, is critical. Mehta could make collective request as in (5) without knowing who is to play what note. He could even make such a request while believing that only one of them was to play, but he didn't know which. All that Mehta need be requesting is for the first chord to be played by the pair of them, however they jointly work out how that is to be done.[10]

Simply put, when Mehta makes a truly collective request of Perlman and Stern, he isn't making elementary requests of each of them separately. His only request is of Perlman-and-Stern as a pair. Now it could be argued that Mehta is, nevertheless, making elementary requests that look something like this: *I request of you, Perlman, that you take part in the joint act in which you and Stern play the first chord.* Elementary requests such as this one, however, cannot account for other collective requests we will take up. Indeed, with the right analysis, they are superfluous in the representation of Mehta's collective request of Perlman and Stern.

Once we eliminate elementary requests from the analysis of collective requests, we have a new and more difficult problem: How can a speaker make a collective request of a pair of people without making elementary requests of each one separately? Before we can offer a solution, we must take a closer look at informatives.

INFORMATIVES

Informatives, we claimed earlier, are a type of illocutionary act that the speaker directs at certain hearers. But are they speech acts at all? Perhaps the speaker isn't directing anything at these hearers. When Mehta simultaneously asks Perlman and Stern to imagine their notes, he considers Perlman and Stern each to be merely overhearers, or eavesdroppers, of the request he is making to the other man, and that is how they become jointly informed. To show that informatives really *are* illocutionary acts, we will consider several possibilities.

The first possibility can be illustrated with (12) and (12′), which are repeated here:

(12) *Mehta, to Perlman:* 'I request of you that you play E.'

(12′) *Mehta, to Stern:* 'I request of you that you play E sharp.'

Let us assume that Perlman and Stern are each fully aware of what is being uttered to the other. Take Perlman's perspective. He recognizes that he has been requested to play E. As an eavesdropper, an overhearer, he also happens to hear that the word *play* has also been directed at Stern. Since he also sees that Stern is overhearing what is uttered to him, he can infer, by the common belief induction schema, that they commonly believe the words Mehta has directed at each of them. Can Perlman now be assured that the joint act of playing the first chord can take place?

No. The reasons are inherent to overhearing. In the general case speakers do not design their utterances so as to guarantee that overhearers will be able to recognize what they mean. They design their utterances so as to guarantee recognition only by specific hearers, generally only the addressees. When you overhear a man on a bus say to a woman, "Let's try your house this week," you may surmise or conjecture that he is proposing an assignation at her house that week, but realize that you can't know for sure. The man may be sug-

gesting her house for the next meeting of Alcoholics Anonymous, or as the next target for their fumigating business. You realize this because you recognize that the man didn't design his utterance in such a way that you, an overhearer, *should* be able to understand what he meant. Thus, if Perlman is merely overhearing Mehta's words to Stern, he could guess that Mehta is making request (12′), but he couldn't know for sure.

However, one type of overhearer *is* intended to be listening in, which leads us to a second possibility. Let us suppose that Perlman believes that Mehta intended him to overhear his words to Stern, and that Mehta intended Perlman to overhear his words to Stern. Perlman could then, with the right assumptions, infer the common belief of Mehta's *intentions* that these words were addressed to both men. This is surely enough to guarantee the joint act of playing the first chord, isn't it?

The answer, however, is again no. Intended overhearers are only somewhat better off than other overhearers. Suppose the man on the bus knew you were listening in and deliberately chose the words "Let's try your house this week" for your benefit. Did he want you to come to the right conclusion in conjecturing that they were having an affair? Did he want to deceive you into thinking that they were having an affair? Or did he merely want to be obscure so that you wouldn't come to *any* coherent conjecture? You still have no *solid* reason to assume that any of these interpretations is the intended one. What you are missing is an essential ingredient for the recognition of a speaker's meaning: the speaker's intention that you recognize his intentions. This is what Grice (1968) has called *m-intention,* and Bach and Harnish (1979) have called *R-intention,* for "reflexive" intention. For you to be sure that the man on the bus believes you have everything you need to know to recognize what he meant, you must believe that he not merely intended, but *m-intended,* that you come to that interpretation.

Informatives, therefore, are a type of illocutionary act. Like illocutionary acts, they are performed by uttering sentences. Like illocutionary acts, they are directed by speakers at particular hearers. Most of all, like illocutionary acts, they require m-intentions and not some simpler form of intentions. They fit

Grice's definition of speaker's meaning and Searle's definition of illocutionary act.

The Firing Squad

In the study of illocutionary acts, one can often sharpen an analytical point by looking at acts that are part of institutional procedures like marriages, christenings and sentencings, as Austin (1962) did. With these, the consequences of breaking one or another requirement are particularly obvious. In this spirit, consider an execution by firing squad in which the commander orders two riflemen, George and Harry, to fire their rifles at a prisoner. Now in the society under consideration, the law requires that one of the riflemen, selected at random without anyone's knowledge, be given a live bullet and the other be given a blank. This way it can be said of each rifleman that it isn't certain whether or not he fired the bullet that killed the prisoner and, therefore, he cannot be held personally responsible for the prisoner's death. Every execution must follow this rule if it is to be considered legal.

What happens when the commander says "Fire!"? George should reason this way: "The commander has ordered us to fire. But that order is not legitimate (indeed, the law forbids me to fire) unless he has ordered us both to fire. Otherwise, I could be held personally liable for the prisoner's death. I must be certain, or as certain as I can be, that Harry is intended to fire too. But before Harry will fire he must assure himself that I am intended to fire, so I must assure myself that Harry has assured himself that I am intended to fire too." And so on. That is, each of the riflemen must mutually believe that the commander has genuinely ordered the two of them jointly to fire now. The commander must j-inform both addressees before his collective order is effectuated.

In this example, it is clear that the j-informatives must be illocutionary acts. The law requires that the commander instruct *both* riflemen to fire at the same time. He must therefore intend both riflemen to recognize his *intentions* that they both fire, since otherwise they are not legally bound, or even allowed, to carry out his order. That is, he must intend them each to recognize that they are both to fire in part by means of their recognition of his intention that they are both to fire. The command would be illegitimate without these m-intentions. Therefore, the j-informatives to George and Harry are illocutionary acts.

Participants and Informatives

Hearers who are targets of informatives ought to be distinguished from mere overhearers, who aren't targets of any illocutionary acts. These hearers we will call *participants*. We can then state the first of three basic hypotheses we wish to defend (see Clark and Carlson, 1980):

> The *participant hypothesis:* Certain illocutionary acts are directed at hearers in their role as addressees, and others are directed at hearers in their roles as participants.

The first class will be called *addressee-directed illocutionary acts,* and the second, *participant-directed illocutionary acts.*

A good deal of evidence has already been provided for the participant hypothesis. Consider the analysis of (5) as provided in (14) and (14′), repeated here:

(14) a. *Mehta, to Perlman:* 'I request of you that you play E.'
     b. *Mehta, to Perlman:* 'I j-inform you and Stern of (14a).'
     c. *Mehta, to Perlman:* 'I j-inform you and Stern of (14′a).'

(14′) a. *Mehta, to Stern:* 'I request of you that you play E sharp.'
     b. *Mehta, to Stern:* 'I j-inform you and Perlman of (14′a).'
     c. *Mehta, to Stern:* 'I j-inform you and Perlman of (14a).'

In traditional terminology, the addressees of requests are the requestees. Perlman plays this role in (14a) and Stern plays this role in (14′a). However, the roles they play in (14b), (14c), (14′b) and (14′c) are very different: they are no longer requestees, but "informees." It is the role of "informee" (an ugly term) that we are calling participant. The participant hypothesis merely says that the roles of addressee and participant are distinct. A hearer can be the target of an illocutionary act in his role as addressee and, simultaneously, the target of a distinct illocutionary act in his role as participant. There is one class of illocutionary acts directed at hearers in their roles as addressees (such acts as requests, promises, assertions and apologies) and there is another class directed at hearers in their roles as participants, such as the acts we have called informatives. Still other hearers are in the role of overhearers. They aren't targets of any illocutionary acts since the speaker has no m-intentions towards them.

The second of our three hypotheses is this:

The informative hypothesis: The fundamental kind of participant-directed illocutionary act is one in which the speaker informs the participants of the addressee-directed illocutionary acts he is performing.

That is, the fundamental illocutionary act directed at participants is the informative. So far, we have only argued that informatives are necessary for collective requests. We will leave the claim that they are fundamental to be demonstrated elsewhere (Clark and Carlson, 1980).

The most far-reaching of our three hypotheses is this:

The informative first hypothesis: All addressee-directed illocutionary acts are performed by means of informatives.

Collective requests provide important evidence that at least *some* addressee-directed illocutionary acts are performed by means of informatives. The argument that *all* such acts are so performed we will leave until later.

Collective Requests Reconsidered

Let us return to Mehta's request in (5) that Perlman and Stern jointly play the first chord of Bartok's "Study 119." In arriving at (14) and (14'), we argued that Mehta's request couldn't be complete without Mehta's j-informatives to the two of them. These informatives, then, are at least a *necessary* condition for the performing of collective requests.

However, the problem with (14) and (14') is that in (5), Mehta isn't asking Perlman to play E and Stern to play E sharp. He is asking the pair of them to play the chord consisting of E and E sharp. He is making not two requests, one of each musician, but a single request of the pair of them, just as if he were asking Perlman alone to play the chord, as in (6). The problem is how to direct a request at Perlman-and-Stern even though Perlman-and-Stern isn't a single individual capable of recognizing

Mehta's intentions in a single act of recognition.

The solution we propose is for Mehta to make the collective request via his informatives. In this analysis, (5) has two levels. It is represented at the level of *elementary* illocutionary acts as the conjunction of (19) and (19'):

(19) *Mehta, to Perlman:* 'I j-inform you and Stern that I am requesting of you-and-Stern that you-and-Stern play the first chord.'

(19') *Mehta, to Stern:* 'I j-inform you and Perlman that I am requesting of you-and-Perlman that you-and-Perlman play the first chord.'

Mehta directs these informatives at Perlman and Stern individually. But by doing so, he m-intends Perlman and Stern to recognize jointly that they as a pair are to play the first chord. By performing the j-informatives, Mehta is, so to speak, turning Perlman and Stern into a joint recognizer as far as his request is concerned. He is thereby, at the level of addressee-directed illocutionary acts, also performing (20):

(20) *Mehta, to Perlman-and-Stern:* 'I request of you that you play the first chord.'

That is, Mehta performs the request in (20) *by means of* the informatives in (19) and (19').

Mehta's request in (20) can be thought of as requiring a single act of recognition, thereby satisfying Grice's and Searle's requirements for illocutionary acts and speaker's meanings. What is special about this act of recognition is that it is itself a type of joint act. It takes Perlman's and Stern's joint act of recognition of Mehta's m-intentions to coordinate successfully the joint act of playing the first chord.

The analysis in (19), (19') and (20) has just the properties we want. First, it satisfies the individual recognition assumption. At the level of elementary illocutionary acts, Perlman and Stern are each to recognize Mehta's m-intentions towards them. Secondly, what is being requested is the *single* joint act of playing the chord, not *two* individual but simultaneous acts of Perlman playing E and Stern playing E sharp. Mehta is making only a single request. And thirdly, the target of the request, namely the pair Perlman-and-Stern, is also the agent who is to do the requested act: to play the first chord.

We will call this sort of analyis the *informative analysis*. If all it accounted for were collective requests like the one in (5), it would be of little use. But it accounts for much more. It makes sense of a network of facts about illocutionary acts when there are two or more participants. It also handles canonical illocutionary acts, those acts that are directed at single namable addressees. To illustrate its power, we turn next to other requests that involve two or more participants.

OTHER COLLECTIVE REQUESTS

So far, we have taken up requests with two or more addressees who could have been referred to by name: Mehta could have said *Itzhak and Pinchas, play*. There are two broad classes of illocutionary acts in which the addressees cannot be referred to by name. In the first, the addressees are designated by indefinite references, such as *someone* or *anyone*. In the second class, they are designated by attributive noun phrases, such as *the person who wins* or *whoever leaves last*. Neither class, we will argue, can be handled by standard speech act theories.

Indefinite Addressees

Consider the requests in (21) and (22):

(21) *David, to Ann, Bonnie and Carol:* Someone, please open the door.

(22) *David, to Ann, Bonnie and Carol:* Anyone wanting to eat, come with me.

These two requests are non-canonical in that they are addressed to indefinite someone's and anyone's, not to single definite people. The reason they cannot be handled by standard speech act theories is obvious. By Searle's essential condition, (21) should be an attempt by David to get the "hearer" to open the door. Yet there are three hearers, and David doesn't have these intentions toward all of them, or even toward any particular one of them. Likewise, (22) should be an attempt by David to get the "hearer" to go with him. However, it is really David's attempt to get any one or more of the three hearers who wants to eat to go with him.

There is an important contrast between (21) and (22). In (21), David wants one of the three

women to open the door, but doesn't specify which one it should be. He leaves it up to Ann, Bonnie and Carol *as a collective* to decide. In (22), David wants any of the three women who wants to eat to go with him. This time he leaves it to each *individual* woman whether or not she is to do the requested act. He doesn't intend them to make a collective decision as in (21).

Although (21) and (22) look very different from Mehta's collective and distributive requests, they work by similar principles. In uttering *Play,* Mehta intended Perlman and Stern to co-ordinate with each other in realizing a result: playing the first chord. Both men were to take part. With *Someone, please open the door,* David similarly intends Ann, Bonnie and Carol to co-ordinate with each other in realizing a result: opening the door. But in this result, only one person is to take part. The way the three women might co-ordinate with each other can take many forms. This contrasts with (22) in which the three women don't have to co-ordinate at all. Without stretching the terms too much, we seem justified in calling (21) and (22) collective and distributive requests, respectively.

There is a clear division in (21) between the two roles that the hearers play. On the one hand, David is speaking to all three women, Ann, Bonnie and Carol. On the other, he is requesting only one of the three (he doesn't care which) to open the door. The set of hearers he is speaking to (Set 1) doesn't coincide with the set of hearers who are being requested to open the door (Set 2). For Mehta's request in (5), these two sets happen to coincide.

There are two arguments for calling Set 2 the "addressees" and Set 1 "participants." First, for all other illocutionary acts, it is the persons specified by the vocative who are considered to be the addressees. In (22), the vocative specifies some one woman and not all three women, and so by this criterion, the addressee is that indefinable someone, Set 2. Secondly, in Searle's characterization of canonical requests, the addressee (whom he labels "the hearer") is the person who is to do the requested act. In (21), the act of opening the door is predicated of only some one of the three women. By this criterion, the addressee is again the indefinitely specified person who is to open the door: the requestee or Set 2. The hearers in Set 1, the "addressees" of the informatives, are better called by another term, namely participants.

Now to the analysis of (21). Since it is a collective request, we might try to divide it up into individual requests and informatives, much as we tried to do in (14) and (14'). Let us consider (21) from just one of the women's point of view: Ann's. The analogue to (14) would be (23):

(23) a. *David, to Ann:* 'I request of one of you that that person open the door.'
   b. *David, to Ann:* 'I j-inform you, Bonnie, and Carol that I am requesting of one of any of you that that person open the door.'

The request in (23a), however, is illegitimate as an elementary request. David isn't making his request of Ann in particular. The only act he is performing toward her in particular is one that *makes it known that* he is requesting some one or other of them to open the door. This is captured in (23b). The question in (23a) must be expunged. The problem here is similar to the one in Mehta's *Play*. The request being made simply cannot be made directly of any single hearer.

The problem is resolved in the informative analysis. Suppose that in uttering (21), David is performing the illocutionary act in (24):

(24) *David, to Ann:* 'I j-inform you, Bonnie, and Carol that I am requesting of any one of you that that person open the door.'

He is simultaneously performing the corresponding j-informatives towards Bonnie and Carol too. By means of these informatives, David is also making a request of some one of the three women: a person of their joint choosing. This might be represented as in (25):

(25) *David, to the person jointly selected by Ann, Bonnie and Carol:* 'I request of you that you open the door.'

David is performing the request in (25) *by means of* the informative in (24). This, therefore, is further evidence for the informative-first hypothesis.

Attributive Addressees

Consider the requests in (26) and (27):

(26) *Ruth, to Tom, Dick and Harry:* The last two of you to leave, please move the piano back into the corner.

(27) *Ruth, to Tom, Dick and Harry:* The last two of you to leave, please go to Room 100.

In both utterances, the addressees (the hearers designated in the vocative to carry out the requested acts) are specified by what Donnellan (1966) has called the attributive use of the definite description. With the phrase *the last two of you to leave,* there aren't two particular people that Ruth intends to designate (say, Tom and Dick) who will in fact be the last two of the three to leave. There might be no way she could know who she is designating, since the three are to leave in the future. Rather, she intends to designate the two people, whoever they turn out to be, who are the last two to leave.

The contrast between (26) and (27) is the by now familiar contrast between collective and distributive readings. In (26), the last two people to leave must carry out the joint act (let us assume) of moving the piano back to the corner. Like other collective requests, this will require Ruth to perform certain joint informatives. In (27), on the other hand, the last two people to leave are each to carry out separate acts (let us assume), and the request is distributive. All Ruth need do is inform each of the two people separately.

Compared to our earlier examples, the collective request in (26) is complicated. As in Mehta's *Play,* the requested act in (26) is a joint act. But as in David's *Someone, please open the door,* any two of the three participants could turn out to be the addressees. This suggests that (26) ought to be analysed like (21). From Tom's point of view, the analysis would go as follows:

(28) *Ruth, to Tom:* 'I j-inform you, Dick and Harry that I am requesting that the last two of you to leave to move the piano back to the corner.'

By performing this informative, Ruth is also performing the request in (29):

(29) *Ruth, to the two people who turn out in fact to be the last two of the three to leave:* 'I request you to move the piano back to the corner.'

As in (21), the request in (29) can only be accomplished by means of the informative in (28) since Ruth's request is not being made of Tom in particular.

The request in (29) is itself collective. It is a request that Ruth cannot make without jointly informing the two addressees, whoever they turn out to be, of what she is requesting. With (28), however, Ruth will already have jointly informed every pair of them, since she has jointly informed all three of them. So the informative in (28) accomplishes all that Ruth needs. It not only makes the request in (29) but also legitimates it as a collective request.

Virtually the same analysis is required for the distributive request in (27). The only difference is that the informatives to Tom, Dick and Harry need not be joint. From Tom's point of view, (27) consists of an e-informative as follows:

(30) *Ruth, to Tom:* 'I e-inform you (*or* j-inform you, Dick, and Harry) that I am requesting the last two of you to leave to go to Room 100.'

Ruth thereby also performs (31):

(31) *Ruth, to the two people who turn out in fact to be the last two of the three to leave:* 'I request each of you to go to Room 100.'

Ruth cannot perform (31) directly since she cannot know who will in fact be the last two to leave. She can only perform (31) by performing (30). This is further evidence in favor of the informative-first hypothesis.

THE INFORMATIVE ANALYSIS

The informative analysis, if it is correct, should also be able to handle the types of requests we have not yet mentioned. It should make sense, too, of such illocutionary acts as promises, assertions, apologies and christenings, whether canonical or not. The claim is that the informative analysis handles all these cases. Here we can only outline the argument in favor of that claim.

The informative analysis divides speech situations up into two parts. First, the speaker *informs* each of the designated participants he has designated that he is performing certain illocutionary acts towards the addressees. And second, he *thereby* performs the illocutionary acts towards those addressees. The informatives are the means by which the addressee-directed illocutionary acts are performed. It is worthwhile reviewing the six major cases of requests we have taken up so far.

Requests

Case 1: Collective requests with namable addressees. When Mehta says to Perlman and Stern *Play,* he cannot request each one directly that the pair of them play. All he can do towards each person individually is inform that person that he is requesting the pair of them to play. He makes the request itself by informing each one that he intends them to believe that they are to play. The informative is not merely a prerequisite for the request. It is the means by which the request is made.

Case 2: Collective requests with indefinite addressees. When David says to Ann, Bonnie and Carol *Someone, please open the door,* he cannot request of each woman individually that someone open the door. Who that someone is is under the joint control of all three women. All David can do is inform each one that he intends them to commonly believe that he is making that request. Since he intends them to recognize the request that logically follows, he thereby makes that request too.

Case 3: Collective request with attributive addressees. When Ruth says to Tom, Dick and Harry *The last two of you to leave, please move the piano back to the corner,* she too cannot make this request of any one individual. It is the circumstances that will determine who this request is being made of. All she can do is inform each man that she intends them to commonly believe that she is making such a request. That will be sufficient for her request to become operative. Collective requests, therefore, offer direct support for the informative analysis. They must be made indirectly, by means of j-informatives.

Case 4: Distributive requests with namable addressees. Let us return to Mehta's request in (15):

(15) *Mehta, to Perlman and Stern:* Imagine the first note.

Recall the three situations in which (15) was uttered:

Situation A. Perlman and Stern each hold a common belief with Mehta about what his own favorite piece is, but they do not know about each other's favorite piece.

Situation B. All three men hold a common belief about what Perlman's favorite piece is, but only

Mehta and Stern hold a common belief about what Stern's favorite is.

Situation C. All three hold common beliefs about Perlman's and Stern's favorite pieces.

Imagining a note, we assumed, was something that Perlman and Stern couldn't do jointly, and so in all three situations, Mehta's request was distributive. Nevertheless, since he was informing Perlman and Stern of different things in the three situations, we needed to bring in informatives in order to distinguish the speech acts Mehta was performing in the three situations. The conclusion was this: Informatives are just as necessary in representing distributive requests as in representing collective requests.

In the informative analysis, however, the informatives are not merely necessary parts of these situations. They are the means by which Mehta makes his requests, even though the requests are distributive. The alternative to this analysis, which we might call the *adjunct model,* makes the weaker assumption that Mehta's informatives are necessary "adjuncts" to his requests but nothing more. They are not the means by which he performs those requests. Which model is better?

The two models can be contrasted in this way. Imagine that Mehta had uttered (32) in the same three situations:

(32) *Mehta, to Perlman and Stern:* Hum the first note.

Let us assume that Perlman and Stern can hum in two ways: (a) individually to themselves, where what the other does is irrelevant; and (b) jointly out loud, where co-ordination is as necessary as ever. Imagine further that Mehta intended, m-intended even, that Perlman and Stern were to hum jointly out loud if all the conditions were right for them to do so jointly, as in Situation C, but that they were to hum to themselves individually if not all the conditions were right, as in Situation B. So by uttering (32) in Situation B, Mehta was making a distributive request, and by uttering it in Situation C, he was making a collective request.

In this example, Mehta's only means for signalling whether his request was distributive or collective was via his informatives. They were the only parts of what he meant that Perlman and Stern could recognize as changing from

Situation B to Situation C. They were the only parts he needed in order to transform his request from distributive to collective. The informatives, then, weren't merely necessary adjuncts to the request being made. They were the means by which the request was intended to be recognized. Such an example favors the informative analysis by Occam's Razor. The analysis, already required for collective requests, accounts for why informatives are not only necessary but the means for making requests such as Mehta's in Situations B and C. It is therefore superfluous to posit a second, weaker, adjunct model, since it would serve no additional purpose.

Case 5: Distributive requests with indefinite addressees. Imagine David saying to Ann, Bonnie and Carol *Anyone, tell me what answer you got.* In one context, he could intend a collective reading, and in another, a distributive reading, where the change from collective to distributive is signalled only by a change in informatives. If so, the arguments made in Case 4 apply to Case 5, giving further evidence for the informative analysis.

Case 6: Distributive requests with attributive addressees. Since Ruth's utterance *The last two of you to leave, please go to Room 100,* could also be changed from a collective to a distributive reading with a change in context, the arguments in Case 4 and Case 5 apply here too. However, an even more fundamental case can be made for the informative analysis whenever the addressees are designated attributively, and this is taken up in Case 7.

Case 7: Singular requests with an attributive addressee. Imagine that Ruth says to Tom, Dick and Harry *The last one of you to leave, please go to Room 100.* Now there is no distributive-collective ambiguity since there is only one addressee. Here, however, it is easy to see that Ruth can only make her request by informing each of the three men of that request either separately or jointly. Ruth can't request of *Tom,* for example, that the last one to leave is to go to Room 100, for he may not be the last to leave. All she can do is *inform* Tom of what she is requesting. If he turns out to be the last one to leave, he will perforce be the addressee. If he isn't the last to leave, the request has still been made, but not of him. So the informative analysis makes the right prediction here too. Ruth can only make her request by means of her informatives to Tom, Dick and Harry.

There can also be mixtures of these seven cases. For a complex example, consider (33):

(33) *Minister, to church gathering:* Those of you here with a spouse, give him or her a hug.

There are many addressees, who are designated attributively, and so we are in Case 5 or Case 6. But (33) is a mixture of the two cases. Each couple is to carry out the joint act of hugging. At the same time, each couple is to do its act separately from the other couples. The request is collective within couples, and distributive across couples. Complicated cases like this aren't difficult to find.

Canonical Requests

What about canonical requests: those with a single namable addressee? In standard speech–act theories, these are performed "directly," without the aid of other illocutionary acts. For example, (34) might be analysed as (35) and nothing more:

(34) *Eve, to Cain:* Bring me a cup of tea.

(35) *Eve, to Cain:* 'I order you to bring me a cup of tea.'

By the informative analysis, canonical orders are like all other addressee-directed illocutionary acts: They are performed by means of informatives. So (34) is analysed as in (36):

(36) a. *Eve, to Cain (as participant):* 'I inform you that I am ordering you to bring me a cup of tea.'
     b. *Eve, to Cain (as addressee):* 'I order you to bring me a cup of tea.'

In uttering (34), Eve performs (36a), and in doing so, she simultaneously performs (36b). Her order is "indirect" to this extent: It is performed by means of her informative. How can we justify this extra step for such simple orders?

One line of argument makes reference again to common beliefs among the hearers. Consider (37), a minor variant of (34):

(37) *Eve, to Cain, in front of Abel:* Bring me a cup of tea.

Let us suppose that Eve intends Abel to be a participant and not just an overhearer. By the

standard theories, (37) would still be analysed as in (35); Cain is still the single, namable addressee. The presence of other participants makes no difference. But in (37), Eve is j-informing both Cain *and* Abel of her order to Cain. That is, she truly means two distinct things in uttering (37):

(38) a. *Eve, to Cain and Abel (as participants):* 'I j-inform you that I am ordering Cain to bring me a cup of tea.'
     b. *Eve, to Cain (as addressee):* 'I order you to bring me a cup of tea.'

By the informative analysis, (34) and (37) receive distinct representations, as they should. Furthermore, the difference between them is located in Eve's informatives, where it belongs. For this distinction to be made, canonical requests must at least be accompanied by informatives.

But the informative analysis claims something stronger. Not only are Eve's orders in (34) and (37) accompanied by informatives, they are performed *by means of* those informatives. Imagine that Eve is in the next room, and yet the three commonly believe that Cain is the one obliged to bring the tea whenever Eve orders it. Suppose that Eve then utters (37). She is still issuing the command in (38b), and she is still informing Cain and Abel of that order, represented in (38a). Cain has all the information he needs to recognize that she is ordering him and not Abel, and so does Abel. Her utterance is just as good as if she had said *Cain, bring me a cup of tea,* using a conventional vocative to designate her addressee. In these circumstances, however, the only way she can order Cain to bring her a cup of tea (38b) is by means of her j-informative (38a).

The reasons are as follows. Since Eve is "speaking to" both Cain and Abel, they must each come to recognize that she is addressing Cain and not Abel. They can't infer this from Eve's gestures or eye gaze, since they cannot see her. They can't infer this from her vocatives, since she isn't using any. Their only route is via Eve's informatives. She is jointly informing them that she is ordering the one of them who is obliged to bring her tea to bring her a cup tea. Since all three commonly believe that Cain is the one who is obliged to bring her tea, both Cain and Abel can recognize that the addressee of the request is Cain and not Abel. Once Cain recognizes this, he can also recognize that Eve is thereby ordering him to bring her a cup of tea. Once Abel recognizes this, he has nothing more to do, since she has not issued any order to him. In terms of logical priority, the first step in computing what Eve meant must be the same for both Cain and Abel. It is only once they recognize what order she is informing them of that Cain sees that he is supposed to bring Eve a cup of tea.[11]

The scenario just described can be viewed differently. When Eve utters *Bring me a cup of tea* in this situation, what she is effectively uttering is *The one of you who is obliged to bring me tea, bring me a cup of tea,* an order with an attributive addressee. This is our Case 7, which we have already argued requires an informative analysis. So even though Eve doesn't utter an attributive vocative, she is designating the addressee in an equivalent way. Let us call this process *designating the addressee by attribution.*

This scenario is just one end of a continuum of scenarios in which addressees are designated in some part by attribution. Virtually every request, we would argue, uses this sort of designation along with such other addressee-designating devices as hand gestures and eye gazes. At the other end of this continuum are the requests in which the addressee is designated by name only, as in *Cain, bring me a cup of tea.* Even this can be viewed as designating the addressee by attribution. What Eve means in using the vocative *Cain* is "the one of you named Cain." Eve couldn't use this vocative if she thought the two participants would be confused about which one was named Cain. Thus, for every case in which there is more than one participant, even requests with single namable addressees must be performed by means of informatives.

Let us return to the contrast between (34) and (37). The orders to Cain in these two utterances are exactly the same. The only difference is in who is being informed of those orders: Cain alone, or Cain and Abel jointly. It would be unparsimonious to claim that Eve is performing those two orders in radically different ways: that she is performing the order in (34) "directly," with the informative merely "accompanying" that order, but that she is performing the order in (37) *via* her informa-

tive. By Occam's Razor, canonical orders too must be performed by means of informatives.

Conclusion: All requests and their kin (orders, questions, prohibitions, authorizations, recommendations, and the like) are performed by means of informatives.

Beyond Requests

For all other addressee-directed illocutionary acts (Searle's (1975) commissives, expressives, declarations, and representatives) the arguments are virtually the same as with requests. There are, however, notable differences in the requirements for common beliefs among the hearers.

Most other types of addressee-directed illocutionary acts can be either distributive or collective. One can promise, apologize to, or fire a group of people either individually or collectively. For the collective acts, however, it doesn't seem necessary to jointly inform all the members of the group. Sam can promise something to Connie and Irene collectively without informing them jointly that he is doing so. One exception perhaps is the marriage act in which the minister or priest says *I now pronounce you husband and wife.* Here it seems that groom and bride must be jointly informed.

What is the status of the informative-first hypothesis with these other illocutionary acts? Although the arguments based on the collective-distributive distinction in requests don't apply to the other acts, the remaining arguments do. Whenever the addressees are designated indefinitely, attributively, or "by attribution," the other illocutionary acts are subject to the same arguments as requests. These arguments show that all such illocutionary acts lie outside the accounts of standard speech act theories, but are properly handled by the informative analysis.

CONCLUSIONS

Since Austin's (1962) *How to Do Things with Words,* there have been many attempts to account for what speakers can do with words. Philosophers such as Grice (1957), Searle (1969), and Bach and Harnish (1979) have focussed on the speaker's intentions in using words and on the hearer's recognition of those intentions. The progess they and others have made on Austin's question has been immense. Yet the only illocutionary acts they have analysed are the canonical ones, those directed at single namable addressees. This oversight has been costly. When there is more than one hearer, these hearers can play several different roles (addressee, participant, and overhearer) and the intentions that the speaker holds toward hearers in each role are different. Standard speech act theories tell us nothing about these differences.

What the standard theories lack, we have argued, is a layer of illocutionary acts that lies just below the standard illocutionary acts: assertions, requests, promises and their kin. The new illocutionary acts, called informatives, are directed at hearers in their roles as participants. They are the direct means, and by hypothesis the only means, by which the speaker can perform assertions, requests, promises and their kin. Without this new layer, it is impossible to account for what speakers do with their words when there is more than one addressee, or participant. For speech-act theories to be complete, they need to add this new layer of informatives.

Our route to this conclusion has taken us through rather foreign territory for most language scientists: the co-ordination of actions. Joint acts, such as playing the first chord of a duet, dancing in a *corps de ballet,* or even shaking hands, make heavy demands on the people taking part in them. For the individual agents to bring off these acts jointly, they must share certain beliefs, and in a rather special way. They must have common or joint beliefs. So if a speaker is to request such an act, he must intend all the individual agents, his addressees, to come to the common or joint beliefs that are needed for the joint acts to come off. To achieve this, he needs informatives.

The general lesson is that speech acts cannot be fully understood without considering the hearers as well as the speakers. Speech acts are directed at real people, whose abilities to recognize put limits on what speakers can do with their utterances. In taking up collective speech acts, we have touched on just one issue in which the hearer is especially important. There are doubtless many more.

ACKNOWLEDGMENTS

The work reported here was supported in part by Grant MH-20021 from the National Institute of Mental Health. We wish to thank Eve V. Clark, Gregory Murphy, Ivan Sag, Amos Tversky and the participants of the Colloquium on Mutual Knowledge for their suggestions and comments on various points in this paper.

NOTES

1. For communication among computers, Yemini and Cohen (1979) and Cohen and Yemini (1979) have provided similar proofs, apparently discovered independently. We wish to thank Amos Tversky for bringing this work to our attention.

2. In this paper, we will skirt the issue of whether we should be using mutual beliefs or mutual knowledge. Schiffer speaks of "mutual knowledge or beliefs." For simplicity, we will use beliefs.

3. At the Colloquium, Grice took a similar stand about the infinite character of m-intentions in the definition of speaker's meaning. As he put it, when the evidence is right, people simply "deem" a speaker's intentions to be of the right kind. They do not need to traverse an infinite series of intentions to find out.

4. This objection was raised by Johnson-Laird both in his comments at the Colloquium and in his written discussion.

5. It is this belief that enables one to settle on the intended referent of *the wick* in *I bought an expensive candle, but the wick wouldn't light.*

6. Schiffer (1972: p.131) also considered mutual knowledge or beliefs within a group, but his formulation is not equivalent to Lewis's common knowledge or beliefs. For one thing, his definition allows for a proposition to be mutually believed within a group without it being mutually believed between two members of the group. Bach and Harnish (1979) give a similar definition, but without the infinite iterations of either Lewis or Schiffer.

7. If Jerry were to ask Richard, with Ruth not present, *Won't you and Ruth come to dinner tonight?*, we would not consider Jerry to be requesting of Richard that Ruth come to dinner, but that Richard bring it about that he and Ruth come.

8. Notice that the e-informative in (16b) is merely a j-informative in which the group G consists of only one person. It could equally well have been called a j-informative.

9. Even this representation isn't complete, since it doesn't include certain "partial informatives," as proposed by Clark and Carlson (1980). They are not needed for the point we are making here.

10. Kempson and Cormack (1981) have noted that for predicates like *destroy, finish,* and *write,* which they call "agent-accomplishment predicates," the agents need only contribute to the accomplishment of the actions. For the assertion *Pat and Mike destroyed six flower beds,* Pat, for example, may have destroyed none, one, or all six flower beds; all he needs to have done is contribute in some way to the total destruction. So when Irving makes a joint request of Pat and Mike to destroy six flower beds, he isn't making *specifiable* requests to Pat and Mike separately. All he is specifying is what they are to accomplish jointly. We are indebted to Ruth Kempson for bringing this point to our attention.

11. Imagine that Abel is the supplier of coffee, so he must be concerned whether she is ordering tea or coffee.

REFERENCES

Austin, J. L. (1962). *How to Do Things with Words.* Oxford: Oxford University Press.

Bach, K., and R. M. Harnish (1979). *Linguistic Communication and Speech Acts.* Cambridge, Mass.: MIT Press.

Chomsky, N. (1965). *Aspects of the Theory of Syntax.* Cambridge, Mass.: MIT Press.

Clark, E. V., and H. H. Clark (1979). "When Nouns Surface as Verbs." *Language* 55:767–811.

Clark, H. H. (1979). "Responding to Indirect Speech Acts." *Cognitive Psychology* 11:430–477. [Reprinted in this volume, Chapter 12]

Clark, H. H., and T. B. Carlson (1980). "Who Are Speech Acts Directed At?" Paper presented at Stanford Conference on Pragmatics, Asilomar, Calif., July 1980.

Clark, H. H., and C. R. Marshall (1981). "Definite Reference and Mutual Knowledge." In A. K. Joshi, I. Sag, and B. Webber (eds.), *Elements of Discourse Understanding.* Cambridge: Cambridge University Press.

Cohen, D., and Y. Yemini (1979). "Protocols for Dating Coordination." In *Proceedings of the Fourth Berkeley Conference on Distributed Data Management and Computer Networks.*

Cohen, P. R., and C. R. Perrault (1979). "Elements of a Plan-Based Theory of Speech Acts." *Cognitive Science* 3:197–212.

Donnellan, K. (1966). "Reference and Definite Description." *Philosophical Review* 75:281–304. [Reprinted in this volume, Chapter 3]

Grice, H. P. (1957). "Meaning." *Philosophical Review* 66:377–388. In D. Steinberg and L. Jakobovits (eds.). (1971). *Semantics.* Cambridge: Cambridge University Press, 53–59; Strawson (ed.) (1967). *Philosophical Logic.* London: Oxford University Press.

Grice, H. P. (1968). "Utterer's Meaning, Sentence-Meaning, and Word-Meaning." *Foundations of Language* 4:225–242. [Reprinted in this volume, Chapter 4]

Harder, P., and C. Kock (1976). *The Theory of Presuppostion Failure.* Copenhagen: Akademisk Forlag.

Karttunen, L., and S. Peters (1975). "Conventional Implicature in Montague Grammar." *Proceedings of the First Annual Berkeley Linguistic Society,* 266–278.

Lewis, D. K. (1969). *Convention.* Cambridge, Mass.: Harvard University Press.

Kempson, R., and A. Cormack (1981). "Ambiguity and Quantification." *Linguistics and Philosophy* 4:259–309.

McCarthy, J. (1979). Untitled manuscript. Stanford University.

Nunberg, G. (1979). "The Non-Uniqueness of Semantic Solutions: Polusemy." *Linguistics and Philosophy* 3:143–184.

Schelling, T. (1960). *The Strategy of Conflict.* Cambridge, Mass.: Harvard University Press.

Schiffer, S. R. (1972). *Meaning.* Oxford: Clarendon Press.

Searle, J. R. (1969). *Speech Acts.* Cambridge: Cambridge University Press.

Searle, J. R. (1975). "A Taxonomy of Illocutionary Acts." In K. Gunderson (ed.), *Language, Mind and Knowledge, Minnesota Studies in the Philosophy of Science,* vol. 3. Minneapolis: University of Minnesota Press, 344–369. Reprinted in J. R. Searle (1979). *Expression and Meaning: Studies in the Theory of Speech Acts.* Cambridge: Cambridge University Press, 1–29.

Stalnaker, R. (1978). "Assertion." In P. Cole (ed.), *Syntax and Semantics.* Vol. 9: *Pragmatics.* New York: Academic Press, 315–332. [Reprinted in this volume, Chapter 17]

Yemini, Y., and D. Cohen (1979). "Some Issues in Distributed Processes Communication." In *Proceedings of the First International Conference on Distributed Computer Systems.*

12

Responding to Indirect Speech Acts

HERBERT H. CLARK

Indirect speech acts, like the request *Do you know the time?,* have both a literal meaning, here "I ask you whether you know the time," and an indirect meaning "I request you to tell me the time." In this paper I outline a model of how listeners understand such speech acts and plan responses to them. The main proposals are these. The literal meaning of indirect speech acts can be intended to be taken *seriously* (along with the indirect meaning) or merely pro forma. In the first case listeners are expected to respond to both meanings, as in *Yes, I do—it's six,* but in the second case only to the indirect meaning, as in *It's six.* There are at least six sources of information listeners use in judging whether the literal meaning was intended seriously or pro forma, as well as whether there was intended to be any indirect meaning. These proposals were supported in five experiments in which ordinary requests for information were made by telephone of 950 local merchants.

Most sentences can be used to convey meanings indirectly. *Is Julia at home?* can be used in its literal sense to ask a question, a *direct* speech act. On the telephone it can also be used as a request to call Julia to the phone, an *indirect* speech act. Although much is known about the linguistic properties of indirect speech acts (see, e.g., Cole and Morgan, 1975), less is known about the processes by which they are produced or understood. In understanding, there are two questions of particular interest. How do listeners decide whether an utterance should be taken directly or indirectly? And if it is to be taken indirectly, how do they decide what its indirect meaning should be?

To get at these questions, I have chosen to study not just indirect speech acts, but also people's responses to them. Take *Is Julia at home?* When it is construed literally, it elicits such responses as *Yes, she is* or *No, she isn't.* But when it is construed as an indirect request,

Herbert H. Clark, "Responding to Indirect Speech Acts." In *Cognitive Psychology* 11: 430–477. Copyright © 1979 by Academic Press, Inc. Reprinted by permission of the publisher.

it elicits two distinct classes of responses. In some contexts it leads to simple responses, like *I'll get her* or *Just a minute,* which respond to the indirect meaning alone. In other contexts it leads to two-part responses, like *Yes, she is—I'll get her,* the first part of which, *Yes, she is,* answers the literal question, and the second part, *I'll get her,* responds to the indirect request. When do the one- and two-part responses occur, and why? These are two questions I will be particularly interested in. I will argue that they bear critically on how indirect speech acts should be characterized and how they are actually understood.

Responses to indirect speech acts, however, are important in their own right. In ordinary conversation, many speech acts, whether direct or indirect, come in what have been called *adjacency pairs.* Requests are responded to by promises of compliance, questions by answers, offers by acceptances or refusals and assertions by acknowledgments. The first half of each adjacency pair is intended to set up its response, and the second half, to satisfy the obligations set up. In conversation, it is these adjacency pairs that enable the participants to coordinate turn taking, the introduction and changing of topics, and the opening and closing of the conversation itself (Goffman, 1976; Sacks, Schegloff, & Jefferson, 1974; Schegloff, 1968; Schegloff, Jefferson, & Sacks, 1977; Schegloff & Sacks, 1973). It is important to learn more about adjacency pairs per se.

This paper, then, is about how people respond to indirect speech acts. It is divided into four parts. In the first, after a review of the major properties of indirect speech acts, I propose a matching set of properties for their responses. In the second part, I outline a model of how people understand indirect speech acts and plan their responses. In the third part, I report five experiments that were designed to refine this model. And in the final discussion, I pull all these refinements together.

INDIRECT SPEECH ACTS AND THEIR RESPONSES

My first goal is to lay out six major properties of indirect speech acts drawn from the philosophical and linguistic literature on the subject, propose a similar set of properties for

their responses, and show how the two sets match. I will speak of A, a generic woman who performs the indirect speech acts, and B, a generic man who responds to her. They can be thought of as Ann and Bob.

Six Properties of Indirect Speech Acts

(1) Multiplicity of meanings. Direct speech acts are intended to have just one meaning, or illocutionary force. In uttering *It's raining out* as a direct speech act, A means simply "I assert to you that it is raining out." Indirect speech acts, according to Searle (1975), always have more than one meaning, or illocutionary force. In uttering *This soup needs salt* in the right circumstances, A may mean both "I assert to you that this soup needs salt" and "I request you to pass the salt." Let us call these meanings M_1 and M_2. M_1, which follows directly from the literal meaning of the sentence, is generally called the speaker's literal or direct meaning. M_2 is generally called the indirect or conveyed meaning. M_1 and M_2 are not meanings of the sentence *This soup needs salt.* Rather, they are the two parts of what A means in uttering the sentence on this occasion. In Grice's (1957, 1968) and Schiffer's (1972) terminology, they are speaker meanings.

(2) Logical priority of meanings. The several meanings of an indirect speech act are not conveyed in parallel. In uttering *This soup needs salt,* A requests B to pass the salt *by virtue of* her assertion to him that the soup needs salt (Searle, 1975). So M_1 and M_2 form a chain of meanings in which M_1 is "logically prior" to M_2, or M_2 is "logically contingent" on M_1. We can refer to M_1 and M_2 as the initial and final meanings of such a chain.[1] Just because M_1 is *logically* prior to M_2, of course, doesn't necessarily imply that M_1 is *temporally* prior to M_2 in any psychological sense. These are two separate issues.

Most indirect speech acts have chains with just two meanings, but longer chains are common too. By uttering *Haven't you forgotten to clean your room?,* for example, A can use her literal question, M_1, to assert that B has forgotten to clean his room, M_2; she can use M_2 to convey another assertion, M_3, that she wants B to clean his room now; and she can use M_3 to request B to clean his room now, M_4. In an independent chain, she can also use M_2 to scold B for not having cleaned his room before, M_5. So there can be more than two meanings in a chain and even more than one chain.

(3) Rationality. The logical contingency between any two meanings of an indirect speech act, according to Gordon and Lakoff (1971), Heringer (Note 1), Searle (1975), and others, has a rational basis. For A to utter *This soup needs salt* and intend both M_1 and M_2, she must first assume that she and B "mutually know" certain background facts (see Lewis, 1969; Schiffer, 1972; Clark & Clark, 1979; Clark & Marshall, 1978, 1980). They may have to share the knowledge, for example, that they are at dinner, that she has just tasted the soup, that there is a salt-shaker near him, and other such facts. She must also observe certain principles of cooperative conversation (Grice, 1975). For one thing, her utterance must be relevant to what is going on at the moment. Finally, she must adhere to certain conventions about the use of sentences in performing direct speech acts. Only then can she be certain that B will be able to infer that she intended both M_1 and M_2.

(4) Conventionality. As part of this rationale, there are conventions about which sentences can be used for which indirect speech acts. One convention of English is that A can indirectly request B to do a particular act by questioning his ability to do that act. A can request the salt, therefore, with *Can you reach the salt?, Are you able yet to pass the salt?,* and *Is it possible for you to pass me the salt?* This type of convention could be called a *convention of means,* since it specifies a semantic device by which an indirect speech act can be performed.

There are also *conventions of form*—conventions about the wording of indirect speech acts. *Can you pass the salt?* and *Could you pass the salt?,* for example, are highly conventional, or idiomatic, forms in English for requesting the salt. *Is it possible for you to pass the salt?* and *Are you able to pass the salt?* are less idiomatic, and *Is it the case that you at present have the ability to pass the salt?* is not at all idiomatic. So idiomaticity, an alternative term for conventionality of form, is a matter of degree. One piece of evidence for this con-

tinuum is that *please* can be inserted at many points in the highly idiomatic indirect requests but at fewer or no points in the less idiomatic ones (Sadock, 1972, 1974). What has come to be the most and least idiomatic forms in English is a result of historical processes, and so the same variation occurs in other areas of syntax and morphology too (Bolinger, 1975, 1976; Clark & Clark, 1979; Morgan, 1978). As Searle put it, there appears to be a conversational maxim that says: Speak idiomatically unless there is some special reason not to.

(5) Politeness. Why are there so many indirect speech acts? The main reason, perhaps, is politeness (Lakoff, 1973a, 1977; Brown & Levinson, 1978; Clark & Schunk, Note 2). Direct requests, for example, presume a certain status of A over B. If he and she are peers, she won't have that status, and so it would be impolite of her to make a bald request like *Loan me $100.* One solution for A is to give B options, or appear to give him options, with an indirect request like *Can you loan me $100?* If he doesn't want to loan her the money, he can duck out with *Sorry, I can't—I don't have that much right now.* Or A can reduce how imposing her request would be, for example, by asking permission to make the request, as in *May I ask you to loan me $100?* On the other hand, A can use *I want you to loan me $100,* which doesn't give options and does impose, to flaunt her authority over him.

(6) Purposefulness. Speech acts are purposeful. They are intended to have a specific effect on the addressee, such as to get him to believe that something is true (as with assertions) or to get him to do something (as with requests). How this is accomplished has been discussed by Grice (1957, 1968), Schiffer (1972), and others. The important point is that speakers ordinarily have goals they want to achieve; they formulate plans for achieving them; and they select their speech acts as parts of these plans. Listeners are intended to infer these speech acts in part by recognizing these goals, these plans, and the roles the speech acts play within the plans (Perrault, Allen, & Cohen, 1978; Allen & Perrault, Note 3; Cohen, Note 4). So far, however, goals and plans have been used very little in explanations of indirect speech acts or their responses. Like Allen, Cohen, and Perrault, I believe they should.

Responses to Indirect Speech Acts

Responses to direct speech acts are, roughly, of three main types. First, there is the class of responses A intended B to give. When she asks him *When does the museum close tonight?*, she intends—that is, she *wants* and *expects*—him to produce an assertion that reveals the time the museum closes, as in *It closes at six* or *At six* or *Just before dark.* If B is fully cooperative and the circumstances are right, he will produce such a response. This class of responses I will call *expected responses.* Of course, A could be wrong in her presuppositions about the situation. If the museum is not open, B will say *It isn't open today.* If B doesn't know the answer, he will respond *Sorry, I don't know.* If B can't figure out which museum she is talking about, he will ask *Which museum?* These are cooperative responses, but not the expected ones, hence I will call them *cooperative but unexpected responses.* And there are a variety of *uncooperative responses.* These three types of responses are elicited by indirect speech acts too. It is the expected responses that I will be most concerned with, although I will touch on the other two types too. I will propose seven properties of such responses.

(1) Multiplicity of moves. Just as indirect speech acts have more than one meaning, their expected responses may contain more than one "move," to use Goffman's (1976) term. *Can you tell me what time it is?* may elicit *Yes, I can—it's six.* If M_1 is the literal question and M_2 the indirect request for the time, then the first move, *Yes, I can,* is an answer to M_1, and the second move, *It's six,* is a response to M_2. Let us call these Move$_1$ and Move$_2$. The point is that they correspond directly to the two meanings of A's indirect request. (Under (2) and (4), I will consider caveats to this notion.) Two-move responses like this are common enough. When Munro (Note 5) asked 61 students on the UCLA campus either *Can you tell me what time it is?* or *Can you tell me the time?*, 31 responded with both of these moves.

Expected responses may also contain more than two moves (see Goffman, 1976). Suppose A said to B *Do you remember who was asking something about Ben?*, intending M_1, "Do you remember the name?," M_2, "Who was ask-

ing?," and M_3, "What did that person ask about?," all in a chain. B's response may consist of three moves: *Yes; Veronica. She was asking where he was.* Each meaning in A's indirect speech act is matched by a move in B's response.

(2) Functions of moves. In actuality, expected responses are often cluttered with extra scraps of information. They may include not only moves that deal with A's intended meanings, but other moves as well. It is convenient to distinguish three functionally different kinds of moves—preliminary moves, expected moves, and added moves.

(a) Preliminary moves: To be cooperative, B must accomplish three things in his response (see Goffman, 1976, p. 300 on). First, he must give A immediate assurance he has received and understood her speech act; otherwise, *What?* or *I didn't hear you* is in order. Second, he must give her immediate assurance that her speech act is legitimate—that he doesn't think it is intrusive, stupid, or otherwise inappropriate. And third, he must deal with the content of the speech act itself as soon as feasible. Ordinarily, he can accomplish all three goals in a single move. For *What time is it?*, he can do it with *It's six.* But if he is delayed in understanding her or in getting the time, he may need to give one or both of these assurances in separate moves, as in *Uh—it's six* or *Let me see—it's six.* The moves *uh* and *let me see* are not necessary parts of the expected response, and so I will call them *preliminary moves.* They can be further classified according to their particular functions (see DuBois, 1974; Lakoff, 1973b; Munro, Note 5).

(b) Expected moves: The moves that specifically deal with A's meanings are the expected moves. For *Can you tell me what time it is?*, there may be two expected moves, *Yes, I can* and *It's six.*

(c) Added moves: For the direct question *Where is Ben?* with just the one meaning B may respond *In the house—he's been there ten minutes.* The first move, *In the house,* is an expected move since it deals with A's direct meaning. The second move, *he's been there ten minutes,* does not deal with any of A's meanings, hence I will call it an *added move.* For indirect speech acts like *Can you tell me what time it is?*, most added moves are tacked on after the expected moves, as in *Yes, I can—*

it's six—we'd better hurry. However, they can be placed elsewhere too, as in *Yes, I can—I just got my watch fixed—it's six.*

(3) Order of moves. When there are two or more expected moves in a response, they must of course be spoken in a chronological order. How is that order determined? The *normal* order, as far as I can tell, is identical to the logical order of the corresponding meanings of the indirect speech act. *Can you tell me what time it is?*, for instance, conveys a question (M_1), which is logically prior to a request for information (M_2). The two expected moves in its response reflect this order: *Yes, I can—it's six.* The reverse order would be very odd indeed: *It's six—Yes, I can.*

The moves of a response can be twisted out of normal order, but only, apparently, for special purposes. Take *Can you give me a dollar?* In the response *Yes, I can—here you are,* the two expected moves are in normal order. In *Here you are, but I can only lend it to you,* there are two similar moves in reverse order, but the second move isn't really an expected move. It merely qualifies how the dollar is to be given and is therefore an added move. And in *Here you are—I can give it to you because I just got paid,* there are also two moves in reversed order, but again the second move isn't really an expected move. It presupposes the literal answer and tells A why B has the ability. It too is an added move. My conjecture is this: The expected moves of a response always follow normal order; when they appear to be twisted out of order, they are always qualified in some way, making them added moves instead.

(4) Selection of moves. Not every expected response exhibits a move for each meaning of the indirect speech act. Which moves are selected, and why? These two questions are a major reason for the experiments I will report later.

For now consider what I will call the *minimum move rule:* An expected response always contains at least the move that responds to the final meaning of the indirect speech act. For *Can you tell me what time it is?*, the expected response can be *Yes, I can—it's six* or merely *It's six,* both of which have moves that respond to M_2. The expected response cannot be *Yes, I can,* which responds to M_1 alone. That would imply either that B didn't take A as

meaning M_2—she was asking about his ability to tell her the time and nothing more—or that he was deliberately being uncooperative.

The minimum move rule has the same basis as the ordering principle for expected moves—logical priority. An expected response is one that deals, explicitly or implicitly, with *all* the meanings of the indirect speech act. The only move that can ever do that by itself is the move that responds to the final meaning in the chain. For *Can you tell me what time it is?*, the response *It's six* deals with M_2 explicitly, but it also implies that the answer to M_1 is yes. Providing the time logically entails being able to provide the time. The response *Yes, I can,* in contrast, answers M_1 explicitly but implies nothing about M_2 and so is not sufficient. Similar reasoning applies to the ordering of two expected moves. The second move must be informative above and beyond the first or else there is no reason to utter it. The second move is informative in this way in *Yes, I can—it's six,* but not in *It's six—yes, I can.* The basis for all this is logical priority. Since M_1 is logically prior to M_2 in this context, $Move_2$ may imply $Move_1$, but not vice versa.[2]

There is one major caveat to the minimum move rule. Responses to many speech acts don't have to be verbal. A request to borrow a dollar may be responded to by a reach for the billfold, which shows the intention to comply. An assertion can be acknowledged with a nod, glance, or smile. Indeed, some speech acts may not require a discrete response at all. Assertions in long narratives, for example, seem to require B's continued attention and little else.

(5) Politeness. For many indirect speech acts, like *Can you tell me what time it is?*, it is logically adequate to respond with one move, *It's six.* Why would B ever respond with more, as in *Yes, I can—it's six,* which is unnecessarily redundant? According to a proposal by Clark & Schunk (Note 1), one reason is politeness. The response *Yes, I can—it's six* is normally taken to be more polite than *It's six.* For a variety of indirect requests tested in several experiments, two-move responses were judged more polite than one-move responses.

(6) Ellipsis. Responses to indirect—as well as direct—speech acts are ordinarily highly elliptical. For *Can you tell me what time it is?*,

Table 12.1. Some Properties of the Indirect Request *Do You Know What Time It Is?* and Its
Expected Response *Yes, I Do—It's Six*

Indirect Request	Expected Response
(1) Multiple meanings	(1) Multiple moves
M_1 = "Do you know the time?"	$Move_1$ = *Yes, I do*
M_2 = "What time is it?"	$Move_2$ = *It's six*
(2) Logical priority in meanings	(2) Temporal order of moves
M_1 is logically prior to M_2	$Move_1$ is temporally prior to $Move_2$
(3) Rationality of meanings	(3) Selection of moves
M_1 is intended to imply M_2	$Move_1$ isn't necessary; $Move_2$ is
(4) Politeness of request	(4) Politeness of response
Including M_1 is polite	Including $Move_1$ is polite

the first expected move could conceivably be *Yes, I can tell you what time it is,* but it would ordinarily be reduced to *Yes, I can* or merely *Yes.* The second expected move could likewise be *The time now is six o'clock,* but it would ordinarily be reduced to *It's six* or merely *Six.* Such ellipsis results in two-move responses like *Yes, it's six* or *Yes, six.* When is ellipsis chosen, and why? These are questions I will take up in the experiments that follow.

By now it should be clear that indirect speech acts and their responses form a special type of adjacency pair. When A takes her turn, she intends B to recognize not just her literal meaning M_1, but also (say) a second indirect meaning M_2. What is crucial here—and a point often missed—is that she *also* intends him to deal with both of these meanings in his very next turn. It isn't enough for him to recognize both and then deal only with the first. He must deal with both. Four main points in the correspondence between A's and B's turns are summarized in Table 12.1. On the left are four properties of the indirect request *Do you know what time it is?*, and on the right are the four matching properties of the expected response *Yes, I do—it's six.*

Yet this characterization is hardly complete. It is easiest to see this by looking at how B understands what A means and then plans his response.

UNDERSTANDING INDIRECT REQUESTS

How does B decide what to respond? Ordinarily, he must first try to understand what A meant. Different interpretations will lead him to make different moves in his response. Then

he must decide what he intends to do based on this understanding—whether he wishes to be cooperative or obstructive, or polite or rude, or what. My main concern is with B's understanding of what A meant. In studying this, I will limit myself to indirect requests conveyed by literal questions, as in *Can you tell me what time it is?* For these, the literal meaning will be called Q, for "question," and the indirect meaning R, for "request." I chose these requests since they lead to such readily identifiable moves as *Yes, I can* for Q and *It's six* for R.

Understanding the Literal and Indirect Meanings

When A makes an indirect request like *Can you tell me the square root of ten?*, she intends both the literal and indirect meaning—both Q and R. At least, this is what Searle (1975) and others have argued. But this cannot be the whole story. Contrast these two situations. In situation 1, B has been looking up square roots in a table for A, and she continues, *Now can you tell me the square root of 10?* In this instance she is asking Q only to convey R. She doesn't intend Q to be taken seriously—she is certain he is *able* to tell her the square root, for he has the table in front of him and has been providing square roots earlier. She is asking him whether he can merely by way of being polite. In situation 2, B is sitting in an easy chair, reading the newspaper, and A, doing a mathematics problem, asks him, *Can you tell me the square root of 10?* Again she is requesting the square root of 10, but this time she is not using Q *merely* to convey R. She is asking Q seriously, since she believes B may well not be able to tell her the square root of 10. Her request is a conditional request. She asks B to tell her the square root of ten if he is able to do so.

Q therefore varies, I propose, in a property I will call *seriousness* (or its inverse *pro-formality*). In situation 1, Q is intended to be taken pro forma. In situation 2, Q is intended to be taken seriously. Since Q is a part of A's full speech act, the seriousness of Q is a property of the speech act. It ought to have a counterpart, therefore, in the expected response to that speech act, and, I suggest, it does. When B takes A as intending Q pro forma, he believes he is *not* intended to respond to Q. In situation 1, he would normally respond simply *It's 3.16.* But when B takes A as intending Q seriously, he believes he *is* intended to respond to Q in a separate move. In situation 2, he would *both* answer Q *and* comply with R, as in *Yes, it's 3.16.* A serious Q gets an expected move in the response; a pro forma Q does not.

Before B can plan his response, he must decide whether Q was intended pro forma or seriously. In general, he won't be able to decide with certainty, since he has to rely on his perception of the situation—as in situations 1 and 2—and on other subjective factors. All he can do is use the evidence at hand to judge the probability that Q was intended seriously. Call this probability q. When B is completely certain Q is pro forma, $q = 0$; when B is completely certain Q is serious, $q = 1$; otherwise, q is somewhere between 0 and 1. How does B estimate q? This is one of the two main empirical questions to be investigated in the experiments that follow.

In trying to understand A's indirect meaning, on the other hand, B has two problems to solve. First, he must select from the many possible things A could mean indirectly the one she most likely meant on that occasion. Call this meaning R. He must then estimate how likely it was that she truly meant R. Because this depends on subjective judgments about the situation and other factors, that estimate can again be only a probability. Call that probability r. When B is absolutely certain A didn't mean R, $r = 0$; when he is absolutely certain she did mean R, $r = 1$; otherwise, r is between 0 and 1. How does B select R and estimate its likelihood r? This is the second main empirical question to be examined in the experiments to be reported.

A Response Model

If B is fully cooperative, he will select his response on the basis of q and r. For *Can you tell me the time?*, he will answer Q with *Yes, I can* when he judges q to be large, and respond to R with *It's six* when he judges r to be large. This will result in one of three responses: (1) *Yes, I can;* (2) *Yes, I can—it's six;* or (3) *It's six.* I will call these three responses, respectively, "answer alone," "answer-plus–information," and "information alone." Note that the fourth possibility—no response at all—is one B can never give, since he knows he is expected to respond in some way. Indeed, for every request I will report, people responded, except for a few clear misunderstandings or misfires, with one of these three responses. What this implies is that B cannot decide on his two moves independently of each other. How, then, does he decide? I will consider three plausible decision schemes.

Scheme 1 consists of two ordered decision rules:

Rule 1. Answer Q with probability q.
Rule 2. If Q was answered, respond to R with probability r; otherwise, respond to R with probability 1.

In this scheme, the responses answer alone, answer-plus-information, and information alone should occur, respectively, with probabilities $q(1 - r)$, qr, and $(1 - q)$. Given this scheme, it is possible to take a group of people's responses to a request and work backwards to discover the estimates of q and r on which their responses were based. Suppose that the responses answer alone, answer-plus-information, and information alone actually occurred for a group of people with proportions a, b, and c, where $a + b + c = 1$. It is easy to show that their responses were based on these estimates; $\hat{q} = a + b$, and $\hat{r} = b/(a + b)$. So for *Can you tell me the time?*, $\hat{q}$ is found by computing the proportion of people who responded *Yes, I can* with or without a second move, and $\hat{r}$ by computing the proportion of this subgroup who went on to respond *It's six.*

Scheme 2 is similar to Scheme 1, except that the two moves are decided on in the reverse order:

Rule 1. Respond to R with probability r.

Rule 2. If R is to be responded to, answer Q with probability q; otherwise, answer Q with probability 1.

This scheme leads to estimates of q and r from people's actual responses as follows: $\hat{q} = b(b + c)$, and $\hat{r} = b + c$.

In Scheme 3 the two moves are decided on simultaneously according to the following two ordered rules:

Rule 1. Answer Q with probability q and, independently, respond to R with probability r.

Rule 2. If nothing results, return to Rule 1.

In this scheme q and r are estimated as follows: $\hat{q} = b/(b + c)$ and $\hat{r} = b/(b + a)$.

Which scheme is best? In the experiments to be reported, the patterns of q and r are so similar for the three schemes that it is empirically impossible to select one scheme over any other. The conclusions I will draw do not depend on which is selected. However, only in Schemes 1 and 2 is there the desirable statistical property that q and r are estimated from the data independently of each other (which does *not* imply, of course, that q and r are themselves independent). And only in Scheme 1 are the two moves decided on in the order in which they are spoken. For these and other reasons I will use Scheme 1.

B's responses, however, should change not only with how he thought A intended him to respond—the expected response—but also with his own additional intentions. Take politeness, for example. For *Can you tell me what time it is?*, he might ordinarily respond as expected with *It's six.* But if he intends to be especially polite, he is more likely to respond, *Yes, I can—it's six.* One way to view this is that he has set for himself a probability p of being completely polite. In Scheme 1, then, he would answer Q not with the probability q as expected, but with probability $q + p(1 - q)$. Whenever he wanted to give merely the expected response, he would set $p = 0$ and respond *Yes, I can* with probability q. Whenever he wanted to enhance politeness half way, he would set $p = 1/2$ and respond *Yes, I can* with probability $(q + 1)/2$. And whenever he wanted to be utterly polite, he would set $p = 1$ and respond *Yes, I can* every time. Politeness can be treated in other ways too.

To take B's intentions into account, however, I would require much more complicated models than could be tested here. For this reason, I have tried to hold the added intentions in these experiments constant; it is natural to assume that for any two requests in the same experiment they were roughly the same. In several places, however, I will note how these sorts of intentions could have affected people's responses.

The Experiments

In the five experiments I will report, I examined spontaneous responses to requests made by telephone. In each experiment a friendly sounding 23-year-old woman with a standard California accent would dial a local merchant's number, wait for the answer (typically *Hello,* or *Green's Pharmacy,* or *Green's Pharmacy, may I help you?*), say *Hi,* and then make a single request the merchant would normally be expected to deal with on the telephone. One typical conversation went like this (the name has been changed for anonymity):

MERCHANT: Green's Pharmacy
    CALLER: Hi. Do you close before seven tonight?
MERCHANT: Uh, no. We're open until nine o'clock.
    CALLER: Thank you very much. Goodbye.
MERCHANT: Goodbye.

During and immediately after the conversation the caller wrote down verbatim the critical part between the request and *thank you,* noting all *uh*'s, hesitations, changes in speakers, and other interruptions.

The merchants were selected from the Yellow Pages of Palo Alto and other San Francisco area telephone books; the category of merchant varied from experiment to experiment. There were two to seven requests per experiment. Within a category, one merchant, chosen roughly at random, was asked the first request; the next one to six merchants listed were asked, in order, the remaining one to six requests; the cycle was repeated until a set number of merchants had responded. The telephoning was done during a time of day appropriate to the merchant and the request. All wrong numbers, merchants out of business, and the like were excluded and replaced by the next merchant in the list. No merchant was called more than once in this series of experiments.

EXPERIMENT 1

Do responses to indirect requests vary at all? Although it has been noted that people sometimes *do* respond to the literal meaning of such requests as *Can you tell me what time it is?* (Green, 1975; Searle, 1975; Munro, Note 5), are there systematic differences in how often they do so? Unless there are, there is no reason to go on. The first issue of Experiment 1, then, is whether *q* and *r* vary systematically from one indirect request to the next.

On the assumption *q* and *r* do vary, how do merchants estimate them? What sources of information—in the caller's utterance or in the situation—do they use to decide how likely Q was intended seriously and how likely R was meant? In this experiment, I will take up three possible sources—conventionality of means, transparency of R, and obviousness of Q's answer.

Conventionality of Means

When A wants to make certain Q will be taken pro forma, I propose, she will want to use a conventional means. Compare *Could you tell me what time you close tonight?* and *Do you close before seven tonight?* Both can be used to request the closing time from a merchant. They differ in that the first uses a conventional means, and the second does not. In selecting the first over the second, all other things being equal, A signals to B that she is requesting the closing time and is asking Q merely to be polite. A's use of a conventional means, then, is evidence that Q may not be intended to be taken seriously—that B should estimate *q* to be small.

A's use of a conventional means is also evidence that R is probably intended. The point of using a conventional means to request something is to make certain B sees it as a request. So when a request is conventional, all other things being equal, *r* should be estimated at or near 1.00. When it is not conventional, it should be estimated at a lower value, with B relying on other factors in his estimating instead.

Transparency

The general form of a request R is this: "I (A) request you (B) to do act C." Example: *I request you to tell me what time you close tonight.* Indirect requests vary in how transparent the three elements A, B, and C are in what is literally said. *Could you tell me what time you close tonight?* is quite transparent, since A, B, and C are each explicitly mentioned. *Do you close before seven tonight?*, used for making the same request, is less transparent, since B and only parts of C ("Tell me what time you close tonight") are specified. And for the same purpose, *Stores seem to close early now* is even less transparent, since A, B, and C are implicit. Specifying act C is probably the most important thing to make transparent, since A and B are always at least clear when A talks to B.

My proposal is this: All other things being equal, the more transparent R is, the lower the estimate of *q* and the higher the estimate of *r*. The logic goes like this. For A to make certain B will see exactly what request she is making, she must make that request transparent in what she says, especially as regards act C. On B's part, he knows that whenever she uses such a request, he can be more certain than otherwise that she intended R. And if she intended R, it is also less likely that she was seriously interested in an answer to Q. The result: a raised estimate of *r*, and a lowered estimate of *q*.

Transparency, however, is correlated with conventionality. Conventional requests tend to be quite transparent, whereas nonconventional ones do not. The connection is probably not accidental. When A wants to make certain B can figure out R precisely, she had better use a transparent indirect request, like *Can you tell me what time you close tonight?* This means that the indirect requests most likely to become conventional are the transparent ones. Indeed, in Experiment 1 there is no way of distinguishing between conventionality and transparency in their effects on *q* and *r*.

Obviousness of Q's Answer

Whenever B believes that the answer to Q is mutually obvious to A and B in the present circumstances, he should take A as *not* intend-

Table 12.2. Percentage of Merchants Giving Answers and Information to Five Requests in Experiment 1

Statement	Answer Alone	Answer Plus Information	Information Alone	Other
(1) What time? (30)[a]	0	0	97	3
(2) Could you? (30)	0	0	97	3
(3) Would you mind? (30)	0	23	70	7
(4) Do you close? (30)	13	57	27	3
(5) I was wondering? (30)	3	60	37	0

[a]Number of merchants asked each request indicated in parentheses.

ing Q seriously and should fix the value of *q* near 0. If he believes that the answer is not mutually obvious, he should take Q as more likely to have been intended seriously and should estimate *q* to be larger than 0. The less obvious the answer, the closer *q* should be to 1. This point was illustrated earlier with situations 1 and 2 for the request *Can you tell me the square root of 10?* But like transparency, the obviousness of Q's answer is correlated with conventionality. Conventional requests tend to have obvious answers to Q, as in *Could you tell me what time you close tonight?,* and nonconventional requests do not. Historically there are good reasons for this correspondence too. So in Experiment 1, it will be impossible to distinguish conventionality from obviousness of Q's answer either.

Yet a small test of this proposal can be made by comparing *Could you tell me what time you close tonight?* and *Would you mind telling me what time you close tonight?,* which for the moment we may assume are equally conventional. It may be mutually obvious to the merchant and caller that she believes he has the ability to tell her the closing time, but not quite so obvious that she believes he wouldn't mind. If so, Q should be taken seriously more often for *Would you mind?* than for *Could you?*

The five requests selected for this experiment, therefore, were the following:

(1) What time do you close tonight?

(2) Could you tell me what time you close tonight?

(3) Would you mind telling me what time you close tonight?

(4) Do you close before seven tonight?

(5) I was wondering whether you close before seven tonight?

For convenience, these will be abbreviated *What time?, Could you?, Would you mind?,*

Do you close?, and *I was wondering.* Each request was asked of 30 merchants for a total of 150 merchants. For this purpose 30 categories of commercial shops were selected from the Yellow Pages with the constraint that the shops be rather small and likely to have regular closing hours—like florist shops, auto repair shops, and delicatessens—and not banks, department stores, or plumbers. Five merchants were selected from each of the 30 categories for the five different requests.

For all five requests, R was intended to be "I request you to tell me what time you close tonight." *What time?* makes this request directly. It has no Q, no yes/no question. *Could you?* and *Would you mind?* have an obvious literal Q by which they make request R, and they use conventional means. *Do you close?* and *I was wondering* both use nonconventional means. Although *Do you close?* has an obvious literal Q, *I was wondering* conveys that same Q indirectly. The caller directly asserts that she is wondering something and by virtue of that assertion asks Q, "Do you close before seven tonight?", and by virtue of this Q makes request R. The assertion, of course, requires no verbal response, so the interest still lies in the merchants' responses to Q and R.

Results

The three main response categories and their percentages of occurrence are shown in Table 12.2. The answers to Q included the affirmative *yes, yeah, ya, uh huh,* and *sure* and the negative *no.* Affirmative and negative answers will be called *yes* and *no,* for short, except when the words themselves are of interest. *Okay* was *not* counted as an affirmative answer since it is really a promise to do what has been requested, as it is in response to the direct request *Open the door.* It occurred only once.

The information provided in response to R included such expressions as *Six, At six,* and *We close at six,* and so the category "answer plus information" included such responses as *No, we close at nine.* The category marked "other" includes all responses that could not be categorized this way or were in some way uncooperative. Only 5 of 150 responses had to be put into this category.

Estimates of q and r. The estimates for each request are shown in Table 12.3. Recall that $\hat{q}$ is the proportion of merchants who answered Q. (This is calculated with the "other" responses excluded.) So for *Do you close?,* $\hat{q}$ is 13% + 57% as a proportion of 97%, or .72. And $\hat{r}$ is the proportion of the merchants who answered Q who also responded with information to R. So for *Do you close?,* $\hat{r}$ is 57% as a proportion of 13% + 57%, or .81. For *What time?* and *Could you?,* there were no answers to Q and so no way in Scheme 1 even to estimate *r.* For these two requests $\hat{r}$ was calculated by Scheme 2, which did allow an estimate. The differences between two proportions will be tested by one of three statistical tests, whichever is appropriate: (1) the usual test for differences in proportions, expressed in z scores; (2) a test of their arcsines, also expressed in z scores; or (3) a χ^2 test.

There is little question that q and r varied from request to request. Note first that there were no *yes* answers for the direct request *What time?* Merchants provided only the information requested, and so $\hat{q} = 0$. This finding is important. It shows that *yes* and its kin aren't automatically used as mere time fillers or appropriateness markers. They are reserved for answers to Q. In the other requests, $\hat{q}$ varied from 0 to .72 and $\hat{r}$ varied from .81 [to] 1.00.

Conventionality was critical. As expected, the value of $\hat{q}$ was smaller for the conventional forms *Could you?* and *Would you mind?,* .00

and .24, than for the nonconventional requests *Do you close?* and *I was wondering?,* .72 and .63. The first two proportions are each significantly smaller than the second two ($z \geqslant$ 2.97, $p < .002$). Also, as expected, $\hat{r}$ was 1.00 for the conventional requests, and smaller for the two nonconventional requests, .81 and .95. Together, the latter two values are significantly less than 1.00 ($z = 2.39, p < .01$); individually, only .81 is ($z = 2.22, p < .02$).

As for obviousness of Q's answer, Q was taken seriously more often for *Would you mind?* than for *Could you?,* .24 to .00. This difference is significant ($z = 2.79, p < .005$).

Ellipsis. The merchants' responses to R varied in ellipsis too. Sometimes they provided their information in complete sentences, like *We close at nine* or *That'd be at nine,* and sometimes in elliptical sentences, like *At nine* or *Nine o'clock.* For these experiments, I will define an elliptical sentence as one without an explicit subject (like *we*) or verb (like *close*) or both. Elliptical sentences were strongly preferred in response to *What time?, Could you?,* and *Would you mind?,* occurring 72, 79, and 79% of the time, respectively. But they were strongly avoided in response to *Do you close?* and *I was wondering,* occurring only 26 and 17% of the time, respectively. The first three percentages are each significantly larger than each of the last two ($z \geqslant 3.50, p < .001$). Furthermore, elliptical sentences were used more often when the information was provided alone than when it followed an answer to Q, 52 to 29%. These percentages are based on *Would you mind?, Do you close?,* and *I was wondering,* the only requests that elicited both categories of responses. This difference is also significant ($\chi^2(1) = 3.93, p < .05$).

Do you close? and *I was wondering* were apparently harder to comprehend than the rest, as suggested by the occasional sign of incomplete or delayed understanding. Some merchants requested a repeat with "What was that?" or "Pardon me?" Others requested clarification with "The time we close?" or "Before seven?" Both types required the caller to respond. Still other merchants repeated part of the request to themselves, such as "The time we close," as if they were trying to get the request straight before responding. These interruptions for clarification, as I will call them, occurred 14 and 17% of the time on *Do you close?* and *I was wondering,* but 0% of the time

Table 12.3. Estimates of q and r for Five Requests in Experiment 1

	Parameters	
Statements	$\hat{q}$	$\hat{r}$
(1) What time?	.00	1.00[a]
(2) Could you tell me?	.00	1.00[a]
(3) Would you mind?	.24	1.00
(4) Do you close?	.72	.81
(5) I was wondering?	.63	.95

[a]These $\hat{r}$s are estimated by Scheme 2.

on the other three requests. The former two percentages are each significantly larger than the latter three ($z \geqslant 2.09$, $p < .02$).

Discussion

Indirect requests, then, do differ systematically in their q's and r's. For conventional requests, Q is seldom taken seriously, and R is always construed as having been meant. For nonconventional requests, Q is often taken seriously, and R is not always construed as having been meant. Yet neither of these findings can be attributed to conventionality alone, for the conventional requests were also the more transparent and had the more obvious answers to Q. One small piece of evidence that the obviousness of Q may have been important on its own, however, was that Q was taken seriously more often for *Would you mind?* than for *Could you?*.

Would you mind?, however, poses a curious problem. Of the seven merchants who answered Q, only one said *no*. The rest answered *yes*.[3] (Actually, four said *yes*, one said *yeah*, and the sixth said *uh huh*.) The problem is this. If, as hypothesized, the reason these seven answered Q was because they thought it might have been intended seriously, they must have determined the import of Q. But if they had determined the import of Q, they should have answered *no*. What is wrong?

Three possibilities suggest themselves. First, merchants could have recognized that *Would you mind?* was a question and that Q was being used to convey R, but they didn't take in Q's content. But if so, why did *Would you mind?* elicit reliably more answers than *Could you?*, which presumably would be treated the same way? Second, merchants could have dealt with *Would you mind?* as in the first case, but considered it more polite than *Could you?* In reciprocating this greater politeness, they would have been more likely to answer Q. But in an unpublished experiment, 100 bank clerks were each asked *Could you tell me the time you close tonight?* For half the clerks the request was preceded by *I'm very sorry to bother you but*. Although the clerks reacted to this polite preface in other appropriate ways, they didn't increase their answers to Q by even 1%. So it doesn't seem plausible that *Would*

you mind? by itself could have changed politeness enough to increase the answers to Q by 24%. Somehow the literal content of *Would you mind?* counts.

The third possibility is the one I prefer. Merchants could have taken the Q of *Would you mind?* as indirectly conveying an intermediate link in the chain, Q', "Will you tell me what time you close tonight?", which in turn indirectly conveyed R. What they were answering, then, was not Q but Q', which takes the answer *yes*. Note how convenient this Q' is. Virtually every other indirect request of this kind—*Can you?, Can't you?, Could you?, Will you?, Won't you?, Would you?, Shouldn't you?, May I ask you?*, and the like—requires the answer yes. By interpreting Q as conveying Q', merchants could rely on a general response strategy in which they answer the Qs of all conventional requests of this sort by *yes*. This strategy would be particularly useful when they have to plan their responses quickly. Under more deliberate circumstances, they might prefer to answer Q instead, as in *No* and *Not at all*. Whatever the explanation, this result emphasizes that *Would you mind?* is a conventional request whose Q is not often construed as having been intended seriously.

Another curious problem can be illustrated for *Do you close?* When merchants answered its Q with *Yes, we do*, they had also given a partial response to R. Information that the shop closes before seven is partial information about the time it actually closes. Many merchants, it might be thought, should therefore not see it necessary to respond to R with a move like *We close at six*. Yet they did—88% of them for *Do you close?* and *I was wondering* combined. So when they took R to be intended, they took their task as providing full and not partial information about R.

As for ellipsis, why were elliptical sentences used so rarely for *Do you close?* and *I was wondering?* One obvious possibility is transparency. Note that the answer to *What time do you close?* has a regular elliptical form— *Nine* or *At nine*. When this question is embedded syntactically in the requests *Could you tell me what time you close?* and *Would you mind telling me what time you close?*, it should allow the same ellipsis. It isn't surprising to find ellipsis 75% of the time for these three requests. *What time do you close?*, however, is not embedded syntactically within *Do you close?* or *I was wondering.* For them it isn't available to "trigger" an elliptical response, and so it isn't surprising to find ellipsis only 20% of the time. But since both these requests are also nonconventional, we cannot tell whether ellipsis is triggered by the transparency of R, the conventionality of the request, or both.

EXPERIMENT 2

While Experiment 1 demonstrated that q and r vary, it only suggested why they might vary. Experiment 2 was designed to pull apart some of these reasons—in particular, obviousness and transparency independent of conventionality.

The requests selected were the following:

(1) Could you tell me the time you close tonight?

(2) Could you tell me the price for a fifth of Jim Beam/Chivas Regal?

(3) Do you have a price for a fifth of Jim Beam/Chivas Regal?

(4) Does a fifth of Jim Beam cost more than $5/$6?

These will be abbreviated *Could you time?, Could you price?, Do you have?,* and *Does a fifth?* Each request, counting the two forms of *Could you price?, Do you Have?,* and *Does a fifth?* separately, was asked of 50 liquor merchants in the San Francisco Bay area for a total of 350 merchants. The two forms of *Could you price?* and *Do you have?* were intended to tax the merchants to different degrees in order to change their assessments of the seriousness of Q. Since Jim Beam is commoner than Chivas Regal, I assumed that the merchants would have the price of Jim Beam more readily available. Since the results revealed no differences between them, the two requests of each pair will be combined and spoken of as if they asked only about Jim Beam. The two forms of *Does a fifth?* were meant to elicit *yes* and *no,* respectively; because of California's so-called fair price law then in effect, almost all stores sold Jim Beam at from $5.59 to $5.79 a fifth. For most analyses, the two forms make little difference, so they will be merged too, except when the difference is of interest. For these requests Q is assumed to be the literal question. R was intended to be "I request you to tell me what

time you close tonight" for *Could you time?,* and "I request you to tell me the price of a fifth of Jim Beam" for the rest.

As in Experiment 1, the conventional requests should differ from the nonconventional ones. *Could you time?, Could you price?,* and *Do you have?* are each conventional forms for making requests, and *Does a fifth?* is not. R should be taken to be meant virtually always for the first three, with r's at or near 1.00, but not for the fourth, where r need not be so large. And on the average, Q should be taken seriously less often for the conventional than for the nonconventional requests, with q smaller for the former than for the latter. Once again, however, the conventional requests are on the whole also the more transparent and have the more obvious answers to Q, so conventionality cannot be distinguished in this way from transparency or obviousness.

Yet among the conventional requests, *Could you price?* and *Do you have?* seem to differ in transparency. *Could you price?* is a conventional and highly transparent means of request. *Do you have?* is also a conventional means of request. One can question the possession of an object in order to request that object, as in *Do you have a match?, Do you have a copy of the Times?,* or *Do you have a watch?* (where, however, the time and not the watch is being requested). But *Do you have?* isn't fully transparent. It doesn't say what the merchant is to do with the price. By the argument offered in Experiment 1, merchants therefore ought to estimate q to be higher for *Do you have?* than for *Could you price?* If she had wanted the price and nothing more, she would have used the more transparent form. Since both requests are highly conventional, on the other hand, merchants ought to estimate r to be at or near 1 for both.

The contrast between *Could you time?* and *Could you price?* seems to offer a relatively clear test of obviousness. The only difference between these two requests is in what is requested, and that in turn should lead to a difference in obviousness of Q's answer. A merchant should assume that it is mutually quite obvious to the caller and him that he should be able to tell her the time the store closes. He should not assume, however, that it is obvious he should be able to tell her the price for Jim Beam. He may not remember it; he may not carry it; or he may not be allowed to give it out over the telephone, as several merchants actually said. In brief, Q's answer should be more obvious for *Could you time?* than for *Could you price?*, and *q* should be correspondingly smaller.

Results

These predictions were generally confirmed. The percentages of the three categories of responses are shown in Table 12.4, and the values of $\hat{q}$ and $\hat{r}$ in Table 12.5. To be counted as an answer alone, the response had to be yes— or no for *Does a fifth of Jim Beam cost more than $6?* The merchant had to have the option of telling the time or price. The few refusals that occurred (like "No, we don't give our prices out on the phone") were relegated to the "other" category along with misunderstandings (like "Yes, we've got fifths" to *Do you have?*) and other failures ("Sorry, we don't have Jim Beam in fifths right now"). These failures, though interesting, were too rare to study here; I will take them up in Experiment 5.

Estimates of q and r. In responding to R, the merchants followed conventionality very closely. For the conventional requests *Could you time?*, *Could you price?*, and *Do you have?*, $\hat{r}$ was .75, 1.00 and .95 (based on 4, 15, and 39 responses, respectively). As expected, these values do not differ significantly from 1.00 either together or separately. (The .75 estimate for *Could you time?* was the result of a single merchant saying *Yes* alone; by Scheme 2, $\hat{r}$ is .98). For the nonconventional *Does a fifth?*, on the other hand, $\hat{r}$ was .58 (based on 53 responses). This is well below 1.00, as expected, and significantly smaller than either 1.00 or .95 for *Could you price?* and *Do you have?* ($z \geqslant 3.53$, $p < .001$).

The answers to Q were expected to follow a more complex pattern, and they did. As predicted on the basis of transparency, $\hat{q}$ was larger for *Do you have?* than for *Could you price?*, .44 to .16. This difference is significant ($z = 4.10$, $p < .001$). As expected on the basis of obviousness, *q* was larger for *Could you price?* than for *Could you time?*, .16 to .08. This difference, however, is only marginally significant ($z = 1.39$, $p < .08$). And as expected on the basis of conventionality, $\hat{q}$ was larger on the average for *Does a fifth?* than for the three conventional requests. Its value of .54 is significantly larger than the $\hat{q}$'s for *Could you time?* and *Could you price?* ($z \geqslant 5.50$, $p < .001$), but only marginally larger than the $\hat{q}$ for *Do you have?* ($z = 1.37$, $p < .09$).

There is further quite unexpected evidence that Q was construed differently for the conventional and nonconventional requests. The 85 affirmative answers to Q in this experiment took four forms: 34 were *yes;* 36 were *yeah* or *ya;* 12 were *sure;* and three were *uh huh.* (The 23 negative answers to *Does a fifth?* were all *no*). Of these four affirmative answers, *yes* is the most formal, while *sure, yeah,* and *uh huh* are all slangier and more informal. As it happened, *yes* was reserved mainly for the nonconventional *Does a fifth?* Of all the affirmative answers to each request, *yes* made up 25% for *Could you time?*, 20% for *Could you price?*, 25% for *Do you have?*, but 70% for *Does a fifth?* These percentages are based on 4, 15, 36, and 30 affirmative answers, respectively. The 70% figure for *Does a fifth?* is significantly larger than the 20 and 25% figures for *Could you price?* and *Do you have?* ($z \geqslant 3.18$, $p < .002$, two-tailed), respectively, but there were too few observations on *Could you time?* for that difference to be significant ($z = 1.69$, $p < .09$). In Experiment 1, by comparison, there was also a high percentage of *yes* answers for the two nonconventional requests *Do you*

Table 12.4. Percentage of Liquor Merchants Giving Answers and Information to Four Requests in Experiment 2

Request	Answer Alone	Answer Plus Information	Information Alone	Other
(1) Could you tell me time? (50)[a]	2	6	92	0
(2) Could you tell me price? (100)	0	15	77	8
(3) Do you have a price? (100)	2	37	49	12
(4) Does a fifth cost more? (100)	22	31	46	1

[a]Number of merchants asked each request indicated in parentheses.

Table 12.5. Estimates of *q* and *r* for Four Requests in Experiment 2

Statement	Parameters	
	$\hat{q}$	$\hat{r}$
(1) Could you tell me the time?	.08	.75
(2) Could you tell me the price?	.16	1.00
(3) Do you have a price?	.44	.95
(4) Does a fifth cost more?	.54	.58

close? and *I was wondering,* with 67% for each. It was as if when the request was not conventional, the caller was often taken to be interested in Q, which should therefore be answered with the more formal *yes.*

Ellipsis. Elliptical moves for R were common. Their percentages are shown in Table 12.6. As in Experiment 1, there was more ellipsis when the information was provided alone than when it was provided along with an answer to Q, 56 to 34%. This difference is significant $(\chi^2(1) = 11.18, p < .001)$. The reversal of this trend for *Could you time?,* the 100% figure, is based on only three responses. Thus, while elliptical responses like *$5.59* were preferred to full responses like *It costs $5.59,* full responses like *Yes, it costs $5.59* were preferred to elliptical responses like *Yes, $5.59.*

The four requests, however, varied in how readily they were responded to elliptically. The percentages of elliptical responses in the answer-plus-information column in Table 12.5 didn't vary significantly among the four requests, probably because they are based on so few responses. The percentages in the information-alone column did. For the first three requests, the percentages hovered around 65%, but for *Does a fifth?,* the percentage was 22%, which is significantly smaller than the other three $(z \geqslant 3.86, p < .001)$. So, as in Experiment 1, the merchants eschewed ellipsis on the request that was nonconventional.

The merchants showed many more signs of difficulty in understanding in Experiment 2 than in Experiment 1. Interruptions for clarification—requests for repeats, requests for clarification, and self-clarifications—occurred 14% of the time on *Could you time?,* but 59, 65, and 62% of the time on the other three requests. To get things straight for the latter requests, the merchants had to register that the caller wanted the price, not the availability, of a fifth, not a quart or half-gallon, of Jim Beam, not Jack Daniels or Cutty Sark. Furthermore, every merchant knew the closing time without checking, but 36% of them had to leave the telephone to check on the price of whiskey. This checking happened equally often for the three requests.

Discussion

As in Experiment 1, conventional and nonconventional requests behaved quite differently. As expected, R was taken to be meant almost invariably for the three conventional requests and less often for the nonconventional one. Also as expected, Q was taken seriously less often for the conventional than for the nonconventional requests. As in Experiment 1, however, these findings cannot be attributed solely to conventionality, transparency, or obviousness, since the conventional and nonconventional requests differ from each other in all three ways.

Transparency and obviousness, however, were tested independently of conventionality in this experiment. As expected on the basis of transparency, Q was taken seriously more often for *Do you have?,* in which R isn't fully transparent, than for *Could you price?,* in which it is. And as expected on the basis of obviousness, Q was taken seriously somewhat

Table 12.6. Percentage of Elliptical Responses for Information Provided for the Four Requests in Experiment 2

Request	Answer Plus Information	Information Alone	Total
(1) Could you tell me time?	100	72	73
(2) Could you tell me price?	33	64	59
(3) Do you have a price?	38	61	51
(4) Does a fifth cost more?	23	22	22
Totals	34	56	50

more often for *Could you price?* than for *Could you time?* This fits the idea that the less obvious Q's answer, the more likely Q was meant seriously.

The last result, however, is problematic. For one thing, it is only marginally significant. For another, it is subject to an alternative account. Recall that when the merchants were asked *Could you time?*, they could all say *yes* and provide the time immediately. But when asked *Could you price?*, 36% of them had to excuse themselves from the telephone, check on the price, return, and then give it. Of the 15 who answered *yes* to this request, 10 left the telephone with such responses as "Yes, hold on a second" and "Sure, just a moment." So these merchants who answered Q may have done so not because its answer was less obvious, but because they wanted to acknowledge they had heard and accepted the request before leaving the telephone. On the other hand, they could have acknowledged the requests with a mere "Hold on a second" or "Just a moment," as many other merchants did. So the alternative account is problematic too. In any case, these interruptions do not affect the comparisons among *Could you price?*, *Do you have?*, and *Does a fifth?*, which were equally often subject to these interruptions.

One striking finding was that the formal *yes* was reserved mainly for the nonconventional request *Does a fifth?*, while the slangier *yeah, sure,* and *uh huh* were reserved mainly for the three conventional requests. Why? It cannot be because *yes* indicates a greater certainty of answer. Surely the answers to the three conventional requests are more certain because they are fore-ordained to be affirmative. A more plausible explanation is that *yes* indicates seriousness of answer. While the Q's for the three conventional requests are generally not intended to be taken seriously, the Q for the nonconventional request is. So the answer to this serious Q is invested with the seriousness it deserves, which is provided by the formal *yes.*

The ellipsis in Experiment 2 bore a strong resemblance to that in Experiment 1. Elliptical responses to R were common for *Could you time?, Could you price?,* and *Do you have?,* but rare for *Does a fifth?* This could be put down to conventionality—the first three are conventional and the last one isn't. It

could also be put down to transparency—the first three are relatively transparent compared to the last one. Or it could be put down to both. At this point we cannot be certain.

EXPERIMENT 3

In Experiments 1 and 2, there was the suggestion that the conventionality of a request may be important to the interpretation of Q and R, but the evidence was far from conclusive. Each comparison of conventional and nonconventional requests was obscured because the conventional requests also had the more transparent R's and the more obvious answers to Q. Experiment 3 was designed to remedy this problem and test for the influence of conventionality uncontaminated by these other two factors.

For this purpose I turned to conventionality of form, or idiomaticity, in selecting the following three requests.

(1) Can you please tell me what the interest is on your regular savings account?

(2) Can you tell me what the interest is on your regular savings account?

(3) Are you able to tell me what the interest is on your regular savings account?

These will be abbreviated *Can you please?, Can you?,* and *Are you able?* Each request was asked of 50 clerks of San Francisco area branch banks for a total of 150 clerks. In each case, Q was intended to be the literal question asked, and R was intended to be "I request you to tell me what the interest is on your regular savings account."

All three requests rely on the same conventional *means* of making a request: Each asks a question with the literal meaning "Do you have the ability to tell me what the interest rate is?" They differ in conventionality of *form. Can you?* is the idiomatic form of expressing this means, whereas *Are you able?* is not. Note, for example, that *Can you?* readily accepts *please,* whereas *Are you able?* does not. When the caller selects the idiomatic form, she says, in effect, "I'm using this question pro forma to make a request. You aren't intended to take Q seriously." When she selects the nonidiomatic form, which emphasizes the literal question, she signals that she

Table 12.7. Percentage of Bank Clerks Giving Answers and Information to Three Requests in Experiment 3

Request	Answer Alone	Answer Plus Information	Information Alone	Other
(1) Can you please tell me? (50)[a]	0	8	92	0
(2) Can you tell me? (50)	0	16	84	0
(3) Are you able to tell me? (50)	4	30	64	2

[a]Number of clerks asked each request indicated in parentheses.

may well be interested in knowing whether the clerk has the ability to tell her the interest rate. So the nonidiomatic *Are you able?* should lead to a larger q than the idiomatic *Can you please?* and *Can you?*, although all three forms should virtually always be taken as meaning request R.

Can you please? was designed to test another factor. Ordinarily, *please* is used to signal, or mark, requests, as in *Tell me please what the interest rate is.* When it is appended to *Can you?*, it should be a further signal that Q was not intended to be taken seriously— that Q is being uttered pro forma. And if there are any doubts about whether or not R was intended, *please* should scotch those doubts too.

Results

The results fell out as predicted. The three response categories and their percentages of occurrence are shown in Table 12.7, and the corresponding estimates of q and r are shown in Table 12.8. As expected, Q was taken seriously more often for the nonidiomatic than for the idiomatic forms. It was answered by 35% of the relevant clerks for *Are you able?*, but by only 12% of them for *Can you please?* and *Can you?* The $\hat{q}$ of .35 is significantly larger than the $\hat{q}$ of .12 ($z = 3.11, p < .001$); it is also significantly larger than the $\hat{q}$'s of .16 and .08 taken separately ($x \geqslant 2.70, p < .02$). As

Table 12.8. Estimates of q and r for Three Requests in Experiment 3

Request	Parameters $\hat{q}$	$\hat{r}$
(1) Can you please tell me?	.08	1.00
(2) Can you tell me?	.16	1.00
(3) Are you able to tell me?	.35	.88

expected, Q was also taken seriously more often for *Can you?* than for *Can you please?*, where Q was answered by 16 and 8% of the clerks, respectively. These two values, however, are based on only 12 clerks altogether, and so the difference isn't quite significant ($z = 1.23, p < .11$). With more respondents it might prove to be reliable. And as expected, R was taken as having been intended by all of the clerks for *Can you please?* and *Can you?* and by all but two of them for *Are you able?* All three values of $\hat{r}$ were at or near 1.00 and don't differ significantly.

The elliptical responses to R fell into a neat pattern too. Their percentages are shown in Table 12.9; *Can you please?* and *Can you?* have been combined since between them there were only 12 responses in the answer-plus-information category. The two conventional forms led to ellipsis 64% of the time, whereas the nonconventional form led to ellipsis only 38% of the time. This difference is significant ($z = 2.94, p < .002$); the difference is also significant when *Can you please?* and *Can you?* are each compared with *Are you able?* ($z \geqslant 1.97, p < .025$). As in Experiments 1 and 2, there was also more ellipsis for the information-alone category than for the answer-plus-information category, 61 to 33%. This difference is also significant ($x^2(1) = 5.69, p < .01$), and it is consistent across the three requests.

Discussion

Conventionality of form matters. Fewer bank clerks took Q seriously when the request was idiomatic than when it wasn't. Even fewer took Q seriously when the idiomatic form had *please* appended. The clerks made these adjustments while still generally taking these forms as conveying R. So with *Can you?*, listeners are ready to believe that the speaker is

Table 12.9. Percentage of Elliptical Responses for Information
Provided for the Four Requests in Experiment 3

Request	Answer Plus Information	Information Alone	Total
(1) Can you (please)?	50	66	64
(2) Are you able?	20	47	38
Totals	33	61	56

requesting information and nothing more. With *Are you able?*, they are more reluctant to do so.

These results also yielded a test of conventionality of form as a source of ellipsis. A priori, there are no syntactic grounds for thinking that the three requests should differ in elliptical responses to R. They are equally transparent to R. All three contain the same WH-question, *What is the interest on your regular savings account?*, embedded as a complement within virtually the same form of yes/no question, *Can you tell me X?* and *Are you able to tell me X?* Yet the three forms did differ. The two idiomatic forms led to ellipsis 64% of the time; the less idiomatic form did so only 38% of the time, a large difference. Since the forms do not differ in conventionality of means or in transparency of R, the cause of this difference must be the conventionality of form. The clearer it is that Q is merely pro forma, the readier a respondent is to provide the information to R elliptically.

One point should be noted here. While these findings show the influence of conventionality of form, they do not bear directly on the influence of conventionality of means, which is what was at issue in Experiments 1 and 2. Indeed, there may be no "pure" test for conventionality of means, since it is almost always correlated with transparency and obviousness. Yet these results suggest that conventionality of means is likely to be a contributing factor to Experiments 1 and 2 above and beyond transparency and obviousness.

EXPERIMENT 4

Experiments 1, 2, and 3 have been mainly concerned with the way indirect requests are expressed linguistically. It was important whether or not the request was conventional in means, was conventional in form, had a transparent R, and was marked with *please.* Another factor that was possibly important was how obvious the answer to Q was in context. With obviousness entered the first major nonlinguistic factor, the fit between A's speech act and the situation in which it was performed. Experiments 4 and 5 were designed to broaden this half of the enterprise. In particular, they bring in A's goals and plans in saying what she did.

Experiment 4 was intended to be a modest demonstration of how the intepretation of a request changes with the manifest reasons for its having been made. The request *Does a fifth of Jim Beam cost more than $5?* was asked of 100 San Francisco area liquor merchants (none the same as in Experiment 2). It was preceded for half of them by one preamble and for the other half by a second preamble. The two preambles were intended to suggest different reasons for the request. The caller's first turn on the telephone, after *Hi,* took one of these two forms:

(1) I want to buy some bourbon. Does a fifth of Jim Beam cost more than $5?

(2) I've got $5 to spend. Does a fifth of Jim Beam cost more than $5?

These two preambles will be abbreviated *Some bourbon* and *Five dollars.* The first was intended to be relatively neutral and uninformative, giving little reason for the caller's request other than the obvious one. *Five dollars* was intended to give more cause for taking Q seriously. It strongly suggests that the caller, because she has only $5 to spend, truly wants to know whether or not she can buy a fifth of Jim Beam with it. Let us consider Q to be the literal question and R to be a request for the price of Jim Beam. Then Q ought to be taken seriously more often for *Five dollars* than for *Some bourbon.* How often R should be taken to have been meant should change little if any.

Results

These predictions were borne out. The three response categories and their percentages are shown in Table 12.10, and the estimates of q and r are shown in Table 12.11. As expected, $\hat{q}$ was larger for *Five dollars* than for *Some bourbon*, .67 to .50. This difference, though not large, is significant ($z = 1.74$, $p < .05$). The difference between the $\hat{r}$'s of .42 and .52 is not ($z = .75$). As a check on the consistency of these two differences, $\hat{q}$ and $\hat{r}$ were also computed according to Scheme 2. The $\hat{q}$ is still larger for *Five dollars* than for *Some bourbon*, .52 to .29, and the difference is still significant ($z = 1.84$, $p < .05$). The direction of $\hat{r}$ reverses, .71 to .67, which is further evidence that r doesn't differ much between the two preambles.

The elliptical responses to R revealed little of interest, since the request itself, *Does a fifth?*, allows little ellipsis in the first place. *Some bourbon* and *Five dollars* each led to ellipsis 18% of the time, and there were no differences between the answer-plus-information and information-alone categories.

Discussion

It isn't surprising that the interpretation of an utterance should change with the manifest reasons for it. But the change induced by the two preambles in this experiment is different from most kinds of change. Typically, one literal meaning is used in different circumstances to convey different *indirect* meanings. But what changed in Experiment 4 was the *literal* meaning Q—how often it was thought to

Table 12.11. Estimates of q and r for the Two Preambles in Experiment 4

Preamble	Parameters	
	$\hat{q}$	$\hat{r}$
(1) Some bourbon	.50	.42
(2) Five dollars	.67	.52

have been intended seriously. In short, the manifest reasons for an utterance can affect both direct and indirect meanings.

EXPERIMENT 5

While the caller in Experiment 4 made her reasons for calling explicit, ordinarily she would not. Instead, she would count on the merchant considering what she said along with the circumstances in which she said it to decide what she meant. But which circumstances, and how are they used to raise or lower q and r? For merchants to combine contextual information with the factors already noted, they must have in their possession a powerful principle of organization. That principle, the evidence suggests, is the merchant's conception of the caller's goals and plans in saying what she said (see Charniak, 1977; Lehnert, 1977; Schank & Abelson, 1977; Allen & Perrault, Note 3; among others).

How does a merchant infer the caller's goals and plans, and how does this conception determine his interpretation of her utterance? Experiment 5 was designed to examine these issues in detail. Four requests were selected.

(1) Do you accept Master Charge cards?
(2) Do you accept American Express cards?
(3) Do you accept credit cards?
(4) Do you accept any kinds of credit cards?

Table 12.10. Percentage of Liquor Merchants in Experiment 4 Giving Answers and Information to *Does a Fifth of Jim Beam Cost More than $5?* When Preceded by Two Preambles

Preamble	Answer Alone	Answer Plus Information	Information Alone	Other
(1) Some bourbon (50)[a]	28	20	48	4
(2) Five dollars (50)	32	34	32	4

[a]Number of merchants asked each request indicated in parentheses.

These will be abbreviated *Master Charge?, American Express?, Credit cards?,* and *Any kinds of credit cards?* Each request was asked of 50 restauranteurs in and around Palo Alto for a total of 200 respondents. Fast food restaurants and restaurant chains were excluded from the sample.

For each request Q is the obvious literal question, and R is stipulated to be "I request you to tell me the names of *all* the credit cards you accept." The restauranteur who responded to any of these requests "Yes, we accept all major credit cards" both answered Q and responded to R. When a restauranteur did not spontaneously name all the credit cards he accepted, he was asked one of the two follow-up questions. For *Master Charge?* and *American Express?,* he was asked *Do you accept any other credit cards?;* for the other two requests, he was asked *Which credit cards do you accept?* The caller always made sure she found out which credit cards the restaurant did accept. Since the first of these follow-up questions is similar to the other four requests, it will be treated as if it were an independent fifth request, abbreviated *Any other credit cards?:*

(5) Do you accept any other credit cards?

Yet it should be kept in mind that this was always a follow-up to a *yes* answer to *Master Charge?* or *American Express?*

The Caller's Plan

In the Palo Alto restaurant world there are five credit cards: Visa (formerly BankAmericard, and often referred to as such), Master Charge, American Express, Diner's Club, and Carte Blanche. These were accepted, respectively, by 72, 71, 38, 12, and 10% of the restaurants in our sample. These percentages probably reflect card ownership. Indeed, it is probably mutual knowledge to restauranteurs and customers that there are about five credit cards, that Visa and Master Charge are the most widely owned and accepted, that Diner's Club and Carte Blanche are the least widely owned and accepted, and that many restaurants accept no credit cards at all.

Why would a caller ask the restauranteur whether he accepted credit cards? He would assume she has a hierarchy of goals. As one goal, she wants to decide whether or not to eat at the restaurant, probably that night. As a subgoal, she wants to know how to pay for the meal. As a subgoal to that, she wants to know if she can pay with any of the credit cards she owns. As next subgoal, she wants to discover whether any of the cards acceptable to the restaurant matches any of hers.

It is the next subgoal down that is critical, for the caller must concoct a plan that will bring out the name of one of her credit cards as efficiently as possible. Her plan will depend on the credit cards she owns. Consider these four cases.

The caller owns exactly one credit card, a Master Charge card. She wants to know whether it is accepted regardless of which others are. To find out efficiently, she should be specific: *Do you accept Master Charge cards?* To ask *Credit cards?* or *Any kinds of credit cards?* would be less efficient. If the merchant answers yes alone, she still has to ask *Master Charge?* If he lists all his acceptable credit cards, she will get a lot of extra information. And to ask *American Express?* would be odd, since a yes answer does not imply he accepts Master Charge cards, and he is unlikely to list the credit cards he accepts. In short, the caller should ask *Master Charge?*

The caller owns two credit cards, Master Charge and Diner's Club. One way to proceed is to ask about the cards in turn, first about the commoner Master Charge and then, if that fails, about Diner's Club. Another way is to ask *Do you accept Master Charge or Diner's Club?* As before, it would be odd to ask *American Express?* But what about *Credit cards?* or *Any kinds of credit cards?* For the first, if the merchant says yes alone, she would have to follow up with specific questions about Master Charge and Diner's Club cards. This is obviously less efficient than the first two routes. But by asking *Any kinds of credit cards?,* which explicitly mentions that there are various kinds of credit cards, she implies that she is interested in specific kinds of credit cards, not just credit cards in general. This is likely to get a listing of the acceptable credit cards without a follow-up question. So while *Master*

Charge? and *Do you accept Master Charge or Diner's Club cards?* are the most efficient, *Any kinds of credit cards?* would probably do the trick too.

The caller owns three credit cards, Master Charge, American Express, and Diner's Club. By now it would be rather inefficient to ask about these cards one at a time, or to ask *Do you accept Master Charge or American Express or Diner's Club?* The first would take too long, and the second would be too tedious if there is a chance no credit cards are accepted at all. For the reasons given before, the most efficient route would be to ask *Any kinds of credit cards?* That would get a quick no if no cards were accepted, and a listing of credit cards if some were. *Credit cards?* is also a possibility. It too would get a quick no if no cards were accepted, and it would be easy to follow up with *Master Charge?* or *American Express?*, the commonest of the credit cards she owns, if the answer was yes. So the caller should ask *Any kinds of credit cards?*, or perhaps *Credit cards?*, but not *Master Charge?* or *American Express?*

The caller owns all five credit cards. Her most efficient strategy would be to ask *Credit cards?*, since it doesn't matter which cards are accepted as long as one is. To ask *Any kinds of credit cards?* would imply concern about specific credit cards and might get a listing of the acceptable ones, which is too much information. And to ask about specific credit cards would be particularly inefficient. She should therefore ask *Credit cards?*, or possibly *Any kinds of credit cards?*, but not *Master Charge?* or *American Express?*

To infer her specific plan, the restauranteur can work backwards from her choice of noun phrase. Her most obvious choices are these, and the inferences he can draw from them follow.

(1) *Master Charge card.* Caller owns this card and perhaps one other.

(2) *Master Charge or Diner's Club cards.* Caller owns these two cards and perhaps one other.

(3) *Any kinds of credit cards.* Caller owns all but one or two cards.

(4) *Credit cards.* Caller probably owns all five cards.

The restauranteur draws these inferences in part by realizing—implicitly—which noun

phrases the caller could have chosen but didn't. By selecting *credit cards,* for example, she doesn't own just one or two cards, for she would have mentioned them explicitly, using (1) or (2). Nor does she own just three, for she would have indicated interest in specific cards, as in (3). Hence she probably owns all five.

The restauranteur can use these predictions to decide what the caller meant by her utterance: whether she intended Q seriously; what R must be, if anything; and whether R was intended. First consider only those restauranteurs—the great majority—who could have answered, or actually did answer, Q with yes. Their decision should go as follows.

(1) *Master Charge?* Since the caller probably has just one card, a yes answer to Q is sufficient, and giving information about R is entirely unnecessary. So Q is intended seriously, and R is not intended, putting *q* at or near 1.00 and *r* at or near 0.

(2) *American Express?* Same as for *Master Charge?*

(3) *Credit cards?* Since the caller probably owns all five cards, a yes answer to Q is probably sufficient, hence Q is probably intended seriously. But because she may not own all of them, she may need a listing to check on her particular cards, and R may have been intended too. So *q* should be high, but not as high as for *Master Charge?* or *American Express?*, and *r* should be low, but not as low as for *Master Charge?* or *American Express?*

(4) *Any kinds of credit cards?* Since the caller probably owns three or so cards but not five, a yes answer to Q is informative, but hardly sufficient. Q may be intended seriously, but R is very likely intended so that she can check on her particular cards. This puts *q* lower than for *Credit cards?* but not 0, and puts *r* much higher than for *Credit cards?* but not 1.00.

(5) *Any other credit cards?* This is an odd question. Since the caller has just received a yes answer to either *Master Charge?* or *American Express?*, she has suggested that she owns an acceptable card. So why ask about *other* cards? She must be asking for a friend, or be inquiring about another card she might like to use, or something similar. A yes answer to Q, then, won't ordinarily be informative, but a

Table 12.12. Percentage of Restaurants Able to Answer Yes Giving Answers and Information to Five Requests in Experiment 5

Requests	Answer Alone	Answer Plus Information	Information Alone	Other
(1) Master Charge cards? (32)[a]	94	6	0	0
(2) American Express cards? (20)	100	0	0	0
(3) Credit cards? (45)	44	38	16	2
(4) Any kinds of credit cards? (39)	10	56	33	0
(5) Any other credit cards? (50)	2	8	88	2

[a]Number of restauranteurs asked each request who could have answered yes indicated in parentheses.

response to R will. So Q is probably pro forma as a way of conveying R to elicit these other cards. This puts q near 0 and r near 1, more extreme in both values than for *Any kinds of credit cards?*

Before planning his response, the restauranteur has one other factor to contend with—the number of credit cards *he* accepts. For *Credit cards?* and *Any kinds of credit cards?*, a yes answer alone would be taken, for reasons discussed by Grice (1975), as implicating that he accepts *any* major credit cards. If he doesn't, a yes answer is misleading, and he should go on to list the several credit cards he does accept. So for these two requests, the fewer credit cards he accepts, the more likely he should respond to R anyway.

What about the restauranteurs for whom the answer to Q was explicitly or implicitly no? Here are the four cases:

(1) *Master Charge?* Since the caller probably has just one card, a no answer to Q is sufficient. Still, she *may* have a second card, and responding to R might be informative. So Q is intended seriously, and R may be intended, putting q at or near 1.00, and r somewhere greater than 0.

(2) *American Express?* Same as for *Master Charge?*

(3) *Credit cards?* Since the caller wants to pay with a credit card, a no answer to Q is highly informative. Q must be intended, putting q at or near 1.00. But with a no answer to Q, R doesn't even make sense, although some other R' may. To decide on R', the merchant must go to the caller's next higher goal—she wants to pay with something besides cash. Indeed, R' could be "Tell me other ways I can pay." The value of r' for this R' should be larger than zero.

(4) *Any kinds of credit cards?* Same as for *Credit cards?*

Results

Affirmative answers. The responses in which Q's answer was explicitly or implicitly yes are summarized in Table 12.12, and the $\hat{q}$'s and $\hat{r}$'s estimated from them are listed in Table 12.13. These are the responses that paved the way for the restauranteur to respond to R too if he chose to.

The expectations about Q were strongly confirmed. The $\hat{q}$'s for *Master Charge?* and *American Express?* were exactly 1.00. For these no restauranteur merely listed the credit cards they accepted. As expected, the $\hat{q}$'s for *Credit cards?* and *Any kinds of credit cards?* were lower at .84 and .67. For these a fair number of restauranteurs merely recited their credit card list. These two $\hat{q}$'s are each significantly smaller than each of the earlier 1.00s ($z \geqslant 1.87$, $p < .05$), and as expected, .67 is significantly smaller than .84 ($z = 1.81$, $p < .05$). Finally, as expected, $\hat{q}$ was virtually nil at .10 for *Any other credit cards?* Almost no restauranteur took Q seriously for this request. This .10 is significantly smaller than each of the others ($z \geqslant 5.46$, $p < .001$).

Table 12.13. Estimates of q and r for Five Requests in Experiment 5

Request	Parameters	
	$\hat{q}$	$\hat{r}$
(1) Master Charge cards?	1.00	.06
(2) American Express cards?	1.00	.00
(3) Credit cards?	.84	.46
(4) Any kinds of credit cards?	.67	.85
(5) Any other credit cards?	.10	.80

The expectations about R were strongly confirmed too. The $\hat{r}$'s for *Master Charge?* and *American Express?* were .06 and .00, respectively. For these two requests, only 2 of 52 restauranteurs followed up their yes answer with a list of their credit cards even though all of them accepted other credit cards and could have done so. In contrast, 46% of the restauranteurs followed up their yes answer on *Credit cards?*, and almost twice as many, 85%, did so on *Any kinds of credit cards?* Among these $\hat{r}$'s, .46 is significantly larger than .06 ($z = 3.78, p < .001$), and .85 is significantly larger than .46 ($z = 3.21, p < .001$). The $\hat{r}$ for *Any other credit cards?*, .80, is roughly the same as that for *Any kinds of credit cards?* But based as it is on only five responses, this $\hat{r}$ is probably an underestimate; by Scheme 2, it is .96.

The restauranteurs who accepted any credit cards accepted from one to five of them. When asked *Credit cards?* or *Any kinds of credit cards?*, as expected, 100% of those accepting just one credit card went on to list it, while only 60% of those accepting five went on to list theirs. The correlation between number of credit cards accepted and the percentage listing them was $-.76, t(77) = 1.94, p < .05$. Part of this correlation could be explained by assuming that it is easier to list one than five credit cards, but this could not be the whole story. Almost all the restauranteurs accepting all five credit cards and responding to R didn't enumerate them but said such things as "Yes, we accept all major credit cards" or "Yes, we have all of them, as a matter of fact." These responses are as short as "Yes, we accept Master Charge cards" and even shorter than an explicit listing of two or more cards, as in "Yes, we accept Master Charge, Visa, and American Express." So although length of response may have been a contributing factor, the restauran-

teurs appear to have been sensitive to the implications of their responses too.

The elliptical responses to R are summarized in Table 12.14. (*Master Charge?* and *American Express?* have been omitted since between them they elicited only two responses to R.) As in Experiments 1, 2, and 3, there was more ellipsis in the information-alone responses than in the answer-plus-information responses, 89 to 60%. This difference is significant ($\chi^2(1) = 10.50, p < .001$). Also, there was less ellipsis for *Any kinds of credit cards?*, 54%, than for either of the other two, 83 and 92%. This percentage is significantly smaller than each of the other two ($z \geqslant 2.36, p < .02$).

As for the 120 affirmative answers in this experiment, 81% were *yes* and the rest were *yeah, uh huh,* or *sure.* The percentage of *yes* answers ranged from 69 to 100% on the five questions, but did not differ significantly or follow any clear pattern.

Negative answers. The expectations about *Master Charge?* and *American Express?* were nicely confirmed. For these there were two types of responses to R. One type asserted that the restaurant didn't accept any credit cards at all. The second type, which occurred only for *American Express?*, listed all the cards that *were* accepted. For the answer-alone, answer-plus-information, and information-alone categories, there were 14, 4, and 0 responses to *Master Charge?* and 18, 10, and 2 such responses to *American Express?*, respectively. So $\hat{q}$ was 1.00 and .93 for *Master Charge?* and *American Express?* This average $\hat{q}$ of .96 obviously doesn't differ from the $\hat{q}$ of 1.00 when the answer to Q was yes. In contrast, $\hat{r}$ was .22 and .36 for these two sentences. This average of .30 is significantly larger than the $\hat{r}$ of .03 for these two sentences. This average of .30 is

Table 12.14. **Percentage of Elliptical Responses to Three Requests in Experiment 5**

Request	Answer Plus Information	Information Alone	Total
(3) Credit cards?	82	86	83
(4) Any kinds of credit cards?	50	62	54
(5) Any other credit cards?	25	98	92
Totals	60	89	78

significantly larger than the $\hat{r}$ of .03 when the answer to Q was yes ($\chi^2(1) = 10.76$, $p < .001$). In brief, *Master Charge?* and *American Express?* were construed as conveying request R only when the answer to Q was no.

The findings for *Credit Cards?* and *Any kinds of credit cards?* also turned out as expected. For these, when the answer to Q is no, that answer should always be made explicit, since it is not implied by any response to an indirect R. It was: $\hat{q}$ was 1.00 for both. This value is almost significantly larger than the average $\hat{q}$ of .76 when the answer to Q was yes ($\chi^2(1) = 3.39$, $p < .07$).

For *Credit cards?* and *Any kinds of credit cards?*, when the answer to Q is no, R makes no sense. As expected, many restauranteurs found an R' that did, namely "Tell me other ways I can pay." Fully 38% of them mentioned personal checks, as in "No. Local checks." This puts $\hat{r}'$ at .38. (A surprising number also mentioned cash—completely redundant information—but almost always along with a mention of personal checks, as in "No, we just take checks or cash.") Even 15% of the restauranteurs answering no to *Master Charge?* and *American Express?* mentioned checks, putting the average $\hat{r}'$ for them at .15. Combining $\hat{r}$ and $\hat{r}'$ for *Master Charge?* and *American Express?*, we get .41, which emphasizes even more how readily they were construed as conveying requests when the answer to Q was no. By comparison, none of the 186 restauranteurs answering in the affirmative in Table 12.12 mentioned checks. They didn't need to, since the affirmative information about credit cards was obviously sufficient.

Discussion

On the surface, these findings show that the interpretation of an interrogative construction can change enormously with small changes in a noun phrase. The five sentences used were all of the form *Do you accept X?* Yet as X went from *Master Charge cards* to *credit cards* to *any kinds of credit cards* to *any other credit cards,* Q was taken seriously less and less often, and R was taken to be meant more and more often. Both $\hat{q}$ and $\hat{r}$ ran the gamut from 0 to 1. Compared to Experiments 1 through 4, these variations are very dramatic indeed.

Beneath the surface, it seems clear that these changes were brought about by the restauranteur's conception of the caller's plan. His assumptions and implicit reasoning went something like this. The caller is a potential customer who wants to pay for a meal at his restaurant with a credit card. Her goal in performing this speech act is knowledge of whether one of her credit cards is accepted by the restaurant and perhaps, failing that, whether some other form of non-cash payment is possible. Her plan for reaching this goal will vary with which credit cards she owns, a plan she intends him to infer from her choice of noun phrase. In short, she expects him to infer her goals and plans in order to see what she meant.

Although the caller's plan, as the restauranteur reconstructs it, may be extensive, he realizes he is expected to deal with only the first one or two steps—for example, answer Q and comply with R. Yet he may also realize that these or other parts of her plan are based on false assumptions, which he will want to correct in a cooperative but unexpected move. The caller's question, for example, suggests that she may patronize the restaurant that night. That assumes that the restaurant is open, and if it isn't, the restauranteur will want to correct this assumption. Indeed, several did, as in "Uh, yes, we accept credit cards. But tonight we are closed." and "Uh uh. We're not open anyways." These cooperative but unexpected moves are further evidence that the restauranteur actively reconstructs the caller's plan as completely as he can and uses it in order to understand her and then plan his response.

GENERAL DISCUSSION

From these five experiments emerges a picture of indirect speech acts and their responses that has several new features. These features fall under four headings: indirect speech acts, understanding indirect speech acts, planning responses, and ellipsis.

Indirect Speech Acts

Indirect speech acts, according to Searle (1975), have at least two meanings—a literal meaning M_1 and an indirect meaning M_2. Furthermore, M_2 is conveyed by virtue of M_1. To these and the other properties listed in the beginning, we can add three important refinements.

Seriousness of the literal meaning. Although M_1 may always be "conveyed" along with M_2, it is not always intended to be taken seriously. For some requests in these experiments, Q was taken as entirely pro forma, merely as a polite means of conveying R, and was not answered with an explicit yes or no. For other requests, it was taken very seriously, as if the caller really wanted to know its answer, and was then answered with an explicit yes or no. That is, a major determinant of whether a merchant answered Q or not was his estimate of how likely it was intended to be taken seriously.

Seriousness is a property of other, perhaps even all, genuine indirect speech acts, although its consequences may vary from one speech act to the next. Take greetings, for example. In English speaking cultures, they are conventionally conveyed indirectly by asking after someone's health. (In other cultures, they are conveyed by other means (Morgan, 1978).) *How are you feeling today?*, for example, is an unidiomatic greeting, and Q would ordinarily be taken quite seriously and might elicit an honest *Okay, except for my knee. How are you?* is highly idiomatic, and Q would ordinarily be taken pro forma. It is likely to elicit the pro forma answer *Fine, thank you*, regardless of health, or even merely the return greeting *How are you?* For historical reasons, the related greeting *How do you do?* has come to convey its greeting directly, even though the fossil of a question is still visible within it. Since this fossil is never answered even with a pro forma *Fine, thank you*, *How do you do?* is a complete idiom—though only a semiopaque one. *Hi*, historically a compressed form of *How are you?* via *Hiya*, doesn't even have a trace of Q left in it, and as an opaque idiom, it also conveys its greetings directly. Similarly continua have been discussed by Clark and Clark (1979) and Morgan (1978).

Uncertainty of meaning. For *Do you accept credit cards?*, about 50% of the merchants responded to R, and the other 50% did not. Were the former merchants *certain* the caller meant R, and the other merchants just as certain she did not? The answer, I believe, is no.

More likely, all the merchants were uncertain to some degree, feeling that the caller may have meant R, but then again may not have. They could only guess at her plans, and that guess was inherently probabilistic.

What, then, are we to make of the responses the merchants did give to R? In their eyes, these responses may have been neither pure "expected moves" nor pure "added moves," as these were distinguished earlier. Rather, they were conditionally expected moves, as if the merchants were saying, "If you were requesting a list of my credit cards, here they are; if you weren't, here is some helpful information anyway." The more certain they were that the caller really did intend R, the more often the best strategy was to respond to R anyway.

A fundamentally different view, however, is that the caller herself intended Q and R to be uncertain. Up to now, I have called q an estimate of how *likely* Q was intended to be taken seriously. Instead, it could be thought of as an estimate of how *seriously* Q was intended to be taken. Similarly, r could be thought of, not as how *likely* R was intended, but as how *seriously* R was intended. This view makes good sense for at least some kinds of indirect speech acts, such as hints. Imagine A asking B, *What did you think of* Vanity Fair?, intending it as an indirect hint for B to return the book to the library. If he understands the hint correctly, he realizes that he could either take the hint *(I liked it—I'll return it today)* or not take the hint *(I liked it—what did you think?)* and that she intended him to have this option and to see that she was leaving him this option. She meant R only half seriously. By making weaker or stronger hints, she could have varied its seriousness from nil to complete. The same rationale could be applied to *Do you accept credit cards?*, where the merchant could see the caller as intending R only half seriously. In short, the uncertainty of meaning could have one of two loci: in what A intended, or in B's recognition of what she intended. For the predictions of these experiments, as it happens, it makes no difference which.

Conditional indirect speech acts. In Experiment 5, several requests were found to convey not just a single pair of meanings Q and R, but one pair of meanings Q + R when Q's answer was yes, and another pair of meanings Q + R' when the answer was no. *Do you accept credit cards?*, for example, was taken to mean R ("List your credit cards") when Q's answer was yes, but R′ ("Say how else ·I can pay") when the answer was no. These, then, are conditional indirect requests. *Credit cards?* would be paraphrased as follows: "I ask you whether or not you accept credit cards and I thereby request you to tell me, if you do accept any, which ones you accept, and if you don't, how else I can pay." Each of these Q's and R's, of course, has its own likelihood or seriousness value.

Most indirect speech acts don't have this conditionality. When A asks B to add salt to the soup by asserting *This soup needs salt,* she intends him to add salt with no possible options. He may try to forestall the request by disputing her assertion—*No, it doesn't*—but that is contrary to her intent. When the literal meaning is a question, however, B is intentionally left with an explicit option, and the indirect speech act is conditional. *Can you add salt to the soup?* says "I ask you whether you are able to add salt to the soup and I request you to add it if you are able and not to add it if you are not able." *Do you want some coffee?*, likewise, is an indirect promise to fill the cup if the answer is yes and not to fill it if the answer is no. What makes *Credit cards?* and *Any kinds of credit cards?* different from these others is that their two options are both positive actions, and each has its own probability.

Understanding Indirect Speech Acts

The merchants in these experiments relied on many different sources of information in estimating q and r. The six I have identified are as follows.

(1) Conventionality of means. In English, some means for making requests are conventional, and others aren't. For conventional means, merchants should be more certain Q was merely pro forma and R was meant, leading them to lower q and increase r. These predictions were confirmed in Experiments 1 and 2, but because they were confounded by other factors, it was impossible to identify conventionality of means as an independent source of information.

(2) Conventionality of form. Similarly, some forms of requests are conventional or idio-

matic, and others are less so. For idiomatic requests, merchants should lower q and, if possible, increase r, and in Experiment 3, they did. Idiomaticity is an important source of information for other indirect speech acts too, as in the greetings cited earlier, which ranged from *How are you feeling today?* to *How are you?* to *How do you do?* to *Hi.*

(3) Special markers. In English, *please* can be used to mark some utterances as requests, and in the right circumstances so can other markers, like *for me* in *Can you open the door for me?* On encountering such markers, merchants should be more certain Q is merely pro forma and R is meant. In Experiment 3, the evidence, though weak, was that they were. Other markers are appropriate to other speech acts and should be a useful source of information too.

(4) Transparency of the indirect meaning. The indirect meaning is more transparent in some indirect speech acts—more completely specified in the words uttered—than it is in others. The more transparent the indirect meaning is, the more confident merchants can be that the literal meaning is pro forma and the indirect meaning is truly intended. This prediction was confirmed in Experiment 2. Also in line with this prediction, conventional requests, which tend to be more transparent than nonconventional ones, had consistently lower q's and higher r's. In general, it is the transparent indirect speech acts that appear most likely to evolve historically into conventional ones.

(5) Implausibility of the literal meaning. For some indirect requests, the answer to Q is obvious to both A and B, but for others, it is not. The more obvious the answer, the more confident merchants can be that Q was not intended seriously and that R was intended. This prediction was confirmed in Experiment 2, though problematically. Yet one mark of most conventional requests is that their Q's have obvious answers, and these requests consistently yielded lower q's and higher r's. Indeed, requests with obvious answers to Q are just the ones that have had the best opportunity historically to evolve into conventional ones.

Implausibility, or irrelevance, of literal meaning is a property of other indirect speech acts too, though in different ways. Most of Grice's (1975) and Searle's (1975) examples of conversational implicature, of which indirect speech acts are but one kind, work in part by the implausibility of their literal meaning alone in context.

(6) The speaker's imputed plans and goals. When A performs an indirect speech act with M_1 and M_2, B assumes that these were intended as two steps in a broader plan for attaining some goal. What is critical is that he further assumes that he is expected to infer her plans, at least to some degree, in order to decide what she meant. This point was demonstrated explicitly in Experiments 4 and 5 yet was also at work in Experiments 1, 2, and 3. The point is very general. Plans and goals are particularly important when they are among the only clues to M_2, as in A's assertion to B, *This soup needs salt,* whose M_2 varies enormously with the context.

By what process is all this information put together? The answer is complicated. Note that the six sources of information are roughly of two kinds. The first four sources consist of linguistic characteristics of the utterance itself—data in the perceived event. The last two sources consist of expectations B has built up based on the circumstances in which the utterance occurred. The process that puts them together, then, must be an interactive process that is both "data driven" and "conceptually driven," to use Norman's (1976) terms. It must work both "bottom up" from the data in the utterance and "top down" from the conceptual base in which the utterance is being processed.

The process must be flexible enough to use whatever pertinent information is available. Imagine A stopping B, a stranger, on a busy street and saying *Will you please take me to Grand Central Station?* To see what she has requested, he will rely mostly on facts about her utterance—that it is a transparent conventional request marked by *please.* The circumstances will be of little help, since they make such a request quite unexpected. Imagine, instead, A stepping into B's taxi and saying the same thing. Since he expects just such a request, he can use both sources of information—the utterance itself and his expectations. In fact, the taxi circumstances are so rich that she would have got by with the minimal *Grand Central Station.* From his expectations, he will infer that she is requesting him to taxi her somewhere and that what she has specified

is the destination. In short, B's understanding is mostly data driven in the first case, half data driven and half conceptually driven in the second, and mostly conceptually driven in the third.

As for speed of processing, understanding M_1 and M_2 should be faster, all other things being equal, the more sources of information converge on them. Evidence for this is found in Schweller's (Note 6) comparison of how long it took people to understand sentences in two contexts, (1) contexts that induced M_1 alone and (2) contexts that induced both M_1 and M_2. Sentences with highly conventional means and forms for making requests—two sources of information that converge on M_2— were understood more quickly when construed as indirect requests than when construed literally. In contrast, sentences not conventionally used for making requests—where the two sources of information converging on M_2 were lacking—were understood more quickly when they were construed literally. So this evidence fits.

In a previous paper (Clark & Lucy, 1975), Lucy and I tentatively proposed that B first computes M_1, then decides whether or not M_1 alone could have been intended in that context, and, if it could not have, goes on to infer M_2. That model, I now believe, is misleading in several respects. First, it treats conventional indirect requests, like *Can you tell me the time?,* as if they conveyed requests directly and were equivalent to the semiopaque idiom *How do you do?* as a greeting. This now seems oversimplified. Second, it assumes that in indirect speech acts M_1 is never intended to be taken seriously. As Experiments 1 through 5 show, this assumption is not correct. And third, it was designed to handle only the fifth source of information—plausibility of literal meaning. As a result, its applicability is limited, and those limits are not well defined. These shortcomings have been taken care of in the present model, though at the expense of simplicity.

In the previous model, for many requests, M_1 was computed before M_2. Once we assume multiple sources of information, this proposal no longer holds much generality. For most requests it makes little sense to speak of one meaning being computed before the other. Imagine A stepping into a taxi and asking B, the driver, *Will you take me to Grand Central*

Station? From the phrase *Grand Central Station* alone, he could guess her request M_2 and then go on to figure out M_1. But this last step is necessary, for if she had said *Is this Grand Central Station?* or *Where is Grand Central Station?* or *Do you pick up people at Grand Central Station?*, he would otherwise have misunderstood her, as children often do in comparable situations (Schatz, 1978). So although the driver guessed M_2 before M_1, he couldn't verify that guess without computing M_1. On the other hand, he had to compute at least part of A's literal meaning—the phrase *Grand Central Station*—before he could even guess at M_2. It seems misleading in this case to talk about either meaning having been computed first.

In the current model, M_1 and M_2 are computed as parts of a single package. The same six sources of information are used in computing both meanings, and they are presumably used by both data driven and conceptually driven processes as they become available. It may happen that a listener will become confident he has recognized one meaning before the other. Yet that doesn't imply that he finished computing one meaning before beginning on the other, although that is possible in certain circumstances.

What is lacking so far is a specification of how the six sources of information interact as they are put together. The present findings give only hints about this process. When an indirect request was conventional, *r* tended to be estimated at the maximum, regardless of other factors, and *q* was determined by the other factors. Otherwise, when Q was intended seriously, R tended not to be, and vice versa. It is as if people prefer speech acts with only one serious meaning, although this preference is anything but perfect. Details about the amalgamation process must wait on future research.

Planning Responses

Once B has understood A's utterance, he must plan his response—though he may start planning and even responding before he has fully understood it. These experiments suggest that B will ordinarily make the expected moves, but he can modify, add to, or even replace these depending on the circumstances.

First, B may add in preliminary moves, like

uh and *just a minute,* which occurred often in these experiments. One special preliminary move was the self-clarification, like "The time we close" (with falling intonation), which appeared when the requests were difficult to understand.

Second, B may see that in A's plan she is presupposing something that isn't true, which he may want to correct in a cooperative but unexpected move. This move may replace an expected move, as when one liquor dealer said "Sorry, we don't have Jim Beam in fifths right now." Or it may be tacked on as an added move, as when one restauranteur said, "Uh, yes, we accept credit cards, but tonight we are closed" (see Kaplan, 1978).

Third, he may modify the expected response to get its implicatures to come out right. When asked *Do you accept credit cards?*, restauranteurs accepting only one or two cards couldn't get away with a mere *yes,* even if they thought that was all that was expected. A *yes* alone would implicate, by Gricean principles, that they accepted credit cards in general, and so these merchants had to go on to say which credit cards they did accept.

Fourth, B may want to answer Q anyway in order to be polite—or not answer it to be impolite. Consider the eight indirect requests in Table 12.15 each of the form *Can* (or *Could*) *you tell me X?* These forms, being highly conventional, were construed by all but one of the 363 respondents as requests. All but one of the $\hat{r}$'s is 1.00. On the other hand, $\hat{Q}$ varied from 0 to .57. The most striking variation seems attributable to politeness. Requests 1 through 5 were all made in an impersonal telephone conversation, only one of many the anonymous merchant would take part in that day. Requests 7 and 8 were made by one student to another, face to face, on the UCLA campus. In that situation the respondent may have felt more responsible for his information—he could be recognized later—and more obligated to treat the requester personally and politely. It was probably this that led to so many more answers to Q. In an informal experiment in which 135 students each asked another student on the Stanford University campus *Could you tell me the time?*, I found similar results, with a $\hat{q}$ of .47. Such politeness isn't confined to UCLA.

Fifth, B may nevertheless lose track and fail to deal with all of A's meanings as he would like. Although Request 6 in Table 12.15 was

Table 12.15. Estimates of q and r for Eight Similar Requests

	Parameters	
Request	$\hat{q}$	$\hat{r}$
(1) Could you tell me what time you close tonight? $(30)^a$	.00	1.00
(2) Could you tell me the time you close tonight? (50)	.08	.75
(3) Could you tell me the price of a fifth of Jim Beam? (50)	.16	1.00
(4) Could you tell me the time you close tonight? (100)	.13	1.00
(5) Can you tell me what the interest is on a regular savings account? (50)	.16	1.00
(6) Can/could you tell me where X is? (22)	.14	1.00
(7) Could you tell me the time? (30)	.57	1.00
(8) Could you tell me what time it is? (31)	.45	1.00

Note. Request 1 is from Experiment 1; 2 and 3 are from Experiment 2; 4 is from an unpublished experiment on bank clerks; 5 is from Experiment 3; and 6, 7, and 8 are from Munro (Note 5).
^{a}Number of people asked each request indicated in parentheses.

asked by Munro of the same population of UCLA students as Requests 7 and 8, it elicited many fewer answers to Q. From Munro's data, the reason seems clear. Many students didn't know the answer to Q right away—they were uncertain where, say, Franz Hall was, as was clear from other things they said. By the time they figured out that they *could* give the directions requested, they may have forgotten the literal question and wanted, in any case, to forge ahead with the directions, which they had already begun to formulate in deciding whether they knew where Franz Hall was.

And finally, of course, B may want to be outright uncooperative. One liquor dealer in Experiment 2 said, "No, we don't give our prices out on the phone." The ways in which B can be uncooperative, and his reasons for doing so, are virtually without limit.

Ellipsis

In planning each response, B has also to decide how elliptical to be. For Q in these experiments, for example, the merchants eschewed long answers like *Yes, I can tell you what time we close tonight* or even *Yes, I can* and went for the minimum *Yes.* Their responses to R, on the other hand, ranged in ellipsis, as I defined it, from 17% on *I was wondering* to 92% on *Any other credit cards? Why?*

Ellipsis is possible only so long as what is missing is reconstructable by the listener. According to Hankamer and Sag (1976), there are two kinds of ellipsis.[4] One requires that the surface structure of the sentence uttered, or something akin to it, be reconstructable from the linguistic context. In *Julia discovered a virus and I did too,* the verb phrase missing

after *did* must be reconstructable from the linguistic context, and it is. The second kind of ellipsis requires only that the *meaning* of the utterance be reconstructable, which can be done from nonlinguistic as well as linguistic contexts. A's elliptical request to the taxi driver, *Grand Central Station,* is of this kind. As for the present experiments, the elliptical responses to Q, like *Yes* and *Yes, I can,* appear to be of the first kind. Since the linguistic context was always present, it isn't surprising such ellipsis occurred 100% of the time. The elliptical responses to R, like *Six* or *About six,* appear to be of the second kind. Since the precision with which R was specified by the context varied enormously from one context to the next, it isn't surprising that their occurrence varied from 17 to 92%.

It is the precise form of R that must be reconstructable from the context, and that was aided in these experiments by two factors— conventionality and transparency. R should be readily reconstructable for requests that are conventional in both means and form. That is what is meant, in effect, by being conventional. In Experiment 3, the conventional *Can you?* led to 64% ellipsis, while the otherwise identical but less conventional *Are you able?* led to only 38% ellipsis. Furthermore, when a request is not conventional, the more transparent R is, the more precisely its form can be recaptured. In Experiment 5, for *Do you accept credit cards?*, it is clear that R is "Tell me which credit cards you accept," but for *Do you accept any kinds of credit cards?* its precise form could be either "Tell me which credit cards you accept" or "Tell me which kinds of credit cards you accept," which leaves R less transparent. Indeed, *Credit cards?* led to 83% ellipsis and *Any kinds of credit cards?* to only

54% ellipsis. Together, these two factors account for the broad pattern of ellipsis in these experiments. The conventional transparent requests generally drew around 75% ellipsis and the nonconventional less transparent requests around 20% ellipsis. Nevertheless, details in this pattern have yet to be accounted for.

There was one other highly consistent finding in these experiments: Whenever the response to R could be elliptical, as for conventional requests, it was elliptical more often when it was a single move, as in *Six o'clock,* than when it followed the answer to Q, as in *Yes, six o'clock.* Why? Several possible explanations suggest themselves. One is that whenever a merchant makes two moves, he needs to make sure they are distinguishable, and so he uses a complete sentence for the second one. Another possibility is that the merchants who took Q seriously and answered it were just those merchants who intended to deal as explicitly as possible with all of the caller's meanings. So when it came to the second move, they tended to be more explicit there too. A third possibility is that planning and executing an answer to Q interferes with the merchant's memory for the precise form of R.

Without the exact form in mind, he cannot be certain that ellipsis is possible and so he is forced to use a complete sentence instead. The merit of this last explanation is that it ties in with the account just offered for the other types of ellipsis. Needless to say, however, the explanation for these findings is still open.

ACKNOWLEDGMENTS

This research was supported in part by Grant MH-20021 from the National Institute of Mental Health, by the Center for Advanced Study in the Behavioral Sciences, and a National Endowment for the Humanities Fellowship. I thank Eve V. Clark, Philip N. Johnson-Laird, Willem J. M. Levelt, Ellen M. Markman, Jerry L. Morgan, Ivan A. Sag, Edward E. Smith, and Ewart A. C. Thomas for their counsel on various aspects of the research and the manuscript. I am most deeply indebted to Susan L. Lyte, who sacrificed her left ear and right index finger to make this research possible. Reprint requests should be sent to Herbert H. Clark, Department of Psychology, Stanford University, Stanford, CA 94305.

NOTES

1. M_1 and M_2 are called the secondary and primary illocutionary acts, respectively, by Searle (1975, p. 62). I have avoided these terms, which are difficult to extend to chains with more than two meanings (see below).

2. According to the minimum move rule, the final move isn't necessarily sufficient to deal with all meanings. For *Can you remember who was asking something about Ben?* with its three meanings, Move₃ *(Where Ben was)* is not sufficient, since it doesn't imply who was asking, whereas Move₂ + Move₃ *(Veronica was asking where Ben was)* is.

3. In an informal experiment in which 135 students each asked a student on the Stanford University campus *Would you mind telling me the time?,* there were 37 affirmative and 26 negative answers to Q, with $\hat{q} = .52$. The merchants' yesses, then, do not appear to be a conspiracy of chance.

4. The term 'ellipsis' here is being used to denote elliptical sentences, as defined in Experiment 1. For Hankamer and Sag, it is a technical term denoting one special kind of incompleteness in sentences.

REFERENCES

Bolinger, D. L. (1975). *Aspects of Language.* 2d ed. New York: Harcourt Brace Jovanovich.
Bolinger, D. L. (1976). "Meaning and Memory." *Forum Linguisticum* 1:1–14.
Brown, P., and S. Levinson (1978). "Universals in Language Usage: Politeness Phenomena." In E. Goody (ed.), *Questions and Politeness.* Cambridge: Cambridge University Press, 56–324.
Charniak, E. (1977). "A Framed PAINTING: The Representation of a Common Sense Knowledge Fragment." *Cognitive Science* 1:355–394.
Clark, E. V., and H. H. Clark (1979). "When Nouns Surface as Verbs." *Language* 55:767–811.

Clark, H. H. (1978). "Inferring What Is Meant." In W.J.M. Levelt and G. B. Flores d'Arcals (eds.), *Studies in the Perception of Language.* London: Wiley, 295–322.

Clark, H. H., and P. Lucy (1975). "Understanding What Is Meant from What Is Said: A Study in Conversationally Conveyed Requests." *Journal of Verbal Learning and Verbal Behavior* 14:56–72.

Clark, H. H., and C. Marshall (1978). "Reference Diaries." In D. L. Waltz (ed.), *Theoretical Issues in Natural Language Processing-2.* New York: Association for Computing Machinery, 57–63.

Clark, H. H., and C. Marshall. (1981). "Definite Reference and Mutual Knowledge." In A. K. Joshi, I. A. Sag, and B. L. Webber (eds.), *Elements of Discourse Understanding.* Cambridge: Cambridge University Press.

Cole, P., and J. L. Morgan (eds.). (1975). *Syntax and Semantics.* Vol. 3: *Speech Acts.* New York: Academic Press.

DuBois, J. W. (1974). "Syntax in Mid-sentence." In *Berkeley Studies in Syntax and Semantics.* Vol. 1. Berkeley: Institute of Human Learning and Department of Linguistics, University of California, III-1-III-25.

Goffman, E. (1976). "Replies and Responses." *Language in Society* 5:257–313.

Gordon, D., and G. Lakoff (1971). "Conversational Postulates." In *Papers from the Seventh Regional Meeting.* Chicago: Chicago Linguistic Society, 63–84.

Green, G. M. (1975). "How to Get People to Do Things with Words: The Whimperative Question." In P. Cole and J. L. Morgan (eds.), *Syntax and Semantics.* Vol. 3: *Speech Acts.* New York: Academic Press, 107–141.

Grice, H. P. (1957). "Meaning." *Philosophical Review* 66:377–388.

Grice, H. P. (1968). "Utterer's Meaning, Sentence-Meaning, and Word-Meaning." *Foundations of Language* 4:225–242. [Reprinted in this volume, Chapter 4]

Grice, H. P. (1975). "Logic and Conversation." In P. Cole and J. L. Morgan (eds.), *Syntax and Semantics.* Vol. 3: *Speech Acts.* New York: Academic Press, 41–58. [Reprinted in this volume, Chapter 19]

Hankamer J., and I. A. Sag (1976). "Deep and Surface Anaphora." *Linguistic Inquiry* 7:391–426.

Kaplan, S. J. (1978). "Indirect Responses to Loaded Questions." In D. L. Waltz (ed.), *Theoretical Issues in Natural Language Processing-2.* New York: Association for Computing Machinery, 202–209.

Lakoff, R. (1973a). "The Logic of Politeness: Or Minding Your p's and q's." In *Papers from the Ninth Regional Meeting.* Chicago: Chicago Linguistic Society, 292–305.

Lakoff, R. (1973b). "Questionable Answers and Answerable Questions." In B. B. Kachru, R. B. Lees, Y. Malkiel, A. Pietrangeli, and S. Saporta (eds..), *Issues in Linguistics: Papers in Honor of Henry and Renee Kahane.* Urbana: University of Illinois Press, 543–567.

Lehnert, W. (1977). "Human and Computational Question Answering." *Cognitive Science* 1:47–73.

Lewis, D. K. (1969). *Convention: A Philosophical Study.* Cambridge, Mass.: Harvard University Press.

Morgan, J. L. (1978). "Two Types of Convention in Indirect Speech Acts." In P. Cole (ed.), *Syntax and Semantics.* Vol. 9: *Pragmatics.* New York: Academic Press, 261–280. [Reprinted in this volume, Chapter 14]

Munro, A. (1979). "Indirect Speech Acts Are Not Strictly Conventional." *Linguistic Inquiry* 10:353–356.

Norman, D. (1976). *Memory and Attention: An Introduction to Human Information Processing.* 2d ed. New York: Wiley.

Perrault, C. R., J. F. Allen, and P. R. Cohen. (1978). "Speech Acts as a Basis of Understanding Dialogue Coherence." In D. L. Watlz (ed.), *Theoretical Issues in Natural Language Processing-2.* New York: Association for Computing Machinery, 125–132.

Sacks, H., E. A. Schegloff, and G. Jefferson (1974). "A Simplest Systematics for the Organization of Turn-taking for Conversation." *Language* 50:696–735.

Sadock, J. M. (1972). "Speech Act Idioms." In *Papers from the Eighth Regional Meeting.* Chicago: Chicago Linguistic Society, 329–339.

Sadock, J. M. (1974). *Toward a Linguistic Theory of Speech Acts.* New York: Academic Press.

Schank, R., and R. Abelson (1977). *Scripts, Plans, Goals, and Understanding: An Inquiry into Human Knowledge Structures.* Hillsdale, N.J.: Erlbaum.

Schatz, M. (1978). "On the Development of Communicative Understandings: An Early Strategy for Interpreting and Responding to Messages." *Cognitive Psychology* 10:271–301.

Schegloff, E. A. (1968). "Sequencing in Conversational Openings." *American Anthropologist* 70:1075–1095.
Schegloff, E. A., G. A. Jefferson, and H. Sacks (1977). "The Preference for Self-correction in the Organization
    of Repair in Conversation." *Language* 53:361–382.
Schegloff, E. A., and H. Sacks. "Opening Up Closings." *Semiotica* 8:289–327.
Schiffer, S. R. (1972). *Meaning.* Oxford: Oxford University Press.
Searle, J. R. (1975). "Indirect Speech Acts." In P. Cole and J. L. Morgan (eds.), *Syntax and Semantics.* Vol.
    3: *Speech Acts.* New York: Academic Press, 59–82. [Reprinted in this volume, Chapter 16]

REFERENCE NOTES

1. J. Herringer (1972). "Some Grammatical Correlates of Felicity Conditions and Presuppositions," *Working Papers in Linguistics* [Ohio State University] 11:1–110.

2. H. H. Clark and D. H. Schunk (1979). "Polite Responses to Polite Requests" (Manuscript, Stanford University).

3. J. F. Allen and C. R. Perrault (1978). "Participating in Dialogue: Understanding via Plan Deduction" (Paper presented at the Second National Conference of the Canadian Society for Studies in Computational Intelligence).

4. P. R. Cohen (1978). "On Knowing What to Say: Planning Speech Acts" (Ph.D. diss., University of Toronto).

5. A. Munro (1977). "Speech Act Understanding in Context" (Ph.D. diss., University of California, San Diego).

6. K. G. Schweller (1978). "The Role of Expectation in the Comprehension and Recall of Direct and Indirect Requests" (Ph.D. diss., University of Illinois, Urbana-Champaign).

13

Linguistic Communication: A Schema for Speech Acts

KENT BACH AND ROBERT M. HARNISH

People don't speak merely to exercise their vocal cords. Generally, the reason people say what they say when they say it is to communicate something to those they are addressing. That is, in saying something a person has a certain intention, and the act of communicating succeeds only if that intention is recognized by the hearer. The intention is recognized partly on the basis of what is said, but only partly. What is said does not fully determine what the speaker is to be taken to be doing. If he says "I'm going to pay you back for that," he could be making a promise or issuing a threat. How does the hearer decide which? And how does the speaker know which way the hearer will take his utterance?

1. COMPONENTS OF SPEECH ACTS

Before taking up those questions, we need to distinguish the different aspects of a speech act. If S is the speaker, H the hearer, e an expression (typically a sentence) in language L, and C the context of utterance, the main constituents of S's speech act can be schematically represented as follows:

Utterance Act: S utters e from L to H in C.

Locutionary Act: S says to H in C that so-and-so.

Illocutionary Act: S does such-and-such in C.

Perlocutionary Act: S affects H in a certain way.[1]

These acts are intimately related. In uttering e, S says something to H; in saying something to H, S does something; and by doing something, S affects H. Moreover, the success of the perlocutionary act depends on H's identifying one of the other acts. Our problem is to specify as precisely as possible the nature of these acts as well as their relations to one another.[2]

Clearly there is more to a speech act than saying something (performing a locutionary act), but our preliminary characterization gives no indication of the difference between illocutionary and perlocutionary acts. Austin's distinction in terms of what is done *in* saying something and what is done *by* saying something (1962, lectures IX and X) is suggestive at best, since it does not explain the distinction it marks.[3] Illocutionary and perlocutionary acts can both produce effects on the hearer, but according to Austin (p. 116) a successful illocutionary act brings about "understanding of the meaning and of the force of the locution," that is, it secures *uptake*. Strawson (1964, 459) suggests that for illocutionary acts, the effectiveness of the speaker's intention requires that the intention be recognized by the hearer: "The illocutionary force of an utterance is essentially something that is intended to be understood." That is, part of the speaker's intention is that the hearer identify the very act the speaker intends to be performing, and successful communication requires fulfillment of that intention.

In general, we cannot rely on our vocabulary of verbs of speech action to mark the distinction between illocutionary and perlocutionary acts. Although Austin's conception of the distinction is different from the one we wish to develop, he himself recognized that "the same word may genuinely be used in both illocutionary and perlocutionary ways and that many illocutionary acts are cases of trying to do some perlocutionary act" (1962, 145–146). For acts like ordering, warning, informing, and assuring, we must distinguish the ultimate perlocutionary effect the speaker is trying to achieve from the illocutionary effect of hearer uptake.

This chapter will be devoted largely to elaborating this conception of illocutionary acts as being performed with the intention that the hearer identify the very act being performed. In particular, since the hearer's primary, but not exclusive, basis for identifying the speaker's illocutionary intention is what the speaker says, we must spell out the connection between the locutionary and the illocutionary act, such that the hearer can reasonably be expected by the speaker to identify the illocutionary act being performed.

2. SIMPLE VERSION OF THE SPEECH ACT SCHEMA (SAS)

We view linguistic communication as an inferential process. The speaker provides, by what he says, a basis for the hearer to infer what the speaker intends to be thereby doing. However, what he says underdetermines what he can reasonably expect to be taken to be intending. Suppose S says "I love you like my brother." There are various ways H could take this, depending on what he can infer S's intention to be under the circumstances, given what

H believes about S and in particular what H believes S to believe H believes about S. Normally, H can assume that if S says "I love you like my brother," S means that he loves H as he (S) loves his own brother. But if a woman says to a man "I love you like my brother," the man can infer (taking himself to be intended to infer) that the woman has a feeling that is more familial than amorous. Perhaps, however, it is not the kind of love but the amount of love that is in question, as, for example, where two wartime buddies are involved. Or "I love you like my brother" might be uttered by one man to another where it is recognized that the speaker hates his brother. In this case H would no doubt take S as informing H that he hates him.

In general, the inference the hearer makes and takes himself to be intended to make is based not just on what the speaker says but also on *mutual contextual beliefs* (MCBs), as we call such salient contextual information. With the example "I love you like my brother," in one case the crucial MCB is that the woman does not have amorous feelings toward her brother, whereas in another it is that the speaker hates his brother. We call such items of information "beliefs" rather than "knowledge" because they need not be true in order to figure in the speaker's intention and the hearer's inference. We call them "contextual" because they are both relevant to and activated by the context of utterance (or by the utterance itself). And we call them "mutual" because S and H not only both have them, they believe they both have them and believe the other to believe they both have them.[4] The contextual beliefs that figure in speakers' intentions and hearers' inferences must be mutual if communication is to take place. Otherwise, it would not be clear to each that the other is taking this belief into account. For instance, if e is ambiguous and S is not punning or otherwise speaking ambiguously, only one meaning of e will be operative; only one will be intended by S to be recognized by H as relevant. Suppose S utters "I had the book stolen," intending to say that he (S) got someone to steal the book for him—a book that S wanted to acquire. For communication to succeed, H must recognize that that is what S intended to say, and not that S intended to say that S had the book stolen from him (S). To reasonably expect his utterance to be taken this way, S must believe not merely that he wanted to acquire the book but also that H believes this and believes that S believes this. And for H to take the utterance as it is intended, H must believe not only that S wanted to acquire the book but also that S believes this and believes that H believes this. Thus, if the belief that S wanted to acquire the book is mutual, S can reasonably intend H to take, and H can reasonably take, S's utterance as saying that S had someone steal the book.

In general, a mutual contextual belief figures in the speaker's intention and the hearer's inference in the following way: if p is mutually believed between S and H, then (1) not only do S and H believe p, but (2) each believes that the other takes it into account in his thinking, and (3) each, supposing the other to take p into account, supposes the other to take him to take it into account. Whether or not p is something previously believed by S and H (much less previously mutually believed), both S and H cannot but think of p, S in making his utterance and H in hearing it, and therefore each supposes that the other cannot fail to take it into account and also that the other cannot fail to suppose that he takes it into account.

The stolen book example illustrates how an MCB can be utilized by H to close the gap between what the speaker utters and what he says. An MCB can be utilized also to determine the intended type of illocutionary act being performed. An utterance of "I love you like my brother" might, depending on the context, have the force of an assurance, an admission, an answer (to a question), or even a promise. Or it might have merely the force of a simple assertion (and by "force" we simply mean 'illocutionary act type'). Whichever way it is to be taken, the speaker must intend the hearer so to take it on the basis of certain MCBs. For example, it might be intended (and be taken) as an assurance if S and H mutually believed that H doubts that S loves him. It would be intended and be taken as an answer if they mutually believed that H has just asked S how he feels about H.

In short, the hearer relies on, and is intended to rely on, MCBs to determine from the meaning of the sentence uttered what the speaker is saying, and from that the force and content of the speaker's illocutionary act. Accordingly, the inference H makes and is intended to make is of roughly the following form:

	Basis
L1. S is uttering e.	hearing S utter e
L2. S means such-and-such by e.	L1, MCBs
L3. S is saying that so-and-so.	L2, MCBs
L4. S is doing such-and-such.	L3, MCBs

Cast in this preliminary form this inference pattern constitutes what we call the *speech act schema* (SAS).

In addition to mutual contextual beliefs, there are two general mutual beliefs that the hearer relies on to make his inference. They are shared not just between S and H but among members of the linguistic community at large. Pervasive as they are, they may seem almost too obvious to mention, but must be included in the SAS. We call them the *linguistic presumption* (LP) *and the communicative presumption* (CP).

Linguistic Presumption (LP): The mutual belief in the linguistic community C_L that

i. the members of C_L share L, and

ii. that whenever any member S utters any e in L to any other member H, H can identify what S is saying, given that H knows the meaning(s) of e in L and is aware of the appropriate background information.

If the LP did not prevail in C_L, and between S and H in particular, then H could not assume that e means to S what it means to himself, and H could not assume that S assumes he (H) assumes this. Similarly, S could not reasonably intend to be saying that so-and-so to H in virtue of the fact that e means so-and-so to L. Thus, in addition to the first two lines of the SAS (L1 and L2), the LP is needed to license H's inference to L3 of the SAS. To license L4 we need the CP.

Communicative Presumption (CP): The mutual belief in C_L that whenever a member S says something in L to another member H, he is doing so with some recognizable illocutionary intent.

If H does not think the CP is operative in a given context—if, for instance, H thinks S is merely reciting a speech—then H has no reason to infer any particular illocutionary intent from what S utters. The CP does not help H determine what S's illocutionary intent is—H must rely on what S says and on the MCBs for that. The CP licenses only H's conclusion that S has some illocutionary intent or other. Accordingly, we may augment our provisional version of the SAS. S intends H to reason as follows:

		Basis
L1.	S is uttering e.	hearing S utter e
L2.	S means such-and-such by e.	L1, LP, MCBs
L3.	S is saying to H that so-and-so.	L2, LP, MCBs
L4.	S is doing such-and-such.	L3, CP, MCBs

In the following section we raise certain issues pertaining to the connection between what S says (L3) and what S means (L2) by what he utters (L1).[5] The relation between the locutionary act (L3) and the illocutionary act (L4) is discussed in section 1.4.

3. SAYING AND THE LINGUISTIC PRESUMPTION

Without mutually believing that they share the language they are using, people would not, and perhaps could not, use the language to communicate: the third step in the SAS (L3) would be blocked. Generally, this mutual belief between S and H arises from the linguistic presumption that prevails among members of the community at large. As a matter of social fact, the LP in a community is so strong that not to know the language is often a sign of nonmembership in the community. People presume that if you belong to the community, you know the language. So when S utters something e in L (the language in question), he expects H to understand it. Indeed he expects this not because he thinks H has heard e before or ever learned the meaning of e in particular, but because he thinks H knows L and will, by virtue of knowing L, understand e.[6] Thus, because the LP applies generally to communication situations in C_L, S and H mutually believe that each will understand almost anything in L uttered by the other; unless something happens to show that the LP does not apply, S and H are each in a position to

reach L3 of the SAS, H to identify what S is saying and S to intend H to identify what he is saying.

Implicit in our discussion of the LP is the distinction between a group's having a language and their sharing that language. However improbable, a group of people could all have a language without mutually believing they do, in which case they probably would not use the language to communicate—no one would have any reason to believe he would be understood. Because of the distinction between having a language and sharing it, we cannot expect linguistic meaning to be explicated in social terms. It is logically possible for a person to know a language without ever having used it (or heard it used) to perform speech acts.[7] Although the concepts of language, of knowing a language, and of sharing a language figure in the linguistic presumption (the mutual belief prevailing in a community that a certain language is known and shared), we need not ascribe theoretical understanding of these concepts to ordinary speakers, who, after all, are not philosophers or linguists. Intuitive understanding is enough for them. Though not pertinent here, characterizing what a language is and what it is to know one (linguistic competence) presents tough philosophical problems.

Recall that in the speech act schema, S's uttering a sentence e and the meaning of e are covered by L1 and L2, while what S says is left for L3. L2 is separate from L1 for two reasons: that S means anything at all by e—that S is doing anything over and above the act of uttering—requires further intentions; moreover, what S means by e may not be wholly determined by the semantics of e, since e may be ambiguous. So whereas S's act of uttering e is reported by direct quotation in L1 of the SAS, the operative meaning of e is given in L2. Because linguistic meaning does not in general determine reference, S's locutionary act is represented separately by L3, in the form of indirect quotation: S said that so-and-so. For this, references must be specified.

As familiar as indirect quotation is, so are the problems it gives rise to.[8] Nevertheless, we will provisionally assume that the notion of indirect quotation can be made philosophically acceptable enough to be used in the SAS. For present purposes let what S means by e be represented by a lacuna of undetermined form, " . . . ," and let what S says in uttering e be represented by a dummy indicator for sentence type "*" and "p" for a proposition: "that *(. . . p . . .)." This notation is meant to indicate that what is said is a function of the intended meaning (" . . .") of the expression e. If e is declarative, then what is said may be specified by truth conditions. For other sentence types it may be feasible to generalize the notion of a truth condition and thereby allow a homogeneous semantics for natural languages and a single style of specification for what is said (see Stenius 1967, Lewis 1969, Strawson 1971, and Katz 1972). If e is imperative, the that-clause specifying what S says (that !(. . . p . . .)) is not itself imperative but of the form, "that H is to A."

As for interrogative sentences, there seem to be two options. On the one hand it could be argued that sentences like "What time is it?" do not express a proposition and their use is to be reported with "ask"—S asked (H) what time it is. In this view (Schiffer 1972, 114ff) interrogative sentences are conventional means for performing illocutionary acts of just one particular kind, namely, asking a question. If this is correct, then the locutionary step in the SAS ("S said that . . .") is simply bypassed in the case of interrogatives, and indirect quotation will be of the form "S asked. . . ." Nevertheless, such sentences need not be used literally (as when used rhetorically to make a statement) and so an adaptation of the SAS must allow for that. On the other hand it might be suggested (as by Katz 1977, 205ff.) that what is said when S uses an interrogative expression like "What time is it?" is: that H is to tell S what time it is. In general, the form of the report will be: S says that H is to tell S ———, where the blank is filled in by some expression determined by e.[9] On this account questions would be a particular case of requests and would be performed normally via the schema. Since either account is compatible with our overall theory, we will leave the matter as it is for now.

4. LITERAL ILLOCUTIONARY ACTS

In the speech act schema L3 represents what the speaker says and L4 what he is thereby doing in saying it. Since the speaker might not be performing any illocutionary act at all, it is only on the presumption that he is (the CP) that the hearer will infer that the speaker is performing some illocutionary act or other. As for identifying what the act is, the hearer relies primarily on what is said, and we find the most straightforward relation between what is said and what is done when the speaker means what he says and nothing else. In this case he is speaking literally and what he does is largely determined by what he says.

Because of nonliteral and indirect illocutionary acts, the slogan "Meaning determines force" is generally false. It is most nearly correct in the case of literal acts—but not quite. Although *what* the speaker does might be determined by what he says, *that* he is performing any illocutionary act at all is not; he could be merely practicing his English or mechanically reciting some lines. Moreover, that he is speaking literally is not determined by what he says. If S says, for example, "The sun is shining on me today," he could be talking either about the weather or about his fortunes, depending on whether or not he is speaking literally. Inasmuch as he can use the same sentence literally or nonliterally, how he intends his utterance to be taken is not determined by what he says.

Even allowing for the fact that the meaning of what is uttered does not determine that some illocutionary act is being performed, much less that it is being performed literally, it is not always true that meaning determines the force of literal illocutionary acts. In general, the meaning merely delimits the force. For example, if someone says that he will return, whether he is making a promise or merely a statement of intention, his illocutionary act is literal. So the force (illocutionary act type) of an utterance need not be explicit to be literal. You do not have to say "I accuse . . ." to make an accusation. For that matter, you can use a performative verb nonliterally, as when posing a threat by saying "I promise."

Let us borrow Searle's (1969, 31) notation for representing an illocutionary act by "$F(P)$," where "F" represents the force and "P" the propositional content of the illocutionary act (lowercase "p" represents the proposition in the locutionary act). Now suppose that S utters e, which means '. . .', and thereby says that *(. . . p . . .). His act is *literal*, and represented by "F*(. . . p . . .),"[10] just in case the proposition that P is the same as the proposition that p and the illocutionary force F of the utterance is *locutionary-compatible (L-compatible)* with the sentence type and meaning of e. Without giving a definition, we can introduce the notion of L-compatibility by examples. An utterance's being a prediction is L-compatible with the sentence used only if the sentence contains future time reference. If that sentence contains an action verb predicated of S, then the force of the utterance is L-compatible with the sentence whether the sentence is used to make a promise or a prediction.[11] An utterance's being a request or an order is L-compatible only with imperative sentences; analogously, an utterance's being a question is L-compatible only with interrogative sentences. If an utterance has a force L-incompatible with the mood and meaning of the sentence used, it is not literal. Notice that our characterization of literal utterances requires what the speaker says to be the same as what he F's, that is, that p be the same proposition as P. Even though an utterance of the sentence, "I am sorry for stepping on your toes," has the L-compatible force of an apology, the speaker can be apologizing nonliterally (say, for preempting the hearer's authority).

Using our notation we can reformulate our provisional version of the SAS. In so doing we will recast L4 in such a way that it is left open for further inference, whether or not S is speaking literally. S intends H to reason as follows:

	Basis
L1. S is uttering e.	hearing S utter e
L2. S means . . . by e.	L1, LP, MCBs
L3. S is saying that $*(\ldots p \ldots)$.	L2, LP, MCBs
L4. S, if speaking literally, is F^*-ing that p.	L3, CP, MCBs

Only after we spell out the details of these steps and present our taxonomy of illocutionary acts will we be in a position to elaborate the SAS to include the further steps whereby H infers, as S intends him to infer, what illocutionary act is in fact being performed, be it literal or otherwise. As we will see, H relies on the *presumption of literalness* (PL):

Presumption of Literalness (PL): The mutual belief in the linguistic community C_L that whenever any member S utters any e in L to any other member

H, if S could (under the circumstances) be speaking literally, then S is speaking literally.

If it is evident to H that S could not be speaking literally, H supposes S to be speaking nonliterally and seeks to identify what that nonliteral illocutionary act is.

5. THE COMMUNICATIVE PRESUMPTION AND ILLOCUTIONARY INTENTIONS

The communicative presumption is the mutual belief prevailing in a linguistic community to the effect that whenever someone says something to somebody, he intends to be performing some identifiable illocutionary act. We say "to the effect that" because, of course, people don't have the technical concept of illocutionary acts and therefore do not have beliefs, much less mutual beliefs, about illocutionary acts. But they do mutually believe that speakers speak with overt intentions, and this mutual belief figures in ordinary communication situations. People do rely on others to have identifiable intentions in their utterances, and they expect others to rely on them to have such intentions.

There are all sorts of effects a speaker can intend an utterance to have on the hearer. S may or may not intend H to recognize S's intention to produce a certain effect, and even if he does so intend, H's recognition of S's intention may be incidental to the production of that effect. In general, hearer recognition of perlocutionary intentions is incidental to the production of perlocutionary effects. Even in the special case where identification of the speaker's intention is necessary to the production of a perlocutionary effect—H might believe something or do something because and only because S wants him to—still there is a distinction between the hearer's recognizing that intention and its being fulfilled. The hearer might recognize what effect is intended without its being produced in him. What distinguishes illocutionary intentions, we suggest, is that their fulfillment consists in their recognition.

This general conception of illocutionary acts and intentions is shared by Searle and Strawson (in detail their views differ radically from ours). Searle (1969, 47) points out the connection between the fulfillment of illocutionary intentions and their recognition when, in contrasting illocutionary with perlocutionary acts, he says,

In the case of illocutionary acts we succeed in doing what we are trying to do by getting our audience to recognize what we are trying to do. But the 'effect' on the hearer is not a belief or a response, it consists simply in the hearer understanding the utterance of the speaker. It is this effect that I have been calling the illocutionary effect.

As Strawson puts it (1964, 459),

The understanding of the force of an utterance in all cases involves recognizing what may be called broadly an audience-directed intention and recognizing it as wholly overt, as intended to be recognized.

Their formulations help to spell out Austin's view that successful communication in performing an illocutionary act consists in uptake, that is, in the hearer identifying the illocutionary act being performed. Our later elaboration of the SAS will detail the pattern of inference by which this is accomplished, but first we must consider precisely what sort of intention is such that its fulfillment consists in its recognition. What sort of intention is distinctively illocutionary and communicative?

Both Searle and Strawson suggest that this intention is essentially reflexive and of the sort discovered by Grice (1957). According to Searle (1969, 43),

In speaking I attempt to communicate certain things to my hearer by getting him to recognize my intention to communicate just those things. I achieve the intended effect on the hearer by getting him to recognize my intention to achieve that effect.

Not just any way of achieving that effect will do. Hypnosis or electrical stimulation might "get" the hearer to recognize the speaker's intention, but for this recognition to be the effect of linguistic communication, it must be achieved by an inference from the speaker's utterance, and normally that is how it is accomplished.

Searle criticizes Grice's account of speaker meaning in terms of reflexive intention, that is, in terms of the intention "to produce some

effect in an audience by means of the recognition of this intention" (Grice 1957, 385). Searle argues that the sorts of effects Grice mentions, such as beliefs, intentions, and actions, are not produced by means of recognition of the intention to produce them. For example, the hearer might recognize that he is to believe something and yet refuse. These sorts of effects are perlocutionary, and the speaker's illocutionary act, whose identity he is trying to communicate, can succeed without the intended perlocutionary effect (if there is one) being produced. So a reflexive intention is involved in communication, just as Grice claimed, but the kinds of intended effects he specified are not of the right sort. Getting the hearer to recognize them does not constitute producing them. In section 6 we consider just what sort of reflexive intention is fulfilled merely by being recognized.

Grice's account of reflexive intentions in communication neglects the role of the communicative presumption when the communication is linguistic.[12] Grice focuses on nonlinguistic examples like drawing a picture and deliberately frowning.[13] When people do things like these, there is no presumption that they have a communicative intention, as there is in the case of linguistic utterances. Because of the CP, when somebody says something to someone, he cannot but expect—he need not intend—the hearer to think he has some identifiable illocutionary intention. Contrary to Grice's nonlinguistic cases, H's reason for thinking S has some such intention is not that he has spotted anything special in S's utterance but, because of the CP, merely that S has uttered something linguistic. S realizes that H routinely assumes that some recognizable intention is there, so no generic intention to be performing some such act is necessary. Indeed, if S were mimicking someone or rehearsing a line and thought this was not evident to H (with the implicit understanding that the CP was inoperative), S would have to have a special intention, one that he could reasonably expect H to recognize, *not* to be performing a full-blown illocutionary act. After all, being a presumption, the CP is operative unless there is indication to the contrary (as ordinarily there is when people mimic or recite).

The difference between linguistic communication and Grice's nonlinguistic cases is the presence of a presumption that there is an inference to be drawn as to what the speaker is doing in issuing his utterance. In Grice's examples part of what the audience has to infer is that *there is an inference to be drawn*. The SAS, which includes the CP, represents the nature of this inference for linguistic cases, and the hearer implements this inference by recognizing what the speaker utters. That it is a sentence in a shared language is enough to implement the inference. So although reflexive intentions (R-intentions) are essential to linguistic communication, not just any sort of R-intention will do. Lingusitic R-intentions are executed pursuant to the communicative presumption, and their fulfillment consists in their recognition. We must now consider what their content can be for this to be true.

6. ILLOCUTIONARY INTENTIONS AND EFFECTS

An illocutionary act is communicatively successful if the speaker's illocutionary intention is recognized by the hearer. These intentions are essentially communicative because the fulfillment of illocutionary intentions consists in hearer understanding. Not only are such intentions reflexive, their fulfillment consists in their recognition. Thus the intended effect of an act of communication is not just any effect produced by means of recognition of the intention to produce a certain effect, it is *the recognition of that effect*. There seems to be a reflexive paradox here, but in fact there is none. The effect, the hearer's recognizing the speaker's intention to produce that effect, is not produced by the hearer's recognizing that intention—that would be worse than a paradox, it would be a miracle. Rather, it is produced by the hearer's recognizing that the speaker has an intention to produce a certain effect in him that he is to identify (and thereby have produced in him) partly by recognizing S's intention to produce an identifiable effect. The hearer has to figure out what that intention—the intended effect—is, on the basis primarily of the speaker's utterance, along the lines of the SAS.

Now what sorts of (intended) illocutionary effects—effects consisting in recognition of R-

intentions—can there be? In other words, what can be the content of communicative intentions? It is a commonplace that linguistic communication consists in putting one's thoughts into words. This cliché is correct as far as it goes; the problem is to go further. In our view, to communicate is indeed to express a thought or, more generally, an attitude, be it a belief, an intention, a desire, or even a feeling; but in saying that to communicate is to express an attitude, we mean something very specific by "express."

Expressing: For S to *express* an attitude is for S to R-intend the hearer to take S's utterance as reason to think S has that attitude.

Accordingly, the intended illocutionary effect (or simply illocutionary intent) is for H to recognize that R-intention. In the taxonomy of communicative acts many types of illocutionary acts are differentiated by types of attitudes expressed.

For now, consider a couple of simple and common types of illocutionary acts: statements and requests. In the case of statements the speaker expresses two attitudes: belief in a certain proposition and the intention that the hearer believe it as well. That is to say, for S's utterance of e to be a statement that P, S must R-intend H to take the utterance as reason to think (a) that S believes that P and (b) that S intends H to believe that P. Correlatively, for H to understand that S is stating that P in uttering e, H must take S's utterance of e as R-intended to be reason to think (a) and (b). For a statement to have been made and to be successful as an act of communication, it is not necessary H actually think that S believes that P or that H believe P himself. These would be perlocutionary effects of S's utterance and are not necessary for the success of the illocutionary act of stating. We might say, speaking loosely, that S's statement was unsuccessful (with respect to a further perlocutionary effect) unless H believed that P (presumably taking S to believe that P); but surely it would be correct to claim that S had successfully made a statement if H understood S's utterance of e, even if H didn't believe that P. It is sufficient that H recognize S's R-intention, S's expressed attitudes. This is what communication is about; anything more is more than just communication.

Similarly, for S's utterance to count as a request that H do A, S must R-intend H to take S's utterance as reason to think (a) that S desires H to do A and (b) that S intends H to do A because of S's desire. His request is successful as an act of communication if H recognizes S's R-intention. Again, anything more—H's actually doing A—is more than just communication.

7. PERLOCUTIONARY ACTS AND EFFECTS

Austin (1962, 101) introduces the notion of a perlocutionary act as follows:

Saying something will often, or even normally, produce certain consequential effects upon the feelings, thoughts, or actions of the audience, or of the speaker, or of other persons: and it may be done with the design, intention, or purpose of producing them ... We shall call the performance of an act of this kind the performance of a *perlocutionary* act.

Since there is virtually no limit to the sorts of things that can result from speech acts—almost anything is possible, from insulting someone to starting a war—it would seem reasonable to restrict the category of perlocutionary acts in whatever ways seem theoretically appropriate. This is a matter of terminological stipulation, of course, but that does not make it arbitrary.

We propose first to limit perlocutionary acts to the *intentional* production of effects on (or in) the hearer. Our reason is that only reference to intended effects is necessary to explain the overall rationale of a given speech act. Utterance, locutionary, and illocutionary acts are all intentional and are generally performed with the primary intention of achieving some perlocutionary effect. To be sure, a speaker can insult, appease, disturb, or excite someone without intending to, but unless this is done intentionally, the fact that it is done does not help explain the speech act. In any case, the vocabulary of verbs of speech actions cannot be relied on to mark the distinction between illocutionary and perlocutionary acts.

We propose further to restrict perlocutionary acts to producing effects from steps of the speech act schema. In our preliminary version of the SAS these steps include the hearer's identification of L1, the utterance of e; L2,

what S meant by e; L3, the locutionary act; and L4, the illocutionary act. We will be interested primarily in perlocutionary effects generated from L4, effects that rely on hearer uptake (of course their production involves more than uptake, more than recognition of the intention to produce them). Perlocutionary effects can be generated from other steps of the SAS as well. The utterance of certain words might be intended to offend someone just by their sound or their manner of pronunciation; or perhaps their meaning is what offends. And the locutionary act might have a distinctive perlocutionary effect, such as reminding the hearer of a person or event referred to. When we refine the SAS, we will see that there are other ways, corresponding to steps in the schema as elaborated, in which perlocutionary effects can be generated. For example, the very fact that an illocutionary act is performed nonliterally or indirectly might have a definite perlocutionary effect, such as protecting the hearer's feelings or making him suspicious.

This second restriction, construing as perlocutionary only those intended effects generated off of steps of the SAS, excludes all sorts of other speech acts . . . . : joking, manipulating, boring, interrupting, and so on. Some of these speech acts are essentially intentional, some even R-intentional. However, they do not work off of the SAS, and in some cases, such as in telling a joke, they presuppose the suspension of the communicative presumption.

Our characterization of the various aspects of speech acts as well as our formulation of the speech act schema itself should be taken as provisional. . . . The SAS is only a schema . . . and can do only so much. It represents the pattern of inference made by the hearer but it does not represent how the inference is made. In particular, even though mutual contextual beliefs are cited in various lines of the schema and are relied on by the hearer to go from one step to the next, the SAS is not equipped to predict which MCBs are activated and so cannot predict precisely how a given hearer will take a given utterance. Moreover, although it represents the pattern of inference in steps, thereby organizing the mass of information available to the hearer, in practice the hearer often works holistically, both looking ahead and backtracking as he goes along. . . .

NOTES

1. In due course we will specify the ranges of the variables *so-and-so, such-and-such,* and *a certain way.* Except for the term *utterance act,* our terminology is Austin's (1962). Utterance acts for us are what Austin calls *phatic acts,* which necessarily involve the performance of what he called *phonetic acts,* a notion unnecessary for our purposes. Utterance acts involve producing certain sounds belonging to (and as belonging to) a certain language, and are reported by direct quotation. Austin characterizes the *rhetic act* as the use of a sentence "or its constitutents with a certain more or less definite 'sense' and a more or less definite 'reference' " (1962, 93), and is reported by the familiar device of indirect quotation. Although Austin speaks of the locutionary act as comprising the phonetic, the phatic, and the rhetic acts, generally what he says about locutionary acts applies to them qua rhetic acts. For us locutionary acts are rhetic acts in Austin's sense.

2. A comprehensive treatment of this second issue would require solving some very hard problems in the (general) theory of action—in particular, problems of identity, individuation, and the part–whole relation of acts. We do not propose (nor presuppose) a general theory, and the reader is invited to try to subsume our discussion of speech action under such a theory, e.g. Goldman (1970) or Thomson (1977).

3. Besides, as Austin noted (lecture X), there are uses of "by" that mark off illocutionary, locutionary, and miscellaneous other redescriptions of an (utterance) act.

4. A and B mutually believe that p if and only if each believes (1) that p, (2) that the other believes that p, and (3) that the other believes that the first believes that p. The idea (as "mutual recognition" and as "mutual expectation") originated with Schelling (1960, ch. 3), who also speaks of a matter of fact as being "obviously obvious."

5. Although there are some questions about how much leeway one has in reporting what has been uttered (can we report "I vant a banana" as "I want a banana"?), differences between utterances of the same sentence do not seem to matter semantically. However, there is an utterance-act difference between whispering something, speaking it, and shouting it, a difference between mumbling something and articulating it clearly, and a difference between uttering something slowly, normally, and fast; each of these utterance-act differences can make an illocutionary difference. A whispered "Leave" might be taken as a plea, a spoken one as a request, and a shouted one as an order or even threat. See Miller and Johnson-Laird (1976, sect. 7.4.1, and references therein) for more discussion.

6. This point does not apply to certain special cases. If S and H are learning a language together, it might well be that S utters e knowing H understands e just because S has seen H use or understand e previously. Or if technical terminology without wide currency is used, then special beliefs to the effect that H is acquainted with that vocabulary are required on the part of S.

7. Even if, as a matter of empirical fact, people have to use or witness the use of a language in order to learn it, our conceptual claim is not affected. Knowledge of a language is one thing, its being mutual in a community is another.

8. For example, in saying that indirect quotation reports the proposition expressed by the utterance of the sentence, we do not mean to hide the philosophically notorious problems of referential opacity and of the identity of propositions.

9. Not all instances of the blank are related in quite the same way to the interrogative uttered. "What time is it?" involves subject–predicate inversion, whereas "Who discovered the calculus?" simply becomes: S says that H is to tell S who discovered the calculus.

10. Not all illocutionary acts (greetings, for example) have propositional content, but we ignore this complication here.

11. Explicit performative utterances are no exception. Literally they are statements and only indirectly do they have the force of the sort named by the performative verb. For example, a typical utterance of "I order you to leave" is literally a statement and only indirectly an order.

12. Grice (1968 [This volume: 69–70]) seems to recognize this important difference when he argues that with meaningful items, the reflexive intention can be replaced by a simple intention. See also Schiffer's discussion of this point (1972, 133ff).

13. The reason for this choice of examples is the strategy of analyzing linguistic meaning in terms of speaker meaning. See Grice (1968), Schiffer (1972, ch. 6), and Bennett (1973, 1976).

REFERENCES

Austin, J. L. (1962). *How to Do Things with Words.* Cambridge, Mass.: Harvard University Press.

Bennett, J. (1973). "The Meaning Nominalist Strategy." *Foundations of Language* 10:141–168.

Goldman, A. (1970). *A Theory of Human Action.* Englewood Cliffs, N.J.: Prentice-Hall.

Grice, H. P. (1957). "Meaning." *Philosophical Review* 66:377–388.

Grice, H. P. (1968). "Utterer's Meaning, Sentence-Meaning, and Word-Meaning." *Foundations of Language* 4:225–242. [Reprinted in this volume, Chapter 4]

Katz, J. J. (1972). *Semantic Theory.* New York: Harper & Row.

Katz, J. J. (1977). *Propositional Structure and Illocutionary Force.* New York: Crowell.

Lewis, D. (1969). *Convention.* Cambridge, Mass.: Harvard University Press.

Miller, G. A., and P. N. Johnson-Laird (1976). *Language and Perception.* Cambridge, Mass.: Harvard University Press.

Schelling, T. (1960). *The Strategy of Conflict.* Cambridge, Mass.: Harvard University Press.

Searle, J. (1969). *Speech Acts.* Cambridge: Cambridge University Press.

Shiffer, S. (1972). *Meaning.* Oxford: Oxford University Press.

Stenius, E. (1967). "Mood and Language Game." *Synthese* 17:254–274.

Strawson, P. (1964). "Intention and Convention in Speech Acts." *Philosophical Review* 73:439–460.

Strawson, P. (1971). "Meaning and Truth." In *Logico-Linguistic Papers.* London: Methuen.

Thomson, J. (1977). *Acts and Other Events.* Ithaca, N.Y.: Cornell University Press.

14

Two Types of Convention in Indirect Speech Acts

J. L. MORGAN

INTRODUCTION

In this paper I want to take up the problem of "indirect speech acts," as exemplified by the infamous case, *Can you pass the salt?,* with the goal of reaching an understanding of its apparently paradoxical nature. In considering the competing analyses of Gordon and Lakoff (1975), Sadock (1974) and Searle (1975), my initial inclination was to reject Searle's discussion as missing the point, in favor of one of the other two. But I have gradually come around to Searle's position, or perhaps I have only constructed a misinterpretation of it that appeals to me. At any rate, in this paper I will be attempting an elaboration of my interpretation of Searle's remarks. I will argue for an account of *Can you pass the salt?* and similar expressions which treats them as CONVENTIONAL but not IDIOMS, by establishing the necessity for distinguishing two kinds of language-related convention: CONVENTIONS OF LANGUAGE, that jointly give rise to the literal meanings of sentences; and CONVENTIONS OF USAGE, that govern the use of sentences, with their literal meanings, for certain purposes.[1] I will suggest, in short, that *Can you pass the salt?* is indeed conventional in some sense, but not an idiom. Rather, it is conventional to USE it (with its literal meaning) for certain purposes. Part of my task will be to dissipate the fog of initial implausibility by establishing on independent grounds the need for this kind of convention.

I hope to end up with a framework that gives a reasonable picture of the diachronic transition from indirectly conveyed to literal meaning and allows the possibility of intermediate points on the natural-conventional scale. I will also argue, contra Searle, for the notion 'conversational postulate', which I have [. . .] argued against (Morgan 1977).

I will proceed as follows: First I will briefly review the nature of the problem involved in expressions like *Can you pass the salt?* This will be followed by a discussion of the role of pragmatics in linguistics, leading up to a discussion of "natural" as opposed to "conventional" and pointing out the difference between two kinds of linguistic convention. I will then offer a schema for describing the less familiar kind of convention, and an account of *Can you pass the salt?* in terms of this kind of convention. I will end with a number of examples of various subtypes of conventionalization.

STATEMENT OF THE PROBLEM

Why are expressions like *Can you pass the salt?* a problem? Why do I say that this expression is apparently paradoxical? The basic fact is this: One can use a sentence like *Can you pass the salt?* to convey a request, though it seems at first glance we would not want to consider the literal meaning of the sentence to be that of a request for the salt.

Grice's (1975) notion of 'conversational implicature' and accompanying maxims offer a potential explanation for this fact (cf. Gordon and Lakoff 1975), but how can we be sure this is the correct analysis? In fact, there are TWO ways to go about giving an account of such cases, and one can construct a case for each that has a certain amount of initial plausibility. The first way, which I will call the NATURAL approach, is to argue that even when I mean to make a REQUEST in uttering *Can you pass the salt?,* I am using the sentence with its literal meaning of a yes/no question; the fact that, by asking this yes/no question, I can manage to convey what amounts to a request is not a matter of knowledge of English, but a consequence of Grice's maxims, which are, roughly, a set of rules for inferring the intentions behind speech acts, or, from the speaker's viewpoint, for selecting one's utterances so as to convey one's intentions, by exploiting the maxims. Given that the need for Grice's maxims has already been clearly demonstrated and that we can show how the request nature of *Can you pass the salt?* is "calculable," that is, can be derived from Grice's maxims, then Occam's Razor dictates that we take this as the correct analysis, lacking strong evidence to the contrary. Further support might be derived from the admittedly vague intuition that it "just FEELS like" one means it in its literal meaning even when using it to make a request, a point that gains some support from the frequently noted fact that the class of possible responses to *Can you . . .* is just about what one would expect from its literal meaning.

Or one can take a conventional approach, saying that *Can you pass the salt?* is an idiom that wears its history on its sleeve, as idioms often do, so that what the expression formerly had as implicature, it now has as literal meaning. As a consequence, *Can you pass the salt?* is now genuinely ambiguous between the literal meaning of a yes/no question and the literal meaning of a request. One can support such an analysis by observing first that *Can you pass the salt?* has some of the grammatical marks of direct requests—the possibility of preverbal *please,* for instance—that not all cases of genuinely indirect requests have. Second, although *Can you pass the salt?* is indeed CALCULABLE, it is not in fact calculated; rather, one gets the point more or less directly, without any inferential processing, which is what we would expect if it has become an idiom, thereby part of knowledge of language. Third, *Can you pass the salt?* is intuitively more direct than its apparent close paraphrases, like *Are you able to . . .* and *Is it possible for you to . . . ,* which do not have the grammatical properties of direct requests, like preverbal *please,* but can, nonetheless, be used to convey indirect requests. Fourth, this kind of conventionalization of indirectly conveyed meaning is in fact clearly attested, which at least increases the plausibility of the idiom approach.

For instance, as Robin Lakoff (1973) has observed, the typical history of euphemisms, expressions the speaker uses to merely hint at what he wants to avoid mentioning directly, is that they eventually take on as literal meaning the very thing they were originally used to avoid. One can see a clear example of this in the expression *to go to the bathroom,* which obviously originated as a euphemism, having a literal meaning like 'to transport oneself to the bathing room,' with the conversational implicature that one actually went there with the purpose of excretion, but at the same time avoiding direct mention of such revolting matters. But now, in at least some American dialects, the implicature has been conventionalized as literal meaning, so that *go to the bathroom* is now an idiom with the meaning 'to excrete'; speakers of these dialects thus can say, nonmetaphorically, *The dog went to the bathroom on the living room rug.* Cole (1975) presents a persuasive discussion of another kind of grammaticalization of implicature, focusing in particular on this as the most reasonable treatment of the expression *let's.*

Then we have the apparent paradox that the expression *Can you . . .* is in some ways natural, in some ways conventional. How can we have both at the same time? I will argue that the answer lies in the following quotation from Searle: "It is by now, I hope, uncontroversial that there is a distinction to be made between meaning and use, but what is less generally recognized is that there can be conventions of usage that are not meaning conventions" [This volume: 274]. Before exploring the idea in this quotation, I need to discuss convention and pragmatics a bit.

PRAGMATICS AND LINGUISTICS

To decide between the "natural" and "conventional" approaches, it is necessary to make clear what these terms mean. To do this, I must begin with a general discussion of pragmatics. As far as I know, the term was until recently applied to the analysis of expressions like indexicals, whose meaning can be fully specified only relative to context of utterance. Recently, though, the term has been extended to cover matters like Grice's conversational implicature that are not part of the literal meaning of sentences. As a result, "pragmatics" may be in danger of becoming a useless catch-all term. But there may be a grain of truth in this lumping together of conversational implicature with the interpretation of indexicals and the like. I think a moment's reflection will show that there is a natural connection, and that the problem of indexicals is naturally subsumed under the problem of the interpretation of intentions behind use of linguistic expressions. If we mean that a pragmatic treatment of demonstrative pronouns and of deictic terms like *here* and *now* should include a recapitulation of the principles we use in determining referents for these terms, then it is clear that it is the same sort of problem, depending on such matters of context as our interpretation of the speaker's goal in the conversation, his intentions, interests, and so on. For example, imagine a jar of sugar with a glass lid, on which the word *sugar* is painted in blue; and imagine that someone puts her fingertip just under the letter *u* of the word *sugar* and says, *What's that?* Our answer might be, among other things, *the letter **u**, the word **sugar**, paint, blue paint, blue, English, a lid, glass, a glass lid, a jar, sugar, a jar of sugar,* and so on, depending on our interpretation of the person's interests—is she learning English, the use of seasoning, physics, or

what? It's clear that there is a natural connection between an account of indexical expressions and the interpretation of intentions. But there is occasional confusion, it seems to me, about the nature of pragmatic principles, so a brief discussion of their nature is in order.

A central question for the study of language is this: How do people understand what's said to them? Linguistics must eventually provide at least a partial answer to this question by saying how much and in what ways knowledge of language per se contributes to the ability to comprehend. It has become fairly obvious in the past few years that a good part of comprehension must be ascribed not to the rules of language that assign meanings to sentences as a function of the meanings of the parts, but to our ability to somehow infer what the speaker's intentions were in saying what he said, with the literal meaning it has. But this ability is not, in general, a strictly linguistic ability—in fact, I think often not a linguistic ability at all, but the application to linguistic problems of very general common-sense strategies for inferring intentions behind all kinds of acts, which may or may not be different in different cultures. And to call them rules of conversation is misleading in the same way that it is misleading to refer to rules of driving as rules of getting to the grocery store and back. It should be clear upon reflection that, unless we are in solitary confinement, we spend most of our waking hours interpreting observed events involving other people in terms of intentions and related notions like purpose and interest—not consciously, of course, but we do it nonetheless. As long as we are able to do it with ease, and to pigeonhole these events in terms of nonthreatening intentions, the matter does not occupy our thoughts. But if a case arises that is not easily classified—we don't understand the intentions involved—it catches our attention, and we may expend some effort to resolve the matter, even if the outcome is of no consequence to the conduct of our affairs. For example, if while studying in the library I notice the person at the opposite carrel slowly and quietly removing pages from a notebook, wadding them up, and putting them in a wastebasket, I probably would ignore him and continue my work. But if he repeatedly removed a sheet of paper, wadded it up, unwadded it, replaced it in the notebook, removed it again, and so on, I would be unable to work until I had provided myself with an explanation of his behavior.

Less bizarre cases confront us constantly. I open the door to find a person standing there who holds out a package, and instantly I interpret her behavior as motivated by the intention that I take the package. Many everyday cases fit Grice's (1957) characterization of "non-natural meaning" of an utterance: "'A meant$_{NN}$ something by x' is (roughly) equivalent to 'A intended the utterance of x to produce some effect in an audience by means of the recognition of this intention'" (p. 385). For example, such everyday acts as holding open a door for somebody or looking daggers at somebody who is on the point of revealing a secret are quite analogous to meaningful utterances under Grice's characterization. And the notion 'conversational implicature' can be naturally extended to nonlinguistic acts. If upon being asked my opinion of a spinach soufflé I have been served, I shovel the contents of my plate into the dog's dish, I have rendered my judgement as clearly as if I had said *It's awful*, though less directly. In interpreting my action the questioner must invoke Grice's maxims just as if I had responded by saying something.

In short, then, conversational pragmatics of the sort Grice discusses is not really conversational at bottom, but the application of general principles of interpreting acts, applied to the subcase of communicative acts, and more particularly, verbal communicative acts. Unless I have misinterpreted him, I am following Grice in this.

Well then, one might object, this is not linguistics, at least not if we narrowly limit the subject matter of linguistics to those abilities that are uniquely linguistic abilities. And the only answer is, of course it's not. But even if we accept this narrow definition of the scope of the field, we are struck with pragmatics on methodological grounds. Semantics is now irretrievably part of linguistics. But our data about semantics are not direct, but really data of comprehension. Comprehension is demonstrably a mixture of pragmatic and semantic matters, and introspection supplies us no simple clue to what's semantic and what's pragmatic in a given case. Our only methodological tool consists of the tests for implicature discussed by Grice, which Sadock shows to be difficult to apply. A major problem for linguists and psycholinguists is the devising of reliable empirical tests for distinguishing sematic properties from matters of implicature in comprehension. But it must be kept constantly in mind that pragmatic "rules" have to do not with linguistic abilities, but with more general ones, so that if it can be shown that a linguistic theory of meaning like Montague grammar or generative semantics can give a unified account of semantics and pragmatics (especially if the account is in terms of formal properties of sentences), we should suspect that there is something wrong with the theory, unless we want to give up the position that there is a difference between the two.

NATURAL VERSUS CONVENTIONAL

One basis of difference between semantics and pragmatics is the distinction between conventional and natural. By NATURAL I mean that kind of "information" that one can reasonably infer as (part of) what the speaker intended to convey, but where the inference is not based DIRECTLY on any kind of linguistic convention but on assumptions about what counts as rational behavior, knowledge of the world, and so on. Let me give a couple of examples of natural inferences, to make clear what I mean.

First a nonlinguistic example. Imagine that I approach a classroom door and turn the knob. The door does not open. I continue turning the knob back and forth, but the door still does not open. A person who has been watching me (and who I have noticed watching me, and who I observe has seen that I have noticed him) approaches and hands me a key. I thank the person, insert the key in the lock on the door, unlock it, and so on. Now there are a number of inferences here, none of them based on any convention save for the conventions involved in the use of *thank you*. The inferences I have in mind are these: The other person inferred from my behavior that I was trying to open the door, and that I was having no success. Notice this is not the sort of inference one would want to consider a matter of COMMUNICATION; it was not my intention that the person make this inference (cf. Grice's definition of "non-natural meaning"). But the next inference is indeed communicative. The person hands me a key, and I am justified in inferring that I am being given the key so that I can open the door with it (thus that it is in fact a key to the door I am trying to open). I am justified in assuming this in that (leaving out many steps), given that the person is rational, and knowing that he has seen me vainly trying the door, and that he knows that I know he saw me, then the most likely interpretation of his behavior is that he is giving me the right key so that I can open the door. Moreover, it is fairly clear that he must be aware that I am very likely to make this inference, and he has done nothing to stop me from making it, so he must intend for me to make it. No doubt this description will call to the reader's mind various points in Grice (1975). It is intended to. Notice that in no way is there any convention involved in this inferential chain, unless one would want to say that there is some cultural convention like "be helpful" involved. At any rate, it is clear that most of the steps in the inference are natural, rather than convention based.

There is an inference involved in the interpretation of my use of *thank you,* on the other hand, that could be described as involving both convention and natural inference. The inference I have in mind is the justified inference by the other person that in saying *thank you,* I mean to thank him for giving me the key. The inference here is in part conventional, in that it is based on knowledge of the English phrase *thank you,* and knowledge of the conventions concerning when one thanks and for what kind of thing. But it also involves natural inference in his figuring out just what it is I'm thanking him for.

As far as communication is concerned, then, I use the term NATURAL in a way that would be appropriately applied to meaning that is conveyed, or at least can be conveyed, via inferences about intentions behind communicative acts, as in the case of conversational implicature. In such cases, the relation between what is said and what is conveyed as natural meaning is not arbitrary, as it is in the case of the literal meanings of words, but can be reasoned out from the literal meaning taken together with the facts surrounding the utterance (i.e., "context").

By CONVENTIONAL, on the other hand, is usually meant the relation between linguistic form and literal meaning, which is arbitrary, a matter of knowledge of language. One cannot reason out from the word *dog* that it is used to refer to a certain kind of animal; one just knows it (or not) as a synchronically arbitrary fact of English. Such knowledge is knowledge of the conventions of English, which jointly constitute all or part of knowledge of language per se.

But as Searle points out in the passage quoted earlier, there is another sort of language-related convention, conventions of usage: "It is by now, I hope, uncontroversial that there is a distinction to be made between meaning and use, but what is less generally recognized is that there can be conventions of usage that are not meaning conventions" [This volume: 274].

Now it is not crystal clear in this passage what Searle has in mind as a case of "conventions of usage that are not meaning conventions," but I think there are cases that can be perspicuously described in these terms: in particular, conventions that are, strictly speaking, not conventions of language, but conventions of usage of language, properly considered conventions of the culture that uses the language. For example, just as in our own culture it is conventional to greet someone by inquiring after the other person's health, so I am told that in some cultures it is conventional to greet by asking after the other person's gastronomic welfare, most likely (but not exclusively) by saying something like *Have you eaten?*, i.e. it's direct translation. Now on the one hand *Have you eaten?* is by virtue of its semantics a natural way of greeting someone by conveying concern for his well-being, given the right conditions in the culture, as opposed to *Seven is prime* or *Your hair is missing;* but at the same time it is entirely arbitrary whether or not a given culture uses *Have you eaten?* as a CONVENTIONAL way of greeting. And I think we would not want to say even when it is a conventional greeting that the expression *Have you eaten?* means the same as *I greet you,* though indeed that kind of linguistic change does occur now and then. Rather, the convention involved here is a cultural convention about the use of language, not part of the language itself—though that is not to say a good language teacher would not teach it.

Another case: according to Webster and Webster (1968), the customary way of opening a conversation among Eskimos is by saying (the direct translation of) *You are obviously*————, where the blank is filled according to what the hearer is doing at the time of the utterance—for example, *You are obviously reading Kant* or *You are obviously skinning a seal.* Again, I think we would not want to say that the conventional literal meaning of the expression is merely a statement of intended effect, namely, to open a conversation. Still there is a convention of some sort here, to the effect that it is customary or conventional to say a certain sentence AND MEAN IT under certain circumstances, with certain purposes.

Still another example: According to Wolff (1966), in Cebu culture one does not knock at a door but says something in the way of greeting, like *good morning.* Both ways—knocking and greeting—would seem to be equally effective as natural ways of getting the attention of the inhabitants and provoking them to open the door. But one way is conventional in Cebu culture, the other in ours. We might be tempted to assign something like 'request for opening' as the literal meaning, so to speak, of the knock, since its use for that purpose is indeed conventional, and seems not to stem from any other "meaning" associated with knocking. But the temptation is less great to say in the Cebu case that the expression translated as 'good morning' is ambiguous between the literal meaning of a morning greeting and that of a request to open the door. Rather, it would seem more appropriate to say that there is a convention to the effect that one announces one's presence at the door, etc., by issuing a greeting to the inhabitants. This is not a convention of the language, but about its use.

In sum, then, I am proposing that there are at least two distinct kinds of convention involved in speech acts: conventions of language [for example, the meaning of *dog,* the fact that in English the subject of a passive sentence is interpreted as (roughly) patient, and so forth] and conventions in a culture of usage of language in certain cases [for example, the fact that to start an auto race one says *Gentlemen, start your engines* (and MEANS it), the fact that one is expected to say something in the way of consolation at funerals, and so on], sometimes

(but sometimes not) with particular expression (with their meanings) mentioned in the convention. The former, conventions OF the language, are what make up the language, at least in part. The latter, conventions of usage, are a matter of culture (manners, religion, law . . .) not knowledge of language per se. And I propose that by looking a little at the STRUCTURE, so to speak, of this second kind of convention, we can derive first an account of the apparent paradox involved in cases like *Can you pass the salt?,* in which they are treated as simultaneously conventional and natural, just as Searle says. Second, we will see that there is a range of possibilities for conventions intermediate between naturalness and conventions of the language. Third, along the way, we will construct a plausible picture of at least one way that expressions can change their status diachronically, by passing from the status of convention about language to the status of convention of language.

CONVENTIONS OF USAGE

As an initial approximation, I think conventions of usage can be considered to contain three kinds of elements: occasion, purpose, and means. As the statement of means becomes more and more specific, the convention approaches a convention of the language, a statement about literal meaning. As the connections between purpose and means become obscured, the relation between them is ripe for reinterpretation as entirely arbitrary, at which point the convention of usage is reinterpreted as a convention of the language.

As an illustration, we might consider various hypothetical versions of a convention concerning departure salutations, proceeding from less to more specific versions. As a rather nonspecific version, we might start with something like a statement of occasion (which not all conventions will have), and purpose, as in (1):

(1) *Upon parting, one expresses one's regard for the other person.*

Then (1) might be made more specific in a given culture by adding various means specifications, as in (2a) or (2b):

(2) a. *by expressing a concern for the welfare of the other person*

b. *by expressing a desire or intention to see the other person again*

These of course can in turn stand as purposes for further specification of means. For example, the alternatives in (3a–c) might stand as means for the purpose (2a):

(3) a. *by expressing a wish for good health*
    b. *by invoking the goodwill of God toward the other person*
    c. *by expressing a wish for peace*

Each of these conventions, of course, could be made more specific, still allowing considerable freedom in choice of utterance to satisfy the convention, including the use of conversational implicature or literal expression of various kinds. Thus, for example, one might conform to the convention jointly defined by (1), (2a), and (3b) by uttering any of the following:

(4) a. *May God be with you.*
    b. *God be with you.*
    c. *I pray to God that He will watch over you.*
    d. *I hope God will be good to you.*

But one further type of specificity leads to a qualitative change in the convention, namely, a specification of means that includes specification of the expression to be used in conforming to the convention, like (5) as a further specification of the parting convention (1)-(2a)-(3b):

(5) *By saying the English sentence "God be with you."*

Notice that in the resulting convention (1)-(2a)-(3b)-(5) the form is specified AS A MEANINGFUL SENTENCE OF ENGLISH, recognizable as such, so that in saying *God be with you* as a way of conforming to the parting convention, one is saying it and MEANING it in its literal meaning, though sincerity may be little more than pretense. The expresison is thus NOT on a par with an idiom like *kick the bucket.* In saying something like *John kicked the bucket,* meaning he died, the word-by-word meaning of the expression plays no role; in fact, one might say that *kicked the bucket* is said (meaning 'died') IN SPITE OF its original literal meaning. But *God be with you* is said, as a way of conforming to the greeting convention, precisely BECAUSE OF its literal meaning; one says it and at least pretends to mean it (an atheist is likely to choose some other expression). Yet it is a matter of convention that one says it (and means it, or at least purports to mean it) under certain circumstances, for certain purposes.

There is a naturalness to the convention in that there is a natural connective chain between the (most general) purpose (1) of the convention and the specification of the means in terms of a particular English sentence. Part of the task of the language learner is to infer the nature of this chain, that is, the purpose-meaning connections between the occasion of usage and the expression used. Insofar as this chain is not fully reconstructed, the connection becomes arbitrary to some degree; once some arbitrariness arises, the relation is ripe for reinterpretation as entirely arbitrary. Thus the original convention (1)-(2a)-(3b)-(5), through failure of language learners to fully reconstruct the occasion-expression chain, might be reinterpreted in the following ways.

(6) *Upon parting, one invokes the good will of God toward the other person by sayng the English sentence **God be with you.***

(7) *Upon parting, one expresses one's regard for the other person by saying the English sentence **God be with you.***

(8) *Upon parting, one says the English sentence **God be with you.***

The most arbitrary version, of course, is (8), where the convention between occasion and expression is stated directly, not via a purpose-means chain. In such cases, the meaning of the literal expresion no longer plays a direct role in the convention; speakers may be aware that the expression has a certain literal meaning, but may be entirely unaware what that meaning has to do with parting.

The use of the expression *break a leg* to wish a performer good luck before a performance is an especially interesting case of a convention of usage that seems headed for eventual status of convention of language. I'm told that this expression originated due to the superstition that it would be bad luck to wish someone good luck—therefore one wished a fellow actor good luck by wishing him bad luck, i.e. a broken leg. But by now the choice of expression is rigidly fixed as part of the convention; none of the plausible paraphrases below will do for the same purpose:

(9) *Fracture a tibia.*

(10) *Break your leg.*

(11) *I hope you break a leg.*

It is likely that newcomers to the theater sub-culture will not be aware of the history of the expression, so that the connection betweeen purpose and means will be direct and arbitrary: Before a performance, to wish a performer good luck in his performance, say *break a leg.* But the expression is not thereby an idiom; if it were we would expect to find it used as if it were an idiom whose literal meaning was 'have good luck', as in (12) as a way of saying (13). But the expression cannot be used this way:

(12) *John really broke a leg last night.*

(13) *John really had good luck/did well in his performance last night.*

The schema I have argued for seems to fit nicely in this case: an occasion, a purpose, and a means, the means specified as the utterance of a particular expression. But the original natural connection between purpose and means has now been lost.

Given this view of conventions of usage, the language learner's task is to discover or reconstruct the details of the connection between occasion and purpose, on the one hand, and linguistic means—the sentence used—on the other. In the case of the literal, nonformulaic use of language, the connection is mediated in a natural way, with the literal meaning of the sentence as one of the links in the connecting chain, as in some of the parting conventions discussed earlier. But these connections, where they are not trivial (e.g. saying *it's raining* to convey that it's raining), must be worked out by the language learner, whose only immediate data are inferences in context about the occasion and/or purpose of the utterance and the expression employed. It may take some time for the language learner to fill in all the missing links in the chain. Accordingly, we might expect to find that children's linguistic competence has typically more of this arbitrary connection than does an adult's. But even in the case of adults there will probably be interpersonal variation on some expressions, describable in terms of the number of missing links in the knowledge of use of the expression. For example, we might find that

knowledge about *Gesundheit* is best captured by (14) for some adults, by (15) or (16) for others:

(14) *When someone sneezes, to express concern for his health, say the German word for healthy, **Gesundheit**.*

(15) *When someone sneezes, to express concern for his health, say **Gesundheit**.*

(16) *When someone sneezes, say **Gesundheit**.*

The third version, (16), if indeed it actually occurs, is of a rare type. The purpose has been entirely lost, so that the speaker knows only the occasion of using the expression, the only purpose for saying it being the purpose of conforming to the convention. It may be that this kind of case is more frequent among children: When such-and-such happens, one is supposed to say so-and-so.

Linguistic change arises when a speaker (or group, or entire generation of speakers) fails to reconstruct all the links of the chain, resulting in greater arbitrariness of the connection between purpose and expression, and potentially leading to use of the expression in situations incompatible with the original literal meaning of the expression. An obvious kind of example is the use of expletives like *for Christ's sake* by non-Christians, or *God damn it* by atheists; but there are more interesting cases as well, ranging from the utterance by German speakers of *auf Wiedersehen* to people whom one knows one will never see again,[2] to eventual change of literal meaning at the lexical level. But this kind of change is inhibited when the expression transparently has a (relevant) literal meaning. When its literal meaning is obscure (as in the case of *Gesundheit*) or becomes obscure due to linguistic change (notice the archaic subjunctive in *God be with you*) speakers may not recognize that the expression has a literal meaning distinct from its purpose or use, and the connection between purpose and form becomes arbitrary. Thus *God be with you* eventually becomes *goodby* by phonological change. In such a case the question arises whether it is the growing arbitrariness that makes the phonological change possible, or the other way around; or do the two reinforce each other?

At any rate, it is clear that a distinction must be made between conventions of language—matters of literal meaning—and conventions of usage. And the descriptive schema I have given for the latter, in terms of occasion-purpose-means chains, allows a plausible account of the change from convention of usage to convention of language.[3] It also gives a picture of things wherein some cases are more arbitrary than others, in that more purpose-means links have been lost in one case than in the other.

Now given this kind of convention, how can it be extended to cases like *Can you pass the salt?* What's needed is a description that says that in using *Can you pass the salt?* to make a request, one is using the sentence with its literal meaning, with the intention of conveying a request via Grice's maxims, but that in doing so one is following a convention about language use, the convention being, roughly: To request someone to do such-and-such indirectly, say the sentence *Can you (do such-and-such)?*, with its literal sense. My proposal, then, goes like this: The expression *Can you . . .* is not an idiom, but has only the obvious literal meaning of a question about the hearer's abilities.[4] One can readily see how the expression could have, via Grice's maxims, the implicature of a request. In fact it has become conventional to use the expression in this way. Thus speakers know not only that *Can you . . .* has a certain literal meaning (a convention of language); they know also that using *Can you . . .* is a standard way of indirectly making a request (a convention of usage). Both are involved in a full understanding by the hearer of what is intended in the use of the expression.

SHORT-CIRCUITED IMPLICATURE

I suspect this will strike some readers as counterintuitive, in that the "feel" of an implicature is lacking. One can see that a request implicature is calculable via Grice's maxims, but the subjective reaction is that the request nature of the speech act is conveyed without the sort of indirect feeling we attribute to the presence of inference; the literal meaning is in some way latent, rather than the basis for an inference. I think this intuition is correct, and that we need a notion of "short-circuited" implicature to account for it. Let me choose another, clearer, illustration to show what I mean by short-circuited implicature.

Suppose I have a stingy friend. One day when asked for a loan, he replies, *Do I look like a rich man?*, intending thereby the conversational implicature of a refusal. Now suppose my friend is not very imaginative, and, impressed by his own wit, he comes to use that sentence for refusing loans as a matter of habit. Still, it is a habit of saying a certain sentence, with its literal meaning, intending thereby to convey a refusal indirectly via Grice's maxims. But in interpreting my friend's utterance, I no longer have to make the inference—his habits are now part of my background knowledge. Upon hearing him say it in the right context, this background knowledge tells me immediately what he is doing. Now suppose my friend's habit spreads, so that it is common throughout the community to refuse loans by saying *Do I look like a rich man?* To be a member of a culture is to some extent to be an observer of the culture; members will thus observe that in this community loans are commonly refused (more specifically, perhaps commonly INDIRECTLY refused) by saying, *Do I look like a rich man?* (though there may be other modes of refusal as well). Thus it becomes "common knowledge" in the community that people refuse loans by saying a certain sentence, with its literal meaning, intending thereby to convey an implicature of refusal. But the inference of the implicature is short-circuited; armed with this common knowledge, I know more or less immediately, WITHOUT CALCULATING THE INFERENCE, that an implicature of a refusal was intended. Nonetheless, a speaker of the language who lacks this bit of common knowledge will understand what is intended if he hears *Do I look like a rich man?*, by the original route of conversational implicature.

SOME MORE CASES

I suspect that the reader will not yet be entirely convinced by my (admittedly counterintuitive) claim that an expression can be conventionalized and at the same time keep its literal meaning. Let me therefore present some more examples, of two kinds: first, cases where a particular expression is part of the convention, and second, some cases where it is a "rule of conversation" that is conventionalized.

Cases abound where it is conventional to use a particular form for a particular purpose, but where the literal meaning of the expression is still involved. A simple example is the forms used for identifying oneself over the telephone. It is conventional, at least in the midwestern United States, to use the forms illustrated in (17) or (18), or a few other expressions:

(17) *This is Edith Thornton.*

(18) *Edith Thornton speaking.*

On the one hand, in using these expressions one means them literally. But on the other hand, it is purely a matter of convention that one uses these particular forms rather than any of (19–22), which are equally appropriate if considered on semantic grounds alone [their literal translations might well be used for this purpose in another language; (20), for example, is used in Hebrew], but just happen not to be conventional English means of identification over the telephone. The slight difference between (18) and (21) is especially interesting as a demonstration of how form-specific such conventions can be:

(19) *Here is Edith Thornton.*

(20) *Here is Edith Thornton speaking.*

(21) *Edith Thornton is speaking.*

(22) *I am Edith Thornton.*

There are many cases that involve implicature, but as a matter of convention, so that the implicature is short-circuited. For example, (23) is commonly used to convey something like (24):

(23) *If you've seen one, you've seen them all.*

(24) *They're all alike, so it's a waste of time to examine them separately.*

It is intuitively clear that (24) could be reasoned out as an implicature of (23), but it is now conventional to use (23) to convey (24). Although one has in mind the literal meaning of (23) in using it to convey (24), the form of the expression is strictly part of the convention. Sentences having precisely the same literal meaning but even slightly different form do not convey (24) with the same immediacy. If one manages to convey (24) by saying (25) or (26), it will be as a fresh implicature, without the short-circuiting that accompanies the conventional form (23):

(25) *If you've seen one, you've seen all of them.*

(26) *You've seen them all if you've seen one.*

Below are some more cases of conventionalized implicature, where a certain expression, with its literal meaning, is used more or less conventionally to convey a certain implicature:

(27) *You can say that again.*
      (cf., You can repeat that.)

(28) *How many times have I told you. . . .*
      (cf., Tell me how many times I've told you. . . .)

(29) *It takes one to know one.*
      (cf., It requires one to recognize one.)

It should be pointed out that another kind of knowledge of usage (not of language) can play an important part in the short-circuiting of implicature: knowledge of previous use of an expression. A kind of common knowledge (not always directly related to literal meaning) about particular expressions can be exploited to bring about a conversational implicature, as in "cliches" like (30–33):

(30) [policeman to motorist] *Where's the fire?*

(31) *. . . no questions asked.*

(32) [spouse to spouse] *I've got a headache.*

(33) *Your place or mine?*

But these expresions are clearly not idioms. One uses them meaning them literally, though their use conveys much besides the literal meaning.

In other cases it is knowledge about particulars of history of use that is exploited for the sake of implicature. One conveys more than literal meaning in saying (34–36) by virtue of the hearer's knowledge of well-known previous uses of these sentences:

(34) *Am I my brother's keeper?*

(35) *I want to be alone.*

(36) *I'd rather be in Philadelphia.*

The hearer will recognize that these are famous lines, will conclude reasonably that the speaker must have known he will make the historical connection but did nothing to stop him from making it, therefore must have intended it to be made, and so on. The allusion, and resulting implicature, are conveyed in the usual Gricean fashion.

Finally, I come to the question of the conventionalization of rules of conversation. Just above I presented cases involving particular expression and the conventionalization of their use of certian implicatures, as in the case of *If you've seen one, you've seen them all,* or the original example, *Can you pass the salt?* I said in the latter case that it had become a convention of usage to use this expression, with its literal meaning, to convey an implicature of a request. The question now arises, can there be this kind of conventionalization of rules of conversation? I think there can. For example, it is more or less conventional to challenge the wisdom of a suggested course of action by questioning the mental health of the suggester, by ANY appropriate linguistic means, as in:

(37) *Are you crazy?*

(38) *Have you lost your mind?*

(39) *Are you out of your gourd?*

and so on. Most Americans have two or three stock expressions usable as answers to obvious questions, as in:

(40) *Is the Pope Catholic?*

(41) *Do bagels wear bikinis?*

But for some speakers the convention does not specify a particular expression, and new ones are manufactured as they are needed. It seems that here a schema for implicature has been conventionalized: Answer an obvious yes/no question by replying with another question whose answer is very obvious and the same as the answer you intend to convey.

In a similar way, most speakers have a small number of expressions usable as replies to assertions, with the implicature that the assertion is transparently false—(42), for example:

(42) *Yes, and I'm Marie the Queen of Romania.*

But again, for some speakers the convention specifies only a general strategy, rather than a particular expression: To convey that an assertion is transparently false, reply with another assertion even more transparently false. Hearers unfamiliar with the convention will take longer, having to calculate as conversational implicature what most Americans (at least) will recognize immediately. But it is

clear that this conventional strategy could have arisen (and probably did arise) as a conversational implicature that became conventionalized. What was formerly a matter of natural inference becomes a convention about language. The result is the hypostaticization of a particular strategy of conversational implicature that one might call a 'conversational postulate'. In Morgan (1977) I criticized Gordon and Lakoff's (1975) exposition of the notion 'conversational postulate' on the grounds that the "postulates" they proposed had no independent status, but could be (or ought to be) derived as consequences of general principles of conversation of the sort proposed by Grice. But the notion 'convention of usage' as I have argued for it here allows for an interpretation of Gordon and Lakoff's proposal in which conversational postulates would have independent status—namely, where implicature strategies become institutionalized as conventions of usage.[5]

CONCLUSION

Here is the moral: There is more to knowing "how to do things with words" than just knowledge of literal meaning. Besides knowledge of the conventions of word meanings and the semantic rules of combination, language users also have knowledge about the use of particular expressions or classes of expressions. This second kind of knowledge sometimes involves convention, but conventions of usage, conventions governing the use of meaning-bearing expressions on certain occasions, for certain purposes. These two kinds of knowledge are not mutually exclusive. They are involved simultaneously in the full understanding of many utterances.

I have left a couple of tough nuts uncracked. First, there is the methodological problem of setting out empirical criteria by which the linguist can determine the status of a given expression vis-à-vis the distinctions I have discussed. Here I have relied heavily on the reader's intuition that the expressions I have discussed work the way I say they do. I expect that psychologists will find it difficult to construct simple relevant experiments.

Second, I have followed hallowed linguistic tradition in carefully avoiding saying what I meant by "convention." Some of the things I have called convention might seem more perspicuously described by phrases like "knowledge of shared habit" or "common knowledge of the way things are done." I think a clearer understanding of these matters will probably strengthen my case.

ACKNOWLEDGMENTS

The research reported herein was supported in part by the National Institute of Education under contract NS-NIE-C-400-76-0116 and grant HEW-NIE-C-74-0007.

NOTES

1. In an earlier version of this paper I had used the term "convention ABOUT language," as opposed to "convention OF language," since I wanted to avoid the meaning-as-use controversy. But the original terminology proved so confusing that I have here used the phrase "convention OF USAGE." It should be clear that these conventions are distinct from conventions of literal meaning (my "conventions OF language"), regardless of whether literal meaning is described in terms of truth conditions or rules of use.

2. Such cases raise questions about the role of habit in this kind of linguistic change. For example, I have noticed in my own behavior the recent annoying habit of using *see you later* when taking leave, even in circumstances where it is clear to everyone involved that I will not see my interlocutor later.

3. As far as I can see, it is logically possible for there to arise changes in the other direction as well, from convention of language to convention of usage. But such a change would require a far more complicated chain of events, and may well never happen.

4. I am ignoring other readings of *Can you . . .* (e.g. deontic and epistemic readings of *can*) that are irrelevant to the present discussion.

5. Given this new sense of 'conversational postulate' as conventionalized strategy of implicature, most of Gordon and Lakoff's analyses of particular cases will have to be reconsidered. For example, their analysis of *Can you . . .* as an instance of a conversational postulate does not mention directly any particular expression, thus predicting incorrectly that literally synonymous expressions (like *Are you able to . . .*) should work the same way as *Can you. . . .* Under the analysis I presented earlier, it is just the use of *Can you . . .* that has been conventionalized as an indirect request. Synonymous expressions work as genuine implicature, not short-circuited as with *Can you . . .* and are thus subjectively more indirect.

REFERENCES

Cole, P. (1975). "The Synchronic and Diachronic Status of Conversational Implicature." In P. Cole and J. L. Morgan (eds.), *Syntax and Semantics.* Vol. 3: *Speech Acts.* New York: Academic Press.

Cole P., and J. L. Morgan (eds.). (1975). *Syntax and Semantics.* Vol. 3: *Speech Acts.* New York: Academic Press.

Gordon, D., and G. Lakoff (1975). "Conversational Postulates." In P. Cole and J. L. Morgan (eds.), *Syntax and Semantics.* Vol. 3: *Speech Acts.* New York: Academic Press.

Grice, H. P. (1957). "Meaning." *Philosophical Review* 66:377–388.

Grice, H. P. (1975). "Logic and Conversation." In P. Cole and J. L. Morgan (eds.), *Syntax and Semantics.* Vol 3: *Speech Acts.* New York: Academic Press. [Reprinted in this volume, Chapter 19]

Lakoff, R. (1973). "Language and Woman's Place." *Language and Society* 1.

Morgan, J. L. (1977). "Conversational Postulates Revisited." *Language* 53:277–284.

Sadock, J. L. (1974). *Toward a Linguistic Theory of Speech Acts.* New York: Academic Press.

Searle, J. (1975). "Indirect Speech Acts." In P. Cole and J. L. Morgan (eds.), *Syntax and Semantics.* Vol. 3: *Speech Acts.* New York: Academic Press. [Reprinted in this volume, Chapter 16]

Webster, D., and T. Webster (1968). *Let's Learn Eskimo.* Fairbanks, Alaska: Summer Institute of Linguistics.

Wolff, J. (1966). *Beginning Cebuano.* New Haven, Conn.: Yale University Press.

15

What Is a Speech Act?

JOHN R. SEARLE

I. INTRODUCTION

In a typical speech situation involving a speaker, a hearer, and an utterance by the speaker, there are many kinds of acts associated with the speaker's utterance. The speaker will characteristically have moved his jaw and tongue and made noises. In addition, he will characteristically have performed some acts within the class which includes informing or irritating or boring his hearers; he will further characteristically have performed some acts within the class which includes referring to Kennedy or Khrushchev or the North Pole; and he will also have performed acts within the class which includes making statements, asking questions, issuing commands, giving reports, greeting, and warning. The members of this last class are what Austin[1] called illocutionary acts and it is with this class that I shall be concerned in this paper, so the paper might have been called 'What is an Illocutionary Act?' I do not attempt to define the expression 'illocutionary act', although if my analysis of a particular illocutionary act succeeds it may provide the basis for a definition. Some of the English verbs and verb phrases as-

sociated with illocutionary acts are: state, assert, describe, warn, remark, comment, command, order, request, criticize, apologize, censure, approve, welcome, promise, express approval, and express regret. Austin claimed that there were over a thousand such expressions in English.

By way of introduction, perhaps I can say why I think it is of interest and importance in the philosophy of language to study speech acts, or, as they are sometimes called, language acts or linguistic acts. I think it is essential to any specimen of linguistic communication that it involve a linguistic act. It is not, as has generally been supposed, the symbol or word or sentence, or even the token of the symbol or word or sentence, which is the unit of linguistic communication, but rather it is the *production* of the token in the performance of the speech act that constitutes the basic unit of linguistic communication. To put this point more precisely, the production of the sentence token under certain conditions is the illocutionary act, and the illocutionary act is the minimal unit of linguistic communication.

I do not know how to *prove* that linguistic communication essentially involves acts but I can think of arguments with which one might attempt to convince someone who was sceptical. One argument would be to call the sceptic's attention to the fact that when he takes a noise or a mark on paper to be an instance of linguistic communication, as a message, one of the things that is involved in his so taking that noise or mark is that he should regard it as having been produced by a being with certain intentions. He cannot just regard it as a natural phenomenon, like a stone, a waterfall, or a tree. In order to regard it as an instance of linguistic communication one must suppose that its production is what I am calling a speech act. It is a logical presupposition, for example, of current attempts to decipher the Mayan hieroglyphs that we at least hypothesize that the marks we see on the stones were produced by beings more or less like ourselves and produced with certain kinds of intentions. If we were certain the marks were a consequence of, say, water erosion, then the question of deciphering them or even calling them hieroglyphs could not arise. To construe them under the category of linguistic communication necessarily involves construing their production as speech acts.

To perform illocutionary acts is to engage in a rule-governed form of behaviour. I shall argue that such things as asking questions or making statements are rule-governed in ways quite similar to those in which getting a base hit in baseball or moving a knight in chess are rule-governed forms of acts. I intend therefore to explicate the notion of an illocutionary act by stating a set of necessary and sufficient conditions for the performance of a particular kind of illocutionary act, and extracting from it a set of semantical rules for the use of the expression (or syntactic device) which marks the utterance as an illocutionary act of that kind. If I am successful in stating the conditions and the corresponding rules for even one kind of illocutionary act, that will provide us with a pattern for analysing other kinds of acts and consequently for explicating the notion in general. But in order to set the stage for actually stating conditions and extracting rules for performing an illocutionary act I have to discuss three other preliminary notions: *rules, propositions,* and *meaning.* I shall confine my discussion of these notions to those aspects which are essential to my main purposes in this paper, but, even so, what I wish to say concerning each of these notions, if it were to be at all complete, would require a paper for each; however, sometimes it may be worth sacrificing thoroughness for the sake of scope and I shall therefore be very brief.

II. RULES

In recent years there has been in the philosophy of language considerable discussion involving the notion of rules for the use of expressions. Some philosophers have even said that knowing the meaning of the word is simply a matter of knowing the rules for its use or employment. One disquieting feature of such discussions is that no philosopher, to my knowledge at least, has ever given anything like an adequate formulation of the rules for the use of even one expression. If meaning is a matter of rules of use, surely we ought to be able to state the rules for the use of expressions in a way which would explicate the meaning of those expressions. Certain other philosophers, dismayed perhaps by the failure of their colleagues to produce any rules, have denied the fashionable view that meaning is a matter of rules and have asserted that there are no semantical rules of the proposed kind at all. I am inclined to think that this scepticism is premature and stems from a failure to distinguish different sorts of rules, in a way which I shall now attempt to explain.

I distinguish between two sorts of rules: Some regulate antecedently existing forms of behaviour; for example, the rules of etiquette regulate interpersonal relationships, but these relationships exist independently of the rules of etiquette. Some rules on the other hand do not merely regulate but create or define new forms of behaviour. The rules of football, for example, do not merely regulate the game of football but as it were create the possibility of or define that activity. The activity of playing football is constituted by acting in accordance with these rules; football has no existence apart from these rules. I call the latter kind of rules constitutive rules and the former kind regulative rules. Regulative rules regulate a pre-existing activity, an activity whose existence is logically independent of the existence of the rules. Constitutive rules constitute (and also regulate) an activity the existence of which is logically dependent on the rules.[2]

Regulative rules characteristically take the form of or can be paraphrased as imperatives, e.g. 'When cutting food hold the knife in the right hand', or 'Officers are to wear ties at dinner'. Some constitutive rules take quite a different form, e.g. a checkmate is made if the king is attacked in such a way that no move will leave it unattacked; a touchdown is scored when a player crosses the opponents' goal line in possession of the ball while play is in progress. If our paradigms of rules are imperative regulative rules, such non-imperative constitutive rules are likely to strike us as extremely curious and hardly even as rules at all. Notice that they are almost tautological in character, for what the 'rule' seems to offer is a partial definition of 'checkmate' or 'touchdown'. But, of course, this quasi-tautological character is a necessary consequence of their being constitutive rules: the rules concerning touchdowns must define the notion of 'touchdown' in the same way that the rules concerning football define 'football'. That, for example, a touchdown can be scored in such and such ways and counts six points can appear sometimes as a rule, sometimes as an analytic truth; and that it can be construed as a tautology is a clue to the fact that the rule in question is a constitutive one. Regulative rules generally have the form 'Do X' or 'If Y do X'. Some members of the set of constitutive rules have this form but some also have the form 'X counts as Y'.[3]

The failure to perceive this is of some importance in philosophy. Thus, e.g., some philosophers ask 'How can a promise create an obligation?' A similar question would be 'How can a touchdown create six points?' And as they stand both questions can only be answered by stating a rule of the form 'X counts as Y'.

I am inclined to think that both the failure of some philosophers to state rules for the use of expressions and the scepticism of other philosophers concerning the existence of any such rules stem at least in part from a failure to recognize the distinctions between constitutive and regulative rules. The model or paradigm of a rule which most philosophers have is that of a regulative rule, and if one looks in semantics for purely regulative rules one is not likely to find anything interesting from the

point of view of logical analysis. There are no doubt social rules of the form 'One ought not to utter obscenities at formal gatherings', but that hardly seems a rule of the sort that is crucial in explicating the semantics of a language. The hypothesis that lies behind the present paper is that the semantics of a language can be regarded as a series of systems of constitutive rules and that illocutionary acts are acts performed in accordance with these sets of constitutive rules. One of the aims of this paper is to formulate a set of constitutive rules for a certain kind of speech act. And if what I have said concerning constitutive rules is correct, we should not be surprised if not all these rules take the form of imperative rules. Indeed we shall see that the rules fall into several different categories, none of which is quite like the rules of etiquette. The effort to state the rules for an illocutionary act can also be regarded as a kind of test of the hypothesis that there are constitutive rules underlying speech acts. If we are unable to give any satisfactory rule formulations, our failure could be construed as partially disconfirming evidence against the hypothesis.

III. PROPOSITIONS

Different illocutionary acts often have features in common with each other. Consider utterances of the following sentences:

(1) Will John leave the room?

(2) John will leave the room.

(3) John, leave the room!

(4) Would that John left the room.

(5) If John will leave the room, I will leave also.

Utterances of each of these on a given occasion would characteristically be performances of different illocutionary acts. The first would, characteristically, be a question, the second an assertion about the future, that is, a prediction, the third a request or order, the fourth an expression of a wish, and the fifth a hypothetical expression of intention. Yet in the performance of each the speaker would characteristically perform some subsidiary acts which are common to all five illocutionary acts. In the utterance of each the speaker *refers* to a particular person John and *predicates* the act of leaving the room of that person. In no case is that all he does, but in every case it is a part of what he does. I shall say, therefore, that in each of these cases, although the illocutionary acts are different, at least some of the non-illocutionary acts of reference and predication are the same.

The reference to some person John and predication of the same thing of him in each of these illocutionary acts inclines me to say that there is a common *content* in each of them. Something expressible by the clause 'that John will leave the room' seems to be a common feature of all. We could, with not too much distortion, write each of these sentences in a way which would isolate this common feature: 'I assert that John will leave the room', 'I ask whether John will leave the room', etc.

For lack of a better word I propose to call this common content a proposition, and I shall describe this feature of these illocutionary acts by saying that in the utterance of each of (1)–(5) the speaker expresses the proposition that John will leave the room. Notice that I do not say that the sentence expresses the proposition; I do not know how sentences could perform acts of that kind. But I shall say that in the utterance of the sentence the speaker expresses a proposition. Notice also that I am distinguishing between a proposition and an assertion or statement of that proposition. The proposition that John will leave the room is expressed in the utterance of all of (1)–(5) but only in (2) is that proposition asserted. An assertion is an illocutionary act, but a proposition is not an act at all, although the act of expressing a proposition is a part of performing certain illocutionary acts.

I might summarize this by saying that I am distinguishing between the illocutionary act and the propositional content of an illocutionary act. Of course, not all illocutionary acts have a propositional content, for example, an utterance of 'Hurrah!' or 'Ouch!' does not. In one version or another this distinction is an old one and has been marked in different ways by authors as diverse as Frege, Sheffer, Lewis, Reichenbach and Hare, to mention only a few.

From a semantical point of view we can distinguish between the propositional indicator in the sentence and the indicator of illocutionary force. That is, for a large class of sentences used to perform illocutionary acts, we can say for the purpose of our analysis that the sentence has two (not necessarily separate) parts, the proposition-indicating element and the function-indicating device.[4] The function-indicating device shows how the proposition is to be taken, or, to put it in another way, what illocutionary force the utterance is to have, that is, what illocutionary act the speaker is performing in the utterance of the sentence. Function-indicating devices in English include word order, stress, intonation contour, punctuation, the mood of the verb, and finally a set of so-called performative verbs: I may indicate the kind of illocutionary act I am performing by beginning the sentence with 'I apologize', ' I warn', 'I state', etc. Often in actual speech situations the context will make it clear what the illocutionary force of the utterance is, without its being necessary to invoke the appropriate function indicating device.

If this semantical distinction is of any real importance, it seems likely that it should have some syntactical analogue, and certain recent developments in transformational grammar tend to support the view that it does. In the underlying phrase marker of a sentence there is a distinction between those elements which correspond to the function-indicating device and those which correspond to the propositional content.

The distinction between the function-indicating device and the proposition-indicating device will prove very useful to us in giving an analysis of an illocutionary act. Since the same proposition can be common to all sorts of illocutionary acts, we can separate our analysis of the proposition from our analysis of kinds of illocutionary acts. I think there are rules for expressing propositions, rules for such things as reference and prediction, but those rules can be discussed independently of the rules for function indicating. In this paper I shall not attempt to discuss propositional rules but shall concentrate on rules for using certain kinds of function-indicating devices.

IV. MEANING

Speech acts are characteristically performed in the utterance of sounds or the making of marks. What is the difference between *just* uttering sounds or making marks and performing a speech act? One difference is that the sounds or marks one makes in the performance of a speech act are characteristically said to *have meaning,* and a second related difference is that one is characteristically said to *mean something* by those sounds or marks. Characteristically when one speaks one means something by what one says, and what one says, the string of morphemes that one emits, is characteristically said to have a meaning. Here, incidentally, is another point at which our analogy between performing speech acts and playing games breaks down. The pieces in a game like chess are not characteristically said to have a meaning, and furthermore when one makes a move one is not characteristically said to mean anything by that move.

But what is it for one to mean something by what one says, and what is it for something to have a meaning? To answer the first of these questions I propose to borrow and revise some ideas of Paul Grice. In an article entitled 'Meaning',[5] Grice gives the following analysis of one sense of the notion of 'meaning'. To say that *A* meant something by *x* is to say that '*A* intended the utterance of *x* to produce some effect in an audience by means of the recognition of this intention.' This seems to me a useful start on an analysis of meaning, first because it shows the close relationship between the notion of meaning and the notion of intention, and secondly because it captures something which is, I think, essential to speaking a language: In speaking a language I attempt to communicate things to my hearer by means of getting him to recognize my intention to communicate just those things. For example, characteristically, when I make an assertion, I attempt to communicate to and convince my hearer of the truth of a certain proposition; and the means I employ to do this are to utter certain sounds, which utterance I intend to produce in him the desired effect by means of his recognition of my intention to produce just that effect. I shall illustrate this with an example. I might on the one hand attempt to get you to believe that I am French by speaking French all the time, dressing in the French manner, showing wild enthusiasm for de Gaulle, and cultivating French acquaintances. But I might on the other hand attempt

to get you to believe that I am French by simply telling you that I am French. Now, what is the difference between these two ways of my attempting to get you to believe that I am French? One crucial difference is that in the second case I attempt to get you to believe that I am French by getting you to recognize that it is my purported intention to get you to believe just that. That is one of the things involved in telling you that I am French. But of course if I try to get you to believe that I am French by putting on the act I described, then your recognition of my intention to produce in you the belief that I am French is not the means I am employing. Indeed in this case you would, I think, become rather suspicious if you recognized my intention.

However valuable this analysis of meaning is, it seems to me to be in certain respects defective. First of all, it fails to distinguish the different kinds of effects—perlocutionary versus illocutionary—that one may intend to produce in one's hearers, and it further fails to show the way in which these different kinds of effects are related to the notion of meaning. A second defect is that it fails to account for the extent to which meaning is a matter of rules or conventions. That is, this account of meaning does not show the connection between one's meaning something by what one says and what that which one says actually means in the language. In order to illustrate this point I now wish to present a counter-example to this analysis of meaning. The point of the counter-example will be to illustrate the connection between what a speaker means and what the words he utters mean.

Suppose that I am an American soldier in the Second World War and that I am captured by Italian troops. And suppose also that I wish to get these troops to believe that I am a German officer in order to get them to release me. What I would like to do is to tell them in German or Italian that I am a German officer. But let us suppose I don't know enough German or Italian to do that. So I, as it were, attempt to put on a show of telling them that I am a German officer by reciting those few bits of German that I know, trusting that they don't know enough German to see through my plan. Let us suppose I know only one line of German, which I remember from a poem I had to memorize in a high-school German course. Therefore I, a captured American, address my Italian captors with the following sentence: 'Kennst du das Land, wo die Zitronen blühen?' Now, let us describe the situation in Gricean terms. I intend to produce a certain effect in them, namely, the effect of believing that I am a German officer; and I intend to produce this effect by means of their recognition of my intention. I intend that they should think that what I am trying to tell them is that I am a German officer. But does it follow from this account that when I say 'Kennst du das Land . . . ' etc., what I mean is, 'I am a German officer'? Not only does it not follow, but in this case it seems plainly false that when I utter the German sentence what I mean is 'I am a German officer,' or even 'Ich bin ein deutscher Offizer,' because what the words mean is, 'Knowest thou the land where the lemon trees bloom?' Of course, I want my captors to be deceived into thinking that what I mean is 'I am a German officer,' but part of what is involved in the deception is getting them to think that that is what the words which I utter mean in German. At one point in the *Philosophical Investigations* Wittgenstein says 'Say "it's cold here" and mean "it's warm here"'.[6] The reason we are unable to do this is that what we can mean is a function of what we are saying. Meaning is more than a matter of intention, it is also a matter of convention.

Grice's account can be amended to deal with counter-examples of this kind. We have here a case where I am trying to produce a certain effect by means of the recognition of my intention to produce that effect, but the device I use to produce this effect is one which is conventionally, by the rules governing the use of that device, used as a means of producing quite different illocutionary effects. We must therefore reformulate the Gricean account of meaning in such a way as to make it clear that one's meaning something when one says something is more than just contingently related to what the sentence means in the language one is speaking. In our analysis of illocutionary acts, we must capture both the intentional and the conventional aspects and especially the relationship between them. In the performance of an illocutionary act the speaker intends to produce a certain effect by means of getting the hearer to recognize his in-

tention to produce that effect, and furthermore, if he is using words literally, he intends this recognition to be achieved in virtue of the fact that the rules for using the expressions he utters associate the expressions with the production of that effect. It is this *combination* of elements which we shall need to express in our analysis of the illocutionary act.

V. HOW TO PROMISE

I shall now attempt to give an analysis of the illocutionary act of promising. In order to do this I shall ask what conditions are necessary and sufficient for the act of promising to have been performed in the utterance of a given sentence. I shall attempt to answer this question by stating these conditions as a set of propositions such that the conjunction of the members of the set entails the proposition that a speaker made a promise, and the proposition that the speaker made a promise entails this conjunction. Thus each condition will be a necessary condition for the performance of the act of promising and taken collectively the set of conditions will be a sufficient condition for the act to have been performed.

If we get such a set of conditions we can extract from them a set of rules for the use of the function-indicating device. The method here is analogous to discovering the rules of chess by asking oneself what are the necessary and sufficient conditions under which one can be said to have correctly moved a knight or castled or checkmated a player, etc. We are in the position of someone who has learned to play chess without ever having the rules formulated and who wants such a formulation. We learned how to play the game of illocutionary acts, but in general it was done without an explicit formulation of the rules, and the first step in getting such a formulation is to set out the conditions for the performance of a particular illocutionary act. Our inquiry will therefore serve a double philosophical purpose. By stating a set of conditions for the performance of a particular illocutionary act we shall have offered a partial explication of that notion and shall also have paved the way for the second step, the formulation of the rules.

I find the statement of the conditions very difficult to do, and I am not entirely satisfied with the list I am about to present. One reason for the difficulty is that the notion of a promise, like most notions in ordinary language, does not have absolutely strict rules. There are all sorts of odd, deviant, and borderline promises; and counter-examples, more or less bizarre, can be produced against my analysis. I am inclined to think we shall not be able to get a set of knock-down necessary and sufficient conditions that will exactly mirror the ordinary use of the word 'promise'. I am confining my discussion, therefore, to the centre of the concept of promising and ignoring the fringe, borderline, and partially defective cases. I also confine my discussion to full-blown explicit promises and ignore promises made by elliptical turns of phrase, hints, metaphors, etc.

Another difficulty arises from my desire to state the conditions without certain forms of circularity. I want to give a list of conditions for the performance of a certain illocutionary act, which do not themselves mention the performance of any illocutionary acts. I need to satisfy this condition in order to offer an explication of the notion of an illocutionary act in general, otherwise I should simply be showing the relation between different illocutionary acts. However, although there will be no reference to illocutionary *acts,* certain illocutionary *concepts* will appear in the analysans as well as in the analysandum; and I think this form of circularity is unavoidable because of the nature of constitutive rules.

In the presentation of the conditions I shall first consider the case of a sincere promise and then show how to modify the conditions to allow for insincere promises. As our inquiry is semantical rather than syntactical, I shall simply assume the existence of grammatically well-formed sentences.

Given that a speaker *S* utters a sentence *T* in the presence of a hearer *H,* then, in the utterance of *T, S* sincerely (and non-defectively) promises that *p* to *H* if and only if:

(1) *Normal input and output conditions obtain.*

I use the terms 'input' and 'output' to cover the large and indefinite range of conditions under which any kind of serious linguistic communication is possible. 'Output' covers the conditions for intelligible speaking and 'input' covers the conditions for understanding. Together they include such things as that the speaker and hearer both know how to speak the language; both are conscious of what they are doing; the speaker is not acting under duress or threats; they have no physical impediments to communication, such as deafness, aphasia, or laryngitis; they are not acting in a play or telling jokes, etc.

(2) *S expresses that p in the utterance of T.*

This condition isolates the propositional content from the rest of the speech act and enables us to concentrate on the peculiarities of promising in the rest of the analysis.

(3) *In expressing that p, S predicates a future act A of S.*

In the case of promising the function-indicating device is an expression whose scope includes certain features of the proposition. In a promise an act must be predicated of the speaker and it cannot be a past act. I cannot promise to have done something, and I cannot promise that someone else will do something. (Although I can promise to see that he will do it.) The notion of an act, as I am construing it for present purposes, includes refraining from acts, performing series of acts, and may also include states and conditions: I may promise not to do something, I may promise to do something repeatedly, and I may promise to be or remain in a certain state or condition. I call conditions (2) and (3) the *propositional content conditions.*

(4) *H would prefer S's doing A to his not doing A, and S believes H would prefer his doing A to his not doing A.*

One crucial distinction between promises on the one hand and threats on the other is that a promise is a pledge to do something for you, not to you, but a threat is a pledge to do something to you, not for you. A promise is defective if the thing promised is something the promisee does not want done; and it is further defective if the promisor does not believe the promisee wants it done, since a non-defective promise must be intended as a promise and not as a threat or warning. I think both halves of this double condition are necessary in order to avoid fairly obvious counter-examples.

One can, however, think of apparent counter-examples to this condition as stated.

Suppose I say to a lazy student 'If you don't hand in your paper on time I promise you I will give you a failing grade in the course'. Is this utterance a promise? I am inclined to think not; we would more naturally describe it as a warning or possibly even a threat. But why then is it possible to use the locution 'I promise' in such a case? I think we use it here because 'I promise' and 'I hereby promise' are among the strongest function-indicating devices for *commitment* provided by the English language. For that reason we often use these expressions in the performance of speech acts which are not strictly speaking promises but in which we wish to emphasize our commitment. To illustrate this, consider another apparent counter-example to the analysis along different lines. Sometimes, more commonly I think in the United States than in England, one hears people say 'I promise' when making an emphatic assertion. Suppose, for example, I accuse you of having stolen the money. I say, 'You stole that money, didn't you?' You reply 'No, I didn't, I promise you I didn't'. Did you make a promise in this case? I find it very unnatural to describe your utterance as a promise. This utterance would be more aptly described as an emphatic denial, and we can explain the occurrence of the function-indicating device 'I promise' as derivative from genuine promises and serving here as an expression adding emphasis to your denial.

In general the point stated in condition (4) is that if a purported promise is to be non-defective the thing promised must be something the hearer wants done, or considers to be in his interest, or would prefer being done to not being done, etc.; and the speaker must be aware of or believe or know, etc., that this is the case. I think a more elegant and exact formulation of this condition would require the introduction of technical terminology.

(5) *It is not obvious to both S and H that S will do A in the normal course of events.*

This condition is an instance of a general condition on many different kinds of illocutionary acts to the effect that the act must have a point. For example, if I make a request to someone to do something which it is obvious that he is already doing or is about to do, then my request is pointless and to that extent defective. In an actual speech situation, listeners, knowing the rules for performing illocutionary acts, will assume that this condition is satisfied. Suppose, for example, that in the course of a public speech I say to a member of my audience 'Look here, Smith, pay attention to what I am saying'. In order to make sense of this utterance the audience will have to assume that Smith has not been paying attention or at any rate that it is not obvious that he has been paying attention, that the question of his paying attention has arisen in some way; because a condition for making a request is that it is not obvious that the hearer is doing or about to do the thing requested.

Similarly with promises. It is out of order for me to promise to do something that it is obvious I am going to do anyhow. If I do seem to be making such a promise, the only way my audience can make sense of my utterance is to assume that I believe that it is not obvious that I am going to do the thing promised. A happily married man who promises his wife he will not desert her in the next week is likely to provide more anxiety than comfort.

Parenthetically I think this condition is an instance of the sort of phenomenon stated in Zipf's law. I think there is operating in our language, as in most forms of human behaviour, a principle of least effort, in this case a principle of maximum illocutionary ends with minimum phonetic effort; and I think condition (5) is an instance of it.

I call conditions such as (4) and (5) *preparatory conditions*. They are *sine quibus non* of happy promising, but they do not yet state the essential feature.

(6) *S intends to do A.*

The most important distinction between sincere and insincere promises is that in the case of the sincere promise the speaker intends to do the act promised, in the case of the insincre promise he does not intend to do the act. Also in sincere promises the speaker believes it is possible for him to do the act (or refrain from doing it), but I think the proposition that he intends to do it entails that he thinks it is possible to do (or refrain from doing) it, so I am not stating that as an extra condition. I call this condition the *sincerity condition*.

(7) *S intends that the utterance of T will place him under an obligation to do A.*

The essential feature of a promise is that it is the undertaking of an obligation to perform a certain act. I think that this condition distinguishes promises (and other members of the same family such as vows) from other kinds of speech acts. Notice that in the statement of the condition we only specify the speaker's intention; further conditions will make clear how that intention is realized. It is clear, however, that having this intention is a necessary condition of making a promise; for if a speaker can demonstrate that he did not have this intention in a given utterance, he can prove that the utterance was not a promise. We know, for example, that Mr. Pickwick did not promise to marry the woman because we know he did not have the appropriate intention.

I call this the *essential condition*.

(8) *S intends that the utterance of T will produce in H a belief that conditions (6) and (7) obtain by means of the recognition of the intention to produce that belief, and he intends this recognition to be achieved by means of the recognition of the sentence as one conventionally used to produce such beliefs.*

This captures our amended Gricean analysis of what it is for the speaker to mean to make a promise. The speaker intends to produce a certain illocutionary effect by means of getting the hearer to recognize his intention to produce that effect, and he also intends this recognition to be achieved in virtue of the fact that the lexical and syntactical character of the item he utters conventionally associates it with producing that effect.

Strictly speaking this condition could be formulated as part of condition (1), but it is of enough philosophical interest to be worth stating separately. I find it troublesome for the following reason. If my original objection to Grice is really valid, then surely, one might say, all these iterated intentions are superfluous; all that is necessary is that the speaker should seriously utter a sentence. The production of all these effects is simply a consequence of the hearer's knowledge of what the sentence means, which in turn is a consequence of his knowledge of the language, which is assumed by the speaker at the outset. I think the correct reply to this objection is that condition (8) explicates what it is for the speaker to 'seriously' utter the sentece, i.e., to utter it and mean it, but I am not completely confident about either the force of the objection or of the reply.

(9) *The semantical rules of the dialect spoken by S and H are such that T is correctly and sincerely uttered if and only if conditions (1)–(8) obtain.*

This condition is intended to make clear that the sentence uttered is one which by the semantical rules of the language is used to make a promise. Taken together with condition (8), it eliminates counter-examples like the captured soldier example considered earlier. Exactly what the formulation of the rules is, we shall soon see.

So far we have considered only the case of a sincere promise. But insincere promises are promises none the less, and we now need to show how to modify the conditions to allow for them. In making an insincere promise the speaker does not have all the intentions and beliefs he has when making a sincere promise. However, he purports to have them. Indeed it is because he purports to have intentions and beliefs which he does not have that we describe his act as insincere. So to allow for insincere promises we need only to revise our conditions to state that the speaker takes responsibility for having the beliefs and intentions rather than stating that he actually has them. A clue that the speaker does take such responsibility is the fact that he could not say without absurdity, e.g., 'I promise to do A but I do not intend to do A'. To say 'I promise to do A' is to take responsibility for intending to do A, and this condition holds whether the utterance was sincere or insincere. To allow for the possibility of an insincere promise then we have only to revise condition (6) so that it states not that the speaker intends to do A, but that he takes responsibility for intending to do A, and to avoid the charge of circularity I shall phrase this as follows:

(6*) *S intends that the utterance of T will make him responsible for intending to do A.*

Thus amended (and with 'sincerely' dropped from our analysandum and from condition (9)), our analysis is neutral on the question whether the promise was sincere or insincere.

VI. RULES FOR THE USE OF THE FUNCTION-INDICATING DEVICE

Our next task is to extract from our set of conditions a set of rules for the use of the function-indicating device. Obviously not all of our conditions are equally relevant to this task. Condition (1) and conditions of the forms (8) and (9) apply generally to all kinds of normal illocutionary acts and are not peculiar to promising. Rules for the function-indicating device for promising are to be found corresponding to conditions (2)–(7).

The semantical rules for the use of any function-indicating device *P* for promising are:

Rule 1. *P* is to be uttered only in the context of a sentence (or larger stretch of discourse) the utterance of which predicates some future act *A* of the speaker *S.* I call this the *propositional-content rule.* It is derived from the propositional-content conditions (2) and (3).

Rule 2. *P* is to be uttered only if the hearer *H* would prefer *S*'s doing *A* to his not doing *A*, and *S* believes *H* would prefer *S*'s doing *A* to his not doing *A*.

Rule 3. *P* is to be uttered only if it is not obvious to both *S* and *H* that *S* will do *A* in the normal course of events.

I call rules (2) and (3) *preparatory rules.* They are derived from the preparatory conditions (4) and (5).

Rule 4. *P* is to be uttered only if *S* intends to do *A.* I call this the *sincerity rule.* It is derived from the sincerity condition (6).

Rule 5. The utterance of *P* counts as the undertaking of an obligation to do *A.* I call this the *essential rule.*

These rules are ordered: rules 2–5 apply only if rule 1 is satisfied, and rule 5 applies only if rules 2 and 3 are satisfied as well.

Notice that whereas rules 1–4 take the form of quasi-imperatives, i.e., they are of the form: utter *P* only if *x*, rule 5 is of the form: the utterance of *P* counts as *Y*. Thus rule 5 is of the kind peculiar to systems of constitutive rules which I discussed in section II.

Notice also that the rather tiresome analogy with games is holding up remarkably well. If we ask ourselves under what conditions a player could be said to move a knight correctly, we would find preparatory conditions, such as that it must be his turn to move, as well as the essential condition stating the ac-

tual positions the knight can move to. I think that there is even a sincerity rule for competitive games, the rule that each side tries to win. I suggest that the team which 'throws' the game is behaving in a way closely analogous to the speaker who lies or makes false promises. Of course, there usually are no propositional-content rules for games, because games do not, by and large, represent states of affairs.

If this analysis is of any general interest beyond the case of promising then it would seem that these distinctions should carry over into other types of speech act, and I think a little reflection will show that they do. Consider, e.g., giving an order. The preparatory conditions include that the speaker should be in a position of authority over the hearer, the sincerity condition is that the speaker wants the ordered act done, and the essential condition has to do with the fact that the utterance is an attempt to get the hearer to do it. For assertions, the preparatory conditions include the fact that the hearer must have some basis for supposing the asserted proposition is true, the sincerity condition is that he must believe it to be true, and the essential condition has to do with the fact that the utterance is an attempt to inform the hearer and convince him of its truth. Greetings are a much simpler kind of speech act, but even here some of the distinctions apply. In the utterance of 'Hello' there is no propositional content and no sincerity condition. The perparatory condition is that the speaker must have just encountered the hearer, and the essential rule is that the utterance indicates courteous recognition of the hearer.

A proposal for further research then is to carry out a similar analysis of other types of speech acts. Not only would this give us an analysis of concepts interesting in themselves, but the comparison of different analyses would deepen our understanding of the whole subject and incidentally provide a basis for a more serious taxonomy than any of the usual facile categories such as evaluative versus descriptive, or cognitive versus emotive.

NOTES

1. J. L. Austin, *How to Do Things with Words* (Oxford: 1962).

2. This distinction occurs in J. Rawls, 'Two Concepts of Rules', *Philosophical Review,* 1955, and J. R. Searle, 'How to Derive "Ought" from "Is"', *Philosophical Review,* 1964.

3. The formulation '*X* counts as *Y*' was originally suggested to me by Max Black.

4. In the sentence 'I promise that I will come' the function-indicating device and the propositional element are separate. In the sentence 'I promise to come', which means the same as the first and is derived from it by certain transformations, the two elements are not separate.

5. *Philosophical Review,* 1957.

6. *Philosophical Investigations* (Oxford: Basil Blackwell, 1953), para. 510.

16

Indirect Speech Acts

JOHN R. SEARLE

INTRODUCTION

The simplest cases of meaning are those in which the speaker utters a sentence and means exactly and literally what he says. In such cases the speaker intends to produce a certain illocutionary effect in the hearer, and he intends to produce this effect by getting the hearer to recognize his intention to produce it, and he intends to get the hearer to recognize this intention in virtue of the hearer's knowledge of the rules that govern the utterance of the sentence. But notoriously, not all cases of meaning are this simple: In hints, insinuations, irony, and metaphor—to mention a few examples—the speaker's utterance meaning and the sentence meaning come apart in various ways. One important class of such cases is that in which the speaker utters a sentence, means what he says, but also means something more. For example, a speaker may utter the sentence *I want you to do it* by way of requesting the hearer to do something. The utterance is incidentally meant as a statement, but it is also meant primarily as a request, a request made by way of making a statement.

In such cases a sentence that contains the illocutionary force indicators for one kind of illocutionary act can be uttered to perform, IN ADDITION, another type of illocutionary act. There are also cases in which the speaker may utter a sentence and mean what he says and also mean another illocution with a different propositional content. For example, a speaker may utter the sentence *Can you reach the salt?* and mean it not merely as a question but as a request to pass the salt.

In such cases it is important to emphasize that the utterance is meant as a request; that is, the speaker intends to produce in the hearer the knowledge that a request has been made to him, and he intends to produce this knowledge by means of getting the hearer to recognize his intention to produce it. Such cases, in which the utterance has two illocutionary forces, are to be sharply distinguished from the cases in which, for example, the speaker tells the hearer that he wants him to do something; and then the hearer does it because the speaker wants him to, though no request at all has been made, meant, or understood. The cases we will be discussing are indirect speech

John R. Searle. "Indirect Speech Acts." In *Syntax and Semantics,* vol. 3: *Speech Acts,* edited by P. Cole and J. L. Morgan, 59–82. New York: Academic Press, 1975. Copyright © 1975 by John Searle. Reprinted by permission of the author.

acts, cases in which one illocutionary act is performed indirectly by way of performing another.

The problem posed by indirect speech acts is the problem of how it is possible for the speaker to say one thing and mean that but also to mean something else. And since meaning consists in part in the intention to produce understanding in the hearer, a large part of that problem is that of how it is possible for the hearer to understand the indirect speech act when the sentence he hears and understands means something else. The problem is made more complicated by the fact that some sentences seem almost to be conventionally used as indirect requests. For a sentence like *Can you reach the salt?* or *I would appreciate it if you would get off my foot,* it takes some ingenuity to imagine a situation in which their utterances would not be requests.

In Searle (1969: chapter 3) I suggested that many such utterances could be explained by the fact that the sentences in question concern conditions of the felicitous performance of the speech acts they are used to perform indirectly—preparatory conditions, propositional content conditions, and sincerity conditions—and that their use to perform indirect speech acts consists in indicating the satisfaction of an essential condition by means of asserting or questioning one of the other conditions. Since that time a variety of explanations have been proposed, involving such things as the hypostatization of 'conversational postulates' or alternative deep structures. The answer originally suggested in Searle (1969) seems to me incomplete, and I want to develop it further here. The hypothesis I wish to defend is simply this: In indirect speech acts the speaker communicates to the hearer more than he actually says by way of relying on their mutually shared background information, both linguistic and nonlinguistic, together with the general powers of rationality and inference on the part of the hearer. To be more specific, the apparatus necessary to explain the indirect part of indirect speech acts includes a theory of speech acts, certain general principles of cooperative conversation [some of which have been discussed by Grice (this volume, Chapter 19)], and mutually shared factual background information of the speaker and the hearer, together with an ability on the

part of the hearer to make inferences. It is not necessary to assume the existence of any conversational postulates (either as an addition to the theory of speech acts or as part of the theory of speech acts) nor any concealed imperative forces or other ambiguities. We will see, however, that in some cases, convention plays a most peculiar role.

Aside from its interest for a theory of meaning and speech acts, the problem of indirect speech acts is of philosophical importance for an additional reason. In ethics it has commonly been supposed that *good, right, ought,* etc. somehow have an imperative or 'action guiding' meaning. This view derives from the fact that sentences such as *You ought to do it* are often uttered by way of telling the hearer to do something. But from the fact that such sentences can be uttered as directives[1] it no more follows that *ought* has an imperative meaning than from the fact that *Can you reach the salt* can be uttered as a request to pass the salt it follows that *can* has an imperative meaning. Many confusions in recent moral philosophy rest on a failure to understand the nature of such indirect speech acts. The topic has an additional interest for linguists because of its syntactical consequences, but I shall be concerned with these only incidentally.

A SAMPLE CASE

Let us begin by considering a typical case of the general phenomenon of indirection:

(1) *Student X: Let's go to the movies tonight.*

(2) *Student Y: I have to study for an exam.*

The utterance of (1) constitutes a proposal in virtue of its meaning, in particular because of the meaning of *Let's.* In general, literal utterances of sentences of this form will constitute proposals, as in:

(3) *Let's eat pizza tonight.*

or:

(4) *Let's go ice skating tonight.*

The utterance of (2) in the context just given would normally constitute a rejection of the proposal, but not in virtue of its meaning. In virtue of its meaning it is simply a statement about Y. Statements of this form do not, in general, constitute rejections of proposals, even in cases in which they are made in response to a proposal. Thus, if Y had said:

(5) *I have to eat popcorn tonight.*

or:

(6) *I have to tie my shoes.*

in a normal context, neither of these utterances would have been a rejection of the proposal. The question then arises, How does X know that the utterance is a rejection of the proposal? and that question is a part of the question, How is it possible for Y to intend or mean the utterance of (2) as a rejection of the proposal? In order to describe this case, let us introduce some terminology. Let us say that the PRIMARY illocutionary act performed in Y's utterance is the rejection of the proposal made by X, and that Y does that by way of performing a SECONDARY illocutionary act of making a statement to the effect that he has to prepare for an exam. He performs the secondary illocutionary act by way of uttering a sentence the LITERAL meaning of which is such that its literal utterance constitutes a performance of that illocutionary act. We may, therefore, further say that the secondary illocutionary act is literal; the primary illocutionary act is not literal. Let us assume that we know how X understands the literal secondary illocutionary act from the utterance of the sentence. The question is, How does he understand the nonliteral primary illocutionary act from understanding the literal secondary illocutionary act? And that question is part of the larger question, How is it possible for Y to mean the primary illocution when he only utters a sentence that means the secondary illocution, since to mean the primary illocution is (in large part) to intend to produce in X the relevant understanding?

A brief reconstruction of the steps necessary to derive the primary illocution from the literal illocution would go as follows. (In normal conversation, of course, no one would consciously go through the steps involved in this reasoning.)

STEP 1: *I have made a proposal to Y, and in response he has made a statement to the effect that he has to study for an exam (facts about the conversation).*

STEP 2: *I assume that Y is cooperating in the conversation and that therefore his remark is intended to be relevant (principles of conversational cooperation).*

STEP 3: *A relevant response must be one of acceptance, rejection, counterproposal, further discussion, etc. (theory of speech acts).*

STEP 4: *But his literal utterance was not one of these, and so was not a relevant response (inference from Steps 1 and 3).*

STEP 5: *Therefore, he probably means more than he says. Assuming that his remark is relevant, his primary illocutionary point must differ from his literal one (inference from Steps 2 and 4).[2]*

This step is crucial. Unless a hearer has some inferential strategy for finding out when primary illocutionary points differ from literal illocutionary points, he has no way of understanding indirect illocutionary acts.

STEP 6: *I know that studying for an exam normally takes a large amount of time relative to a single evening, and I know that going to the movies normally takes a large amount of time relative to a single evening (factual background information).*

STEP 7: *Therefore, he probably cannot both go to the movies and study for an exam in one evening (inference from Step 6).*

STEP 8: *A preparatory condition on the acceptance of a proposal, or on any other commissive, is the ability to perform the act predicated in the propositional content condition (theory of speech acts).*

STEP 9: *Therefore, I know that he has said something that has the consequence that he probably cannot consistently accept the proposal (inference from Steps 1, 7, and 8).*

STEP 10: *Therefore, his primary illocutionary point is probably to reject the proposal (inference from Steps 5 and 9).*

It may seem somewhat pedantic to set all of this out in 10 steps; but if anything, the example is still underdescribed—I have not, for example, discussed the role of the assumption of sincerity, or the *ceteris paribus* conditions that attach to various of the steps. Notice, also, that the conclusion is probabilistic. It is and ought to be. This is because the reply does not necessarily constitute a rejection of the proposal. Y might have gone on to say:

(7) *I have to study for an exam, but let's go to the movies anyhow.*

(8) *I have to study for an exam, but I'll do it when we get home from the movies.*

The inferential strategy is to establish, first, that the primary illocutionary point departs from the literal, and second, what the primary illocutionary point is.

The argument of this chapter will be that the theoretical apparatus used to explain this case will suffice to explain the general phenomenon of indirect illocutionary acts. That apparatus includes mutual background information, a theory of speech acts, and certain general principles of conversation. In particular, we explained this case without having to assume that sentence (2) is ambiguous or that it is 'ambiguous in context' or that it is necessary to assume the existence of any 'conversational postulates' in order to explain X's understanding the primary illocution of the utterance. The main difference between this case and the cases we will be discussing is that the latter all have a generality of FORM that is lacking in this example. I shall mark this generality by using bold type for the formal features in the surface structure of the sentences in question. In the field of indirect illocutionary acts, the area of directives is the most useful to study because ordinary conversational requirements of politeness normally make it awkward to issue flat imperative sentences (e.g., *Leave the room*) or explicit performatives (e.g., *I order you to leave the room*), and we therefore seek to find indirect means to our illocutionary ends (e.g., *I wonder if you would mind leaving the room*). In directives, politeness is the chief motivation for indirectness.

SOME SENTENCES 'CONVENTIONALLY' USED IN THE PERFORMANCE OF INDIRECT DIRECTIVES

Let us begin, then, with a short list of some of the sentences that could quite standardly be used to make indirect requests and other directives such as orders. At a pretheoretical level these sentences naturally tend to group themselves into certain categories.[3]

GROUP 1 *Sentences concerning H's ability to perform A:*
   Can you reach the salt?
   Can you pass the salt?
   Could you be a little more quiet?
   You could be a little more quiet.

You can go now (this may also be a permission = *you may go now*).
Are you able to reach the book on the top shelf?
Have you got change for a dollar?

GROUP 2 *Sentences concerning S's wish or want that H will do A:*
   I would like you to go now.
   I want you to do this for me, Henry.
   I would/should appreciate it if you would/could do it for me.
   I would/should be most grateful if you would/could help us out.
   I'd rather you didn't do that any more.
   I'd be very much obliged if you would pay me the money back soon.
   I hope you'll do it.
   I wish you wouldn't do that.

GROUP 3 *Sentences concerning H's doing A:*
   Officers **will** henceforth wear ties at dinner.
   Will you quit making that awful racket?
   Would you kindly get off my foot?
   Won't you stop making that noise soon?
   Aren't you going to eat your cereal?

GROUP 4 *Sentences concerning H's desire or willingness to do A:*
   Would you be willing to write a letter of recommendation for me?
   Do you want to hand me that hammer over there on the table?
   Would you mind not making so much noise?
   Would it be convenient for you to come on Wednesday?
   Would it be too much (trouble) for you to pay me the money next Wednesday?

GROUP 5 *Sentences concerning reasons for doing A:*
   You ought to be more polite to your mother.
   You should leave immediately.
   Must you continue hammering that way?
   Ought you to eat quite so much spaghetti?
   Should you be wearing John's tie?
   You had better go now.
   Hadn't you better go now?
   Why not stop here?
   Why don't you try it just once?
   Why don't you be quiet?
   It would be better for you (for us all) if you **would** leave the room.
   It wouldn't hurt if you left now.
   It might help if you shut up.
   It would be better if you gave me the money now.
   It would be a good idea if you left town.
   We'd all be better off if you'd just pipe down a bit.

This class also contains many examples that have no generality of form but obviously, in an appropriate context, would be uttered as indirect requests, e.g.:

You're standing on my foot.
I can't see the movie screen while you have that hat on.

Also in this class belong, possibly:

How many times have I told you (must I tell you) *not to eat with your fingers?*
I must have told you a dozen times not *to eat with your mouth open.*
If I have told you once I have told you a thousand times not to *wear your hat in the house.*

GROUP 6 *Sentences embedding one of these elements inside another; also, sentences embedding an explicit directive illocutionary verb inside one of these contexts.*

Would you mind awfully if I asked you if you could *write me a letter of recommendation?*
Would it be too much if I suggested that you could possibly *make a little less noise?*
Might I ask you *to take off your hat?*
I hope you won't mind if I ask you if you could *leave us alone.*
I would appreciate it if you could *make less noise.*[4]

This is a very large class, since most of its members are constructed by permitting certain of the elements of the other classes.

SOME PUTATIVE FACTS

Let us begin by noting several salient facts about the sentences in question. Not everyone will agree that what follows are facts; indeed, most of the available explanations consist in denying one or more of these statements. Nonetheless, at an intuitive pretheoretical level each of the following would seem to be correct observations about the sentences in question, and I believe we should surrender these intuitions only in the face of very serious counterarguments. I will eventually argue that an explanation can be given that is consistent with all of these facts.

FACT 1: *The sentences in question do not have an imperative force as part of their meaning.* This point is sometimes denied by philosophers and linguists, but very powerful evidence for it is provided by the fact that it is possible without inconsistency to connect the literal utterance of one of these forms with the denial of any imperative intent, e.g.:

I'd like you to do this for me, Bill, but I am not asking you to do it or requesting that you do it or ordering you to do it or telling you to do it.

I'm just asking you, Bill: Why not eat beans? But in asking you that I want you to understand that I am not telling you to eat beans; I just want to know your reasons for thinking you ought not to.

FACT 2: *The sentences in question are not ambiguous as between an imperative illocutionary force and a nonimperative illocutionary force.* I think this is intuitively apparent, but in any case, an ordinary application of Occam's Razor places the onus of proof on those who wish to claim that these sentences are ambiguous. One does not multiply meanings beyond necessity. Notice, also, that it is no help to say they are 'ambiguous in context,' for all that means is that one cannot always tell from what the sentence means what the speaker means by its utterance, and that is not sufficient to estalish sentential ambiguity.

FACT 3: *Notwithstanding Facts 1 and 2, these are standardly, ordinarily, normally— indeed, I shall argue, conventionally—used to issue directives.* There is a systematic relation between these and directive illocutions in a way that there is no systematic relation between *I have to study for an exam* and rejecting proposals. Additional evidence that they are standardly used to issue imperatives is that most of them take *please,* either at the end of the sentence or preceding the verb, e.g.:

I want you to stop making that noise, please.
Could you please lend me a dollar?

When *please* is added to one of these sentences, it explicitly and literally marks the primary illocutionary point of the utterance as directive, even though the literal meaning of the rest of the sentence is not directive.

It is because of the combination of Facts 1, 2, and 3 that there is a problem about these cases at all.

FACT 4: *The sentences in question are not, in the ordinary sense, idioms.*[5] An ordinary example of an idiom is *kicked the bucket* in *Jones kicked the bucket.* The most powerful evidence I kow that these sentences are not idioms is that in their use as indirect directives they admit of literal responses that presuppose that they are uttered literally. Thus, an utterance of *Why don't you be quiet, Henry?* admits as a response an utterance of *Well, Sally, there are several reasons for not being quiet. First, ...* Possible exceptions to this are occurrences of *would* and *could* in indirect speech acts, and I will discuss them later.

Further evidence that they are not idioms is that, whereas a word-for-word translation of *Jones kicked the bucket* into other languages will not produce a sentence meaning 'Jones died,' translations of the sentences in question will often, though by no means always, produce sentences with the same indirect illocutionary act potential of the English examples. Thus, e.g., *Pourriez-vous m'aider?* and *Können Sie mir helfen?* can be uttered as indirect requests in French or German. I will later discuss the problem of why some translate with equivalent indirect illocutionary force potential and some do not.

FACT 5: *To say they are not idioms is not to say they are not idiomatic.* All the examples given are idiomatic in current English, and—what is more puzzling—they are idiomatically used as requests. In general, nonidiomatic equivalents or synonyms would not have the same indirect illocutionary act potential. Thus, *Do you want to hand me the hammer over there on the table?* can be uttered as a request, but *Is it the case that you at present desire to hand me that hammer over there on the table?* has a formal and stilted character that in almost all contexts would eliminate it as a candidate for an indirect request. Furthermore, *Are you able to hand me that hammer?*, though idiomatic, does not have the same indirect request potential as *Can you hand me that hammer?* That these sentences are IDIOMATIC and are IDIOMATICALLY USED AS DIRECTIVES is crucial to their role in indirect speech acts. I will say more about the relations of these facts later.

FACT 6: *The sentences in question have literal utterances in which they are not also indirect requests.* Thus, *Can you reach the salt?* can be uttered as a simple question about your abilities (say, by an orthopedist wishing to know the medical progress of your arm injury). *I want you to leave* can be uttered simply as a statement about one's wants, without any directive intent. At first sight, some of our examples might not appear to satisfy this condition, e.g.:

Why not stop here?

Why don't you be quiet?

But with a little imagination it is easy to construct situations in which utterances of these would be not directives but straight-forward questions. Suppose someone had said *We ought not to stop here.* Then *Why not stop here?* would be an appropriate question, without necessarily being also a suggestion. Similarly, if someone had just said *I certainly hate making all this racket,* an utterance of *(Well, then) Why don't you be quiet?* would be an appropriate response, without also necessarily being a request to be quiet.

It is important to note that the intonation of these sentences when they are uttered as indirect requests often differs from their intonation when uttered with only their literal illocutionary force, and often the intonation pattern will be that characteristic of literal directives.

FACT 7: *In cases where these sentences are uttered as requests, they still have their literal meaning and are uttered with and as having that literal meaning.* I have seen it claimed that they have different meanings 'in context' when they are uttered as requests, but I believe that is obviously false. The man who says *I want you to do it* means literally that he wants you to do it. The point is that, as is always the case with indirection, he means not only what he says but something more as well. What is added in the indirect cases is not any additional or different SENTENCE meaning, but additional SPEAKER meaning. Evidence that these sentences keep their literal meanings when uttered as indirect requests is that responses that are appropriate to their literal utterances are appropriate to their indirect speech act utterances (as we noted in our discussion of Fact 4), e.g.:

Can you pass the salt?

No, sorry, I can't, it's down there at the end of the table.

Yes, I can. (Here it is.)

FACT 8: *It is a consequence of Fact 7 that when one of these sentences is uttered with the primary illocutionary point of a directive, the literal illocutionary act is also performed.* In every one of these cases, the speaker issues a directive BY WAY OF asking a question or making a statement. But the fact that his primary illocutionary intent is directive does not alter the fact that he is asking a question or making a statement. Additional evidence for Fact 8 is that a subsequent report of the utterance can truly report the literal illocutionary act.

Thus, e.g., the utterance of *I want you to leave now, Bill* can be reported by an utterance of *He told me he wanted me to leave, so I left.* Or, the utterance of *Can you reach the salt?* can be reported by an utterance of *He asked me whether I could reach the salt.* Similarly, an utterance of *Could you do it for me, Henry; could you do it for me and Cynthia and the children?* can be reported by an utterance of *He asked me whether I could do it for him and Cynthia and the children.*

This point is sometimes denied. I have seen it claimed that the literal illocutionary acts are always defective or are not 'conveyed' when the sentence is used to perform a nonliteral primary illocutionary act. As far as our examples are concerned, the literal illocutions are always conveyed and are sometimes, but not in general, defective. For example, an indirect speech act utterance of *Can you reach the salt?* may be defective in the sense that S may already know the answer. But even this form NEED not be defective. (Consider, e.g., *Can you give me change for a dollar?.*) Even when the literal utterance is defective, the indirect speech act does not depend on its being defective.

AN EXPLANATION IN TERMS OF THE THEORY OF SPEECH ACTS

The difference between the example concerning the proposal to go to the movies and all of the other cases is that the other cases are systematic. What we need to do, then, is to describe an example in such a way as to show how the apparatus used on the first example will suffice for these other cases and also will explain the systematic character of the other cases.

I think the theory of speech acts will enable us to provide a simple explanation of how these sentences, which have one illocutionary force as part of their meaning, can be used to perform an act with a different illocutionary force. Each type of illocutionary act has a set of conditions that are necessary for the successful and felicitous performance of the act. To illustrate this, I will present the conditions on two types of acts within the two genuses, directive and commissive (Searle, 1969: chap. 3).

A comparison of the list in Table 16.1 of felicity conditions on the directive class of illocutionary acts and our list of types of sentences used to perform indirect directives show that Groups 1–6 of types can be reduced to three types: those having to do with felicity conditions on the performance of a directive illocutionary act, those having to do with reasons for doing the act, and those embedding one element inside another one. Thus, since the ability of H to perform A (Group 1) is a preparatory condition, the desire of S that H perform A (Group 2) is the sincerity condition, and the predication of A of H (Group 3) is the propositional content condition, all of Groups 1–3 concern felicity conditions on directive illocutionary acts. Since wanting to do something is a reason par excellence for doing it, Group 4 assimilates to Group 5, as both concern reasons for doing A. Group 6 is a special class only by courtesy, since its elements either are performative verbs or are already contained in the other two categories of felicity conditions and reasons.

Ignoring the embedding cases for the moment, if we look at our lists and our sets of

Table 16.1. Directive and Commissive Felicity Conditions

	Directive (request)	Commissive (promise)
Preparatory condition	H is able to perform A.	S is able to perform A. He wants S to perform A.
Sincerity condition	S wants H to do A.	S intends to do A.
Propositional content condition	S predicates a future act A of H.	S predicates a future act A of S.
Essential condition	Counts as an attempt by S to get H to do A.	Counts as the undertaking by S of an obligation to do A.

conditions, the following generalizations naturally emerge:

GENERALIZATION 1: *S can make an indirect request (or other directive) by either asking whether or stating that a preparatory condition concerning H's ability to do A obtains.*

GENERALIZATION 2: *S can make an indirect directive by either asking whether or stating that the propositional content condition obtains.*

GENERALIZATION 3: *S can make an indirect directive by stating that the sincerity condition obtains, but not by asking whether it obtains.*

GENERALIZATION 4: *S can make an indirect directive by either stating that or asking whether there are good or overriding reasons for doing A, except where the reason is that H wants or wishes, etc., to do A, in which case he can only ask whether H wants, wishes, etc., to do A.*

It is the existence of these generalizations that accounts for the systematic character of the relation between the sentences in Groups 1–6 and the directive class of illocutionary acts. Notice that these are generalizations and not rules. The rules of speech acts (or some of them) are stated in the list of conditions presented earlier. That is, for example, it is a rule of the directive class of speech acts that the directive is defective if the hearer is unable to perform the act, but it is precisely not a rule of speech acts or of conversation that one can perform a directive by asking whether the preparatory condition obtains. The theoretical task is to show how that generalization will be a consequence of the rule, together with certain other information, namely, the factual background information and the general principles of conversation.

Our next task is to try to describe an example of an indirect request with at least the same degree of pedantry we used in our description of the rejection of a proposal. Let us take the simplest sort of case: At the dinner table, X says to Y, *Can you pass the salt?* by way of asking Y to pass the salt. Now, how does Y know that X is requesting him to pass the salt instead of just asking a question about his abilities to pass the salt? Notice that not everything will do as a request to pass the salt. Thus, if X had said *Salt is made of sodium chloride* or *Salt is mined in the Tatra mountains*, without some special stage setting, it is very unlikely that Y would take either of these

utterances as a request to pass the salt. Notice further that, in a normal conversational situation, Y does not have to go through any conscious process of inference to derive the conclusion that the utterance of *Can you pass the salt?* is a request to pass the salt. He simply hears it as a request. This fact is perhaps one of the main reasons why it is tempting to adopt the false conclusion that somehow these examples must have an imperative force as part of their meaning or that they are 'ambiguous in context,' or some such. What we need to do is offer an explanation that is consistent with all of Facts 1–8 yet does not make the mistake of hypostatizing concealed imperative forces or conversational postulates. A barebones reconstruction of the steps necessary for Y to derive the conclusion from the utterance might go roughly as follows:

STEP 1: *Y has asked me a question as to whether I have the ability to pass the salt (fact about the conversation).*

STEP 2: *I assume that he is cooeprating in the conversation and that therefore his utterance has some aim or point (principles of conversational cooperation).*

STEP 3: *The conversational setting is not such as to indicate a theoretical interest in my salt-passing ability (factual background information).*

STEP 4: *Furthermore, he probably already knows that the answer to the question is yes (factual background information). (This step facilitates the move to Step 5, but is not essential.)*

STEP 5: *Therefore, his utterance is probably not just a question. It probably has some ulterior illocutionary point (inference from Steps 1, 2, 3, and 4). What can it be?*

STEP 6: *A preparatory condition for any directive illocutionary act is the ability of H to perform the act predicated in the propositional content condition (theory of speech acts).*

STEP 7: *Therefore, X has asked me a question the affirmative answer to which would entail that the preparatory condition for requesting me to pass the salt is satisfied (inference from Steps 1 and 6).*

STEP 8: *We are now at dinner and people normally use salt at dinner; they pass it back and forth, try to get others to pass it back and forth, etc. (background information).*

STEP 9: *He has therefore alluded to the satisfaction of a preparatory condition for a request whose obedience conditions it is quite likely he wants me to bring about (inference from Steps 7 and 8).*

STEP 10: *Therefore, in the absence of any other plausible illocutionary point, he is probably requesting me to pass him the salt (inference from Steps 5 and 9).*

The hypothesis being put forth in this chapter is that all the cases can be similarly analyzed. According to this analysis, the reason I can ask you to pass the salt by saying *Can you pass the salt?* but not by saying *Salt is made of sodium chloride* or *Salt is mined in the Tatra mountains* is that your ability to pass the salt is a preparatory condition for requesting you to pass the salt in a way that the other sentences are not related to requesting you to pass the salt. But obviously, that answer is not by itself sufficient, because not all questions about your abilities are requests. The hearer therefore needs some way of finding out when the utterance is just a question about his abilities and when it is a request made by way of asking a question about his abilities. It is at this point that the general principles of conversation (together with factual background information) come into play.

The two features that are crucial, or so I am suggesting, are, first, a strategy for establishing the existence of an ulterior illocutionary point beyond the illocutionary point contained in the meaning of the sentence, and second, a device for finding out what the ulterior illocutionary point is. The first is established by the principles of conversation operating on the information of the hearer and the speaker, and the second is derived from the theory of speech acts together with background information. The generalizations are to be explained by the fact that each of them records a strategy by means of which the hearer can find out how a primary illocutionary point differs from a secondary illocutionary point.

The chief motivation—though not the only motivation—for using these indirect forms is politeness. Notice that, in the example just given, the *Can you* form is polite in at least two respects. Firstly, X does not presume to know about Y's abilities, as he would if he issued an imperative sentence; and, secondly, the form gives—or at least appears to give—Y the option of refusing, since a yes–no question allows *no* as a possible answer. Hence, compliance can be made to appear a free act rather than obeying a command.[6]

SOME PROBLEMS

It is important to emphasize that I have by no means demonstrated the thesis being argued for in this chapter. I have so far only suggested a pattern of analysis that is consistent with the facts. Even supposing that this pattern of analysis could be shown to be successful in many more cases, there are still several problems that remain:

PROBLEM 1: The biggest single problem with the foregiong analysis is this: If, as I have been arguing, the mechanisms by which indirect speech acts are meant and understood are perfectly general—having to do with the theory of speech acts, the principles of cooperative conversation, and shared background information—and not tied to any particular syntactical form, then why is it that some syntactical forms work better than others? Why can I ask you to do something by saying *Can you hand me that book on the top shelf?* but not, or not very easily, by saying *Is it the case that you at present have the ability to hand me that book on the top shelf?*

Even within such pairs as:

Do you want to do A?

Do you desire to do A?

and:

Can you do A?

Are you able to do A?

there is clearly a difference in indirect illocutionary act potential. Note, for example, that the first member of each pair takes *please* more readily than the second. Granting that none of these pairs are exact synonyms, and granting that all the sentences have some use as indirect requests, it is still essential to explain the differences in their indirect illocutionary act potential. How, in short, can it be the case that some sentences are not imperative idioms and yet function as forms for idiomatic requests?

The first part of the answer is this: The theory of speech acts and the principles of conversational cooperation do, indeed, provide a framework within which indirect illocutionary acts can be meant and understood. However, within this framework certain forms will tend to become conventionally established as the standard idiomatic forms for indirect speech acts. While keeping their literal meanings, they will acquire conventional uses as, e.g., polite forms for requests.

It is by now, I hope, uncontroversial that there is a distinction to be made between meaning and use, but what is less generally recognized is that there can be conventions of usage that are not meaning conventions. I am suggesting that *can you, could you, I want you to,* and numerous other forms are conventional ways of making requests (and in that sense it is not incorrect to say they are idioms), but at the same time they do not have an imperative meaning (and in that sense it would be incorrect to say they are idioms). Politeness is the most prominent motivation for indirectness in requests, and certain forms naturally tend to become the conventionally polite ways of making indirect requests.

If this explanation is correct, it would go some way toward explaining why there are differences in the indirect speech forms from one language to another. The mechanisms are not peculiar to this language or that, but at the same time the standard forms from one language will not always maintain their indirect speech act potential when translated from one language to another. Thus, *Can you hand me that book?* will function as an indirect request in English, but its Czech translation, *Můžete mi podat tu Knížku?* will sound very odd if uttered as a request in Czech.

A second part of the answer is this: In order to be a plausible candidate for an utterance as an indirect speech act, a sentence has to be idiomatic to start with. It is very easy to imagine circumstances in which: *Are you able to reach that book on the top shelf?* could be uttered as a request. But it is much harder to imagine cases in which *Is it the case that you at present have the ability to reach that book on the top shelf?* could be similarly used. Why?

I think the explanation for this fact may derive from another maxim of conversation having to do with speaking idiomatically. In general, if one speaks unidiomatically, hearers assume that there must be a special reason for it, and in consequence, various assumptions of normal speech are suspended. Thus, if I say, archaically, *Knowest thou him who calleth himself Richard Nixon?,* you are not likely to respond as you would to an utterance of *Do you know Richard Nixon?*

Besides the maxims proposed by Grice, there seems to be an additional maxim of conversation that could be expressed as follows: *Speak idiomatically unless there is some special reason not to.* For this reason, the normal conversational assumptions on which the possibility of indirect speech acts rests are in large part suspended in the nonidiomatic cases.

The answer, then, to Problem 1 is in two parts. In order to be a plausible candidate at all for use as an indirect speech act, a sentence has to be idiomatic. But within the class of idiomatic sentences, some forms tend to become entrenched as conventional devices for indirect speech acts. In the case of directives, in which politeness is the chief motivation for the indirect forms, certain forms are conventionally used as polite requests. Which kinds of forms are selected will, in all likelihood, vary form one language to another.

PROBLEM 2: Why is there an asymmetry between the sincerity condition and the others such that one can perform an indirect request only by asserting the satisfaction of a sincerity condition, not by querying it, whereas one can perform indirect directives by either asserting or querying the satisfaction of the propositional content and preparatory conditions?

Thus, an utterance of *I want you to do it* can be a request, but not an utterance of *Do I want you to do it?* The former can take *please,* the latter cannot. A similar asymmetry occurs in the case of reasons: *Do you want to leave us alone?* can be a request, but not *You want to leave us alone.*[7] Again, the former can take *please,* the latter cannot. How is one to explain these facts?

I believe the answer is that it is odd, in normal circumstances, to ask other people about the existence of one's own elementary psychological states, and odd to assert the existence of other people's elementary psychological states when addressing them. Since normally you are never in as good a position as I am to assert what I want, believe, intend, and so on, and since I am normally not in as good a position as you to assert what you want, believe, intend, and so on, it is, in general, odd for me to ask you about my states or tell you about yours. We shall see shortly that this asymmetry extends to the indirect performance of other kinds of speech acts.

PROBLEM 3: Though this chapter is not intended as being about English syntactical forms, some of the sentences on our lists are of enough interest to deserve special comment. Even if it should turn out that these peculiar cases are really imperative idioms, like *how about . . . ?*, it would not alter the general lines of my argument; it would simply shift some examples out of the class of indirect speech acts into the class of imperative idioms.

One interesting form is *why not plus verb,* as in *Why not stop here?* This form, unlike *Why don't you?*, has many of the same syntactical constraints as imperative sentences. For example, it requires a voluntary verb. Thus, one cannot say **Why not resemble your grandmother?* unless one believes that one can resemble someone as a voluntary action, whereas one can say *Why not imitate your grandmother?* Furthermore, like imperative sentences, this form requires a reflexive when it takes a second-person direct object, e.g., *Why not wash yourself?* Do these facts prove that the *Why not . . . ?* (and the *why . . . ?*) forms are imperative in meaning? I think they are not. On my account, the way an utterance of *why not?* works is this: In asking *Why not stop here?* as a suggestion to stop here, S challenges H to provide reasons for not doing something on the tacit assumption that the absence of reasons for not doing something is itself a reason for doing it, and the suggestion to do it is therefore made indirectly in accordance with the generalization that alluding to a reason for doing something is a way of making an indirect directive to do it. This analysis is supported by several facts. First, as we have already seen, this form can have a literal utterance in which it is not uttered as a suggestion; second, one can respond to the suggestion with a response appropriate to the literal utterance, e.g., *Well, there are several reasons for not stopping here. First. . . .* And third, one can report an utterance of one of these, without reporting any directive illocutionary forces, in the form *He asked me why we shouldn't stop there.* And here the occurrence of the practical *should* or *ought* (not the theoretical *should* or *ought*) is sufficient to account for the requirement of a voluntary verb.

Other troublesome examples are provided by occurrences of *would* and *could* in indirect speech acts. Consider, for example, utterances of *Would you pass me the salt?* and *Could you hand me that book?* It is not easy to analyze

these forms and to describe exactly how they differ in meaning from *Will you pass me the salt?* and *Can you hand me that book?* Where, for example, are we to find the *if* clause, which, we are sometimes told, is required by the so-called subjunctive use of these expressions? Suppose we treat the *if* clause as *if I asked you to.* Thus, *Would you pass me the salt?* is short for *Would you pass me the salt if I asked you to?*

There are at least two difficulties with this approach. First, it does not seem at all plausible for *could,* since your abilities and possibilities are not contingent on what I ask you to do. But second, even for *would* it is unsatisfactory, since *Would you pass me the salt if I asked you to?* does not have the same indirect illocutionary act potential as the simple *Would you pass me the salt?* Clearly, both forms have uses as indirect directives, but, equally clearly, they are not equivalent. Furthermore, the cases in which *would* and *could* interrogative forms DO have a nondirect use seem to be quite different from the cases we have been considering, e.g., *Would you vote for a Democrat?* or *Could you marry a radical?* Notice, for example, that an appropriate response to an utterance of these might be, e.g., *Under what conditions?* or *It depends on the situation.* But these would hardly be appropriate responses to an utterance of *Would you pass me the salt?* in the usual dinner table scene we have been envisaging.

Could seems to be analyzable in terms of *would* and possibility or ability. Thus, *Could you marry a radical* means something like *Would it be possible for you to marry a radical? Would,* like *will,* is traditionally analyzed either as expressing want or desire or as a future auxiliary.

The difficulty with these forms seems to be an instance of the general difficulty about the nature of the subjunctive and does not necessarily indicate that there is any imperative meaning. If we are to assume that *would* and *could* have an imperative meaning, then it seems we will be forced to assume, also, that they have a commissive meaning as well, since utterances of *Could I be of assistance?* and *Would you like some more wine?* are both normally offers. I find this conclusion implausible because it involves an unnecessary proliferation of meanings. It violates Occam's Razor regarding concepts. It is more economical to assume that *could* and *would* are univocal in *Could you pass the salt?*, *Could I be of assistance?*, *Would you stop making that noise?*, and *Would you like some more wine?*. However, a really satisfactory analysis of these forms awaits a satisfactory analysis of the subjunctive. The most plausible analysis of the indirect request forms is that the suppressed *if* clause is the polite *if you please* or *if you will*.

EXTENDING THE ANALYSIS

I want to conclude this chapter by showing that the general approach suggested in it will work for other types of indirection besides just directives. Obvious examples, often cited in the literature, are provided by the sincerity conditions. In general, one can perform any illocutionary act by asserting (though not by questioning) the satisfaction of the sincerity condition for that act. Thus, for example:

I am sorry I did it. (an apology)

I think/believe he is in the next room. (an assertion)

I am so glad you won. (congratulations)

I intend to try harder next time, coach. (a promise)

I am grateful for your help. (thanks)

I believe, however, that the richest mine for examples other than directives is provided by commissives, and a study of the examples of sentences used to perform indirect commissives (especially offers and promises) shows very much the same patterns that we found in the study of directives. Consider the following sentences, any of which can be uttered to perform an indirect offer (or, in some cases, a promise).

I. Sentences concerning the preparatory conditions:
   A. that S is able to perform the act:
      Can I help you?
      I can do that for you.
      I could get it for you.
      Could I be of assistance?
   B. that H wants S to perform the act:
      Would you like some help?
      Do you want me to go now, Sally?
      Wouldn't you like me to bring some more next time I come?
      Would you rather I came on Tuesday?

II. Sentences concerning the sincerity condition:
      I intend to do it for you.
      I plan on repairing it for you next week.

III. Sentences concerning the propositional content condition:
      I will do it for you.
      I am going to give it to you next time you stop by.
      Shall I give you the money now?

IV. Sentences concerning S's wish or willingness to do A:
      I want to be of any help I can.
      I'd be willing to do it (if you want me to).

V. Sentences concerning (other) reasons for S's doing A:
      I think I had better leave you alone.
      Wouldn't it be better if I gave you some assistance?
      You need my help, Cynthia.

Notice that the point made earlier about the elementary psychological states holds for these cases as well: One can perform an indirect illocutionary act by asserting, but not by querying, one's own psychological states; and one can perform an indirect illocutionary act by querying, but not by asserting, the presence of psychological states in one's hearer.

Thus, an utterance of *Do you want me to leave?* can be an offer to leave, but not *You want me to leave*. (Though it can be, with the tag question *You want me to leave, don't you?*) Similarly, *I want to help you out* can be uttered as an offer, but not *Do I want to help you out?*

The class of indirect commissives also includes a large number of hypothetical sentences:

If you wish any further information, just let me know.

If I can be of assistance, I would be most glad to help.

If you need any help, call me at the office.

In the hypothetical cases, the antecedent concerns either one of the preparatory conditions, or the presence of a reason for doing A, as in *If it would be better for me to come on Wednesday, just let me know.* Note also that, as well as hypothetical sentences, there are iterated cases of indirection. Thus, e.g., *I think I ought to help you out* can be uttered as an indirect offer made by way of making an indirect assertion. These examples suggest the following further generalizations:

GENERALIZATION 5: *S can make an indirect commissive by either asking whether or stating that the preparatory condition concerning his ability to do A obtains.*

GENERALIZATION 6: *S can make an indirect commissive by asking whether, though not by stating that, the preparatory condition concerning H's wish or want that S do A obtains.*

GENERALIZATION 7: *S can make an indirect commissive by stating that, and in some forms by asking whether, the propositional content condition obtains.*

GENERALIZATION 8: *S can make an indirect commissive by stating that, but not by asking whether, the sincerity condition obtains.*

GENERALIZATION 9: *S can make an indirect commissive by stating that or by asking whether there are good or overriding reasons for doing A, except where the reason is that S wants or desires to do A, in which case he can only state but not ask whether he wants to do A.*

I would like to conclude by emphasizing that my approach does not fit any of the usual explanatory paradigms. The philosopher's paradigm has normally been to get a set of logically necessary and sufficient conditions for the phenomena to be explained; the linguist's paradigm has normally been to get a set of structural rules that will generate the phenomena to be explained. I am unable to convince myself that either of these paradigms is appropriate for the present problem. The problems seem to me somewhat like those problems in the epistemological analysis of perception in which one seeks to explain how a perceiver recognizes an object on the basis of imperfect sensory input. The question, How do I know he has made a request when he only asked me a question about my abilities? may be like the question, How do I know it was a car when all I perceived was a flash going past me on the highway? If so, the answer to our problem may be neither 'I have a set of axioms from which it can be deduced that he made a request' nor 'I have a set of syntactical rules that generate an imperative deep structure for the sentence he uttered.'

ACKNOWLEDGMENTS

I am indebted for comments on earlier drafts of this study to Julian Boyd, Charles Fillmore, Dorothea Franck, Georgia Green, George Lakoff, Dagmar Searle, and Alan Walworth.

NOTES

1. The class of 'directive' illocutionary acts includes acts of ordering, commanding, requesting, pleading, begging, praying, entreating, instructing, forbidding, and others. See Searle (1975) for an explanation of this notion.

2. For an explanation of the notion of 'illocutionary point' and its relation to illocutionary force, see Searle (1975).

3. In what follows, I use the letters *H, S,* and *A* as abbreviations for 'hearer,' 'speaker,' and 'act' or 'action.'

4. This form is also included in Group 2.

5. There are some idioms in this line of business, however, for example *How about* as used in proposals and requests: *How about going to the movies tonight? How about giving me some more beer?*

6. I am indebted to Dorothea Franck for discussion of this point.

7. This point does not hold for the etymologically prior sense of *want* in which it means 'need.'

REFERENCES

Searle, J. R. (1975). "A Taxonomy of Illocutionary Acts." In K. Gunderson (ed.), *Language, Mind, and Knowledge: Minnesota Studies in the Philosophy of Science.* Minneapolis: University of Minnesota Press.

Searle, J. R. (1969). *Speech Acts.* New York: Cambridge University Press.

17

Assertion

ROBERT C. STALNAKER

Let me begin with some truisms about assertions. First, assertions have content; an act of assertion is, among other things, the expression of a proposition—something that represents the world as being a certain way. Second, assertions are made in a context—a situation that includes a speaker with certain beliefs and intentions, and some people with their own beliefs and intentions to whom the assertion is addressed. Third, sometimes the content of the assertion is dependent on the context in which it is made, for example, on who is speaking or when the act of assertion takes place. Fourth, acts of assertion affect, and are intended to affect, the context, in particular the attitudes of the participants in the situation; how the assertion affects the context will depend on its content.

My aim in this paper is to sketch some theoretical concepts with which to develop these truisms, and to show how these concepts can be used to explain some linguistic phenomena. I want to suggest how content and context might be represented in a theory of speech, and how the interaction of content and context to which the above mentioned

truisms point might be described. I will not propose an analysis of assertion, but I will make some modest claims about the way assertions act on the contexts in which they are made, and the way contexts constrain the interpretation of assertions. In conclusion, I will look briefly at an example of a phenomenon which I think these modest claims help to explain.

Three notions will play a central role in the theory I will sketch: the notion of a PROPOSITION, the notion of a PROPOSITIONAL CONCEPT, and the notion of SPEAKER PRESUPPOSITION. Each of these three notions will be defined or explained in terms of the notion of a POSSIBLE WORLD, or a possible state of the world, so one might think it important to begin with the question, what is a possible world? This is a good question, but I will not try to answer it here, and I am not sure that an abstract theory of speech should say very much in answer to it. In particular inquiries, deliberations, and conversations, alternative states of the subject matter in question are conceived in various different ways depending on the interests and attitudes of the partici-

Robert C. Stalnaker, "Assertion." In *Syntax and Semantics*, vol. 9: *Pragmatics*, edited by P. Cole, 315–322. Copyright © 1978 by Academic Press, Inc. Reprinted by permission of the publisher.

Assertion

hing that is
essential to
:k to distin-
'hat things
may be that
ial structure
vhat is done
native states
ns about the
ves. The de-
possible sit-
a theory of
,udes does
,itment to
)f the uni-
heorize at a

erms of pos-
the context
logic.[2] The
a function
from possible worlds into truth values (true or
false). More roughly and intuitively, a proposition is a rule for determining a truth value as
a function of the facts—of the way the world
is. Or, a proposition is a way—any way—of
picking out a set of possible states of affairs—
all those for which the proposition takes the
value true.

The intuitive motivation for this analysis is
something like the following. A proposition—
the content of an assertion or belief—is a representation of the world as being a certain
way. But for any given representation of the
world as being a certain way, there will be a
set of all the possible states of the world which
accord with the representation—which *are*
that way. So any proposition determines a set
of possible worlds. And, for any given set of
possible worlds, to locate the actual world in
that set is to represent the world as being a certain way. So every set of possible worlds determines a proposition. Furthermore, any two assertions or beliefs will represent the world as
being the SAME way if and only if they are true
in all the same possible worlds. If we assume,
as seems reasonable, that representations
which represent the world as being the same
way have the same content (express the same
proposition), then we can conclude that there
is a one-one correspondence between sets of
possible worlds and propositions. Given this

correspondence, it seems reasonable to use
sets of possible worlds, or (equivalently) functions from possible worlds into truth values, to
play the role of propositions in our theory.
The analysis defines propositions in terms of
their essential function—to represent the
world.[3]

Supposing for convenience of exposition
that there is just a small finite number of possible states of the world, we might represent a
proposition by enumerating the truth values
that it has in the different possible worlds, as
in the following matrix:

$$A \qquad \begin{array}{ccc} i & j & k \\ \hline \boxed{\text{T}} & \text{F} & \text{T} \end{array}$$

i, j, and *k* are the possible worlds—the different possible sets of facts that determine the
truth value of the proposition.

But there is also a second way that the facts
enter into the determination of the truth value
of what is expressed in an utterance: It is a
matter of fact that an utterance has the content which it has. What one says—the proposition he expresses—is itself something that
might have been different if the facts had been
different; and if one is mistaken about the
truth value of an utterance, this is sometimes
to be explained as a misunderstanding of what
was said rather than as a mistake about the
truth value of what was actually said. The difference between the two ways that truth values
depend on facts is exploited in the familiar rid-
dle, *If you call a horse's tail a leg how many
legs does a horse have?* The answer, of course,
is four, since calling a tail a leg does not make
it one, but one can see a different way to take
the question.

Let me give a simple example: I said *You
are a fool* to O'Leary. O'Leary IS a fool, so
what I said was true, although O'Leary does
not think so. Now Daniels, who is no fool and
who knows it, was standing nearby, and he
thought I was talking to him. So both O'Leary
and Daniels thought I said something false:
O'Leary understood what I said, but disagrees
with me about the facts; Daniels, on the other
hand, agrees with me about the fact (he knows
that O'Leary is a fool), but misunderstood
what I said. Just to fill out the example, let me
add that O'Leary believes falsely that Daniels

is a fool. Now compare the possible worlds, *i*, *j*, and *k*. *i* is the world as it is, the world we are in; *j* is the world that O'Leary thinks we are in; and *k* is the world Daniels thinks we are in. If we ignore possible worlds other than *i*, *j*, and *k*, we can use matrix *A* to represent the proposition I actually expressed. But the following TWO-DIMENSIONAL matrix also represents the second way that the truth value of my utterance is a function of the facts:

$$
\begin{array}{c|ccc}
B & i & j & k \\
\hline
i & T & F & T \\
j & T & F & T \\
k & F & T & F \\
\end{array}
$$

The vertical axis represents possible worlds in their role as context—as what determines what is said. The horizontal axis represents possible worlds in their role as the arguments of the functions which are the propositions expressed. Thus the different horizontal lines represent WHAT IS SAID in the utterance in various different possible contexts. Notice that the horizontal line following *i* is the same as the one following *j*. This represents the fact that O'Leary and I agree about what was said. Notice also that the vertical column under *i* is the same as the one under *k*. This represents the fact that Daniels and I agree about the truth values of both the proposition I in fact expressed and the one Daniels thought I expressed.

In a sense, I said something true at *i* and false at *j* and *k*, even though in none of these worlds did I express the proposition that is true in *i* and false in *j* and *k*. Although not expressed in any of the contexts, this proposition is represented in the matrix. I will call it the DIAGONAL PROPOSITION since it is the function from possible worlds into truth values whose values are read along the diagonal of the matrix from upper left to lower right. In general, this is the proposition that is true at *i* for any *i* if and only if what is expressed in the utterance at *i* is true at *i*. I shall say more about diagonal propositions later.

I will call what a matrix like *B* represents a PROPOSITIONAL CONCEPT. A propositional concept is a function from possible worlds into propositions, or, equivalently, a function from an ordered pair of possible worlds into a

truth value. Each concrete utterance token can be associated with the propositional concept it determines, and, I will suggest below, some of the principles constraining the interpretation and evaluation of assertions are constraints on propositional concepts determined by assertive utterances rather than simply on the propositions expressed. This is my motivation for introducing propositional concepts, but one can study this kind of structure from an abstract point of view, independently of utterances or contexts of utterance. The abstract theory of what I am calling propositional concepts has received some attention from logicians recently under the name TWO-DIMENSIONAL MODAL LOGIC.[4] The theory focusses on the notion of a two-dimensional modal operator.

A two-dimensional modal operator is an operator which takes a propositional concept into a propositional concept. If *o* is such an operator, then the meaning of *o* will be a rule that gives you the propositional concept expressed by *oP* in terms of the one expressed by *P*, for any *P*. I will describe one such operator, and contrast it with more traditional extensional and intensional sentence operators.[5]

The dagger is an operator which takes the diagonal proposition and projects it onto the horizontal. If φ is the diagonal proposition determined by *P*, then †*P* expresses φ relative to all contexts. So if *B* is the propositional concept determined by my statement to O'Leary in the example above, the following matrix gives the propositional concept, †*B*:

$$
\begin{array}{c|ccc}
\dagger B & i & j & k \\
\hline
i & T & F & F \\
j & T & F & F \\
k & T & F & F \\
\end{array}
$$

What †*B* says is roughly this: *What is said in S's utterance of* **You are a fool** *is true,* where the definite description, *What is said in S's utterance of* **You are a fool** may be a nonrigid designator—a description that refers to different propositions in different worlds. Notice that the dagger always yields a constant propositional concept as its value. That is, whatever the case with *P*, †*P* will always express the same proposition relative to every context. If *P* itself is already a constant propositional concept in this sense, then $\dagger P$ will express the same propositional concept as P.[6]

Compare this operator with a more familiar modal operator, propositional necessity. $\Box P$ expresses in any world the proposition that is true at that world if and only if the proposition expressed by P at that world is the necessary proposition—the one that is true in all possible worlds. Propositional necessity is a one-dimensional operator in the following sense: The proposition expressed by $\Box P$ at any point depends only on the proposition expressed by P at that point. To evaluate $\Box P$ on any horizontal line, one need look only at the values of P on that line. This distinction between one- and two-dimensional operators parallels, on the next level up, the distinction between extensional and intensional operators. Compare the extensional negation operator: to evaluate $\sim P$ at any point, one need look only at the value of P at that point. Extensional operators take points (truth values) into points; one-dimensional operators take horizontal lines (propositions) into horizontal lines; two-dimensional operators take the whole matrix (the propositional concept) into another whole matrix. Each kind of operator is a generalization of the kind preceding it.[7]

Let me mention one complex operator, square-dagger, which says that the diagonal proposition is necessary. This can be understood as the A PRIORI TRUTH operator, observing the distinction emphasized in the work of Saul Kripke between a priori and necessary truth. An a priori truth is a statement that, while perhaps not expressing a necessary proposition, expresses a truth in every context. This will be the case if and only if the diagonal proposition is necessary, which is what the complex operator says. I will illustrate this with a version of one of Kripke's own examples (1971: 273–275). Suppose that in worlds i, j, and k, a certain object, a metal bar, is one, two, and three meters long, respectively, at a certain time t. Now suppose an appropriate authority fixes the reference of the expression *one meter* by making the following statement in each of the worlds i, j, and k: *This bar is one meter long.* Matrix C below represents the propositional concept for this statement. Matrix $\Box \dagger C$ represents the propositional concept for the claim that this statement is a priori true:

C	i	j	k		$\Box \dagger C$	i	j	k
i	T	F	F		i	T	T	T
j	F	T	F		j	T	T	T
k	F	F	T		k	T	T	T

The proposition expressed by the authority is one that might have been false, although he couldn't have expressed a false proposition in that utterance.

I have said how propositions are to be understood, and what propositional concepts are. The third notion I need is the concept of speaker presupposition. This, I want to suggest, is the central concept needed to characterize speech contexts. Roughly speaking, the presuppositions of a speaker are the propositions whose truth he takes for granted as part of the background of the conversation. A proposition is presupposed if the speaker is disposed to act as if he assumes or believes that the proposition is true, and as if he assumes or believes that his audience assumes or believes that it is true as well. Presuppositions are what is taken by the speaker to be the COMMON GROUND of the participants in the conversation, what is treated as their COMMON KNOWLEDGE or MUTUAL KNOWLEDGE.[8] The propositions presupposed in the intended sense need not really be common or mutual knowledge; the speaker need not even believe them. He may presuppose any proposition that he finds it convenient to assume for the purpose of the conversation, provided he is prepared to assume that his audience will assume it along with him.

It is PROPOSITIONS that are presupposed—functions from possible worlds into truth values. But the more fundamental way of representing the speaker's presuppositions is not as a set of propositions, but rather as a set of possible worlds, the possible worlds compatible with what is presupposed. This set, which I will call the CONTEXT SET, is the set of possible worlds recognized by the speaker to be the "live options" relevant to the conversation. A proposition is presupposed if and only if it is true in all of these possible worlds. The motivation for representing the speaker's presuppositions in terms of a set of possible worlds in this way is that this representation is appropriate to a description of the conversational process in terms of its essential purposes. To engage in conversation is, essentially, to distinguish among alternative possible ways that things may be. The purpose of expressing propositions is to make such distinctions. The presuppositions define the limits of the set of alternative possibilities among which speakers intend their expressions of propositions to distinguish.

Each participant in a conversation has his own context set, but it is part of the concept of presupposition that a speaker assumes that the members of his audience presuppose everything that he presupposes. We may define a NONDEFECTIVE CONTEXT as one in which the presuppositions of the various participants in the conversation are all the same. A DEFECTIVE CONTEXT will have a kind of instability, and will tend to adjust to the equilibrium position of a nondefective context. Because hearers will interpret the purposes and content of what is said in terms of their own presuppositions, any unnoticed discrepancies between the presuppositions of speaker and addressees [are] likely to lead to a failure of communication. Since communication is the point of the enterprise, everyone will have a motive to try to keep the presuppositions the same. And because in the course of a conversation many clues are dropped about what is presupposed, participants will normally be able to tell that divergences exist if they do. So it is not unreasonable, I think, to assume that in the normal case contexts are nondefective, or at least close enough to being nondefective.

A context is CLOSE ENOUGH to being nondefective if the divergences do not affect the issues that actually arise in the course of the conversation. Suppose for example that you know that Jones won the election, believe mistakenly that I know it as well, and are prepared to take the truth of this proposition for granted if the occasion should arise, say by using it as a suppressed premiss in an argument, or by using the description *the man who won the election* to refer to Jones. On my dispositional account of speaker presupposition, if you are prepared to use the proposition in this way, then you DO presuppose that Jones won the election, even if you never have the opportunity to display this disposition because the subject does not come up. Since I do not know that Jones won the election, I do NOT presuppose it, and so the context is defective. But the defect may be harmless.

It will not necessarily be harmless: If the news is of sufficiently urgent interest, your failure to raise the subject may count as a display of your disposition to take its truth for granted. There will not be exactly a failure of communication, but there will be a misperception of the situation if I infer from the fact that you do not tell me who won that you do not know either.

A conversation is a process taking place in an ever-changing context. Think of a state of a context at any given moment as defined by the presuppositions of the participants as represented by their context sets. In the normal, nondefective case, the context sets will all be the same, so for this case we can talk of the context set of the conversation. Now how does an assertion change the context? There are two ways, the second of which, I will suggest, should be an essential component of the analysis of assertion. I will mention the first just to set it apart from the second: The fact that a speaker is speaking, saying the words he is saying in the way he is saying them, is a fact that is usually accessible to everyone present. Such observed facts can be expected to change the presumed common background knowledge of the speaker and his audience in the same way that any obviously observable change in the physical surroundings of the conversation will change the presumed common knowledge. If a goat walked into the room, it would normally be presupposed, from that point, that there was a goat in the room. And the fact that this was presupposed might be exploited in the conversation, as when someone asks, *How did **that** thing get in here?*, assuming that others will know what he is talking about. In the same way, when I speak, I presuppose that others know I am speaking, even if I do not assume that anyone knew I was going to speak before I did. This fact, too, can be exploited n the conversation, as when Daniels says *I am bald,* taking it for granted that his audience can figure out who is being said to be bald.

I mention this commonplace way that assertions change the context in order to make clear that the context on which an assertion has its ESSENTIAL effect is not defined by what is presupposed before the speaker begins to speak, but will include any information which the speaker assumes his audience can infer from the performance of the speech act.

Once the context is adjusted to accommodate the information that the particular utterance was produced, how does the CONTENT of an assertion alter the context? My suggestion is a very simple one: To make an assertion is to reduce the context set in a particular way, provided that there are no objections from the other participants in the conversation. The particular way in which the context set is reduced is that all of the possible situations incompatible with what is said are eliminated. To put it a slightly different way, the essential effect of an assertion is to change the presuppositions of the participants in the conversation by adding the content of what is asserted to what is presupposed. This effect is avoided only if the assertion is rejected.

I should emphasize that I do not propose this as a DEFINITION of assertion, but only as a claim about one effect which assertions have, and are intended to have—an effect that should be a component, or a consequence, of an adequate definition. There are several reasons why one cannot define assertion in terms of this effect alone. One reason is that other speech acts, like making suppositions, have and are intended to have the same effect. A second reason is that there may be various indirect, even nonlinguistic, means of accomplishing the same effect which I would not want to call assertions. A third reason is that the proposed essential effect makes reference to another speech act—the rejection of an assertion,[9] which presumably cannot be explained independently of assertion.

Our proposed effect is clearly not a sufficient condition for assertion. Is it even a necessary condition? It might be objected that a person who makes an assertion does not necessarily intend to get his audience to accept that what he asserts is true. The objector might argue as follows: Take one of your own examples, your statement to O'Leary that he is a fool. You knew in advance that O'Leary would not accept the assertion, so according to your account, you knew in advance that your assertion would fail to achieve its essential effect. That example should be anomalous if your account were correct, but it is not anomalous. Would it not be more plausible to characterize assertion as trying to get the audience to accept THAT THE SPEAKER ACCEPTS the content of the assertion?[10] But this Gricean twist is not required. My suggestion about the essential effect of assertion does not imply that speakers INTEND to succeed in getting the addressee to accept the content of the assertion, or that they believe they will, or even might succeed. A person may make an assertion knowing it will be rejected just as Congress may pass a law knowing it will be vetoed, a labor negotiator may make a proposal knowing it will be met by a counterproposal, or a poker player may place a bet knowing it will cause all the other players to fold. Such actions need not be pointless, since they all have secondary effects, and there is no reason why achieving the secondary effects cannot be the primary intention of the agent performing the action. The essential effects will still be relevant even when it is a foregone conclusion that the assertion, legislative act, proposal, or bet will be rejected, since one generally explains why the action has the secondary effects it has partly in terms of the fact that it would have had certain essential effects had it not been rejected.

One may think of a nondefective conversation as a game where the common context set is the playing field and the moves are either attempts to reduce the size of the set in certain ways or rejections of such moves by others. The participants have a common interest in reducing the size of the set, but their interests may diverge when it comes to the question of how it should be reduced. The overall point of the game will of course depend on what kind of conversation it is—for example, whether it is an exchange of information, an argument, or a briefing.

The game could be expanded by introducing other kinds of moves like making stipulations, temporary assumptions, or promises, asking questions, and giving commands and permissions.[11] Each of these kinds of linguistic action is presumably performed against a background of presuppositions, and can be understood partly in terms of the effect that it has, or is intended to have, on the presuppositions, and on the subsequent behavior, of the other participants in the conversation.

This is a very abstract, and a very simple, sketch of what goes on when someone says something to someone else. But there is enough in it to motivate some principles that are useful for explaining regularities of linguistic usage. I will mention three such rules which illustrate the interaction of context and content. Given the framework of propositions, presupposition, and assertion, the principles are all pretty obvious, which is as it should be. They are not intended as empirical generalizations about how particular languages or idiosyncratic social practices work. Rather, they are proposed as principles that can be defended as essential conditions of rational communication, as principles to which any rational agent would conform if he were engaged in a practice that fits the kind of very abstract and schematic sketch of communication that I have given.[12]

I will list the three principles and then discuss them in turn.

1. A proposition asserted is always true in some but not all of the possible worlds in the context set.

2. Any assertive utterance should express a proposition, relative to each possible world in the context set, and that proposition should have a truth value in each possible world in the context set.

3. The same proposition is expressed relative to each possible world in the context set.

The first principle says that a speaker should not assert what he presupposes to be true, or what he presupposes to be false. Given the meaning of presupposition and the essential effect ascribed to the act of assertion, this should be clear. To assert something incompatible with what is presupposed is self-defeating; one wants to reduce the context set, but not to eliminate it altogether. And to assert something which is already presupposed is to attempt to do something that is already done.

This rule, like the others, can be applied in several ways. If one could fix independently what was presupposed and what was said on a given occasion, then one could use the rule to evaluate the speaker's action. If he failed to conform to the rule, then he did something that, from the point of view of the conversation, was unreasonable, inefficient, disorderly, or uncooperative. But one can also use the rule, or the presumption that the speaker is conforming to the rule, as evidence of what was presupposed, or of what was said. Perhaps as more than just evidence. The rules may be taken to define partially what is presupposed and what is said in a context by constraining the relation between them. So, if a speaker says something that admits of two interpretations, one compatible with the context set and one not, then the context, through the princi-

ple, disambiguates. If the speaker says something that seems prima facie to be trivial, one may take it as a clue that the speaker's context set is larger than was realized—that the context was defective—or one may look for another interpretation of what he said. There are thus three ways to react to an apparent violation of the rule: First, one may conclude that the context is not as it seems. Second, one may conclude that the speaker didn't say (or didn't mean) what he seemed to say (or to mean). Third, one may conclude that the rule was indeed violated. Since there is usually a lot of flexibility in both the context and the interpretation of what is said, the third reaction will be an unusual one, although it will not be unusual to use the rule to explain why some utterance would have been deviant if it had occurred in a given context.

The second principle concerns truth value gaps, and connects semantic presupposition with pragmatic speaker presupposition. The principle implies that that if a sentence x semantically presupposes a proposition φ (in the sense that x expresses a truth or a falsehood only if φ is true), then φ is presupposed by the speaker in the sense of presupposition discussed above.

There are two different ways that a truth value gap may arise: a sentence may fail to express a proposition at all in some possible situation, or it may succeed in expressing a proposition, but express one that is a PARTIAL function—one that is undefined for certain possible worlds. Both kinds of truth value gap are excluded from the context set by this rule.

The rationale for this rule is as follows: The point of an assertion is to reduce the context set in a certain determinate way. But if the proposition is not true or false at some possible world, then it would be unclear whether that possible world is to be included in the reduced set or not. So the intentions of the speaker will be unclear.

Again this principle can be used in any of the three ways: to interpret what is said, as a clue to what is presupposed, or as a basis for evaluating the action of a speaker.

The third principle, which says that an utterance must express the SAME proposition relative to each possible world in the context set, is closely related in its motivation to a fundamental assumption of the logical atomists and the logical empiricist tradition. In Wittgenstein's terminology the assumption is this: Whether a proposition (read: sentence) has sense cannot depend on whether another proposition is true (cf. *Tractatus;* Proposition 2.0211). Meaning and truth must be sharply divided, according to this tradition, in order that one be able to use language to communicate in a determinate way. One must be able to tell what a statement says independently of any facts that might be relevant to determining its truth. Now it has always been clear that this kind of principle requires qualification, since it is a matter of fact that words mean what they mean. And the phenomena of context dependence are evidence of other ways in which what is said is a function of what is true. The framework of presupposition and assertion at once provides a natural way to qualify this traditional assumption so as to make it compatible with the phenomena, and a clear explanation of why it must hold in the qualified version. To see why the principle must hold, look at the matrix for the propositional concept *D*. Suppose the context set consists of *i, j,* and *k,* and the speaker's utterance determines *D*. What would he be

$$
\begin{array}{c|ccc}
D & i & j & k \\
\hline
i & T & T & T \\
j & F & F & T \\
k & F & T & T \\
\end{array}
$$

asking his audience to do? Something like this: If we are in world *i,* leave the context set the same: if we are in world *j,* throw out worlds *i* and *j,* and if we are in world *k,* throw out just world *i.* But of course the audience does not know which of those worlds we are in, and if it did the assertion would be pointless. So the statement, made in that context, expresses an intention that is essentially ambiguous. Notice that the problem is not that the speaker's utterance has failed to determine a unique proposition. Assuming that one of the worlds *i, j,* or *k* is in fact the actual world, then that world will fix the proposition unambiguously. The problem is that since it is unknown which proposition it is that is expressed, the expression of it cannot do the job that it is supposed to do.[13]

As with the other principles, one may respond to apparent violations in different ways.

One could take an apparent violation as evidence that the speaker's context set was smaller than it was thought to be, and eliminate possible worlds relative to which the utterance receives a divergent interpretation. Or, one could reinterpret the utterance so that it expresses the same proposition in each possible world. Consider an example: hearing a woman talking in the next room, I tell you, *That is either Zsa Zsa Gabor or Elizabeth Anscombe.* Assuming that both demonstrative pronouns and proper names are rigid designators—terms that refer to the same individual in all possible worlds—this sentence comes out expressing either a necessary truth or a necessary falsehood, depending on whether it is one of the two mentioned women or someone else who is in the next room. Let *i* be the world in which it is Miss Gabor, *j* the world in which it is Professor Anscombe, and *k* a world in which it is someone else, say Tricia Nixon Cox. Now if we try to bring the initial context set into conformity with the third principle by shrinking it, say by throwing out world *k,* we will bring it into conflict with the first principle by making the assertion trivial. But if we look at what is actually going on in the example, if we ask what possible states of affairs the speaker would be trying to exclude from the context set if he made that statement, we can work backward to the proposition expressed. A moment's reflection shows that what the speaker is saying is that the actual world is either *i* or *j,* and not *k.* What he means to communicate is that the diagonal proposition of the matrix *E* exhibited below, the proposition expressed by †*E,* is true.

$$
\begin{array}{c|ccc}
E & i & j & k \\
\hline
i & T & T & T \\
j & T & T & T \\
k & F & F & F \\
\end{array}
\qquad
\begin{array}{c|ccc}
\dagger E & i & j & k \\
\hline
i & T & T & F \\
j & T & T & F \\
k & T & T & F \\
\end{array}
$$

I suggest that a common way of bringing utterances into conformity with the third principle is to interpret them to express the diagonal proposition, or to perform on them the operation represented by the two-dimensional operator DAGGER. There are lots of examples. Consider: *Hesperus is identical with Phosphorus, it is now three o'clock, an ophthalmologist is an eye doctor.* In each case, to construct a context which conforms to the first principle, a context in which the proposition expressed is neither trivial nor assumed false, one must include possible worlds in which the sentence, interpreted in the standard way, expresses different propositions. But in any plausible context in which one of these sentences might reasonably be used, it is clear that the diagonal proposition is the one that the speaker means to communicate. The two-dimensional operator DAGGER may represent a common operation used to interpret, or reinterpret, assertions and other speech acts so as to bring them into conformity with the third principle constraining acts of assertion.

To conclude, let me show how this last suggestion can help to explain a puzzle concerning singular negative existential statements. The puzzle arises in the context of a causal or historical explanation theory of reference according to which proper names refer to their bearers, not in virtue of the fact that the bearer has certain properties expressed in the sense of the name, but rather in virtue of certain causal or historical connections between the referent and the speaker's use of the name.[14] According to this theory, the PROPOSITION expressed by a simple singular statement containing a proper name, like *O'Leary is a fool,* is the one that is true if and only if the individual who is in fact causally connected in the right way with the speaker's use of the name has the property expressed in the predicate. So the proposition is determined as a function of the individual named rather than as a function of the name, or the sense of the name.

What does this theory say about statements like *O'Leary does not exist?* If the statement is true (which this one happens to be), then there is no individual appropriately related to the speaker's use of the name, and thus no proposition determined as a function of such an individual. So at least for TRUE negative existential statements, it seems that proper names must play a different role in the determination of the proposition expressed from the role they play in ordinary predicative statements.

Perhaps a negative existential statement says, simply, that there is no individual standing in the right causal relation to the speaker's use of the name.[15] This does seem to get the truth conditions right for negative existential ASSERTIONS, but it clearly gets them wrong for some other kinds of singular negative existen-

tial constructions. Consider, for example, counterfactual suppositions, as in the antecedent of the conditional *If Aristotle hadn't existed, the history of philosophy would have been very different from the way it was.*[16] Clearly the proposition expressed in the antecedent of this conditional is not the proposition that our use of the name *Aristotle* is not appropriately connected with any individual. THAT proposition is compatible with Aristotle's existence. Furthermore, if Aristotle hadn't existed, then our uses of his name probably would not have existed either. The proper name seems to function in the antecedent of the counterfactual more like the way it functions in ordinary predicative statements: The proposition is determined as a function of the PERSON Aristotle; it is true in possible worlds where HE does not exist, and false in possible worlds where HE does exist.

So it seems that not only do proper names act differently in negative existential assertions than they do in singular predicative assertions, they also act differently in negative existential ASSERTIONS than they do in negative existential SUPPOSITIONS. What one asserts when he says *Aristotle does not exist* seems to be different from what one supposes when he says *Suppose Aristotle hadn't existed.*

Let us see how the pragmatic principle can account for these facts. Begin with the most straightforward semantic account of negative existential constructions: *Aristotle does not exist,* like *Aristotle was wise,* is a proposition about Aristotle. It is true in possible worlds whose domains contain the person WE call Aristotle and false in possible worlds whose domains do not contain that person. What if the name does not, in fact, refer? Suppose for example the statement is *Sherlock Holmes does not exist.* Then the proposition will be necessarily false, by the same rule, since the domain of no possible world contains the actual person WE call Sherlock Holmes.[17] Now let us use this straightforward semantic account to construct a propositional concept for an utterance of *Sherlock Holmes does not exist.* Let the world *i* be the actual world. Let *j* be a world in which a famous detective named *Sherlock Holmes* lived in nineteenth century London, and Sir Arthur Conan Doyle wrote a series of historical accounts of his cases. Let world *k* be a possible world in which Sir Arthur Conan

Doyle was a famous detective named *Sherlock Holmes* who wrote a series of autobiographical accounts of his own cases under the pseudonym *Sir Arthur Conan Doyle*. These stipulations determine the following two-dimensional matrix for the utterance:

	i	*j*	*k*
i	T	T	T
j	T	F	T
k	F	F	F

G appears above the matrix.

Now suppose *i, j,* and *k* are a context set (say a person has heard these three rumors about the origin of the Sherlock Holmes stories and does not know which is true). As the matrix shows, the utterance violates the third principle, and so a reinterpretation is forced on it. Diagonalization, or the dagger operation, brings the utterance into line with the principle, and yields the intuitively right result:

	i	*j*	*k*
i	T	F	F
j	T	F	F
k	T	F	F

But now contrast the case of the counterfactual. To interpret the statement *If Aristotle hadn't existed, the history of philosophy would have been very different from the way it was,* we do not need to diagonalize, since in any possible context appropriate to THAT statement, it will be presupposed that Aristotle does exist. So the proposition supposed is the one obtained by the straightforward rule.[18] Again, this is intuitively the right result.

We have not escaped the conclusion that the content of the assertion *Aristotle did not exist* is different from the content of the supposition *suppose Aristotle hadn't existed.* But we have explained that consequence using a single SEMANTIC account of singular negative existential constructions—the account which is most natural, given the causal theory of names—together with independently motivated pragmatic principles.

The general strategy which this explanation illustrates is to use pragmatic theory—theory of conversational contexts—to take some of the weight off semantic and syntactic theory. Some other problems where I think this strategy and this theory will prove useful are the explanation of presupposition phenomena,[19] the explanation of the differences between subjunctive and indicative conditionals,[20] the analysis of definite descriptions, and the behavior of deictic and anaphoric pronouns. My hope is that by recognizing the interaction of some relatively simple contextual factors with the rules for interpreting and evaluating utterances, one can defend simpler semantic and grammatical analyses and give more natural explanations of many linguistic phenomena.

ACKNOWLEDGMENTS

The development of the ideas in this paper was stimulated by David Kaplan's lectures, some years ago, on the logic of demonstratives. The influence of Paul Grice's ideas about logic and conversation will also be evident. I have benefited from discussions of earlier versions of this paper with both of these philosophers and many others, including David Lewis, Zeno Vendler, and Edmund Gettier. I am indebted to the John Simon Guggenheim Memorial Foundation for research support.

NOTES

1. I argued in Stalnaker (1976a) that one can take possible worlds seriously without accepting an implausible metaphysics.

2. The possible worlds analysis of propositions was suggested originally by Saul Kripke in the early 1960s.

3. I recognize that I am skating quickly over large problems here. In particular, the identity conditions which the analysis assigns to propositions have some extremely paradoxical consequences (such as that there is only one necessary proposition) which seem to make the analysis particularly unsuited for an account of the objects of propositional attitudes. I discuss some of these problems, inconclusively, in Stalnaker (1976b).

4. The most general discussion of two-dimensional modal logic I know of is in Segerberg (1973). See also Aqvist (1973) and Kamp (1971). The earliest investigations of two-dimensional operators were, I believe, carried out in the context of tense logic by Frank Vlach and Hans Kamp at UCLA.

5. The tense logic analogue of the dagger operator was, according to David Lewis, invented by Frank Vlach and is discussed in his UCLA Ph.D. dissertation (1974). The notation is Lewis's. See Lewis (1973a:63–64n).

6. Another operator which has intuitive application is represented by Lewis as an upside-down dagger. What it does is to project the diagonal proposition onto the VERTICAL, which, in effect, turns contingent truths into necessary truths and contingent falsehoods into necessary falsehoods. Hans Kamp (1971) proposed the temporal analogue of this operator as a representative of the sentence adverb *now*. *It is **now** true that A* said at time t expresses a proposition that is true at all times just in case A is true at t. The operator makes a difference when *now* is embedded in the context of other temporal modifiers. Using it, one can represent sentences like *Once, everyone now alive hadn't yet been born* without object language quantifiers over times. David Lewis and David Kaplan have suggested that this operator shows the semantic function of expressions like *actually* and *in fact,* as in *If I had more money than I in fact have, I would be happier.*

7. Although the dagger and the upside-down dagger are defined as operators on propositional concepts, they can be generalized to any kind of two-dimensional intension. For example, they may be interpreted as operators on two-dimensional individual concepts, or on property concepts. Let a represent a definite description, say *the President of the United States,* and let $i, j,$ and k be three times, say 1967, 1971, and 1975. Matrix (i) below represents the two-dimensional intension of this definite description relative to these times. Matrix (ii) represents the rigid description, *the person who is **in fact**, or **now**, the President of the United States.* This is the two-dimensional intension of ⬇a. David Kaplan, in "DTHAT," discusses this operator on singular terms and compares it with Keith Donnellan's account of the referential use of definite descriptions.

(i)

	i	j	k
i	LJ	RN	GF
j	LJ	RN	GF
k	LJ	RN	GF

(ii)

	i	j	k
i	LJ	LJ	LJ
j	RN	RN	RN
k	GF	GF	GF

8. I have discussed this concept of presupposition in two earlier papers, Stalnaker (1973) and Stalnaker (1974). Stephen Schiffer (1972:30–42) and David Lewis (1969:52–60) have discussed concepts of mutual knowledge and common knowledge which resemble the notion of presupposition I have in mind. Paul Grice spoke, in the William James Lectures, of propositions having COMMON GROUND STATUS in a conversation (published in part in Grice 1975 [Reprinted in this volume, Chapter 19]).

9. It should be made clear that to reject an assertion is not to assert or assent to the contradictory of the assertion, but only to refuse to accept the assertion. If an assertion is rejected, the context remains as it was. (More exactly, rejection of an assertion blocks the SECOND kind of effect that assertions have on the context. The first kind of effect cannot be blocked or withdrawn.)

10. David Kaplan, in discussion, raised this objection.

11. David Lewis (1973b) outlined a language game of commanding and permitting which would fit into this framework.

12. The influence of Grice's theory of conversation should be clear from my discussion of the application of these principles.

13. A clarification is needed to resolve an ambiguity. The third principle says that the proposition expressed in any possible world in the context set must coincide WITHIN THE CONTEXT SET with the proposition expressed in any other possible world in the context set. So, for example, if the context set is $\{i, j\}$, then an utterance determining the propositional concept represented below will not violate the principle. Even though the proposition expressed in i diverges from the proposition expressed in j, the divergence is outside the context set. David Lewis pointed out the need for this clarification.

	i	*j*	*k*
i	T	F	T
j	T	F	F
k	F	T	T

14. The causal account of reference is defended, in general, in Kripke (1971) and Donnellan (1971). Donnellan (1974) discusses the problem of singular negative existential statements in the context of this account of reference.

15. Donnellan's explanation of the TRUTH CONDITIONS for singular negative existential statements is roughly in accord with this suggestion, but he cautions that the rule he proposes "does not provide an ANALYSIS of such statements: it does not tell us what such statements mean, or what propositions they express. This means that in this case we are divorcing truth conditions from meaning" (1974:25). According to Donnellan, "no obvious way of representing propositions expressed by existential statements suggests itself" (1974:30).

16. Kripke, in talks on this subject, has made this point about counterfactuals with negative existential antecedents.

17. I believe this straightforward semantic account is the one that Kripke has defended in the talks mentioned in note 16.

18. It is interesting to note that if the conditional were in the indicative mood, the result would have been different. This is because an indicative conditional is appropriate only in a context where it is an open question whether the antecedent is true. So to say *If Aristotle didn't exist* is to suppose just what is asserted when one asserts *Aristotle didn't exist.*

19. This is discussed in Stalnaker (1973).

20. This is discussed in Stalnaker (1976c).

REFERENCES

Aqvist, L. (1973). "Modal Logic with Subjunctive Conditionals and Dispositional Predicates." *Journal of Philosophical Logic* 2:1–76.

Donnellan, K. (1971). "Proper Names and Identifying Descriptions." In D. Davidson and G. Harman (eds.), *Semantics of Natural Language.* Dordrecht: Reidel.

Donnellan, K. (1974). "Speaking of Nothing." *Philosophical Review* 83:3–31.

Grice, H. P. (1975). "Logic and Conversation." In P. Cole and J. L. Morgan (eds.), *Syntax and Semantics.* Vol. 3: *Speech Acts.* New York: Academic Press. [Reprinted in this volume, Chapter 19]

Kamp, H. (1971). "Formal Properties of 'Now'." *Theoria* 37:227–273.

Kripke, S. (1971). "Naming and Necessity." In D. Davidson and G. Harman (eds.), *Semantics of Natural Language.* Dordrecht: Reidel.

Lewis, D. (1969). *Convention.* Cambridge, Mass.: Harvard University Press.

Lewis, D. (1973a). *Counterfactuals.* Oxford: Basil Blackwell.

Lewis, D. (1973b). "A Problem about Permission." Manuscript, Princeton University.

Schiffer, S. (1972). *Meaning.* Oxford: Clarendon Press.

Segerberg, K. (1973). "Two-dimensional Modal Logic." *Journal of Philosophical Logic* 2:77–96.

Stalnaker, R. C. (1973). "Presuppositions." *Journal of Philosophical Logic* 2:447–457.

Stalnaker, R. C. (1974). "Pragmatic Presuppositions." In M. K. Munitz and P. K. Unger (eds.), *Semantics and Philosophy.* New York: New York University Press. [Reprinted in this volume, Chapter 27]

Stalnaker, R. C. (1976a). "Possible Worlds." *Nous* 10:65–75.

Stalnaker, R. C. (1976b). "Propositions." In A. F. MacKay and D. D. Merrill (eds.), *Issues in the Philosophy of Language.* New Haven, Conn.: Yale University Press.

Stalnaker, R. C. (1976c). "Indicative Conditionals." In A. Kasher (ed.), *Language in Focus: Foundations, Methods, and Systems* [essays in honor of Y. Bar-Hillel]. Dordrecht: Reidel.

Vlach, F. (1973). ["'Now' and 'Then'; A Formal Study in the Logic of Tense Anaphora"]. Ph.D. diss., University of California, Los Angeles.

Wittgenstein, L. (1961). *Tractatus Logico-Philosophicus.* New York: Routledge and Kegan Paul. (Originally published in 1921)

18

Intention and Convention in Speech Acts

P. F. STRAWSON

I

In this paper I want to discuss some questions regarding J. L. Austin's notions of the illocutionary force of an utterance and of the illocutionary act which a speaker performs in making an utterance.[1]

There are two preliminary matters I must mention, if only to get them out of the way. Austin contrasts what he calls the 'normal' or 'serious' use of speech with what he calls 'etiolated' or 'parasitical' uses. His doctrine of illocutionary force relates essentially to the normal or serious use of speech and not, or not directly, to etiolated or parasitical uses; and so it will be with my comments on his doctrine. I am not suggesting that the distinction between the normal or serious use of speech and the secondary uses which he calls etiolated or parasitical is so clear as to call for no further examination; but I shall take it that there is such a distinction to be drawn and I shall not here further examine it.

My second preliminary remark concerns another distinction, or pair of distinctions, which Austin draws. Austin distinguishes the illocutionary force of an utterance from what he calls its 'meaning' and distinguishes between the illocutionary and the locutionary acts performed in issuing the utterance. Doubts may be felt about the second term of each of these distinctions. It may be felt that Austin has not made clear just what abstractions from the total speech act he intends to make by means of his notions of meaning and of locutionary act. Although this is a question on which I have views, it is not what the present paper is about. Whatever doubts may be entertained about Austin's notions of meaning and of locutionary act, it is enough for present purposes to be able to say, as I think we clearly can, the following about their relation to the notion of illocutionary force. The meaning of a (serious) utterance, as conceived by Austin, always embodies some limitation on its possible force, and sometimes—as, for example, in some cases where an explicit performative formula, like 'I apologize', is used—the meaning of an utterance may exhaust its force; that is, there may be no more to the force than there is to the meaning; but very often the meaning, though it limits, does not exhaust, the force. Similarly, there may sometimes be no more to say about the illocution-

P. F. Strawson, "Intention and Convention in Speech Acts," *Philosophical Review* 73 (1974): 439–460. Copyright © 1974 by The Philosophical Review. Reprinted by permission of the publisher and the author.

ary force of an utterance than we already know if we know what locutionary act has been performed; but very often there is more to know about the illocutionary force of an utterance than we know in knowing what locutionary act has been performed.

So much for these two preliminaries. Now I shall proceed to assemble from the text some indications as to what Austin means by the force of an utterance and as to what he means by an illocutionary act. These two notions are not so closely related that to know the force of an utterance is the same thing as to know what illocutionary act was actually performed in issuing it. For if an utterance with the illocutionary force of, say, a warning is not understood in this way (that is, as a warning) by the audience to which it is addressed, then (it is held) the illocutionary act of warning cannot be said to have been actually performed. 'The performance of an illocutionary act involves the securing of uptake'; that is, it involves 'bringing about the understanding of the meaning and of the force of the locution' (pp. 115–116).[2] Perhaps we may express the relation by saying that to know the force of an utterance is the same thing as to know what illocutionary act, *if any,* was actually performed in issuing it. Austin gives many examples and lists of words which help us to form at least a fair intuitive notion of what is meant by 'illocutionary force' and 'illocutionary act'. Besides these, he gives us certain general clues to these ideas, which may be grouped, as follows, under four heads:

1. Given that we know (in Austin's sense) the meaning of an utterance, there may still be a further question as to *how what was said was meant* by the speaker, or as to *how the words spoken were used,* or as to *how the utterance was to be taken* or *ought to have been taken* (pp. 98–99). In order to know the illocutionary force of the utterance, we must know the answer to this further question.

2. A locutionary act is an act *of* saying something; an illocutionary act is an act we perform *in* saying something. It is what we *do, in* saying what we *say.* Austin does not regard this characterization as by any means a satisfactory test for identifying kinds of illocutionary acts since, so regarded, it would admit many kinds of acts which he wishes to exclude from the class (p. 99 and Lecture X).

3. It is a sufficient, though not, I think, a necessary, condition of a verb's being the name of a *kind* of illocutionary act that it can figure, in the first person present indicative, as what Austin calls an explicit performative. (This latter notion I shall assume to be familiar and perspicuous.)

4. The illocutionary act is 'a conventional act; an act done as conforming to a convention' (p. 105). As such, it is to be sharply contrasted with the producing of certain effects, intended or otherwise, by means of an utterance. This producing of effects, though it too can often be ascribed *as an act* to the speaker (his *perlocutionary* act), is in no way a conventional act (pp. 120–121). Austin reverts many times to the 'conventional' nature of the illocutionary act (pp. 103, 105, 108, 115, 120, 121, 127) and speaks also of 'conventions of illocutionary force' (p. 114). Indeed, he remarks (pp. 120–121) that though acts which can properly be called by the same names as illocutionary acts—for example, acts of warning—can be brought off nonverbally, without the use of words, yet, in order to be properly called by these names, such acts must be *conventional* nonverbal acts.

II

I shall assume that we are clear enough about the intended application of Austin's notions of illocutionary force and illocutionary act to be able to criticize, by reference to cases, his general doctrines regarding those notions. It is the general doctrine I listed last above—the doctrine that an utterance's having such and such a force is a matter of convention—that I shall take as the starting point of inquiry. Usually this doctrine is affirmed in a quite unqualified way. But just once there occurs an interestingly qualified statement of it. Austin says, of the use of language with a certain illocutionary force, that 'it may . . . be said to be *conventional* in the sense that at least it could be made explicit by the performative formula' (p. 103). The remark has a certain authority in that it is the first explicit statement of the conventional nature of the illocutionary act. I shall refer to it later.

Meanwhile let us consider the doctrine in its unqualified form. Why does Austin say that the illocutionary act is a conventional act, an act done as conforming to a convention? I must first mention, and neutralize, two possible sources of confusion. (It may seem an excess of precaution to do so. I apologize to those who find it so.) First, we may agree (or not dispute) that any speech act is, as such, at least in part a conventional act. The performance of any *speech* act involves at least the observance or exploitation of some *linguistic* conventions, and every illocutionary act is a speech act. But it is absolutely clear that this is not the point that Austin is making in declaring the illocutionary act to be a conventional act. We must refer, Austin would say, to linguistic conventions to determine what *locutionary* act has been performed in the making of an utterance, to determine what the *meaning* of the utterance is. The doctrine now before us is the further doctrine that where force is *not* exhausted by meaning, the fact that an utterance has the further unexhausted force it has is also a matter of convention; or, where it is exhausted by meaning, the fact *that* it is, is a matter of convention. It is not just as being a speech act that an illocutionary act—for example, of warning—is conventional. A nonverbal act of warning is, Austin maintains, conventionally such in just the same way as an illocutionary—that is, verbal—act of warning is conventionally such.

Second, we must dismiss as irrelevant the fact that it can properly be said to be a matter of convention that an act of, for example, warning is correctly called by this name. For if this were held to be a ground for saying that illocutionary acts were conventional acts, then any describable act whatever would, as correctly described, be a conventional act.

The contention that illocutionary force is a matter of convention is easily seen to be correct in a great number of cases. For very many kinds of human transaction involving speech are governed and in part constituted by what we easily recognize as established conventions of procedure additional to the conventions governing the *meanings* of our utterances. Thus the fact that the word 'guilty' is pronounced by the foreman of the jury in court at the proper moment constitutes his utterance as the act of bringing in a verdict; and that this is so is certainly a matter of the conventional procedures of the law. Similarly, it is a matter of convention that if the appropri-

ate umpire pronounces a batsman 'out', he thereby performs the act of *giving the man out,* which no player or spectator shouting 'Out!' can do. Austin gives other examples, and there are doubtless many more which could be given, where there clearly exist statable conventions, relating to the circumstances of utterance, such that an utterance with a certain meaning, pronounced by the appropriate person in the appropriate circumstances, has the force it has *as* conforming to those conventions. Examples of illocutionary acts of which this is true can be found not only in the sphere of social institutions which have a legal point (like the marriage ceremony and the law courts themselves) or of activities governed by a definite set of rules (like cricket and games generally) but in many other relations of human life. The act of *introducing,* performed by uttering the words 'This is Mr. Smith', may be said to be an act performed as conforming to a convention. The act of surrendering, performed by saying *'Kamerad!'* and throwing up your arms when confronted with a bayonet, may be said to be (to have become) an act performed as conforming to an accepted convention, a conventional act.

But it seems equally clear that, although the circumstances of utterance are always relevant to the determination of the illocutionary force of an utterance, there are many cases in which it is not as conforming to an accepted *convention* of any kind (other than those linguistic conventions which help to fix the meaning of the utterance) that an illocutionary act is performed. It seems clear, that is, that there are many cases in which the illocutionary force of an utterance, though not exhausted by its meaning, is not owed to any *conventions* other than those which help to give it its meaning. Surely there may be cases in which to utter the words 'The ice over there is very thin' to a skater is to issue a warning (is to say something with the *force* of a warning) without its being the case that there is any statable convention at all (other than those which bear on the nature of the *locutionary* act) such that the speaker's act can be said to be an act done as conforming to that convention.

Here is another example. We can readily imagine circumstances in which an utterance of the words 'Don't go' would be correctly described not as a request or an order, but as an entreaty. I do not want to deny that there may be conventional postures or procedures for entreating: one can, for example, kneel down, raise one's arms and *say,* 'I entreat you.' But I do want to deny that an act of entreaty can be performed only as conforming to some such conventions. What makes *X*'s words to *Y* an *entreaty* not to go is something—complex enough, no doubt—relating to *X*'s situation, attitude to *Y,* manner, and current intention. There are questions here which we must discuss later. But to suppose that there is always and necessarily a convention conformed to would be like supposing that there could be no love affairs which did not proceed on lines laid down in the *Roman de la Rose* or that every dispute between men must follow the pattern specified in Touchstone's speech about the countercheck quarrelsome and the lie direct.

Another example. In the course of a philosophical discussion (or, for that matter, a debate on policy) one speaker *raises an objection* to what the previous speaker has just said. *X* says (or proposes) that *p* and *Y objects* that *q.* *Y*'s utterance has the force of an objection to *X*'s assertion (or proposal) that *p.* But where is the *convention* that constitutes it an objection? That *Y*'s utterance has the force of an objection may lie partly in the character of the dispute and of *X*'s contention (or proposal) and it certainly lies partly, in *Y*'s *view* of these things, in the bearing which he takes the proposition that *q* to have on the doctrine (or proposal) that *p.* But although there may be, there does not have to be, any convention involved, other than those linguistic conventions which help to fix the meanings of the utterances.

I do not think it necessary to give further examples. It seems perfectly clear that, if at least we take the expressions 'convention' and 'conventional' in the most natural way, the doctrine of the conventional nature of the illocutionary act does not hold generally. Some illocutionary acts are conventional; others are not (except in so far as they are locutionary acts). Why then does Austin repeatedly affirm the contrary? It is unlikely that he has made the simple mistake of generalizing from some cases to all. It is much more likely that he is moved by some further, and fundamental, feature of illocutionary acts, which it must be our business to discover. Even though we may decide that the description 'conventional' is not appropriately used, we may presume it worth our while to look for the reason for

using it. Here we may recall that oddly qualified remark that the performance of an illocutionary act, or the use of a sentence with a certain illocutionary force, 'may be said to be conventional in the sense that at least it *could* be made explicit by the performative formula' (p. 103). On this we may first, and with justice, be inclined to comment that there is no such *sense* of 'being conventional', that if this is a *sense* of anything to the purpose, it is a sense of 'being *capable* of being conventional'. But although this is a proper comment on the remark, we should not simply dismiss the remark with this comment. Whatever it is that leads Austin to call illocutionary acts in general 'conventional' must be closely connected with whatever it is about such acts as warning, entreating, apologizing, advising, that accounts for the fact that *they* at least *could* be made explicit by the use of the corresponding first-person performative form. So we must ask what it is about them that accounts for this fact. Obviously it will not do to answer simply that they are acts which can be performed by the use of words. So are many (perlocutionary) acts, like convincing, dissuading, alarming, and amusing, for which, as Austin points out, there is no corresponding first-person *performative* formula. So we need some further explanation.

III

I think a concept we may find helpful at this point is one introduced by H. P. Grice in his valuable article on *Meaning (Philosophical Review,* LXVII, 1957), namely, the concept of *someone's nonnaturally meaning something by an utterance.* The concept does not apply only to speech acts—that is, to cases where that by which someone nonnaturally means something is a *linguistic* utterance. It is of more general application. But it will be convenient to refer to that by which someone, *S,* nonnaturally means something as *S*'s *utterance.* The explanation of the introduced concept is given in terms of the concept of intention. *S* nonnaturally means something by an utterance *x* if *S* intends (i_1) to produce by uttering *x* a certain response (r) in an audience *A* and intends (i_2) that *A* shall recognize *S*'s intention (i_1) and intends (i_3) that this recognition on the part of *A* of *S*'s intention (i_1)

shall function as A's reason, or a part of his reason, for his response r. (The word 're-sponse', though more convenient in some ways than Grice's 'effect', is not ideal. It is intended to cover cognitive and affective states or attitudes as well as actions.) It is, evidently, an important feature of this definition that the securing of the response r is intended to be mediated by the securing of another (and always cognitive) effect in A; namely, recognition of S's intention to secure response r.

Grice's analysis of his concept is fairly complex. But I think a little reflection shows that it is not quite complex enough for his purpose. Grice's analysis is undoubtedly offered as an analysis of a situation in which one person is trying, in a sense of the word 'communicate' fundamental to any theory of meaning, to communicate with another. But it is possible to imagine a situation in which Grice's three conditions would be satisfied by a person S and yet, in this important sense of 'communicate', it would not be the case that S could be said to be trying to communicate by means of his production of x with the person A in whom he was trying to produce the response r. I proceed to describe such a situation.

S intends by a certain action to induce in A the belief that p; so he satisfies condition (i_1). He arranges convincing-looking 'evidence' that p, in a place where A is bound to see it. He does this, knowing that A is watching him at work, but *knowing also that A does not know that S knows that A is watching him at work*. He realizes that A will not take the *arranged* 'evidence' as genuine or natural evidence that p, but realizes, and indeed intends, that A will take his arranging of it as grounds for thinking that he, S, intends to induce in A the belief that p. That is, he intends A to recognize his (i_1) intention. So S satisfies condition (i_2). He knows that A has general grounds for thinking that S would not wish to make him, A, think that p unless it were known to S to be the case that p; and hence that A's recognition of his $(S's)$ intention to induce in A the belief that p will in fact seem to A a sufficient reason for believing that p. And he intends that A's recognition of his intention (i_1) should function in just this way. So he satisfies condition (i_3).

S, then, satisfies all Grice's conditions. But this is clearly not a case of attempted *com-munication* in the sense which (I think it is fair to assume) Grice is seeking to elucidate. A will indeed take S to be trying to bring it about that A is aware of some fact; but he will not take S as trying, in the colloquial sense, to 'let him know' something (or to 'tell' him something). But unless S at least brings it about that A takes him (S) to be trying to let him (A) know something, he has not succeeded in communicating with A; and if, as in our example, he has not even *tried* to bring this about, then he has not even *tried* to communicate with A. It seems a minimum further condition of his trying to do this that he should not only intend A to recognize his intention to get A to think that p, but that he should also *intend A to recognize his intention to get A to recognize his intention* to get A to think that p.

We might approximate more closely to the communication situation if we changed the example by supposing it not only clear to both A and S that A was watching S at work, but also clear to them both that it *was* clear to them both. I shall content myself, however, with drawing from the actually considered example the conclusion that we must add to Grice's conditions the further condition that S should have the further intention (i_4) that A should recognize his intention (i_2). It is possible that further argument could be produced to show that even adding this condition is not *sufficient* to constitute the case as one of attempted communication. But I shall rest content for the moment with the fact that this addition at least is necessary.

Now we might have expected in Grice's paper an account of what it is for A to *understand* something by an utterance x, an account complementary to the account of what it is for S to *mean* something by an utterance x. Grice in fact gives no such account, and I shall suggest a way of at least partially supplying this lack. I say 'at least partially' because the uncertainty as to the sufficiency of even the modified conditions for S's nonnaturally *meaning* something by an utterance x is reflected in a corresponding uncertainty in the sufficiency of conditions for A's understanding. But again we may be content for the moment with necessary conditions. I suggest, then, that for A (in the appropriate sense of 'understand') to understand *something* by utterance x, it is necessary (and perhaps sufficient) that there should be *some* complex intention of the (i_2) form, described above, which A takes S to have, and that for A to understand the utterance correctly, it is necessary that A should take S to have *the* complex intention of the (i_2) form which S does have. In other words, if A is to understand the utterance correctly, S's (i_4) intention and hence his (i_2) intention must be fulfilled. Of course it does not follow from the fulfillment of these intentions that his (i_1) intention is fulfilled; nor, consequently, that his (i_3) intention is fulfilled.

It is at this point, it seems, that we may hope to find a possible point of connection with Austin's terminology of 'securing uptake'. If we do find such a point of connection, we also find a possible starting point for an at least partial analysis of the notions of illocutionary force and of the illocutionary act. For to secure uptake is to secure understanding of (meaning and) illocutionary force; and securing understanding of illocutionary force is said by Austin to be an essential element in bringing off the illocutionary act. It is true that this doctrine of Austin's may be objected to.[3] For surely a man may, for example, actually have made such and such a bequest, or gift, even if no one ever reads his will or instrument of gift. We may be tempted to say instead that at least *the aim, if not the achievement,* of securing uptake is an essential element in the performance of the illocutionary act. To this, too, there is an objection. Might not a man really have made a gift, in due form, and take some satisfaction in the thought, even if he had no expectations of the fact ever being known? But this objection at most forces on us an amendment to which we are in any case obliged[4]: namely, that the aim, if not the achievement, of securing uptake is essentially *a standard, if not an invariable,* element in the performance of the illocutionary act. So the analysis of the aim of securing uptake remains an essential element in the analysis of the notion of the illocutionary act.

I V

Let us, then, make a tentative identification— to be subsequently qualified and revised—of

Austin's notion of uptake with that at least partially analysed notion of understanding (on the part of an audience) which I introduced just now as complementary to Grice's concept of somebody nonnaturally meaning something by an utterance. Since the notion of audience understanding is introduced by way of a fuller (though partial) analysis than any which Austin gives of the notion of uptake, the identification is equivalent to a tentative (and partial) analysis of the notion of uptake and hence of the notions of illocutionary act and illocutionary force. If the identification were correct, then it would follow that to say something with a certain illocutionary force is at least (in the standard case) to have a certain complex intention of the (i_4) form described in setting out and modifying Grice's doctrine.

Next we test the adequacy and explanatory power of this partial analysis by seeing how far it helps to explain other features of Austin's doctrine regarding illocutionary acts. There are two points at which we shall apply this test. One is the point at which Austin maintains that the production of an utterance with a certain illocutionary force is a conventional act in that unconventional sense of 'conventional' which he glosses in terms of general suitability for being made explicit with the help of an explicitly performative formula. The other is the point at which Austin considers the possibility of a general characterization of the illocutionary act as what we *do, in* saying what we say. He remarks on the unsatisfactoriness of this characterization in that it would admit as illocutionary acts what are not such; and we may see whether the suggested analysis helps to explain the exclusion from the class of illocutionary acts of those acts falling under this characterization which Austin wishes to exclude. These points are closely connected with each other.

First, then, we take the point about the general suitability of an illocutionary act for performance with the help of the explicitly performative formula for that act. The explanation of this feature of illocutionary acts has two phases; it consists of, first, a general, and then a special, point about intention. The first point may be roughly expressed by saying that in general a man can speak of his intention in performing an action with a kind of authority which he cannot command in predicting its outcome. What he intends in doing something is up to him in a way in which the results of his doing it are not, or not only, up to him. But we are concerned not with just any intention to produce any kind of effect by acting, but with a very special kind of case. We are concerned with the case in which there is not simply an intention to produce a certain response in an audience, but an intention to produce that response by means of recognition on the part of the audience of the intention to produce that response, this recognition to serve as part of the reason that the audience has for its response, and the intention that this recognition should occur being itself intended to be recognized. The speaker, then, not only has the general authority on the subject of his intention that any agent has; he also has a motive, inseparable from the nature of his act, for making that intention clear. For he will not have secured understanding of the illocutionary force of his utterance, he will not have performed the act of communication he sets out to perform, unless his complex intention is grasped. Now clearly, for the enterprise to be possible at all, there must exist, or he must find, means of making the intention clear. If there exists any conventional linguistic means of doing so, the speaker has both a right to use, and a motive for using, those means. One such means, available sometimes, which comes very close to the employment of the explicit performative form, would be to attach, or subjoin, to the substance of the message what looks like a force-elucidating *comment* on it, which may or may not have the form of a self-ascription. Thus we have phrases like 'This is only a suggestion' or 'I'm only making a suggestion'; or again 'That was a warning' or 'I'm warning you'. For using such phrases, I repeat, the speaker has the *authority* that anyone has to speak on the subject of his intentions and the *motive* that I have tried to show is inseparable from an act of communication.

From such phrases as these—which have, *in appearance,* the character of comments on utterances other than themselves—to the explicit performative formula the step is only a short one. My reason for *qualifying* the remark that such phrases have the character of comments on utterances other than themselves is this. We are considering the case in which the subjoined quasi-comment is addressed to the same audience as the utterance on which it is a quasi-comment. Since it is *part* of the speaker's audience-directed intention to make clear the character of his utterance as, for example, a warning, and since the subjoined quasi-comment directly subserves this intention, it is better to view the case, appearances notwithstanding, *not* as a case in which we have two utterances, one commenting on the other, but as a case of a single unitary speech act. Crudely, the addition of the quasi-comment 'That was a warning' is *part* of the total act of warning. The effect of the short step to the explicitly performative formula is simply to bring appearances into line with reality. When that short step is taken, we no longer have, even in appearance, two utterances, one a comment on the other, but a single utterance in which the first-person performative verb *manifestly* has that peculiar logical character of which Austin rightly made so much, and which we may express in the present context by saying that the verb serves not exactly to *ascribe* an intention to the speaker but rather, in Austin's phrase, to *make explicit* the type of communication intention with which the speaker speaks, the type of force which the utterance has.

The above might be said to be a deduction of the general possibility and utility of the explicitly performative formula for the cases of illocutionary acts not essentially conventional. It may be objected that the deduction fails to show that the intentions rendered explicit by the use of performative formulae *in general* must be of just the complex form described, and hence fails to justify the claim that just this kind of intention lies at the core of all illocutionary acts. And indeed we shall see that this claim would be mistaken. But before discussing why, we shall make a further application of the analysis at the second testing point I mentioned. That is, we shall see what power it has to explain why some of the things we may be *doing, in* saying what we say, are not illocutionary acts and could not be rendered explicit by the use of the performative formula.

Among the things mentioned by Austin which we might be doing in saying things, but which are not illocutionary acts, I shall consider the two examples of (1) showing off and

(2) insinuating. Now when we show off, we are certainly trying to produce an effect on the audience: we talk, indeed, for effect; we try to impress, to evoke the response of admiration. But it is no part of the intention to secure the effect *by means of* the recognition of the intention to secure it. It is no part of our total intention to secure recognition of the intention to produce the effect at all. On the contrary: recognition of the intention might militate against securing the effect and promote an opposite effect, for example, disgust.

This leads on to a further general point not explicitly considered by Austin, but satisfactorily explained by the analysis under consideration. In saying to an audience what we do say, we very often intend not only to produce the primary response *r* by means of audience recognition of the intention to produce that response, but to produce further effects by means of the production of the primary response *r*. Thus my further purpose in informing you that *p* (that is, aiming to produce in you the primary cognitive response of knowledge or belief that *p*) may be to bring it about thereby that you adopt a certain line of conduct or a certain attitude. In saying what I say, then, part of what I am *doing* is trying to influence your attitudes or conduct in a certain way. Does this part of what I am doing in saying what I say contribute to determining the character of the illocutionary act I perform? And if not, why not? If we take the first question strictly as introduced and posed, the answer to it is 'No'. The reason for the answer follows from the analysis. We have no complex intention (i_4) that there should be recognition of an intention (i_2) that there should be recognition of an intention (i_1) that the further effect should be produced; for it is no part of our intention that the further effect should be produced by way of recognition of our intention that it should be; the production in the audience of belief that *p* is intended to be itself the means whereby his attitude or conduct is to be influenced. We secure uptake, perform the act of communication that we set out to perform, if the audience understands us as *informing* him that *p*. Although it is true that, in saying what we say, we are in fact *trying* to produce the further effect—this is part of what we are doing, whether we succeed in producing the effect or not—yet this does not enter into the characterization of the illocutionary act. With this case we have to contrast the case in which, instead of aiming at a primary response and a further effect, the latter to be secured through the former alone, we aim at a complex primary response. Thus in the case where I do not simply inform, but warn, you that *p*, among the intentions I intend you to recognize (and intend you to recognize as intended to be recognized), are not only the intention to secure your belief that *p*, but the intention to secure that you are on your guard against *p*-perils. The difference (one of the differences) between showing off and warning is that your recognition of my intention to put you on your guard may well contribute to putting you on your guard, whereas your recognition of my intention to impress you is not likely to contribute to my impressing you (or not in the way I intended).[5]

Insinuating fails, for a different reason, to be a type of illocutionary act. An essential feature of the intentions which make up the illocutionary complex is their overtness. They have, one might say, essential avowability. This is, in one respect, a logically embarrassing feature. We have noticed already how we had to meet the threat of a counterexample to Grice's analysis of the communicative act in terms of three types of intention—(i_1), (i_2), and (i_3)—by the addition of a further intention (i_4) that an intention (i_2) should be recognized. We have no proof, however, that the resulting enlarged set of conditions is a complete analysis. Ingenuity might show it was not; and the way seems open to a regressive series of intentions that intentions should be recognized. While I do not think there is anything necessarily objectionable in this, it does suggest that the complete and rounded-off set of conditions aimed at in a conventional analysis is not easily and certainly attainable in these terms. That is why I speak of the feature in question in these terms. That is why I speak of the feature in question as logically embarrassing. At the same time it enables us easily to dispose of insinuating as a candidate for the status of a type of illocutionary act. The whole point of insinuating is that the audience is to *suspect*, but not more than suspect, the intention, for example, to induce or disclose a certain belief. The intention one has in insinuating is essentially nonavowable.

Now let us take stock a little. We tentatively laid it down as a necessary condition of securing understanding of the illocutionary force of an utterance that the speaker should succeed in bringing it about that the audience took him, in issuing his utterance, to have a complex intention of a certain kind, namely the intention that the audience should recognize (and recognize as intended to be recognized) his intention to induce a certain response in the audience. The suggestion has, as we have just seen, certain explanatory merits. Nevertheless we cannot claim general application for it as even a partial analysis of the notions of illocutionary force and illocutionary act. Let us look at some reasons why not.

V

I remarked earlier that the words 'Don't go' may have the force, *inter alia,* either of a request or of an entreaty. In either case the primary intention of the utterance (if we presume the words to be uttered with the *sense* 'Don't go *away*') is that of inducing the person addressed to stay where he is. His staying where he is is the primary response aimed at. But the only other intentions mentioned in our scheme of partial analysis relate directly or indirectly to recognition of the primary intention. So how, in terms of that scheme, are we to account for the variation in illocutionary force between requests and entreaties?

This question does not appear to raise a major difficulty for the scheme. The scheme, it seems, merely requires supplementing and enriching. *Entreaty,* for example, is a matter of trying to secure the primary response not merely through audience recognition of the intention to secure it, but through audience recognition of a complex attitude of which this primary intention forms an integral part. A wish that someone should stay may be held in different ways: passionately or lightly, confidently or desperately; and it may, for different reasons, be part of a speaker's intention to secure recognition of *how* he holds it. The most obvious reason, in the case of entreaty, is the belief, or hope, that such a revelation is more likely to secure the fulfillment of the primary intention.

But one may not only request and entreat; one may *order* someone to stay where he is. The words 'Don't go' may have the illocutionary force of an order. Can we so simply accommodate in our scheme *this* variation in illocutionary force? Well, we can accommodate it; though not so simply. We can say that a man who issues an order typically intends his utterance to secure a certain response, that he intends this intention to be recognized, and its recognition to be a reason for the response, that he intends the utterance to be recognized as issued in a certain social context such that certain social rules or conventions apply to the issuing of utterances in this context and such that certain consequences may follow in the event of the primary response not being secured, that he intends *this* intention too to be recognized, and finally that he intends the recognition of these last features to function as an element in the reasons for the response on the part of the audience.

Evidently, in this case, unlike the case of entreaty, the scheme has to be extended to make room for explicit reference to social convention. It can, with some strain, be so extended. But as we move further into the region of institutionalized procedures, the strain becomes too much for the scheme to bear. On the one hand, one of its basic features—namely, the reference to an intention to secure a definite response in an audience (over and above the securing of uptake)—has to be dropped. On the other, the reference to social conventions of procedure assumes a very much greater importance. Consider an umpire giving a batsman out, a jury bringing in a verdict of guilty, a judge pronouncing sentence, a player redoubling at bridge, a priest or a civil officer pronouncing a couple man and wife. Can we say that the umpire's primary intention is to secure a certain response (say, retiring to the pavilion) from a certain audience (say, the batsman), the jurymen's to secure a certain response (say, the pronouncing of sentence) from a certain audience (say, the judge), and then build the rest of our account around this, as we did, with some strain, in the case of the order? Not with plausibility. It is not even possible, in other than a formal sense, to isolate, among all the participants in the procedure (trial, marriage, game) to which the utterance belongs, a particular audience to whom the utterance can be said to be addressed.

Does this mean that the approach I suggested to the elucidation of the notion of illocutionary force is entirely mistaken? I do not think so. Rather, we must distinguish types of case; and then see what, if anything, is common to the types we have distinguished. What we initially take from Grice—with modifications—is an at least partially analytical account of an act of communication, an act which might indeed be performed nonverbally and yet exhibit all the essential characteristics of a (nonverbal) equivalent of an illocutionary act. We gain more than this. For the account enables us to understand how such an act may be linguistically conventionalized right up to the point at which illocutionary force is exhausted by meaning (in Austin's sense); and in this understanding the notion of wholly overt or essentially avowable intention plays an essential part. Evidently, in these cases, the illocutionary act itself is not *essentially* a conventional act, an act done as conforming to a convention; it may be that the act is conventional, done as conforming to a convention, only in so far as *the means used to perform it* are conventional. To speak only of those conventional means which are also *linguistic* means, the extent to which the act is one done as conforming to conventions may depend solely on the extent to which conventional linguistic meaning exhausts illocutionary force.

At the other end of the scale—the end, we may say, from which Austin began—we have illocutionary acts which *are* essentially conventional. The examples I mentioned just now will serve—marrying, redoubling, giving out, pronouncing sentence, bringing in a verdict. Such acts could have no existence outside the rule- or convention-governed practices and procedures of which they essentially form parts. Let us take the standard case in which the participants in these procedures know the rules and their roles, and are trying to play the game and not wreck it. Then they are presented with occasions on which they have to, or may, perform an illocutionary act which forms part of, or furthers, the practice or procedure as a whole; and sometimes they have to make a decision within a restricted range of alternatives (for example, to pass or redouble,

to pronounce sentence of imprisonment for some period not exceeding a certain limit). Between the case of such acts as these and the case of the illocutionary act not essentially conventional, there is an important likeness and an important difference. The likeness resides in the fact that, in the case of an utterance belonging to a convention-governed practice or procedure, the speaker's utterance is standardly *intended* to further, or affect the course of, the practice in question in some one of the alternative ways open, and intended to be recognized as so intended. I do not mean that such an act could *never* be performed *unintentionally.* A player might let slip the word 'redouble' without *meaning* to redouble; but if the circumstances are appropriate and the play strict, then he *has* redoubled (or he may be *held* to have redoubled). But a player who continually did this sort of thing would not be asked to play again, except by sharpers. Forms can take charge, in the absence of appropriate intention; but when they do, the case is *essentially* deviant or nonstandard. There is present in the standard case, that is to say, the same element of wholly overt and avowable intention as in the case of the act not essentially conventional.

The difference is a more complicated affair. We have, in these cases, an act which is conventional in two connected ways. First, if things go in accordance with the rules of the procedure in question, the act of furthering the practice in the way intended is an act required or permitted by those rules, an act done as falling under the rules. Second, the act is identified as the act it is just because it is performed by the utterance of a form of words conventional for the performance of that act. Hence the speaker's utterance is not only *intended* to further, or affect the course of, the practice in question in a certain conventional way; in the absence of any breach of the conventional conditions for furthering the procedure in this way, it cannot fail to do so.

And here we have the contrast between the two types of case. In the case of an illocutionary act of a kind not essentially conventional, the act of communication is performed if *uptake* is secured, if the utterance is taken to be issued with the complex overt intention with which it is issued. But even though the act of communication is performed, the wholly overt intention which lies at the core of the intention complex may, *without any breach of rules or conventions,* be frustrated. The audience response (belief, action, or attitude) may simply not be forthcoming. It is different with the utterance which forms part of a wholly convention-governed procedure. Granted that uptake is secured, then any frustration of the wholly overt intention of the utterance (the intention to further the procedure in a certain way) must be attributable to a breach of rule or convention. The speaker who abides by the conventions can avowably have the intention to further the procedure in the way to which his current linguistic act is conventionally appropriated *only* if he takes it that the conventional conditions for so furthering it are satisfied and hence takes it *that his utterance will not only reveal his intentions but give them effect.* There is nothing parallel to this in the case of the illocutionary act of a kind not essentially conventional. In both cases, we may say, speakers assume the responsibility for making their intentions overt. In one case (the case of the convention-constituted procedure) the speaker who uses the explicitly performative form also explicitly assumes the responsibility for making his overt intention effective. But in the other case the speaker cannot, in the speech act itself, explicitly assume any such responsibility. For there are no conditions which can conventionally guarantee the effectiveness of his overt intention. Whether it is effective or not is something that rests with his audience. In the one case, therefore, the explicitly performative form *may* be the name of the very act which is performed if and only if the speaker's overt intention is effective; but in the other case it cannot be the name of this act. But of course—and I shall recur to this thought—the sharp contrast I have here drawn between two extreme types of case must not blind us to the existence of intermediate types.

Acts belonging to convention-constituted procedures of the kind I have just referred to form an important part of human communication. But they do not form the whole nor, we may think, the most fundamental part. It would be a mistake to take them as the model for understanding the notion of illocutionary force in general, as Austin perhaps shows

some tendency to do when he both insists that the illocutionary act is essentially a conventional act and connects this claim with the possibility of making the act explicit by the use of the performative formula. It would equally be a mistake, as we have seen, to generalize the account of illocutionary force derived from Grice's analysis; for this would involve holding, falsely, that the complex overt intention manifested in any illocutionary act always includes the intention to secure a certain definite response or reaction in an audience over and above that which is necessarily secured if the illocutionary force of the utterance is understood. Nevertheless, we can perhaps extract from our consideration of two contrasting types of cases something which is common to them both and to all the other types which lie between them. For the illocutionary force of an utterance is essentially something that is intended to be understood. And the understanding of the force of an utterance in all cases involves recognizing what may be called broadly an audience-directed intention and recognizing it as wholly overt, as intended to be organized. It is perhaps this fact which lies at the base of the general possibility of the explicit performative formula; though, as we have seen, extra factors come importantly into play in the case of convention-constituted procedures.

Once this common element in all illocutionary acts is clear, we can readily acknowledge that the types of audience-directed intention involved may be very various and, also, that different types may be exemplified by one and the same utterance.

I have set in sharp contrast those cases in which the overt intention is simply to forward a definite and convention-governed practice (for example, a game) in a definite way provided for by the conventions or rules of the practice and those cases in which the overt intention includes that of securing a definite response (cognitive or practical) in an audience over and above that which is necessarily secured if uptake is secured. But there is something misleading about the sharpness of this contrast; and it would certainly be wrong to suppose that all cases fall clearly and neatly into one or another of these two classes. A speaker whose job it is to do so may offer information, instructions, or even advice, and yet be overtly indifferent as to whether or not his information is accepted as such, his instructions followed, or his advice taken. His wholly overt intention may amount to no more than that of making available—in a 'take it or leave it' spirit—to his audience the information or instructions or opinion in question; though again, in some cases, he may be seen as the mouthpiece, merely, of another agency to which may be attributed at least general intentions of the kind that can scarcely be attributed, in the particular case, to him. We should not find such complications discouraging; for we can scarcely expect a general account of linguistic communication to yield more than schematic outlines, which may almost be lost to view when every qualification is added which fidelity to the facts requires.

NOTES

1. All references, unless otherwise indicated, are to *How To Do Things with Words* (Oxford: Oxford University Press, 1962).

2. I refer later to the need for qualification of this doctrine.

3. I owe the objections which follow to Professor Hart.

4. For an illocutionary act *may* be performed *altogether* unintentionally. See the example about redoubling at bridge [This volume: 299].

5. Perhaps trying to impress might sometimes have an illocutionary character. For I might try to impress you with my *effrontery,* intending you to recognize this intention and intending your recognition of it to function as part of your reason for being impressed, and so forth. But then I am not *merely* trying to impress you; I am *inviting* you to be impressed. I owe this point to Mr. B. F. McGuinness.

FURTHER READING

Austin, J. L. (1962). *How to Do Things with Words.* Oxford: Oxford University Press.

Bach, K., and R. M. Harnish (1982). *Linguistic Communication and Speech Acts.* Cambridge, Mass.: MIT Press.

Clark, H. H., and T. B. Carlson (1982). "Hearers and Speech Acts." *Language* 58:332–373.

Cohen, L. J. (1964). "Do Illocutionary Forces Exist?" *Philosophical Quarterly* 14:118–137.

Cole, P., and J. Morgan (eds.). (1975). *Syntax and Semantics.* Vol. 3: *Speech Acts.* New York: Academic Press.

Davison, S. (1975). "Indirect Speech Acts and What to Do with Them." In P. Cole and J. Morgan (eds.), *Syntax and Semantics.* Vol. 3: *Speech Acts.* New York: Academic Press, 143–185.

Holdcroft, D. (1978). *Words and Deeds: Problems in the Theory of Speech Acts.* Oxford: Clarendon Press.

Sadock, J. M. (1975). *Toward a Linguistic Theory of Speech Acts.* New York: Academic Press.

Searle, J. R. (1970). *Speech Acts: An Essay in the Philosophy of Language.* Cambridge: Cambridge University Press.

Searle, J. R. (1979). "The Classification of Illocutionary Acts." In *Expression and Meaning.* Cambridge: Cambridge University Press.

Searle, J. R., F. Kiefer, and M. Bierwisch (eds.). (1980). *Speech Act Theory and Pragmatics.* Dordrecht: Reidel.

Warnock, G. J. (1973). "Some Types of Performative Utterance." In I. Berlin et al. (eds.), *Essays on J. L. Austin.* Oxford: Oxford University Press, 69–89.

V

Conversational Implicature and Relevance

19

Logic and Conversation

H. P. GRICE

It is a commonplace of philosophical logic that there are, or appear to be, divergences in meaning between, on the one hand, at least some of what I shall call the formal devices— $\sim$, $\wedge$, $\vee$, $\supset$, $(\forall x)$, $(\exists x)$, (ιx) (when these are given a standard two-valued interpretation)— and, on the other, what are taken to be their analogs or counterparts in natural language— such expressions as *not, and, or, if, all, some* (or *at least one*), *the*. Some logicians may at some time have wanted to claim that there are in fact no such divergences; but such claims, if made at all, have been somewhat rashly made, and those suspected of making them have been subjected to some pretty rough handling.

Those who concede that such divergences exist adhere, in the main, to one or the other of two rival groups, which I shall call the formalist and the informalist groups. An outline of a not uncharacteristic formalist position may be given as follows: Insofar as logicians are concerned with the formulation of very general patterns of valid inference, the formal devices possess a decisive advantage over their natural counterparts. For it will be possible to construct in terms of the formal devices a sys-

tem of very general formulas, a considerable number of which can be regarded as, or are closely related to, patterns of inferences the expression of which involves some or all of the devices: Such a system may consist of a certain set of simple formulas that must be acceptable if the devices have the meaning that has been assigned to them, and an indefinite number of further formulas, many of which are less obviously acceptable and each of which can be shown to be acceptable if the members of the original set are acceptable. We have, thus, a way of handling dubiously acceptable patterns of inference, and if, as is sometimes possible, we can apply a decision procedure, we have an even better way. Furthermore, from a philosophical point of view, the possession by the natural counterparts of those elements in their meaning, which they do not share with the corresponding formal devices, is to be regarded as an imperfection of natural languages; the elements in question are undesirable excrescences. For the presence of these elements has the result both that the concepts within which they appear cannot be precisely or clearly defined, and that at least some state-

Reprinted by permission of Harvard University Press from *Studies in the Way of Words,* by Paul Grice, © 1968, 1975 by H. P. Grice, © 1989 by The President and Fellows of Harvard College.

ments involving them cannot, in some circumstances, be assigned a definite truth value; and the indefiniteness of these concepts is not only objectionable in itself but also leaves open the way to metaphysics—we cannot be certain that none of these natural language expressions is metaphysically 'loaded'. For these reasons, the expressions, as used in natural speech, cannot be regarded as finally acceptable, and may turn out to be, finally, not fully intelligible. The proper course is to conceive and begin to construct an ideal language, incorporating the formal devices, the sentences of which will be clear, determinate in truth value, and certifiably free from metaphysical implications; the foundations of science will now be philosophically secure, since the statements of the scientist will be expressible (though not necessarily actually expressed) within this ideal language. (I do not wish to suggest that all formalists would accept the whole of this outline, but I think that all would accept at least some part of it.)

To this, an informalist might reply in the following vein. The philosophical demand for an ideal language rests on certain assumptions that should not be conceded; these are, that the primary yardstick by which to judge the adequacy of a language is its ability to serve the needs of science, that an expression cannot be guaranteed as fully intelligible unless an explication or analysis of its meaning has been provided, and that every explication or analysis must take the form of a precise definition that is the expression or assertion of a logical equivalence. Language serves many important purposes besides those of scientific inquiry; we can know perfectly well what an expression means (and so a fortiori that it is intelligible) without knowing its analysis, and the provision of an analysis may (and usually does) consist in the specification, as generalized as possible, of the conditions that count for or against the applicability of the expression being analyzed. Moreover, while it is no doubt true that the formal devices are especially amenable to systematic treatment by the logician, it remains the case that there are very many inferences and arguments, expressed in natural language and not in terms of these devices, which are nevertheless recognizably valid. So there must be a place for an unsimplified, and so more or less unsystematic, logic

of the natural counterparts of these devices; this logic may be aided and guided by the simplified logic of the formal devices but cannot be supplanted by it. Indeed, not only do the two logics differ, but sometimes they come into conflict; rules that hold for a formal device may not hold for its natural counterpart.

On the general question of the place in philosophy of the reformation of natural language, I shall, in this essay, have nothing to say. I shall confine myself to the dispute in its relation to the alleged divergences. I have, moreover, no intention of entering the fray on behalf of either contestant. I wish, rather, to maintain that the common assumption of the contestants that the divergences do in fact exist is (broadly speaking) a common mistake, and that the mistake arises from inadequate attention to the nature and importance of the conditions governing conversation. I shall, therefore, inquire into the general conditions that, in one way or another, apply to conversation as such, irrespective of its subject matter. I begin with the characterization of the notion of 'implicature'.

IMPLICATURE

Suppose that A and B are talking about a mutual friend, C, who is now working in a bank. A asks B how C is getting on in his job, and B replies, *Oh quite well, I think; he likes his colleagues, and he hasn't been to prison yet.* At this point, A might well inquire what B was implying, what he was suggesting, or even what he meant by saying that C had not yet been to prison. The answer might be any one of such things as that C is the sort of person likely to yield to the temptation provided by his occupation, that C's colleagues are really very unpleasant and treacherous people, and so forth. It might, of course, be quite unnecessary for A to make such an inquiry of B, the answer to it being, in the context, clear in advance. It is clear that whatever B implied, suggested, meant in this example, is distinct from what B said, which was simply that C had not been to prison yet. I wish to introduce, as terms of art, the verb *implicate* and the related nouns *implicature* (cf. *implying*) and *implicatum* (cf. *what is implied*). The point of this maneuver is to avoid having, on each occasion, to choose between this or that member of the family of verbs for which *implicate* is to do general duty. I shall, for the time being at least, have to assume to a considerable extent an intuitive understanding of the meaning of *say* in such contexts, and an ability to recognize particular verbs as members of the family with which *implicate* is associated. I can, however, make one or two remarks that may help to clarify the more problematic of these assumptions, namely, that connected with the meaning of the word *say*.

In the sense in which I am using the word *say,* I intend what someone has said to be closely related to the conventional meaning of the words (the sentence) he has uttered. Suppose someone to have uttered the sentence *He is in the grip of a vice.* Given a knowledge of the English language, but no knowledge of the circumstances of the utterance, one would know something about what the speaker had said, on the assumption that he was speaking standard English, and speaking literally. One would know that he had said, about some particular male person or animal *x,* that at the time of the utterance (whatever that was), either (1) *x* was unable to rid himself of a certain kind of bad character trait or (2) some part of *x*'s person was caught in a certain kind of tool or instrument (approximate account, of course). But for a full identification of what the speaker had said, one would need to know (a) the identity of *x,* (b) the time of utterance, and (c) the meaning, on the particular occasion of utterance, of the phrase *in the grip of a vice* [a decision between (1) and (2)]. This brief indication of my use of *say* leaves it open whether a man who says (today) *Harold Wilson is a great man* and another who says (also today) *The British Prime Minister is a great man* would, if each knew that the two singular terms had the same reference, have said the same thing. But whatever decision is made about this question, the apparatus that I am about to provide will be capable of accounting for any implicatures that might depend on the presence of one rather than another of these singular terms in the sentence uttered. Such implicatures would merely be related to different maxims.

In some cases the conventional meaning of the words used will determine what is impli-

cated, besides helping to determine what is said. If I say (smugly), *He is an Englishman; he is, therefore, brave,* I have certainly committed myself, by virtue of the meaning of my words, to its being the case that his being brave is a consequence of (follows from) his being an Englishman. But while I have said that he is an Englishman, and said that he is brave, I do not want to say that I have *said* (in the favored sense) that it follows from his being an Englishman that he is brave, though I have certainly indicated, and so implicated, that this is so. I do not want to say that my utterance of this sentence would be, *strictly speaking,* false should the consequence in question fail to hold. So *some* implicatures are conventional, unlike the one with which I introduce this discussion of implicature.

I wish to represent a certain subclass of nonconventional implicatures, which I shall call *conversational* implicatures, as being essentially connected with certain general features of discourse; so my next step is to try to say what these features are. The following may provide a first approximation to a general principle. Our talk exchanges do not normally consist of a succession of disconnected remarks, and would not be rational if they did. They are characteristically, to some degree at least, cooperative efforts; and each participant recognizes in them, to some extent, a common purpose or set of purposes, or at least a mutually accepted direction. This purpose or direction may be fixed from the start (e.g., by an initial proposal of a question for discussion), or it may evolve during the exchange; it may be fairly definite, or it may be so indefinite as to leave very considerable latitude to the participants (as in a casual conversation). But at each stage, *some* possible conversational moves would be excluded as conversationally unsuitable. We might then formulate a rough general principle which participants will be expected *(ceteris paribus)* to observe, namely: Make your conversational contribution such as is required, at the stage at which it occurs, by the accepted purpose or direction of the talk exchange in which you are engaged. One might label this the Cooperative Principle (CP).

On the assumption that some such general principle as this is acceptable, one may perhaps distinguish four categories under one or another of which will fall certain more specific maxims and submaxims, the following of which will, in general, yield results in accordance with the Cooperative Principle. Echoing Kant, I call these categories Quantity, Quality, Relation, and Manner. The category of Quantity relates to the quantity of information to be provided, and under it fall the following maxims:

1. Make your contribution as informative as is required (for the current purposes of the exchange).

2. Do not make your contribution more informative than is required.

(The second maxim is disputable; it might be said that to be overinformative is not a transgression of the CP but merely a waste of time. However, it might be answered that such overinformativeness may be confusing in that it is liable to raise side issues; and there may also be an indirect effect, in that the hearers may be misled as a result of thinking that there is some particular *point* in the provision of the excess of information. However this may be, there is perhaps a different reason for doubt about the admission of this second maxim, namely, that its effect will be secured by a later maxim, which concerns relevance.)

Under the category of Quality falls a supermaxim—'Try to make your contribution one that is true'—and two more specific maxims:

1. Do not say what you believe to be false.

2. Do not say that for which you lack adequate evidence.

Under the category of Relation I place a single maxim, namely, 'Be relevant.' Though the maxim itself is terse, its formulation conceals a number of problems that exercise me a good deal: questions about what different kinds and focuses of relevance there may be, how these shift in the course of a talk exchange, how to allow for the fact that subjects of conversation are legitimately changed, and so on. I find the treatment of such questions exceedingly difficult, and I hope to revert to them in a later work.

Finally, under the category of Manner, which I understand as relating not (like the previous categories) to what is said but, rather, to *how* what is said is to be said, I include the supermaxim—'Be perspicuous'—and various maxims such as:

1. Avoid obscurity of expression.

2. Avoid ambiguity.

3. Be brief (avoid unnecessary prolixity).

4. Be orderly.

And one might need others.

It is obvious that the observance of some of these maxims is a matter of less urgency than is the observance of others; a man who has expressed himself with undue prolixity would, in general, be open to milder comment than would a man who has said something he believes to be false. Indeed, it might be felt that the importance of at least the first maxim of Quality is such that it should not be included in a scheme of the kind I am constructing; other maxims come into operation only on the assumption that this maxim of Quality is satisfied. While this may be correct, so far as the generation of implicatures is concerned it seems to play a role not totally different from the other maxims, and it will be convenient, for the present at least, to treat it as a member of the list of maxims.

There are, of course, all sorts of other maxims (aesthetic, social, or moral in character), such as 'Be polite', that are also normally observed by participants in talk exchanges, and these may also generate nonconventional implicatures. The conversational maxims, however, and the conversational implicatures connected with them, are specially connected (I hope) with the particular purposes that talk (and so, talk exchange) is adapted to serve and is primarily employed to serve. I have stated my maxims as if this purpose were a maximally effective exchange of information; this specification is, of course, too narrow, and the scheme needs to be generalized to allow for such general purposes as influencing or directing the actions of others.

As one of my avowed aims is to see talking as a special case or variety of purposive, indeed rational, behavior, it may be worth noting that the specific expectations or presumptions connected with at least some of the foregoing maxims have their analogues in the sphere of transactions that are not talk exchanges. I list briefly one such analog for each conversational category.

1. *Quantity.* If you are assisting me to mend a car, I expect your contribution to be neither more nor less than is required. If, for example, at a particular stage I need four screws, I expect you to hand me four, rather than two or six.

2. *Quality.* I expect your contributions to be genuine and not spurious. If I need sugar as an ingredient in the cake you are assisting me to make, I do not expect you to hand me salt; if I need a spoon, I do not expect a trick spoon made of rubber.

3. *Relation.* I expect a partner's contribution to be appropriate to the immediate needs at each stage of the transaction. If I am mixing ingredients for a cake, I do not expect to be handed a good book, or even an oven cloth (though this might be an appropriate contribution at a later stage).

4. *Manner.* I expect a partner to make it clear what contribution he is making and to execute his performance with reasonable dispatch.

These analogies are relevant to what I regard as a fundamental question about the CP and its attendant maxims, namely, what the basis is for the assumption which we seem to make, and on which (I hope) it will appear that a great range of implicatures depends, that talkers will in general (*ceteris paribus* and in the absence of indications to the contrary) proceed in the manner that these principles prescribe. A dull but, no doubt at a certain level, adequate answer is that it is just a well-recognized empirical fact that people do behave in these ways; they have learned to do so in childhood and have not lost the habit of doing so; and, indeed, it would involve a good deal of effort to make a radical departure from the habit. It is much easier, for example, to tell the truth than to invent lies.

I am, however, enough of a rationalist to want to find a basis that underlies these facts, undeniable though they may be; I would like to be able to think of the standard type of conversational practice not merely as something that all or most do *in fact* follow but as something that it is *reasonable* for us to follow, that we *should not* abandon. For a time, I was attracted by the idea that observance of the CP and the maxims, in a talk exchange, could be thought of as a quasi-contractual matter, with parallels outside the realm of discourse. If you pass by when I am struggling with my stranded car, I no doubt have some degree of expectation that you will offer help, but once you join me in tinkering under the hood, my expectations become stronger and take more specific forms (in the absence of indications that you are merely an incompetent meddler); and talk exchanges seemed to me to exhibit, characteristically, certain features that jointly distinguish cooperative transactions:

1. The participants have some common immediate aim, like getting a car mended; their ultimate aims may, of course, be independent and even in conflict—each may want to get the car mended in order to drive off, leaving the other stranded. In characteristic talk exchanges, there is a common aim even if, as in an over-the-wall chat, it is a second-order one, namely, that each party should, for the time being, identify himself with the transitory conversational interests of the other.

2. The contributions of the participants should be dovetailed, mutually dependent.

3. There is some sort of understanding (which may be explicit but which is often tacit) that, other things being equal, the transaction should continue in appropriate style unless both parties are agreeable that it should terminate. You do not just shove off or start doing something else.

But while some such quasi-contractual basis as this may apply to some cases, there are too many types of exchange, like quarreling and letter writing, that it fails to fit comfortably. In any case, one feels that the talker who is irrelevant or obscure has primarily let down not his audience but himself. So I would like to be able to show that observance of the CP and maxims is reasonable (rational) along the following lines: that any one who cares about the goals that are central to conversation/communication (such as giving and receiving information, influencing and being influenced by others) must be expected to have an interest, given suitable circumstances, in participation in talk exchanges that will be profitable only on the assumption that they are conducted in general accordance with the CP and the maxims. Whether any such conclusion can be reached, I am uncertain; in any case, I am fairly sure that I cannot reach it until I am a good deal clearer about the nature of relevance and of the circumstances in which it is required.

It is now time to show the connection between the CP and maxims, on the one hand, and conversational implicature on the other.

A participant in a talk exchange may fail to fulfill a maxim in various ways, which include the following:

1. He may quietly and unostentatiously *violate* a maxim; if so, in some cases he will be liable to mislead.

2. He may *opt out* from the operation both of the maxim and of the CP; he may say, indicate, or allow it to become plain that he is unwilling to cooperate in the way the maxim requires. He may say, for example, *I cannot say more; my lips are sealed.*

3. He may be faced by a *clash:* He may be unable, for example, to fulfill the first maxim of Quantity (Be as informative as is required) without violating the second maxim of Quality (Have adequate evidence for what you say).

4. He may *flout* a maxim; that is, he may blatantly fail to fulfill it. On the assumption that the speaker is able to fulfill the maxim and to do so without violating another maxim (because of a clash), is not opting out, and is not, in view of the blatancy of his performance, trying to mislead, the hearer is faced with a minor problem: How can his saying what he did say be reconciled with the supposition that he is observing the overall CP? This situation is one that characteristically gives rise to a conversational implicature; and when a conversational implicature is generated in this way, I shall say that a maxim is being *exploited.*

I am now in a position to characterize the notion of conversational implicature. A man who, by (in, when) saying (or making as if to say) that *p* has implicated that *q,* may be said to have conversationally implicated that *q,* provided that (1) he is to be presumed to be observing the conversational maxims, or at least the Cooperative Principle; (2) the supposition that he is aware that, or thinks that, *q* is required in order to make his saying or making as if to say *p* (or doing so in *those* terms) consistent with this presumption; and (3) the speaker thinks (and would expect the hearer to think that the speaker thinks) that it is within

the competence of the hearer to work out, or grasp intuitively, that the supposition mentioned in (2) is required. Apply this to my initial example, to B's remark that C has not yet been to prison. In a suitable setting A might reason as follows: "(1) B has apparently violated the maxim 'Be relevant' and so may be regarded as having flouted one of the maxims conjoining perspicuity, yet I have no reason to suppose that he is opting out from the operation of the CP; (2) given the circumstances, I can regard his irrelevance as only apparent if, and only if, I suppose him to think that C is potentially dishonest; (3) B knows that I am capable of working out step (2). So B implicates that C is potentially dishonest."

The presence of a conversational implicature must be capable of being worked out; for even if it can in fact be intuitively grasped, unless the intuition is replaceable by an argument, the implicature (if present at all) will not count as a conversational implicature; it will be a conventional implicature. To work out that a particular conversational implicature is present, the hearer will reply on the following data: (1) the conventional meaning of the words used, together with the identity of any references that may be involved; (2) the CP and its maxims; (3) the context, linguistic or otherwise, of the utterance; (4) other items of background knowledge; and (5) the fact (or supposed fact) that all relevant items falling under the previous headings are available to both participants and both participants know or assume this to be the case. A general pattern for the working out of a conversational implicature might be given as follows: "He has said that *p*; there is no reason to suppose that he is not observing the maxims, or at least the CP; he could not be doing this unless he thought that *q*; he knows (and knows that I know that he knows) that I can see that the supposition that he thinks that *q* is required; he has done nothing to stop me thinking that *q*; he intends me to think, or is at least willing to allow me to think, that *q*; and so he has implicated that *q*."

EXAMPLES OF CONVERSATIONAL IMPLICATURE

I shall now offer a number of examples, which I shall divide into three groups.

GROUP A: *Examples in which no maxim is violated, or at least in which it is not clear that any maxim is violated*

A is standing by an obviously immobilized car and is approached by B; the following exchange takes place:

(1) A: *I am out of petrol.*
    B: *There is a garage round the corner.*

(Gloss: B would be infringing the maxim 'Be relevant' unless he thinks, or thinks it possible, that the garage is open, and has petrol to sell; so he implicates that the garage is, or at least may be open, etc.)

In this example, unlike the case of the remark *He hasn't been to prison yet,* the unstated connection between B's remark and A's remark is so obvious that, even if one interprets the supermaxim of Manner, 'Be perspicuous,' as applying not only to the expression of what is said but also to the connection of what is said with adjacent remarks, there seems be no case for regarding that supermaxim as infringed in this example. The next example is perhaps a little less clear in this respect:

(2) A: *Smith doesn't seem to have a girlfriend these days.*
    B: *He has been paying a lot of visits to New York lately.*

B implicates that Smith has, or may have, a girlfriend in New York. (A gloss is unnecessary in view of that given for the previous example.)

In both examples, the speaker implicates that which he must be assumed to believe in order to preserve the assumption that he is observing the maxim of Relation.

GROUP B: *Examples in which a maxim is violated, but its violation is to be explained by the supposition of a clash with another maxim*

A is planning with B an itinerary for a holiday in France. Both know that A wants to see his friend C, if to do so would not involve too great a prolongation of his journey:

(3) A: *Where does C live?*
    B: *Somewhere in the South of France.*

(Gloss: There is no reason to suppose that B is opting out; his answer is, as he well knows, less informative than is required to meet A's needs. This infringement of the first maxim of Quantity can be explained only by the supposition that B is aware that to be more informative would be to say something that infringed the second maxim of Quality. 'Don't say what you lack adequate evidence for', so B implicates that he does not know in which town C lives.)

GROUP C: *Examples that involve exploitation, that is, a procedure by which a maxim is flouted for the purpose of getting in a conversational implicature by means of something of the nature of a figure of speech*

In these examples, though some maxim is violated at the level of what is said, the hearer is entitled to assume that that maxim, or at least the overall Cooperative Principle, is observed at the level of what is implicated.

(1a) *A flouting of the first maxim of Quantity*

A is writing a testimonial about a pupil who is a candidate for a philosophy job, and his letter reads as follows: 'Dear Sir, Mr. X's command of English is excellent, and his attendance at tutorials has been regular. Yours, etc.' (Gloss: A cannot be opting out, since if he wished to be uncooperative, why write at all? He cannot be unable, through ignorance, to say more, since the man is his pupil; moreover, he knows that more information than this is wanted. He must, therefore, be wishing to impart information that he is reluctant to write down. This supposition is tenable only if he thinks Mr. X is no good at philosophy. This, then, is what he is implicating.)

Extreme examples of a flouting of the first maxim of Quantity are provided by utterances of patent tautologies like *Women are women* and *War is war.* I would wish to maintain that at the level of what is said, in my favored sense, such remarks are totally noninformative and so, at that level, cannot but infringe the first maxim of Quantity in any conversational context. They are, of course, informative at the level of what is implicated, and the hearer's identification of their informative content at this level is dependent on his ability to explain the speaker's selection of this particular patent tautology.

(1b) *An infringement of the second maxim of Quantity, 'Do not give more information than is required', on the assumption that the existence of such a maxim should be admitted*

A wants to know whether *p*, and B volunteers not only the information that *p*, but information to the effect that it is certain that *p*, and that the evidence for its being the case that *p* is so-and-so and such-and-such.

B's volubility may be undesigned, and if it is so regarded by A it may raise in A's mind a doubt as to whether B is as certain as he says he is ('Methinks the lady doth protest too much'). But if it is thought of as designed, it would be an oblique way of conveying that it is to some degree controversial whether or not *p*. It is, however, arguable that such an implicature could be explained by reference to the maxim of Relation without invoking an alleged second maxim of Quantity.

(2a) *Examples in which the first maxim of Quality is flouted*

Irony. X, with whom A has been on close terms until now, has betrayed a secret of A's to a business rival A and his audience both know this. A says *X is a fine friend.* (Gloss: It is perfectly obvious to A and his audience that what A has said or has made as if to say is something he does not believe, and the audience knows that A knows that this is obvious to the audience. So, unless A's utterance is entirely pointless, A must be trying to get across some other proposition than the one he purports to be putting forward. This must be some obviously related proposition; the most obviously related proposition is the contradictory of the one he purports to be putting forward.)

Metaphor. Examples like *You are the cream in my coffee* characteristically involve categorial falsity, so the contradictory of what the speaker has made as if to say will, strictly speaking, be a truism; so it cannot be *that* that such a speaker is trying to get across. The most likely supposition is that the speaker is attributing to his audience some feature or features in respect of which the audience resembles (more or less fancifully) the mentioned substance.

It is possible to combine metaphor and irony by imposing on the hearer two stages of interpretation. I say *You are the cream in my coffee,* intending the hearer to reach first the metaphor interpretant 'You are my pride and joy' and then the irony interpretant 'You are my bane.'

Meiosis. Of a man known to have broken up all the furniture, one says *He was a little intoxicated.*

Hyperbole. Every nice girl loves a sailor.

(2b) Examples in which the second maxim of Quality, 'Do not say that for which you lack adequate evidence', is flouted are perhaps not easy to find, but the following seems to be a specimen. I say of X's wife, *She is probably deceiving him this evening.* In a suitable context, or with a suitable gesture or tone of voice, it may be clear that I have no adequate reason for supposing this to be the case. My partner, to preserve the assumption that the conversational game is still being played, assumes that I am getting at some related proposition for the acceptance of which I do have a reasonable basis. The related proposition might well be that she is given to deceiving her husband, or possibly that she is the sort of person who would not stop short of such conduct.

(3) *Examples in which an implicature is achieved by real, as distinct from apparent, violation of the maxim of Relation* are perhaps rare, but the following seems to be a good candidate. At a genteel tea party, A says *Mrs. X is an old bag.* There is a moment of appalled silence, and then B says *The weather has been quite delightful this summer, hasn't it?* B has blatantly refused to make what he says relevant to A's preceding remark. He thereby implicates that A's remark should not be discussed and, perhaps more specifically, that A has committed a social gaffe.

(4) *Examples in which various maxims falling under the supermaxim 'Be perspicuous' are flouted*

Ambiguity. We must remember that we are concerned only with ambiguity that is deliberate, and that the speaker intends or expects to be recognized by his hearer. The problem the hearer has to solve is why a speaker should, when still playing the conversational game, go out of his way to choose an ambiguous utterance. There are two types of cases:

(a) Examples in which there is no difference, or no striking difference, between two interpretations of an utterance with respect to straightforwardness; neither interpretation is notably more sophisticated, less standard, more recondite or more far-fetched than the other. We might consider Blake's lines: 'Never seek to tell thy love, Love that never told can be.' To avoid the complications introduced by the presence of the imperative mood, I shall consider the related sentence, *I sought to tell my love, love that never told can be.* There may be a double ambiguity here. *My love* may refer to either a state of emotion or an object of emotion, and *love that never told can be* may mean either 'Love that cannot be told' or 'love that if told cannot continue to exist.' Partly because of the sophistication of the poet and partly because of internal evidence (that the ambiguity is kept up), there seems to be no alternative to supposing that the ambiguities are deliberate and that the poet is conveying both what he would be saying if one interpretation were intended rather than the other, and vice versa; though no doubt the poet is not explicitly saying any one of these things but only conveying or suggesting them (cf. 'Since she [nature] pricked thee out for women's pleasure, mine be thy love, and thy love's use their treasure').

(b) Examples in which one interpretation is notably less straightforward than another. Take the complex example of the British General who captured the province of Sind and sent back the message *Peccavi.* The ambiguity involved ('I have Sind'/'I have sinned') is phonemic, not morphemic; and the expression actually used is unambiguous, but since it is in a language foreign to speaker and hearer, translation is called for, and the ambiguity resides in the standard translation into native English. Whether or not the straightforward interpretant ('I have sinned') is being conveyed, it seems that the nonstraightforward interpretant must be. There might be stylistic reasons for conveying by a sentence merely its nonstraightforward interpretant, but it would be pointless, and perhaps also stylistically objectionable, to go to the trouble of finding an expresion that nonstraightforwardly conveys that *p*, thus imposing on an audience the effort involved in finding this interpretant, if this interpretant were otiose so far as communication was concerned. Whether the straightforward interpretant is also being conveyed seems to depend on whether such a supposition would conflict with other conversational

requirements, for example, would it be relevant, would it be something the speaker could be supposed to accept, and so on. If such requirements are not satisfied, then the straightforward interpretant is not being conveyed. If they are, it is. If the author of *Peccavi* could naturally be supposed to think that he had committed some kind of transgression, for example, had disobeyed his orders in capturing Sind, and if reference to such a transgression would be relevant to the presumed interests of the audience, then he would have been conveying both interpretants; otherwise he would be conveying only the nonstraightforward one.

Obscurity. How do I exploit, for the purposes of communication, a deliberate and overt violation of the requirement that I should avoid obscurity? Obviously, if the Co-operative Principle is to operate, I must intend my partner to understand what I am saying despite the obscurity I import into my utterance. Suppose that A and B are having a conversation in the presence of a third party, for example, a child, then A might be deliberately obscure, though not too obscure, in the hope that B would understand and the third party not. Furthermore, if A expects B to see that A is being deliberately obscure, it seems reasonable to suppose that, in making his conversational contribution in this way, A is implicating that the contents of his communication should not be imparted to the third party.

Failure to be brief or succinct. Compare the remarks:

(a) *Miss X sang 'Home Sweet Home.'*

(b) *Miss X produced a series of sounds that corresponded closely with the score of 'Home Sweet Home.'*

Suppose that a reviewer has chosen to utter (b) rather than (a). (Gloss: Why has he selected that rigmarole in place of the concise and nearly synonymous *sang*? Presumably, to indicate some striking difference between Miss X's performance and those to which the word *singing* is usually applied. The most obvious supposition is that Miss X's performance suffered from some hideous defect. The reviewer knows that this supposition is what is likely to spring to mind, so that is what he is implicating.)

GENERALIZED CONVERSATIONAL IMPLICATURE

I have so far considered only cases of what I might call 'particularized conversational implicature'—that is to say, cases in which an implicature is carried by saying that p on a particular occasion in virtue of special features of the context, cases in which there is no room for the idea that an implicature of this sort is normally carried by saying that p. But there are cases of generalized conversational implicature. Sometimes one can say that the use of a certain form of words in an utterance would normally (in the absence of special circumstances) carry such-and-such an implicature or type of implicature. Noncontroversial examples are perhaps hard to find, since it is all too easy to treat a generalized conversational implicature as if it were a conventional implicature. I offer an example that I hope may be fairly noncontroversial.

Anyone who uses a sentence of the form X *is meeting a woman this evening* would normally implicate that the person to be met was someone other than X's wife, mother, sister, or perhaps even close platonic friend. Similarly, if I were to say *X went into a house yesterday and found a tortoise inside the front door,* my hearer would normally be surprised if some time later I revealed that the house was X's own. I could produce similar linguistic phenomena involving the expressions *a garden, a car, a college,* and so on. Sometimes, however, there would normally be no such implicature ('I have been sitting in a car all morning'), and sometimes a reverse implicature ('I broke a finger yesterday'). I am inclined to think that one would not lend a sympathetic ear to a philosopher who suggested that there are three senses of the form of expression *an X:* one in which it means roughly 'something that satisfies the conditions defining the word X,' another in which it means approximately 'an X (in the first sense) that is only remotely related in a certain way to some person indicated by the context,' and yet another in which it means 'an X (in the first sense) that is closely related in a certain way to some person indicated by the context.' Would we not much prefer an account on the following lines (which, of course, may be incorrect in detail): When someone, by using the form of expression *an X*, implicates that the X does not belong to or is not otherwise closely connected with some identifiable person, the implicature is present because the speaker has failed to be specific in a way in which he might have been expected to be specific, with the consequence that it is likely to be assumed that he is not in a position to be specific. This is a familiar implicature situation and is classifiable as a failure, for one reason or another, to fulfill the first maxim of Quantity. The only difficult question is why it should, in certain cases, be presumed, independently of information about particular contexts of utterance, that specification of the closeness or remoteness of the connection between a particular person or object and a further person who is mentioned or indicated by the utterance should be likely to be of interest. The answer must lie in the following region: Transactions between a person and other persons or things closely connected with him are liable to be very different as regards their concomitants and results from the same sort of transactions involving only remotely connected persons or things; the concomitants and results, for instance, of my finding a hole in my roof are likely to be very different from the concomitants and results of my finding a hole in someone else's roof. Information, like money, is often given without the giver's knowing to just what use the recipient will want to put it. If someone to whom a transaction is mentioned gives it further consideration, he is likely to find himself wanting the answers to further questions that the speaker may not be able to identify in advance; if the appropriate specification will be likely to enable the hearer to answer a considerable variety of such questions for himself, then there is a presumption that the speaker should include it in his remark; if not, then there is no such presumption.

Finally, we can now show that, conversational implicature being what it is, it must possess certain features:

1. Since, to assume the presence of a conversational implicature, we have to assume that at least the Cooperative Principle is being observed, and since it is possible to opt out of the observation of this principle, it follows that a generalized conversational implicature can be canceled in a particular case. It may be explicitly canceled, by the addition of a clause

that states or implies that the speaker has opted out, or it may be contextually canceled, if the form of utterance that usually carries it is used in a context that makes it clear that the speaker is opting out.

2. Insofar as the calculation that a particular conversational implicature is present requires, besides contextual and background information, only a knowledge of what has been said (or of the conventional commitment of the utterance), and insofar as the manner of expression plays no role in the calculation, it will not be possible to find another way of saying the same thing, which simply lacks the implicature in question, except where some special feature of the substituted version is itself relevant to the determination of an implicature (in virtue of one of the maxims of Manner). If we call this feature nondetachability, one may expect a generalized conversational implicature that is carried by a familiar, nonspecial locution to have a high degree of nondetachability.

3. To speak approximately, since the calculation of the presence of a conversational implicature presupposes an initial knowledge of the conventional force of the expression the utterance of which carries the implicature, a conversational implicatum will be a condition that is not included in the original specification of the expression's conventional force. Though it may not be impossible for what starts life, so to speak, as a conversational implicature to become conventionalized, to suppose that this is so in a given case would require special justification. So, initially at least, conversational implicata are not part of the meaning of the expressions to the employment of which they attach.

4. Since the truth of a conversational implicatum is not required by the truth of what is said (what is said may be true—what is implicated may be false), the implicature is not carried by what is said, but only by the saying of what is said, or by 'putting it that way.'

5. Since, to calculate a conversational implicature is to calculate what has to be supposed in order to preserve the supposition that the Cooperative Principle is being observed, and since there may be various possible specific explanations, a list of which may be open, the conversational implicatum in such cases will be disjunction of such specific explanations; and if the list of these is open, the implicatum will have just the kind of indeterminacy that many actual implicata do in fact seem to possess.

20

Logical Form and Implicature

ROBERT M. HARNISH

In another work (1972, Chap. I), I presented the doctrine of logical form as a program committing one, at least in part, to representing those features of a sentence that play an essential role in entailments. Of course the notion of entailment, as well as its analysis, is not uncontroversial. However, it seems fairly central to the notion of entailment that if a sentence S entails a sentence S', then S' would, in virtue of its meaning,[1] have to be true if S were true (Massey, 1970, p. 3). If this is even in part the province of a theory of logical form, then such a theory will, in the long run, be affected by the correctness of proposals as to the presence or absence of entailments between sentences in the language to which that theory of logical form applies.

In this paper I investigate some proposals that bear directly on the issue of the logical form of certain kinds of sentences in English by way of their claim (or assumption) that a relation of entailment does or does not hold between certain kinds of sentences. In one case I want to argue that a relation of implication, not entailment, holds. In another group of cases I want to argue that entailment, not presupposition, holds.

CONJUNCTION REDUCTION: THE PROBLEM

'Tom and William arrived' does not mean the same as 'Tom arrived and William arrived'; for the first suggests 'together' and the second an order of arrival.

Strawson (1952, p. 80)

If I can call the same object red and green with equal right, it is a sure sign that the object named is not what really has the green colour, for that we must get a surface which is green only.

Frege (1884, § 22)

It has been known for a long time that there are certain verbs for which the deprivation of a sentence with conjoined subjects from conjoined sentences is implausible (Strawson, 1952, p. 79; Lakeoff and Peters, 1969). Sentence (1) is not derived from (2):

(1) John and Bill met.[2]

(2) John met and Bill met.

because the conjoined simple sentences 'John met' and 'Bill met' are not well formed. However, along with such examples are those of another sort that require a slightly different argument, and it is on these examples that I want to focus my attention. The cases divide into at least two classes, verbs and adjectives, but I think it will be obvious that the same phenomena is illustrated by both classes.

Verbs

It is sometimes claimed that (3) has problems in its derivation analogous to the proposed derivation of (1) from (2):

(3) Russell and Whitehead wrote *Principia*.

On the standard account, (3) would come from (4i) and (4ii):

(4) (i) Russell wrote *Principia*.
    (ii) Whitehead wrote *Principia*.

The argument against deriving (3) from (4) goes as follows:

(5) (i) Sentence (4i) is false.
    (ii) Sentence (4ii) is false.
    (iii) Therefore, sentence (4) is false.
    (iv) Two sentences with the same meaning cannot have different truth values at the same time with the same referents.
    (v) Since (3) is true and (4) is false they cannot have the same meaning.
    (vi) Transformations do not change meaning.
    (vii) Therefore (3) cannot be derived from (4).

Clearly, there are a number of places at which one could challenge this argument, but I want to challenge steps (5i) and (5ii). That is, I want to deny that (4i) and (4ii) are false.

The first thing to ask is why one might think that (4i) and (4ii) are false. Although I have no proof, I think the reason is as follows. If someone else asks

(6) Who wrote *Principia?*

and someone answers,

(7) Russell and Whitehead wrote *Principia*.

it is claimed that (7) *entails*

(8) Russell and Whitehead wrote *Principia* together.

If someone asks (6) and someone answers,

(9) Russell wrote *Principia*.

then (9) is also taken to *entail* that

(10) Russell wrote *Principia* alone.

However, this reading of (9) is inconsistent with the favored reading of (7), and since the favored reading of (7) is deemed true, (9) must be false.

The argument as stated turns on (7) entailing (8) and (9) entailing (10). Since I want to challenge the claim that the correct relation both between (7) and (8) and between (9) and (10) is entailment, we need some term for the whole family of relations that hold between sentences of these types—as well as perhaps between other things. For this I (hesitantly) settle on 'implies' and its cognates ('implication') mainly because it has in the philosophical literature the proper ambiguity. It has been used (by Russell) to mean 'entail' and it has been used by others to mean 'suggest,' 'indicate', etc. I will use IMPLICATION for this generic relation, reserving 'Implication' for a more specific class of IMPLICATIONS which exclude entailments. I call a person who maintains that the relation of IMPLICATION in question is entailment a 'strong theorist.'[3] To break the strong theorist's argument we need only establish (11):

(11) Either (7) does not entail (8), or (9) does not entail (10).

In the end, I will try to establish (11).

As a first step in this direction, we should attempt to isolate what part of sentences (7) and (9) support the purported entailments. Clearly, the subject expressions here play no favored role. It must then be all or part of the predicate expressions that support the purported entailments. We call IMPLICATIONS of the sort alleged between (7) and (8) 'together-IMPLICATIONS' and those between (9) and (10) 'alone-IMPLICATIONS'. How are we to understand (A) and (B)?

(A) *A* ϕ-ed *C* alone.

(B) *A* and *B* ϕ-ed *C* together.

As it stands, (A) is multiply ambiguous[4] for most substitution instances of 'ϕ'. Consider the instance: '*A* moved that table alone'. We do not want to take it that *that* table was the only thing he moved (ever) or even on some occasion. Nor do we want to take it that *A* was the only person ever to move that table. Rather we take it as

(A') *A* alone ϕ-ed *C*.

on the occasion in question. This reading is similar to

(A″) *A* φ-ed *C* by himself.

But this is still ambiguous. Here we do not mean 'by himself' in the sense in which one may want to 'be by himself' for a while. We want to read (A″) as either

(A‴) (i) *A* φ-ed *C* by himself. (not jointly with anyone)

(ii) *A* φ-ed *C* by himself. (without anyone else's help)

I will not distinguish between (A‴i) and (A‴ii) here, as either of these will do as the sense I want for (A). It is very hard to distinguish a joint enterprise from one person's enterprise aided by another.[5] As for (B), most instances of this also are ambiguous. However, I do not want to consider the reading of (B) as in: *A* and *B* added the numbers together—that is, *A* and *B* added together the numbers. Rather, I want it in the sense of

(B′) *A* and *B* together φ-ed *C*.

But here again I do not want it to be understood as simple concurrence. It is not that they each φ-ed *at the same time*. If that was so, there would be two φ-ings at some time. But in the sense I want, there was only one φ-ing— and *A* and *B* were both doing it.[6] Unfortunately, this is not too helpful since I do not know the principle for counting most acts. I want to say that for *A* and *B* to travel together (to *C*), it is not sufficient that they both be traveling to *C* at the same time. Nor even on the same vehicle. In some sense they must be intending to spend most of their time together *while* traveling to *C*. At the moment I cannot make this more precise.

Even though it is the predicate that supports the IMPLICATION there are a number of differences among predicates, as can be illustrated with some examples. In testing one's intuition here it is important to keep a number of things in mind. First, it must be remembered that we are trying to discover the contribution of the predicate expressions as abstracted from all *particular* contexts of utterance. Second, that it takes place in a communication situation. Imagine, then, what I shall call the 'minimal context': where someone asks 'who φ-ed?'

with no stage setting and the answer is an instance of one of the schemata that follows. If this is not observed, it is easy to construct situations when the IMPLICATIONS of all of these forms vary wildly. Where the schematic letter '*C*' appears in a predicate, it is to stand in for some noun phrase that identifies a particular token of the type appropriate to the verb. For example, ⌜*A* and *B* read *C*⌝ could be ⌜*A* and *B* read *War and Peace*.⌝ Third, the cases often break down into two groups that I have not distinguished. For instance, with ⌜*A* and *B* remembered *C*⌝ as opposed to ⌜*A* and *B* read *C*⌝ it is not possible for logical reasons that *A* and *B* remembered *C* in any stronger sense than temporal concurrence. Thus, the absence of a together-IMPLICATION is a degenerate or limiting case. This is not so with the second example. It is logically possible for two people to read the same book (token). I would think that this knowledge about 'remember' on the part of language users is what keeps this kind of utterance from having the IMPLICATION in question. Nevertheless, it is still *true* that there is no such IMPLICATION. Consider the following examples:[7]

(12) No Alone-IMPLICATIONS:
    (i) *A* sidled up to *C*.
    (ii) *A* remembers *C*.
    (iii) *A* ignored *C*.
    (iv) *A* raved about *C*.
    (v) *A* promised to *C*.
    (vi) *A* belongs to *C*.
    (vii) *A* scratched the *C*.
    (viii) *A* went to *C*.
    (ix) *A* left for *C*.

(13) No Together-IMPLICATIONS:
    (i) *A* and *B* remembered *C*.
    (ii) *A* and *B* ignored *C*.
    (iii) *A* and *B* raved about *C*.
    (iv) *A* and *B* promised *C*.
    (v) *A* and *B* read *C*.
    (vi) *A* and *B* ran the mile.
    (vii) *A* and *B* drew circles.

(14) Weak Together-IMPLICATIONS:
    (i) *A* and *B* left for *C*.
    (ii) *A* and *B* sidled up to *C*.
    (iii) *A* and *B* invited *C* over.
    (iv) *A* and *B* scratched *C*.
    (v) *A* and *B* went to *C*.
    (vi) *A* and *B* shot the *C*s.
    (vii) *A* and *B* replied to *C*.
    (viii) *A* and *B* discovered *C*.
    (ix) *A* and *B* crossed *C*.

(15) Weak Alone-IMPLICATIONS:
    (i) *A* replied to *C*.
    (ii) *A* shot the *C*s.
    (iii) *A* invited *C* over.
    (iv) *A* sang to *C*.
    (v) *A* sold *C* to *B*.
    (vi) *A* accepted *C*.
    (vii) *A* argued with *C*.
    (viii) *A* called *C*.
    (ix) *A* caught *C*.

(16) Strong Together-IMPLICATIONS:
    (i) *A* and *B* moved *C*.
    (ii) *A* and *B* washed *C*.
    (iii) *A* and *B* cleaned *C*.
    (iv) *A* and *B* painted *C*.[8]
    (v) *A* and *B* drew *C*.
    (vi) *A* and *B* wrote *C*.
    (vii) *A* and *B* pushed *C*.
    (viii) *A* and *B* bought *C*.

(17) Strong Alone-IMPLICATIONS:
    (i) *A* moved *C*.
    (ii) *A* washed *C*.
    (iii) *A* cleaned *C*.
    (iv) *A* painted *C*.
    (v) *A* drew *C*.
    (vi) *A* wrote *C*
    (vii) *A* pushed *C*.
    (viii) *A* threw *C* to *B*.
    (ix) *A* answered *C*.
    (x) *A* confessed to *C*.
    (xi) *A* ate the *C*.[9]

Notice that most cases use the schematic letter '*C*' for the object phrase. This suggests that in many cases the internal structure of the object plays no role in the IMPLICATION. Consider (16i) again. It seems to me that the following C-variants of (16i) have the same strong together-IMPLICATION:

(18) A and B moved
    (i) this table.
    (ii) a table (specific).
    (iii) the tables.
    (iv) some of the tables.
    (v) all of the tables.
    (vi) a few of the tables,
      etc.

However, in some cases the object plays a crucial role via its interactions with the contribution to the truth conditions of the verb:

(18) (a) (i) Who drew a circle? (must be nonspecific)
      (ii) *A* and *B* drew a circle. (implies specific?)
(18) (b) (i) Who drew that circle? (token)
      (ii) *A* and *B* drew that circle. (token)

(18) (c) (i) Who wrote *The Butterfly?*
      (ii) *A* and *B* wrote *The Butterfly.*

(18) (d) (i) Who discovered the calculus?
      (ii) Newton and Leibnitz discovered the calculus.

In (18a, ii), both *A* and *B* *could* have drawn different circles, but this is not so in (18b, ii).[10] Likewise, it is *possible,* but highly *improbable,* that in (18c, ii), both *A* and *B* happened to write the same book, in the same way that Newton and Leibniz made the same discovery. Indeed, it is probably this very improbability that helps give rise to the IMPLICATION that *A* and *B* wrote *The Butterfly* together. This is legitimate because some IMPLICATIONS can be a function of (shared) background knowledge. There are many more complications here that I am not going to go into.

At the moment it seems to me that the verbs listed as having strong IMPLICATIONS form a natural class. I call these 'chore' verbs for obvious reasons. It would be interesting to see how this class of verbs (when filled out with more examples) relates to the taxonomies of Ryle, Vendler, and Kenny. Unfortunately, these taxonomies are in no better shape than mine—some are worse, since they are contradictory.[11] Most of the strong IMPLICATIONS look as if they are what Kenny calls performances, but this needs further work.

Adjectives

A perfectly analogous argument to (5) can be constructed using certain adjectives. It could be claimed that

(19) The flag is red and white.

cannot be derived from (20i) and (20ii):

(20) (i) The flag is red.
    (ii) The flag is white.

because

(21) (i) Sentence (20i) is false.
    (ii) Sentence (20ii) is false.
    (iii) Therefore (20) is false.
    (iv) Two sentences with the same meaning cannot have different truth values at the same time with the same referents.
    (v) Since (19) is true and (20) is false they cannot have the same meaning.
    (vi) Transformations do not change meaning.

(vii) Therefore (19) cannot be derived from (20).

A version of this argument has been put forward recently in a discussion of the assignment of logical form. Ackermann writes: "Consider this argument: 'The flag is black and white. Therefore, the flag is black.' An appropriate flag would provide a counterexample, since we assert 'The flag is black' only where the flag is plain black or nearly so" (1970, p. 64). While I would agree that this is the normal implication when making the assertion, I do not agree that this has to be a part of the meaning of the statement, nor does it have to affect its logical form.

Returning to the grammatical version of the point, there are many places where one could challenge argument (21), but I will focus only on (21i) and (21ii). Again we must ask why one might think (20i) and (20ii) false. The strong theorist might reason as follows. Suppose someone asks,

(22) What color is the flag?

and I answer

(23) (The flag is) red and white.

But if someone asks (22) and I answer,

(24) (The flag is) red.

then (24) entails that

(25) (The flag is) all (only?) red.

Since (25) is inconsistent with (23) and (23) is (supposedly) true, (24) which entails (25) must be false. The reasoning again turns on (24) entailing (25). To block the strong theorist we need only establish (26):

(26) Sentence (24) does not entail (25).

In the end I will try to establish (26).

The question of what elements in the sentence support the purported entailment is, in the case of adjectives, easy—it is the adjective. To see this we need only exhibit adjectives which fail to support this IMPLICATION. I call the IMPLICATION between (24) and (25) a case of 'all-IMPLICATION.' Now consider the following:

(27) No All-IMPLICATION:
    (i) X is spotted.
    (ii) X is dirty.
    (iii) X is stained.

    (iv) X is torn.
    (v) X is patched.
    (vi) X is dented.
    (vii) X is wet.
    (viii) X is on fire.

(28) Weak All-IMPLICATION:[12]
    (i) X is twisted.
    (ii) X is curved.
    (iii) X is steep.

It will be a condition of adequacy on a complete account of this phenomena in verbs and adjectives that one be able to explain why the expressions fit into the category they do vis-a-vis these IMPLICATIONS. With IMPLICATIONS we cannot *assume* that differences between verbs and so on turn (solely) on differences in their logical (semantic) representation, because IMPLICATIONS turn also on contextual knowledge and *shared background information.* This means that it is possible that non-essential properties of the referents can contribute to IMPLICATIONS. With verbs this distinction is harder to make clear because it is not clear in what sense verbs refer. Nevertheless, it could be the case that the reason, for example, that

(29) A and B imagined C.

does not have a together-IMPLICATION is simply our shared belief that the event token specified by the verb in uttering (29) is not the type of token which ever is a shared "activity." Although it may be a logical truth that two people cannot perform the same act token of *imagining C,* it may not be—and this is all that I want to illustrate.

In the rest of this section I want to argue for two things. First, that the strong theorist is wrong in thinking that the IMPLICATIONS mentioned are *entailments,* and second, that the relationship really is one of *implication* in a specific sense (to be specified shortly). I want to argue, moreover, that the theory that the relationship is one of implication can explain phenomena that the strong theorist cannot explain. I will now present some evidence for thinking the strong theorist wrong.

PRIMA FACIE EVIDENCE FOR A MISTAKE

I want to claim that in supposing there to be an entailment between (7) and (8), (9) and (10), and (24) and (25), the strong theorist has mistaken entailment for implication. I have two kinds of arguments to suggest that it is not entailment.

First Kind of Argument

For verbs:

(30)　(i) Suppose that Russell and Whitehead wrote *Principia*.
　　(ii) Suppose that 'Russell wrote *Principia*' is false.
　　(iii) Suppose that 'Whitehead wrote *Principia*' is false.
　　(iv) Then 'Russell did not write *Principia*' is true.
　　(v) And 'Whitehead did not write *Principia*' is true.
　　(vi) By conjunction, 'Russell did not write *Principia* and Whitehead did not write *Principia*' is true.
　　(vii) Therefore neither Russell nor Whitehead wrote *Principia*.[13]
　　(viii) But this conflicts with (i), so suppositions (ii) and (iii) must be false.

For adjectives:

(31)　(i) Suppose that the flag is red and white.
　　(ii) Suppose 'the flag is red' is false.
　　(iii) Suppose 'the flag is white' is false.
　　(iv) Then 'the flag is not red' is true.
　　(v) And 'the flag is not white' is true.
　　(vi) Then 'the flag is not red and the flag is not white' is true.
　　(vii) So the flag is neither red nor white (see note 13).
　　(viii) But this conflicts with (i), so assumptions (ii) and (iii) must be false.

Second Kind of Argument If P entails Q, then it cannot be the case that ⌜P and not Q⌝ is true; ⌜P and not Q⌝ is a contradiction.

For verbs, suppose that

(32)　(i) 'Russell wrote *Principia*' entails 'Russell wrote *Principia* alone'.

then it should be the case that

　　(ii) 'Russell wrote *Principia*, and he did not write it alone'.[14]

is a contradiction. But it doesn't seem to be, so (32) is false and not a case of entailment.

For adjectives, suppose that

(33)　(i) 'the flag is red' entails 'the flag is all red'.

then it should be the case that

　　(ii) 'the flag is red, but it is not all red'.

is a contradiction. But it does not seem to be, so (33i) is false and not a case of entailment.

A Potential Objection

One way the previous arguments could be stopped is by claiming that the crucial expression 'write' is *ambiguous* as between, say, 'write collectively' and 'write singly'. Thus, in (32i) if true, 'wrote' means 'wrote singly' whereas (32ii) is false if the first occurrence of 'wrote' means 'wrote collectively' and contradictory if not. Argument (30) would then just be invalid by equivocation on 'wrote'.

No philosopher has made this move that I know of. However, McCawley (1968) has taken this line with an example sufficiently close to mine that I think the points on both sides will carry over.

McCawley says, (I have renumbered the examples),

Consider now another class of sentences which has been proposed as an argument for deriving some conjoined noun phrases from conjoined sentences, namely sentences such as

(34) John and Harry went to Cleveland
　　This sentence is ambiguous, allowing the two paraphrases

(35) John and Harry each went to Cleveland

(36) John and Harry went to Cleveland together
　　　　　　　　　　　　　　(1968, pp. 152ff.)

It is not clear from the text how we are to think McCawley takes (35) and (36). They are not themselves perfectly precise. How then do we answer such (nonindependent) questions as

(Q1) Does (36) entail (35)?

(Q2) Are (35) and (36) compatible?

(Q3) Are (35) and (36) contradictories?

Although McCawley does not go on to discuss (34), he does discuss the sentence

(37) Those men went to Cleveland.

which he claims has "exactly the same ambiguity as" (34), and so we can assume that whatever is required to represent the ambiguity of (39) will be required for (34). Thus McCawley's analysis of (37) can serve as the basis for answering our questions about (34). McCawley's proposal is to

(38) subcategorize noun phrases which have set indices into two types, which I will call joint and nonjoint. Joint noun phrases allow adjuncts such as *together;* nonjoint noun phrases allow

adjuncts such as *each*. Attached to each set index in deep structure will be a specification of [+ joint] or [− joint]. Some verbs allow only a nonjoint subject, for example, *erudite;* some allow either a joint or a nonjoint subject, for example *go.* . . . Semantically, the distinction between joint and nonjoint relates to the order of quantifiers. In the one reading (joint) of [37], the meaning is that there was an event of 'going to Cleveland' in which each of the men participated; in the other reading (nonjoint), the meaning is that for each man there was an event of 'going to Cleveland' in which he participated; symbolized very roughly,

(39) (a) Joint: $\exists\ \forall$ 'go to Cleveland' (x, y)
$\quad\quad\quad\quad\quad$ y $x\in M$

$\quad\quad$ (b) Nonjoint: $\forall\ \exists$ 'go to Cleveland' (x, y_x)
$\quad\quad\quad\quad\quad\quad\quad\quad$ $x\in M$ yx

$\quad\quad\quad\quad\quad\quad\quad\quad$ (1968, pp. 152–153)

I do not see that we will get much help from (39).[15] Rather, we must turn to the informal remarks for help in answering questions (Q1)–(Q3). On the one hand, the choice of 'nonjoint' instead of 'disjoint' as the label for (35) suggests that (35) and (36) could both be true (of the same occasion). On the other hand, toward the end of (38) we are told that the joint reading of (34), that is, (36), would read something like

(40) There is an event of going to Cleveland in which John and Harry participated.

For the nonjoint reading of (34), that is, (35), we get something like

(41) For each of John and Harry there is an event of going to Cleveland in which he participated.

I take it that if (41) is true (and John ≠ Harry) then it follows that there are at least two events of the type: going to Cleveland. However, (40) entails only that there is one event of this type. So (40) could be true and (41) false. But since (40) and (41) were supposed to be translations of (36) and (35) respectively, we have an answer to (Q1): (36) does not entail (35) on McCawley's way of taking them. It is also clear that both (40) and (41) could be true, so the answer to (Q2) is "yes" and to Q3 is "no"—for John and Harry might have gone to Cleveland twice, once satisfying (40) and once satisfying (41). But suppose that they have been to Cleveland only once. Then if (40) is true, (41) is false. How about the converse? (41) entails that there were two events of going to Cleveland, and (40) that there was

one such event. It seems plausible to argue that if there are *two* such events, then there is not *one* such event. But this would be to move too fast, for all we can conclude so far is that there is not *just one* such event. If we can establish (42),

(42) 'There are two events of going to Cleveland' entails 'It is not the case that there is one event of going to Cleveland',

we could establish that if (41) is true, then (40) is false. Is (42) true? Consider the following:

(43) (i) There are two people here.
$\quad\quad$ (ii) Therefore, there is one person here.

(44) (i) The number of people here is two.
$\quad\quad$ (ii) Therefore, the number of people here is one.

(45) (i) Two people are in the room.
$\quad\quad$ (ii) Therefore, one person is in the room.

Are these valid? First, suppose you bet me that there will be 20 people at the talk tonight. We arrive and there are 25 people 'there. Who wins? There may be some temptation in both directions, but that seems to be because the question is underdetermined. It seems that the sentence

(46) There will be 20 people there.

can be used to make the following claims:

(47) (i) There will be at most 20 people there.
$\quad\quad$ (ii) There will be exactly 20 people there.
$\quad\quad$ (iii) There will be at least 20 people there.

Of course I do *not* want to claim that (46) is ambiguous and has (47) as its senses. Suppose that in the situation imagined, I had been complaining about the poor attendance at talks and you reply with (46)—against the mutual understanding that 20 people is a good turnout. In this context, what you said could have been paraphrased as (47iii), and so you would win the bet. Another context could have changed the force of my utterance to either of the other two.[16] So questions and examples like the previous one will not decide the validity of (43)–(45).

Second, notice that the standard logicist translations of sentences like (44) render the arguments invalid. For instance, Hempel writes:[17]

(48) Let us now express precisely the meaning of the assertion that a certain class *C* [e.g., of peo-

ple in the room] has the number 2, or briefly, that $n(C) = 2$. Brief reflection will show that the following definition is adequate in the sense of the customary meaning of the concept 2: there is some object x and some object y such that (1) $x \in C$ ... and $y \in C$, (2) $x \neq y$ and (3) if z is any object such that $z \in C$, then either $z = x$ or $z = y$.

(1964, p. 375)

Applying this to (45) we get

(49) (i) $(\exists x)(\exists y)(x$ is in the room & y is in the room & $x \neq y$ & $(z)(z$ is in the room $\supset (z = x \lor z = y)))$

(ii) $(\exists x)(x$ is in the room & $(y)(y$ is in the room $\supset y = x))$.

and (i) is true iff (ii) is false. Of course the fact that various philosophers have chosen to translate sentences this way does not show that this is the *correct* translation. However, I will accept these translations provisionally,[18] and so will accept (42). This in turn shows that if (41) is true, (40) is false. And this, in conjunction with its converse established earlier, yields the conclusion

(50) If John and Harry have only been to Cleveland once, then (40) is true iff (41) is false.

Recall that (40) was McCawley's explication of what he meant by (36) and (41) was his explication of what he meant by (35). Consequently, we can substitute into (50), yielding

(51) If John and Harry have only been to Cleveland once, then (36) is true iff (35) is false.

If we could discharge the antecedent in (51) we could answer (Q2) as "no" and (Q3) as "yes," which in turn will give us some grip on the logical force of the purported senses of (51). Can the antecedent of (51) be discharged? I do not see any natural way to do it.[19] So in all that follows I will make the assumption (which could be true) that the antecedent is true and thus

(52) (36) is true iff (35) is false.

The questionable antecedent could be carried along as a premise and my arguments would not be affected. However, (52) is more convenient to work with.

Given (52), we can now answer (Q2), as "no" and (Q3) as "yes." But this raises serious doubts as to the adequacy of (35) for saying what (41) says. That is, if McCawley wants

(34) to be ambiguous, and to have one of its senses be such as to require that if true, then (41) is the case, then, (35) is a poor way of stating it. On most people's understanding of (35), it need only be the case that both Harry and John traverse some distance and arrive in Cleveland. Nothing more is claimed, although of course more may in fact be true. So (35) does not seem to have the right logical properties to make (41) a translation of it. A more accurate rendition of the sense that (41) is supposed to capture would be

(53) John and Harry went to Cleveland separately.

One advantage that (53) has over (35) is that it fairly clearly has the properties we determined (41) to have (and which it was not clear that (35) had):

(54) (i) (53) entails that there were (at least) two events of going to Cleveland.

(ii) On the assumption that John and Harry have been to Cleveland only once, our questions (Q1)–(Q3) get answered as before.

I call this an advantage of (53) over (35) because although (40) explicates (36) and we have concluded that (40) entails the falsity of (41), it is not at all clear that (36) entails the falsity of (35). In fact I think that (36) entails (35).

In summary, McCawley claims that (34) is ambiguous. It has a joint and a nonjoint reading. As explications of what he takes the ambiguity to be, McCawley has offered (40) and (41), which he seems to think are captured by (36) and (35) respectively. I have argued that the nonjoint reading, i.e. (41), is better captured by (53) than (35). I conclude that Mc-Cawley's claim is that (34) can mean either (36) or (53).

Replies

I do not think that McCawley is correct in claiming that (34) is *ambiguous* as between (36) and (53)—or between (36) and (35), if (35) $\neq$ (53). I want to contend that what McCawley gives as two readings for (34) are simply two of the most common kinds of circumstances that do *in fact* satisfy (34). That is, (34) is certainly *vague* or *indeterminate*,[20] but that it is *ambiguous* requires some argument. That it is *not* ambiguous also requires some arguments. Here are a few.

Suppose, as McCawley suggests, that (34) is ambiguous as between (36) ($\equiv$(40)) and (53) ($\equiv$(41)). Assume the following two sets of circumstances:

C 1: the circumstances such that John and Harry meet halfway to Cleveland and continue there together.

C 2: the circumstance such that John and Harry meet a quarter of the way to Cleveland and continue there together.

I. *First Argument*

1. Since *C 1* obtains, (34) is true. Certainly it can be said of both of them that they went to Cleveland.
2. *C 1* makes (34) true iff either it makes (36) or (53) true, because these are the possible readings of (34).
3. If *C 1* makes (36) true it is because they went at least part of the way together.
4. But, then, by parity of reason, *C 1* will make (53) true also, for they traveled at least part of the way separately
5. But we established earlier that (36) and (53) were contradictories, so no circumstance can make them both true at the same time.
6. So, if *C 1* cannot make (36) true without making (53) true, it cannot make (36) true, and the same for (53).
7. But, then by 2, *C 1* cannot make (34) true.
8. But this contradicts our assumptions *C 1* and 1.
9. But since *C 1* could be true and 1 is true, our assumption that (34) is ambiguous must be rejected.

II. *Second Argument*

1. Same as I.1.
2. A sentence is true only if one of its senses 'represents' circumstances that obtain.
3. So one of the senses of (34) must represent *C 1* (from 1, 2, assumption). Call this sense 'S_3'.
4. Either S_3 = the sense of (36) or (53), or it does not.
5. But $S_3 \neq$ the sense of (36) nor the sense of (53) because *C 1* makes S_3 true, but not the sense of (36) nor (53) (from 3–6, argument I.)
6. So S_3 is a new sense of (34).
7. But now consider *C 2*.
8. *Mutatis mutandis,* reapply steps 1–6.
9. So there is a new sense S_4 of (34).
10. Reapply steps 1–9 for as many times as there are rational numbers.
11. Therefore, on McCawley's assumptions,

(34) has at least as many senses as there are rational numbers.

III. *Third Argument*[21]

If (34) is ambiguous, it should have two senses each of which can have semantic properties and relations such as analyticity, redundancy, contradictoriness, etc. For instance, the sentence

(55) He fed her dog biscuits.

is ambiguous between

(56) He fed her (dog biscuits).

(57) He fed (her dog) biscuits.

Consequently, if we add information to (56) or (57) that is contained in the sentence already, we will produce a redundancy. Moreover, it should be possible to construct a sentence that is redundant on one sense but not on the other—given the knowledge we might have of those senses.[22] Thus the sentence

(58) He fed her dog biscuits for dogs.

will be redundant on the sense of (56), that is,

(59) He fed her (dog biscuits) for dogs.

but not on the sense of (57):

(60) He fed (her dog) biscuits for dogs.

Now consider McCawley's proposed ambiguity again. Since one of the senses of (34) is supposed to be (36), it should be *redundant* on one sense to say,

(61) John and Harry went to Cleveland and they went together.

That is, given that (34) is supposed to be able to mean (36), then (61) should be able to mean,

(62) John and Harry went to Cleveland together and they went together.

Native informants have unanimously rejected (62) as a reading for (61). Moreover, on McCawley's analysis, we ought to be able to get (61) as contradictory[23] that is, as

(63) John and Harry went to Cleveland separately and they went together.

Again, native informants unanimously reject (63) as a possible sense of (61).

By now it should be getting clearer that the addition of 'separately' or 'together' to (34) does not constitute a more adequate formulation of one of its *senses,* but is rather a more *specific* statement. The relation of (34) to (36) and (53) is more like genus to species than a sentence to its paraphrases.

In summary, I take it that the original arguments against the strong theorist stand, so far, and we turn now to an alternate account of the relationship.

GRICE'S THEORY OF IMPLICATION

In this section I present what is the main point of the first parts of this paper: reasons for believing that the relationship in question is one of implication. Since this is an empirical hypothesis and one of the best ways of challenging a theory is to provide a more adequate alternative, I shall try to make this part as persuasive as possible.

In an important series of papers, published and unpublished, H. P. Grice has been developing a theory of the relationship among an expression, its meaning, the speaker's meaning, the implications, and so on, of the utterance. Some of this structure is indicated in (64):[24]

(64) total content (signification) of an utterance (remark)

One convenient way of investigating Grice's theory is by tracking down various branches of this tree.[25]

In a number of places (1965, p. 444; 1967; 1971, p. 54), Grice has attempted to draw, both pretheoretically and theoretically, a distinction between what someone stated or said on an occasion, and what was implied or implicated.[26] To focus our attention on saying and implicating, Grice invites us to consider the following dialogue:

(65) (i) *S* (to *H*): How is *C* getting on in his job at the bank?
   (ii) *H* (to *S*): Quite well, he likes his colleagues and he hasn't been sent to prison yet.
       (1967, II, p. 4)

Grice wants to claim that *H* did not *say* that *C* is the sort of person who might yield to monetary temptations, but *S*'s saying (65ii) suggested, indicated, implied it—that is, his saying what he did *implicated* it.

This raises two related problems. One, how does one tell whether something is said or (just?) implied on a given occasion? Two, what is it to say or imply something? If we had necessary or sufficient conditions for saying or for implying, then we might be able to answer the first question, and if we had a way of assigning cases, we might be able to construct necessary or sufficient conditions. So anybody's discussion of one question is likely to include probes into the other, and Grice is no exception. What is true in Grice's case, I think, is that the different problems get different emphasis in these various discussions. The

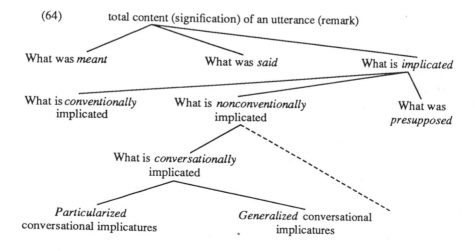

(64)   total content (signification) of an utterance (remark)

What was *meant*   What was *said*   What is *implicated*

What is *conventionally*   What is *nonconventionally*   What was
implicated   implicated   *presupposed*

What is *conversationally*
implicated

Particularized   *Generalized* conversational
conversational implicatures   implicatures

first question gets more emphasis in the earlier works, the second in the latter. We can take them up in this order.

In an early paper Grice (1965) discusses four cases "in which . . . something might be said to be implied as distinct from being stated." Although his main purpose seems to be to decide on the "vehicle" of the implication in each case, in the course of this Grice suggests some useful diagnostic tests:

1. *Nondetachability* (of the implication from what is asserted): "*Any* way of asserting what is asserted . . . involves the implication in question" (1965, p. 446).
2. *Noncancelability* (of the implication without canceling the assertion): "One cannot take . . . [another] form of words for which both what is asserted and what is implied is the same as [the first] . . . and *then* add a further clause withholding commitment from what would otherwise be implied, with the idea of annulling the implication without annulling the assertion" (1965, p. 446).
3. "If accepting that the implication holds involves one in accepting a hypothetical 'if *p* then *q*' where '*p*' represents the original statement and '*q*' represents what is implied, then what the speaker said (or asserted) is a vehicle of implication, otherwise not" (1965, p. 445–6).

These tests will be of assistance only to the extent we are able to tell when the conditions mentioned in them are met. However, the first two conditions appeal to the notion of two statements being the same, while the third appeals to the notion of 'involving one in accepting,' and one may protest that these notions are less clear than the notions we were testing for. Still, if we do not press too hard I think they can be of some utility. This does perhaps indicate that progress is more likely to be made by turning to the second set of problems mentioned earlier. We can conveniently reformulate that set as the following triple question:

(Q1) What is it for someone to *say that p?*
(Q2) What is it for someone (or something) to *implicate that q?*
(Q3) What are the main kinds of implicature?

We take these up in turn.

Saying that *p*

Without further remarks, (Q1) as stated blurs an important distinction—or rather, can be taken as asking two nonequivalent questions—depending on whether we view '*p*' as a variable or as a schematic letter. Taking it as a variable is to take (Q1) to be equivalent to

(Q1a) What is it to *say* something?

Taking it as a schematic letter or place holder shifts the emphasis to the place held: What is it to say *p*? This is better put: Given that something was said,

(Q1b) *What* was said? (How do we identify (or specify) what goes into the place held?)

We can put these questions as requests that the theorist fill out the following two schemas correctly:

(Q1a′) *Saying Attribution:* (*x*) (*x* said something if and only if *x* . . .).
(Q1b′) *Saying Specification:* (*x*) (If *x* said that *p*, then one identifies *p* if and only if one specifies . . .).

What does Grice have to say that bears on (Q1a) and (Q1b)?

Saying Specification. Grice does not say too much about this question. At one point (1967, II, p. 5) he does remark that, "for a full identification of what the speaker had said one would need to know (a) the identity of *x* [the referent(s)], (b) the time of utterance, (c) the meaning, on the particular occasion of utterance, of the phrase . . . [uttered]." Although Grice is here talking about a particular example, there is no indication that any of (a)–(c) are peculiar to it. So we can perhaps generalize this remark to the following Gricean instantiation of (Q1b′):

(66) To identify what *x* said [within the total significance of the utterance] (on some occasion) one must identify (specify)
   (a) The identity of the referents (if there was reference).
   (b) The time of utterance (if there was temporal specification).
   (c) The meaning of the expression uttered on that occasion of utterance.

Clause (c) has the effect of insuring that

(67) "In the sense in which I am using the word 'say', I intend what someone has said to be closely related to the conventional meaning of the words (the sentence) which he has uttered."

Thus, a person who understood English and supposed the speaker to be speaking literally, but knew nothing of the context, could only know that in uttering "He's in the grip of a vice" the speaker had *said* of some male that at the time of utterance (whenever that was) either he was unable to rid himself of some bad character trait, or he was caught in a particular kind of tool. Clause (a) is left vague on purpose, since Grice wants to leave it open "whether a man who says (today) 'Harold Wilson is a great man' and another who says (also today) 'The British Prime Minister is a great man' would, if each knew that the two singular terms had the same reference, have said the same thing" (1967, II, p. 5). However, there is *some* tension now with (c), for the two sentences certainly do not mean the same thing (in English), on any reading. But then it is not clear what the status of (c) is in the identification of what is said. Since that is the most natural way of reading the quotation, some additional elucidation is called for.

Saying Attribution. The saying specification (66) does not, of course, tell us under what circumstances it will be true that someone has said something. In his later works Grice has taken a number of steps toward an analysis of '*U* said that *p*'. One of the first things Grice wants to say (1967, V, p. 13) is that

(68) '*U* said that *p*' entails '*U* did something *x*':
   (1) by which *U* meant that *p*
   (2) which is an occurrence of an utterance type (sentence) S such that
     (i) S *means* '*p*'
     (ii) S consists of a sequence of elements (e.g., words) ordered in a way licensed by a system of rules (syntactic rules)
     (iii) S means '*p*' in virtue of the particular meaning of the elements of S, their order, and their syntactic character.

Grice abbreviates (68, 2) to read

(2') which is an occurrence of a type S which means '*p*' in some linguistic system.
                         (1967, V, p. 14)

From this it *looks* like we will get a definition of 'saying' like the following:

(69) *U* said that *p* iff
   (1) By uttering *X*, *U* meant that *p*
   (2) When uttered by *U*, *X* meant '*p*'.

But Grice does *not* want to subscribe to (69). Grice considers (69, 1,2) to be the definiens for '*U conventionally meant* that *p*' which is introduced as a technical term (1971, p. 57). Why does Grice think that '*U* said that *p*' is not equivalent to the coincidence of utterer's occasion-meaning and applied timeless meaning? Apparently because

(70) There are, I think, at least some sentences whose timeless meaning is not adequately specificable by a statement of the exemplary form.
                         (1971, p. 56)

If this were not the case, Grice seems to think that it would be possible to defend (69). Grice gives as an example of such a sentence:

(S1) Bill is a philosopher and he is, therefore, brave.

A specification of timeless meaning for (S1) might go,

(71) One meaning of (S1) includes 'Bill is occupationally engaged in philosophical studies' and 'Bill is courageous' and 'That Bill is courageous follows from his being occupationally engaged in philosophical studies' and that is all that is included
                         (1971, p. 57)

But rather than argue that (71) does *not* exemplify the schema for (applied) timeless meaning specification, and so is not exemplary, Grice *seems* to accept it as a good specification of timeless meaning and then he *goes on* to argue that even though

(i) By uttering (S1), *U* meant that Bill is . . .

and

(ii) When uttered by *U*, (S1) meant "Bill is . . ." . . .

it may *not* be the case that

(iii) *U said* that Bill is . . . and that his being courageous *follows from* his being a philosopher . . .

This is because Grice wants to claim that *U indicated,* but did not *say* (in his favored sense) that Bill's being courageous follows from his being a philosopher:

(72) I wish to maintain that the semantic function of the word 'therefore' is to enable the speaker

to *indicate*, though not to *say*, that a certain consequence holds.

(1971, p. 57)

Thus, Grice contends that concordance of (applied) timeless meaning and occasion-meaning is not *sufficient* for 'saying that'. Quite simply, if metaphorically, a person (and a sentence) can mean more than they *say*. But I think it is misleading to pin *this* disparity on the nonexemplariness of a certain meaning specification—or at least we need to be told how/why the said specification is not exemplary. What (72) indicates is that the utterance-meaning/speaker-meaning   distinction cuts across the saying/implying distinction. That is, if (69) were correct, then in diagram (64), what the speaker meant by uttering *x*, and what *x* has meant, would determine what was said. But this may not be correct, since it seems that what is *implicated* can be a part of what is meant (by *U*, or *X*, or both). Since what is said may be only a *part* of what is meant, Grice needs some way of factoring out a central core of meaning that will help determine what is said. Grice wants to

(73)   be able to explain or talk about what (within what *U* meant) *U* *centrally* meant: to give sense to 'in meaning that *p*, *U* centrally meant that *q*'.

(1967, V, p. 14)

As far as I know, Grice has not yet produced an analysis of 'centrally meant,' but he does suggest one role that it will play in the *definition* of *said that:*

(74)   '*U* said that *p*' is true iff *U* did something *x*:
(1) by which *U* *centrally* meant that *p*.
(2) which is an occurrence of a type S, part of the meaning of which is '*p*'.

(1967, V, p. 14)

In (1971, p. 57), Grice expands on his program for getting an analysis of 'saying that'. It includes

(75)   (i) specifying conditions for a limited range of central or fundamental speech acts: *Y*-ing;
(ii) Defining each *Y*-ing that **p* in terms of occasion-meaning, or important elements in the analysis thereof;
(iii) Stipulating that
In uttering *X*, *U* will have *said that *p* if
(1) *U* has *Y*-ed that **p*;
(2) *X* embodies some conventional de-

vice the meaning of which is such that its presence in *X* indicates that its utterer is *Y*-ing that **p*.

It would seem that one defect of all these preliminary analyses, ((68), (74), (75))—insofar as they are *necessary* conditions—is that the clause requiring that the speaker mean that *p* (or **p*) is too strong.[27] Suppose that someone thought that 'hoi polloi' meant 'the upper classes'. Then, by uttering 'he likes to associate with (the) hoi polloi' he would have meant that he likes to associate with the upper classes. But of course this is not what he *said*. When his mistake is pointed out to him, he agrees that he hadn't said what he meant—he had said that *p*, but meant that *q*, when *q* was in fact incompatible with *p*. Grice could, of course, say that his 'favored' sense of 'say' is not the sense above, but without more in the way of independent characterization of this sense (or use) of 'say' the move is not helpful. It is interesting to note that in his earlier paper (1965, p. 444) Grice drew the contrast not between *saying* and implicating, but between *stating* and implicating (he then used 'implying'). This may have been better since I find it more plausible to deny that I *stated* (or *asserted*) that *p* when I meant that *q*. However, this move would rule out all 'nonindicative' central speech acts.

Implicating that *q*

I think that the same distinctions made for 'saying' carry over to 'implicating'. We get

(Q2a)   *Implicature Attribution:* (*x*) (*x* implicated something iff . . . *x* . . .)

(Q2b)   *Implicature Specification:* (*x*) (if *x* implicated that *q*, then one specifies *q* iff one specifies . . .)

To my knowledge, Grice has not attempted either to formulate necessary and jointly sufficient conditions for implicating nor to give a general procedure for identifying, on an occasion, what has been implicated—although at one point ("Conditionals," p. 4) he does offer the following partial characterization:

(76)   *S implicates* that *q* (to *H*) if:
(i) *S* says that *p* (to *H*)
(ii) *S* does not say that *q* (to *H*)

(iii) By saying that *p* (to *H*) *S* meant, conveyed, implied, suggested, indicated that *q* (to *H*).

Rather, Grice has turned his attention mainly to sorting out different kinds of implicature and analyzing their modes of operation.

Some Kinds of Implicature

In his work so far, Grice distinguishes three major species of implicature: conventional implicature, conversational implicature, and presupposition. Since Grice has very little to say about the last category, we can look at it first.

Presupposition. Grice's main example of presupposition is (77):

(77) (a) 'Smith has left off beating his wife' presupposes that
     (b) Smith has been beating his wife.

Moreover, Grice is working with the 'semantic' notion of presupposition in the sense that "the truth of what is implied is a necessary condition of the original statement's being either true or false" (1965, p. 445). However, he also is willing to allow that in this case the *speaker* can be said to have presupposed (implied) that (77b). Presumably this is either a derived use of 'presupposition', or the speaker is said to have implied it in some way *because* what he said presupposed it. Grice does not spell this out, but he does say one curious thing about this case. He says that we should have "at least some inclination to say that the presence of the implication was a matter of the meaning of some of the words in the sentence, but we should be in some difficulty when it came to specifying precisely which this word or words are, of which this is true" (1965, p. 447). What is curious is that it seems clear that the guilty words are "left off." Synonyms preserve the presupposition (e.g., "quit"), and nonsynonyms do not (e.g., "started" or "begun thinking about").

Conventional Implicatures. In conventional implicatures:

(78) The conventional meaning of the words used will determine what is implicated, besides helping to determine what is said.
(1967, II, p. 6)

What is conventionally implicated is part of the meaning/force of the utterance.
(1967, III, p. 1)

One of our earlier examples falls under this category. Consider:

(79) He is a philosopher; he is, therefore, brave.

Grice comments,

(80) I would wish to maintain that the semantic function of the word 'therefore' is to enable the speaker to *indicate* though not to *say,* that a certain consequence holds ... I would adopt the same position with regards to words like 'but' and 'moreover'.
(1971, p. 57)

(81) The presence of this implicative is clearly a matter of the meaning of the word 'therefore'
("Conditionals," p. 4).

Later (1967, III, p. 8) Grice entertains the idea that

(82) a model case for a word which carries a conventional implicature is 'but.'

In his early paper (1965), Grice considers the example "[2] She was poor but she was honest" which is said to imply some contrast between *poverty* and *honesty.* Grice wants to claim the following:

(83) (i) It would be ... incorrect to say in the case of [2] that what he said (or asserted) implied that there was a contrast between, e.g., honesty and poverty.
    (ii) I should be inclined to say ... that the speaker could be said to have implied whatever it is that is implied; that in the case of [2] it seems fairly clear that the speaker's words could be said to imply a contrast ...
    (iii) The implication is *detachable:* had I said 'she is poor and she is honest' I would assert just what I would have asserted if I had used the original sentence; but there would now be no implication of a contrast between, e.g., poverty and honesty.
    (iv) as regards [2], the fact that the implication obtains is a matter of the meaning of the word 'but' ...
(pp. 445–447)

We have, then, the following cases of conventional implicature:

(a) *p* therefore *q* : *q* follows from *p* (perhaps: *p* provides good reasons for believing *q*).

(b) *p* but *q* : *p* contrasts with *q*.

One might question the correctness of with-holding some of this from what is said. Sup-pose someone says, "Sartre is a philosopher; he is, therefore, brave." Now, it might very well be true that Sartre is a philosopher and that he is brave, but that the *reason* we are willing to say he is brave has nothing at all to do with his being a philosopher, but rather with his work in the Resistance. Thus I would reject the statement above as false, but to do this it would have to be the case that what was said comprises the notion of his being a phi-losopher providing grounds for thinking him to be brave, because the other two clauses are true.

This is not the case with 'but'. If one says that Jackie is wealthy, but a brunet, one im-plies a contrast between wealth and hair color. However, in this case one is inclined to say that the statement is true even though the im-plicate is (probably) false, indicating that it is not a part of what was said.

I do not want to deny there is a class of con-ventional implicatures, but I will continue to be suspicious until more examples are ad-duced, and their conventionality is explicated.

Conversational Implicature. In contrast with conventional implicatures (which turn on the meaning of the words used) there is a class of implicatures that turn not only on what a per-son says but also on principles governing dis-course. As such, Grice's theory is the latest, and most sophisticated, in a line of attempts to account for what has variously been called *contextual* or *pragmatic* implication.[28] These implications turn on saying what is said in a discourse of a certain kind. The kind of dis-course at issue is one governed by the *Coop-erative Principle* (CP):[29]

(84) Make your conversational contribution such as is required, at the stage at which it occurs, by the accepted purpose or direction of the talk-exchange in which you are engaged.
                                  (1967, II, p. 7)

Under this principle come the following *max-ims.*[30] The first are those relating to *what is said:*

(85) *Quantity*
   (1) Make your contribution as informative as necessary.
   (2) Do not make it too informative.

(86) *Quality* (supermaxim: "try to make your con-tribution one that is true").
                                  (1967, II, p. 8)
   (1) Do not say what you believe to be false.[31]
   (2) Do not say what you lack adequate evi-dence for.[32]

(87) *Relation:* Be relevant.[33]

Relating to *how* what is said to be *said:*

(88) *Manner* (supermaxim: "Be perspicuous")
   (1) Avoid obscurity of expression.
   (2) Avoid ambiguity.
   (3) Be brief.
   (4) Be orderly.

And Grice observes (1967, II, p. 9) that there will need to be other kinds of maxims, e.g., es-thetic, social (politeness), moral.[34]

From these maxims it is obvious that the purpose mentioned in the Cooperative Prin-ciple is *here* taken to be the exchange of infor-mation. But there are, as Grice acknowledges (1969, II, p. 9), many other purposes of a talk exchange such as to influence the actions of others. Thus these maxims must be general-ized and supplemented for a complete the-ory.[35]

According to Grice, participants in a talk exchange may fail to fulfill a maxim in many ways. Since Grice is not always completely consistent in the use of his terminology, we adopt the neutral term 'infringement' for any failure to fulfill a maxim (or the CP). Saying that *A* infringed a certain maxim simply means he failed to fulfill it. This use commits us to nothing regarding the *way* the maxim was not fulfilled or the *consequences* of not fulfilling it. Of the four ways discussed, only three of them gave rise to implicatures: (90), (91), and (92).[36]

(89) seems to be the only infringement that does not give rise to implicature:

(89) One may *opt out* by indicating plainly that he is unwilling to cooperate. ("I cannot say any-thing more.")

In violating a maxim one is likely to mislead. Grice does not say very much about this as a way of infringing a maxim distinct from the others to follow. In fact, sometimes he uses 'vi-olate' where I have picked 'infringe'.

(90) One may quietly and unostentatiously *violate* a maxim.

These two infringements, (89) and (90), seem to be logically distinct. That is, if A opts out of a maxim, he does not infringe it "quietly and unostentatiously" and thus violate it. Conversely, if A violates a maxim, he has not indicated plainly that he is "unwilling to cooperate" and thus opted out. In (91), a maxim may be infringed, but its infringement is explained by supposing it to conflict with another maxim.

(91) One may be faced with a *clash* between one maxim and another.

Consider Grice's example. Suppose A is planning with B an itinerary for a holiday in France. Both know that A wants to visit his friend C. A: "Where does C live?" B: "Somewhere in the south of France."

GLOSS: (1) B is not opting out. (2) B has infringed the first maxim, Quantity (say as much as necessary). (3) (2) can be explained only by supposing that B is aware that to be more informative would be to infringe the second maxim, Quality (have evidence for what you say). (4) So B implicates that he does not know which town C lives in.

Notice first that it seems to be in the nature of the clash that in the particular circumstances the speaker cannot fulfill both of the maxims in question at once. However, it is not in the nature of the clash that any *particular* maxim must override the other. In this case, the second maxim of Quality overrides the first maxim of Quantity. Notice also in (3) Grice claims that this is the only supposition that would explain (2), but he gives no reason to believe this to be true—although it may be.

There are two ways of viewing this clash. From the speaker's point of view he must, in the circumstances, either infringe the first maxim of Quantity or the second maxim of Quality, and he must make a choice—between giving not enough information and giving groundless information. If the speaker does not opt out of the second maxim of quality (by saying "I do not know exactly") then the hearer is faced with an infringement he can explain (or explain away) by positing that there was a clash and that the speaker opted for fulfilling the second maxim of Quality.

On the speaker's side, this suggests an ordering or weighting of the maxims and it is not too hard to find a plausible explanation. If it

can be assumed that the speaker S is observing at least the CP, then S will pick quality over quantity if only because truly groundless information has at least as good a chance of being wrong as right, and as such would probably not be helpful—thereby violating the CP.

On the hearer's side, this suggests that there is a metaprinciple at work, which I will call the Principle of Charity:

(*PC*) Other things being equal, construe the speaker's remark so as to violate as few maxims as possible.

Since, however, some maxims may be more highly weighted than others we need the Weighted Principle of Charity (for pairs of maxims):

(*WPC*) Other things being equal, construe the speaker's remark so that it is consistent with the maxim of higher weight.

or

If the speaker has infringed one or other of a pair of maxims, other things being equal, assume that he has chosen to infringe the lowest valued maxim.

Now we can reconstruct Grice's Gloss in more detail and perhaps eliminate the appeal to "explanations" in favor of an appeal to a sufficient condition. We will assume that B knows that A is observing the maxims, CP and the metaprinciples:

GLOSS: (0) B said that p. (1) B has not opted out. (2) B's saying that p in this context infringes Quantity-1. (3) So some p' (more informative than p) would not have infringed Quantity-1. (4) So B could have said that p', but if he had said that p' then under the (ex hypothesi) assumption that B is obeying Quality-2, he would had to have had evidence for p'. (5) If B had no evidence for p' and said that p', he would have violated Quality-2. (6) Assume that B has no evidence for p'. (7) Then: (i) If B says that p, he infringes Quantity-1. (ii) If B says that p', he infringes Quality-2. (8) Apply the WPC to (7): Do not infringe Quality over Quantity, so do not say that p'. (9) B said that p (and not p') thereby satisfying (8). (10) So (6) (plus general principles) is sufficient for (9), so B has no evidence for p'. (11) So B has implicated that he does not know which town C lives in.

The final infringement of a maxim that Grice discusses is flouting:

(92) The speaker may *flout* a maxim—he may blatantly fail to fulfill it.

It is this class of infringements that gives rise to conversational implicatures. The speaker *S* *exploits* a maxim when *S* flouts a maxim, with the consequence that the hearer *H* knows that *S*'s utterance does not fall under (89)–(91) and so *H* must reconcile *S*'s saying what he said with the supposition that *S* is obeying the conversational maxims and/or the cooperative principle.

Here (as indicated by '□') are some examples of Grice's (1967, II) that involve exploitation, the procedure by which a maxim is flouted for the purpose of getting in a conversational implicature. Though a maxim is infringed at the level of *what is said,* the hearer is entitled to assume that the maxims (or the CP) is being observed at the level of *what is implicated.*

Quantity-1 Make your contribution as informative as necessary.

□ *A* is writing a recommendation for his philosophy pupil *C* to *B*. It reads: "Mr. *C*'s command of English is excellent and his attendance at tutorials has been regular. Yours, etc."

GLOSS: (of *B*'s reasoning): (1) *A* cannot be opting out, for he need not have written at all. (2) *A* cannot be unable, through ignorance, to say more since *C* was *A*'s pupil. (3) Therefore, *A* must be wishing to impart some information that he is unwilling to write down. (4) This supposition is tenable only on the assumption that *A* thinks that *C* is no good at *X*-ing. (5) Therefore, this is what he is implicating.

The end of a review of a sleazy American novel is an analogous case: "The print is tolerably readable and all the pages in the last two chapters are correctly numbered" (*Punch,* 1969, p. 354). Although this carries a definite implication of worthlessness, it would have been quite strong had this been the total review. The mechanism behind this implication may well underlie the force of the slogan 'damn with faint praise'.

□ Tautologies like: "war is war" and "boys will be boys" flout the first maxim of Quantity.

GLOSS: These are totally uniformative at the level of what is said, but they are informative at the level of what is implicated. The hearer's identification of their information content at this level depends on his ability to explain the speaker's selection of this *particular* patent tautology.

I do not find this completely satisfactory. We still need some argument to show that these are not idiomatic, for instance. Notice that if this was *purely* conversational, it ought to work appropriately for almost any tautology of the relevant type. But consider: "Tables are tables"; "Pencils will be pencils." These simply do not have the requisite implicature *except* as being read (by the hearer) as conscious plays by the speaker on the standard tautologies. As such, the principles that yield the requisite implicatures in the standard cases yield the requisite implicatures in these cases (e.g. pencils usually break or have some characteristic defect). Notice how hard it is to figure out what the first of the tautologies above would implicate even in the appropriate contexts. This application of Quantity-1 still needs more work, since the mechanism generating the specific implications is still obscure.[37]

Although Grice does not mention contradictions, since they also carry no information it might be supposed that they can function the same way as tautologies in generating implicatures. Cases are hard to find, however, the following might be considered: "Contemporary philosophers are not (really?) philosophers." "It is raining and it isn't." "Fairest Cordelia, that art most rich being poor" (*King Lear,* 1, i).

Quantity-2 Do not give more information than is required.

□ *A* asks "Is it the case that p? and *B* answers: "It is certain that p" or "*p*, and I am certain of it, every body knows it."

GLOSS: (of *A*'s reasoning): (1) if *B*'s volubility is undesigned it may raise doubt whether *B* is as certain as he says ("The lady doth protest too much"). (2) If it is thought of as designed, it would be an oblique way of conveying that it is to some degree controversial whether or not p.

I find these very suspicious. The gloss does not exhibit any of the structural complexity of the working-out schema.

Quality-1 Do not say what you believe to be false.

□ Irony: *A* and *B* both know that *A*'s friend *X* has just sold *A*'s business secrets. A: "X is a fine friend."(*P*).

GLOSS: (by *B*) (1) *A* has flouted the first maxim of quality. (2) *A* knows that I know this. (3) *A* has not opted out, nor is there any obvious clash. (4) Therefore, *A* must be trying to get across some other proposition *Q*. (5) For me to be successful it must be some obviously related propositions. (6) The most obviously related proposition is the contradictory of the purported one. (7) Therefore, this is the proposition that *A* is trying to get across.

I find this suspicious for two reasons. First, why should we suppose that the contradictory is the most obviously related proposition and not, say, the Existential Generalization of *P*, or the result of substituting the name of *B*'s mother for the subject expression in *P*, etc? Second, the contradictory of *P* is "*X* is not a fine friend" and it at least has to be argued that this *entails* that *X* is not a friend at all. It is at least possible that without stress on "fine" I might still only be denying him a certain *rank* as a friend. But suppose it does entail that *X* is not a friend, this does not, certainly, entail that he is an enemy, rival, villain. Presumably many people are not *A*'s friends who also are not *A*'s enemies. Notice, I am *not* denying that in the context, there is the implication that *X* is a cad; rather I am complaining that this fact has not been captured by the description Grice gives of both the upshot and the way it is achieved.

☐ Metaphor: A: "You are the cream in my coffee."(P).

GLOSS: (1) P is categorically false. (2) Therefore the contradictory of what *A* has made as if to say will strictly speaking be a truism. (3) Therefore, it cannot be *that*, that *A* is trying to get across. (4) The most likely supposition is that *A* is attributing to his audience some feature in respect of which the audience resembles (more or less fancifully) the mentioned substance. (5) Therefore, this is what is implicated.

Again, why is (4) supposed to be true? Why is *this* the "most likely" supposition? I take it that Grice would like to *explain* metaphor along these lines rather than appeal to some sort of loose 'metaphor-conventions' to sanction the move to (4)—that is, the move to (4), and others like it, is to *explain* metaphorical use of language. But then we need some principles to guide our search for the correct supposition. I do not see why the proposition Grice gives is the "most likely."

Quality-2 Do not say what you lack adequate evidence for.

☐ Grice's only example of this is where some-

one says, in suitable circumstances, "She is probably deceiving him this evening," thereby implicating that she is (the sort of person who is) given to deceiving her husband. The implicature is supposed to be off of the contextually determined fact that the speaker has no evidence for what he said, so the hearer must find a proposition that the speaker might have sufficient evidence for, such as the above.[38]

Relation Be relevant.

☐ At a genteel tea-party, A: "Mrs. X is an old bag." (Appalled silence). B: "The weather has been quite delightful this summer, hasn't it?"

GLOSS: (1) *B* has flouted the maxim of relation—it is not relevant to *A*'s remark. (2) He thereby implicates that *A*'s remark should not be discussed or that *A* has committed a social gaffe.

I find this case suspect because it is not at all obvious how to fill in the reasoning between flouting the maxim and the implication, which must be possible if it is to be a conversational implicature.

We can now try to characterize conversational implicatures as follows (1967, II, p. 13):[39]

(93) *S conversationally implicates* that *q* to *H* iff:
    (1) *S* implicates that *q* to *H*;
    (2) *H* presumes that *S* is observing the conversational maxims (or CP) when *S* says that *p* to *H*;
    (3) If *S*'s saying that *p* is *S*'s total contribution to the conversation at that point, then *S*'s saying that *p* is not consistent with the presumption that *S* is observing the conversational maxims (or CP);
    (4) The supposition that *S* *things, is aware,* that *q* is required to make *S*'s saying (or making as if to say) that *p* consistent with the presumption that *S* is observing the conversational maxims (or CP);
    (5) *S* thinks (and would expect *H* to think that *S* thinks) that it is within the competence of *H* to work it out or grasp intuitively that (4).

Working-Out Schema. Since it is a necessary condition on something being a conversational implicature that it at least be capable of being worked out, we should be able to schematize this working out as follows (1967, II, p. 14):[40]

(94) (1) *S* said that *p*.
    (2) If *S*'s saying that *p* is his total contribution to the conversation at this point, it is not

consistent with the presumption that S is observing the conversational maxims (or CP).

(3) There is no reason to suppose that S is not observing the conversational maxims (or CP).

(4) The supposition that S thinks that q is required to make S's saying that p consistent with the presumption that S is observing the conversational maxims (or CP).

(5) S knows that I can see that (4).

(6) S has done nothing to block (5).

(7) Therefore S intends me to think that q.

(8) So, S has implicated that q.

In this reasoning H makes use of at least the following information:

(95) (1) the conventional meaning of the words;

(2) The identity of the referents;

(3) The conversational maxims (or CP);

(4) The context of utterance;

(5) Background knowledge;

(6) The mutual belief that S and H share knowledge of (1)–(5).

At this point we must notice that the implicature that q has been carried by S's saying that p on a particular occasion in virtue of special features of the context. These kinds of conversational implicatures Grice calls *particularized* conversational implicatures. As he says: "There is no room for the idea that an implicature of this sort is *normally* carried by saying that P" (1967, II, p. 21).

Generalized Conversational Implicature. Grice coins the category of *generalized* conversational implicatures for cases where saying that p would *normally* carry such and such an implicature. The fact that a generalized conversational implicature carries a normal implicature is liable to make it appear similar to a conventional implicature. As examples of generalized conversational implicatures, Grice gives the following:

(96) 'x is meeting a woman this evening'[41] implicates 'the woman is not his sister, mother, wife, or close platonic friend'.

(97) 'x went into a house yesterday and found a tortoise inside the front door' implicates 'the house was not his own'. The same could be said of 'a car,' 'a garden, 'a college'.

Grice claims that sometimes there is no such implicature. For example,

(98) I've been sitting in a car all morning.

If this is correct it is an interesting question why there is no implicature in (98), but there is in the following:

(99) x climbed into a car yesterday and found a tortoise behind the seat.

Notice that the explanation cannot turn on a difference in the verbs in (99) and (98), because the same verb in different VP's can have or fail to have the requisite implicature. Consider the following:

(100) (i) 'I slept in a chair last night' does not imply 'the chair is not mine'.

(ii) 'I slept under a table last night' does not imply 'the table is not mine'.

(iii) 'I slept $\begin{Bmatrix} \text{in a house last night} \\ \text{on a boat last night} \end{Bmatrix}$' does not imply 'the house/boat is not mine'.

(iv)? 'I slept in a car last night' does imply 'the car is not mine'.

(v) 'I slept in a small room last night' does not imply 'the small room is not mine'.

(101) (i) 'I found a ring yesterday' does imply 'the ring is not mine.'

(ii) 'I found an error yesterday' does not imply 'the error was not mine'.

(102) (i) 'I read a book yesterday' does not imply 'the book is mine.'

(ii)? 'I lost a book yesterday' does imply 'the book is mine.'

I have as yet no explanation for these differences.

Grice concludes that a conversational implicature possesses certain features:

(103) (1) Since observance of the conversational maxims is a necessary condition for calculating a conversational implicature, a generalized conversational implicature can be *canceled* by either *explicitly or contextually opting out.*

(2) Since calculation of a conversational implicature requires only:

(i) Contextual information

(ii) Background information

(iii) What is said

and not the *manner* in which it is said, then any way of saying what is said is likely to have the same conversational implicature. Since a generalized conversational implicature is fairly insensitive to context and background information, it should have a high degree of nondetachability.

(3) Since calculation of the conversational implicature requires prior knowledge of

what is said, the conversational implicature is not a part of the meaning-force of what is said.

(4) Since what is said may be true and what is conversationally implicated is false, the implicature is not carried by what is said, but only by, "The saying of what is said or by 'putting it that way'".

(1967, II, p. 25)

Clause (4) is not at all clearly true and seems to conflict with the claim in (103, 2). In (4) Grice seems to be invoking his old criteria of cancelability as the test for whether *what is said* is the vehicle of the implication. But since implicature is not entailment and can always be canceled, it is not clear what truth or falsity has to do with it at all.

(103) (5) In many cases the conversational implicature will be a disjunction.

A Problem with This Account

The possibility of (103, 5) raises some questions about the completeness or adequacy of Grice's characterization of the generalized conversational implicature. Reconsider Grice's examples:

(104) I found a tortoise in a house yesterday.

is said to conversationally implicate

(105) The house was not mine.

How would we get this implicature on Grice's scheme? Presumably, the first maxim of quantity is being exploited. 'A house' conveys less information than might be desired. In normal circumstances the speaker might legitimately suppose that the hearer would like him to be more specific. But there are many ways of being more specific here:

$$(106)\ \text{I found a tortoise in} \left\{ \begin{array}{l} \text{my} \\ \text{Nixon's} \\ \text{Aunt Martha's} \end{array} \right\} \text{house}$$
yesterday.

Again, feature (103, 5) predicts that my saying that I found a tortoise in a house yesterday should implicate an open disjunction of the form

(107) The house was mine or the house was Nixon's, or the house was Aunt Martha's . . .

However, none of these are implicated. All that *is* implicated is that it is *not* my house. Fortunately for Grice's theory, the description above does not satisfy all of his conditions for a conversational implicature. In particular, it doesn't satisfy condition (1): that S implicates that q to H, because it does not satisfy condition (iii) on Implicature: that by saying that p to H, S implied, suggested, indicated, etc., that q (to H).

Since it is false that I implicated that

$$(108)\ \text{The house was} \left\{ \begin{array}{l} \text{mine.} \\ \text{Nixon's.} \\ \text{not Nixon's.} \\ \text{Aunt Martha's.} \\ \text{not Aunt Martha's.} \end{array} \right.$$

it is false that I *conversationally* implicated that (108). For this reason we must assume that the *range* of the possible disjunction in (5) is determined by what is implicated. However, the theory now cannot explain why the implicature is there in the first place.[42] One way to get the requisite implicature might be as follows. We distinguish between a *primary* and a *secondary* implicature. A secondary implicature is whatever can be reasonably inferred by the hearer (given shared background knowledge and beliefs) from the primary implicature in the context. In the case above the hearer reasons as follows:

(109) (1) X said he found a tortoise in a house yesterday.

(2) We both know (and know that we both know) that the conversational maxims are being observed.

(3) Therefore, the first maxim of Quantity is being observed.

(4) The speaker should assume that I am interested in knowing what house it was found in.

(5) Therefore, he is flouting the first maxim of Quantity.

(6) Since the speaker is obeying the conversational maxims, he is observing the maxim of Relation: be relevant. Thus the most charitable assumption consistent with the exploitation of the first maxim of Quantity is that he doesn't know anything more about the house (that he thinks is relevant).

(7) Therefore, he *primarily implicates* that he doesn't have any more pertinent information about the house.

(8) Since one usually knows what houses one

possesses, we may reasonably infer that this was not one of them.

(9) Therefore, he *secondarily implicates* that the house was not his.

Notice that this way of handling the case has the advantage that it explains why, in a conversation about, say, Aunt Martha's house, the speaker would be taken to implicate that the tortoise was not in Aunt Martha's house. This is because the gap between the primary and secondary implicature is bridged by background knowledge and beliefs—and in the course of a conversation various pieces of information that influence the inference can be conveyed. It seems to me that there is liable to be a complex interaction here (and other places, of course) among various pieces of information and the different maxims—although I have no clear data to support this hunch. This also suggests that the terminology 'generalized' implicature is misleading. What appears to happen is that such implicatures stand unless they are explicitly or contextually cancelled. Such 'standing' conversational implicatures are presumably sustained by a variety of mutual beliefs among participants in the talk-exchange.

FIRST SOLUTION TO THE PROBLEM PROPOSED

We now return to our problem cases. We have decided that the IMPLICATION is not entailment, is not a *part* of what is said. The question then becomes, what kind of implicature they are: conventional, particularized conversational, or generalized conversational. Here we must be careful, for although we have been given five features of conversational implicatures, we do not have and may never have a decision procedure to settle the question of whether q—which is a part of the total signification of the utterance of a sentence—is a conversational implicate or an element in the conventional meaning of the sentence (1967, III, p. 3). To make any case for the existence of a conversational implication, it is necessary (and perhaps not sufficient) to exhibit the reasoning that generates it. As Grice says:

(110) "Any such case [for the existence of a conversational implicature] would at least have

to be supported by a demonstration of the way in which what is putatively implicated could have come to be implicated (by a derivation of it from conversational principles and other data); and even this may not be sufficient to provide a decisive distinction between a conversational implicature and a case in which what was originally a conversational implicature has become conventionalized."

(1967, III, p. 4)

Thus, to make even a plausible case for our favored relation being a nonconventional implicature, the exact steps for its generation must be specified. This is a requirement I will try to strictly observe.

Our earlier results showed that the implications were cancelable, but not (easily) detachable. Since these are two of the properties of the generalized conversational implicature, it is plausible that this is the correct category. However, if we try to apply the paradigm it is not clear how it is supposed to work. The main problem is to find an adequate sense in which one *exploits* a conversational maxim in uttering our sentences. This should make us suspicious. Nevertheless, we will try to construct an explanation along these lines.

Adjectives

The only plausible maxim to be exploited is Quantity-1: be as informative as is necessary. Suppose Jones asks: "what color is the flag?" and Smith replies: "(the flag is) red." Thus

(111) (1) (i) Smith said that the flag was red.
        (ii) Smith did not say that the flag was red all over.
        (iii) Smith's saying that the flag was red suggested or implied that it was red all over.
        (iv) Therefore, Smith implicated that the flag was red all over.
     (2) Smith supposes that Jones is aware that Smith is observing the general maxims.
     (3) The supposition that the flag is red all over is required to make Smith's saying that the flag is red consistent with the first maxim of quantity.
     (4) Jones is aware that Smith knows it is within Jones' competence to work it out that (3).
     (5) Smith has done nothing to block (3).
     (6) Therefore Smith thinks that the flag is red all over.

The exploitation of the first maxim of Quantity comes about by having the choice of sentences:

(112) The flag is $\left\{\begin{array}{l}\text{(i) } \phi \\ \text{(ii) partly} \\ \text{(iii) all}\end{array}\right\}$ red.[43]

But if we read 'the flag is red' as I want to— 'the flag is at least partly red', then *both* 'the flag is partly red' and 'the flag is all red' are *more* informative than 'the flag is red'. The problem is why it implies 'all' rather than 'partly' since they are both compatible with the first maxim of Quantity. This is a case like the one we mentioned earlier as raising questions about the completeness of Grice's characterization of the generalized conversational implicature. According to feature (103, 5), in many cases the conversational implicature will be a disjunction and that is just what we have here. However, only the 'all' statement is really implicated—whereas the theory predicts that both will be.

Our difficulty here is analogous to our difficulty with 'a house'. With the house example we saw that saying 'I found a tortoise in a house yesterday' did not conversationally implicate (via exploitation of the first maxim of quantity) that the house was Aunt Martha's or Nixons's—even though these were assumptions that would make what I said compatible with the maxims—because I didn't implicate these at all. Likewise with 'the flag'; I do not implicate at all that the flag is partly red, so I don't conversationally implicate it. But analogous to the house example, we still need to explain how the implicature arises in the first place. With the house example, we got the implicature through the distinction between primary and secondary implication. How can we get it with the flag example? It might go the same way as follows. Recall that we introduced our sentence in response to the question, 'What color is the flag?' (what I earlier called the 'minimal context'). It can reasonably be supposed that when a person asks a question of the form

(113) What ϕ is the X?

he wants enough information about the ϕ of the X so that if he wanted to pick out X with respect to ϕ, he could. To say that the flag is at least red is to provide less identificatory information than that it is all red.[44]

Given this, we can account for the implicature stated as a blunt fact in (111, 1) (iii) and shortcircuit the unwanted implicatures of (107). The hearer's (questioner's) reasoning is as follows:

(114) (1) Jones said that the flag is (at least) red.
       (2) Jones did not say that the flag is all red.
       (3) We both are observing the conversational maxims, etc.
       (4) Therefore, Jones is observing the first maxim of Quantity.
       (5) Under the circumstances, Jones can reasonably assume (and assume that I assume him to assume) that I would like ϕ-identifying information about x.
       (6) Given assumption (5), Jones has flouted the first maxim of Quantity.
       (7) The most charitable assumption consistent with (4) and (5) is that no further information is needed (for ϕ-identification).
       (8) Therefore, Jones *primarily implicates* that no further information is needed (for ϕ-identification).
       (9) But if the flag were other colors besides red, other information would be needed, but since (7), then there are no other colors.
       (10) Therefore, Jones *secondarily implicates* that the flag is *all* red.

Notice that one advantage of treating 'the flag is all red' as a conversational implicature and not as an entailment is that in a conversation requiring the identification of a certain color, one can point to an American flag and say 'that flag is magenta' without implicating that it is all red. In this case, the implicature is *contextually* canceled. This is analogous to the first feature Grice gives of a general conversational implicature—that its implication can be canceled by either explicitly or contextually *opting out*.

Verbs

We turn now to sentences like

(115) Russell wrote *Principia*.

(116) Smith and Jones moved the table.

Again there is a certain difficulty in seeing how to apply the theory. Rather than assume that the explanation for the IMPLICATIONS will be the same for both (115) and (116), I will attack them one at a time.

Consider the following dialogue again:

(117) (i) *H*: Who wrote *Principia*?
(ii) *S*: Russell wrote *Principia*.

The most obvious way of handling the implication in our theory is to appeal again to the first maxim of Quantity. Again, we can suppose that the hearer-*cum*-questioner is requesting ϕ-identifying information about *Principia*. The hearer-*cum*-questioner (*H*) upon hearing the answer reasons as follows:

(118) (1) *S* said that (at least) Russell wrote *Principia*.
(2) *S* did not say that Russell alone wrote *Principia*.
(3) We are both obeying (and know that we both know we are obeying) the conversational maxims.
(4) *H* supposes that *S* knows that *H* is requesting authorship-identifying information, and that all information *necessary* for this is relevant.
(5) Since *H* supposes *S* to fulfill (3), *H* supposes *S* to be obeying the maxim of Relation: be relevant.
(6) Since *H* supposes *S* to fulfill (3), *H* supposes *S* to be obeying the first maxim of Quantity.
(7) But on supposition (5), *S* is flouting the first maxim of Quantity by uttering (117 ii) (in this context).
(8) To make *S*'s saying that (117 ii) consistent with supposition (6), the most charitable assumption is that no further information is needed for ϕ-identification.
(9) Therefore, *S primarily implicates* that no further information is necessary for ϕ-identification.
(10) But if Russell wrote *Principia* with someone else, (8) would be false.
(11) Since *H* is supposing (8) is true, Russell did not write *Principia* with someone else.
(12) Therefore *S secondarily implicated* that Russell alone wrote *Principia*.

Consider the following dialogue:

(118) (i) *H*: Who moved the table?
(ii) *S*: Smith and Jones moved the table.

Besides the implication that no one else helped them move the table, there is the implication that they moved it together. It is this latter implication that I want to investigate.

Unfortunately, here there seems to be no obvious way of appealing to the first maxim of

Quantity. As a clue to what is going on, notice what kinds of cases would make the implication false. For example,

(119) First Smith moved the table, then Jones moved the table.

This suggests to me that it is possible that the single temporal specification in (118ii) could be playing a role in the implication. Notice that the conjoined sentence

(120) (i) Smith moved the table and (ii) Jones moved the table.

tends, if anything, to imply that they did *not* move it together. Again it is possible that picking twin temporal specification contributes to carrying the implication of two separate act-tokens. This phenomenon is similar to Strawson's examples (1952, p. 80):

(121) (i) They got married and had a child.
(ii) They had a child and got married.

Some logicians have claimed that these two sentences are equivalent (that 'and' is the English analogue of the standard connective '&') while other logicians (among them Strawson) have claimed that (121) is a counterexample to such a view. Grice, subscribing to the former view, has tried to explain the *prima facie* difference between (121i) and (121ii) as due to an implicature, not to the meaning of 'and'. Grice handles this case by appealing to a submaxim of Manner, to the effect that one should make the order of telling reflect the order of the events.

In an analogous fashion, choosing the conjoined-subject sentence (118, ii) over the conjoined-sentence sentence (120), or vice versa, implies something about the nature of the event. The problem is finding the necessary feature of the sentence and finding a suitable submaxim. In Grice's account of Strawson's example there was an appeal to similarity of temporal order. What can I appeal to? As a start consider the following:

Super Submaxim: Be representational; in so far as possible, make your sayings "mirror" the world.

With this *Tractatus*-like maxim available, we can see Grice's submaxim as fitting one "dimension" of mirroring, *time:*

Submaxim of Time: In so far as possible, make the order of saying reflect the order of events.

Another dimension of mirroring might be *space:*

Submaxim of Space: In so far as possible, if objects *a, b, c, . . . φ* together, put their names together when reporting this *φ*-ing.

These may not be as farfetched as they seem. At times we seem to utilize in our sayings the parallelism between our sayings and the world. Consider: "Sam read Plato, Aristotle and Descartes in that order." What order is *that* order? Clearly it is not the left-to-right order of the words 'Plato', 'Aristotle', and 'Descartes', but rather the temporal order in speech which the left-to-right order represents in English. The use of 'that' in this way here requires that the temporal order of saying mirror that of the reading.

Does the submaxim of space contain a pun on 'together'? Consider the difference in implication between the following:

(122) (i) Sam was in New York last week, and John was in New York last week, and Fred was in New York last week.
(ii) Sam and John and Fred were in New York last week.

For me, (122ii) implies that they were in New York together, while (122i) does not. In fact (122, i) weakly implies that they were not together in New York last week. The question is what (122ii) shares with (118ii) such that an implication is generated, but which (122i) and (120i) lack. At the moment, only the condition specified by the applied submaxim seems to sort these cases. Using this submaxim we can, perhaps, account for the implicature in (118ii) that they moved the table together in a way that resembles (114) and (118).

PROBLEMS WITH THE FIRST PROPOSAL

Besides the obvious deficiencies of vagueness, overhasty generalization, one-sided diet of examples, and so on, the explanation sketched in the previous section has at least the following limitations. One, the theory so far does not explain why some adjectives and verbs contribute to an implicature and others do not. Two, previously I said that we ought to be suspicious of our difficulty in identifying the appropriate maxim for exploitation and utilization in the working-out schema. I think those suspicions were justified. In fact, not all of the working-out schema was utilized, as a glance back at (94) will show. In particular, clause (94, 4) requires that the output of the schema have the form

(123) *S* thinks (is aware) that *q.*

whereas our implicata had the form

(124) *q* (e.g., 'The flag is all red.')

But clause (94, 4) is a reflex of a condition on conversational implicature—it is the supposition (123) that is required for maxim consistency. Thus technically our cases were not cases of conversational implicature. In a way this is good, for certainly when I say 'The flag is red' I am not trying to get you to work it out that I think that the flag is all red. I may be being coy or noncommittal, but I need neither think that the flag is all red nor need I be trying to get you to think that I think that the flag is all red. Nevertheless, I want to claim that something like this implication *is* generated by saying that *p*. In this respect our cases [differ] from some of the paradigmatic examples with which Grice introduces and illustrates the notion of conversational implicature. In cases like (65ii) and (96), the probable context is one where the speaker wants to *communicate* a certain belief or piece of information without *saying* it—as if he might want to leave the 'I didn't *say* that' bridge unburned. But notice that I did not cite Grice's example (97) in the list above. All along I have been working off of the parallelisms between the house example (97) and my examples, and it strikes me that the house example falls under criticisms above, too. In saying 'I found it in a house', I am not trying to get you to work it out that (I think that) the house was not mine. The implication is carried regardless of this. It is not something I might care to avoid *saying* but nevertheless want to *communicate*. The conclusion that the working-out schema does not (completely) apply has serious consequences. As Grice says:

(125) The presence of a conversational implicature must be capable of being worked out; for even if it can in fact be intuitively grasped, unless the intuition is replaceable by an argument, this implicature will not count as a

conversational implicature; it will be a *conventional* implicature

(1967, II, p. 13).

This might lead us to believe that the phenomena I am trying to explain is conventional, but it cannot be—first, since the implications are cancelable, and, second, because there is no obvious way to tie the implication to the words in question without creating difficulties. Thus, even if conventional implication is distinguished from entailment, it cannot be *attached directly* to the adjective because conjoined predicates like 'red and white' would then have incompatible conventional implications. But if the implication is not conventional and not conversational, what is it? There are at least two alternatives. First, we could either modify the definition of conversational implicature and the working-out schema by (*a*) making the appropriate condition *disjunctive,* i.e., ⌜*S* thinks that *q,* or *q̄*⌝; or (*b*) we could simply replace ⌜*S* thinks that *q̄*⌝ by *q* in the definition, and let ⌜*S* thinks that *q̄*⌝ be inferred by the hearer via the first maxim of Quality: do not say what you believe to be false. But since *q* is not a part of what is *said,* the maxim does not literally apply. The second alternative is to attempt to isolate another kind of implicature that does not necessitate the use of exploitation and the fullblown working-out schema. This kind of implication would lie 'between' conventional implication and generalized conversational implication.

Second Solution Proposed: Direct and Indirect Implicature

Recall that we earlier noted that Grice distinguished four ways in which a maxim could be infringed: by opting out, by violation, by clash, and by flouting. Grice *seems* to reserve the title 'conversational implicature' for those aroused by flouting a maxim. What then of the others? Since they also turn on supposing the maxims to be in effect thay can be said to be broadly 'conversational' too. If all nonconventional implicatures should turn out to be conversational (in the sense of turning on maxims of conversation), then we could adopt some other term like 'pragmatic' for the genus, and reserve 'conversational' for those

gotten by flouting. However, this generalization is by no means clearly true. So I will adopt the terminology of *direct* and *indirect* (conversational) implicatures. *Indirect* implicatures require that a maxim be flouted, whereas *direct* implicatures require that the highest-valued maxims are intended to be observed, at the level of what is said. Nonconventional, but nonconversational implicatures might be called 'contextual'.

These two kinds of implicature seem to have at least one important difference. With indirect conversational implicature, the hearer is intended to reason from the speaker's saying that *p* to his implicating that *q,* that it would be reasonable (on Grice's theory of utterer's occasion-meaning[45]) to say that the speaker meant that *q.* This will not be the case with direct implicature since the speaker need not be aware that the hearer is making the inference generating the implicature. Consider again

(126) The flag is red.

On the assumption that the speaker is obeying the conversational maxims, the speaker is obeying the following maxims:

(127) (i) Be as informative as necessary.
        (ii) Be relevant.
        (iii) Have evidence for what you say.

These obviously can interact in various ways and for this reason it is useful to state them separately. However, I want to suggest[46] another maxim that combines them in a specific way:

(128) *Maxim of Quantity-Quality:* Make the strongest relevant claim justifiable by your evidence.

This maxim is ordered with respect to the other three—it applies unless one of the others overrides it (either explicitly or contexually).

On hearing (126), the Hearer reasons as follows:

(129) (1) *S* is obeying all the maxims, so he is obeying Quantity-Quality.
       (2) The claim that the flag is red and some other color would be stronger than the claim that it is red, because ⌜*p* and *q̄*⌝ entails *p,* but not conversely.
       (3) Therefore *S* is directly implying that the flag is not red *and* some other color, and therefore that the flag is only red.

The same reasoning will work for "Russell wrote *Principia*." And the nonconventional implicature branch of (64) should look something like (130):

(130)

	Nonconventional Implicature		
	Conversational		Contextual
	Direct	Indirect	?
Particular			
Standing (Generalized)			

CONCLUSIONS

I want to emphasize exactly how weak my conclusions are even on the assumption that all of my arguments are sound. I am *not* claiming that I have shown that sentences like the ones I have been interested in are correctly gotten by conjunction reduction. Indeed, I think that evidence will eventually turn up that will show that they are *not* gotten by conjunction reduction—but this is presently just a hunch. Nor am I claiming that there are not other arguments besides (5) and (21) that would show that the sentences at issue could not come from conjunction reduction. Finally, I am not claiming that there is nothing wrong with these arguments except the steps that I have isolated for discussion. All I claim to have shown is that one argument in support of two of the premises of (5) and (21) is not sound because it has a false premise—that (7) entails (8) and (9) entails (10). I have given two sets of considerations against that view: direct counterargument and a theory of why one might have thought the relation was entailment. Now, it might turn out that my use of Grice's theory here is incorrect, and it might be that some more obviously adequate explanation can be found. Still, this paper will have the value of having demonstrated that in that case Grice's theory is simply too strong, that it can be applied very naturally to a domain that should be explained some other way. This would tell us that (and perhaps to some extent how) we must constrain the theory. This is one of the reasons that I have been at special pains to keep my examples and explanations as close to Grice's examples and explanations as possible.

FURTHER APPLICATIONS

If, contrary to my suspicions, the general mode of explanation investigated in this paper holds up and even is confirmed by independent arguments, then I think it would be profitable to take seriously the possibility of extending this kind of explanation to other data uncovered by linguists and philosophers and to their proposals.

Presupposition

Consider the following observation of Chomsky's:

(131) Two of my five children are in elementary school.

The statement of [131] presupposes that I have five children; if I have six children, the statement is without truth value. In quite another sense, [131] presupposes that three of my five children are not in elementary school. That is, it would be natural for the hearer to assume this, on the basis of the statement [131]. On the other hand, if, in fact, three are in elementary school, [131] is not devoid of truth value; in fact it is true. Hearing [131], one is entitled to assume that three of my children are not in elementary school, perhaps by virtue of general conditions on discourse of a sort that have been discussed by Paul Grice in his work on 'conversation implicature' (1972, p. 112).

I agree with the substance of these remarks and I think that I can apply Grice's theory to the example. However, I will not subscribe to the current practice of distinguishing various 'senses' of presupposition. I will always use 'presuppose' as a relation between two statements such that if p presupposes q, then q is a necessary condition for the truth or falsity of p.[47] Now I want to reconstruct Chomsky's remarks in an explicitly Gricean framework. But first notice that the claim that (131) presupposes that I have five children, together with the usual account of presupposition, entails that a certain plausible account of its logical form is incorrect. That is, one might think that (131) has, on one level of analysis, the form

(132) I have five children and two of them are in elementary school.

But whereas (131) was said to lack a truth value if

(133) I have five children.

is false, (132) would be false if (133) were false. So if Chomsky and the usual accounts were right about (131), it could not have the form of (132).[48]

I am not at all confident about the correct ascription of logical form to (131), but for our purposes it is sufficient to assume that it is not (132) and that "two of my five children" is, on some level of analysis, a complex referring expression. Next we assume that the grammar can assign some representation of conceptual as well as logical (in the narrow sense) structure to (131). We can provisionally identify this as what a sentence literally and standardly/conventionally means. Further, let's assume that an expression means, on the occasion of its utterance, what it standardly means (this need not always be the case, see Grice (1969), Schiffer (1972)). Now, given a time of utterance, we can follow (66) and identify *what is said.* We suppose the hearer to be able to do this. If the hearer believes that the conversational maxims are being observed, then in particular the hearer believes that the maxim of Quantity-Quality is being observed. Thus, the hearer reasons:

(134) (1) *S* is obeying all the maxims so he is obeying Quantity-Quality.
  (2) The claim that three (or more) of *S*'s five children are in elementary school would be stronger than the claim that two are— because the first entails the second but not vice versa.
  (3) Therefore, given (1), *S* is directly implying that it is not the case that three or more of *S*'s five children are in elementary school.
  (4) Therefore, *S* is directly implying that three of *S*'s five children are not in elementary school.

It strikes me as plausible that much of what has been said in the recent literature on presupposition can be reinterpreted in terms of implicature. Whether it all can, and whether this would result in the best overall theory of language, is a matter for future research and present faith.

Indirect Speech Acts

Consider again the sentence given earlier:

(135) Who has a (the) key?

Notice that in uttering (135), one could be performing the act of questioning, but one could also be performing the act of requesting a key. No doubt some philosophers (and linguists) would be inclined by this to the view that (135) is ambiguous.[49] I have referred to this kind of case as 'speech-act' indeterminacy or 'force' indeterminacy, to distinguish it from the usual kind of ambiguity. It is very common. For instance, the sentence

(136) I will be at your party tonight.

can be used to make a promise, make a threat, vow prediction, express intention, and so on. When one considers these kinds of cases, one is no longer quite so tempted to say that (135) is ambiguous, because by parity of reasoning, (136) would be five ways ambiguous. The mistake is to attach the force of the utterance too tightly to the meaning of the sentence uttered. These considerations lead me to think that (135) is not in fact ambiguous, but rather that the difference in the force of its utterance is to be accounted for contextually.

The conversion of questions into requests is quite widespread in English speech. One of the most powerful classes of these is simple yes/no questions. Consider the following examples:

(137)   (i) Will you pass the salt?
        (ii) Won't you pass the salt?
       (iii) Would you pass the salt?
        (iv) ?Wouldn't you pass the salt?
         (v) Can you pass the salt?
        (vi) ?Can't you pass the salt?
       (vii) Could you pass the salt?
      (viii) ?Couldn't you pass the salt?
        (ix) *Should you pass the salt?
         (x) ?Shouldn't you pass the salt?

Notice two things. First, all of the sentences without initial question marks or star will take 'please' appended to them, while none of those with question marks or star prefixed will take 'please' appended to them. It is sometimes suggested that the possibility of so placing 'please' is a necessary (and perhaps sufficient) condition for a sentence being imperative. This may or may not be correct for the sentence type 'imperative', but if it is meant to suggest that if a sentence will not take 'please' it cannot be used to make a request or give an order then it must be mistaken: (137x) will not take 'please' but can be used to make a request. So also can "Should you be pulling the kitty's tail, Johnny?", which clearly can have the force of a request to stop. I think that this can be explained. Second, there is a natural hierarchy of 'strength' or politeness in the examples. The ordering for me and others of (137) from weakest (most polite) to strongest (most rude) is: (vii), (iii), (v), (i), (ii). Since conversations will also be governed by maxims of politeness, this data will have to be explained. One would like to find some (semantic?) property that correlates with this ordering. I have no indisputable candidate.

Returning to our original concern, we want to explain the conversion of interrogatives like 'who has a key?' and 'Will you pass the salt?' into requests like 'Somebody, give me a key' and 'Pass the salt'. Or, to put it another way, how do we get to what the speaker meant (to communicate) on that occasion from what the sentence means? The general form of the conversion (for these examples) is from (138) to (139):

(138) He requested information about $\begin{Bmatrix} \text{the key.} \\ \text{the salt.} \end{Bmatrix}$

(139) He requested $\begin{Bmatrix} \text{the key.} \\ \text{the salt.} \end{Bmatrix}$

What precisely is the question asked on these occasions? We have already spelled out the key example. For the salt example, the question is harder, for some people claim that 'will' is ambiguous. This is analogous to the sentence: 'I will be at your party tonight'. The basic senses seem to be: 'intend to' and 'predict that'. It should not be too hard to get the force of a promise, threat, and vow contextually off of the intend-reading. For the moment I am content to work with the assumption that 'will you pass the salt' is two ways ambiguous: (roughly) 'Do you intend to pass the salt?' and 'Do you think your passing the salt will come about?' I will work off of the intention reading because its connection with the request is more direct.[50] In effect what the hearer does is ignore part of the object of the request—the request *for information*. Instead, it is taken as

a request for what the information is *about*. What would warrant this on Grice's account? Most plausibly it is the maxim of Relevance. The hearer must suppose that it is not *really* information that the speaker wants. It is of course easy to construct cases where it is *prima facie* obvious that the person does not want information and so must want something else (presumably). Consider Katz's case (personal communication) where the speaker says:

"Can you lift the log that is crushing my leg?"

One might then argue, on the assumption that 'can' here means 'ability':

Surely the addressee must ask himself how it could be relevant to the speaker's immediate needs to have the addressee provide information about his physical prowess. Surely, too, the addressee must conclude that the speaker's utterance is only an apparent violation of the maxim, not a real one, since he knows that the speaker is in no position to indulge in irrelevancies. Given this, it can be shown that the speaker's utterance conversationally implicates a proposition expressing a request for aid.

But of course if we are to get this implication conversationally, then the maxim of Relevance must be flouted, but to be flouted, it must be flagrantly violated—or as Grice puts it, *X* flouts a maxim if he "*blatantly* fails to fulfill it." So it is not the case that the speaker can just 'apparently' violate the maxim—he must really do so, and for a reason.

Now, although it can be the case in certain circumstances that it is obvious that the maxim of Relevance is being exploited, this is not so with my two examples. In Katz's example, the context is loaded so heavily toward a request for aid that the working-out schema seems almost otiose. If the speaker had simply mumbled something unintelligible we would have taken it to be a plea for help. The problem with my examples, on the other hand, is that the context does not have this kind of weight and so we still need an explanation of how the content of the question is related to the content of the request. To put it another way, the speaker asks a question (about *x*), the hearer understands this question (about *x*) and for some reason supposes it to flout the maxim of Relevance, and he then (somehow) concludes that it is a request (about *x*). Why does he assume it is a request about *x* and not about y? It may be obvious that it is, but so far all the hearer need supply is some z that would make requesting z conversationally relevant. Why should he suppose $z = x$?[51] The best reason I can think of is that what the questioner says is *more* relevant if the content of his utterance is considered relevant and only its *force* irrelevant. The hearer's job is then lightened in that he need only find the relevant speech-act type. However, we should not be overly impressed by the fact that a question is a request for information about x. This seems to suggest that a request *tout court* is the simplest hypothesis consistent with the supposition that the speaker is obeying the maxims. But this might only be an accident. Nevertheless, one can wonder why questions have been favored as forms of polite request—although there certainly are other kinds:

(140) I sure would like some salt.
      I wish I had some salt.

Either of these could count (on occasion) as a request for salt. These are expressions of desire (notice that they will not take 'please'), but the way they could generate a request is fairly straightforward on Gricean lines. It would be interesting to know what the limits to this kind of speech-act conversion are, if there are any.[52]

Moore's Paradox

Given the second maxim of quality it would be natural to try to account for the oddity of such sentences as

(141) Snow is white, but I don't believe it.

by appealing in some way to conflict between what is said and what should be implicated, etc. And *if* this were to be the sort of account offered, it would have to be direct implicature that is appealed to, not indirect, since the maxim is not flouted.

Interestingly enough, Grice does not want to explain Moore's paradox conversationally: "On my account, it will not be true that when I say that p, I conversationally implicate that I believe that p . . . the natural thing to say is that he has *expressed* (or at least purported to express) the belief that p . . . the nature of the

connection will, I hope, become apparent when I say something about the function of the indicative mood" (1967, III, p. 2).

This strikes me as a better line to take. The oddity of sentences like (141) do not seem to turn on the accidents of conversation. It seems like a much tighter relationship. Moreover, given Grice's early remarks on implication it would seem that it should not be implicature at work. If the relation between p and ⌜I believe that p⌝ were one of implication, then one should be able to cancel it. But Moore-type sentences just *are* such an attempt. This suggests the implication is not cancelable and so not conversational at all. What then of Grice's proposal? According to his later theory of meaning, indicative mood indicators are correlated (by 'procedures') to speakers' beliefs. For example, Grice imagines the following procedure:

(P) To utter the indicative version of σ [an indicative sentence] if (for some A) U wants/intends A to think U thinks . . . (the blank being filled in by the infinitive version of σ).

                                        (1971, p. 65)

Furthermore, according to definition D.2, this would specify the meaning of the mood indicator for U (and for those who shared the procedure).

Turning again to sentences like (141), we can see that it is in the indicative mood and so applying (P) to it yields the result that it is to be U's policy:

(142) To utter (141) if U intends A to think U thinks that snow is white, but that U does not believe that snow is white.

Now, one might suggest that the oddity of (141) be accounted for on the basis of the oddity of the belief expressed in (142). After all, A is to think the following schema to be truly instantiated by U:

(143) UBp & $UB(\sim UBp)$

The problem with this line is that it may be *unusual,* but it does not seem odd in the *way* that the Moore sentences are. For a person could believe that p and not believe that he believes it: a person might believe that such and such a race is inferior, but not believe that he believes it. Not to allow this would force all racism to be explicit, and that seems very implausible. So we really do not yet have an account of the oddity of Moore's sentences. If this is correct, then we must turn to either a speech-act explanation (one like Searle's, 1969), or try to make the conversational hypothesis work. Perhaps when (or if) Grice develops a theory of speech acts we can look there for an account of Moore's Paradox.

Factives

The Kiparskys, in their interesting paper "Fact," claim that there is a set of 'predicates' such that sentences containing them have the property that speakers presuppose that the complement sentence is true. Thus, for the Kiparskys, presupposition is a relation between a person, a sentence, and a truth value (truth). But what is this relation? The Kiparskys do not say very much about it. They do distinguish it from both assertion and belief, and they note its traditional property (due to Frege) of being invariant under negation. However, this is not an analysis. We want a definiens for (144).

(144) In uttering S (S'), x *presupposes* that S' is true iff . . .

I do not know how to complete (144), but I think there are some wrong ways of putting the Kiparsky's point.
1. Someone first encountering the Kiparsky's relation of presupposition might be tempted to fashion it into something more familiar—say, a relation between a sentence and a belief. They might propose that

(145) S(S') presupposes that x believes that S'.

But there are serious problems with (145) if we mean by 'presuppose' what it has been taken to mean since Frege and Strawson (1952):

(146) X's belief that S' is a necessary condition for the truth-or-falsity of S(S').

The problems arise as follows. First, it makes the truth value of what one says depend on one's beliefs, even when what is said is not about those beliefs. For suppose that x utters S(S') and does not believe that S'. Since the presupposition is false, S(S') has no truth value (by (146)). Second, the analysis in (145) makes

it almost impossible to lie with factives. To lie is at least to (intentionally) assert that p, while believing that p is false. But on the account above, if I believe that S' is false, this is sufficient to guarantee that S(S') has no truth value, and so cannot be asserted to be true, except from ignorance or by mistake. These cases are bound to be rare, however, since people usually know what sentences they believe to be false.
2. Suppose that someone were to say that factive sentences presuppose their complements in the Strawsonian sense that

(147) S(S') *presupposes* S' iff the truth of S' is a necessary condition for the truth-or-falsity of S(S').[53]

Now, one of the interesting things about (147) is that it conflicts with the standard philosophical analysis of many factives, so if this is what the Kiparskys were to mean, the standard accounts would be wrong if the Kiparskys were right. The standard analysis of 'know', for instance, is

(148) x knows that p if and only if
(i) x believes that p.
(ii) p is true.
(iii) x is justified in believing that p.

On this analysis, if any of (i)–(iii) are false, then ⌜x knows that p⌝ is false. But if the relationship were one of presupposition, then if any of (i)–(iii) were false, then ⌜x knows that p⌝ would lack a truth value. How do we decide which is correct? Here are some considerations in favor of the standard analysis, as against the presuppositional view.

First Argument

1. Assume: 'I know that the earth is flat' presupposes 'The earth is flat.'
2. 'The earth is flat' is false.
3. So, 'I know that the earth is flat' has no truth value.
4. So, 'I do not know that the earth is flat' has no truth value.
5. So 'I know that the earth is flat' and 'I do not know that the earth is flat' each have no truth value.
6. So 'I know and I do not know that the earth is flat' has no truth value.

7. But 6 seems just false, so we must reject assumption 1.

Second Argument[54]

1. If my car has not been stolen, then I cannot know that it has been stolen.

2. Assume: my car has not been stolen.

3. Then I cannot know that my car has been stolen.

4. Then it is not possible that I know that my car has been stolen.

5. Then it is necessary that I do not know that my car has been stolen.

6. Then I do not know that my car has been stolen.

But now, from the assumption that 'My car has been stolen' is false we derived the result that I do not know that my car has been stolen. But then it must be true, not neither true nor false, as the presuppositionalist would have it.

One weakness of the standard analysis is that it fails to account for the fact that embedded sentences in both positive and negative factives are held to be true by the speaker, or at least this is implied. Consider the following;

(Affirmative Factives)
John knows that his car has been stolen.
    "   remembers   "
    "   realizes   "
    "   regrets (it)   "

(Negative Factives)
John doesn't know that his car has been stolen.
    "   remember   "
    "   realize   "
    "   regret   "

The presuppositional theory can, at one level at least, handle this, since presupposition has traditionally been taken to be invariant under negation. But how can the standard 'entailment' theorist account for this? Is it perhaps some form of implication? In the case of positive factives, the answer is straightforward entailment. It is the class of negative factives that gives the entailment view trouble.

A Bracketing Proposal. In the middle lectures, Grice introduces what he calls a 'bracketing device' used to "indicate the assignation of common ground status" to some of the clauses in the anlysis of indicative conditionals (1967 IV, p. 10). He then illustrates its utility in a variety of cases. I would like to try to bend

this device to our present concerns.[55] As a first step we could claim that what has been considered 'presupposition' is really 'common ground' on Grice's story. If we suppose (148) to have the standard analysis as in (149a), then the bracketed analysis would be as indicated in (149b), thus representing that the truth of p is to be common ground:

(149) (a) $x\mathrm{K}p$ iff $x\mathrm{B}p$ & $x\mathrm{JB}p$ & p
       (b) $x\mathrm{B}p$ & $x\mathrm{JB}p$ $[\&p]$

The denial of (149b) would then be as in (150):

(150) $\sim(x\mathrm{B}p$ & $x\mathrm{JB}p$ $[\&p])$

Being common ground, p will not be affected by operators like negation, and so the negated version of (149b) would be (151):

(151) $\sim x\mathrm{B}p \vee \sim x\mathrm{JB}p$ $[\&p]$

On this view, negative factives would have the force of an assertion of the disjunction above. But this does not seem correct. Negative factives are not normally taken that way. They normally have the force of a denial of the belief condition. We can get this result by imposing more structure on (149) as follows:

(152) $x\mathrm{K}p$ iff $x\mathrm{B}p$ $[\& \ x\mathrm{JB}p \ [\&p]]$

Using the principle (0),

(0) Operators go to the least deeply embedded condition first

we get the result that the denial of (152) would be required (153):

(153) $\sim x\mathrm{B}p$ $[\& \ x\mathrm{JB}p \ [\& \ p]]$

The principle (0) suggests that the brackets are penetrable, and that an operator can attach itself to one of these embedded conditions. To say how this can happen, what makes it happen, and what all this machinery means is to give the beginnings of a genuine theory.

If the bracketing does not reflect the truth-conditional semantics of the expression, then what does it reflect? So far, I have hedged on this by talking of indicating common ground in the utterance of the expression. What I want to suggest about the bracketing is that it is somehow a part of a system that relates what an expression means in the dialect to what the speaker means in uttering it. Where exactly it goes, and what its exact interpretation is, remains a bit of a mystery to me. We can start with the idea that the least deeply embedded condition specifies what the speaker primarily meant in uttering the expression, while the rest of the conditions are proposed as shared suppositions, in order to get to the point of the remark. That is, the speaker is indicating that he assumes that he and the hearer will both assume that such-and-such is true for the purposes of discussion.

But now that justification clause is in the way. It is not proposed as common ground that x is justified (in believing that p) when one utters a negative factive. We are in a dilemma. The standard analysis requires this clause to be there in the positive cases, but by the bracketing device it will be there in the negative cases as well where we do not want it. But to eliminate it from the negative cases it seems necessary to eliminate it from the positive cases as well or be *ad hoc*.

There are at least a couple of ways out. We could, one, argue that the justification clause is *not* in the positive cases either, or, two, argue that there is a reason for excluding it from the negative cases.

1. If we were to take the first way out we then need to see how we can distinguish 'knows that' from 'be aware that' and 'realize that,' for the previously present justification clause seemed to do just that. Also, we need to explain how evidence and justification *can* be the topic of discussion without much stage setting when ascribing knowledge or ignorance (especially if we stress 'know' in these ascriptions), but not, for example, awareness that p.

One way of supplying this information might be to say that there is a generalized conversational implicature of justification when one ascribes knowledge that p. On this view the 'analysis' of knowledge would be

(154) (a) Truth conditions: xBp & p.
      (b) Generalized implicature: $xJBp$.

The *saying* that xKp would *implicate* that x was justified in believing that p.

To make this line plausible one would have to give some sort of reason why the implicature is there with 'know' and not with 'aware' (maybe it is conventional implicature and not generalized conversational), and also one would have to explain how we can (or seem to) deny the justification clause in making the

negative ascriptions. How can denial go to the implicature?

2. If we take the second way out and let the justification clause remain in the positive cases, then we need to find some way of 'removing' it from the total content of the remark in the negative cases. One way to do this would be to read the justification clause as something like

(155) $xJBp$ iff x is justified in believing that p

Then we could say that if denial goes to the belief clause (by bracketing), then that entails that it is not the case that $xJBp$. Of course this does not entail that x has no evidence for p, just that if x does not believe that p, then x is not justified in believing that p. We would then get the result we want if we required common ground to be consistent with what was meant (as well as shared beliefs about the context; we will make this more explicit shortly).

In sum, I do not know exactly what is the best way of handling these facts, and I have sketched a pair of proposals that might be pursued. Assuming some reasonable account can be given, what more can be said about the basis and justification of the bracketing?

Let us first agree that many conversations are governed by maxims that enjoin us from being overly ambiguous and nonspecific. On the standard analysis of negative factives, they have the form of disjoined negations. Thus, if this is what the speaker meant to communicate, he might well be cited for violating a maxim; if the bracketing of the positive case were left as in (149b), the denial would still be unspecific or ambiguous:

(156) $\sim xBp \lor \sim xJBp$ [& p]

The bracketing convention (in the negative cases) comes in to reduce ambiguity and increase specificity. The negative operator goes to just one condition. So with negation, (149a) is interpreted as (152); the ordering of constituent conditions is *completed* so that ambiguity or equivocation is avoided.

What is the status of this bracketing device? Is it a part of the language, a conventional device that serves a purpose like the one sketched above? Or is it just a principle of interpretation based on conversation or discourse? I don't know, but the latter seems more plausible to me. On this account we

Table 20.1.

Context	Operator	Factive	Force of Negative Factive
1. ϕ(None of the conditions clearly antecedently true)	'not'	'know'	$\sim xBp\ [\&\ \phi\ [\&\ p]]$
2. xBp	"	"	$[xBp\ \&]\ \sim xJBp\ [\&\ p]$
3. $xBp\ \&\ p$	"	"	same
4. $xBp\ \&\ xJBp$	"	"	$[xBp\ \&\ xJBp\ \&]\ \sim p$

could say the bracketing reflects our expectations about what a speaker will mean based mainly on our previous experience with the point or topic of such remarks in the past. If these experiences were to change, our expectations would change and so the bracketing would change. This account has the virtue of meshing in an obvious way with our earlier justification for the device, but it also meshes with a fact we alluded to earlier—the fact that in certain circumstances, context can force a change in bracketing. In a context in which it is obvious that xBp, the negative factive will not be interpreted as the denial of xBp. The general principle seems to be

(0') If C is a condition in the analysis of an expression E, and C is contextually satisfied, then the operator is taken as going to the next most deeply embedded condition consistent with what is meant and context.

Thus, if the context is such that it is clear that xBp, then (0') predicts that the negative factive will be taken as a denial that $xJBp$. And if the context is such that it is clear that both xBp and $xJBp$, then the negative factive would be taken as the denial of p. This would explain why negative factives seem to be arranged on a scale of difficulty with regard to what they will be taken to mean, as well as why the scale of Table 20.1 is the way it is.[56]

There remain a host of questions conerning this proposal, and two are of some immediate concern. First, what are the rules or principles besides (0) and (0') that give us Table 20.1 as output from the initial bracketings as input, plus context? Second, what accounts for the fact (assuming it to be one) that negative factives of this sort are taken as denial of the *belief* condition? If this is explained on the basis of expectation on the basis of experience, then

why did it develop this way in the beginning? Of course it could be that it just happened that way. But as we will see shortly, it does not seem to be a fact just about 'know', but other factives as well, and this requires some explanation, if only an account in terms of what the speaker is more likely to have evidence for (in accordance with the maxims of Quality) and will therefore be supposed to mean.

Extending the Proposal. With some reservations it looks like the proposal above can be extended in two directions: to other operators besides negation, and to other factives besides 'know.'

Other Operators. It seems to me that, at least in an unbiased context, the sentences reflected in Table 20.2 would be taken primarily as remarks about belief.

Other Factives. The same sort of analysis and bracketing seems to work with other factives like

(157) realize; recognize; remember; be aware; admit

For instance, if we suppose the following to be roughly right:

(158) x is aware that p iff $xBp\ [\&\ p]$

then the denial of (158) has just the force we take it to have—as the denial that x believes that p. The same seems to hold for 'realize,' and for one common propositional use of 'rec-

Table 20.2.

Context	Operator	Factive	Force
ϕ	possibly	know	possibly xBp ...
ϕ	unlikely	know	unlikely that xBp ...
ϕ	uncertain	know	uncertain that xBp ...
ϕ	must	know	x must Bp ...
ϕ	hopefully	know	hopefully xBp ...
ϕ	finally	know	finally xBp ...

ognize.' Also, if we suppose 'admit' to have an analysis something like (159):

(159) x admits that p iff x says that p [& p]

then the negative factive: x didn't admit that p, comes out right, as primarily a denial that x said (or would say) that p. Perhaps other cases could be handled as these.

Illocutionary Generalizations

At the end of Chapter 3 of *Speech Acts,* Searle gives a number of "generalizations" over speech acts (1969, p. 65). We can summarize two of them as follows:

(EXP) "Whenever there is a psychological state specified in the sincerity condition, the performance of the act counts as an *expression* of that psychological state."

(IMP) "In the performance of any illocutionary act, the speaker *implies* that the preparatory conditions of the act are satisfied."

Given a tentative analysis of various illocutionary acts, these principles can be used to do some work. For instance, fairly plausible accounts can be given for Moore's Paradox and various cases of contextual implication. However, Searle does note something he may not appreciate the importance of: "If it really is the case that the other rules are functions of the essential rule, and if some of the others tend to recur in consistent patterns, then these recurring ones ought to be eliminable" (1969, p. 69). Searle suggests that these regularities may go into the general theory of illocutionary acts, but it would be worthwhile to explore the possibility that these generalizations might be special cases of a theory superordinate even to the general theory of illocutionary acts; say, the general theory of conversations.

Before we can do this, we must be clearer about the force of these principles. I am not sure how Searle intends us to take these remarks: as (contextual) *definitions* of the notions of expressing and implying, in performing a speech act, or as *empirical* generalizations over expressings and implyings. By using such phrases as 'counts as' he suggests the former, but by calling these 'ten-

tative generalizations' he suggests the latter. I think the latter is what he wants, or should want. This is because the notions of 'expressing' and 'implying' are pulling some weight in these generalizations. This can be seen by substituting 'exponentiation' for 'expression' and 'diagonalizes' for 'implies' in these generalizations. If these really were contextual definitions, it should make no difference what word we decided to define, but clearly we have lost a great deal of explanatory utility in these substitutions. But if these are really generalizations then the antecedent meaning of the words 'expresses' and 'implies' will be important. To test these generalizations we need to know what it is to express a psychological state or to imply that a certain condition is satisfied. As far as I can tell Searle never does this.

With both expressing[57] and implying[58] there is a range of characteristic circumstances in which we would say that something has been expressed and implied. I think that ones that come the closest to what Searle may have in mind are the following:

(E) (S's) doing ϕ (timelessly-) *expresses* (the psychological state) ψ if:
　(i) If S were to ϕ, then if
　(ii) H were aware that S had ϕ-ed, then
　(iii) Probably H would conclude that S was in ψ, at least partly on the basis of the awareness in (ii).

(I) (S's) doing ϕ (timelessly-) *implies* that p if:
　(i) If S were to ϕ, then if
　(ii) H were aware that S had ϕ-ed, then
　(iii) Probably H would conclude that p, at least partly on the basis of the awareness in (ii).

Notice that in these definitions, expressing a psychological state is just implying that you are in that state. This is not implausible.

We can now give at least sufficient conditions for (EXP) and (IMP), and I will call these analyses (EXP') and (IMP'):

(EXP') If there is a psychological state ψ mentioned in the sincerity condition of ϕ-ing, then ϕ-ing *expresses* that state ψ if: S ϕ-es and
　(i) If H were aware that S had ϕ-ed, then
　(ii) Probably H would conclude that S was in ψ, at least partly on the basis of the awareness in (i).

(IMP') In the performance of an illocutionary act of ϕ-ing the speaker S *implies* that the preparatory conditions p of the act are satisfied if: S ϕ-es and

(i) If H were aware that S had ϕ-ed, then
(ii) Probably H would conclude that p, at least partly on the basis of the awareness in (i).

We now turn to the task of deriving (EXP) and (IMP) via deriving (EXP') and (IMP') from facts and principles not specifically illo-cutionary and constitutive. We will start with (IMP') since (EXP') may require material that Grice has not yet developed.

1. (IMP)

We can get (IMP') without using any special illocutionary constitutive rules given a fact and two plausible principles:

Fact: On Searle's account, preparatory conditions are necessary for the performance of the illo-cutionary act they are conditions for.

P 1. If ψ is a necessary condition for having ϕ-ed, then being aware that S has ϕ-ed is a basis for concluding that ψ.

P 2. If 'ψ is an immediate consequence of ϕ and one is aware that ϕ, then one will probably conclude that ψ.[59]

We can now argue thus:

1. Suppose that S has ϕ-ed.
2. Suppose H were aware that S had ϕ-ed.
3. Then H probably will conclude that p (from *Fact*, 2, and *P 2*)
4. Then H probably will conclude that p at least partly on the basis of 2 (from *Fact*, 2, and *P 1*)
5. Then probably H would conclude that p, at least partly on the basis of 2 (from 3 and 4)
6. So given *Fact*, *P 1* and *P 2*, then if 1 then if 2 then 5 (conditional proof from above)
7. But 'If 1 then if 2, then 5' is the sufficient con-dition for (IMP')
8. So given *Fact*, *P 1* and *P 2* we can conclude that

In the performance of an illocutionary act of ϕ-ing, the speaker implies that the preparatory conditions of the act are satisfied.

2. (EXP)

Before turning to this argument it should be noted that the 'counts as' phrase has dropped out of (EXP'). This is in keeping with its em-pirical character as well as reflecting my belief that the relationship between the psychologi-cal state and the act is *not* conventional.

We cannot derive (EXP') on the model of

the derivation of (IMP') because the sincerity condition is not a necessary condition for the performance of the act. The obvious question is: what might support the hearer's inference from the fact that the speaker performed the act to his being in a certain psychological state? There are at least three ways it could go. First, we might try to get (EXP') just using some other generalization about action and reasoning. Second, we might try to get it by concocting a 'Gricean' theory of illocutionary acts that would not appeal to the notion of special illocutionary constitutive rules, and then try to state the generalizations over *this* theory. Of course, some combination of these might be necessary. I want to take a quick look at the prospects and problems associated with these suggestions.

Generalization about Action and Reasoning. We might suppose that most speakers count among their everyday beliefs something like (G):

(G) People usually believe (want, intend to do, . . . ψ . . .) what they state (request, promise, . . . ϕ . . .)

(We postpone the question of why and on what basis might people hold such a general belief.) Then given (G) we could argue roughly:

1. Suppose that S has ϕ-ed.
2. Suppose H were aware that S had ϕ-ed.
3. Suppose S believed (G).
4. Then H would probably conclude that S was in ψ, at least partly on the basis of 2. (from above, *P 2* and (G))
5. So we have it that given *P 2* and (G), if 1, then if 2, then 4.
6. But this is sufficient for (EXP').

To this there are a number of immediate ob-jections.

One could object that this is no advance on Searle because we have *lost* a generalization, since (EXP) was of the form

For any illocutionary act, if . . . then ————.

and (G) is just a list, pairing certain acts with certain states. But I think that the contrast is illusory. This is because Searle has no *general* procedure for determining the necessity for, or content of, the sincerity condition for each act. Thus the universal quantifier is just a summary for a conjunction of particular facts about a particular analysis. For the purposes of the theory it would have been no different had the 'generalization' been formulated as

If S performs an act n, then S expresses the psychological state n.

Given that we had some pairing between acts and states the only difference between this (and (G)) and Searle is that it refers to the pairing via a number rather than some rubric like 'sincerity condition'. The work this rubric does could equally be done on the scheme above by saying simply,

If S performs act n, then if n is paired with a psychological state n, then S performs n *sincerely* iff S is then in state n.

In the absence of a deduction of the sincerity condition from the essential condition or illocutionary purpose of the act, both 'generalizations' are essentially lists.

One may also object that we have given no account of how or why people might come to hold a belief like (G). I suspect that such a belief could arise from at least two sources: projections from one's own case, and observations of and inferences concerning others. Both of these could interact and support each other and become more refined over time, giving rise to the often highly specific expectations we have of others and expect others to have of us.

Finally, it may be objected that we have given no reason to suppose that (G) might be the *basis* of the inference to the psychological state. Here is one slight consideration on its behalf. Suppose that a study was indicating that (G) was wildly wrong, that people most often lied, requested what they didn't want, and so on, and it also gave an account of why we thought the opposite. Suppose it was very convincing. Under these circumstances, any H who had been persuaded of this would surely be reluctant to infer from S's having ϕ-ed that S was in state ψ.

A Special Consequence of Conversational Maxims. One may find the first proposal implausible, and it may be false. It could be that the basis of the inference to ψ is not anything like (G), but rather the belief that S is obeying some general conversational principles. One problem here is that Grice's theory of conver-

sation is geared to the accepted purpose of the talk exchange (at that point). So to make the connection between Grice and Searle we must connect the illocutionary act with the accepted purpose of the talk exchange (at that point). So to make the connection between Grice and Searle we must connect the illocutionary act with the accepted purpose of the talk exchange. But there may be no *accepted* purpose to the talk exchange at that point, though the *speaker* may have a purpose at that point. Indeed, the conversation may be *given* purpose at a point *by* the speaker's purpose(s) in making the utterance he makes. If we view (most sorts of) conversations as a sequence of illocutionary acts, governed by certain principles of cohesion, relevance, and the like, then the move to conversations will *not* bypass illocutionary acts in providing an account of (EXP).

A "Gricean" Theory of Illocutionary Acts. I think the most promising thing to do here is to first find a natural and general way of categorizing the purposes of a talk exchange (both at a point and over time), and then try to correlate these with illocutionary acts that might be performed in fulfilling those purposes. Since maxims of Quality seem to be a function of the purpose of the talk exchange, it should be possible to get the sincerity conditions on illocutionary acts via the maxim of Quality for the correlated sort of conversation. Such a project is clearly beyond the scope of this study.

GLIMPSES BEYOND

There are a number of (kinds of) cases not so far discussed that might yield to a Gricean analysis of one sort or another. Certainly this possibility should be pursued. I shall just mention and gloss a few of them briefly.

Intentional Verbs

If I say that John kicked the dog this morning I imply that he kicked the dog intentionally (and voluntarily). Certainly this does not *entail* that John kicked the dog intentionally (or voluntarily) because one can say without contradiction that John kicked the dog, but he did it accidentally or unintentionally. With some other verbs this is not the case. If I say that John stumbled on the dog this morning I do not imply that he did it intentionally or voluntarily. The generalization seems to be

If it is possible to ϕ intentionally (or voluntarily) then in saying that x ϕ-ed, one will imply that x ϕ-ed intentionally (or voluntarily).

What is the basis of this generalization? Is it a generalized conversational implicature? Perhaps it is no more than the general belief that acts that can be so performed usually are so performed.

Opaque Simplification

It is sometimes said that if Jones wants (hopes that, etc.) p and q, it does not follow that Jones wants p, nor does it follow that Jones wants q. For instance, if Jones wants ham and eggs for breakfast, it is claimed that it does not follow that Jones wants ham for breakfast nor that he wants eggs for breakfast.

However, I think that this case should be handled just as we handled the earlier cases of conjunction reduction. We could well contend that the *reason* one thinks that it does not follow is that the conclusion commits one to the view that Jones wants *only* ham for breakfast, etc. However, by the maxim of Quantity-Quality and the inference outlined earlier, we could contend that the commitment is via implicature, not entailment.

Completion Verbs

It is often claimed that remarks like (160a) presuppose (160b, c):

(160) (a) x has not stopped ϕ-ing.
     (b) x was ϕ-ing.
     (c) x (had) started ϕ-ing.

There are other cases as well:

(161) (a) x (has) finished ϕ-ing.
     (b) x was ϕ-ing.
     (c) x (had) started ϕ-ing.

The reason for supposing this to be presupposition is mainly invariance under negation:

(162) (a) x has not stopped ϕ-ing.
     (b) x was ϕ-ing.
     (c) x (had) started ϕ-ing.

There are at least two possible nonpresuppositional treatments available in Gricean terms: a bracketing theory and a conversational theory.

Bracketing. Suppose that at some level of representation the analysis of (160a) was something like (163):[60]

(163) [x started (or was) ϕ-ing &] x is not now ϕ-ing.

Then (160a) would *entail* (160b, c). But the denial of (163), i.e. (162a), would be (164):

(164) $\sim x$ started ϕ-ing $\vee$ x is now ϕ-ing

although by bracketing it would have the force of (165):

(165) x started ϕ-ing & x is now ϕ-ing.

Conversational. Suppose the analysis of (161a) is, at some level of representation,

(166) x started ϕ-ing & x terminated ϕ-ing.

Then we have it that saying that x finished is a stronger remark than saying that x started, since finishing entails starting, but not vice versa. Consequently, the denial of finishing should be a weaker remark than the denial of starting.[61] The denial of (166) would be (167):

(167) $\sim x$ started ϕ-ing $\vee$ $\sim x$ terminated ϕ-ing.

But if the first disjunct is taken as sufficient for the truth of (167), then the speaker will have produced a weaker remark than is relevant and suitable. So he will have implicated that the first disjunct of (167) is not true, i.e., that x (has) started ϕ-ing.

Subject-oriented Adverbs

It has been noticed (Lehrer, 1975) that there are adverbs that have the property that combined with certain nonfactive verbs like 'believe' they *imply* that the complement of the verb is true, or is false (or perhaps just that the speaker believes it):

(168) (a) Wisely, cleverly John believes that p.
     (b) p (or perhaps, x B p).

(169) (a) Foolishly, John believes that p.
     (b) not p (or perhaps, $xB\sim p$).

However, these adverbs combined with factives like 'know' produce oddity:

(170) ?Wisely, cleverly John knows that p.

(171) ?Foolishly John knows that p.

These adverbs are to be distinguished from another group like 'correctly', 'erroneously', and 'falsely', which have the property that combined with certain nonfactive verbs like 'believes' *entail* that the complement is true, or that it is false:

(172) a. Correctly John believes that p.
   b. p.

(173) a. Falsely, erroneously John believes that p.
   b. not p.

When these are combined with certain factives like 'know', they produce oddity:

(174) ?John correctly knows that p.

(175) ?John falsely, erroneously knows that p.

Suppose that semantically these groups of adverbs are operators that have an effect on logical syntax, and that the effect of 'foolishly' and 'cleverly' as opposed to 'falsely' and 'correctly' is the following:

(176) Foolishly $(x\mathrm{B}p) \Rightarrow x\mathrm{B}p$ & $(\sim x\mathrm{JB}p \lor \sim p)$

(177) Falsely $(x\mathrm{B}p) \Rightarrow x\mathrm{B}p$ & $\sim p$

(178) Cleverly $(x\mathrm{B}p) \Rightarrow x\mathrm{B}p$ & $(x\mathrm{JB}p \lor p)$

(179) Correctly $(x\mathrm{B}p) \Rightarrow x\mathrm{B}p$ & p

Next, suppose part of the communicative force of an operator is to emphasize what is contributed by the operator, and to subordinate what is inherited from the operand to something like common ground. Then the bracketed result for the above would be:

(176′) $[x\mathrm{B}p$ &$] (\sim x\mathrm{JB}p \lor \sim p)$

(177′) $[x\mathrm{B}p$ &$] \sim p$

(178′) $[x\mathrm{B}p$ &$] (x\mathrm{JB}p \lor p)$

(179′) $[x\mathrm{B}p$ &$] p$

We can get the entailments recorded in (172) and (173) from (177) and (179) by elementary logic. How can we get the implications recorded in (168) and (169), and the remaining oddities? Suppose that (169a) has the bracketed semantic representation of (176′) (repeated):

(176′) Foolishly $x\mathrm{B}p$: $[x\mathrm{B}p$ &$] (\sim x\mathrm{JB}p \lor \sim p)$.

Now, given the conversational maxims to avoid equivocation we might suppose that the primary content of the remark will be taken to

be one of the disjuncts left unbracketed. Given the maxim of Quality-2, the speaker is to say (mean) only what he has adequate evidence for. But other things being equal, it is much more likely that the speaker has evidence that $\sim p$ than that he has evidence that x has insufficient evidence that p—what do most speakers know about the epistemic biographies of others? So, by charity, the speaker will be taken to primarily mean that $\sim p$, and also imply, that $x\mathrm{B}p$.

Suppose that (168a) has the semantic representation of (178′) (repeated):

(178′) Cleverly $x\mathrm{B}p$: $x\mathrm{B}p$ & $(x\mathrm{JB}p \lor p)$

By the same reasoning as above we have it the speaker will be taken to mean that p, and also to imply, that $x\mathrm{B}p$.

Notice that this explanation leans heavily on there being or not being certain shared beliefs between speaker and hearer. For instance, if it is common knowledge that nobody is in any position to be able to claim that p, then the speaker will (be taken to) primarily mean that x is not justified in believing that p in saying that foolishly $x\mathrm{B}p$, as for example in (180b) as opposed to (180a):

(180) (a) Foolishly $x\mathrm{B}$ that the earth is flat.
   (b) Foolishly $x\mathrm{B}$ that there were exactly five trillion mosquitoes in Panama in 1903.

We can account for the oddities recorded in (174), (175) and (170), (171) along the same lines.

The oddity of (174) arises from the redundancy of the operation, since the knowledge claim already commits one to the truth of p. The oddity of (175) arises from the conflict between the commitment to the truth of p via 'knows' and the falsity of p via the operator.

The oddity of (171) arises from the implication by the operator that $\sim p$, and the commitment to p via 'knows'. The oddity of (170) can be accounted for by the redundancy of the implication of the operator, given the commitment to the truth of p via 'knows'. Notice finally that (182) is not odd;

(181) Foolishly x does not know that p

since on this account by bracketing (182) becomes $\sim x\mathrm{B}p$, and 'foolishly' will go with 'believe'.

Repeaters

It is sometimes said that among sentences like those of (182)–(184), the (a) sentences presuppose the (b) sentences:

(182) (a) John kicks it again.
　　　(b) John kicked it previously.
(183) (a) John kicks it too, also.
　　　(b) Somebody (else?) kicked it.
(184) (a) John kicks it a second (nth) time.
　　　(b) Somebody (John?) kicked it a first (n − 1) time.

The reason for calling this presupposition is again the invariance under negation.

(185) (a) John did not kick it again.
　　　(b) John kicked it prevously.

Suppose that (182a) is represented something like (186):

(186) [x kicked it before t_0 &] x kicks it at t_0

Then the denial of (186), i.e. (185a), would be (187), though the conversational force of (185a) would be (188):

(187) $\sim x$ kicked it before t_0 ∨ $\sim x$ kicks it at t_0.

(188) x kicked it before t_0 & $\sim x$ kicks it at t_0.

Depending on larger issues, one could view 'again' as the surface remnant of the second conjunct, or as an operator on the main clause forming a second conjunct semantically.

However, we still need an acount of why the bracketing favors the conjunct indexed (by t) earliest in time. Perhaps this is just a part of the meaning of expressions like 'again' as opposed to 'before'.

It might be objected to this proposal that it cannot be a general account of repeater words. The reason sometimes given is that we have sentences like (189) which cannot, it is claimed, be given a conjunctive analysis as in (190):

(189) I promise not to do it again.

(190) I did it before t_0 and I promise not to do it after t_0.

It is not clear why (190) cannot be the analysis of (189), but apparently it is thought that conjunction can connect only constatives. But this is false as can be seen by the felicity of (191):

(191) I did it before, but I promise never to do it again.

An adequate semantics must reflect the fact that connectives can connect nonconstatives, but that is not my obligation here.

Miscellaneous

Finally, I should just mention some additional cases that pose an interesting range of challenges to this sort of explanation.

☐ "Not all the tables are round" seems to imply that (the speaker believes that) most of the tables are round.

☐ Many euphemisms may have their origin in uses of language governed by conversational principles similar to Grice's discussion of metaphor. Consider the likely origins of such phrases as:[62] 'go to the bathroom'; 'sleep(ing) with'; 'going to be sick'.

☐ "I used to like spinach" seems to imply that I do not now like spinach. In fact, to a lesser extent, the use of the past tense often carries the implication that the activity or state indicated by the verb no longer is present: "I wanted to live in Rome"; "I lived in Rome"; I believed that p.

☐ "He walked halfway to New York" seems to imply that he did not walk all the way to New York. "He lifted his arm halfway to his head" seems to imply that he did not lift his arm to his head. These implications can be canceled, as when one prefixes the above with "In the course of walking all the way to New York. . . ."

☐ "I haven't played tennis for ten years"[63] seems to imply that I had played tennis before that.

☐ "Have you mastered the topspin lob yet?" seems to imply that I expect you to (try to) master the topspin lob. "I haven't mastered the topspin lob yet" seems to imply that I expect (or will try) to. Perhaps this is simply a case of conventional implicature off of 'yet'—though notice that it is cancelable: "I haven't ϕ-ed yet, and I don't ever expect to."[64]

In this essay I have tried to make plausible the application of major portions of Grice's framework for the analysis of the total content of an utterance. I have also used this as an opportunity to raise certain questions about, and suggest various extension of, that theory. No doubt my execution has been defective in detail, even in major detail. Nevertheless, I do remain fairly convinced that the Gricean vision is basically correct, and it is just a matter of more work and further elaboration to make that conviction stick.

ACKNOWLEDGMENTS

The main parts of this essay were written in 1969 and slightly revised and expanded as Chapter III of my thesis. This version is essentially that of my thesis, with minor revision. I have held off publishing these thoughts on Grice until he released at least some of his own material. I want to thank Kent Bach, Sylvain Bromberger, Noam Chomsky, Jerry Fodor, Bruce Fraser, Paul Grice, Jerrold J. Katz, and Judith Jarvis Thomson for the many helpful discussions I have had on the topics of this paper. Needless to say, not everyone agrees with everything I say.

NOTES

1. This clause cannot be dropped on pain of allowing statements true by 'physical necessity' to be sufficient for entailment.

2. Displayed sentences are to be interpreted in the usual manner. Where necessary I will use corners.

3. I borrow the term from Grice (1967), though I am not sure he would agree with its application here.

4. These remarks are the result of a very helpful discussion of these cases with Judith Jarvis Thomson.

5. By far the most interesting and compelling discussion of these matters I have seen is in Ware. As far as I can tell, Ware's study reinforces my belief in the necessity of drawing the distinctions mentioned.

6. This locution must be watched, because I think that 'Jones and Smith both moved the table' itself implies that they did *not* move it together.

7. Carole Taylor is to be thanked for her assistance with these, and with (27).

8. As in 'painting a wall' vs. 'painting a portrait.'

9. Contrast this with 'John tasted the cake'. Sentence (17 xi) implies that John ate the whole cake. But 'John tasted the cake' does not imply he was the only one to have tasted the cake or that he tasted the whole cake. This might be related to what have been called 'unit concepts' like 'see', 'touch', etc. One can be said to have seen the car even if one saw only (strictly?) the left side. See Clark (1965) for an extended discussion of this.

10. What if A and B both held the pencil?

11. See Harnish (1975a) for additional discussion.

12. Sylvain Bromberger is thanked for suggesting the first of these for me.

13. This should strike one as at least suspicious. Unfortunately, I do not at the moment see how to decide if it is valid *in English* or not. The standard treatments of translation in logic texts which allow us to render ⌜neither Fx nor Fy⌝ as ⌜not Fx and not Fy⌝ and to render ⌜Fx and Fy⌝ for ⌜F x and y⌝ are of no help. This is because rejecting (30) amounts to rejecting at least one of these translations—and pretty clearly the last one, since it looks equivalent to what I want to conclude.

14. Sylvain Bromberger suggests: "Russell wrote *Principia* and Whitehead wrote *Principia* and they wrote it together."

15. It is not clear how "rough" (39) is supposed to be—which is unfortunate because of the fanfare which usually accompanies the introduction of logic into syntax (usually only logical *notation* at that). Now, it is clear that there is nothing magical about the explanatory power of expressions like 'x', '∃', '$x \in$ M' in themselves. Either they must be explained upon introduction or we must be allowed to assume that they are being used with the force conventional in the relevant literature. Since we are told almost nothing about the expressions in (39) we must assess it as standard. But then it is just gibberish. Among its defects are:

It is not well-formed. (a) says literally: there is a y such that for all x's in the set M the expression 'go to Cleveland.' (b) is just as bad.

(39) is supposed to say something about events, but nothing indicates that this is so.

Even if we add event predicates, the use of quotes precludes a going-to-Cleveland event.

And what exactly *is* a going-to-Cleveland event? Is it a type or a particular? How is John's going-to-Cleveland related to it? The serious use of logical notation should at least indicate what direction our translation would take us, but we get precious little from (39).

Even if we get the quotes out and solve the previous problems, do we want to say that 'go to Cleveland' is two-place predicate—as seems to be required by the notation '(x, y)'? Why not say it is a one-place predicate or a three-place predicate?

I leave deciphering '$x \in M$,' 'x_y' and '(x, y_x)' as an exercise to the reader.

16. But it is at least very odd to say,

(a) There wasn't one person there.

when there were two people there, because (a) at least suggests or implies that nobody was there. Also notice that

(b) There weren't 10 people there.

suggests, implies, etc., that there were less than 10 people there. It would again be odd at least, to say (b) if there were 15 people there. Since $0 < 1$, the generalization to be captured from (a) and (b) is that sentences of the form

(c) There weren't n G's there.

imply sentences of the form

(d) There were less than n G's there.

I expect that this can be explained along Gricean lines explored in this paper.

17. See also Quine (1959, § 39) for a similar analysis of 'the Apostles are twelve'.

18. It does have some merits, as Hempel points out. For the defects of logicism see *inter alia* Benacerraf (1965). Notice that even if the critics of logicism can make their claim that numbers are not sets stick, this in itself does not show that the translations offered for numerical statements are wrong, since they do not entail that view nor are they entailed by it.

19. For instance, it might be thought that we can just build the uniqueness condition into the sentences themselves and thereby dispense with the troublesome antecedent. But how would this go? Consider.

(a) John and Harry went to Cleveland once in their lives.

This may, on the proposal above, be said to have the readings of (b) and (c):

(b) John and Harry each went to Cleveland once in their lives.
(c) John and Harry went to Cleveland together once in their lives.

Unfortunately, (b) and (c) can both be true, because the scope of the adverb is 'went . . . together' and 'went . . .' and they may have done each of these once in their lives. Another proposal might be to add on the phrase 'and John and Harry only visited Cleveland once in their lives' to (34), (35) and (36). It looks like this would support the requisite entailments and allow us to drop the antecedent, but I have not thought it out. Again, it is very unnatural.

20. I do not think that these are the same: 'father' is *ambiguous* as between (at least) 'biological father' and 'member of a religious organization who . . .', 'grandfather' is *indeterminate* as between 'maternal grandfather' and 'paternal grandfather,' and 'paternal grandfather' is *vague* (do hermaphrodites count? etc.). However, for my purposes I need not distinguish this last pair of properties.

21. The first of these is due to Jerrold J. Katz (in conversation)—who also suggested Bever's ambiguity example, "He fed her dog biscuits." This conversation prompted me to make (and aided me in making) my arguments more explicit.

22. This is because to be two senses they must differ in some way. One then picks one's predicate to reflect this semantic difference.

23. Again assuming that they went just once.

24. This diagram is meant to be only suggestive. There is no readily apparent interpretation of the domination lines that is coherent. It is an interesting and important question how these notions are related. The dotted line will be filled in.

25. I will not be concerned here with Grice's theory of meaning. But it is important to know how utterer's meaning and utterance type meaning are related to saying and implying. Especially vexing is the relationship between utterer's meaning and implicature. One strong supposition worth looking at is that what one implicates (as well as what one says) is always a species of what was meant, differences being traceable to different ways in which various intentions are to function and different reasons the audience is intended to have. It would be important for this strong view that one not be able to imply that *p* and not mean that *p*, and to get at this one might need to know if one could imply unintentionally (as might a Republican who said that Nixon was the best president that money could buy).

26. The reason for the disjunction is that Grice's terminology has shifted from the first pair to the second. The shift to 'implicature' frees him from the unwanted 'logical' use of 'implies', and the shift to 'said' is a generalization from 'state'. I can report what someone said in cases besides what they stated, for instance, when I report that he said that you are to leave the room.

27. I owe this version of the complaint to a conversation with Anthony Woozley. An earlier version of this complaint (mine) was met by Jerrold Katz in conversation.

28. For a survey discussion up to 1960, see Hungerland (1960) and the references there.

29. Some have been misled by Grice's remarks. For instance, Elinor Keenan's interesting paper (1974) is somewhat marred by the supposition that her data from Madagascar are counterexamples to Grice's theory of conversation. Keenan's mistake is to assume that for maxims to be universal, they must be *categorically* observed. But this need not be so. Grice's theory of implicature requires just that the speaker and hearer(s) be observing the cooperative maxims. This assumption is necessary for Grice's theory of implicature to work, but it is also sufficient. Grice nowhere says, nor would want to say, that all conversations are governed by the cooperative maxims. There are too many garden-variety counterexamples: social talk between enemies, diplomatic encounters, police interrogation of a reluctant suspect, most political speeches, and many presidential news conferences. These are just some of the cases in which the maxims of cooperation are not in effect and are known not to be in effect by the participants.

Since Grice's theory is basically conditional (if any conversation is governed by the cooperative maxims, then we can explain such and such implicatures in such and such a way), it will not do for falsifying it just to show that the antecedent is false. What must be done to falsify this theory, and what Keenan does not report doing, is to find examples of cooperative exchanges where the maxims are violated in the requisite way and none of the predicted implicatures are present.

However, Keenan does ask the important question: why don't the Malagasy cooperate with information? And to this question she has an interesting suggestion. Apparently the Malagasy are so closely knit that possessing information another lacks gives one status over them. Thus, reluctance to cooperate on information could be viewed as a natural consequence of the general reluctance to relinquish advantages in status.

30. This raises the general question of how to discover new maxims and how to justify the claim that some maxim 'governs' discourse. A rough and ready principle I have used is the following: the supposition that maxim *M* governs conversations affords the best available explanation for the (pretheoretically identifiable) implication that *p*, in such and such contexts.

31. It is interesting to note that Sir David Ross considers this a *prima facie* duty arising from: "The implicit understanding not to tell lies, which seems to be implied in the act of entering into conversation" (Ross, 1930, p. 21). A slightly stronger version of this can be found in Urmson (1963, p. 224): "Whenever anyone utters a sentence which could be used to convey truth or falsehood there is an implied claim to truth by that person, unless the situation shows that this is not so (he is acting or reciting or incredulously echoing the remarks of another) . . . it is understood that no one will utter a sentence of a kind which can be used to make a statement unless he is willing to claim that the statement is true . . . The word 'implies' is being used in such a way that if there is a convention that *X* will be done in circumstances *Y*, a man implies that *Y* holds if he does *X*." I say that this account is slightly stronger because stated as a maxim it enjoins one to speak (what one believes to be) the truth (and not just to *refrain* from speaking what one believes to be falsehoods), and because it appeals to the existence of a *convention* to explain the implication. However, if I understand Grice correctly, the maxims are not conventions at all. They are a "part" of what it is to be verbally cooperative and so lose the feature of arbitrariness so dear to most accounts of conventions (See e.g., Lewis, 1969, for a more adequate statement. For a critique and reformulation, see Schiffer, 1972, Chap. V.).

32. Urmson (1963, pp. 229–230) again notes that "Whenever we make a statement in a standard context

there is an implied claim to reasonableness . . . it is, I think, a presupposition of communication that people will not make statements, thereby implying their truth, unless they have some ground, however tenuous, for those statements . . . There is a convention that we will not make statements unless we are prepared to claim and defend their reasonableness."

33. This maxim turns out to be so central and important in conversational implicature that it is not clear that it belongs on equal footing with the rest. I suspect that maxims are (at least partially) ordered with respect to weight, etc. and that relevance is at the top, controlling most of the others.

34. I find this a bit misleading. It is easy to see how the maxims given might fall under the cooperative principle, but it is not at all obvious that esthetic, social, or moral maxims need contribute to rational cooperation. Indeed, moral maxims may well preclude obedience to other maxims. (Presumably, one was not obliged to give all necessary information when the Gestapo came calling.) Part of the problem here is that we have no suggestions as to what any of these new maxims might look like. Grice's only example of a social maxim is: be polite! Moreover, it is not clear what Grice has in mind as an "esthetic" maxim. Perhaps the best research strategy to adopt is first to imagine ideally cooperative conversations, ideally esthetic (?) conversations, etc. Then turn to the project of seeing how these maxims interact in actual contexts.

35. The project of supplementing and generalizing *these* maxims to nonconstative cases is distinct from the project mentioned earlier of finding other sorts of maxims. Generalizing these maxims, or finding special cases for other (classes of) speech acts, presumably yields maxims falling under the cooperative principle. The only maxims mentioned so far that are specifically constative are the maxims of Quantity and Quality, so these are likely candidates for supplementation or generalization. Analogues for requesting (as a type of speech act, asking a question might fall under this) could be:

Quantity' (a) Do not request too little ("Breathe.")
       (b) Do not request too much. ("Bring me the moon.")
 Quality' (a) Do not request what you do not want. ("Leave the room, but I don't want you to.")
       (b) Do not request what you do not have a reason for requesting. ("Leave the room." "Why?" "I don't know.")

Furthermore, the original maxims of Quanity and Quality should probably be generalized for just *saying*. This is because implicatures can work off of what is presupposed but not said, as well as what is said.

36. I want to emphasize that these are not exclusive ways of infringing a maxim. As far as I can tell, clashes are just a special subclass of violations—where the violation is forced, or seen as forced, by having in the circumstances competing maxims.

37. Consider a remark like "Church's discussion may or may not be helpful here." Clearly this can (would) be taken as a certain suggestion, not as just the utterance of a tautology. Or, "There are movies and there are movies" is used to stress that there are certain (contextually determined) differences between movies.

38. This example is complicated by the fact that we do not know from the description of the case whether 'deceiving him' is meant literally or is a general euphemism for (the more specific euphemism) 'sleeping with someone.' (For the record, note that within the context of a discussion about said wife, a person remarking "She probably is sleeping with someone tonight" would normally be taken to mean that she is probably sleeping with someone *else* (other than her husband) tonight. Presumably this is because otherwise the remark would have added no new relevant information to the talk exchange.) I find the example more plausible but more complicated on the euphemistic reading. The complication is that the hearer must first recover what the speaker more specifically meant, then, given that, determine what was implicated. Much of the same machinery and pattern of inference are involved in both steps.

39. Grice mentions all but (3).

40. Grice mentions all but (2).

41. But does '*x* is meeting an adult human female this evening' carry the *same* implication? It seems not, and this creates the following difficulty (emphasized by Chomsky, in conversation); Grice wants to say that any *way* or *manner* of saying the same thing is likely to have the same generalized implicature. So if the above does not (in all likelihood) have the requisite implicature it should not count as another way or manner of saying (the same thing as) the original. And this would be the case if either (i) these two expressions did not count as 'saying the same thing' when uttered in the appropriate context, or (ii) these were not different 'ways' or 'manners' of saying the same thing. There is reason to deny both (i) and (ii). First, recall that 'what is said' was in part a function of (or at least 'closely related to') the conventional meaning of the words uttered (1967,

II, p. 5) and presumably the two expressions in question are paraphrases. So, other things being equal, one would expect the same thing to have been said. Second, under the maxim of Manner (relating *how* what is said is to be said) we find: "be brief." And clearly we could generate an implicature off of the expanded paraphrase. (For instance, *A* says, "I'm goint to meet Bobby," *B* says, "Is Bobby a man or a woman?" *A* says, "(Well) Bobby's an adult human female." I would think that *A* implied something like the opinion that he did not view Bobby as particularly attractive or desirable in a feminine way, and he did this by conspicuously picking this verbose equivalent thereby (conspicuously) avoiding the word 'woman' and so disavowing some of its usual suggestions in these contexts. That it has these suggestions cannot be doubted in view of pairs like: 'She is a real (good, etc.) woman' vs. 'She is a real (good, etc.) adult human female'.)

42. The point can be put more precisely as follows:

(1) Feature (5) allows for the possibility of many implicata *Q*, *R*, etc.

(2) (i) Either (2)–(5) define conversational implicata *Q*, *R*, etc. or,

    (ii) (1)–(5) define conversational implicata *Q*, *R*, etc.

(3) Suppose (2i): then by definition, the set of implicata (on a particular occasion) is determined by the predicate (roughly):
    (a) *X* is required to make *S*'s-saying-that-*P*, consistent with the supposition that *S* is observing the conversational maxims.

(4) thus, (3a) can explain (via the working-out schema) how *P*, etc., get implicated. But,

(5) (3a) predicts that
    (b) The house was Aunt Martha's.
    is an implication of "I found it in a house."

(6) But (5b) is not such an implication, so (3a) cannot be sufficient.

(7) Suppose (2ii): Then by definition the set of implicata (on a particular occasion) is determined by the predicate:
    (c) (i) *x* is implicated (i.e., suggested, implied, but not said) and (ii) *x* is required to make *S*'s-saying-that-*P*, consistent with the supposition that *S* is observing the conversational maxims.

(8) Then (7c) does not predict that (5b) is an implicata of "I found it in a house," because (5b) does not satisfy condition (i) on the predicate (c).

(9) However, now condition (ii) on the predicate (c) does not provide us with an explanation of why
    (d) The house was not mine.
    gets conversationally implicated, because it does not provide us with an explanation of why (d) gets implicated at all.

(10) This result seems counter to the whole point of Grice's discussion of conversational implicature.

Although it is true that conversational implication is a species of implication, its relationship to the genus is not the usual one of having the properties of the genus *plus* some new property essential to the species. Rather a conversational implication is an implication *generated in a certain way:* by exploiting a maxim on the assumption that the hearer will be able to apply the working out schema. For our part, we want to see if we can find an explanation for the implicature on the basis of exploitation and working out.

43. Notice that 'the flag is red' does not *mean* 'the flag is partly red' because this entails that it is not all red. As evidence for this entailment consider

(a) The flag is partly red and it is all red.

Since this is a contradiction, 'the flag is partly red' entails 'the flag is not all red'. As further evidence notice that contraposition seems to hold: if the flag is all red it follows that that flag is not partly red. Furthermore, Chomsky has pointed out (in conversation) the following curiosity. Suppose that I am right about the meaning of 'the flag is red'. Consider

(b) The red flag (is on the table).

Here, in prenominal position, we feel disinclined to say that a flag so picked out need only have *some* red in it. Rather it should be distinctively or predominantly red. But if prenominal adjectives are gotten in a grammar by Rel-Clause Reduction and Adjective-Preposing, then transformations seem to change meaning. Alternately, if they do not change meaning, then either 'The flag is red' does not mean 'The flag is at least partly red,' or 'The red flag is . . .' does not mean 'The flag which is predominantly red is . . . ,' but only implies it. I am more inclined toward the latter way out. But then one needs to explain why 'The flag that is red . . .' seems not to carry the same implication. One proposal might be along the lines that the attributive use is in some way more characteristically referential and so would carry more of an implication because of maximum identificatory power. Unfortunately, there are many nonreferential occurrences of prenominal adjectives where the difference still seems to show up: 'I am looking for a red flag' versus 'I am looking for a flag that is red'.

44. Fodor observed (in conversation) that questions of the form (a) 'Who ϕ-ed?' do not always ask for a complete specification of X with respect to ϕ. For example, (b): 'Who has a key?' can be used to ask for a specification of *someone* with a key, not *everyone* with a key. Now, on the Katz-Postal (1964) theory of interrogatives, (b) has the deep structure shown in (c):

(c)

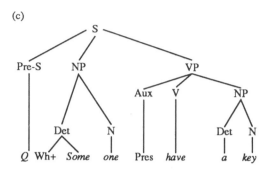

The reading of 'Q' expresses the fact that the utterance of (b) counts as a request that a hearer provide a sentence synonymous with what is dominated by S, except that more semantic information should be included in the constituent which in the interrogative is in the scope of Wh, and which the answerer believes to be true. (Unfortunately, unless Frege is right, the answer 'John' will not count as an answer to the question since proper names have no sense and so do not contribute markers to the reading of the answer.) Ignoring this, it is clear that something like the proper interpretation is assigned to (b) by this theory since it in effect asks for substitution instances on 'someone'. The problem is, rather, that it is not clear how we get the other interpretation of (b), i.e., give me identifying expressions for all the people with keys. This is the common reading one finds in exam questions: 'who holds that all *a priori* statements are analytic?' Here I am asking for *everyone* (within the scope of the discussion) who held that all *a priori* statements are analytic. Now, do we want to say that (most) questions of form (a) are *ambiguous* as between a 'someone' and an 'everyone' reading. If one takes this line, it is difficult to specify the underlying structure for the 'everyone' reading. I do not think that we can simply substitute 'every' for 'some' in (c). I do not know how to interpret 'Wh+ everyone' in a way that guarantees what we want. Notice that if 'who' can come from 'Wh+ everyone,' then we could not define a rejected question as before. If I ask 'who has a ϕ?' I can answer (and not reject) the question by replying 'everyone has a ϕ'. Rather, I think that the most plausible line for a person to take (who thinks that questions like (a) are *ambiguous*) is to offer two interpretations of 'Q'; one asks for at least *some* additional semantic information, the other asks for *all* additional semantic information. This approach, however, has its own obvious drawbacks.

I would prefer to assume that questions of form (a) have only the one sense, but that the context determines when the scope of the question is stronger than (or is intended to be taken as stronger than) the minimal as determined by the meaning of the sentence. Unfortunately, I have no theory of how the context can determine the force of the utterance in the appropriate way.

45. See for instance Grice (1969), redefinition IV (B).

46. In his earlier paper, Grice makes use of a similar principle: "One should not make a weaker statement rather than a stronger one unless there is a good reason for so doing" (1965, p. 451). In his interesting study of this principle, O'Hair ends up with the following version: "Unless there are outweighing good reasons to the contrary, one should not make a weaker statement rather than a stronger one if the audience is interested in the extra information that could be conveyed by the latter" (1969a, p. 45). This can be viewed as spelling out what "strongest relevant" might come to in my maxim.

We have been assuming that if p entails q, and q does *not* entail p, then p is stronger than, more informative than, q. This was supposed to be a sufficient condition on relative strength of information. One problem is that, on this account, if p is contradictory or logically false, then it will (trivially) entail any contingent statement q, but q will not entail it. So by this criterion contradictions will be stronger than, more informative than, any contingent statement, and this does not seem right. One way out might be to analyze entailment along the lines of recent work in 'relevance' logic (see Anderson and Belnap, 1968).

Nor can the suggested criterion be turned into a necessary condition. This would preclude the possibility of independent statements bearing relations of strength. Yet we feel that a statement to the effect that Jones' phone number is 1213 is more informative than that someone has been happy. So we want an account that meets the following conditions (if possible):

(1) Logical truths and falsehoods are least informative and get rank 0. (If logicism is correct, then mathematical statements would be uninformative. Perhaps we could say that what is informative is not the statement that p, but the realization that p is a mathematical truth.)

(2) If p, q are not of rank 0, then if p entails q, but q does not entail p, then p is stronger than q.

(3) Logically independent statements can bear relations of strength.

I have no analysis that meets these, but see Smokler (1966) and O'Hair (1969b) for some relevant discussion.

Another line of attack might be to postpone the search for a general criterion of information strength, and turn instead to more specific submaxims of information. Steps in this direction have been taken by Fogelin (1967, I.6). There he considers statements related by the traditional square of opposition and offers us two principles that range over them:

(P 1) Do not employ an I or an O proposition in a context where you can legitimately employ an A or an E proposition (p. 21).

And its 'corollary':

(P 2) Do not affirm one subcontrary if you are willing to deny the other (p. 21).

It is convenient to restate (and perhaps generalize) (P 2) as (P 2'):

(P 2') Affirm one subcontrary iff you are willing to affirm the other.

Give (P 2') it is clear that the use of one subcontrary will suggest that one would affirm the other as well, and that "subcontraries tend to collapse together" (p. 22). To say that some As are B is conversationally taken to mean that some are and some are not; likewise, with saying that some As are not B. It is important to note that this implication is contextually dependent. Consider Fogelin's case of a prison guard who announces that some of his prisoners have escaped, when they all have. The implication is dependent on the presumption that if more were missing, he would know. Contrast this with another case (due to Merrilee Salmon): I am driving past Jones' house, the light is on, and I say: 'Somebody must be home.' I certainly do not imply that somebody is not; and this is because (I contend) I am not supposed by the hearer to be in any position to know.

47. This is slightly inaccurate, since I am tempted to follow Katz and others in 'extending' logical relations to sentences not conventionally used to make statements, but used to ask questions, issue commands, and so on.

48. Unless some way can be found for 'bracketing' off certain clauses in a conjunction and marking them for this logical property (see Grice, 1967, later lectures, and the last sections of this work).

49. W. Alston (1963, IV) says, for instance, "'Can you reach the salt?' sometimes means *please pass the salt*, sometimes *Are you able to pass the salt?* and perhaps sometimes *I challenge you to try to reach as far as the salt*."

50. It is not fair asking now for a principle by which the hearer selects that reading (over the prediction reading) before performing the requisite reasoning. It might be the case that the reasoning at issue will contribute to the determination of which the hearer selects. It is not implausible, for instance, that selection is made in accordance with the maxim of Relevance, so if Relevance is used in working out the implication, the possibility of such a working-out can confirm the original selection. The picture I am suggesting, then, is that in the communication situation the hearer forms hypotheses as to what the speaker meant on the basis of what 'what he uttered' means, and tests each hypothesis contextually in some vaguely understood way, being guided by the maxims. In this procedure the maxim of Relevance seems to play a uniquely central role. This is reflected by its similarity to the Cooperative Principle.

51. Recently, I understand, this problem has gone under the title of the problem of 'Whimperatives.' This is of course just one case of a very general phenomenon (see Searle, (1975) for an interesting discussion and a speech-act solution to this problem).

52. It is interesting to note that an opinion close to mine was reached by Robert Heinlein, who probably can be said not to have any philosophical/linguistic axes to grind. In his book *Stranger in a Strange Land,* a Martian (Mike Smith) is brought to Earth. His instruction in English is underdescribed, but apparently it consists mainly of memorizing a dictionary (he has total recall of course) and an old-fashioned grammar. He uses his (memorized) dictionary to translate English into Martian when possible. E.g., 'Smith used English as one might use a code book, with tedious and imperfect translation" (p. 14). Because of the way he understands English, Smith understands sentences quite *literally,* and many humorous situations develop because "He knows a number of words, but . . . he doesn't have any cultural context to hang them on" (p. 37). Under this description of Smith's linguistic competence, it is instructive to consider the following episode. Smith is suspected of having the ability to levitate objects. He is being put to the test by Jubal and Jill. The dialogue (with slight alterations) is as follows:

JUBAL: "Mike, sit at my desk. Now, can you pick up that ash tray? Show me."
MIKE: "Yes, Jubal." Smith reached out and took it in his hand.
JUBAL: "No, no!"
MIKE: "I did it wrong?"
JUBAL: "No, it was my mistake. I want to know if you can lift it *without* touching it?"
MIKE: "Yes, Jubal."
JUBAL: "Well, are you tired?"
MIKE: "No, Jubal."
JILL: "Jubal, you haven't *told* him to—you just asked if he could."
JUBAL: (looking sheepish) "Mike, will you please, without touching it, lift that ash tray a foot above the desk?"
MIKE: "Yes, Jubal." (The ash tray raised, floated above the desk) (p. 112).

I think that Heinlein is right here. A person who learns English from a dictionary and a grammar would need some "cultural context" to justifiably take the *prima facie* question as a request.

Or consider the (unconsciously) interesting example from Frederic Brown:

Carmody grinned. "You want me to get graphic, but I'll fool you. I'll just ask you this—should I see her again?" "No," said Junior mechanically, but implacably. Carmody's eyebrows went up. "The devil you say. And may I ask why, since you haven't met the lady, you say that?" "Yes. You may ask why." That was one trouble with Junior; he always answered the question you actually asked, not the one you implied (p. 8).

53. It is not to be thought that this definition is unproblematic. In fact, it can be shown that 'necessary condition' cannot mean 'logically necessary condition' in the sense of standard logic, for all presuppositions would then be logical truths, by a familiar argument.

54. A variant of this argument appears in Wilson (1972). As far as I know, these were arrived at independently.

55. Although Wilson (1970) does not mention this device in her discussion of negative factives and offers a slightly different account, she may have had some of this material in mind also.

56. It is not too difficult to find a context in which 2 and 3 are true. Many a situation from epistemology will do. It is harder to construct one for 4, but consider the following dialogue:

s: I didn't know that you were married.
h: You still don't.

Here I think it plausible to say that the force of *H*'s remark was that of a denial that he was married; a denial that *p*. It is a very instructive exercise to try to figure out exactly how this comes about.

57. Among the variety of circumstances that would make it true to say that someone expresses a psychological state would be

(A) *S* expresses ψ if
   (i) (optional for achievement sense) *S* is in state ψ.
   (ii) *S* does something ϕ such that:
      (a) if *H* were aware the *S* had ϕ-ed, then
      (b) *H* probably would conclude that *S* was in ψ, at least partly on the basis of the awareness in (a).

(B) S (intentionally) expresses ψ if
    (i) (optional for success sense) S is in state ψ.
    (ii) S does something ϕ with the intention that:
        (a) if H were aware that S had ϕ-ed, then
        (b) H probably would conclude the S was in ψ, at least partly on the basis of the awareness in (a).

58. Among the variety of circumstances that would make it true to say that someone implies something would be

(A) S's doing ϕ implied that p if
    (i) S ϕ-ed.
    (ii) H is aware the S has ϕ-ed.
    (iii) H concluded that p, at least partly on the basis of the awareness in (ii).
(B) In doing ϕ, S implied that p (to H) if
    (i) S does ϕ.
    (ii) S does ϕ with the intention that:
        (a) H be aware that S has ϕ-ed.
        (b) H conclude that p, at least partly on the basis of the awareness in (a).

59. For the purposes of the argument it is sufficient that q is an immediate consequence of p if q is a logical consequence of p and q may be inferred from p by a single intuitively correct principle of inference (like simplification or *modus ponens*).

60. For instance see Ayer, 1946, p. 76.

61. This does not follow truth functionally from our working definition of strength, but it is a reasonable requirement.

62. Some more common euphemisms clustering around the usual taboo subjects of sex, excrement, death, and related interest are: make love to (with?), lost her virtue/honor, loose woman, ?do it, streetwalker (Boston: working girl), ?gay, birthday suit/clothes, house of ill repute, little girls' room, senior citizen, passed on, etc. It is important to distinguish euphemisms ('passed on') from clinical or technical terminology ('expired', 'deceased') and both of these from the common terms ('die'), slang ('croaked'), and idioms ('kicked the bucket'). I am not sure how to do this in general, but for various particular semantic fields it seems moderately clear how it should go.

63. Perhaps this sentence is just ambiguous as between: "It has been ten years since I last played tennis." and "It is not true that I have been playing tennis (as an activity) for ten years." However, I think that the former is not a sense of the sentence; rather the sense is "I have not played tennis during the last ten years" and the first sense can be seen as being implied in a way that should now be clear.

64. Glenn Ross brought these last two examples to my attention. See Wilson (1975) and Harnish (1975b) for further remarks.

REFERENCES

Ackermann, R. (1970). *Modern Deductive Logic.* New York: Doubleday.

Alston, W. (1963). "Meaning and Use." *Philosophical Quarterly* 13:107–124.

Anderson, A., and N. Belnap (1968). "Entailment." In G. Iseminger (ed.), *Logic and Philosophy.* New York: Applcton-Century-Crofts.

Ayer, A. (1946). *Language, Truth and Logic.* 2d ed. New York: Dover Books.

Benacerraf, P. (1965). "What Numbers Could Not Be." *Philosophical Review* 74:47–73.

Brown, F. (1948). *Honeymoon in Hell.* New York: Bantam Books.

Chomsky, N. (1972). "Some Empirical Issues in the Theory of Transformational Grammar." In S. Peters (ed.), *Goals of Linguistic Theory.* Englewood Cliffs, N.J.: Prentice-Hall.

Clark, T. (1965). "Seeing Surfaces and Seeing Objects." In M. Black (ed.), *Philosophy in America.* Ithaca, N.Y.: Cornell University Press.

Davidson, D., and G. Harman (eds.). (1975). *The Logic of Grammar.* Encino, Calif.: Dickenson.

Fogelin, R. (1967). *Evidence and Meaning.* Atlantic Highlands, N.J.: Humanities Press.

Frege, G. (1884). *Grundlagen der Arithmetic.* Translated by J. Austin as *The Foundations of Arithmetic* (1953). New York: Harper & Row.

Grice, H. P. (1965). "The Causal Theory of Perception." In R. Shwartz (ed.), *Perceiving, Sensing, and Knowing.* New York: Doubleday.

Grice, H. P. (1967). "William James Lectures." Photocopy. Lecture II, "Logic and Conversation." In D. Davidson and G. Harman (eds.), (1975). *The Logic of Grammar.* Encino, Calif.: Dickenson. [Reprinted in this volume, Chapter 19]

Grice, H. P. (1969). "Utterer's Meaning and Intentions." *Philosophical Review* 78:147–177.

Grice, H. P. (1971). "Utterer's Meaning, Sentence-Meaning and Word-Meaning." In J. Searle (ed.), *The Philosophy of Language.* Oxford: Oxford University Press. [Reprinted in this volume, Chapter 4]

Grice, H. P. (Undated). "Conditionals." Photocopy.

Harnish, R. (1972). "Studies in Logic and Language." Ph.D. diss., Massachusetts Institute of Technology.

Harnish, R. (1975a). "Verb Taxonomies and Entailment." University of Arizona. Photocopy.

Harnish, R. (1975b). "Review of Wilson (September, 1975)." *Times Literary Supplement.*

Heinlein, R. (1961). *Stranger in a Strange Land.* New York: Putnam.

Hempel, C. (1964). "The Nature of Mathematical Truth." In P. Benacerraf and H. Putnam (eds.), *Philosophy of Mathematics.* Englewood Cliffs, N.J.: Prentice-Hall.

Hungerland, I. (1960). "Contextual Implication." *Inquiry* 3:211–258.

Katz, J., and P. Postal (1964). *An Integrated Theory of Linguistic Descriptions.* Cambridge, Mass.: MIT Press.

Keenan, E. (1974). "The Universality of Conversational Implicatures." Photocopy.

Kiparsky, P., and C. Kiparsky (1971). "Fact." In D. Steinberg and L. Jakobovits (eds.), *Semantics.* Cambridge: Cambridge University Press.

Lakoff, G., and S. Peters. (1969). "Phrasal Conjunction and Symmetric Predicates." In D. Reibel and S. Schane (eds.), *Modern Studies in English.* Englewood Cliffs, N.J.: Prentice-Hall.

Lehrer, A. (1975). "Interpreting Certain Adverbs: Semantics or Pragmatics?" *Journal of Linguistics* 11:239–248.

Lewis, D. (1969). *Convention: A Philosophical Study.* Cambridge, Mass.: Harvard University Press.

Massey, G. (1970). *Understanding Symbolic Logic.* New York: Harper & Row.

McCawley, J. (1968). "The Role of Semantics in a Grammar." In E. Bach and R. Harms (eds.), *Universals in Linguistic Theory.* New York: Holt, Rinehart and Winston.

O'Hair, S. G. (1969a). "Meaning and Implication." *Theoria* 35:38–54.

O'Hair, S. G. (1969b). "A Definition of Information Content." *Journal of Philosophy* 66:132–133.

Punch (1969). 257:27.

Quine, W.V.O. (1959). *Methods of Logic.* New York: Holt, Rinehart and Winston.

Ross, D. (1930). *The Right and the Good.* Oxford: Oxford University Press.

Schiffer, S. (1972). *Meaning.* Oxford: Oxford University Press.

Searle, J. (1969). *Speech Acts.* Cambridge: Cambridge University Press.

Searle, J. (1975). "Indirect Speech Acts." In P. Cole and J. Morgan (eds.), *Syntax and Semantics.* Vol. 3: *Speech Acts.* New York: Academic Press. [Reprinted in this volume, Chapter 16].

Smokler, H. (1966). "Information Content: A Problem of Definition." *Journal of Philosophy* 63:201–211.

Strawson, P. (1952). *Introduction to Logical Theory.* London: Methuen.

Urmson, J. (1963). "Parenthetical Verbs." In C. Caton (ed.), *Philosophy and Ordinary Language.* Champaign: University of Illinois Press.

Ware, R. (Undated). "Two Models of the Mental Life of Groups." University of Calgary. Photocopy.

Wilson, D. (1970). "Presupposition." Massachusetts Institute of Technology. Photocopy.

Wilson, D. (1972). "Presuppositions on Factives." *Linguistic Inquiry* 3:405–410.

Wilson, D. (1975). *Presuppositions and Non-Truth-Conditional-Semantics.* New York: Academic Press.

21

On Testing for Conversational Implicature

JERROLD M. SADOCK

H. P. Grice's (1975) suggestions concerning the relationship between natural language and logic provide the outline of a system for explaining certain aspects of what utterances convey without claiming that they are part of the conventional force of the uttered sentence. The notion of conversational implicature makes it possible to claim that a sentence with two quite distinct effects is nevertheless unambiguous from the point of view of its conventional content, and that two sentences that can convey practically the same thing are nevertheless not logically or linguistically equivalent.

There is, then, a serious methodological problem that confronts the advocate of linguistic pragmatics. Given some aspect of what a sentence conveys in a particular context, is that aspect part of what the sentence conveys in virtue of its meaning (in the generative semanticist's sense) or should it be "worked out" on the basis of Gricean principles of conversation from the rest of the meaning of the sentence and relevant facts of the context of utterance? Obviously, the problem of deciding whether a certain bit of conveyed information is attributable to the grammar or to pragmat-

ics can be attacked from either direction. Either we can try to decide how one recognizes essentially grammatical facts and establish a rigorous methodology leading from surface structure down to meaning, or we could establish a pragmatic methodology that leads from what is conveyed in contexts up to meaning. The first approach has been followed fairly extensively, e.g., in Zwicky and Sadock 1975. But at present a rigorous pragmatic methodology is lacking. This chapter examines the problems pervading the methodology of linguistic pragmatics.

According to Grice's much-followed precepts, what an utterance conveys in context falls into two parts; what is SAID is the logical content, the minimum necessary to specify the truth conditions of the sentence. For the remainder, Grice coined the term IMPLICATURE. Thus the class of implicatures is defined negatively as what is conveyed less what is said. It is often the case that negatively defined classes are not uniform classes; their only common defining property is that none of the members of the class has one particular property. I suspect this is also true of Grice's class of implicatures.

Implicatures themselves come in two varieties, conventional and conversational. Conventional implicatures include all non-truth-conditional aspects of what is conveyed by an utterance solely due to the words or forms the sentence contains. These include, then, most of what have been called by linguists the presuppositions of a sentence; they are closely allied to what is said in the strict sense, at least in that the same clause can determine either the truth conditions of a sentence or a set of conventional implicatures. In (1), the clause *that Bill is a linguist* enters into the evaluation of the truth of the sentence, but in (2) it does not. In Grice's system, example (2) would be considered true in case the proposition that Bill is a linguist is surprising, regardless of whether that proposition is true or false:

(1) *It is true that Bill is a linguist.*

(2) *It is surprising that Bill is a linguist.*

Conventional implicatures thus should be and have been handled in a way that closely parallels the treatment of semantic content (see, for example, Karttunen and Peters 1975).

In contrast, however, conversational implicatures are only indirectly associated with the linguistic content of utterances. They are derived from the content of the sentences used and owe their existence, according to Grice, to the fact that participants in a conversation are constrained by the common goal of communication to be cooperative. Nonconventional implicatures come in two varieties: first the important class of conversational implicatures that involve the Cooperative Principle and its maxims, and then a poorly described class of nonconventional, nonconversational implicatures that are calculated in context on the basis of the conventional meaning, knowledge of the context of utterance, and background knowledge, but which depend crucially for their existence on nonconversational maxims that are "aesthetic, social, or moral in character" (Grice 1975:47). Grice gives as an example the maxim *Be polite.* I have some trouble understanding exactly why it is that such maxims differ from those that fall under the Cooperative Principle, for, on the one hand, it would be uncooperative to be gratuitously impolite, antisocial, or unpleasant, and, on the other, the requirement that we make our contributions true and that we tell the whole truth could easily be construed as moral principles as well as, or instead of, cooperative principles. At any rate, for our purposes the class of nonconversational, nonconventional implicatures belongs with conversational implicatures rather than with conventional implicatures. In the case of either kind, what is conveyed is conveyed nonconventionally. I will speak only of conversational implicatures in what follows, but because my remarks are addressed to the problem of discriminating between information that is conventionally conveyed and that which is not, what I say should carry over to implicatures based on maxims such as *Be polite.*

Conversational implicatures themselves divide into two classes, particularized and generalized. The former are crucially dependent not only on the content of the utterance and the Cooperative Principle, but also on the context of utterance. The latter are relatively in-

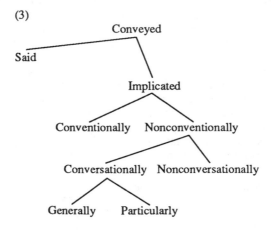

(3)

Conveyed

Said

Implicated

Conventionally Nonconventionally

Conversationally Nonconversationally

Generally Particularly

(4)

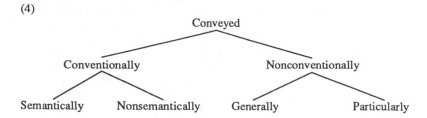

dependent of context and therefore can rather easily be confused with conventional implicatures since they are constantly associated with particular linguistic forms.

The various ways in which, according to Grice, utterances can convey information are represented schematically in (3). Because of the close similarity between what is said and what is conventionally implicated, and because of the similarity between conversational and nonconversational, nonconventional implicature, I would prefer a schematization such as that in (4). For the purposes of this paper, however, the difference may be considered merely terminological.

Regardless of which of these categorizations gives the more accurate picture of the ways in which utterances can convey messages, it appears that there is an important distinction between the conventional and the nonconventional aspects of the import of what we say. This dichotomy concerns the grammarian in a fundamental way, for it is the grammar of a language that is the repository of the conventional aspects of language use. The nonconventional, while surely of interest to students of language, does not need to be, and indeed should not be, mentioned in the description of the language, which is the conventional sign system. Rather, the account of conversational implicature is best understood as a partial description of the USERS of the language, and hence truly deserves the name "pragmatics." Therefore, given the fact that the utterance of a particular linguistic form on a particular occasion conveys some particular submessage, the grammarian must be able to decide whether that submessage is conveyed conventionally or nonconventionally.

But how can we make this decision in a reasoned and reasonable way? Grice provides some guidelines which it is my purpose to examine here. Let us assume for the moment that we know in a particular case what is said

(in the special sense of Grice). Then our job consists of separating the conventional implicatures in the residue from the conversational implicatures. Grice (1975) provides six characteristics of conversational implicature, the first on p. 50, and the remainder, in a block, at the end of the chapter. Briefly stated:

(a) *Conversational implicata are capable of being "worked out" on the basis, inter alia, of the Cooperative Principle. That is, they are* CALCULABLE.

(b) *Conversational implicata are* CANCELLABLE.

(c) *Conversational implicata are* NONDETACHABLE.

(d) *Conversational implicata are not part of the meaning of the uttered forms. They are* NONCONVENTIONAL.

(e) *Conversational implicata are not carried by what is said, but by the saying of it.*

(f) *Conversational implicata may be* INDETERMINATE.

Of these, only the first three are reasonable candidates for practical tests that could be used in settling the matter in particular instances. The fourth, (d), is completely circular. Conversational implicata are by definition nonconventional and if it were possible to tell in some intuitive way what is and what is not conventional, then there would be no need for other criteria. But of course it is not possible. Characteristic (e), if coherent at all, seems to me to be a version of (d). What is conventional is the meaning of the utterance ("what is said"), but nonconventional effects can be triggered only by uttering something with a particular form and a particular meaning on a particular occasion. Thus to use (e) as a practical criterion, it would be necessary to know the solution to the problem in advance, which would, of course, make tests irrelevant. The last test is seriously weakened by the modal. Some conversational implicata are fully determinate, I take it. Furthermore, if reference is part of meaning, then what is said in using a definite pronoun or a demonstrative is also indeterminate.

Characteristics (a–c), however, do deserve closer scrutiny. First let us consider (a). It certainly makes sense that, if a particular piece of conveyed information is conveyed pragmatically rather than purely linguistically, there is some available scheme that allows the addressee to figure out what is being conveyed and allows the speaker to figure out that the addressee might figure it out. I think that some version of (a) must surely be a necessary characteristic of conversational implicatures. But I think that two separate considerations indicate that (a) criterion of derivability is not a sufficient condition. First of all, the Cooperative Principle with its maxims of Quality, Quantity, Relation, and Manner is so vague that almost anything can be "worked out" on the basis of almost any meaning. Let me briefly rehash the maxims in an effort to prove my point:

1. The maxim of Quantity has two parts that require the cooperative speaker to say as much but no more than is required for his particular purposes in the "talk exchange";

2. The maxim of Quality also has two parts, and demands that the speaker say only what he believes to be true and on that for which he has sufficient evidence;

3. The maxim of Relation urges the speaker to make his contribution relevant; and

4. The maxim of Manner cautions the speaker to be methodical and to avoid ambiguity, prolixity, and obscurity.

So powerful is each of the maxims that at times they vie for the privilege of explaining the same facts. It is not clear to me, for example, how one could both be relevant and say either less or more than is required. In what way is the avoidance of prolixity different from saying only as much as is required? If a particular contribution is obscure does it not also lack relevance? While it is perhaps possible to eliminate some of the redundancy in the maxims, I feel that the extreme power of the system is in fact an unavoidable characteristic. Grice says that metaphor, for example, is partially explained by the Cooperative Principle since metaphors are often literally and patently false. If someone tells me

that Bill is the Rock of Gibraltar, and if, as seems reasonable, I don't believe that Bill actually IS the Rock of Gibraltar, but if I believe that the speaker is not being deliberately uncooperative, and in particular that he is not violating the maxim of Quality, then I am forced to search for a communicative intent, other than the literal meaning of what has been said, that can eliminate the clash. Now the literal meaning of metaphors and what they are intended to communicate can differ fairly widely. In fact, I believe it is the case that the conceptual distance between the literal meaning of a metaphorical expression and the meaning it is intended to convey and might actually convey can be as large as one chooses. Metaphor might lack aptness if the communicative intent is far-fetched but then it is simply a poor metaphor and not no metaphor at all. If the cooperative principle is to handle this discrepancy, between literal meaning and metaphorical intent, as I believe it should, it is going to have to be pretty powerful.

Indirect speech acts provide another example with the same force. The Cooperative Principle has been very believably invoked, e.g., by Searle (1975), to account for the fact that an utterance of *It's cold in here* can convey a request to close a door. But it can also convey a request to open a door, or to bring a blanket, or to pay a gas bill. In fact it's difficult to think of a request that the utterance could NOT convey in the right context. My point is that if the Cooperative Principle is strong enough to do this, then it is going to have to be strong enough to do certain things it shouldn't.

Consider the following fairly improbable example. Suppose someone says to me, *Bernstein studies hard.* Under fairly ordinary circumstances, the communicated import of the utterance could be that of an exhortation to me to study hard, too. Similarly, *Wright letters well* could be an exhortation to reproduce the alphabet neatly. Since well-motivated conversational principles are available to explain the contextual force of the utterance, there is no need to postulate that this sentence is ambiguous between a meaning that only conversationally implicates an exhortation to letter well and one that IS an exhortation to letter well. But we know, of course, that the *Wright* example IS ambiguous while the *Bernstein* example is not, for while one can say, *I shall [rajt] letters,* saying *I shall [bʌrnstijn] letters* would cause a bit of consternation. The Cooperative Principle must therefore be strong enough to work out certain implicatures where in fact what is conveyed is conveyed directly by meaning. Thus the mere fact that something conveyed by an utterance CAN be worked out according to pragmatic principles is not enough to guarantee that it is in fact a conversational implicature.

There is, as I indicated earlier, a second consideration which leads to the conclusion that calculability is not a sufficient condition for conversational implicature. I have argued at length elsewhere (Sadock 1972 and 1975a) that conversational implicatures can become conventionalized by stages. That is, what starts life as a metaphor can grow into an idiom. Euphemisms fairly rapidly come to MEAN what they were originally intended to circumlocute and so cease to be euphemisms, and indirect speech acts can in time metamorphose into direct forms. But except for the limiting case in which the original meaning is entirely lost, conversational principles can always be called upon to explain the force of an originally indirect form, since those principles were indeed important in the history of the reanalyzed forms. An idiom such as *spill the beans* displays its idiomaticity in the form of peculiar syntax. One can say without oddity, *Dean spilled the beans to Congress.* Similarly, the fact that the expression *go to the bathroom* no longer means just what one would suspect from the words in the expression is reflected by the fact (pointed out to me by Jerry Morgan) that the sentence *My dog went to the bathroom on the living room carpet* is not contradictory. But if these phrases had just been coined there would still be the possibility of understanding them in the way we do with the assistance of the rules of conversation. The rules don't cease to exist when their work is taken over by the grammar. Rather, through something like a principle of least resistance, a direct route is taken to a conventionalized, idiomatic sense of an expression in order to spare unnecessary pragmatic calculation. There is no need to figure out anew what is intended by *spill the beans* or *go to the bathroom* since they have come to mean (roughly) 'divulge the secret' and 'perform a bodily

function', respectively. Yet the principles that ORIGINALLY allowed these expressions to have metaphorical senses are still vital and therefore these conventionalized implicatures are also cases where the Cooperative Principle could be invoked, but where it should not be.

Therefore the fact that conversational implicatures are calculable with the aid of the Cooperative Principle is a necessary but not sufficient characterization. And in fact it is not even a very interesting necessary condition since, as we have seen, the maxims need to have such great power that nearly anything can be worked out with them on the basis of nearly any meaning. If nearly anything that is conveyed is calculable, it is not especially tantalizing to find calculability in some particular instance.

I turn next to Grice's claim that conversational implicatures are not detachable. What this means is the following: If X is an expression with meaning M and C_K is a conversational implicature based on an utterance of X in context K, then it should not be possible to find an expression X' that shares meaning M with X but is not associated with the conversational implicature C_K. The rationale for the doctrine of nondetachability is that, as defined, conversational implicatures are worked out on the basis of meaning. In other words, the Cooperative Principle is supposed to be blind to form, and preservation of meaning should imply the preservation of conversational implicature.

An important exception that Grice mentions and that already severely diminishes the value of this test arises from the fact that certain conversational implicatures are in fact based on the WAY what is said is said—on how it is put. Such implicatures make use of the maxim of Manner for their effect and will, of course, be detachable. For such cases, the nondetachability test will be useless. But how good is nondetachability as a criterion for other examples of conversational implicature? Is it necessary? Or both? I shall argue that it is neither.

It should be plain that nondetachability is not a sufficient test for conversational implicature. For one thing, nondetachability is not strict enough to distinguish between entailment and conversational implicature, as Grice himself points out (Grice 1969). It is not possible to paraphrase *Bill and Harry left* without conveying *Harry left*. Yet this is clearly not an example of conversational implicature, but of logical inference.

In this example, it might be argued, no confusion can arise, for the inference in question is based upon what is said (in Grice's sense) and I have assumed that we somehow know in advance what a particular expression says and that our task is simply to distinguish between conventional and conversational implicature. Perhaps the doctrine of nondetachability could be brought one step closer to being a sufficient test for conversational implicature in something like the following way: If C_K is conveyed by an utterance of X in context K and C_K is not entailed by what is said in uttering X, then C_K is a conversational implicature. But this will not work either because, as I claimed earlier, conventional implicature is so very like what is said. Consider a sentence like *Since birds have hair, most politicians are dishonest*. I think it is reasonable to suppose that this sentence is true just in case most politicians are dishonest. In other words, all that the clause *since birds have hair* contributes to the sentence is a set of conventional implicatures; that clause is not part of the semantic content of the sentence, not part of what is said. Now consider the sentence *Since Bill and Harry left, most politicians are dishonest*. Let us consider in particular the relationship between an utterance of this sentence and the conveyed information that the utterer believes Harry to have left. I think it is clear that we do not want to claim to be dealing with a conversational implicature here, but rather with a logical deduction based on nonsemantic content or, in Gricean terms, conventional implicature. But the conveyed proposition is totally nondetachable. Anything that means (taking meaning to be the sum of what is said and what is conventionally implicated) what the original sentence means will have to convey the speaker's belief that Harry left. The only noncircular way of saving nondetachability as a sufficient distinguishing feature between conventional and conversational implicature would be to exclude conventional implicature from the meaning that is substituted for in the test. In the present example, then, detachability would be demonstrated by adducing a simple sentence like *Most politicians are dishonest*, a

sentence that means (excluding conventional implicature) what the more complex example means but does not (ordinarily) convey the speaker's belief that Harry left, and thereby demonstrates that the original example conventionally implicates it. But excluding conventional implicature from what is substituted for in the nondetachability test is tantamount to claiming that conversational implicatures can be based only on semantic content and not on conventional implicatures, a claim that can easily be shown to be false. Consider the sentence *Since it's cold in here, there must be a north wind*. An uttering of this sentence could easily, if sneakily, conversationally implicate something on the order of *Close the door*, BECAUSE IT CONVENTIONALLY IMPLICATES *It's cold in here*. Therefore conventional implicature cannot be excluded from what is kept constant in the nondetachability test, and nondetachability fails to distinguish conversational implicature and cases of entailments of conventional implicatures. Both are quite reasonably nondetachable.

As a further demonstration of the nonsufficiency of nondetachability as a test for conversational implicature, consider the fact that there are bound to be expressions in any natural language that cannot be paraphrased, expressions whose supposed synonyms actually differ in meaning in significant ways. In fact it has been suggested that no two expressions have precisely the same meaning. At any rate, in the clear case of a lexical *hapax*, EVERYTHING conveyed by the expression is trivially nondetachable since there are no paraphrases at all.

Whether there are absolutely equivalent paraphrases or not, the fact that it is difficult to tell if two expressions have the same meaning makes the nondetachability test less useful in practice. Suppose the claim is made that a sentence such as *Can you open the door?* does not conversationally implicate a request to open the door but rather conventionally implicates it and that this claim is backed up by the observation that the implicature fails to go through if the synonymous periphrastic modal *be able* is substituted for *can*. Since the paraphrase detaches the implicature, the argument goes, it cannot be conversational. This claim can all too easily be countered with the claim that *can* and *be able* are not synonymous and that in fact this example PROVES that they are not.

This vicious circle really shows that the nondetachability test, as stated, does not make sense. It is supposed to bring out the difference between the case where the meaning of an expression X includes C_K as a conventional implicature and the case where C_K is related to the uttering of X through the Cooperative Principle. But if C_K is part of the meaning of X, then any expression X' that means the same thing as X will also mean C_K (among other things), and uttering X' will therefore convey C_K. On the other hand, if uttering X' does not convey C_K then X' cannot include C_K as part of its meaning and therefore X' does not mean what X means and detachability has not been shown.

Thus, strictly speaking, detachability and nondetachability don't show anything at all. Nevertheless, the test is a pretty good one, at least in extreme cases. Detachability in the absence of obvious meaning differences of the right kind is a suspicious fact, and the more apparent paraphrases there are that succeed in detaching an implicature, the more it looks as if the implicature must be conventional. On the other hand, the more apparently synonymous expressions there are that fail to detach an implicature, the less the situation looks accidental and the more it looks as if some principle, such as the Cooperative Principle, is in force.

Another practical problem with nondetachability as a touchstone for conversational implicature relates to the foregoing discussion of calculability. The Cooperative Principle is potent enough to allow almost any, and perhaps all, requests (to choose one sort of example) to be worked out on the basis of almost any utterance. Since this is so, how could ANY implicated request, conventional or conversational, be detached by a reasonable facsimile of a synonym? Take the last example I discussed. *Are you able to close the door?* does not in fact succeed in detaching the implicated request. It is quite easy to imagine circumstances under which the uttering of that sentence would convey a request. But this is not particularly surprising in view of the fact that practically any question can convey this request under the right circumstances. I am led to wonder whether anything is detachable

from anything. Surprisingly, this very serious difficulty has not caused much anguish. The claim that the *be able* sentence does not carry the implicature that the *can* sentence does, while strictly speaking false, has for the most part been taken in the right spirit. While *Are you able to open the door?* can convey a request to open the door, it does so in a much less direct manner than the supposed near synonym *Can you open the door?* But this notion of directness is very vague and not at all serviceable as a litmus for conventional versus conversational implicature.

As if the inconsistencies mentioned above were not enough to eliminate nondetachability as an important test for conversational implicature, there is another extremely serious contradiction that appears when we consider the doctrine of cancellability. As I will explain shortly, this principle assumes that it is possible to deny a conversational implicature without contradiction, whereas denial of a conventional implicature, or part of what is said in making an utterance, results in infelicity or contradiction. But if this is so, why should it not be possible to find two expressions that differ just in that one contains the denial of what the other conversationally implicates? It has been claimed, for example in Horn 1973 that my saying *I ate some of the cake* conversationally implicates that I did not eat all of the cake. Now the doctrine of nondetachability claims that if this is a bona fide case of conversational implicature, then there should be a lexical item that means just what *some* does but which, when substituted for *some* in the sentence above, detaches the implicature. This happens to be true for English, but the cancellability doctrine would seem to indicate that it does not need to be true. Why could there not be a word that happened to mean 'some and perhaps all'? Admittedly, such a lexical item would be redundant in that *some* in the theory under discussion MEANS just 'some and perhaps all.' But we can SAY things like *Bill ate some, and perhaps all of the cake* without being guilty of any egregious redundancy. As a matter of fact, that is just what the doctrine of cancellability predicts. What principle, then, prevents a lexical item IN A NATURAL LANGUAGE from having a partially redundant literal sense? I know of none and doubt that any such principle would turn out to be tenable. Here are two examples where such an analysis seems reasonable.

It frequently occurs in the law that a word is given a more specific definition than it usually has, just so that it will not drag along with it any unwanted implicatures. For example, meals eaten while doing business away from home are tax deductible. Now *home* is a very vague word in English. To people abroad, the United States is my home. I call Chicago home when I am speaking to people from Boston. The Lakeview neighborhood is my home to other Chicagoans and for some purposes 1140 West George, Apartment 2, is home. I think it is reasoanble to claim that each of these more specific understandings of *home* is only conversationally implicated by the demand for relevance. But am I allowed to claim as a deduction the cheese sandwich that I bought in the Classics Building? No, because, "For traveling purposes, your HOME is your place of business, employment, or post of duty . . ." (Greisman 1975:17). This definition cancels certain implicatures that I would like to have been able to draw.

As a second example, consider the well-known property of English *or* that it can, but need not, be used in an exclusive understanding. Now McCawley (1973) has shown that binary exclusive disjunction does not correspond to the exclusive understanding of its natural language counterpart. Rather, *or* is taken as 'exactly one of . . .' when it is used exclusively. Furthermore, McCawley suggested the assimilation of *or* to the existential quantifier. Since the existential quantifiers can be used in an apparently exclusive sense (e.g. *some but not all*), whatever treatment suffices for them can also suffice for disjunction. In other words, *or* need not be treated as an ambiguous lexical item but may be assigned a conventional meaning exactly like logical (inclusive) disjunction. The fact that it often suggests the exclusion of conjunction would then be a conversational implicature generated on the basis of (among other things) the maxim of Relation.

But in English we have a form *and/or*. Logically speaking, this has just the same meaning as *or*, but, because of a redundancy it contains, it has the property of cancelling the implicature from PVQ to $\sim (P \wedge Q)$. The Latin disjunctions *aut*, which is supposedly an exclusive disjunction, and *vel*, which is supposedly an inclusive disjunction, could be handled in a parallel fashion. *Aut* would be a simple, logical disjunction, and *vel* would differ from it in containing material that cancels an otherwise frequent conversational implicature. These analyses are very much in the spirit of Grice's program, since they claim that the logical basis of language is very much like classical logic. But adopting them involves giving up the claim that nondetachability is a necessary characteristic of conversational implicature.

Last on Grice's list of earmarks of conversational implicature is cancellability, and it is the best of the tests. The test is based on the notion that conversational implicatures are not part of the conventional force of utterances but are figured out in context. It ought to be the case, therefore, that a speaker may freely include, or append to his utterance, material that indicates that the implicature in question is not to be drawn. Contradicting any part of the conventional meaning of an utterance, on the other hand, will amount to logical contradiction (in the case of semantic content) or to internal infelicity (in the case of nonsemantic content). There are no circumstances under which the sentence *It's odd that dogs eat cheese even though they don't* is not bizarre. The reason is this: Conventional implicatures are felicitous only if their propositions are "part of the context." The factive predicate *be odd* conventionally implicates the truth of its complement and therefore requires for its felicitous use that the complement be presumed true in the context in which it is uttered. But in the example above the complement is denied and therefore cannot be presumed true, so that the uttering of the sentence would be invariably infelicitous. In an indubitable case of conversational implicature, cancellation does not produce oddity. One can perfectly well say, *I don't want you to close the door, but it is cold in here.*

The cancellability test, good as it is in the clear cases, is not perfect. There is one large fly in the ointment, and a gnat. Before putting these insects under glass I would like to make a small caveat as to applying the test of cancellability. It is not a problem with the test itself but simply a confusion that I have observed. As Horn (1972) has pointed out, cancellability is not the same thing as suspendibility. Certain conventional implicatures can be called into question without producing infelicity, but none can be denied. While there is nothing wrong with saying, *It's odd that dogs eat cheese if in fact they do,* thus calling the conventional implicature associated with the factive predicate into question, this implicature may not be contradicted openly. It is not proper to conclude, then, that the sentence *Only Muriel voted for Humphrey, if even she did* shows the cancellability of an implicature and therefore confirms its conversational status. This is an instance of suspension. The implicature in question is not cancellable and therefore must be conventional: **Only Muriel voted for Humphrey and even she didn't.*

Now for the above-mentioned gnat. Grice states explicitly that generalized conversational implicatures, those that have little to do with context, are cancellable. But is it not possible that some conversational implicatures are so little dependent on context that cancellation of them will result in something approaching invariable infelicity? In Sadock 1981 I argue that sentences of the form *almost P* only conversationally entail *not P,* contrary to the claim made by Karttunen and Peters (1975). The implicature is straightforwardly calculable and highly nondetachable but, unfortunately for my thesis, just about uncancellable. The sentence *Gertrude not only almost swam the English Channel, in fact she swam it* is, I admit, pretty strange. The reason that this particular dipteran is merely a gnat is that an obviously conventional implicature of the same kind is much less cancellable: *Gertrude not only just barely failed to swim the English Channel, in fact she swam it* is close to being contradictory. The discrepancy can be explained, I think, by claiming that *not P* is a highly generalized conversational implicature based on the uttering of *almost P.* Under all ordinary circumstances the implicature will go through, and it takes pretty unusual contexts to block it. Conventional implicatures, in contrast, reside in the conventional meaning of the utterance and just can't be blocked.

Here is the bigger bug in the theory of cancellability: The test does not distinguish cases of ambiguity from cases of univocality plus possible conversational implicature. One of the senses of a grammatically ambiguous sentence may always be contradicted. This would merely disambiguate the utterance. Let us take as an example the familiar sentence *Everyone speaks one language.* It is usually said that such a sentence is ambiguous (see, for example, Reichenbach 1947:98–99). But it can be, and even has been, perversely claimed (Sadock 1975b) that the sentence is univocal and that one of the apparent senses is, in fact, a conversational implicature. The claim would be that the only meaning the sentence has solely in virtue of its form is 'For each person, there is a language that he/she speaks.' The more specific reading under which it is the same language that everyone speaks is claimed to be a conversational implicature based on the first meaning and the maxim of Quantity. Now I do not believe this treatment for reasons that need not concern us here. All that is important for the methodological purposes at hand is to realize that the cancellability test could be used to strengthen the apparently bogus claim that the reading of the sentence where the existential quantifier has wide scope is a conversational implicature, since it is, in fact, cancellable. That is, one can say without contradiction or oddity, *Everyone speaks one language although no one language is spoken by everyone.* But it shouldn't come as a surprise that the example sentence gives the impression of allowing a more specific interpretation to be cancelled since the more specific interpretation is one pole of an ambiguity.

In Searle (1975) we find an instance of just this sort of misapplication of the principle of cancellability. Searle is at pains to argue that sentences such as *Can you pass the salt?* are not ambiguous between a question sense and an imperative sense. He argues instead that they always and only have the sense of a question and that any requests that they may convey are conversational implicatures. In order to prove his point he says (p. 67): "This point is sometimes denied by philosophers and linguists, but very powerful evidence for it is provided by the fact that it is possible without inconsistency to connect the literal utterance of one of these forms with the denial of any imperative intent." But of course this is exactly what we should expect if the disputed examples were ambiguous.

The sad fact is that in the very cases where

argument is likely to arise as to whether something conveyed by an utterance is conversationally implicated, the competing claim would be that the utterance is ambiguous. But since one sense of a grammatically ambiguous sentence can be denied or contradicted, these are exactly the cases where the cancellability test is of no use whatever.

These two problems with the doctrine of cancellability indicate that it is not a sufficient test, and may not be a necessary test, for conversational implicature.

Cancellability is related to another possible test, not mentioned by Grice. Since conversational implicatures are not part of the conventional import of utterances, it should be possible to make them explicit without being guilty of redundancy. Conversational implicatures, that is, ought to be reinforceable, whereas conventional implicatures should not. In the clear cases, this test accords well with intuition. Thus the second clause of *It's odd that dogs eat cheese and they do* is redundant because it restates what is conventionally implicated by the first clause. But no redundancy shows up when a clearly conversational implicature is made explicit, as in *Maggie ate some, but not all, of the cheddar.*

Just as it was the case with the cancellability test, though, reinforceability will not distinguish conversational additions from privative ambiguities. The fact that the following sentence is unobjectionable is not sufficient evidence to warrant the conclusion that a conversational implicature is involved in the stronger understanding of the unadorned first clause: *Everyone speaks one language and it is the same language.*

For reasons that I do not understand, reinforceability seems to be a more sensitive test in the borderline cases than is cancellability. What I have claimed to be a generalized conversational implicature associated with *almost* is easily reinforceable in *Gertrude almost, but didn't quite, swim the English Channel,* but it is not, as we have seen, so readily cancelled.

Another difference is that the reinforcement test is sensitive to the order of the reinforcing expression and the implicature-bearing expression. A cancelling expression may either precede or follow an implicature-bearing expression without affecting the validity of the test. Because of the pragmatic function of con-

ventional implicatures, these may quite freely be preceded by an expression that establishes the implicature, as in *Dogs eat cheese and it's odd that they do.* Conventional implicatures must, as Karttunen and Peters (1975) have shown, already be part of (i.e. be entailed by) the common ground (roughly, the background information available to both speaker and hearer) to be used appropriately. Therefore, no expression that asserts a proposition P may appropriately follow one that conventionally implicates P without redundantly restating part of the common ground. On the other hand, asserting P BEFORE conventionally implicating P makes P part of the common ground and thus legitimizes the succeeding conventional implicature. It follows also that only assertions are valid test expressions for the reinforcement test while any expression that unequivocally indicates that a speaker holds a certain belief, whether it does so by conventional implicature or assertion, can function properly in testing for cancellability.

Aside from these two caveats, however, reinforceability ought to be about as good—and about as poor—a test for conversational implicature as cancellability.

SUMMARY

Grice (1975) gave six characteristics of conversational implicature that were supposed to distinguish examples of this phenomenon from examples of conventional implicature. Of these, only three seem to merit serious consideration as practical tests in unclear cases.

Only one feature, calculability, is clearly a necessary property of conversational implicature. But calculability is trivially necessary since nearly anything can be "worked out" with the aid of the Cooperative Principle on the basis of nearly any meaning in some context. Nondetachability fails to be a necessary feature of conversational implicature since there does not seem to be any principled reason why two lexical items could not differ just in that one includes a cancellation of a conversational implicature that might be associated with the other. In such a case, substitution of the more specific lexical item for the less specific one would amount to detaching a conversational implicature. Cancellability is probably a necessary feature of conversational implicature, but it gets progressively harder to cancel any implicature the more generalized it is.

There are no sufficient tests for conversational implicature and no group of tests that together are sufficient. Because of the necessarily great power of Grice's pragmatic calculus, many things can be calculated that are not conversational implicatures. Nondetachability cannot be a sufficient test because, for one thing, certain meanings can probably be rendered in only one way. Everything that the application of such a meaning could implicate would be trivially nondetachable since there are no precise paraphrases for it at all. Worse, everything that is entailed by the logical form and by the conventional implicatures of a sentence is nondetachable. Cancellability and reinforceability fail to be sufficient for recognizing conversational implicature because, in the very important case of grammatical ambiguity, any one sense is obviously cancellable or reinforceable.

There is, then, given the existing methodology, no way of knowing for sure whether an implicature is conversational. In the extreme cases a particular implicature will either pass all three tests with flying colors or fail all three miserably. But there is rarely any argument in these cases and the tests are more or less superfluous. To solve the problem of the thorny cases and shore up the foundations of linguistic pragmatics, more powerful tools will have to be developed.

We encountered all of the difficulties above even though it was assumed that we knew where to make the first cut—that we knew what is semantic content and what is not. But that assumption is false. There are arguments as to whether a certain bit of what is conveyed is semantically contained or not. Karttunen and Peters and I agree, at least, that whatever the relation between *almost P* and *not P,* the latter is not part of the semantic content of the former. We agree that *Gertrude almost swam the English Channel* is not false, in the strict sense, if Gertrude made it all the way to Calais. But Grice (personal communication) holds the opposite view. Whether one considers the sentence *Maggie went to the bathroom* false if Maggie didn't even come near the little room with the ceramic fixtures in it, but happened to soil the living room rug, depends on whether one considers the semantic content of the sentence always to include a reference to bathrooms. But at present this seems to be a matter of preference. Even if reliable criteria could be found that tell us what is and what is not part of semantic content, the problems that I have sketched would still remain to haunt the practitioner of linguistic pragmatics.

ACKNOWLEDGMENTS

This is a revised and expanded version of Sadock 1976. Subsequent to writing that paper, I discovered that many of the points I made are also made in Walker 1975.

REFERENCES

Greisman, B. (ed.). (1975). *J. K. Lasser's Your Income Tax.* New York: Simon and Schuster.

Grice, H. P. (1969). "Utterer's Meaning and Intentions." *Philosophical Review* 78:147–177.

Grice, H. P. (1975). "Logic and Conversation." In P. Cole and J. L. Morgan (eds.), *Syntax and Semantics.* Vol. 3: *Speech Acts.* New York: Academic Press, 41–58. [Reprinted in this volume, Chapter 19]

Horn, L. R. (1972). "On the Semantic Properties of Logical Operators in English." Ph.D. diss., University of California, Los Angeles. (Reprinted by Indiana University Linguistics Club, 1976)

Horn, L. R. (1973). "Greek Grice." In C. Corum, T. Smith-Stack, and A. Weiser (eds.), *Papers from the Ninth Regional Meeting of the Chicago Linguistic Society,* Chicago: Chicago Linguistic Society.

Karttunen, L., and S. Peters (1975). "Conventional Implicature." In C. Cogen et al. (eds.), *Proceedings of the First Annual Meeting of the Berkeley Linguistics Society.* Berkeley: University of California.

McCawley, J. D. (1973). "Semantic Representation." In J. D. McCawley, (ed.). *Grammar and Meaning,* Tokyo: Taishukan.

Reichenbach, H. (1947). *Elements of Symbolic Logic.* New York: Free Press.

Sadock, J. M. (1972). "Speech Act Idioms." In P. Peranteau, J. Levi, and G. Phares (eds.). *Papers from the Eighth Regional Meeting of the Chicago Linguistic Society.* Chicago: Chicago Linguistic Society.

Sadock, J. M. (1975a). *Toward a Linguistic Theory of Speech Acts.* New York: Academic Press.

Sadock, J. M. (1975b). "Larry Scores a Point." *Pragmatics Microfiche* I, Fiche 1.4, G 10.

Sadock, J. M. (1976). "Methodological Problems in Linguistic Pragmatics." In *Problems in Linguistic Metatheory: 1976 Conference Proceedings,* Dept. of Linguistics, Michigan State University, East Lansing, Mich.

Sadock, J. M. (1981). "Almost." In P. Cole (ed.), *Radical Pragmatics.* New York: Academic Press.

Searle, J. (1975). "Indirect Speech Acts." In P. Cole and J. L. Morgan (eds.), *Syntax and Semantics.* Vol. 3: *Speech Acts.* New York: Academic Press, 59–82. [Reprinted in this volume, Chapter 16]

Walker, R. (1975). "Conversational Implicatures." In S. Blackburn (ed.), *Meaning, Reference and Necessity.* London: Cambridge University Press.

Zwicky, A., and J. M. Sadock (1975). "Ambiguity Tests and How to Fail Them." In J. Kimball (ed.), *Syntax and Semantics.* Vol. 4. New York: Academic Press.

22

Inference and Implicature

DEIRDRE WILSON AND DAN SPERBER

Recent accounts of utterance interpretation have tended to downplay the role of deductive reasoning in comprehension. Here are two illustrations from current textbooks on discourse analysis. Brown and Yule say: 'It may be the case that we are capable of drawing a specific conclusion . . . from specific premises . . . via deductive inference, but we are rarely asked to do so in the everyday discourse we encounter. . . . We are more likely to operate with a rather loose form of inferencing.'[1] Similar views are expressed by de Beaugrande and Dressler: 'Humans are evidently capable of intricate reasoning processes that traditional logics cannot explain: jumping to conclusions, pursuing subjective analogies, and even reasoning in the absence of knowledge. . . . The important standard here is not that such a procedure is logically unsound, but rather that the procedures work well enough in everyday affairs.'[2]

The implication of these remarks is that any element of deductive reasoning in the 'loose' or 'unsound' inference processes involved in utterance interpretation can safely be ignored. Our own researches have led us to a quite different conclusion. We do believe that non-demonstrative inference plays a crucial role in

utterance interpretation. We also believe, however, that deductive reasoning makes a crucial contribution to the non-demonstrative inference processes spontaneously used in utterance interpretation. In this chapter we will offer a partial justification of these claims by illustrating the contribution of deductive reasoning to just one aspect of utterance interpretation in which non-demonstrative inference is generally agreed to play a major role: the recovery of implicatures. A fuller justification would deal with other aspects of interpretation—disambiguation, reference assignment, the recovery of illocutionary force and the interpretation of figurative language, for example—and would not merely illustrate the contribution of deductive reasoning to spontaneous non-demonstrative inference processes but would provide a psychologically adequate account of these non-demonstrative inference processes themselves.[3]

THE CALCULABILITY REQUIREMENT ON IMPLICATURES

Grice distinguishes two main types of implicit content or implicature that an utterance can convey.[4] *Conventional implicatures* are determined by particular lexical items or linguistic constructions occurring in the utterance. *Conversational implicatures* follow from general maxims of truthfulness, informativeness, relevance and clarity that speakers are assumed to observe. For Grice, the important difference between conventional and conversational implicature is that the conventional implicatures of an utterance are arbitrarily stipulated, whereas its conversational implicatures should be recoverable by a reasoning process. 'The presence of a conversational implicature must be capable of being worked out; for even if it can in fact be intuitively grasped, unless the intuition is replaceable by an argument, the implicature (if present at all) will not count as a *conversational* implicature: it will be a *conventional* implicature.'[5] Grice regards this calculability requirement as fundamental: 'The final test for the presence of a conversational implicature had to be, as far as I could see, a derivation of it. One has to produce an account of how it could have arisen and why it is there. And I am very much opposed to any kind of sloppy use of this philosophical tool in which this condition is not fulfilled.'[6] However, his own account of the derivation process is rather sketchy, and although the idea of conversational implicature has had enormous appeal and been used in an informal way to account for a wide range of pragmatic phenomena, little progress has been made in specifying the exact nature of the inference process by which conversational implicatures are 'worked out'.

Grice suggests that the conversational implicatures of an utterance might be derived by arguments of the following form:[7]

(1) (a) He has said that *p*.
    (b) There is no reason to suppose that he is not observing the maxims.
    (c) He could not be doing this unless he thought that *q*.
    (d) He knows (and knows that I know that he knows) that I can see that the supposition that he thinks that *q is* required.
    (e) He had done nothing to stop me thinking that *q*.
    (f) He intends me to think, or is at least willing to allow me to think, that *q*.
    (g) And so, he has implicated that *q*.

It is unclear what sort of argument this is meant to be; it is not even clear which of (1a–g) are meant to be premises and which conclusions. What does seem clear is that (1c), in which the content of the implicature is introduced for the first time, is not directly deducible from (1a–b). Either (1c) is simply an independent premise, or it is meant to be derivable from (1a–b) with the aid of some supplementary premises whose nature has been left unspecified. What (1) really offers is not a method for working out the content of the propositions that the speaker, in producing an utterance, implicitly commits himself to, but rather a method for working out which of these commitments the speaker *meant,* in Grice's special technical sense.[8] An adequate pragmatic theory should also provide some method of recovering the content of the implicatures themselves: that is, some method of deriving not (1g) but (1c).

It is becoming a commonplace of the pragmatic literature that deductive inference plays little if any role in the recovery of implicatures. Leech says that implicatures are 'probabilistic,' and that the process by which they are recovered 'is not a formalized deductive logic, but an informal rational problem-solving strategy'.[9] Levinson says that implicatures 'appear to be quite unlike logical inferences, and cannot be directly modelled in terms of some semantic relation like entailment'.[10] Bach and Harnish say that the form of inference by which implicatures are recovered 'is not deductive but what might be called an inference to a plausible explanation'.[11] Brown and Yule, who as we saw above claim that utterance comprehension rarely involves deductive processes, add that in the recovery of implicatures 'we are more likely to operate with a rather loose form of inferencing.'[12] These remarks can be taken in a number of ways.

In a sense, they follow directly from Grice's characterization of implicature, and some of these authors may be making a purely definitional point. Consider (2b), for example:

(2) (a) *He:* Will you have some coffee?
    (b) *She:* Coffee would keep me awake.

In normal circumstances, the speaker of (2b) would implicate (3):

(3) She won't have any coffee.

Now (3) is not deducible from the content of (2b) alone: (4) is not a contradiction:

(4) Coffee would keep her awake, and she will have some coffee.

Indeed, if (3) *were* deducible from (2b) it would not be an implicature in Grice's sense, since according to him 'the truth of a conversational implicature is not required for the truth of what is said (what is said may be true—what is implicated may be false).'[13] If this is taken as a defining feature of implicature, no implicature will be deducible from the explicit content of an utterance alone.

However, to show that (3) is not directly deducible from (2b) is not to show that deduction plays no significant role in its derivation. Grice himself claims that background knowledge must play a role in the process by which conversational implicatures are 'worked out'. Why should the hearer not simply supply the background assumptions in (5) and use them, together with the content of (2b), to deduce the conclusion in (3)?

(5) (a) She doesn't want to be kept awake.
    (b) She won't have anything that would keep her awake.

We will argue that deduction processes of this type play a central role in the recovery of implicatures. This is not, of course, to tell the whole story about how implicatures are derived. It is also necessary to show how appropriate premises for the deduction process are selected and potential conclusions evaluated: why does the hearer of (2b) supply the background assumptions (5) and accept the conclusion (3) rather than, say, supplying the assumptions (6) and deriving the conclusion (7)?

(6) (a) She wants to be kept awake.
    (b) She will have anything on offer that would keep her awake.

(7) She will have some coffee.

However, there is no reason in principle why an account of implicature in which deduction is a central element should not be adequate to deal with the interpretation of (2b) and other examples of implicature-carrying utterances.

Some of the authors cited above seem to be making not just the definitional point that implicatures cannot be deduced from the content of the utterance alone, but the stronger claim that deduction plays no significant role in their derivation, and in particular that an account like the one just suggested cannot be correct.[14] To be able to evaluate this claim we would have to have not only a clearer idea of the deduction-based account, but also some idea of possible alternatives to it. By what non-deductive inference processes might the hearer of (2b) arrive at the conclusion in (3), and how would the alternative conclusion in (7) be ruled out?

It is now fairly widely recognized that there can be no non-demonstrative inference *rules* (in the sense that there are deductive inference rules) which, given a set of premises, simply enumerate a set of valid conclusions. Instead, the process of reaching valid non-demonstrative conclusions is standardly broken down into two distinct stages: hypothesis formation and hypothesis confirmation. For example, the hearer of (2b) would have first to form the hypothesis in (3), or the hypothesis that the speaker was trying to communicate (3), and second to confirm or disconfirm this hypothesis.

As Fodor points out,[15] we are very far from having an adequate account of the psychology of hypothesis formation and confirmation. It is well known that from the purely logical point of view any empirical proposition confirms or disconfirms an infinity of others. For example, (8) is logically equivalent to (9), and any proposition that confirms the latter confirms the former:

(8) All snow is white.

(9) Anything that is not white is not snow.

Proposition (9) is confirmed by anything that is not white and not snow: for example, a green apple. Hence, (10) confirms the claim that all snow is white:

(10) This is a green apple.

Someone who says (10) would not normally, of course, be construed as encouraging the hearer to derive either (8) or (9) as a conclusion. The problem is that there is as yet no principled account capable of explaining which of the infinite set of possible conclusions that the hearer of a given utterance *could* draw will actually be drawn.

Hypothesis formation, according to Fodor, is a creative process involving analogical reasoning, about which virtually nothing is known. Once formed, a given hypothesis will be accepted or rejected on a basis which is again very little understood. As Fodor sees it, the difficulties with hypothesis formation and confirmation arise from the fact that they are *global* as opposed to *local* processes. The distinction between global and local processes corresponds roughly to a distinction between processes which have free access to contextual information and those which do not. A global process is one in which any item of information, however remote and unrelated to the information being processed, may legitimately be used. So, for example, in creating a scientific hypothesis to account for a certain range of data it is legitimate to rely on analogies with other domains of knowledge, seemingly random association of ideas, and any other source of inspiration that comes to hand. Once a hypothesis has been formed, the extent to which it is regarded as confirmed will depend on how well it fits not only with neighbouring domains of knowledge but with one's whole overall conception of the world. A local process, by contrast, is one which needs to take nothing into account apart from the information actually being processed. For example, deductive reasoning from fixed premises is a purely local process in which no attention need be paid to information not contained in the premises themselves. Fodor's argument is that although we have a fair understanding of a variety of local processes, the working of global processes remains a mystery.

Given the haziness of our understanding both of the psychology of hypothesis formation and confirmation and of the effects of context on information processing, it is perhaps not surprising that pragmatists who express scepticism about the role of deductive reasoning in comprehension have said little about the process by which implicatures are recovered. Bach and Harnish, after establishing that the working out schema is not deductive, add:

Our empirical thinking in general is rife with generalizations and inference principles that we are not conscious of when we use them, if we are conscious of them at all. It would take us well beyond present-day cognitive psychology to speculate on the details

of any of this. . . . Whatever these processes are, whatever activates them, whatever principles or strategies are involved, they work, and work well.[16]

But the fact that these processes work well enough in everyday utterance comprehension does not absolve us from saying what they are. If anything, the lack of any existing framework for describing them should make us more, not less, interested in their nature. Given the 'probabilistic' nature of implicatures as illustrated in (2b) above, an adequate theory of how implicatures are recovered might shed light not just on utterance comprehension but on the more general psychological problem of hypothesis formation and confirmation which, for the reasons Fodor has given, has proved to be so intractable.

The claim that pragmatics must be based on *either* deductive *or* non-demonstrative inferential systems, or that the adoption of one type of system must inevitably lead to the rejection of the other, seems to us to be unfounded. For the last few years we have been working on a theory of spontaneous non-demonstrative inference in utterance comprehension and other cognitive domains, in which deductive reasoning plays a central role. In previously published work[17] we have concentrated on the central, deductive element of the theory, which will be outlined briefly in the next section. In the remainder of this paper we will sketch in some of the broader background against which this central deductive element is set, and show how 'probabilistic' implicatures would be handled in this framework.

RELEVANCE THEORY

Grice's work on the maxims of conversation[18] can be seen as providing the elements of a pragmatic hypothesis confirmation system. Given (a) a source of hypotheses about the speaker's communicative intentions and (b) an adequate account of what it is for a speaker to observe the conversational maxims, it seems reasonable to claim that the most favoured hypothesis, the one the hearer should choose, would be the one which best satisfies the maxims. In at least a few cases, it is easy to see how this proposal might work. Consider disambiguation, for example. Here the source of hypotheses is the grammar, which assigns a range of possible senses to an utterance. On the approach now being considered, the sense the hearer should assume that the speaker wanted to communicate is the one which best accords with the assumption that Grice's maxims have been observed.

Or consider how a hearer might decide which of the deductive consequences of an utterance the speaker wanted to communicate. Here the source of hypotheses is the deductive inference rules. On the approach now being considered, the hearer should assume that the speaker wanted to communicate any subset of consequences needed to satisfy him that the maxims have been observed. Consider, for example, the exchange in (11):

(11) (a) *He:* Is Jacques a good cook?
    (b) *She:* He's French, and all the French are good cooks.

Here, in order to satisfy himself that the speaker of (11b) is observing the maxims of relevance and informativeness, the hearer must assume that she wanted him to deduce from her utterance the conclusion in (12):

(12) Jacques is a good cook.

In these two types of case, Grice's maxims can thus be used, if not to generate a set of hypotheses about the speaker's communicative intentions, at least to choose among them.

To provide an adequate account of implicature along these lines, two questions would have to be answered. First, what is the source of hypotheses about the possible implicatures of an utterance? Second, is it possible to show more precisely what it is for a speaker to observe Grice's maxims? In previously published work[19] we have offered, in outline, an answer to the second of these questions. We have proposed a definition of relevance and suggested what factors might be involved in assessments of degrees of relevance. We have also argued that all Grice's maxims can be replaced by a single principle of relevance—that the speaker tries to be as relevant as possible in the circumstances—which, when suitably elaborated, can handle the full range of data that Grice's maxims were designed to explain.

We treat relevance as a relation between a proposition P and a set of contextual assumptions $\{C\}$. In previously published work we have made the simplifying assumption that the only propositions used in the comprehension process are those believed to be true. On the basis of this assumption we defined relevance as follows:

(13) A proposition P is relevant in a context $\{C\}$ if and only if P has at least one contextual implication in $\{C\}$.

A contextual implication is a special type of logical implication, derived by the use of a restricted set of deductive rules which derive at most a finite set of conclusions from any finite set of premises.[20] The contextual implications of a proposition P in a context $\{C\}$ are all those conclusions deducible from the union of P with $\{C\}$, but from neither P alone nor $\{C\}$ alone. For example, (2b) above contextually implies (3) in a context containing (5), and contextually implies (7) in a context containing (6); it would thus, by our definitions, be relevant in a context containing either (5) or (6).

The intuitive idea behind these definitions is that relevance is achieved when the addition of a proposition to a context modifies the context in a way that goes beyond the mere incrementation of that context with the proposition itself and all its logical implications. As we will show, the production of contextual implications is a special case of a more general notion of contextual modification which emerges once we drop the assumption that the only propositions used in comprehension are those believed to be true. For the moment we will continue to assume that a hearer who wants to establish the relevance of an utterance should be looking for a context with which it will interact to yield contextual implications.

Consider, in this framework, how a hearer might set about processing the information in (14):

(14) *She:* Susan doesn't drink alcohol.

One possible line of interpretation would be to think of the names of some alcoholic drinks, as in (15), and conclude that Susan doesn't drink them, as in (16):

(15) (a) Sherry is alcoholic.
    (b) Gin is alcoholic.
    (c) Whiskey is alcoholic.
    . . .

(16) (a) Susan doesn't drink sherry.
    (b) Susan doesn't drink gin.
    (c) Susan doesn't drink whisky.
    . . .

One of the conclusions in (16) might in turn combine with further contextual assumptions to yield a range of further contextual implications, which could in turn combine with further contextual assumptions, and so on indefinitely.

Another line of interpretation would be to think of conditional premises with (14) as antecedent, as in (17), and derive their consequents as conclusions, as in (18):

(17) (a) If Susan doesn't drink alcohol, she may prefer a soft drink.
    (b) If Susan doesn't drink alcohol, she probably disapproves of getting drunk.
    (c) If Susan doesn't drink alcohol, she never has hangovers.
    . . .

(18) (a) Susan may prefer a soft drink.
    (b) Susan probably disapproves of getting drunk.
    (c) Susan never has hangovers.
    . . .

Again, one of the conclusions in (18) may combine with further contextual assumptions to yield further contextual implications, and so on indefinitely.

We assume that in processing a proposition the hearer begins by systematically searching for contextual implications in a small, immediately accessible context consisting of the propositions that have most recently been processed. To these, further assumptions may be added subject to the following constraint. We assume that information is stored in memory in encyclopaedic entries attached to concepts, and that the information in a given encyclopaedic entry can only be accessed via the presence in the set of propositions currently being processed of the concept to which it is attached. For example, an utterance mentioning alcohol makes accessible (to varying degrees) the set of propositions in the encyclopaedic entry attached to the concept *alcohol;* these in turn give access to the encyclopaedic entries attached to the concepts they contain, and so on indefinitely.

It can be seen that in this framework not all the contextual implications of a given proposition will be equally easy to obtain. Those derived from small, easily accessible contexts will be relatively cheap in processing terms. Those derived from larger, less easily accessible contexts will be relatively expensive in processing terms, because of the additional effort required to access the contexts needed to derive them and to search these contexts systematically for contextual implications. We assume that the universal aim in processing is to obtain the maximum of contextual implications in return for any processing effort expended. However, at a certain point in processing—which will vary from person to person and situation to situation—the cost of obtaining any further contextual implications will become too high, and processing will stop.

Let us say that, other things being equal, the relevance of a proposition increases with the number of contextual implications it yields and decreases as the amount of processing needed to obtain them increases. Maximizing the relevance of a proposition is thus a matter of accessing, as quickly as possible, a context in which it will yield the maximum of contextual implications in return for the available processing effort. The most relevant propositions will be those which yield a wide range of contextual implications in a small, immediately accessible context.

We assume that the universal goal in cognition is to acquire relevant information, and the more relevant the better. We also assume that a speaker who thinks it worth speaking at all will try to make his utterance as relevant as possible. A hearer should therefore bring to the processing of every utterance the standing assumption that the speaker has tried to be as relevant as possible in the circumstances. It is this assumption that we call the principle of relevance.

A speaker cannot observe the principle of relevance without believing that his utterance will convey some relevant information to the hearer. Sometimes, he may have only the most general grounds for thinking so. For example, if I know you follow the pop music charts, I can reasonably assume that it will be relevant to you to know the name of the new number one hit, even though I may have no idea what specific implications this information will have for you. At other times, however, a speaker may have a much more specific idea of the sort of context that will be brought to bear and the sort of conclusions derived. It is in situations like this that we believe implicatures arise.

Consider, for example, the exchange in (19):

(19) (a) *He:* Does Susan drink whisky?
(b) *She:* She doesn't drink alcohol.

On what grounds might the speaker of (19b) have thought her utterance would be relevant to the hearer? What sort of context might she have expected him to supply that would be both accessible enough and rich enough in contextual implications for it to be worth his while to process her utterance? The answer is clear. He has just asked her whether Susan drinks whisky. In our framework, he would not have asked this question if he had not had immediately accessible a context in which the information that she did (or did not) drink whisky would be relevant—and indeed more relevant than any other information he thinks she will be able to provide. By providing this information directly, she would therefore be sure of satisfying the principle of relevance.

In fact, her utterance does not provide the information directly: the hearer has first to supply the contextual assumption in (15c) and then to derive the conclusion in (16c):

(15) (c) Whisky is alcoholic.

(16) (c) Susan doesn't drink whisky.

However, the speaker can reasonably expect him to do this. On the one hand, her utterance gives him immediate access to his encyclopaedic entry for *alcohol,* which should in turn provide access to propositions of the form (15a–c). On the other hand, on normal assumptions about the organization of memory, the immediately preceding mention of whisky should act as a prompt, making (15c) more accessible than other propositions of this form. It would therefore be reasonable to assume that one of the grounds on which the speaker of (19b) thought her utterance would be relevant was that she expected it to be processed in a context which contained (15c) as an assumption and yielded (16c) as a contextual implication.

We want to say that the speaker of (19b) implicates both (15c) and (16c). On this approach, the implicatures of an utterance are those contextual assumptions and implications which the hearer has to recover in order to satisfy himself that the speaker has observed the principle of relevance. Here, (15c) is a nec-

essary precondition on the recovery of (16c), and (16c) is a necessary precondition on the recovery of the whole range of contextual implications on which the main relevance of (19b) depends. We will call (15c) an *implicated assumption* and (16c) an *implicated conclusion* of (19b).

In fact, as we have described it, the interpretation of (19b) does not conform to the principle of relevance. The speaker could have conveyed the whole of this interpretation more economically by producing the direct answer (16c). Instead, she has forced the hearer to process the proposition expressed by (19b), to access (15c) and to deduce (16c) as a contextual implication, each step requiring some processing effort which would not have been required by the direct answer (16c). Suppose the hearer asks himself why she might have thought that the indirect answer (19b) would be more relevant to him than a direct answer. The only possible explanation is that she must have expected it to yield some additional contextual implications, not derivable from the direct answer (16c), which would more than compensate for the extra processing cost. In other words, the only possible explanation is that she believed that the surplus of information she was providing had some relevance in its own right.

As always, the speaker must have some reason for thinking that this surplus of information will be relevant, and more relevant than any alternative information she could provide. She may know, for example, that the hearer is wondering what drink to offer Susan. In these circumstances, her response in (19b) would encourage him to derive conclusions along the lines of (16) and (18c) above: that she doesn't drink sherry, gin, etc., and that she may prefer a soft drink. Or he may be wondering whether to invite Susan to his party. In these circumstances, the response in (19b) would encourage him to derive conclusions along the lines of (18b) above: that Susan may disapprove of getting drunk, that he should maybe not bother inviting her to his party, and so on.

Grice suggests that many implicatures are indeterminate:

Since to calculate a conversational implicature is to calculate what has to be supposed in order to preserve the supposition that the Co-Operative Principle is being observed, and since there may be various possible specific explanations, a list of which may be open, the conversational implicatum in such cases will be a disjunction of such specific explanations; and if the list of these is open, the implicatum will have just the kind of indeterminacy that many actual implicata do in fact seem to possess.[21]

His commentators have been divided in their reaction to this suggestion. Some, realizing the difficulty of providing an explicit treatment of indeterminacy, have largely ignored it. Gazdar, for example, notes the existence of indeterminacy, but adds: 'Because indeterminacy is hard to handle formally, I shall mostly ignore it in the discussion that follows. A fuller treatment of implicatures would not be guilty of this omission, which is really only defensible on formal grounds.'[22] Others, less interested in explicit treatment of the processes by which implicatures arise, tend to use the indeterminacy of implicatures as an argument against deductive models of the recovery process and in favour of 'informal', 'loose' or 'probabilistic' models.[23] In our framework, the indeterminacy of implicatures can be dealt with without losing the explicitness of the deductive approach.

Sometimes, as we have shown, a speaker can observe the principle of relevance without having any idea of the sort of context the utterance will be processed in, or the sort of conclusions that will be derived. In these cases, the utterance will have no implicatures at all. In other cases, as with (19b) and its implicatures (15c) and (16c), it is impossible to see how the speaker could have observed the principle of relevance without expecting a specific contextual assumption to be supplied and a specific conclusion derived. In these cases the utterance will have fully determinate implicatures. Between these two extremes lie a whole range of intermediate cases. We have discussed a situation where the indirect answer (19b) would encourage the hearer to think of assumptions along the lines of (15) or (17) and conclusions along the lines of (16) or (18). Here, the speaker has a general idea of the type of assumption to be supplied and the type of conclusion to be derived, but may not know or care which specific assumptions and conclusions of this type will be supplied. The clearer an idea the speaker must have had of the specific assumptions and conclusions to be supplied, the more determinate the implica-

tures will be; the vaguer an idea he could have had and still have been observing the principle of relevance, the less determinate the implicatures will be, up to the point where they vanish altogether and the choice of contexts and conclusions is left solely up to the hearer.

In every case, the method of processing is the same. The hearer supplies specific contextual assumptions and derives specific contextual implications. What varies is not the specificity of the assumptions and conclusions derived, or the formality of the reasoning processes involved, but simply the amount of foreknowledge the speaker must be taken to have had of the way the utterance would be processed, and with it the degree of responsibility he must take for the particular conclusions derived. Suppose, for instance, that I could not have observed the principle of relevance without expecting you to supply a certain assumption and derive a certain conclusion in processing my utterance. Then by encouraging you to supply them, I take as much responsibility for their truth as for the truth of the proposition I have explicitly expressed.

To take an example, suppose that after the exchange in (19) has taken place it turns out that Susan does drink whisky. Although (19b) does not *entail* that Susan does not drink whisky (the additional assumption that whisky is alcoholic is needed), the speaker could be quite rightly accused of having misled the hearer by allowing him to suppose that she did. Similarly, a speaker who secretly believed that whisky was not alcoholic could be accused at least of having *tried* to mislead the hearer by uttering (19b) and thus encouraging him to suppose that whisky was alcoholic. In other words, the speaker is committed to the truth of all determinate implicatures conveyed by her utterance, just as much as if she had expressed them directly.

With less determinate implicatures, the speaker cannot be held solely responsible for their truth. Suppose, for example, that the exchange in (19) takes place in the circumstances described above, where the speaker of (19a) is wondering whether to invite Susan to his party. Here, (19b) would clearly carry implicatures to the effect that Susan may disapprove of getting drunk, is unlikely to enjoy rowdy behaviour, may inhibit the proceedings, and is thus not a suitable person to invite to a party. However, it would be a little strong to say that the speaker of (19b) had specifically indicated that the hearer should not invite Susan to his party: this is only one among a range of roughly equivalent conclusions that the hearer could have drawn, any of which would have satisfied him that the speaker had observed the principle of relevance by providing some information with a bearing on his deliberations. The weaker the implicature—that is, the wider the range of roughly equivalent alternative assumptions and conclusions that would have satisfied the hearer that the speaker had observed the principle of relevance—the weaker the speaker's responsibility for its truth, up to the point where the implicature disappears altogether and the responsibility for the assumptions used and the conclusions drawn from them lies solely on the side of the hearer.

Talk of degrees of responsibility for the truth of implicated assumptions and conclusions takes us outside the simplified framework we have been assuming so far—a framework which abstracts away from the fact that a proposition can be expressed by the speaker with a stronger or weaker guarantee of truth, and that this guarantee may be more or less trusted by the hearer.[24] In the next section we will outline only as much as is needed to account for the 'probabilistic' nature of implicatures.

AN EXTENSION TO THE THEORY

What would happen, in our simplified framework, if the hearer of (20) tried to process it in a context such as (21a–d), which directly contradicts it?

(20) *She:* Peter is not coming to the party.

(21) (a) Peter is coming to the party.
   (b) If Peter is coming to the party, Jane will come.
   (c) Jane will come to the party.
   (d) If Peter is not coming to the party, Harry will not come.

We assume that no contextual implications at all are derivable from a contradictory set of assumptions.[25] The hearer of (20) must therefore

either reject the utterance as irrelevant, or modify his assumptions in (21). By eliminating (21a) he could, in the simplified system outlined above, establish the relevance of (20) in a context consisting of the remaining assumptions (21b–d), deriving (22) as a contextual implication:

(22) Harry will not come to the party.

However, this is a rather unsatisfactory account, for two reasons. First, it implies that if (21d) had not been present in the context to enable (22) to be derived, (20) could not have been relevant at all. Yet intuitively it is always relevant to discover that one has been mistaken. In such cases, our original intuition that a proposition achieves relevance by interacting with, or modifying, the context in which it is processed, is not matched by our formal definition. Second, it is clear that a hearer in real life might neither reject (20) and retain (21a) nor accept (20) and reject (21a). He might decide that on the whole (20) is more likely to be true than (21a), or that (21a) is more likely to be true than (20), or that he has no idea which of (20) and (21a) is true. To account for these facts we must abandon the assumption that the only way a proposition can modify a context is by yielding contextual implications, and that the only propositions which play a role in processing are those regarded as certainly true.

A proposition may be put forward, and accepted, with varying degrees of confidence. Some account of how this can happen must be provided by any adequate theory of cognition. We argue elsewhere that a logical theory of confirmation, involving the assignment of numerical confirmation values, is not the best starting point for such an account.[26] For the purposes of this paper, however, let us say that when a proposition is processed it is assigned some form of gross absolute confirmation value representing its estimated likelihood of being true. Positive values represent the estimate that it is more likely to be true than false; the highest positive value, *true*, represents it as certainly true. Negative values represent the estimate that it is more likely to be false than true; the lowest negative value, *false*, represents it as certainly false. The absence of a value represents the absence of an opinion either way. When (20) is added to the context in

(21), some complementary assignment of values to (20) and (21a) must be achieved: for example, by giving (20) the value *true* and (21a) the value *false,* or by giving (20) some positive value less than *true* and (21a) some negative value greater than *false.* The greatest possible effect that (20) could have would be to make the hearer entirely abandon his former assumption (21a), assigning (20) the value *true* and (21a) the value *false.* Let us assume that this readjustment takes place.

The deductive rules must now be applied to a context in which one premise, (21a), is *false.* Moreover, (21a) combines with (21b) to yield (21c) as a conclusion. What happens to this conclusion now that one of the premises used to derive it is *false?* Let us say that only conclusions based on premises with positive confirmation values can have confirmation values of their own, so that once (21a) is assigned the value *false,* (21c) automatically loses its own value. Any further conclusions involving (21c) will in turn be affected. Let us also assume that (21d) has some positive value less than *true.* How does this affect the value of (22), a contextual implication based on (20) and (21d) as premises? Let us say (simplifying slightly) that a conclusion based on a mixture of premises with positive values will inherit at most the lowest value of any premise used in deriving it. Thus (22) will inherit at most the value of (21d).

The total effect of a proposition on a context can now be assessed by answering the following questions. First, did it directly affect the value of any proposition already present in the context, as (20) affected the value of (21a)? If so, how large was the change? Second, did it indirectly affect the value of any proposition already present in the context, as the modification of (21a) indirectly affected the value of (21c)? If so, how many propositions were affected, and how large was the change? Third, did its addition to the context yield any new contextual implications, as (20) yielded (22)? If so, how many were there, and how high were their values? We assume that the higher the value of any new contextual implication, the greater the modification to the context, and that a new contextual implication which lacks a confirmation value does not modify the context at all. With this extension to the

framework, the recovery of contextual implications becomes just a special case of a more general notion of contextual modification in terms of which relevance can be redefined.

Let us say, then, that the proposition P is relevant in a context $\{C\}$ if and only if it modifies $\{C\}$ in one of the ways described above. Let us say that other things being equal, the more P modifies the context the more relevant it is, but that other things being equal, the greater the amount of processing required to bring about this modification, the *less* relevant it is. As before, the aim of the hearer in processing P will be to access a context which makes the best possible use of the available processing resources—that is, a context that maximizes the relevance of P.

From this very brief account, one or two general principles emerge. In particular, the only new contextual implications worth deriving will be those based on assumptions with positive values, the higher the better. The use of other assumptions will incur processing costs, but without leading to any reward in terms of contextual modification, since no new contextual implication based on them will be assigned a confirmation value at all. The use of such assumptions will thus detract from the relevance of any proposition being processed. Retrieval strategies geared to the maximization of relevance should therefore be aimed at retrieving, as quickly as possible, assumptions with positive confirmation values, the higher the better, and this fact should be known to any speaker. The hearer should also be able to infer, from the fact that the speaker is observing the principle of relevance, that he must have believed that all implicated conclusions, and all assumptions needed to derive them, had positive confirmation values, even if the hearer, of his own knowledge, would have been inclined to treat them as *false.*

Let us return, in the light of this discussion, to (2b) and its implicature (3):

(2) (a) *He:* Will you have some coffee?
    (b) *She:* Coffee would keep me awake.

(3) She won't have any coffee.

We can now answer the two questions raised earlier: how is (3) derived, and how is the alternative derivation of (7) ruled out?

(7) She will have some coffee.

The answer to the first question is that (3) is a contextual implication of (2b) in a context containing (5):

(5) (a) She doesn't want to be kept awake.
     (b) She won't have anything that would keep her awake.

Moreover, (5a–b) are implicated assumptions, and (3) is an implicated conclusion. By parallel arguments to those used in the discussion of relevance theory, the hearer knows that a speaker observing the principle of relevance must have expected him to supply the assumptions in (5) and derive the conclusion in (3). A question we have not yet considered is what confirmation value the speaker expects the hearer to assign to the implicated assumptions and conclusion.

If the exchange was taking place in the evening, the hearer could no doubt, of his own knowledge, assign some positive confirmation value less than *true* to (3) and (5). Under normal assumptions, it would be no more than a probability that the speaker does not want to be kept awake, and will not have anything that would keep her awake, and hence no more than a probability that she won't have any coffee. In the circumstances, however, the information that the speaker probably won't have any coffee would not be relevant enough. In the first place, she ought to know whether she will or will not have any coffee, and if she knows, she should have told him, since he has indicated that this information would be relevant to him. In the second place, she must realize that the hearer would have been aware that she *might* not want any coffee when he asked his question. What he indicated by asking it was that a categorical answer would be relevant to him. Therefore, if she has this information and is observing the principle of relevance, she ought to have given it. Is there any way of construing (2b) as giving a categorical answer to the question in (2a)? Certainly: all the hearer has to do is upgrade the values of (3) and (5) to *true*. To preserve the assumption that the speaker has observed the principle of relevance, this is what he must do. By the arguments of relevance theory, the speaker, who has encouraged him to do this, will be held just as responsible for the truth of (3) and (5)

as if she had expressed these propositions directly.

To complete the interpretation, some justification has to be found for the fact that the speaker has chosen an indirect rather than a direct form of answer. Failure to find such a justification would be *prima facie* evidence that this line of interpretation was not correct. Here, at least on an informal level, the reason is easy to see. A direct refusal, with no explanation, would be likely to raise all sorts of questions in the hearer's mind about why his offer has been refused. The indirect answer (2b) simultaneously refuses the offer of coffee and explains the refusal, thus saving the hearer the time he might have spent speculating on the reasons behind it. This line of interpretation is thus confirmed as satisfying the principle of relevance.

By contrast, an interpretation based on the contextual assumptions in (6) and the conclusion in (7) is unlikely to be considered at all. If considered, it should be rejected as not conforming to the principle of relevance:

(6) (a) She wants to be kept awake.
     (b) She will have anything on offer that would keep her awake.

(7) She will have some coffee.

In the first place, if the exchange was taking place in the evening, the hearer of (2b) would no doubt, of his own knowledge, assign a lower confirmation value to (6) than to (5). On the assumption that retrieval strategies give preferential access to higher-valued assumptions, (5) should be retrieved before (6); and since it gives rise to a satisfactory interpretation, there is no reason why (6) should not be considered at all. However, suppose it is. The interpretation it gives rise to should still be rejected as not conforming to the principle of relevance. There is no reason why a speaker observing the principle of relevance should have preferred the indirect answer (2b), construed in this way, to the direct answer that she wants some more coffee. An acceptance, unlike a refusal, normally needs no justification; it normally raises no questions in a hearer's mind about the reasons behind it. Moreover, a speaker who attempted to justify her acceptance on the grounds that she wanted to stay awake and would accept anything on offer that would keep her awake *would* raise a number of questions in her hearer's mind, and cost him valuable processing time if she did not go on immediately to answer them. Hence, the line of interpretation based on (6) and (7) is ruled out at a number of points as failing to conform to the principle of relevance.

Many standard examples of implicature fit quite straightforwardly into this framework. For example, Clark discusses a class of 'bridging' implicatures needed to establish the reference of the referring expressions in (23b)–(25b):[27]

(23) *She:* (a) I went into   (b) The window was
          the room.   open.

(24) *She:* (a) I went into   (b) Both windows
          the room.   were open.

(25) *She:* (a) I went into   (b) All three windows
          the room.   were open.

As Clark points out, in normal circumstances the hearer of these utterances would supply assumptions (26)–(28) respectively, even if there had been no previous mention of the number of windows in the room:

(26) The room had a window.

(27) The room had two windows.

(28) The room had three windows.

Consider how this might happen in the case of (24b). Given the immediately preceding mention of a room, the hearer of (24b) would no doubt, of his own knowledge, have relatively easy access to each of the assumptions in (26)–(28), and be able to assign each of them some confirmation value less than *true*. On the assumption that the speaker has observed the principle of relevance, he will take it that he must upgrade the value of (27) to *true* and use it to establish the reference of the referring expression *both windows* in (24b). As long as this assignment leads to a satisfactory range of contextual implications, he will accept it as correct. The role of the implicated assumption here is not to yield any particular contextual implication, but to establish the referential content of the utterance, which is a necessary precondition to recovering any contextual implications at all.

There may, of course, be many other logically possible assumptions that the hearer of (24b) could have used: for example, the windows might have been in the house opposite, or mentioned in a letter the speaker found in the room. However, in normal circumstances, unless the existence of these windows had already been established, these assumptions would be much less accessible than those in (26)–(28) above, and a speaker observing the principle of relevance could not normally have expected the hearer to supply them. The general principle, for bridging implicatures as for all other implicated assumptions, is that they should—at least in the estimation of the speaker—be virtually instantaneously accessible, and more accessible than any alternative assumption likely to lead to an acceptable interpretation. If not, a speaker observing the principle of relevance should have done something to increase their accessibility—for example by directly mentioning them in the utterance—and thus save the hearer some unnecessary processing costs.

Grice is unsure whether the implicatures carried by (29b) would be categorical or merely probable:

(20) (a) *A:* I am out of petrol.
      (b) *B:* There is a garage round the corner.

He claims that 'B would be infringing the maxim 'Be relevant' unless he thinks, or thinks it possible, that the garage is open and has petrol to sell; so he implicates that the garage is, or at least may be open, etc.'[28]

We can shed some light on his uncertainty. A speaker observing the principle of relevance should expect the hearer, among other things, to supply the contextual assumption in (30) and derive the conclusion in (31):

(30) If there's a garage round the corner, I can get some petrol there.

(31) I can get some petrol round the corner.

However, if it occurs to the hearer that garages may be closed or out of petrol, he will be unable of his own knowledge to assign more than a fairly high degree of probability to (30) or (31). In other words, he will only be able to derive the conclusion that he *may* be able to get some petrol round the corner. So far, the case is exactly like the two previous ones discussed in this section. The difference is that in this case, even the information that he *may* be able to get petrol round the corner might be relevant enough for a speaker who could not make a more categorical claim to think this information worth offering.

More precisely, what the speaker of (29b) indicates is that *as far as he knows* (30) and (31) are true, and therefore that *as far as he knows* the garage is open and selling petrol, etc. In some circumstances—for example if the speaker is coming from the direction of the garage with a full petrol can in his hand—the hearer would be justified in assuming that he knew with certainty; in this case the implicatures (30) and (31), and their necessary conditions that the garage is open and selling petrol, would be regarded as categorical. In different circumstances only a weaker attribution of confirmation value would be justified. The general principle is thus that when a less than categorical implicature would conform to the principle of relevance, the hearer is not entitled to assume that the speaker expected a categorical implicature to be supplied.

All the implicatures considered so far have arisen in processing the explicit content of the utterance, or in Grice's terms 'what was strictly speaking said.' As Grice points out, many implicatures arise not so much from the content of what was said as from the saying of it, in those circumstances, to that audience, and so on. Consider (32), for example:

(32) (a) *A*: Where does *C* live?
     (b) *B*: Somewhere in the South of France.

In normal circumstances, *B* would implicate that he does not know more precisely where *C* lives. We would analyse this implicature as resulting not from the explicit content of (32b) but from the fact, which the hearer is expected to notice and process, that the speaker has failed to give more precise information when, in the circumstances, more precise information would have been more relevant. To reconcile this fact with the assumption that the speaker has observed the principle of relevance, the hearer would have to access something like the contextual assumption in (33) and derive something like the conclusion in (34):

(33) If *B* has failed to give more precise information on *C*'s whereabouts, he has no more precise information to give.

(34) *B* has no more precise information to give.

Here, (34) is a contextual implication, not of the content of (32b), but of (35):

(35) *B* has failed to give more precise information on *C*'s whereabouts.

This is a proposition which may, and in this case clearly does, have some relevance in its own right. It would therefore be a mistake to think of a speaker as providing relevant information only through the explicit content of his utterance. An act of utterance may draw the hearer's attention to a number of propositions other than explicitly expressed, and these may contribute to the overall relevance of the utterance.

Grice analyses (32b) as involving a clash between the maxims of informativeness and truthfulness; the desire to give precise information about *C*'s whereabouts is sacrificed to the demands of truthfulness. He says little to explain why the supposed clash is not resolved in the opposite direction, which is a weakness of his system. Any system with more than one pragmatic principle must provide some account of their interaction—an account which is rarely provided. In our framework, with its single principle, there is no possibility of clashes. Notice, too, that there is no appeal to a violation of the principle of relevance, real or apparent, in our account of (32b). The speaker has been as relevant as he can in the circumstances—more relevant, for example, than if he had merely said 'I don't know.' His failure to provide more detailed information is explained not by appeal to deliberate violation of the principle of relevance, but by the assumption that he did not have more detailed information to provide.

We would like to make the more general claim that the recovery of implicatures *never* involves an appeal to deliberate violation of the principle of relevance. Grice himself remarks that it is hard to find cases in which his maxim of relevance is deliberately violated, but offers the following as a candidate example:

At a genteel tea party, *A* says 'Mrs *X* is an old bag.' There is a moment of appalled silence, and then *B* says 'The weather has been quite delightful this summer, hasn't it?' *B* has blatantly refused to make what *he* says relevant to *A*'s preceding remark. He therefore implicates that *A*'s remark should not be discussed and, perhaps more specifically, that A has committed a social gaffe.[29]

However, the fact that B's utterance is not relevant to the immediately preceding remark does not mean that it is not relevant at all. Most of its relevance would be achieved, not through its content, but by drawing the hearers' attention to the fact that B is deliberately ignoring A's remark. To reconcile this with the assumption that the principle of relevance has been observed, they would have to access assumptions along the lines of (36a–b) and derive conclusions along the lines of (37a–b):

(36) (a) If B is deliberately ignoring A's remark, he believes it should not be discussed.
     (b) If B believes A's remark should not be discussed, he believes it was a social gaffe.

(37) (a) B believes A's remark should not be discussed.
     (b) B believes A's remark was a social gaffe.

In our framework these would be implicatures, since they are needed to reconcile the fact that B is deliberately ignoring A's remark with the assumption that he is being as relevant as he can. They would, however, be relatively weak implicatures, since a variety of roughly equivalent assumptions could be made, all of which would reconcile B's behaviour with the assumption that he is observing the principle of relevance. By the arguments outlined above, the speaker could therefore not be held solely responsible for their truth.

Relevance theory thus makes a number of specific claims about the role of implicatures in comprehension and the processes by which they are recovered. First, they are either contextual assumptions or contextual implications which the hearer is expected to supply in satisfying himself that the speaker has observed the principle of relevance. Implicated assumptions are recovered by the same processes used to retrieve other contextual assumptions, with ease of accessibility playing a decisive role; implicated conclusions are recovered by deduction.

Second, the hearer may be expected to upgrade the confirmation value of an implicated assumption to the point where the conclusions it yields conform to the principle of relevance. The speaker is held responsible for the truth (or degree of confirmation) of any assumptions and conclusions upgraded in this way.

The hearer may thus acquire new information, not only from the explicit content of an utterance and its implicated conclusions, but also from its implicated assumptions.

Third, implicatures may be recovered either in the course of processing the explicit content of an utterance, or in the course of processing some higher-level description of it which the hearer is expected to construct. It is important, therefore, that relevance is defined not as a relation between utterances, but as a relation between propositions or sets of propositions.

Fourth, there is no essential connection between the recovery of an implicature and the assumption that the speaker has deliberately violated the principle of relevance. On the contrary: in this aspect of comprehension as in every other, it is the assumption that the speaker has *not* violated the principle of relevance that makes all the difference between processing an item of information that has been deliberately communicated and one that has not.

Within this framework, utterance comprehension is ultimately a matter of hypothesis formation and confirmation: the best hypothesis about the speaker's communicative intentions is the one that best satisfies the principle of relevance. However, it does not follow that deductive inference plays no role in the formation and confirmation of pragmatic hypotheses. On the contrary, because relevance is itself defined in partly deductive terms, the description of pragmatic hypothesis formation and confirmation makes essential reference to deductive processing. In particular, the class of possible implicated assumptions must be of a form capable of combining with information derived from the utterance to undergo deductive inference rules, and the class of possible implicated conclusions is itself deductively determined. The assumption that the overall framework in which comprehension takes place is ultimately non-demonstrative is not incompatible with the assumption that deductive processing plays a central role in comprehension.

CONCLUDING REMARK

As we have described them, the processes of pragmatic hypothesis formation and confirmation are clearly context dependent. But to what extent are they global processes in Fodor's sense? They are global in principle because, as we have shown, the interpretation of a given utterance can proceed, in ever expanding contexts, just as long as the hearer thinks that the rewards are likely to outweigh the processing costs. With certain types of utterance, for example a sacred text or a fortune-teller's prophecy, a hearer might be willing to devote a lifetime's effort to the interpretation process. In practice, however, expectations of relevance are generally much lower; there are other demands on the hearer's processing time; and he generally satisfies himself with establishing relevance in the most immediately accessible context, and leaves it at that.

The same point applies to the formation and confirmation of scientific hypotheses. At one extreme are major theories, which may take a lifetime to develop and confirm. At the other extreme are such minor hypotheses as that there is a bird on the grass, or that spring is on the way, which are formulated in passing, processed in the most immediately accessible context and either abandoned or stored for future use.

We see little reason to think that there are differences of principle between relatively local and relatively global processes of pragmatic or scientific hypothesis formation and confirmation. In particular, the role of context and the goal of maximizing relevance are the same for both types of process, although the principle of relevance, of course, applies only to deliberately communicated information. What distinguishes the two types of process is simply a relative difference, in practice not in principle, in their freedom of access to contextual information. We therefore suggest that the most useful way of gaining insight into fully global processes in Fodor's sense is to look at the relatively more local processes of everyday utterance interpretation and the interpretation of everyday sights and sounds, and work on the assumption that other, more global processes of hypothesis formation and confirmation involve the same cognitive principles and goals.

ACKNOWLEDGMENTS

We are grateful to Rose Maclaran for a number of helpful comments on an earlier version.

NOTES

1. G. Brown and G. Yule, *Discourse Analysis* (CUP, Cambridge, 1983), p. 33.

2. R. de Beaugrande and W. Dressler, *Introduction to Text Linguistics* (Longman, London, 1981), pp. 93–94.

3. This fuller justification is attempted in D. Sperber and D. Wilson, *Relevance: Communication and Cognition* (Basil Blackwell, Oxford, 1986).

4. H. P. Grice, 'Logic and Conversation', in *Syntax and Semantics* 3: *Speech Acts,* ed. P. Cole and J. Morgan (Academic Press, New York, 1975), pp. 41–58. [Reprinted in this volume, Chapter 19]

5. Ibid. [This volume: 310]

6. H. P. Grice, 'Presupposition and Conversational Implicature', in *Radical Pragmatics,* ed. P. Cole (Academic Press, New York, 1981), pp. 183–98, at p. 187.

7. Grice, 'Logic and Conversation'. [This volume: 310]

8. For discussion, see H. P. Grice, 'Utterer's Meaning, Sentence-Meaning and Word-Meaning', *Foundations of Language,* 4 (1968), pp. 1–18. [Reprinted in this volume, Chapter 4]

9. G. N. Leech, *Principles of Pragmatics* (Longman, London, 1983), pp. 30–31.

10. S. C. Levinson, *Pragmatics* (CUP, Cambridge, 1983), pp. 115–16.

11. K. Bach and R. M. Harnish, *Linguistic Communication and Speech Acts* (MIT Press, Cambridge, Mass., 1979), pp. 92–93.

12. Brown and Yule, *Discourse Analysis,* p. 33.

13. Grice, 'Logic and Conversation'. [This volume: 315]

14. See, for example, Levinson, *Pragmatics,* p. 116; and Brown and Yule, *Discourse Analysis,* pp. 33–35.

15. J. Fodor, *The Modularity of Mind* (MIT Press, Cambridge, Mass., 1983).

16. Bach and Harnish, *Linguistic Communication*, p. 83.

17. See, for example, D. Sperber and D. Wilson, 'Mutual Knowledge and Relevance in Theories of Comprehension', in *Mutual Knowledge*, ed. N. V. Smith (Academic Press, London, 1982), pp. 61–87; and D. Wilson and D. Sperber, 'On Defining Relevance', in *Philosophical Grounds for Rationality*, ed. R. Grandy and R. Warner (OUP, Oxford, 1986).

18. Grice, 'Logic and Conversation'.

19. For example, D. Wilson and D. Sperber, 'On Grice's Theory of Conversation', in *Conversation and Discourse*, ed. P. Werth (Croom Helm, London, 1981), pp. 152–77; and Wilson and Sperber, 'On Defining Relevance'.

20. The details of this system will not concern us here. See, for discussion, D. Sperber and D. Wilson, 'Reply to Gazdar and Good', in Smith, ed., pp. 101–10; Wilson and Sperber, 'On Defining Relevance'; Sperber and Wilson, *Relevance*.

21. Grice, 'Logic and Conversation'. [This volume: 315].

22. G. Gazdar, *Pragmatics: Implicature, Presupposition and Logical Form* (Academic Press, New York, 1979).

23. See, for example, Leech, *Principles of Pragmatics*, chapters 2 and 7.

24. The full framework is developed in detail elsewhere. See Sperber and Wilson, *Relevance*.

25. See ibid. for discussion.

26. Ibid.

27. H. H. Clark, 'Bridging', in *Thinking: Readings in Cognitive Science*, ed. P. N. Johnson-Laird and P. C. Wason (CUP, Cambridge, 1977), pp. 411–420.

28. Grice, 'Logic and Conversation'. [This volume: 311].

29. Ibid. [This volume: 312].

FURTHER READING

Bertolet, R. (1983). "Where Do Implicatures Come From?" *Canadian Journal of Philosophy* 13:181–192.

Grice, H. P. (1978). "Further Notes on Logic and Conversation." In P. Cole (ed.), *Syntax and Semantics.* Vol. 9: *Pragmatics.* New York: Academic Press, 113–127.

Horn, L. R., and S. Bayer (1984). "Short-Circuited Implicature: A Negative Contribution." *Linguistics and Philosophy* 7:397–414.

Kasher, A. (1976). "Conversational Maxims and Rationality." In A. Kasher (ed.), *Language in Focus.* Dordrecht: Reidel, 197–216.

Sperber, D., and D. Wilson (1982). "Mutual Knowledge and Relevance in Theories of Comprehension." In N. V. Smith (ed.), *Mutual Knowledge.* London: Academic Press, 61–82.

Sperber, D., and D. Wilson (1986). *Relevance: Communication and Cognition.* Cambridge, Mass.: Harvard University Press.

Walker, R.C.S. (1975). "Conversational Implicature." In S. Blackburn (ed.), *Meaning, Reference and Necessity.* Cambridge: Cambridge University Press, 133–181.

Wilson, D., and D. Sperber (1981). "On Grice's Theory of Conversation." In P. Werth (ed.), *Conversation and Discourse.* London: Croom Helm, 155–178.

VI

Presupposition

23

On the Projection Problem
for Presuppositions

IRENE HEIM

The projection problem is the problem of predicting the presuppositions of complex sentences in a compositional fashion from the presuppositions of their parts. A simple illustration is provided by the following three sentences.

(1) The king has a son.

(2) The king's son is bald.

(3) If the king has a son, the king's son is bald.

Restricting our attention to existence presuppositions resulting from definite descriptions, we observe that (3) inherits the presupposition that there is a king, which both of its constituents carry, but doesn't inherit the presupposition that the king has a son, which its right constituent carries. The solution I will advocate was in some sense already arrived at by Karttunen (1974), but its full potential was not realized at the time, perhaps because an appropriately sophisticated view of context change and its relation to truthconditional meaning was not available then.

1. COMPLEMENTARY STRENGTHS AND WEAKNESSES OF TWO RECENT THEORIES

I start with a brief comparison between two well-known recent treatments of the problem, one due to Gazdar (henceforth G.), the other to Karttunen and Peters (henceforth K.&P.).

1.1 Explanation vs. Mere Description

G.'s strongest objection to K.&P.'s theory is that it merely describes the projection facts instead of explaining them. Recall what we just observed about (3). To predict this observation, K.&P. appeal to the assumption that the grammar of English supplies three pieces of information for each lexical item: The first piece pertains to the item's purely truthconditional content. For the word "if," let's say this is the information that "if" is material implication.[1] The second piece specifies what the

Irene Heim, "On the Projection Problem for Puppositions." In *Proceedings of the Second West Coast Conference on Formal Linguistics*, edited by D. Flickinger et al., 114–125. Stanford, Calif.: Stanford University Press, 1988. Copyright © 1988 by Irene Heim. Reprinted by permission of the author.

item contributes in the way of presuppositions. E.g., for the word "the," this includes at least the information that "the" contributes the presupposition that the noun it combines with has a non-empty extension. (For "if," we presumably have the information that it contributes nothing.) The third piece of information becomes relevant only for items that are functors rather than arguments, and it concerns the item's permeability for the presuppositions of its arguments. E.g., for "if" (a functor taking two propositional arguments), this is the information that "if" lets through the full presupposition of its left argument, as well as as much of the presupposition of its right argument as doesn't follow from the left argument. In other words:

(4) If A has p as its truthconditional content and p′ as its presupposition, and B has content q and presupposition q′, then the presupposition of "If A, B" is p′ & (p → q′).

Let's refer to these three pieces of information as the "content property," "presupposition property," and "heritage property" of the item in question. G.'s point of criticism is that the K.&P.-theory treats these three properties as mutually independent. None of them is derived from the other two. The theory thus implies—implausibly—that someone who learns the word "if" has to learn not only which truthfunction it denotes and that it contributes no presupposition, but moreover that it has the heritage property specified in (4). It also implies that there could well be a lexical item—presumably not attested as yet—whose content and presupposition properties are identical to those of "if," while its heritage property is different.[2] We have to agree with G. that a more explanatory theory would not simply stipulate (4) as a lexical idiosyncrasy of "if," but would somehow derive it on the basis of general principles and the other semantic properties of "if."

G. further claims that his own theory is explanatory in just this respect. While he, too, takes every basic expression to be lexically specified for a content and a presupposition property, he manages to get away without heritage properties. In their stead, he invokes a general and quite simple theory of how utterances change the context in which they occur. In the case of (3), for instance, G. assumes that one of the existence presuppositions of the consequent gets cancelled by a conflicting conversational implicature of (3): (3) implicates that, for all the speaker knows, the king may not have a son, which is not consistent with a presupposition to the effect that the king must have a son. The cancellation that ensues is dictated by a completely general strategy of maintaining consistency during context change; it does not depend upon a heritage property or other idiosyncratic property of "if."

1.2 Differing Predictions

It has been observed[3] that G. systematically makes inadequate predictions for examples of the following two types.

(5) If John has children, then Mary will not like his twins.

(6) If John has twins, then Mary will not like his children.

Intuitively, (6) as a whole presupposes nothing, in particular not that John has children. (5), by contrast, is slightly strange, at least out of context. It somehow suggests that it is a matter of course that someone with children will have twins among them. K.&P. predict just these judgments. But G. unfortunately predicts the opposite, i.e., that (5) presupposes nothing while (6) carries a substantial presupposition, viz. that John has children. These examples suggest to me that there is something fundamentally wrong with G.'s idea that presupposition projection in conditionals is a matter of cancellation.

The literature also contains a battery of examples designed to show that G.'s predictions are superior to those of K.&P. One group of such examples is supposed to discredit K.&P.'s assumption that conditionals presuppose the conditional p → q′ (cf. (4) above) rather than q′ simpliciter. I agree with Soames (1982) that none of these examples are convincing. The remaining groups of genuine counterexamples to K.&P. are disjunctions whose disjuncts carry contradictory presuppositions (e.g., "He either just stopped or just started smoking.") and conditionals in which a presupposition of the antecedent fails to sur vive (e.g., "If I later realize I haven't told the truth, I will tell you.").

1.3 Subsentential Constituents and Quantification

In computing the presuppositions of sentences from the presuppositions of their parts, one must eventually attend to parts that are not complete sentences themselves. This presents no difficulty to K.&P., since their theory assigns presuppositions to expressions of any syntactic category and semantic type and employs projection rules above and below the sentence level that are not different in kind. G. remains silent about presupposition projection below the sentence level, and it is not obvious how he would handle it. Presumably, nonsentential phrases don't have presuppositions that are propositions; in the extended sense that they have any presuppositions at all, those are of other semantic types. But then G.'s mechanism of context change is not applicable to them: presuppositions that are not propositions are not the sort of thing that can get added to a context, at least not with contexts construed as sets of propositions. Given that G.'s main point is that presupposition projection is an epiphenomenon of the laws governing context change, his solution to the projection problem remains incomplete until this issue is addressed.

Quantified sentences provide a particularly interesting illustration of the task that G. faces here. Consider (7).

(7) Every nation$_i$ cherishes its$_i$ king.

The parts of (7), at the relevant level of analysis (logical form), are something like the following three:

(8) every x_i, x_i (is a) nation, x_i cherishes x_i's king

The third part of (8) contains the definite description "x_i's king," which one might want to say carries the existence presupposition expressed in (9).

(9) x_i has a king

But whatever (9) expresses is not a proposition: the free variable in it makes it incomplete. Would G. say that (9) expresses a poten-

tial presupposition of a part of (7) and hence of (7) as a whole? If so, what would it mean for this presupposition to get added to the context?

2. THE CONCEPTUAL PRIORITY OF CONTEXT CHANGE

The following is an attempt to combine the descriptive coverage of the K.&P.-theory with the explanatory adequacy demanded by G.

2.1 Admittance Conditions

We start by reformulating the heritage property of "if," currently stated as in (4). As Karttunen (1974) has shown, a stipulation like (4) is reducible to a stipulation like (10) combined with a general principle along the lines of (11).

(10) If "If A, B" is uttered in context c, then c is the local context for A, and c + A (read: "c incremented by A") is the local context for B.

(11) A context c admits a sentence S just in case each of the constituent sentences of S is admitted by the corresponding local context.

A context is here construed more or less like in G.'s theory, i.e., as a set of propositions, or more simply, as a proposition, namely that proposition which is the conjunction of all the elements of the set. (See e.g., Stalnaker (1979).) (11) appeals to a relation of "admittance" which is to hold between contexts and sentences. This relation is taken to be interdefinable with the relation "presuppose" that relates sentences to the propositions they presuppose, under the following equivalence:

(12) S presupposes p iff all contexts that admit S entail p.

Given their interdefinability, either relation can be used in the formulation and treatment of the projection problem. Following Karttunen (1974), we approach the problem in terms of the "admit" relation: How do the admittance conditions of a complex sentence derive from the admittance conditions of its parts? E.g., we want to predict that for a context c to admit (3), c has to entail that there is a king, but needn't entail that the king has a son. (10) in conjunction with (11) tells us that c will admit (3) just in case (i) c admits (1), and (ii) c + (1) admits (2). Given that we already know the admittance conditions for (1) and (2), this amounts to the following: (i) c has to entail that there is a king, and (ii) c conjoined with the proposition that the king has a son has to entail that there is a king and he has a son. Requirement (ii) will hold automatically whenever (i) does, so the admittance condition for sentence (3) is merely (i). We have now shown that (10) together with (11) can do the job of the previous stipulation (4).

2.2 Context Change Potentials

The general principle (11) need not worry us any further, but (10) is still a stipulation specifically about "if" and is apparently independent of that item's content and presupposition properties. G.'s objection, as reported in 1.1 above, therefore still applies. Next I will show that (10) is actually nothing but an incomplete specification of what I call the "context change potential" (henceforth CCP) of "if." I will suggest that, while the CCP of "if" cannot be derived from its other properties, one *can* derive the content property from the CCP. More generally, the truthconditional aspect of the meaning of any expression is predictable on the basis of its CCP. Since the CCP also determines the heritage property, I can then answer G.'s objection: A two-fold lexical specification of each item, in terms of CCP and presupposition property, can replace the three-fold specification that appeared to be needed in the K.&P.-theory.

What are CCPs? Intuitively, they are instructions specifying certain operations of context change. The CCP of "It is raining," for instance, is the instruction to conjoin the current context with the proposition that it is raining. (If we construe propositions as sets of possible worlds, as we will here, "conjoin" means "intersect.") The CCPs of complex sentences can be given compositionally on the basis of the CCPs of their constituents. We will illustrate this shortly. We will always write "c + S" to designate the result of executing the CCP of sentence S on context c.

There is an intimate connection between the CCP of a sentence and its truthconditional content:

(13) Suppose c is true (in w) and c admits S. Then S is true (in w) with respect to c iff c + S is true (in w).

(Informally: To be a true sentence is to keep the context true.) Something like (13) has occasionally been used to define CCP in terms of truthconditional content (see e.g., Stalnaker (1979)). I want to exploit it for the opposite purpose: to give an—albeit only partial—definition of truth of a sentence in terms of the CCP of that sentence. The partiality results from the fact that (13) says nothing about the truth of S when c is false. I believe, without offering justification here,[4] that (13) is nevertheless good enough as a truth-definition for sentences. If this is so, then a compositional assignment of CCPs to the sentences of a language can fully replace a compositional assignment of truthconditions of the sort normally envisaged by semanticists, without any loss of empirical coverage.

I indicated that, by specifying the CCP of an expression, the need for a separate specification of its heritage property is obviated. Suppose, e.g., the CCP of "if" is as described in (14).

(14) c + If A, B = c\(c + A\c + A + B)

("M\N" stands for the intersection of M with the complement of N, as usual.) Suppose further, as seems natural, that admittance conditions are conditions on the definedness of the CCP, i.e., that c + S is defined iff c admits S. It is apparent from (14) that c + If A, B is only defined when both c + A and c + A + B are. Under our assumptions, this means that c admits "If A, B" only if c admits A and c + A admits B. In this way, the heritage property of "if" falls out from its CCP (14).

To give another example: If (15) describes the CCP of "not," we can read off immediately that c will admit "Not S" only if it admits S.

(15) c + Not S = c\c + S

In other words, (15) determines that negation is a "hole" in the sense of Karttunen (1973).

Of course, (14) and (15) are motivated independently of the heritage properties of "if" and "not." They are just the CCPs that one would be led to assume if one's only goal were to arrive via (13) at the standard truthconditions for "if"- and "not"-sentences. (The reader should convince herself of this.) So it is fair to say that we have reduced two seemingly independent semantic properties, the content and the heritage property, to just one, the CCP. The current theory no longer implies that content and heritage properties will vary independently across lexical items, or that they need be learned separately, and it is hence no less explanatory than G.'s.

2.3 Accommodation

Suppose S is uttered in a context c which doesn't admit it. We have said that this makes c + S undefined. What does that mean in practice? Does it mean that context change simply comes to a halt at this point and communication breaks down? That would be an unrealistic assumption. In real-life conversations, people deal with this kind of situation effortlessly: They simply amend the context c to a slightly richer context c', one which admits S and is otherwise like c, and then proceed to compute c' + S instead of c + S. Following Lewis (1979), I call this adjustment "accommodation." Accommodation accounts for the common observation that utterances can convey their presuppositions as new information.

The informal characterization of accommodation that I just gave contains a hidden ambiguity, which comes to light when we look at an example: Suppose S presupposes p, and "Not S" is uttered in a context c which fails to entail p, hence doesn't admit "Not S." Some sort of accommodation is called for. One can imagine two quite different ways in which it might occur: (A) The "global" option: Amend c to c & p and, instead of c + Not S, calculate c & p + Not S. Following (15), you will end up with c & p\c & p + S. (B) The "local" option: Amend c to c & p so that you can calculate c & p + S instead of c + S. Then substitute the result of this calculation in the place of "c + S" in (15), so that you end up with c\c & p + S. A is more like pretending that c & p obtained instead of c all along (hence the word "global"). B is rather like adjusting the context only for the immediate purpose of evaluating the constituent sentence S (hence "local"). The results are obviously different, so which way do people proceed in real life? I

suggest that the global option is strongly preferred, but the local option is also available in certain circumstances that make it unavoidable. Consider a concrete example.

(16) The king of France didn't come,

uttered in a context which is compatible with France having no king. By the global option, we end up with a context that entails that France has a king; this is presumably how we tend to read (16) in isolation. Under the local option, the resulting context will only entail that either France has no king or he didn't come. We will read (16) this way if we are for some reason discouraged from assuming France to have a king, e.g., if the speaker continues (16) with "because France doesn't have a king." Note that by stipulating a *ceteris paribus* preference for global over local accommodation, we recapture the effect of G.'s assumption that presupposition cancellation occurs only under the threat of inconsistency.[5]

I am here stopping far short of a general and precise formulation of the laws governing accommodation and their interaction with the instructions contained in the CCPs.

3. THE INTERPRETATION OF VARIABLES

While the theory I have sketched builds in many ways on that of K.&P., it also shares a problematic feature with G.'s: It treats presupposition projection as a side-effect of the rules governing context change. It is therefore not straightforwardly applicable below the level of complete sentences (cf. 1.3). Like G., I am faced with the difficulty of assigning CCPs to constituent sentences with variables free in them, i.e., to expressions that don't express propositions.

3.1 Contexts as Sets of Sequence-World-Pairs

We can solve our problem if we abandon the identification of contexts with propositions. The information accumulated in a context need not all be propositional; much of it is rather like information as one finds it represented in a card file, i.e., a collection of cards with a (more or less informative) description

[on] each card. Depending on the facts, such a file may be true or false: true if there is at least one collection of individuals that can be lined up with the cards so that each individual fits the description on the corresponding card; false otherwise. If contexts are like files, then context changes in response to utterances are like updating operations: additions of further cards and/or additions of further entries on already established cards. This metaphor is naturally applicable to utterances containing variables: The context change induced by, say, "x_7 is a nation" consists of writing the entry "is a nation" onto card number 7, where this card is either created on the occasion or found among the already established cards, as the case may be.[6]

Technically, files and, I suggest, contexts can be identified with properties of sequences of individuals, i.e., with sets of pairs $\langle g,w \rangle$, where g is a sequence of individuals (a function from the set of natural numbers into the domain of individuals), and w is a world. Since each such set of pairs determines uniquely a proposition:

(17) Let c be a set of sequence-world-pairs. Then the proposition determined by c is {w: for some g, $\langle g,w \rangle \in$ c}.

we don't give up any of the advantages of identifying contexts with propositions when we identify them with properties of sequences instead. In particular, we can still evaluate contexts in terms of truth and falsity, as shown in (18), and can retain the truth definition for sentence (13) which relies on that.

(18) c is true in w iff for some g, $\langle g,w \rangle \in$ c.

We can now assign CCPs to sentences with free variables, e.g., to sentence (9):

(19) c + (9) = c $\cap$ {$\langle g,w \rangle$: g(i) has a king in w}

(As for the CCPs for "if" and "not" that I formulated earlier, (14) and (15) carry over just as they stand into the new framework.) We can also formulate admittance conditions for sentences with free variables. E.g., in order to admit (20):

(20) x_i cherishes x_i's king,

a context must, informally speaking, "entail that x_i has a king." By this I mean that it has to be a context c such that, for every $\langle g,w \rangle \in$ c, g(i) has a king in w.

3.2 Presuppositions of Quantified Sentences

So how are we going to predict the presuppositions of a sentence like (7)? We have almost everything we need, except for the CCP of "every." Considering the truthconditions to be captured, the following formulation suggests itself.

(21) c + Every x_i, A, B = {$\langle g,w \rangle \in$ c: for every a, if $\langle g^i/a,w \rangle \in$ c + A, then $\langle g^i/a,w \rangle \in$ c + A + B}

("$g^i/_a$" stands for the sequence that is like g, except that $g^i/_a(i)$ = a.) We need a further stipulation to ensure that (21) always yields adequate truthconditions: x_i must somehow be required to be a "new" variable at the time when "every x_i" is uttered. In terms of the file metaphor, we want to require that the file which obtains prior to the utterance doesn't yet contain a card number i, so that a fresh card will be set up when x_i is encountered in the evaluation of A. More technically, the stipulation we need is this:

(22) For any two sequences g and g' that differ at most in their i-th member, and for any world w: $\langle g,w \rangle \in$ c iff $\langle g',w \rangle \in$ c.

Given (22), (21) will derive the intended truthconditions for a sentence like (7), but not without (22). (The reader should verify this for himself by computing c + (8) for a choice of c that violates (22), e.g., c = {$\langle g,w \rangle$: g(i) = France}.) For our present purposes, we take (22) to be a lexical property of "every," i.e., part of its presupposition property. In other words, we stipulate that no context that violates (22) will admit a sentence of the form "Every x_i, A, B."[7]

Back to the issue of presupposition projection in "every"-sentences. (21) determines that c + "Every x_i, A, B" can only be defined if c + A and c + A + B are. Applied to (8), this means that c will not admit (8) unless (i) c admits "x_i is a nation," and (ii) c + "x_i is a nation" admits (20). We suppose (i) to be trivially satisfied. As for (ii), we determined in the previous section that c + "x_i is a nation" = c $\cap$ {$\langle g,w \rangle$: g(i) is a nation in w}, and furthermore that this will admit (20) just in case the following entailment holds:

(ii) For every $\langle g,w \rangle \in$ c $\cap$ {$\langle g,w \rangle$: g(i) is a nation in w}, g(i) has a king in w.

Now suppose that in every world in which c is true, every nation has a king. This is clearly a sufficient condition for (ii) to hold. It turns out that it is also a necessary condition; one can prove this by exploiting (22). We therefore conclude that a context that is to admit (8) must entail that every nation has a king. In other words: (7) presupposes that every nation has a king. The reasoning by which we arrived at this prediction may strike you as somewhat complicated. But bear in mind that all the machinery we had to invoke (in particular (21) and (22)) was needed independently to predict the truthconditions.

For the type of example discussed so far, i.e., universally quantified sentences with the presupposition-inducing element (here: a definite description) in the "consequent" (i.e., in the B-part of "Every x_i, A, B"), our predictions coincide with those of Karttunen and Peters (1979): If B presupposes X, "Every x_i, A, B" presupposes "Every x_i, A, X." But when the presupposition-inducing element is in the "antecedent," i.e., in A, as in (23), my claims differ from theirs.

(23) Everyone who serves his king will be rewarded.

According to K.&P. (1979), (23) presupposes nothing. I am committed, by the assumptions I have introduced so far, to the claim that (23)—normally, at any rate—presupposes that everyone has a king. I say "normally," because the prediction stands only to the extent that there is no local accommodation. As we observed in connection with (16), local accommodation may produce what looks like presupposition cancellation. Limitations of space prevent me from exploring the implications this might have for cases like (23). I can only hope the reader will agree with my impression that a theory which assigns a universal presupposition to (23) as the unmarked case is tolerably close to the actual facts, or at least as close as K.&P.'s analysis or any other simple generalization that comes to mind.

What about quantifiers other than universal? Concerning "no," we find conflicting factual claims in the literature. According to Cooper (1983), (24) should presuppose that every nation (in the relevant domain of discourse) has a king; for Lerner & Zimmermann (1981), it presupposes merely that some nation does.

(24) No nation cherishes its king.

Here as elsewhere, the theory I am advocating gives me no choice: Once I have assigned "no" a CCP that will take care of its truthconditional content, it turns out that I have to side with Cooper. But again, this applies only for the "ordinary" cases which don't involve any local accommodation. When the latter is brought into play, the universal presupposition will appear to be weakened in various ways or even cancelled.

3.3 Indefinites

Karttunen and Peters (1979) point out a difficulty with sentences like (25).

(25) A fat man was pushing his bicycle.

Their rules assign to (25) a presupposition that they admit is too weak: that some fat man had a bicycle. On the other hand, a universal presupposition that every fat man had a bicycle would be too strong. What one would like to predict is, vaguely speaking, a presupposition to the effect that the same fat man that verifies the content of (25) had a bicycle. But it is neither clear what exactly that means nor how it could be worked into K.&P.'s theory.[8]

I have argued elsewhere[9] that indefinites are not quantifying. The logical form of (25) thus lacks the part corresponding to "every x_i" in (8):

(26) x_i (was a) fat man, x_i was pushing x_i's bicycle

(26) is just a sequence of two open sentences with free occurrences of x_i, which are interpreted as though conjoined by "and." The CCP of (26) is simply:

(27) c + (26) = (c + x_i was a fat man) + x_i was pushing x_i's bike

This gives adequate truthconditions—provided that x_i is a new variable. We therefore stipulate that a context must conform to (22) if it is to admit a sentence containing an indefinite indexed i.

Now what about presupposition projection? (27) shows that for c to admit (26), c + "x_i was a fat man" must entail that x_i had a bicycle. It turns out that, due to (22), this entailment will hold just in case every fat man in any world compatible with c had a bicycle. So we are prima facie committed to an unintuitively strong universal presupposition for (25).

I suggest that our actual intuitions are accounted for by the ready availability of a certain kind of accommodation in the evaluation of indefinite sentences. In the case of (25), when c fails to entail that every fat man had a bicycle, the following appears to happen: First, $c + $ "x_i is a fat man" is computed, call the result of this c'. Then c' is found not to admit "x_i was pushing x_i's bicycle." So it is amended to c'', which presumably is c' & x_i has a bicycle. From there, $c'' + $ "x_i was pushing x_i's bicycle" is calculated. The net result is a context which entails that x_i was a fat man, had a bicycle, and was pushing it, but entails nothing about fat men having bicycles in general.

This sort of accommodation seems to happen with the ease typical of global, rather than local, accommodation. In fact, it *is* global accommodation if we take the defining feature of globality to be that the accommodated piece of information (here that x_i had a bicycle) remains in the context *for good.* (Notice that this criterion distinguishes appropriately between the global and local accommodation options as exemplified above for example (16).) In other words, I speculate that the relative ease with which a missing presupposition is accommodated in the midst of evaluating an indefinite sentence can be subsumed under the general observation that global accom-

modation is more common than local accommodation. Incidentally, this speculation relies crucially on the non-quantificational analysis of indefinites: only because x_i remains free in (26) does the information that x_i had a bicycle end up being entailed by the context ever after.

4. FINAL REMARK

Many non-trivial aspects of presupposition projection could not even be alluded in this paper, e.g., the heritage properties of "or," modal operators, and propositional attitude verbs. As for the latter two, I expect that the present approach will make reasonable predictions when combined with a treatment of modality in terms of quantification over possible worlds.[10] But I don't expect my readers to take this on faith.

ACKNOWLEDGMENTS

This work is supported by the Center for Cognitive Science of M.I.T. under a grant from the Sloan Foundation's particular program in Cognitive Science. I thank Stanley Peters, Lauri Karttunen, Robin Cooper, and Thomas "Ede" Zimmermann for illuminating conversations on the material.

NOTES

1. I don't believe that, but it doesn't matter here.

2. G.'s point is not affected by the fact that Karttunen and Peters (1979) use a "heritage function" which assigns heritage properties to pairs consisting of the content and presupposition properties. For notice that this function is defined point by point, not as a general procedure.

3. Peters, personal communication. G.'s problem with (6) is also pointed out by Soames (1982), whose proposal, however, continues to be affected by the problem with (5).

4. I discuss this point somewhat further in Heim (1982).

5. The examples mentioned at the end of section 1.2 may also be amenable to a treatment in terms of local accommodation.

6. For a more explicit motivation of the file metaphor and the corresponding technical concepts, see Heim (1983).

7. This stipulation is derived from the indefiniteness of quantifying NPs in Heim (1982) and (1983).

8. A solution very different from the one sketched below is developed in Cooper (1983).

9. See Heim (1982) and (1983) for details.

10. E.g. along the lines of Kratzer (1981).

REFERENCES

Cooper, R. (1983). *Quantification and Syntactic Theory.* Dordrecht: Reidel.

Heim, I. (1982). "The Semantics of Definite and Indefinite Noun Phrases." Ph.D. diss., University of Massachusetts.

Heim, I. (1983). "File Change Semantics and the Familiarity Theory of Definiteness." In A. von Stechow, R. Bauerle, and C. Schwarze (eds.), *Meaning, Use and Interpretation.* Berlin: W. de Gruyter.

Karttunen, L. (1973). "Presuppositions of Compound Sentences." *Linguistic Inquiry* 4:169–193.

Karttunen, L. (1974). "Presupposition and Linguistic Context." *Theoretical Linguistics* 1:181–194. [Reprinted in this volume, Chapter 24]

Karttunen, L., and S. Peters (1979). "Conventional Implicature." In Ch.-K. Oh and D. Dinneen (eds.), *Syntax and Semantics.* Vol. 11: *Presupposition.* New York: Academic Press.

Kratzer, A. (1981). "The Notional Category of Modality." In H. Riesser and J. Eikmeyer (eds.), *Words, Worlds and Contexts,* Berlin: W. de Gruyter.

Lewis, D. (1979). "Scorekeeping in a Language Game." In R. Bauerle, V. Egli, and A. von Stechow (eds.), *Semantics from Different Points of View.* Berlin: Springer-Verlag. [Reprinted in the volume, Chapter 25]

Lerner, J., and T. Zimmermann (1981). "Mehrdimensionale Semantik: Die Prasupposition and die Kontextabhangigkeit von 'nur.'" Working paper 50, SFB 99.

Soames, S. (1982). "How Presuppositions Are Inherited: A Solution to the Projection Problem." *Linguistic Inquiry* 13:483–545.

Stalnaker, R. (1979). "Assertion." In P. Cole (ed.), *Syntax and Semantics.* Vol. 9: *Pragmatics.* New York: Academic Press. [Reprinted in this volume, Chapter 17]

24

Presupposition and Linguistic Context

LAURI KARTTUNEN

According to a pragmatic view, the presuppositions of a sentence determine the class of contexts in which the sentence could be felicitously uttered. Complex sentences present a difficult problem in this framework. No simple "projection method" has been found by which we could compute their presuppositions from those of their constituent clauses. This paper presents a way to eliminate the projection problem. A recursive definition of "satisfaction of presuppositions" is proposed that makes it unnecessary to have any explicit method for assigning presuppositions to compound sentences. A theory of presuppositions becomes a theory of constraints on successive contexts in a fully explicit discourse.

What I present here is a sequel to a couple of my earlier studies on presuppositions. The first one is the paper "Presuppositions of Compound Sentences" (Karttunen 1973a), the other is called "Remarks on Presuppositions" (Karttunen 1973b). I won't review these papers here, but I will start by giving some idea of the background for the present paper.

Earlier I was concerned about two things. First, I wanted to show that there was no adequate notion of presupposition that could be defined in purely semantic terms, that is, in terms of truth conditions. What was needed was a pragmatic notion, something along the lines Stalnaker (1972) had suggested, but not a notion of the speaker's presupposition. I had in mind some definition like the one given under (1).

(1) Surface sentence A pragmatically presupposes a logical form L, if and only if it is the case that A can be felicitously uttered only in contexts which entail L.

The main point about (1) is that presupposition is viewed as a relation between sentences, or more accurately, as a relation between a surface sentence and the logical form of another.[1] By "surface sentence" I mean expressions of a natural language as opposed to sentences of a formal language which the former are in some manner associated with. "Logical forms" are expressions of the latter kind. "Context" in (1) means a set of logical forms that describe the set of background assumptions, that is, whatever the speaker chooses to regard as being shared by him and his intended audience. According to (1), a sentence can be felicitously uttered only in contexts that entail all of its presuppositions.

Lauri Karttunen, "Presupposition and Linguistic Context," *Theoretical Linguistics* 1 (1974): 181–194. Copyright © 1974 by Walter de Gruyter & Co. Reprinted by permission of the publisher and the author.

Secondly, I argued that, if we look at things in a certain way, presupposition turns out to be a relative notion for compound sentences. The same sentence may have different presuppositions depending on the context in which it is uttered. To see what [that] means, let us use "X" as a variable for contexts (sets of logical forms), "A" and "B" stand for (surface) sentences, and "P_A" and "P_B" denote the set of logical forms presupposed by A and B, respectively. Let us assume that A and B in this instance are simple sentences that contain no quantifiers and no sentential connectives. Furthermore, let us assume that we know already what A and B presuppose, that is, we know the elements of P_A and P_B. Given all that, what can we say about presuppositions of complex sentences formed from A and B by means of embedding and sentential connectives? This is the notorious "projection problem" for presuppositions (Morgan 1969, Langendoen & Savin 1971). For instance, what are the presuppositions of "If A then B"?

Intuitively it would seem that sentential connectives such as *if . . . then* do not introduce any new presuppositions. Therefore, the set $P_{if\ A\ then\ B}$ should be either identical to or at least some proper subset of the combined presuppositions of A and B. This initially simple idea is presented in (2).

(2) $P_{if\ A\ then\ B} \subseteq P_A \cup P_B$

However, I found that when one pursues this line of inquiry further, things become very complicated. Consider the examples in (3).

(3) (a) If Dean told the truth, Nixon is guilty too.
    (b) If Haldeman is guilty, Nixon is guilty too.
    (c) If Miss Woods destroyed the missing tapes, Nixon is guilty too.

In all of these cases, let us assume that the consequent clause "Nixon is guilty too" is interpreted in the sense in which it presupposes the guilt of someone else. The question is: does the compound sentence as a whole carry that presupposition? In the case of (3a), the answer seems to be definitely *yes*, in the case of (3b) definitely *no*, and in the case of (3c) a *maybe*, depending on the context in which the sentence is used. For example, if the destruction of the tapes is considered a crime, then Miss Woods would be guilty in case she did it, and (3c) could be a conditional assertion that

Nixon was an accomplice. In this context the sentence does not presuppose that anyone is guilty. But in contexts where the destruction of the tapes in itself would not constitute a crime (3c) apparently does presuppose the guilt of someone other than Nixon.

These examples show that if we try to determine the presuppositions of "If A then B" as a particular subset of the joint presuppositions of A and B, the initial simplicity of that idea turns out to be deceptive. In reality it is a very complicated enterprise. The kind of recursive principle that seems to be required is given in (4a) in the form it appears in Karttunen (1973b). (4b) says the same in ordinary English.

(4) (a) $P_{if\ A\ then\ B/X} = P_{A/X} \cup (P_{B/X \cup A} - (E_{X \cup A} - E_X))$ where E_X is the set of logical forms entailed (in the standard sense) by X, and $X \cup A$ is the result of adding the logical form of A to X.
    (b) The presuppositions of "If A then B" (with respect to context X) consist of
    (i) all of the presuppositions of A (with respect to X) and
    (ii) all of the presupposition[s] of B (with respect to $X \cup A$) except for those entailed by the set $X \cup A$ and not entailed by X alone.

One would like to find a better way to express this, but I am not sure there is one.[2] It really is a complicated question.

So much for the background. What I want to show now is that there is another way to think about these matters, and about presuppositions of complex sentences in particular. Let us go back for a moment to the attempted pragmatic definition in (1). The point of that definition is that the presuppositions of a sentence determine in what contexts the sentence could be felicitously used. A projection method, such as (4a), associates a complex sentence with a class of such contexts by compiling a set of logical forms that must be entailed in any context where it is proper to use the sentence. Thus we say that the sentence "If A then B" can be felicitously uttered in context X only if X entails all of the logical forms in the set $P_{if\ A\ then\ B/X}$, defined in (4a).

There is another, much simpler, way to associate complex sentences with proper contexts of use. Instead of characterizing these contexts by compiling the presuppositions of the sentence, we ask what a context would have to be like in order to satisfy those presuppositions. Of course, it is exactly the same problem but, by turning it upside down, we get a surprisingly simple answer. The reason is that we can answer the latter question directly, without having to compute what the presuppositions actually are.

The way we go about this is the following. We start by defining, not presupposition, but a notion of *satisfaction of presuppositions*. This definition is based on the assumption that we can give a finite list of basic presuppositions for each simple sentence of English. For all cases where A is a simple, non-compound sentence, satisfaction is defined as in (5).

(5) Context X *satisfies-the-presuppositions-of* A just in case X entails all of the basic presuppositions of A (that is, $P_A \subseteq E_X$).

The basic presuppositions of a simple sentence presumably can be determined from the lexical items in the sentence and from its form and derivational history, say, the application of certain transformations such as Pseudo-Clefting. To give a somewhat oversimplified example, consider the word *too* that occurs in the examples under (3). As a first approximation to the meaning of *too* we could give a condition like the one in (6), which is based on Green (1968).

(6) Context X satisfies-the-presuppositions-of "a is P too" only if either (i) X entails "b is P" for some b ($\neq$ a), or (ii) X entails "a is Q" for some Q ($\neq$ P).

This in turn is equivalent to saying that a simple sentence like "Nixon is guilty too" either has a presupposition that someone else is guilty or that Nixon has some other property.[3] One or the other must be entailed in context.

For compound sentences we define satisfaction recursively by associating each part of the sentence with a different context. The basic idea behind this was independently suggested in both Stalnaker (1973) and Karttunen (1973b). For conditionals, satisfaction is defined in (7).

(7) Context X satisfies-the-presuppositions-of "If A then B" just in case (i) X satisfies-the-presuppositions-of A, and (ii) X $\cup$ A satisfies-the-presuppositions-of B.

As before, the expression "X $\cup$ A" denotes the set that results from incrementing X with

the logical form of A.[4] For conjunctions, that is, sentences of the form "A and B", satisfaction is defined just as in (7). For disjunctions, sentences of the form "A or B", we have "$\sim$A" instead of "A" in part (ii). Examples that illustrate and support these principles can be found in my earlier papers.[5]

Note that *satisfies-the-presuppositions-of* is a relation between contexts and sentences. As I have tried to indicate orthographically, we are defining it here as a primitive, irreducible locution. Eventually it would be better to replace this clumsy phrase with some simple verb such as "admits", which has the right pragmatic connotations. I keep the former term only to bring out the connection between (4) and (7) more clearly. At the end, of course, it comes down to having for each simple sentence a set of logical forms that are to be entailed (in the standard logical sense) by a certain context. What is important is that we define satisfaction for complex sentences directly without computing their presuppositions explicitly. There is no need for a projection method. Secondly, in case a sentence occurs as part of a larger compound, its presuppositions need not always be satisfied by the actual conversational context, as long as they are satisfied by a certain local extension of it. For example, in order to admit "If A then B" a context need only satisfy-the-presuppositions-of A, provided that the presuppositions of B are satisfied by the context as incremented with the logical form of A.

It can be shown that the new way of doing things and the old way are equivalent. They sanction the use of any sentence in the same class of contexts. Although it may not be obvious at first, the statement in (8) is true just in case (9) holds, and vice versa.

(8) X satisfies-the-presuppositions-of "If A then B."

(9) $P_{\text{if A then B}/X} \subseteq E_X$

The proof is straight-forward and will not be presented in detail. Here it suffices to note that, by (4a), (9) is equivalent to the conjunction of (10) and (11).

(10) $P_A \subseteq E_X$

(11) $P_B - (E_{X \cup A} - E_X) \subseteq E_X$

Similarly, by (7), (8) is equivalent to the conjunction of (12) and (13).

(12) X satisfies-the-presuppositions-of A.

(13) X ∪ A satisfies-the-presuppositions-of B.

Given our basic definition of satisfaction in (5) and that A and B are simple sentences, it follows that (10) and (12) are equivalent. So it remains to be shown that (11) and (13) also amount to the same thing. This can be done with simple set-theoretic means by proving the equivalence of (11) and (14). (Note that $E_X \subseteq E_{X \cup A}$).

(14) $P_B \subseteq E_{X \cup A}$

(14) in turn says the same thing as (13) provided that B is a simple sentence, as we have assumed here. In short, (8) and (9) are equivalent by virtue of the fact that (10) is equivalent to (12) and (11) is equivalent to (13). Consequently, the class of contexts that satisfy-the-presuppositions-of "If A then B" by principle (7) is the same class of contexts that entail all of the presuppositions assigned to this sentence by (4a).[6]

As we move on to more complicated sentences, the advantages of (7) over (4) become more and more clear. For example, consider sentences of the form (15).

(15) If (A and B) then (C or D).

It is a very cumbersome undertaking to compute the set of logical forms presupposed by (15) by means of rules like (4a). But it is a simple matter to tell by principles like (7) what is required of a context in which (15) is used. This is shown in (16). Note that (16) is not a new definition but a statement that directly follows from (7) and the corresponding principles for conjunctions and disjunctions.

(16) Context X satisfies-the-presuppositions-of "If (A and B) then (C or D)" just in case
  (i) X satisfies-the-presuppositions-of A,
  (ii) X ∪ A satisfies-the-presuppositions-of B,
  (iii) X ∪ A & B satisfies-the-presuppositions-of C, and
  (iv) X ∪ A & B ∪ ∼C satisfies-the-presuppositions-of D.

As we study complex cases such as this one, we see that we could look at satisfaction of presuppositions in an even more general way. As illustrated in (16), by our definition a given initial context satisfies-the-presuppositions-of a complex sentence just in case the presuppositions of each of the constituent sentences are satisfied by a certain specific extension of that initial context. For example, the presuppositions of D in (15) must be satisfied by a set of logical forms that consists of the current conversational context as incremented with the logical forms of "A and B" and the negation of C. In compound sentences, the initial context is incremented in a left-to-right fashion giving for each constituent sentence a *local context* that must satisfy its presuppositions.[7] We could easily define a notion of local context separately and give the following general definition of satisfaction for all compound sentences.

(17) Context X satisfies-the-presuppositions-of S just in case the presuppositions of each of the constituent sentences in S are satisfied by the corresponding local context.

Note that in this new framework the earlier question of how it comes about that presupposition is a relative notion for compound sentences does not arise at all. Also, the distinction between cases like (3a) and (3b) is of no particular importance. What is required in both cases is that the presupposition of the consequent clause contributed by the word *too* be entailed by the current conversational context as incremented with the logical form of the antecedent. In case of (3b), we recognize that this condition is met, no matter what the initial context is like, by virtue of the particular antecedent. In (3a) it appears that the antecedent does not contribute anything towards satisfying the presuppositions of the consequent, at least, not in contexts that immediately come to mind. Hence we can be sure that the presuppositions of the consequent are satisfied in the incremented context just in case they are already satisfied initially. It seems to me now that this is a much better way of putting it than to talk about a presupposition being "shared" by the compound in (3a) and being "cancelled" or "filtered away" in (3b), as I did in the earlier papers. Such locutions can be thrown out with the projection method that gave rise to them.

So far I have only discussed complex sentences that are formed with sentential connectives. However, satisfaction of presuppositions can easily be defined for all kinds of complex sentences. Without going into any great detail,

I will try to outline how this is done for sentences with sentential subjects or objects.

Let us represent such sentences with the expression "v(... A ...)" where "v" stands for a complementizable verb and "A" for an embedded subject or object clause. Sentences with verbs like *believe* and *want* that require non-sentential subjects are represented with "v(a,A)" where "a" stands for the underlying subject. In this connection we have to distinguish three kinds of complementizable verbs, as shown in (18).

(18)   I Verbs of saying: *say, ask, tell, announce,* etc. (including external negation).
II Verbs of propositional attitude: *believe, fear, think, want,* etc.
III All other kinds of complementizable verbs: factives, semi-factives, modals, one- and two-way implicatives, aspectual verbs, internal negation.

Essentially this amounts to a distinction between verbs that are "transparent" with respect to presuppositions of their complements (type III) and verbs that are "opaque" to one degree or another (types I and II).[8] These distinctions of course are not arbitrary but presumably follow from the semantics of verb complementation in some manner yet to be explained.

For sentences where the main verb is of the last type, we need the condition in (19).

(19) If v is of type III, context X satisfies-the-presuppositions-of "v(... A ...)" only if X satisfies-the-presuppositions-of A.

Thus in a case such as (20), where *may, force,* and *stop* all are of type III, a context satisfies-the-presuppositions-of the whole sentence only if it satisfies those of all the nested complements.[9]

(20) The courts may force Nixon to stop protecting his aides.

For example, a context for (20) ought to entail that Nixon has or will have been protecting his aides.

For verbs of propositional attitude we need a condition such as (21), where the expression "$B_a(X)$" stands for the set of beliefs attributed to a in X.

(21) If v is of type II, context X satisfies-the-presuppositions-of "v(a,A)" only if $B_a(X)$ satisfies-the-presuppositions-of A.[10]

The condition says that sentences such as (22) require that the subject of the main sentence be understood to have a set of beliefs that satisfy-the-presuppositions-of-the complement.

(22) John fears that Nixon will stop protecting his aides.

To satisfy the presuppositions of (22), a context must ascribe to John a set of beliefs that satisfy-the-presuppositions-of "Nixon will stop protecting his aides."

Finally, with verbs of type I a complex sentence does not necessarily require that the presuppositions of the complement be satisfied, as we can observe by contemplating examples such as (23).

(23) Ziegler announced that Nixon will stop protecting his aides.

(23) can be spoken felicitously, perhaps even truly, no matter what the facts are understood to be or whether anyone is supposed to hold a set of beliefs that satisfy the presuppositions of the complement.

As a final example of complementation, consider the sentence in (24).

(24) John thinks that, if Rosemary believes that Nixon has been protecting his aides, she is afraid that Nixon will stop protecting them.

By applying the principles in (21) and (7) recursively, we arrive at the conclusion that, if a given context, X, satisfies the presuppositions of (24), then the presuppositions of the last clause in (24), "Nixon will stop protecting his aides", are satisfied by the set (25).

(25) $B_{Rosemary}$ (B_{John} (X) ∪ Rosemary believes that Nixon has been protecting his aides).

This set contains all of the beliefs attributed to Rosemary in a context that consists of all of the beliefs attributed to John in X and the logical form of the given sentence. By virtue of its last-mentioned ingredient, this set in (25) is guaranteed to entail that Nixon has been protecting his aides. Therefore, (24) does not require that this particular presupposition of the last clause be entailed in contexts where (24) is used, or by the set of beliefs that in those contexts are attributed to John or to Rosemary. As far as I am able to tell, this is the correct result.

This concludes what I have to say about satisfaction of presuppositions. What we are interested in is associating sentences with proper contexts of use. We can achieve this goal directly by defining a notion of satisfaction as a relation between contexts and sentences. In this way we avoid the many complications that have to be built into a projection method that does the same by associating each sentence with a set of presuppositions. The efforts by Langendoen and Savin (1971), Morgan (1969, 1973), Keenan (1973), Lakoff and Railton (1971), Herzberger (1973), myself (1973a, 1973b), and many others to find such a method now seem misplaced to me. The best solution to the projection problem is to do away with it. The moral of this paper is: do not ask what the presuppositions of a complex sentence are, ask what it takes to satisfy them.

I will conclude with a few comments about the notion of *context*. It is implicit in what I have said about satisfaction that a conversational context, a set of logical forms, specifies what can be taken for granted in making the next speech act. What this common set of background assumptions contains depends on what has been said previously and other aspects of the communicative situation. In a fully explicit discourse, the presuppositions of the next sentence uttered are satisfied by the current context. This guarantees that they are true in every possible world consistent with the context. Of course, it is possible that the actual world is not one of them, since people may be talking under various misapprehensions. Satisfaction of presuppositions is not a matter of what the facts really are, just what the conversational context is.

Once the new sentence has been uttered, the context will be incremented to include the new shared information. Viewed in this light, a theory of presuppositions amounts to a theory of a rational order of contexts from smaller to larger sets of shared information. At each step along the way that a fully explicit discourse proceeds, the current context satisfies the presuppositions of the next sentence that in turn increments it to a new context.

There are definitions of pragmatic presupposition, such as (1), which suggest that there is something amiss in a discourse that does not proceed in this ideal, orderly fashion. Those definitions make it infelicitous to utter sentences whose presuppositions are not satisfied by the current conversational context. They

outlaw any leaps and shortcuts. All things considered, this is an unreasonable view. Consider the examples in (26).

(26) (a) We *regret* that children cannot accompany their parents to commencement exercises.
(b) There are *almost* no misprints in this book.
(c) I would like to introduce you to *my wife.*
(d) John lives in *the third brick house down the street from the post office.*
(e) It has been *pointed out* that there are counter examples to my theory.

The [italicized] items in these sentences bring in a certain presupposition. Thus (26a) presupposes that its complement is true. Yet the sentence could readily be used in a conversational context that does not satisfy this presupposition. Perhaps the whole point of uttering (26a) is to let it be known that parents should not bring their kids along. Similarly, (26d) might be used to give directions to a person who up to that point had no idea that there are at least three brick houses down the street from the post office, which is a presupposition for the sentence by virtue of the [italicized] definite description. The same goes for the other examples in (26).

What do we say here? I am not all sure we want to say that, in these cases, a sentence has been used infelicitously. I am sure that there is no advantage in saying that sentences like (26a) sometimes do and sometimes do not presuppose their complements. A notion of "part-time presupposition" is not going to help; on the contrary. Had we defined presupposition as a relation between a sentence and its speaker, we would be tempted to talk about some presuppositions being optional.

I think the best way to look at this problem is to recognize that ordinary conversation does not always proceed in the ideal orderly fashion described earlier. People do make leaps and shortcuts by using sentences whose presuppositions are not satisfied in the conversational context. This is the rule rather than the exception, and we should not base our notion of presupposition on the false premiss that it does not or should not happen. But granting that ordinary discourse is not always fully explicit in the above sense, I think we can maintain that a sentence is always taken to be an increment to a context that satisfies its presuppositions. If the current conversational context does not suffice, the listener is entitled and expected to extend it as required. He must determine for himself what context he is supposed to be in on the basis of what was said and, if he is willing to go along with it, make the same tacit extension that his interlocutor appears to have made.[11] This is one way in which we communicate indirectly, convey matters without discussing them.

When we hear a sentence such as (26a), we recognize that it increments contexts which entail that children are not permitted at commencement exercises. These are the only contexts that satisfy the presuppositions of (26a). So if we have not realized already that we are supposed to be in that kind of context, the sentence lets us know that indirectly. Perhaps the whole point of uttering (26a) was to make us conclude this for ourselves so that we would not have to be told directly.[12]

One must be careful not to confuse presuppositions with features of contexts that satisfy those presuppositions. Consider a sentence such as (27), which is a modified version of an example discussed by Lakoff (1971).

(27) John called Mary a Republican and then she insulted him back.

Because of the word *back,* the second conjunct of (27) presupposes that John has insulted Mary. The principle (17) tells us that this presupposition ought to be satisfied by the corresponding local context. In this case, the local context consists of the initial context for (27) incremented with the logical form of "John called Mary a Republican". Let us suppose that this context in fact satisfies the presupposition that John has insulted Mary, and that the initial context by itself would not satisfy it. This state of affairs could come about in several ways. The most obvious one is that the initial context entails that calling someone a Republican constitutes an insult.

Note that there is nothing in (27) which presupposes that "Republican" is a dirty word. It is not a necessary feature of every context that satisfies the presuppositions of (27). But there are some contexts in which the presuppositions of (27) are satisfied only because of it. Sometimes we can exploit this fact by uttering (27) in a context which does not satisfy its presuppositions. In that case we expect the listener to notice what extension we have in

mind. This is similar to what can be done with the examples in (26), except that here the piece of information that is passed along under the counter is neither presupposed nor entailed by any part of (27).

As a final example, consider a case of the kind first discussed in Liberman (1973).

(28) Bill has met either the King or the President of Slobovia.

The two disjuncts that constitute (28) have conflicting presuppositions: Slobovia is a monarchy/Slobovia is a republic. Yet, (28) as a whole is not contradictory. It seems to assert that Bill has met the Slobovian Head of State and indicates that the speaker does not know much about Slobovia. What sort of context does it take to satisfy-the-presuppositions-of (28)?

Assuming that the condition for "or" is symmetric (see note 5), we find that, according to our principles, (28) can be admissible at least in contexts which entail the logical forms of the three sentences in (29).

(29) (a) Slobovia is either a monarchy or a republic.
     (b) If Slobovia is a monarchy, Bill has met the King of Slobovia.
     (c) If Slobovia is a republic, Bill has met the President of Slobovia.

Such a context can satisfy the presuppositions of (28) for the following reason. By incrementing it with the negation of the first disjunct, "Bill has not met the King of Slobovia", we get a context which entails that Slobovia is a republic, which is what the second disjunct presupposes. By incrementing the original context with the negation of the second disjunct, we get a context which entails that Slobovia is a monarchy, which is a presupposition for the first disjunct. Given that both constituent sentences in (28) are admissible in their respective local contexts, (28) as a whole is admissible.

If our way of looking at presuppositions is correct, it should be in principle possible to utter (28) to someone who has never even heard of Slobovia and leave it up to him to conclude that the speaker assumes (29). It seems to me that this is a desirable result.

In this paper I have argued that a theory of presuppositions is best looked upon as a theory of constraints on successive contexts in a fully explicit discourse in which the current conversational context satisfies-the-presuppositions-of, or let us say from now on, *admits* the next sentence that increments it. I have outlined a recursive definition of admittance, based on the assumption that we can give a finite list of presuppositions for each simple sentence. In this approach we do not need an explicit projection method for assigning presuppositions to complex sentences. A theory of presuppositions of the kind advocated here attempts to achieve both less and more than has been expected of such a theory: less in the sense that it is not a theory of how ordinary discourse does or ought to proceed; more in the sense that it tries to explain some of the principles that we make use of in communi-cating indirectly and in inferring what someone is committed to, although he did not exactly say it.

ACKNOWLEDGMENTS

Presented at the 1973 Winter Meeting of the Linguistic Society of America in San Diego. This work was supported in part by the 1973 Research Workshop on Formal Pragmatics of Natural Language, sponsored by the Mathematical Social Science Board. I acknowledge with special gratitude the contributions of Stanley Peters to my understanding of the problems in this paper. Any remaining confusions are my own.

NOTES

1. There is some question over whether this notion of presupposition is properly labeled "pragmatic." For Stalnaker (1972, 1973), pragmatic presupposing is a propositional attitude of the speaker. However, I will follow Thomason (1973) and others who would like to reserve the term "presupposes" for relations (semantic or pragmatic) between sentences. The idea that it is important to distinguish in this connection between surface sentences and their logical forms is due to Lakoff (1972, 1973).

2. Peters has pointed out to me that, under certain conditions, (4a) is equivalent to the following projection principle.

$$P_{if \ A \ then \ B} = P_A \cup \{\ulcorner A \supset C \urcorner | C \in P_B\}$$

Peters' principle has the advantage that it assigns the same set of presuppositions to "If A then B" irrespective of any context. Note that this set is not a subset of $P_A \cup P_B$, as required by my initial assumption in (2). Peters' principle says that, for each presupposition of B, "If A then B" presupposes a conditional with that presupposition as the consequent and the logical form of A as the antecedent. In addition, "If A then B" has all of the presuppositions of A. I realize now that some of the complexity in (4a) comes from trying to state the principle in such a way that (2) holds. If this is not worth doing, Peters' way of formulating the rule is superior to mine. However, in the following I will argue that we can just as well do without any explicit projection method at all, hence the choice is not crucial.

3. It appears to me that the only contribution *too* makes to the meaning of a sentence is that it introduces a presupposition whose form depends on the sentence as a whole and the particular constituent *too* focuses on. If this is so, there is no reason to assume that *too* is represented in the logical form of the sentence. As far as the truth conditions are concerned, "Nixon is guilty too" seems equivalent to "Nixon is guilty", therefore, it is possible to assign the same logical form to them. The same point has been raised in Lakoff and Railton (1971) with regard to two-way implicative verbs, such as *manage*, whose only function also seems to be to bring in a presupposition.

4. In simple cases, incrementing a context consists of adding one more logical form to it. If the context entails the negation of what is to be added to it, as in counterfactual conditionals, other changes are needed as well to keep the resulting set consistent. This is a difficult problem, see Lewis (1973) for a general discussion of counterfactuals.

5. It is possible that the principle for disjunctions, and perhaps that for conjunctions as well, should be symmetric. This depends on how we want to deal with sentences like "Either all of Jack's letters have been

help up, or he has not written any" (see Karttunen 1973a; note 11). A symmetric condition for "or" would read [as] follows

X satisfies-the-presuppositions-of "A or B" iff X $\cup$ {~A}
   satisfies-the-presuppositions-of "B" and X $\cup$ {~B}
   satisfies-the-presuppositions-of "A". For "and", substitute "A" for "~A" and "B" for "~B".

6. The same holds in case we choose Peters' principle (see note 2) over (4a). In demonstrating this, what we prove equivalent to (14) is not (11), of course, but that $\{\ulcorner A \supset C \urcorner | C \in P_B\} \subseteq E_X$. This equivalence follows straight-forwardly from the fact that $\ulcorner A \supset C \urcorner \in E_X$ just in case $C \in E_{X \cup A}$.

7. Lakoff has pointed out to me that a notion of local context is also needed for transderivational constraints that make the well-formedness of derivations in which a certain transformation has applied dependent on the context. In compound sentences, it is the local context these constraints must refer to, not the overall conversational context.

8. One of the mistakes in Karttunen (1973a) was the claim that verbs of saying and propositional attitude verbs are all "plugs".

9. Since ordinary negation is a sentential operator of type III, it also follows from (19) that a context satisfies-the-presuppositions-of "Nixon won't stop protecting his aides" just in case it satisfies-the-presuppositions-of "Nixon will stop protecting his aides". This is an important fact, but there is no need to make it part of the definition of pragmatic presupposition, as Thomason (1973) does, presumably for historical reasons because the semantic notion of presupposition is traditionally defined in that way.

10. It is implicit in this treatment that every individual's beliefs are considered to be closed under entailment. I am not sure whether this is a defect.

11. Many things can of course go wrong. First of all, the listener may refuse to go along with the tacit extension that the speaker appears to be suggesting. In case of the classical example: "Have you already stopped beating your wife?" he may have a good reason to balk. The listener may also be unable to comprehend what tacit extension of the current context the speaker has in mind. Some types of presupposition are especially unsuited for conveying anything indirectly. For example, "Nixon is guilty too" is not a good vehicle for suggesting that Agnew is guilty, although the presuppositions of the sentence are satisfied in all contexts where the latter is the case. Finally, the listener may extend the context in some way other than what was intended by the speaker. To what extent we actually can and do make use of such shortcuts depends on pragmatic considerations that go beyond the presuppositions themselves.

Note also that there are certain expressions in current American English that are almost exclusively used to convey matters indirectly, hence it is a moot question whether there is anything indirect about them any more. One is likely never to hear "Don't you realize it's past your bedtime" in a context entailing that the addressee ought to be in bed.

12. I owe this example to an official MIT bulletin about the spring 1973 commencement.

REFERENCES

Davidson, D., and G. Harman (eds.). (1972). *Semantics of Natural Language.* Dordrecht: Reidel.

Fillmore, C. J., and D. T. Langendoen (eds.). (1971). *Studies in Linguistic Semantics.* New York: Holt, Rinehart and Winston.

Green, G. (1968). "On *Too* and *Either,* and Just on *Too* and *Either,* Either." In B. Darden et al. (eds). *Papers From the Fourth Regional Meeting of the Chicago Linguistic Society.* Chicago: University of Chicago Press.

Herzberger, H. G. (1973). "Dimensions of Truth." *Journal of Philosophical Logic* 2:535–556.

Karttunen, L. (1973a). "Presuppositions of Compound Sentences." *Linguistic Inquiry* 4:169–193.

Karttunen, L. (1973b). "Remarks on Presuppositions." In J. Murphy, A. Rogers, and R. Wall (eds.). (1977). *Proceedings of the Texas Conference on Performatives, Presuppositions, and Conversational Implicatures.* Washington, D.C.: Center for Applied Linguistics.

Keenan, E. (1973). "Presupposition in Natural Logic." *The Monist* 57:344–370.

Lakoff, G. (1971). "The Role of Deduction in Grammar." In C. J. Fillmore and D. T. Langendoen (eds.), *Studies in Linguistic Semantics.* New York: Holt, Rinehart and Winston.

Lakoff, G. (1972). "Linguistics and Natural Logic." In D. Davidson and G. Harman (eds.), *Semantics of Natural Language.* Dordrecht: Reidel.

Lakoff, G. (1973). "Pragmatics and Natural Logic." In J. Murphy, A. Rogers, and R. Wall (eds.) (1977). *Proceedings of the Texas Conference on Performatives, Presuppositions, and Conversational Implicatures.* Washington, D.C.: Center for Applied Linguistics.

Lakoff, G., and P. Railton (1971). "Some Types of Presupposition and Entailment in Natural Language." Manuscript.

Langendoen, D. T., and H. B. Savin (1971). "The Projection Problem for Presuppositions." In C. J. Fillmore and D. T. Langendoen (eds.), *Studies in Linguistic Semantics.* New York: Holt, Rinehart and Winston.

Lewis, D. (1973). *Counterfactuals.* Cambridge, Mass.: Harvard University Press.

Liberman, M. (1973). "Alternatives." In *Papers from the Ninth Regional Meeting of the Chicago Linguistic Society.* Chicago: University of Chicago Press.

Morgan, J. L. (1973). "Presupposition and the Representation of Meaning." Ph.D. diss., University of Chicago.

Murphy, J., A. Rogers, and B. Wall (eds.). (1977) *Proceedings of the Texas Conference on Performatives, Presuppositions, and Conversational Implicatures.* Washington, D.C.: Center for Applied Linguistics.

Stalnaker, R. C. (1972). "Pragmatics." In D. Davidson and G. Harman (eds.), *Semantics of Natural Language.* Dordrecht: Reidel.

Stalnaker, R. C. (1973). "Presuppositions." *Journal of Philosophical Logic* 2:447–457.

Thomason, R. H. (1973). "Semantics, Pragmatics, Conversation, and Presupposition." In J. Murphy, A. Rogers, and R. Wall (eds.), (1977). *Proceedings of the Texas Conference on Performatives, Presuppositions, and Conversational Implicatures.* Washington, D.C.: Center for Applied Linguistics.

25

Scorekeeping in a Language Game

DAVID LEWIS

EXAMPLE 1: PRESUPPOSITION[1]

At any stage in a well-run conversation, a certain amount is presupposed. The parties to the conversation take it for granted; or at least they purport to, whether sincerely or just "for the sake of the argument". Presuppositions can be created or destroyed in the course of a conversation. This change is rule-governed, at least up to a point. The presuppositions at time t' depend, in a way about which at least some general principles can be laid down, on the presuppositions at an earlier time t and on the course of the conversation (and nearby events) between t and t'.

Some things that might be said require suitable presuppositions. They are acceptable if the required presuppositions are present; not otherwise. "The king of France is bald" requires the presupposition that France has one king, and one only; "Even George Lakoff could win" requires the presupposition that George is not a leading candidate; and so on.

We need not ask just what sort of unacceptability results when a required presupposition is lacking. Some say falsehood, some say lack

of truth value, some just say that it's the kind of unacceptability that results when a required presupposition is lacking, and some say it might vary from case to case.

Be that as it may, it's not as easy as you might think to say something that will be unacceptable for lack of required presuppositions. Say something that requires a missing presupposition, and straightway that presupposition springs into existence, making what you said acceptable after all. (Or at least, that is what happens if your conversational partners tacitly acquiesce—if no one says "But France has *three* kings!" or "Whadda ya mean, '*even* George'?") That is why it is peculiar to say, out of the blue, "All Fred's children are asleep, and Fred has children." The first part requires and thereby creates a presupposition that Fred has children; so the second part adds nothing to what is already presupposed when it is said; so the second part has no conversational point. It would not have been peculiar to say instead "Fred has children, and all Fred's children are asleep."

I said that presupposition evolves in a more or less rule-governed way during a conversa-

David Lewis, "Scorekeeping in a Language Game," *Journal of Philosophical Language* 8 (1979): 339–359. Copyright © 1979 by D. Reidel Publishing Company. Reprinted by permission of Kluwer Academic Publishers.

tion. Now we can formulate one important governing rule: call it the *rule of accommodation for presupposition.*

If at time *t* something is said that requires presupposition *P* to be acceptable, and if *P* is not presupposed just before *t*, then—*ceteris paribus* and within certain limits—presupposition *P* comes into existence at *t*.

This rule has not yet been very well stated, nor is it the only rule governing the kinematics of presupposition. But let us bear it in mind nevertheless, and move on to other things.

EXAMPLE 2: PERMISSIBILITY[2]

For some reason—coercion, deference, common purpose—two people are both willing that one of them should be under the control of the other. (At least within certain limits, in a certain sphere of action, so long as certain conditions prevail.) Call one the *slave,* the other the *master.* The control is exercised verbally, as follows.

At any stage in the enslavement, there is a boundary between some courses of action for the slave that are permissible, and others that are not. The range of permissible conduct may expand or contract. The master shifts the boundary by saying things to the slave. Since the slave does his best to see to it that his course of action is a permissible one, the master can control the slave by controlling what is permissible.

Here is how the master shifts the boundary. From time to time he says to the slave that such-and-such courses of action are impermissible. Any such statement depends for its truth value on the boundary between what is permissible and what isn't. But if the master says that something is impermissible, and if that would be false if the boundary remained stationary, then straightway the boundary moves inward. The permissible range contracts so that what the master says is true after all. Thereby the master makes courses of action impermissible that used to be permissible. But from time to time also the master relents, and says to the slave that such-and-such courses of action are permissible. Or perhaps he says that some of such-and-such courses of action are permissible, but doesn't say just which ones.

Then the boundary moves outward. The permissible range expands, if need be (and if possible), so that what the master says is true. Thereby the master makes courses of action permissible that used to be impermissible.

The truth of the master's statements about permissibility—one aspect of their acceptability—depends on the location of the boundary. The boundary shifts in a rule-governed way. The rule is as follows; call it the *rule of accommodation for permissibility.*

If at time *t* something is said about permissibility by the master to the slave that requires for its truth the permissibility or impermissibility of certain courses of action, and if just before *t* the boundary is such as to make the master's statement false, then—*ceteris paribus* and within certain limits—the boundary shifts at *t* so as to make the master's statement true.

Again, this is not a very satisfactory formulation. For one thing, the limits and qualifications are left unspecified. But more important, the rule as stated does not say exactly how the boundary is to shift.

What if the master says that some of such-and-such courses of actions are permissible, when none of them were permissible before he spoke. By the rule, some of them must straightway become permissible. Some—but which ones? The ones that were closest to permissibility beforehand, perhaps. Well and good, but now we have a new problem. At every state there is not only a boundary between the permissible and the impermissible, but also a relation of comparative near-permissibility between the courses of action on the impermissible side. Not only do we need rules governing the shifting boundary, but also we need rules to govern the changing relation of comparative near-permissibility. Not only must we say how this relation evolves when the master says something about absolute permissibility, but also we must say how it evolves when he says something—as he might—about comparative near-permissibility. He might say, for instance, that the most nearly permissible courses of action in a class *A* are those in a subclass *A'*; or that some courses of action in class *B* are more nearly permissible than any in class *C*. Again the rule is a rule of accommodation. The relation of comparative near-permissibility changes, if need be, so that what the master says to the slave is true. But again, to say that is not enough. It does not suffice to determine just what the change is. Those were Examples 1 and 2. Examples of what? I'll say shortly; but first, a digression.

SCOREKEEPING IN A BASEBALL GAME

At any stage in a well-run baseball game, there is a septuple of numbers $\langle r_v, r_h, h, i, s, b, o \rangle$ which I shall call the *score* of that game at that stage. We recite the score as follows: the visiting team has r_v runs, the home team has r_h runs, it is the hth half (h being 1 or 2) of the ith inning; there are s strikes, b balls, and o outs. (In another terminology, the score is only the initial pair $\langle r_v, r_h \rangle$, but I need a word for the entire septuple.) A possible codification of the rules of baseball would consist of rules of four different sorts.

(1) *Specifications of the kinematics of score.* Initially, the score is $\langle 0, 0, 1, 1, 0, 0, 0 \rangle$. Thereafter, if at time t the score is **s**, and if between time t and time t' the players behave in manner m, then at time t' the score is **s**′, where **s**′ is determined in a certain way by **s** and **m**.

(2) *Specifications of correct play.* If at time t the score is **s**, and if between time t and time t' the players behave in manner m, then the players have behaved incorrectly. (Correctness depends on score: what is correct play after two strikes differs from what is correct play after three.) What is not incorrect play according to these rules is correct.

(3) *Directive requiring correct play.* All players are to behave, throughout the game, in such a way that play is correct.

(4) *Directives concerning score.* Players are to strive to make the score evolve in certain directions. Members of the visiting team try to make r_v large and r_h small, members of the home team try to do the opposite.

(We could dispense with rules of sorts (2) and (3) by adding an eighth component to the score which, at any stage of the game, measures the amount of incorrect play up to that stage. Specifications of correct play are then included among the specifications of the kinematics of score, and the directive requiring correct play becomes one of the directives concerning score.)

Rules of sorts (1) and (2) are sometimes called *constitutive rules.* They are said to be akin to definitions, though they do not have the form of definitions. Rules of sorts (3) and (4) are called *regulative rules.* They are akin to the straightforward directives "No smoking!" or "Keep left!"

We could explain this more fully, as follows. Specifications of sorts (1) and (2) are not themselves definitions of "score" and "correct play". But they are consequences of reasonable definitions. Further, there is a systematic way to construct the definitions, given the specifications. Suppose we wish to define the *score function:* the function from game-stages to septuples of numbers that gives the score at every stage. The specifications of the kinematics of score, taken together, tell us that the score function evolves in such-and-such way. We may then simply define the score function as that function which evolves in such-and-such way. If the kinematics of score are well specified, then there is one function, and one only, that evolves in the proper way; and if so, then the score function evolves in the proper way if and only if the suggested definition of it is correct. Once we have defined the score function, we have thereby defined the score and all its components at any stage. There are two outs at a certain stage of a game, for instance, if and only if the score function assigns to that game-stage a septuple whose seventh component is the number 2.

Turn next to the specifications of correct play. Taken together, they tell us that correct play occurs at a game-stage if and only if the players' behavior at that stage bears such-and-such relation to score at that stage. This has the form of an explicit definition of correct play in terms of current behavior. If current score has already been defined in terms of the history of the players' behavior up to now, in the way just suggested, then we have defined correct play in terms of current and previous behavior.

Once score and correct play are defined in terms of the players' behavior, then we may eliminate the defined terms in the directive requiring correct play and the directives concerning score. Thanks to the definitions constructed from the constitutive rules, the regulative rules become simply directives to strive to see to it that one's present behavior bears a certain rather complicated relation to the history of the players' behavior in previous stages of the game. A player might attempt to conform to such a directive for various reasons: contractual obligation, perhaps, or a conventional understanding with his fellow players based on their common interest in enjoying a proper game.

The rules of baseball could in principle be formulated as straightforward directives concerning behavior, without the aid of definable terms for score and its components. Or they could be formulated as explicit definitions of the score function, the components of score, and correct play, followed by directives in which the newly defined terms appear. It is easy to see why neither of these methods of formulation has found favor. The first method would pack the entire rulebook into each directive; the second would pack the entire rulebook into a single preliminary explicit definition. Understandably averse to very long sentences, we do better to proceed in our more devious way.

There is an alternative analysis—the baseball equivalent of operationalism or legal realism. Instead of appealing to constitutive rules, we might instead claim that the score is, by definition, whatever some scoreboard says it is. Which scoreboard? Various answers are defensible: maybe the visible scoreboard with its arrays of light bulbs, maybe the invisible scoreboard in the head umpire's head, maybe the many scoreboards in many heads to the extent that they agree. No matter. On any such view, the specifications of the kinematics of score have a changed status. No longer are they constitutive rules akin to definitions. Rather, they are empirical generalizations, subject to exceptions, about the ways in which the players' behavior tends to cause changes on the authoritative scoreboard. Under this analysis, it is impossible that this scoreboard fails to give the score. What is possible is that the score is an abnormal and undesired relation to its causes, for which someone may perhaps be blamed.

I do not care to say which analysis is right for baseball as it is actually played. Perhaps the question has no determinate answer, or perhaps it has different answers for formal and informal baseball. I only wish to distinguish the two alternatives, noting that both are live options.

This ends the digression. Now I want to propose some general theses about language—theses that were examplified by Examples 1 and 2, and that will be exemplified also by several other examples.

CONVERSATIONAL SCORE

With any stage in a well-run conversation, or other process of linguistic interaction, there are associated many things analogous to the components of a baseball score. I shall therefore speak of them collectively as the *score* of that conversation at that stage. The points of analogy are as follows.

(1) Like the components of a baseball score, the components of a conversational score at a given stage are abstract entities. They may not be numbers, but they are other set-theoretic constructs: sets of presupposed propositions, boundaries between permissible and impermissible courses of action, or the like.

(2) What play is correct depends on the score. Sentences depend for their truth value, or for their acceptability in other respects, on the components of conversational score at the stage of conversation when they are uttered. Not only aspects of acceptability of an uttered sentence may depend on score. So may other semantic properties that play a role in determining aspects of acceptability. For instance, the constituents of an uttered sentence—subsentences, names, predicates, etc.—may depend on the score for their intension or extension.

(3) Score evolves in a more-or-less rule-governed way. There are rules that specify the kinematics of score:

If at time t the conversational score is s, and if between time t and time t' the course of conversation is c, then at time t' the score is s', where s' is determined in a certain way by s and c.

Or at least:

... then at time t' the score is some member of the class S of possible scores, where S is determined in a certain way by s and c.

(4) The conversationalists may conform to directives, or may simply desire, that they strive to steer certain components of the conversational score in certain directions. Their efforts may be cooperative, as when all participants in a discussion try to increase the amount that all of them willingly presuppose. Or there may be conflict, as when each of two debaters tries to get his opponent to grant him—to join with him in presupposing— parts of his case, and to give away parts of the contrary case.

(5) To the extent that conversational score is determined, given the history of the conversation and the rules that specify its kinematics, these rules can be regarded as constitutive rules akin to definitions. Again, constitutive rules could be traded in for explicit definitions: the conversational score function could be defined as that function from conversation-stages to n-tuples of suitable entities that evolves in the specified way.

Alternatively, conversational score might be operationally defined in terms of mental scoreboards—some suitable attitudes—of the parties to the conversation. The rules specifying the kinematics of conversational score then become empirical generalizations, subject to exceptions, about the causal dependence of what the scoreboards register on the history of the conversation.

In the case of baseball score, either approach to the definition of score and the status of the rules seems satisfactory. In the case of conversational score, on the other hand, both approaches seem to meet with difficulties. If, as seems likely, the rules specifying the kinematics of conversational score are seriously incomplete, then often there may be many candidates for the score function, different but all evolving in the specified way. But also it seems difficult to say, without risk of circularity, what are the mental representations that comprise the conversationalists' scoreboards.

It may be best to adopt a third approach— a middle way, drawing on both the alternatives previously considered. Conversational score is, by definition, whatever the mental scoreboards say it is; but we refrain from try-ing to say just what the conversationalists' mental scoreboards are. We assume that some or other mental representations are present that play the role of a scoreboard, in the following sense: what they register depends on the history of the conversation in the way that score should according to the rules. The rules specifying the kinematics of score thereby specify the role of a scoreboard; the scoreboard is whatever best fills this role; and the score is whatever this scoreboard registers. The rules specifying the kinematics of score are to some extent constitutive, but on this third approach they enter only in a roundabout way into the definition of score. It is no harm if they underdetermine the evolution of score, and it is possible that score sometimes evolves in a way that violates the rules.

RULES OF ACCOMMODATION

There is one big difference between baseball score and conversational score. Suppose the batter walks to first base after only three balls. His behavior would be correct play if there were four balls rather than three. That's just too bad—his behavior does not at all make it the case that there *are* four balls and his behavior *is* correct. Baseball has no rule of accommodation to the effect that if a fourth ball is required to make correct the play that occurs, then that very fact suffices to change the score so that straightway there are four balls.

Language games are different. As I hope my examples will show, conversational score does tend to evolve in such a way as is required in order to make whatever occurs count as correct play. Granted, that is not invariable but only a tendency. Granted also, conversational score changes for other reasons as well. (As when something conspicuous happens at the scene of a conversation, and straightway it is presupposed that it happened.) Still, I suggest that many components of conversational score obey rules of accommodation, and that these rules figure prominently among the rules governing the kinematics of conversational score.

Recall our examples. Example 1: presupposition evolves according to a rule of accommodation specifying that any presuppositions that are required by what is said straightway come into existence, provided that nobody objects. Example 2: permissibility evolves according to a rule of accommodation specifying that the boundaries of the permissible range of conduct shift to make true whatever is said about them, provided that what is said is said by the master to the slave, and provided that there does exist some shift that would make what he says true. Here is a general scheme for rules of accommodation for conversational score.

If at time t something is said that requires component s_n of conversational score to have a value in the range r if what is said is to be true, or otherwise acceptable; and if s_n does not have a value in the range r just before t; and if such-and-such further conditions hold; then at t the score-component s_n takes some value in the range r.

Once we have this scheme in mind, I think we will find many instances of it. In the rest of this paper I shall consider some further examples. I shall have little that is new to say about the individual examples. My interest is in the common pattern that they exhibit.

EXAMPLE 3: DEFINITE DESCRIPTIONS[3]

It is not true that a definite description "the F" denotes x if and only if x is the one and only F in existence. Neither is it true that "the F" denotes x if and only if x is the one and only F in some contextually determined domain of discourse. For consider this sentence: "The pig is grunting, but the pig with floppy ears is not grunting" (Lewis). And this: "The dog got in a fight with another dog" (McCawley). They could be true. But for them to be true, "the pig" or "the dog" must denote one of two pigs or dogs, both of which belong to the domain of discourse.

The proper treatment of descriptions must be more like this: "the F" denotes x if and only if x is the most salient F in the domain of discourse, according to some contextually determined salience ranking. The first of our two sentences means that the most salient pig is grunting but the most salient pig with floppy ears is not. The second means that the most salient dog got in a fight with some less salient dog.

(I shall pass over some complications. Never mind what happens if two F's are tied for maximum salience, or if no F is at all salient. More important, I shall ignore the possibility that something might be highly salient in one of its guises, but less salient in another. Possibly we really need to appeal to a salience ranking not of individuals but rather of individuals-in-guises—that is, of individual concepts.)

There are various ways for something to gain salience. Some have to do with the course of conversation, others do not. Imagine yourself with me as I write these words. In the room is a cat, Bruce, who has been making himself very salient by dashing madly about. He is the only cat in the room, or in sight, or in earshot. I start to speak to you:

The cat is in the carton. The cat will never meet our other cat, because our other cat lives in New Zealand. Our New Zealand cat lives with the Cresswells. And there he'll stay, because Miriam would be sad if the cat went away.

At first, "the cat" denotes Bruce, he being the most salient cat for reasons having nothing to do with the course of conversation. If I want to talk about Albert, our New Zealand cat, I have to say "our other cat" or "our New Zealand cat." But as I talk more and more about Albert, and not any more about Bruce, I raise Albert's salience by conversational means. Finally, in the last sentence of my monologue, I am in a position to say "the cat" and thereby denote not Bruce but rather the newly-most-salient cat Albert.

The ranking of comparative salience, I take it, is another component of conversational score. Denotation of definite descriptions is score-dependent. Hence so is the truth of sentences containing such descriptions, which is one aspect of the acceptability of those sentences. Other aspects of acceptability in turn are score-dependent: non-triviality, for one, and possibility of warranted assertion, for another.

One rule, among others, that governs the kinematics of salience is a rule of accommodation. Suppose my monologue has left Albert more salient than Bruce; but the next thing I say is "The cat is going to pounce on you!" If Albert remains most salient and "the cat" denotes the most salient cat, then what I say is patently false: Albert cannot pounce all the way from New Zealand to Princeton. What I have said requires for its acceptability that "the cat" denote Bruce, and hence that Bruce be once again more salient than Albert. If what I say requires that, then straightway it is so. By saying what I did, I have made Bruce more salient than Albert. If next I say "The cat prefers moist food", that is true if Bruce prefers moist food, even if Albert doesn't.

The same thing would have happened if instead I had said "The cat is out of the carton" or "The cat has gone upstairs". Again what I say is unacceptable unless the salience ranking shifts so that Bruce rises above Albert, and hence so that 'the cat' again denotes Bruce. The difference is in the type of unacceptability that would ensue without the shift. It is trivially true, hence not worth saying, that Albert is out of the carton. ("The carton" denotes the same carton as before; nothing has been done to raise the salience of any carton in New Zealand.) It may be true or it may be false that Albert has gone upstairs in the Cresswells' house in New Zealand. But I have no way of knowing, so I have no business saying that he has.

We can formulate a *rule of accommodation for comparative salience* more or less as follows. It is best to speak simply of unacceptability, since it may well be that the three sorts of unacceptability I have mentioned are not the only sorts that can give rise to a shift in salience.

If at time t something is said that requires, if it is to be acceptable, that x be more salient than y; and if, just before t, x is no more salient than y; then—*ceteris paribus* and within certain limits—at t, x becomes more salient than y.

Although a rule of accommodation, such as this one, states that shifts of score take place when they are needed to preserve acceptability, we may note that the preservation is imperfect. It is not good conversational practice to rely too heavily on rules of accommodation. The monologue just considered illustrates this. Because "the cat" denotes first Bruce, then Albert, then Bruce again, what I say is to some extent confusing and hard to follow. But even if my monologue is not perfectly acceptable, its flaws are much less serious than the flaws that are averted by shifts of

salience in accordance with our rule of accommodation. Confusing shifts of salience and reference are not as bad as falsity, trivial truth, or unwarranted assertion.

(It is worth mentioning another way to shift comparative salience by conversational means. I may say "A cat is on the lawn" under circumstances in which it is apparent to all parties to the conversation that there is some one particular cat that is responsible for the truth of what I say, and for my saying it. Perhaps I am looking out the window, and you rightly presume that I said what I did because I saw a cat; and further (since I spoke in the singular) that I saw only one. What I said was an existential quantification; hence, strictly speaking, it involves no reference to any particular cat. Nevertheless it raises the salience of the cat that made me say it. Hence this newly-most-salient cat may be denoted by brief definite descriptions, or by pronouns, in subsequent dialogue: "No, it's on the sidewalk." "Has Bruce noticed the cat?" As illustrated, this may happen even if the speaker contradicts my initial existential statement. Thus although indefinite descriptions—that is, idioms of existential quantification—are not themselves referring expressions, they may raise the salience of particular individuals in such a way as to pave the way for referring expressions that follow.)

EXAMPLE 4: COMING AND GOING[4]

Coming is a movement toward a point of reference. Going is movement away from it. Sometimes the point of reference is fixed by the location of speaker and hearer, at the time of conversation or the time under discussion. But sometimes not. In third-person narrative, whether fact or fiction, the chosen point of reference may have nothing to do with the speaker's or the hearer's location.

One way to fix the point of reference at the beginning of a narrative, or to shift it later, is by means of a sentence that describes the direction of some movement both with respect to the point of reference and in some other way. "The beggars are coming to town" requires for its acceptability, and perhaps even for its truth, that the point of reference be in town. Else the beggars' townward movement is not properly called "coming". This sentence can be used to fix or to shift the point of reference. When it is said, straightway the point of reference is in town where it is required to be. Thereafter, unless something is done to shift it elsewhere, coming is movement toward town and going is movement away. If later we are told that when the soldiers came the beggars went, we know who ended up in town and who did not.

Thus the point of reference in narrative is a component of conversational score, governed by a rule of accommodation. Note that the rule must provide for two sorts of changes. The point of reference may simply go from one place to another, as is required by the following text:

When the beggars came to town, the rich folk went to the shore. But soon the beggars came after them, so they went home.

But also the point of reference is usually not fully determinate in its location. It may become more or less determinate, as is required by the following:

After the beggars came to town, they held a meeting. All of them came to the square. Afterwards they went to another part of town.

The first sentence puts the point of reference in town, but not in any determinate part of town. The second sentence increases its determinacy by putting it in the square. The initial fixing of the point of references is likewise an increase in determinacy—the point of reference starts out completely indeterminate and becomes at least somewhat more definitely located.

EXAMPLE 5: VAGUENESS[5]

If Fred [has] a borderline case of baldness, the sentence "Fred is bald" may have no determinate truth value. Whether it is true depends on where you draw the line. Relative to some perfectly reasonable ways of drawing a precise boundary between bald and not-bald, the sentence is true. Relative to other delineations, no less reasonable, it is false. Nothing in our use of language makes one of these delineations right and all the others wrong. We cannot pick a delineation once and for all (not if we are interested in ordinary language), but must consider the entire range of reasonable delineations.

If a sentence is true over the entire range, true no matter how we draw the line, surely we are entitled to treat it simply as true. But also we treat a sentence more or less as if it is simply true, if it is true over a large enough part of the range of delineations of its vagueness. (For short: if it is *true enough*.) If a sentence is true enough (according to our beliefs) we are willing to assert it, assent to it without qualification, file it away among our stocks of beliefs, and so forth. Mostly we do not get into any trouble this way. (But sometimes we do, as witness the paradoxes that arise because truth-preserving reasoning does not always preserve the property of being true enough.)

When is a sentence true enough? Which are the "large enough" parts of the range of delineations of its vagueness? This is itself a vague matter. More important for our present purposes, it is something that depends on context. What is true enough on one occasion is not true enough on another. The standards of precision in force are different from one conversation to another, and may change in the course of a single conversation. Austin's "France is hexagonal" is a good example of a sentence that is true enough for many contexts, but not true enough for many others. Under low standards of precision it is acceptable. Raise the standards and it loses its acceptability.

Taking standards of precision as a component of conversational score, we once more find a rule of accommodation at work. One way to change the standards is to say something that would be unacceptable if the standards remained unchanged. If you say "Italy is boot-shaped" and get away with it, low standards are required and the standards fall if need be; thereafter "France is hexagonal" is true enough. But if you deny that Italy is boot-shaped, pointing out the differences, what you have said requires high standards under which "France is hexagonal" is far from true enough.

I take it that the rule of accommodation can go both ways. But for some reason raising of standards goes more smoothly than lowering. If the standards have been high, and something is said that is true enough only under lowered standards, and nobody objects, then indeed the standards are shifted down. But what is said, although true enough under the lowered standards, may still seem imperfectly acceptable. Raising of standards, on the other hand, manages to seem commendable even when we know that it interferes with our conversational purpose. Because of this asymmetry, a player of language games who is so inclined may get away with it if he tries to raise the standards of precision as high as possible—so high, perhaps, that no material object whatever is hexagonal.

Peter Unger has argued that hardly anything is flat. Take something you claim is flat; he will find something else and get you to agree that it is even flatter. You think the pavement is flat— but how can you deny that your desk is flatter? But "flat" is an *absolute term:* it is inconsistent to say that something is flatter than something that is flat. Having agreed that your desk is flatter than the pavement, you must concede that the pavement is not flat after all. Perhaps you now claim that your desk is flat; but doubtless Unger can think of something that you will agree is even flatter than your desk. And so it goes.

Some might dispute Unger's premise that "flat" is an absolute term; but on that score it seems to me that Unger is right. What he says is inconsistent does indeed sound that way. I take this to mean that on no delineation of the correlative vagueness of "flatter" and "flat" is it true that something is flatter than something that is flat.

The right response to Unger, I suggest, is that he is changing the score on you. When he says that the desk is flatter than the pavement, what he says is acceptable only under raised standards of precision. Under the original standards the bumps on the pavement were too small to be relevant either to the question whether the pavement is flat or to the question whether the pavement is flatter than the desk. Since what he says requires raised standards, the standards accommodatingly rise. Then it is no longer true enough that the pavement is flat. That does not alter the fact that it *was* true enough *in its original context.* "The desk is flatter than the pavement" said under raised standards does not contradict "The pavement is flat" said under unraised standards, any more than "It is morning" said in the morning contradicts "It is afternoon" said in the after-

noon. Nor has Unger shown in any way that the new context is more legitimate than the old one. He can indeed create an unusual context in which hardly anything can acceptably be called "flat", but he has not thereby cast any discredit on the more usual contexts in which lower standards of precision are in force.

In parallel fashion Unger observes, I think correctly, that "certain" is an absolute term; from this he argues that hardly ever is anyone certain of anything. A parallel response is in order. Indeed the rule of accommodation permits Unger to create a context in which all that he says is true, but that does not show that there is anything whatever wrong with the claims to certainty that we make in more ordinary contexts. It is no fault in a context that we can move out of it.

EXAMPLE 6: RELATIVE MODALITY[6]

The "can" and "must" of ordinary language do not often express absolute ("logical" or "metaphysical") possibility. Usually they express various relative modalities. Not all the possibilities there are enter into consideration. If we ignore those possibilities that violate laws of nature, we get the physical modalities; if we ignore those that are known not to obtain, we get the epistemic modalities; if we ignore those that ought not to obtain—doubtless including actuality—we get the deontic modalities; and so on. That suggests that "can" and "must" are ambiguous. But on that hypothesis, as Kratzer has convincingly argued, the alleged senses are altogether too numerous. We do better to think of our modal verbs as unambiguous but relative. Sometimes the relativity is made explicit. Modifying phrases like "in view of what is known" or "in view of what custom requires" may be present to indicate just which possibilities should be ignored.

But sometimes no such phrase is present. Then context must be our guide. The boundary between the relevant possibilities and the ignored ones (formally, the accessibility relation) is a component of conversational score, which enters into the truth conditions of sentences with "can" or "must" or other modal verbs. It may change in the course of conversation. A modifying phrase "in view of such-and-such" does not only affect the sentence in which it appears, but also remains in force until further notice to govern the interpretation of modal verbs in subsequent sentences.

This boundary may also shift in accordance with a rule of accommodation. Suppose I am talking with some elected official about the ways he might deal with an embarrassment. So far, we have been ignoring those possibilities that would be political suicide for him. He says: "You see, I must either destroy the evidence or else claim that I did it to stop Communism. What else can I do?" I rudely reply: "There is one other possibility—you can put the public interest first for once!" That would be false if the boundary between relevant and ignored possibilities remained stationary. But it is not false in its context, for hitherto ignored possibilities come into consideration and make it true. And the boundary, once shifted outward, stays shifted. If he protests "I can't do that", he is mistaken.

Take another example. The commonsensical epistemologist says: "I *know* the cat is in the carton—there he is before my eyes—I just *can't* be wrong about that!" The sceptic replies: "You might be the victim of a deceiving demon." Thereby he brings into consideration possibilities hitherto ignored, else what he says would be false. The boundary shifts outward so that what he says is true. Once the boundary is shifted, the commonsensical epistemologist must concede defeat. And yet he was not in any way wrong when he laid claim to infallible knowledge. What he said was true with respect to the score as it then was.

We get the impression that the sceptic, or the rude critic of the elected official, has the last word. Again this is because the rule of accommodation is not fully reversible. For some reason, I know not what, the boundary readily shifts outward if what is said requires it, but does not so readily shift inward if what is said requires that. Because of this asymmetry, we may think that what is true with respect to the outward-shifted boundary must be somehow more true than what is true with respect to the original boundary. I see no reason to respect this impression. Let us hope, by all means, that the advance toward truth is irreversible. That is no reason to think that just any change that resists reversal is an advance toward truth.

EXAMPLE 7: PERFORMATIVES[7]

Suppose we are unpersuaded by Austin's contention that explicit performatives have no truth value. Suppose also that we wish to respect the seeming parallelism of form between a performative like "I hereby name this ship the *Generalissimo Stalin*" and such non-performative statements as "Fred thereby named that ship the *President Nixon*". Then we shall find it natural to treat the performative, like the non-performative, as a sentence with truth conditions. It is true, on a given occasion of its utterance, if and only if the speaker brings it about, by means of that very utterance, that the indicated ship begins to bear the name "Generalissimo Stalin". If the circumstances are felicitous, then the speaker does indeed bring it about, by means of his utterance, that the ship begins to bear the name. The performative sentence is therefore true on any occasion of its felicitous utterance. In Lemmon's phrase, it is a sentence verifiable by its (felicitous) use.

When the ship gets its name and the performative is verified by its use, what happens may be described as a change in conversational score governed by a rule of accommodation. The relevant component of score is the relation that pairs ships with their names. The rule of accommodation is roughly as follows.

If at time t something is said that requires for its truth that ship s bear name n; and if s does not bear n just before t; and if the form of circumstances of what is said satisfy certain conditions of felicity; then s begins at t to bear n.

Our performative sentence does indeed require for its truth that the indicated ship bear the name "Generalissimo Stalin" at the time of utterance. Therefore, when the sentence is felicitously uttered, straightway the ship bears the name.

The sentence has other necessary conditions of truth: the ship must not have borne the name beforehand, the speaker must bring it about that the ship begins to bear the name, and he must bring it about by uttering the sentence. On any felicitous occasion of utterance, these further conditions take care of themselves. Our rule of accommodation is enough to explain why the sentence is verified by its felicitous use, despite the fact that the rule deals only with part of what it takes to make the sentence true.

A similar treatment could be given of many other performatives. In some cases the proposal may seem surprising. "With this ring I thee wed" is verified by its felicitous use, since the marriage relation is a component of conversational score governed by a rule of accommodation. Is marriage then a *linguistic* phenomenon? Of course not, but that was not implied. The lesson of performatives, on any theory, is that use of language blends into other social practices. We should not assume that a change of conversational score has its impact only within, or by way of, the realm of language. Indeed, we have already seen another counterexample: the case of permissibility, considered as Example 2.

EXAMPLE 8: PLANNING

Suppose that you and I are making a plan—let us say, a plan to steal some plutonium from a reprocessing plant and make a bomb of it. As we talk, our plan evolves. Mostly it grows more and more complete. Sometimes, however, parts that had been definite are revised, or at least opened for reconsideration.

Much as some things said in ordinary conversation require suitable presuppositions, so some things we say in the course of our planning require, for their acceptability, that the plan contain suitable provisions. If I say "Then you drive the getaway car up to the side gate", that is acceptable only if the plan includes provision for a getaway car. That might or might not have been part of the plan already. If not, it may become part of the plan just because it is required by what I said. (As usual the process is defeasible. You can keep the getaway car out of the plan, for the time being at least, by saying "Wouldn't we do better with mopeds?") The plan is a component of conversational score. The rules governing its evolution parallel the rules governing the kinematics of presupposition, and they include a rule of accommodation.

So good is the parallel between plan and presupposition that we might well ask if our plan simply *is* part of what we presuppose. Call it that if you like, but there is a distinction to be made. We might take for granted, or

purport to take for granted, that our plan will be carried out. Then we would both plan and presuppose that we are going to steal the plutonium. But we might not. We might be making our plan not in order to carry it out, but rather in order to show that the plant needs better security. Then plan and presupposition might well conflict. We plan to steal the plutonium, all the while presupposing that we will not. And indeed our planning may be interspersed with commentary that requires presuppositions contradicting the plan. "Then I'll shoot the guard (I'm glad I won't really do that) while you smash the floodlights." Unless we distinguish plan from presupposition (or distinguish two levels of presupposition) we must think of presuppositions as constantly disappearing and reappearing throughout such a conversation.

The distinction between plan and presupposition is not the distinction between what we purport to take for granted and what we really do. While planning that we will steal the plutonium and presupposing that we will not, we might take for granted neither that we will nor that we won't. Each of us might secretly hope to recruit the other to the terrorist cause and carry out the plan after all.

One and the same sentence may require, and if need be create, both provisions of the plan and presuppositions. "Then you drive the getaway car up to the side gate" requires both a getaway car and a side gate. The car is planned for. The gate is more likely presupposed.

ACKNOWLEDGMENTS

I am doubly grateful to Robert Stalnaker: first, for his treatment of presupposition, here summarized as Example 1, which I have taken as the prototype for parallel treatments of other topics; and second, for valuable comments on a previous version of this paper. I am also much indebted to Stephen Isard, who discusses many of the phenomena that I consider here in his 'Changing the Context' in Edward L. Keenan, ed., *Formal Semantics of Natural Language* (Cambridge University Press, 1974). Proposals along somewhat the same lines as mine are to be found in Thomas T. Ballmer, 'Einführung und Kontrolle von Diskurswelter', in Dieter Wunderlich, ed., *Linguistische Pragmatik* (Athenäum-Verlag, 1972), and Ballmer, *Logical Grammar: With Special Consideration of Topics in Context Change* (North-Holland, 1978).

An early version of this paper was presented to the Vacation School in Logic at Victoria University of Wellington in August 1976; I thank the New Zealand–United States Educational Foundation for research support on that occasion. The paper also was presented at a workshop on pragmatics and conditionals at the University of Western Ontario in May 1978, and at a colloquium on semantics at Konstanz University in September 1978.

NOTES

1. This treatment of presupposition is taken from two papers of Robert Stalnaker: 'Presuppositions,' *Journal of Philosophical Logic* 2 (1973), 447–457, and 'Pragmatic Presuppositions', in Milton K. Munitz and Peter K. Unger, eds., *Semantics and Philosophy* (New York University Press, 1974), pp. 197–213. [Reprinted in this volume, Chapter 27]

2. This treatment of permissibility is discussed more fully in my paper 'A Problem about Permission', in Esa Saarinen et al., *Essays in Honour of Jaakko Hintikka* (Reidel).

3. Definite descriptions governed by salience are discussed in my *Counterfactuals* (Blackwell, 1973), pp. 111–117; and in James McCawley, 'Presupposition and Discourse Structure', in David Denneen and Choon-Kyu Oh, eds., *Syntax and Semantics,* Vol. 11 (Academic Press, 1979). A similar treatment of demonstratives is found in Isard, *op. cit.*

Manfred Pinkal, 'How to Refer with Vague Descriptions' (presented at the Konstanz colloquium on semantics, September 1978) notes a further complication: if some highly salient things are borderline cases of *F*-hood, degree of *F*-hood and salience may trade off.

Indefinite descriptions that pave the way for referring expressions are discussed in Charles Chastain, 'Reference and Context', *Minnesota Studies in the Philosophy of Science* 7 (1975), 194–269, and in Saul Kripke, 'Speaker's Reference and Semantic Reference', *Midwest Studies in Philosophy* 2 (1977), 255–276. [Reprinted in this volume, Chapter 5]

4. See Charles Fillmore, 'How to Know Whether You're Coming or Going', in Karl Hyldgaard-Jensen, ed., *Linguistik 1971* (Athenäum-Verlag, 1972), and 'Pragmatics and the Description of Discourse', in Siegfried J. Schmidt, ed., *Pragmatik/Pragmatics II* (Wilhelm Fink Verlag, 1976).

5. See the treatment of vagueness in my 'General Semantics', *Synthese* 22 (1970), 18–67. For arguments that hardly anything is flat or certain, see Peter Unger, *Ignorance* (Oxford University Press, 1975), pp. 65–68. For another example of accommodating shifts in resolution of vagueness, see the discussion of backtracking counterfactuals in my 'Counterfactual Dependence and Time's Arrow', *Noûs* 13 (1979).

6. See Angelika Kratzer, 'What "Must" and "Can" Must and Can Mean', *Linguistics and Philosophy* 1 (1977), 337–355. The accessibility semantics considered here is equivalent to a slightly restricted form of Kratzer's semantics for relative modality.

Knowledge and irrelevant possibilities of error are discussed in Alvin I. Goldman, 'Discrimination and Perceptual Knowledge', *Journal of Philosophy* 73 (1976), 771–791.

7. See J. L. Austin, 'Performative Utterances', in his *Philosophical Papers* (Oxford University Press, 1961) for the original discussion of performatives. For treatments along the lines here preferred, see E. J. Lemmon, 'On Sentences Verifiable by Their Use', *Analysis* 22 (1962), 86–89; Ingemar Hedenius, 'Performatives', *Theoria* 29 (1963), 1–22; and Lennart Aqvist, *Performatives and Verifiability by the Use of Language* (Filosofiska Studier, Uppsala University, 1972). Isard *(op. cit.)* suggests as I do that performative utterances are akin to other utterances that 'change the context'.

26

How Presuppositions Are Inherited:
A Solution to the Projection Problem

SCOTT SOAMES

1. INTRODUCTION

It isn't Lauri Karttunen, or Stan Peters, or Gerald Gazdar who has solved the projection problem for presuppositions. In saying this, I am *asserting* that Lauri and Stan and Gerald haven't solved the projection problem, and *presupposing* that someone has. I am also giving an example of the problem I wish to discuss.

The example I gave was the negation of the positive cleft sentence (1).

(1) It is Lauri Karttunen or Stan Peters or Gerald Gazdar who has solved the projection problem for presuppositions.

Now, it is a fact about cleft sentences of the form (2) that they regularly give rise to presuppositions of the form (3):

(2) It was NP who VP^{ed}

(3) Someone (something) has VP^{ed}

Moreover, it is a fact about presupposition that the grammatical negation of a sentence typically gives rise to the presuppositions of its positive counterpart. Thus, utterances of both (1) and (4) presuppose (5).

(4) It isn't Lauri Karttunen or Stan Peters or Gerald Gazdar who has solved the projection problem for presuppositions.

(5) Someone has solved the projection problem.

One way of thinking about this is to see the presupposition of the positive sentence as *projected onto,* and, hence, *inherited by,* utterances of its negative counterpart. Such projection is by no means limited to negation. Typically, utterances of interrogatives, epistemic modals, indicative conditionals, disjunctions, conjunctions, and sentences with certain complementizable verbs inherit the presuppositions of their sentential constituents. This can be seen by comparing the sentences in (6) with those in (7).

(6) a. Maybe it's Lauri who has solved the projection problem.
   b. Either it is Lauri who has solved the projection problem or they have awarded the Nobel Prize for Linguistics to the wrong person.
   c. If the projection problem is as crucial to the study of presupposition as they say it is, then it is probably Lauri who has solved it.
   d. That it is Lauri who has solved the projection problem isn't very likely.

Scott Soames, "How Presuppositions Are Inherited: A Solution to the Projection Problem," *Linguistic Inquiry* 13 (1982): 483–545. Copyright © 1982 by The Massachusetts Institute of Technology. Reprinted by permission of The MIT Press.

(7) a. Maybe Lauri has solved the projection problem.
b. Either Lauri has solved the projection problem, or they have awarded the Nobel Prize for Linguistics to the wrong person.
c. If the projection problem is as central to the study of presupposition as they say it is, then Lauri has probably solved it.
d. That Lauri has solved the projection problem isn't very likely.

The difference between these two sets of sentences is that (6a–d) contain the cleft sentence (8) as a sentential constituent, whereas (7a–d) contain its noncleft counterpart (9).

(8) It is Lauri who has solved the projection problem.

(9) Lauri has solved the projection problem.

Although (8) and (9) both entail (5), only (8) presupposes it. The utterances in (6) inherit this presupposition. Those in (7) have nothing to inherit.

This sort of projection is all but ubiquitous. Standardly, presuppositions of a sentential constituent become presuppositions of an utterance of the whole sentence, of which the constituent is a part. Standardly, but not always. For example, utterances of the sentences in (10) do not presuppose (5), even though they contain constituents that do.

(10) a. If the problem has been solved, then it is Lauri who solved it.
b. Someone has solved the problem and it's Lauri who has solved it.
c. Either it is Lauri who has solved the problem or the problem hasn't been solved.

The contrast between these examples and those in (6) gives rise to three fundamental questions which, in broadest terms, make up the projection problem.

Q_1. *Which* utterances inherit the presuppositions of their constituents and which do not?

Q_2. *Why* do some utterances inherit presuppositions whereas others do not?

Q_3. *What sort* of phenomenon is presupposition projection—semantic, pragmatic, conversational, or a combination of these?

My aim is to answer Question 1 by producing a descriptively adequate mechanism for predicting presuppositions, and to answer Questions 2 and 3 by relating the descriptive apparatus to a model of discourse which explains presuppositions in terms of broader conversational goals and strategies.[1]

2. DEFINING PRESUPPOSITION

Accomplishing these tasks requires first a little more precision regarding what it means to say that a speaker, utterance, or sentence presupposes something.

(11) *Speaker Presupposition*
A member S of a conversation presupposes a proposition P at a time t iff at t S believes or assumes
a. P;
b. that the other members of the conversation also believe or assume P; and
c. that the other members of the conversation recognize that S believes or assumes (a) and (b).

Roughly speaking, a person presupposes a proposition at a given point in a conversation just in case he believes that proposition to be one that the conversational participants already accept as part of the shared background information against which the conversation takes place. Although this relation is often called *speaker presupposition,* it is not limited to speakers, but rather is defined for conversational participants generally. Moreover, in order for a person to presuppose a proposition P, it is not necessary that he have said or done anything to indicate that P is being presupposed.[2] Propositions that are generally regarded to be matters of common knowledge are presuppositions, in this sense, for most participants in most conversations.

There are various means by which a presupposition may come into play in guiding a conversation and rendering it intelligible. A speaker may indicate that he is presupposing P by saying something that has a point only if P is already accepted, by presenting an argument that relies on P as a suppressed premise, or by producing an utterance that presupposes P. It is this last means of expressing presuppositions that is of most direct concern to theories of natural language.

The central idea is that the form and content of certain sentences constitute conventional means for indicating that the utterer is taking certain propositions for granted. This idea can be made more precise by defining general notions of utterance and sentential presupposition and specifying their semantic and syntactic sources.

An essential ingredient in this enterprise is the concept of a conversational context at a time t.

(12) *Conversational Context*
The conversational context at t = the set of propositions P such that at t speakers and hearers
a. believe or assume P; and
b. recognize this about each other.

The conversational context at a moment of utterance constitutes the background information, common to speakers and hearers, against which the utterance is evaluated. The notions of utterance and sentential presupposition are then characterized as follows:[3]

(13) *Utterance Presupposition*
An utterance U presupposes P (at t) iff one can reasonably infer from U that the speaker S accepts P and regards it as uncontroversial, either because
a. S thinks that it is already part of the conversational context at t, or because
b. S thinks that the audience is prepared to add it, without objection, to the context against which U is evaluated.

(14) *Sentential Presupposition*
A sentence S presupposes P iff normal utterances of S presuppose P.

The primary notion here is that of an utterance presupposition, which is used to characterize sentential presupposition and which, in turn, is closely related to speaker presupposition. Often, when an utterance presupposes P, the conversational context at the time of the utterance already contains P. Thus, a speaker whose utterance presupposes P often himself presupposes P in the sense I have indicated.

Sometimes, however, speakers use utterance presuppositions to introduce new information. In such cases the status of the information as a presupposition indicates that the speaker expects, or wishes, it to be regarded as uncontroversial. For example, a speaker might utter (15)

(15) My son is living proof that there is no species-universal innate linguistic knowledge.

in a conversation in which he realizes that his hearers do not already know that which (15) presupposes—namely, that the speaker has a

son. The status of this proposition as a presupposition indicates that the speaker does not regard *it* as potentially controversial—no matter how much he may expect his hearers to object to his remark as a whole.

In this example, the point of introducing new information in the form of a presupposition, rather than an explicit assertion, is simply brevity and convenience. In other cases, the point of using presuppositions in this way may involve a kind of pretense which serves special conversational purposes.[4] For example, one can easily imagine contexts in which an utterance of (16)

(16) Yes, and his wife is very attractive, too.

might be intended to convey information about someone's marital status, without explicitly acknowledging an embarrassing ignorance or interest on the part of the hearer. The utterance succeeds in this task precisely because the information regarding marital status is presupposed.

In both of these cases, (15) and (16), a speaker's utterance presupposes a proposition, even though the speaker himself does not presuppose it in the sense I have defined. Nevertheless, understanding these cases involves recognizing that utterance presuppositions are standard devices for indicating propositions that the speaker intends to have the status of common background assumptions among the conversational participants. In each case the speaker utters a sentence that presupposes P, knowing that his audience will reason as follows:

(a) The speaker's utterance presupposes P.

(b) Since the speaker knows that the actual conversational context at the time of his utterance does not include P, he must expect me not to take issue with P, but to add it to the context and treat it on a par with propositions we have been presupposing all along.[5]

Since an utterance that presupposes P does not always license hearers to conclude that the speaker presupposes P, it is convenient to introduce explicit terminology for stating the conclusion that is warranted.

(17) *Taking P to Be Uncontroversial*[6]
A speaker S takes a proposition P to be uncontroversial at t (or, equivalently, takes P for granted at t) iff at t, S accepts P and thinks

a. that P is already part of the conversational context at t; or
b. that the other members of the conversation are prepared to add P to the context without objection.

An utterance that presupposes P *often* indicates that the speaker presupposes P; it *always* indicates (i.e., provides hearers with a warrant for concluding) that the speaker is taking P for granted.[7]

This account of speaker, uttterance, and sentential presupposition is avowedly pragmatic. I want to emphasize, however, that the explanation of why certain utterances and sentences bear certain presuppositions may well be semantic or syntactic. For example, I take it to be a fact deriving from the syntax and semantics of the following sentences that they presuppose the corresponding propositions P:

(18) Bill regrets lying to his parents.   (Factive)
     P: Bill has lied to his parents.

(19) Ivan has stopped beating his wife.   (Aspectual)
     P: Ivan has beaten his wife.

(20) Andy met with the PLO again today.   (Iterative)
     P: Andy has met with the PLO before.

(21) It was in August that we left Connecticut.   (Cleft)
     P: We left Connecticut.

(22) What John destroyed was his typewriter.   (Pseudocleft)
     P: John destroyed something.

(23) *Billy* is guilty, too.   (Too)
     P: Someone other than Billy is guilty.

(24) All of John's children are asleep.   (Certain Quantifiers)
     P: John has children.

(25) The King of France is in hiding.   (Referential)
     P: There is a King of France.

Identifying and explaining the semantic and syntactic facts that give rise to these sentential presuppositions is part of the job of giving a complete account of English.[8]

However, this is not the primary task involved in solving the projection problem. In posing the projection problem, theorists take it as given that examples like (18)–(25) bear presuppositions. Their problem is to predict when, and explain why, these presuppositions are inherited by more complex examples in which (18)–(25) are embedded. Of course, insofar as a solution to this problem sheds light on the nature of presupposition, it may contribute to an explanation of why even elementary examples like those just cited presuppose what they do. However, that is a potential dividend of solving the projection problem, not a prerequisite for doing so.

3. THE PROJECTION PROBLEM

Let us now turn to that problem. The descriptive task is to specify how the presuppositions of constituents of compound sentences contribute to the presuppositions of utterances of those sentences. Noticing examples like (6), the first linguists to study the problem proposed the Cumulative Hypothesis as its solution.[9] This hypothesis can be expressed as the conjunction of two main claims:

(26) *The Cumulative Hypothesis*
     Claim 1: Compound (multiclause) sentences inherit all of the presuppositions of their constituent clauses.
     Claim 2: If a sentence S presupposes P, then assertive utterances of S also presuppose P.

Claim 1 proposes a simple cumulative algorithm for computing the presuppositions of compound sentences from those of their parts. Claim 2 characterizes those presuppositions as sentential, in the sense already defined.[10] Together, the two claims account for a variety of cases, including those in (6). However, since they incorrectly predict that the sentences in (10) inherit the presuppositions of their constituents, linguists have come to recognize that they must either be modified or rejected.

Two main strategies have been developed for doing this. Strategy 1 retains the cumulative projection method of Claim 1, but rejects the characterization of presuppositions given in Claim 2. Instead of thinking of projected presuppositions as sentential (and hence invariant from context to context), proponents of Strategy 1 characterize them as *potential presuppositions* that can be canceled by conversational and contextual means. Strategy 2, on the other hand, retains noncancelable sentential presuppositions while rejecting the cumulative projection mechanism in favor of a set of more complicated projection algorithms.

(27) *Strategy 1* (Gazdar–Soames)
     Cumulative projection algorithm
     Cancelable potential presuppositions

(29) *Strategy 2* (Karttunen–Peters)
     Noncumulative algorithms
     Uncancelable, sentential presuppositions

Strategy 1 has been advocated, with different degrees of commitment, by Gerald Gazdar and by me.[11] Strategy 2 is the work of Lauri Karttunen and Stan Peters.[12] The two strategies conflict most clearly and interestingly in their treatments of conjunctions, disjunctions, and indicative conditionals. I will use these constructions to show that although neither strategy is correct, both contain elements needed to solve the projection problem. My own solution will be a synthesis which attempts to preserve the positive contributions of both strategies while avoiding their defects.

4. TWO STRATEGIES

4.1. Strategy 1[13]

Let S be a negation, epistemic modal, conjunction, disjunction, or indicative conditional. Let P be presupposed by one of S's constituents. As a first approximation, Strategy 1 can be taken to make the claim given in (29).

(29) An utterance of S in a (consistent) conversational context C presupposes P unless
     a. P is incompatible with C; or
     b. the utterance conversationally implicates that the speaker is not taking P for granted.

Clause (29a) accounts for cases like (30) in which (b) is uttered immediately after (a) (by the same or a different speaker).

(30) a. There is no King of France.
     b. Therefore, the King of France isn't in hiding.

After (30a) has been added to the conversational context, an utterance of (30b) will not be taken as committing the speaker to (30c):

(30) c. There is a King of France.

Clause (29a) accounts for this by allowing the context to cancel this constituent presupposition.

Clause (29b) handles a variety of cases, including those in (10). Where A^P and B^P stand for the (relevant) presuppositions of A and B, the examples in (10) are represented by their counterparts in (31).

(31) a. If B^P then B $(A = B^P)$
     b. B^P and B $(A = B^P)$
     c. A or $\sim A^P$ $(B = \sim A^P)$

In each case, for a speaker to take the constituent presupposition to be uncontroversial would be for him to take the truth value of one of the constituents of his sentence for granted. However, someone who assertively utters such a disjunction, conjunction, or indicative conditional implicates that he is not doing this. For example, a speaker who took B^P for granted, and who had sufficient evidence to warrant asserting the conditional (31a), would be in a position to make a stronger statement by asserting B. Since he does not do this, he conversationally implicates that he is not taking B^P for granted. Analogous arguments can be given for (31b,c).[14]

We have now seen how Strategy 1 handles counterexamples to the original Cumulative Hypothesis. The problem is to explain why utterances of these sentences do not indicate that the speaker is taking certain propositions P for granted. The answer given by Strategy 1 is that these utterances *do not indicate* that the speaker is taking P for granted because they conversationally implicate that he *is not* doing so.

This idea can be given a more perspicuous, and perhaps more familiar, formulation in terms of Gerald Gazdar's notion of potential presupposition. This notion may be thought of as being defined by two components of Strategy 1 theories.

(32) *Defining Potential Presuppositions*
     a. A specification of the potential presuppositions of positive sentences like (18)–(25).
     b. A cumulative projection algorithm.[15]

This characterization of potential presupposition is purely formal; it simply pairs sentences with propositions and attaches the label "potential presupposition." A third component is needed to give the theory empirical content—one that uses potential presuppositions to make predictions about utterance presuppositions in the sense I have defined.[16] This component can be expressed, roughly, as follows:

(32) *Giving Empirical Content to Potential Presuppositions*
    c. If P is entailed by some potential presupposition Q of S, then an utterance of S in a (consistent) context C presupposes P unless
      i. Q is incompatible with C; or
      ii. uttering S in C conversationally implicates that the speaker is not taking Q for granted.[17]

This says that actual presuppositions are those entailed by uncanceled potential presuppositions.

The components of this theory are relatively unproblematic. (32b) is our familiar projection mechanism; (32a) is something every theory needs in one form or another. The only novelty introduced by formulating (32a) in terms of potential, rather than actual, presuppositions is a requirement that sets of potential presuppositions not be routinely closed under entailment. This requirement is crucial if conversational and contextual canceling are to work correctly.

This point is illustrated by (33) and (34).

(33) The King of France is in hiding.
    Q: There is a King of France.
    P: There is at least one king (of something).

(34) Either the King of France is in hiding or there is no King of France.

Q is a potential presupposition of (33). Since Q entails both P and Q, our theory predicts that utterances of (33) presuppose both. More generally, utterances with uncanceled potential presuppositions presuppose every proposition entailed by those presuppositions. This is just what we want, if, following Karttunen, Peters, and Gazdar, we adopt an idealization in which the beliefs of speaker–hearers are recognized to be closed under entailment.

Next consider (34), to which the cumulative algorithm assigns Q as a potential presupposition. Since utterances of (34) conversationally implicate that the speaker is not taking Q

for granted (via Grice's maxim of quantity), this presupposition is canceled. P is also eliminated, provided that it is not a potential presupposition in its own right. If it were, it would be inherited, but *not* canceled, since taking P for granted while asserting (34) would not violate conversational maxims. The way to avoid this is to prevent P from becoming a potential presupposition of (33) in the first place. This is accomplished by not closing sets of potential presuppositions under entailment, but reinstating such entailments when uncanceled potential presuppositions become actual.

The result is a theory designed to avoid the generation of too many actual presuppositions. Although the cumulative algorithm still generates superfluous potential presuppositions, these are canceled by conversational and contextual means. In this way Strategy 1 is able to handle the initial counterexamples to the old Cumulative Hypothesis.[18]

4.2. Strategy 2

Proponents of Strategy 2 have taken a different tack. Instead of generating superfluous presuppositions that can later be canceled, they have tried to find projection algorithms that generate the right presuppositions directly. In their latest formulation of this strategy,[19] Karttunen and Peters state these algorithms in terms of noncancelable sentential presuppositions (which they call *conventional implicatures*).

The algorithms for negations, epistemic modals, and many sentences with complementizable verbs remain the same as before; that is, these sentences inherit all of the presuppositions of their constituents. The algorithms for indicative conditionals, conjunctions, and disjunctions are given in (35).[20]

(33) a. $(\text{If A, then B})^P = (A^P \ \& \ (A^T \supset B^P))$
    b. $(\text{A and B})^P = (A^P \ \& \ (A^T \supset B^P))$
    c. $(\text{A or B})^P = ((A^T \vee B^P) \ \& \ (B^T \vee A^P) \ \& \ (A^P \vee B^P))$

These inheritance conditions can be illustrated by considering (35a) more closely. First notice that the maximal sentential presupposition of the antecedent is carried over as one conjunct of the maximal sentential presupposition assigned to the entire conditional. Since Karttunen and Peters assume an idealization in which the set of *sentential* presuppositions of a sentence is closed under entailment, (35a) predicts that indicative conditionals always inherit the presuppositions of their antecedents. This accounts for examples like (36):

(36) If it is Lauri who has solved the projection problem, then he will probably be awarded the Nobel Prize for Linguistics.
   A^P: Someone has solved the projection problem.

Next consider (37), which carries no corresponding substantive presupposition.

(37) If the projection problem has been solved, then Lauri is the one who has solved it.
   $A^T = B^P$: The projection problem has been solved.

According to the inheritance algorithm, the presupposition that (37) inherits from its consequent is $(A^T \supset B^P)$. Since in this case A^T and B^P express the *same* proposition, the inherited presupposition is trivially true. Thus, Strategy 2 correctly predicts that no substantive presupposition is inherited from the consequent.

This case contrasts with sentence (38).

(38) If the problem was difficult, then Morton isn't the one who solved it.

Although the inheritance condition assigns (39)

(39) The problem was $\supset$ Someone has
   difficult   solved it
        A^T $\supset B^P$

as its *sentential* presupposition, Karttunen and Peters acknowledge that in many contexts *utterances* of (38) would presuppose B^P. Their explanation of this stronger presupposition is based on the speaker's *grounds* for assuming (39). Since finding out that a problem is difficult normally would not provide grounds for thinking that it has been solved, Karttunen and Peters argue that in most contexts we may presume that the speaker's grounds for (39) are not non–truth-functional. Since the antecedent A^T of the *presupposition* is also the antecedent of the proposition *asserted,* they maintain that we may also presume that the speaker is not assuming (39) to be true by falsity of antecedent. Thus, he must be assuming

the truth of the consequent, B^P. Hence, the predicted *utterance* presupposition of (38).[21]

Analogous arguments are given for the inheritance conditions for conjunctions and disjunctions. The only significant twist is that the algorithm for disjunction is *symmetric* regarding the contributions made by the disjuncts to the presuppositions of the entire disjunction. The reason for this symmetry is illustrated by (40).

(40) a. Either there is no King of France, or the King of France is in hiding.
   b. Either the King of France is in hiding, or there is no King of France.

Neither of these sentences presupposes that there is a King of France. The first two conjuncts of condition (35c) handle these sentences by assigning them the tautologous presupposition (40c):

(40) c. Either there isn't a King of France or there is a King of France.

The final conjunct of the condition for disjunctions ensures that presuppositions common to both disjuncts are always inherited.[22]

5. DIFFERING PREDICTIONS

We have so far been considering examples which Strategies 1 and 2 can both handle. To see where they go wrong, we need to look at cases in which they conflict. There are two kinds of cases to consider: those in which Strategy 1 predicts an utterance presupposition that Strategy 2 does not; and those in which Strategy 2 predicts an utterance presupposition that Strategy 1 does not. The fact of the matter regarding these two cases is roughly this: whenever one strategy predicts an utterance presupposition that the other does not, the strategy predicting the presupposition is wrong. In effect, each strategy contains a mechanism for blocking presupposition inheritance which the other lacks and which is needed to solve the projection problem.

6. THE INSUFFICIENCY OF STRATEGY 1[23]

The problem with Strategy 1 can best be brought out by distinguishing three different possibilities regarding what a speaker's utterance shows about that which he is, or is not, assuming.

Possibility 1 (Positive Case)

The utterance presupposes P. Typically, this indicates that the speaker is taking P for granted.

(41) It is Bill who has just opened a savings account.
     P: Someone has just opened a savings account.

Possibility 2 (Negative Case)

The utterance does not presuppose P. Moreover, it conversationally implicates that the speaker is not taking P for granted.

(42) Either Bill doesn't have a savings account or he has just opened one.
     P: Bill has a savings account.[24]

Possibility 3 (Neutral Case)

The utterance does not presuppose P, but it also does not conversationally implicate that the speaker is not taking P for granted. It is simply neutral, or noncommittal, regarding whether or not he is.[25]

(43) Bill may have put a lot of the money into those special, high-interest, savings accounts.
     P: Bill has at least one savings account.

(43) can be used appropriately both in situations in which the speaker assumes P and in situations in which he is not sure of its truth value. In some of these situations, other things said in the conversation may clarify whether he is taking P for granted. In other situations, nothing said in the conversation may settle the matter. The point about (43) is that *it* is noncommittal. There is nothing inherent in an utterance of it which indicates either that the speaker does, or that he does not, accept P, or take it to be uncontroversial.

With these three possibilities in mind, let us now turn to cases in which S is a compound sentence one of whose constituents presupposes P. A priori one might expect the same three possibilities to be illustrated. However, Strategy 1 is unable to accommodate them all.

According to Strategy 1, a potential presupposition P of a constituent becomes an actual presupposition of an utterance, unless the context plus the conversational implicatures of the utterance entail that the speaker is *not* taking P for granted. Thus, it is impossible for an utterance to be noncommittal with respect to a potential presupposition P. If there is no contextual or conversational canceling, then Strategy 1 predicts that the utterance indicates that the speaker takes P for granted. If there is

such canceling, it predicts that the utterance indicates that the speaker does not take P for granted. This means that where P is a potential presupposition, Strategy 1 makes no provision for Possibility 3.

The error in this can be shown by considering utterances of conditionals that meet three conditions.

(44) *Utterances Falsifying Strategy 1 (indicative conditionals: If A, then B)*
     a. B^P is compatible with the conversational context.
     b. The utterance, in this context, does not conversationally implicate $\sim TG_s : B^P$ (not the speaker takes B^P for granted).
     c. The context plus the antecedent, A^T, entail B^P (though the context alone does not).

Strategy 1 predicts that an utterance satisfying these conditions presupposes B^P. Strategy 2 treats such an utterance on the model of (37). Since the context plus antecedent entail B^P, the *sentential* presupposition assigned by Strategy 2, $(A^T \supset B^P)$, is trivially true with respect to the context. Thus, Strategy 2 predicts that such an utterance inherits no substantive presupposition from its consequent. In effect, Strategy 1 treats the utterance as an instance of Possibility 1 (a positive presupposition), whereas Strategy 2 treats it as an instance of Possibility 3 (the neutral case).

Examples of this type can be constructed using (45)–(49).

(45) If the Poles defeat the Russians, then the Hungarians will defeat the Russians, too.
     B^P: Someone other than the Hungarians will defeat the Russians.

(46) If Andy met with the PLO last week to discuss diplomatic recognition, then he will probably meet with them again this week.
     B^P: Andy has met with the PLO.

(47) If Bill has any high-interest, timed savings accounts, then all of his savings accounts will be taxed at the maximum rate.
     B^P: Bill has savings accounts.

(48) If France has an intelligent king, then the King of France is the only intelligent monarch in Europe.
     B^P: There is a King of France.

(49) If someone at the conference solved the problem, it was Julius who solved it.
     B^P: Someone has solved the problem.

In each case, one can imagine the sentence being uttered in a context that does not already include either B^P or its negation. Since B^P is compatible with the context, and the utterance does not conversationally implicate that the speaker is not taking it for granted, Strategy 1 predicts that the utterance does presuppose B^P.

This prediction is wrong. For example, consider (45). If uttering it indicated that the speaker thought that someone other than the Hungarians would defeat the Russians, then it would be natural to ask who this might be.[26] Since the utterance conversationally implicates that the speaker is not assuming the antecedent, it cannot be the Poles. Nor is anyone else specified. Of course, there could be some third parties (say the Afghans) who the speaker assumes will win their freedom from Moscow. However, *the utterance* gives no indication whether or not this is so. Thus, it does not presuppose that someone other than the Hungarians will defeat the Russians. Exactly analogous results hold for each of the other examples, as well as for corresponding utterances involving disjunctions and conjunctions. For instance:

(50) Maybe Mary proved the theorem and John proved it, too.
     B^P: Someone other than John proved the theorem.[27]

There is no way for a pure Strategy 1 theory to avoid being falsified by these results. Since there are utterances which are neutral regarding the speaker's attitude toward a constituent presupposition, any theory that fails to accommodate them is wrong, not just in some computational detail, but in principle.[28]

Such a theory fails to recognize the reasons why a speaker may produce an utterance that is neutral in the sense I have defined. He may think, perhaps mistakenly, that the conversational status of the putative presupposition has already been settled; he may judge that settling its status is not important to the conversation; or he may simply be waiting for the proper time to comment on it. In any case, the speaker who utters one of the sentences (45)–(49) knows that once his hearers add the antecedent of his assertion to the conversational context, the constituent presupposition B^P will be entailed and hence satisfied by the enlarged

context, *whether or not* it was present in the context immediately preceding his utterance. Since he relies on his hearers to evaluate the consequent of his assertion relative to this enlarged context, his utterance commits him to the claim that *it* entails B^P. Since the enlarged context is just the initial context plus antecedent, this claim is tantamount to the claim that the initial context entails $(A^T \supset B^P)$. This, in effect, is what the utterance presupposes.

It is also what Strategy 2 predicts. In examples (45)–(49) this presupposition is, of course, trivial. Thus, Strategy 2 correctly accounts for the fact that these utterances do not inherit substantive presuppositions from their consequents, whereas Strategy 1 incorrectly predicts that the utterances inherit B^P. This is just one example of a general rule mentioned earlier: whenever Strategy 1 predicts a substantive presupposition that Strategy 2 does not, Strategy 2 is right and Strategy 1 is wrong.[29] In every case, the reason for the error is that Strategy 1 treats an utterance that is neutral regarding a potential presupposition P as if it positively presupposed P. What these cases show is that conversational and contextual canceling cannot be the only mechanisms for blocking presupposition inheritance. Rather, some means is needed for suspending presuppositions without revealing the speaker's attitude toward them. The main strength of Strategy 2 is that it provides such a means.

7. THE INSUFFICIENCY OF STRATEGY 2

However, Strategy 2 also has a corresponding weakness—namely, not allowing conversational implicatures to play *any* significant role in the cancellation of presuppositions. Since the Strategy 2 inheritance conditions are stated in terms of uncancelable, sentential presuppositions, cancellation by conversational implicature is impossible. This leads to a number of incorrect results, most notably to a conflict between the Strategy 2 inheritance conditions and the theory of conversational implicature.

This conflict is due to the fact that there are cases in which an account of conversational implicature predicts (51), whereas the Strategy 2 inheritance conditions predict (52).

(51) An utterance U of a sentence S in a context C indicates that the speaker is *not* assuming P.

(52) a. S presupposes P.
   b. An utterance U of S in C presupposes P.
   c. An utterance U of S in C indicates that the speaker is assuming P.

In every such case, the conversational implicature (51) is genuine and the prediction made by Strategy 2 is incorrect. I will illustrate this with three examples.

The first involves disjunctions whose disjuncts bear conflicting presuppositions.[30]

(53) Either Bill has just started smoking or he has just stopped smoking.
   A^P: Bill hasn't smoked in the recent past.
   B^P: Bill has smoked in the recent past.

The inheritance condition for disjunctions predicts that a disjunction (A or B) presupposes (54).

(54) $(A^T \lor B^P) \& (B^T \lor A^P) \& (A^P \lor B^P)$

However, where A^P and B^P are inconsistent, as they are in (53), (54) entails (55):

(55) $A^T \lor B^T$

But (55) is just the proposition expressed by the speaker's utterance. Thus, where the constituent presuppositions are contradictory, Strategy 2 incorrectly predicts that the utterance presupposes the very proposition that it asserts.

One way of showing that this prediction is false is to embed (53) in larger linguistic contexts. For example, consider (56).

(56) a. If Bill has either just started smoking or just stopped smoking, his colleagues will probably notice a big change in him.
   b. It may be that Bill has either just started smoking or just stopped smoking.
   c. No, he didn't. (Said in response to (53))
   d. Are you sure? (Said in response to (53))

According to Strategy 2, the presuppositions of (53) are inherited by the examples in (56). Thus, if (53) presupposes itself, Strategy 2 predicts that a speaker who utters the sentences in (56) indicates that he is assuming (53). However, this is clearly wrong, since these utterances *conversationally implicate* that the speaker is *not* assuming (53).

These examples are cases in which the Strategy 2 inheritance conditions make a predic-tion of the form (52) that conflicts with the prediction of the form (51) made by an account of conversational implicature. Since the implicatures are genuine, the Strategy 2 presuppositions are not.

A second example of this type is (57), first discussed by Gazdar.

(57) It is possible that John has children and it is possible that his children are away.
   A^T: $\Diamond$ John has children.
   B^T: $\Diamond$ John's children are away.
   B^P: John has children.

The Strategy 2 inheritance condition for conjunctions predicts that (57) presupposes (58).

(58) $\Diamond B^P \supset B^P$ (Note, $A^T = \Diamond B^P$)

Since (57) entails (59),

(59) $\Diamond B^P$

which is one of its conjuncts, Strategy 2 predicts that a speaker who utters (57) is committed to the claim that John has children. However, this is obviously false. A speaker who utters an epistemic modal $\Diamond \phi$ implicates he does not know ϕ or its negation. Thus, a speaker who utters (57) implicates that he is not assuming that John has children.

My final example of this type is the widely discussed (60).[31]

(60) If I realize later that I have not told the truth, I will confess it to everyone.
   A^T: I will realize later that I have not told the truth.
   A^P: I have not told the truth.

In this case, if the speaker knew that he had not told the truth, then presumably he would know the truth value of the antecedent. Since he conversationally implicates that he does not know this, he conversationally implicates that he is not assuming A^P. The Strategy 2 prediction that the utterance does presuppose A^P conflicts with this, and is therefore incorrect.

It is instructive to compare (60) with (61).

(61) If I regret later that I have not told the truth, I will confess it to everyone.
   A^T: I will regret later that I have not told the truth.
   A^P: I have not told the truth.

Here it is quite conceivable that the speaker might know that he has not told the truth without knowing whether he will regret it later, and hence without knowing the truth value of the antecedent. As a result there is no conversational implicature that the speaker is not assuming A^P (or taking it for granted), and A^P is inherited as a presupposition of the utterance of the conditional. Thus, if presuppositions are conversationally cancelable, the difference between (60) and (61) is easily explained.

This illustrates the main respect in which Strategy 1 is superior to Strategy 2. Since Strategy 1 makes presuppositions conversationally cancelable, its account of presuppositions cannot conflict with the predictions made by a theory of conversational implicature. Moreover, Strategy 1 can handle all of the counterexamples to Strategy 2. We have just seen how it accounts for (60) and (61). In the case of (53), the speaker conversationally implicates, via the maxim of quantity, that he does not know the truth value of either disjunct, and hence cannot be assuming either A^P or B^P. In the case of (57) he implicates that he is not assuming that John has children. In each case, the constituent presupposition is canceled by a conversational implicature. Although we have seen that such cancellation cannot be the *only* means of blocking the inheritance of presuppositions, examples like these show that it is *one* means of doing so. The fact that Strategy 2 does not recognize this shows that it, too, is wrong, not just in computational detail, but in principle.

8. A POSITIVE SYNTHESIS

8.1. First Attempt

The defects I have pointed out in Strategies 1 and 2 are complementary. Everything that is a problem for one of them is handled by the other. This suggests the possibility of solving the projection by synthesizing the positive contributions of the two strategies. But how should this be done?

A natural thought would be to reinterpret the Strategy 2 inheritance conditions as issuing in cancelable potential presuppositions. The resulting theory would then be exactly like Strategy 1 except that the cumulative al-

gorithm would be replaced by noncumulative inheritance conditions.

Despite the naturalness of this proposed synthesis, there are some troublesome details regarding its proper formulation. For example, in order to account for sentences like (62), the inheritance conditions would have to assign *sets* of potential presuppositions, on the model of (63), rather than single, *maximal* potential presuppositions, on the model of (64).

(62) If Mary's boss doesn't have children, then it wasn't his child who won the fellowship.
    A^T: $\smile$Mary's boss has a child.
    A^P: Mary has a boss.
    B^{P1}: Mary has a boss.
    B^{P2}: Mary's boss has a child. ($\smile B^{P2} = A^T$)
    B^{P3}: Someone won the fellowship.

(63) a. A^P
    b. $\smile B^{P2} \supset B^{P1}$
    c. $\smile B^{P2} \supset B^{P2}$
    d. $\smile B^{P2} \supset B^{P3}$
    (63c) is logically equivalent to B^{P2}, which is conversationally canceled.
    (63a,b,d) remain as actual presuppositions.

(64) $(A^P \& (\smile B^{P2} \supset (B^{P1} \& B^{P2} \& B^{P3})))$
    Second conjunct is logically equivalent to B^{P2}. Since it is canceled, the entire conjunction (64) is wrongly canceled as well.

However, once the inheritance conditions have been formulated in this way, disjunctions whose disjuncts bear conflicting presuppositions become problematic. We may take it that a speaker who utters such a disjunction

(65) A or B
    a. $A^T \vee B^P$
    b. $B^T \vee A^P$
    c. $A^P \vee B^P$

conversationally implicates that he is not taking A^T, B^T, A^P, or B^P for granted. However, is it clear that obedience to conversational maxims entails that he is not taking for granted the putative potential presuppositions (65a), (65b), or (65c)? If there are no such canceling implicatures, then (65a–c) are *not* conversationally canceled and (wrongly) become actual presuppositions of the utterance. Since the set of actual presuppositions of an utterance is assumed to be closed under logical consequence (see note 18), this leads to the intuitively incorrect result that the utterance presupposes the proposition it is used to assert.[31]

This difficulty poses a challenge for a theory

which replaces the cumulative algorithm in Strategy 1 with the Strategy 2 inheritance conditions. However, the real problem with this synthesis is more general: its inheritance conditions simply generate the wrong presuppositions. This can best be seen by considering cases like (66) in which the putative presuppositions are not conversationally canceled.

(66) a. John has children and his sons are bald.
    b. Maybe John has children and his sons are bald.
    c. If John has children and his sons are bald, then baldness is probably hereditary.

(67) (John has children ⊃ John has sons)
    $(A^T \quad \supset \quad B^P)$

According to the inheritance conditions, each of the sentences in (66) bears the potential presupposition (67). This presupposition is not conversationally canceled. In each case, the speaker conversationally implicates that he is not assuming (66a) to be false. Since (66a) entails (67), this means that he conversationally implicates that he is not assuming the falsity of (67). However, this leaves it open that he *might* be taking its truth for granted. As a result, the potential presupposition is not conversationally canceled, and the proposed synthesis predicts that (67) becomes an actual presupposition of the utterance.

The falsity of this prediction is most evident for utterances of (66b) and (66c). A speaker who assertively utters one of these sentences commits himself to the *possibility* that (67) is true; he does not commit himself to its *actual* truth. Rather, his remark leaves it open whether he believes (67) or is unsure of its truth value, and hence believes neither it nor its negation. Thus, a reasonable hearer will not conclude from an utterance of one of these sentences that the speaker must be assuming (67).

In the terminology used in my original criticism of Strategy 1, these utterances are *neutral* regarding the speaker's attitude toward the putative presupposition (67). The present synthesis errs in treating them as instances of positive presupposition. The source of the error lies in the assignment of a potential presupposition (67) that is too weak to be conversationally canceled but too strong to be carried by the relevant utterances. These examples show that the synthesis we are looking for can-

not be the result of simply construing the Strategy 2 inheritance conditions in terms of potential presuppositions and substituting them for the cumulative algorithm.

8.2. A Descriptively Adequate Theory

Nevertheless, the idea of a synthesis is correct; there are two mechanisms for blocking the inheritance of presuppositions. What I have just shown is that one hypothesis regarding how these mechanisms interact is wrong. According to that hypothesis, Strategy 2 is employed first, filtering out certain constituent presuppositions in favor of weaker ones to which the Strategy 1 cancellation mechanism is then applied. This won't do.

Suppose, however, that the order in which the blocking mechanisms are applied is reversed. Suppose that the Strategy 1 cancellation method is applied first, yielding a set of remaining uncanceled potential presuppositions. Next, the Strategy 2 inheritance conditions are employed to filter out still more potential presuppositions in favor of weaker ones. This is, in fact, how presupposition suspension operates.

This synthesis requires two crucial elements: a definition of the *remaining potential presuppositions* of a sentence relative to an utterance, and a reinterpretation of the Strategy 2 inheritance conditions that relativizes them to utterances.

(68) *Definition: The Remaining Potential Presuppositions of a Sentence S Relative to an Utterance U*[33]
    P is a remaining potential presupposition of S relative to U iff
    a. P is a potential presupposition of S;
    b. P is not contextually canceled (P is consistent with the context in which the utterance U was produced);
    c. P is not conversationally canceled (U does not conversationally implicate that the speaker is not taking P for granted).

(69) *Recursive Definition: The Actual Presuppositions of S Relative to U*[34]
    a. If S is an affirmative, single-clause sentence, then the actual presuppositions of S relative to U are those entailed by the remaining potential presuppositions of S relative to U.
    b. If S ≈ ⌜∼A⌝, ⌜M_EA⌝, ⌜It is verb $_{+hole}$ A⌝,[35] then the actual presuppositions of S relative

to U = the actual presuppositions of A relative to U.

c. If S ≈ ⌈A and B⌉ or ⌈If A, then B⌉, then the actual presuppositions of S relative to U are those entailed by
$$(A^{AP/U} \& (A^T \supset B^{AP/U}))$$
(where $\phi^{AP/U}$ represents a maximal actual presupposition of ϕ relative to U—one equivalent to the set of actual presuppositions of ϕ relative to U).

d. If S ≈ ⌈A or B⌉, then the actual presuppositions of S relative to U are those entailed by
$$(A^{AP/U} \vee B^T) \& (B^{AP/U} \vee A^T) \& (A^{AP/U} \vee B^{AP/U}).$$

(70) *Prediction*
An utterance U of a sentence S presupposes a proposition P, if P is an actual presupposition of S relative to U.

A few examples should suffice to illustrate how the proposal works. In the case of (53),

(53) Either Bill has just started smoking or he has just stopped smoking.
A^P: Bill hasn't smoked in the recent past.
B^P: Bill has smoked in the recent past.

the utterance conversationally implicates, via the maxim of quantity, that the speaker is not assuming A^P or B^P.[36] Thus, A^P is not included among the remaining potential presuppositions of A relative to the utterance of the entire disjunction. The same is true for B and B^P. Supposing, for the sake of argument, that A and B have no other potential presuppositions, this means that A$^{AP/U}$ and B$^{AP/U}$ can be represented by a tautology T (see note 20). The actual presuppositions assigned to the utterance are those entailed by (69d′) (corresponding to clause (d) in the recursive definition):

(69) d′. $(T \vee B^T) \& (T \vee A^T) \& (T \vee T)$

Since (69d′) is itself a tautology, the theory correctly blocks the inheritance of substantive presuppositions from A^P and B^P.

In the case of (45),

(45) If the Poles defeat the Russians, then the Hungarians will defeat the Russians, too.
A^T: The Poles will defeat the Russians.
B^P: Someone other than the Hungarians will defeat the Russians.

the utterance does not conversationally implicate that the speaker is not taking B^P for granted. Thus, B^P is a remaining potential presupposition of B relative to the utterance (pro-

vided the context does not already contain $\sim$B^P). The actual presuppositions assigned to the utterance are those entailed by (69c′) (corresponding to clause (c) in the recursive definition).

(69) c′. $A^{AP/U} \& (A^T \supset B^P)$

Given the nonidentity of Poland and Hungary, the right conjunct of (69c′) is trivially true and the theory correctly blocks the inheritance of a substantive presupposition arising from B^P.

A contrasting case, in which a substantive presupposition is inherited, is provded by (38).

(38) If the problem was difficult, then Morton isn't the one who solved it.
A^T: The problem was difficult.
B^P: Someone solved the problem.

Here, there is no conversational canceling and the utterance presupposition emerging from the recursive definition plus the predictive principle is (39).

(39) The problem was $\supset$ Someone has solved
      difficult   the problem
                    A^T $\supset$ B^P

A stronger utterance presupposition, B^P, can be explained, as in section 4.2, on the presumption that the speaker's grounds for (39) are not non–truth-functional.[37]

As examples like these illustrate, the proposed synthesis accounts for all of the data presented in this article.[38] It does so by blocking the inheritance of every presupposition that is blocked by either Strategy 1 or Strategy 2. Since this is just what is needed to solve the projection problem, my solution can be given the following form:

(71) *Proposed Solution to Projection Problem*
a. Characterization of constructions that give rise to potential presuppositions (assignment of potential presuppositions)
b. Definition of *remaining potential presuppositions* of S relative to U (contribution of Strategy 1)
c. Definition of *actual presuppositions* of S relative to U (contribution of Strategy 2)
d. Predictive principle

My solution can also be given another, roughly equivalent, but more revealing formulation. This involves replacing (71c) with a definition modeled on an earlier formulation of Strategy 2.[39] The alternative definition is that of a context X satisfying the remaining potential presuppositions of S relative to U. As before, the definition is recursive.

(72) *Definition: A Context X Satisfies the Remaining Potential Presuppositions of S Relative to U*

(X Sat–S–U) iff

a. S is an affirmative, single-clause sentence and X entails (includes) all of the remaining presuppositions of S relative to U; or

b. S ≈ $\ulcorner \sim A \urcorner$, $\ulcorner M_E A \urcorner$, $\ulcorner$It is verb $_{+hole}$ A$\urcorner$ and X Sat–A–U; or

c. S ≈ $\ulcorner$A and B$\urcorner$ or $\ulcorner$If A, then B$\urcorner$ and
   i. X Sat–A–U; and
   ii. X ∪ {A^T} Sat–B–U; or

d. S ≈ $\ulcorner$A or B$\urcorner$ and
   i. X ∪ {$\sim$A^T} Sat–B–U; and
   ii. X ∪ {$\sim$B^T} Sat–A–U; and
   iii. for all propositions P, if P is entailed by every context Y such that Y Sat–A–U and Y Sat–B–U, then X entails P. (Note: where A and B are affirmative, single-clause sentences, (iii) says that X entails all remaining potential presuppositions, relative to U, that are common to both A and B. The point is to make sure that remaining potential presuppositions common to both disjuncts are not eliminated by clauses (i) and (ii).[40]

If this definition is employed, then the predictive principle that I formulated earlier in terms of *actual presuppositions* will be replaced with the corresponding alternative:

(73) *Alternative Predictive Principle*

A speaker who assertively utters a sentence S indicates to his hearers that he believes there is a set C′ of propositions which

a. satisfies the remaining presuppositions of S relative to U; and

b. differs from the conversational context immediately prior to U at most in the addition of true propositions that the hearers are prepared to treat as uncontroversial.

We may even think of this prediction as resulting from a maxim governing speakers' contributions to conversations: Assertively utter a sentence S only if you think that the conversational context, augmented with uncontroversial propositions, satisfies the remaining potential presuppositions of S relative to U. The solution to the projection problem incorporating this maxim makes essentially the same predictions as does the ear-

lier formulation involving actual presuppositions. Both account for all of the examples I have presented and, I believe, approach descriptive adequacy.

9. WHY THE SYNTHESIS WORKS

9.1. Overview

However, descriptive adequacy is not enough. It is one thing to be able to predict what utterances of compound sentences presuppose; it is another to explain why those utterances bear the presuppositions they do. I believe that my proposed synthesis does provide the basis for such an explanation. However, this needs showing.

The basic idea expressed by the synthesis is that a speaker who utters a compound sentence, one of whose constituents presupposes P, creates a defeasible presumption that he is taking P for granted. This presumption remains in force unless it is defeated by one or the other of two different means. One involes conversational and contextual cancellation, which indicate that the speaker *is not* taking P for granted. The other involves the relativized Strategy 2 inheritance conditions, which remove the presumption that P is being taken for granted without creating the opposite presumption that it is not being taken for granted by the speaker.[41]

Since conclusions about what the speaker is or is not assuming arise automatically from independently motivated conversational principles, the fact that the presumptive presupposition can be defeated by conversational and contextual canceling requires no further explanation. All that remains to be explained is why it can also be removed by the relativized inheritance conditions.

9.2. Stalnaker's Explanation for Conjunctions and Conditionals

The beginnings of such an explanation have been given by Robert Stalnaker in an important but too little heeded paper, "Pragmatic Presupposition." There Stalnaker compares the behavior of conjunctions and conditionals such as (74a,b) with discourses such as the ones in (75).

(74) a. Joan proved the theorem and *Martha proved it, too.*
   b. If Joan proved the theorem, then *Martha proved it, too.*
   B^P: Someone other than Martha proved the theorem.

(75) a. Joan proved the theorem. What's more, *Martha proved it, too.*
   b. Suppose Joan proved the theorem. In that case, *Martha must have proved it, too.*
   B^P: Someone other than Martha proved the theorem.

First consider the discourses. Let t_0 be the time immediately prior to the utterance of the first sentence, and let t_1 be the time immediately prior to the utterance of the second. The speaker asserts in the case of (75a), and supposes in the case of (75b), that Joan proved the theorem. After the assertion or supposition has been made, that proposition enters the conversational context. The speaker builds on this incremented context by uttering the second, italicized sentence. This utterance indicates that *at t_1* the speaker was taking B^P for granted. However, this does not commit him to anything new, since the earlier assertion or supposition has already guaranteed the presence of B^P in the context at t_1.

It is because of this guarantee that the utterance of the second sentence does not license an inference that the speaker was taking B^P for granted at the earlier time t_0. On noting that the speaker is taking B^P for granted at t_1, the hearer must ask whether this is due to the way in which the context has just been incremented, or to his having taken B^P for granted prior to the incrementation. Since the discourse leaves these alternatives open, it results neither in a presumption that the speaker was taking B^P for granted at t_0, nor in a presumption that he was not. It is neutral in that respect.

Stalnaker points out that this explanation carries over to conjunctions and conditionals, like those in (74). If we imagine conversational contexts being incremented in mid-utterance, then these utterances as wholes do not presuppose B^P for the same reason that the discourses do not. The only additional assumptions needed are that antecedents of conditionals constitute suppositions and that assertions of conjunctions are assertions of both conjuncts. General conversational prin-

ciples regarding the incrementation of contexts do the rest.

9.3. Extending Stalnaker's Analysis

The purpose of Stalnaker's analysis is to explain the asymmetric inheritance algorithm for conjunctions and conditionals in terms of broader, independently motivated conversational principles. In both cases, the asymmetry results from the fact that the context against which the utterance of the B-sentence is evaluated is richer than the context relevant to the A-sentence. However, the reason for this richness is different in the two cases. The relevant pragmatic principle at work in discourses like (75a) and conjunctions like (74a) is a temporal one regarding the way in which the conversational context grows over time.

(76) *The Past Is Prologue*
   Once something is asserted, it is added to the conversational context against which subsequent utterances are evaluated.

By contrast, the pragmatic principle at work in (75b) and (74b) is not strictly temporal, but rather concerns the nature of supposition.

(77) *The Pragmatics of Supposition*
   When an utterance U is to be evaluated relative to the supposition of P, the context against which U is evaluated is one to which P has been added.

The difference between these two principles is best illustrated by examples in which the supposition follows, rather than precedes, that which it is relevant to evaluating.

(78) a. Andy will probably meet with the PLO again this week, if he met with them last week.
   b. Andy will probably meet with the PLO again this week, provided that he met with them last week.
   c. Andy will probably meet with the PLO again this week. Supposing, of course, that he met with them last week.

   Suspended (neutralized) presupposition B^P: Andy has met with the PLO.

(79) Dialogue:
   The Russians are having a hard time of it.
   Yes.

a. The Hungarians will probably defeat them, too, if the Poles do.
b. The Hungarians will probably defeat them, too, provided that the Poles do.
c. The Hungarians will probably defeat them, too. Supposing that the Poles do.

Suspended (neutralized) presupposition B^P: Someone other than the Hungarians will defeat the Russians.

The explanation of these cases parallels that of (74b) and (75b). In each instance, the addition of the supposition to the context suspends the presupposition of the consequent. What these examples show is that for this to occur it is not necessary for the supposition to precede the consequent.[42]

The most interesting aspect of this analysis is that the independently motivated pragmatic principle which explains the discourses (75b), (78c), and (79c) automatically explains the suspension of presuppositions in indicative conditionals. This suggests that, as in the case of conjunctions, the inheritance condtiion is not an ad hoc, idiosyncratic device, but rather is a special case of a broader pragmatic principle relating utterances to conversational contexts.

Once it is clear that the explanation of Strategy 2 type presupposition suspension does not depend on which clause of a compound sentence is uttered first, we can extend the Stalnaker analysis to cases which heretofore have seemed more problematic. For example, sentences of the form (80) behave like indicative conditionals of the form (81):

(80) B unless ⌐A
It was probably Mary who solved the problem, unless no one at the conference did.
Suspended presupposition B^P: Someone has solved the problem.

(81) B, if A
It was probably Mary who solved the problem, if anyone at the conference did.
Suspended presupposition B^P: Someone has solved the problem.

In each case the utterance of B is intended to increment a context to which A has been added. Thus, presupposition suspension in (80) will parallel that in (81). *Unless* is novel only in that even though the supposition against which B is evaluated involves A, the sentence uttered is not A, but its negation.

However, this has nothing special to do with pragmatics or presupposition. It is simply part of the truth-conditional semantics of *unless*.

Presupposition suspension involving sentences with *or* parallels that in sentences with *unless*.

(82) a. Either no one at the conference solved the problem, or it was Mary who solved it.
b. Either it was Mary who solved the problem or no one at the conference did.

Suspended presupposition: Someone solved the problem. (B^P in the case of (a), A^P in the case of (b).)

(82b) can be explained on the model of *unless*. Here the utterance of the first disjunct is considered as incrementing a context to which the negation of the second has been added. In (82a), the order of incrementation is reversed. In general, utterances of disjunctions are seen as cases in which the speaker intends either (i) the second disjunct to be evaluated against a context that includes the negation of the first; or (ii) the first disjunct to be evaluated against a context that includes the negation of the second; or both. Hence, the symmetric inheritance condition.

This analysis of disjunction raises a question that has been implicit all along. In examples like (83a–c),

(83) a. If A, then B
b. B, if A
c. B unless ⌐A

it is plausible to hold that the truth conditions of these sentences are to be explained roughly along the lines suggested by Robert Stalnaker, David Lewis, and Wayne Davis—namely, these sentences are true iff B is true in an A-world which is maximally close to the actual world.[43] If so, then a pragmatic analysis of how discourses are augmented by utterances of these sentences will closely parallel their semantics.[44]

In the case of disjunction, this close parallel breaks down. I assume that *or* in English is the standard, inclusive *or* of the propositional calculus. To determine the truth value of a sentence ⌐A or B⌐ it is sufficient to determine the truth value of the disjuncts. Evaluation of A relative to a supposition of ⌐~B⌐, or of B relative to a supposition of ⌐~A⌐, need not be involved. Why then are the pragmatic inheritance conditions for disjunctions stated as if disjunctions involved such suppositons?

The answer, I think, involves not the truth conditions for disjunctions, but the grounds for asserting them. A speaker obeying Grice's conversational maxims will assert a disjunction only when his grounds are non-truth-functional—that is, only when he believes that the falsity of one disjunct would provide good grounds for the truth of the other. If he does believe this, then he will be willing to accept one disjunct relative to a supposition of the negation of the other. Recognizing this, the hearer responds by incrementing the context with the relevant negation and using the enlarged context to evaluate the other disjunct. In this way an utterance of a sentence like (84) might have the same pragmatic effect as an utterance of (85), even though the truth conditions of the two assertions may be different.

(84) Either the Russians won't invade Poland or the Poles will defeat them.

(85) If the Russians invade Poland, then the Poles will defeat them.

Another utterance that might share this pragmatic effect is an utterance of (86):

(86) Either the Poles will defeat the Russians or the Russians won't invade them.

As in the case of (84), we may presume that a speaker uttering this sentence believes that the falsity of the disjunct *the Russians won't invade the Poles* would provide good grounds for the truth of the other disjunct. These examples demonstrate the symmetry of *or* regarding possible non-truth-functional grounds for asserting a disjunction. I conjecture that it is this symmetry which underlies and explains the symmetric inheritance condition for utterances of disjunctions.

9.4. A Final Set of Examples

The descriptive apparatus I have advocated for suspending constituent presuppositions[45] involves evaluating the presuppositions carried by one clause of a compound sentence relative to a context that has been augmented as a function of another clause of that sentence. In extending Stalnaker's explanation of

this apparatus, I have tried to show that the mechanisms at work in sentences of the form (87)

(87) a. A and B
     b. If A, then B
     c. A or B
     d. B, if A; B, provided that A; B unless $\neg A$[46]

are reflections of general, independently motivated principles for incrementing contexts in discourses.

A final set of examples confirming this view is given in (88) and (89).

(88) a. If Haldeman is guilty, then Nixon is (guilty), too.
     b. Nixon is guilty, too, if Haldeman is (guilty).
     B^P: Someone other than Nixon is guilty.

     Suspended in both cases.

(89) a. If Nixon is guilty, too, then Haldeman is (guilty).
     b. Haldeman is guilty, if Nixon is (guilty), too.
     A^P: Someone other than Nixon is guilty.

     Inherited in (89a); suspended in (89b).

The suspension of B^P in (88a) and inheritance of A^P in (89a) are correctly predicted by clause (c) of the definition of *A Context X Satisfying the Remaining Potential Presuppositions of S Relative to U* (X Sat–S–U) (72). These predictions are explained by the different contexts that are relevant to evaluating suppositions and their consequents: consequents are evaluated relative to contexts to which suppositions have been added; suppositions are evaluated relative to contexts at the time the suppositions are made.

The suspension of B^P in (88b) is analogous to the suspension in (88a). The interesting case is (89b). Examples like this demonstrate that the presuppositions of an antecedent can be suspended by a prior utterance of a consequent. This means that the clause in the definition of X Sat–S–U for sentences of the form (90) cannot be the same as the one for sentences of the form (91).

(90) B, if A

(91) If A, then B

Noting that suspension occurs in both (88b) and (89b), one can give a partial formulation of the needed clause as follows:

(92) If $S \approx \ulcorner B$, if $A \urcorner$,[47] then X Sat–S–U only if
    a. $X \cup \{A^T\}$ Sat–B–U; and
    b. $X \cup \{B^T\}$ Sat–A–U[48]

The different clauses for (90) and (91) provide an argument against taking the machinery for presupposition suspension to represent aspects of meaning (as is done in Karttunen and Peters (1979)). Since sentences of the form $\ulcorner B$, if $A \urcorner$ are synonymous with those of the form $\ulcorner$If A, then $B \urcorner$, the differences exhibited in presupposition suspension cannot be due to differences in meaning (truth-conditional or otherwise). Rather, they are the result of general pragmatic principles regulating how contexts change in discourses.[49]

An informal explanation of (92b) can be given in these terms as follows: In the cases covered by this clause, the consequent, B, is uttered first. Since initially there is no indication that B is anything other than an assertion, it is added to the conversational context, just as if it had been asserted.[50] Uttering the antecedent has two effects on this newly enlarged context: the antecedent is added as a supposition; and the status of B is changed from that of a previously established fact to that of something accepted only conditionally. Since A carries a presupposition, A^P, its utterance indicates that the speaker believes the enlarged context (following the utterance of B) to entail A^P.[51] However, this does not commit him to anything new, since

(a) the prior addition of B guarantees the entailment of A^P; and

(b) the ultimate status of B is not that of something the speaker accepts as fact, but merely that of something he is prepared to grant relative to a supposition.

As a result, utterances of (89b) (and other sentences covered by (92b)) do not commit the speaker to A^P.

This account does more than correctly predict the different behaviors of sentences of the form (90) and (91); it explains why this difference exists in terms of the interaction of utterance presuppositions and context incrementation. The plausibility and generality of this explanation provide significant support for the pragmatic, discourse-based conception of presupposition projection and suspension elaborated here.

9.5. Conclusion

This completes my explanation of why the descriptive synthesis that I have proposed is successful in predicting the presuppositions that it does. My goal has been to show how the descriptive apparatus needed to solve the projection problem can be seen as arising from independently motivated semantic and pragmatic principles. Doubtless, more could and should be said about this. For example, nothing in this discussion explains why the inheritance conditions are able to operate recursively and in embedded sentences in the way that they do.[52] Nevertheless, I hope that enough has been said to indicate that the descriptive apparatus I have employed is not arbitrary.[53]

In my opinion, any adequate solution to the projection problem must include three major components:

(a) a definition of presupposition;

(b) a set of principles for predicting which utterances bear which presuppositions; and

(c) a plausible explanation of the status of one's descriptive principles.

By and large, philosophers have tended to focus on the first and third components, linguists on the second. What is needed is a comprehensive view encompassing all three. The synthesis I have proposed is intended as a step in that direction.

APPENDIX

A1. TOPICS TO BE COVERED

In this appendix I will demonstrate that my criticisms of the Strategy 1 approach to presupposition projection apply to Gazdar's (1979a,b) formalization of this approach. I will also present broader criticisms of Gazdar's system and discuss certain alleged counterexamples to Karttunen and Peters (1979) which would be counterexamples to my proposed synthesis, if they were genuine.

A2. GAZDAR'S IDEALIZATION

Gazdar is concerned with the situation in which a sentence is uttered against a background context of propositions assumed by the speaker prior to the utterance. The information conveyed by the utterance alters the context in certain ways. Gazdar's problem is to specify for each sentence and context how an utterance of the sentence would alter the context.

In trying to solve this problem, Gazdar imposes the following simplifying assumptions.

(a) The initial context of background assumptions is consistent.

(b) The method by which an utterance alters a context is always by adding propositions to it.

(c) If an utterance U_j by a speaker X immediately follows an utterance U_i of X in a conversation, the initial context of background assumptions for U_j = the enlarged context that results from U_i.

(d) Propositions are represented as sets of possible worlds.

(e) Where the proposition expressed by ϕ entails the proposition expressed by ψ, the proposition expressed by $\ulcorner\alpha$ knows that $\phi\urcorner$ entails the proposition expressed by $\ulcorner\alpha$ knows that $\psi\urcorner$.

A3. GAZDAR'S STRATEGY FOR CONTEXT INCREMENTATION

According to Gazdar, the incrementation of a context by an utterance proceeds in several stages. First, a *quality implicature* is added which states that the speaker knows that which he asserted. Next, *conversational implicatures* resulting from Grice's maxim of quantity are added. *Presuppositions* are added last. At each stage (except the first) a relevant proposition is added only if it is consistent (in a sense to be defined) with the context as it exists at that stage. Thus, propositions added at earlier stages can prevent the addition of propositions at later stages (if the latter are inconsistent with the former). Since conversational implicatures are added before presuppositions, the former can "cancel" the latter, but not vice versa.

Formalizing this strategy involves giving precise specifications of

(a) the notion of consistency that is required for context incrementation;

(b) the quality implicature that the speaker knows that which he asserted;

(c) the class of quantity implicatures that are candidates for addition to the context (potential quantity implicatures);

(d) the class of presuppositions that are candidates for addition (potential presuppositions).

Each of these is defined independently of variations from one context to another. The contents of (b)–(d) are determined by the semantic and syntactic structure of sentences considered in isolation from all contexts. Roughly speaking, these contents are supposed to capture the total potential information that an utterance of S might convey. When S is uttered in a particular context, the constraints imposed by the context (in conjunction with (a)) filter out some of this potential information to yield the actual information conveyed by the utterance in this context. The solution to the projection problem embodied in this system is one which claims that the potential presuppositions of a compound *sentence* are (roughly) those of its constituents; and the *actual* presuppositions of an *utterance* are those that survive the process of cancellation involved in context incrementation.

A4. FORMALIZING THE STRATEGY

A4.1. Consistency and Consistent Incrementations

Propositions are sets of possible worlds. A set X of propositions is consistent iff $\cap X$ (i.e., the intersection of all of its members) is not empty. Intuitively, a set X of propositions is consistent iff there is at least one world W such that each member of X is true in (i.e., contains) W.

Gazdar uses the notion of consistency to define the notion of *the satisfiable incrementation of a (consistent) set X of propositions by a set Y of propositions*. This definition can be stated informally as follows:

(A1) The satisfiable incrementation of X by Y consists of every proposition of X, plus each proposition of Y that preserves consistency when added to any consistent set of propositions drawn from X and Y.

Using $X \cup! Y$ for *the satisfiable incrementation of X by Y*, we can express (A1) symbolically as follows:

(A2) $X \cup! Y = X \cup \{y : y \in Y \ \& \ \forall Z((Z \subseteq (X \cup Y) \ \& \ \mathrm{con}(Z)) \supset \mathrm{con}(Z \cup \{y\}))\}$

One consequence of this definition is that if the set PP of propositions expressed by potential presuppositions of S contains inconsistent propositions Q and R, then neither Q nor R is in $X \cup!$ PP.

A4.2. The Quality Implicature

Where S is any (declarative) sentence, let KS be ⌜The speaker knows that S⌝. Where ϕ is any (declarative) sentence, let $[\phi]$ be the proposition expressed by ϕ. Gazdar, then, defines the *quality implicature* of an utterance of a sentence S to be [KS]. In other words, someone who assertively utters a sentence implicates that he knows that which he has asserted.

A4.3. Potential Quantity Implicatures

A4.3.1. Two Types. Grice's maxim of quantity directs speakers to make the strongest (relevant) statement they can. Where P is the proposition the speaker asserts and Q is "stronger" than P, the speaker's utterance typically carries the implicature that, roughly, the speaker was not in a position to assert Q.

Gazdar divides *quantity implicatures* into two types, according to the source of the implicatures in the sentence uttered. *Scalar implicatures* are those based on the presence in a sentence of an element that forms part of a quantitative scale; for example:

(A3) all, most, many, some, . . .
Ten, nine, eight, . . .
necessarily, possibly, . . .
must, may, . . .

Clausal implicatures are those based on the content of clauses of compound sentences. Gazdar gives clausal implicatures priority over scalar implicatures by stipulating that they be added, as a group, to context before the scalar implicatures are. Thus, clausal implicatures

are able to cancel (potential) scalar implicatures, but not vice versa.

A4.3.2. Potential Scalar Implicatures.
Someone who assertively utters one of the following (a)-sentences is normally taken to indicate that he is not in a position to assert the proposition expressed by the corresponding (b)-sentence.

(A4) a. *Some of the boys* were at the party.
     b. *All of the boys* were at the party.

(A5) a. *Possibly* prices will rise.
     b. *Necessarily* prices will rise.

(A6) a. Osmosis *may* involve porosity.
     b. Osmosis *must* involve porosity.

(A7) a. Mary *tried* to cash a check.
     b. Mary *succeeded* in cashing a check.

(A8) a. Bill *believes* he is ill.
     b. Bill *knows* he is ill.

(A9) a. ϕ *or* ψ
     b. ϕ *and* ψ

Gazdar's formal characterization of potential scalar implicatures is an attempt to capture these facts.

That characterization is stated in terms of the notion of a *quantitative scale* which, in turn, requires two preliminary definitions.

(A10) A sentence ϕ (of semantic representation) is *simple with respect to an occurrence of a component expression α* iff ϕ contains no logical functors[54] having wider scope than α.[55]

(A11) Sentences ϕ_α and ϕ_β are *expression alternatives with respect to α and β* iff ϕ_α is identical with ϕ_β except that ϕ_β has β in (exactly) one place where ϕ_α has α.

(A12) An n-tuple Q of expressions is a *quantitative scale* iff
    a. $Q = \langle \alpha_0, \alpha_1, \ldots \alpha_{n-1} \rangle$, where $n > 1$ and each constituent of Q has the same domain of (sortal) applicability[56] as every other constituent; and
    b. $[\phi_{\alpha_i}]$ entails[57] but is not entailed by $[\phi_{\alpha_j}]$, where ϕ_{α_j} and $\phi_{\alpha_{j+1}}$ are any pair of simple[58] expression alternatives with respect to $\alpha_i, \alpha_{i+1} \in Q$.[59]

Examples of quantitative scales that Gazdar takes to be in accord with this definition are

(A13) a. all of the, some of the
     b. necessarily, possibly
     c. must, may
     d. succeed, try
     e. know, believe
     f. and, or

The set of potential scalar implicatures of a sentence ψ can now be characterized in terms of a function f_s, defined as follows:

(A14) $f_s(\psi) = \{\gamma : \gamma = K \smallfrown \phi_{\alpha_i}\}$ for all ϕ_{α_i} such that for some Q, α_i, $\alpha_{i+1} \in Q$ and
  a. $\psi = X \overbrace{\phi_{\alpha_{i+1}}} Y$ (X, Y possibly null)
  b. $[\psi]$ entails $[\phi_{\alpha_{i+1}}]$

For simple cases like the (a)-examples of (A4)–(A9), this says, roughly, that the potential scalar implicatures of a sentence ψ are *sentences*[60] of the form (A15),

(A15) The speaker knows that $\smallfrown \phi$

where ϕ differs minimally from ψ and entails it by virtue of containing an element on a quantitative scale that is stronger than the corresponding element contained by ψ.[61]
  Applying this definition to (A4)–(A9) yields the following potential scalar implicatures.

(A4) c. K $\smallfrown$ all of the boys were at the party.

(A5) c. K $\smallfrown$ necessarily prices will rise.

(A6) c. K $\smallfrown$ osmosis must involve porosity.

(A7) c. K $\smallfrown$ Mary succeeded in cashing a check.

(A8) c. K $\smallfrown$ Bill knows he is ill.

(A9) c. K $\smallfrown$ (ϕ and ψ)

Thus, Gazdar implicitly claims that the reason why someone who utters one of the (a)-sentences normally indicates that he is not in a position to assert (b) is that Grice's maxim of quantity gives rise to an even stronger implicature: namely, that the speaker knows that (b) is not true.

A4.3.3. Potential Clausal Implicatures.
Paradigm examples of clausal, quantity implicatures are those arising from utterances of sentences of the following form:

(A16) a. ϕ or ψ
  b. If ϕ, then ψ
  c. If ϕ and ψ, then Γ

Utterances of these sentences conversationally implicate (A17).

(A17) $\smallfrown K\phi$, $\smallfrown K\smallfrown\phi$, $\smallfrown K\psi$, $\smallfrown K\smallfrown\psi$ ((c) also implicates $\smallfrown K\Gamma$, $\smallfrown K\smallfrown\Gamma$)

These implicatures can be explained by the following informal reasoning. Consider an utterance of (A16a). If the speaker had known the truth value of one of the disjuncts, he would have been in a position to make a stronger statement. If he had known that ϕ were true, he could have asserted it. If he had known that $\ulcorner\smallfrown\phi\urcorner$ were true, and also had sufficient evidence to warrant asserting (A16a) in the first place,[62] then he would have been in a position to assert ψ. Since both ϕ and ψ entail, but are not entailed by, (A16a), they are stronger than (A16a). Since the speaker chose to assert only the latter, the assumption that he was obeying the maxim of quantity requires us to conclude that he was not in a position to assert either disjunct. Thus, he must not have known the truth value of either. Hence, the implicatures.[63]
  Gazdar proposes to replace this informal reasoning by a formal characterization of the set of potential, clausal, quantity implicatures of a sentence S. This is done by defining a function f_c from sentences (of semantic representation) to sets of sentences (of semantic representation) that represent the implicatures.

(A18) $f_c(\phi) = \{\gamma : \gamma \in \{\smallfrown K\psi,\ \smallfrown K \smallfrown\psi\}\}$ for all sentences ψ such that
  a. $\phi = X \overbrace{\psi} Y$, where X and Y are possibly null (roughly, ψ is a clause of ϕ); and
  b. $[\phi]$ does not entail $[\psi]$; and
  c. $[\phi]$ does not entail $[\smallfrown\psi]$;[64] and
  d. ψ occurs in ϕ in at least one nonpresuppositional position—that is, ϕ has some expression alternative ϕ_α with respect to ψ and α, where α is a sentence such that
    i. $\alpha \neq \psi$; and
    ii. neither Kα nor K $\smallfrown$ α is a potential presupposition of ϕ_α.[65]

Application of (A18) to the sentences in (A16) produces the desired (potential) implicatures in (A17).
  It also produces many more, for which informal Gricean arguments cannot always be constructed; for example:[66]

(A19) a. Aquinas said that ϕ.
  b. Either Aquinas said that ϕ or he said that ψ.
  c. Aquinas said that if ϕ, then ψ.
  d. Aquinas said that Aristotle wondered whether ϕ.

(A20) Potential clausal, quantity, implicatures generated by (A18).
  $\{\smallfrown K\phi,\ \smallfrown K\smallfrown\phi\}$ for (a), (d)
  $\{\smallfrown K\phi,\ \smallfrown K\smallfrown\phi,\ \smallfrown K\psi,\ \smallfrown K\smallfrown\psi\}$ (b), (c)

Gazdar recognizes that there are contexts in which an utterance of (A19a–d) would not implicate the corresponding potential implicature in (A20). However, he limits such contexts to those that already contain, prior to the addition of potential clausal implicatures, propositions inconsistent with those implicatures. In effect, Gazdar predicts that if the speaker has not already established his knowledge of ϕ, or its negation, prior to uttering (A19a–d), then his utterance will implicate that he does not know either. (If he hasn't said, he doesn't know.)

A4.3.4. Potential Presuppositions.

Potential presuppositions of *sentences* are candidates for becoming actual presuppositions of *utterances* of those sentences. Potential presuppositions are completely determined by the form and content of sentences. Whether or not they become actual depends on the context at the time of incrementation.

According to Gazdar, all potential presuppositions have the form (A21):

(A21) $K\phi$

This allows them to be canceled by conversational implicatures on the basis of simple, logical incompatibility.

Examples of constructions that give rise to potential presuppositions are those given in (18)–(25). Gazdar does not attempt to specify all constructions that give rise to potential presuppositions or to give formal characterizations of the presuppositions corresponding to each construction he does consider. However, he does present a conception of the general form of such a theory together with some illustrative components.

For each construction that gives rise to potential presuppositions, there is a corresponding function yielding these presuppositions.

(A22) *Factives*
$$f_1(\phi) = \{\psi : \psi = K\gamma \ \& \ \phi = X \ \widehat{\upsilon \ \text{that}} \ \widehat{\gamma} \ Y\}$$
where υ is factive or semifactive, ϕ and γ are sentences, X and Y possibly null.
(Sentences containing factive verbs potentially presuppose that the speaker knows the factive complement to be true.)

(A23) *Definite Descriptions*
$$f_2(\phi) = \{\psi : \psi = K\gamma \ \& \ \phi = X \ \widehat{\text{the } \alpha} \ Y \ \& \ \gamma = \text{there is a } \widehat{\alpha}\}$$

where $\widehat{\text{the } \alpha}$ is the longest string, having that occurrence of *the* as its initial element, which is an NP; ϕ and ψ are sentences, X and Y possibly null.
(Sentences containing definite descriptions carry the relevant potential, existential presuppositions.)

(A24) *Before*
$$f_3(\phi) = \{\psi : \psi = K\gamma \ \& \ \phi = X \ \widehat{\text{before}} \ \widehat{\gamma} \ Y\} \cdot \phi, \gamma \text{ sentences; X, Y possibly null.}$$
(Sentences containing *before* potentially presuppose any clause immediately following *before*.)

Gazdar envisions a complete account of potential presupposition as specifying such a function for each presupposition-yielding construction.[67] The set F of all of these functions is then used to define a comprehensive function f_p, which characterizes the complete set of potential presuppositions of an arbitrary sentence ϕ.

(A25) $f_p(\phi) = \bigcup_{f_i \in F} f_i(\phi)$

This says that the complete set of potential presuppositions of ϕ is the sum of the results of applying each subfunction (corresponding to a distinct presupposition-yielding construction) to ϕ.

It should be noted that the functions assigning potential presuppositions to sentences operate without respect to the complexity of the sentences they apply to. For example, f_2 above assigns potential existential presuppositions on the basis of an occurrence of a definite description anywhere in the sentence. Thus, no projection machinery for assigning potential presuppositions to compound sentences on the basis of those of their clauses is needed.[68] The same functions that assign potential presuppositions to simple sentences apply to compound sentences as well.

A4.3.5. The Formula for Context Incrementation.

Let C be the conversational context prior to the speaker's utterance of ϕ. Let $\{f_s(\phi)\}$, $\{f_c(\phi)\}$, $\{f_p(\phi)\}$ be the sets of propositions expressed by members of $f_s(\phi)$, $f_c(\phi)$, $f_p(\phi)$, respectively (e.g., $\{f_s(\phi)\} = \{p \mid \exists s \ ([s] = p \ \& \ s \in f_s(\phi))\}$). The context C' resulting from the utterance is then characterized as follows:

(A26) $C' = (((C \cup \{[K\phi]\}) \cup! \{f_c(\phi)\}) \cup! \{f_p(\phi)\}$

In other words, Gazdar predicts the resulting context to contain

(a) every member of the initial context;

(b) the proposition that the speaker knows that which he asserted (the quality implicature);

(c) all potential clausal, quantity implicatures that can consistently be added[69] to the result of combining (a) and (b);

(d) all potential scalar, quantity implicatures that can consistently be added to the result achieved at stage (c);

(e) all potential presuppositions that can consistently be added to the result achieved at stage (d).

A good way of testing Gazdar's predictions is by considering utterances of sentences in contexts that do not already contain a given proposition P, or its negation. If (A26) predicts that P would be added to the context on the basis of the utterance, then it predicts that the utterance commits the speaker to P. If it predicts that P would not be added, then it predicts that the utterance does not commit the speaker to P. Thus, we can test Gazdar's system by consulting our intuitions about what various utterances commit a speaker to.

A5. FALSE PREDICTIONS ABOUT PRESUPPOSITION PROJECTION

A5.1. The Nature of the Problem

The central problem facing Gazdar's account of presupposition projection is that it commits the speaker to too much by predicting actual presuppositions where none exist. The source of the problem is a failure to recognize that potential presuppositions can be suspended without being canceled. As a result, the problem cannot be solved by any technical adjustments within Gazdar's basic framework.

A5.2. Some Counterexamples

All of the counterexamples to Strategy 1 theories cited in the main text ((45)–(50), (88), (89)) are counterexamples to Gazdar's analysis. For present purposes, (88a)—here renumbered as (A27)—can be used to represent all of them.

(A27) If Haldeman is guilty, then Nixon is guilty, too.

(A28) *Potential Presupposition* (as characterized by Gazdar)
K $(\exists x)(x \neq$ n & Gx) (The speaker knows that someone other than Nixon is guilty)

(A29) *Potential Clausal, Quantity Implicatures*
$\sim$KG(h), $\sim$K$\sim$G(h), $\sim$KG(n), $\sim$K$\sim$G(n)

Let C be a context that does not already contain (entail) either (A28) or its negation. Since (A28) is compatible with (A29), and since there are no relevant scalar implicatures to consider, Gazdar's principle of context incrementation—(A26)—adds (A28) to C in producing the context C′ resulting from the utterance. Thus, Gazdar wrongly predicts that an utterance of (A27) in C would commit the speaker to the truth of (A28).

A5.3. Why the Problem Cannot Be Solved

In Gazdar's system, the only way to prevent a potential presupposition from being inherited is to cancel it, using the initial context, the quality implicature of the utterance, the scalar implicatures, the clausal implicatures, or another potential presupposition. In the examples we are concerned with, there are no relevant scalar implicatures or additional potential presuppositions capable of doing the canceling. Contexts can always be chosen that are compatible with the problematic potential presupposition, and there is no question of attributing the cancellation to the quality implicature. Thus, the only candidate for revision is (A18)—the formal characterization of the class of clausal, quantity implicatures of a sentence.

What is needed is a modification of (A18) that assigns (A30) to (A27).

(A30) $\sim$K $\exists x(x \neq n$ & Gx)

The reason (A18) does not now do this is that the italicized portion of (A30) is not a clause of (A31), which we may take to be the semantic representation of (A27).

(A31) G(h) $\rightarrow$ G(n)[70]

What is needed is a liberalized version of (A18) which produces potential quantity implicatures that are *based on* the clauses of the semantic representation of the sentence uttered, without being *part of* that representation.

Although it is easy to produce reformulations of (A18) that have this characteristic, it is equally easy to see that no such reformulation will solve the problem. There are two reasons for this. First, any reformulation capable of canceling (A28) would have to generate (A30) as a conversational implicature of (A27).[71] However, someone who utters (A27) does not implicate this.[72] Thus, the price of blocking a nonexistent presupposition is the generation of a nonexistent conversational implicature.

The second reason why no such reformulation will solve the problem is illustrated by the contrast between (89a) and (89b)—here renumbered (A32) and (A33).

(A32) If Nixon is guilty, too, then Haldeman is (guilty).

(A33) Haldeman is guilty, if Nixon is guilty, too.

These sentences express the same proposition and have the same potential presuppositions. Since Grice's quantity implicatures are based on the statement made by an utterance, utterances of these sentences also have the same quantity implicatures. Gazdar's formalization reflects this by making potential quantity implicatures depend on semantic representations.[73] Presumably, (A32) and (A33) have the same semantic representations. Thus, any reformulation of (A18) will assign these sentences the same potential, clausal implicatures.

It follows that no such reformulation is capable of accounting for the different presuppositional behavior of these sentences. As Gazdar's system now stands, it incorrectly predicts that utterances of (A33), as well as (A27), presuppose (A28). If (A18) were modified so as to produce a canceling implicature, the presupposition in (A32) would be eliminated and a case of actual presupposition inheritance would be missed. Either way, it is impossible to account for all of these examples in Gazdar's framework.

A5.4. A Case in Point

A5.4.1. Landman's Proposal.
The futility of trying to handle Strategy 2 type presupposition suspension within Gazdar's framework can be illustrated by considering an attempt to do so. Landman (1981) acknowledges that the formalization in Gazdar (1979a,b) is falsified by the examples presented in Soames (1979)—examples which include (A27). He also sees that the only move available is to modify Gazdar's characterization of clausal quantity implicatures so as to produce the requisite canceling implicatures (e.g., (A30)). Thus, he sets himself the task of modifying (A18).

Landman's proposed replacement is (A34).

(A34) *Revised Characterization of Potential Clausal Quantity Implicatures*
$f_c(\phi) = \{\gamma : \gamma \in \{-K\psi, -K\sim\psi\}\}$
for all ψ such that for some Δ
   a. $\phi = X \frown \Delta \frown Y$; X and Y possibly null
   b. $[\Delta]$ entails $[\psi]$
   c. $[\phi]$ does not entail $[\psi]$
   d. $[\phi]$ does not entail $[\sim\psi]$

As Landman notes, this amounts to taking the logical consequences of clauses, rather than the clauses themselves, as that about which a speaker implicates ignorance. This is a natural modification. The counterexamples presented in Soames (1979) (and in section 6 above) are ones in which the relevant potential presupposition is entailed by (the context plus) one of the clauses of the sentence uttered, without itself being a clause of that sentence. Landman's proposal is designed to block presupposition inheritance in just such cases.

Nevertheless, Landman has not solved the problem, but simply moved it elsewhere. This is shown by the following five falsifying counterarguments.

A5.4.2. Argument 1: Nonexistent Conversational Implicatures.
A speaker who assertively utters (A27) does not conversationally implicate (A30).[74] Similarly, a speaker who assertively utters (45)–(50) does not conversationally implicate that he does not know B^p. Thus, for every nonexistent presupposition blocked by (A34), there is a corresponding nonexistent conversational implicature

that is generated. As a result, the only achievement of (A34) is to replace false predictions about presuppositions with false predictions about conversational implicatures.

This dilemma is inevitable for every Strategy 1 theory. It is created by the existence of utterances which are neutral (in the sense characteized in section 6) regarding a speaker's attitude toward a potential presupposition. Since pure Strategy 1 theories cannot, in principle, recognize the existence of such cases, they cannot be saved by any technical modifications.

A5.4.3. Argument 2: The Asymmetry of Presupposition Suspension.

Gazdar (1979a,b) incorrectly predicts that utterances of (A27) and (A33) presuppose (A28). Landman's (A34) blocks these precitions by assigning (A30) as a (canceling) conversational implicature in these cases. However, it also assigns (A30) to (A32), thereby missing the fact that (A32) inherits its potential presupposition. As a result, an incorrect account of one set of cases is replaced by an incorrect account of another.

As before, this dilemma is inevitable as long as one fails to recognize Strategy 2 presupposition suspension and relies instead on cancellation via quantity implicatures. Since quantity implicatures are dependent on the statement made by an utterance of a sentence, they ought to be insensitive to the order in which the clauses in (A32) and (A33) are uttered. Consequently, such implicatures cannot discriminate between these examples.[75]

A5.4.4. Argument 3: An Uncanceled Instance of Suspension.

Consider (A35)–(A37):

(A35) If the dress Mary bought is powder blue and the dress Susan bought is, too, then Mary will regret having bought a dress that is the same color as Susan's.

(A36) If the dress Mary bought is powder blue, then if the dress Susan bought is also powder blue, Mary will regret having bought a dress that is the same color as Susan's.

(A37) Mary bought a dress that is the same color as Susan's.

Although (A37) is embedded beneath the factive verb *regret,* utterances of (A35) and

(A36) do not presuppose (A37) or commit the speaker to (A38).

(A38) K(A37)

Since Gazdar counts (A38) as a potential presupposition, he predicts that it is inherited unless it is conversationally canceled. However, in his theory there is no way of canceling it. The clause (A37) does not occur in nonpresuppositional position in (A35) or (A36). Thus, (A18) does not assign a canceling implicature,

(A39) ¬K(A37)

and Gazdar's theory wrongly predicts (A38) to be inherited.

Landman's (A34) takes the logical consequence of clauses, rather than the clauses themselves, to generate the relevant implicatures. Since the antecedent of (A35) entails (A37), (A34) blocks the inheritance of (A38). However, it cannot do this in the case of (A36). If the semantic representation of this sentence is (A40),

(A40) (A → (B → C))

then none of the clauses in its representation entails (A37). Thus, Landman's modification of Gazdar (1979a,b) retains the incorrect prediction that utterances of (A36) commit the speaker to (A38).[76]

A5.4.5. Argument 4: The Wholesale Elimination of Genuine Presuppositions.

A5.4.5.1. A Problem. Let S be a sentence that entails P and potentially presupposes KP in Gazdar's system. Examples include the following.

(A41) The Crown Prince of Sri Lanka is in hiding.
   K *There is a Crown Prince of Sri Lanka.*

(A42) Sam is the one who solved the problem.
   K *Someone solved the problem.*

(A43) Harry sold his car before he left town.
   K *Harry left town.*

(A44) Martha regrets taking the job.
   K *Martha took the job.*

Now form a compound sentence by embedding S under negation, epistemic modals, verbs like *likely* (which are holes for presuppositions), *or, if, then,* etc. This produces examples like the following.

(A45) a. The Crown Prince of Sri Lanka isn't in hiding.
      b. Maybe the Crown Prince of Sri Lanka is in hiding.
      Pot. Presupp.: K *There is a Crown Prince of Sri Lanka.*

(A46) a. It is likely that Sam is the one who solved the problem.
      b. If the problem is difficult, then Sam is the one who solved it.
      Pot. Presupp.: K *Someone solved the problem.*

(A47) a. Maybe Harry sold his car before he left town.
      b. Either Harry sold his car before he left town, or he withdrew all the money from his savings account.
      Pot. Presupp.: K *Harry left town.*

(A48) a. If Martha regrets taking the job, then she is probably not easy to get along with.
      b. Maybe Martha regrets taking the job.
      Pot. Presupp.: K *Martha took the job.*

Finally, let ϕ be one of the (a)- or (b)-sentences above, ψ the italicized part of its potential presupposition, and Δ the clause of ϕ corresponding to the relevant example in (A41)–(A44). Landman's characterization of potential clausal quantity implicatures—(A34)—incorrectly predicts conversational implicatures of the form $\frown K\psi$ in these cases. Since these implicatures cancel the corresponding potential presupposition, Landman's modification of Gazdar's framework fails to account for paradigm cases of presupposition inheritance of the kind illustrated by (A45)–(A48) above.

A5.4.5.2. A Modification. In presenting his modification of Gazdar's (A18), Landman (1981, 468) notes that he is "leaving aside that part of the definition not relevant to our purpose." The part of the definition he does not consider is condition (d) of (A18) which requires that the clause upon which the potential clausal implicature is based must occur in ϕ in at least one nonpresuppositional position. Adding this requirement as a fifth condition to Landman's (A34) results in (A34'):

(A34') *Revised Characterization of Potential Clausal Quantity Implicatures*
$$f_c(\phi) = \{\gamma : \gamma \in \{\frown K\psi, \frown K \frown \psi\}\}$$
for all ψ such that for some Δ
    a. $\phi = X \frown \Delta \frown Y$, X and Y possibly null

    b. [Δ] entails [ψ]
    c. [ϕ] does not entail [ψ]
    d. [ϕ] does not entail [$\frown\psi$]
    e. Δ occurs in ϕ in some nonpresuppositional position—that is, ϕ has some expression alternative ϕ_α with respect to Δ and α, where α is a sentence such that
      i. $\alpha \neq \Delta$; and
      ii. neither K α nor K $\frown \alpha$ is a potential presupposition of ϕ_α

Addition of clause (e) does nothing to block the canceling implicatures predicted for (A45)–(A48).[77] Thus, it does not save Landman's proposal from misconstruing paradigmatic instances of presupposition inheritance.

Perhaps an extension of (A34') will do the job. In each of the above examples, the clause Δ which is allowed to generate the canceling implicature is a clause that carries the potential presupposition itself. This suggests the need for a further condition (f) to rule out this possibility.

(A34") Same as (A34') except for the addition of (f)
    f. Kψ, and K $\frown \psi$, $\in f_p(\Delta)$

Although baroque, (A34") correctly predicts presupposition inheritance in (A45)–(A48).[78]

A5.4.5.3. Falsifying Counterexamples: The Problem Recreated. Consider (A49) and (A50):

(A49) a. If John didn't say that Mary solved the problem, then Mary didn't solve it.
      b. If John didn't say that Mary solved the problem, then it wasn't Mary who solved it.
      Inherited presupposition of (b): K *Someone solved the problem.*

(A50) a. If John doubts that Martin proved the theorem, then Martin may not have proved it.
      b. If John doubts that Martin proved the theorem, then Martin may not be the one who proved it.
      Inherited presupposition of (b): K *Someone has proved the theorem.*

Where ϕ is either one of the (b)-sentences above, Δ is the complement of *say/doubt,* and ψ is the italicized part of the potential presupposition, all of the conditions of (A34") are met. Consequently, this modification of Gazdar's system incorrectly generates conversational implicatures --Kψ which cancel the potential presuppositions of (A49b) and (A50b). Since these presuppositions are in fact inherited by utterances of the (b)-sentences, the system continues to misconstrue innumerable instances of presupposition inheritance.[79]

The source of the problem lies in the interaction of two factors:

(a) Gazdar's conception of potential, clausal, quantity implicatures as arising from clauses generally, no matter what semantic content is carried by the matrix structures in which they are embedded;[80]

(b) Landman's revision of the characterization of clausal quantity implicatures to allow entailments of clauses to generate canceling potential implicatures.

(b) was needed to avoid false predictions about examples like (A27). What (A49) and (A50) show is that the cost of avoiding those predictions is the generation of a different set of false predictions. Falsifying instances have simply been shifted from one part of the theory to another.[81]

A5.4.6. Argument 5: Too Many Implicatures. Landman's modification of Gazdar falsely characterized (A49b) and (A50b) as failing to inherit the relevant potential presuppositions. It did this by predicting conversational implicatures that do not exist. Thus, these examples illustrate two problems: the elimination of genuine presuppositions and the generation of nonexistent conversational implicatures.

The distinctness of these problems is illustrated by (A49a) and (A50a). A speaker who utters these sentences does not conversationally implicate (A51) and (A52), respectively.

(A51) –K Someone solved the problem.

(A52) –K Someone proved the theorem.

Here, the problem is not that the theory blocks the inheritance of genuine presuppositions, but simply that it generates the wrong implicatures. Thus, even if some way could be found of reinstating the presuppositions of (A49b) and (A50b) within the Landman–Gazdar framework, the generation of too many implicatures would still falsify the theory. It is simply not true that speakers conversationally implicate that they do not know the truth

value of *any* entailment of *any* clause of *any* sentence that they utter.[82]

A6. PROBLEMS WITH GAZDAR'S FORMALIZATION OF CONVERSATIONAL IMPLICATURES

A6.1. Overview

I take it to have been shown that Strategy 1 theories, like Gazdar's, cannot provide a complete account of presupposition projection. In addition to the cancellation of potential presuppositions by context and conversational implicatures, an adequate account must make room for the suspension of potential presuppositions by Strategy 2 type means. If this is granted, then some of the pressure on the theory of conversational implicature is removed. Since conversational implicatures are no longer seen as responsible for blocking the inheritance of potential presuppositions in cases like (A27), these cases provide no motivation for substituting Landman's problematic (A34) for Gazdar's more plausible (A18).

Recognizing this limitation on the theoretical role of conversational implicature does not diminish the interest of formalizing this notion. Gazdar's proposed formalization consists of three main elements:

(a) a proposed formalization of potential scalar, quantity implicatures—(A14);

(b) a proposed formalization of potential, clausal, quantity implicatures—(A18);

(c) the proposed priority of clausal implicatures in canceling potential scalar implicatures—incorporated in (A26).

I will argue that the scalar implicatures generated by (a) are too strong, that the priority of clausal over scalar implicatures posited by (c) is unnecessary, and that the clausal quantity implicatures aimed at by (b) resist formalization.

A6.2. Scalar, Quantity Implicatures

A6.2.1. Counterclaims. According to Gazdar, the (a)-sentences in (A4)–(A9) conversationally implicate that the speaker knows the negation of the proposition expressed by the

corresponding (b)-sentence. Let us use (A4a,b) and, in general, sentences of the form (A53a,b) to represent the issues raised by all such examples.

(A4) a. Some of the boys were at the party.
      b. All of the boys were at the party.

(A53) a. Some of the NPs VP
      b. All of the NPs VP

My counterclaims are the following:

(a) The potential, scalar quantity implicatures of sentences of the form (A53a) are not of the form K⌐(A53b), but rather of the form ⌐K(A53b).

(b) Utterances of sentences of the form (A53a) give rise to particularized conversational implicatures of the form K⌐(A53b) when
    (i) the generalized[83] scalar implicature, ⌐K(A53b), is uncanceled and hence actual; and
    (ii) the context contains the propositions expressed by
         (A53b) ⊃ K(A53b)
         ⌐(A53b) ⊃ K⌐(A53b)

If these claims are correct, then Gazdar's characterization of the class of potential scalar implicatures of a sentence ψ should be modified in the manner of (A14′).[84]

(A14′) $f_s(\psi) = \{\gamma : \gamma = K\phi_{\alpha_j}\}$
        for all ϕ_{α_j} such that for some quantitative scale Q, $\alpha_i, \alpha_{i+1} \in Q$ and
        a. $\psi = X \overbrace{\phi_{\alpha_{i+1}}} Y$ (X,Y possibly null)
        b. $[\psi]$ entails $[\phi_{\alpha_{i+1}}]$

A6.2.2. The Argument.

Grice's maxim of quantity requires speakers to make the strongest statement they can (that is relevant to the conversation). If P and Q are both relevant, and Q entails, but is not entailed by, P, then Q is stronger than P. Let us assume, with Gazdar, that propositions expressed by sentences of the form (A53b) entail those expressed by sentences of the form (A53a). Then, when both are relevant to the conversation, Grice's maxim of quantity requires the speaker to assert (A53b) if he is in a position to do so.

To be in a position to assert a proposition is to be in a position to assert it *without violating other conversational maxims*—in particular the maxim of quality.

(A54) *Maxim of Quality*
      Try to make your contribution one that is true.

a. Do not say what you believe to be false.
b. Do not say that for which you lack adequate evidence.

Since the notion of adequate evidence is here left vague, it is not obvious that this maxim requires one to assert only those propositions one knows. Nevertheless, Gazdar's strengthened version (A55)

(A55) Assert only what you know.

is a reasonable idealization of the maxim of quality that may be adopted for the purpose of argument.

This means that when (A53a) and (A53b) are both relevant to the conversation, Grice's maxim of quantity requires the speaker to assert the stronger, (A53b), *provided that he knows it to be true*. Thus, if he chooses to assert only (A53a), he conversationally implicates that he does not know (A53b). There is no general argument that he must know the negation of (A53b). Thus, utterances of sentences of the form (A53a) carry generalized implicatures of the form ⌐K(A53b), rather than K⌐(A53b).

In cases in which the speaker can be presumed to know the truth value of (A53b), these generalized implicatures can be used to derive stronger, particularized implicatures. For example, consider (A56).

(A56) a. Some of the books on my shelf are paperbacks.
      b. All of the books on my shelf are paperbacks.

In most contexts, someone who asserts (A56a) can be presumed to know the truth value of (A56b). In other words, it can be presumed that (A57) is true.

(A57) (A56b) ⊃ K(A56b)
       ⌐(A56b) ⊃ K⌐(A56b)

The particularized implicature K⌐(A56b) is derived from the generalized implicature ⌐K(A56b) together with (A57).

Whether or not a speaker who utters a sentence of the form (A53a) can be presumed to know the truth value of (A53b) depends on the context and the content of (A53b). For example, it is easy to imagine contexts in which someone who uttered (A58a) would not be presumed to know the truth value of (A58b),

even if he were presumed to be obeying conversational maxims.

(A58) a. Some of the birds we tagged last summer
          have migrated to California.
       b. All of the birds we tagged last summer
          have migrated to California.

In such a context, an utterance of (A58a)
would conversationally implicate $\smile$K(A58b)
without implicating K$\smile$(A58b).[85]

The way to account for the difference between these examples is to assign potential
scalar quantity implicatures, $\smile$K(A53b), to all
sentences of the form (A53a), and to derive
stronger particularized implicatures when the
context justifies the presumption that the
speaker knows the truth value of (A53b). This
means that (A14′) must be substituted for
Gazdar's (A14).

A6.3. Eliminating the Priority of Clausal over Scalar Implicatures

A6.3.1. Strategy.
Gazdar's claim that
clausal implicatures have priority over scalar
implicatures lacks an independent explanation. (Why should one have priority over the
other?) It is made necessary by his inaccurate
account of scalar implicatures. Once (A14′) is
substituted for (A14), no such priority is
needed.

A6.3.2. Gazdar's Argument.
Gazdar's ar-
gument for the priority of clausal over scalar
implicatures is based on two examples.

(A59) a. John did it or Mary did it.
       b. John did it or Mary did it or both of them
          did it.
       c. John did it and Mary did it.

(A60) a. Some of the students were there.
       b. Some, if not all, of the students were
          there.[86]
       c. All of the students were there.

Consider (A59). According to (A14) and
(A18), (A59a) and (A59b) carry the following
potential quantity implicatures:

(A61) a. Alleged Potential Implicatures of (A59a)
          Scalar: K$\smile$(A59c)
          Clausal: $\smile$K John did it, $\smile$K $\smile$John
                   did it, $\smile$K Mary did it, $\smile$K
                   $\smile$Mary did it

       b. Alleged Potential Implicatures of (A59b)
          Scalar: K$\smile$(A59c)
          Clausal: Same as (A59a) plus
                   $\smile$K(A59c), $\smile$K$\smile$(A59c)

Given these implicatures plus his strategy of
context incrementation, Gazdar has no choice
but to accord clausal implicatures priority
over their scalar counterparts. To give scalar
implicatures priority would be to incorrectly
characterize utterances of (A59b) as implicating that the speaker knows the third disjunct
of his utterance—(A59c)—to be false.[87] To
give neither priority would be to fail to characterize utterances of (A59b) as implicating
that the speaker does not know the truth value
of (A59c).[88] Gazdar's only alternative is to give
clausal implicatures priority, thereby canceling the scalar implicature of (A59b) and leaving its clausal implicatures intact. The pragmatic difference between (A59a) and (A59b) is
then claimed to be this: utterances of (A59b)
implicate that the speaker does not know the
truth value of (A59c), whereas utterances of
(A59a) implicate that he knows it to be false.
(A60) is treated analogously.[89]

A6.3.3. Rebuttal.
Gazdar's argument rests
on the false assumption that the potential scalar implicature of (A59a) and (A59b) is K$\smile$
(A59c) rather than $\smile$K(A59c). When the latter is substituted for the former, the argument
collapses. The potential scalar implicature, $\smile$
K(A59c), is entailed by the clausal implicatures common to both sentences,[90] and hence
can be disregarded. Thus, the pragmatic difference between (A59a) and (A59b) results entirely from their different clausal implicatures.
(A59b) implicates $\smile$K$\smile$(A59c); (A59a) does
not. The pragmatic difference between the two
sentences is, therefore, this: utterances of
(A59b) implicate that for all the speaker
knows, (A59c) may be true;[91] whereas utterances of (A59a) are compatible with the possibility that he knows it to be false. In general,
one uses a sentence ⌜φ or ψ or both⌝ when one
wants to make explicit one's ignorance about
the possibility that φ and ψ might both be true.
One uses ⌜φ or ψ⌝ when one does not wish to
do this.[92]

(A60) parallels (A59).[93] In both cases, the
pragmatic differences between the (a)- and (b)-
sentences can be explained, and incorrect pre-

dictions avoided, without giving either scalar or clausal implicatures priority over the other.

A6.4. Clausal, Quantity Implicatures

In section 4.3.3, I pointed out that Gazdar's characterization of potential, clausal, quantity implicatures—(A18)—assigns the potential implicatures in (A20) to the sentences in (A19).

(A19) a. Aquinas said that ϕ.
   b. Either Aquinas said that ϕ or he said that ψ.
   c. Aquinas said that if ϕ, then ψ.
   d. Aquinas said that Aristotle wondered whether ϕ.

(A20) $\sim K\phi, \sim K\sim\phi$ (a),(d)
      $\sim K\phi, \sim K\sim\phi, \sim K\psi, \sim K\sim\psi$ (b),(c)

Let C be a context that does not already contain $K\phi$, $K \sim \phi$, $K\psi$, $K \sim \psi$. If it is clear from the nature of C that the point of uttering (A19a–d) is to adduce evidence for or against ϕ (or ψ), then utterances of (A19a–d) will conversationally implicate the propositions in (A20). The reason is simple. If the conversational participants are trying to determine the truth value of ϕ (or ψ), it will be more informative for the speaker to assert ϕ (or ψ) than to assert (A19a–d). Since he in fact asserts only the latter, the presumption that he is obeying the maxim of quantity leads to the conclusion that he does not know the truth value of the former. Hence, the implicatures in (A20).

There are also contexts C in which the point of assertively uttering (A19a–d) is not to adduce evidence for or against ϕ (or ψ), but rather to present a historically accurate account of the views of Aquinas. In such contexts, determining the truth value of ϕ (or ψ) may be irrelevant to the conversation. If it is, then utterances of (A19a–d) will not carry the implicatures in (A20)—even though they are not inconsistent with anything in C. Gazdar's theory—which includes (A18)—predicts just the opposite. Thus, his characterization of potential, clausal, quantity implicatures cannot be accepted.

Since the notion of informativeness used in the maxim of quantity seems to be closely related to the notion of conversational relevance, formalizing the former would seem to

require formalizing the latter. At present, I see no way of doing this and hence will not offer a substitute for (A18).

A7. SOME PUTATIVE COUNTEREXAMPLES TO STRATEGY 2 PRESUPPOSITION SUSPENSION

A7.1. Two Kinds of Examples

Gazdar (1979a,b) presents two types of alleged counterexamples to the Strategy 2 theory of Karttunen and Peters.

(A62) Type A: Examples in which Karttunen and Peters predict presuppositions that are nonexistent because of conversational and contextual canceling.
   Type B: Examples in which Karttunen and Peters eliminate presuppositions that should remain.

Examples of type A are generally genuine and are accounted for by my synthesis of Strategies 1 and 2. Examples of type B would be counterexamples to my theory if they were genuine counterexamples to the theory of Karttunen and Peters. Fortunately, they are not.

A7.2. Example One

A7.2.1. Gazdar's Criticism.   Consider examples (A63a–c).

(A63) a. If all countries are now republics, then it is unlikely that the President of France still feels lonely.
   b. There is a President of France.
   c. All countries are $\supset$ There is a
      now republics   President
                           of
                           France

We are to imagine (A63a) being uttered in a context that alraedy contains (A64).

(A64) All republics have presidents.

Gazdar makes two claims about these utterances:

(a) They presuppose (A63b).

(b) Karttunen and Peters wrongly predict that they do not presuppose this, but instead presuppose only the trivial (A63c).

These claims are intended to show that there are utterance presuppositions that are incorrectly eliminated (reduced to trivialities) by Strategy 2 inheritance algorithms. They fail to do this because claim (b) is false.

A7.2.2. An Analogous Example.

First consider an analogous case in which Strategy 2 mechanisms actually do suspend presuppositions.

(A65) a. If all countries have presidents, then the President of France probably regards himself as their cultural leader.
   b. There is a President of France.
   c. All countries have ⊃ There is a
      presidents   President
                         of
                         France

If (A65b) is not already in the context, then an utterance of (A65a) would not result in its being added. Someone hearing (A65a) would, of course, conclude that the speaker does not know whether or not all countries have presidents. (This is conversationally implicated.) Thus, he would also conclude that the speaker does not know that there is no President of France ($\backsim K \backsim (A65b)$). However, this leaves it open whether the speaker knows for a fact that France has a president ($K(A65b)$), or whether he has no such knowledge ($\backsim K(A65b)$). Either way, the speaker's remark makes sense as a comment on the cultural pretensions of the French. Thus, it is *neutral* regarding whether or not the speaker assumes (A65b), and no utterance presupposition is heard.

Strategy 2 accounts for this with no difficulty. The antecedent of (A65a), together with the background assumption that France is a country, entails the potential presupposition—(A65b)—of the consequent. Thus, Strategy 2 correctly predicts that no substantive presupposition is inherited from the consequent.

It is Strategy 1 that cannot accommodate the facts. Since $K(A65b)$ is compatible with (A66),

(A66) $\backsim K$ All countries have presidents.
       $\backsim K \backsim$ All countries have presidents.

Gazdar's theory incorrectly predicts that utterances of (A65a) inevitably commit the speaker to (A65b).[94]

A7.2.3. The Source of the Presupposition

of (A63a). The suspension of (A65b) raises a question about why (A63b) is not also suspended. The difference between the two cases has nothing to do with the difference in their antecedents. Utterances of (A67)

(A67) If all countries are republics, then the President of France probably regards his republic as superior to all the others.

in contexts in which (A64) is taken for granted receive the same analysis as utterances of (A65a). Similarly, utterances of (A68)

(A68) If all countries now have presidents, it is unlikely that the President of France is still lonely.

raise the same question as utterances of (A63a). Namely, why is the existential presupposition of the consequent not eliminated?

The answer is that the consequent contains a presupposition-creating constituent, *still,* which we have so far ignored. Roughly speaking, a clause

(A69) ... still ...

containing *still* gives rise to a potential presupposition of the form

(A70) In the past it has been the case that ...

The matter is complicated by the different possible scopes that *still* can take with respect to other logical operators. For example, the clause embedded beneath *unlikely* in (A68) can carry the potential presupposition (A71) or (A72), depending on the relative scopes of *still* and the definite description.

(A71) In the past the President of France has been lonely.

(A72) The President of France is such that in the past he has been lonely.

The important point is that, under either interpretation, the potential presupposition arising from *still* entails an existential claim about the President of France. (A71) entails (A73); (A72) entails (A74).

(A73) In the past France had a president.

(A74) France (now) has a president.

This means that if the potential presupposition arising from *still,* on a given interpretation, is not suspended, then its existential consequence will enter the context along with it as an utterance presupposition.

Typically, neither (A71) nor (A72) will be suspended. Since they are not entailed by the antecedent of (A68), the Strategy 2 conditional presuppositions to which they give rise will be nontrivial.

(A75) All countries now have presidents ⊃ (A71)

(A76) All countries now have presidents ⊃ (A72)

Since the antecedent of these conditionals normally would not provide strong grounds for believing the consequent, the speaker's grounds for assuming (A75) or (A76) can normally be presumed to be truth functional. The conversational implicature that someone who utters (A68) does not know the truth value of its antecedent rules out the possibility that the speaker is assuming (A75)–(A76) to be true by falsity of antecedent. Thus, the speaker may be presumed to be assuming the consequent ((A71) or (A72)).

In other words, the presupposition arising from *still* is inherited by an utterance of (A68). Since all of its logical consequences are also inherited, the utterance carries an existential presupposition about the President of France.

This analysis can be carried out using either version of the Strategy 2 inheritance mechanisms discussed in the main text. No matter which version is used, examples like these illustrate an important point. In some cases a given utterance presupposition can be inherited from a variety of potential sources. Where P is a potential presupposition of S, Strategy 2 allows it to be inherited provided that it follows from *at least one* presupposition Q which is itself inherited. In particular, where S = ⌈If A, then B⌉, a potential presupposition B^P, entailed by A, may nevertheless be inherited by an utterance of S, if it follows from another, unsuspended potential presupposition B^Q, which has nothing to do with A.

A7.3. Example 2

(A77) Speaker and addressee both know that John is a policeman who is always getting drunk, picking fights, and having to be dragged off by his colleagues.

(A78) If John came to the party, then the hostess must have been really glad that there was a policeman present.

B^P: There was a policeman present.

Gazdar is concerned with utterances of (A78) in contexts containing (A77), where "*a policeman* [in (A78) 'refers' to some other policeman (who, we may assume, would have kept John in check)" (1979a, 114). Gazdar notes that in such contexts, utterances of (A78) presuppose B^P, even though the corresponding Strategy 2 conditional presupposition (A79) is trivial.

(A79) John came to the party ⊃ B^P

The implication here is that a theory incorporating Strategy 2 inheritance conditions cannot explain how such utterances inherit a nontrivial presupposition from B.

Examples like this do raise serious questions—but not, primarily, about presuppositions. Gazdar indicates that he is interested in uses of (A78) in which what the speaker asserts/conveys by his utterance is

(A80) If John came to the party, then the hostess must have been really glad that there was a policeman other than John present.

The interesting question is how an utterance of (A78) can succeed in asserting/conveying this.

One answer might be that (A78) is ambiguous, having (A80) as one of its semantic interpretations. If so, then the potential presupposition arising from the factive verb *glad,* on this interpretation, will be (A81):

(A81) Some policeman other than John was present.

Since this presuppositon is not trivially satisfied by the addition of the antecedent of (A78) to the context, Strategy 2 inheritance conditions allow the utterance to inherit a substantive presupposition from its consequent.

The problem with this view is not what it says about presupposition, but what it says about meaning. It seems unlikely that (A78) is ambiguous, having (A80) as one of its semantic interpretations. Indeed, it seems unlikely that the "reference" of *a policeman* in (A78) to someone other than John is a semantic fact at all (see Kripke (1977)). In my opinion, the most attractive account of the semantics of indefinite descriptions is the one given by Russell, in which they are not referring expressions at all. On this account, (A78) has the same semantic interpretation as (A82).

(A82) If John came to the party, then the hostess must have been really glad that there was at least one policeman present.

Hence, the question: if (A78) means (A82), how do utterances of it succeed in asserting/conveying (A80)?

The answer to this question must await a detailed account of the semantics and pragmatics of indefinite descriptions. Nevertheless, it is reasonable to suppose that whatever answer is forthcoming will be one that accommodates a theory of presupposition incorporating Strategy 2 inheritance conditions. If the assertions made by uttering (A78) are somehow dependent on context, then it seems natural to suppose that both the potential and actual presuppositions of such utterances are similarly dependent.[95] Thus, whatever explains how utterances of (A78) can succeed in asserting/conveying (A80) should also explain how these utterances come to have the potential presupposition (A81). Once this potential presupposition is generated, it will not be suspended by the addition of the antecedent of (A78) to the context. Hence, (A78) will not provide a counterexample to theories incorporating Strategy 2 inheritance conditions.

A7.4. Example 3

(A83) a. If I go to bed with her, then *Maria's children* get jealous.
  b. Maria has children.
  c. I go to bed with her ⊃ Maria has children

Gazdar notes that an utterance of (A83a) would typically presuppose (A83b). He claims that a theory incorporating Strategy 2 inheritance conditions cannot account for this, but instead generates the unwanted presupposition (A83c).

This is unfair. What these examples show is that temporal reference must somehow be incorporated into the statement of presuppositions. Note that the potential presupposition corresponding to the definite description in (A84a) is not (A84b), but rather (A84c).

(A84) a. If Maria has a baby next month, then *her child* may be part of the medical school's longitudinal study.
  b. Maria (now) has a child.
  c. Maria will have a child.[96]

Similarly, the correct interpretation of the Strategy 2 conditional presupposition (A83c) is (A85), not (A86).

(A85) I go to bed with Maria ⊃ Maria already
      at time t has children at
                                      t

(A86) I go to bed with Maria ⊃ Maria will have
      at time t children later

The only reasonable grounds for believing (A85) are truth functional. Since the speaker cannot be regarding its antecedent to be false, a theory of presupposition incorporating Strategy 2 mechanisms correctly predicts utterances of (A83a) to presuppose that Maria (now) has children.[97]

A7.5. Example 4

(A87) a. If gold is missing from Fort Knox, then the crooked accountants in the U.S. Treasury will be worried.

  b. There are crooked accountants in the U.S. Treasury.

  c. Gold is missing ⊃ There are crooked
     from Fort   accountants in
     Knox   the
                          U.S. Treasury

Gazdar notes that an utterance of (A87a) might easily be heard as presupposing (A87b). The challenge for a theory incorporating Strategy 2 inheritance conditions is to explain this. My synthesis theory claims that someone who utters (A87a) indicates that he assumes the context of the utterance (perhaps augmented with uncontroversial propositions) to satisfy its (remaining) presuppositions. There are two possible reasons why a speaker might assume this.

(a) He may regard (A87b) as already in the context (or as something his hearers will find uncontroversial).

(b) He may think that (A87b) is not in the context (and would not be uncontroversial), but that (A87c) is in the context (or would be uncontroversial).

On hearing an utterance of (A87a), one must decide which of these alternatives is the most plausible representation of the speaker's attitudes. If (a) seems to be the most plausible, then the utterance will be heard as presupposing (A87b). If (b) is the most plausible, then this presupposition should not be heard. As far as I can tell, this characterization is correct.[98]

ACKNOWLEDGMENTS

The idea for this article was first presented at the Sloan Conference on Semantics for Natural Languages at Stanford University, April 1980. Preliminary versions of the article were read at MIT, April 1981; Princeton, May 1981; Stanford, July 1981.

NOTES

1. My discussion of Question 1 will be limited primarily to examples involving connectives that Karttunen (1973) originally characterized as filters *(and, or, if—then, unless)*. I assume the usual classification of expressions like *likely* and *possible* as holes and *regret* and *discover* as factives. However, I will have nothing to say about whether verbs such as *believe* and *say* should be treated as plugs, in the manner of Karttunen (1973; 1974), or as holes (for pre-suppositions), in the manner of Gazdar (1979a,b). Thus, the solution I offer to the projection problem is only partial.

2. See Stalnaker (1973).

3. These definitions differ slightly from those of Soames (1979) and supersede them.

4. Stalnaker (1974) has stressed this point.

5. The addition of presuppositions to the conversational context of an utterance is noted in Stalnaker (1974), Gazdar (1979a,b), and Lewis (1979) (in his rule of accommodation for presupposition). Such addition undermines all definitions which make the presence of presupposed propositions in the conversational context prior to an utterance a necessary condition for the appropriateness of the utterance.

The addition of presuppositions to conversational contexts reflects the fact that a speaker commits himself to the proposition that his utterance presupposes. However, it is important to recognize that there is more to presupposition than just this commitment. Presupposing P and asserting P are both ways of committing oneself to P. However, when one's utterance presupposes P, one indicates that one regards P as uncontroversial, and hence not subject to questioning in the way that a straightforward assertion is. It is this special attitude taken toward presuppositions that makes them so useful for conversational purposes involving pretense, indirection, rhetorical bullying, etc.

There are then, two features of utterance presuppositions that any adequate definition must take account of.

(i) The ability to use them to increment a context by adding new information.

(ii) The special, privileged status accorded this information.

6. This should be taken as a stipulative definition of a technical notion, not an attempt to capture the ordinary meanings of *uncontroversial* or *take for granted*.

7. The notion of *taking P for granted* cannot simply replace that of *a speaker presupposing P* in all theoretical contexts, as is shown by the utility of the latter in formulating the conversational rule: Don't assert what you are presupposing (since such an assertion would be redundant). Although it would be desirable to have a single concept that could somehow do the work of both notions, I know of no clearly successful attempt to formulate one. See Stalnaker (1974, note 3), for an illuminating discussion of this point. For my purposes, *taking P for granted* will be the more central notion.

8. Not all utterance presuppositions arise from the semantic and syntactic structure of the sentence uttered. For example, Gazdar's (1979a) (i) may well be a presupposition of most utterances, regardless of the semantic or syntactic structure of the sentence uttered.

(i) The addressee can understand what the speaker is saying.

Although the *definition* of utterance presupposition does not distinguish such cases from examples like (18)–(25), a substantive *theory* of how presuppositions arise (including apparatus for solving the projection problem) will.

9. Langendoen and Savin (1971).

10. Although Langendoen and Savin did not use the terminology adopted here, there are good reasons to think that any presupposition in their sense is a sentential presupposition in the sense defined above (though not vice versa). See Soames (1979, note 3).

11. There are several significant differences in the positive theories of Gazdar (1979a,b) and Soames (1979). Whereas Gazdar's theory is formalized and extended to all complex sentences, my (1979) theory is presented relatively informally in a discussion of sentential connectives (Karttunen's filters). More important, whereas Gazdar claims that Strategy 1 constitutes a complete solution to the projection problem, I argued that it is incapable of handling a certain class of examples, and hence must be modified or supplemented in any adequate solution to the projection problem.

12. Karttunen (1973; 1974); Karttunen and Peters (1979); Peters (1977).

13. The sketch of Strategy 1 presented below is an informal composite, drawing on elements of both Soames (1979) and Gazdar (1979a,b). The strengths and weaknesses of the strategy pointed out below apply to these earlier versions. However, the form and terminology in which the points are put require some adjustments in applying them to the earlier works. For more on this, see the appendix to this chapter.

14. In the case of (31b) the argument is a bit tricky. Certainly, someone who asserts a conjunction implicates that he is not presupposing either conjunct. However, in the present case, we need to go beyond this to argue that he is not taking the first conjunct, B^P, to be uncontroversial, either.

The implication in question can be seen as arising from a consequence, (i), of Grice's maxim "Be Brief."

(i) Assertively utter a sentence S only if there is no sentence S', significantly shorter than S, which would convey the same thing.

To assertively utter the righthand conjunct of (31b) by itself would be to convey that Lauri solved the problem and that the speaker regards it as uncontroversial that someone did (recall that (31b) represents (10b)). To assertively utter the entire conjunction, (31b), for the purpose of conveying the same thing would be to violate (i). The speaker's reason for explicitly asserting B^P can therefore be presumed to be a recognition that it is at least potentially controversial, and hence subject to possible questioning in a way in which utterance presuppositions generally are not. As a result, the utterance of (31b) conversationally implicates that the speaker is not taking its first conjunct for granted.

15. Strictly speaking, it is not necessary to separate (32a) and (32b) into different mechanisms (see the appendix). However, for present purposes there is no harm in doing so.

16. Gazdar (1979a,b) does not use any notion of presupposition to cash the empirical content of his theory. Rather, he constructs a mechanism for predicting when assertions, conversational implicatures, and potential presuppositions are added to a speaker's "commitment slate." Roughly speaking, uncanceled potential presuppositions are among the propositions added, and hence are things that the speaker commits himself to.

A problem with this approach is that it fails to account for the special status of the commitments that arise from presuppositions (see note 5). Thus, I prefer an account which employs some principle like (32c), together with a general rule (here unspecified) for adding each of the various sorts of speaker commitments to the conversational context (in the absence of objections from other conversational participants).

17. This may also be expressed as follows:

(i) For all sentences S, consistent contexts C, and propositions P,
  If $\exists Q$ (Q is a potential presupposition of S; Q is compatible with C; uttering S in C does not conversationally implicate that the speaker is not taking Q for granted; and Q entails P)
 then an utterance of S in C presupposes P.

18. Although (32a–c) account for all data considered so far, there is a minor difficulty with the present formulation of (32c). Let $Q_1 \ldots Q_n$, be uncanceled potential presuppositions of S. Let P be a proposition that is entailed by $Q_1 \ldots Q_n$ but not by any single Q_i. As it stands, (32c) fails to predict that utterances of S presuppose P. This prediction is needed in an idealization in which speaker–hearers' beliefs are closed under entailment, and in which speaker–hearers recognize this about each other.

This difficulty can be eliminated by reformulating (32c) as follows:

(i) For all propositions P, sets Q of propositions, sentences S, and consistent contexts C,
 If every member of Q is a potential presupposition of S, and Q entails P, then an utterance of S in C presupposes P provided that

a. Q is compatible with C; and
b. uttering S in C does not conversationally implicate that the speaker is not taking Q for granted.

One might wonder whether (i) could be further strengthened by recasting it as a biconditional.

(ii) For all propositions P, sentences S, and consistent contexts C, an utterance of S in C presupposes P iff there is a set Q of potential presuppositions of S such that
a. Q entails P; and
b. Q is compatible with C; and
c. uttering S in C does not conversationally implicate that the speaker is not taking Q for granted.

Whether or not this strengthening is possible depends on whether or not there are utterance presuppositions which arise from sources other than potential presuppositions—for example, from general preconditions for successful communication (see note 8). If there are no such presuppositions, (ii) can stand as an explication of Strategy 1. If there are such presuppositions, and if T is a theory of them, then (ii) can be replaced by (iii).

(iii) For all sentences S, consistent contexts C, and propositions P, an utterance of S in C presupposes P iff
a. P is one of the propositions characterized by T; or
b. there is a set Q of potential presuppositions of S such that . . . (as in (ii)).

Since I am concerned only with projected and projectible presuppositions arising from the form and content of specific sentences, I will not be concerned with the difference between (i) and (iii). For my purposes, (i) characterizes Strategy 1 perfectly well. When the entailments of multiple potential presuppositions are not a concern, even (32c) can be used for expository purposes without fear of confusion.

19. Karttunen and Peters (1979).

20. The notation in (35) can be understood as follows: A and B are metalinguistic variables that range over English sentences. P is a function that assigns to each English sentence a metalanguage expression that is equivalent to the conjunction of all of its sentential presuppositions (i.e., a maximal sentential presupposition). (Where ϕ carries no presuppositions, we let ϕ^P be a tautology.) T is a function that assigns to each English sentence a metalanguage expression that represents its truth conditions. &, $\vee$, and $\supset$ are here treated as denoting functions from pairs of metalanguage formulas to metalanguage formulas. Similarly for the English words *and, or,* and *if, then,* except that the domains and ranges of the functions they represent consist of English sentences.

21. See Karttunen and Peters (1979, 37–39) for a discussion of an analogous example.

22. Karttunen and Peters neglect this conjunct. For a demonstration that their strategy for solving the projection problem requires it, see Soames (1979, 636–640).

23. An earlier version of the critique made here can be found in Soames (1979).

24. In this case, the utterance conversationally implicates (via the maxim of quantity) that the speaker does not believe, or at any rate is not in a position to assert, P. It follows from this that he is not taking P for granted.

25. Not only is the utterance noncommittal regarding whether or not the speaker takes P for granted, it is also noncommittal regarding whether he believes P, or is in a position to assert it.

26. This is not to say that anyone who assumed that someone other than the Hungarians will defeat the Russians necessarily must have some particular people in mind (it is possible to assume $\exists x \phi x$ without assuming anything of the form ϕa). However, if the utterance did presuppose that someone other than the Hungarians would defeat the Russians, then the question of who that might be would be a natural one to ask in response to the utterance. Since, in fact, this is not a natural response to the utterance, there is no such presupposition.

27. According to Strategy 1, B^P is a potential presupposition of (50). Since utterances of (50) do not conversationally implicate that the speaker is not assuming B^P, Strategy 1 predicts that these utterances presuppose it (provided $-B^P$ was not in the context prior to the utterance). This prediction is incorrect. Such utterances are not instances of positive presupposition, but rather are neutral with respect to the speaker's attitude toward B^P.

28. See the appendix for an explicit application of this argument to Gazdar (1979a,b). There I present Gazdar's formalization of Strategy 1, demonstrate its susceptibility to the above argument, and relate its failure to account for "neutral cases" to other problems facing his system.

29. See the appendix for a defense of this general rule against alleged counterexamples in Gazdar (1979a,b).

30. See Soames (1979) for further examples.

31. See Stalnaker (1974), Gazdar (1979a,b).

32. There is no conversational injunction against asserting that which one takes to be uncontroversial. However, except for bizarre examples like (i),

(i) The King of France is a king.

assertive utterances do not *indicate* that the speaker takes that which he asserts to be uncontroversial (whether or not he actually does). Hence, assertive utterances (and in particular assertive utterances of (65)) generally do not presuppose that which they assert.

33. Although we may restrict U to complete assertive utterances—utterances that are not parts of larger assertive utterances—we do not restrict the relation here defined to cases in which U is a complete utterance of S.

34. This definition covers only the constructions I have been discussing. In a complete theory, it would be replaced by a similar definition with recursive clauses covering every construction in the language.

35. The three constructions covered by this clause are negations of A, epistemic modals like ⌜Maybe A⌝ and ⌜It is possible that A⌝, and cases in which A is the complement of a verb which is a hole for presuppositions. In a complete account, some obvious refinements will be needed—for example, a distinction between holes which are factives and those which are not (plus a separate clause for the former). Since my present aim is to sketch the form of a solution to the projection problem, I will not be concerned with such complications here.

36. To assume that A^P is true would be to assume that B^T is false. A speaker who assumed this, and who had sufficient evidence to warrant asserting (53), would be in a position to make a stronger statement by asserting the left disjunct. Since the speaker did not make the stronger statement, he conversationally implicated that he was not assuming A^P. (The same holds for B^P.)

37. The need to appeal to this presumption is one reason, among several, for not making the predictive principle a biconditional. Where no such presumption is justified, the theory predicts (I think correctly) that the utterance does not presuppose B^P. For a discussion of some alleged counterexamples to this claim, see the final section of the appendix.

38. The reader can gain an understanding of the treatment of more complex examples, involving multiple embedding, by working through (i) and (ii).

(i) If Martha bought a blue dress and Susan bought a blue dress, too, then Martha will regret having bought a dress that is the same color as the one Susan bought.
   If A and B, then C
   A^T: Martha bought a blue dress.
   B^P: Someone other than Susan bought a blue dress.
   $(A \& B)^T$: Martha bought a blue dress and Susan bought a blue dress.
   C^P: Martha bought a dress that is the same color as the one Susan bought.
(ii) If I discover that I haven't told the truth, I will be embarrassed; and if I regret that I haven't told the truth, I will confess it to everyone.
   (If A, then B) and (If C, then D)
   $A^P C^P$: I didn't tell the truth.

In the case of (i), suspension can occur, without conversational canceling, solely as a result of the recursive definition of actual presupposition. In the case of (ii), the left conjunct gives rise to a conversational implicature of the entire utterance that cancels both A^P and C^P (i.e., A^P is not a remaining presupposition of A relative to U and C^P is not a remaining presupposition of C relative to U).

The same result is obtained if the order of the conjuncts in (ii) is reversed; although the sentence is a bit odd because of the awkwardness of uttering a presupposition-bearing conjunct prior to a conjunct whose utterance gives rise to a canceling conversational implicature. The same oddity would be found if *and* were deleted and the conjuncts were uttered as separate, complete sentences.

39. Karttunen (1974).

40. See Soames (1976) and (1979) for discussions.

41. This approach has a certain plausibility. Imagine being confronted with a speaker who has uttered a

compound sentence, one of whose constituents presupposes P. One asks oneself why the speaker chose such a sentence rather than a logically equivalent one with no constituent presupposition. I suggest that the null hypothesis is that he used the sentence because he was taking P for granted. This presumption remains in force unless something special about the utterance removes it.

42. This does not mean that temporal order is irrelevant to explaining the presuppositional behavior of sentences, and discourses, of the form (i) and (ii).

(i) a. B, if A.
     b. B, provided that A.
     c. B. Supposing A.

(ii) a. If A, then B.

     b. Suppose that A. In that case, B.

See section 9.4 for discussion of the different presuppositional behavior of these two classes of cases.

43. Stalnaker (1968), Lewis (1973), Davis (1979). See Davis for an account of the differences among these proposals plus a defense of this kind of analysis for indicative, as well as subjunctive, conditionals.

44. In evaluating the truth value of the speaker's remark, the hearer augments his present conception of the actual world, which includes the propositions in the conversational context, with the supposition of A. He then tries to determine whether B is true in a world that satisfies these propositions, while differing minimally from the actual world. On this analysis, the process that one goes through in evaluating the truth value of certain sentences mirrors the pragmatic augmentation of the context needed to explain presuppositon.

45. As opposed to canceling them via the mechanisms of Strategy 1.

46. The mechanisms for (87a–c) are found in clauses (c) and (d) of the recursive definition of *A Context X Satisfying the Remaining Potential Presuppositions of S Relative to U* (72). The mechanisms for (87d) are given below.

47. Or ⌜B provided that A⌝, or ⌜B unless ⌐A⌝.

48. The symmetry of (92a) and (92b) requires the addition of (c) to (92) in order to prevent presupposition suspension in cases in which there is some P that is presupposed by both A and B, as well as entailed by both.

(92) c. For all propositions P, if P is entailed by every context Y, such that Y Sat–A–U and Y Sat–B–U, then X entails P.

See Soames (1976, 344–352; 1979, section 3 and note 40).

49. This argument can easily be generalized to cover Gazdar's attempt to explain all failures to inherit potential presuppositions in terms of the *cancellation* of such presuppositions. If sentences of the form (90) and (91) give rise to the same Gricean implicatures (as they do in the case of the quantity and quality implicatures used by Gazdar), then the different inheritance characteristics of these sentences cannot be explained by Gazdar's machinery. See the appendix for an elaboration of this point.

50. Unchallenged assertions (or what are taken to be assertions) are added to the context against which the next utterance is evaluated.

51. Suppositions are evaluated relative to the context at the time the supposition is made.

52. For instance, although my descriptive apparatus correctly predicts presupposition suspension in (i),

(i) It isn't likely that the Poles will defeat the Russians and the Hungarians will, too.

I have offered no pragmatic explanation of why principles of discourse incrementation should have been generalized to apply to these cases.

53. There are a number of respects in which this apparatus is incomplete. For example, my explanation of why the prior utterance of a consequent can suspend the presupposition of an antecedent contained two features not found in its descriptive counterpart (92):

(i) A distinction between two ways in which a proposition can be represented as part of a conversational context—as an established fact or as a provisional assumption.

(ii) The ability of an utterance to change the status of something already in a context from one of these poles to the other.

Although (92) makes the right predictions about (89b), it does so without mentioning (i) and (ii). For that reason, it fails to give a full account of the mechanisms involved in presupposition suspension and is best regarded as a close approximation to the actual facts. (I am indebted to David Lewis for pointing out the importance of (i) and (ii).)

Another way in which my descriptive apparatus is incomplete involves (88a) and (88b). Although my apparatus correctly predicts presupposition suspension in these cases, it fails to indicate a significant difference between the two. Utterances of the latter, but not the former, typically indicate that B^p was somehow already a live option (perhaps accepted by some members of the conversation) prior to the utterance of the conditional. That is what allows the speaker to put the presupposition-bearing constituent first—even when the speaker himself wishes to avoid explicit commitment to B^p and does so by uttering the antecedent. The clauses in the definition of X Sat–S–U are too coarse-grained to capture this fact.

Finally, I want to emphasize the need to give formal and precise statements of the general pragmatic principles for incrementing contexts that I have appealed to:

(i) Unchallenged assertions are added to the context preceding the next utterance.

(ii) Suppositions are evaluated relative to the context at the time the supposition is made.

(iii) Consequents are evaluated relative to contexts that include the relevant suppositions, etc.

Until this is done we have not completed our explanation of presupposition projection, but have provided a sort of interim explanation scheme.

54. Functors include negation, connectives, quantifiers, modal operators.

55. Gazdar does not give a formal characterization of scope.

56. This notion is intended to express the requirement that constituents of the scale be qualitatively similar. Gazdar does not define this notion in (1979a) or (1979b).

57. Gazdar defines entailment for propositions, and for sentences, as follows: Proposition P entails proposition Q iff Q is true in every world in which P is true (i.e., $P \subseteq Q$). A sentence ϕ entails a sentence ψ iff the proposition $[\phi]$ expressed by ϕ entails the proposition $[\psi]$ expressed by ψ.

These definitions, together with a theory of direct reference, have the consequence that the sentence (i) entails the sentence (ii), given that Cicero was Tully.

(i) Cicero was a Roman.

(ii) Tully was a Roman.

This seems unfortunate, if we want entailment to be a *logical* relation. Thus, I would define entailment for sentences via the usual appeal to models: A sentence ϕ entails a sentence ψ iff for all models M $[\phi]_M \subseteq [\psi]_M$.

Fortunately, this qualm about Gazdar's characterization of entailment does not affect the examples of projection and cancellation discussed [in A5.2.].

58. Without the requirement of *simple* expression alternatives, examples like (i) and (ii)

(i) $\frown$all of the As are Bs.

(ii) $\frown$some of the As are Bs.

would prevent ⟨*all of the, some of the*⟩ from being a quantitative scale.

59. Gazdar (1979b, 60, note 2) notes that this definition is not adequate for certain cases, and formulates it in (1979a) so as to provide only a necessary condition for being a quantitative scale. The issues involved in this change are not directly relevant to the present discussion.

60. The sentences in the domains and ranges of all of Gazdar's implicature and presupposition functions are sentences of semantic representation. Thus, Gazdar assumes that whenever two sentences differ in their potential implicatures or potential presuppositions, they have different semantic *representations*. Whether or not they have different semantic *interpretations* is an open question.

61. Strictly speaking, the definition requires $\phi_{\alpha i}$ to entail ψ only when X and Y in clause (a) are null. In other cases, it requires $\phi_{\alpha i}$ to entail a subpart $\phi_{\alpha i+1}$ of ψ, which is itself entailed by ψ. Note that (b) of (A14) prevents (ib) from being a potential scalar implication of (ia).

(i) a. John believes that some of the boys were at the party.
     b. The speaker knows that not all of the boys were at the party.

However, it does not prevent (iib) from being a potential scalar implicature of (iia).

(ii) a. John knows that some of the boys were at the party.
     b. The speaker knows that not all of the boys were at the party.

This failure to exclude (iib) seems wrong, as the unproblematic discourse (iii) illustrates.

(iii) John knows that some of the boys were at the party. What he doesn't know is that all of the boys were there.

62. Here we rely on the assumption that the speaker was obeying the maxim of quality.

63. If natural language conditionals are not material conditionals, then this informal reasoning will have to be supplemented in some way to cover (A16b).

64. Clauses (b) and (c) block $-K\phi$, $-K-\phi$ as potential quantity implicatures of $\ulcorner\phi$ and ψ, $\ulcorner-\phi\urcorner$, $\ulcorner\alpha$ knows that $\phi\urcorner$, $\ulcorner\alpha$ knows that $-\phi\urcorner$, etc.

65. Clause (d) is needed to prevent presupposed clauses like the one in (i)

(i) If John tells Margaret, he will regret *seeing me.*

from giving rise to quantity implicatures that would cancel the presupposition (by implicating that the speaker does not know whether or not the clause is true (false)). In effect, clause (d) is needed to prevent the cancellation of every clausal presupposition of a compound sentence that is not entailed by it. Cases like (ii),

(ii) If *John sees me,* he will regret *seeing me.*

in which the presupposed clause also occurs in a nonpresuppositional position, do give rise to canceling implicatures. Gazdar accounts for this by allowing (in fact, (A11) requires) expression alternatives, with respect to α, to differ at only one position.

66. In order for an informal quantity argument to be constructed, the propositions implicated not to be known must be "stronger" than the proposition asserted. The problem is in characterizing strength. One-way entailment is often a useful guide, as it was with (A16a). However, no such entailment connects (A19) with (A20). In these cases the intuitive notion of strength seems to depend heavily on the point of the conversation. In cases in which the purpose of the utterance is to adduce evidence for or against ϕ, ϕ and $\ulcorner-\phi\urcorner$ are clearly stronger than the corresponding assertions (A19a–d) and the predicted implicatures will be heard. In cases in which the point of the conversation is not to decide ϕ, but to present an accurate account of Aquinas's (Aristotle's) beliefs, no clear relation of strength obtains and no implicature is present (even when the prior context contains no canceling propositions). It is a weakness of Gazdar's account that it does not make this distinction, and hence incorrectly predicts clausal, quantity implicatures in some contexts where there are none.

67. Although these functions merely list potential presuppositions, they should not be thought of as precluding independent explanations of why various constructions give rise to presuppositions.

68. Though the resulting system is equivalent to one employing the cumulative projection algorithm.

69. The notion of a consistent addition here is that of a satisfiable incrementation in the sense of (A1) and (A2).

70. Where '$\rightarrow$' represents the semantic content of *If, then,* whatever that may be. I here ignore the semantic representation of 'too.'

71. Note that the conversational implicature would have to be actual, rather than merely potential, in order for it to be capable of canceling the potential presupposition.

72. To test this, imagine (A27) being uttered in a context that does not already contain (i):

(i) $K\exists x(x \neq n \& Gx)$

On hearing (A27), would one automatically conclude that the speaker does not know whether Dean or Mitchell or Ehrlichman is guilty? It seems obvious that one would not. (Note, to say that (i) is not in the context already is not to say that its negation is. Otherwise, every context C would be such that for every proposition P, either P or its negation would be in C, and *any* incrementation would result in inconsistency.)

73. See Gazdar (1979a, 56–57) for a discussion of the difference between formulating implicatures in terms of semantic representations and formulating them in terms of propositions expressed.

74. See note 72.

75. The persistent dispute over the symmetry vs. asymmetry of presupposition inheritance has been much confused by the failure to distinguish Strategy 1 type cancellation from Strategy 2 type suspension. The former is symmetric; the latter is asymmetric, in the case of some conditionals.

76. Unlike the failures noted in the previous two arguments, this one is not an inevitable consequence of

Strategy 1. For example, (A34) could be modified by allowing any set of (propositions expressed by) clauses to entail [ψ]. The inheritance of (A38) by utterances of (A36) would then be blocked. Nevertheless, two objections would remain. First, the set of nonexistent conversational implicatures generated by the theory would be greatly expanded. Second, the theory would still be without any means of accounting for presupposition suspension in the case of disjunctions of the form (i):

(i) Either α will ϕ after all or β won't ϕ, either.

This sentence carries a potential presupposition of the form (ii).

(ii) $\exists X(X \neq \beta \ \& \ X$ won't $\phi)$

which is not entailed by any set of clauses of (i). Thus, the above modification of (A34), in conjunction with the rest of Gazdar's theory, would incorrectly predict that utterances of (i) commit the speaker to (iii):

(iii) K $\exists X(X \neq \beta \ \& \ X$ won't $\phi)$

The right way to account for all of these cases—(A35), (A36), (i)—is recursively, using the descriptive apparatus given earlier in section 8.2.

77. In (A48a,b) clause (e) prevents Δ from being the clause embedded beneath *regret*. However, it does not prevent Δ from being (A44), which entails the clause embedded beneath *regret* in Gazdar's system.

78. Note that the addition of (f) does not allow the deletion of (e). In (A48a,b) clause (f) prevents Δ from being (A44). Clause (e) is needed to prevent Δ from being identical with ψ.

79. Note that the failure of (i) to inherit the potential presupposition (ii)

(i) If John said that someone solved the problem, then it was Mary who solved it.

(ii) Someone solved the problem.

can be explained as an instance of Strategy 2 presupposition suspension in contexts in which what John says can be trusted, and which contain (iii):

(iii) John said that someone solved the problem $\supset$ Someone solved the problem

80. With the minor exception of those cases covered by (b) and (c) of (A18).

81. In section A6.4, I will argue that (a) itself is a source of false predictions. However, adding (b) compounds the problem, as is shown by the fact that Gazdar's original system allowed the potential presuppositions of (A49b) and (A50b) to be inherited.

82. Subject to the qualifications in (A34'').

83. For discussions of the distinction between particularized and generalized conversational implicatures, see Grice (1975, 56), Gazdar (1979a, 38–39), Karttunen and Peters (1979, 2–11).

84. Problems independent of those considered here prevent (A14') from being fully adequate (see notes 59, 61). However, it does correctly account for paradigmatic cases like (A4)–(A9) and is an improvement on (A14).

85. Another example of this type is provided by the following dialogue.

A: Did the students in your seminar understand what you were saying?
B: Some of them did.
A: What about the others?
B: I'm not sure. They didn't say anything.

86. (A60b) is assumed to have the semantic representation (i):

(i) If not all of the students were there, then some of the students were there.

Gazdar claims that (A60a) and (A60b) have the same truth conditions.

87. The scalar implicature cancels the potential clausal implicature $\smallfrown$K$\smallfrown$(A59c).

88. The scalar implicature, K$\smallfrown$(A59c), and the clausal implicature, $\smallfrown$K$\smallfrown$(A59c), cancel one another. This incorrectly leaves it open that a speaker obeying Grice's maxims might know (A59c) to be false, while nevertheless uttering (A59b).

89. According to (A14) and (A18), the potential implicatures of (A60a) and (A60b) are as follows:

(i) *(A60a)*
   Scalar: K~(A60c)

(ii) *(A60b)*
   Scalar: K~(A60c)
   Clausal: ~K~(A60c), ~K~ ~(A60c)

The priority of clausal over scalar implicatures results in the cancellation of the scalar implicature of (A60b). Thus, someone who assertively utters (A60a) is characterized as knowing that (A60c) is false; whereas someone who utters (A60b) is characterized as being ignorant of its truth value.

90. Subject to the idealization that where ϕ entails ψ, Kϕ entails Kψ.

91. To say that for all X knows ϕ may be true is to say that $-$X knows ϕ to be false.

92. Either because one is not ignorant, or because one's ignorance of this possibility is irrelevant to the conversation.

93. Utterances of (A60a) and (A60b) both implicate $-$K(A60c). They differ in that the latter, but not the former, also implicates $-$K $-$(A60c). Thus, using (A60b) makes explicit one's ignorance about the possibility that (A60c) might be true. Using (A60a) does not.

94. Except when the preceding context results in cancellation.

95. Gazdar himself implicitly relativizes potential presuppositions to contexts in dealing with (i)–(iii):

(i) If Carter invites George Wallace's wife to the White House, then the President will regret having invited a black militant to his residence.

(ii) If Carter invites Angela Davis to the White House, then the President will regret having invited a black militant to his residence.

(iii) The President will invite a black militant to his residence.

Gazdar notes (1979a, 151–152) that, intuitively, (i) presupposes (iii), whereas (ii) does not—in a context in which it is assumed that Carter is President, the White House is the President's residence, Mrs. Wallace is not a black militant, and Angela Davis is. In such a context, (i) and (ii) conversationally implicate (iv) and (v), respectively.

(iv) $-$K The President will invite George Wallace's wife to his residence.

(v) $-$K The President will invite Angela Davis to his residence.

The problem for Gazdar's theory is that (iv) and (v) are compatible with the potential presupposition (iii). Hence, his formula for context incrementation will wrongly allow for presupposition inheritance in *both* cases. To avoid this he says we need "a rule of anaphora for 'a'." Although he does not commit himself to a specific formulation of this rule, he said "it will have to provide for the fact that (i) is an acceptable sentence even though *a black militant* cannot 'refer' to Governor Wallace's wife, whereas the *ceteris paribus* interpretation of (ii) is one in which *a black militant* does 'refer' to Angela Davis. Given such a rule, the inconsistency required for pre-supposition suspension is derivable from the context and (ii), but not from the context and (i)" (1979a, 152).

Note that this inconsistency will be derivable only if the rule for anaphora provides different interpretations of the potential presuppositon (iii) in the two cases—with the potential presupposition in the case of (ii) being (iii′):

(iii′) The President will invite a black militant—namely Angela Davis—to his residence.

96. This potential presupposition is suspended by the antecedent of (A84a).

97. Similar remarks apply to three other examples cited by Gazdar (1979a, 115).

(i) If I torture him, Boris regrets laughing at me.

(ii) If I pull this handle, the explosion is inhibited.

(iii) If I scold him, Boris regrets sulking.

98. Note that for someone who does not assume (A87b), (A87c) may not be very plausible. It is not obvious that if gold is missing the accountants must be guilty. (Couldn't someone else—say, the guards—have taken it?) This fact, together with the widespread cynicism about government officials, may be responsible for the preference for (a)—and hence the presupposition of (A87b)—above.

REFERENCES

Davis, W. (1979). "Indicative and Subjunctive Conditionals," *Philosophical Review* 88:544–564.

Gazdar, G. (1979a). *Pragmatics: Implicature, Presupposition, and Logical Form.* New York: Academic Press.

Gazdar G. (1979b). "A Solution to the Projection Problem." In Ch.-K. Oh and D. Dinneen (eds.), *Syntax and Semantics.* Vol. 11: *Presupposition.* New York: Academic Press.

Grice, H. P. (1975). "Logic and Conversation." In D. Davidson and G. Harman (eds.), *The Logic of Grammar.* Encino, Calif.: Dickenson, 64–75. [Reprinted in this volume, Chapter 19]

Karttunen, L. (1973). "Presupposition of Compound Sentences." *Linguistic Inquiry* 4:169–193.

Karttunen, L. (1974). "Presupposition and Linguistic Context." *Theoretical Linguistics* 1:181–194. [Reprinted in this volume, Chapter 24]

Karttunen, L., and S. Peters (1979). "Conventional Implicature." In Ch.-K. Oh and D. Dinneen (eds.), *Syntax and Semantics,* Vol. 11: *Presupposition.* New York: Academic Press.

Kripke, S. (1977). "Speaker's Reference and Semantic Reference," *Midwest Studies in Philosophy* 2:255–276. [Reprinted in this volume, Chapter 5]

Landman, F. (1981). "A Note on the Projection Problem." *Linguistic Inquiry* 12:467–471.

Langendoen, D. T., and H. B. Savin (1971). "The Projection Problem for Presuppositions." In C. J. Fillmore and D. T. Langendoen (eds.), *Studies in Linguistic Semantics,* New York: Holt, Rinehart and Winston, 55–60.

Lewis D. (1973). *Counterfactuals.* Cambridge, Mass.: Harvard University Press.

Lewis, D. (1979). "Scorekeeping in a Language Game," *Journal of Philosophical Logic* 8:339–359. [Reprinted in this volume, Chapter 25]

Peters, S. (1977). "A Truthconditional Formulation of Karttunen's Account of Presupposition," *Texas Linguistic Forum* 6, Department of Linguistics, University of Texas at Austin, 137–149.

Soames, S. (1976). "A Critical Examination of Frege's Theory of Presupposition and Contemporary Alternatives." Ph.D. diss., Massachusetts Institute of Technology.

Soames, S. (1979). "A Projection Problem for Speaker Presuppositions." *Linguistic Inquiry* 10:623–666.

Stalnaker, R. (1968). "A Theory of Conditionals." In N. Rescher (ed.), *Studies in Logical Theory.* Oxford: Basil Blackwell, 98–112.

Stalnaker, R. (1973). "Presuppositions." *Journal of Philosophical Logic* 2:447–457.

Stalnaker, R. (1974). "Pragmatic Presuppositions." In M. K. Munitz and P. K. Unger (eds.), *Semantics and Philosophy.* New York: New York University Press, 197–214. [Reprinted in this volume, Chapter 27]

27

Pragmatic Presuppositions[1]

ROBERT C. STALNAKER

There is a familiar intuitive distinction between what is *asserted* and what is *presupposed* in the making of a statement. If I say that the Queen of England is bald, I presuppose that England has a unique queen, and assert that she is bald. If I say that Sam regrets that he voted for Nixon, I presuppose that Sam voted for Nixon, and assert that he feels bad about it. If I say that Ted Kennedy is the only person who could have defeated Nixon in 1972, I presuppose that Ted Kennedy could have defeated Nixon in 1972, and assert that no one else could have done so. Philosophers have discussed this distinction mainly in the context of problems of reference. Linguists have discussed it in many other contexts as well. They have argued that the phenomenon of presupposition is a pervasive feature of the use of natural language, one that must play a role in the semantic analysis of many words and phrases.

The principal criterion that has been used to identify presuppositions can be stated in the following way: Q is presupposed by an assertion that P just in case under normal conditions one can reasonably infer that a speaker believes that Q from either his assertion or his denial that P. One who denies the example statements listed above—who says that the Queen of England is *not* bald, that Sam does *not* regret that he voted for Nixon, or that Ted Kennedy is *not* the only person who could have defeated Nixon in 1972, normally makes the same presuppositions as the person who makes the affirmative statements. Linguists have used this criterion to identify many examples of the phenomenon. The criterion, and many of the examples, are relatively clear and uncontroversial; it is clear that there is a phenomenon to be explained. But it is much less clear what kind of explanation of it should be given. Granted that either the statement that the Queen of England is bald, or the speaker who makes it, presupposes that England has a unique queen. But what is it about the statement, or the speaker, which constitutes this fact? There are two very different kinds of answers to this question.

The first answer is that presupposition is a semantic relation holding between sentences or propositions. This kind of account draws the distinction between presupposition and as-

Robert C. Stalnaker, "Pragmatic Presuppositions." Reprinted by permission of New York University Press from *Semantics and Philosophy*, edited by Milton K. Munitz and Peter K. Unger. Copyright © 1974 by New York University.

sertion in terms of the content or truth-conditions of the sentence uttered or the proposition expressed. Here is an example of such a definition: a proposition that P presupposes that Q if and only if Q must be true in order that P have a truth-value at all. The presuppositions of a proposition, according to this definition, are necessitated by the truth, and by the falsity, of the proposition. When any presupposition is false, the assertion lacks a truth-value.

The second answer is that presupposition should be given a pragmatic analysis. The distinction between presupposition and assertion should be drawn, not in terms of the content of the propositions expressed, but in terms of the situations in which the statement is made—the attitudes and intentions of the speaker and his audience. Presuppositions, on this account, are something like the background beliefs of the speaker—propositions whose truth he takes for granted, or seems to take for granted, in making his statement.

The pragmatic account is closer to the ordinary notion of presupposition, but it has frequently been assumed that the semantic account is the one that is relevant to giving a rigorous theoretical explanation of the linguistic phenomena. I want to argue that this assumption is wrong. I will suggest that it is important for correctly understanding the phenomena identified by linguists to give the second kind of analysis rather than the first. In terms of the pragmatic account, one can give intuitively natural explanations of some facts that seem puzzling when presupposition is viewed as a semantic relation. The pragmatic account makes it possible to explain some particular facts about presuppositions in terms of general maxims of rational communication rather than in terms of complicated and ad hoc hypotheses about the semantics of particular words and particular kinds of constructions. To argue this, I will sketch an account of the kind I want to defend, and then discuss some of the facts identified by linguists in terms of it.

Let me begin by rehearsing some truisms about communication. Communication, whether linguistic or not, normally takes place against a background of beliefs or assumptions which are shared by the speaker and his audience, and which are recognized by them to be

so shared. When I discuss politics with my barber, we each take the elementary facts of the current political situation for granted, and we each assume that the other does. We assume that Richard Nixon is the President, that he recently defeated George McGovern by a large margin, that the United States has recently been involved in a war in Vietnam, which is a small country in Southeast Asia, and so forth. That we can reasonably take these facts for granted obviously makes our communication more efficient. The more common ground we can take for granted, the more efficient our communication will be. And unless we could reasonably treat *some* facts in this way, we probably could not communicate at all.

Which facts or opinions we can reasonably take for granted in this way, as much as what further information either of us wants to convey, will guide the direction of our conversation—will determine what is said. I will not say things that are already taken for granted, since that would be redundant. Nor will I assert things incompatible with the common background, since that would be self-defeating. My aim in making assertions is to distinguish among the possible situations which are compatible with all the beliefs or assumptions that I assume that we share. Or it could be put the other way around: the common background is defined by the possible situations which I intend to distinguish among with my assertions, and other speech acts. Propositions true in all of them are propositions whose truth is taken for granted.

Although it is normally inappropriate because unnecessary for me to assert something that each of us assumes the other already believes, my assertions will of course always have consequences which are part of the common background. For example, in a context where we both know that my neighbor is an adult male, I say "My neighbor is a bachelor," which, let us suppose, entails that he is adult and male. I might just as well have said "my neighbor is unmarried." The same information would have been conveyed (although the nuances might not have been exactly the same). That is, the *increment of information,* or of content, conveyed by the first statement is the same as that conveyed by the second. If the asserted proposition were accepted, and added to the common background, the resulting situation would be the same as if the second assertion were accepted and added to the background.

This notion of common background belief is the first approximation to the notion of pragmatic presupposition that I want to use. A proposition P is a pragmatic presupposition of a speaker in a given context just in case the speaker assumes or believes that P, assumes or believes that his addressee assumes or believes that P, and assumes or believes that his addressee recognizes that he is making these assumptions, or has these beliefs.

I do not propose this as a definition or analysis, first since it is far from clear what it is to believe or assume something, in the relevant way and second since even assuming these notions to be clear, the definition would need further qualification. My aim is not to give an analysis but rather to point to a familiar feature of linguistic contexts which, I shall argue, is the feature in terms of which a certain range of linguistic phenomena should be explained. The notion has, I think, enough intuitive content to enable us to identify a lot of particular cases, and the general outlines of the definition are clear enough to justify some generalizations about presuppositions which help to explain the facts. Before defending this claim by discussing some of the facts, I will make two remarks about the general notion.

First, note that it is persons rather than sentences, propositions or speech acts that have or make presuppositions. This goes against the prevailing technical use of the term, according to which presuppositions, whether semantic or pragmatic, are normally taken to relate two linguistic things. One might define such a relation in terms of the pragmatic notion in something like one of the following ways: (a) One might say that a sentence x presupposes that Q just in case the use of x to make a statement is appropriate (or normal, or conversationally acceptable) only in contexts where Q is presupposed by the speaker, or (b) one might say that the statement that P (made in a given context) presupposes that Q just in case one can reasonably infer that the speaker is presupposing that Q from the fact that the statement was made; or (c) one might say that the statement that P (made in a given context) presupposes that Q just in case it is necessary

to assume that the speaker is presupposing that Q in order to understand or interpret correctly the statement. As stated, these suggested definitions are vague, and each is different from the other. But I do not think it would be fruitful to refine them, or to choose one over the others. It is true that the linguistic facts to be explained by a theory of presupposition are for the most part relations between linguistic items, or between a linguistic expression and a proposition. They are, as I interpret them, facts about the constraints, of one kind or another, imposed by what is said on what is appropriately presupposed by the speaker, according to various different standards of appropriateness. But I think all the facts can be stated and explained directly in terms of the underlying notion of speaker presupposition, and without introducing an intermediate notion of presupposition as a relation holding between sentences (or statements) and propositions.

This last point is a strategic recommendation, and not a substantive claim. As I said, one *could* define such a notion in various ways; I just doubt the theoretical utility of doing so. My purely strategic motive for emphasizing this point is that I want to avoid what I think would be a fruitless debate over which of various explications of the notion of pragmatic sentence presupposition best accords with the use of the term "presupposition" by linguists. I do not want to deny that, in an adequate theory of conversation, one will need a notion or notions of conversational acceptability, and that once one has such a notion one has all the material for a definition of pragmatic sentence presupposition. A rough definition of "conversational acceptability" might be something like this: a speech act is conversationally acceptable in the relevant sense just in case it can reasonably be expected to accomplish its purpose in the normal way in which the normal purposes of such speech acts are accomplished. But such a notion would get its content from an account of the mechanisms by which the normal purposes of speech acts are accomplished, and the notion of speaker presupposition is intended to be one theoretical concept useful for giving such an account. It is in this way that it is a more basic concept than the concept of conversational acceptability.

Second, let me suggest one way that the def
inition given above needs to be qualified. In
normal, straightforward serious conversational contexts where the overriding purpose
of the conversation is to exchange information, or conduct a rational argument, what is
presupposed by the speaker, in the sense intended, is relatively unproblematic. The presuppositions coincide with the shared beliefs,
or the presumed common knowledge. The difficulties in applying the notion come with contexts in which other interests besides communication are being served by the conversation.
If one is talking for some other purpose than
to exchange information, or if one must be polite, discreet, diplomatic, kind, or entertaining
as well as informative, then one may have reason to act as if the common background were
different than one in fact knows it to be. For
example, when I talk to my barber, neither of
us expects to learn anything; we are talking
just to be civil, and to pass the time. If we hav-
en't much to say, we may act as if the background of common knowledge is smaller than
it really is. "Cold today, isn't it?" "Sure is,
windy too." "Well, spring will be here before
long." Although there is little actual communication going on here, it is clear that what is
going on is to be understood in terms of genuine communication. We are pretending to
communicate, and our pretense can be explained in terms of the same categories as a
serious exchange of information.

In other cases, a speaker may act as if certain propositions are part of the common
background when he knows that they are not.
He may want to communicate a proposition
indirectly, and do this by presupposing it in
such a way that the auditor will be able to infer
that it is presupposed. In such a case, a speaker
tells his auditor something in part by pretending that his auditor already knows it. The pretense need not be an attempt at deception. It
might be tacitly recognized by everyone concerned that this is what is going on, and recognized that everyone else recognizes it. In
some cases, it is just that it would be indis-
creet, or insulting, or tedious, or unnecessarily
blunt, or rhetorically less effective to openly
assert a proposition that one wants to communicate.[2]

Where a conversation involves this kind of
pretense, the speaker's presuppositions, in the
sense of the term I shall use, will not fit the
definition sketched above. That is why the definition is only an approximation. I shall say
that one actually does make the presuppositions that one seems to make even when one
is only pretending to have the beliefs that one
normally has when one makes presuppositions. Presupposing is thus not a mental attitude like believing, but is rather a linguistic
disposition—a disposition to behave in one's
use of language as if one had certain beliefs, or
were making certain assumptions.[3]

The presumed background information—
the set of presuppositions which in part define
a linguistic context—naturally imposes constraints on what can reasonably or appropriately be said in that context. Where the constraints relate to a particular kind of
grammatical construction, or to a particular
expression or category of expressions, one has
a linguistic fact to be explained. This is the
case with the sample sentences with which I
began. One of the facts could be stated like
this: it is inappropriate to say "The Queen of
England is bald" (or to say "the Queen of England is not bald") except in a context in
which it is part of the presumed background
information that England has a queen. Compare this with a description that interprets the
phenomena in terms of a semantic concept of
presupposition: the proposition expressed by
"the Queen of England is bald" has a truth-
value only if England has a unique queen. The
first description, in contrast to the second,
makes no claim at all about the content of the
statement—about the truth-conditions of
what is said. The description in terms of the
pragmatic notion does not rule out a semantic
explanation for the fact that a certain presupposition is required when a certain statement
is made, but neither does it demand such an
explanation. That is, one *might* explain why it
is appropriate for a speaker to say "the Queen
of England is bald" only if he presupposes that
England has a queen in terms of the following
two assumptions: first, that the statement
lacks a truth-value unless England has a
queen, and second, that one normally presupposes that one's statements have a truth-value.
But one also might explain the fact in a different way. The *facts* about presuppositions, I am
suggesting, can be separated from a particular
kind of semantic explanation of those facts.

This separation of the account of presupposition from the account of the content of what is said will allow for more diversity among presupposition phenomena than would be possible if they all had to be forced into the semantic mold. Let me suggest, more specifically, four of the advantages of making this move.

First, if presupposition is defined independently of truth-conditions, then it is possible for the constraints on presuppositions to vary from context to context, or with changes in stress or shifts in word order, without those changes requiring variation in the semantic interpretation of what is said. This should make possible a simpler semantic theory; at the very least, it should allow for more flexibility in the construction of semantic theories. For example, D. T. Langendoen points out in a paper on presupposition and assertion that normally, if one said "my cousin isn't a boy anymore" he would be asserting that his cousin had grown up, presupposing that he is male. But one might, in a less common context, use the same sentence to assert that one's cousin had changed sexes, presupposing that she is young.[4] If a semantic account of presupposition is given of this case, then one must say that the sentence is therefore ambiguous. On the pragmatic account, one just points to two different kinds of situations in which a univocal sentence could be used.

Second, if presupposition is defined independently of truth-conditions, then one can separate the question of entailment relations from the question of presupposition. On the semantic account, presupposition and entailment are parallel and incompatible semantic relations. A presupposes that B if and only if B is necessitated by *both* A and its denial. A entails B if and only if B is necessitated by A but *not* by its denial. Thus the claim that the sentence, "Sam realizes that P" *entails* that P conflicts with the claim that that sentence presupposes, in the semantic sense, that P. But using the pragmatic account, one may say that sometimes when a presupposition is required by the making of a statement, what is presupposed is also entailed, and sometimes it is not. One can say that "Sam realizes that P" entails that P—the claim is false unless P is true. "Sam does not realize that P," however, does not entail that P. That proposition may be true even when P is false. All this is compatible with the claim that one is required to presuppose that P whenever one asserts or denies that Sam realizes it.

Third, the constraints imposed by a statement on what is presupposed seem to be a matter of degree, and this is hard to explain on the semantic account. Sometimes no sense at all can be made of a statement unless one assumes that the speaker is making a certain presupposition. In other cases, it is mildly suggested by a speech act that the speaker is taking a certain assumption for granted, but the suggestion is easily defeated by countervailing evidence. If a speaker says to me, "Sam was surprised that Nixon lost the election," then I have no choice but to assume that he takes it for granted that Nixon lost. But if he says, "If Eagleton hadn't been dropped from the Democratic ticket, Nixon would have won the election" (without an "even" before the "if" or a "still" after the "Nixon"), there is a suggestion that the speaker presupposes that Nixon in fact did not win, but if the statement is made in the right context, or with the right intonation, the suggestion is overruled. This difference in degree, and variation with context is to be expected on the pragmatic account, since it is a matter of the strength of an inductive inference from the fact that a statement was made to the existence of a background assumption or belief.

Fourth, and perhaps most important, the pragmatic analysis of presupposition, because it relates the phenomena to the general communication situation, may make it possible to explain some of the facts in terms of general assumptions about rational strategy in situations where people exchange information or conduct argument. One way to explain the fact that a particular assertion requires or suggests a certain presupposition is to hypothesize that it is simply a fact about some word or construction used in making the assertion. In such a case, the fact about the presupposition requirement must be written into the dictionary, or into the semantics. But since we have an account of the *function* of presuppositions in conversations, we may sometimes be able to explain facts about them without such hypotheses. The propositions that P and that Q may be related to each other, and to common beliefs and intentions, in such a way that it is hard to think of a reason that anyone would raise the question whether *P*, or care about its answer, unless he already believed that *Q*. More generally, it might be that one can make sense of a conversation as a sequence of rational actions only on the assumption that the speaker and his audience share certain presuppositions. If this kind of explanation can be given for the fact that a certain statement tends to require a certain presupposition, then there will be no need to complicate the semantics or the lexicon.

For example, consider the word "know." It is clear that "*x* knows that *P*" entails that *P*. It is also clear that in most cases when anyone asserts or denies that *x* knows that *P*, he presupposes that *P*. Can this latter fact be explained without building it into the semantics of the word? I think it can. Suppose a speaker were to assert that *x* knows that *P* in a context where the truth of *P* is in doubt or dispute. He would be saying in one breath something that could be challenged in two different ways. He would be leaving unclear whether his main point was to make a claim about the truth of *P*, or to make a claim about the epistemic situation of *x* (the knower), and thus leaving unclear what direction he intended or expected the conversation to take. Thus, given what "*x* knows that *P*" means, and given that people normally want to communicate in an orderly way, and normally have some purpose in mind, it would be unreasonable to assert that *x* knows that *P* in such a context. One could communicate more efficiently by saying something else. For similar reasons, it would normally be inappropriate to say that *x* does not know that *P* in a context where the truth of *P* was in question. If the speaker's reason for believing his assertion were that he thought that *P* was false, or that he thought that *x* didn't believe that *P*, or didn't have reason to believe that *P*, then his statement would be gratuitously weak. And it would be unusual for a speaker to be in a position to know that one of these situations obtained, without knowing which.

This is a tentative and incomplete sketch of an explanation. Much more would have to be said to make it convincing. My point is to make it plausible that, in some cases at least, such explanations might be given, and to argue that where they can be given, there is no reason to build specific rules about presuppositions into the semantics.

I want now to illustrate these advantages of the pragmatic account by looking at some linguistic facts in terms of it. The two sets of facts I will consider are taken from two papers by Lauri Karttunen.[5]

First, on a distinction between two kinds of factive verbs. It is well known that among verbs which take a nominalized sentence complement (for example *believe, know, intend, see*) one can distinguish a subclass known as factive verbs (*know, regret, discover, see,* as contrasted with *believe, intend, assert, claim*). A number of syntactic and semantic criteria are used to draw the distinction, but the distinguishing mark that is relevant here is the following: If *V* is a factive verb, then *x V's that P* presupposes (and, I would say, entails as well) that *P*. If I assert or deny that Jones regrets, realizes, or discovers that Nixon won the election, then I presuppose that Nixon did in fact win. Karttunen has drawn a further distinction among two kinds of factive verbs which, he argues, requires a distinction between two kinds of presupposition relations. One kind of factive verb (labeled the *full factives*) includes *regret, forget* and *resent*. The basis for the distinction is as follows: with full factives, it is not only an assertion or denial of the proposition *x V's that P* that requires the presupposition that *P*, but also the *supposition* that *x V's* that *P* in the antecedent of a conditional, or the claim that the proposition *might* be true. With semi-factives, it is only the assertion or denial that require the presupposition. For example, consider the two statements

Sam may regret that he voted for Nixon.

If Sam regrets that he voted for Nixon, then he is a fool.

Because these two statements clearly require the presupposition that Sam voted for Nixon, *regret* is seen to be a full factive.

The following is Karttunen's example to illustrate the contrast between full factives and semi-factives. Compare

$$\textit{If I} \begin{cases} \textit{regret} \\ \textit{realize} \\ \textit{discover} \end{cases} \textit{later that I have not told the truth,}$$

I will confess it to everyone.

In the first statement, the speaker clearly pre-supposes that he has not told the truth. In the other two cases, he clearly does not presup-pose this. Thus *realize* and *discover* are seen to be semi-factives.

To explain the difference, Karttunen pos-tulates a distinction between a strong and a weak kind of semantic presupposition. If *P* is necessitated by *Possibly Q*, and by *Possibly not-Q*, then *Q* strongly presupposes that *P*. Weak semantic presuppositions are defined in the usual way.

In discussing this example, I want to dispute both the data, and the theoretical account of them. I agree that there is a sharp contrast in the particular example given, but the matter is less clear if one looks at other examples. Con-sider:

If Harry discovers that his wife is playing around, he will be upset.

If Harry had discovered that his wife was playing around, he would have been upset.

If Harry had realized that his wife was playing around, he would have been upset.

Harry may realize that his wife has been playing around.

Harry may never discover that his wife has been playing around.

There is, I think, in all these cases a presump-tion that the speaker presupposes that Harry's wife is, or has been, playing around. The pre-sumption is stronger in some of the examples than in others, but it seems to me that in some of them it is as strong as with *regret*. Further, if we assume that with the so-called semi-fac-tives like *discover* and *realize,* there is *always* a presumption that the speaker presupposes the truth of the proposition expressed in the complement, we can still explain why the pre-sumption is defeated in Karttunen's particular example. The explanation goes like this: if a speaker explicitly supposes something, he thereby indicates that he is not *pre*supposing it, or taking it for granted. So when the speaker says "if I realize later that *P*," he in-dicates that he is not presupposing that he will realize later that *P*. But if it is an open ques-tion for a speaker whether or not he will at some future time have come to realize that *P*, he can't be assuming that he already knows that *P*. And if he is not assuming that he him-

self knows that *P*, he can't be assuming that *P*. Hence *P* cannot be presupposed. A roughly parallel explanation will work for *discover,* but not for *regret.*

One can explain another of Karttunen's ex-amples in a similar way. Consider the three questions:

$$Did\ you \begin{cases} regret \\ realize \\ discover \end{cases} that\ you\ had\ not\ told\ the\ truth?$$

Here *realize* seems to go with *regret* and not with *discover.* The first two questions seem to require that the speaker presuppose that the auditor did not tell the truth, while the third does not. Again, we can explain the difference, even while assuming that there is a presump-tion that the presupposition is made in all three cases. The reason that the presumption is defeated in the third case is that the speaker could not make that presupposition without assuming an affirmative answer to the ques-tion he is asking. But in general, by asking a question, one indicates that one is not presup-posing a particular answer to it. This expla-nation depends on the particular semantic properties of *discover,* and will not work for *realize* or *regret.*[6] It also depends on the fact that the subject of the verb is the second-per-son pronoun. Hence if the explanation is right, one would expect the presupposition to reappear in the analogous third-person ques-tion, "Did Sam discover that he hadn't told the truth?" It seems that it does.

Since on the pragmatic account, the con-straints on presuppositions can vary without the truth-conditions changing, we can allow presupposition differences between first- or second-person statements and questions and the corresponding third-person statements and questions without postulating separate se-mantic accounts of propositions expressed from different points of view. So, while we have noted differences in the presuppositions required or suggested by the following two statements,

If Harry discovers that his wife has been playing around, he will be upset.

If I discover that my wife has been playing around, I will be upset (said by Harry).

This difference does not prevent us from say-ing that the two statements both have the same semantic content—that the same proposition is expressed in both cases. It would not be possible to say this on a semantic account of presupposition.

If the explanations I have sketched are on the right track, then we can account for at least some of the differences between factive and semi-factive verbs without distinguishing between two different kinds of presupposition relations. We can also account for some differences among semi-factives, and differences between first- and third-person statements without complicating the semantics. The explanation depends on just two things: first, some simple and very general facts about the relation between pragmatic presuppositions and assertions, questions, and suppositions; second, on the ordinary semantic properties of the particular verbs involved.[7]

The second set of facts that I will discuss concerns the presuppositions of compound sentences. How do the presuppositions required by a conditional or conjunctive statement relate to the presuppositions that would be required by the component parts, stated alone? In general, what is the relation between the presuppositions required by an assertion that *A* and the assertion that *B* on the one hand, and by an assertion that *A and B* or that *if A, then B* on the other? Karttunen defends the following answer to the question: Let *S* be a sentence of the form *A and B* or *If A, then B*. *S* presupposes that *C* if and only if either *A* presupposes that *C, or B* presupposes that *C* and *A* does not semantically entail that *C*. In other words, the presuppositions of a conjunction are the presuppositions required by either of the conjuncts, *minus any required by the second conjunct which are entailed by the first.* The presuppositions of a conditional are the presuppositions of either antecedent or consequent minus those required by the consequent and entailed by the antecedent. So if I say "Harry is married, and Harry's wife is a great cook," I assert, and do not presuppose, that Harry is married. But the second conjunct, stated alone *(Harry's wife is a great cook),* would require the presupposition that Harry is married. The sentence with conjuncts in reverse order would be unacceptable in any normal context *(Harry's wife is a great cook, and Harry is married).*

Now if we regard Karttunen's generalization as a generalization about *semantic* presuppositions, then we will interpret it as a hypothesis about the way the truth-value (or lack of it) of a conjunction or conditional relates to the truth-values of the parts. The hypothesis has the consequence that the conjunction *and* is not truth-functional, since the truth-value of a conjunctive statement will in some cases depend on entailment relation between the conjuncts. It has the consequence that *and* is not symmetric. *A and B* may be false while *B and A* lacks a truth-value. Finally, it has the consequence that the simple conjunction *and* is governed by mysteriously complicated rules.

On the other hand, if we regard Karttunen's generalization as a generalization about *pragmatic* presuppositions, then we can reconcile it with the standard truth-functional account of *and,* and we can explain the generalization without postulating any ad hoc semantic or pragmatic rules. The explanation goes like this: first, once a proposition has been asserted in a conversation, then (unless or until it is challenged) the speaker can reasonably take it for granted for the rest of the conversation. In particular, when a speaker says something of the form *A and B,* he may take it for granted that *A* (or at least that his audience recognizes that *he* accepts that *A*) after he has said it. The proposition that *A* will be added to the background of common assumptions before the speaker asserts that *B.* Now suppose that *B* expresses a proposition that would, for some reason, be inappropriate to assert except in a context where *A,* or something entailed by *A,* is presupposed. Even if *A* is *not* presupposed initially, one may still assert *A and B* since by the time one gets to saying that *B,* the context has shifted, and it is by then presupposed that *A.*[8]

As with the explanation sketched in the earlier discussion, this explanation rests on just two things: first, a simple pragmatic assumption about the way presuppositions shift in the course of a conversation—an assumption that says, roughly, that a speaker may build on what has already been said; second, an uncontroversial assumption about the semantic properties of the word *and*—in particular, that when one asserts a conjunction, he asserts both conjuncts. If we interpret presupposition to mean *pragmatic* presupposition, then we can deduce Karttunen's generalization from these two almost trivial assumptions.

The analogous generalization about conditional statements is explainable on equally simple assumptions. Here we need first the assumption that what is explicitly *supposed* becomes (temporarily) a part of the background of common assumptions in subsequent conversation, and second that an *if* clause is an explicit supposition. Again, Karttunen's generalization can be derived from these obvious assumptions.

I have been arguing in this paper for the fruitfulness of separating semantic from pragmatic features of linguistic expressions and situations, and of explaining a certain range of phenomena in terms of pragmatic rather than semantic principles. This goes against the trend of the work of generative semanticists such as George Lakoff and John Ross, who have emphasized the difficulty of separating syntactic, semantic, and pragmatic problems, and who have sometimes suggested that such distinctions as between syntactic and semantic deviance or semantic and pragmatic regularities are of more use for avoiding problems than for solving them. Partly to respond to this concern, I will conclude with some general remarks about the distinction between semantics and pragmatics, and about what I am *not* recommending when I suggest that the distinction be taken seriously.

First remark: semantics, as contrasted with pragmatics, can mean either the study of *meaning* or the study of *context.* The contrast between semantic and pragmatic claims can be either of two things, depending on which notion of semantics one has in mind. First, it can be a contrast between claims about the particular conventional meaning of some word or phrase on the one hand, and claims about the general structure or strategy of conversation on the other. Grice's distinction between conventional implicatures and conversational implicatures is an instance of this contrast. Second, it can be a contrast between claims about the truth-conditions or *content* of what is said—the proposition expressed—on the one hand, and claims about the *context* in which a statement is made—the attitudes and interests of speaker and audience—on the other. It is the second contrast that I am using when I argue for a pragmatic rather than a semantic account of presuppositions. That is, my claim is that constraints on the presuppositions are constraints on the contexts in which statements can be made, and not constraints on the truth-conditions of propositions expressed in making the statements. I also made use of the other contrast in arguing for this claim. I conjectured that one can explain many presupposition constraints in terms of general conversational rules without building anything about presuppositions into the meanings of particular words or constructions. But I make no general claim here. In some cases, one may just have to write presupposition constraints into the dictionary entry for a particular word. This would make certain presupposition requirements a matter of *meaning,* but it would not thereby make them a matter of *content.* There may be facts about the meaning of a word which play no role at all in determining the truth-conditions of propositions expressed using the word.

Second remark: in recommending a separation of content and context I am not suggesting that there is no interaction between them. Far from it. The semantic rules which determine the content of a sentence may do so only relative to the context in which it is uttered. This is obviously the case with sentences using personal pronouns, demonstratives, quantifiers, definite descriptions, or proper names. I suspect it happens in less obvious cases as well. But this interaction does not prevent us from studying the features which define a linguistic context (such as a set of pragmatic presuppositions) in abstraction from the propositions expressed in such contexts, or from studying the relationships among propositions in abstraction from the contexts in which they might be expressed.

A final remark: in some cases, distinctions such as that between semantic and pragmatic features may be used as a way to set problems aside. Some linguists have accused other linguists of using the distinction between syntax and semantics in this way. Deviant sentences which seem to conflict with syntactic generalizations are not treated as counterexamples, but instead are thrown into a "semantic wastebasket" to be explained away by some future semantic theory. In the same way, some may be suspicious that I am setting up a pragmatic wastebasket, and recommending that all the interesting problems be thrown away.

I do not think that this is always a bad procedure, but it is not what I am suggesting here. I am recommending instead the development and application of a pragmatic theory in which detailed explanations of phenomena relating to linguistic contexts can be given. It is true that traditionally the more well-developed and the more rigorous linguistic theories have focused on questions of grammar and content, while the discussions which emphasized the role of conversational content have been more informal and less theoretical. But there is no necessity in this. Potentially at least, a theory of pragmatics, and the notion of pragmatic presupposition can be as precise as any of the concepts in syntax and semantics. Although the explanations I have sketched in this paper are informal and incomplete, I think they suggest a strategy for giving explanations of linguistic phenomena relating to contexts which are both rigorous and intuitively natural.[9]

NOTES

1. This paper was read at the University of Texas conferences on performatives, conversational implicature, and presupposition in March, 1973, as well as at New York University. I, and I hope the paper, benefited from stimulating comments by linguists and philosophers at both places.

2. This is a special case of what Grice has called *exploitation,* since the speaker exploits the rules governing normal conversation in order to communicate something which is not explicitly said. See H. P. Grice, "Logic and Conversation," In *Studies in the Way of Words,* Cambridge, Mass.: Harvard University Press, 1989), 1–144.

3. It was suggested by Jerry Sadock (personal communication) that the definition should be modified in another way to account for examples of the following kind: I am asked by someone who I have just met, "Are you going to lunch?" I reply, "No, I've got to pick up my sister." Here I seem to *presuppose* that I have a sister even though I do not assume that the speaker knows this. Yet the statement is clearly acceptable, and it does not seem right to explain this in terms of pretense, or exploitation. To meet this problem, Sadock suggests replacing the clause in the definition, "speaker assumes or believes that the addressee assumes or believes that P" with the clause, "speaker assumes or believes that the addressee *has no reason to doubt* that P."

The reason I resist this suggestion, even though I recognize the force of the example, is that some basic generalizations about speaker presuppositions would fail if it were adopted. For example, one important generalization, alluded to above, is that it is unnecessary, in fact inappropriate, to assert what is presupposed. But consider a routine lecture or briefing by an acknowledged expert. It may be that everything he says is something that the audience has no reason to doubt, but this does not make it inappropriate for him to speak. The problem is that the modification would work only for cases where the addressee could infer what was being presupposed from the overt speech act. But this is not the only case where speaker presuppositions are important.

Two alternative responses to the example are possible: (a) one can explain it in terms of exploitation; (b) one can deny that there is a presupposition made at all in this kind of example.

To respond in the first way is, I admit, to stretch the notion of exploitation, first because the example lacks the flavor of innuendo or diplomatic indirection which characterizes the clearest cases of communication by pretense, and second because in the best cases of exploitation, it is the main point of the speech act to communicate what is only implied, whereas in this example, the indirectly communicated material is at best only a minor piece of required background information. Nevertheless, the explanation of how communication takes place in this example may be thought to be similar in form to explanations of how it takes place in the more familiar cases: the addressee infers that the speaker accepts that Q from the fact that he says that P because normally one says that P only when it is common background knowledge that Q.

To take the second option is to deny the generalization that the speaker *always* presupposes the existence of a unique referent (in the relevant domain of discourse) fitting any definite description (like "my sister") which he uses. To make this plausible, one would have to give an explanation of why one is *usually* expected to presuppose the existence of a unique referent when one uses a definite description—an explanation which also explains the exceptions to the rule.

4. D. Terence Langendoen, "Presupposition and Assertion in the Semantic Analysis of Nouns and Verbs in English," in *Semantics: An Interdisciplinary Reader in Philosophy, Linguistics and Psychology,* ed. by Danny D. Steinberg and Leon A. Jakobovits (Cambridge, England: Cambridge University Press, 1971).

5. Lauri Karttunen, "Some Observations on Factivity" and "Presuppositions of Compound Sentences," *Linguistic Inquiry,* IV (1973).

6. The relevant difference between *realize* and *discover* is this: because *realize* is a stative verb, a past tense statement of the form *x didn't realize that P* must be about some particular time in the past (determined by the context), and not about *all* times in the past. This means that *x didn't realize that P* may be true, even though *x now* knows that *P*. Therefore, a speaker may assume that his addressee knows or assumes that *P* without prejudging the question whether or not he realized (at the relevant past time) that *P*. In contrast, because *discover* is an inchoative verb, *x didn't discover that P* may be about *all* times in the past. For this reason, normally, *x didn't discover that P* implies that x has not *yet* discovered that *P*, and so does not now know that *P*. Therefore, if a speaker presupposes that *P*, he assumes that *x has* discovered that *P*, and so assumes a particular answer to the question he is asking.

7. Two disclaimers: First, I do not want to leave the impression that I think I have explained very much here. I have not made any attempt to explain the source of the presumption that the complements of both factive and semi-factive verbs are presupposed. I have tried to explain only how the presumption is canceled in certain cases. Also, the presumption is clearly harder to defeat in some cases than in others: harder with *realize* than with *discover,* and harder with full factives than with semi-factives. I have said nothing that would explain this. My hope, however, is that such explanations can be given using the general strategy which I am recommending. Second, I do not want to deny that there are systematic differences between factives and semi-factives. One difference is that full factives all require not only the presupposition that the proposition expressed in the complement is true, but also the presupposition that the subject of the verb knows or knew that it is. None of the semi-factives require or suggest this second presupposition; in fact, they rule it out.

8. In a paper given at the Texas conference on performatives, conversational implicatives, and presuppositions, Karttunen put forward an explanation of his generalization which is very similar to this. Our accounts were developed independently.

9. I have been accused, partly on the basis of this concluding paragraph, of being overly optimistic about the possibility of a formal theory of pragmatics which is both rigorous and sufficiently detailed to provide substantive explanations of linguistic phenomena. This accusation may be just, but my main point here is independent of this. However easy or difficult it proves to be to develop an adequate theory of conversation, one cannot simplify the task by building conversational rules into a semantic theory of the content of what is said.

FURTHER READING

Caton, C. E. (1981). "Stalnaker on Pragmatic Presupposition." In P. Cole (ed.), *Radical Pragmatics*. New York: Academic Press, 83–100.

Donnellan, K. S. (1981). "Intuitions and Presuppositions." In P. Cole (ed.), *Radical Pragmatics*. New York: Academic Press, 129–142.

Grice, H. P. (1981). "Presupposition and Conversational Implicature." In P. Cole (ed.), *Radical Pragmatics*. New York: Academic Press, 183–198.

Karttunen, L. (1973). "Presuppositions of Compound Sentences." *Linguistic Inquiry* 4:169–193.

Katz, J., and D. Langendoen (1976). "Pragmatics and Presupposition." *Language* B 52:1–17.

Keenan, E. L. (1971). "Two Kinds of Presupposition in Natural Language." In C. Fillmore and D. Langendoen (eds.), *Studies in Linguistic Semantics*. New York: Holt, Rinehart and Winston, 44–52.

Kempson, R. (1975). *Presupposition and the Delimitation of Semantics*. Cambridge: Cambridge University Press.

Langendoen, D., and H. Savin (1971). "The Projection Problem for Presuppositions." In C. Fillmore and D. Langendoen (eds.), *Studies in Linguistic Semantics*. New York: Holt, Rinehart and Winston, 54–60.

Oh, Ch.-K., and D. Dinneen (eds.). (1979). *Syntax and Semantics*. Vol. 11: *Presupposition*. New York: Academic Press.

Soames, S. (1979). "A Projection Problem for Speaker Presupposition." *Linguistic Inquiry* 10:623–666.

Stalnaker, R. (1973). "Presuppositions." *Journal of Philosophical Logic* 2:447–457.

Van Der Auwera, J. (1979). "Pragmatic Presupposition: Shared Beliefs in a Theory of Irrefutable Meaning." In Ch.-K. Oh and D. Dinneen (eds.), *Syntax and Semantics*. Vol. 11: *Presuppositions*. New York: Academic Press, 249–264.

Wilson, D. (1975). *Presuppositions and Non–Truth-Conditional Semantics*. New York: Academic Press.

VII

Non-Literal Uses of Language:
Metaphor and Irony

28

Metaphorical Assertions

MERRIE BERGMANN

I

Metaphors can be used, and used successfully, to make assertions. The claim that there is such a use of metaphor seems obvious enough, and many authors have treated it as such. Yet the claim is incompatible with, even flatly denied by, numerous other accounts of the "nature" of metaphor. Although the antagonists hail from diverse philosophical quarters, they share a concern with one aspect of metaphor: this is the "richness," or the "pregnancy" or "expansiveness," of metaphor. There are those who maintain outright that the richness of metaphor precludes its use in the making of assertions. And there are those who stop short of this conclusion but nevertheless maintain that because of their richness, what we say when we use metaphors is in some way different in kind from what can be said literally: for example, we use metaphors to say things that are "wildly" or "mythically" true.[1]

In this paper, I provide a theoretical account of the assertive use of metaphor. One of the consequences of the account is this: not only is the richness of metaphor *compatible* with its

use in making assertions; but in addition our assessments of the richness of metaphors are based on the workings of *the same linguistic mechanism* which enables us to make and understand specific assertions with metaphors. Once this mechanism is understood, there is no need to maintain that the contents of metaphorical assertions, or their truth-values, are different in kind from those of literal assertions. First, though, I shall explain how concern with the richness of metaphor has led to the conclusion that assertive use is precluded, and state why the general strategy of reasoning is mistaken.

The claim that metaphors are rich means that they invite many readings, or suggest many things, and diverse ones. Consider Romeo's "Juliet is the sun." Since Shakespeare wrote that line many plausible and interesting readings have been attributed to the metaphor. There are two reasons why this richness of metaphor might be thought to preclude assertion. First, assertions presumably have fairly well-defined contents (with fuzzy edges, perhaps, due to vagueness); and when we examine a metaphor to determine all the readings it invites, we find that what the metaphor

Merrie Bergmann, "Metaphorical Assertions," *Philosophical Review* 91 (1982): 229–245. Copyright © 1982 by The Philosophical Review. Reprinted by permission of the publisher and the author.

"means" is difficult to contain. Second, if metaphors are rich in the sense of conveying endlessly many things to us, it is hard to see how anyone making an assertion with a metaphor could have a good grasp on what, exactly or *even roughly,* is being asserted. While it is true that sometimes we are not fully aware of the content of our assertions, or of what we mean when we assert something, usually we are aware enough.[2]

Thus it is tempting to draw a conclusion like Donald Davidson's:

. . . the thesis that associated with a metaphor is a cognitive content that its author wishes to convey and that the interpreter must grasp if he is to get the message . . . is false, whether or not we call the purported cognitive content a meaning.

It should make us suspect the theory that it is so hard to decide, even in the case of the simplest metaphors, exactly what the cognitive content is supposed to be. . . . [I]n fact, there is no limit to what a metaphor calls to our attention. . . . When we try to say what a metaphor "means", we soon realize there is no end to what we want to mention.[3]

The fact that metaphors "generate" further and further readings does not, however, conflict with the claim that an author *can* successfully use a metaphor to convey a fairly specific cognitive content. For a person who uses a metaphor to make an assertion typically does not intend to assert *everything* that we can "read into" the metaphor. Nor does the audience typically attribute all of those readings to the author.

Let me illustrate. Suppose I say to you, after hearing the latest report on Three Mile Island, "As far as I'm concerned, nuclear reactors are time bombs." You correctly interpret my remark as an assertion to the effect that nuclear reactors are likely to fail, at any moment—of course, with disastrous consequences. A while later you say, "That was an interesting metaphor: nuclear reactors being time bombs. Although I don't think that the guys responsible for those things *want* people to get killed by them, still it seems that, like people who use time bombs, they have a frightening disregard for human lives." This, then, is something else that I could have used the metaphor to assert. But it does not follow, from the possibility of using a metaphor to make different assertions, that anyone who *does* use that metaphor *is* making all of those assertions. You and I may

both recognize that I could have used the metaphor to make a comment about the people responsible for nuclear reactors, and at the same time recognize that I was not doing so. The richness, or suggestiveness, of metaphors does not forestall their use in making fairly specific assertions, and it is a mistake to argue otherwise.

The grain of truth in Davidson's claim about richness is this: without knowing the context in which a metaphor occurs and who its author is, it is impossible to state conclusively what the metaphor "means" without drawing out all that it *could* mean. And here the process does seem endless. Dwell on a metaphor long enough, even a relatively uninteresting one, and numerous and varied interpretations come to mind.

But bring in a well-defined context and a real author, and matters may change drastically. Although there may be *prima facie* reasons for denying the status of assertion to certain metaphors in certain contexts—as when they occur in poetry, if we do not believe that the point of poetry is assertion—there are good reasons to give the status of assertion to others. These are the metaphors that occur in everyday conversation, and in many varieties of prose.

II

My claim is that the author of a metaphor can use that metaphor to assert something, and can do so with success. In this section I provide a theoretical account of this linguistic act. First, I characterize the assertive use of metaphor; and second, I explain what is involved in the success of this use of language. For even when an author intends to assert something with metaphor, the communicative enterprise, just like any other attempt at communication, may fail. Some of the reasons for failure are peculiar to metaphor, but others are not.

It should be clear from my remarks in the last section that I do not maintain that metaphors are *always* used to make assertions. The account that follows paves the way for a theoretical description of other uses of metaphor as well. For although I develop an account of the assertive use, I characterize metaphor independently of any particular illocutionary force.

To simplify matters, I focus on assertive metaphors that occur in conversational contexts. What counts as a metaphor, and what we should regard the metaphor as doing, both involve questions of *use*. Asking of a sentence itself—say, 'Smith is a Communist'—whether it is a metaphor is like asking of the sentence itself whether it is a lie, or whether it is a warning or an insult. In each case the question is, illegitimate. What we can legitimately ask is whether the the sentence is, on a particular occasion, being used as a metaphor. And an answer to this question relies on recognizing, or assuming, something about the *intentions* of the person who uses the sentence.[4] The sentence 'Smith is a Communist' is not itself either literal or metaphorical; it may be used either way.

But the classification of a sentence as a metaphor does not settle the other questions of use. The uses of a sentence as a metaphor and as a lie are not mutually exclusive; and so it is with metaphor and warning, metaphor and criticizing, metaphor and asserting. Concerning lying, it suffices to note that metaphor may be used with or without intent to deceive. And when we decide that a sentence is a metaphor we are not classifying it according to illocutionary force. Here we have three dimensions of use, distinguished from one another by the sorting criterion that operates within each dimension: sincerity (truth-telling or lying), purpose (illocutionary force), and manner: the systematic relation between the words used and the content of the illocutionary act. Identification of a sentence as metaphor is classification according to manner, and manner may be literal, metaphoric, ironic, hyperbolic, and so on. In the case of the assertive metaphor, then, we must make two distinct identifications as to use: the sentence is being used *as* a metaphor, and *to* assert.

Further, when a sentence is used as a metaphor with the intention of assertion, various propositions may be intended or conveyed, depending on the author and the context. The point of 'Smith is a Communist' used as a metaphor may be to assert that Smith is unpatriotic, that Smith advocates abolition of the nuclear family, or that Smith opposes religious freedom. What is a proposition? I take a proposition to be what the best linguistic the-

ory available says it is: something that can be represented as a function from possible worlds into truth-values, or, equivalently, a set of possible worlds (those worlds to which the function assigns the value TRUE).[5] This concept of a proposition—one that has been applied successfully to a variety of linguistic and logical problems—has a particular virtue in the analysis of metaphor: propositions are language-independent entities. So in developing a theory of what different metaphors can be used to assert, we need not assume that we must "translate" the metaphors into language used literally, as if that were the only way to get at propositions.[6]

Whereas a proposition represents the world as being a certain way, an act of asserting a proposition is an act of saying that the world *is* the way the proposition represents it as being.[7] When language is used literally to assert a proposition, there is an intimate connection between the words used and the proposition asserted: the words literally *express* the proposition. Or, to put it another way, the proposition is the *meaning* of the sentence used.[8] But a person who uses a sentence metaphorically does not use it to assert the proposition that is literally expressed by the sentence. In the case of assertive metaphor, we must distinguish between sentence meaning and speaker's meaning.[9]

If the use is to count as *metaphor,* however, rather than as some other figure like irony or even as nonsense, a particular sort of relation must hold between the sentence used and the proposition asserted. What is distinctive of all metaphorical uses of language (whether the purpose is to assert or to do something else) is that the content of what is communicated is a *direct* function of salient characteristics associated with (at least) part of the expression—rather than of the literal meaning of that part.[10] The concept of a salient characteristic associated with an expression is a technical one, which I develop in a companion to this article, and its definition will vary with the grammatical category of the expression. Here I'll just give examples for some simple sorts of expressions.[11]

Characteristics include properties and relations. *Salience* of characteristics is partially a function of commonplaces and stereotypes. The salient characteristics of a thing include those characteristics which we would typically list on the spot if asked to state what we believe is *distinctive* of that thing.[12] So the salient characteristics associated with a name include properties that are commonly attributed to the thing named (perhaps incorrectly). Salient characteristics associated with the name 'Einstein' include the properties of being a scientist, and of being brilliant. In virtue of these characteristics, I may use 'John is an Einstein' to say that John is a brilliant scientist. The proposition I have asserted is then a function of the literal meaning of 'John' and of salient characteristics associated with 'Einstein'. I may also use 'Einstein' to *refer* to John, if he is a brilliant scientist: 'Einstein is on his lunch break'.

The salient characteristics associated with a common noun or intransitive verb include properties commonly believed to be characteristic of the things—possible or actual—the noun or verb applies to, properties that are part of the stereotype of that sort of thing.[13] One salient characteristic associated with 'encyclopedia' is the property of being a source of information. Thus I can use 'Marie is an encyclopedia' to attribute that property to Marie, to assert that Marie knows lots of things. A salient characteristic associated with 'smile' is benevolence and consequently I can use 'Uncle George was smiling at us when he wrote his will' to assert that Uncle George decided to leave us something after all. The salient characteristics associated with a transitive verb include relations that are commonly thought to hold between things standing in the relation literally expressed by the verb. A salient characteristic associated with 'cook' is the relation *prepare*. Thus I can assert that Roger has become a poet by saying 'Roger is cooking poems these days.'[14]

Salience is also sensitive to context—to matters of ongoing concern, information that has just been shared. Thus the salient characteristics associated with a name also include properties that, in the context in which the name is used, have been made conspicuous by some means or other. A certain context may bring the property of being eccentric to the status of a salient characteristic associated with 'Einstein'—for example, one in which I have just been telling anecdotes (mostly false) about Einstein. In such a context, 'John is an Einstein' may be used to assert the proposition

that John is eccentric, as well as (or instead of) the proposition that he is a brilliant scientist. Or perhaps you have been complaining about the exorbitant price you just paid for a cord of wood, lamenting that you will now have to watch your budget closely. I pick up on this when the conversation turns to my new refrigerator, saying 'That refrigerator is *my* cord of wood' to indicate that it, too, was expensive and that I will be on a tight budget as well.

I want to stress that properties or relations may be *ephemerally* rather than eternally salient. By telling anecdotes about Einstein I have managed to make eccentricity a salient characteristic of the man; but tomorrow this may be forgotten. And what is salient for one person may not be salient for another. A third party who did not hear your complaint will not understand why I called my refrigerator, rather than my electric space heater, a 'cord of wood.'

Salience, then, is context-dependent. And a context, when the understanding of metaphor is at issue, is a context for a person. We may think of the context that a person brings to the interpretation of a metaphor as the set of prominent beliefs that determine salience— beliefs that may vary from person to person and from situation to situation. The context includes the linguistic exchange in which the metaphor occurs—what propositions have been asserted, what the topics are.[15] The context also includes background knowledge about parties to the conversation.

While certain salience-making factors vary from context to context, however, there are still the culturally shared beliefs—the stereotypes—that stay with us. The description of contexts as person- and situation-specific is not intended to suggest that stereotypes play no role in the understanding of metaphor; they do. Rather, it is intended to draw attention to those beliefs which are not stereotypical, or which are lately acquired, that contribute to our assessments of salience along with those beliefs which are habitual.

In metaphorical assertion, then, the proposition that we take to be asserted is a direct function of salient characteristics associated with (at least) part of the expression. And as what is salient varies, so do the propositions that a sentence, taken as metaphor, may successfully be used to assert. It is a trivial consequence of my account that metaphors may be used to make true or false assertions, where an assertion is true if the proposition asserted is true and false otherwise. But it is important that truth and falsehood be tied to the assertion made, rather than to the sentence used. For a metaphor may be used to make different assertions, and typically some of these will be true and others false. Propositions themselves, at any rate, are true or false in the same sense whether metaphorically or literally asserted; so there is no need to call the contents of metaphorical assertions "wildly" true. It is not the content of what is said, but the manner of saying it, that distinguishes metaphorical assertions from literal ones.

What can be said in favor of accepting the salience relation as the basis for determining the content of metaphorical assertions? It works. Take an assertive metaphor, and take what you assume is the content of the metaphor—and you will find that content *is* determined by salient characteristics you associate with expressions in the metaphor. Moreover, the account based on salience corresponds nicely to what we do when we set out to *explicate* metaphors. A typical way to explicate 'Life is a game' as a metaphor about life is to draw attention to our beliefs about what characteristics are distinctive of games and to attribute these characteristics to life.[16]

Now we may state the conditions for success in the case of assertive metaphor. First, the audience must recognize the author's utterance as *metaphor*. There are several familiar ways in which this may happen. The speaker may explicitly indicate that he or she is using metaphor. The expression used may be either semantically or contextually anomalous if taken literally. Following Grice,[17] we may say that in this case a conversational maxim has apparently been violated: Quality (the sentence 'Men are wolves,' taken literally, is false), Quantity (you may say of our mutual friend who has long lived in California, 'Hayward is a Californian, all right'), Relation (you may answer my questions about your new automobile's road performance and gas mileage by replying 'It seems I have a mule with an insatiable appetite'). In each case, the literal content of the sentence is conversationally inappropriate. Or recognition of metaphor may just involve recognition of the appropriateness

of a particular reading of the expression as metaphor, rather than recognition of inappropriateness of the literal reading.

Second, the audience must recognize the author's utterance as an *assertion*. And third, the audience must properly identify the proposition the author intended to assert. The audience must identify which component expressions (if any) are to be taken literally— and will use clues from the context (for example, the topic of discussion) to do so. And the audience must identify the correct salient characteristics for fixing the content of the assertion. Here the audience will typically choose characteristics the salience of which is believed to be mutual knowledge in the conversational setting.[18] Of course, not all the propositions the audience may arrive at on the basis of salient characteristics will be *plausible* in the context; and those that are not will be rejected or ignored. Grice's maxims thus help us to choose between a metaphor's possible contents, as well as to recognize metaphor.

The responsibility for the success of a metaphorical assertion is the author's; he or she must ensure that the audience can figure out *what* proposition is being asserted. Here Grice's maxim of Manner, "Be perspicious," is relevant: the audience must have access to the salient characteristics necessary for retrieving the intended content of the assertion.[19] The author, in short, is responsible for preventing the "richness" of a metaphor from interfering with its efficacy in asserting a specific proposition. Principles of cooperative discourse are in effect here as well as in literal discourse. This is just as one would expect, if metaphors can be used to make assertions.

III

Finally, I shall use my account to address some important issues in the literature on metaphor, and I shall substantiate the claim that I made at the beginning of this paper concerning the relation between the richness of metaphor and its assertive use.

1. *The salience relation distinguishes metaphor from other tropes.* The relations involved in figuration differ from trope to trope. For example, the relation in irony is one of inversion: what is meant is the *opposite* of what is

literally expressed; the relation in hyperbole is one of exaggeration: what is literally expressed is an exaggeration of what is meant. In this paper, the examples I have given are cases of "pure" metaphor—the use of the expression involves only the figure of metaphor. Metaphor does not interfere with other tropes or figures; but it should not be *confused* with them. 'You are the cream in my coffee' may be used at once ironically and metaphorically; 'It's the Empire State Building' may involve both metaphor and hyperbole.[20]

2. *Understanding metaphor requires more than understanding word meaning.* A while back, various attempts were made to show how metaphorical "meanings" could be generated on the basis of deleted selection restrictions of semantic features (components of literal meanings). Thus L. Jonathan Cohen and Avishai Margalit write:

> The metaphorical meanings of a word or phrase in a natural language are all contained, as it were, within its literal meaning or meanings. They are reached by removing any restrictions in relation to certain variables from the appropriate section or sections of its semantical hypothesis. For example, *baby* has as one of its metaphorical meanings the sense of *very small of its kind:* cf. *baby airplane* as against *baby daughter.* Here it is obviously the age and human/animal/artificial/etc. variables that are being treated as if they imposed no restriction, while a restriction of size is still retained. Or if this is considered an example of already dead metaphor, consider *That old man is a baby,* where on the most straightforward interpretation the age and size variables are presumably being treated as if they imposed no restriction, and other attributes of babies are being ascribed, such as mental incapacity.[21]

Such a theory requires a broad conception of literal meanings—most of us wouldn't normally think of mental incapacity as contributing to the literal meaning of 'baby'. This objection has been raised often enough.

But there is a more severe problem with the theory. For *ephemerally* salient characteristics may not be commonplace at all; yet, as I have suggested, they can play an important role in the interpretation of metaphors. Consider:

JOHN: Look at how blue the sky is today!
  JOE: Sure is. What a great color . . . and not a cloud in sight. When the sky is that blue, the air seems fresher . . . crisper . . . it really makes you feel good.
JOHN: Yeah, it sure is a good feeling. Like every-

thing's gonna be great, when the sky is that blue.
  JOE: Mmm. . . . Hey—even the news report was blue today for a change—lotsa good stuff.

What has happened during this brief exchange is that 'blue,' which under somewhat conventional usage has the associated salient characteristic *sad* or *depressing,* has picked up a very different associated characteristic: one that will likely be lost shortly in John's and Joe's conceptual schemes. In basing my account of assertive metaphor on the concept of associated salient characteristics I have developed a theory that is sensitive to those interpretations which clearly rest on context rather than on lexical knowledge, as well as to those interpretations which are dependent on community-wide beliefs.[22]

3. *A metaphor used assertively may not admit of simple paraphrase.* The claim has often been made that metaphors are not paraphrasable in literal language. Sometimes the claim is trivial, as when we are then told that even literal expressions cannot be paraphrased. When it is not trivial, the claim takes one of three forms:

(i) There is a lexical gap in our vocabulary; there are some things that can be said by metaphor for which we have no literal words.

(ii) No literal paraphrase can capture the suggestiveness of a metaphor.

(iii) No literal paraphrase can give the "insight" a metaphor gives.[23]

I shall comment on (ii) and (iii) below; it is (i) that interests me here. My theory is consistent with both (i) and its denial.

It is important to distinguish two versions of the gap mentioned in (i):

(ia) There is some proposition that, given the available resources of our language, is not literally expressed by any sentence or set of sentences.

I have not seen any convincing example supporting the existence of a gap of this sort that has been successfully plugged by a *metaphor.* Stipulation and theoretical introduction of terms, as in scientific inquiry, may fill such gaps—but this is not metaphor.

(ib) There is some meaning of a nonpropositional sort that, given the available resources of our language, is not literally expressed by any single word.

This claim seems to be true. For example, I know of no single word that means the same as what 'brilliant and eccentric scientist' literally expresses. Yet, under appropriate circumstances, this may be a metaphorical interpretation of 'an Einstein.'

4. *There is no one answer to the question 'Why do we use metaphors?'* Although I have focused on the use of metaphor in making assertions, we must not forget that metaphors can be used nonassertively: for example, we may question or command with metaphors. But even when the use of a metaphor *is* assertive, there may be purposes beyond that of conveying a proposition. The metaphor may be used for aesthetic reasons (it conjures up a pleasing or disturbing image), or rhetorical ones (an expression in the metaphor has strong emotive connotations). Or the metaphor may be used because it is believed to be rich, to be fecund, or to have considerable organizing power.

A metaphor is *fecund* if it suggests other, related, metaphors. From 'John is a child' we may move to talk of playing to characterize John metaphorically, or we may move to characterizing other people metaphorically as adolescents, as middle-aged, or as elderly. And we may, in the process, discover a useful new vocabulary for a certain subject matter.[24]

A metaphor has *organizing power* if it influences our orientation toward a subject matter. Organizing power is what Susan Sontag notes in metaphors about artistic style:

Take ... Whitman's very material metaphor. By likening style to a curtain, he has of course confused style with decoration and for this would be speedily faulted by most critics. To conceive of style as a decorative encumbrance on the matter of the work suggests that the curtain could be parted and the matter revealed; or, to vary the metaphor slightly, that the curtain could be rendered transparent. But this is not the only erroneous implication of the metaphor. What the metaphor also suggests is that style is a matter of more or less (quantity), thick and thin (density). And ... this is just as wrong as the fancy that an artist possesses the genuine option to have or not to have a style. Style is not quantitative, any more than it is superadded. ... .[25]

The organizing power of a metaphor concerns the *directedness* and *restrictedness* of what it suggests. A metaphor may highlight certain aspects of a subject while obscuring others. Here, I think, is the heuristic value in thinking of the understanding of certain metaphors as being akin to "seeing-as": metaphors sometimes give us a new orientation toward a familiar subject matter, making us revise, ignore, or even forget, the beliefs that went along with the old orientation.[26]

5. *Our assessments of the richness of metaphors are based on the workings of the same linguistic mechanism that enables us to make specific assertions with metaphor.* The mechanism is, of course, the manner of metaphor: the salience relation between the expression used and the content of what is communicated.

A metaphor is *rich* if it is one that causes us to notice many things. Richness is not something inherent in a metaphor; rather our judgments as to richness are based on the effects the metaphor has on us. Our perceptions of the richness of a metaphor, like those of fecundity and organizing power, may vary with time and with concentration.

Take 'John is a child' as metaphor. I may use this to assert that John is naive, but it may cause you to notice (and I may have intended this) that John has other, perhaps less salient, characteristics of children: he is small, he giggles a lot. If I had just said 'John is naive' you would probably not, as a result of my utterance, notice these other things about John. In this sense, the literal paraphrase of my assertion does not have the suggestive power of the metaphor I used.

What you are noticing are salient characteristics associated with 'child'. I have already explained how salience can vary from context to context, and this is true whether the point of metaphor is assertion, heuristic guidance, or poetry. But there is another way in which salience won't stay fixed. Namely, the act of dwelling on a metaphor long enough, teasing out all that it can "mean," will affect salience of characteristics associated with component expressions. Specifically, if we repeatedly ask of a metaphor 'What *else* might it mean?', after the propositions based on some highly salient characteristics have been noted we may begin to notice, or to *focus upon,* characteristics that initially were not salient—and this very focusing raises the salience of those characteristics.

Thus, it is not surprising, to echo Davidson, that when we dwell on a metaphor we realize that there is no end to what it can "mean." And here we find one of the makings of poetry. For the poetic context invites us to dwell, to go beyond the *immediately* salient. But the poetic metaphor does not differ from the street variety in kind, for both do their work through salient characteristics. The difference lies in the practice rather than in the principle, in the ways we allow or disallow the immediate context to determine salience and hence interpretations. The underlying mechanism is the same in both cases. And it is reliance on this mechanism, rather than the purpose for which an expression is used—be it simple assertion, the sharing of profound insight, or poetry— that makes a linguistic act a metaphorical one.

ACKNOWLEDGMENTS

Research for this paper was supported by a Faculty Fellowship from Dartmouth College. I am grateful to my colleagues Robert Fogelin, Bernard Gert, and James Moor for valuable criticisms and suggestions prompted by an earlier version of this paper.

NOTES

1. See, for example, Stanley Cavell, "Aesthetic Problems in Modern Philosophy," in his *Must We Mean What We Say?* (New York: Cambridge University Press, 1976), pp. 73–96; and Ted Cohen, "Notes on Metaphor," *Journal of Aesthetics and Art Criticism,* Vol. 34 (1976), 669–84.

2. Arne Naess discusses definiteness of intention in literal language use in *Interpretation and Preciseness* (Oslo: I Kommisjon Hos Jacob Dybwad, 1953).

3. "What Metaphors Mean," *Critical Inquiry,* 5 (1978), 46. [Reprinted in this volume, Chapter 27] Davidson argues that metaphors mean only what they literally mean. So the cognitive content at issue in the quotation is something different from literal meaning—a "metaphorical meaning." Israel Scheffler makes a claim similar to the one in this quotation, in *Beyond the Letter* (Boston: Routledge and Kegan Paul, 1979), pp. 128–30.

4. The nonexclusive contrast with lying is Davidson's. The inadequacies of purely semantic characterizations of metaphor are discussed in my "Metaphor and Formal Semantics," *Poetics,* 8 (1979), 213–30, in Ted Cohen, "Notes on Metaphor" and in Ina Loewenberg, "Identifying Metaphors," *Foundations of Language,* 12 (1975), 315–38.

5. Thus Robert Stalnaker writes:

The intuitive motivation for this analysis is something like the following. A proposition—the content of an assertion or belief—is a representation of the world as being a certain way. But for any given representation of the world as being a certain way, there will be a set of all the possible states of the world which accord with the representation—which *are* that way. So any proposition determines a set of possible worlds. And, for any given set of possible worlds, to locate the actual world in that set is to represent the world as being a certain way. So every set of possible worlds determines a proposition.

"Assertion," in *Syntax and Semantics.* Vol. 9: *Pragmatics* ed. Peter Cole (New York: Academic Press, 1978), 315–32. [Reprinted in this volume, Chapter 17]

6. Whether metaphors are "paraphrasable" has long been a live issue, and I'll briefly comment on it in Section III. Here my point is simply that, using intensional concepts like propositions as sets of possible worlds, we needn't beg the quesion as to the paraphrasability of assertive metaphors.

7. Cf. Stalnaker, "Assertion."

8. Strictly speaking, this needs qualification of a sort that need not concern us here: qualification concerning, for example, ambiguity and the use of indexicals.

9. I agree with Davidson on this point:

Once we understand a metaphor we can call what we grasp the "metaphorical truth" and (up to a point) say what the "metaphorical meaning" is. But simply to lodge this meaning in the metaphor is like explaining why a pill puts you to sleep by saying it has a dormative power. Literal meaning and literal truth conditions can be assigned to words and sentences apart from particular contexts of use. This is why adverting to them has genuine explanatory power. ("What Metaphors Mean," p. 33.)

The fact that an expression can be used as a metaphor does not point to, or create, an *ambiguity* in the expression. When metaphors die, to be sure, we may be left with new ambiguities. But that is the point of calling a metaphor 'dead'—it has become common currency.

10. The "direct" indicates that the proposition expressed may (and indeed will) depend on the literal meaning of the expression at issue; but it does so only insofar as the salient characteristics associated with an expression are partially a function of its literal meaning.

11. The companion is "The Formal Semantics of Metaphorical Assertions."

The concept of salience has appeared now in several accounts of metaphor. In particular, I am indebted to the work of Andrew Ortony for detailed discussions of this concept. See his "Beyond Literal Similarity," *Psychological Review*, 86 (1976), 161–80, and "The Role of Similarity in Similes and Metaphors," in *Metaphor and Thought*, ed. Andrew Ortony (New York: Cambridge University Press, 1979), pp. 186–201.

12. The "distinctive" part is important. Israel Scheffler has pointed out that an account of metaphor that appeals to commonplaces with no restrictions will allow unacceptable interpretations of metaphors:

That wolves are larger than mushrooms is not only true but also commonly held to be true by laymen within our culture. These laymen also normally hold that wolves have eyes, occupy space and have weight; they are persuaded that no wolf is a tree or an umbrella or identical with Mount Everest. Does [such an account] then imply that to call men wolves is to say that men too are larger than mushrooms, have eyes, and so forth? (*Beyond the Letter*, p. 114.)

13. Max Black's description of a 'system of associated commonplaces' amplifies the notion of a stereotype:

Imagine some layman required to say, without taking special thought, those things he held to be true about wolves; the set of statements resulting would approximate to what I am here calling the system of commonplaces associated with the word 'wolf.' I am assuming that in any given culture the responses made by different persons to the test suggested would agree rather closely, and that even the occasional expert, who might have unusual knowledge of the subject, would still know "what the man in the street thinks about the matter." From the expert's standpoint, the system of commonplaces may include half-truths or downright mistakes (as when a whale is classified as a fish); but the important thing for the metaphor's effectiveness is not that the commonplaces shall be true, but that they should be readily and freely evoked ("Metaphor," *Proceedings of the Aristotelian Society*, 55 (1954–55), 287.)

See also Hilary Putnam's account of stereotypes in "The Meaning of 'Meaning'," in *Language, Mind, and Knowledge*, Minnesota Studies in the Philosophy of Science, Vol. 7, ed. Keith Gunderson (Minneapolis: University of Minnesota Press, 1975), 131–93.

14. Sometimes the salient characteristics we associate with a general expression such as a common noun or a verb are characteristics thought typical or distinctive of some *prominent subclass* of the extension of the word. Consider 'He had a green thought.' I can't think of any distinctive characteristics associated with the *entire* collection of green things, save that they are green. In interpreting the sentence as metaphor we may focus on a subcollection of green things—plants, perhaps, or unripe fruit. Then we have the characteristics on the one hand of growing, or thriving; and on the other of being immature or underdeveloped.

15. This includes the topics of the metaphorical sentence. Although I do not ordinarily take their lacking consciousness as a distinctive property of vegetables, in the context of the sentence 'John's grandfather is a vegetable' the property *does* become a prominent, noticeable characteristic. (The example is Andrew Ortony's.)

16. I should also add, for those who have qualms about resting an account of metaphor on the context-sensitive concept of salience, that statements of comparison and counterfactual statements are in the same boat as metaphor in this respect. See David Lewis' *Counterfactuals* (Cambridge, Mass.: Harvard University Press, 1973), pp. 91–95 and 114–17; and also his "Counterfactual Dependence and Time's Arrow," *Nous*, 13 (1979), 466–67.

There is, of course, a long tradition of semantically analyzing metaphors *as* comparisons; and there has also been an attempt to analyze metaphors as elliptical counterfactuals. For the latter, see Teun A. van Dijk, "Formal Semantics of Metaphorical Discourse," *Poetics*, 4 (1975), 173–98. I prefer the account based on salience since the comparison and counterfactual accounts are going to have to rely on salience anyway if they are to give fairly specific content to metaphorical assertions. Once the necessity of recourse to salience is granted, there seems to be little point in taking the intermediate step of converting a metaphor into either a statement of comparison or a counterfactual.

17. "Logic and Conversation," in *The Logic of Grammar*, Donald Davidson and Gilbert Harman (Encino, Calif.: Dickenson, 1975) [Reprinted in this volume, Chapter 19]

18. See Stephen Schiffer, *Meaning* (Oxford: Clarendon Press, 1972) and Stalnaker, "Assertion," on mutual knowledge.

19. Considerations of perspicuity enter in another way: we should use metaphorical expressions *consistently.* If I say 'Bob is a bird and Julie is a bird,' intending to assert that Bob is a light eater and Julie sings beautifully, you will probably *not* get what I intended to convey.

If you do succeed in switching salience of characteristics midsentence along with me, it may be because we mutually know that Julie is no light eater and that she has been studying opera. Cf. the "rule of accommodation for comparative salience" in David Lewis, "Scorekeeping in a Language Game," *Journal of Philosophical Logic,* 8 (1979), 339–59. [Reprinted in this volume, Chapter 25]

20. And some *dead* metaphors may not, when live, have been pure ones. On this point see Nelson Goodman, *Languages of Art* (New York: Bobbs-Merrill, 1968), pp. 76–77.

21. "The Role of Inductive Reasoning in the Interpretation of Metaphor," in *Semantics of Natural Language, ed.* Donald Davidson and Gilbert Harman (Dordrecht: D. Reidel, 1972) p. 735.

22. Ted Cohen has argued in "Figurative Speech and Figurative Acts," *Journal of Philosophy,* 72 (1975), pp. 669–84 that because what a metaphor "means" is not a function of its literal meaning, metaphorical meaning is therefore not rule-governed and is hence unpredictable. I have been arguing that interpretation of metaphor *is* rule-governed; but the output depends on salience determined by the context as well as on literal meanings. It is this reliance on *context,* rather than the lack of a rule, that makes for unpredictability: as what is salient changes, so do the interpretations we read into metaphors.

23. The first form has been attributed to Aristotle (the *Poetics*); an example of the second is found in Charles L. Stevenson, *Ethics and Language* (New Haven: Yale University Press, 1944); and an example of the third is found in Black's "Metaphor."

24. Cf. Goodman, *Languages of Art,* pp. 74 ff.

25. *Against Interpretation* (New York: Dell, 1966), pp. 17–18.

26. There is extensive discussion of what I have called the *organizing power* of metaphor in George Lakoff and Mark Johnson, *Metaphors We Live By* (Chicago: University of Chicago Press, 1980).

Some authors have characterized or *defined* metaphor as a linguistic act of a special sort: as an invitation to "see-as" or to view the world in a new way. Loewenberg, for example, says: ". . . I believe that 'making a proposal' distinguishes metaphorical utterances more effectively than merely 'saying something' does" ("Identifying Metaphors," p. 335). The distinction is not at all effective, for two reasons. First, metaphors can be used simply to "say something"—these are the assertive metaphors; and, second, language can be used *literally* to make proposals. Any attempt to define metaphor in terms of purpose or illocutionary force is bound to fail. The points of using metaphor, like the points of using language literally, are varied; and there is no "point" that is the exclusive domain of either.

29

What Metaphors Mean

DONALD DAVIDSON

Metaphor is the dreamwork of language and, like all dreamwork, its interpretation reflects as much on the interpreter as on the originator. The interpretation of dreams requires collaboration between a dreamer and a waker, even if they be the same person; and the act of interpretation is itself a work of the imagination. So too understanding a metaphor is as much a creative endeavor as making a metaphor, and as little guided by rules.

These remarks do not, except in matters of degree, distinguish metaphor from more routine linguistic transactions: all communication by speech assumes the interplay of inventive construction and inventive construal. What metaphor adds to the ordinary is an achievement that uses no semantic resources beyond the resources on which the ordinary depends. There are no instructions for devising metaphors; there is no manual for determining what a metaphor "means" or "says"; there is no test for metaphor that does not call for taste.[1] A metaphor implies a kind and degree of artistic success; there are no unsuccessful metaphors, just as there are no unfunny jokes. There are tasteless metaphors, but these are turns that nevertheless have brought something off, even if it were not worth bringing off or could have have been brought off better.

This paper is concerned with what metaphors mean, and its thesis is that metaphors mean what the words, in their most literal interpretation, mean, and nothing more. Since this thesis flies in the face of contemporary views with which I am familiar, much of what I have to say is critical. But I think the picture of metaphor that emerges when error and confusion are cleared away makes metaphor a more, not a less, interesting phenomenon.

The central mistake against which I shall be inveighing is the idea that a metaphor has, in addition to its literal sense or meaning, another sense or meaning. This idea is common to many who have written about metaphor: it is found in the works of literary critics like Richards, Empson, and Winters; philosophers from Aristotle to Max Black; psychologists from Freud and earlier, to Skinner and later; and linguists from Plato to Uriel Weinreich and George Lakoff. The idea takes many forms, from the relatively simple in Aristotle to the relatively complex in Black. The idea appears in writings which maintain that a literal paraphrase of a metaphor can be produced, but it is also shared by those who hold that typically no literal paraphrase of a metaphor can be found. Some stress the special insight metaphor can inspire and make much of the fact that ordinary language, in its usual functioning, yields no such insight. Yet this view too sees metaphor as a form of communication alongside ordinary communication; it conveys truths of falsehoods about the world much as plainer language does, though the message may be considered more exotic, profound, or cunningly garbed.

The concept of metaphor as primarily a vehicle for conveying ideas, even if unusual ones, seems to me as wrong as the parent idea that a metaphor has a special meaning. I agree with the view that metaphors cannot be paraphrased, but I think this is not because metaphors say something too novel for literal expression but because there is nothing there to paraphrase. Paraphrase, whether possible or not, is appropriate to what is *said:* we try, in paraphrase, to say it another way. But if I am right, a metaphor doesn't say anything beyond its literal meaning (nor does its maker say anything, in using the metaphor, beyond the literal). This is not, of course, to deny that a metaphor has a point, nor that that point can be brought out by using further words.

In the past those who have denied that metaphor has a cognitive content in addition to the literal have often been out to show that metaphor is confusing, merely emotive, unsuited to serious, scientific, or philosophic discourse. My views should not be associated with this tradition. Metaphor is a legitimate device not only in literature but in science, philosophy, and the law: it is effective in praise and abuse, prayer and promotion, description and prescription. For the most part I don't disagree with Max Black, Paul Henle, Nelson Goodman, Monroe Beardsley, and the rest in their accounts of what metaphor accomplishes, except that I think it accomplishes more and that what is additional is different in kind.

My disagreement is with the explanation of how metaphor works its wonders. To anticipate: I depend on the distinction between what words mean and what they are used to do. I think metaphor belongs exclusively to

the domain of use. It is something brought off by the imaginative employment of words and sentences and depends entirely on the ordinary meanings of those words and hence on the ordinary meanings of the sentences they comprise.

It is no help in explaining how words work in metaphor to posit metaphorical or figurative meanings, or special kinds of poetic or metaphorical truth. These ideas don't explain metaphor, metaphor explains them. Once we understand a metaphor we can call what we grasp the "metaphorical truth" and (up to a point) say what the "metaphorical meaning" is. But simply to lodge this meaning in the metaphor is like explaining why a pill puts you to sleep by saying it has a dormative power. Literal meaning and literal truth-conditions can be assigned to words and sentences apart from particular contexts of use. This is why adverting to them has genuine explanatory power.

I shall try to establish my negative views about what metaphors mean and introduce my limited positive claims by examining some false theories of the nature of metaphor.

A metaphor makes us attend to some likeness, often a novel or surprising likeness, between two or more things. This trite and true observation leads, or seems to lead, to a conclusion concerning the meaning of metaphors. Consider ordinary likeness or similarity: two roses are similar because they share the property of being a rose; two infants are similar by virture of their infanthood. Or, more simply, roses are similar because each is a rose, infants, because each is an infant.

Suppose someone says "Tolstoy was once an infant." How is the infant Tolstoy like other infants? The answer comes pat: by virtue of exhibiting the property of infanthood, that is, leaving out some of the wind, by virtue of being an infant. If we tire of the phrase "by virtue of," we can, it seems, be plainer still by saying the infant Tolstoy shares with other infants the fact that the predicate "is an infant" applies to him; given the word "infant," we have no trouble saying exactly how the infant Tolstoy resembles other infants. We could do it without the word "infant"; all we need is other words that mean the same. The end result is the same. Ordinary similarity depends on groupings established by the ordinary meanings of words. Such similarity is natural and unsurprising to the extent that familiar ways of grouping objects are tied to usual meanings of usual words.

A famous critic said that Tolstoy was "a great moralizing infant." The Tolstoy referred to here is obviously not the infant Tolstoy but Tolstoy the adult writer; this is metaphor. Now in what sense is Tolstoy the writer similar to an infant? What we are to do, perhaps, is think of the class of objects which includes all ordinary infants and, in addition, the adult Tolstoy and then ask ourselves what special, surprising property the members of this class have in common. The appealing thought is that given patience we could come as close as need be to specifying the appropriate property. In any case, we could do the job perfectly if we found words that meant exactly what the metaphorical "infant" means. The important point, from my perspective, is not whether we can find the perfect other words but the assumption that there is something to be attempted, a metaphorical meaning to be matched. So far I have been doing no more than crudely sketching how the concept of meaning may have crept into the analysis of metaphor, and the answer I have suggested is that since what we think of as garden variety similarity goes with what we think of as garden variety meanings, it is natural to posit unusual or metaphorical meanings to help explain the similarities metaphor promotes.

The idea, then, is that in metaphor certain words take on new, or what are often called "extended," meanings. When we read, for example, that "the Spirit of God moved upon the face of the waters," we are to regard the word "face" as having an extended meaning (I disregard further metaphor in the passage). The extension applies, as it happens, to what philosophers call the extension of the word, that is, the class of entities to which it refers. Here the word "face" applies to ordinary faces, and to waters in addition.

This account cannot, at any rate, be complete, for if in these contexts the words "face" and "infant" apply correctly to waters and to the adult Tolstoy, then waters really do have faces and Tolstoy literally was an infant, and all sense of metaphor evaporates. If we are to think of words in metaphors as directly going about their business of applying to what they

properly do apply to, there is no difference between metaphor and the introduction of a new term into our vocabulary: to make a metaphor is to murder it.

What has been left out is any appeal to the original meaning of the word. Whether or not metaphor depends on new or extended meanings, it certainly depends in some way on the original meanings; an adequate account of metaphor must allow that the primary or original meanings of words remain active in their metaphorical setting.

Perhaps, then, we can explain metaphor as a kind of ambiguity: in the context of a metaphor, certain words have either a new or an original meaning, and the force of the metaphor depends on our uncertainty as we waver between the two meanings. Thus when Melville writes that "Christ was a chronometer," the effect of metaphor is produced by our taking "chronometer" first in its ordinary sense and then in some extraordinary or metaphorical sense.

It is hard to see how this theory can be correct. For the ambiguity in the word, if there is any, is due to the fact that in ordinary contexts it means one thing and in the metaphorical context it means something else: but in the metaphorical context we do not necessarily hesitate over its meaning. When we do hesitate, it is usually to decide which of a number of metaphorical interpretations we shall accept; we are seldom in doubt that what we have is a metaphor. At any rate, the effectiveness of the metaphor easily outlasts the end of uncertainty over the interpretation of the metaphorical passage. Metaphor cannot, therefore, owe its effect to ambiguity of this sort.[2]

Another brand of ambiguity may appear to offer a better suggestion. Sometimes a word will, in a single context, bear two meanings where we are meant to remember and to use both. Or, if we think of wordhood as implying sameness of meaning, then we may describe the situation as one in which what appears as a single word is in fact two. When Shakespeare's Cressida is welcomed bawdily into the Grecian camp, Nestor says, "Our general doth salute you with a kiss." Here we are to take "general" two ways: once as applying to Agamemnon, who is the general; and once, since she is kissing everyone, as applying to no one in particular, but everyone in general. We really have a conjunction of two sentences: our general, Agamemnon, salutes you with a kiss; and everyone in general is saluting you with a kiss.

This is a legitimate device, a pun, but it is not the same device as metaphor. For in metaphor there is no essential need of reiteration; whatever meanings we assign the words, they keep through every correct reading of the passage.

A plausible modification of the last suggestion would be to consider the key word (or words) in a metaphor as having two different kinds of meaning at once, a literal and a figurative meaning. Imagine the literal meaning as latent, something that we are aware of, that can work on us without working in the context, while the figurative meaning carries the direct load. And finally, there must be a rule which connects the two meanings, for otherwise the explanation lapses into a form of the ambiguity theory. The rule, at least for many typical cases of metaphor, says that in its metaphorical role the word applies to everything that it applies to in its literal role, and then some.[3]

This theory may seem complex, but it is strikingly similar to what Frege proposed to account for the behavior of referring terms in modal sentences and sentences about propositional attitudes like belief and desire. According to Frege, each referring term has two (or more) meanings, one which fixes its reference in ordinary contexts and another which fixes its reference in the special contexts created by modal operators or psychological verbs. The rule connecting the two meanings may be put like this: the meaning of the word in the special contexts makes the reference in those contexts to be identical with the meaning in ordinary contexts.

Here is the whole picture, putting Frege together with a Fregean view of metaphor: we are to think of a word as having, in addition to its mundane field of application or reference, two special or supermundane fields of application, one for metaphor and the other for modal contexts and the like. In both cases the original meaning remains to do its work by virtue of a rule which relates the various meanings.

Having stressed the possible analogy between metaphorical meaning and the Fregean

meanings for oblique contexts, I turn to an imposing difficulty in maintaining the analogy. You are entertaining a visitor from Saturn by trying to teach him how to use the word "floor." You go through the familiar dodges, leading him from floor to floor, pointing and stamping and repeating the word. You prompt him to make experiments, tapping objects tentatively with his tentacle while rewarding his right and wrong tries. You want him to come out knowing not only that these particular objects or surfaces are floors but also how to tell a floor when one is in sight or touch. The skit you are putting on doesn't *tell* him what he needs to know, but with luck it helps him to learn it.

Should we call this process learning something about the world or learning something about language? An odd question, since what is learned is that a bit of language refers to a bit of the world. Still, it is easy to distinguish between the business of learning the meaning of a word and using the word once the meaning is learned. Comparing these two activities, it is natural to say that the first concerns learning something about language, while the second is typically learning something about the world. If your Saturnian has learned how to use the word "floor," you may try telling him something new, that *here* is a floor. If he has mastered the word trick, you have told him something about the world.

Your friend from Saturn now transports you through space to his home sphere, and looking back remotely at earth you say to him, nodding at the earth, "floor." Perhaps he will think this is still part of the lesson and assume that the word "floor" applies properly to the earth, at least as seen from Saturn. But what if you thought he already knew the meaning of "floor," and you were remembering how Dante, from a similar place in the heavens, saw the inhabited earth as "the small round floor that makes us passionate"? Your purpose was metaphor, not drill in the use of language. What difference would it make to your friend which way he took it? With the theory of metaphor under consideration, very little difference, for according to that theory a word has a new meaning in a metaphorical context; the occasion of the metaphor would, therefore, be the occasion for learning the new meaning. We should agree that in some ways it makes relatively little difference whether, in a given context, we think a word is being used metaphorically or in a previously unknown, but literal way. Empson, in *Some Versions of Pastoral,* quotes these lines from Donne: "As our blood labours to beget / Spirits, as like souls as it can, . . . / So must pure lover's soules descend. . . ." The modern reader is almost certain, Empson points out, to take the word "spirits" in this passage metaphorically, as applying only by extension to something spiritual. But for Donne there was no metaphor. He writes in his *Sermons,* "The spirits . . . are the thin and active part of the blood, and are a kind of middle nature, between soul and body." Learning this does not matter much; Empson is right when he says, "It is curious how the change in the word [that is, in what we think it means] leaves the poetry unaffected."[4]

The change may be, in some cases at least, hard to appreciate, but unless there is a change, most of what is thought to be interesting about metaphor is lost. I have been making the point by contrasting learning a new use for an old word with using a word already understood; in one case, I said, our attention is directed to language, in the other, to what language is about. Metaphor, I suggested, belongs in the second category. This can also be seen by considering dead metaphors. Once upon a time, I suppose, rivers and bottles did not, as they do now, literally have mouths. Thinking of present usage, it doesn't matter whether we take the word "mouth" to be ambiguous because it applies to entrances to rivers and openings of bottles as well as to animal apertures, or we think there is a single wide field of application that embraces both. What does matter is that when "mouth" applied only metaphorically to bottles, the application made the hearer *notice* a likeness between animal and bottle openings. (Consider Homer's reference to wounds as mouths.) Once one has the present use of the word, with literal application to bottles, there is nothing left to notice. There is no similarity to seek because it consists simply in being referred to by the same word.

Novelty is not the issue. In its context a word once taken for a metaphor remains a metaphor on the hundredth hearing, while a word may easily be appreciated in a new lit-eral role on a first encounter. What we call the element of novelty or surprise in a metaphor is a built-in aesthetic feature we can experience again and again, like the surprise in Haydn's Symphony no. 94, or a familiar deceptive cadence.

If metaphor involved a second meaning, as ambiguity does, we might expect to be able to specify the special meaning of a word in a metaphorical setting by waiting until the metaphor dies. The figurative meaning of the living metaphor should be immortalized in the literal meaning of the dead. But although some philosophers have suggested this idea, it seems plainly wrong. "He was burned up" is genuinely ambiguous (since it may be true in one sense and false in another), but although the slangish idiom is no doubt the corpse of a metaphor, "He was burned up" now suggests no more than that he was very angry. When the metaphor was active, we would have pictured fire in the eyes or smoke coming out of the ears.

We can learn much about what metaphors mean by comparing them with similes, for a simile tells us, in part, what a metaphor merely nudges us into noting. Suppose Goneril had said, thinking of Lear. "Old fools are like babes again"; then she would have used the words to assert a similarity between old fools and babes. What she did say, of course, was "Old fools are babes again," thus using the words to intimate what the simile declared. Thinking along these lines may inspire another theory of the figurative or special meaning of metaphors; the figurative meaning of a metaphor is the literal meaning of the corresponding simile. Thus "Christ was a chronometer" in its figurative sense is synonymous with "Christ was like a chronometer," and the metaphorical meaning once locked up in "He was burned up" is released in "He was like someone who was burned up" (or perhaps "He was like burned up").

There is, to be sure, the difficulty of identifying the simile that corresponds to a given metaphor. Virginia Woolf said that a highbrow is "a man or woman of thoroughbred intelligence who rides his mind at a gallop across country in pursuit of an idea." What simile corresponds? Something like this, perhaps: "A highbrow is a man or woman whose intelligence is like a thoroughbred horse and who persists in thinking about an idea like a rider galloping across country in pursuit of . . . well, something."

The view that the special meaning of a metaphor is identical with the literal meaning of a corresponding simile (however "corresponding" is spelled out) should not be confused with the common theory that a metaphor is an elliptical simile.[5] This theory makes no distinction in meaning between a metaphor and some related simile and does not provide any ground for speaking of figurative, metaphorical, or special meanings. It is a theory that wins hands down so far as simplicity is concerned, but it also seems too simple to work. For if we make the literal meaning of the metaphor to be the literal meaning of a matching simile, we deny access to what we originally took to be the literal meaning of the metaphor, and we agreed almost from the start that *this* meaning was essential to the working of the metaphor, whatever else might have to be brought in the way of a nonliteral meaning.

Both the elliptical simile theory of metaphor and its more sophisticated variant, which equates the figurative meaning of the metaphor with the literal meaning of a simile, share a fatal defect. They make the hidden meaning of the metaphor all too obvious and accessible. In each case the hidden meaning is to be found simply by looking to the literal meaning of what is usually a painfully trivial simile. This is like that—Tolstoy like an infant, the earth like a floor. It is trivial because everything is like everything, and in endless ways. Metaphors are often very difficult to interpret and, so it is said, impossible to paraphrase. But with this theory, interpretation and paraphrase typically are ready to the hand of the most callow.

These simile theories have been found acceptable, I think, only because they have been confused with a quite different theory. Consider this remark by Max Black:

When Schopenhauer called a geometrical proof a mousetrap, he was, according to such a view, *saying* (though not explicitly): "A geometrical proof is *like* a mousetrap, since both offer a delusive reward, entice their victims by degrees, lead to disagreeable surprise, etc." This is a view of metaphor as a condensed or elliptical *simile.*[6]

Here I discern two confusions. First, if metaphors are elliptical similes, they say *explicitly*

what similes say, for ellipsis is a form of abbreviation, not of paraphrase or indirection. But, and this is the more important matter, Black's statement of what the metaphor says goes far beyond anything given by the corresponding simile. The simile simply says a geometrical proof is like a mousetrap. It no more *tells* us what similarities we are to notice than the metaphor does. Black mentions three similarities, and of course we could go on adding to the list forever. But is this list, when revised and supplemented in the right way, supposed to give the *literal* meaning of the simile? Surely not, since the simile declared no more than the similarity. If the list is supposed to provide the figurative meaning of the simile, then we learn nothing about metaphor from the comparison with simile—only that both have the same figurative meaning. Nelson Goodman does indeed claim that "the difference between simile and metaphor is negligible," and he continues, "Whether the locution be 'is like' or 'is,' the figure *likens* picture to person by picking out a certain common feature. . . ."[7] Goodman is considering the difference between saying a picture is sad and saying it is like a sad person. It is clearly true that both sayings liken picture to person, but it seems to me a mistake to claim that either way of talking "picks out" a common feature. The simile says there is a likeness and leaves it to us to pick out some common feature or features; the metaphor does not explicitly assert a likeness, but if we accept it as a metaphor, we are again led to seek common features (not necessarily the same features the associated simile suggests; but that is another matter).

Just because a simile wears a declaration of similitude on its sleeve, it is, I think, far less plausible than in the case of metaphor to maintain that there is a hidden second meaning. In the case of simile, we note what it literally says, that two things resemble one another; we then regard the objects and consider what similarity would, in the context, be to the point. Having decided, we might then say the author of the simile intended us—that is, meant us—to notice that similarity. But having appreciated the difference between what the words meant and what the author accomplished by using those words, we should feel little temptation to explain what has happened by endowing the words themselves with a second, or figurative, meaning. The point of the concept of linguistic meaning is to explain what can be done with words. But the supposed figurative meaning of a simile explains nothing; it is not a feature of the word that the word has prior to and independent of the context of use, and it rests upon no linguistic customs except those that govern ordinary meaning.

What words do do with their literal meaning in simile must be possible for them to do in metaphor. A metaphor directs attention to the same sorts of similarity, if not the same similarities, as the corresponding simile. But then the unexpected or subtle parallels and analogies it is the business of metaphor to promote need not depend, for their promotion, on more than the literal meanings of words.

Metaphor and simile are merely two among endless devices that serve to alert us to aspects of the world by inviting us to make comparison. I quote a few stanzas of T. S. Eliot's "The Hippopotamus":

The broad-backed hippopotamus
Rests on his belly in the mud;
Although he seems so firm to us
He is merely flesh and blood.

Flesh and blood is weak and frail,
Susceptible to nervous shock;
While the True Church can never fail
For it is based upon a rock.

The hippo's feeble steps may err
In compassing material ends,
While the True Church need never stir
To gather in its dividends.

The 'potamus can never reach
The mango on the mango-tree;
But fruits of pomegranate and peach
Refresh the Church from over sea.

Here we are neither told that the Church resembles a hippopotamus (as in simile) nor bullied into making this comparison (as in metaphor), but there can be no doubt the words are being used to direct our attention to similarities between the two. Nor should there be much inclination, in this case, to posit figurative meanings, for in what words or sentences would we lodge them? The hippopotamus really does rest on his belly in the mud; the True Church, the poem says literally, never can fail. The poem does, of course, intimate much that goes beyond the literal

meanings of the words. But intimation is not meaning.

The argument so far has led to the conclusion that as much of metaphor as can be explained in terms of meaning may, and indeed must, be explained by appeal to the literal meanings of words. A consequence is that the sentences in which metaphors occur are true or false in a normal, literal way, for if the words in them don't have special meanings, sentences don't have special truth. This is not to deny that there is such a thing as metaphorical truth, only to deny it of sentences. Metaphor does lead us to notice what might not otherwise be noticed, and there is no reason, I suppose, not to say these visions, thoughts, and feelings inspired by the metaphor, are true or false.

If a sentence used metaphorically is true or false in the ordinary sense, then it is clear that it is usually false. The most obvious semantic difference between simile and metaphor is that all similes are true and most metaphors are false. The earth is like a floor, the Assyrian did come down like a wolf on the fold, because everything is like everything. But turn these sentences into metaphors, and you turn them false; the earth is like a floor, but it is not a floor; Tolstoy, grown up, was like an infant, but he wasn't one. We use a simile ordinarily only when we know the corresponding metaphor to be false. We say Mr. S. is like a pig because we know he isn't one. If we had used a metaphor and said he was a pig, this would not be because we changed our mind about the facts but because we chose to get the idea across a different way.

What matters is not actual falsehood but that the sentence be taken to be false. Notice what happens when a sentence we use as a metaphor, believing it false, comes to be thought true because of a change in what is believed about the world. When it was reported that Hemingway's plane had been sighted, wrecked, in Africa, the New York *Mirror* ran a headline saying, "Hemingway Lost in Africa," the word "lost" being used to suggest he was dead. When it turned out he was alive, the *Mirror* left the headline to be taken literally. Or consider this case: a woman sees herself in a beautiful dress and says, "What a dream of a dress!"—and then wakes up. The point of the metaphor is that the dress is like a dress one would dream of and therefore isn't a dream-dress. Henle provides a good example from *Anthony and Cleopatra* (2.2):

The barge she sat in, like a burnish'd throne
Burn'd on the water

Here simile and metaphor interact strangely, but the metaphor would vanish if a literal conflagration were imagined. In much the same way the usual effect of a simile can be sabotaged by taking the comparison too earnestly. Woody Allen writes, "The trial, which took place over the following weeks, was like a circus, although there was some difficulty getting the elephants into the courtroom."[8]

Generally it is only when a sentence is taken to be false that we accept it as a metaphor and start to hunt out the hidden implication. It is probably for this reason that most metaphorical sentences are *patently* false, just as all similes are trivially true. Absurdity or contradiction in a metaphorical sentence guarantees we won't believe it and invites us, under proper circumstances, to take the sentence metaphorically.

Patent falsity is the usual case with metaphor, but on occasion patent truth will do as well. "Business is business" is too obvious in its literal meaning to be taken as having been uttered to convey information, so we look for another use; Ted Cohen reminds us, in the same connection, that no man is an island.[9] The point is the same. The ordinary meaning in the context of use is odd enough to prompt us to disregard the question of literal truth.

Now let me raise a somewhat Platonic issue by comparing the making of a metaphor with telling a lie. The comparison is apt because lying, like making a metaphor, concerns not the meaning of words but their use. It is sometimes said that telling a lie entails saying what is false; but this is wrong. Telling a lie requires not that what you say be false but that you think it false. Since we usually believe true sentences and disbelieve false, most lies are falsehoods; but in any particular case this is an accident. The parallel between making a metaphor and telling a lie is emphasized by the fact that the same sentence can be used, with meaning unchanged, for either purpose. So a woman who believed in witches but did not think her neighbor a witch might say, "She's a witch," meaning it metaphorically; the same woman, still believing the same of witches and her neighbor but intending to deceive, might use the same words to very different effect. Since sentence and meaning are the same in both cases, it is sometimes hard to prove which intention lay behind the saying of it; thus a man who says "Lattimore's a Communist" and means to lie can always try to beg off by pleading a metaphor.

What makes the difference between a lie and a metaphor is not a difference in the words used or what they mean (in any strict sense of meaning) but in how the words are used. Using a sentence to tell a lie and using it to make a metaphor are, of course, totally different uses, so different that they do not interfere with one another, as say, acting and lying do. In lying, one must make an assertion so as to represent oneself as believing what one does not; in acting, assertion is excluded. Metaphor is careless to the difference. It can be an insult, and so be an assertion, to say to a man "You are a pig." But no metaphor was involved when (let us suppose) Odysseus addressed the same words to his companions in Circe's palace; a story, to be sure, and so no assertion—but the word, for once, was used literally of men.

No theory of metaphorical meaning or metaphorical truth can help explain how metaphor works. Metaphor runs on the same familiar linguistic tracks that the plainest sentences do; this we saw from considering simile. What distinguishes metaphor is not meaning but use—in this it is like assertion, hinting, lying, promising, or criticizing. And the special use to which we put language in metaphor is not—cannot be—to "say something" special, no matter how indirectly. For a metaphor *says* only what shows on its face—usually a patent falsehood or an absurd truth. And this plain truth or falsehood needs no paraphrase—it is given in the literal meaning of the words.

What are we to make, then, of the endless energy that has been, and is being, spent on methods and devices for drawing out the content of a metaphor? The psychologists Robert Verbrugge and Nancy McCarrell tell us that:

Many metaphors draw attention to common systems of relationships or common transformations, in which the identify of the participants is secondary. For example, consider the sentences: *A car is like an animal, Tree trunks are straws for thirsty leaves and branches.* The first sentence directs attention to systems of relationships among energy consumption, respiration, self-induced motion, sensory systems, and, possibly, a homunculus. In the second sentence, the resemblance is a more constrained type of transformation: suction of fluid through a vertically oriented cylindrical space from a source of fluid to a destination.[10]

Verbrugge and McCarrell don't believe there is any sharp line between the literal and metaphorical uses of words; they think many words have a "fuzzy" meaning that gets fixed, if fixed at all, by a context. But surely this fuzziness, however it is illustrated and explained, cannot erase the line between what a sentence literally means (given its context) and what it "draws our attention to" (given its literal meaning as fixed by the context). The passage I have quoted is not employing such a distinction: what it says the sample sentences direct our attention to are facts expressed by paraphrases of the sentences. Verbrugge and McCarrell simply want to insist that a correct paraphrase may emphasize "systems of relationships" rather than resemblances between objects.

According to Black's interaction theory, a metaphor makes us apply a "system of commonplaces" associated with the metaphorical word to the subject of the metaphor: in "Man is a wolf" we apply commonplace attributes (stereotypes) of the wolf to man. The metaphor, Black says, thus "selects, emphasizes, suppresses, and organizes features of the principal subject by implying statements about it that normally apply to the subsidiary subject."[11] If paraphrase fails, according to Black, it is not because the metaphor does not have a special cognitive content, but because the paraphrase "will not have the same power to inform and enlighten as the original. . . . One of the points I most wish to stress is that the loss in such cases is a loss in cognitive content; the relevant weakness of the literal paraphrase is not that it may be tiresomely prolix or boringly explicit; it fails to be a translation because it fails to give the insight that the metaphor did."[12]

How can this be right? If a metaphor has a special cognitive content, why should it be so difficult or impossible to set it out? If, as Owen Barfield claims, a metaphor "says one thing

and means another," why should it be that when we try to get explicit about what it means, the effect is so much weaker—"put it that way," Barfield says, "and nearly all the tarning, and with it half the poetry, is lost."[13] Why does Black think a literal paraphrase "inevitably says too much—and with the wrong emphasis"? Why inevitably? Can't we, if we are clever enough, come as close as we please?

For that matter, how is it that a simile gets along without a special intermediate meaning? In general, critics do not suggest that a simile says one thing and means another—they do not suppose it *means* anything but what lies on the surface of the words. It may make us think deep thoughts, just as a metaphor does; how come, then, no one appeals to the "special cognitive content" of the simile? And remember Eliot's hippopotamus; there there was neither simile nor metaphor, but what seemed to get done was just like what gets done by similes and metaphors. Does anyone suggest that the *words* in Eliot's poem have special meanings?

Finally, if words in metaphor bear a coded meaning, how can this meaning differ from the meaning those same words bear in the case where the metaphor *dies*—that is, when it comes to be part of the language? Why doesn't "he was burned up" as now used and meant mean *exactly* what the fresh metaphor once meant? Yet all that the dead metaphor means is that he was very angry—a notion not very difficult to make explicit.

There is, then, a tension in the usual view of metaphor. For on the one hand, the usual view wants to hold that a metaphor does something no plain prose can possibly do and, on the other hand, it wants to explain what a metaphor does by appealing to a cognitive content—just the sort of thing plain prose is designed to express. As long as we are in this frame of mind, we must harbor the suspicion that it *can* be done, at least up to a point.

There is a simple way out of the impasse. We must give up the idea that a metaphor carries a message, that it has a content or meaning (except, of course, its literal meaning). The various theories we have been considering mistake their goal. Where they think they provide a method for deciphering an encoded content, they actually tell us (or try to tell us) something about the *effects* metaphors have on us. The common error is to fasten on the contents of the thoughts a metaphor provokes and to read these contents into the metaphor itself. No doubt metaphors often make us notice aspects of things we did not notice before; no doubt they bring surprising analogies and similarities to our attention; they do provide a kind of lens or lattice, as Black says, through which we view the relevant phenomena. The issue does not lie here but in the question of how the metaphor is related to what it makes us see.

It may be remarked with justice that the claim that a metaphor provokes or invites a certain view of its subject rather than saying it straight out is a commonplace; so it is. Thus Aristotle says metaphor leads to a "perception of resemblances." Black, following Richards, says a metaphor "evokes" a certain response: "a suitable hearer will be led by a metaphor to construct a . . . system."[14] This view is neatly summed up by what Heraclitus said of the Delphic oracle: "It does not say and it does not hide, it intimates."[15]

I have no quarrel with these descriptions of the effects of metaphor, only with the associated views as to *how* metaphor is supposed to produce them. What I deny is that metaphor does its work by having a special meaning, a specific cognitive content. I do not think, as Richards does, that metaphor produces its result by having a meaning which results from the interaction of two ideas; it is wrong, in my view, to say, with Owen Barfield, that a metaphor "says one thing and means another"; or with Black that a metaphor asserts or implies certain complex things by dint of a special meaning and *thus* accomplishes its job of yielding an "insight." A metaphor does its work through other intermediaries—to suppose it can be effective only by conveying a coded message is like thinking a joke or a dream makes some statement which a clever interpreter can restate in plain prose. Joke or dream or metaphor can, like a picture or a bump on the head, make us appreciate some fact—but not by standing for, or expressing, the fact.

If this is right, what we attempt in "paraphrasing" a metaphor cannot be to give its meaning, for that lies on the surface; rather we attempt to evoke what the metaphor brings to

our attention. I can imagine someone granting this and shrugging it off as no more than an insistence on restraint in using the word "meaning." This would be wrong. The central error about metaphor is most easily attacked when it takes the form of a theory of metaphorical meaning, but behind that theory, and statable independently, is the thesis that associated with a metaphor is a cognitive content that its author wishes to convey and that the interpreter must grasp if he is to get the message. This theory is false, whether or not we call the purported cognitive content a meaning.

It should make us suspect the theory that it is so hard to decide, even in the case of the simplest metaphors, exactly what the content is supposed to be. The reason it is often so hard to decide is, I think, that we imagine there is a content to be captured when all the while we are in fact focusing on what the metaphor makes us notice. If what the metaphor makes us notice were finite in scope and propositional in nature, this would not in itself make trouble; we would simply project the content the metaphor brought to mind onto the metaphor. But in fact there is no limit to what a metaphor calls to our attention, and much of what we are caused to notice is not propositional in character. When we try to say what a metaphor "means," we soon realize there is no end to what we want to mention.[16] If someone draws his finger along a coastline on a map, or mentions the beauty and deftness of a line in a Picasso etching, how many things are drawn to your attention? You might list a great many, but you could not finish since the idea of finishing would have no clear application. How many facts or propositions are conveyed by a photograph? None, an infinity, or one great unstatable fact? Bad question. A picture is not worth a thousand words, or any other number. Words are the wrong currency to exchange for a picture.

It's not only that we can't provide an exhaustive catalogue of what has been attended to when we are led to see something in a new light; the difficulty is more fundamental. What we notice or see is not, in general, propositional in character. Of course it *may* be, and when it is, it usually may be stated in fairly plain words. But if I show you Wittgenstein's duck-rabbit, and I say, "It's a duck," then with luck you see it as a duck; if I say, "It's a rabbit," you see it as a rabbit. But no proposition expresses what I have led you to see. Perhaps you have come to realize that the drawing can be seen as a duck or as a rabbit. But one could come to know this without ever seeing the drawing as a duck or as a rabbit. Seeing as is not seeing that. Metaphor makes us see one thing as another by making some literal statement that inspires or prompts the insight. Since in most cases what the metaphor prompts or inspires is not entirely, or even at all, recognition of some truth or fact, the attempt to give literal expression to the content of the metaphor is simply misguided.

The theorist who tries to explain a metaphor by appealing to a hidden message, like the critic who attempts to state the message, is then fundamentally confused. No such explanation or statement can be forthcoming because no such message exists.

Not, of course, that interpretation and elucidation of a metaphor are not in order. Many of us need help if we are to see what the author of a metaphor wanted us to see and what a more sensitive or educated reader grasps. The legitimate function of so-called paraphrase is to make the lazy or ignorant reader have a vision like that of the skilled critic. The critic is, so to speak, in benign competition with the metaphor-maker. The critic tries to make his own art easier or more transparent in some respects than the original, but at the same time he tries to reproduce in others some of the effects the original had on him. In doing this the critic also, and perhaps by the best method at his command, calls attention to the beauty or aptness, the hidden power, of the metaphor itself.

NOTES

1. I think Max Black is wrong when he says, "The rules of our language determine that some expressions must count as metaphors." He allows, however, that what a metaphor "means" depends on much more: the speaker's intention, tone of voice, verbal setting, etc. "Metaphor," in his *Models and Metaphors* (Ithaca, N.Y.: 1962), p. 29.

2. Nelson Goodman says metaphor and ambiguity differ chiefly "in that the several uses of a merely ambiguous term are coeval and independent" while in metaphor "a term with an extension established by habit is applied elsewhere under the influence of that habit"; he suggests that as our sense of the history of the "two uses" in metaphor fades, the metaphorical word becomes merely ambiguous (*Languages of Art* [Indianapolis, Ind.: 1968]. p. 71). In fact in many cases of ambiguity, one use springs from the other (as Goodman says) and so cannot be coeval. But the basic error, which Goodman shares with others, is the idea that two "uses" are involved in metaphor in anything like the way they are in ambiguity.

3. The theory described is essentially that of Paul Henle. Metaphor, in *Language, Thought and Culture,* ed. Henle (Ann Arbor, Mich: 1958).

4. William Empson, *Some Versions of Pastoral* (London: 1935), p. 133.

5. J. Middleton Murray says a metaphor is a "compressed simile," *Countries of the Mind,* 2d ser. (Oxford: 1931), p. 3. Max Black attributes a similar view to Alexander Bain, *English Composition and Rhetoric,* enl. ed. (London: 1887).

6. Black, p. 35.

7. Goodman, pp. 77–78.

8. Woody Allen, *New Yorker,* 21 November 1977, p. 59.

9. Ted Cohen, "Figurative Speech and Figurative Acts," *Journal of Philosophy* 72 (1975): 671. Since the negation of a metaphor seems always to be a potential metaphor, there may be as many platitudes among the potential metaphors as there are [absurdities].

10. Robert R. Verbrugge and Nancy S. McCarrell, "Metaphoric Comprehension: Studies in Reminding and Resembling." *Cognitive Psychology* 9 (1977): 499.

11. Black, pp. 44–45.

12. Ibid., p. 46.

13. Owen Barfield, "Poetic Diction and Legal Fiction," in *The Importance of Language,* ed. Max Black (Englewood Cliffs, N.J.: 1962), p. 55.

14. Black, p. 41.

15. I use Hannah Arendt's attractive translation of "σημαινει": it clearly should not be rendered as "mean" in this context.

16. Stanley Cavell mentions the fact that most attempts at paraphrase end with "and so on" and refers to Empson's remark that metaphors are "pregnant" (*Must We Mean What We Say?* (New York: 1969). p. 79). But Cavell doesn't explain the endlessness of paraphrase as I do, as can be learned from the fact that he thinks it distinguishes metaphor from some ("but perhaps not all") literal discourse. I hold that the endless character of what we call the paraphrase of a metaphor springs from the fact that it attempts to spell out what the metaphor makes us notice, and to this there is no clear end. I would say the same for any use of language.

30

A Theory for Metaphor

A. P. MARTINICH

A lot of interesting work has been done recently on the concept of a metaphor, and any adequate theory of metaphor will have to take account of much of this work, accommodating what is true and explaining where this recent work goes wrong. (Typically, this work errs either by overgeneralizing or by mistaking an essential but subordinate feature of metaphor for the whole or the most central feature.) However, as interesting as much of this work is, it lacks something essential to an adequate theory of metaphor, namely, a place within a more general theory of language or language use. The reason metaphor needs to be placed within a more general theory is that metaphor itself is a logically derivative phenomenon and, derivative, in particular, from some aspect of language use. In this paper, I will place metaphor within such a theory. Specifically, I will explain metaphor in terms of H. P. Grice's theory of conversation. By extending Grice's theory to account for metaphor, I am holding in effect that metaphor is pragmatically and not semantically based. Although there is a sense in which the sentence used metaphorically has a metaphorical meaning, this meaning is itself a consequence of the mechanisms that give rise to the metaphor and are not what makes the metaphor possible. In Grice's terminology, the metaphorical meaning of an utterance is an instance of utterance occasion meaning and not (applied) timeless utterance meaning.

I. PRELIMINARY THEORETICAL DISTINCTIONS

Grice distinguishes a number of different elements within the total content of what a speaker signifies.[1] The first division he makes is into what the speaker says (or makes-as-if-to-say) and what he implies. Both of these elements come into play in the explanation of metaphor. Let's begin with the former notion. There are various senses of the word "say." A parrot can say, "Polly wants a cracker" and yet not mean anything by what he says. We are not interested in this sense of "say." An actor, rehearsing his lines for a play can say, "All the world's a stage," and mean those words to have their normal meaning without meaning that all the world's a stage. We are not interested in this sense of "say" either. The

A. P. Martinich, "A Theory for Metaphor," *Journal of Literary Semantics* 13 (1984): 35–56. Copyright © 1984 by Julius Groos Verlag. Reprinted by permission of the publisher.

sense of "say" in which we are interested involves more than simply uttering words and intending them to be perceived as having a meaning. In order to count as an instance of saying something, the words uttered must be used to refer to something or predicate something and have some force, directly or indirectly. A citizen, discussing a proposed governmental budget, might utter the sentence, "There will be a 100 billion dollar deficit this year," and thereby *say that* there will be a 100 billion dollar deficit. We can correctly report the citizen to be *saying that* such and such, while we cannot correctly report the parrot or the actor as saying anything in our sense, because neither the parrot nor the actor uses the utterance to communicate anything. Because of the legitimacy of using the "say that" locution in indirect speech to report what a speaker says, let's use the portmanteau expression "saying-that" to express this sense of "say." This sense of "say" is closely tied to the words actually uttered and their ordinary meanings; but more, it includes all the references and predications that result from that utterance, and whatever force, direct or indirect, it might have.

Connected with saying-that is the notion of making-as-if-to-say. This notion is more difficult to characterize than saying-that. But it is easily illustrated. A disgruntled worker in a financially depressed, politically repressive country utters the sentence, "This is a *fine* country" sarcastically. The worker does *not* say-that his is a fine country. He intends to communicate by implication that his is *not* a fine country by flouting the maxim of quality. What he does is to make-as-if-to-say that his is a fine country.

One of the most difficult and important issues for a theory of metaphor to get right concerns the question of whether a person who utters a sentence metaphorically says-that anything or only makes-as-if to say something. On the one hand, it is correct to hold that a speaker who utters a sentence metaphorically, for example, "My love is a red rose," is not asserting that his love is a red rose. For, if he were, then he would be saying something false, and, surely, a person who utters a metaphor typically is not speaking falsely, *pace* Plato. A person who speaks metaphorically aims at the truth. To hold that a person who speaks met-

aphorically is speaking falsely is a kind of philistinism. These considerations incline one to say that a person who speaks metaphorically does not say-that anything but only makes-as-if-to-say something. On the other hand, a metaphor can contain its literal reference or its literal predication (though not both). Suppose the parents of an ebullient young woman are disturbed by her reckless social life. Her Dutch uncle might say to them, "I will clip the wings of the butterfly" and refer to himself while also speaking metaphorically. Or he might say, "That butterfly will be home by 10:00 p.m." and predicate being home by 10:00 p.m. It is also important to recognize that some metaphorical utterances have their literal illocutionary forces. The Dutch uncle might say, "I promise that I will clip that butterfly's wings," and thereby make a promise. Since a metaphorical utterance can have its literal illocutionary force, and its literal reference or predication, one is inclined to think that a person who speaks metaphorically is saying what would normally be said by a sentence. I think the truth lies in between these two extreme positions. A person who speaks metaphorically does succeed in performing some of the subacts that together constitute a complete act of saying-that, namely, reference, predication and illocutionary force. However, a person who speaks metaphorically does not say-that what he would normally be taken to have said-that if he were speaking literally; further, he does not represent himself as saying-that such and such, but only makes-as-if to say it by flouting a maxim of quality.

It is very important to distinguish what a speaker says (or makes-as-if-to-say) from what he communicates in some other way. Merrie Bergmann has conflated these elements and has consequently come up with a defective theory of metaphor. She holds that metaphors are typically used successfully to make true assertions.[2] The falsity of her view is evidenced by typical metaphors: Mary is a butterfly; The Middle East is a time bomb. If someone were actually asserting these sentences, he would be asserting respectively that Mary is a butterfly and that the Middle East is a time bomb. Both assertions are patently false. What is not false is what a speaker might be implying by uttering the sentences in question metaphorically. Bergmann holds that what the speaker communicates by such utterances are assertions; but she is mistaken. For what a person asserts must be explicit and determined by the rules governing the use of the words uttered; but what a person, speaking metaphorically, means by the sentence in question is not explicit in the utterance, but implicit, and is not governed by the rules for the use of those words. What the speaker communicates, he communicates by some kind of implication. This notion of implication returns us to Grice's second main element of what a speaker signifies.

Grice distinguishes two different kinds of implication: conventional and nonconventional. These terms are a bit misleading and I prefer to call them "linguistic" and "nonlinguistic" implication, respectively. What a speaker says linguistically implies what it does in virtue of the meanings of the words used. Thus, saying that *even Bill likes Mary* linguistically implies *people other than Bill like Mary* in virtue of the meaning of the word "even," just as "John loves Mary and Mary is happy" entails "John loves Mary" in virtue of the meaning of "and." Linguistic implication is not crucial to the understanding of metaphor, and is mentioned only to distinguish it from nonlinguistic implication. There are several types of nonlinguistic implication, of which the most important is conversational implication, and it is this type that is crucial to the understanding of metaphor.

Saying that *p* conversationally implies that *q* just in case (a), a speaker has said (or made-as-if-to-say) that *p*; (b), the speaker is observing the conversational maxims or, at least, the cooperative principle; and (c), the satisfaction of conditions (a) and (b) jointly make it highly plausible that the speaker means that *q*. The crucial element in this notion of conversational implication is that of a conversational maxim. Grice has pointed out that conversation is regulated by certain global conventions, which he calls conversational maxims and which he divides into four categories: quantity, quality, relation and manner. The maxims of quantity are "Make your contribution as informative as is necessary," and "Do not make your contribution more informative than is necessary." The maxims of quality are, "Do not say what is false" and "Do not say that for which you lack sufficient evidence."

The maxim of relation is, "Be relevant." The maxims of manner are "Be clear," "Avoid ambiguity," "Be brief," and "Be orderly." I should also mention that an important feature of a conversational implication is that in order to understand what has been implicated the audience must draw an inference, and the audience must go through a characteristic and more or less complex pattern of reasoning in order to calculate what implication has been made. For example, suppose Professor Wisdom is supposed to write a letter of recommendation for his student Nullset. Wisdom writes "Nullset is a very well-groomed young man, who has beautiful handwriting." If Wisdom says nothing more than this, then he does not say, but conversationally implies that Nullset is not a very good candidate. For the addressee reasons: Wisdom has said that Nullset is well-groomed, etc.; he is observing the cooperative principle; and, by the maxim of quantity, he would be making a stronger claim about Nullset's philosophical ability if he were able to. Since he has not made a stronger claim, he must be unable to, and that implies that he thinks that Nullset is not a very good philosopher.

II. FLOUTING THE MAXIM OF QUALITY

Conversational maxims regulate our discourse and usually are observed by interlocutors; usually, not always. Grice distinguishes four different ways in which a maxim might be contravened and thereby go unfulfilled. First, a speaker might violate a maxim; that is, he might quietly and unostentatiously contravene a maxim. Liars contravene a maxim of quality of course; but it is important to recognize that not all violations are sinister. Any honest mistake violates a maxim of quality. Moreover, a good teacher often says what is false in order to help his students learn more easily, because the literal and unadulterated truth about something is often too difficult or even impossible for them to understand. Second, a speaker might opt out of a maxim. A person who is asked for the details of a private meeting might say, "I'm sorry; I cannot say. That information is privileged," thereby opting out of a maxim of quantity. A person who is asked to explain Einstein's theory of relativity briefly might reply, "There is no brief explanation," thereby opting out of a maxim of manner. Third, a speaker might flout a maxim. Our disgruntled laborer who said, "This is a fine country," provided an example of flouting a maxim of quality. Grice claims there is also a fourth way of not fulfilling a maxim: by being faced with a clash of maxims. However, a moment's reflection should reveal that this alleged fourth way is not a genuine way of not fulfilling a maxim but a reason for not doing so. A person might violate or opt out of or flout a maxim if he is faced with a clash of maxims; but the clash itself is not a way of contravening them. A person who is required to speak both truly and briefly about a complicated subject may be faced with a clash and may either violate one of the maxims, opt out of one or, what is least likely in this case, flout one. Of the three remaining ways of contravening a maxim, flouting is the one most relevant to the analysis of metaphor.

If we accept Grice's formulation of the maxims of quality, then a central thesis about metaphors can be stated simply and in nontechnical language:[3] Every metaphor either is (or is thought to be) literally false or is supposed to be false. This disjunction reflects a genuine division of two types of metaphor. I shall call metaphors that are literally false *standard* metaphors; and those that are supposed to be false *nonstandard* metaphors. By "supposed," I do not mean that the metaphor is intended to be false but that the metaphor is *treated as if* or *entertained as if* it were false in order to consider the consequences, as when, in a *reductio ad absurdum* argument, the proposition to be proved is *supposed* to be false in order to show that the consequences of such a supposition are absurd. Most of this article will be devoted to standard cases of metaphor because the nonstandard cases are derivative, rare and merely an unavoidable complication to the theory. Until further notice, then, by "metaphor" I will mean "standard metaphor."

Every metaphorical proposition is false. Every metaphor flouts the *first* maxim of quality. This is not to say or imply that the point of a metaphor (what the speaker intends to communicate) is false. On the contrary, the point of a metaphor is typically true. Further, the point of a metaphor is conversationally implied in virtue of the fact that the speaker *flouts* the first maxim of quality. This is not to say or imply that any metaphorical proposition is a lie. Indeed, no metaphor *can* be a lie. It can be inapt or inept, imaginative or dull, cheery or morbid or any number of other things. But no metaphor is a lie. The reason is that every lie, by definition, must be unostentatious; it violates the first maxim of quality. A metaphor, in contrast, flouts the maxim. A hearer relies upon the open and ostentatious falsity of the utterance as one important clue that the speaker is speaking metaphorically.

III. ANALYSIS OF A METAPHOR

Let's now see how the foregoing applies to the analysis of a particular metaphor. Suppose someone writes the sentence, "My love is a red rose," in the context of a poem, singing the praises of his lover. The audience reads the sentence and tries to interpret it. If the audience takes the poet to be saying-that his love is a red rose, then the audience must take the poet to be uttering a patent falsehood, and not fulfilling the maxim of quality. "Do not say that which is false." But the audience knows that the poet cannot be intending to utter a patent falsehood, because a falsehood would make sense in the context only if it were disguised and the audience is justified in believing that the poet is observing the conversational maxims. Consequently, the audience infers that the poet is not saying-that his love is a red rose, but only making-as-if-to-say that she is. Once the audience has determined that the speaker is only making-as-if-to-say something, it is then able to begin calculating the actual content of what the speaker has signified. Since the poet is signifying by implication, he must believe that the audience is able to work out the implication. For this reason, the features of the rose that are exploited will be those that the audience is as likely to know as the poet. They will be held mutually, or, as we might say, commonly. Max Black saw this point, more or less clearly, and made it part of his theory of metaphor. He calls such features "related commonplaces."[4] Typically, metaphors do exploit "related commonplaces." (Jones is a dog (gorilla); my love is a red rose (a doll)). Yet, it is also true that some metaphors do not trade on commonplaces, such as "The fog came in on tiny cat's feet." Such metaphors are, however, exceptional, the work of poets or poetic spirits. Such metaphors force the audience to explore the concepts introduced by the metaphor in order to come up with terms that, working in conjunction with the metaphor, will yield the meaning the poet intends, the metaphorical truth. Nonetheless, even in such "creative" metaphors it must be possible for the audience to determine which properties of the metaphorical term the speaker is thinking of and which the speaker thinks that the audience will think that the speaker thinks the audience will think of. And these features we call salient.[5] What features these will be cannot be specified in advance of extensive knowledge of the context: who the speakers are, what their mutual beliefs are; what has been said earlier in the conversation, etc.

Not all salient properties are meant by the speaker; there are too many of them. Thus the set of salient properties must be further reduced. There are two further principles that limit the properties the speaker intends to be operative in the metaphor. One concerns a conversational requirement. Since the speaker has flouted a maxim of quality, he is exploiting that maxim and thereby conversationally implying something. The pattern of inference involved in calculating what the speaker conversationally implies typically involves the maxim of relation: Be relevant. In order to interpret what the poet means, it is necessary to understand his utterance as relevant to the context. The poet is comparing his lover to a rose and hence, given that his comparison is apt, only those salient properties will be considered that are relevant to the poet's attitude towards his love.

The other principle that limits the salient properties is this: the properties intended are only those that contribute to a true conclusion. One plausible statement of the salient features of a rose, relevant to the context of utterance and leading to a true conclusion, is that a red rose is beautiful, or sweet-smelling, or highly-valued. ... Putting the poet's sentence and the statement of salience together and drawing an obvious inference, we construct the following argument:

My love is a red rose.

A red rose is beautiful, or sweet-smelling, or highly-valued. . . .

Therefore, my love is beautiful, or sweet-smelling or highly-valued, . . .

There are at least four things to notice about this argument as it relates generally to the analysis of metaphors. First, the conclusion is presumably true. People who use metaphors aim at the truth, even in those cases in which they fall wide or short of the mark. The premise expressing the salient features of the rose, the major premise, is also true and typically such premises will be true, though not always. Some metaphors can trade on false but commonly held beliefs or false beliefs mutually held by speaker and audience, even when they alone hold the false beliefs; other metaphors can trade on myths or folklore that the community knows to be false. Take for example the folklore that elephants have infallible memories. Someone might exploit this folkloric belief and say, "Jones has the memory of an elephant" without believing that elephants have prodigious memories.[6] Also notice that the argument about the rose is valid, and typically such arguments will be valid although again they may not, and need not always be. There is no reason why a good metaphor cannot trade on some subtle or not so subtle fallacious pattern of reasoning. Consider the metaphor, "Mary is a block of ice." As John Searle has argued, there if no similarity between Mary, in the sense in which she is cold, and a block of ice, in the sense in which it is cold. Thus, the comparison theory of metaphor is false because it holds that all metaphors trade on similarity and not just most of them. Nonetheless, the sentence "Mary is a block of ice" can be used successfully as a metaphor. The explanation, I think, is that the metaphor trades on an equivocation on "cold":

Mary is a block of ice.

Blocks of ice are cold.

Therefore, Mary is cold.

"Cold" is equivocal; it means "low in temperature" in the major premise and "unresponsive" in the conclusion.

The second thing to notice about the argument we are considering is that the first premise has its literal meaning. If "My love is a red rose" did not have its literal meaning, then it would not play its proper role in the argument. If, in the first premise, "red rose" did not mean what it normally does, then the first premise jointly with the second premise would not entail the conclusion and the point of the metaphor would not be conveyed. Moreover, if "red rose" did not have its normal meaning, then there would be no way for the audience to determine what form the second premise of the argument should take. Donald Davidson has argued at length that sentences used metaphorically retain their literal meaning.[7] Davidson also holds that sentences used metaphorically say what they literally mean. He does not, however, commit himself on the more difficult issue of whether a speaker who utters a metaphor says anything. I have argued that such a speaker does not say-that s completely, but does perform some acts that count as parts of saying-that.

Third, notice that the second or major premise expressing the salient features of the rose ends with an ellipsis. Peter Geach distinguishes between two kinds of pronouns: pronouns of laziness and others. We can make an analogous distinction for types of ellipsis: dots of laziness and others. Dots of laziness are a kind of abbreviation. They mark a context that could be filled out if it were desired or necessary, as in the sentence, "The fifty states of the USA are Alabama, Alaska, Arkansas, . . ." The other kind of dots indicate a context that cannot be completed, as in "The natural numbers are 1, 2, 3, . . ." All sentences of natural languages are finite in length and there are an infinite number of natural numbers, so no sentence can specify them all. The dots at the end of the major premise are not dots of laziness. There is no way to fill out the sentence completely and determinately. What a person means by an utterance is not always, if ever, wholly determinate. Usually, the border of what a speaker means is penumbral. Also, since a speaker and his audience are likely to differ about how many features of a rose should be included in the major premise and people will differ about which proposed features are actual features of roses, it is to the communicative advantage of both speaker and audience to leave the major premise disjunctively indeterminate. This kind of indeter-

minacy does not constitute a defect in our analysis of metaphor. Just the opposite. Most metaphors, and, more generally, most cases of conversational implication, exhibit just this kind of indeterminateness and for the reasons given above. Grice thinks that conversational implications generally should be formulated as open disjunctions of propositions and this seems to me to be largely correct. The disjunctive sentences are clearly inclusive disjunctions; so it is possible, indeed, it is intended, that more than one of the disjuncts are true; yet, should one turn out to be false or should the audience either dispute the truth of one of the disjuncts or not take one as partially constituting the premise, the truth of the premise is still safeguarded by the other disjuncts. The view that the supplied premise (or premises) is an open disjunction also helps us pinpoint one objectionable feature of the comparison view of metaphor. According to the comparison view, the meaning of every metaphor can be rendered by some literal paraphrase. Further, it implies, if it does not say, that the literal paraphrase is a determinate and precise sentence. It is this part of the theory that is objectionable. Metaphors are typically vague and indeterminate. This is not a defect. This indeterminateness is one of the more intriguing features of metaphors; it is what encourages the audience to play with and explore the concepts involved; to look for relationships between things not previously countenanced.[8]

Fourth, the argument about the metaphor involving the red rose can be used to answer a criticism against the interaction view of metaphor. That criticism briefly is that the key term employed in that view is metaphorical, and hence defective as an analysis. What literal sense, to put the objection interrogatively, can be given to the notion that the terms of a metaphor interact?[9] Our theory supplies an answer: Notice first that understanding a metaphor requires that the audience must supply one or more premises that will work in conjunction with the metaphor that will (seem to) entail the conclusion, that is, the proposition that expresses the point of the metaphor. Further, and more importantly, such an argument will often be a syllogism, and what will allow the two premises to work jointly is the metaphor term, which occurs as the middle term of the syllogism. Middle terms are those that mediate the two other terms of the syllogism or, we might say, interact with both premises. There is, perhaps, a stronger sense of interaction to be noted; it concerns the principle of selecting the missing premise. In formulating the missing premise, the audience must take into account the following constraints: whatever term is selected, it must be relevant to the topic, salient and contribute to yielding a true conclusion.

IV. METAPHOR AND OTHER FIGURES OF SPEECH

Metaphor is a figure of speech, and it may be instructive to compare it to three other figures of speech. One crucial mark of a metaphor, I have claimed, is that [it] would be false, if it were asserted. However, a speaker who uses a metaphor does not assert it, but, by flouting the second maxim of quality, only makes-as-if-to-say what the metaphor expresses. The correct treatment of hyperbole is strictly analogous to metaphor. Hyperboles, like metaphors, are cases of flouting the second maxim of quality. A person who speaks hyperbolically, that is, who consciously and intentionally exaggerates what he knows to be the truth and intends his audience to recognize this, does not say-that but only makes-as-if-to-say.

Hyperbole should be contrasted with simple overstatement, by which a person who unconsciously or unintentionally expresses a proposition that is stronger than the evidence warrants. The same proposition can be overstatement in one person's mouth and hyperbole in another's. A person who states "Every American who wants to be successful can be" without realizing that circumstances of nature and society prevent some people from achieving their full potential has simply overstated the truth. However, a person who both realizes the truth and intends his audience will understand it may express the same proposition and thereby speak hyperbolically for effect. Hyperbole is a rhetorical device; overstatement is a mistake. Hyperbole differs from metaphor in that the expressed hyperbolic proposition always entails the proposition that should have been expressed and does not require any additional premises as metaphors do. If someone says, "Jones has never

been late to anything in his life," he probably means, "Jones is almost never late for anything" and the former entails the latter.

There is a curious asymmetry between metaphor and hyperbole on the one hand, and meiosis on the other, in two ways. First, meiosis unlike hyperbole and metaphor, does not contravene a maxim of quality but a maxim of quantity: Contribute as much to the conversation as is required. Meiosis contributes too little. While an hyperbolic proposition entails what ought to be said, meiosis is entailed by what ought to be said. Second, because the proposition the speaker expresses is not false, there is no need to interpret it as not being said-that.

Finally, consider irony. Ironical utterances, like metaphors and hyperboles, appear to contravene a maxim of quality. The contravention is, however, only apparent and not genuine. A person who speaks ironically is not saying what is obviously false; for if he were, he would be conveying something that is explicitly contradictory. For example, if the disgruntled worker who uttered the sentence, "This is a *fine* country," and meant that his country is not a fine country, were saying that his is a fine country, then he would be contradicting himself. Ironical utterances, like metaphors and hyperboles, constitute cases of making-as-if-to-say; the speaker means just the opposite of what he makes-as-if-to-say.

V. NONSTANDARD METAPHORS

I have now concluded my treatment of standard metaphors, that is, those metaphorical propositions which would be false if asserted and which, by flouting the second maxim of quality, are cases of making-as-if-to-say. (Thus, "metaphor" no longer means "standard metaphor.") I need now to discuss the nature of nonstandard metaphors, that is, metaphorical propositions, which, if asserted, would be literally true. The first thing to say about such metaphors is that they are rare. The second thing is that they must be treated, because they are genuine cases of metaphor. The third thing is that treatment is more complicated than that of standard metaphors. It is difficult to think of good examples of nonstandard metaphors. Here is the best that I have been able to come up with. Suppose Princess Grace of Monaco is speaking with an American friend about her daugher Caroline. She might say, "Caroline is our princess." Here we have a case of a nonstandard metaphor. Since Caroline is a princess by virtue of her birth to a princely family, Grace's utterance, if asserted, would be literally true. Grace means it, however, metaphorically. The metaphor operates in the following way. When Grace utters "Caroline is our princess," the American must interpret what Grace means. The American reasons that, if Grace means (or means only) that Caroline is the daughter of a prince, then her utterance is defective because it flouts the first maxim of quantity since it is mutually obvious to Grace and the American that Caroline is the daughter of a prince. Consequently, the American reasons that, since Grace is not (simply) stating the obvious, she must be implying something. Since the assumption that the proposition expressed is (simply) true would make it defective, the audience supposes that the proposition is false in order to test the consequences. If Grace intends the American to suppose the proposition is false, then the second maxim of quality is being flouted in that way. Hence, Grace must mean her utterance to be construed metaphorically. Using a folkloric belief as the major premise, the American constructs the following syllogism:

Caroline is a princess.

Princesses are beautiful or admired or well-loved or slightly spoiled or . . .

Therefore, Caroline is beautiful or admired or well-loved or slightly spoiled or . . .

What unites the standard and nonstandard cases of metaphor are the role that falsity plays in generating the metaphor and the characteristic form of conversational implication, leaning on either true or folkloric or mythic or communal beliefs.

A less clearcut case of a nonstandard metaphor is provided by Julia Driver's poem, "The Prostitute," which begins

I am stripped,
an old screw.

Taking "stripped" literally to mean "deprived of clothes" and "screw" as "woman who engages in sexual intercourse," we can suppose

the sentence is literally true but in this sense plays little or no part in its metaphorical interpretation. The metaphorical interpretation depends upon another interpretation of the meaning of the sentence. In addition to the meaning already cited, the sentence can mean, "I am an old metal fastener with a defective spiral ridge running around it." In this latter sense, it is patently false of the speaker, flouts the first maxim of quality and invites a standard metaphorical interpretation. This example is interesting, however, because the first and second sense of the sentence are not independent. The two senses of "screw" in the poem are etymologically related. The reading of the sentence, "I am stripped, an old screw," that is literally true invites, at least by association, the reading of the sentence that is patently false and metaphorical. (Much more could be said about the metaphor; for example, a stripped metal fastener is virtually useless as is an old prostitute.)

I have claimed that nonstandard metaphors are genuine metaphors but rare and derivative upon standard ones. My view is importantly different from the view that the comparatively rare metaphors that are or would be literally true if asserted are not importantly different from the statistically more numerous cases of metaphors that are or would be literally false if asserted. This latter view is defective for two reasons, one positive and one negative. Positively, this view cannot adequately explain how speakers can expect their audience to understand that a metaphor is being broached. On my view, an audience knows that a standard metaphor is being broached largely by the patent falsity of the metaphorical proposition. And if a metaphorical proposition does not appear to be patently false, then there must be some other mechanism that eventually leads the audience to suppose that the literally true proposition must be supposed to be false in order to understand what the speaker means. On my view this other mechanism is the flouting of some conversational maxim— it might be any of the maxims other than the first maxim of quality—that forces the audience to suppose that the utterance is patently false and hence to be interpreted as a standard metaphor would be.

Negatively, the view that some literally true metaphors are merely statistically rare and not conceptually derivative has led some theorists mistakenly to classify as metaphors utterances that are not metaphors. I shall use some of Ted Cohen's work as an example. Cohen gives three examples of allegedly true metaphors: "No man is an island"; "Jesus was a carpenter"; and "Moscow is a cold city."[10] Each of these sentences must be given a different treatment.

As for "No man is an island," my view is that it is not a metaphor at all. It is true and not false that no man is an island. This is not to imply that Donne's line is not a figure of speech. It is. "No man is an island" is trivially true, and for that reason it is a case of meiosis. One might wonder how such a trivial truth could be so poetically powerful? The answer is that it is powerful in the richness of its associations, conveyed by conversational implication. In saying, "No man is an island," Donne is saying something trivial. The reader must, consequently, muse about the relevance of a triviality; he reasons, presumably, in a way analogous to a case of metaphor:

No man is an island.

Every island is separated from every other thing of its own kind, does not depend upon any other thing of its own kind for its existence or well-being, and is not diminished by the destruction of any other of its own kind; . . .

Therefore, no man is separated from every other thing of its own kind, does not depend upon any other thing of its own kind for its existence or well-being, and is not diminished by the destruction of any other of its own kind; . . . .

This argument is invalid; yet not the less effective as poetry for all that. In short, while what Donne has said is trivial, what he has linguistically communicated *via* conversational implication is not at all trivial; but, on the contrary, profound.

Concerning "Jesus was a carpenter," a speaker who says this speaks truly. Perhaps, however—and this seems to be Cohen's point—the speaker might well mean more than he says. He might mean that Jesus fashions valuable things out of unfashioned worthless things. If this statement of what the speaker additionally means seems itself metaphorical, it can be paraphrased in ways to eliminate those elements: Jesus causes things that have no value in themselves to become things that do have value in themselves. What is important to notice is that we have specified what the speaker means by specifying that the speaker *means what he says* and *means more than what he says.* And this specification does not commit us to holding that "Jesus is a carpenter" is a metaphor. For, to appeal to the classic formula, "to utter a metaphor is to say one thing and to mean something else" (i.e., something inconsistent with what you say.) In the case under consideration, the speaker does not mean something inconsistent with what he said, merely something additional, just as anyone conversationally implying something means something additional to what he says.

Finally, "Moscow is a cold city" is not a metaphor; it is ambiguous, perhaps, a pun. It has two literal readings: "Moscow is a city that often has low temperatures" and "Moscow is not a cordial city." "Cold," in the latter sentence is a dead metaphor; but dead metaphors are not metaphors.

VI. GENERALIZING THE THEORY

In section II, I said that *if* we accept Grice's formulation of the maxim of quality, then every metaphor is (or is thought to be) literally false or is supposed to be false. However, Grice's formulation of the maxim of quality is not correct. The principal problem with it is that it is too narrow. As Grice formulates them, "Do not say that which is false," and "Do not say that for which you lack evidence," the maxims apply only to speech acts that have truth values, for example, statements and assertions. Many speech acts do not have a truth value, for example, questions, promises and requests. All of this is important for our theory because many metaphors are embedded in utterances that would not have a truth value if uttered literally, e.g., the Dutch uncle's utterance, "I promise I will clip that butterfly's wings." So, such simple cases cannot be explained in our original formulation about standard and nonstandard metaphors. However, the problem is easily corrected by replacing Grice's too narrow maxims of quality with a sufficiently broad one and generalizing our initial formulation to accord with the broader maxim of quality.

In another article, I have argued that Grice's

maxims of quality should be replaced by this one: Do not participate in a speech act unless you satisfy all the conditions required for its successful and nondefective performance.[11] This maxim is obviously broad enough to cover the entire spectrum of speech acts. The question now is, what was the intuition behind the distinction between standard and nonstandard metaphors? We can get at it if we consider the following sentences that might be uttered in the Dutch uncle situation.

I state that Mary will have her wings clipped.

I promise that Mary will have her wings clipped.

I ask whether Mary will have her wings clipped.

I insist that Mary will have her wings clipped.

In each case, the same proposition is involved: that Mary will have her wings clipped. Yet, in each case the force of the utterance would be different if the sentence were uttered literally. Searle would say that each utterance involves the same propositional content and each attempted speech act would be defective for the same reason if the relevant sentence were uttered literally. In each case, what Searle calls "the propositional content condition" would be flouted. These are cases of standard metaphors. That is, a standard metaphor is one in which the propositional content condition is flouted. Nonstandard metaphors are those in which the propositional content is supposed to be flouted. This formulation of the distinction between standard and nonstandard metaphors is unavoidably stated in technical terms in order to describe the phenomenon of metaphor correctly and with the required generality.

VII. A COMPARISON WITH SEARLE'S THEORY OF METAPHOR

There are some important similarities between my theory of metaphor and that of John Searle. The spirit is the same. Both are pragmatic theories that exploit features of Grice's theory of linguistic communication. We also differ in several significant respects. My theory is logically stronger than Searle's in three important ways. First, Searle claims that the stimulus to treat a sentence as being uttered metaphorically is the result of "false-

hood, semantic nonsense, violations of the rules of speech acts, or violations of conversational principles of communication."[12] My view is stronger in that I claim that all standard metaphors must be supposed to contravene it. Second, Searle does not make clear whether, when a speaker utters a sentence s metaphorically, he is saying-that s or only making-as-if-to-say it. I have argued for the latter view, while also explaining how a speaker communicates some parts of what he says. Third, I have specified that the premises that are added to the metaphor, in order to infer what the point of the metaphor is, are constrained by three principles: they must involve features or properties that are salient to the metaphorical term; they must fulfill the maxim of relation by being relevant to the topic of the conversation; and they must help form a premise that ends to yield a true conclusion.

There is one respect in which Searle's theory has a superficial appearance of being stronger than mine. In contrast with my principles of salience and relevance and truth-producing premises, Searle specifies nine supposed principles for computing the features relevant to the metaphor. Yet, upon reflection, these nine principles turn out to be vacuous. Searle intends his nine principles to constitute at least a partial answer to the question. How is it possible for the hearer who hears the utterance "S is P" to know that the speaker means "S is R"[?][13] I want to show that Searle's nine principles fail to answer this question in any part, because the principles are so weak as to permit any possible feature or property of a thing to be a value of R.

Any feature or property will either be true of an object or false of it; and Searle allows any feature or property whether true or false of an object to play a role in the interpretation of a metaphor. This is objectionable because it fails to limit the possible features or properties of an object to those that are relevant to a metaphorical interpretation of a sentence. A theory of metaphor must provide principles that specify which features or properties might be relevant to a metaphor in order to allow the audience to know which features or properties the speaker means to imply by the metaphor. We can see this argument against Searle's principles more clearly by considering what he says about the metaphorical applicability of all those features or properties that are true of an object and then all those features or properties that are false of an object. According to Principle 1, a feature or property could be true of the object by definition; according to Principle 2, a feature or property could be contingently true of an object. Since every feature that is true of an object is either necessarily true, that is, true by definition, or contingently true, Searle has in no way restricted the actual features of an object to those that might play a role in a metaphor.

What about features that are not true of an object? Again, Searle allows such a latitude that no feature is excluded from possibly playing a role in a metaphor. Citing Principles 3 and 4 is sufficient to show this. Principle 3 allows features that are often said of or believed to be true of an object; Principle 4 allows features that a thing does not have as well as those that are not even like any feature it has. In short, Searle's theory suffers from being too weak for failing to explain when a feature or property might play a role in a metaphor and when it would not.

VIII. REPLY TO OBJECTIONS TO A PRAGMATIC THEORY OF METAPHOR

The theory of metaphor I have been advancing is blatantly pragmatic. Since some distinguished theorists have claimed that metaphor is a semantic phenomenon, their claims should be discussed, if only briefly. Max Black is perhaps the most distinguished philosophical proponent of this view. He says that in a metaphor, the focal or metaphorical term "obtains a new meaning, which is not quite its meaning in literal uses, not quite the meaning which any literal substitute would have."[14] This is in line with his general view that metaphor is a semantic phenomenon: " 'metaphor' must be classified as a term belonging to 'semantics' and not to 'syntax'...."[15] When Black expressed this view, there was no well-developed pragmatic theory such as Searle's revision of Austin's theory of speech acts and Grice's theory of linguistic communication; so it is not surprising that Black opts for a semantic theory against a syntactic theory and does not consider the possibility of a pragmatic the-

ory. And it is not surprising that his arguments in behalf of a semantic treatment are not very telling against a pragmatic theory. He holds that "The chairman plowed though the discussion" and "The poor are the negroes of Europe" (attributed to Chamfort) are "unmistakeably *instances* of metaphor."[16] They are such only in context. We can imagine a crazed chairman driving a plow through a meeting of his committee; in which case the first sentence, if asserted, would be literally true. And we can imagine a slightly different history of Europe, in which the statement made by "The poor are the negroes of Europe" would be literally true and not a metaphor. The upshot is that whether a sentence is used literally or metaphorically depends upon the context of its use; and is, I maintain, a fit subject for a pragmatic theory.

Recently, L. Jonathan Cohen has also urged that metaphor be given a semantic treatment.[17] Since Peter Lamarque has acutely criticized Cohen's views [...], it is not necessary for me to provide an extended response.[18] Lamarque correctly notes several respects in which metaphors do not parallel genuine illocutionary acts, and this is sufficient to undermine Cohen's case. There is just one issue about which I disagree with Lamarque. He holds that Tom's ironical utterance of

(5) That was a brilliant thing to do.

can be correctly reported by

(7) Tom said that that was a brilliant thing to do.

And he holds that Tom's metaphorical utterance of

(9) The rats have driven me out of the house.

can be correctly reported as

(10) Tom said that the rats have driven him out of his house.

I have already explained why I think sentences (7) and (10) do not correctly report Tom's actions. Ironical and metaphorical utterances are not cases of *saying-that* something, but of *making-as-if-to-say* something. This objection to Lamarque does not diminish the force of his criticisms of Cohen's views. So, the objections of Black and Cohen do not seem to stand in the way of the kind of pragmatic theory I have presented.

NOTES

1. H. P. Grice, "Logic and Conversation," in *Syntax and Semantics,* vol. 3, ed. Peter Cole and Jerry L. Morgan (New York: Academic Press, 1975), 44–45. [Reprinted in this volume, Chapter 19]

2. Cf. Merrie Bergmann, "Metaphorical Assertions," *Philosophical Review* 91 (1982), 225–245. [Reprinted in this volume, Chapter 28]

3. Bergmann in "Metaphorical Assertions," 234, confuses what is conversationally implied by a metaphor, the point of the metaphor, with what a speaker asserts by a metaphor. What a speaker asserts must be closely tied to the conventional meaning of the words he utters, but what Bergmann calls the metaphorical assertion is either loosely tied or not tied at all to the conventional meaning.

4. Max Black, "Metaphor," in *Models and Metaphors* (Ithaca: Cornell University Press, 1954), 41; see also Max Black, "More on Metaphor," in *Metaphor and Thought,* ed. Andrew Ortony (New York: Cambridge University Press, 1979), 28–29.

5. For more about salience, see Andrew Ortony, "Beyond Literal Similarity," *Psychological Review* 86 (1976), 161–180, and "The Role of Similarity in Similes and Metaphors," in *Metaphor and Thought,* ed. Andrew Ortony (New York: Cambridge University Press, 1979), 186–201; and Merrie Bergmann, "Metaphorical Assertions," 234–239.

6. See also John Searle, "Metaphor," in his *Expression and Meaning* (Cambridge: Cambridge University Press, 1979), 88–90. [Reprinted in this volume, Chapter 31]

7. See his "What Metaphors Mean," *Critical Inquiry* 5 (1978), 31–47 [Reprinted in this volume, Chapter 29]. John Searle in "Metaphor," p. 77, and Ted Cohen in "Figurative Speech and Figurative Acts," *The Journal of Philosophy* 72 (1975), 670, hold the same view.

8. I think that my treatment of the role played by open disjunctive propositions is the theoretical counterpart of Black's "implicative complex"; see "More on Metaphor," 28.

9. Searle hints at this criticism; see his "Metaphor," 92.

10. "Figurative Speech and Figurative Acts," 671.

11. A. P. Martinich, "Conversational Maxims and Some Philosophical Problems," *Philosophical Quarterly* 30 (1980), 215–228.

12. Searle, "Metaphor," 105.

13. Searle, "Metaphor," 134.

14. Black, "Metaphor," 39.

15. Black, "Metaphor," 39.

16. Black, "Metaphor," 26.

17. "The Semantics of Metaphor," in *Metaphor and Thought,* 65.

18. Peter Lamarque, "Metaphor and Reported Speech: In Defence of a Pragmatic Theory," *Journal of Literary Semantics* 11 (1982), 14–18.

31

Metaphor

JOHN R. SEARLE

FORMULATING THE PROBLEM

If you hear somebody say, "Sally is a block of ice," or "Sam is a pig," you are likely to assume that the speaker does not mean what he says literally but that he is speaking metaphorically. Furthermore, you are not likely to have very much trouble figuring out what he means. If he says, "Sally is a prime number between 17 and 23," or "Bill is a barn door," you might still assume he is speaking metaphorically, but it is much harder to figure out what he means. The existence of such utterances—utterances in which the speaker means metaphorically something different from what the sentence means literally—poses a series of questions for any theory of language and communication: What is metaphor, and how does it differ from both literal and other forms of figurative utterances? Why do we use expressions metaphorically instead of saying exactly and literally what we mean? How do metaphorical utterances work, that is, how is it possible for speakers to communicate to hearers when speaking metaphorically inasmuch as they do not say what they mean? And why do some metaphors work and others not?

In my discussion, I propose to tackle this latter set of questions—those centering around the problem of how metaphors work—both because of its intrinsic interest, and because it does not seem to me that we shall get an answer to the others until this fundamental question has been answered. Before we can begin to understand it, however, we need to formulate the question more precisely.

The problem of explaining how metaphors work is a special case of the general problem of explaining how speaker meaning and sentence or word meaning come apart. It is a special case, that is, of the problem of how it is possible to say one thing and mean something else, where one succeeds in communicating what one means even though both the speaker and the hearer know that the meanings of the words uttered by the speaker do not exactly and literally express what the speaker meant. Some other instances of the break between speaker's utterance meaning and literal sentence meaning are irony and indirect speech acts. In each of these cases, what the speaker means is not identical with what the sentence means, and yet what he means is in various ways dependent on what the sentence means.

It is essential to emphasize at the very beginning that the problem of metaphor concerns the relations between word and sentence meaning, on the one hand, and speaker's meaning or utterance meaning, on the other. Many writers on the subject try to locate the metaphorical element of a metaphorical utterance in the sentence or expressions uttered. They think there are two kinds of sentence meaning, literal and metaphorical. However, sentences and words have only the meanings that they have. Strictly speaking, whenever we talk about the metaphorical meaning of a word, expression, or sentence, we are talking about what a speaker might utter it to mean, in a way that departs from what the word, expression, or sentence actually means. We are, therefore, talking about possible speaker's intentions. Even when we discuss how a non-sense sentence, such as Chomsky's example, "Colorless green ideas sleep furiously," could be given a metaphorical interpretation, what we are talking about is how a speaker could utter the sentence and mean something by it metaphorically, even though it is literally nonsensical. To have a brief way of distinguishing what a speaker means by uttering words, sentences, and expressions, on the one hand, and what the words, sentences, and expressions mean, on the other, I shall call the former *speaker's utterance meaning,* and the latter, *word,* or *sentence meaning.* Metaphorical meaning is always speaker's utterance meaning.

In order that the speaker can communicate using metaphorical utterances, ironical utterances, and indirect speech acts, there must be some principles according to which he is able to mean more than, or something different from, what he says, whereby the hearer, using his knowledge of them, can understand what the speaker means. The relation between the sentence meaning and the metaphorical utterance meaning is systematic rather than random or ad hoc. Our task in constructing a theory of metaphor is to try to state the principles which relate literal sentence meaning to metaphorical utterance meaning. Because the knowledge that enables people to use and understand metaphorical utterances goes beyond their knowledge of the literal meanings of words and sentences, the principles we seek are not included, or at least not entirely in-

cluded, within a theory of semantic competence as traditionally conceived. From the point of view of the hearer, the problem of a theory of metaphor is to explain how he can understand the speaker's utterance meaning given that all he hears is a sentence with its word and sentence meaning. From the point of view of the speaker, the problem is to explain how he can mean something different from the word and sentence meaning of the sentence he utters. In light of these reflections, our original question, How do metaphors work? can be recast as follows: What are the principles that enable speakers to formulate, and hearers to understand, metaphorical utterances? and How can we state these principles in a way that makes it clear how metaphorical utterances differ from other sorts of utterances in which speaker meaning does not coincide with literal meaning?

Because part of our task is to explain how metaphorical utterances differ from literal utterances, to start with we must arrive at a characterization of literal utterances. Most—indeed all—of the authors I have read on the subject of metaphor assume that we know how literal utterances work; they do not think that the problem of literal utterances is worth discussing in their account of metaphor. The price they pay for this is that their accounts often describe metaphorical utterances in ways that fail to distinguish them from literal ones.

In fact, to give an accurate account of literal predication is an extremely difficult, complex, and subtle problem. I shall not attempt anything like a thorough summary of the principles of literal utterance but shall remark on only those features which are essential for a comparison of literal utterance with metaphorical utterance. Also, for the sake of simplicity, I shall confine most of my discussion of both literal and metaphorical utterance to very simple cases, and to sentences used for the speech act of assertion.

Imagine that a speaker makes a literal utterance of a sentence such as

(1) Sally is tall

(2) The cat is on the mat

(3) It's getting hot in here.

Now notice that in each of these cases, the literal meaning of the sentence determines, at least in part, a set of truth conditions; and because the only illocutionary force indicating devices (see Searle, 1969) in the sentences are assertive, the literal and serious utterance of one of these sentences will commit the speaker to the existence of the set of truth conditions determined by the meaning of that sentence, together with the other determinants of truth conditions. Notice, furthermore, that in each case the sentence only determines a definite set of truth conditions relative to a particular context. That is because each of these examples has some indexical element, such as the present tense, or the demonstrative "here," or the occurrence of contextually dependent definite descriptions, such as "the cat" and "the mat."

In these examples, the contextually dependent elements of the sentence are explicitly realized in the semantic structure of the sentence: One can see and hear the indexical expressions. But these sentences, like most sentences, only determine a set of truth conditions against a background of assumptions that are not explicitly realized in the semantic structure of the sentence. This is most obvious for (1) and (3), because they contain the relative terms "tall" and "hot." These are what old-fashioned grammarians called "attributive" terms, and they only determine a definite set of truth conditions against a background of factual assumptions about the sort of things referred to by the speaker in the rest of the sentence. Moreover, these assumptions are not explicitly realized in the semantic structure of the sentence. Thus, a woman can be correctly described as "tall" even though she is shorter than a giraffe that could correctly be described as "short."

Though this dependence of the application of the literal meaning of the sentence on certain factual background assumptions that are not part of the literal meaning is most obvious for sentences containing attributive terms, the phenomenon is quite general. Sentence (2) only determines a definite set of truth conditions given certain assumptions about cats, mats, and the relation of being on. However, these assumptions are not part of the semantic content of the sentence. Suppose, for example, that the cat and mat are in the usual cat-on-mat spatial configuration, only both cat and mat are in outer space, outside any gravitational field relative to which one could be said to be "above" or "over" the other. Is the cat still *on* the mat? Without some further assumptions, the sentence does not determine a definite set of truth conditions in this context. Or suppose all cats suddenly became lighter than air, and the cat went flying about with the mat stuck to its belly. Is the cat still on the mat?

We know without hesitation what are the truth conditions of, "The fly is on the ceiling," but not of, "The cat is on the ceiling," and this difference is not a matter of meaning, but a matter of how our factual background information enables us to apply the meanings of sentences. In general, one can say that in most cases a sentence only determines a set of truth conditions relative to a set of assumptions that are not realized in the semantic content of the sentence. Thus, even in literal utterances, where speaker's meaning coincides with sentence meaning, the speaker must contribute more to the literal utterance than just the semantic content of the sentence, because that semantic content only determines a set of truth conditions relative to a set of assumptions made by the speaker, and if communication is to be successful, his assumptions must be shared by the hearer (for further discussion of this point, see Searle, 1978).

Notice finally that the notion of similarity plays a crucial role in any account of literal utterance. This is because the literal meaning of any general term, by determining a set of truth conditions, also determines a criterion of similarity between objects. To know that a general term is true of a set of objects is to know that they are similar with respect to the property specified by that term. All tall women are similar with respect to being tall, all hot rooms similar with respect to being hot, all square objects similar with respect to being square, and so on.

To summarize this brief discussion of some aspects of literal utterance, there are three features we shall need to keep in mind in our account of metaphorical utterance. First, in literal utterance the speaker means what he says; that is, literal sentence meaning and speaker's utterance meaning are the same; second, in general the literal meaning of a sentence only determines a set of truth conditions relative to a set of background assumptions which are not part of the semantic content of the sentence; and third, the notion of similarity plays an essential role in any account of literal predication.

When we turn to cases where utterance meaning and sentence meaning are different, we find them quite various. Thus, for example, (3) could be uttered not only to tell somebody that it is getting hot in the place of utterance (literal utterance), but it could also be used to request somebody to open a window (indirect speech act), to complain about how cold it is (ironical utterance), or to remark on the increasing vituperation of an argument that is in progress (metaphorical utterance). In our account of metaphorical utterance, we shall need to distinguish it not only from literal utterance, but also from these other forms in which literal utterance is departed from, or exceeded, in some way.

Because in metaphorical utterances what the speaker means differs from what he says (in one sense of "say"), in general we shall need two sentences for our examples of metaphor—first the sentence uttered metaphorically, and second a sentence that expresses literally what the speaker means when he utters the first sentence and means it metaphorically. Thus (3), the metaphor (MET):

(3) (MET) It's getting hot in here.

corresponds to (3), the paraphrase (PAR):

(3) (PAR) The argument that is going on is becoming more vituperative

and similarly with the pairs:

(4) (MET) Sally is a block of ice

(4) (PAR) Sally is an extremely unemotional and unresponsive person

(5) (MET) I have climbed to the top of the greasy pole (Disraeli)

(5) (PAR) I have after great difficulty become prime minister

(6) (MET) Richard is a gorilla

(6) (PAR) Richard is fierce, nasty, and prone to violence.

Notice that in each case we feel that the paraphrase is somehow inadequate, that something is lost. One of our tasks will be to explain this sense of dissatisfaction that we have with paraphrases of even feeble metaphors. Still, in some sense, the paraphrases must approximate what the speaker meant, because in each case the speaker's metaphorical assertion will be true if, and only if, the corresponding assertion using the PAR sentence is true. When we get to more elaborate examples, our sense of the inadequacy of the paraphrase becomes more acute. How would we paraphrase

(7) (MET) My Life had stood—a Loaded Gun—
In Corners—till a Day
The Owner passes—identified
And carried Me away—
(Emily Dickinson)?

Clearly a good deal is lost by

(7) (PAR) My life was one of unrealized but readily realizable potential (a loaded gun) in mediocre surroundings (corners) until such time (a day) when my destined lover (the owner) came (passed), recognized my potential (identified), and took (carried) me away.

Yet, even in this case, the paraphrase or something like it must express a large part of speaker's utterance meaning, because the truth conditions are the same.

Sometimes we feel that we know exactly what the metaphor means and yet would not be able to formulate a literal PAR sentence because there are no literal expressions that convey what it means. Thus even for such a simple case as

(8) (MET) The ship ploughed the sea,

we may not be able to construct a simple paraphrase sentence even though there is no obscurity in the metaphorical utterance. And indeed metaphors often serve to plug such semantic gaps as this. In other cases, there may be an indefinite range of paraphrases. For example, when Romeo says:

(9) (MET) Juliet is the sun,

there may be a range of things he might mean. But while lamenting the inadequacy of paraphrases, let us also recall that paraphrase is symmetrical relation. To say that the paraphrase is a poor paraphrase of the metaphor is also to say that the metaphor is a poor paraphrase of its paraphrase. Furthermore, we should not feel apologetic about the fact that some of our examples are trite or dead metaphors. Dead metaphors are especially interesting for our study, because, to speak oxymoronically, dead metaphors have lived on. They have become dead through continual use, but their continual use is a clue that they satisfy some semantic need.

Confining ourselves to the simplest subject–predicate cases, we can say that the general form of the metaphorical utterance is that a speaker utters a sentence of the form "S is P" and means metaphorically that S is R. In analyzing metaphorical predication, we need to distinguish, therefore, between three sets of elements. Firstly, there is the subject expression "S" and the object or objects it is used to refer to. Secondly, there is the predicate expression "P" that is uttered and the literal meaning of that expression with its corresponding truth conditions, plus the denotation if there is any. And thirdly, there is the speaker's utterance meaning "S is R" and the truth conditions determined by that meaning. In its simplest form, the problem of metaphor is to try to get a characterization of the relations between the three sets, S, P, and R,[1] together with a specification of other information and principles used by speakers and hearers, so as to explain how it is possible to utter "S is P" and mean "S is R," and how it is possible to communicate that meaning from speaker to hearer. Now, obviously, that is not all there is to understand about metaphorical utterances; the speaker does more than just assert that S is R, and the peculiar effectiveness of metaphor will have to be explained in terms of how he does more than just assert that S is R and why he should choose this roundabout way of asserting that S is R in the first place. But at this stage we are starting at the beginning. At the very minimum, a theory of metaphor must explain how it is possible to utter "S is P" and both mean and communicate that S is R.

We can now state one of the differences between literal and metaphorical utterances as applied to these simple examples: In the case of literal utterance, speaker's meaning and sentence meaning are the same; therefore the assertion made about the object referred to will be true if and only if it satisfies the truth conditions determined by the meaning of the general term as applied against a set of shared background assumptions. In order to understand the utterance, the hearer does not require any extra knowledge beyond his knowledge of the rules of language, his awareness of the conditions of utterance, and a set of shared background assumptions. But, in the case of the metaphorical utterance, the truth conditions of the assertion are not determined by the truth conditions of the sentence and its general term. In order to understand the metaphorical utterance, the hearer requires something more than his knowledge of the language, his awareness of the conditions of the utterance, and background assumptions that he shares with the speaker. He must have some other principles, or some other factual information, or some combination of principles and information that enables him to figure out that when the speaker says, "S is P," he means "S is R." What is this extra element?

I believe that at the most general level, the question has a fairly simple answer, but it will take me much of the rest of this discussion to work it out in any detail. The basic principle on which all metaphor works is that the utterance of an expression with its literal meaning and corresponding truth conditions can, in various ways that are specific to metaphor, call to mind another meaning and corresponding set of truth conditions. The hard problem of the theory of metaphor is to explain what exactly are the principles according to which the utterance of an expression can metaphorically call to mind a different set of truth conditions from the one determined by its literal meaning, and to state those principles precisely and without using metaphorical expressions like "call to mind."

SOME COMMON MISTAKES ABOUT METAPHOR

Before attempting to sketch a theory of metaphor, I want in this section and the next to backtrack a bit and examine some existing theories. Roughly speaking, theories of metaphor from Aristotle to the present can be divided into two types.[2] Comparison theories assert that metaphorical utterances involve a *comparison* or *similarity* between two or more *objects* (e.g., Aristotle, 1952a, 1952b; Henle, 1965), and semantic interaction theories claim that metaphor involves a *verbal opposition* (Beardsley, 1962) or *interaction* (Black, 1962b) between two *semantic contents,* that of the expression used metaphorically, and that of the surrounding literal context. I think that both of these theories, if one tries to take them quite literally, are in various ways inadequate; nonetheless, they are both trying to say something true, and we ought to try to extract what is true in them. But first I want to show some of the common mistakes they contain and some further common mistakes made in discussions of metaphor. My aim here is not polemical; rather, I am trying to clear the ground for the development of a theory of metaphor. One might say the endemic vice of the comparison theories is that they fail to distinguish between the claim that the statement of the comparison is part of the *meaning,* and hence the *truth conditions,* of the metaphorical statement, and the claim that the statement of the similarity is the *principle of inference,* or a step in the process of *comprehending,* on the basis of which speakers produce and hearers understand metaphor. (More about this distinction later.) The semantic interaction theories were developed in response to the weaknesses of the comparison theories, and they have little independent argument to recommend them other than the weakness of their rivals: Their endemic vice is the failure to appreciate the distinction between sentence or word meaning, which is never metaphorical, and speaker or utterance meaning, which can be metaphorical. They usually try to locate metaphorical meaning in the sentence or some set of associations with the sentence. In any event, here are half a dozen mistakes, which I believe should be noted:

It is often said that in metaphorical utterances there is a change in meaning of at least one expression. I wish to say that on the contrary, strickly speaking, in metaphor there is never a change of meaning; diachronically speaking, metaphors do indeed initiate semantic changes, but to the extent that there has been a genuine change in meaning, so that a word or expression no longer means what it previously did, to precisely that extent the locution is no longer metaphorical. We are all familiar with the processes whereby an expression becomes a dead metaphor, and then finally becomes an idiom or acquires a new meaning different from the original meaning. But in a genuine metaphorical utterance, it is only because the expressions have not changed their meaning that there is a metaphorical utterance at all. The people who make this claim seem to be confusing *sentence* meaning with *speaker's* meaning. The metaphorical utterance does indeed mean something different from the meaning of the words and sentences, but that is not because there has been any change in the meanings of the lexical elements, but because the speaker means something different by them; speaker meaning does not coincide with sentence or word meaning. It is essential to see this point, because the main problem of metaphor is to explain how speaker meaning and sentence meaning are different and how they are, nevertheless, related. Such an explanation is impossible if we suppose that sentence or word meaning has changed in the metaphorical utterance.

The simplest way to show that the crude versions of the comparison view are false is to show that, in the production and understanding of metaphorical utterances, there need not be any two objects for comparison. When I say metaphorically

(4) (MET) Sally is a block of ice,

I am not necessarily quantifying over blocks of ice at all. My utterance does not entail literally that

(10) $(\exists x)$ (x is a block of ice),

and such that I am comparing Sally to x. This point is even more obvious if we take expressions used as metaphors which have a null extension. If I say

(11) Sally is a dragon

that does not entail literally

(12) $(\exists x)$ (x is a dragon).

Or, another way to see the same thing is to note that the negative sentence is just as metaphorical as the affirmative. If I say

(13) Sally is not a block of ice,

that, I take it, does not invite the absurd question: Which block of ice is it that you are comparing Sally with, in order to say that she is not like it? At its *crudest,* the comparison theory is just muddled about the referential character of expressions used metaphorically.

Now, this might seem a somewhat minor

objection to the comparison theorists, but it paves the way for a much more radical objection. Comparison theories which are explicit on the point at all, generally treat the statement of the comparison as part of the meaning and hence as part of the truth conditions of the metaphorical statement. For example, Miller is quite explicit in regarding metaphorical statements as statements of similarity, and indeed for such theorists the meaning of a *metaphorical* statement is always given by an explicit *statement* of similarity. Thus, in their view, I have not even formulated the problem correctly. According to me, the problem of explaining (simple subject–predicate) metaphors is to explain how the speaker and hearer go from the literal sentence meaning "*S* is *P*" to the metaphorical utterance meaning "*S* is *R*." But, according to them, that is not the utterance meaning; rather the utterance meaning must be expressible by an explicit statement of similarity, such as "*S* is like *P* with respect to *R*," or in Miller's case, the metaphorical statement "*S* is *P*" is to be analyzed as, "There is some property *F* and some property *G* such that *S*'s being *F* is similar to *P*'s being *G*." I will have more to say about this thesis and its exact formulation later, but at present I want to claim that though similarity often plays a role in the *comprehension* of metaphor, the metaphorical assertion is not necessarily an *assertion* of similarity. The simplest argument that metaphorical assertions are not always assertions of similarity is that there are true metaphorical assertions for which there are no objects to be designated by the *P* term, hence the true metaphorical statement cannot possibly presuppose the existence of an object of comparison. But even where there are objects of comparison, the metaphorical assertion is not necessarily an assertion of similarity. Similarity, I shall argue, has to do with the production and understanding of metaphor, not with its meaning.

A second simple argument to show that metaphorical assertions are not necessarily assertions of similarity is that often the metaphorical assertion can remain true even though it turns out that the statement of similarity on which the inference to the metaphorical meaning is based is false. Thus, suppose I say,

(6) (MET) Richard is a gorilla

meaning

(6) (PAR) Richard is fierce, nasty, prone to violence, and so forth.

And suppose the hearer's inference to (6 PAR) is based on the belief that

(14) Gorillas are fierce, nasty, prone to violence, and so forth,

and hence (6 MET) and (14), on the comparison view, would justify the inference to

(15) Richard and gorillas are similar in several respects; *viz.,* they are fierce, nasty, prone to violence, and so forth,

and this in turn would be part of the inference pattern that enabled the hearer to conclude that when I uttered (6 MET) I meant (6 PAR). But suppose ethological investigation shows, as I am told it has, that gorillas are not at all fierce and nasty, but are in fact shy, sensitive creatures, given to bouts of sentimentality. This would definitely show that (15) is false, for (15) is as much an assertion about gorillas as about Richard. But would it show that when I uttered (6 MET), what I said was false? Clearly not, for what I meant was (6 PAR), and (6 PAR) is an assertion about Richard. It can remain true regardless of the actual facts about gorillas; though, of course, what expressions we use to convey metaphorically certain semantic contents will normally depend on what we take the facts to be.

To put it creduely, "Richard is a gorilla," is just about Richard; it is not literally about gorillas at all. The word "gorilla" here serves to convey a certain semantic content other than its own meaning by a set of principles I have yet to state. But (15) is literally about both Richard and gorillas, and it is true if and only if they both share the properties it claims they do. Now, it may well be true that the hearer employs something like (15), as a step in the procedures that get him from (6 MET) to (6 PAR), but it does not follow from this fact about his *procedures of comprehension* that this is part of the *speaker's utterance meaning* of (6 MET); and, indeed, that it is not part of the utterance meaning is shown by the fact that the metaphorical statement can be *true* even if it turns out that gorillas do not have the traits that the metaphorical occurrence of "gorilla" served to convey. I am not saying that a metaphorical assertion can *never* be equivalent in meaning to a statement of similarity—whether or not it is would depend on the intentions of the speaker; but I am saying that it is not a necessary feature of metaphor—and is certainly not the point of having metaphor—that metaphorical assertions are equivalent in meaning to statements of similarity. My argument is starkly simple: In many cases the metaphorical statement and the corresponding similarity statement cannot be equivalent in meaning because they have different truth conditions. The difference between the view I am attacking and the one I shall espouse is this. According to the view I am attacking, (6 MET) *means* Richard and gorillas are similar in certain respects. According to the view I shall espouse, similarity functions as a comprehension strategy, not as a component of meaning: (6 MET) says that Richard has certain traits (and to figure out what they are, look for features associated with gorillas). On my account the P term need not figure literally in the statement of the truth conditions of the metaphorical statement at all.

Similar remarks apply incidentally to similes. If I say,

(16) Sam acts like a gorilla

that need not commit me to the truth of

(17) Gorillas are such that their behavior resembles Sam's.

For (16) need not be about gorillas at all, and we might say that "gorilla" in (16) has a metaphorical occurrence. Perhaps this is one way we might distinguish between figurative similes and literal statements of similarity. Figurative similes need not necessarily commit the speaker to a literal statement of similarity.

The semantic interaction view, it seems to me, is equally defective. One of the assumptions behind the view that metaphorical meaning is a result of an interaction between an expression used metaphorically and other expressions used literally, is that all metaphorical uses of expressions must occur in sentences containing literal uses of expressions, and that assumption seems to me plainly false. It is, incidentally, the assumption behind the terminology of many of the contemporary discussions of metaphor. We are told, for example, that every metaphorical sentence contains a "tenor" and a "vehicle" (Richards, 1936) or

a "frame" and a "focus" (Black, 1962b). But it is not the case that every metaphorical use of an expression is surrounded by literal uses of other expressions. Consider again our example (4): In uttering, "Sally is a block of ice," we referred to Sally using her proper name literally, but we need not have. Suppose, to use a mixed metaphor, we refer to Sally as "the bad news." We would then say, using a mixed metaphor

(18) The bad news is a block of ice.

If you insist that the "is" is still literal, it is easy enough to construct examples of a dramatic change on Sally's part where we would be inclined, in another mixed metaphor, to say

(19) The bad news congealed into a block of ice.

Mixed metaphors may be stylistically objectionable, but I cannot see that they are necessarily logically incoherent. Of course, most metaphors do occur in contexts of expressions used literally. It would be very hard to understand them if they did not. But it is not a logical necessity that every metaphorical use of an expression occurs surrounded by literal occurrences of other expressions and, indeed, many famous examples of metaphor are not. Thus Russell's example of a completely nonsensical sentence, "Quadrilaterality drinks procrastination," is often given a metaphorical interpretation as a description of any postwar four-power disarmament conference, but none of the words, so interpreted, has a literal occurrence; that is, for every word the speaker's utterance meaning differs from the literal word meaning.

However, the most serious objection to the semantic interaction view is not that it falsely presupposes that all metaphorical occurrences of words must be surrounded by literal occurrence of other words, but rather, that even where the metaphorical occurrence is within the context of literal occurrences, it is not in general the case that the metaphorical speaker's meaning is a result of any interaction among the elements of the sentence in any literal sense of "interaction." Consider again our example (4). In its metaphorical utterances, there is no question of any interaction between the meaning of the "principal subject" ("Sally") and the "subsidiary subject" ("block of ice"). "Sally" is a proper name; it does not have a meaning in quite the way in which "block of ice" has a meaning. Indeed, other expressions could have been used to produce the same metaphorical predication. Thus,

(20) Miss Jones is a block of ice

or

(21) That girl over there in the corner is a block of ice

could have been uttered with the same metaphorical utterance meaning.

I conclude that, as general theories, both the object comparison view and the semantic interaction view are inadequate. If we were to diagnose their failure in Fregean terms, we might say that the comparison view tries to explain metaphor as a relation between references, and the interaction view tries to explain it as a relation between senses and beliefs associated with references. The proponents of the interaction view see correctly that the mental processes and the semantic processes involved in producing and understanding metaphorical utterances cannot involve references themselves, but must be at the level of intentionality, that is, they must involve relations at the level of beliefs, meanings, associations, and so on. However, they then say incorrectly that the relations in question must be some unexplained, but metaphorically described, relations of "interaction"[3] between a literal frame and a metaphorical focus.

Two final mistakes I wish to note are not cases of saying something false about metaphors but of saying something true which fails to distinguish metaphor from literal utterance. Thus it is sometimes said that the notion of similarity plays a crucial role in the analysis of metaphor, or that metaphorical utterances are dependent on the context for their interpretation. But, as we saw earlier, both of these features are true of literal utterances as well. An analysis of metaphor must show how similarity and context play a role in metaphor different from their role in literal utterance.

A FURTHER EXAMINATION OF THE COMPARISON THEORY

One way to work up to a theory of metaphor would be to examine the strengths and weaknesses of one of the existing theories. The obvious candidate for this role of stalking horse is a version of the comparison theory that goes back to Aristotle and can, indeed, probably be considered the common-sense view—the theory that says all metaphor is really literal simile with the "like" or "as" deleted and the respect of the similarity left unspecified. Thus, according to this view, the metaphorical utterance, "Man is a wolf," means "Man is like a wolf in certain unspecified ways"; the utterance, "You are my sunshine," means "You are like sunshine to me in certain respects," and "Sally is a block of ice," means "Sally is like a block of ice in certain but so far unspecified ways."

The principles on which metaphors function, then, according to this theory are the same as those for literal statements of similarity together with the principle of ellipsis. We understand the metaphor as a shortened version of the literal simile.[4] Since literal simile requires no special extralinguistic knowledge for its comprehension, most of the knowledge necessary for the comprehension of metaphor is already contained in the speaker's and hearer's semantic competence, together with the general background knowledge of the world that makes literal meaning comprehensible.

We have already seen certain defects of this view, most notably that metaphorical statements cannot be equivalent in meaning to literal statements of similarity because the truth conditions of the two sorts of statements are frequently different. Furthermore, we must emphasize that even as a theory of metaphorical comprehension—as opposed to a theory of metaphorical meaning—it is important for the simile theory that the alleged underlying similes be literal statements of similarity. If the simile statements which are supposed to explain metaphor are themselves metaphorical or otherwise figurative, our explanation will be circular.

Still, treated as theory of comprehension, there does seem to be a large number of cases where for the metaphorical utterance we can construct a simile sentence that does seem in some way to explain how its metaphorical meaning is comprehended. And, indeed, the fact that the specification of the values of R is left vague by the simile statement may, in fact, be an advantage of the theory, inasmuch as metaphorical utterances are often vague in precisely that way: it is not made *exactly* clear what the R is supposed to be when we say that S is P, meaning metaphorically that S is R. Thus, for example, in analyzing Romeo's metaphorical statement, "Juliet is the sun," Cavell (1976, pp. 78–79) gives as part of its explanation that Romeo means that his day begins with Juliet. Now, apart from the special context of the play, that reading would never occur to me. I would look for other properties of the sun to fill in the values of R in the formula. In saying this I am not objecting to either Shakespeare or Cavell, because the metaphor in question, like most metaphors, is open-ended in precisely that way.

Nonetheless, the simile theory, in spite of its attractiveness, has serious difficulties. First, the theory does more—or rather, less—than fail to tell us how to compute the value of R exactly: So far it fails to tell us how to compute it at all. That is, the theory still has almost no explanatory power, because the task of a theory of metaphor is to explain how the speaker and hearer are able to go from "S is P" to "S is R," and it does not explain that process to tell us that they go from "S to P" to "S is R" by first going through the stage "S is like P with respect to R" because we are not told how we are supposed to figure out which values to assign to R. Similarity is a vacuous predicate: any two things are similar in some respect or other. Saying that the metaphorical "S is P" implies the literal "S is like P" does not solve our problem. It only pushes it back a step. The problem of understanding literal similes with the respect of the similarity left unspecified is only a part of the problem of understanding metaphor. How are we supposed to know, for example, that the utterance, "Juliet is the sun," does not mean "Juliet is for the most part gaseous," or "Juliet is 90 million miles from the earth," both of which properties are salient and well-known features of the sun.

Yet another objection is this: It is crucial to the simile thesis that the simile be taken literally; yet there seem to be a great many metaphorical utterances where there is no relevant literal corresponding similarity between S and P. If we insist that there are always such similes, it looks as if we would have to interpret them metaphorically, and thus our account

would be circular. Consider our example (4), "Sally is a block of ice." If we were to enumerate quite literally the various distinctive qualities of blocks of ice, none of them would be true of Sally. Even if we were to throw in the various beliefs that people have about blocks of ice, they still would not be literally true of Sally. There simply is no class of predicates, R, such that Sally is literally like a block of ice with respect to R where R is what we intended to predicate metaphorically of Sally when we said she was a block of ice. Being unemotional is not a feature of blocks of ice because blocks of ice are not in that line of business at all, and if one wants to insist that blocks of ice are literally unresponsive, then we need only point out that that feature is still insufficient to explain the metaphorical utterance meaning of (4), because in that sense bonfires are "unresponsive" as well, but

(22) Sally is a bonfire

has a quite different metaphorical utterance meaning from (4). Furthermore, there are many similes that are not intended literally. For example, an utterance of "My love is like a red, red rose" does not mean that there is a class of literal predicates that are true both of my love and red, red roses and that express what the speaker was driving at when he said his love was like a red, red rose.

The defender of the simile thesis, however, need not give up so easily. He might say that many metaphors are also examples of other figures as well. Thus, "Sally is a block of ice" is not only an example of metaphor, but of hyperbole as well.[5] The metaphorical utterance meaning is indeed derived from the simile, "Sally is like a block of ice," but then both the metaphor and the simile are cases of *hyperbole;* they are exaggerations, and indeed, many metaphors are exaggerations. According to this reply, if we interpret both the metaphor and the simile hyperbolically, they are equivalent.

Furthermore, the defender of the simile thesis might add that it is not an objection to the simile account to say that some of the respects in which Sally is like a block of ice will be specified metaphorically, because for each of these metaphorical similes we can specify another underlying simile until eventually we reach the rock bottom of literal similes on which the whole edifice rests. Thus "Sally is a block of ice" means "Sally is like a block of ice," which means "She shares certain traits with a block of ice, in particular she is very cold." But since "cold" in "Sally is very cold" is also metaphorical, there must be an underlying similarity in which Sally's emotional state is like coldness, and when we finally specify these respects, the metaphor will be completely analyzed.

There are really two stages to this reply: First, it points out that other figures such as hyperbole sometimes combine with metaphor, and, secondly, it concedes that some of the similes that we can offer as translations of the metaphor are still metaphorical, but insists that some recursive procedure of analyzing metaphorical similes will eventually lead us to literal similes.

Is this reply really adequate? I think not. The trouble is that there do not seem to be any literal similarities between objects which are cold and people who are unemotional that would justify the view that when we say metaphorically that someone is cold what we mean is that he or she is unemotional. In what respects exactly are unemotional people like cold objects? Well, there are some things that one can say in answer to this, but they all leave us feeling somewhat dissatisfied.

We can say, for example, that when someone is physically cold it places severe restrictions on their emotions. But even if that is true, it is not what we meant by the metaphorical utterance. I think the only answer to the question, "What is the relation between cold things and unemotional people?" that would justify the use of "cold" as a metaphor for lack of emotion is simply that as a matter of perceptions, sensibilities, and linguistic practices, people find the notion of coldness associated in their minds with lack of emotion. The notion of being cold just is associated with being unemotional.

There is some evidence, incidentally, that this metaphor works across several different cultures: It is not confined to English speakers (cf. Asch, 1958). Moreover, it is even becoming, or has become, a dead metaphor. Some dictionaries (for example, the *Oxford English Dictionary*) list lack of emotion as one of the meanings of "cold." Temperature metaphors for emotional and personal traits are in fact quite common and they are not derived from any literal underlying similarities. Thus we speak of a "heated argument," "a warm welcome," "a lukewarm friendship," and "sexual frigidity." Such metaphors are fatal for the simile thesis, unless the defenders can produce a literal R which S and P have in common, and which is sufficient to explain the precise metaphorical meaning which is conveyed.

Because this point is bound to be contested, it is well to emphasize exactly what is at stake. In claiming that there are no sufficient similarities to explain utterance meaning, I am making a negative existential claim, and thus not one which is demonstrable from an examination of a finite number of instances. The onus is rather on the similarity theorist to state the similarities and show how they exhaust utterance meaning. But it is not at all easy to see how he could do that in a way that would satisfy the constraints of his own theory.

Of course, one can think of lots of ways in which any S is like any P, e.g., ways in which Sally is like a block of ice, and one can think of lots of F's and G's such that Sally's being F is like a block of ice's being G. But that is not enough. Such similarities as one can name do not exhaust utterance meaning and if there are others that do, they are certainly not obvious.

But suppose with some ingenuity one could think up a similarity that would exhaust utterance meaning. The very fact that it takes so much ingenuity to think it up makes it unlikely that it is the underlying principle of the metaphorical interpretation, inasmuch as the metaphor is obvious: There is no difficulty for any native speaker to explain what it means. In "Sam is a pig," both utterance meaning and similarities are obvious, but in "Sally is a block of ice," only the utterance meaning is obvious. The simpler hypothesis, then, is that this metaphor, like several others I shall now discuss, functions on principles other than similarity.

Once we start looking for them, this class of metaphors turns out to be quite large. For example, the numerous spatial metaphors for temporal duration are not based on literal similarities. In "time flies," or "the hours crawled by," what is it that time does and the hours did which is literally like flying or crawling? We are tempted to say they went rapidly or slowly respectively, but of course "went rapidly" and "went slowly" are further spatial metaphors. Similarly, taste metaphors for personal traits are not based on properties in common. We speak of a "sweet disposition" or a "bitter person," without implying that the sweet disposition and the bitter person have literal traits in common with sweet and bitter tastes which exhaust the utterance meaning of the metaphorical utterance. Of course, sweet dispositions and sweet things are both pleasant, but much more is conveyed by the metaphor than mere pleasantness.

So deeply embedded in our whole mode of sensibility are certain metaphorical associations that we tend to think there *must* be a similarity, or even that the association itself is a form of similarity. Thus, we feel inclined to say that the passage of time *just is like* spatial movement, but when we say this we forget that "passage" is only yet another spatial metaphor for time and that the bald assertion of similarity, with no specification of the respect of similarity, is without content.

The most sophisticated version of the simile thesis I have seen is by George Miller, and I shall digress briefly to consider some of its special features. Miller, like other simile theorists, believes that the meanings of metaphorical statements can be expressed as statements of similarity, but he offers a special kind of similarity statement (rather like one of Aristotle's formulations, by the way) as the form of "reconstruction" of metaphorical statements. According to Miller, metaphors of the form "*S* is *P*," where both *S* and *P* are noun phrases, are equivalent to sentences of the form

(23) $(\exists F)(\exists G) \{ \text{SIM} [F(S), G(P)] \}$.

Thus, for example, "Man is a wolf," according to Miller would be analyzed as

(24) There is some property F and some property G such that man's being F is similar to a wolf's being G.

And when we have metaphors where a verb or predicate adjective F is used metaphorically in a sentence of the form "*x* is *F*" or "*xF*'s," the analysis is of the form

(25) $(\exists G)(\exists y) \{ \text{SIM} [G(x), F(y)] \}$.

Thus, for example, "The problem is thorny" would be analyzed as

(26) There is some property G and some object y such that the problem's being G is similar to y's being thorny.

I believe this account has all the difficulties of the other simile theories—namely, it mistakenly supposes that the use of a metaphorical predicate commits the speaker to the existence of objects of which that predicate is literally true; it confuses the truth conditions of the metaphorical statement with the principles under which it is comprehended; it fails to tell us how to compute the values of the variables (Miller is aware of this problem, he calls it the problem of "interpretation" and sees it as different from the problem of "reconstruction"); and it is refuted by the fact that not all metaphors have literal statements of similarity underlying them. But it has some additional problems of its own. In my view, the most serious weakness of Miller's account is that according to it the semantic contents of most metaphorical utterances have too many predicates, and, in fact, rather few metaphors really satisfy the formal structure he provides us with. Consider, for example, "Man is a wolf." On what I believe is the most plausible version of the simile thesis, it means something of the form

(27) Man is like a wolf in certain respects R.

We could represent this as

(28) SIM_R (man, wolf).

The hearer is required to compute only one set of predicates, the values for R. But according to Miller's account, the hearer is required to compute no less than three sets of predicates. Inasmuch as similarity is a vacuous predicate, we need to be told in which respect two things are similar for the statement that they are similar to have any informative content. His formalization of the above metaphorical utterance is

(29) $(\exists F)(\exists G) \{ \text{SIM} [F(\text{man}), G(\text{wolf})] \}$.

In order to complete this formula in a way that would specify the respect of the similarity we would have to rewrite it as

(30) $(\exists F)(\exists G)(\exists H) \{ \text{SIM}_H [F(\text{man}), G(\text{wolf})] \}$.

But both the reformulation (30), and Miller's original (29), contain too many predicate variables: When I say, "Man is a wolf," I am not saying that there are some *different* sets of properties that men have from those that wolves have, I am saying they have the *same* set of properties (at least on a sympathetic construal of the simile thesis, that is what I am saying). But according to Miller's account, I am saying that man has one set of properties F, wolves have a different set of properties G, and man's having F is similar to wolves having G with respect to some other properties H. I argue that this "reconstruction" is (a) counterintuitive, (b) unmotivated, and (c) assigns an impossible computing task to the speaker and hearer. What are these F's, G's and H's supposed to be? and, How is the hearer supposed to figure them out? It is not surprising that his treatment of the interpretation problem is very sketchy. Similar objections apply to his accounts of other syntactical forms of metaphorical utterances.

There is a class of metaphors, that I shall call "relational metaphors," for which something like his analysis might be more appropriate. Thus, if I say

(8) The ship ploughed the sea

or

(31) Washington is the father of his country,

these might be interpreted using something like his forms. We might treat (8) as equivalent to

(32) There is some relation R which the ship has to the sea and which is similar to the relation that ploughs have to fields when they plough fields;

and (31) as

(33) There is some relation R which Washington has to his country and which is like the relation that fathers have to their offspring.

And (32) and (33) are fairly easily formalized *à la* Miller. However, even these analyses seem to me to concede too much of his approach: (8) makes no reference either implicitly or explicitly to fields and (31) makes no reference to offspring. On the simplest and most plausible version of the simile thesis (8) and (31) are equivalent to:

(34) The ship does something to the sea which is like ploughing

and

(35) Washington stands in a relation to his country which is like the relation of being a father.

And the hearer's task is simply to compute the intended relations in the two cases. By my account, which I shall develop in the next section, similarity does not, in general, function as part of the truth conditions either in Miller's manner or in the simpler version; rather, when it functions, it functions as a strategy for interpretation. Thus, very crudely, the way that similarity figures in the interpretation of (8) and (31) is given by

(36) The ship does something to the sea (to figure out what it is, find a relationship like ploughing)

and

(37) Washington stands in a certain relationship to his country (to figure out what it is, find a relationship like that of being a father).

But the hearer does not have to compute any respects in which these relations are similar, inasmuch as that is not what is being asserted. Rather, what is being asserted is that the ship is doing something to the sea and that Washington stands in a certain set of relations to his country, and the hearer is to figure out what it is that the ship does and what the relations are that Washington stands in by looking for relations similar to ploughing and being a father of.

To conclude this section: The problem of metaphor is either very difficult or very easy. If the simile theory were true, it would be very easy, because there would be no separate semantic category of *metaphors*—only a category of *elliptical utterances* where "like" or "as" had been deleted from the uttered sentence. But alas, the simile theory is not right, and the problem of metaphor remains very difficult. I hope our rather lengthy discussion of the simile theory has been illuminating in at least these respects. First, there are many metaphors in which there is no underlying literal similarity adequate to explain the metaphorical utterance meaning. Second, even where there is a correlated literal statement of similarity, the truth conditions, and hence the meaning of the metaphorical statement and the similarity statement, are not, in general, the same. Third, what we should salvage from the simile theory is a set of strategies for producing and understanding metaphorical utterances, using similarity. And fourth, even so construed, that is, construed as a theory of interpretation rather than of meaning, the simile theory does not tell us how to compute the respects of similarity or which similarities are metaphorically intended by the speaker.

THE PRINCIPLES OF METAPHORICAL INTERPRETATION

The time has now come to try to state the principles according to which metaphors are produced and understood. To reiterate, in its simplest form, the question we are trying to answer is, How is it possible for the speaker to say metaphorically "S is P" and mean "S is R," when P plainly does not mean R; furthermore, How is it possible for the hearer who hears the utterance "S is P" to know that the speaker means "S is R"? The short and uninformative answer is that the utterance of P calls to mind the meaning and, hence, truth conditions associated with R, in the special ways that metaphorical utterances have of calling other things to mind. But that answer remains uninformative until we know what are the principles according to which the utterance calls the metaphorical meaning to mind, and until we can state these principles in a way which does not rely on metaphorical expressions like "calls to mind." I believe that there is no single principle on which metaphor works.

The question, "How do metaphors work?" is a bit like the question, "How does one thing remind us of another thing?" There is no single answer to either question, though similarity obviously plays a major role in answering both. Two important differences between them are that metaphors are both restricted and systematic; restricted in the sense that not every way that one thing can remind us of something else will provide a basis for metaphor, and systematic in the sense that metaphors must be communicable from speaker to hearer in virtue of a shared system of principles.

Let us approach the problem from the hear-er's point of view. If we can figure out the principles according to which hearers understand metaphorical utterances, we shall be a long way toward understanding how it is possible for speakers to make metaphorical utterances, because for communication to be possible, speaker and hearer must share a common set of principles. Suppose a hearer hears an utterance such as, "Sally is a block of ice," or "Richard is a gorilla," or "Bill is a barn door." What are the steps he must go through in order to comprehend the metaphorical meaning of such utterances? Obviously an answer to that question need not specify a set of steps that he goes through consciously; instead it must provide a rational reconstruction of the inference patterns that underlie our ability to understand such metaphors. Furthermore, not all metaphors will be as simple as the cases we shall be discussing; nonetheless, a model designed to account for the simple cases should prove to be of more general application.

I believe that for the simple sorts of cases we have been discussing, the hearer must go through at least three sets of steps. First, he must have some strategy for determining whether or not he has to seek a metaphorical interpretation of the utterance in the first place. Secondly, when he has decided to look for a metaphorical interpretation, he must have some set of strategies, or principles, for computing possible values of R, and third, he must have a set of strategies, or principles, for restricting the range of R's—for deciding which R's are likely to be the ones the speaker is asserting of S.

Suppose he hears the utterance, "Sam is a pig." He knows that that cannot be literally true, that the utterance, if he tries to take it literally, is radically defective. And, indeed, such defectiveness is a feature of nearly all of the examples that we have considered so far. The defects which cue the hearer may be obvious falsehood, semantic nonsense, violations of the rules of speech acts, or violations of conversational principles of communication. This suggests a strategy that underlies the first step: *Where the utterance is defective if taken literally, look for an utterance meaning that differs from sentence meaning.*

This is not the only strategy on which a hearer can tell that an utterance probably has a metaphorical meaning, but it is by far the most common. (It is also common to the interpretation of poetry. If I hear a figure on a Grecian urn being addressed as a "still unravish'd bride of quietness," I know I had better look for alternative meanings.) But it is certainly not a necessary condition of a metaphorical utterance that it be in any way defective if construed literally. Disraeli might have said metaphorically

(5) (MET) I have climbed to the top of the greasy pole,

though he had in fact climbed to the top of a greasy pole. There are various other cues that we employ to spot metaphorical utterances. For example, when reading Romantic poets, we are on the lookout for metaphors, and some people we know are simply more prone to metaphorical utterances than others.

Once our hearer has established that he is to look for an alternative meaning, he has a number of principles by which he can compute possible values of R. I will give a list of these shortly, but one of them is this: *When you hear "S is P," to find possible values of* R *look for ways in which* S *might be like* P, *and to fill in the respect in which* S *might be like* P, *look for salient, well known, and distinctive feature[s] of* P *things.*

In this case the hearer might invoke his factual knowledge to come up with such features as that pigs are fat, gluttonous, slovenly, filthy, and so on. This indefinite range of features provides possible values of R. However, lots of other features of pigs are equally distinctive and well known, for example, pigs have a distinctive shape and distinctive bristles. So, in order to understand the utterance, the hearer needs to go through the third step where he restricts the range of possible R's. Here again the hearer may employ various strategies for doing that but the one that is most commonly used is this: *Go back to the* S *term and see which of the many candidates for the values of* R *are likely or even possible properties of* S.

Thus, if the hearer is told, "Sam's car is a pig," he will interpret that metaphor differently from the utterance, "Sam is a pig." The former, he might take to mean that Sam's car consumes gas the way pigs consume food, or that Sam's car is shaped like a pig. Though, in one sense, the metaphor is the same in the two cases, in each case it is restricted by the S term

in a different way. The hearer has to use his knowledge of S things and P things to know which of the possible values of R are plausible candidates for metaphorical predication.

Now, much of the dispute between the interaction theories and the object comparison theories derives from the fact that they can be construed as answers to different questions. The object comparison theories are best construed as attempts to answer the question of stage two: "How do we compute the possible values of R?" The interaction theories are best construed as answers to the question of stage three: "Given a range of possible values of R, how does the relationship between the S term and the P term restrict that range?" I think it is misleading to describe these relations as "interactions," but it seems correct to suppose that the S term must play a role in metaphors of the sort we have been considering. In order to show that the interaction theory was also an answer to the question of stage two, we would have to show that there are values of R that are specifiable, given S and P together, that are not specifiable given P alone; one would have to show that S does not *restrict* the range of R's but in fact, creates new R's. I do not believe that can be shown, but I shall mention some possibilities later.

I said that there was a variety of principles for computing R, given P—that is, a variety of principles according to which the utterance of P can call to mind the meaning R in ways that are peculiar to metaphor. I am sure I do not know all of the principles that do this, but here are several (not necessarily independent) for a start.

Principle 1

Things which are P are by definition R. Usually, if the metaphor works, R will be one of the salient defining characteristics of P. Thus, for example,

(38) (MET) Sam is a giant

will be taken to mean

(38) (PAR) Sam is big,

because giants are by definition big. That is what is special about them.

Principle 2

Things which are P are contingently R. Again, if the metaphor works, the property R should be a salient or well known property of P things.

(39) (MET) Sam is a pig

will be taken to mean

(39) (PAR) Sam is filthy, gluttonous, sloppy, and so on.

Both principles 1 and 2 correlate metaphorical utterances with literal similes, "Sam is like a giant," "Sam is like a pig," etc. Notice in connection with this principle and the next that small variations in the P term can create big differences in the R terms. Consider the differences between "Sam is a pig," "Sam is a hog," and "Sam is a swine."

Principle 3

Things which are P are often said or believed to be R, even though both speaker and hearer may know that R is false of P. Thus,

(7) (MET) Richard is a gorilla

can be uttered to mean

(7) (PAR) Richard is mean, nasty, prone to violence, and so on,

even though both speaker and hearer know that in fact gorillas are shy, timid, and sensitive creatures, but generations of gorilla mythology have set up associations that will enable the metaphor to work even though both speaker and hearer know these beliefs to be false.

Principle 4

Things which are P are not R, nor are they like R things, nor are they believed to be R, nonetheless it is a fact about our sensibility, whether culturally or naturally determined, that we just do perceive a connection, so that utterance of P is associated in our minds with R properties.

Thus,

(4) (MET) Sally is a block of ice

(40) (MET) I am in a black mood

(41) (MET) Mary is sweet

(42) (MET) John is bitter

(43) (MET) The hours $\left\{ \begin{array}{l} \text{crept} \\ \text{crawled} \\ \text{dragged} \\ \text{sped} \\ \text{whizzed} \end{array} \right\}$ by as we waited for the plane

are sentences that could be uttered to mean metaphorically that: Sally is unemotional; I am angry and depressed; Mary is gentle, kind, pleasant, and so on; John is resentful; and the hours seemed (of varying degrees of duration) as we waited for the plane; even though there are no literal similarities on which these metaphors are based. Notice that the associations tend to be scalar: degrees of temperature with ranges of emotion, degrees of speed with temporal duration, and so forth.

Principle 5

P things are not like R things, and are not believed to be like R things, nonetheless the condition of being P is like the condition of being R. Thus, I might say to someone who has just received a huge promotion

(44) You have become an aristocrat,

meaning not that he has personally become *like* an aristocrat, but that his new status or condition is like that of being an aristocrat.

Principle 6

There are cases where P and R are the same or similar in meaning, but where one, usually P, is restricted in its application, and does not literally apply to S. Thus, "addled" is only said literally of eggs, but we can metaphorically say

(45) This soufflé is addled

(46) That parliament was addled

and

(47) His brain is addled.

Principle 7

This is not a separate principle but a way of applying principles 1 through 6 to simple cases which are not of the form "S is P" but relational metaphors, and metaphors of other syntactical forms such as those involving verbs and predicate adjectives. Consider such relational metaphors as

(48) Sam devours books

(8) The ship ploughs the sea

(31) Washington was the father of his country.

In each case, we have a literal utterance of two noun phrases surrounding a metaphorical utterance of a relational term (it can be a transitive verb, as in (48) and (8) but it need not be, as in (31)). The hearer's task is not to go from "S is P" to "S is R" but to go from "S P-relation S'" to "S R-relation S'" and the latter task is formally rather different from the former because, for example, our similarity principles in the former case will enable him to find a property that S and P things have in common, namely, R. But in the latter, he cannot find a relation in common, instead he has to find a relation R which is different from relation P but similar to it in some respect. So, as applied to these cases, principle 1, for example, would read

P-relations are by definition *R*-relations.

For example, *ploughing* is by definition partly a matter of moving a substance to either side of a pointed object while the object moves forward; and though this definitional similarity between the *P*-relation and the *R*-relation would provide the principle that enables the hearer to infer the *R*-relation, the respect of similarity does not exhaust the context of the *R*-relation, as the similarity exhausts the content of the *R* term in the simplest of the "S is P" cases. In these cases, the hearer's job is to find a relation (or property) that is similar to, or otherwise associated with, the relation or property literally expressed by the metaphorical expression P; and the principles function to enable him to select that relation or property by giving him a respect in which the *P*-relation and the *R*-relation might be similar or otherwise associated.

Principle 8

According to my account of metaphor, it becomes a matter of terminology whether we want to construe metonymy and synecdoche as special cases of metaphor or as independent tropes. When one says, "S is P," and means that "S is R," P and R may be associated by such relations as the part–whole relation, the container–contained relation, or even the clothing and wearer relation. In each case, as in metaphor proper, the semantic content of the P term conveys the semantic content of the R term by some principle of association. Since the principles of metaphor are rather various anyway, I am inclined to treat metonymy and synecdoche as special cases of metaphor and add their principles to my list of metaphorical principles. I can, for example, refer to the British monarch as "the Crown," and the executive branch of the U.S. government as "the White House" by exploiting systematic principles of association. However, as I said, the claim that these are special cases of metaphor seems to me purely a matter of terminology, and if purists insist that the principles of metaphor be kept separate from those of metonymy and synecdoche, I can have no nontaxonomical objections.

In addition to these eight principles, one might wonder if there is a ninth. Are there cases where an association between P and R that did not previously exist can be created by the juxtaposition of S and P in the original sentence? This, I take it, is the thesis of the interaction theorists. However, I have never seen any convincing examples, nor any even halfway clear account, of what "interaction" is supposed to mean. Let us try to construct some examples. Consider the differences between

(49)
$$\text{Sam's voice is} \begin{Bmatrix} \text{mud} \\ \text{gravel} \\ \text{sandpaper} \end{Bmatrix}$$

and

(50) Kant's second argument for the transcendental

$$\text{deduction is so much} \begin{Bmatrix} \text{mud} \\ \text{gravel} \\ \text{sandpaper} \end{Bmatrix}$$

The second set clearly gives us different metaphorical meanings—different values for R—than the first trio, and one might argue that this is due not to the fact that the different S terms restrict the range of possible R's generated by the P terms, but to the fact that the different combinations of S and P create new R's. But that explanation seems implausible. The more plausible explanation is this. One has a set of associations with the P terms, "mud," "gravel," and "sandpaper." The principles of these associations are those of principles 1 through 7. The different S terms restrict the values of R differently, because different R's can be true of voices than can be true of arguments for transcendental deductions. Where is the interaction?

Because this section contains my account of metaphorical predication, it may be well to summarize its main points. Given that a speaker and a hearer have shared linguistic and factual knowledge sufficient to enable them to communicate literal utterance, the following principles are individually necessary and collectively sufficient to enable speaker and hearer to form and comprehend utterances of the form "S is P," where the speaker means metaphorically that S is R (where $P \neq R$).

First, there must be some shared strategies on the basis of which the hearer can recognize that the utterance is not intended literally. The most common, but not the only strategy, is based on the fact that the utterance is obviously defective if taken literally.

Second, there must be some shared principles that associate the P term (whether the meaning, the truth conditions, or the denotation if there is any) with a set of possible values of R. The heart of the problem of metaphor is to state these principles. I have tried to state several of them, but I feel confident that there must be more.

Third, there must be some shared strategies that enable the speaker and the hearer, given their knowledge of the S term (whether the meaning of the expression, or the nature of the referent, or both), to restrict the range of possible values of R to the actual value of R. The basic principle of this step is that only those possible values of R which determine possible properties of S can be actual values of R.

METAPHOR, IRONY, AND INDIRECT SPEECH ACTS

To conclude, I wish to compare briefly the principles on which metaphor works with those on which irony and indirect speech acts work. Consider first a case of irony. Suppose you have just broken a priceless K'ang Hsi vase and I say ironically, "That was a brilliant thing to do." Here, as in metaphor, the speaker's meaning and sentence meaning are different. What are the principles by which the hearer is able to infer that the speaker meant, "That was a stupid thing to do," when what he heard was the sentence, "That was a brilliant thing to do"? Stated very crudely, the mechanism by which irony works is that the utterance, if taken literally, is obviously inappropriate to the situation. Since it is grossly inappropriate, the hearer is compelled to reinterpret it in such a way as to render it appropriate, and the most natural way to interpret it is as meaning the *opposite* of its literal form.

I am not suggesting that this is by any means the whole story about irony. Cultures and subcultures vary enormously in the extent and degree of the linguistic and extralinguistic cues provided for ironical utterances. In English, in fact, there are certain characteristic intonational contours that go with ironical utterances. However, it is important to see that irony, like metaphor, does not require any conventions, extralinguistic or otherwise. The principles of conversation and the general rules for performing speech acts are sufficient to provide the basic principles of irony.

Now consider a case of an indirect speech act. Suppose that in the usual dinner-table situation, I say to you, "Can you pass the salt?" In this situation you will normally take that as meaning, "Please pass the salt." That is, you will take the question about your ability as a request to perform an action. What are the principles on which this inference works? There is a radical difference between indirect speech acts, on the one hand, and irony and metaphor, on the other. In the indirect speech act, the speaker means what he says. However, in addition, he means something more. Sentence meaning is part of utterance meaning, but it does not exhaust utterance meaning. In

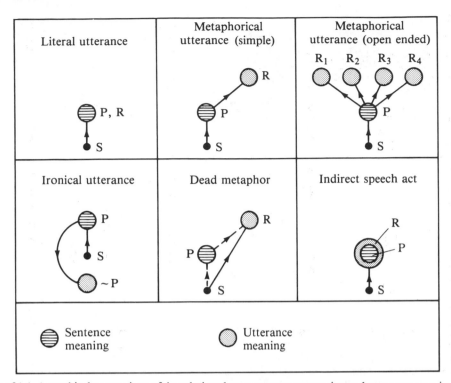

Figure 31.1 A graphical comparison of the relations between sentence meaning and utterance meaning where the sentence meaning is S is P and the utterance meaning is S is R, that is, where the speaker utters a sentence that means literally that the object S falls under the concept P, but where the speaker means by his utterance that the object S falls under the concept R.

a. *Literal Utterance.* A speaker says S is P and he means S is P. Thus the speaker places object S under the concept P, where P = R. Sentence meaning and utterance meaning coincide.

b. *Metaphorical Utterance (simple).* A speaker says S is P but means metaphorically that S is R. Utterance meaning is arrived at by going through literal sentence meaning.

c. *Metaphorical Utterance (open ended).* A speaker says S is P, but means metaphorically an indefinite range of meanings, S is R₁, S is R₂, etc. As in the simple case, utterance meaning is arrived at by going through literal meaning.

d. *Ironical Utterance.* A speaker means the opposite of what he says. Utterance meaning is arrived at by going through sentence meaning and then doubling back to the opposite of sentence meaning.

e. *Dead Metaphor.* The original sentence meaning is bypassed and the sentence acquires a new literal meaning identical with the former metaphorical utterance meaning. This is a shift from the metaphorical utterance (simple), *b* above, to the literal utterance, diagram *a*.

f. *Indirect Speech Act.* A speaker means what he says, but he means something more as well. Thus utterance meaning includes sentence meaning but extends beyond it.

a very simplified form (for a more detailed account, see Searle, 1975), the principles on which the inference works in this case are: First, the hearer must have some device for recognizing that the utterance might be an indirect speech act. This requirement is satisfied by the fact that in the context, a question about the hearer's ability lacks any conversational point. The hearer, therefore, is led to seek an alternative meaning. Second, since the hearer knows the rules of speech acts, he knows that the ability to pass the salt is a preparatory condition on the speech act of requesting him to do so. Therefore, he is able to infer that the question about his ability is likely to be a polite request to perform the act. The differences and similarities between literal utterances, metaphorical utterances, ironical utterances, and indirect speech acts are illustrated in Figure 31.1.

The question of whether all metaphorical utterances can be given a literal paraphrase is one that must have a trivial answer. Interpreted one way, the answer is trivially yes; interpreted another way, it is trivially no. If we interpret the question as, "Is it possible to find or to invent an expression that will exactly express the intended metaphorical meaning R, in the sense of the truth conditions of R, for any metaphorical utterance of 'S is P,' where what is meant is that S is R?" the answer to that question must surely be yes. It follows trivially from the Principle of Expressibility (see Searle, 1969) that any meaning whatever can be given an exact expression in the language.

If the question is interpreted as meaning, "Does every existing language provide us exact devices for expressing literally whatever we wish to express in any given metaphor?" then the answer is obviously no. It is often the case that we use metaphor precisely because there is no literal expression that expresses exactly what we mean. Furthermore, in metaphorical utterances, we do more than just state that S is R; as Figure 31.1 shows, we state that S is R by way of going through the meaning of "S is P." It is in this sense that we feel that

metaphors somehow are intrinsically not paraphrasable. They are not paraphrasable, because without using the metaphorical expression, we will not reproduce the semantic content which occurred in the hearer's comprehension of the utterance.

The best we can do in the paraphrase is reproduce the truth conditions of the metaphorical utterance, but the metaphorical utterance does more than just convey its truth conditions. It conveys its truth conditions by way of another semantic content, whose truth conditions are not part of the truth conditions of the utterance. The expressive power that we feel is part of good metaphors is largely a matter of two features. The hearer has to figure out what the speaker means—he has to contribute more to the communication than just passive uptake—and he has to do that by going through another and related semantic content from the one which is communicated. And that, I take it, is what Dr. Johnson meant when he said metaphor gives us two ideas for one.

ACKNOWLEDGMENTS

I am indebted to several people for helpful comments on earlier drafts of this article, and I especially want to thank Jerry Morgan, Andrew Ortony, Paul Rauber, and Dagmar Searle.

NOTES

1. It is essential to avoid any use–mention confusions when talking about these sets. Sometimes we will be talking about the words, other times about meanings, other times about references and denotations, and still other times about truth conditions.

2. I follow Beardsley (1962) in this classification.

3. Even in Black's clarification of interaction in terms of "implication-complexes" there still does not seem to be any precise statement of the principles on which interaction works. And the actual example he gives, "Marriage is a zero-sum game," looks distressingly like a comparison metaphor: "Marriage is *like* a zero-sum game in that it is an adversary relationship between two parties in which one side can benefit only at the expense of the other." It is hard to see what the talk about interaction is supposed to add to this analysis.

4. By "literal simile," I mean literal statements of similarity. It is arguable that one should confine "simile" to nonliteral comparisons, but that is not the usage I follow here.

5. Furthermore, it is at least arguable that "block of ice" functions metonymously in this example.

REFERENCES

Aristotle. (1952a). [*Rhetoric*]. Translated by W. R. Roberts. In W. D. Ross (ed.), *The Works of Aristotle*. Vol. 11: *Rhetorica, De rhetorica ad Alexandrum, Poetica*. Oxford: Clarendon Press.

Aristotle. (1952b). [*Poetics*]. Translated by I. Bywater. In W. D. Ross (ed.), *The Works of Aristotle*. Vol. 11: *Rhetorica, De rhetorica ad Alexandrum, Poetica*. Oxford: Clarendon Press.

Asch, S. E. (1958). "The Metaphor: A Psychological Inquiry." In R. Tagiuri and L. Petrullo (eds.), *Person Perception and Interpersonal Behavior*. Stanford, Calif.: Stanford University Press.

Beardsley, M. C. (1962). "The Metaphorical Twist." *Philosophy and Phenomenological Research* 22:293–307.

Black, M. (1962). "Metaphor." In M. Black (ed.), *Models and Metaphors*. Ithaca, N.Y.: Cornell University Press.

Cavell, S. (1976). *Must We Mean What We Say?* Cambridge: Cambridge University Press.

Henle, P. (ed.). (1965). *Language, Thought, and Culture*. Ann Arbor: University of Michigan Press.

Richards, I. A. (1936). *The Philosophy of Rhetoric*. London: Oxford University Press.

Searle, J. R. (1969). *Speech Acts*. Cambridge: Cambridge University Press.

Searle, J. R. (1975). "Indirect Speech Acts." In P. Cole and J. L. Morgan (eds.), *Syntax and Semantics*. Vol. 3: *Speech Acts*. New York: Academic Press. [Reprinted in this volume, Chapter 16]

Searle, J. R. (1978). "Literal Meaning." *Erkenntnis* 13:207–224.

32

Loose Talk

DAN SPERBER AND DEIRDRE WILSON

Literal talk, loose talk and metaphorical talk are often seen as different in kind. We want to argue that they differ not in kind but only in degree of looseness, and that they are understood in essentially the same way. The literature on literalness, looseness (or vagueness) and metaphor is vast; we will not attempt to review it here. Our discussion, which will be both brief and untechnical, is based on a view of human communication developed in greater detail in our book *Relevance: Communication and cognition* (Sperber and Wilson 1986).

I

The Issue

Suppose Mary believes that the car is in the garage and intends Peter to share this belief. One way she can fulfil her intention is by informing him of it: knowing her intention, he will have good reason for fulfilling it provided that he trusts her. One way she can inform Peter of her intention is by saying to him:

(1) The car is in the garage.

This utterance expresses just the proposition and propositional attitude that Mary intends Peter to share with her.

As it stands, this commonplace account leaves several questions unanswered. In particular, it does not explain why Peter should take utterance (1) as evidence that Mary has, and intends him to adopt, the propositional attitude expressed. One generally accepted answer is that there is a rule (or norm, or principle, or maxim, or convention, or presumption) of literal truthfulness whereby the utterer of a declarative sentence, in expressing a certain proposition, automatically vouches for its truth (similar rules of literal commitment can be formulated for non-declarative utterances). This accounts well enough for examples such as (1). It is tempting to go on to treat these examples as paradigmatic of verbal communication in general.

However, there are various exceptions to a hypothetical rule of literal truthfulness. Some exceptions (e.g., quotations) involve declarative sentences whose literal meaning is conveyed, but not asserted. We will not consider these today. Others involve a departure from literalness: the speaker is apparently vouching

Dan Sperber and Deirdre Wilson, "Loose Talk," *Proceedings of the Aristotelian Society* 86 (1985–86): 153–171.

for the truth of *some* proposition, but not for the truth of the proposition literally expressed. The most blatant exceptions of this second type are metaphors such as (2):

(2) *Mother to child:* You're a piglet.

The mother who says to her child that he is a piglet is certainly not committed to the literal truth of her utterance. She seems, rather, to be vouching for the truth of some proposition such as (3):

(3) He is a dirty child.

Metaphors, and tropes in general, are classically described as departures from a norm of literalness: a 'figurative meaning' such as (3) is said to be substituted for the literal meaning of (2). But, as romantic critics of classical rhetoric have pointed out, ordinary discourse is shot through with metaphors; if anything, it is a long stretch of strictly literal discourse that should be seen as a departure from a norm. The initial implausibility of any hypothetical rule of literal truthfulness might be overlooked if the appeal to such a rule had useful theoretical consequences; if it helped to explain how not only literal talk, but also loose talk and metaphor are understood. But in this respect, modern accounts are neither essentially different from, nor superior to, classical rhetorical accounts.

For instance, Grice's brief account of figurative language (Grice 1975:53; Grice 1978:123–125) is very much in the classical rhetorical tradition. He treats irony, metaphor, hyperbole and litotes as departures from a norm, the norm in this case being obedience to a 'maxim' of truthfulness. According to Grice, when a speaker says, or makes as if to say, something which would blatantly violate the maxim of truthfulness, the hearer will assume that the maxim is being observed on another level, and will try to recover as an implicature some related proposition which a speaker observing the maxims might have wanted to convey. For instance, in example (2)–(3) above, the child would infer from the fact that his mother could not have intended to assert truthfully and literally that he is a piglet, that she must have implicated the related proposition that he is a dirty child.

What is classically treated as a figurative meaning is thus reanalysed by Grice as an im-

plicature. Both approaches assume that when the literal interpretation is inappropriate, the appropriate figurative interpretation somehow comes to the hearer's mind. Both resort, implicitly or explicitly, to some form of associationist psychology: trains of thought are seen as guided by contiguity, part-whole relations, resemblance and antinomy. Such views are no longer considered adequate to account for other cognitive abilities, but are still called upon, for want of any alternative, when it comes to explaining what is evoked by a metonymy, a synecdoche, a metaphor, or an irony. No other explanation is given of how figurative interpretations are recovered. Grice's account merely adds an inferential step of confirmation to these mysteriously retrieved figurative interpretations. Yet by Grice's own criteria, an implicature should be not only confirmable, but also calculable.

Many modern pragmatic accounts, including Grice's, are vulnerable to another criticism raised by the romantics against classical rhetoricians. The romantics challenged the classical view, shared by many modern pragmatists, that any trope has a literal paraphrase which is cognitively synonymous. Against this, the romantics maintained that a felicitous trope cannot be paraphrased. Thus Coleridge argues that the 'infallible test of a blameless style' is:

its *untranslateableness* in words of the same language without injury to the meaning. Be it observed, however, that I include in the *meaning* of a word not only its correspondent object but likewise all the associations which it recalls. (Coleridge: *Biographia Literaria,* Ch. XXII)

In her modest way, the mother who calls her child a piglet achieves some unparaphrasable effects: for instance, she seems more indulgent than if she had called him a dirty child. More generally, utterances in which all the speaker wants to do is to inform the hearer of a simple fact are untypical of communication in general. Quite often, the speaker wants to communicate not a single atomic proposition, but a complex thought made up of many atomic thoughts, some of which are salient while others are not consciously spelled out in her mind. The speaker does not expect the hearer to entertain exactly the same complex thought. Rather, she intends him to entertain the proposition(s) most salient in her mind and to construct around it (or them) a complex thought which merely bears some similarity to her own. For instance, the mother wants the child to realise quite clearly that she thinks he is dirty, and to get at least an inkling of her accompanying thoughts. Some implicatures, we will claim, are strongly conveyed, others are weakly conveyed: implicatures come in varying degrees of strength.

The romantic critics were unquestionably right to draw attention to the richness and importance of those effects of figures of speech which are not maintained under paraphrase. These effects have merely been noted by classical rhetoricians and modern pragmatists alike; they have not been described, let alone explained, and have been treated without further discussion as cognitively negligible ornaments. But for all their justified criticisms and subtle observations, the romantics and their modern descendants have been content to talk about metaphor in metaphorical terms, and have proposed no explicit theory of their own; if anything, they have cast doubt on the very possibility of a non-metaphorical theory of metaphor by rejecting outright both the notion of a literal meaning—the 'proper meaning superstition' as I. A. Richards calls it—and the framework of truth-conditional semantics.

Our aim here is to give a brief sketch of a theory which differs from both the classical and romantic approaches and from their modern counterparts. Unlike romantic theorists, we will accept the idea that utterances express a literal truth-conditional meaning which is partly determined by the semantics of the sentence uttered; unlike classical theorists, we will challenge the idea that the speaker normally communicates the literal meaning of her utterance.

II

Resemblance

An utterance expresses a proposition. In consequence, it represents a state of affairs: the state of affairs which must obtain for the proposition expressed to be true. We would like to suggest, though, that utterances are not restricted to representing states of affairs. Any object in the world can, in principle, be used

to represent any other object that it resembles. For instance, a piece of rope can be used to represent a snake which it resembles in shape. An utterance can be used to represent another utterance which it resembles in meaning—either closely, as in the case of a paraphrase or translation, or more distantly, as in the case of a summary. Generally speaking, an utterance can be used to represent any representation which it resembles in content, whether a public representation such as another utterance, or a mental representation such as a thought.

To distinguish these two modes of representation—representation in virtue of truth-conditions and representation in virtue of resemblance—we will call the former *description,* and the latter *interpretation.* We will say that an utterance *descriptively* represents the state of affairs which makes the proposition it expresses true, and *interpretively* represents a representation which it resembles in content. While resemblance in general is a notoriously vague notion, we are only interested here in resemblance in content between representations, a relationship which we will call *interpretive resemblance* and which is easier to define.

In isolation, a proposition P (and, by extension, a representation with P as its content) has a number of analytic implications. However, propositions are entertained not in isolation but in a context of background assumptions. In a context {*C*}, a proposition P may have what we call *contextual implications.* A contextual implication of P in the context {*C*} is a proposition implied neither by {*C*} alone, nor by P alone, but by the union of {*C*} and P. We will say that two propositions P and Q (and, by extension, two representations with P and Q as their propositional content) interpretively resemble one another in a context {*C*} to the extent that they share their analytic and contextual implications in the context {*C*}.

We are thus defining interpretive resemblance as a context-dependent notion: two propositions P and Q may resemble one another closely in one context and less closely or not at all in another context. Let us briefly illustrate this with an artificially simple example. Consider:

(4) It is winter.

(5) It is freezing cold.

(6) (*a*) If it is winter, then it is cold.
    (*b*) If it is cold, then we should stay at home.

(7) (*a*) If it is winter, there are no flowers in the garden.
    (*b*) If it is freezing cold, we should heat the greenhouse.

(8) It is cold.

(9) We should stay at home.

By our definition, propositions (4) and (5) resemble one another more in context (6a–b) than in context (7a–b): in (6a–b) they share implication (8), which is contextually implied by (4) and analytically implied by (5), and implication (9), which is contextually implied by both; whereas in (7a–b), (4) and (5) share no implications at all. This seems to match our intuitions, insofar as intuitions are possible given the artificiality of the example.

Interpretive resemblance is a comparative notion with two extremes: no resemblance at all (i.e., no shared implications) at one end, and full propositional identity at the other. If two representations have the same propositional content, and hence share all their analytic implications, they also, of course, share all their contextual implications in every context. Let us say that when one representation is interpretively used to represent another, all of whose implications it shares, it is a *literal* interpretation of that other representation. On this account, literalness is just a limiting case of interpretive resemblance.

We began this section by suggesting that utterances can in principle represent something other than the states of affairs they describe. We now want to claim that they do. Every utterance used in verbal communication interpretively represents a thought entertained by the speaker—the very thought that the speaker wants to communicate. That much the hearer is entitled to expect; that much is necessary for verbal communication to be possible at all. However, the hearer is not invariably entitled to expect a literal interpretation of the speaker's thought, nor is such an interpretation always necessary for successful communication to take place. A less-than-literal interpretation of the speaker's thought may be good enough: may indeed be better on some occasions than a strictly literal one.

At this point, someone might raise the following objection. A rule of literal truthfulness at least explains how literal utterances are understood. Merely to assume that utterances interpret thoughts, without fixing the degree of resemblance required, may indeed put literal talk, loose talk, and metaphorical talk on a level, but it is a level on which all three are obscure. How is the hearer to assess the intended degree of resemblance? How is he to decide which of the implications of the utterance are shared with the speaker's thought, and which are not? This is, of course, a genuine problem. But before offering a solution, let us point out that it is one that already exists in the study of cognition in general, and of communication in particular.

A great many representations used by humans are representations in virtue of resemblance. Not all the properties of such a representation need, or generally even could, be shared by the original. For instance, when I draw you a diagram of how to get to my house, you do not infer that I intend you to travel across white paper, in two dimensions, past landmarks clearly labelled CHURCH and NEWSPAPER SHOP, a distance of 8 inches from door to door. You have to make some assumption about which properties of the representation carry over to the original. Or if I summarize in my own terms an article I have just read, you have to decide how close my summary is to the article, and in what respects.

So the problem of how intended resemblances are recognized is not an artifact of our approach. Any account of human communication will have to offer a solution to it. Since we believe we have a solution, we have no qualms about acknowledging the role of resemblance in communication.

III

Relevance

Human information processing requires some mental effort and achieves some cognitive effect. Some effort of attention, memory and reasoning is required. Some effect is achieved in terms of alterations to the individual's beliefs: the addition of new beliefs, the cancellation of old beliefs, or merely a change in his degree of confidence in old beliefs. We may characterise a comparative notion of *relevance* in terms of effect and effort as follows:

(10) (a) Other things being equal, the greater the cognitive effect achieved by the processing of a given piece of information, the greater its relevance for the individual who processes it.
(b) Other things being equal, the greater the effort involved in the processing of a given piece of information, the smaller its relevance for the individual who processes it.

We claim that humans automatically aim at maximal relevance, i.e. maximal cognitive effect for minimal processing effort. This is the single general factor which determines the course of human information processing. It determines which information is attended to, which background assumptions are retrieved from memory and used as context, which inferences are drawn. Subjectively, of course, it seems that it is particular interests, transient or long-term, which guide our thoughts and determine the relevance of new information. We claim that interests are simply by-products of the general search for relevance: as a result of our cognitive history, some topics in our memory are richer in information and, either temporarily or permanently, more accessible than others, so that information relating to them is likely to produce greater effect for less effort, i.e., be more relevant as defined.

To communicate is, among other things, to claim someone's attention, and hence to demand some expenditure of effort. People will not pay attention unless they expect to obtain information that is rich enough in effects to be relevant to them. Hence, to communicate is to imply that the stimulus used (e.g., the utterance) is worth the audience's attention. Any utterance addressed to someone automatically conveys a presumption of its own relevance. This fact, we call the *principle of relevance.*

The principle of relevance differs from every other principle, maxim, convention or presumption proposed in modern pragmatics in that it is not something that people have to know, let alone learn, in order to communicate effectively; it is not something that they obey or might disobey: it is an exceptionless generalization about human communicative behaviour. What people do have to know, and always do know when they recognize an utterance as addressed to them, is that the speaker intends that particular utterance to seem relevant enough to them to be worth their attention. At this moment, you know that we intend this paper to seem relevant to you. In other words, what people have to recognize is not the principle of relevance in its general form, but the particular instantiations of it that they encounter.

Speakers may try hard or not at all to be relevant to their audience; they may succeed or fail; they still convey a presumption of relevance: that is, they convey that they have done what was necessary to produce an adequately relevant utterance.

Relevance, we said, is a matter of cognitive effect and processing effort. On the effect side, it is in the interest of hearers that speakers offer the most relevant information they have. However, speakers have their own legitimate aims, and as a result may choose to offer some other information which is less than maximally relevant. Even so, to be worth the hearer's attention, this information must yield at least adequate effects, and the speaker manifestly intends the hearer to assume that this is so. On the effort side, there may be different ways of conveying the same information, all equally easy for the speaker to produce, but requiring different amounts of processing effort from the hearer. Here, the speaker manifestly intends the hearer to assume that the formulation chosen is the one that is easiest to process. In other words, the presumption of relevance has two parts: a presumption of adequate effect on the one hand, and a presumption of minimally necessary effort on the other.

As is well known, linguistic structure grossly underdetermines the interpretation of an utterance: the linguistic meaning is generally ambiguous, it may be elliptical or vague, it contains referential expressions with undetermined referents, the intended illocutionary force is often not fully specified, and implicatures are not linguistically encoded at all. There are still other sources of underdetermination: one is that the strictly literal interpretation need not be the one intended, and, if we are right, is not even a preferred interpretation.

Various pragmatic theories appeal to complex sets of rules, maxims, or conventions to explain how this linguistic underdetermination is contextually overcome. We claim that the principle of relevance is enough on its own to explain how linguistic structure and background knowledge interact to determine verbal comprehension.

In a nutshell, for an utterance to be understood, it must have one and only one interpretation consistent with the fact that the speaker intended it to seem relevant to the hearer—adequately relevant on the effect side and maximally relevant on the effort side. We will say that in this case the interpretation is *consistent with the principle of relevance,* meaning consistent with the particular instantiation of the principle. The speaker's task is to make sure that the thought she intends to convey is consistent with the principle of relevance; otherwise, she runs the risk of not being properly understood. The hearer's task is to find the interpretation which is consistent with the principle of relevance; otherwise, he runs the risk of misunderstanding the utterance or not understanding it at all. In our book and several articles (see, for example, Sperber and Wilson 1981, 1982; Wilson and Sperber 1985, forthcoming), we have illustrated how this criterion of consistency with the principle of relevance works for various aspects of linguistic underdetermination. Here, we will show how it works to determine the intended resemblance between the utterance and the thought it is used to communicate.

IV

Loose Talk

Loose talk is appropriate in the following, quite ordinary circumstances. The speaker wants to communicate to her hearer a certain set of propositions $P_1 \ldots P_n$. They are all quite easily derivable as logical or contextual implications of a proposition Q whose truth she does not believe and does not want to guarantee. The best way of conveying this information may be to express the single proposition Q, as long as the hearer has some way of selecting those of its logical and contextual implications that the speaker intends to convey, and ignoring the others.

Our claim is that such a selection process is always at work: is part of the process by which

every utterance is understood. Whenever a proposition is expressed, the hearer takes for granted that some subset of its logical and contextual implications are also logical or contextual implications of the thought being communicated, and aims to identify this subset. He assumes (or at least assumes that the speaker assumed) that this subset will have enough cognitive effects to make the utterance worth his attention. He also assumes (or at least assumes that the speaker assumed) that there was no obvious way of achieving these effects with less processing effort. He aims for an interpretation consistent with these assumptions, i.e., consistent with the principle of relevance. When this criterion selects a single interpretation (or closely similar interpretations with no significant differences between them), communication succeeds.

Suppose Marie lives in Issy-les-Moulineaux, a block away from the city limits of Paris. At a party in London, she meets Peter. He asks her where she lives, and she answers:

(11) I live in Paris.

Marie's answer is literally false, but in ordinary circumstances it is not misleading. Peter will be able to infer from it a substantial amount of true or plausible information: that Marie spends most of her time in the Paris area, that she knows Paris, that she lives an urban life, that he might try to meet her on his next trip to Paris, and so on. It is such implications which make Marie's utterance relevant enough to be worth his attention, in a way Marie manifestly might have foreseen; moreover, there was no obviously more economical way of conveying these implications. Hence, Peter is entitled to assume that Marie intended him to interpret her utterance in this way, which is consistent with the principle of relevance.

Peter would be misled by Marie's answer only if he were to conclude from it that she lives within the city limits of Paris rather than in a suburb. However, it is clear that Marie had no reason to think that Peter would have to derive such a conclusion in order to establish the relevance of her utterance. Therefore her utterance does not warrant it.

Suppose, now, that Marie had answered instead:

(12) I live near Paris.

This time her answer is literally true, but it might well be misleading. The qualification '*near* Paris' demands some processing effort, which, given the presumption of relevance, should be offset by some cognitive effect. Peter might thus infer from this answer that Marie probably has to travel, say by suburban transport, to get to Paris, that she lives a suburban life and so on, which is not the case. In other words, it is not just that Marie's first answer, 'I live in Paris', is effective enough to convey just what she wants; it may be more effective than the literally true second answer, 'I live near Paris'.

There will be cases where the subset of implications selected by the criterion of consistency with the principle of relevance will include the proposition actually expressed. Suppose Marie is asked where she lives, not at a party in London, but at an electoral meeting for a Paris local election. If she answers that she lives in Paris, the proposition expressed will itself be crucially relevant; hence the utterance will be understood literally, and Marie will have lied.

Our approach handles loose uses without abandoning truth-conditional semantics. If we are right, loose uses are non-literal uses in the sense described above: they are based on resemblance relations among representations, and involve interpretive rather than descriptive dimensions of language use. When a proposition or concept is loosely understood, it is not (or at least it need not be) that it is a vague concept or proposition; it is not that a guarantee of approximate truth is given to the proposition expressed: no guarantee of truth is given to this proposition at all. Instead, certain of its logical and contextual implications are taken to be accompanied by regular guarantees of truth, whereas others are simply ignored. Thus the truth-conditional relation between propositions and the states of affairs they represent remains unaltered: what varies is how closely the proposition expressed is taken to represent the speaker's thought.

We would like to suggest that much of the attraction of appeals to fuzzy concepts is that they seem to offer an account of data at least some of which might be better handled along the lines just described. The issue is whether we have well-defined classificatory concepts such that every object either does or does not fall under them, or whether our concepts are inherently fuzzy or open-ended, with no well-defined satisfaction conditions or clear boundaries between them. Does it make sense, for example, to ask whether a certain drinking vessel that seems to fall midway between being a cup and a mug is *really* a cup or a mug, or are these concepts fuzzy in such a way that either can accommodate our vessel as a marginal case, low, so to speak, in cuppiness or mugginess?

Once the interpretive dimension of language use is taken into account, it is possible to suggest a rather different solution. In at least some cases, what is analysed as a literal use of a fuzzy concept might instead be analysed as a loose use of a classificatory concept, the looseness being motivated by the pursuit of relevance. In the above case, 'cup' and 'mug' may well have clear-cut boundaries and still be used loosely to refer to an object which falls outside these boundaries.[1]

This approach, incidentally, suggests a solution to the so-called baldness paradox. One is led into this paradox by agreeing, first, that a man with no hair is bald, next, that if a man with no hair is bald then a man with one hair is bald, and then, via the general principle that if a man with n hairs is bald then a man with n + 1 hairs is bald, to the conclusion that a man with a full head of hair is bald. One way of avoiding this paradox is to treat *bald* as a classificatory concept with a necessary and sufficient condition: having no hair. Thus, to describe a man with one hair as bald is strictly speaking false, though of course perfectly appropriate as a loose use: virtually every conclusion that would be drawn from the fact that he was bald would apply to someone with only a single hair, and in most circumstances calling such person not bald, though literally true, would be grossly misleading. The same is true of somebody with very little hair. However, there comes a degree of looseness where not enough implications of calling someone bald are maintained. The point at which looseness becomes unacceptable varies with the context and is therefore not well defined in the abstract. On this approach, the claim that a man with one hair is bald is just as false as the claim that a man with a full head of hair is bald. What distinguishes them is not the fact that one is true and the other false, but the fact that one is an acceptable loose use because many of its logical and contextual implications are true, whereas the other is unacceptable since a hearer would be able to derive from it virtually no true descriptive information about the state of affairs it purports to represent.

V

Metaphor

We want to claim that there is no discontinuity between loose uses and the most characteristic cases of poetic metaphor. In both instances the proposition expressed departs from full literalness. In both instances, however, the hearer must assume that the speaker is prepared to endorse some subset of the logical and contextual implications of the proposition expressed. In this way, information will be assertively conveyed by expressing a proposition which itself receives no guarantee of truth.

There is no discontinuity either between metaphor and a variety of other figures such as hyperbole, synecdoche or metonymy. Some of these provide intermediate cases between ordinary loose talk and typical metaphors. Consider an example of hyperbole. The speaker expresses the proposition in (13) and communicates a belief not in this proposition but in the weaker (14):

(13) Bill is the nicest person there is.

(14) Bill is a very nice person.

How can this be? Let us assume that by expressing (14) directly the speaker would not exhaust her thoughts about Bill: its contextual implications would fall short of what she wants to convey. Nor is there any obvious combination of adverbs and adjectives that would exactly express her thoughts. Perhaps they are too vague: there are a lot of aspects of Bill's niceness that she is not thinking about with equal clarity at the time, and to access these thoughts and make them more precise would involve more work than she is prepared to do. By expressing (13), she can be sure that all the propositions which make up the thought she does want to convey are among its contextual implications. Perhaps (13) has other contextual implications which she does

not want to endorse. As long as she can rely on the hearer to ignore them, (13) will be a much more adequate representation of her thought than the weaker (14).

What exactly does (13) convey? The speaker is certainly guaranteeing the truth of (14), which is thus a strong implicature of (13). However, if this were all she had wanted to convey, she could have saved the hearer some processing effort by expressing (14) directly. The greater effort imposed indicates that greater effect is intended. By uttering (13), the speaker thus encourages the hearer to look for a range of further contextual implications not shared by (14), and to assume that within this range there are some that she is prepared to endorse. He might conclude that the speaker finds Bill nicer than any of their common acquaintances; he might conclude that Bill has behaved in ways which show extraordinary niceness, and so on. Unlike (14), which is strongly implicated by (13), these further conclusions are only weakly implicated. That is, the hearer is encouraged to derive them, he can find some degree of confirmation for them in the utterance; however, this degree of confirmation may not be enough by itself and he must share the responsibility for deriving them. Thus (13) conveys a range of propositions, some, such as (14), very strongly and distinctly, others less so: a range of propositions which should closely resemble the complex thought that the speaker intended to share with the hearer. Conveying such a range of partly weak, partly strong implicatures is typical of the better-known figures of speech.

Metaphors vary in their degree of creativity. At one extreme are highly standardized examples such as (15):

(15) Jeremy is a lion.

Typically, such examples have one very strong implicature which constitutes the main point of the utterance: thus (15) implicates, in the context of stereotypical assumptions about lions, that Jeremy is brave. The fact that such metaphors are so regularly used with the same clearly defined implicature makes them relatively cheap to process, which in turn compensates for their relative poverty of content as compared to genuine creative metaphors. Nonetheless, they must suggest *some* further line of thought if their relative indirectness and its extra processing cost is to be justified. The speaker must be taken to have had in mind, however, dimly, something more than Jeremy's bravery; and the hearer is encouraged to explore other contextual implications of (15), having to do, say, with the type of bravery Jeremy exhibits, or with his physical appearance. Thus even these highly standardized examples cannot be paraphrased without loss.

Our example (2) was that of a marginally more creative metaphor:

(2) *Mother to child:* You're a piglet.

While calling somebody a pig is quite standard, calling a child a piglet requires some extra processing effort, which should be offset by added effect. For instance, young animals are endearing, even when the adults of the species are not; so the child may feel encouraged to derive not only the obvious contextual implication that he is dirty, but also the further contextual implication that he is, nevertheless, endearing.

The most creative metaphors require of the hearer a greater effort in building an appropriate context, and deriving a wide range of implications. In general, the wider the range of potential implicatures and the greater the hearer's responsibility for constructing them, the more creative the metaphor. In the richest and most successful cases, the hearer can go beyond just exploring the immediate context and the background knowledge directly invoked, accessing a wider area of knowledge, entertaining ad hoc assumptions which may themselves be metaphorical, and getting more and more very weak implicatures, with suggestions for still further processing. The result is a quite complex picture, for which the hearer has to take a large share of the responsibility, but the discovery of which has been triggered by the speaker. The surprise or beauty of a successful creative metaphor lies in this extreme condensation, in the fact that a single expression which has itself been loosely used will determine a very wide range of acceptable weak implicatures.

For example, take Prospero's words to his daughter Miranda:

The fringed curtains of thine eyes advance
And say what thou see'st yond.

> (Shakespeare: *The Tempest* I ii)

Coleridge argues, against Pope and Arbuthnot, that these words should not be taken as equivalent in meaning to 'Look what is coming yonder'. They are uniquely appropriate to the characters and situation:

Prospero sees Ferdinand and wishes to point him out to his daughter not only with great but with scenic solemnity . . . Something was to appear to Miranda on the sudden, and as unexpectedly as if the hearer of a drama were to be on the stage at the instant when the curtain is elevated . . . Turning from the sight of Ferdinand to his thoughtful daughter, his attention was first struck by the downcast appearance of her eyes and eyelids . . . (Coleridge: Notes on *The Tempest*)

Coleridge's comments are indeed illuminating, but they invite an objection and a question. The objection is that it is possible to appreciate Shakespeare's metaphor without understanding it exactly as Coleridge does. The question is how such an understanding is arrived at.

Our answer to the question also takes account of the objection. To understand Prospero's metaphor, the hearer must construct a context which will involve, on the one hand, his knowledge of the appearance of eyelids, and, on the other hand, his knowledge of curtains, and theatre curtains in particular. Merely retaining the implication that Prospero is telling Miranda to raise her eyelids—no doubt the strongest implicature—would result in an interpretation requiring too much effort for too little effect. A more creative hearer will invest a little more effort and get much more effect. This extra effort may consist in creating a metaphor of his own—for instance Coleridge's metaphor of the hearer of a drama being brought on stage—and adopting some of the joint implications of Prospero's metaphor and his. In such a process, the hearer is taking a large share of the responsibility for the conclusions he arrives at. As a result, different hearers with different background knowledge and different imaginations will follow somewhat different routes. However, they are all encouraged and guided by the text, and they all proceed by exploring its analytic and contextual implications as relevantly as they can.

In conclusion, let us consider how this approach to metaphor compares with the classical and romantic accounts. In many ways, we are on the romantic side. If we are right, metaphors are based on fundamental psychological mechanisms which are both natural and universal. They are in no sense departures from a norm or breaches of a rule or maxim of communication. They are simply creative and evocative exploitations of a basic feature of all verbal communication: the fact that every utterance resembles, with a degree of closeness determined by considerations of relevance, a thought of the speaker's.

We also reject the classical claim that tropes in general, and metaphor in particular, have a purely decorative function. For us, as for the romantics, metaphor has a genuine cognitive content which, particularly with the more creative metaphors, is not paraphrasable without loss. This content we have proposed to analyse in terms of an indefinite array of weak implicatures whose recovery is triggered by the speaker, but whose content the hearer actively helps to determine.

Despite our general sympathy with the romantic view of metaphor, we differ sharply from the romantics on the nature of language and logic. We have tried to show that the existence of loose uses does not mean that language is irremediably fuzzy, and that the fact that language use is shot through with metaphor does not make metaphor an aspect of word and sentence meaning. Our aim has been to reconcile the view that looseness and metaphor belong to the most basic level of language use with a truth-conditional view of semantics.

Our main claim has been that hearers generally approach utterances without fixed expectations as to their literalness, looseness or metaphorical nature. They merely expect there to be an interpretative resemblance between the proposition expressed by the utterance and the thought that the speaker intends to convey. This expectation itself derives from, and is warranted by, a more basic expectation: an expectation of relevance. Such an expectation of relevance is automatically encouraged by any act of communication. This fact—the principle of relevance—is enough to explain how contextual information can be brought to bear on a linguistically underdetermined utterance, underdetermined in particular as regards its degree of literalness or looseness, and uniquely determine its interpretation.

NOTE

1. There are, however, independent reasons for thinking that not all utterances are fully truth-conditional.

REFERENCES

Grice, H. P. (1975). "Logic and Conversation." In P. Cole and J. Morgan (eds.), *Syntax and Semantics.* Vol. 3: *Speech Acts.* New York: Academic Press, 41–58. [Reprinted in this volume, Chapter 19]

Grice, H. P. (1978). "Further Notes on Logic and Conversation." In P. Cole (ed.), *Syntax and Semantics.* Vol. 9: *Pragmatics.* New York: Academic Press, 113–128.

Sperber, D., and D. Wilson (1981). "Irony and the Use–Mention Distinction." In P. Cole (ed.), *Syntax and Semantics.* Vol. 9: *Pragmatics.* New York: Academic Press, 295–318. [Reprinted in this volume, Chapter 33]

Sperber, D., and D. Wilson (1982). "Mutual Knowledge and Relevance in Theories of Comprehension." In N. V. Smith (ed.), *Mutual Knowledge.* London: Academic Press, 61–131.

Sperber, D., and D. Wilson (1986). *Relevance: Communication and Cognition.* Oxford: Basil Blackwell; Cambridge, Mass.: Harvard University Press.

Wilson, D., and D. Sperber (1985). "On Choosing the Context for Utterance Interpretation." In J. Allwood and E. Hjelmquist (eds.), *Foregrounding Background.* Lund: Doxa, 51–64.

Wilson, D., and D. Sperber (1986). "Inference and Implicature." In C. Travis (ed.), *Meaning and Interpretation.* Oxford: Basil Blackwell 45–75. [Reprinted in this volume, Chapter 22]

33

Irony and the Use–Mention Distinction

DAN SPERBER AND DEIRDRE WILSON

1. INTRODUCTION

An ironical utterance is traditionally analyzed as literally saying one thing and figuratively meaning the opposite. Thus the ironical remark *What lovely weather* would have the figurative meaning "What awful weather," and so on.[1] An explicit semantic theory designed to incorporate such an account would have to provide, first, a definition of figurative meaning; second, a mechanism for deriving the figurative meaning of a sentence; and third, some basis for explaining why figurative utterances exist: why a speaker should prefer the ironical utterance *What lovely weather* to its literal counterpart *What awful weather* which, on this analysis, means exactly the same thing. It is because they provide no answers to such questions that traditional semantic accounts of irony ultimately fail.

At first sight, Grice's (1975, 1978) pragmatic approach to irony looks more promising than the traditional semantic approach. Grice attempts to reanalyze the notion of figurative meaning in terms of his independently motivated category of conversational implicature. Thus, for Grice, ironical utterances

would conversationally implicate, rather than figuratively mean, the opposite of what they literally say: *What lovely weather* would have no figurative meaning, but would conversationally implicate that the weather was awful. Grice's proposal would relieve semantic theory of the problems of defining figurative meaning and deriving the figurative meaning of an utterance. However, these problems are not solved simply by transferring them from the semantic to the pragmatic domain. It still has to be shown how the interpretation of ironical utterances can be successfully integrated into Grice's pragmatic framework. In this chapter we shall argue that it cannot, and that existing pragmatic accounts of irony are as seriously defective as earlier semantic accounts.

Grice's departure from the traditional account of irony is not a radical one. It is based on the same assumption—the assumption that what the speaker of an ironical utterance intends to get across is the opposite of what he has literally said. In fact the only disagreement between Grice and more traditional theorists is over whether the substitution mechanisms involved are semantic or pragmatic. Grice's

Dan Sperber and Deirdre Wilson, "Irony and the Use–Mention Distinction." In *Radical Pragmatics,* edited by P. Cole, 295–318. Copyright © 1981 by Academic Press, Inc. Reprinted by permission of the publisher.

account, like the traditional one, fails to explain why an ironical utterance should ever be preferred to its literal counterpart: why someone should choose to say *What lovely weather* rather than the more transparent *What awful weather*. As will be seen, it also fails to make explicit exactly how the move from literal meaning to conversational implicature is made in the case of irony. Finally, it fails to show that the "conversational implicatures" involved in irony are of the same type as the more standard cases of conversational implicature to which they are supposed to be assimilated. For these reasons, Grice's purely pragmatic account of irony also fails.

In this chapter, we offer an account of irony that goes some way toward solving the problem raised by both traditional semantic and pragmatic approaches. In particular, it explains why ironical utterances are made, and why they occasionally (but not always) implicate the opposite of what they literally say. Unlike the traditional theory, it makes no reference to the notion of figurative meaning. Unlike both the traditional theory and Grice's account, it involves no substitution mechanism, whether semantic or pragmatic. Unlike Grice's theory, it assumes that there is a necessary (though not sufficient) semantic condition for an utterance to be ironical. Furthermore, the crucial fact that ironical utterances convey not only propositions (which can be accounted for in terms of meaning and implicature), but also vaguer suggestions of images and attitudes, finds a natural description in the framework we propose.

2. SOME METHODOLOGICAL PRELIMINARIES

There are a number of obvious similarities between linguistics and the study of rhetoric. Rhetorical judgments, like linguistic judgments, are ultimately based on intuition; rhetoric, like linguistics, is a branch of cognitive psychology. It is well known that linguistic judgments may be affected by explicit teaching or conscious theorizing; the same is true of rhetorical judgments, only much more so, because many rhetorical categories such as "metaphor," "figurative," or "irony" are part of everyday speech. Because of this, informant

work in rhetoric must be approached with a certain amount of methodological caution.

For example, suppose we ask an informant whether (1) or (2) could be ironical when said by someone caught in a downpour:

(1) *What lovely weather.*

(2) *It seems to be raining.*

Anyone who has been taught the traditional definition of irony, that ironical utterances say one thing and mean the opposite, will naturally say that (1), but not (2), is ironical. He will say this even though he may notice that both (1) and (2) could be said in the same (wry) tone of voice which a naive informant would precisely call ironical. Given enough responses of this type, we might well take the traditional definition of irony as being strongly confirmed; however, this would be a mistake, since it is the definition itself that is directly responsible for the judgments which "confirm" it.

The best way of avoiding these pitfalls is to ask questions that have no stereotyped response. The ultimate goal is to find intuitive relationships among the data, intuitive ways of grouping them, which do not simply reflect conscious, explicitly defined categories. This is not because stereotyped responses or conscious categories are uninteresting, but because they only provide insight into cultural peculiarities or idiosyncrasies. A GENERAL theory of rhetoric should be concerned with basic psychological and interpretative mechanisms which remain invariant from culture to culture.

There is another, closely related point. The traditional study of rhetoric, which dates back 2000 years, offers a rich and subtle set of analytical concepts. These concepts are interesting in themselves; it is possible that some of them will have a necessary role to play in any future theory of rhetoric. However, it would be a mistake to prejudge the issue. It should not be taken for granted that even the major rhetorical categories, such as alliteration, ellipsis, hyperbole, metaphor, metonymy, irony, and so on, correspond to genuine natural classes of facts, playing clearly defined and distinguishable roles in speech production and perception. It is possible that the whole idea of tropes and their classification is destined to go the same way as the notion of humors in medicine; it is possible that verbal irony and its associated attitude have about as much claim on our attention as black bile and the atrabilious temperament.

The notion of irony is an abstract one, based on a rather arbitrary range of examples which have themselves been rather inadequately described. Because of this, it seems to us to be a mistake to take IRONY itself as the object of investigation, and to limit one's attention to its more standard cases. There is a whole range of utterance-types that can be more or less loosely called ironical. The basic facts to be accounted for are the particular effects produced by particular utterances, and the perceived similarities among them. We should be looking for psychological mechanisms that can account for these effects and their interrelationships. When we have found some, it might be interesting to make some comparisons between the resulting (provisional) conceptual scheme and the framework of classical rhetoric, to see which notion of irony emerges, if any; but the existence of a unified category of irony should not be taken for granted.

Quite independently of the existence of irony, there are already strong grounds for rejecting the notion of figurative meaning itself. For example, consider the treatment of disambiguation, which is a major problem for any pragmatic theory. Every hearer (or reader) almost instantaneously disambiguates each of the utterances he hears. Even if we ignore figurative meanings, and consider only the literal senses of an utterance, narrowly defined, almost every utterance is ambiguous. In fact, almost every utterance is multiply ambiguous, with possible semantic interactions among its individual ambiguous constructions. Most utterances also contain referential expressions which may have a wide range of possible referents, even when the shared knowledge of speaker and hearer is taken into account. It is thus quite typical for an utterance to have dozens, or even hundreds, of possible propositional interpretations. However, speaker and hearer are normally able to select a single one of these interpretations without even realizing that they have made a choice. It is generally agreed that this choice is a function of the context; but to define the function, as opposed to simply claiming that it exists, is no easy task.

As long as we only have to choose among the literal senses of an utterance, the task is still an approachable one; the set of possible interpretations remains finite, and will be specifiable on the basis of a fairly restricted range of semantic and referential variables. One can think of several types of explicit procedures that could be used to eliminate all but one of the possible interpretations. The difficulty lies not so much in conceiving of such a procedure in principle, as in choosing and justifying the right one. On the other hand, suppose that we have to take into account not only the literal senses of an utterance, but also the whole range of figurative senses that are loosely based on them via relations of resemblance, contiguity, inclusion or inversion; in this case, the set of possible interpretations becomes to all intents and purposes nonenumerable. And if this is so, it is hard to see how one could even set about giving an account of disambiguation, which is not, we repeat, a rare and marginal phenomenon, but a basic factor in the interpretation of every utterance.

Thus the notion of figurative meaning, whatever its value for the analysis of figures of speech, becomes a real source of difficulty as soon as we look at other aspects of the interpretation of utterances. The question is whether these difficulties are caused by the complexity of the data—which cannot be ignored—or whether they result from some inadequacy in the concepts being used to analyze them.

Obviously, a speaker may sometimes intend to convey something other than one of the literal senses of his utterance. When he wants to convey something IN ADDITION TO one of the literal senses, the notion of conversational implicature is relevant. This presents no problem for a theory of disambiguation; on the contrary, it has a role to play in such a theory. If figurative meaning could be analyzed in terms of conversational implicature, as Grice has proposed, disambiguation would be fairly straightforward. However, in the case of figurative language, the speaker normally intends to convey something INSTEAD OF one of the literal senses of his utterance; the implicature has to be seen as SUBSTITUTING FOR the literal sense. The idea that an implicature could actually contradict the literal sense of an utterance—as it would in the case of irony—does not square with Grice's central claim that implicatures act as premises in an argument designed to establish that the speaker has observed the maxims of conversation in saying what he said. It follows that the interpretation of ironical utterances cannot be reduced to the search for conversational implicatures without grossly distorting the notion of implicature itself. Grice does not succeed in integrating figurative interpretations into his overall pragmatic theory.[2]

This being so, if the substitution theory of irony is correct, some notion of figurative meaning seems called for, and the problems it gives rise to seem to be forced on us by the data themselves. However, if it were possible to give just as good an account of the data, but without any appeal to the notion of figurative meaning, and using only independently motivated concepts (literal sense, implicature, etc.), it is clear that this would be preferable to the traditional account. An approach along these lines has already been suggested for the cases of metaphor, synecdoche and metonymy in Sperber (1975b); in this chapter we attempt to extend the analysis to irony. The problem will be taken up in more detail in Sperber and Wilson (1979).

3. SOME BASIC DATA

Consider the utterances in (1) and (2) (repeated here for convenience) and (3)–(8), exchanged between two people caught in a downpour in circumstances that are otherwise normal:

(1) *What lovely weather.*

(2) *It seems to be raining.*

(3) *I'm glad we didn't bother to bring an umbrella.*

(4) *Did you remember to water the flowers?*

(5) *What awful weather.*

(6) *It seems to be thundering.*

(7) *I'm sorry we didn't bother to bring an umbrella.*

(8) *Did you remember to bring in the washing?*

There are two obvious ways of grouping these examples. First, there are close syntactic and lexical parallels between (1) and (5), (2) and (6), (3) and (7), and (4) and (8). Second, in a less straightforwardly definable way, (1)–(4) have something in common which distin-

guishes them from (5)–(8). Consider (1)–(4) in turn.

What lovely weather. In the circumstances described, it is inconceivable that the speaker meant to get across the literal meaning of his utterance. In fact, it is certain that he believes the opposite of what he has said. However, it is not so obvious that it was this belief that he primarily intended to get across, as would be claimed by both the semantic and pragmatic accounts of irony referred to above. In the first place, suppose this WAS his primary intention: How would it be recognized? Ironical utterances are not always distinguishable by intonation from their literal counterparts. When there is no distinctive intonation, it is clear that the choice between literal and ironical interpretation must be based on information external to the utterance—contextual knowledge and other background assumptions—rather than the form or content of the utterance itself. Where such external information is lacking—for example where (1) is said in the course of a long distance telephone call—then the utterance would certainly be taken as literal. In other words, knowing the speaker's beliefs about the weather is a precondition for, rather than a consequence of, recognizing that his utterance was ironical. The standard approach to irony, which claims that the main point of an ironical utterance is to convey the opposite of what is said, would thus make every ironical utterance uninformative, both on the level of what is said and on the level of what is implicated. The speaker would be intending to communicate a certain belief, but, in the absence of any special intonation, his intention would only be recognized by someone who already knew that he held that belief.

We have already mentioned another problem with this account. If the speaker of (1) meant to indicate that he thought the weather was awful, why not say so directly? What is the point of the indirect approach? What difference is there between saying *What lovely weather* ironically, and *What awful weather* literally? On both standard semantic and pragmatic accounts, there is nothing to choose between these two remarks, and therefore no particular reason for ever being ironical.[3] This is clearly not right. Moreover, the data do not entirely support the standard description of ironical utterances.

The only clear intuition is that the speaker of (1) does not mean what he has literally said, and lets it be understood that what he has literally said is the opposite of what he really believes. Obviously, his real beliefs can be deduced from this, but we cannot necessarily conclude that his main intention—or even a subsidiary intention—was to get these beliefs across. He might instead have been trying to express an opinion, not about the weather, but about the content of (1) itself—to indicate, for example, that it had been ridiculous to hope that the weather would be lovely.

It seems to be raining. This clearly does not express the opposite of what the speaker thinks; it just expresses LESS than what he thinks. Whereas (1) was odd because the speaker did not believe what he said, (2) is odd because its truth is so patently obvious. Although it might have been relevant or informative as the first few drops of rain were falling, in the middle of a downpour it could never be seriously made except by someone with incredibly slow reactions. The speaker is not trying to pretend that he is such a person; nor is he parodying anyone in particular. What he is trying to do is to bring to mind just this exaggerated slowness of reaction which would itself be worth remarking on in the circumstances. For an utterance to have this effect, it must be obvious that the speaker is drawing attention to its content, while at the same time dissociating himself from it. What is important is the content of the utterance, rather than what it is about.

I'm glad we didn't bother to bring an umbrella. Like (1), this is a case where the utterance does not directly reflect the speaker's views; where in fact he believes the opposite of what he says. One could imagine (3) being used to echo an earlier remark made to, or by, the speaker or hearer before setting off: *Don't bother to take an umbrella,* or *Let's not bother to take an umbrella,* for example. By repeating this advice in the pouring rain, the speaker of (3) underlines its futility.

Clearly someone who asks *Did you remember to water the flowers?* cannot mean the opposite of what he says. Indeed it is hard to see what would BE the opposite of (4), or of most other ironical questions. This is a further argument against both standard semantic and pragmatic accounts of irony. The question in

(4) is odd because, like (2), it is so obviously irrelevant in the circumstances. The speaker is not interested in the answer; he is much more likely to have asked the question precisely to highlight its irrelevance and the pointlessness of asking or answering it in the circumstances. If we also suppose that the hearer is fanatical about keeping his flowers watered, (3) will have the further implication that the question is USUALLY pointless, and that the hearer's obsession is ridiculous. Thus, what the speaker actually communicates is not question (4) itself, but an attitude to it and to the state of mind that might give rise to it.

Although incomplete and imprecise, these observations about (1)–(4) do at least make clear what these utterances have in common that distinguishes them from (5)–(8). Someone who utters (1)–(4) cannot but dissociate himself from the content of his utterance, either because it is clearly false, as in (1) and (3), or because it is clearly irrelevant, as in (2) and (4). The only way to understand him is to assume that he is expressing a belief ABOUT his utterance, rather than BY MEANS of it. What (1)–(4) express is an attitude of the speaker to his utterance, whereas what (5)–(8) express is an attitude of the speaker to what his utterance is about: the weather, the rain, and the appropiate steps for dealing with them. This distinction between two basic types of utterance is entirely missed by both standard semantic and pragmatic accounts of irony. On both standard accounts, the ironical utterance of (1) is about the wather, and is thus indistinguishable from the literal utterance *What awful weather.* On our account, there is a crucial difference between the two utterances, because one expresses an attitude to the content of an utterance, whereas the other expresses an attitude to the weather.

4. THE USE–MENTION DISTINCTION

The intuitive distinction we have just illustrated using (1)–(4) and (5)–(8) as examples is closely related to the distinction drawn in philosophy between the USE and MENTION of an expression. USE of an expression involves reference to what the expression refers to; MENTION of an expression involves reference to the expression itself. Thus *marginal* is used in

(9) to refer to the doubtful grammatical status of certain examples:

(9) *These examples are rare and marginal.*

It is mentioned in (10a) and (10b), where reference is made to the word *marginal* itself:

(10) a. *"Marginal" is a technical term.*
   b. *Who had the nerve to call my examples marginal?*

When the expression mentioned is a complete sentence, it does not have the illocutionary force it would standardly have in a context where it was used. Thus, the remark in (11a) is uttered in (11b) without actually being made, the question in (12a) is uttered in (12b) without actually being asked, and the order in (13a) is uttered in (13b) without actually being given:

(11) a. *What a shame!*
   b. *Don't just say "What a shame"; do something.*
(12) a. *What is irony?*
   b. *"What is irony?" is the wrong question.*
(13) a. *Be quiet!*
   c. *"Be quiet! Be quiet!" And suppose I feel like talking?*

This may be used as a test for distinguishing between use and mention of sentences.

The use–mention distinction is a logical one. In formal languages, mention is distinguished from use in a conventional way, and there can be no question about whether a formula contains a mention, nor about what is being mentioned. In natural languages, mentions take a variety of forms, some of which might seem to be intermediate cases, falling somewhere between use and mention. Moreover, cases of mention in natural languages are not usually studied in their own right, but only for the role they play within the frameworks of either "reported speech" or "opaque contexts." Both framewords are inappropriate for the study of mention; they are too broad in some respects and too narrow in others.

The reported speech framework is too broad because there are standard cases of indirect speech such as (14), where the indirectly reported proposition (15) is part of a larger proposition, and there is no demarcation line, explicit or implicit, to set it off as a case of mention:

(14) *They say that it is going to rain.*
(15) *It is going to rain.*

The reported speech framework is also too narrow, because a number of clear cases of mention do not involve any report of speech, even in the very loose usual acceptation. Sentences (16) and (17) are examples:

(16) *A yellow flag means "stay away."*
(17) *"Stay away" is a grammatical sentence.*

The opaque context framework is too broad because it covers cases of indirect speech such as (14), (18) and (19), which clearly fall outside the scope of any notion of mention, however extended:

(18) *Oedipus wanted to marry Jocasta.*
(19) *Oedipus wanted to marry his mother.*

The contexts in (18) and (19) are opaque, since the substitution of the coreferential expressions *Jocasta* and *his mother* is not truth-preserving. However, we would not want to say that these expressions are mentioned. The notion of opaque context, as usually understood, is also too narrow, because it does not account for cases such as (13b) (where *"Be quiet! Be quiet!"* is certainly mentioned, but where no opaque context is involved; see also (27)–(30) in what follows). One could of course say that the null context is opaque under certain conditions, but the conditions would have to be defined.

There is a real need for a comprehensive account of mention in natural language, which would cover not only mention of an expression, as in (11)–(13), but also mention of a proposition, as in what is usually referred to as "free indirect style."[4] In free indirect style, an independent proposition is reported with an optional comment in a parenthetical phrase, as in (20):

(20) *He will come at five, he says.*

It seems clear that (20) is equivalent in logical structure to (21) rather than (22), and is therefore a genuine case of mention:

(21) *"I will come at five," he says.*
(22) *He says that he will come at five.*

There are thus two properties that may be used to distinguish various types of mention in natural language; looking at these, one can see why it is sometimes felt that there are intermediate cases between the poles of pure use and pure mention. On the one hand, we can contrast explicit mention, as in (23) and (25), with implicit mention, as in (24) and (26). On the other hand, we can contrast the two different types of object that may be mentioned: linguistic expressions, as in (23) and (24), and propositions, as in (25) and (26):

(23) *The master began to understand and to share the intense disgust which the archdeacon always expressed when Mrs Proudie's name was mentioned. "What am I to do with such a woman as this?" he asked himself.*

(24) *The master began to understand and to share the intense disgust which the archdeacon always expressed when Mrs Proudie's name was mentioned. "What am I to do with such a woman as this?"*

(25) *The master began to understand and to share the intense disgust which the archdeacon always expressed when Mrs Proudie's name was mentioned. What was he to do with such a woman as this, he asked himself.*

(26) *The master began to understand and to share the intense disgust which the archdeacon always expressed when Mrs Proudie's name was mentioned. What was he to do with such a woman as this?*

Trollope, Barchester Towers

In formal language, only the explicit mention of an expression is possible; this is illustrated in (23). However, implicit mention of an expression, as in (24), explicit mention of a proposition, as in (25), and implicit mention of a proposition, as in (26), are equally clear cases of mention from a logical point of view, unless the concept of mention is arbitrarily restricted to mention of expressions. It is from a linguistic point of view that mention of a proposition is harder to identify than mention of an expression, and implicit mention harder to identify than explicit mention; hence the impression that there are mixed forms. The most difficult cases to identify are those where a proposition is implicitly mentioned. When the context gives no indication that the free indirect style is being used for reporting speech—as in (26), for example—it is often possible to process an utterance quite satisfactorily without consciously noticing that it is an utterance of a particular logical type, closely related to quotation. When the mention does not involve reported speech proper, it is less easily identifiable still, and it would not be too much of a surprise to come across whole classes of implicit mention of propositions that have so far been overlooked or misinterpreted. Ironical utterances are a case in point.

5. IRONY AS ECHOIC MENTION

Consider the following exchanges:

(27) a. *I've got a toothache.*
     b. *Oh, you've got a toothache. Open your mouth, and let's have a look.*

(28) a. *Where can I buy pretzels at this time of night?*
     b. *Where can you buy pretzels? At this time of night? At Barney's, of course.*

(29) a. *I'm tired.*
     b. ***You're** tired. And what do you think **I** am?*

(30) a. Doolittle: *Listen here, Governor. You and me is men of the world, ain't we?*
     b. Higgins: *Oh! Men of the world, are we? You'd better go, Mrs. Pearce.*

G. B. Shaw, *Pygmalion*

In these examples, the propositions used in (a) are implicitly mentioned in the responses in (b). These cases of mention are clearly not reported speech, in the sense that they are not intended to inform anyone of the content of a preceding utterance (such an intention would be pointless, since the utterance has only just occurred). Rather, they are meant to indicate that the preceding utterance has been heard and understood, and to express the hearer's immediate reaction to it. Apart from this instant echoing of a preceding utterance, there are also cases of echoic mention that are less directly related to what has gone before—for instance, where the proposition mentioned is not the one just uttered but what the hearer takes to be one of its pragmatic implications:

(31) a. *I'm a reasonable man.*
     b. *Whereas I'm not (is what you're implying).*

There are cases where what is echoed is not an immediately preceding utterance, but one that occurred some time ago:

(32) *It absolutely poured. I know, it was going to rain (you told me so). I should listen to you more often.*

There are cases of echoing where the sources are very distant indeed:

(33) *Jack elbowed Bill, and Bill punched him on the nose. He should have turned the other cheek (as it says in the Bible). Maybe that would have been the best thing to do.*

There are also what one might call anticipatory echoes:

(34) *You're going to do something silly. You're free to do what you want (you'll tell me). Maybe so. But you still ought to listen to me.*

Such cases of echoic mention are extremely common in ordinary conversation, and considerably more varied than we have time to show here. In each case, the speaker's choice of words, his tone (doubtful, questioning, scornful, contemptuous, approving, and so on), and the immediate context, all play a part in indicating his own attitude to the proposition mentioned. In particular, the speaker may echo a remark in such a way as to suggest that he finds it untrue, inappropriate, or irrelevant:

(35) *'You take an eager interest in that gentleman's concerns,' said Darcy in a less tranquil tone, and with a heightened colour.*
'Who that knows what his misfortunes have been, can help feeling an interest in him?'
'His misfortunes!' repeated Darcy contemptuously, 'yes, his misfortunes have been great indeed.'
Jane Austen, *Pride and Prejudice*

(36) *'Now just attend to me for a bit, Mr. Pitch, or Witch, or Stitch, or whatever your name is.'*
'My name is Pinch,' observed Tom. 'Have the goodness to call me by it.'
'What! You mustn't ever be called out of your name, mustn't you?' cried Jonas. 'Pauper 'prentices are looking up, I think. Ecod, we manage 'em a little better in the city!'
Charles Dickens, *Martin Chuzzlewit*

There are also cases where what is echoed is not a proposition expressed by an utterance, but a thought imputed by the speaker to the hearer:

(37) *Elinor looked at him with greater astonishment than ever. She began to think he must be in liquor; . . . and with this impression she immediately rose, saying,*
'Mr. Willoughby, I advise you at present to return to Combe—I am not at leisure to remain with you longer.—Whatever your business may be with me, it will be better recollected and explained tomorrow.'
'I understand you,' he replied, with an expressive smile, and a voice perfectly calm, 'yes, I am very drunk.—A pint of porter with my cold beef at Marlborough was enough to overset me.'
Jane Austen, *Sense and Sensibility*

We have presented examples (35)–(37) as cases of echoic mention; we could equally well have presented them as cases of irony. The utterances in question are patently ironical: The speaker mentions a proposition in such a way as to make clear that he rejects it as ludicrously false, inappropriate, or irrelevant. For the hearer, understanding such an utterance involves both realizing that it is a case of mention rather than use, and also recognizing the speaker's attitude to the proposition mentioned. The whole interpretation depends on this double recognition. Recovery of the implicatures (38) for (35), (39) for (36) and (40) for (37) will follow automatically:

(38) *He has not been the victim of misfortunes.*

(39) *You have no right to demand that I call you by your proper name.*

(40) *I am not drunk.*

Not only it is unnecessary to appeal to the notion of figurative meaning in dealing with the interpretation of (35)–(37) [and their implicatures (38)–(40)], any account in terms of figurative meaning will actually be incomplete. Suppose we treat (38)–(40) along traditional lines, as figurative senses rather than implicatures of (35)–(37). Then either the proposition that constitutes the figurative meaning must be understood as USED, and the status of the utterance as echoic mention will disappear; or it will be understood as MENTIONED, and since it is not patently false, inappropriate or irrelevant, there will be no way of explaining the speaker's attitude of mockery or disapproval. Either way, an account in terms of figurative meaning will necessarily overlook a central and obvious aspect of the interpretation of the utterance.

The analysis we are proposing, although it involves implicatures, differs from Grice's in at least two important respects. Grice sees violation of the maxim of truthfulness as both a necessary and a sufficient condition for ironical interpretation. When an utterance is patently false, he argues the hearer interprets it as implicating the contradictory of what was literally said. We have already mentioned one problem with this account: Unlike standard implicatures, the "implicature" carried by an ironical utterance must be substituted for, rather than added to, what was literally said, because otherwise the total message conveyed would be a contradiction. A more general problem is that violation of the maxim of truthfulness is in fact neither necessary nor sufficient for ironical interpretation. It is not necessary because of the existence of ironical questions, ironical understatements, and ironical references to the inappropriateness or irrelevance of an utterance rather than to the fact that it is false. Numerous illustrations have been given earlier in the chapter. Furthermore, as Grice himself points out (1978), patent falsehood or irrelevance is not a sufficient condition for irony—not every false or irrelevant utterance can be interpreted as ironical. What is missing from Grice's account is precisely the fact that ironical utterances are cases of mention, and that the propositions mentioned are ones that have been, or might have been, actually entertained by someone.

On our analysis, recognition of an ironical utterance as a case of mention is crucial to its interpretation. Once the hearer has recognized this, and has seen the speaker's attitude to the proposition mentioned, the implicatures in (38)–(40) follow by standard reasoning processes. They are typical cases of conversational implicature, and not problematic in any way. Our account of irony thus fits more naturally into Grice's overall framework than the account he himself proposes.

It might be suggested that there are two distinct types of irony: "echoic" irony, as illustrated earlier, whose interpretation involves a recognition of its status as mention, and "standard" irony, whose interpretation involves a recovery of its figurative meaning.[5] The problem with this suggestion is that there is a whole range of intermediate cases between the clear cases of echoic irony and the "standard" cases (see below). If there were two totally distinct processes, one based on mention and the other on figurative meaning, each resulting in a different type of irony, such intermediate cases should not exist.

It seems more accurate to say that all ex-

amples of irony are interpreted as echoic mentions, but that there are echoic mentions of many different degrees and types. Some are immediate echoes, and others delayed; some have their source in actual utterances, others in thoughts or opinions; some have a real source, others an imagined one; some are traceable back to a particular individual, whereas others have a vaguer origin. When the echoic character of the utterance is not immediately obvious, it is nevertheless suggested. Within this framework, we return to our original examples of irony, sentences (1)–(4).

What lovely weather. Suppose that, as we were deciding to set off on our walk, someone told us that the weather was going to be lovely. It is quite clear that (1) is an ironical echo of this remark. Or suppose we have spent a rainy winter talking about the walks we will have in the summer sun. The echoic quality of (1), though its source is more distant, is nonetheless clear. Even when there is no prior utterance some vague echoing is still involved. One normally sets off for a walk in the hope or expectation of good weather: *What lovely weather* may simply echo these earlier high hopes. In all these cases the remark in (1) is interpreted along exactly the same lines. There is no question of a move from one figure of speech to another, or one type of irony to another, with quite different interpretation processes being involved; the only move is from obvious cases of echoic mention to much vaguer (and duller) varieties of the same thing.

It seems to be raining. Suppose someone had originally made this remark just as the rain was starting. By repeating it in the middle of a downpour, the speaker of (2) shows how laughable it was, in retrospect, to be in any doubt about whether it was really raining. Even when there is no prior utterance, (2) would have a similar effect: By pretending a degree of hesitancy which is completely inappropriate in the circumstances, it conjures up a picture of a quite ludicrous degree of inattention or failure to react.

It should be obvious without further contextualization that (3) *(I'm glad we didn't bother to bring an umbrella)* and (4) *(Did you remember to water the flowers?)* are naturally interpreted as ironical echoes of advice on the one hand, and obsession on the other, which are both totally irrelevant in the circumstances.

Whether the advice was actually given or not, whether the obsession was put into words or not, does not affect the status of the utterance as echoic mention, but only its degree of pointedness.

What we are claiming is that all standard cases of irony, and many that are nonstandard from the traditional point of view, involve (generally implicit) mention of a proposition. These cases of mention are interpreted as echoing a remark or opinion that the speaker wants to characterize as ludicrously inappropriate or irrelevant. This account makes it possible to give a more detailed description of a much wider range of examples of irony than the traditional approach can handle. In particular, it provides a unified treatment of ironical antiphrasis and meiosis, which are traditionally regarded as two quite different things. Moreover, it makes no appeal to the notion of figurative meaning, nor to any other notion not fully justified in independent grounds.[6]

6. SOME FURTHER ASPECTS OF IRONY

Our analysis sheds some light on a number of further problems with the treatment of irony. We shall mention five of them here. Four we shall deal with rather briefly: the relation between irony and parody, the "ironical tone of voice," the shifts in style or register that often occur in ironical utterances, and the moralistic overtones that they sometimes have. The last problem, which we shall look at in more detail, has to do with the fact that ironical utterances often seem to be aimed at a particular target or victim.

1. According to the traditional analysis, irony and parody involve quite different production and interpretation processes: Irony involves change of meaning, whereas parody involves imitation. There is no necessary relation between the two, and any similarities that exist must result from similarities in the attitudes of ironist and parodist. If irony is a type of mention, however, it is easy to account for the similarities and differences between irony and parody, and for the fact that intermediate cases exist. Both irony and parody are types of mention: Irony involves mention of propositions; parody involves mention of linguistic expressions. In other words, parody is

related to direct discourse as irony is to free indirect discourse.

2. Within the traditional framework, the existence of an "ironical tone of voice" is rather puzzling. Why not also a "metaphorical tone of voice," a "synecdochical tone of voice," and so on? When irony is seen as a type of mention, the ironical tone of voice falls quite naturally into place: It is merely one of the variety of tones (doubtful, approving, contemptuous, and so on) that the speaker may use to indicate his attitude to the utterance or opinion mentioned.

3. It is well known that ironical utterances often involve a switch in style or register. For example, it is quite common to show that one's utterance is ironical by changing to a more formal or pompous style:

(41) *That's done it—you've broken the vase. I hope you're satisfied, my lady.*

There is nothing in the traditional account of irony that would lead one to expect such shifts. However, they can be quite easily explained on the assumption that irony involves echoic mention of a real or imagined utterance or opinion. [In (41) the speaker is echoing the sort of deferential remark that he implies the hearer is expecting.] As in free indirect discourse, the implicit mention of a proposition sometimes involves mention of an expression.

4. From the point of view of the traditional theory, there is a strange asymmetry in the uses of irony. One is much more likely to say *How clever* to imply "How stupid," or *How graceful* to imply "How clumsy," than the other way round. This connection of irony with implications of failure to reach a certain standard has often been noted. There is no explanation for it in terms of the traditional process of meaning-inversion, which should be able to work just as well in one direction as in the other. However, on our account there is a straightforward explanation. Standards or rules of behavior are culturally defined, commonly known, and frequently invoked; they are thus always available for echoic mention. On the other hand, critical judgments are particular to a given individual or occasion, and are thus only occasionally available for mention. Hence, it is always possible to say ironically of a failure *That was a great success,*

since it is normal to hope for the success of a given course of action. However, to say of a success *That was a failure* without the irony falling flat, the speaker must be able to refer back to prior doubts or fears, which he can then echo ironically. In the face of an imperfect reality, it is always possible to make ironical mention of the norm. In the face of a perfect reality, there must be past doubts or fears to echo if the mention of a critical judgment is to count as ironical.

5. The claim that ironical utterances are aimed at a particular target or victim is based on a variety of intuitions, sometimes clear-cut, sometimes less so. Within the traditional framework, there are two quite separate processes that might account for this aspect of irony.

On the one hand, every utterance whose literal sense would carry overtones of approval will have a corresponding figurative sense with critical overtones. The intended victim, on this account, would be the object of the criticism. For example, if (42) has the figurative meaning (43), then Fitzgerald would be the victim of the irony in (42):

(42) *Fitzgerald plays by the rules.*

(43) *Fitzgerald cheats.*

On the other hand, the person to whom the ironical utterance was apparently addressed may fail to detect its figurative meaning. The immediate result will be that any third parties present (who immediately detect the figurative meaning and are thus revealed as the true addressees of the irony) will feel drawn into a conspiracy with the speaker, at the expense of the person to whom the remark was overtly made. For example, if (44) has the figurative meaning (45), and if Billy fails to notice this, then on this account Billy becomes the intended victim of the irony in (44):

(44) *Go on, Billy, you're nearly there!*

(45) *Go on, Billy, you're nowhere near!*

These two processes may on occasion select the same victim. This would happen, for example, if (46) has the figurative meaning (47), and Jeremy fails to detect it:

(46) *Go on, Jeremy, your story's really interesting.*

(47) *Don't go on, Jeremy. Your story's really boring.*

Someone who restricts himself to examples of this last type, as happens rather too often, would get the misleading impression that the traditional theory can provide a unified account of how an ironical utterance chooses its victim. However, anyone who looks at the differences between examples like (42) and (44) will immediately see that two quite different processes are involved, and that they are not necessarily related at all.

Moreover, it is easy to think of quite ordinary examples that are not accounted for in terms of either process. Suppose the following remark is made ironically to someone who dislikes classical music:

(48) *Of course all classical music sounds the same!*

On the one hand, the figurative meaning of this remark has no critical content; on the other hand, in normal circumstances the hearer is unlikely to mistake the speaker's intentions. In this case, neither process will apply and there is no immediate explanation within the traditional framework for the clear intuition that the hearer of (48) is also its intended victim.

Within our framework it would be possible to define two processes that would correspond closely to those used in the traditional account. Instead of figurative meanings, there would be pragmatic implications or implicatures which might carry critical overtones; instead of a failure to distinguish literal from figurative meanings there would be a failure to distinguish use from mention. The framework we are proposing is thus at least as explanatory in this respect as the traditional framework.

However, the analysis of irony as a type of mention does involve a quite central claim which has no equivalent in the traditional framework, and which by itself provides a more satisfactory explanation for a much wider range of intuitions. Within our framework, an ironical remark will have as natural target the originators, real or imagined, of the utterances or opinions being echoed. If the remark also carries critical overtones, or if the hearer fails to detect the speaker's ironical intent, the ironical effect may of course be reinforced, but it may equally well be achieved when neither of these conditions is present.

In example (46) the victim is Jeremy, because the utterance echoes an opinion of himself that he expects to hear. In (44) the target is Billy, because the utterance echoes an opinion imputed to him, that he is nearly there. In (42) the victims are all those who think or claim that Fitzgerald plays by the rules: Fitzgerald himself, and in certain circumstances the hearer too, will be a victim in the virtue of this. In (48), it is the hearer who is the victim, because the utterance echoes an opinion he is believed to hold. In (1), if the weather forecast has predicted good weather, it is this forecast that is echoed in the remark *"What lovely weather"*; on the other hand, if no one in particular has actually made such a prediction, our account correctly predicts that the irony is not aimed at any particular victim.

The analysis of irony as a type of mention thus makes it possible to predict which ironical utterances will have a particular victim, and who that victim will be. When the utterance or opinion echoed has no specific originator, there will be no victim; when there is a specific, recognizable originator, he will be the victim. Thus, when the speaker echoes himself, the irony will be self-directed; when he echoes his hearer, the result will be sarcasm. In the traditional framework, the ad hominem character of irony is a function of the propositional content of the utterance; in our framework, it is a function of the ease with which some originator of the opinion echoed can be recognized. The many cases where these two accounts make different predictions, as in (48), should make it possible to choose between them.

and from then on it increases in intensity. In the traditional framework, we would have to say that at the second or third repetition the literal meaning is replaced by the opposite figurative meaning—there can be no intermediate stage between literal and figurative interpretation.

In our framework, Mark Antony has to be seen from the very first as MENTIONING the proposition that Brutus is an honorable man. He first mentions it in a conciliatory tone of voice. No doubt it is not his own most personal opinion, but he is prepared to put it forward in a spirit of appeasement, echoing the sentiments of Brutus's supporters. Then, each time he repeats it, he mentions it in the context of further facts which make it clear that he is dissociating himself from it, more strongly each time: The irony is first hinted at, then strengthened, then forced home. Mark Antony carries his audience with him, through a series of successively more hostile attitudes to a proposition which itself remains unchanged from start to finish. At every stage the proposition is mentioned, and not used.

This example brings us back to our preliminary remark that the concept of irony itself is open to reconsideration, not just in its intension but also in its extension. In classical terms an utterance either is ironical or it is not. The picture we are suggesting is different: Although an utterance either is or is not a mention, a mention may be more or less ironical, with many intermediary and complex shades between stereotypical cases of irony and other kinds of echoic mention.

7. A FINAL EXAMPLE

In Shakespeare's *Julius Caesar*, act 3, scene 2, Mark Antony says six times that Brutus is an honorable man. This is frequently cited as an example of irony, but on closer examination it raises a number of problems for the traditional theory. The first time Mark Antony says "Brutus is an honorable man," there is no perceptible irony; the inclination is to take it as a propitiatory remark, suitable to an occasion where Mark Antony is about to give Caesar's funeral oration with Brutus's permission. It is not until he says it for the third time that the ironical interpretation is really forced on us,

8. CONCLUSION

As an undersized boy trips over his own feet while coming in last in the school sports, one spectator turns to another and remarks:

(49) *It's a bird—it's a plane—it's Superman.*

This remark is clearly ironical. Because it is an actual quotation, it fits quite straightforwardly into our framework as a case of echoic mention; however, it poses considerable problems for both standard semantic and pragmatic accounts of irony. Within these frameworks, it would have to be analyzed as carrying the figurative meaning or conversational implicature in (50):

(50) *It's not a bird, it's not a plane, it's not Superman.*

But if (49) figuratively means or conversationally implicates (50)—which is literally true—it is hard to see why it would also be taken as a joke. There is a further problem for Grice's approach, since the implicature in (50) is completely uninformative in the context, and would itself violate the maxims of conversation. Our proposed analysis, by virtue of its ability to handle (49) and similar examples, proves both more explanatory and more general than either of the traditional alternatives.

Compared with traditional semantic approaches, Grice's approach to irony is radically pragmatic: The proper interpretation of an ironical utterance is assumed to consist solely of conversational implicatures, logically derived according to pragmatic patterns of inference. If what we have been arguing in this chapter is correct, then Grice's and other similar approaches to irony (and more generally to figures of speech) are too "radical" in one respect, and not "radical" enough in another.

In the first place, ironical utterances do have one essential semantic property: They are cases of mention, and are thus semantically distinguishable from cases where the same proposition is used in order to make an assertion, ask a question, and so on. As has been seen, this semantic distinction is crucial to the explanation of how ironical utterances are interpreted, and indeed why they exist. Without this distinction the echoic character of irony will be overlooked, and it will thus be impossible to make the correct prediction that where no echoing is discernible, an utterance, however false, uninformative or irrelevant, will never be ironical. In this respect, then, a purely logical-pragmatic approach to irony is too radical.

In a second respect, though, a logical-pragmatic approach to irony remains too close to a semantic one. In both cases it is assumed that the interpretation of an ironical utterance consists solely of propositions (whether entailments or implicatures) intended by the speaker and recoverable by the hearer. Now it has long been recognized that the understand-

ing of figures of speech, and of irony in particular, has nonpropositional, nondeductive aspects. An ironical utterance carries suggestions of attitude—and sometimes, as in (49), of images—which cannot be made entirely explicit in propositional form. In this respect a logical-pragmatic model does not provide a better description—let alone a better explanation—than a semantic model. On the other hand, our analysis of irony as a case of echoic mention crucially involves the evocation of an attitude—that of the speaker to the proposition mentioned. This attitude may imply a number of propositions, but it is not reducible to a set of propositions. Our analysis thus suggests that a logical-pragmatic theory dealing with the interpretation of utterances as an inferential process must be supplemented by what could be called a "rhetorical-pragmatic," or "rhetorical" theory dealing with evocation.[7]

To conclude: The value of current pragmatic theory, as inspired by Grice's work, lies mainly in the fact that it relieves semantics of a number of problems for which it can provide a more general and explanatory treatment. However, in the case of figurative utterances, the move from semantics to logical pragmatics merely creates a number of new problems, without providing solutions to many of the problems raised by the traditional semantic approach. Taking irony as an example, we have tried to show that, given an adequate semantic analysis of ironical utterances as echoic mentions, the problems with both the traditional semantic account and Grice's pragmatic account dissolve away. A number of problems still remain; what we are suggesting is that logical pragmatics must in turn be relieved of these problems, which can be given a more general and explanatory treatment within the rhetorical component of a radically extended pragmatic theory.

ACKNOWLEDGMENT

A shorter version of this chapter appeared in French in *Poétique, 36,* 399–412. We would like to thank Diane Brockway, Robyn Carston, and Julius Moravcsik for a number of helpful suggestions.

NOTES

1. For example, Quintilian defines irony in terms of the fact that "we understand something which is the opposite of what is actually said [Quintilian IX, II, p. 44]." See also Turner (1973, p. 216).

2. For more detailed discussion of Grice's treatment of figurative language, see Wilson and Sperber (1979).

3. A similar point is made in Harnish (1976).

4. For recent work on free indirect style, see Banfield (1973) and McHale (1978).

5. See for example Cutler (1974), who distinguishes between "spontaneous" (standard) and "provoked" (echoic) irony.

6. It is widely accepted, though not entirely uncontroversial, that free indirect speech may be used to ironic effect (see McHale 1978, pp. 275–276 and references therein). What is lacking in the extensive literature on this subject is any attempt, on the one hand, to explain why this connection should exist, and on the other hand, to construct a unified theoretical account of irony around it. In this article, we hope to have shown that such an attempt is worth making.

7. The psychological basis of this rhetorical theory is discussed in Sperber (1975a), and Sperber and Wilson (forthcoming).

REFERENCES

Banfield, A. (1973). "Narrative Style and the Grammar of Direct and Indirect Speech." *Foundations of Language* 10:1–39.

Cutler, A. (1974). "On Saying What You Mean Without Meaning What You Say." In *Papers from the Tenth Regional Meeting of the Chicago Linguistics Society.* Department of Linguistics, University of Chicago, 117–127.

Grice, H. P. (1975). "Logic and Conversation." In P. Cole and J. Morgan (eds.), *Syntax and Semantics.* Vol. 3: *Speech Acts.* New York: Academic Press, 41–58. [Reprinted in this volume, Chapter 19]

Grice, H. P. (1978). "Further Notes on Logic and Conversation." In P. Cole (ed.), *Syntax and Semantics.* Vol. 9: *Pragmatics.* New York: Academic Press, 113–127.

Harnish, R. M. (1976). "Logical Form and Implicature." In T. Bever, J. J. Katz, and D. T. Langendoen (eds.), *An Integrated Theory of Linguistic Ability.* New York: Crowell, 313–391. [Reprinted in this volume, Chapter 20]

McHale, B. (1978). "Free Indirect Discourse: A Survey of Recent Accounts." *PTL: A Journal for Descriptive Poetics and the Theory of Literature* 3:249–287.

Quintilian. (1966). *Institutio Oratoria.* Translated by H. E. Butler. Loeb Classical Library. London: Heinemann.

Sperber, D. (1975a). *Rethinking Symbolism.* Cambridge: Cambridge University Press.

Sperber, D. (1975b). "Rudiments de rhétorique cognitive." *Poétique* 23:389–415.

Sperber, D., and D. Wilson (forthcoming). *Foundations of Rhetorical Theory.*

Turner, G. W. (1973). *Stylistics.* London: Penguin Books.

Wilson, D., and D. Sperber (1981). "On Grice's Theory of Conversation." In P. Werth (ed.), *Conversation and Discourse.* London: Croom Helm, 155–178. (French version in *Communications* 30: 80–94).

FURTHER READING

Cohen, T. (1975). "Figurative Speech and Figurative Acts." *Journal of Philosophy* 72:669–684.

Lamarque, P. (1982). "Metaphor and Reported Speech: In Defence of a Pragmatic Theory." *Journal of Literary Semantics* B 11:14–18.

Morgan, J. L. (1979). "Observations on the Pragmatics of Metaphor." In A. Ortony (ed.), *Metaphor and Thought.* Cambridge: Cambridge University Press, 136–147.

Ortony, A. (ed.). (1979). *Metaphor and Thought.* Cambridge: Cambridge University Press.

Stern, J. (1985). "Metaphor as Demonstrative." *Journal of Philosophy* 82:677–710.

Tanaka, R. (1973). "The Concept of Irony: Theory and Practice." *Journal of Literary Semantics* 2:43–56.

VIII

Psychology and Pragmatics

34

Pragmatics and the Modularity of Mind

ASA KASHER

1

Natural languages, in the everyday sense, seem rather evasive. Take, for example, the label 'Hebrew.' You will find it attached to what was spoken, about three thousand years ago, by Absalom, son of King David. You will find it attached also to what is spoken these days by my two-year-old son, Avshalom. Thus, on the one hand, big Absalom and little Avshalom are both taken to be speakers of Hebrew, a shared language, "something essentially social, a practice in which many people engage" (Dummett [1975:135]). On the other hand, could that treacherous Absalom and this innocent Avshalom meet here, their utterances would be mutually incomprehensible, for more than one linguistic reason. Consequently, they could hardly be taken to be speakers of the same language. Indeed, similar difficulties emerge when other "super-languages," such as English, or German and Dutch, are considered (Chomsky [1980: 118ff]). There is, therefore, something evasive, if not utterly wrong, in our naive concept of natural language, where it gives rise to such simple but conflicting depictions of the facts.

Such evasiveness is much reduced when the study of natural language, in the everyday sense of "something essentially social," is being replaced by the study of related systems of rules. All the more so, when the study of natural language in general takes the form of studying characteristic properties of systems of linguistic rules.

There is an important conceptual difference between the everyday notion of natural language and the linguistic notions of rule systems. Whereas "language is not one of the things in the real world" (Chomsky [1984:26]), linguistic systems of rules "have to have a real existence" (Chomsky [1982:107]), in a sense to be clarified presently.

For a system of rules 'to have a real existence,' we take it, an entity (be it a human being, a robot, a computer or what have you) has to be shown that has properties or bears relations which are best described or explained by a theory which posits those rules. Thus, a system of norms can be shown to exist not only when a person is shown who follows them, in some strict sense of being aware of their content and being intentionally guided by their prescription, but also when a person

Asa Kasher, "Pragmatics and the Modularity of Mind," *Journal of Pragmatics* 8 (1984): 539–557. Copyright © 1984 by Elsevier Science Publishers. Reprinted by permission of the publisher and the author.

is shown who manifests a competence which is best explained in terms of that system of norms being in some way mentally represented. In other words, such a system of rules is taken 'to have a real existence' by virtue of its forming an essential part of the best available theoretical explanation of some facts.

Interesting facts are usually amenable to different descriptions and explanations, in natural sciences as well as in studies of linguistic competences. Hence, different systems of linguistic rules may well be introduced within competing theoretical explanations of the same family of linguistic facts. The question then arises of the 'existential import' of these explanations: If the related systems of rules are not simply notational variants of each other and if they are not mutually compatible, then it would be implausible to grant all of them the same kind of 'real existence' on the grounds of their each serving a crucial role in some explanation of the facts. Therefore, under such quite ordinary circumstances, one is inclined to look for some form of methodological or empirical adjudication.

Methodological selection among rival theoretical explanations of the same family of facts involves 'internal' considerations of coherence, explanatory power, simplicity and the like. A natural and powerful method of empirical selection involves putting those explanations to some 'external' tests, ones that determine the extent to which each of the explanations is compatible with certain 'external' theories. The latter are theories which have been successfully and independently used as theoretical explanations of some other families of facts.

To be sure, resort to such 'external' tests is not confined to cases of selection among alternative theories. Even when just one major theory is under consideration, "[w]e will always search for more evidence and for deeper understanding of given evidence which also may lead to change of theory" (Chomsky [1980:109]), studies of language being no exception. 'Adjacent theories,' ones that have been developed in related though clearly disparate areas, form a natural possible source of new observations and explanations. Attempts to integrate such 'adjacent' theoretical explanations may well lead to enhanced understanding, most probably by some appropriate change of theory.

A simple case of a linguistic theoretical claim being put to a crucial 'external' test appears in Miller and Chomsky (1963:429–430). The authors discuss a certain type of finite state automaton (viz. k-limited Markov sources) and show that if such an automaton is meant to serve "as a serious proposal for the way people create and interpret their communicative utterances," it must have at least 109 parameters, each being a certain estimated probability. The objections raised by Miller and Chomsky are simple: First, "an enormous amount of text would have to be scanned and tabulated in order to provide a satisfactory empirical basis for a model of this type," and secondly, "we cannot seriously propose that a child learns the values of 109 parameters in a childhood lasting only 108 seconds." One is, then, in a position to reject a theoretical proposal on the grounds that it is incompatible with some 'external' observations, assumptions or theoretical explanations.

In the present paper we discuss some of the results of putting pragmatic theories to some 'external' test. Our main concern here is how well does pragmatics fare with a certain general, psychological conception of the nature of human mind, viz. that of the modular approach, as put forward and discussed by Chomsky ([1980], [1984], for example) and Fodor ([1983] in particular).

Although our project of putting a linguistic theory to a psychological test involves a distinction between 'internal,' linguistic observations, assumptions and theoretical explanations, and 'external,' psychological ones, it definitely does not subsume any distinction between 'apparent linguistic reality' and 'genuine psychological reality.' There is nothing in the nature of psychological studies or linguistic studies that should lead us to hold that psychological observations or explanations are, as such, more powerful than linguistic ones. Indeed, linguistic theories suffice to establish 'real existence' to the same extent that physical, biological or psychological theories do. No special category of evidence is required for supporting claims to reality. There is "no reason not to take our theories tentatively to be true [under certain framework assumptions] at the level of description at which we are working, then proceeding to refine and evaluate them and to relate them to other levels of description" (Chomsky [1980:107]. See also, Bruner [1986], e.g., pp. 87–88]).

2

The scope of what is called "pragmatics" depends on one's view of the nature of pragmatics. However, our arguments with respect to the possible integration of pragmatics and the modular approach to the study of mental competences will not hinge on any delineation of pragmatics which rests on a certain full-fledged pragmatic theory. Instead of following, say, our own view of the nature of pragmatics (Kasher [1977], for example) or any other conception of it,[1] we assume that a list can be easily compiled of linguistic phenomena, such that no theory in pragmatics could be adequate, in an elementary, descriptive sense, if it does not capture, in an appropriate way, the major facts with respect to all of these phenomena. Such a list of phenomena is introduced with one qualification, though: a descriptively adequate theory in pragmatics may still fall short of capturing the facts about some phenomenon on the list, provided that this omission is supported by some general, methodological or empirical consideration.

Our list includes, for the present purposes, six items, each consisting of some family of phenomena: (1) deixis; (2) lexical pragmatical presuppositions; (3) forces (of speech acts); (4) performatives; (5) conversation implicatures; and (6) politeness principles.

Indeed, these are imprecise labels of linguistic families of phenomena: in most of the cases it takes at least a little theory to introduce the very family of facts to be under consideration. Hence, in order to obviate difficulties that might arise as to the identity of some of the phenomena, we specify an introductory theory whenever it seems required.

3

It would be useful to draw in outline part of the psychological background of the present project, namely the modular approach to the study of mental competences, that will be used in the sequel to put pragmatics to an 'external' test of compatibility and integration.

The following assumptions form the core of the modular approach:

(1) The mind manipulates symbols, in the sense used when symbol manipulation is ascribed to computer programs.

(2) The symbols that the mind manipulates have formal properties.

(3) Operations of the mind's mechanisms take the form of computations, in some broad sense of the term. These computations are driven according to the formal properties of their data.[2]

(4) The mind includes several faculties, which may show various degrees of independence. A faculty of mind has access to propositional content in a certain domain, whether innately or by acquisition, and it uses this propositional content in its computational processes.

(5) The mind has parts which are mental mechanisms, but which are not faculties, in the present sense of the term.[3]

(6) There are faculties of mind which are, to use Fodor's term, 'cognitive modules' (Fodor [1983:36ff]). These modules are domain-specific, primary (in the sense of not being composed of more elementary mechanisms, 'not assembled,' in Fodor's terms), computationally autonomous (in the sense of not sharing mental resources, such as memory, with other congnitive systems), and innately specified, their structure not having been determined by some learning process solely.[4]

(7) Cognitive modules of the mind, such as its input systems, are informationally encapsulated (Fodor [1983:64–86]). That is to say, they have no access to information of certain kinds, even if it is mentally represented and accessible to other cognitive systems.

(8) In addition to cognitive modules, the mind includes cognitive systems which are neither domain specific nor informationally encapsulated. Such 'central systems' (Fodor [1983:101–119]) are related to general mental capacities of belief formation and problem solving.

(To be sure, doubts can be cast on such assumptions within several philosophical or psychological frameworks. However, the present context of discussion is different: those assumptions form part of our framework of scrutiny, rather than its object.)

Notice that conditions (1)–(8) can be taken to serve as a psychological elaboration of the standard Finite Representability Constraint, imposed on cognitive theories in philosophy of language (Davidson [1965] being the locus classicus) and generative linguistics. Most of the time, it has been the finiteness component of the finite representability constraint which has done the methodological work of casting grave doubts on prevalent theories (e.g., in Kasher [1979] and Gochet [1980], in the context of semantic theories. For a formal semantic theory which, in a way, does take finite representability seriously, see Barwise and Perry [1983], e.g., p. 52]). Presently, however, it is the representability component of the constraint which is going to play the major role in our discussion. Conditions (1)–(8) are, actually, psychological restrictions imposed on any claim with respect to the structure, content and operation of the mind. How such restrictions are put to use will be seen in the sequel.

4

The notion of 'deixis' has been used in two different ways. In its narrow sense this term applies to phenomena related to a certain group of lexical or syntactical devices, in each of the natural languages. Personal pronouns, some tenses and honorifics are often used as prime examples of the ways natural languages reflect spatio-temporal and social coordinates of typical contexts of utterance, by using deictic devices. (For a discussion of deixis in this narrow sense, see for example Lyons [1968:7.2]). In its broad sense, 'deixis' is related to a more general phenomenon, namely the dependence of full understanding of produced sentences on their respective contexts of utterance, including much which is beyond a restricted class of spatiotemporal and similar indexical elements. (For such a view of indexicality, see Bar-Hillel [1970] and Kaplan [1988]. Causal theories of proper names, as proposed by Donellan and Kripke involve an interesting type of such a dependence.)

There have not been too many theoretical discussions of deixis in the narrow sense. Most conspicuous are the attempts to incorporate indices into formal semantics. David Lewis, for example, defined 'appropriate intension

for a sentence' as "any function from indices to truth-values," where the indices are taken to be finite sequences of coordinates. Some of the latter David Lewis called 'contextual,' e.g., time, place, speaker, audience, etc. (Lewis [1972:174–176]).

A theory of deixis has been offered by David Kaplan. In his logic of demonstratives (Kaplan [1979]) Kaplan introduced the useful distinction between 'contents' and 'characters,' where content (intensions, in Carnap's terms, or propositions) are functions from possible worlds to extensions, whereas characters are functions from contexts to contents, i.e., "that component of the sense of an expression which determines how the content is determined by the context" ([1979:403]. See also his [1988].)

Assuming that a theory of deixis should be included in pragmatics, it turns out that an intensional logic of one type or another has to be subsumed by a full-fledged pragmatic theory. Hence, the results of putting pragmatics to the 'external' test of the modular approach depend on the results of putting the related intensional logic to such a test.

There seems to be an obvious way to formulate an adequacy condition that would have to be fulfilled by indexical semantics of the formal brand if a claim is made as to its compatibility with conditions of finite representability in general and of the modular approach in particular. The semantic value that a standard intensional framework ascribes to any of its terms is a function. A natural restriction to be imposed on these functions, on grounds of finite representability and the modular approach, would be that they are computable. (See Kasher [1979:262–265], for some elaboration.)

The problem here is that such an adequacy condition may be rendered vacuous, because of being trivially satisfied when the functions and contexts related to indexical terms are appropriately construed. For instance, the contextual coordinates of Lewis (1972) are things which are given as values of free variables marked by indexical expressions such as I, you, $here$, $today$, $that$ P and the like. Thus, given that in a certain context of utterance the speaker is John, a genuine occurence of the word I in the uttered sentence will create no problem when the intension of the sentence is considered in order to determine its value for the given context, i.e., for the given values of the coordinates.

The same adequacy condition would be rendered much less trivial, if a given context is not taken to consist of a given pairing of variables with their present values, but rather of a given class of propositions, e.g., perceptual information and some background beliefs. Under such a construal of contexts of utterance, a new class of functions is revealed, namely functions that determine, for any context of utterance given as an appropriate class of propositions, the values of those variables which are marked by indexical terms. Here a real computational process takes place, one which derives from the given class of perceptual and belief propositional items, say, a characterization of the place of utterance, marked by 'here' in the uttered sentence. In order to satisfy the above-mentioned adequacy condition these functions have to be computable, in an appropriate sense. There is no reason to assume that this condition is trivially satisfied.

Pondering over the nature of such functions, one encounters a consideration which might influence us in forming a view of pragmatics or even natural language in general. Consider, for example, the indexical term *she,* which has counterparts in various additional languages. In order to comprehend what is said with the words *She is clever* when uttered under certain circumstances, one has to apply some mental device which will identify a human female, other than the speaker and oneself, who is somehow present in the same context of utterance. Such a device will no doubt use both background beliefs and perceptual information for detecting the referent of *she* in that utterance. Just a slight stretch of imagination is required for realizing that any type of background information may be used by such a mental device. Thus, there is no reason to assume that the latter device is informationally encapsulated. Given, as a psychological background assumption, that the input systems of the mind are informationally encapsulated, cognitive modules, it follows that there is no pragmatic input system that pairs a given occurrence of the indexical term *she* in an uttered sentence with an appropriate female.

If the rules which govern these pairing functions fall within a pragmatic theory which, in turn, serves as a component of a grammar of a natural language, on a par with, say, syntax, then it turns out that the rules of language itself include ones which essentially rest on utterly non-linguistic information, such as the one required for identifying a certain female at the context of utterance. Not willing to give up hope for a decent distinction between linguistic rules and non-linguistic ones, we are left with the following alternatives: to exclude the study of those pairing functions from pragmatics, to exclude pragmatics from the theoretical study of language, or to draw some internal distinction within pragmatics such that part of it will fall under theory of language while the rest won't. We opt for the third alternative, which we apply along the following line. Consider again the indexical term *she.* If on some level of a linguistic representation this term is construed as a variable the value of which is determined in a certain way by the context of utterance each time the word is used in some sentence, this variable must be a restricted one and the restrictions are imposed on it by the language. Thus, the relation between appropriate use of the word *she* and the referent of it being a female is part of what is acquired when English is mastered, whereas identification of an appropriate female in the context of utterance is achieved by using a device which is mostly non-linguistic in nature. Put differently, indexical terms play the pragmatic role of referential schemes. The study of such schemes is part of the study of the pragmatic aspects of language, but the study of the ways in which such schemes are supplemented by successful identification devices falls outside the study of language itself. Perhaps the term 'peri-pragmatics' should be used for the latter kind of study, while the former one would fall within the confines of pragmatics proper.

Another problem to be tackled by an adequate pragmatic theory of deixis would be to characterize possible indexical expressions, where possibility is taken to be tantamount to being compatible with the given psychological background.

Notice, first, that a distinction can be drawn between two types of indexical expressions. We dub them 'acquaintance indexicals' and 'description indexicals,' after Russell's famous distinction between knowledge by acquaintance and knowledge by description (Russell [1918], cf. Hintikka [1974]). Thus, on the one hand there are expressions such as *the afore-mentioned painting of Rembrandt, my late uncles, your third degree* and *yesteryear.* These and similar expressions render their referential services by combining some indexical element with an independently understood, explicitly given descriptive expression. On the other hand there are indexical expressions such as *I, here* and *now,* the functioning of which does not seem to hinge on any independently understood, explicitly given descriptive expression. It can, indeed, be shown that the indexical core of any description indexical, whether explicit or implicit, is directly related to one of the few acquaintance indexicals. Thus, it is reasonable to assume that a characterization of the possible acquaintance indexicals is a major part of any characterization of possible indexical expressions, in the psychological sense of possibility.

As a first approximation to an analysis of the psychologically possible acquaintance indexicals, we make a peri-pragmatic suggestion: the pairing of such an indexical with the appropriate element of a context of utterance must be made by a perceptual input system, without recourse to the background beliefs accessible only to the central cognitive systems. On the plausible assumption that not too many aspects of any context of utterance are grasped by such informationally encapsulated systems, our suggestion imposes a psychological restriction on the class of possible acquaintance indexicals.[5]

5

We turn now to a brief discussion of the broader notion, or family of notions of context. Roughly speaking, context in any of these senses is taken "to be any background knowledge assumed to be shared by *s* (speaker) and *h* (hearer) and which contributes to *h*'s interpretation of what *s* means by a given utterance" (Leech [1983:13]).

What does it take for a speaker and a hearer to share some knowledge with each other? Some arguments have been put forward to the effect that such shared knowledge involves an infinite set of propositions. For example, assume that speaker *s* and hearer *h* sit face to face and that on the table between them is a conspicuous garland of flowers. They share the knowledge that there is a garland on the table, if and only if,

(1) Speaker *s* knows that there is a garland on the table.

(2) Hearer *h* knows that there is a garland on the table.

(3) Speaker *s* knows that (2).

(4) Hearer *h* knows that (1).

. . . and so on *ad infinitum.* (Cf. Schiffer [1972:30–36]).

Some authors have used the additional notions of mutual belief and mutual supposition, both being analyzed on a par with mutual knowledge as defined above (cf., for example, Clark and Carlson [1982]).

In order to accommodate an infinite set of propositions into a theory which claims compatibility with the modular brand of the finite representability constraint, several problems have to be solved first. To be sure, the infinite set of propositions which defines any case of, say, mutual belief is of course finitely representable, but this trivial observation carries much less than what is required when modular finite representability is sought. If the context of utterance and comprehension is identified with the mutual knowledge, beliefs and suppositions of speaker and hearer, then the infinite sets involved are thereby held to play an active role in every speech event. One problem we face is, then, how such an infinite set of propositions is represented in the mind in a way which enables cognitive devices to put it to use. Notice that using such an infinite set of propositions might mean using the whole set at once, in some appropriate sense, or using single elements of it, however remote they appear in the natural order of the set under consideration. Furthermore, since whatever proposition appears in the set of propositions defining a particular case of mutual belief (or supposition)[6] does not logically follow from previous elements of the set, the problem arises of the formation of such a set of propositions in one's mind. In other words, for pragmatics not to fail the 'external' test of the modularity approach, or even the weaker test of finite representability, what enables us to form an infinite set of independent beliefs or suppositions must be compatible with the the-oretical assumptions of the modularity ap-proach, or, in the weaker case, with those of finite representability. What, then, could it be?

Clark and his associates have suggested that an 'induction schema' is used in order to allow for an inference of a mutual belief (Clark and Marshall [1981]; Clark and Carlson [1982]). One insight we gain from this suggestion into the nature of mutual belief is its being hypo-thetical, in the sense that it involves evidence and support rather than proof and certainty. Secondly, grounds for any particular case of mutual belief are of a collective rather than a distributive nature, in the sense that except for the very first elements of the related infinite set, all its propositions are inductively sup-ported, at least under ordinary conditions, at one and the same time.

Furthermore, Clark and his associates sug-gest that there are three basic kinds of evi-dence for mutual belief, generally in combi-nation, viz. 'physical co-presence, linguistic co-presence, and community membership' (Clark and Carlson [1982:6]), the latter kind being also dubbed 'cultural co-presence' (Johnson-Laird [1982]). Physical co-presence involves the speaker and the hearer each being aware both of the presence of some physical object and of each other attending to it. Thus, evidence for physical co-presence can be es-tablished by a perceptual module. Similarly, linguistic co-presence involves the speaker and the hearer each being aware both of their pres-ence, so to speak, of the speaker's utterance, and of each other attending to it as a speech act of a language they share. Given that signif-icant parts of the comprehension of utterances are carried out by cognitive modules, part of the evidence for linguistic co-presence can be established by a linguistic module. However, as we have seen, full-fledged understanding is sometimes achieved only by recourse to infor-mation accessible just to the central cognitive systems. Consequently, part of linguistic co-presence sometimes depends for supportive evidence on more than some cognitive mod-ules. Clearly, cultural co-presence is mostly within the informational domain of the cen-tral systems of the mind. If evidence for mu-tual belief is of these kinds generally in com-

bination, there seems to be no reason to ascribe the co-presence heuristics operative in forming mutual belief to the cognitive mod-ules or to the central cognitive systems. How-ever, the whole process of forming a mutual belief is in any case one that includes also the induction schema which uses the evidence produced by the co-presence heuristics and it might be interesting to see whether such a schema can be accommodated into an infor-mationally encapsulated, cognitive module, or alternatively, should by its nature be part of some central system to which many kinds of information are available.

The answer to this question is perhaps re-lated to the following consideration. On many occasions we opt for a certain course of action on the ground of an appropriate presumption we hold. The interesting point about acting on presumptions is not that we take something for granted though we have no evidence that would establish that it holds, but rather that we govern some of our actions by rules which allocate the burden of proof in a nonsymmet-rical way. For example, having no evidence at all or just weak evidence to the effect that John murdered Bill, we act on the presumption that John is not guilty unless the opposite is estab-lished by a due process of law.

Under ordinary circumstances, it seems rea-sonable to assume, evidence of some kind is sufficient for producing a new presumption of common belief (or knowledge or supposition). Physical co-presence, for example, creates a presumption of common belief on the part of both speaker and hearer that certain physical objects are present and are being attended to. Thus, each proposition in the infinite set which defines a certain mutual belief is pre-sumed to hold, given appropriate evidence about physical, linguistic or cultural co-pres-ence. Such a proposition is dropped and the whole presumption revised when counter-evi-dence emerges and is brought to bear on that presumption.

When the evidence triggering the produc-tion of such a presumption of mutual belief is related to physical co-presence or linguistic co-presence of certain kinds, that is to say, when that evidence can be obtained by using just cognitive modules, whether perceptual or lin-guistic, the related presumption of the formed mutual belief is perhaps produced without any significant recourse to the central cognitive systems.

Our discussion of deixis leads us to the suggestion that certain phenomena of language use are, in a sense, a result of the psychological devices of utterance and understanding being of a certain nature, viz. resting on the operation of informationally encapsulated, input modules. The introduction of presumptions is directly due to the psychological background. The use of indexical schemes is also directly related to it. The two linguistic devices seem to be solutions of problems raised by the psychological setting.

6

We turn now to an examination of several aspects of the problem of the compatibility of pragmatic theories of presupposition with the modular approach. Under the appellation of 'presupposition', a host of utterly different phenomena, explanations and difficulties have been discussed. It seems that without confining our attention to a particular class of phenomena, one which shows a sufficient extent of homogeneity, it would be pointless to raise problems of compatibility and integration.

Thus, we consider just what might be dubbed 'lexical pragmatic presuppositions.' We use the term 'pragmatic presupposition' not only to mark the distinction between pragmatic and semantic presuppositions, but also to stress an essential feature of the presuppositions we are presently interested in, namely that the basic notion to be used in specifying these presuppositions is the relation between a speaker, an utterance and a proposition: roughly speaking, a speaker s, uttering u, pragmatically presupposes that proposition p holds, if and only if, by utter u speaker s has committed himself or herself to the belief or the assumption that proposition p holds.[7] Among the pragmatic presuppositions we are particularly interested in those which are created by lexical elements rather than by syntactic or logical form. For example, an ordinary utterance of the sentence *John managed to drive the car* commits the speaker to holding that John tried to drive the car, and clearly it is the lexical item marked by the words 'managed to' which triggers this pragmatic presup-

position. Our discussion is, then, mainly related to lexical pragmatic presuppositions, i.e., to pragmatic presuppositions which are triggered by lexical elements. (For critical surveys of studies of presuppositions in general and pragmatic presuppositions in particular, see Gazdar [1979] and Levinson [1983].

Much of the linguistic discussion of presupposition has been related to the projection problem of presuppositions, i.e., to the problem of specifying the set of presuppositions associated with a complex sentence in terms of the sets of presuppositions associated with its simpler parts. The underlying idea, that presuppositions are compositional, is of double significance when problems of finite representability and modularity are under consideration.

Compositionality provides a simple solution to the problem of finite representability, since the number of primitive elements is finite. Secondly, and much less self-evidently, compositionality is closely related to cognitive modules rather than to central cognitive systems, because it satisfies the requirement of enabling a cognitive system which operates on its grounds to be informationally encapsulated. Hence, specification of the lexical pragmatic presuppositions accompanying a given utterance seems to be an appropriate task for a module which has access to the lexical information and the syntactic interpretation of utterances. If there were such a cognitive module, it would have been a pragmatic module. This would have enhanced possible claims as to the psychological tenability of pragmatics, within a modular framework, but as it happens there is enough evidence to show that specificiation of lexical pragmatic presuppositions is beyond the power of cognitive modules.

What has led us to the conclusion that specification of lexical pragmatic presuppositions is not an informationally encapsulated process is a certain trait of some of these presuppositions, viz. that they are sometimes defeasible. If, for example, participants in a conversation are assumed by the speaker to know that John failed to get into a doctoral course, he or she can utter the sentence *At least John won't have to regret that he did a Ph.D.*, without thereby having committed oneself to the belief that John did a Ph.D., though such a pragmatic presupposition is triggered by the lexical element marked by the word 'regret.' 'The presupposition is simply cancelled by prevailing assumptions.' (Levinson [1983:187]). How a cancelling mechanism which produces such effects does work is presently of less concern to whoever is interested in problems of compatibility of pragmatics with the modular approach to the study of mental competences than is the source of information which triggers off the cancellation, viz. background information of the type which is available to central cognitive systems only. Now, since cancellation of some lexical pragmatic presupposition is an essential part of specifying the lexical pragmatic presuppositions accompanying speakers' speech acts, the task of specifying those presuppositions is beyond the power of cognitive modules, having to use whatever beliefs a person might entertain at the context of utterance and understanding. Thus, the most a module can do in service of the process of specifying the lexical pragmatic presuppositions in a context of utterance and understanding is to provide input for some central cognitive device which is to use both this input and the classes of present beliefs, assumptions and the like, as grounds for establishing the current class of pragmatic presuppositions. Note that though the output of such a cognitive module is an intermediate representation it might be of some theoretical significance, marking the analytical, lexical contribution to the specification of pragmatic presuppositions.

7

The study of speech acts is, in a sense, the most basic component of pragmatics: here we try to understand how we use words to do things. Theories of speech acts have borne some insights into the fundamentals of language, e.g., into the nature of the rules governing speech acts in natural language, but some of these theories have also led their followers into blind alleys commonly marked by classifications which serve no clear purpose. However, none of these theories has failed to draw attention to some interesting phenomena, that is to say, facts which are not only the subject of seemingly interesting questions, but also

such that no theory can claim empirical adequacy and explanatory respectability, so to speak, if it does not make at least a significant attempt at solving them in a general way. One such phenomenon, we believe, is that of indirect speech acts.

There seem to be indefinitely many different ways of requesting someone to shut the door, but only very few of them are direct ones, such as *Please close the door.* The indirect requests range from, say, *Would you mind closing the door* or *Can you close the door,* through *It might help to close the door* or *The door is still open,* to as far as *Now Johnny, what do big people do when they come in?* or even *Okay Johnny, what am I going to say next?* (Levinson [1983:264ff]). The problem of such indirect speech acts is, in a nutshell, how to obviate the apparent incompatibility of two simple observations on such a range of requesting acts, viz. that they all serve as requests and that almost all of them have syntactic and semantic properties of questions or assertions.

One way of clearing away a dilemma is by denying one of its horns. Thus, one might try to deny the very existence of literal forces, as ascribed to sentences rather than to utterances or to speech acts. Since such literal forces are tagged to certain syntactic forms (e.g., that of the imperative in English) or to certain lexical elements as well (e.g., performative verbs, 'please' and, in a way, 'hereby'), the possiblity of ascribing to any speech act a force on grounds of straightforward syntactic and semantic considerations would also be denied.

Obviously, the mental device which determines the force of an utterance or of a speech act under such an approach could not be informationally encapsulated. Recall the utterance, which serves as a request (though indirect one) to close the door, of the sentence *Okay Johnny, what am I going to say next?* There is no reason to assume that there is a way to bridge the gap between the literal meaning of the latter sentence and the force of the former request without recourse to beliefs accessible to just the central systems of the mind (or some of them) and not to the linguistic, informationally encapsulated modules. In other words, according to that approach to indirect speech acts, understanding the forces of speech acts (or utterances) is the task of a central system of the mind, in the operation of which the input from the linguistic modules, which represents a certain syntactic structure, does not play a major role. The role it probably does play is that of imposing some general restriction on the central process of specifying forces of speech acts (or utterances). For example, where the input coming from the linguistic modules represents the syntactic form of a *wh*-question, the central device may take it to stand for a certain open formula ($Q(x)$) related to a certain domain of appropriate entities (the possible answers). The force of the utterance under consideration has yet to be determined, because several speech acts fit in with such a pair of an open formula and a range of possible values, e.g., requests for information, offers, threats and many others.

Given our assumptions about the psychological background, another solution of the problem of indirect speech acts turns out to be more appealing. The linguistic modules determine a literal force using the syntactic properties of the utterance under analysis and the semantic properties of lexical or other elements of the utterance. Thus, the basic syntactically defined forms of the declarative, the interrogative, the imperative and perhaps some other ones too, as well as the performative elements (of the form *I hereby apologize for,* for example) play a major role in specifying literal forces. Now, these literal forces are taken by the related central device to presumably be the forces of the utterances under consideration. Recall that any presumption is held unless there is enough evidence to deem it wrong. Indeed, many of the presumptions that the linguistic modules create for the central systems of understanding are left intact by it: the force of many declarative sentences, for example, is that of assertion. On other occasions these presumptions are not retained, because beliefs available to the central device are found to be incompatible with them. A presumable assertion, for example, may thus turn out to be a promise, when there is reason to assume that speaker *s* does not have any grounds for a prediction that *s* will act in a certain way, specified in *s*'s utterance, except for *s*'s having undertaken an obligation to act so.

On still other occasions, the input presumption with respect to the force of a given utterance is not discarded but rather used and dismissed, so to speak. Consider the typical example of an ordinary request for information which is commonly taken to be an indirect request to close the door: *Could you close the door?* Under fairly common conditions there would be no reason to assume that such a request for information is posed for the sake of some remote future possible use of the answer or for gaining knowledge of the answer for the sake of itself. Usually (though not always), questions are put in order to serve some going concern, on the nature of which a central cognitive system forms a belief. Such a belief forms a hypothetical explanation of the speech act of *s* having been performed under the circumstances. The most natural explanation of that question would, in many cases, be that *s* is interested in the addressee's closing the door and this is why such a question is taken by many to serve as an indirect request for closing the door. In one sense it is and in another sense it isn't: it is intended to trigger an act of closing the door to be performed by the addressee, but the process of understanding that intention is not purely linguistic, resting on a central device for explaining intentional acts of speakers, well beyond what is literally said in the utterances used.[8]

We prefer the latter explanation of indirect speech acts over the former one, because it renders the module-center interface much more cogent. To be sure, the nature of the interface with respect to indirect speech acts is empirical and what we have done is just to outline some theoretical possibility for further consideration.

To be sure, there have been quite a number of empirical studies of indirect speech acts, but their results have not been used for the present purpose of putting pragmatics to the 'external' test of the modularity approach.

We saw earlier that an explanation of indirect speech acts seems plausible in terms of presumed, literal forces, as determined by a linguistic module on grounds of strictly linguistic information, and of eventual forces, as determined by some central device on grounds of the presumed, literal forces as well as additional, non-linguistic information. The distinction we use, between literal and eventual forces, is meant to apply on an abstract level of description and explanation, where the major claims are couched in terms of relations between different types of information. It is of course not assumed that this distinction is or should be directly reflected in processes as studied on other, 'lower' levels, by using common experimental paradigms, measuring accuracy, response time and the like. This is no reason to assume that explanatory distinctions on one level are simply detectable on any 'lower' level.

This is why some experimental work, interesting as it might be found out to be for other purposes, sheds no light on our problems of compatibility and integration. For example, even if one follows Raymond Gibbs in interpreting his interesting results as supporting the view that complete processing of the literal meaning of a sentence, in a context of its utterance, is not required, say, for proper understanding of the indirect force of its utterance (e.g., Gibbs [1979], [1983]), we are still under no commitment to accept his conclusion that abstract distinctions between literal elements and non-literal ones have "little psychological validity" (Gibbs [1984:275]). Actually, it seems plausible to assume that models of processing could be suggested, for example, by way of improving upon some fruitful suggestions (Clark [1979], Clark and Schunk [1980]), which would employ the distinction between a presumed, literal force and an eventual one.

Moreover, without a distinction between literal elements and non-literal ones, one could hardly make any sense of many interesting observations made with respect to brain damaged patients of various types (Gardner et al. [1983], Hirst et al. [1984], Foldi [1987], Weylman et al. [1989] and Zaidel and Kasher [1988]). In all of these studies the distinction between literal and non-literal elements is employed on the simplest level of description and none of them seems to motivate any attempt at describing the same data without recourse to that distinction.

From our present point of view, these neuropsychological studies are of additional interest, because they show that what supports an integration of certain explanations in pragmatics with the modular approach, seems to suggest an integration of those explanations with an additional level of description and explanation, viz. a neuropsychological one.

8

Grice's philosophical theory of implicatures, both conversational and conventional, has attracted much linguistic attention in attempts to explain a variety of intricate observations on language use and understanding. The basic pattern of establishing a conversational implicature, whether according to Grice's original suggestion (in Grice [1975]) or according to some revised versions of it, as well as several conversational maxims that have been suggested by Grice and others, have been rightly considered as paradigms of theoretical insight that can be gained into the nature of language by pragmatic theories.

From the present perspective there is one basic remark that we would like to make. As we argued elsewhere (in Kasher [1976, 1982]), the philosophical foundations on which Grice's theory of conversational implicature rests is a general theory of rational action. Thus, every conversational implicature that can be derived by a Gricean pattern, on the presumption that his cooperative principle holds for the conversation under analysis, can be derived by a similar pattern, where the dubious cooperative principle is replaced by a general rationality principle, viz. 'Where there is no reason to assume the contrary, take the speaker s to be a rational agent; s's ends and beliefs in a context of utterance should be assumed to supply a complete justification of s's behavior, unless there is evidence to the contrary.' In the present context, being rational is tantamount to following a principle of effective means, viz. 'Given a desired end, one is to choose that action which most effectively, and at least cost, attains that end, *ceteris paribus*'.

One merit of the present approach is that it does not have to invoke any practical principle which holds just for speech activity. Indeed, the principles of general rationality and of effective means apply to any case of presumably intentional behavior, speech acts not excluded. It is not difficult to demonstrate that from these general principles there follow not only conversational maxims and patterns for establishing conversational implicatures, but also the explanation of various insights that have been made into the nature of language use and which otherwise seem to hover over the theory as if having flown in from nowhere. To mention just two examples, Sperber and Wilson have proposed "the single principle governing every aspect of comprehension, the principle of relevance: The speaker tries to express the proposition which is the most relevant one possible to the hearer" (1982:75). With respect to the notorious notion of relevance they assume, first, "that other things being equal, the more contextual implications a proposition has, the more relevant it is" (p. 103) and secondly, "that other things being equal, the smaller the amount of processing, the greater the relevance of the proposition" (p. 105). A plausible version of these two facets of that principle of relevance follows from general considerations of rationality. The same holds for the observation on indirect speech acts made by Gordon and Lakoff (1975), namely that "[o]ne can convey a request by (a) asserting a speaker-based sincerity condition or (b) questioning a hearer-based sincerity condition" (p. 86), which is an instance of a more general claim about the direct relation between asserting or questioning a felicity condition of a speech act and its indirect production.

Obviously, our principles of general rationality and of effective means are not domain specific in any reasonable sense and hence, if they constitute the principles of operation of some mental device, then the latter must be a central cognitive system which employs the former principle in forming beliefs and in planning action, not only when language plays an overt role.

This rather simple observation has an interesting consequence regarding the very nature of pragmatics. It turns out that one of the most important areas of pragmatics is not purely linguistic, in an interesting sense. Some of the most impressive insights into the operation of language use are found not to capture an essential property of language use per se, but rather reflect an intrinsic property of intentional activity in general. In terms of cognitive processing it means that the explanatory power of pragmatic theories hinges on central cognitive systems of a highly abstract nature,

abstract to the extent required for the formulation and employment of the principles of general rationality and of effective means.

9

It has been noticed for a long time now that certain social relations between speaker and hearer are sometimes marked in utterances the former addresses to the latter, but the related deference principles have played at most a marginal role in any general theory of language use. Recently, however, an attempt has been made, in Leech (1983), to show that politeness principles, in a very broad sense of the term, play a central role in explaining a variety of language uses, on a par with and in a way which is closely related to Grice's maxims. Leech's theory deserves philosophical scrutiny but we will address ourselves to it on another occasion. Presently we take the principles of this theory for granted and assume that they do not follow from the rationality principles we mentioned in the previous section.[9]

Leech's most general politeness principle commends minimizing the expression of 'impolite beliefs,' i.e., ones which are 'unfavourable . . . on some scale of values' (p. 131). Different scales give rise to different politeness maxims. Thus, what Leech calls 'the tact maxim,' in impositives and commissives, minimizes 'cost to *other*,' his 'generosity maxim,' in the same types of speech act, minimizes 'benefit to *self*,' while what he dubbed 'the approbation maxim' minimizes 'dispraise to *other*,' in expressives and assertives. Similarly, Leech's maxim minimizes 'disagreement between *self* and *other*,' in assertives (p. 132).

Notice that though these and other maxims are taken by Leech to be "the general 'imperatives' of human communication" and hence "are more or less universal," "their relative weights will vary from one cultural, social, or linguistic milieu to another" (p. 150). To be sure, what counts, for example, as cost to *other* or benefit to *self* varies not only with the general facets of the context of utterance, such as the background social milieu, but also with much more particular facets of it. Consequently, the information required by a speaker *s* for applying politeness maxims to *s*'s own speech could not be considered encapsulated in any interesting sense. What regulates certain aspects of speech and understanding are, then, principles by which some central cognitive system operates on varied data.

10

So far we have discussed only 'local' problems, i.e., ones which pertain to certain theoretical explanations within pragmatics. With respect to each of these parts of pragmatics, we tried to find out how it fares within a modular framework for the study of mental competences. In conclusion of this paper, we would like to briefly address the 'global' problem of compatibility and integration, viz. how does pragmatics, as a whole family of theoretical explanations, fare within the modular framework.[10]

The 'global' picture which emerges from our 'local' discussions seems to involve a division of the core of pragmatics into three parts—two different competences and an interface:

(a) The first part is a pragmatic, purely linguistic competence, embodying, first and foremost knowledge of certain speech act types.

(b) The second part is a pragmatic, non-linguistic competence, governing aspects of intentional action in general, including linguistic activity, which is intentional in nature. This competence produces conversational implicatures, for example, and is thereby also involved in politeness considerations as applied to speech activity. There are also reasons to assume that this competence is involved in producing the integrated understanding of what has been said in a given context of utterance, as a function of the presumed linguistic interpretation of what has been said and additional information with respect to the intentional activity under consideration.

(c) The third part is not a competence, but rather a class of various interface features. Indexicals, for instance, involve the output of a language module and its integration with some output of a perception module, where both serve as input for the same central cognitive device which produces the integrated understanding of what has been said in a given context of utterance. Lexical pragmatical presuppositions involve another type of interface between a lanuage module and that central device.

Summarizing what has so far been said about pragmatics in the mind, within the framework of the modular approach to the study of mental competences, we put forward the following "basic formula of the modular structure of pragmatics":

Pragmatics in the mind = a pragmatic module
+ a pragmatic part of the center
+ pragmatic interface

Two features of this 'formula' should be mentioned. First, there is a natural relationship between the pragmatic module and the pragmatic part of the center. The specific domain of this module is that of speech acts, while the pragmatic part of the center governs general aspects of intentional activity, including that of performing and understanding speech acts. Moreover, some features of pragmatic interface actually involve the interface of the pragmatic module with the pragmatic part of the center.

However, secondly, one should notice that not all the features of pragmatic interface are related to this pragmatic module. As is clear from our discussion of indexicals, there are features of interface of linguistic elements with the context of utterance, which seem to be of a different nature. Expressions such as "she" or "there" involve interface of linguistic and nonlinguistic modules with the center, whereas the former type of interface involves the interface of just linguistic modules with the center.

The distinction between these two types of interface could suggest a division of pragmatics into two fields, viz. the study of pragmatic aspects of word meaning and the study of pragmatic aspects of sentence use, or in other words, into the study of context dependence and a study of speech acts.

There seem to be two important reasons for not accepting this suggestion. First, speech acts too involve certain forms of context dependence. Commands, for example, are performed within a certain hierarchy, whether formal or not, which grants certain speakers with some authority with respect to others. The identity of such a background hierarchy of a particular command does, of course, depend on the context of utterance.[11]

Secondly, according to our own conception of pragmatics, this part of the study of language has in its focus appropriateness conditions of sentences with contexts of their utterance. (Kasher [1977] and [1988a]). Accordingly, both the study of context dependence and the study of speech acts belong to pragmatics, since both play the major roles in linguistic considerations of appropriateness of sentences to contexts.

ACKNOWLEDGMENTS

This chapter is an extensively revised version of the author's "On the Psychological Reality of Pragmatics," *Journal of Pragmatics* 8 (1984):539–557.

NOTES

1. See, for example, Gazdar (1979), Leech (1983) and Levinson (1983). Our own conception is closely related to that of Chomsky (1980). On Chomsky's views of pragmatics and our related conception, see Kasher (1988a).

2. Notice that by assuming (1)–(3), we have not committed ourselves to the view that the mind is just a 'purely formal' device, a 'syntactic' symbol manipulator, a system of 'computational' programs. An identification of the mind with such entities would leave room for arguments of the Chinese Room variety (Searle [1984] and [1987]). Cf. Fodor (1987:166, fn 3).

3. Memory is an example. See Fodor (1983:7ff).

4. Fodor (1983) mentions additional properties of cognitive modules. One will be mentioned in the next assumption and serves a major role in our discussion. The others are presently less significant. For a discussion of the latter properties in the context of pragmatics, see Kasher [1988a] and [1988b].

5. Russell used to think that what he called 'egocentric particulars,' such as 'I,' 'you,' 'here,' 'there,' 'now,' 'then,' 'past,' 'present,' 'future' and tenses in verbs, can all be defined in terms of 'this.' See, for example, Russell (1962:102ff). We don't have space for evaluating this claim presently.

6. When mutual knowledge, rather than belief or supposition, is under consideration the situation is slightly different, but we don't have to go into that now.

7. The utterance u can be analysed as an ordered pair of sentence s and a context of utterance c. See Kasher (1971) and Cresswell (1973:113) for slightly different suggestions.

8. The problem arises of why speakers should ever opt for such indirect forms of speech. Allusion to politeness effects won't count as an explanation, because the problem remains of why politeness should be marked by indirectness. At least part of the explanation is related to the intermediate notion of optionality: a question which serves as an indirect request leaves the addressee more open options and most probably the more options one leaves open to the addressee the better, as far as politeness is concerned (and all other things being equal). I owe this explanation to Franck (1980). See also Leech (1983:109ff).

9. The exact relations that politeness considerations bear to rationality principles is outlined in our Kasher (1986), where we show that politeness serves as a parameter in a rationality ends/means principle, which prescribes maximization of certain parameters (related to achievement of ends) and minimization of some other parameters (such as ones related to expenditures). Politeness considerations usually introduce a minimization parameter into applications of the rationality principle.

10. This problem is addressed in Kasher (1988a) and (1988b).

11. For a detailed discussion of such context dependence and a general framework for its accommodation within pragmatics, see our [1988b].

REFERENCES

Bar-Hillel, Y. (1970). "Indexical Expressions." In Y. Bar-Hillel (ed.), *Aspects of Language.* Jerusalem: Magnes Press, 69–88.
Barwise, J., and J. Perry (1983). *Situations and Attitudes.* Cambridge, Mass., and London: MIT Press.
Bruner, J. (1986). "Psychological Reality." In J. Bruner (ed.), *Actual Minds, Possible Worlds.* Cambridge, Mass., and London: Harvard University Press, 79–92.
Chomsky, N. (1980). *Rules and Representations.* Oxford: Basil Blackwell.
Chomsky, N. (1982). *The Generative Enterprise: A Discussion with R. Huybregts and H. van Riemsdijk.* Dordrecht: Foris.

Chomsky, N. (1984). *Modular Approaches to the Study of Mind.* San Diego: San Diego State University.

Chomsky, N. (1988). "Language and Interpretation: Philosophical Reflections and Empirical Inquiry." Manuscript.

Clark, H. H. (1979). "Responding to Indirect Speech Acts." *Cognitive Psychology* 11:430–477. [Reprinted in this volume, Chapter 12]

Clark, H. H., and T. B. Carlson (1982). "Speech Acts and Hearers' Beliefs." In N. V. Smith (ed.), *Mutual Knowledge.* London and New York: Academic Press, 1–36. [Reprinted in this volume, Chapter 11]

Clark, H. H., and C. R. Marshall (1981). "Definite Reference and Mutual Knowledge." In A. K. Joshi, I. Sag, and B. Webber (eds.), *Elements of Discourse Understanding.* Cambridge: Cambridge University Press.

Clark, H. H., and D. Schunk (1980). "Polite Responses to Polite Requests." *Cognition* 8:111–143.

Cresswell, M. J. (1973). *Logics and Languages.* London: Methuen.

Davidson, D. (1965). "Theories of Meaning and Learnable Languages." In Y. Bar-Hillel (ed.), *Logic, Methodology and Philosophy of Science.* Amsterdam: North-Holland, 383–394.

Dummet, M. (1975). "What Is a Theory of Meaning? I." In S. Guttenplan (ed.), *Mind and Language.* Oxford: Clarendon Press, 97–138.

Fodor, J. A. (1983). *The Modularity of Mind,* Cambridge, Mass., and London: MIT Press.

Fodor, J. A. (1987). *Psychosemantics,* Cambridge, Mass., and London: MIT Press.

Foldi, N. S. (1987). "Appreciation of Pragmatic Interpretations of Indirect Commands: Comparison of Right and Left Hemisphere Brain-damaged Patients." *Brain and Language* 31:88–108.

Franck, D. (1980). *Grammatik und Konversation.* Konigstein: Scriptor.

Gardner, H., H. H. Brownell, W. Wapner, and D. Michelow (1983). "Missing the Point: The Role of the Right Hemisphere in the Processing of Complex Linguistic Materials." In E. Perecman (ed.), *Cognitive Processes in the Right Hemisphere.* New York: Academic Press, 169–191.

Gazdar, G. (1979). *Pragmatics.* New York and London: Academic Press.

Gibbs, R. W. (1979). "Contextual Effects in Understanding Indirect Requests." *Discourse Processes* 2:1–10.

Gibbs, R. W. (1983). "Do People Always Process the Literal Meanings in Indirect Requests?" *Journal of Experimental Psychology: Learning, Memory and Cognition* 9:524–533.

Gibbs, R. W. (1984). "Literal Meaning and Psychological Theory." *Cognitive Science* 8:275–304.

Gochet, P. (1980). *Outline of a Nominalist Theory of Propositions.* Dordrecht: Reidel.

Gordon, D., and G. Lakoff (1975). "Conversational Postulates." In P. Cole and J. L. Morgan (eds.), *Syntax and Semantics.* Vol. 3: *Speech Acts.* New York: Academic Press, 83–106.

Grice, H. P. (1975). "Logic and Conversation." In P. Cole and J. L. Morgan (eds.), *Syntax and Semantics.* Vol. 3: *Speech Acts.* New York: Academic Press, 41–58. [Reprinted in this volume, Chapter 19].

Hintikka, J. (1974). "Knowledge by Acquaintance—Individuation by Acquaintance." In J. Hintikka (ed.), *Knowledge and the Known.* Dordrecht: Reidel. 212–233.

Hirst, W., J. LeDoux, and S. Stein. (1984). "Constraints on the Processing of Indirect Speech Acts: Evidence from Aphasiology." *Brain and Language* 23:26–33.

Johnson-Laird, P. N. (1982). "Mutual Ignorance: Comments on Clark and Carlson." In N. V. Smith (ed.), *Mutual Knowledge.* London and New York: Academic Press, 40–45.

Kaplan, D. (1979). "On the Logic of Demonstratives." In P. A. French, T. E. Uehling, and H. K. Wettstein (eds.), *Contemporary Perspectives in the Philosophy of Language.* Minneapolis: University of Minnesota Press, 401–412. [Reprinted in this volume, Chapter 8]

Kaplan, D. (1989). "Afterthoughts." In J. Perry, H. K. Wettstein, and J. Almog (eds.), *Themes from Kaplan.* New York: Oxford University Press.

Kasher, A. (1971). "A Step Toward a Theory of Linguistic Performance." In Y. Bar-Hillel (ed.), *Pragmatics of Natural Languages.* Dordrecht: Reidel, 84–93.

Kasher, A. (1976). "Conversational Maxims and Rationality." In A. Kasher (ed.), *Language in Focus: Foundations, Methods and Systems.* Dordrecht: Reidel, 197–216.

Kasher, A. (1977). "What Is a Theory of Use?" *Journal of Pragmatics* 1:105–120.

Kasher, A. (1979). "Logical Rationalism and Formal Semantics of Natural Languages: On Conditions of Adequacy." In F. Heny and H. S. Schnelle (eds.), *Selections from the Third Groningen Round Table.* New York and London: Academic Press, 257–273.

Kasher, A. (1982). "Gricean Inference Revisited." *Philosophica* (Ghent) 29:25–44.

Kasher, A. (1986). "Politeness and Rationality." In J. Dines and H. Sonne (eds.), in collaboration with H. Haberland, *Pragmatics and Linguistics: Festschrift for Jacob L. Mey.* Odense: Odense University Press, 103–114.

Kasher, A. (1987). "Justification of Speech, Acts, and Speech Acts." In E. LePore (ed.), *New Directions in Semantics.* London: Academic Press, 281–303.

Kasher, A. (1988a). "Pragmatics and Chomsky's Research Program." In *The Chomskyan Turn: Generative Linguistics, Philosophy, Mathematics and Psychology.*

Kasher, A. (1988b). "The Pragmatic Module." In *Text and Context: Cognitive Studies in Language Use.*

Leech, G. (1983). *Principles of Pragmatics.* London and New York: Longman.

Levinson, S. (1983). *Pragmatics.* Cambridge: Cambridge University Press.

Lewis, D. (1972). "General Semantics." In D. Davidson and G. Harman (eds.), *Semantics of Natural Language.* Dordrecht: Reidel, 169–218.

Lyons, J. (1968). *Introduction to Theoretical Linguistics.* Cambridge: Cambridge University Press.

Miller, G., and N. Chomsky (1963). "Finitary Models of Language Users." In R. D. Luce, R. B. Bush, and E. Galanter (eds.), *Handbook of Mathematical Psychology II.* New York and London: Wiley, 419–491.

Russell, B. (1918). "Knowledge by Acquaintance and Knowledge by Description." In B. Russel (ed.), *Mysticism and Logic.* London: Allen and Unwin, 209–232.

Russell, B. (1962). *An Inquiry into Meaning and Truth.* London: Penguin.

Schiffer, S. (1972). *Meaning.* Oxford: Clarendon Press.

Searle, J. R. (1984). *Minds, Brains and Science.* London: BBC Publications.

Searle, J. R. (1987). "Minds and Brains Without Programs." In C. Blakemore and S. Greenfield (eds.), *Mindwaves.* Oxford: Basil Blackwell, 209–233.

Sperber, D., and D. Wilson (1982). "Mutual Knowledge and Relevance in Theories of Comprehension." In N. V. Smith (ed.), *Mutual Knowledge.* London and New York: Academic Press, 61–85.

Weylman, S. T., H. H. Brownell, M. Roman, and H. Gardner (1989). "Appreciation of Indirect Requests by Left and Right Brain-damaged Patients: The Effects of Verbal Context and Conventionality of Wording." *Brain and Language* 36:580–591.

Zaidel, D., and A. Kasher (1988). "The Right Hemisphere Communication Battery: Performance of Commissurotomy and Hemispherectomy Patients."

35

Pragmatics and Modularity

DEIRDRE WILSON AND DAN SPERBER

1. INTRODUCTION

Grammar and pragmatics are alike in two respects: they fall within the domain of cognitive
psychology, and they have to do with language. Apart from that, we will argue, they
have virtually nothing in common. Grammar
is a special-purpose modular system; pragmatics is not a cognitive system at all. There are
no special-purpose pragmatic principles, maxims, strategies or rules; pragmatics is simply
the domain in which grammar, logic and
memory interact. Modular grammatical processes offer little direct insight into the nature
of non-modular pragmatic processes. Indeed,
the more we model pragmatics on grammar,
the more mistaken we are likely to be.

2. WHY PRAGMATICS IS NOT A MODULE

Utterance interpretation involves a variety of
processes, grammatical and pragmatic. By
'grammatical processes,' we mean the processes used to recover the semantic represen-

tation of the sentence uttered (or in the case of
ambiguity, its set of semantic representations).
By 'pragmatic processes,' we mean the processes used to bridge the gap between the semantic representations of sentences and the
interpretation of utterances in context. The
goal of the hearer, and, by extension, of the
pragmatic processes, is to recover not just
some arbitrary interpretation, but the interpretation intended by the speaker: this is the
only interpretation it is worth the hearer's effort to recover.

Pragmatic processs are involved in every aspect of utterance interpretation: in the recovery of explicit propositional content, implicit
import and illocutionary force. Often, the sentence uttered is ambiguous or ambivalent, as
in (1):

(1) His food is not hot enough.

The hearer of (1) must not only recover the
semantic representation of the sentence uttered, but decide who the referential expression 'he' refers to, whether the ambiguous
word 'hot' means *very warm* or *spicy,* whether
the vague expression 'his food' refers to the

Deirdre Wilson and Dan Sperber, "Pragmatics and Modularity." In *The Chicago Linguistic Society Parassession
on Pragmatics and Grammatical Theory,* edited by Anne M. Farley, Peter T. Farley, and Karl-Erik McCullough.
Copyright © 1986 by the Chicago Linguistic Society. Reprinted by permission of the publisher.

food he cooked, the food he brought, the food he served, the food he is eating, etc., and what this food is claimed to be not hot enough *for*.

Utterances have not only propositional content but illocutionary force, and ambiguities or ambivalences may arise at this level, as in (2):

(2) You're not leaving.

The hearer of (2) must not only recover its explicit propositional content, but also decide whether it is intended as a statement, a question or an order.

Utterances have not only explicit content but implicit import, as in (3):

(3) a. *Peter:* Do you want some coffee?
    b. *Mary:* Coffee would keep me awake.

The hearer of (3b) must recover not only its explicit content but also the implicature that Mary doesn't want any coffee (or, in some circumstances, that she does).

Utterances may be metaphorical or ironical, as in (4) and (5):

(4) Their friendship blossomed.

(5) I've never had such a lovely meal.

The hearer of (4) or (5) must not only recover its explicit content but also decide whether it was literally or figuratively intended, and what its figurative interpretation was intended to be.

More generally, the style of an utterance may affect its interpretation—compare the mildly witty (6) with its heavy-handed explicit paraphrase (7):

(6) Two taxis collided and 30 Scotsmen were taken to hospital.

                                         [Woody Allen]

(7) Scotsmen are very mean. They travel in enormously overcrowded taxis to avoid paying full fare. Once two taxis containing 30 Scotsmen collided. The passengers were taken to hospital.

These stylistic effects on the hearer must be described and explained. Pragmatics, then, is a theory of the cognitive principles and abilities involved in utterance interpretation, and of their cognitive effects.

Is pragmatics a module? For Fodor (1983), the paradigm example of a modular system is the linguistic system. By hypothesis, this incorporates a grammar, i.e. a code, which re-

lates phonetic representations of sentences to semantic representations of sentences. Here, we will simply assume that there is a necessary connection between the modularity of the linguistic system and the fact that it incorporates a grammar or code. The claim that pragmatics is a module is thus essentially equivalent to the claim that there is a pragmatic code.

Many linguists have assumed without question that speakers of English know a pragmatic code, analogous to a grammar, which enables them to recover the intended interpretation of utterances in English. They have assumed, in other words, that pragmatics is a module, an extension of the grammar. Underlying this assumption is a more general assumption about the nature of communication: that communication necessarily involves the use of a code. Both assumptions seem to us to be false.

In the first place, pragmatic processes are highly context dependent. Different contextual assumptions lead to different pragmatic interpretations. If utterance interpretation is a matter of decoding the speaker's intentions, there must be some algorithm for selecting the appropriate set of contextual assumptions, the ones the hearer was intended to use. Yet there are at least two types of case[s] which suggest that no such algorithm exists.

Sometimes, a hearer is simply unable to access a contextual assumption he was intended to use in interpreting an utterance. Consider (8):

(8) a. *Peter:* Ozzy Osbourne's coming to dinner.
    b. *Mary:* I'll bring a bat.

To disambiguate the word 'bat' in (8b), the hearer would need access to the information that Ozzy Osbourne is a rock musician mainly known for having bitten the head off a live bat on stage. What algorithm could he use to recover this assumption from the exchange in (8)?

More often, a hearer has access to a variety of alternative contextual assumptions, which yield a variety of incompatible interpretations, only one of which could have been intended by the speaker. Suppose that as I give a lecture, I make a slip of the tongue. You turn to your neighbour and whisper:

(9) That was interesting.

What algorithm could your neighbour use to decide that you intended to refer to the slip of the tongue I had just made, rather than, say, to the example I had just been discussing, the theoretical claim I had just made, or the fact that a strange bird had just flown past the window? But if there is no algorithm for identifying the intended set of contextual assumptions, there can be no algorithm for recovering the intended overall interpretation of an utterance.

A more general problem for modular approaches to pragmatics is their failure to deal with indeterminacies in interpretation. According to the code model, the speaker's thoughts, encoded into an utterance, should be replicated in the hearer by a decoding process. The result of verbal communication should be an exact reproduction in the hearer of the thoughts the speaker intended to convey. However, the most cursory examination of ordinary conversation reveals that in the case of implicit import, figurative interpretation and stylistic effects, such reproduction is rarely intended or achieved. The existence of indeterminacies in interpretation suggests a fundamental inadequacy in modular approaches to pragmatics. Where indeterminacy is involved, it seems that the most that communication can achieve is to bring about some similarity between the thoughts of communicator and audience; but the code model can provide no interesting account of those cases where similarity, rather than identity, is intended and achieved.

Finally, it is easy to show that communication is possible in the absence of a code. Consider (10):

(10) a. *Peter:* How are you feeling today?
  b. *Mary:* [Takes a bottle of aspirin out of her bag and shows it to Peter.]

Here, Mary communicates that she is not feeling very well, even though there is no code or convention which says that showing someone a bottle of aspirin means that one is not feeling well. Intuitively, Peter does not need a code to understand Mary's behavior in (10) because he can use his knowledge of the world and his general reasoning abilities to *work out* what she must have intended to convey. On this account, communication is achieved not by coding and decoding messages, but by providing evidence for an intended inference about the communicator's intentions. Might this not be the case for verbal communication too?

The assumption that pragmatic processes are modular thus seems to us neither necessary nor plausible. But what exactly does it mean to claim that they are not modular? According to Fodor, the paradigm example of a non-modular process is scientific theorizing. Scientific theorizing is a non-demonstrative inference process. Like all such processes, it can be broken down into two stages: hypothesis formation and hypothesis confirmation. Both stages exhibit what Fodor regards as the defining feature of non-modular processes: they are *informationally unencapsulated.* That is, they have free access to contextual information. There is no piece of evidence, however remote, no hypothesis, however implausible, that might not turn out to have a bearing on their outcome. Grammatical processes, by contrast, have highly restricted access to contextual information: they are unaffected by the hearer's non-linguistic beliefs.

Pragmatic interpretation seems to us to resemble scientific theorizing in essential respects. The speaker's intentions are not decoded but non-demonstratively inferred, by a process of hypothesis formation and confirmation which, like scientific theorizing and unlike grammatical analysis, has free access to contextual information. The hearer's aim is to arrive at the most plausible hypothesis about the speaker's intentions; but the most plausible hypothesis, in pragmatic interpretation as in science, may still be wrong.

There is thus a fundamental difference between the modular and the non-modular approaches to pragmatics. A fundamental assumption of the non-modular approach is that the interpretation of communicative behaviour, like the interpretation of evidence in general, is always subject to risk. There are always alternative ways of interpreting a given piece of evidence, even when all the correct procedures for interpretation are applied. These procedures may yield a best hypothesis, but even the best hypothesis may not be the correct, i.e., the intended, one. By contrast, decoding procedures, when correctly applied to an undistorted signal, guarantee the recovery not only of *an* interpretation, but of the *correct,* i.e. the intended interpretation. The two approaches start from radically different assumptions about the nature of communication itself.

Fodor is sceptical about the amenability of non-modular processes to scientific study:

> ... the limits of modularity are also likely to be the limits of what we are going to be able to understand about the mind, given anything like the theoretical apparatus currently available. (Fodor 1983:126)

As he rightly points out, virtually nothing is known about either the logic or the psychology of scientific hypothesis formation and confirmation. If pragmatic interpretation is just a special case of scientific theorizing, it seems that the search for an explanatory pragmatic theory is doomed to fail.

Certainly, recent work in pragmatics gives little cause for optimism. Formal pragmatists simply assume that pragmatics is a module, and provide mechanical analyses for a severely restricted range of data. Gricean pragmatists, who approach pragmatics in inferential terms, often fall back on the assumptions of the code model, and offer nothing approaching an explicit theory. In the last few years, we have been trying to develop an explicit, explanatory theory of pragmatic interpretation. We will try to show that it offers interesting solutions to a variety of empirical problems arising from more traditional accounts. (For a full account of this theory, and the assumptions behind it, see Sperber and Wilson 1986).

3. COGNITION: RELEVANCE

Grice made two major contributions to pragmatics. First, he outlined an inferential alternative to the code model of communication. Second, he suggested a method by which pragmatic hypotheses might be confirmed or disconfirmed. The idea was that, given a range of hypotheses about the communicator's intentions, the hearer should discard any that are incompatible with the assumption that the co-operative principle and maxims of truthfulness, informativeness, relevance and brevity have been observed. For a variety of reasons, this suggestion does not amount to an explanatory theory: crucial terms such as 'relevance,' 'co-operation,' 'brevity,' 'required informa-

tion,' 'purposes of the exchange' were left undefined; no account of the role of contextual information, nor of the processes of pragmatic hypothesis formation, were offered, and the origin of the maxims themselves was left unexplained. However, it does indicate what we should be trying to do. We should be trying to develop an explicit criterion powerful enough to eliminate all but a single hypothesis about the communicator's intentions. The rest of this paper will be devoted to developing such a criterion and showing how it works.

We believe that this criterion has its source in some basic facts about human cognition. Humans pay attention to some phenomena rather than others; they represent these phenomena to themselves in one way rather than another; they process these representations in one context rather than another. What is it that determines these choices? Our suggestion is that humans tend to pay attention to the most relevant phenomena available; that they tend to construct the most relevant possible representations of these phenomena, and to process them in a context that maximises their relevance. Relevance, and the maximisation of relevance, is the key to human cognition.

This has an important consequence for the theory of communication. A communicator, by the very act of claiming an audience's attention, suggests that the information he is offering is relevant enough to be worth the audience's attention. We would like to show that this simple idea—that communicated information comes with a guarantee of relevance—is enough on its own to yield an explanatory pragmatic theory.

But what is relevance? We claim that information is relevant to you if it interacts in a certain way with your existing assumptions about the world. Here are three examples of the type of interaction we have in mind.

Case A

You wake up with the following thought:

(11) a. If it's raining, I'll stay at home.

You look out of the window and discover:

(11) b. It's raining.

In this case, from your existing assumption (11a) and the new information (11b), you can deduce some further information not deducible from either the existing assumption or the new information alone:

(11) c. I'll stay at home.

To deduce (11c), you have to use both old and new information as joint premises in an inference process. Intuitively, the new information (11b) would be relevant in a context containing assumption (11a). We claim that it is relevant precisely because it enables such a joint inference process to take place. Let us say that assumption (11a) is the *context* in which the new information (11b) is processed, and that (11b) *contextually implies* (11c) in the context (11a). Then we claim that new information is relevant in any context in which it has contextual implications, and the more contextual implications it has, the more relevant it will be.

Assumptions about the world may vary in their strength: you may have more or less evidence for, more or less confidence in, your assumption that it is raining. New information may affect the strength of your existing assumptions, as in the following case.

Case B

You wake up, hearing a pattering on the roof, and form the hypothesis that:

(12) a. It's raining.

You open your eyes, look out of the window, and discover that:

(12) b. It is raining.

Here, the new information (12b) strengthens, or confirms, your existing assumption (12a). It would also, intuitively, be relevant to you in a context containing assumption (12a). We claim that (12b) is relevant precisely because it strengthens an existing assumption of yours. New information is relevant in any context in which it strengthens an existing assumption; and the more assumptions it strengthens, and the more it strengthens them, the more relevant it will be.

If new information can achieve relevance by strengthening an existing assumption, it

should also achieve relevance by contradicting, and eliminating, an existing assumption, as in the following case.

Case C

You wake up, as in case B, hearing a pattering on the roof, and form the hypothesis that:

(13) a. It's raining.

This time, when you open your eyes and look out of the window, you discover that the sound was made by leaves falling on the roof, and that acutally:

(13) b. It's not raining.

Let us assume that when new and old assumptions contradict each other, the weaker of the two assumptions is abandoned. Here, the new information (13b) would provide conclusive evidence against the old assumption (13a), which would therefore be abandoned. Intuitively, (13b) would be relevant in these circumstances. We claim that new information is relevant in any context in which it contradicts, and leads to the elimination of, an existing assumption; and the more assumptions it eliminates, and the stronger they were, the more relevant it will be.

These cases illustrate the three ways in which new information can interact with, and be relevant in, a context of existing assumptions: by combining with the context to yield contextual implications; by strengthening existing assumptions; and by contradicting and eliminating existing assumptions. Let us group these three types of interaction[s] together and call them *contextual effects*. Then we claim that new information is relevant in any context in which it has contextual effects, and the greater its contextual effects, the more relevant it will be.

This comparative definition of relevance is inadequate in one respect, as the following example shows:

Case D

You wake up, thinking:

(14) a. If it rains, I'll stay at home.

Then EITHER:
You look out of the window and see:

(14) b. It's raining.

OR:
You look out of the window and see:

(14) c. It's raining and there's grass on the lawn.

Intuitively, (14b) would be more relevant to you than (14c) in the context (14a). Yet (14b) and (14c) have exactly the same contextual effects in this context: they both have the contextual implication (14d), and no other contextual effect at all:

(14) d. I'll stay at home.

If comparisons of relevance are based solely on contextual effects, then the difference in relevance between (14b) and (14c) is inexplicable.

This difference, we suggest, can be explained in terms of the intuition underlying Grice's Manner maxims, which itself derives from some basic facts about cognition. The intuition is that speakers should make their utterances easy to understand: in our terms, that speakers should make the contextual effects of their utterances easy to recover. Now it is clear that though (14b) and (14c) above have exactly the same contextual effects in the context (14a), you would have to work harder to recover them from (14c) than from (14b): since (14c) includes (14b) as a subpart, (14c) will require all the effort needed to process (14b), and more besides. This extra processing effort detracts from the relevance of the information in (14c), and of any utterance used to communicate it.

We thus propose the following comparative definition of relevance (developed in more detail in Sperber and Wilson 1986):

Relevance:
(a) Other things being equal, the greater the contextual effects, the greater the relevance.
(b) Other things being equal, the smaller the processing effort, the greater the relevance.

An individual with finite processing resources, who is aiming to maximise relevance, should pay attention to the phenomena which, when represented in the best possible way, and processed in the best possible context, seem likely to yield the greatest possible contextual effects

in return for the available processing effort. Relevance, and the aim of maximising relevance, is the key to cognition.

4. COMMUNICATION: THE PRINCIPLE OF RELEVANCE

If humans pay attention only to relevant information, a communicator, by claiming an audience's attention, gives a guarantee of relevance. He guarantees, in particular, that the information he is attempting to convey, when processed in a context he believes the audience has accessible, will be relevant enough to be worth the audience's attention. But how relevant is that? What exactly is the guarantee of relevance that accompanies each act of inferential communication?

On the contextual effect side, the guarantee is one of adequacy. In the most straightforward cases of verbal communication, the speaker guarantees that the proposition he intends to express, when processed in a context he expects the hearer to have accessible, will yield enough contextual effects to be worth the hearer's attention. How much is required in the way of contextual effects will vary from individual to individual and occasion to occasion. How the level of adequacy is fixed and varies is an interesting question, but intuitions about particular examples are clear enough.

On the processing effort side, as Grice's Manner maxims suggest, the guarantee is of more than adequacy. A speaker who wants to achieve a certain range of contextual effects must make sure that they are as easy as possible for the hearer to recover: that is, he must make sure that his utterance puts the hearer to no unjustifiable processing effort. This is in the speaker's interest as well as the hearer's, for two reasons: firstly, the speaker wants to be understood, and any increase in unjustifiable processing effort required of the hearer is an increase in risk of misunderstanding; secondly, any increase in processing effort detracts from overall relevance, and might cause the overall relevance of the utterance to fall below an acceptable level.

Let us say that an utterance (or more generally an act of inferential communication) which, on the one hand, achieves an adequate range of contextual effects, and on the other hand, achieves it for the minimum justifiable processing effort, is *optimally relevant*. Then Grice's maxim of relevance can be replaced by the following *principle of relevance:*

Principle of relevance
Every act of inferential communication carries a guarantee of optimal relevance.

We believe that this single principle (or rather a more technical version developed in Sperber and Wilson 1986) is enough on its own to yield an explanatory pragmatic theory.

The fact that an utterance carries a guarantee of optimal relevance does not mean that it will actually be optimally relevant to the hearer. A guarantee may be given mistakenly or in bad faith: I may tell you something in the mistaken belief that you do not already know it, or speak simply to distract your attention from relevant information elsewhere. In this case, you will be unable to find an interpretation which satisfies the guarantee.

Let us say that an utterance on a given interpretation is *consistent with the principle of relevance* if a rational communicator might have expected it to be optimally relevant to the hearer, i.e., to achieve an adequate range of contextual effects as economically as possible. Then it is easy to show that every utterance has at most one interpretation which is consistent with the principle of relevance.

We will show this using our example of disambiguation, (8b), with possible interpretations (15a) and (15b):

(8) b. *Mary:* I'll bring a bat.
(15) a. Mary will bring a flying rodent.
    b. Mary will bring a hitting instrument.

Logically speaking, there are two routes that the disambiguation process might follow: one interpretation may be more accessible than the other, and be tested first for consistency with the principle of relevance; or both interpretations may be equally accessible, and be tested in parallel. We consider each possibility in turn.

Suppose that interpretation (15a) is more accessible to Peter than (15b), and is therefore the first to be tested for consistency with the principle of relevance. Suppose, moreover, that there is an easily accessible context in which this interpretation would have a manifestly adequate range of contextual effects, and

that there would have been no obviously cheaper way of obtaining them. Then as long as Mary could have foreseen this situation, interpretation (15a) is consistent with the principle of relevance, and is the only interpretation consistent with the principle of relevance, as the following argument shows.

Imagine that Mary had wanted to convey interpretation (15b), but had foreseen that interpretation (15a) would be both more accessible and consistent with the principle of relevance. By reformulating her utterance to eliminate this unwanted interpretation—for example, saying 'I'll bring a baseball bat', thus eliminating interpretation (15a) entirely—she could have spared her hearer the effort of first accessing and processing interpretation (15a), then accessing and processing interpretation (15b), and then engaging in some form of inference process to choose between them. In other words, she could have achieved the intended range of contextual effects at a much reduced processing cost, and at a much smaller risk of misunderstanding, by rephrasing her utterance. On this interpretation, although Mary's utterance (8b) may achieve an adequate range of contextual effects, it would put her hearer to some unjustifiable processing effort in recovering them, and is not consistent with the principle of relevance.

What would happen if interpretations (15a) and (15b) were equally accessible, and were thus simultaneously tested for consistency with the principle of relevance? Suppose that Peter has easy access to a context in which interpretation (15a) has an adequate range of contextual effects, while a comparable context for (15b) is much less accessible or not accessible at all. As long as Mary could rationally have foreseen this situation, (15a) is consistent with the principle of relevance, and is the only interpretation consistent with the principle of relevance. If Mary had intended to convey interpretation (15b), she could manifestly have spared Peter some processing effort by rephrasing her utterance to eliminate the unwanted interpretation (15a). For example, by saying 'I'll bring a baseball bat,' she could have spared Peter the effort of accessing and processing both (15a) and (15b), and then engaging in some inference process to choose between them. On this interpretation, Mary's utterance (8b) would [put] Peter to some unjustifiable processing effort, and is not consistent with the principle of relevance.

Finally what would happen if interpretations (15a) and (15b) were equally accessible, and, moreover, yielded comparable contextual effects at comparable processing costs? Then there would be no way of choosing between them, the ambiguity would remain unresolved, and neither interpretation would be consistent with the principle of relevance, since each could only be preferred, if at all, after an effort of comparison which Mary could easily have spared Peter. Thus the principle of relevance provides an account, not just of successes, but also of failures of disambiguation.

This example shows that, whatever the procedures used in disambiguation, the first interpretation—if any—tested and found consistent with the principle of relevance is the only interpretation consistent with the principle of relevance. A speaker who does not intend this interpretation should rephrase her utterance to eliminate it. This general principle applies to every aspect of utterance interpretation, shedding light on a number of long-standing pragmatic problems, as our next section is designed to show.

5. PRAGMATICS AND RELEVANCE THEORY

Grice has a maxim 'Be brief.' There are a number of problems attaching to the maxim of brevity. One is that brevity itself is left undefined: should it be measured in terms of phoneme counts, syllable counts, word counts, or what? Another is that there are clear counterexamples. Compare (16a) and (16b):

(16) a. I have no brothers or sisters.
     b. I have no siblings.

By any intuitive measure of brevity, (16b) is shorter than (16a), which is thus predicted as stylistically inappropriate on Grice's account. The fact is, though, that it is (16b) rather than (16a) which is the stylistically inappropriate member of this pair.

Relevance theory offers a solution to both these problems. There is no maxim of brevity. The intuitions Grice wanted to explain are intuitions about processing effort, and in parti

ular, about the fact that a speaker aiming at optimal relevance should spare her hearer any unnecessary processing effort. Whereas 'brevity' is an ad hoc linguistic category, processing effort is a psychological category whose empirical causes and consequences are at least to some extent known. In particular, it is known that word frequency affects processing effort: in general, the rarer the word, the greater the processing effort. Now 'sibling' is a very rare word indeed. The differences between (16a) and (16b) are straightforwardly explained on the assumption that the relative brevity of the word 'sibling' is not enough to offset the increase in processing cost resulting from its infrequency, so that (16a) is more economical overall.

Relevance theory also offers solutions to a variety of problems raised by traditional accounts of implicature. In our framework, implicatures are the contextual assumptions and implications which form part of the intended interpretation of an utterance. Consider (3) above:

(3)   a. *Peter:* Do you want some coffee?
      b. *Mary:* Coffee would keep me awake.

On what grounds might Mary have thought her utterance (3b) would be optimally relevant to Peter? In the circumstances, Peter can reasonably assume that Mary intended him *either* to supply the contextual assumption (17) and derive (18) as a contextual implication, *or* to supply the contextual assumptions in (19a–b) and derive (20) as a contextual implication:

(17) Mary does not want to stay awake.

(18) Mary does not wany any coffee.

(19) a. Mary wants to stay awake.
     b. Mary wants anything that will keep her awake.

(20) Mary wants some coffee.

But which of these possible interpretations did Mary have in mind?

The answer follows from the principle of relevance. Suppose that in the circumstances, assumption (17) is more accessible to Peter than assumptions (19a–b), and that Mary could have foreseen this. Then the interpretation based on (17) and (18) is the only one consistent with the principle of relevance. Suppose that Mary did not intend this interpretation: then she could have spared Peter the unnecessary effort of first accessing the interpretation based on (17) and (18), then accessing the interpretation based on (19) and (20), and then engaging in some inference process to choose between them. For example, by adding 'And I want to stay awake,' she could have eliminated the interpretation based on (17) and (18). In this situation, the interpretation based on (17) and (18) is the only one consistent with the principle of relevance. It follows that in the recovery of implicatures, as in disambiguation, the first interpretation tested and found consistent with the principle of relevance is the *only* interpretation consistent with the principle of relevance.

In fact, if Mary had merely intended to implicate that she didn't want any coffee, she could have conveyed this information more economically by simply saying 'No'. A speaker aiming at optimal relevance, who wanted to spare her hearer any unnecessary processing effort, must have intended to achieve some additional contextual effects, not derivable from the direct answer 'No.' Here, the most natural assumption for Peter to make is that she is refusing the coffee *because* it keeps her awake—rather than, say, because he makes horrible coffee, or because she doesn't want to spend a moment longer with him. Thus, (3b), unlike the direct answer 'No,' simultaneously conveys a refusal and an explanation of that refusal. The principle of relevance explains both when an implicature is needed, and what the best hypothesis about its content will be.

Often, as in (4)–(6) above, the implicatures of an utterance are less determinate than this. The problem of providing an explicit account of the indeterminacy of implicatures has defeated many pragmatists. Relevance theory offers a solution. The implicatures of an utterance are the contextual assumptions and implications that a speaker aiming at optimal relevance must have expected the hearer to supply. Sometimes, as with (17) and (18) above, there is only a single possible hypothesis about what these implicatures might be. Let us call (17) and (18) *strong* implicatures of (3b). Sometimes, however, there is a range of alternative hypotheses, all compatible with each other and roughly comparable in accessibility and contextual effects. Here, the utterance provides a certain amount of evidence

for each alternative hypothesis, and the hearer is free to adopt whichever he chooses, and regard it as weakly confirmed by the speaker. The more alternative hypotheses there are, the weaker the implicatures will be, up to the point where the utterance provides no evidence at all for a certain assumption or conclusion, and all the responsibility for supplying it rests with the hearer. Although we have no space here for an analysis of stylistic and figurative effects, the notion of weak implicature plays a decisive role in our account, as it does in our account of the vaguer aspects of both verbal and non-verbal communication.

A speaker aiming at optimal relevance should leave implicit everything that the hearer can be trusted to access for himself with less effort than would be required to process an explicit prompt. In (1) above, for example, the speaker does not explicitly specify what the food is too hot for, trusting the hearer to access this information for himself and use it to enrich the explicit content of the utterance to the point where it is consistent with the principle of relevance. This aspect of utterance interpretation has been largely ignored in the pragmatic literature, which tends to equate the domain of pragmatics with the domain of what we have been calling strong implicatures. We believe that a number of pragmatic problems have arisen directly from the fact that a variety of phenomena which have been standardly analysed as typical strong implicatures are not implicatures at all, but pragmatically determined aspects of explicit content.

Here is an example. Grice (1989) argued that the connectives 'and,' 'or' and 'if . . . then' were not ambiguous between truth-functional and non-truth-functional senses. According to him, an utterance of the form 'P and Q' would be true if and only if both its conjuncts were true. The occasional temporal and causal connotations of conjoined utterances did not result from extra senses of the word 'and,' but were implicatures arising from the co-operative principle and maxims. A major problem for this account is that the alleged 'implicatures' fall within the scope of logical operators such as negation, disjunction, comparison and conditionals, contributing to the truth conditions of complex utterances in which they occur. Thus, (21a) and (21b) are not, respectively, tautologous and contradictory, as they

should be if the temporal connotations of conjoined utterances are not part of truth-conditional content, but merely implicatures:

(21) a. It's always the same at parties: either you
get drunk and no one will talk to you, or no
one will talk to you and you get drunk.
b. If the old king died of a heart attack and a
republic was declared Sam will be happy,
but if a republic was declared and the old
king died of a heart attack Sam will be unhappy.

[Adapted from Cohen 1971]

Grice himself seems to have regarded this objection as decisive. After discussing a parallel
objection to his analysis of 'if,' he concludes:

I'm afraid I do not see what defence (if any) can be
put up against this objection.

[Lecture V, p. 10]

For Grice, as for most pragmatists, there
seemed to be only two possibilities: either
'and' is ambiguous between truth-functional,
temporal and causal senses, or 'and' has a single, truth-functional sense, and the temporal
and causal connotations of conjoined utterances arise at the level of implicature. However, as Carston (1984, 1985) has pointed out,
relevance theory offers a third possibility: it
may be that 'and' has a single, truth-functional
sense, but that the temporal and causal connotations of conjoined utterances are pragmatically determined aspects of explicit propositional content, and not implicatures at all.

Within relevance theory, the recovery of explicit content is not necessarily a simple matter of decoding, disambiguation and reference
assignment. To obtain an interpretation consistent with the principle of relevance, the explicit content of the utterance may have to be
enriched in certain ways. As always, this enrichment is severely constrained: the first accessible enrichment consistent with the principle of relevance is the *only* enrichment
consistent with the principle of relevance. By
assuming that the temporal and causal connotations of conjoined utterances are pragmatically determined aspects of explicit content, we can preserve Grice's arguments
against the ambiguity of 'and', while still
maintaining that the temporal and causal connotations of conjoined utterances contribute
to truth conditions, and thus fall within the
scope of logical operators.

We will end by showing that relevance theory eliminates the need for a maxim of truthfulness, the maxim that Grice himself regarded as the most important of the maxims,
and without which Horn (1985:12) believes
that 'the entire conversational and implica-
tural apparatus collapses.' We will argue that
the assumption that there is a maxim, or
norm, or principle, or convention of literal
truthfulness creates unnecessary and insoluble
problems for pragmatic theory.

A speaker observing the maxim of truthfulness should express only propositions she believes to be true, or at least propositions which
she has some reason to believe are true. There
are glaring counterexamples to the maxim of
truthfulness, some familiar from the literature, others rarely considered: they include fic-
tions, fantasies, idle speculations, guesses,
rough approximations, metaphors, ironies
and free indirect speech. Griceans have a set
of labels for classifying these counterexamples:
'deliberate violation', 'opting out', 'clash of
maxims', 'making as if to say', and so on.
Thus, metaphor and irony are analysed as 'deliberate violations' of the maxim of truthfulness, from which the hearer is supposed to recover some logically related proposition as in
implicature. However, nothing approaching
an explanatory theory is proposed; and indeed, there are quite ordinary counterexamples to the maxim of truthfulness which the
Gricean framework cannot deal with at all.

Consider the exchange in (22):

(22) a. *Peter:* What does the election pamphlet
say?
b. *Mary:* We'll all be rich and happy if we vote
for them.

In a framework with a maxim of truthfulness,
in saying (22b), Mary must be understood as
expressing a belief that we will all be rich and
happy if we vote for that particular party.
However, it would often be quite natural to
understand her not as expressing her own belief, but as representing or reporting the belief
expressed in the manifesto. All we need to do
to account for this interpretation is to drop the
maxim of truthfulness and assume that an utterance may achieve optimal relevance by representing *either* the beliefs of the speaker *or*
those of someone other than the speaker
which it would be relevant to the hearer to

know. The correct assumption about whose views are being represented is, as always, the first one tested and found consistent with the principle of relevance.

Irony fits quite straightforwardly into this framework. There is nothing to stop Mary, in representing the beliefs expressed in the manifesto, from communicating her own attitude to those beliefs. For example, she may indicate by facial expression or tone of voice, or simply trust Peter to realize from his knowledge of her, that she dissociates herself from the views she is representing, and indeed regards them as ridiculous or contemptible. The result is irony. Irony, on this account, does not involve a deliberate violation of any pragmatic principle or maxim: it is merely one means among others of communicating relevant information.

Another range of counterexamples to the maxim of truthfulness is the class of utterances intended and understood as rough approximations. Compare the alternative answers (23b) and (23c) to the question in (23a):

(23) a. *Peter:* How far is Nottingham from London?
   b. *Mary:* 120 miles.
   c. *Mary:* 118 miles.

According to the maxim of truthfulness, Mary should not say that Nottingham is 120 miles from London unless she believes that it is exactly 120 miles from London. If she believes that the true distance is in fact 118 miles, then she would violate the maxim of truthfulness by answering as in (23b). However, there are many situations in which a speaker aiming at optimal relevance should prefer the rough approximation (23b) to the strictly truthful (23c). Suppose Peter, who normally drives at about 60 miles an hour, is trying to decide when he should leave London for dinner in Nottingham. From both (23b) and (23c) he can recover the contextual implication that it will take him about two hours to drive to Nottingham, and that he should plan his journey accordingly. However, given that mental calculation is easier to do in round numbers, it will cost him less effort to recover these implications from (23b) than from (23c), and a speaker aiming at optimal relevance should prefer (23b) to (23c), as long as Peter has some way of knowing that the contextual effects she

intends her utterance to achieve are only a subset of those he could in principle derive from her utterance (23b). We will argue that this is a possibility to which hearers are quite generally alert.

An utterance, we have seen, can be used to represent the thought of the speaker, or of someone other than the speaker. But why should we assume that the proposition expressed by an utterance must be identical to the thought it represents? Representation involves the exploitation of resemblances, and two objects resemble each other to the extent that they have properties in common. However, a representation can achieve its aim without sharing *all* its properties with the original it represents. For example, a bust of Napoleon may be made of white plaster, have no arms and legs, be found in a certain museum, and have been bought for a certain price. No rational addressee would attribute these properties to Napoleon himself. Nor should he. In this, as in every other aspect of interpretation, the minimal assumption—that is, the first accessible assumption—consistent with the principle of relevance is the only assumption consistent with the principle of relevance. If a communicator aiming at optimal relevance could have intended to convey an adequate idea of Napoleon *without* intending to suggest that Napoleon was made of white plaster, lacked arms and legs, etc., then he must be credited with this minimal intention: it is the only intention which a communicator aiming at optimal relevance could have hoped to achieve.

The proposition expressed by an utterance resembles the thought it is used to represent to the extent that they share logical properties, i.e. logical and contextual implications. Let us say that if they share all their logical and contextual implications, the utterance is a *literal* representation of the speaker's thought. Then it follows from the maxim of truthfulness that an utterance should always be a literal representation of the speaker's thought. By contrast, it follows from the principle of relevance that the hearer should take the utterance to be a literal representation of the speaker's thought only if this is the minimal assumption, i.e. the first accessible assumption, consistent with the principle of relevance. In the case of rough approximations such as (23b),

since, as we have seen, there is an easily accessible less-than-literal interpretation of (23b)
which is consistent with the principle of relevance, there is no need for the hearer to consider the literal interpretation at all.

Metaphorical utterances such as (4) fit
straightforwardly into this pattern:

(4) Their friendship blossomed.

By processing (4) in the context of his encyclopaedic knowledge of blossoming, the hearer
might derive a number of contextual implications. Some, for instance the implication that
their friendship belonged to the plant king-
dom, carry no plausible information and
could hardly have been intended by the
speaker to contribute to the relevance of her
utterance. Other contextual implications, by
contrast, do contribute to the relevance of the
utterance and can therefore be assumed to
have been· at least weakly implicated by the
speaker, in the sense that the speaker intended
the hearer to derive some such implications, if
not exactly these. Thus, the hearer might conclude that the friendship in question grew
from small beginnings, in a favourable environment, by a natural process, into something
beautiful, that was perhaps destined to fade.
As with most metaphors, there is a substantial
element of indeterminacy in the interpretation
of (4), and its associated implicatures will be
relatively weak. For a speaker who wanted to
achieve a range of effects along these lines, (4)
would be the most economical way of achieving them. Since (4) has an easily accessible
non-literal interpretation which is consistent
with the principle of relevance, there is no
need for the hearer to consider the literal interpretation at all. By assuming that speakers
aim not at literal truthfulness but at optimal
relevance, an explanatory insight into metaphor, irony and a variety of related phenomena can be achieved.

6. CONCLUDING REMARK

In this paper, we have tried to show that considerations of relevance play a decisive role
both in communication and cognition. Notice, though, that the principle of relevance,
and the criterion of consistency with the principle of relevance, apply only to the recognition of communicators' intentions: other non-
demonstrative inference processes are under
no such constraint. The consequences are
considerable.

As we have shown, every utterance has at
most a single interpretation which is consistent with the principle of relevance. Moreover,
it is in the speaker's interests to make sure that
this interpretation, and the contextual assumptions needed to obtain it, are instantly
accesssible to the hearer: otherwise she is wast-
ing her breath. It is an interesting question
whether any comparable criterion applies to
other non-demonstrative inference processes.
Certainly, there is no criterion which is powerful enough to eliminate all but a single scientific hypothesis on the basis of immediately
accessible contextual information. For this
reason, pragmatic processes are more amenable than scientific theorising to scientific
study. For this reason too, the search for an
adequate pragmatic theory is doubly worthwhile: not just for its own sake, but for the
light it may shed on other non-modular processes, about which, as Fodor has rightly em-
phasised, so little is so far known.

REFERENCES

Carston, R. (1984). "Semantic and Pragmatic Analyses of 'And'." Paper delivered to the Linguistics Associ-
    ation of Great Britain, April 1984.
Carston, R. (1985). "Saying and Implicating." Paper delivered to the Cumberland Lodge Conference on Log-
    ical Form, April 1985.
Cohen, L. J. (1971). "The Logical Particles of Natural Language." In Y. Bar-Hillel (ed.), *Pragmatics of Nat-
    ural Language.* Dordrecht: Reidel.
Fodor, J. (1983). *The Modularity of Mind.* Cambridge, Mass.: MIT Press.
Grice, H. P. (1989). *Studies in the Way of Words.* Cambridge, Mass.: Harvard University Press.
Horn, L. R. (1985). "Metalinguistic Negation and Pragmatic Ambiguity." *Language* 61:121–174.
Sperber, D., and D. Wilson (1986). *Relevance: Communication and Cognition.* Cambridge, Mass.: Harvard
    University Press; Oxford: Basil Blackwell.

FURTHER READING

Bates, R. (1976). *Language and Context.* New York: Academic Press.

Brewer, W. (1977). "Memory for the Pragmatic Implications of Sentences." *Memory and Cognition* 5:673–678.

Clark, H., and R. Gerring (1975). "On the Pretense Theory of Irony." *Journal of Experimental Psychology* 113:56–72.

Clark, H., and P. Lucy (1975). "Inferring What Is Meant from What Is Said: A Study in Conversationally Conveyed Requests." *Journal of Verbal Learning and Verbal Behavior* 14:56–72.

Fodor, J. A. (1981). *Representations.* Cambridge, Mass.: MIT Press.

Fodor, J. A. (1983). *The Modularity of Mind.* Cambridge, Mass.: MIT Press.

Harris, R., and G. Monaco (1978). "Psychology of Pragmatic Implication: Information Processing Between the Lines." *Journal of Experimental Psychology* 107:1–22.

Jorgensen, J., G. Miller, and D. Sperber (1984). "Test of the Mention Theory of Irony." *Journal of Experimental Psychology* 113:112–120.

Ochs, E., and B. S. Schieffelin (eds.). (1979). *Developmental Pragmatics.* New York: Academic Press.

Sperber, D. (1984). "Verbal Irony: Pretense or Echo Mention?" *Journal of Experimental Psychology* 113:130–136.